Chapter Title	Chapter Focus Company	Company Logo	Type of Company	Contrast Companies	Key Ratios
8 Reporting and Interpreting Inventories	Oakley, Inc.	**Oakley, Inc.**	Eyewear, apparel, and footwear manufacturer	Nortel The Hockey Company Mega Brands Sleeman Breweries Hudsons Bay Company	Inventory Turnover
9 Reporting and Interpreting Long-Lived Tangible and Intangible Assets	ClubLink Corporation	CLUBLINK ONE MEMBERSHIP *more golf*	Owner and operator of golf courses	CN Purolator Fairmont Hotels & Resorts Petro-Canada Air Canada	Fixed Asset Turnover
10 Reporting and Interpreting Liabilities	Rogers Communication Inc.	ROGERS CENTRE	Wireless, cable, and media communications	BCE Telus Hydro One Forzanie Group Sears Canada CIBC Greater Toronto Transit Authority Tim Hortons	Current Ratio Times Interest Earned
11 Reporting and Interpreting Shareholders' Equity	Danier Leather, Inc.	DANIER LEATHER	Leather apparel and accessories	Reitmans (Canada) Le Chateau RIM Telus Barrick Gold Suncor Energy	Earnings per Share (EPS) Return on Equity (ROE)
12 Reporting and Interpreting the Statement of Cash Flows	Magnotta Winery Corporation	MAGNOTTA *The Award Winning Winery*	Producer of wine, beer, and juice	Vincor Andrew Peller Sleeman Breweries Humpty Dumpty CHC Helicopter Loblaws Sobeys Maple Leaf Foods Leon's Furniture	Quality of Income Cash Coverage Capital Acquisitions
13 Measuring and Evaluating Financial Performance	High Liner Foods Incorporated	High Liner	Food processor	Sun-Rype Products Shell Canada Canadian Tire Forzani Group Gildan Activewear HBC Mega Brands	Summary of Preceding Ratios (Exhibit 13.4) Price/Earnings Ratio

FUNDAMENTALS OF
Financial Accounting

Second Canadian Edition

Fred Phillips
University of Saskatchewan

Robert Libby
Cornell University

Patricia A. Libby
Ithaca College

Teresa Anderson
University of Ottawa

McGraw-Hill
Ryerson

Toronto Montréal Boston Burr Ridge, IL Dubuque, IA Madison, WI New York
San Francisco St. Louis Bangkok Bogotá Caracas Kuala Lumpur Lisbon London
Madrid Mexico City Milan New Delhi Santiago Seoul Singapore Sydney Taipei

McGraw-Hill
Ryerson

FUNDAMENTALS OF FINANCIAL ACCOUNTING
Second Canadian Edition

ISBN-13: 978-0-07-096819-6
ISBN-10: 0-07-096819-5

3 4 5 6 7 8 9 CTPS 1 9 8 7 6 5 4 3 2 1

Printed and bound in China

Care has been taken to trace ownership of copyright material contained in this text; however, the publisher will welcome any information that enables them to rectify any reference or credit for subsequent editions.

Vice President, Editor-in-Chief: Joanna Cotton
Senior Sponsoring Editor: Rhondda McNabb
Executive Marketing Manager: Joy Armitage Taylor
Senior Developmental Editor: Suzanne Simpson Millar
Senior Editorial Associate: Christine Lomas
Supervising Editor: Graeme Powell
Copy Editor: Carol Fordyce
Production Coordinator: Lena Mastromarco
Cover Design: Liz Harasymczuk
Cover Image: © Corbis Premium RF/Alamy
Illustrator: Rose Zgodzinski
Interior Design: Liz Harasymczuk
Page Layout: Laserwords
Printer: China Translation & Printing Services Ltd.

Library and Archives Canada Cataloguing in Publication
    Fundamentals of financial accounting / Fred Phillips ... [et al.].—2nd Canadian ed.

Includes index.
ISBN 978-0-07-096819-6

    1. Accounting–Textbooks. 2. Accounting–Canada.
    I. Phillips, Fred, 1964-

HF5636.F85 2009   657   C2008-904474-6.

About the Authors

Fred Phillips

Fred Phillips is a Professor and the George C. Baxter Chartered Accountants of Saskatchewan Scholar at the University of Saskatchewan, where he teaches introductory financial accounting. He also has taught introductory accounting at the University of Texas at Austin and the University of Manitoba. Fred has an undergraduate accounting degree, a professional accounting designation, and a PhD from the University of Texas at Austin. He previously worked as an audit manager at KPMG.

Fred's main interest is accounting education. He has won 11 teaching awards, including three national case-writing competitions. Recently, Fred won the 2007 Alpha Kappa Psi Outstanding Professor award at The University of Texas at Austin and, in 2006, he was awarded the title Master Teacher at the University of Saskatchewan. He has published instructional cases and numerous articles in journals such as *Issues in Accounting Education, Journal of Accounting Research,* and *Organizational Behavior and Human Decision Processes.* He received the American Accounting Association's Outstanding Research in Accounting Education Award in 2006 and 2007 for one of his articles. Fred is a past associate editor of *Issues in Accounting Education*, and a current member of the Teaching & Curriculum and Two-Year College sections of the American Accounting Association. In his spare time, he likes to work out, play video games, and drink iced cappuccinos.

Robert Libby

Robert Libby is the David A. Thomas Professor of Accounting at Cornell University, where he teaches the introductory financial accounting course. He previously taught at the University of Illinois, Pennsylvania State University, the University of Texas at Austin, the University of Chicago, and the University of Michigan. He received his B.S. from Pennsylvania State University and his M.A.S. and PhD from the University of Illinois; he also is a CPA.

Bob is a widely published author specializing in behavioural accounting. He was selected as the AAA Outstanding Educator in 2000 and received the AAA Outstanding Service Award in 2006. His prior text, *Accounting and Human Information Processing* (Prentice Hall, 1981), was awarded the AICPA/AAA Notable Contributions to the Accounting Literature Award. He received this award again in 1996 for a paper. He has published numerous articles in *The Accounting Review, Journal of Accounting Research, Accounting, Organizations, and Society;* and other accounting journals. He has held a variety of offices in the American Accounting Association and is a member of the American Institute of CPAs and the editorial boards of *The Accounting Review, Accounting, Organizations, and Society, Journal of Accounting Literature,* and *Journal of Behavioral Decision Making.*

Patricia A. Libby

Patricia Libby is Associate Professor of Accounting and Coordinator of the Financial Accounting course at Ithaca College, as well as Faculty Advisor to Beta Alpha Psi, Ithaca College Accounting Association, and Ithaca College National Association of Black Accountants. She previously taught graduate and undergraduate financial accounting at Eastern Michigan University and the University of Texas at Austin . Before entering academe, she was an auditor with Price Waterhouse (now PricewaterhouseCoopers) and a financial administrator at the University of Chicago. She received her BS from Pennsylvania State University, her MBA from DePaul University, and her PhD from the University of Michigan; she also is a CPA.

Pat conducts research on using cases in the introductory course and other parts of the accounting curriculum. She has published articles in *The Accounting Review, Issues in Accounting Education,* and *The Michigan CPA.* She has also conducted seminars nationwide on active learning strategies, including cooperative learning methods.

Teresa Anderson

M. Teresa Anderson, PhD, FCA is an adjunct professor of accounting at the University of Ottawa. She received her bachelor's degree from Loyola of Montreal, her master's degree from the University of Ottawa, and her doctorate from Queen's University. She worked as a chartered accountant in public practice in both Montreal and Bermuda. Professor Anderson's research interests encompass various aspects of financial reporting and audit services, and she has written articles for both academic and professional journals. Professor Anderson has actively served the Institute of Chartered Accountants of Ontario, primarily on its examination subcommittee and as an elected member of its governing council. She has been a vice-president of the Canadian Academic Accounting Association and a director for a number of private organizations. Professor Anderson has been active in curriculum review and course development and has been nominated by the School of Management three times for the University of Ottawa Excellence in Teaching Award. In 2006, Professor Anderson was named a Fellow of the Institute of Chartered Accountants of Ontario.

Brief Table of Contents

Chapter 1

Reporting and Interpreting the Financial Results of Business Activities   1
Focus Company: Mattel, Inc.

Chapter 2

Reporting and Interpreting Investing and Financing Results on the Balance Sheet   41
Focus Company: First Choice Haircutters

Chapter 3

Reporting and Interpreting Operating Results on the Income Statement   85
Focus Company: First Choice Haircutters

Chapter 4

Adjustments, Financial Statements, and the Quality of Financial Reporting   130
Focus Company: First Choice Haircutters

Chapter 5

Understanding Financial Statements and the Financial Reporting Environment   189
Focus Company: Reitmans (Canada) Limited

Chapter 6

Financial Reporting Controls for Merchandising Operations   231
Focus Company: Shoppers Drug Mart

Chapter 7

Reporting and Interpreting Receivables   287
Focus Company: Sony Corporation

Chapter 8

Reporting and Interpreting Inventories   329
Focus Company: Oakley Inc.

Chapter 9

Reporting and Interpreting Long-Lived Tangible and Intangible Assets   377
Focus Company: ClubLink Corporation

Chapter 10

Reporting and Interpreting Liabilities   428
Focus Company: Rogers Communications

Chapter 11

Reporting and Interpreting Shareholders Equity   479
Focus Company: Danier Leather

Chapter 12

Reporting and Interpreting the Statement of Cash Flows   522
Focus Company: Magnotta Winery

Chapter 13

Measuring and Evaluating Financial Performance   577
Focus Company: High Liner Foods

Appendix A

High Liner Foods Incorporated 2007 Annual Report   616

Appendix B

Present and Future Value Concepts   634

Appendix C

Reporting and Interpreting Investments in Other Corporations   652

Appendix D

Sun-Rype Products Ltd Annual Report 2007. Online Learning Centre.

Glossary   671

Photo Credits   677

Name Index   678

Topical Index   681

Table of Contents

About the Authors   iii

Preface   xi

Getting the most from this book   xii

Your Personal Coach in Financial Accounting   xiii

Stay focused on the Real World   xv

A book with its own Teaching Assistant included   xvi

End-of-chapter material   xviii

How do we get students to practise?   xix

Digital Learning Solutions   xx

Instructor Resources   xxii

What's new in the 2nd Canadian Edition?   xxiv

Acknowledgments   xxvi

Chapter 1

Reporting and Interpreting the Financial Results of Business Activities   1

Mattel, Inc.   1

Understand the Basic Activities of Businesses   2

The Development of Mattel's Business   2

Study How Financial Results Are Reported in Financial Statements   4

Financial Statements   4

Generally Accepted Accounting Principles (GAAP)   16

Evaluate Results from the Perspective of Financial Statement Users   17

Who Cares?   17

Reconsider How Financial Statement Reporting Informs Users   20

The Glimpse Inside   20

A Glance Outside   20

What's Coming Up   20

For Your Review   21

Demonstration Case   21

Chapter Summary   23

Key Terms to Know   23

Supplement A: Accounting Careers   23

For Your Practice   24

Questions   24

Multiple Choice   24

Mini-Exercises   26

Exercises   30

Coached Problems   35

Group A Problems   35

Group B Problems   36

Skills Development Cases   37

Chapter 2

Reporting and Interpreting Investing and Financing Results on the Balance Sheet   41

First Choice Haircutters   41

Understand What a Balance Sheet Means to Users   42

Business Activities and Common Balance Sheet Accounts   42

Study How to Analyze Transactions   44

Transaction Analysis   44

The Ideas behind Transaction Analysis   46

DECIDE: A Systematic Approach to Transaction Analysis   48

Evaluate Transactions Using the Debit/Credit Framework   52

T-Accounts: Separating Increases and Decreases in the Basic Accounting Equation   53

Journal Entries   54

Transaction Analysis Revisited   55

Unadjusted Trial Balance   59

Preparing a Balance Sheet   60

Reconsider the Balance Sheet Concepts That Users Rely On   61

The Effects of a Transaction Focus   61

What's Coming Up   63

For Your Review   63

Demonstration Case   63

Chapter Summary   65

Key Terms to Know   66

For Your Practice   67

Questions   67

Multiple Choice   67

Mini-Exercises   69

Exercises   72

Coached Problems   77

Group A Problems   78

Group B Problems   80

Skills Development Cases   81

Chapter 3

Reporting and Interpreting Operating Results on the Income Statement   85

First Choice Haircutters   85

Understand What an Income Statement Means to Users   86

Revenues and Expenses   86

Study How to Analyze Operating Transactions   88

Cash-Based Measurements   88

Accrual-Based Measurement of Revenues   90

Accrual-Based Measurement of Expenses   92

Evaluate Transactions Using the Debit/Credit Framework   94

Including Revenues and Expenses in the Transaction Analysis Model   94

Using the DECIDES Approach with Revenues and Expenses   94

Calculating Account Balances   100

Preparing the Unadjusted Trial Balance   100

Summarizing How to Account for Revenues and Expenses   101

Reconsider the Income Statement Concepts That Users Rely On   103

The Revenue Principle   104

The Matching Principle   104

Unethical Violations of the Revenue Principle and the Matching Principle   104

What's Coming Up   105

For Your Review   105

Demonstration Case   105

Chapter Summary   109

Key Terms to Know   110

For Your Practice   110

Questions   110

Multiple Choice   110

Mini-Exercises   112

Exercises   114

Coached Problems   120

Group A Problems   122

Group B Problems   124

Skills Development Cases   125

Chapter 4

Adjustments, Financial Statements, and the Quality of Financial Reporting   130

First Choice Haircutters   130

Understand Why Adjustments Are Needed   131

1. Deferral Adjustments

2. Accrual Adjustments

Study How Adjustments Are Made   133

Examples of Deferral Adjustments   133

Examples of Accrual Adjustments   139

Evaluate the Quality of Adjusted Financial Statements   142

Adjustments for Good, Not Evil   142

Reconsider the Accounting Process   143

Preparing the Adjusted Trial Balance   145

Preparing the Income Statement and Statement of Retained Earnings   146

Preparing the Balance Sheet   147

Preparing the Statement of Cash Flows and Notes to the Financial Statements   147

Closing the Income Statement and Dividend Accounts   148

Post-Closing Trial Balance   149

What's Coming Up   151

For Your Review   152

Demonstration Case   152

Chapter Summary   158

Key Terms to Know   159

For You Practice   159

Questions   159

Multiple Choice   159

Mini-Exercises   161

Exercises   165

Coached Problems   174

Group A Problems   178

Group B Problems   181

Skills Development Cases   184

Chapter 5

Understanding Financial Statements and the Financial Reporting Environment   189

Reitmans (Canada) Limited   189

Understand the Financial Reporting Environment   190

Who Are the Main Users and What Do They Need?   190

What Do Users Get?   191

Why Would Management Misrepresent the Financial Results?

Why Would Management Not Represent the Financial Results?

The Role of Auditors, Directors, and Analysts

Study How to Analyze Financial Statements

A Model of Reitmans' Business

Comparing Results with Benchmarks

Financial Statement Ratio Analysis

Evaluate Sources of Information Other Than Annual Financial Statements   203

Financial News

Annual and Quarterly Reports

Canadian Securities Administrators (CSA) Filings

Investor Information Web Sites

Reconsider the Financial Reporting Environment

Investor Beware

For Your Review   207

Demonstration Case   207

Chapter Summary   209

Financial Statement Analysis Tips   210
Key Terms to Know   211
For Your Practice   211
Questions   211
Multiple Choice   211
Mini-Exercises   212
Exercises   215
Coached Problems   219
Group A Problems   221
Group B Problems   223
Skills Development Cases   225

Chapter 6

Financial Reporting Controls for Merchandising Operations   231

Shoppers Drug Mart   231

Understand Financial Reporting Controls
Principles of Internal Control   233

Study Control and Accounting for Cash, Purchases, and Sales   234
Cash Control and Reporting   234
Operating Cycles   240
Operating Activities and Cycles   240
Inventory Controls and Tracking Systems   241
Purchases, Purchase Returns and Allowances, and Purchase Discounts   244
Sales, Sales Returns and Allowances, and Sales Discounts   246
A Final Word on Internal Control   249

Evaluate the Operating Results of Merchandisers
Drilling Down in a Multi-Step Income Statement   250

Gross Profit Percentage   251

Reconsider the Impact of Operating Cycles on Financial Results   252
Comparing Operating Results across Companies and Industries   252
Be on the Alert   253
What's Coming Up   253
For Your Review   254
Demonstration Case A   254
Demonstration Case B   254
Chapter Summary   256
Financial Statement Analysis Tip   257
Key Terms to Know   257

Supplement A: Periodic Inventory Systems   257
For Your Practice   211
Questions   259
Multiple Choice   260
Mini-Exercises   261
Exercises   263

Coached Problems   271
Group A Problems   275
Group B Problems   278
Skills Development Cases   262

Chapter 7

Reporting and Interpreting Receivables   287

Sony Corporation   287

Understand Key Receivables Management Decisions   288
Cash Management   288
Extending Credit to Customers   288
Study How to Account for Receivables   289
The Allowance Met hod of Accounting for Accounts Receivable and Bad Debts   289
Other Methods of Accounting for Accounts Receivable and Bad Debts   296
Accounting for Notes Receivable   296
Evaluate Receivables Management Practices   299
Speeding Up the Collection Process   299
Receivables Turnover Analysis   300
Reconsider How Receivables Reporting Affects Analyses   302
The Impact of Estimation   302
What's Coming Up   304
For Your Review   304
Demonstration Case   304
Chapter Summary   306
Financial Statement Analysis Tip   307
Key Terms to Know   307
Supplement A: Direct Write-Off Method   308
For Your Practice   308
Questions   308
Multiple Choice   309
Mini-Exercises   310
Exercises   312
Coached Problems   316
Group A Problems   318
Group B Problems   321
Skills Development Cases   324

Chapter 8

Reporting and Interpreting Inventories   329

Oakley Inc.   329

Understand Key Inventory Management Decisions   330
The Business of Inventory Management   330
Study Inventory Costing and Reporting Decisions   330
Types of Inventory   330
Inventory Cost   332

Cost of Goods Sold   333

Inventory Costing Methods   334

Additional Inventory Cost Flow Computations   342

Reporting Inventory at the Lower of Cost or Market   343

Evaluate Inventory Management Practices   344

Interpreting Changes in Inventory Levels   344

Reconsider How Inventory Numbers Affect Analyses   347

The Impact of Inventory Costing Methods   347

The Impact of Errors in Ending Inventory   347

What's Coming Up

For Your Review   349

Demonstration Case   349

Chapter Summary   350

Financial Statement Analysis Tip   351

Key Terms to Know   352

Supplement A: Applying FIFO, LIFO, and Weighted-Average in a Perpetual Inventory System   352

For Your Practice   353

Questions   353

Multiple Choice   354

Mini-Exercises   355

Exercises   357

Coached Problems   363

Group A Problems   366

Group B Problems   369

Skills Development Cases   372

Chapter 9

Reporting and Interpreting Long-Lived Tangible and Intangible Assets   377

ClubLink Corporation   377

Understand the Types of Long-Lived Assets Used in Business   378

Defining and Classifying Long-Lived Assets   379

Study How to Account for Long-Lived Assets   379

Acquisition of Tangible Assets   379

Use of Tangible Assets   382

Asset Impairment Losses   389

Disposal of Tangible Assets   390

Types of Intangible Assets   391

Acquisition, Use, and Disposal of Intangible Assets   392

Bricks and Clicks   394

Natural Resources   395

Evaluate the Effectiveness of Long-Lived Asset Management Decisions   395

What's an Optimal Level of Investment?   395

To Lease or Buy?   395

Evaluate the Use of Long-Lived Tangible Assets   396

Amortization and Cash Flow   397

Reconsider How Reporting Decisions Affects Analyses   397

The Impact of Amortization Differences   397

The Role of Judgment   399

What's coming Up   400

For Your Review   400

Demonstration Case   400

Chapter Summary   403

Financial Statement Analysis Tip   404

Key Terms to Know   404

Supplement A: Change in Amortization Estimates   405

For Your Practice   406

Questions   406

Multiple Choice   406

Mini-Exercises   408

Exercises   410

Coached Problems   416

Group A Problems   418

Group B Problems   420

Skills Development Cases   422

Chapter 10

Reporting and Interpreting Liabilities   428

Rogers Communications   428

Understand Decisions That Involve Liabilities   429

Classification of Liabilities   430

Study How to Account for and Report Liabilities   430

Measurement of Liabilities   430

Current Liabilities   430

Long-Term Liabilities   437

Evaluate the Likelihood That Liabilities Will Be Repaid in Full   445

Analyzing the Ability to Pay Amounts Currently Owed   446

Analyzing the Ability to Generate Resources to Pay Future Amounts Owed   447

Understanding Common Features of Debt   449

Reconsider How Liability Decisions Can Be Affected by Unrecorded Debt   449

Unrecorded Liabilities   450

What's Coming Up   452

For Your Review   452

Demonstration Case A   452

Demonstration Case B   453

Chapter Summary   454

Financial Statement Analysis Tips   455

Key Terms to Know   455

Supplement A: Effective -Interest Amortization of Bond Discount and Premium 455

For Your Practice 460

Questions 460

Multiple Choice 460

Mini-Exercises 462

Exercises 463

Coached Problems 467

Group A Problems 470

Group B Problems 473

Skills Development Cases 475

Chapter 11

Reporting and Interpreting Shareholders' Equity 479

Danier Leather 479

Understand Forms of Business Organization 480

Understanding Corporations 480

Ownership of a Corporation 481

Study How to Account for Equity Transactions 483

Common Share Transactions 484

Dividends on Common Shares 485

Stock Dividends and Stock Splits 487

Preferred Shares 489

Retained Earnings 491

Evaluate the Return to Shareholders 491

Earnings per Share (EPS) 491

Return on Equity (ROE) 493

Reconsider Decisions That Affect Measures of Shareholder Returns 494

Equity versus Debt 494

Retained Earnings Restrictions 495

Stock Options and Diluted Earnings per Share 495

Be on the Alert for Stock Repurchases 496

What's Coming Up 406

For Your Review 496

Demonstration Case A 496

Demonstration Case B 497

Chapter Summary 498

Financial Statement Analysis Tips 499

Key Terms to Know 499

Supplement A: Accounting for Equity in Sole Proprietorships and Partnerships 500

For Your Practice 504

Questions 504

Multiple Choice 504

Mini-Exercises 505

Exercises 507

Coached Problems 513

Group A Problems 515

Group B Problems 517

Skills Development Cases 519

Chapter 12

Reporting and Interpreting the Statement of Cash Flows 522

Magnotta Winery 522

Understand What a Statement of Cash Flows Reports 523

The Need for a Statement of Cash Flows 523

Classifications in the Statement of Cash Flows 523

Study How to Prepare a Statement of Cash Flows 526

Relationships to the Balance Sheet and Income Statement 526

Reporting Cash Flows from Operating Activities 528

Reporting Cash Flows from Investing Activities 537

Format for the Statement of Cash Flows 540

Additional SCF Information 540

Evaluate Financial Results in a Statement of Cash Flows 541

Interpreting C ash Flow from Operating Activities 541

Interpreting Cash Flows from Investing Activities 642

Interpreting Cash Flows from Financing Activities 543

Reconsider Financial Performance in the Light of Cash Flows 544

Using Net Operating Cash Flows to Evaluate Net Income 544

What's Coming Up 545

For Your Review 546

Demonstration Case A 546

Demonstration Case B 547

Chapter Summary 548

Financial Statement Analysis Tips 549

Key Terms to Know 549

Supplement A: Reporting Sales of Property, Plant, and Equipment 550

For Your Practice 551

Questions 551

Multiple Choice 552

Mini-Exercises 553

Exercises 556

Coached Problems 563

Group A Problems 564

Group B Problems 568

Skills Development Cases 572

Chapter 13

Measuring and Evaluating Financial Performance 577

High Liner Foods 577

Understand Techniques Used to Evaluate Financial Performance 578

Study How to Evaluate Financial Performance (Using High Liner) 579

Trend Analysis of High Liner's Financial Statements 581

Ratio Analyses Using High Liner's Financial Statements 581

Other Considerations 589

Evaluate Financial Results in Relation to Stock Price 590

The Relationship between Earnings and Stock Prices 590

Reconsider the Conceptual Framework for Financial Accounting 591

The Objective of Financial Reporting 591

For Your Review 594

Demonstration Case 594

Chapter Summary 594

Financial Statement Analysis Tips 595

Key Terms to Know 596

Supplement A: Non-Recurring and Other Items 596

For Your Practice 597

Questions 597

Multiple Choice 597

Mini-Exercises 598

Exercises 599

Coached Problems 603

Group A Problems 606

Group B Problems 610

Skills Development Cases 614

Appendix A

High Liner Foods Incorporated 2007 Annual Report 616

Appendix B

Present and Future Value Concepts 634

Computing Future and Present Values of a Single Amount 635

Future Value of a Single Amount 635

Present Value of a Single Amount 635

Computing Future and Present Values of an Annuity 637

Future Value of an Annuity 637

Present Value of an Annuity 638

Interest Rates and Interest Periods 639

Accounting Applications of Present Values 639

Case A—Present Value of a Single Amount 640

Case B—Present Value of an Annuity 641

Case C—Present Value of a Single Amount and an Annuity 642

Future and Present Value Tables 644

For Your Review 648

Key Terms to Know 648

For Your Practice 648

Questions 648

Multiple Choice 648

Mini-Exercises 650

Exercises 650

Coached Problem 651

Group A Problem 651

Group B Problem 651

Appendix C

Reporting and Interpreting Investments in Other Corporations 652

Why Does a Company Invest in Other Corporations? 652

Consolidation Method for Investments Involving Control 653

Equity Method for Investments Involving Significant Influence 654

Market Value Methods for Passive Investments 657

For Your Review 561

Demonstration Case A—Equity Method for Significant Influence Investments 661

Demonstration Case B—Market Value Method for Securities Available for Sale 662

Demonstration Case C—Market Value Method for Trading Securities 663

Key Terms to Know 664

For Your Practice 664

Questions 664

Multiple Choice 664

Mini-Exercises 665

Exercises 667

Coached Problems 668

Group A Problems 69

Appendix D

Sun-Rype Products Ltd Annual Report 2007.
Online Learning Centre.

Glossary 671

Photo Credits 677

Name Index 678

Topical Index 681

Preface

Fundamentals of Financial Accounting, 2nd Canadian edition

The Student-Centred Approach

Phillips, Libby, Libby, and Anderson's *Fundamentals of Financial Accounting,* 2nd Canadian edition arms students with a secret weapon for success in financial accounting: the best personal coach on the market. The following are highlights of Phillips' innovative student-centred approach:

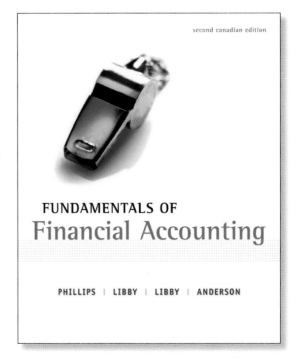

Writing that students can read. What does it mean to say that a book is "readable"? In the case of *Fundamentals of Financial Accounting,* 2nd Canadian edition, it simply means the most enjoyable accounting textbook your students have ever read. Through a mix of conversational wording, humour, and everyday examples, *Fundamentals of Financial Accounting* achieves a style that maintains rigour without sacrificing student engagement. Open this textbook to any page and read for yourself; *Fundamentals of Financial Accounting* offers **the most engaging read** of any financial text.

Student-friendly coverage of difficult topics. Written with students in mind, *Fundamentals of Financial Accounting* handles difficult concepts in a way that reflects the balance of preparer and user concepts and keeps students from being overwhelmed.

- **Financial statement analysis** is covered in two chapters (5 and 13) rather than one.

- **Ratios** are introduced throughout the chapters and then pulled together at the end.

- **Individual concepts** are introduced throughout the text as needed to explain specific accounting practices, and then pulled together at the end.

- **The Accounting Process** is covered in three chapters (2, 3, and 4) rather than two.

- The purpose of a **Statement of Cash Flows** is introduced at the beginning of the text, but the mechanics of preparing one are studied at the end.

Getting the most from this book

We're tired of people saying that accounting is deadly boring. So we wrote this textbook to show just how interesting it can be. Here are a few tips to help you get the most from this book and this course.

- **Read the book.** Seriously.

- **Get the point.** Even though you're going to read all the assigned chapters (right?), you'll want to know what's important and likely to be on your test. The learning objectives tell you. Find them on the first page of each chapter.

- **Consult the coach.** Each Coach's Tip will walk you through tough problems and give you advice on improving your game.

- **Keep on track.** The self-study quizzes gauge whether you've been thinking hard enough as you read. There's no point in blasting through the chapter just to finish. Cover the self-study quiz answers with your thumb and give the questions a try.

- **Practise, practise, practise.** We can't say it enough. You can't just read about accounting; you have to do it. So be sure to do all the questions you've been assigned. If you're assigned the Group A problems, you can do the Group B problems for extra practice and use the coached problems when reviewing for tests and exams.

- **Get extra help.** The Online Learning Centre is full of digital tools that will help you pull it all together: www.mcgrawhill.ca/olc/phillips.

Enjoy yourself. Ask questions. Share the cartoons with friends who aren't even taking this course. Discover for yourself that accounting isn't boring.

Your Personal Coach in Financial Accounting

Having a great personal coach means having the ongoing support, direction, and motivation necessary to ensure success. The second Canadian edition of *Fundamentals of Financial Accounting* is your personal coach. It provides students with the tools needed to make sense of business activities, and to help them prepare and interpret financial information in an accurate and relevant way.

The cover of this text is the quintessential representation of a coach: a whistle. Simple, maybe, but this whistle captures the essence of this text as your coach.

Fundamentals of Financial Accounting 2nd Canadian edition provides an engaging, balanced, and appropriately paced analysis of the fundamentals of financial accounting. Its conversational writing style makes it easy to read and understand, while the selection of real focus companies reinforces the relevance of accounting by introducing students to accounting and business activities in the context of their favourite companies. Balance between preparer and user orientations is achieved throughout the text, by studying both the accounting activities that take place inside the company, as well as evaluating the impact of accounting activities on decisions made by users of the financial statements. Topic coverage is paced appropriately for students new to accounting, and is thoroughly reinforced every step of the way with an ample variety of innovative pedagogical tools.

Clearly understandable, relevant, and accessible, *Fundamentals of Financial Accounting* is simply the most student-friendly financial accounting book on the market and provides the tools for students to grasp financial accounting from the ground up.

Welcome to your personal coach.

Stay focused...

The best way to learn to prepare and use financial statements is to study accounting in real business contexts. This is the key idea behind the **focus company** approach, which is introduced in the first chapter and integrates each chapter's material around a focus company, its decisions, and its financial statements.

In choosing **focus companies** to use in *Fundamentals of Financial Accounting,* Second Canadian Edition, we took care that our companies' products and services are used by students and will appeal to their curiosity. We further heighten student engagement by injecting our discussions with issues and questions that actually matter in the real world. *What decisions does ClubLink make when investing in and reporting its golf courses and other long-lived assets? How does Magnotta Winery monitor and manage its fluctuating cash flows during the pre- and post-harvest seasons?* These are but a couple of the companies and issues discussed over the course of this book.

Students often feel they lack the real-world experience needed to understand accounting, a subject they believe has little impact on their daily lives. *Fundamentals of Financial Accounting'*s **chapter openers** provide entertaining analogies that illustrate how accounting principles can inform even the most seemingly mundane things, from making peanut-butter sandwiches to catching a roommate stealing snacks. There's no better way to help students feel comfortable with accounting topics and to trigger an interest that invites them into the chapter. (To see how peanut-butter sandwiches relate to amortization, take a look at Chapter 9.)

CHAPTER

6 Financial Reporting Controls for Merchandising Operations

Understand internal control.
LO1 Describe the purpose of internal controls.

Study financial reporting controls related to cash, inventory, purchases, and sales.
LO2 Perform a key cash control by reconciling to bank statements.
LO3 Describe an operating cycle, and explain the use of a perpetual inventory system as a control in a merchandising operation.
LO4 Account for and analyze purchase and sales transactions under a perpetual inventory system.
LO5 (Supplement) Account for inventory under a periodic inventory system.

Evaluate the operating results of merchandisers.
LO6 Analyze a merchandiser's multi-step income statement.

Reconsider the impact of operating cycles on financial results.
LO7 Explain factors to consider when comparing across industries.

INSIDE LOOKING OUT
OUTSIDE LOOKING IN

This chapter focuses on how merchandisers track and report operating activities related to cash, product purchases, and sales. We focus on Shoppers Drug Mart Corporation, Canada's only nationwide, as well as its largest, drugstore chain.

During a long night of studying, there's nothing like a revitalizing snack to perk you up, right? Imagine your disappointment if you went to snack on a stack of Pringles™ chips but discovered the container was empty. How could this have happened? Did you forget that you already ate them, or did that sneaky roommate of yours pilfer them? Oh well, there's always the yogurt you've got in the fridge. Oh, wait, it's mouldy. Looks like you'll have to go to the ATM so you can buy more goodies at a nearby convenience store. But what if you found that someone had emptied almost all of your bank account last month? What an unpleasant surprise that would be! All of these problems could have been avoided had you exercised tighter control over your day-to-day activities.

Good controls are needed, not only by individuals, but also by every business, ranging from small convenience stores to massive box supercentres. At a very basic level, these businesses face many of the same potential problems as you did in our opening example. They need to ensure that they have inventory on hand to meet their customers' needs, but they don't want too much inventory hanging around because it can become spoiled, stale, damaged, obsolete, or stolen before it is sold to customers. To combat these potential problems, most businesses, including **SHOPPERS DRUG MART**, use special accounting systems to track and control inventory purchases and sales. These companies also implement strict controls to monitor their cash levels because, like many inventory items, cash is

Outside Looking In/Inside Looking Out

Different people use accounting information in different ways: Those within the firm must choose when and how to report events, while those outside it rely on those reports to make their own decisions. Instances of this dual nature of accounting information are highlighted in the Outside Looking In/ Inside Looking Out feature, using an analogy from students' own experiences to highlight the personal relevance of the chapter's topics.

INSIDE LOOKING OUT
OUTSIDE LOOKING IN

In every chapter, we introduce a key accounting decision that is made inside a real-world company, and, later in the chapter, we show how people outside the company are affected by it. This chapter features Mattel, Inc., the company that makes toys and games that everyone has enjoyed at one time in their lives. As you will see in this chapter, this industry isn't child's play—toys are one of the riskiest of all businesses to manage.

Ethical Issues

ETHICAL ISSUES

We've seen all too plainly what can happen when accounting data are distorted or used inappropriately. *Fundamentals of Financial Accounting* ensures your students start off with a solid grounding in ethics. Ethical Issues in each chapter prompt your students to think about tough ethical decisions and to practise making these decisions in the end-of-chapter cases.

Point of Interest

It always helps to take a little break now and then and the Point of Interest icon provides attention-grabbing diversions for students as they read. From the financial performance of the Toronto Maple Leafs, to bogus investment opportunities, Point of Interest icons illuminate the topic at hand with amusing and unusual facts that introduce a breath of fresh air into students' reading.

POINT OF INTEREST

Mattel executives have learned the importance of honest financial reporting. Three decades earlier, six Mattel executives were charged with including fictitious sales in the company's financial statements. The fun and games ended with the Mattel execs paying over $30 million to settle lawsuits filed by angry investors and creditors. As the saying goes, today's good decisions come from experience, which itself comes from yesterday's bad decisions.

A book with its own...

Fundamentals of Financial Accounting, 2nd Canadian Edition, is loaded with so many innovative pedagogical features you'd swear we sent a TA along with the book. From quick review tools to head-scratching ethical dilemmas, this text's pedagogy gives students every opportunity to reinforce and expand on what they're learning.

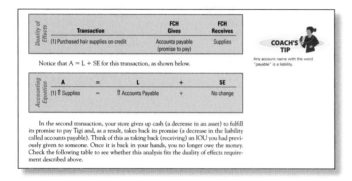

Coach's Tip

Virtually every student has been inspired by a great coach at some point or another. Throughout the chapters, Coach's Tips provide students with advice and guidance on learning the material. Coach's Tips appear again in the problem material to offer encouragement as students work to reinforce what they've learned.

Coached Problems

Every chapter includes three problem sets: Coached Problems, Group A Problems, and Group B Problems. The **Coached Problems** go beyond the traditional check figures to advise students on the *process* of solving a problem rather than just its outcome.

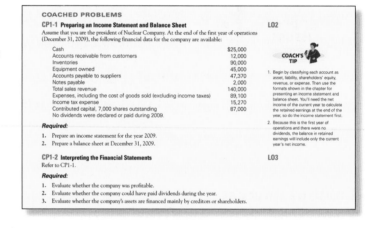

How's It Going?

Nothing helps like a quiz for mastering tricky subjects, so *Fundamentals of Financial Accounting* provides plenty of these innovative review boxes throughout each chapter. "How's It Going?" boxes pose a review question about the recent material and provide the answer right there on the page, printed sideways so that students don't accidentally read it before answering the question.

Teaching Assistant included

CHAPTER 1
Reporting and Interpreting the Financial Results of Business Activities

Understand the basic activities of businesses.
LO1 Distinguish operating, investing, and financing activities.

Study how financial results are reported in financial statements.
LO2 Describe the purpose, set-up, and content of the four basic financial statements.

Evaluate results from the perspective of financial statement users.
LO3 Explain the primary goals of financial statement users.

Reconsider how financial statement reporting informs users' decision-making.
LO4 Describe the importance of ethics and reputation in accounting.

INSIDE LOOKING OUT

OUTSIDE LOOKING IN

In every chapter, we introduce a key accounting decision that is made inside a real-world company, and, later in the chapter, we show how people outside the company are affected by it. This chapter features Mattel, Inc., the company that makes toys and games that everyone has enjoyed at one time in their lives. As you will see in this chapter, this industry isn't child's play—toys are one of the riskiest of all businesses to manage.

The USER Framework

The USER framework provides a "roadmap" to each chapter, delineating how accounting functions work at all levels of the firm. Students learn to **U**nderstand the business decisions that managers make, **S**tudy the accounting methods used, **E**valuate the reported results from the viewpoint of financial statement users, and **R**econsider how the accounting methods affect the evaluation of results, which indicate the quality of managers' decisions.

A Good Accountant DECIDES

The DECIDES decision model provides students with the structure they need to tackle challenging topics. This model helps students to decide on the accounting effects of transactions by thinking through the following steps:

1. **D**oes a transaction exist? Go to step 2 only if your answer is "yes."
2. **E**xamine it for the accounts affected. Put a name on what is given and received.
3. **C**lassify each account as asset (A), liability (L), or shareholders' equity (SE).
4. **I**dentify the direction and amount of the effects. By how much does each asset, liability, and shareholders' equity account increase or decrease?
5. **D**ebit and credit the accounts affected.
6. **E**nsure that the basic accounting equation still balances and that debits equal credits.
7. **S**ummarize the transaction effects in T-accounts.

The DECIDES model is introduced in Chapter 2, expanded in Chapter 3, and reinforced throughout the remaining chapters.

exhibit 2.7   Transaction Analysis: The DECIDES Approach

1. **D**oes a transaction exist?
2. **E**xamine it for accounts affected.
3. **C**lassify each account affected.
4. **I**dentify direction and amount.
5. **D**ebit and credit the accounts affected.
6. **E**nsure the equation still balances and debits = credits.
7. **S**ummarize the transaction effects in T-accounts.

End-of-chapter material...

The end-of-chapter material is traditionally where students go from reading to doing: answering review questions, solving problems, and wrestling with issues that help them to assimilate the material and apply it in a realistic context. *Fundamentals of Financial Accounting,* 2nd Canadian edition, doesn't see reading as a passive process—our pedagogy does more to maintain student interest and engagement than any competing book—so the end-of-chapter material offers a wealth of opportunities for students to connect to the material, and for you to enliven your class with a variety of assignments and discussion questions.

For Your Review:

Demonstration Cases, with Suggested Solutions directly after (or following)

Chapter Summary, cross-referenced with Learning Objectives and including page references

Key Terms, including page references

For Your Practice

Questions Students are likely to see these kinds of questions on tests and exams, so give them some practice with these quick checks of basic concepts.

Multiple-Choice Quizzes

Mini-Exercises Exercises which focus on one concept, or one learning objective. Cross-referenced to Learning Objectives.

Exercises More than one concept/Learning Objective. Cross-referenced to LOs.

Practise practise practise?

Problems With (and Without) the Coach's Help Instructors tell us how important decision-making skills are for students entering the accounting profession, and we have recognized this through an innovative approach to problem solving. Every chapter includes three problem sets: Coached Problems, Group A Problems, and Group B Problems. The **Coached Problems** advise students on the *process* of solving a problem rather than just its outcome. When students can solve the Coached Problems, they'll be ready to tackle the **Group A and Group B problems**, which echo the content without the advice offered by the Coach.

Skills Development Cases

Ethical Issues: The last decade has seen controversies that brought the ethics of the accounting profession to the forefront of public debate. Young people entering the business world, whether as accountants or other business majors, simply must have a strong ethical grounding, so two ethics cases are included in each chapter.

Team Cases: Every chapter also includes a team case that directs groups to search the Internet for companies to analyze, using the tools covered in that chapter. Students not only learn useful research skills, but gain valuable practice solving accounting problems in group settings.

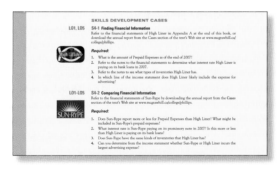

Annual Report Cases: There's no substitute for working on real-world data, so the 2007 Annual Report for High Liner Foods is reproduced in Appendix A. The end-of-chapter cases make extensive use of these data, showing students how to draw information from an annual report and providing them with a valuable perspective on how financial accounting information is used in decision-making.

Spreadsheets: Why do the same calculations over and over again when you can enter them once, and then just copy and paste? Every chapter includes one spreadsheet problem that allows students to skip the tedium of repetitive number-crunching and focus instead on "what if" analyses and interpretations. And don't worry if your students haven't had formal training with spreadsheets; each problem includes relaxed, student-friendly advice.

In partnership with Youthography, a Canadian youth research company, and hundreds of students from across Canada, McGraw-Hill Ryerson conducted extensive student research on student study habits, behaviours, and attitudes—we asked questions and listened … and we heard some things we didn't expect. We had two goals: to help faculty be more efficient in and out of the classroom by providing a study tool that would help them improve student engagement, and to help students learn their course material and get better grades. Through this research, we gained a better understanding of how students study—and how we could make vast improvements to our current online study tools. The result is a study tool that students overwhelming said is *better* and there's *nothing else like it out there*. *i*Study really is the first study tool built by students for students.

Getting better grades really is only a click away!

www.mcgrawhill.ca/olc/phillips/iStudy

Study Plan

An innovative tool that helps students customize their own learning experience. Students can diagnose their knowledge pre- and post-test, identify the areas where they are weak, search contents of the entire learning package for content specific to the topic they're studying, and add these resources to their study plan. Students told us the act of creating a study plan is how they actually study, and that having the opportunity to have everything in one place, with the ability to search, customize, and prioritize the class resources, was critical. Students told us, without a doubt, the "Study Plan" feature is the most valuable tool they have used to help them study.

eText

Now students can search the textbook online, too! When struggling with a concept or reviewing for an exam, students can conduct key word searches to find quickly the content they need, and text pages will appear for them to view.

Homework Assessment

*i*Study assessment activities don't stop with students. There is material for instructors to leverage as well. For Financial Accounting, this includes quizzes you can use in class, assign as homework, or add to exams.

Online Learning Centre resources: *www.mcgrawhill.ca/olc/phillips*

As your students study, they can visit the OLC and work with a multitude of helpful tools:

- Learning Objectives
- Links to focus companies and annual reports
- Excel templates for selected assignments (noted in the text by an icon in the margin)
- Quizzes

Lyryx Assessment for Financial Accounting.

A Complete Online Assessment System

LYRYX LEARNING INC
Online Learning and Assessment
lyryx.com

Lyryx Assessment for *Fundamentals of Financial Accounting*, 2nd Canadian Edition, is a Web-based teaching, learning, and assessment tool that has captured the attention of higher education institutions across the country while improving student success in financial accounting. The assessment takes the form of a homework assignment called a Lab, which corresponds to the chapters in the text.

The Labs are automatically graded, so students get instant scores and feedback—no need to wait until the next class to find out how well they did!

New Labs are randomly generated each time, providing the student with unlimited opportunities to try a type of question. After they submit a Lab for marking, students receive extensive feedback on their work, thus promoting their learning experience. Student motivation is high with these Labs, because they can be tied to assessment and they can be tried as many times as wanted prior to the due date, with only their best grade being recorded.

Instructors can create Labs of their choice by selecting problems from our test bank, and setting a deadline for each one. Instructors have access to all the students' marks, and can download the class grades at any time to analyze individual and class performance.

If students do their financial accounting practice and homework, they will improve their performance in the course. Recent research regarding the use of Lyryx has shown that when Labs are tied to assessment, even if worth only a small percentage of the total grade for the course, students will do their homework—and more than once!

Instructor Resources

Online Learning Centre for instructors www.mcgrawhill.ca/olc/phillips

A secured Instructor Resource Centre stores your essential course materials to save you prep time before class. Everything you need to run a lively classroom and an efficient course is included, and cross-referenced to the Learning Objectives in each chapter.

- **Downloadable Computerized Test Bank:**
This electronic test-generating engine is stocked with thousands of true/false, multiple choice, and short answer questions; generating quizzes and tests is as easy as clicking a mouse. All questions have been revised to reflect this new edition and technical-checked for accuracy. For secure online testing, exams can be exported to WebCT or Blackboard.

- **Microsoft® PowerPoint® Presentations:**
These offer a great visual complement to your lectures. A complete set of slides covers the key concepts presented in each chapter.

- **Instructors Manual:** This robust supplement is a definite asset to your own course. It follows the text, but adds in additional teaching tips, as well as further information about the subject. An effective addition to your teaching needs.

- **Solutions Manual:** Provides solutions for all end of chapter material.

- **Solutions to Excel Template assignments:**
Some problems include spreadsheet templates for students to work with. The solutions for all of these are included in the Instructor's Centre of the OLC.

iLearning Sales Specialist

Your Integrated Learning Sales Specialist is a McGraw-Hill Ryerson representative who has the experience, product knowledge, training, and support to help you assess and integrate any of our products, technology, and services into your course for optimum teaching and learning performance. Whether it's using our test banks software, helping students improve their grades, or putting your entire course online, your iLearning Sales Specialist is there to help you do it.

i-Learning
ADVANTAGE
McGraw-Hill Ryerson

Superior Service

Service takes on a whole new meaning with McGraw-Hill Ryerson and *Fundamentals of Financial Accounting*, Second Canadian Edition. More than just bringing you the textbook, we have raised the bar for innovation and educational research. These investments in learning and the academic community have helped us understand the needs of students and educators across the country, and allowed us to foster the growth of integrated learning.

Teaching, Technology, and Learning Conference Series

The educational environment has changed tremendously in recent years, and McGraw-Hill Ryerson continues to be committed to helping you acquire the skills you need to succeed in this new milieu. Our innovative Teaching, Technology, and Learning Conference Series brings faculty together from across Canada with 3M Teaching Excellence award winners to share teaching and learn best practices in a collaborative and stimulating environment. Pre-conference workshops on general topics, such as teaching large classes and technology integration, are also offered. We will also work with you at your own institution to customize workshops that best suit the needs of your faculty at your institution.

Primis Online

Primis Online gives you access to our resources in the best medium for your students: printed textbooks or electronic e-books. There are over 350,000 pages of content available from which you can create customized learning tools from our online database at www.mhhe.com/primis.

Course Management

Content cartridges are available for course management systems such as WebCT and Blackboard. These platforms provide instructors with user-friendly, flexible teaching tools. Please contact your iLearning Sales Specialist for details.

CourseSmart

CourseSmart brings together thousands of textbooks across hundreds of courses in an eTextbook format providing unique benefits to students and faculty. By purchasing an eTextbook, students can save up to 50 percent off the cost of a print textbook, reduce their impact on the environment, and gain access to powerful Web tools for learning, including full-text search, notes, and highlighting, and e-mail tools for sharing notes between classmates. For faculty, CourseSmart provides instant access to review and compare textbooks and course materials in their discipline area without the time, cost, and environmental impact of mailing print exam copies. For further details contact your iLearning Sales Specialist or go to www.coursesmart.com.

What's new in the 2nd Canadian Edition?

The financial statement figures for the focus companies in this text have been updated to the most recent numbers available at the time of writing (December 31, 2007 or later). We have expanded the end-of-chapter (EOC) material and this new edition includes over 200 examples of real Canadian and international companies. The accounting practices in this edition reflect generally-accepted accounting principles in Canada as of December 31, 2008. References to Canada's transition to IFRS by 2011 have been made where appropriate and at a level that reflects the introductory focus of the text.

Ch 1: Rewritten to include Mattel toy recalls in 2007. Added supplement on careers in accounting. Added epilogue on Conrad Black to Skills problem. Added four new problems. Updated dates for all companies and real company figures to most recent (December 31, 2006 or later) in EOC material.

Ch 2: Updated dates and story in text and EOC material. Updated numbers for real companies. Added one new problem.

Ch 3: Updated dates and story in text and EOC material. Made Exhibit 3.2 consistent with Exhibit 2.3. Updated fraud convictions (Exhibit 3.13), revised two coached problems and deleted cost of goods sold. Added one new comprehensive problem (E3-16).

Ch 4: Revised Exhibit 4.7 to refer students to other exhibits that show each step in the reporting phase. Updated dates and story in text and EOC material. Updated real company data to most recent numbers (December 31, 2006 or later). Added two new questions and three exercises.

Ch 5: Reorganized chapter to make topics flow more easily and to make connections among topics clearer. Changed focus and two comparison companies to Reitmans, Le Château, and Danier Leather. Rewrote story to accommodate new numbers, years, and companies. Expanded the discussion of accounting fraud. Made reference to SOX and its Canadian counterparts. Explained the role directors play in keeping information from being misstated. Moved vertical analysis from coached problems to chapter material. Changed Learning Objectives to reflect revisions. Added one question and one mini-exercise. Updated EOC material. Updated real company data to most recent numbers in EOC material (December 31, 2006 or later).

Ch 6: Changed title to Financial Reporting Controls for Merchandising Operations to better reflect the chapter coverage. Reorganized topics in chapter based on market feedback. Expanded discussion of internal control principles and fraud. Combined Learning Objectives 4&5. Updated real company data to most recent numbers in EOC material (December 31, 2006 or later); added five questions, three mini-exercises, one exercise.

Ch 7: Changed title to Reporting and Interpreting Receivables to better reflect chapter coverage. Expanded discussion of accrual accounting/matching for bad debts. Expanded discussion of write-offs and recoveries. Moved details of income smoothing to OLC. Updated dates and story in text and EOC material. Updated real company data to most recent numbers (December 31, 2006 or later). Added one new question, one mini-exercise, and two problems.

Ch 8: Changed title to Reporting and Interpreting Inventories to better reflect chapter coverage. Expanded discussion of inventory types and what to include in cost. Moved discussion of inventory errors from a supplement to the body of the chapter. Added an illustration that explains FOB terms. Updated dates and story in text and EOC material. Updated real company data to most recent numbers (December 31, 2006 or later). Added one new question and three mini-exercises.

Ch 9: Added discussion of expensing immaterial items. Now chapter shows amortization credited directly to intangible asset (no contra-account). Updated dates and story in text and EOC material. Updated real company data to most recent numbers (December 31, 2006 or later). Added one new question, two new exercises, three new problems, and added additional questions to three existing exercises.

Ch 10: Moved supplement on Straight-Line Amortization of Discounts and Premiums to OLC. Updated dates and story in text and EOC material. Updated real company data to most recent numbers (December 31, 2006 or later). Expanded discussion in many areas to improve clarity and links among topics in response to reviewers' comments. Added two new problems and one new skills development case.

Ch 11: Expanded discussion of forms of business organization. Added a section on Retained Earnings. Scaled back discussion of financial leverage and moved the calculations to the OLC. Updated dates and story in text and EOC material. Updated real company data to most recent numbers (December 31, 2006 or later). Added one new exercise, two new problems and one new skills development case.

Ch 12: Changed the introduction to relate to student cash flows. Changed Exhibit 12.1 to show only the headings of the three sections to make it easier for students to see. The complete SCF is shown later in Exhibit 12.10. Added the Chapter 1 definitions of the three business activities to the beginning of Chapter 12. Added 5 more Coach's Tips. Added a summary of all the steps in preparing the SCF. Updated dates and story in text and EOC material. Updated real company data to most recent numbers (December 31, 2006 or later). Added three new mini-exercises, one new exercise, and new requirements to six existing problems.

Ch 13: All financial data and information have been updated to reflect the 2007 Annual Report.

Acknowledgments

To the Second Canadian Edition

I am extremely grateful to all the reviewers who provided such valuable comments and suggestions for improvements to the first edition of this text. The whole process has been a rewarding and pleasurable experience, due in large part to the talents, commitment, and professionalism of the team at McGraw-Hill Ryerson, from the Sponsoring Editor, Rhondda McNabb, to the Developmental Editor, Suzanne Simpson Millar, and the production staff under the leadership of Graeme Powell. I am grateful to our copy editor, Carol Fordyce, and our technical checkers, Susan Cohlmeyer and Don Smith, whose careful attention to detail was so valuable, and to our illustrator, Rose Zgodzinski, whose playful illustrations give the text a special appeal. I am deeply grateful to all of you for your insights, your patience, and your dedication. Working with you was a real treat.

Also, to the authors of our supplemental material, we are thankful for your creativity, attention to detail, and accuracy. Sandra Daga, University of Toronto at Scarborough, has developed the ever-helpful Instructor's Manual once again. Jennifer Li, Brock University, has revised the Computerized Test Bank to ensure the right coverage, at the right level. All of which has then been technically-checked for accuracy by Ross Meacher. Penny Parker at Fanshawe College has been busy compiling all the student and instructor Excel templates for this edition, and University of Western Ontario professor Melissa Jean's PowerPoint lectures will be enjoyed by hundreds across the country. Also thanks to the two authors of this textbook's online study guide, iStudy: Angela Davis at University of Winnipeg, who leads and challenges students with the quiz material, and Carol Meissner from Georgian College, who uses her creative eye (and voice!) to keep pace with students' need for visual material to help learn accounting. Thanks go out to all.

Teresa Anderson

Reviewers for the Second Canadian Edition

Ron Baker, University of Regina
Paul Berry, Mount Allison University
Andrea Chance, George Brown College, University of Guelph
Gerry Dupont, Carleton University
George Gekas, Ryerson University
Colin Haime, Malaspina University College
Gordon Holyer, Malaspina University College
Melissa Jean, University of Western Ontario
Glen Kobussen, University of Saskatchewan
Walter Krystia, Ryerson University
Carol Meissner, Georgian College

Robert C. Nichols, Capilano College
John Siambanopoulos, University of Western Ontario
Glenys Sylvestre, University of Regina
Shu-Lun Wong, Memorial University of Newfoundland
Richard Wright, Fanshawe College

Reviewers for the Canadian Edition

Hilary Becker, Carleton University
Catherine Byers, Seneca College of Applied Arts & Technology
Sandra Daga, University of Toronto at Scarborough
Angela Davis, University of Winnipeg
Han Donker, University of Northern British Columbia
Ian Feltmate, Acadia University
Elizabeth Grasby, University of Western Ontario
Mahlon Harvey, University of Winnipeg
Gordon Holyer, Malaspina University-College
Rafik Kurji, Mount Royal College
Marie Madill-Payne, George Brown College
Muriel McKenna, Seneca College of Applied Arts & Technology
Shu-Lin Wong, Memorial University of Newfoundland
Elisa Zuliani, University of Toronto

To the U.S. Edition

We received invaluable input and support from present and former colleagues and students, in particular Jocelyn Allard, Anders Bergstrom, Shari Boyd, Kara Chase, Shana M. Clor, Nicole Dewan, Erin Ferguson, Aaron Ferrara, Robin Harrington, Lee Harris, Blair Healy, Carrie Hordichuk, Lorraine Hurst, Jennifer Johnson, Nancy Kirzinger, Paul Knepper, Deborah Loran, Diana Mark, Roger Martin, Jason Matshes, Jennifer Millard, Kimberley Olfert, Ryan Olson, David Pooler, Jessica Pothier, Emery Salahub, Bailey Schergevitch, Marie Tait, and Kory Wickenhauser.

We thank the extraordinary efforts of a talented group of individuals at McGraw-Hill/Irwin, including Stewart Mattson, our editorial director; Alics Harra, our sponsoring editor; Daniel Silverberg, director of marketing, Scott Bishop, our marketing manager, Kimberly Hooker, our developmental editor; Mary Conzachi, our project manager, Artermio Ortiz, our designer; Debra Sylvester, our production supervisor; Matthew Perry and Susan Lombard, our media project managers; Lori Kramer, our photo research coordinator; David Tietz, our photo researcher; and Marcy Lunetta, our permissions researcher, for her patience and persistance.

We also want to recognize the valuable input of all those who helped guide our developmental decisions.

CHAPTER 1

Reporting and Interpreting the Financial Results of Business Activities

Understand the basic activities of businesses.

LO1 Distinguish operating, investing, and financing activities.

Study how financial results are reported in financial statements.

LO2 Describe the purpose, set-up, and content of the four basic financial statements.

Evaluate results from the perspective of financial statement users.

LO3 Explain the primary goals of financial statement users.

Reconsider how financial statement reporting informs users' decision-making.

LO4 Describe the importance of ethics and reputation in accounting.

OUTSIDE LOOKING IN
INSIDE LOOKING OUT

In every chapter, we introduce a key accounting decision that is made inside a real-world company, and, later in the chapter, we show how people outside the company are affected by it. This chapter features Mattel, Inc., the company that makes toys and games that everyone has enjoyed at one time in their lives. As you will see in this chapter, this industry isn't child's play—toys are one of the riskiest of all businesses to manage.

It's never easy to break bad news to someone. Just how do you tell your best friend that you lost his car keys last night or that his girlfriend is planning to break up with him? You want to convince him that it won't happen again and that things will get better, but that's not going to be easy. It's also difficult to be in your friend's position on the receiving end of bad news, because it's tough to know for sure what happened and who's to blame.

The same thing is true in the business world. Just imagine the problems faced by the executives at **MATTEL, INC.,** the maker of Barbie® dolls and Hot Wheels® cars, in the last few years. In 2007, Mattel had to tell the public that they were recalling more than 20 million of their toys for safety reasons. A few years before that, they had to break the news to investors that their company had lost $431 million on an investment they had made. It's tough to convince investors that things aren't so bad when the company just lost more than a million dollars a day. Also imagine yourself on the other side of this news, as one of Mattel's investors. Would you be happy with these results? Would you believe what the executives were telling you? Would you think the sparkle had faded from Barbie's eyes and sell your shares? These are the kinds of questions that come up when reporting and interpreting the financial results of business activities.

Wait a second. Did you just skip over the inside/outside feature story for Mattel? We suspect that you're used to seeing stories like it in textbooks for other courses, and that you may even have developed a habit of skipping them in a rush to get to the "important" part of those courses. We urge you not to do so with the stories in this book because we frequently refer to them throughout the chapters, so skipping over them would be like arriving late to a movie. Plus, you'd miss one of the most interesting parts of accounting. The glimpse inside the company reveals some of the key decisions that accountants make and sets the stage for topics that will be discussed in greater detail in the chapter. The glance outside the company should help you to understand how business people use accounting information and why they consider it so important in their decision-making.

To complement this inside/outside approach, the text organizes its Learning Objectives (LO1–LO4) using the USER framework to provide the framework for each chapter. This USER framework, shown on the first page of each chapter, encourages students to Understand the business decisions that managers make, Study the accounting methods used to record these decisions, Evaluate the reported results from the viewpoint of financial statement users, and Reconsider how accounting and decision-making are linked.

Financial statements are reports that summarize the financial results of business activities.

As you read the first part of this chapter, which begins with a look inside Mattel, focus on understanding how and where the financial results of Mattel's business activities are presented in accounting reports called the **financial statements.** In the second part of the chapter, after you have learned about what is reported in the financial statements, we describe how outsiders use Mattel's financial statements to make important business decisions, such as determining whether to invest in or lend money to Mattel. In this part, your main goal should be to understand the information these **financial statement users,** as they are often called, use when making their decisions. At the end of the chapter, we'll return to Mattel's costly problems to let you test whether you understand how, on the inside, Mattel's managers deal with these problems in the company's financial statements, and how, on the outside, users use this financial statement information in their decision making.

Financial statement users are people who base their decisions, in part, on information reported in a company's financial statements.

UNDERSTAND _____
The Basic Activities of Businesses

Operating activities include day-to-day events involved in running a business.

THE DEVELOPMENT OF MATTEL'S BUSINESS

Mattel's history provides an interesting look at how a business can change in form as it grows. Its history also provides a good context for introducing the three main types of business activities: **operating, investing,** and **financing.** You will find that one of the first steps to understanding accounting is to start thinking about business activities in terms of these three main categories. When Mattel started out, its first steps were to raise money (a financing activity) and then buy manufacturing equipment (an investing activity). Only then could it begin to make and sell its toys (its operating activity). Look for the operating, investing, and financing activities in the following paragraph that describes how Mattel developed into an international toy monster.

Investing activities involve buying or selling long-term items such as land, buildings, and equipment.

Financing activities involve raising money from lenders and owners or paying it back.

Sole proprietorships are business organizations owned by one person who is personally liable for the debts of the business.

There are a number of different forms of business organization: the most common are **sole proprietorships,** partnerships, and corporations. The toy company that claims to sell a couple of Barbie dolls every second started its business in 1945 as a **partnership.** Two friends, Harold "Matt" Matson and Elliot Handler, combined their names, money, and artistic skills to form a business to produce picture frames and dollhouse furniture. Matt left the business soon after it was started and was replaced by Elliot's wife Ruth. With the picture frame business struggling and opportunities growing in the dollhouse business, the Handlers decided they needed to get serious about toys. They changed their business from a partnership to a **corporation** in 1948, and borrowed money from a bank to expand their company. After a decade of satisfactory but not stellar performance, Mattel struck it big in 1959 with the introduction of Barbie. She

Partnerships are business organizations owned by two or more people. Each partner is often personally liable for debts that the partnership cannot pay.

Corporations operate as businesses separate from their owners. Owners of corporations (often called shareholders) are not personally responsible for debts of the corporation.

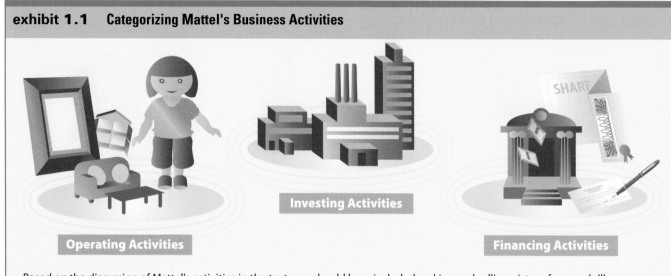

exhibit 1.1   Categorizing Mattel's Business Activities

Operating Activities

Investing Activities

Financing Activities

Based on the discussion of Mattel's activities in the text, you should have included making and selling picture frames, dollhouse furniture, and toys as operating activities. Investing activities would have included the purchase of production facilities during Mattel's expansion. Mattel's financing activities consisted of borrowing money from the bank, and obtaining money from investors in exchange for a share in the ownership of the business.

was an instant success, selling over 350,000 dolls in the first year, and eventually became an icon in North American pop culture. The Handlers quickly realized that Mattel needed to expand the production facilities to try to keep up with growing worldwide toy demand. The money for financing the expansion this time didn't come from a bank loan. Instead, Elliot and Ruth decided Mattel should become a **public company,** which attracted hordes of investors who gave money to Mattel in exchange for a share of its ownership.

Like most public companies, Mattel started out small but continually evolved from one type of business organization to another. As the business grew, so did the variety of its activities. Were you able to slot the business activities into their operating, investing, and financing categories? Check whether you were on track by reading Exhibit 1.1.

In reality, companies like Mattel become involved in hundreds of different types of operating, investing, and financing activities. Rather than bombard you with all possible examples in this course, we'll stick to the main business activities that affect almost all of today's companies. Although we'll focus on how these activities affect the company in terms of dollars and cents, we don't want you to get the impression that this financial information is all that matters. In fact, to run a company successfully, business managers also need information about other aspects of their business, such as how much time Mattel's production line takes to roll out a Magic 8 Ball®. To ensure this other information is available, most modern businesses install sophisticated computer systems (called accounting information systems, or, more broadly, management information systems) that monitor business activities in both financial and nonfinancial terms. This information then is reported in either the financial statements or other reports.

Exhibit 1.2 shows how these different aspects of **accounting** fit together and what courses you'll take to learn more about them. Accounting Information Systems courses focus on how to design systems to capture and report the information that is needed in financial statements and other accounting reports. Financial Accounting courses (like this one) focus on preparing and using the financial statements that are made available by public companies to anyone who's interested in reading them. Managerial Accounting courses focus on other accounting reports that are not released to the general public, but instead are prepared and used by accountants and managers who run the business.

Public companies have their shares bought and sold on stock exchanges. (Private companies' shares are bought and sold privately.)

COACH'S TIP

Researchers have found that people learn more from exhibits when they look at the pictures in them, then read the explanations in their captions, and then look again at the pictures.

Accounting is the process of capturing and reporting the results of a business's operating, investing, and financing activities.

POINT OF INTEREST

Accounting has been around for over 6,000 years. The ancient civilization of Mesopotamia used clay tablets for record-keeping.

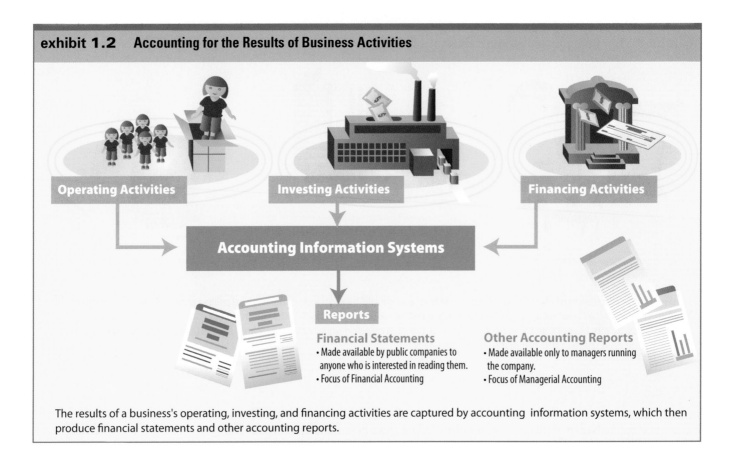

exhibit 1.2   Accounting for the Results of Business Activities

Operating Activities   **Investing Activities**   **Financing Activities**

Accounting Information Systems

Reports

Financial Statements
- Made available by public companies to anyone who is interested in reading them.
- Focus of Financial Accounting

Other Accounting Reports
- Made available only to managers running the company.
- Focus of Managerial Accounting

The results of a business's operating, investing, and financing activities are captured by accounting information systems, which then produce financial statements and other accounting reports.

STUDY _____

How Financial Results Are Reported in Financial Statements

FINANCIAL STATEMENTS

The term "financial statements" typically refers to the following four accounting reports:

1. Balance Sheet
2. Income Statement
3. Statement of Retained Earnings
4. Statement of Cash Flows

COACH'S TIP

The balance sheet is also known as the statement of financial position. The income statement is also known as the statement of income, the statement of operations, the statement of earnings, or the statement of profit and loss.

One of the most confusing things for people first learning about accounting (or anything new, for that matter) is that different people use different terms to mean exactly the same thing. We will avoid doing this, but we can't stop others from doing it. So look to the coach for help with interpreting alternative names that people use in accounting.

Financial statements can be prepared at any time during the year, although they are most commonly prepared monthly, every three months (known as *quarterly reports*), and at the end of the year (known as *annual reports*). Companies are allowed to choose any date for the end of their accounting (or *fiscal*) year. Mattel chose a December 31 year-end because this is the start of its slow business period. Fewer toys are sold in January through May than in the first three weeks of December. Hudson's Bay Company (HBC), Canada's oldest corporation and its largest department store chain, ends its financial year on January 31, after its post-holiday clear-out sales are finished.

COACH'S TIP

Rather than memorizing detailed definitions for every financial statement item, try to understand the purpose, set-up, and content of the four basic financial statements.

Each of the four statements has a specific and unique purpose, so we will begin by studying them one at a time. Later you will see how the four statements fit together, but for now just focus on learning what goes into each individual financial statement. Specifically, look for the answers to these questions:

a. **Purpose.** What is each statement attempting to explain?

b. **Set-up.** How is the information on each statement organized?

c. **Content.** What kind of information is found on each statement?

Remember that this chapter is intended to provide an overview of financial statements, so focus on the "big picture." You will have the opportunity to learn details about specific financial statement items when we discuss them in depth in Chapters 2 through 5.

1. The Balance Sheet

a. **Purpose.** The balance sheet reports *at a point in time* what a business owns (**assets**), what it owes to outsiders (**liabilities**), and what is left over for the owners of the company's shares (**shareholders' equity**). In effect, the balance sheet asks, Does a business have enough resources to pay its bills and still have something left for its owners? The business itself, not the individual shareholders who own the business, is viewed as owning the assets and owing the liabilities on its balance sheet. This is also the idea behind the **separate entity** assumption, which requires that a business's balance sheet include the assets, liabilities, and shareholders' equity of only that business and not those of the shareholders. In accounting language, assets are the resources owned by the business, and liabilities and shareholders' equity represent the claims that interested parties have over the assets. These claims exist because the interested parties have provided the financing for the business to buy the assets.

> **Assets** are the resources (things of value) owned by a business.
>
> **Liabilities** are amounts owed by the business.
>
> **Shareholders' equity** is the amount invested in the business by its owners.
>
> The **separate entity** assumption states that the financial statements of a company are assumed to include the results of only that company's business activities.

b. **Set-up.** The balance sheet, like the other three basic financial statements, starts with a *heading* that answers three questions: (*i*) who—the name of the company, (*ii*) what—the name of the financial statement, and (*iii*) when—the date of the financial statement. The heading is followed by a *body* that lists dollar amounts for various aspects of the business. The body of every balance sheet contains three interrelated parts: assets, liabilities, and shareholders' equity. The relationship that unites these three parts of the balance sheet is often called the **basic accounting equation,** and it is represented by the following:

> The **basic accounting equation** is A = L + SE.

The body of the balance sheet always shows that assets equal liabilities plus shareholders' equity. This basic accounting equation is true by definition because each asset on the balance sheet has been financed by either **creditors** or shareholders. Financing provided by creditors creates a liability. Financing provided by shareholders creates shareholders' equity.

> **Creditors** are those to whom a business owes money.

c. **Content.** Now that you know the purpose and set-up for the balance sheet, you can probably predict its content. The balance sheet should have a heading that is followed by a body, which lists the business's assets, liabilities, and shareholders' equity at a particular point in time. You can learn lots about the balance sheet just by reading it from the top. As you read the following paragraphs, glance at Mattel's balance sheet in Exhibit 1.3, which we have adapted from the "investors" section of Mattel's Web site at www.mattel.com.

The heading indicates *who* (Mattel, Inc.), *what* (Balance Sheet), and *when* (At December 31, 2007). The balance sheet is like a snapshot indicating the financial position of a company at a particular point in time. Like most big companies, our Mattel example in Exhibit 1.3 rounds to the nearest million dollars, which involves dropping the last six digits.

---

exhibit 1.3   **Sample Balance Sheet and Explanation of Items**

MATTEL, INC.
Balance Sheet
At December 31, 2007

Who: Name of the business
What: Title of the statement
When: Accounting period (at a point in time)

Assets

	(in millions)	
Cash	$ 901	The amount of cash in the company's bank accounts
Accounts Receivable	991	Amounts owed to Mattel by customers for prior credit sales
Inventories	429	Toys being made and finished toys ready to be sold
Property, Plant, and Equipment	519	Land, factories, and production machinery
Other Assets	1,965	Trademarks, brand names, and other assets bought by Mattel
Total Assets	**$4,805**	Total must equal total liabilities and shareholders' equity below.

Liabilities

Accounts Payable	$1,570	Amounts owed by Mattel for prior purchases on credit
Notes Payable	928	Amounts owed based on written debt contracts
Total Liabilities	2,498	

Shareholders' Equity

Contributed Capital	505	Amounts invested in the business by shareholders
Retained Earnings	1,802	Past earnings minus past distributions to shareholders
Total Shareholders' Equity	2,307	
Total Liabilities and Shareholders' Equity	$4,805	Total must equal total assets above.

Accounts are records that summarize the items a company wants to keep track of, such as its cash.

COACH'S TIP

Assets are listed on the balance sheet in order of how quickly they are used up or converted into cash. This is called order of liquidity.

Let's move on to the body of the balance sheet, focusing first on the Assets section. The five items listed there are common names that many companies use to describe the assets that they own and use in their business activities. If these **accounts,** as they are often called, don't adequately describe the company's assets, then the list would be expanded.

Assets.   The first three assets (*Cash*, *Accounts Receivable*, and *Inventories*) relate to Mattel's main operating activities. The amount shown for the *Cash* account indicates that Mattel has over $900 million in its bank accounts (remember that the amounts in the exhibit are rounded to the nearest million dollars, so $901 is actually $901,000,000). The second asset account, *Accounts Receivable*, indicates the total amount of money that Mattel expects to collect from its customers for toys it has sold on credit. Think of this as an IOU that gives Mattel the right to collect cash from customers in the future. The third asset account, *Inventories*, reports the cost of all toys that Mattel has on hand.

Mattel's remaining asset accounts relate to its investing activities. The fourth asset account listed, *Property, Plant, and Equipment,* indicates that Mattel has invested a great deal of money in the land, factories, and production machinery that are used to make toys. The final asset shown, *Other Assets*, is a catch-all that includes a variety of assets, including trademarks and brand names (like View-Master® and Matchbox®) that Mattel has bought from other companies. The figures shown for *Property, Plant, and Equipment* and *Other Assets* are the cost of the assets less an amount for wear and tear and general decline in usefulness. How that amount is calculated is discussed in Chapter 9.

Liabilities. Financing for Mattel to buy its assets has come from liabilities and share-holders' equity. Under the Liabilities category, Mattel's balance sheet in Exhibit 1.3 lists two items. *Accounts Payable* includes amounts owed to other companies for purchases of goods or services on credit. For example, when Mattel buys the material for Barbie's hair, which is the very same as that used to make Saran Wrap™,[1] it doesn't pay cash upfront. Instead, Mattel promises to pay within a short interest-free period of 60 days or less. The amount owed is included in accounts payable. If Mattel were to need a longer period of time to pay, the accounts payable could be converted to *Notes Payable*—the next liability listed on Mattel's balance sheet. Notes payable are like accounts payable except that they (*a*) are not interest-free, (*b*) will not be paid as soon as accounts payable, and (*c*) are documented using formal written debt contracts known as "notes." So, if your friend buys a DVD for you with the understanding that you'll pay her back right away, you would have an account payable. If you arrange and sign for a car loan through your bank, you would have a note payable.

Shareholders' Equity. The Shareholders' Equity section of the balance sheet is called *shareholders'* equity to emphasize that Mattel is a corporation owned by shareholders. This section lists two accounts, both of which represent financing provided by share-holders. *Contributed Capital* reports the amount of cash injected into the business by shareholders who bought shares directly from the company. *Retained Earnings* represents the company's total earnings (and losses) less all **dividends** paid to the shareholders since the formation of the corporation. We'll discuss this account in more detail later in this chapter when we get to the statement of retained earnings.

Dividends are payments a company periodically makes to its shareholders as a return on their investment.

HOW'S IT GOING? A Self-Study Quiz

1. Mattel's *assets* are listed in one section of the balance sheet and *liabilities* and *shareholders' equity* are in other sections. Notice that, according to the basic accounting equation, these sections must balance. In the following chapters, you will learn that this basic accounting equation is the main building block for the entire accounting process. Your task in this quiz is to show that Mattel's reported assets of $4,805 (million) are correct, by using the numbers for liabilities and shareholders' equity presented in Exhibit 1.3. Fill in the blanks in the basic accounting equation:

$$\textbf{Assets} = \textbf{Liabilities} + \textbf{Shareholders' Equity}$$
$$\$4,805 = \boxed{} + \boxed{}$$

(amounts rounded to the nearest million)

2. Learning which items belong in each of the balance sheet categories is an important first step in understanding their meaning. Without referring to Exhibit 1.3, mark each balance sheet item in the following list with letters to show it as an <u>A</u>sset, <u>L</u>iability, or <u>S</u>hareholders' Equity account.

☐	Accounts Payable	☐	Inventories
☐	Accounts Receivable	☐	Property, Plant, and Equipment
☐	Cash	☐	Notes Payable
☐	Contributed Capital	☐	Retained Earnings

When working on these questions, cover up the solutions in the margin with your thumb. After you're finished, check the answers in the margin.

COACH'S TIP

If you're thinking of leaving out the self-study quiz just to "get through" the chapter, don't. The best way to know whether you've been reading the chapter carefully enough is to see how well you do on the self-study quiz.

Quiz Answers
1. Assets $4,805 = Liabilities $2,498 + Shareholders' Equity $2,307.
2. Column 1: L, A, A, SE; Column 2: A, A, L, SE.

2. THE INCOME STATEMENT

a. **Purpose.** In the same way that your personal tax return shows how much you made during the year, the income statement reports whether a business made a profit (**net income**) from selling goods and providing services (**revenues**) after subtracting the costs of doing business (**expenses**). The income statement summarizes these financial results *over a particular time period*, such as one month, a quarter (three months), or an entire year.

b. **Set-up.** Like the balance sheet, the income statement starts with a heading that shows *who*, *what*, and *when*. Following this is a body, which reports the various operating activities of the business along with related dollar amounts. These operating activities are classified as revenues or expenses. The amount by which revenues exceed expenses is reported as net income. (It's called a net loss if expenses are greater than revenues.) These three main parts of the income statement are connected through the following relationship:

Revenues   −   Expenses   =   Net Income

c. **Content.** As you can see from Exhibit 1.4, the heading of the income statement indicates that it covers a period of time ("For the Year Ended"). This means that the net income of $600 million shown in the body is the amount by which Mattel's revenues exceeded its expenses during the period from January 1 through December 31, 2007. The specific types of revenues and expenses reported in the body of the income statement depend on the nature of the business, as discussed below.

Revenues. Mattel's (adapted) income statement in Exhibit 1.4 reports only one type of revenue (*Sales*), which implies they only sell goods. If you were to look instead at Blockbuster's income statement, you would see three types of revenues: movie rentals, merchandise sales, and the ever-mysterious "other revenues." The main rule of all reported revenues, whether they relate to Blockbuster's DVD rentals or Mattel's sales of Survivor™ games, is that revenues are reported when the product or service is given to a customer *whether or not they are paid for in that period*. Some companies may collect cash at the time a sale is made, like when Blockbuster rents you a video, but others do not (such as when Mattel sells toys to The Bay on credit). Either way, revenues include all sales (cash and credit) made during the period.

Expenses. In addition to sales revenue, we see from Mattel's income statement in Exhibit 1.4 that its operating activities result in several types of expenses, which are the costs of running the business. The biggest expense is the $3.2 billion cost of making the toys that were sold in 2007 (called *Cost of Goods Sold Expense*). Another big expense for Mattel was the $709 million in *Advertising and Promotion Expenses*. It's pretty easy for Mattel to run up costs like this because it sells about 100 different lines of toys, and a single full-page ad for only one product in a popular magazine can cost over $75,000. We could go on, but you probably already get the point: companies, like Mattel, have to take on many different kinds of expenses in order to generate revenues. All expenses are reported on the income statement.

Throughout this course, you will learn that some expenses involve immediate cash payments, while others involve payments at a later date. Expenses also can arise from selling or using assets that have been paid for in a prior period. We'll sort through all of

---

exhibit 1.4   Sample Income Statement and Explanation of Items

MATTEL, INC. Income Statement For the Year Ended December 31, 2007		*Who:* Name of the business *What:* Title of the statement *When:* Accounting period (for the year)
	(in millions)	
Revenues		
Sales Revenue	$5,970	Revenue earned from selling toys
Total Revenues	5,970	
Expenses		
Cost of Goods Sold Expense	3,193	Costs to make the toys that were sold
Advertising and Promotion Expenses	709	Expenses to run ads and provide coupons
Other Selling and Administrative Expenses	1,338	Expenses to sell toys and manage the business
Interest Expense	27	Cost of using borrowed funds
Income Tax Expense	103	Cost of taxes charged on income earned
Total Expenses	5,370	Total of all expenses
Net Income	**$ 600**	Total of all revenues minus all expenses

this in Chapters 2 to 4, but for now you should note that expenses are reported in the same period in which they help to generate revenues *whether or not they are paid for in cash during that period.*

HOW'S IT GOING? A Self-Study Quiz

1. Learning which items belong in each of the income statement categories is an important first step in understanding their meaning. Without referring to Exhibit 1.4, mark each income statement item in the following list with a letter to indicate whether it is a <u>R</u>evenue or an <u>E</u>xpense.

   ☐ Cost of goods sold   ☐ Sales

   ☐ Advertising and promotion   ☐ Selling and administrative

2. During 2007, Mattel delivered toys for which customers paid or promised to pay amounts totalling $5,970 (million). During the same period, it collected $5,986 (million) in cash from its customers. Without referring to Exhibit 1.4, pick which of these two amounts will be shown on Mattel's income statement as *sales revenue* for 2007. Why did you pick this answer?

3. During 2007, Mattel *produced* toys with a total cost of production of $3,176 (million). During the same period, it *delivered* to customers toys that cost a total of $3,193 (million) to produce. Without referring to Exhibit 1.4, pick which of the two numbers will be shown on Mattel's income statement as *cost of goods sold expense* for 2007. Why did you pick this answer?

   After you're finished, check your answers with the solutions in the margin.

Net Income.   To understand how successful Mattel was in generating a profit from its business operations, we need to consider both the revenues and the expenses at the same time. *Net Income* does this by meshing revenues and expenses into a single number. This combined (or "net") number indicates whether the inflow of resources from making sales (revenues) was greater or less than the outflow of resources (expenses) to generate those sales. In Mattel's case in 2007, the net income (or "bottom line") was $600 million. Nice.

3. The Statement of Retained Earnings

a.   **Purpose.** The statement of retained earnings shows the amount of earnings that have been retained in the business and the amount of the company's resources paid out to shareholders as dividends.

b.   **Set-up.** As shown in Exhibit 1.5, Mattel's (adapted) statement of retained earnings has the customary heading and is followed by a body that reports the way that net income and dividends affected the company's financial position during the accounting period. The equation for the statement of retained earnings is:

A **dividend** is said to be **declared** when a company formally promises to pay out some of its resources to its owners.

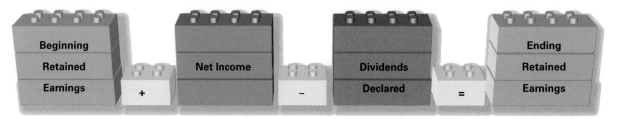

Net income earned during the period increases the retained earnings balance. When a company **declares** dividends during the period, *Retained Earnings* decreases.

c.   **Content.** The statement begins with Mattel's beginning-of-year *Retained Earnings* balance of $1,477 million. This beginning balance indicates the total net income of the company that has not been distributed to shareholders, added up from when the corporation was formed in 1948 to the beginning of the current year. The current year's *Net Income* of $600 million (which we saw earlier on the income statement in Exhibit 1.4) is then added to the beginning retained earnings balance. The next line subtracts *Dividends* totalling $275 million that were declared in 2007 to be paid to shareholders. The last line reports the new end-of-year retained earnings balance, which for Mattel was $1,802 million at December 31, 2007.

COACH'S TIP

Notice that dividends are reported in the statement of retained earnings, not the income statement. Dividends are not an expense. They are a distribution of profits to shareholders.

Notice that the ending retained earnings balance in Exhibit 1.5 is the same as the amount reported for *Retained Earnings* on Mattel's balance sheet in Exhibit 1.3. Thus, the

---

exhibit 1.5   Sample Statement of Retained Earnings and Explanation of Items

<table>
<tr><td colspan="2" align="center">MATTEL, INC.
Statement of Retained Earnings
For the Year Ended December 31, 2007</td><td>*Who:* Name of the business
What: Title of the statement
When: Accounting period (for the year)</td></tr>
<tr><td></td><td align="center">(in millions)</td><td></td></tr>
<tr><td>Retained Earnings, January 1, 2007</td><td align="center">$1,477</td><td>Balance carried forward from previous year</td></tr>
<tr><td>Net Income for 2007</td><td align="center">600</td><td>"Bottom line" from the income statement</td></tr>
<tr><td>Dividends Declared for 2007</td><td align="center">(275)</td><td>Declared distributions to shareholders</td></tr>
<tr><td>Retained Earnings, December 31, 2007</td><td align="center">$1,802</td><td>Balance at the end of this year</td></tr>
</table>

statement of retained earnings shows how the income statement (and net income, in particular) links to the balance sheet (and retained earnings). We'll talk about this link in more detail later in this chapter.

4. The Statement of Cash Flows

a. **Purpose.** Most people are keenly interested in monitoring the balance in their own bank accounts, often asking questions such as: Why do I have only $23 left? Didn't my paycheque get deposited? Where did I spend all that money? These are precisely the kinds of questions that a statement of cash flows answers. The purpose of the statement of cash flows is to summarize how a business's operating, investing, and financing activities caused its cash balance to change over a particular period of time.

b. **Set-up.** The statement of cash flows contains the now-familiar heading and a body. The body, unlike your personal bank statement, classifies cash increases (inflows) and decreases (outflows) into the three categories of business activities (operating, investing, and financing). As you can see from Mattel's (adapted) statement of cash flows in Exhibit 1.6, cash inflows are shown as positive numbers and cash outflows appear as negative numbers (i.e., in parentheses). A subtotal (called *net cash flow*) is reported at the bottom of each of the three main categories, and these three subtotals are added together to yield a total *Net Change in Cash*. When this total change is added to the *Beginning-of-Year Cash* balance, an *End-of-Year Cash* balance pops out. This end-of-year cash balance is precisely the amount reported for the asset account *Cash* on the balance sheet.

COACH'S TIP

Negative amounts are reported in parentheses in the financial statements. The Statement of Cash Flows presented in Exhibit 1.6 has been prepared using a format called the Direct Method. As you will learn in Chapter 12, there is another common format for the statement, called the Indirect Method. The direct method is presented here because students usually find it easier to understand.

---

exhibit 1.6   Sample Statement of Cash Flows and Explanation of Items

MATTEL, INC.
Statement of Cash Flows
For the Year Ended December 31, 2007

Who: Name of the business
What: Title of the statement
When: Accounting period (for the year)

	(in millions)	
Cash Flows from Operating Activities		
Cash collected from customers	$5,986	
Cash paid to suppliers and employees	(3,505)	
Cash paid for other operating activities	(1,921)	
Net cash flow from operating activities	560	Cash flow from making and selling toys
Cash Flows from Investing Activities		
Cash paid to purchase equipment and other assets	(286)	
Cash received from selling equipment and other assets	1	
Net cash flow from investing activities	(285)	Cash flow from buying/selling long-term assets
Cash Flows from Financing Activities		
Cash paid on notes payable and other financing	(307)	
Cash paid for dividends	(272)	
Net cash flow from financing activities	(579)	Cash flow from dealings with lenders/shareholders
Net Change in Cash during the Year	(304)	Change in cash (560 – 285 – 579)
Cash at Beginning of Year	1,205	Last period's ending cash balance
Cash at End of Year	$ 901	This period's ending cash on the balance sheet

c. **Content.** *Cash Flows from Operating Activities* are cash flows that are directly related to earning income. For example, when The Bay and other customers pay Mattel for the toys delivered to them, the statement of cash flows lists the amounts collected as "cash collected from customers." From the first line of the operating activities section of the statement of cash flows in Exhibit 1.6, you can see that Mattel received nearly $6 billion in cash from its customers during 2007. When Mattel pays salaries to its employees at its Design Centre, or pays bills received from supply companies like Dow Chemical, the statement of cash flows includes the amounts as "cash paid to suppliers and employees," as shown in the second line of the operating activities section. Other cash outflows for operating activities are shown in a similar manner.

Cash Flows from Investing Activities include cash flows related to the acquisition or sale of the company's long-term assets. Exhibit 1.6 reports only one cash outflow from investing activities, the purchase of additional tools, properties, and equipment to meet growing demand for Mattel's toys. The company also reported a cash inflow of $1 million, which it received from selling some equipment and other long-term assets.

Cash Flows from Financing Activities are directly related to financing the company itself. These cash flows involve receiving money from or paying money back to lenders and shareholders. We see from Exhibit 1.6 that Mattel paid down $307 million of its notes payable and other financing, and it also paid out $272 million in dividends to shareholders in 2007.

HOW'S IT GOING?   A Self-Study Quiz

1. During 2007, Mattel delivered toys to customers who paid or promised to pay amounts totalling $5,970 (million). During the same period, Mattel collected $5,986 (million) in cash from its customers. Without referring to Exhibit 1.6, indicate which of the two amounts will be shown on Mattel's cash flow statement for 2007.

2. Learning which items belong in each cash flow statement category is an important first step in understanding their meaning. Without referring to Exhibit 1.6, use a letter to mark each item in the following list as a cash flow from <u>O</u>perating, <u>I</u>nvesting, or <u>F</u>inancing activities. **Put parentheses around the letter if it is a cash *outflow* and use no parentheses if it's an *inflow*.**

☐ Cash paid to suppliers and employees	☐ Cash paid to purchase equipment
☐ Cash paid on note payable	☐ Cash collected from customers
☐ Cash paid for dividends	☐ Cash received from selling equipment

After you're finished, check your answers with the solutions in the margin.

Relationships among the Four Basic Financial Statements

The goal for this section is to show how the four statements fit together. Exhibit 1.7 presents one way to picture this, by reminding you that a balance sheet reports a snapshot of the company at a *point* in time whereas the other three statements cover a *period* of time. Think of the balance sheet on December 31, 2006, as the starting point for 2007, and the other three statements as explanations of what happened during the year (2007), ending on December 31, 2007, with a new balance sheet that presents an updated picture of the company.

In the real world, most companies do, in fact, present balance sheets which provide figures for the two points in time shown in Exhibit 1.7. Rather than create two separate reports, though, they report the data from two years by using two columns of numbers on a single report. One column displays the balances at the end of the previous period (which is the starting point for the current period), and the other displays balances at

COACH'S TIP

Learning how the four statements fit together is very important. Slow down and spend a little extra time on the next couple of pages.

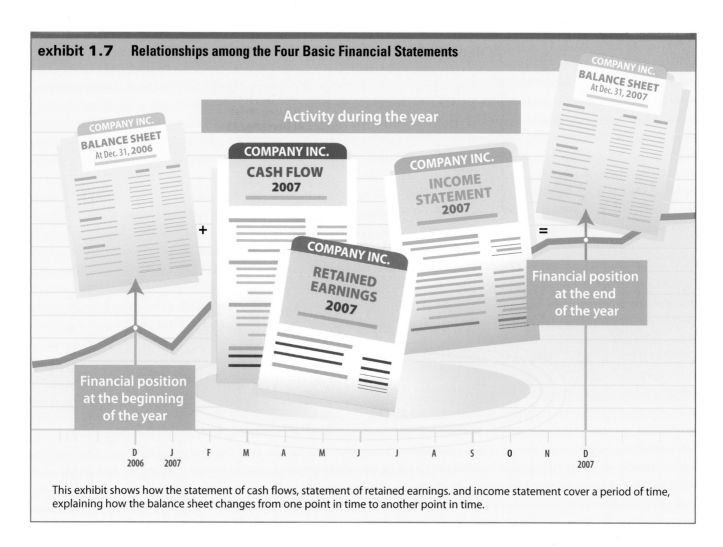

exhibit 1.7   Relationships among the Four Basic Financial Statements

This exhibit shows how the statement of cash flows, statement of retained earnings. and income statement cover a period of time, explaining how the balance sheet changes from one point in time to another point in time.

the end of the current period. An example of this **comparative** balance sheet format is shown in Exhibit 1.8. This comparative balance sheet acts as our starting point for showing how the financial statements connect together in the real world.

Think of actually splitting the balance sheet apart to form two points on a timeline, with one end on the far left side of the page and the other on the far right. Imagine that, for *Cash* and *Retained Earnings*, there are lines linking their beginning and ending balance sheet amounts. If you click on the cash link, the statement of cash flows would pop up, showing how the cash balance changed during the year. If you click on the retained earnings link, the statement of retained earnings would pop up, showing how the retained earnings balance changed during the year. If you were to click on the net income number within the statement of retained earnings, the income statement would pop up, explaining how the company's operations improved or harmed Mattel's financial position during the year. Exhibit 1.9 shows the end result of these clicks and pop-ups.

In addition to the four reports that we've just described, the financial statements include two additional parts that you should know about: assurance statements and notes to the financial statements.

Assurance Statements

There are two assurance statements that generally appear directly before the four financial statements in a company's annual report:

1. *The Management's Statement of Responsibility for Financial Reporting* states that management is responsible for the integrity of the information contained in the statements and that they have taken steps to ensure that they can stand behind them.

Comparative financial statements report numbers for two or more periods to make it easy for users to compare account balances from one period to the next.

POINT OF INTEREST

If you want to see what these assurance statements look like, refer to Appendix A at the back of this book.

COACH'S TIP

Financial statements are prepared using common formatting styles:

- List assets in order of ease of conversion to cash.
- List liabilities in order of their due dates.
- Place a dollar sign next to the first dollar amount listed.
- Place a single underline below the last item in a group before a subtotal or total (e.g., total shareholders' equity).
- Place a double underline below and a dollar sign beside totals for complete groups (e.g., total assets).

exhibit 1.8   Comparative Balance Sheet

MATTEL, INC.
Balance Sheet
At December 31

	(in millions)	
Assets	**2007**	**2006**
Cash	$901	$1,205
Accounts Receivable	991	944
Inventories	429	383
Property, Plant, and Equipment	519	537
Other Assets	1,965	1,887
Total Assets	$4,805	$4,956
Liabilities		
Accounts Payable	$1,570	1,583
Notes Payable	928	940
Total Liabilities	2,498	2,523
Shareholders' Equity		
Contributed Capital	505	956
Retained Earnings	1,802	1,477
Total Shareholders' Equity	2,307	2,433
Total Liabilities and Shareholders' Equity	$4,805	$4,956

2. *The Independent Auditors' Report* states that external accountants, who are independent of management and are called auditors, have examined the statements and believe that they follow the rules of accounting.

Notes to the Financial Statements

Notes provide additional information about the financial condition of a company, without which the financial statements cannot be fully understood.

The **notes** to the financial statements (or "footnotes") appear on the pages immediately *after* the four financial statements.

There are three types of financial statement notes:

1. *Accounting policies.* This type of note describes the accounting decisions that were made when preparing financial statements. For example, Mattel's accounting policy note for advertising and promotion describes how (and when) these costs are reported in Mattel's financial statements.

2. *Contents included.* This type of note presents additional detail about what's included in certain financial statement account balances. For example, Mattel's notes tell us that its "other assets" include the costs of trademarks and brand names.

3. *Additional information.* The third type of note provides additional financial disclosures about items not listed on the statements themselves. For example, Mattel rents warehouse space, and the terms of these rental agreements (also known as leases) are disclosed in a note.

We've covered a lot of material to this point in the chapter. Exhibit 1.10 on page 16 summarizes the main points for each of the four basic financial statements. Notice that the fourth column provides examples of items included in each financial statement. For more formal definitions of these financial statement items, see the key terms presented in the margins of this chapter.

COACH'S TIP

Unlike the footnotes in some articles and books, which you might gloss over, don't overlook the footnotes to the financial statements.

exhibit 1.9 Linking the Four Basic Statements

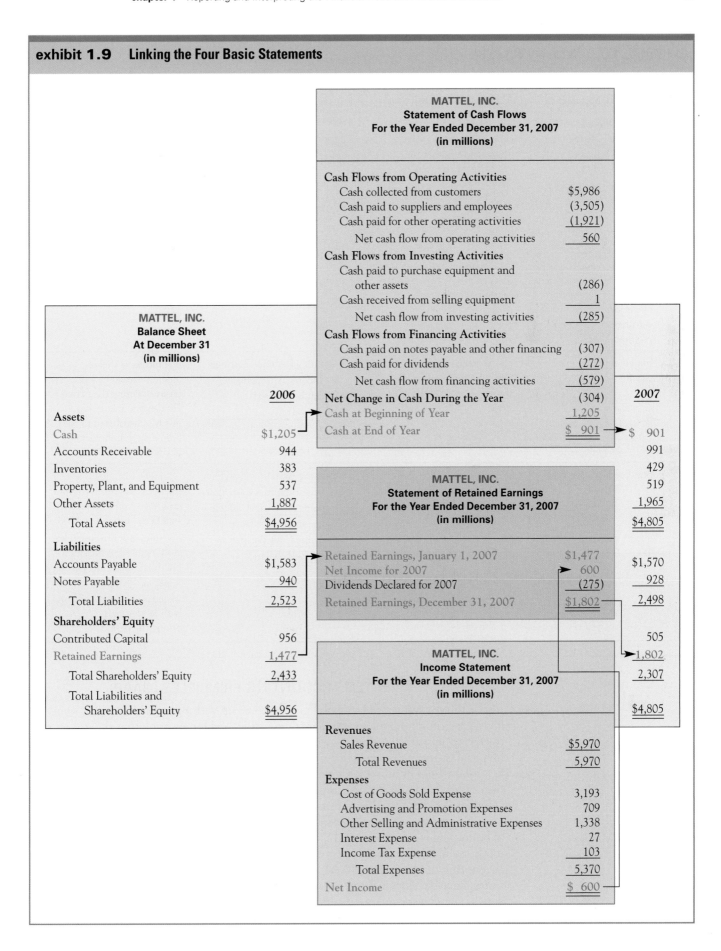

MATTEL, INC.
Statement of Cash Flows
For the Year Ended December 31, 2007
(in millions)

Cash Flows from Operating Activities
Cash collected from customers	$5,986
Cash paid to suppliers and employees	(3,505)
Cash paid for other operating activities	(1,921)
Net cash flow from operating activities	560

Cash Flows from Investing Activities
Cash paid to purchase equipment and other assets	(286)
Cash received from selling equipment	1
Net cash flow from investing activities	(285)

Cash Flows from Financing Activities
Cash paid on notes payable and other financing	(307)
Cash paid for dividends	(272)
Net cash flow from financing activities	(579)
Net Change in Cash During the Year	(304)
Cash at Beginning of Year	1,205
Cash at End of Year	$ 901

MATTEL, INC.
Balance Sheet
At December 31
(in millions)

	2006	2007
Assets		
Cash	$1,205	$ 901
Accounts Receivable	944	991
Inventories	383	429
Property, Plant, and Equipment	537	519
Other Assets	1,887	1,965
Total Assets	$4,956	$4,805
Liabilities		
Accounts Payable	$1,583	$1,570
Notes Payable	940	928
Total Liabilities	2,523	2,498
Shareholders' Equity		
Contributed Capital	956	505
Retained Earnings	1,477	1,802
Total Shareholders' Equity	2,433	2,307
Total Liabilities and Shareholders' Equity	$4,956	$4,805

MATTEL, INC.
Statement of Retained Earnings
For the Year Ended December 31, 2007
(in millions)

Retained Earnings, January 1, 2007	$1,477
Net Income for 2007	600
Dividends Declared for 2007	(275)
Retained Earnings, December 31, 2007	$1,802

MATTEL, INC.
Income Statement
For the Year Ended December 31, 2007
(in millions)

Revenues
| Sales Revenue | $5,970 |
| Total Revenues | 5,970 |

Expenses
Cost of Goods Sold Expense	3,193
Advertising and Promotion Expenses	709
Other Selling and Administrative Expenses	1,338
Interest Expense	27
Income Tax Expense	103
Total Expenses	5,370
Net Income	$ 600

Exhibit 1.10   Summary of Key Points

Financial Statement	Purpose: To report . . .	Set-up	Examples of Content
1. Balance sheet (also called the statement of financial position)	. . . what the business owns at a particular point in time, and whether they were financed by creditors or shareholders.	Assets = Liabilities + Shareholders' Equity	*Assets* include cash in the bank, production equipment, and toys Mattel has made but not yet sold. *Liabilities* include amounts owed but not yet paid. *Shareholders' Equity* shows the amount owners have invested in the company.
2. Income statement (also called the statement of income, statement of operations, statement of earnings, statement of profit and loss)	. . . what the business has earned from its operating activities *over a period of time.*	Revenues − Expenses = Net Income	*Revenues* include what Mattel earns from selling toys. *Expenses* include Mattel's costs of running its business.
3. Statement of retained earnings	. . . the accumulated earnings retained in the business *over a period of time.*	Beginning Retained Earnings + Net Income (this period) − Dividends Declared (this period) = Ending Retained Earnings	*Net Income* is the net amount earned by the business during the period. *Dividends* indicate how much is distributed to the business's shareholders during the period.
4. Statement of cash flows	. . . the cash received and paid out by the business *over a period of time.*	Operating Activities Cash Flow + Investing Activities Cash Flow + Financing Activities Cash Flow = Change in Cash Balance + Beginning Cash Balance = Ending Cash Balance	*Operating* cash flow includes cash received from customers and cash paid to suppliers during the period. *Investing* cash flow includes cash used to buy factory buildings during the period. *Financing* cash flow includes exchanges of cash with lenders and owners during the period.

GENERALLY ACCEPTED ACCOUNTING PRINCIPLES (GAAP)

Just as the inventors of Monopoly® had to come up with rules for that game, someone has to determine the rules for financial reporting, and for ensuring that the accounting rules keep up with the ever-changing nature of business. As it turns out, the system of financial statement reporting in use today has a long history—all the way back to a publication in 1494 by an Italian monk and mathematician, Luca Pacioli. Despite this long history, few hard-and-fast accounting rules existed until the 1930s. Until that time, most companies decided for themselves how and what to report in their financial statements. Following the dramatic stock market crash of 1929 in North America, the governments of both Canada and the United States enacted legislation designed to improve financial reporting and to protect investors. Since that time, rules called **generally accepted accounting principles,** or **GAAP** for short (pronounced like the name of the clothing store), have developed. To ensure accountants follow GAAP when preparing their company's financial statements, securities legislation requires that each public company hire independent **auditors** to scrutinize its financial records. Following rules called **generally accepted auditing standards (GAAS),** the Auditors' Report mentioned on page 14

GAAP (generally accepted accounting principles) are the rules for financial reporting.

GAAS (generally accepted auditing standards) are the rules used by **auditors,** who report on whether a company's financial statements are, in fact, prepared following GAAP.

states whether, in their opinion, the financial statements represent what they claim to represent and whether they comply with GAAP. In a sense, GAAP are to auditors and accountants what the criminal code is to lawyers and the public.

Who sets these accounting rules? Well, that depends on where your company operates. Most industrialized countries have their own national organization for setting accounting rules. In Canada, the Canadian Institute of Chartered Accountants (CICA) has this responsibility.[2] In the United States, it is the Financial Accounting Standards Board (FASB). Because so many companies operate internationally, there is also an International Accounting Standards Board (IASB) that has been instrumental in harmonizing accounting rules around the world. In 2005, the CICA declared its intention to phase out Canadian-made accounting rules for public companies and to adopt the IASB rules (called International Financial Reporting Standards, or IFRS) by 2011. The CICA will, however, continue to set accounting rules for non-public entities in Canada.

Chartered accountants may dominate the standard-setting process in Canada, but they are only one of the many professional designations that students interested in accounting may pursue. The supplement to this chapter (see page 23) briefly describes the wide range of careers available to those in this fast-growing field.

POINT OF INTEREST

Harmonization does not mean accounting rules are identical across countries. Investors who want to compare the financial statements of an American company with those of a Canadian company, for example, have to be aware of differences that exist between the two sets of accounting rules.

EVALUATE

Results from the Perspective of Financial Statement Users

WHO CARES?

Now that you see what goes into financial statements, it's time to ask *who cares?* As Exhibit 1.11 shows, lots of people care. Financial statements are used by people inside the company and those outside it. In this course, we focus on decisions made by two important groups of external financial statement users: *investors* and *creditors*.

In general, investors and creditors use the four basic financial statements (and notes) to:

1. *Understand the current state of the business.*
2. *Predict how the business is likely to do in the future.*

1. Using the Balance Sheet

Investors and creditors look at the balance sheet to see whether the company owns enough (assets) to pay all that it owes to creditors (liabilities) and still have enough left to distribute as dividends to shareholders and fund future operations (shareholders' equity). If assets are barely enough to cover liabilities, the company's future is at risk because, if it does not pay its creditors on time, it can be forced to sell its assets to pay its liabilities. When this happens, the law requires that creditors be paid before investors receive any money, as illustrated in Exhibit 1.12.

2. Using the Income Statement

Investors and creditors are eager to analyze the income statement because it indicates whether a company made a profit during the current period. Also, by looking for a trend in a company's net income from year to year, users can get clues about the company's future earnings. Estimated future earnings are important to investors because they buy shares when they believe that future earnings will improve and lead to higher dividends and/or share prices. These estimates also are important to creditors because future earnings provide the resources to repay loans.

3. Using the Statement of Retained Earnings

Creditors closely monitor the retained earnings statement because a company's policy on dividend payments to shareholders affects its ability to repay its debts. Every dollar from

Balance Sheet

Assets

Liabilities

Shareholders' Equity

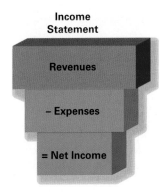

Income Statement

Revenues

– Expenses

= Net Income

---

[2] The CICA receives input from a variety of interested groups in making these decisions and is further overseen by various boards set up to protect the public interest.

exhibit **1.11** Financial Statement Users

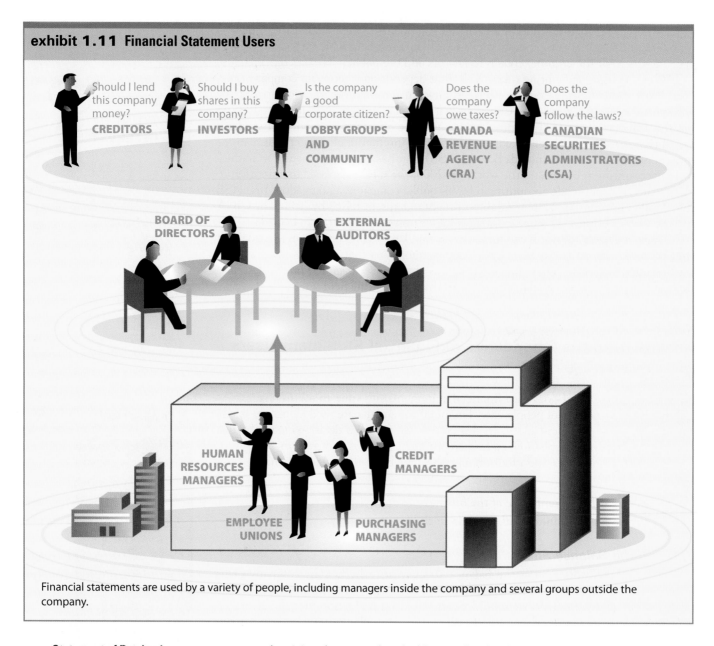

Should I lend this company money?
CREDITORS

Should I buy shares in this company?
INVESTORS

Is the company a good corporate citizen?
LOBBY GROUPS AND COMMUNITY

Does the company owe taxes?
CANADA REVENUE AGENCY (CRA)

Does the company follow the laws?
CANADIAN SECURITIES ADMINISTRATORS (CSA)

BOARD OF DIRECTORS

EXTERNAL AUDITORS

HUMAN RESOURCES MANAGERS

CREDIT MANAGERS

EMPLOYEE UNIONS

PURCHASING MANAGERS

Financial statements are used by a variety of people, including managers inside the company and several groups outside the company.

Statement of Retained Earnings

Retained earnings, 1/1/07

+ Net income (2007)

– Dividends declared (2007)

= Retained earnings, 12/31/07

earnings that Mattel pays to shareholders as dividends is not available to use in paying back its debt to banks and other creditors. Investors, on the other hand, use the statement of retained earnings to evaluate whether the company favours paying out dividends or retaining its earnings to support future growth. There are two ways that an investor can make money owning shares in a company: (1) the company can pay dividends to the investors, or (2) if the company keeps profits in the business instead and uses them wisely, this should cause the company's share price to increase, and the investor can sell the shares for more than the purchase price. Some investors, perhaps your grandparents, prefer steady dividends, whereas others prefer that every dollar that Mattel makes in profit is kept for investing in additional factories and the latest manufacturing equipment.

4. Using the Statement of Cash Flows

The statement of cash flows indicates to investors and creditors how the company obtained and spent its money during the accounting period. The Operating Activities section indicates the company's ability to generate cash from sales to meet its current cash needs, and the Investing and Financing Activities sections indicate whether any

exhibit 1.12 Creditor and Shareholder Claims

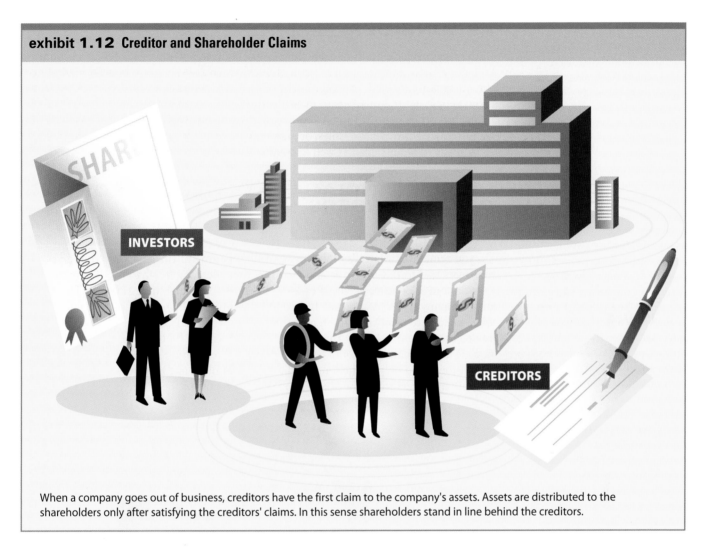

When a company goes out of business, creditors have the first claim to the company's assets. Assets are distributed to the shareholders only after satisfying the creditors' claims. In this sense shareholders stand in line behind the creditors.

money left over from operations was used to expand the company, pay back the bank debt, or pay dividends to shareholders. By comparing Mattel's statement of cash flows from year to year, users can see that in 2007 Mattel generated less cash from operations but increased the dividends it paid to its shareholders.

Using the Notes and Other Reports

All financial statement users need to understand the rules used in computing the numbers on the financial statements. A swim coach would never try to evaluate a swimmer's time in the 100 freestyle without first asking if the time was for a race in metres or in yards. Likewise, a financial statement user should never attempt to use accounting information without reading the notes that describe the rules used to prepare the financial statements. Information in the notes can dramatically influence your interpretation of the main statements. Consider them the equivalent of the fine print in an insurance policy.

In addition to reading the notes to the financial statements, users also consider the information reported in the auditors' report. This report describes whether the financial statements present a fair picture of the company, and whether they are prepared using methods allowed by GAAP. The purpose of the auditors' report isn't to tell you if a company is about to go broke—you have to make that assessment—but it is the best protection against having a company's accountants and executives unintentionally or intentionally prepare misleading financial reports.

Statement of Cash Flows

Operating Cash Flows | Investing Cash Flows | Financing Cash Flows

Net Change in Cash

+ Beginning Cash

= Ending Cash

RECONSIDER _____

In the Reconsider section of each chapter, we go from a worm's eye view of accounting (the nitty-gritty practical number-crunching) to a bird's eye view (a broader view of how the information is used, or sometimes misused). This section will help you see that, because people use the numbers to make decisions, accounting matters, and that accounting is not as black-and-white as you may have thought before taking this course. Often we introduce controversial issues, or ones that are difficult to understand, in this section, so be ready to be intrigued as well as challenged.

HOW FINANCIAL STATEMENT REPORTING INFORMS USERS

THE GLIMPSE INSIDE

ETHICAL ISSUES

Do you remember Mattel's problems from the opening of this chapter? In one year, its managers had to tell investors and creditors that the company had recalled millions of toys, and, in another year, that they lost $431 million on their investment in The Learning Company (TLC)[3], and they had to tell them this bad news without alarming them. They needed to be ethical and report the bad news honestly and, at the same time, convey to users the good news that Mattel was still strong. By being honest with the bad news, Mattel's managers could begin to develop a reputation for honest reporting. This reputation could help in the long run because it would make users more likely to believe Mattel's managers when they have good news to report in the future.

POINT OF INTEREST

Mattel executives have learned the importance of honest financial reporting. Three decades earlier, six Mattel executives were charged with including fictitious sales in the company's financial statements. The fun and games ended with the Mattel execs paying over $30 million to settle lawsuits filed by angry investors and creditors. As the saying goes, today's good decisions come from experience, which itself comes from yesterday's bad decisions.

© 1997 Randy Glasbergen.

"The bad news is, you do less work than anyone in this office. The good news is, you make the fewest mistakes."

A GLANCE OUTSIDE

How did users take the news when Mattel issued press releases describing their problems? Not well. In both of the situations mentioned in this chapter, Mattel's stock price fell about 30 per cent. But the good news is that customers continued to buy Mattel products. The strength of its toy sales and its reputation allowed Mattel not only to survive, but also to thrive, despite the problems they faced.

WHAT'S COMING UP

In this chapter, you studied the basic financial statements that give external users an idea of how things are doing inside the company. The next chapter will take you deep inside a company to learn about the detailed steps involved in determining the amounts reported in each financial statement. To get ready for Chapter 2, use the materials in the following sections to review and practise what we covered in this chapter.

---

[3] TLC was a business that produced kids' computer software under the Reader Rabbit® brand name. Within three months of buying it, Mattel ran into big losses from TLC. After a year and a half, Mattel finally admitted defeat and sold TLC, confirming what some analysts called one of the biggest acquisition failures of all time.

_____ **FOR YOUR REVIEW**

DEMONSTRATION CASE

The introductory case presented here reviews the items reported on the income statement and balance sheet, using the financial statements of Tim Hortons. Tim Hortons® opened its first coffee and doughnut shop in Ontario in 1964. Founded by NHL hockey player Tim Horton, and expanded under the direction of Ron Joyce, the highly successful chain was sold to Wendy's International in 1995. Wendy's subsequently sold off 18 per cent of Tim Hortons in a red-hot stock offering to the public in March 2006. Tim Hortons currently has over 3,000 stores and has passed McDonald's to become Canada's favourite fast-food operator. Following is a list of the financial statement items and amounts adapted from a recent Tim Hortons Inc. balance sheet and income statement. The numbers are presented in millions of dollars for the year ended December 31, 2006.

COACH'S TIP

At the end of most chapters, one or more demonstration cases are presented. These cases show you how to apply the material from the chapter to a problem similar to what you are likely to be asked to do as homework. It's worth your effort to do the demo case before studying the suggested solution.

Accounts payable	$ 116
Accounts receivable	110
Cash	176
Contributed capital	844
Income tax expense	101
Inventories	54
Net income	260
Notes payable	451
Operating expenses	937
Other assets	240
Other expenses	361
Other liabilities	160
Property and equipment	1,165
Retained earnings	174
Sales revenues	1,072
Total assets	1,745
Total expenses	1,399
Total liabilities	727
Total liabilities and shareholders' equity	1,745
Franchise revenues	587
Total shareholders' equity	1,018

Required:

1. Prepare a balance sheet and an income statement for the year, following the formats in Exhibits 1.3 and 1.4.
2. Describe the content of these two statements.
3. Name the other two statements that Tim Hortons would include in its financial statements.
4. Did financing for Tim Hortons' assets come primarily from liabilities or shareholders' equity?
5. Explain why Tim Hortons would subject its statements to an independent audit.

Suggested Solution

1.

TIM HORTONS INC.
Balance Sheet
At December 31, 2006
(in millions of dollars)

Assets	
Cash	$ 176
Accounts receivable	110
Inventories	54
Property and equipment	1,165
Other assets	240
Total assets	**$ 1,745**
Liabilities	
Accounts payable	$ 116
Notes payable	451
Other liabilities	160
Total liabilities	727
Shareholders' Equity	
Contributed capital	844
Retained earnings	174
Total shareholders' equity	1,018
Total liabilities and shareholders' equity	**$ 1,745**

TIM HORTONS INC.
Income Statement
For the Year Ended December 31, 2006
(in millions of dollars)

Revenues	
Sales revenues	$ 1,072
Franchise revenues	587
Total revenues	1,659
Expenses	
Operating expenses	937
Other expenses	361
Income tax expense	101
Total expenses	1,399
Net income	**$ 260**

2. The balance sheet reports the amount of assets, liabilities, and shareholders' equity of a business at a point in time. The income statement reports the most common measure of financial performance for a business: net income (revenues minus expenses during the accounting period).

3. Tim Hortons would also present a statement of retained earnings and a statement of cash flows.

4. Financing for Tim Hortons' assets is provided more from shareholders' equity ($1,018) rather than liabilities ($727).

5. Users will have greater confidence in the accuracy of financial statement information if they know that it has been audited, particularly because the people who audited the statements are required to meet professional standards of ethics and competence. In addition, an audit is required, because Tim Hortons is a public company.

CHAPTER SUMMARY

Distinguish operating, investing, and financing activities. p. 2   **LO1**

- *Operating activities* include day-to-day events involved in making and delivering goods and services.
- *Investing activities* involve buying or selling longer-term assets such as land and buildings.
- *Financing activities* are related to exchanging money with lenders or owners.

Describe the purpose, set-up, and content of the four basic financial statements. p. 4   **LO2**

- The *balance sheet* reports what the business owns (reported as assets) at a particular point in time, and whether the financing for these assets came from creditors (reported as liabilities) or shareholders (reported as shareholders' equity).
- The *income statement* reports the net amount that a business earned (net income) over a period of time by subtracting the costs of running the business (expenses) from the total amount earned (revenues).
- The *statement of retained earnings* explains changes in the retained earnings account over a period of time by considering increases (from net income) and decreases (from dividends to shareholders).
- The *statement of cash flows* explains changes in the cash account over a period of time by reporting inflows and outflows of cash from the business's operating, investing, and financing activities.

Explain the primary goals of financial statement users. p. 17   **LO3**

- Although the particular interests of the various financial statement users differ somewhat, they ultimately are interested in using the financial statements to
  1. Understand the current state of the business.
  2. Predict how the business is likely to do in the future.

Describe the importance of ethics and reputation in accounting. p. 20   **LO4**

- Users have confidence in the accuracy of financial statement numbers when the people associated with their preparation and audit have reputations for ethical behaviour and competence.

KEY TERMS TO KNOW

Accounting p. 3

Accounts p. 6

Assets p. 5

Auditors p. 16

Basic Accounting
  Equation p. 5

Comparative Information
  p. 13

Corporations p. 2

Creditors p. 5

Declaration of Dividend p. 10

Dividends p. 7

Expenses p. 8

Financial Statements p. 2

Financial Statement Users p. 2

Financing Activities p. 2

Generally Accepted
  Accounting Principles
  (GAAP) p. 16

Generally Accepted Auditing
  Standards (GAAS) p. 16

Investing Activities p. 2

Liabilities p. 5

Net Income p. 8

Notes (Footnotes) p. 14

Operating Activities p. 2

Partnerships p. 2

Public Companies p. 3

Revenue p. 8

Separate-Entity
  Assumption p. 5

Shareholders' Equity p. 5

Sole Proprietorships p. 2

SUPPLEMENT A: ACCOUNTING CAREERS

The financial services sector employs over 750,000 Canadians, representing 4 per cent of Canada's employment and 6 per cent of Canada's gross domestic product, with wages and salaries well above the national average. Accountants are in high demand these days. In 2006, the financial services sector added 61,000 new jobs.

The accounting field includes a wide range of work in both private and public accounting. Accountants employed by a single organization are in private accounting, and may work in general accounting, budgeting, cost accounting, taxation, internal auditing, finance, or information systems. Accountants who provide professional services to a number of organizations are in public accounting and may provide services in assurance, taxation, business valuation, fraud investigation, management controls, or other consulting areas.

Students interested in a career in the financial sectior can pursue a number of designations, including the CA (Chartered Accountant), CMA (Certified Management Accountant), CGA (Certified General Accountant), and CFA (Chartered Financial Analyst), among others.

FOR YOUR PRACTICE _____

QUESTIONS

1. Define *accounting*.
2. Briefly distinguish financial accounting from management accounting.
3. The accounting process generates financial reports for both internal and external users. Describe some of the specific groups of internal and external users.
4. Briefly distinguish investors from creditors.
5. Explain what the separate entity concept means when it says a business is treated as separate from its owners for accounting purposes.
6. Complete the following:

Name of Statement	Alternative Title
a. Income statement	*a.* _____
b. Balance sheet	*b.* _____

7. What information should be included in the heading of each of the four primary financial statements?
8. What are the purposes of (*a*) the balance sheet, (*b*) the income statement, (*c*) the statement of retained earnings, and (*d*) the statement of cash flows?
9. Explain why the income statement, statement of retained earnings, and statement of cash flows would be dated "For the Year Ended December 31, 2009," whereas the balance sheet would be dated "At December 31, 2009."
10. Briefly explain the importance of assets and liabilities to the decisions of investors and creditors.
11. Briefly define the following: *net income* and *net loss*.
12. Describe the basic accounting equation that underlies the balance sheet. Define the three major components reported on the balance sheet.
13. Describe the equation that underlies the income statement. Explain the three major items reported on the income statement.
14. Describe the equation that underlies the statement of retained earnings. Explain the four major items reported on the statement of retained earnings.
15. Describe the equation that underlies the statement of cash flows. Explain the three major types of activities reported on the statement.
16. Who is responsible for developing accounting rules (generally accepted accounting principles) in Canada?

MULTIPLE CHOICE

Select the one alternative that best answers the question or completes the sentence.

1. Which of the following is *not* one of the four basic financial statements?
a. The balance sheet	*c.* The income statement
b. The audit report	*d.* The statement of cash flows
2. Which of the following is true regarding the income statement?
   a.   The income statement is sometimes called the statement of earnings.
   b.   The income statement reports revenues, expenses, and liabilities.
   c.   The income statement only reports revenue for which cash was received at the point of sale.
   d.   The income statement reports the financial position of a business at a particular point in time.

3. Which of the following is false regarding the balance sheet?

   a. The accounts shown on a balance sheet represent the basic accounting equation for a particular business.

   b. The retained earnings balance shown on the balance sheet must agree with the ending retained earnings balance shown on the statement of retained earnings.

   c. The balance sheet summarizes the net changes in specific account balances over a period of time.

   d. The balance sheet reports the amount of assets, liabilities, and shareholders' equity of a business at a point in time.

4. Which of the following regarding retained earnings is false?

   a. Retained earnings is increased by net income.

   b. Retained earnings is a component of shareholders' equity on the balance sheet.

   c. Retained earnings is an asset on the balance sheet.

   d. Retained earnings represents earnings not distributed to shareholders in the form of dividends.

5. Which of the following is not one of the items required to be shown in the heading of a financial statement?

   a. The financial statement preparer's name

   b. The title of the financial statement

   c. The financial reporting date or period

   d. The name of the business entity

6. How many of the following statements regarding the statement of cash flows are true?

   • The statement of cash flows separates cash inflows and outflows into three major categories: operating, investing, and financing.

   • The ending cash balance shown on the statement of cash flows must agree with the amount shown on the balance sheet at the end of the same period.

   • The total increase or decrease in cash shown on the statement of cash flows must agree with the "bottom line" (net income or net loss) reported on the income statement.

   a. None

   b. One

   c. Two

   d. Three

7. Which of the following is not a typical footnote included in an annual report?

   a. A note describing the auditors' opinion of the management's past and future financial planning for the business

   b. A note providing more detail about a specific item shown in the financial statements

   c. A note describing the accounting rules applied in the financial statements

   d. A note describing financial disclosures about items not appearing in the financial statements

8. Which of the following regarding GAAP is true?

   a. GAAP is an abbreviation for Goodie, Another Accounting Problem.

   b. Changes in GAAP do not affect the amount of income reported by a company.

   c. GAAP is the abbreviation for generally accepted accounting principles.

   d. Changes to GAAP must be approved by the federal government.

9. Which of the following is true?

   a. CICA creates IASB.

   b. GAAP creates CICA.

   c. GAAP creates CRA.

   d. CICA creates GAAP.

10. Which of the following would *not* be a goal of external users reading a company's financial statements?

   a. Understanding the current financial state of the company

   b. Assessing the company's contribution to social and environmental policies

   c. Predicting the company's future financial performance

   d. Evaluating the company's ability to generate cash from sales

11. If a company's liabilities are \$65,000 and its total assets are \$135,000, what is the company's shareholders' equity?

    a.   \$200,000 (\$135,000 + \$65,000)

    b.   \$70,000 (\$135,000 − \$65,000)

    c.   \$0 (Since assets are larger than liabilities, there is no shareholders' equity.)

    d.   Cannot be determined from the information given

12. If a company's retained earnings at the beginning of the year and at the end of the year are \$245,000 and \$280,000 respectively, and its net income for the year is \$63,500, what was the amount of dividends declared by the company during the year?

    a.   \$35,000

    b.   \$98,500

    c.   \$28,500

    d.   \$0

MINI-EXERCISES

L03   **M1-1 Identifying Definitions with Abbreviations**

The following is a list of important abbreviations used in the chapter. These abbreviations also are used widely in business. For each abbreviation, give the full name. The first one is an example.

	Abbreviation	Full Name
1.	IASB	International Accounting Standards Board
2.	GAAP	_____
3.	CICA	_____
4.	CSA	_____

L01–L03   **M1-2 Matching Definitions with Terms or Abbreviations**

Match each definition with its related term or abbreviation by entering the appropriate letter in the space provided.

	Term or Abbreviation		Definition
F	1. Investing activities	A.	A system that collects and processes financial information about an organization and reports that information to decision makers
D	2. Private company		
E	3. Corporation		
A	4. Accounting	B.	The financial statements of a company include only the results of that company's business activities
I	5. Audit report		
C	6. Partnership	C.	An unincorporated business owned by two or more persons
J	7. CICA		
G	8. Financing activities	D.	A company that sells its shares privately and does not release its financial statements to the public
B	9. Separate entity		
L	10. GAAP	E.	An incorporated business that issues shares as evidence of ownership
K	11. Public company		
H ~~G~~	12. Operating activities	F.	Purchases and disposals of long-term assets
		G.	Transactions with lenders (borrowing and repaying cash) and shareholders (selling company shares and paying dividends)
		H.	Day-to-day activities related to a company's core business
		I.	A report that describes the auditors' opinion of the fairness of the financial statement presentations and the evidence gathered to support that opinion
		J.	Canadian Institute of Chartered Accountants
		K.	A company that has its shares bought and sold by investors on established stock exchanges
		L.	Generally accepted accounting principles

M1-3 Matching Items to Balance Sheet and Income Statement Categories

LO2

According to its Web site, Sun-Rype Products Ltd. is a leading Canadian manufacturer and marketer of juice-based beverages and all-natural fruit snacks, including Blue Label Apple Juice and Fruit to Go snacks. Based in the Okanagan Valley of British Columbia, Sun-Rype operates one of the most sophisticated processing plants in North America. The following are items taken from its recent balance sheet and income statement. Mark each item in the following list with letters to indicate whether it would be reported as an Asset, Liability, or Shareholders' Equity account on the balance sheet or a Revenue or Expense account on the income statement.

_L_ 1. Accounts payable   _e_ 7. Interest expense
_A_ 2. Accounts receivable   _A_ 8. Inventories
_A_ 3. Cash   _e_ 9. Selling and administrative expenses
_e_ 4. Cost of goods sold expense   _R_ 10. Sales revenue
_A_ 5. Property, plant, and equipment   _L_ 11. Notes payable
_e_ 6. Income tax expense   _A_ 12. Retained earnings

M1-4 Matching Financial Statement Items to Balance Sheet and Income Statement Categories

LO2

Mark each item in the following list with letters to indicate whether it would be reported as an Asset, Liability, or Shareholders' Equity account on the balance sheet or a Revenue or Expense account on the income statement.

_____ 1. Retained earnings   _____ 5. Cost of goods sold expense
_____ 2. Accounts receivable   _____ 6. Inventories
_____ 3. Sales revenue   _____ 7. Advertising expense
_____ 4. Property, plant, and equipment _____ 8. Accounts payable

M1-5 Matching Financial Statement Items to Balance Sheet and Income Statement Categories

LO2

McCain Foods is the number one French fry maker in the world, processing about a million pounds of French fries and other potato products per hour. The McCain family began producing French fries in 1957 and they still own the New Brunswick company. For the following items that would typically appear in McCain's financial statements, mark each item from the balance sheet as an Asset, Liability, or Shareholders' Equity, and each item from the income statement as a Revenue or Expense.

_____ 1. Accounts payable   _____ 7. Cash
_____ 2. Accounts receivable   _____ 8. Machinery
_____ 3. Cost of goods sold expense   _____ 9. Promotion and advertising expenses
_____ 4. Selling and administrative expenses   _____ 10. Sales revenue
_____ 5. Income tax expense   _____ 11. Notes payable to banks
_____ 6. Inventories   _____ 12. Retained earnings

M1-6 Matching Financial Statement Items to Balance Sheet and Income Statement Categories

LO2

Maple Leaf Foods is a Canadian manufacturer of food products, operating under a number of banners, including Maple Leaf, Olivieri, and Dempster's brands. The following items were presented in the company's financial statements. Mark each item from the balance sheet as an Asset, Liability, or Shareholders' Equity, and each item from the income statement as a Revenue or Expense.

_____ 1. Inventories   _____ 7. Cash
_____ 2. Accounts payable   _____ 8. Retained earnings

_____ 3. Contributed capital   _____ 9. Operating expenses

_____ 4. Property, plant, and equipment   _____ 10. Interest expense

_____ 5. Accounts receivable   _____ 11. Income tax expense

_____ 6. Notes payable   _____ 12. Sales revenue

LO2   **M1-7 Matching Financial Statement Items to Balance Sheet and Income Statement Categories**

Shell Canada is one of the largest integrated petroleum companies in Canada. The following items were presented in the company's financial statements. Mark each item from the balance sheet as an <u>A</u>sset, <u>L</u>iability, or <u>S</u>hareholders' Equity, and each item from the income statement as a <u>R</u>evenue or <u>E</u>xpense.

_____ 1. Accounts payable   _____ 7. Contributed capital

_____ 2. Inventories   _____ 8. Accounts receivable

_____ 3. Cash   _____ 9. Sales revenue

_____ 4. Retained earnings   _____ 10. Selling and administration expenses

_____ 5. Property, plant, and equipment   _____ 11. Exploration expense

_____ 6. Notes payable   _____ 12. Cost of goods sold expense

LO1, LO2   **M1-8 Matching Financial Statement Items to the Four Basic Financial Statements**

Match each element with its financial statement by entering the appropriate letter in the space provided.

Element	Financial Statement
_____ 1. Expenses	A. Balance sheet
_____ 2. Cash flows from investing activities	B. Income statement
_____ 3. Assets	C. Statement of retained earnings
_____ 4. Dividends declared	D. Statement of cash flows
_____ 5. Revenues	
_____ 6. Cash flows from operating activities	
_____ 7. Liabilities	
_____ 8. Cash flows from financing activities	

LO1, LO2   **M1-9 Matching Financial Statement Items to the Four Basic Financial Statements**

Oakley, Inc., manufactures sunglasses, goggles, shoes, watches, footwear, and clothing. Recently, the company reported the following items in its financial statements. Indicate whether these items appeared on the balance sheet (B/S), income statement (I/S), statement of retained earnings (SRE), or statement of cash flows (SCF).

_____ 1. Total shareholders' equity

_____ 2. Sales revenue

_____ 3. Total assets

_____ 4. Cash flows from operating activities

_____ 5. Total liabilities

_____ 6. Net income

_____ 7. Cash flows from financing activities

_____ 8. Dividends declared

M1-10 Reporting Amounts on the Income Statement

LO2

During a recent year, Maple Leaf delivered boxes of hot dogs, buns, and other products for which customers paid or promised to pay amounts totalling $6,364,983,000. During the same period, it collected $6,314,827,000 in cash from its customers. Indicate which of these two amounts will be shown on Maple Leaf's income statement as *sales revenue*.

M1-11 Reporting Amounts on the Income Statement

LO2

During a recent year, Shell Canada delivered gas, oil, and other products for which customers paid or promised to pay amounts totalling $11,228,000,000. During the same period, it collected $10,510,000,000 in cash from its customers. Indicate which of these two amounts will be shown on Shell Canada's income statement as *sales revenue*.

M1-12 Reporting Amounts on the Income Statement

LO2

During a recent year, assume that Maple Leaf *produced* sliced meats, bread, and other products with a total cost of production of $5,568,231,000. During the same period, it *delivered* to customers sliced meats, bread, and other products that cost a total of $5,574,034,000 to produce. Indicate which of the two numbers will be shown on Maple Leaf's income statement as *cost of goods sold expense*.

M1-13 Reporting Amounts on the Income Statement

LO1

During a recent year, Shell Canada *produced* petroleum products with a total cost of production of $6,590,000,000. During the same period, it *delivered* to customers petroleum products that cost a total of $6,068,000,000 to produce. Indicate which of the two numbers will be shown on Shell Canada's income statement as *cost of goods sold expense*.

M1-14 Reporting Amounts on the Statement of Cash Flows

LO1

During a recent year, Maple Leaf delivered hot dogs, buns, and other products to customers who paid or promised to pay amounts totalling $6,364,983,000. During the same period, Maple Leaf collected $6,314,827,000 in cash from its customers. Indicate which of the two amounts will be shown on Maple Leaf's cash flow statement.

M1-15 Reporting Amounts on the Statement of Cash Flows

LO1

During a recent year, Shell Canada delivered gas, oil and other products to customers who paid or promised to pay amounts totalling $11,228,000,000. During the same period, Shell Canada collected $10,510,000,000 in cash from its customers. Indicate which of the two amounts will be shown on Shell Canada's cash flow statement.

M1-16 Reporting Amounts on the Statement of Cash Flows

LO1

Learning which items belong in each cash flow statement category is an important first step in understanding their meaning. Use a letter to mark each item in the following list as a cash flow from Operating, Investing, or Financing activities. **Put parentheses around the letter if it is a cash *outflow* and use no parentheses if it's an *inflow*.**

_____ 1.   Cash paid for dividends   _____ 4.   Cash paid to suppliers and employees

_____ 2.   Cash collected from customers   _____ 5.   Cash paid to purchase equipment

_____ 3.   Cash received from notes payable   _____ 6.   Cash received from issuing shares

M1-17 Reporting Amounts on the Statement of Cash Flows

LO1

Learning which items belong in each category of the statement of cash flows is an important first step in understanding their meaning. Use a letter to mark each item in the following list as a cash flow from Operating, Investing, or Financing activities. **Put parentheses around the letter if it is a cash *outflow* and use no parentheses if it's an *inflow*.**

_____ 1.   Cash paid to purchase equipment   _____ 4.   Cash paid for dividends

_____ 2.   Cash collected from customers   _____ 5.   Cash paid to suppliers and employees

_____ 3.   Cash received from selling equipment _____ 6.   Cash received from issuing shares

EXERCISES

LO2   ### E1-1 Reporting Amounts on the Four Basic Financial Statements

Using the figures listed in the table below and the equations underlying each of the four basic financial statements, show (*a*) that the balance sheet is in balance, (*b*) that net income is properly calculated, (*c*) what caused changes in the retained earnings account, and (*d*) what caused changes in the cash account.

Assets	$18,200	Beginning Retained Earnings	$3,500
Liabilities	13,750	Ending Retained Earnings	4,300
Shareholders' Equity	4,450	Cash Flows from Operating Activities	1,600
Revenue	10,500	Cash Flows from Investing Activities	(1,000)
Expenses	9,200	Cash Flows from Financing Activities	(900)
Net Income	1,300	Beginning Cash	1,000
Dividends	500	Ending Cash	700

LO2   ### E1-2 Reporting Amounts on the Four Basic Financial Statements

Using the figures listed in the table below and the equations underlying each of the four basic financial statements, show (*a*) that the balance sheet is in balance, (*b*) that net income is properly calculated, (*c*) what caused changes in the retained earnings account, and (*d*) what caused changes in the cash account.

Assets	$79,500	Beginning Retained Earnings	$20,500
Liabilities	18,500	Ending Retained Earnings	28,750
Shareholders' Equity	61,000	Cash Flows from Operating Activities	15,700
Revenue	32,100	Cash Flows from Investing Activities	(7,200)
Expenses	18,950	Cash Flows from Financing Activities	(5,300)
Net Income	13,150	Beginning Cash	3,200
Dividends	4,900	Ending Cash	6,400

LO2, LO3   ### E1-3 Preparing a Balance Sheet

Dave & Buster's Inc. is a restaurant/entertainment company. Founded in 1982, D&B provides high-quality food and beverage items, combined with an extensive array of interactive entertainment attractions such as pocket billiards, shuffleboard, state-of the-art simulators, and virtual reality and traditional carnival-style amusements and games of skill. A recent balance sheet contained the following items (in thousands).

Cash	$ 7,582
Contributed capital	125,783
Accounts payable	64,436
Inventories	12,469
Notes payable	153,406
Property and equipment	351,883
Other assets	51,128
Retained earnings	79,437
Total assets	423,062
Total liabilities and shareholders' equity	?

Required:

1. Prepare the balance sheet, solving for the missing amount.
2. What is Dave & Buster's biggest asset?
3. Did most of the financing for assets come from creditors or shareholders?

E1-4 Completing a Balance Sheet and Inferring Net Income

Terry Lloyd and Jean Dupuis organized Read More Store as a corporation; each contributed $50,000 cash to start the business and received 4,000 shares. The store completed its first year of operations on December 31, 2008. On that date, the following financial items for the year were determined: cash on hand and in the bank, $48,900; amounts due from customers from sales of books, $26,000; property and equipment, $48,000; amounts owed to publishers for books purchased, $8,000; one-year note payable to a local bank for $2,120. No dividends were declared or paid to the shareholders during the year.

Required:

1. Complete the following balance sheet as of the end of 2008.

Assets			Liabilities		
Cash	$ _____		Accounts payable	$ _____	
Accounts receivable	_____		Note payable	_____	
Property, plant, and equipment	_____		Total liabilities		$ _____
			Shareholders' Equity		
			Contributed capital	_____	
			Retained earnings	12,780	
			Total shareholders' equity	_____	
			Total liabilities and shareholders' equity		
Total assets	$ _____				$ _____

2. Using the retained earnings equation and an opening balance of $0, compute the amount of net income for the year.
3. As of December 31, 2008, did most of the financing for assets come from creditors or shareholders?

E1-5 Analyzing Revenues and Expenses and Preparing an Income Statement

Assume that you are the owner of The Sports Shop, which specializes in selling sports T-shirts and caps. At the end of January 2009, you find (for January only) this information:

a. Sales, per the cash register tapes, of $120,000, plus one sale on credit (a special situation) of $1,000
b. With the help of a friend, you determine that all of the goods sold during January had cost $40,000 to purchase.
c. During the month, according to the cheque book, you paid $38,000 for selling, administration, interest, and other expenses; however, you have not yet paid the $600 monthly advertising expense for January.

Required:

On the basis of the data given (and ignoring income taxes), what was the amount of net income for January? Show computations.

E1-6 Preparing an Income Statement and Inferring Missing Values

Leon's Furniture, which sells home furnishings, major appliances, and home entertainment items in nine provinces, was founded in 1909 in Weston, Ontario. It is still owned and operated by the Leon family. A recent annual income statement contained the following items (in millions):

Cost of goods sold expense	$206.5
Net income	?
Sales revenue	352.5
Selling and administrative expenses	98.9
Income tax expense	17.1
Total expenses	?

COACH'S TIP

Hint: First put the items in the order in which they would appear on the income statement, and then solve for the missing values.

Required:

1. Solve for the missing amounts and prepare an income statement for the year ended December 31.
2. What is Leon's biggest expense?
3. What is Leon's markup percentage? Markup is the difference between what an item costs Leon's to buy and what it sells the item for. This is also called the gross profit or gross margin. (*Hint:* Use Leon's numbers above to determine the percentage. Express the markup as a percentage of cost.)

LO2

E1-7 Analyzing Revenues and Expenses and Completing an Income Statement

Home Realty, Incorporated, has been operating for three years and is owned by three investors. J. Doe owns 60 per cent of the 9,000 shares outstanding and is the managing executive in charge. On December 31, 2009, the following financial items for the entire year were determined: sales revenue earned and collected in cash, $150,000, plus $16,000 not yet collected; selling expenses paid, $97,000; interest expense paid, $5,775 (not including December interest of $525, yet to be paid); promotion and advertising expenses paid, $9,025; and income tax expense paid, $18,500. There were no other unpaid expenses at December 31. Also, during the year, the company declared and paid the owners dividends amounting to $12,000. Complete the following income statement:

_____		
_____		
_____		
Revenues		
Sales revenue		$ _____
Expenses		
Selling expenses	$ _____	
Interest expense	_____	
Promotion and advertising expenses	_____	
Income tax expense	_____	
Total expenses		_____
Net income		$ 35,175

LO2

E1-8 Inferring Values Using the Income Statement and Balance Sheet Equations

Review the chapter explanations of the income statement and the balance sheet equations. Apply these equations in each of the following independent cases to compute the two missing amounts for each case. Assume that it is the end of 2009, the first full year of operations for the company.

COACH'S TIP

Hint: In E1-8, first identify the numerical relations among the columns, using the balance sheet and income statement equations. Then compute the missing amounts.

Independent Cases	Total Revenues	Total Expenses	Net Income (Loss)	Total Assets	Total Liabilities	Shareholders' Equity
A	$100,000	$82,000	$_____	$150,000	$70,000	$_____
B	_____	80,000	12,000	112,000	_____	60,000
C	80,000	86,000	_____	104,000	26,000	_____
D	50,000	_____	13,000	_____	22,000	77,000
E	_____	81,000	(6,000)	_____	73,000	28,000

LO2, LO3

E1-9 Preparing an Income Statement and Balance Sheet

Five individuals organized Clay Corporation on January 1, 2009. At the end of January 2009, the following monthly financial data are available:

Total revenues	$130,000
Other expenses (excluding income taxes)	80,000
Income tax expense (all paid as of January 31)	15,000
Cash balance, January 31, 2009	30,000
Accounts receivable from customers (all considered collectible)	15,000
Inventory (by inventory count at cost)	42,000
Accounts payable to suppliers for merchandise purchased from them (will be paid during February 2009)	26,000
Contributed capital (2,600 shares)	26,000

No dividends were declared or paid during January.

Required:

1. Complete the following balance sheet and income statement for the month of January.

CLAY CORPORATION
Income Statement
For the Month of January 2009

Total revenues	$ _____
Other expenses (excluding income tax)	_____
Income tax expense	_____
Net income	$ _____

CLAY CORPORATION
Balance Sheet
At January 31, 2009

Assets	
Cash	$ _____
Accounts receivable	_____
Inventory	_____
Total assets	$ _____
Liabilities	
Accounts payable	$ _____
Total liabilities	_____
Shareholders' Equity	
Contributed capital	_____
Retained earnings	_____
Total shareholders' equity	_____
Total liabilities and shareholders' equity	$ _____

2. Discuss whether Clay Corporation will be able to pay its liabilities.

E1-10 Analyzing and Interpreting an Income Statement　　LO3

Three individuals organized Pest Away Corporation on January 1, 2009, to provide insect extermination services. At the end of 2009, the following income statement was prepared:

PEST AWAY CORPORATION
Income Statement
For the Year Ended December 31, 2009

Revenues		
Sales revenue (cash)	$192,000	
Sales revenue (credit)	24,000	
Total revenues		$216,000
Expenses		
Cost of goods sold expense	76,000	
Selling expense	33,000	
Advertising expense	14,000	
Interest expense	8,000	
Income tax expense	21,000	
Other expenses	25,000	
Total expenses		177,000
Net income		$ 39,000

Required:

1. What was the amount of average monthly revenue?
2. What was the average amount of monthly selling expense?

3. Explain why cost of goods sold is reported as an expense.
4. Explain why interest is reported as an expense.
5. Can you determine how much cash the company had on December 31, 2009? Answer yes or no, and explain your reasoning.

LO1   **E1-11**   **Matching Cash Flow Statement Items to Business-Activity Categories**

Tech Data Corporation is a leading distributor of computer peripherals and network solutions, and recently was ranked by *Fortune* as the second most admired company in its industry category. The following items were taken from its recent cash flow statement. Mark each item in the following list with a letter to indicate whether it is a cash flow from Operating, Investing, or Financing activities. **Put parentheses around the letter if it is a cash *outflow* and use no parentheses if it's an *inflow*.**

_____ 1.   Cash paid to suppliers and employees
_____ 2.   Cash received from customers
_____ 3.   Cash received from borrowing long-term debt
_____ 4.   Cash received from issuing shares
_____ 5.   Cash paid to purchase equipment

LO1   **E1-12**   **Matching Cash Flow Statement Items to Business-Activity Categories**

Clearly Canadian Beverage, headquartered in West Vancouver, B.C., is a producer of premium beverages. It is best known for its sparkling flavoured water and was among the first to tap the alternative beverage craze. Mark each item in the following list with a letter to indicate whether it is a cash flow from Operating, Investing, or Financing activities. **Put parentheses around the letter if it is a cash *outflow* and use no parentheses if it's an *inflow*.**

_____ 1.   Purchases of property, plant, and equipment
_____ 2.   Cash received from customers
_____ 3.   Cash received from issuing shares
_____ 4.   Cash paid to suppliers and employees
_____ 5.   Cash paid on notes payable
_____ 6.   Cash received from selling equipment

LO2   **E1-13**   **Preparing an Income Statement, Statement of Retained Earnings, and Balance Sheet**

The following accounts are taken from the December 31, 2006, financial statement of WestJet Airlines Ltd.

Cash	$377,517,000
Interest expense	70,176,000
Accounts receivable	12,645,000
Sales and marketing expense	154,734,000
Supplies	8,200,000
Contributed capital	489,904,000
Other revenue	215,215,000
Property and equipment	2,158,746,000
Income tax expense	49,805,000
Other assets	169,419,000
Other operating expenses	626,504,000
Aircraft fuel expense	425,506,000
Repairs and maintenance expense	69,975,000
Accounts payable	121,157,000
Other liabilities	508,207,000
Notes payable	1,291,136,000
Retained earnings (as of December 31, 2006)	316,123,000
Ticket revenues	1,558,471,000
Airport operations expense	262,310,000
No dividends were declared or paid during 2006.	

Required:

1. Prepare an income statement for the year ended December 31, 2006. Round the reported amounts to thousands.

2. Prepare a statement of retained earnings for the year ended December 31, 2006. Assume the balance in retained earnings was $201,447,000 at January 1, 2006.

3. Prepare a balance sheet as at December 31, 2006.

4. Using the balance sheet, indicate whether the total assets of WestJet Airlines at the end of 2006 were financed primarily by liabilities or shareholders' equity.

COACHED PROBLEMS

CP1-1 Preparing an Income Statement and Balance Sheet

LO2

Assume that you are the president of Nuclear Company. At the end of the first year of operations (December 31, 2009), the following financial data for the company are available:

COACH'S TIP

Cash	$25,000
Accounts receivable from customers	12,000
Inventories	90,000
Equipment owned	45,000
Accounts payable to suppliers	47,370
Notes payable	2,000
Total sales revenue	140,000
Expenses, including the cost of goods sold (excluding income taxes)	89,100
Income tax expense	15,270
Contributed capital, 7,000 shares outstanding	87,000

No dividends were declared or paid during 2009.

1. Begin by classifying each account as asset, liability, shareholders' equity, revenue, or expense. Then use the formats shown in the chapter for presenting an income statement and balance sheet. You'll need the net income of the current year to calculate the retained earnings at the end of the year, so do the income statement first.

2. Because this is the first year of operations and there were no dividends, the balance in retained earnings will include only the current year's net income.

Required:

1. Prepare an income statement for the year 2009.
2. Prepare a balance sheet at December 31, 2009.

CP1-2 Interpreting the Financial Statements

LO3

Refer to CP1-1.

Required:

1. Evaluate whether the company was profitable.
2. Evaluate whether the company could have paid dividends during the year.
3. Evaluate whether the company's assets are financed mainly by creditors or shareholders.

GROUP A PROBLEMS

PA1-1 Preparing an Income Statement and Balance Sheet

LO2

Assume that you are the president of McClaren Corporation. At the end of the first year of operations (June 30, 2009), the following financial data for the company are available:

Cash	$13,150
Accounts receivable from customers	9,500
Inventories	57,000
Equipment owned	36,000
Accounts payable to suppliers	31,500
Notes payable	1,500
Total sales revenue	90,000
Expenses, including the cost of goods sold (excluding income taxes)	60,500
Income tax expense	8,850
Contributed capital, 5,000 shares outstanding	62,000

No dividends were declared or paid during fiscal 2009.

Required:

1. Prepare an income statement for the year ended June 30, 2009.
2. Prepare a balance sheet at June 30, 2009.

PA1-2 Interpreting the Financial Statements

LO3

Refer to PA1-1.

Required:

1. Evaluate whether the company was profitable.
2. Evaluate whether the company could have paid dividends during the year.
3. Evaluate whether the company's assets are financed mainly by creditors or shareholders.

LO2   **PA1-3 Preparing a Balance Sheet and Income Statement**

Canadian Tire started out in Toronto in 1922, and now operates almost 500 of its own stores, as well as almost 400 Mark's Work Wearhouse stores, across the country. It is Canada's largest independent gasoline retailer. More than 60 per cent of this company is still owned by the daughter of one of its original founders. Below is a list of the financial statement items and amounts adapted from a recent Canadian Tire Corporation balance sheet and income statement.

Accounts payable	$1,580
Accounts receivable	341
Cash	741
Contributed capital	704
Interest expense	76
Income tax expense	201
Inventories	667
Net income	355
Notes payable	1,168
Operating expenses	7,637
Other assets	1,175
Other liabilities	271
Property and equipment	2,881
Retained earnings	2,082
Sales revenues	8,269
Total assets	5,805
Total expenses	7,914
Total liabilities	3,019
Total liabilities and shareholders' equity	5,805
Total revenues	8,269
Total shareholders' equity	2,786

Required:

1. Prepare a balance sheet and income statement for the year, following the formats in Exhibits 1.3 and 1.4.
2. What other two statements would Canadian Tire include in its financial statements?
3. Does Canadian Tire rely more or less on shareholders for financing than does Tim Hortons? (See the Demonstration Case on pages 21 to 22.)

GROUP B PROBLEMS

PB1-1 Preparing an Income Statement and Balance Sheet

Assume that you are the president of Riterong Corporation. At the end of the first year of operations (April 30, 2009), the following financial data for the company are available:

Cash	$39,150
Accounts receivable from customers	27,500
Inventories	135,000
Equipment owned	108,000
Accounts payable to suppliers	57,800
Notes payable	3,500
Total sales revenue	270,000
Expenses, including the cost of goods sold (excluding income taxes)	180,500
Income tax expense	27,150
Contributed capital, 5,000 shares outstanding	186,000

No dividends were declared or paid during fiscal 2009.

Required:

1. Prepare an income statement for the year ended April 30, 2009.
2. Prepare a balance sheet at April 30, 2009.

PB1-2 Interpreting the Financial Statements

LO3

Refer to PB1-1.

Required:

1. Evaluate whether the company was profitable.
2. Evaluate whether the company could have paid dividends during the year.
3. Evaluate whether the company's assets are financed mainly by creditors or shareholders.

SKILLS DEVELOPMENT CASES

S1-1 Finding Financial Information

LO1–LO3

Refer to the financial statements of High Liner Foods in Appendix A at the end of this book, or download the annual report from the *Cases* section of the text's Web site at www.mcgrawhill.ca/college/phillips. (High Liner's year-end is December 29, 2007.)

Required:

1. What is the amount of net income for 2007?
2. What amount of revenue was earned in 2007?
3. How much inventory does the company have at the end of 2007?
4. How much cash is on hand at the end of 2007?
5. High Liner's shares are traded on the Toronto Stock Exchange under the symbol HLF. What kind of company does this make High Liner?
6. Which public accounting firm signed High Liner's Auditors' Report?

S1-2 Comparing Financial Information

LO1–LO3

Refer to the financial statements of Sun-Rype Products by downloading the annual report from the *Cases* section of the text's Web site at www.mcgrawhill.ca/college/phillips. Note that High Liner ends its fiscal year on December 29, 2007, which doesn't perfectly match Sun Rype's year ended December 31, 2007. In the questions that follow, assume both financial statements are for the year ended December 31, 2007. (This is a reasonable assumption, since there is only a two-day difference.)

Required:

1. Was Sun-Rype's net income for 2007 greater or less than High Liner's?
2. Was Sun-Rype's revenue for 2007 greater or less than High Liner's?
3. Did Sun-Rype have more or less inventories than High Liner at the end of 2007?
4. Did Sun-Rype have more or less cash than High Liner at the end of 2007?
5. Is Sun-Rype the same type of business organization as High Liner? Does it use the same firm of external auditors?
6. On an overall basis, was Sun-Rype or High Liner more successful in 2007?

S1-3 Internet-Based Team Research: Examining an Annual Report

LO1–LO3

As a team, select an industry to analyze. Go to the Web site for the System for Electronic Document Analysis and Retrieval (SEDAR) at www.SEDAR.com to search for information about Canadian public companies. The Canadian Securities Administrators (CSA) and CDS INC, a subsidiary of The Canadian Depository for Securities Limited, have operated the SEDAR Web site since 1997 to make Canadian public securities filings easily accessible. Click on Search Database and Public Company and run your search by industry group to find companies in your chosen industry. Each group member should acquire the annual report for one Canadian publicly traded company in the industry, with each member selecting a different company. In addition to SEDAR's and the company's own Web sites, corporate and industry information can be found on

TEAM CASE

a number of other Web sites, such as www.hoovers.com and www.fin-info.com. The United States runs a service similar to SEDAR called EDGAR. For American company data, go to www.edgarscan.pwcglobal.com.

Required:

1. On an individual basis, each team member should write a short report that lists the following information:
    a.   What type of business organization is it?
    b.   What types of products or services does it sell?
    c.   On what day of the year does its fiscal year end?
    d.   For how many years does it present complete balance sheets? Income statements? Cash flow statements?
    e.   Are its financial statements audited by independent auditors? If so, by whom?
    f.   Did its total assets increase or decrease over the last year?
    g.   Did its net income increase or decrease over the last year?

2. Then, as a team, write a short report comparing and contrasting your companies using these attributes. Discuss any patterns across the companies that you as a team observe and, in particular, compare the level of reporting detail. Provide potential explanations for any differences discovered.

LO2–LO4

ETHICAL ISSUES

S1-4 Ethical Decision Making: A Real-Life Example

In January 2004, Lord Conrad Black and other executives at Hollinger International Inc (HII) were hit with a lawsuit accusing them of defrauding investors and lenders of over $1.25 billion. To understand the charges, let's look a bit at HII's and Black's history. Conrad Black, born in Montreal and educated at Carleton and McGill, began buying newspapers after graduation and built a publishing empire that included the *Daily Telegraph* in London and the *Chicago Sun-Times*. Black and his wife became well-known for their love of the good life, owning lavish homes worth close to $100 million in London, Palm Beach, Toronto, and New York. Black gave up his Canadian citizenship in 2001 so that he could be inducted into England's House of Lords under the sponsorship of then-British Prime Minister Margaret Thatcher. A percentage of HII's shares traded publicly on the Toronto and New York Stock Exchanges, but Black still controlled the company through his holdings. The lawsuit claimed that HII executives took money from HII in a conspiracy to enrich themselves improperly at the expense of the other shareholders. It alleged that during the late 1990s, when HII was selling off many of its assets, HII paid part of the money received from the sale to insiders and then falsified the accounting records to hide what they had done. For example, in 2000 HII sold Canadian newspaper assets to CanWest Global for $1.8 billion. On top of this, CanWest paid $28 million to Black and three other executives plus another $25 million to a Toronto-based company controlled by Black. In 2005, United States law enforcement authorities filed criminal charges against Conrad Black and a number of HII executives.[4]

1. What is the accounting concept that Lord Black was accused of violating?
2. Based on the information provided above, can you determine which of HII's dealings are clearly inappropriate and which are clearly appropriate?
3. As a shareholder, how might you attempt to ensure that this kind of behaviour does not occur or, at least, does not occur without your knowing about it?
4. Aside from HII's shareholders, who else might have been harmed by the actions allegedly committed by HII executives?

Epilogue: In 2007, Lord Black was convicted on four counts of fraud and obstruction of justice and was sentenced to 6½ years in prison, a fine of U.S.$125,000 and forfeiture of another U.S.$6.1 million.

LO4

S1-5 Ethical Decision Making: A Mini-Case

You are one of three partners who own and operate Mary's Maid Service. The company has been operating for seven years. One of the other partners has always prepared the company's annual financial statements. Recently, you proposed that the statements be audited each year because it would benefit the partners and prevent possible disagreements about the division of profits. The

---

[4] *The Globe and Mail*, May 8, 2004; *Ottawa Citizen*, August 20, 2005; *Canadian Business*, Nov. 21–Dec. 4, 2005.

partner who prepares the statements proposed that his Uncle Ray, who has a lot of financial experience, can do the job and at little cost. Your other partner remained silent.

Required:

1. What position would you take on the proposal? Justify your response.
2. What would you strongly recommend? Give the basis for your recommendation.

S1-6 Critical Thinking: Developing a Balance Sheet and Income Statement

LO2, LO3

On September 30, Jill and Jack started arguing about who was better off. Jack said he was better off because he had the latest PlayStation console that he bought last year for $350. Jill, on the other hand, argued that she was better off because she had $1,000 and a '75 Mustang that she bought two years ago for $800. Jack countered that Jill still owed $250 on her car and that Jack's dad promised to buy him a Porsche if he gets a great grade in his accounting class. Jill pointed out that she inherited a collection of trading cards that she figured she could sell for about $250. Jack said he had $6,000 in his bank account right now because he just received a $4,800 student loan. Jill knows that Jack still owes an instalment of $800 on this term's tuition.

Jill and Jack met again in early November. They asked each other how they were doing. Jill claimed that she'd become much more successful than Jack. She had a part-time job, where she earned $500 per month. Jack laughed at Jill because he had won $950 on a lottery ticket he bought in October, and that was merely for the "work" of standing in line for a minute. It was just what he needed because his apartment costs $450 each month. Jill, on the other hand, pays $120 for her share of the rent. Both Jill and Jack have other normal living costs that total $300 each month.

1. Prepare a report that compares what Jill and Jack each own and owe on September 30. Note any decisions you had to make when preparing your report. Which of the two is better off?
2. Prepare a report that compares what Jill and Jack each earned during October. Note any decisions you had to make when preparing your report. Which of the two is more successful?

S1-7 Preparing an Income Statement and Balance Sheet

LO2

Electronic Arts is the world's leading developer and publisher of interactive entertainment software for personal computers and advanced entertainment systems made by Sony, Nintendo, and Microsoft. Assume that the company is revising its methods for displaying its financial statements, and the controller in the accounting department has asked you to create electronic worksheets that they can use as their standard format for financial statement reporting. The controller has provided you with an alphabetical list of statement categories and account names (below), with corresponding balances (in millions) as of September 30. She has asked you to use a spreadsheet program to create two worksheets that organize the accounts into a properly formatted balance sheet and income statement, and use formulas to compute amounts marked by a ? below.

Accounts Payable	$171	Other Liabilities	587
Accounts Receivable	328	Promotion Expense	107
Assets		Property, Plant, and Equipment	364
Cash	2,412	Retained Earnings	1,998
Contributed Capital	986	Revenue	
Cost of Goods Sold Expense	284	Sales Revenue	675
Expenses		Selling Expense	223
Income Tax Expense	9	Shareholders' Equity	
Inventories	367	Total Assets	?
Liabilities		Total Expenses	?
Net Income	?	Total Liabilities	?
Notes Payable	12	Total Liabilities and Shareholders' Equity	?
Other Assets	283	Total Shareholders' Equity	?
Other Expenses	1		

Not knowing quite where to start, you e-mailed your friend Billy for advice on using a spreadsheet. Billy is an extreme Type A personality, which explains his very detailed reply, as shown on the next page.

Required:

Follow Billy's advice to create a balance sheet and income statement, with each statement saved on a separate worksheet in a file called *me*EA.xls where the *me* part of the file name uniquely identifies you.

From:	BillyTheTutor@yahoo.com
To:	Overwhelmed@hotmail.com
Cc:	
Subject:	Excel Help

Hey pal. Long time, no chat. Here's the scoop on creating those worksheets, with a screen shot that shows how to go. If you need more help, let me know and I'll submit an application for your position there. ☺

1. Start-up Excel to open a new spreadsheet file. You'll need only two worksheets for this assignment, so delete the third worksheet by clicking on the *Sheet3* tab at the bottom of the worksheet and selecting Edit/Delete Sheet in the pull-down menu. While you're at it, rename *Sheet1* and *Sheet2* to *Balance Sheet* and *Income Statement* by double-clicking on the worksheet tabs and typing in the new names.
2. Plan the layout for your reports. Use the first column as a blank margin, the second column for account names and their headings, and the third column for the numbers corresponding to each account name or total. If you want to apply the same format to all worksheets, begin by right-clicking on the tab at the bottom of a worksheet and choosing Select All Sheets. Next, resize the first column by clicking on the A at the top of that column, selecting Format/Column/Width . . . from the pull-down menu, and choosing a width of 2. Using this same procedure, resize columns B and C to 50 and 15, respectively.
3. Starting with cell B1, enter the company's name. Enter the report name and date in cells B2 and B3. To merge cells so these headings span more than one column, select the cells to be merged and then click on ⊞. Continue with the body of the report in cell B5, entering any necessary amounts in column C.
4. To use formulas to compute subtotals and totals, the equals sign = is entered first into the cell and is followed immediately by the formula. So, to subtract cell C16 from C13, enter =C16−C13. To add a series of amounts, say C6 through C10, use a formula like =SUM(C6:C10), as shown in the screen shot below.
5. After you get all the data entered and totals calculated, be sure to save the file. To do this, just click on File/Save As . . . and enter the file name.
6. If you need to print the worksheets, it might be best to highlight what you want printed; then click File/Print . . . and choose Selection in the dialogue box that pops up.
7. Go to it, you accounting guru!

COACH'S TIP

To apply different formats (such as dollar signs, centre alignment, single- or double-underlined borders, boldface), select the cell(s), click on Format/Cells . . . in the pull-down menu, and choose the desired options.

	A	B	C
1		**Electronic Arts, Inc.**	
2		**Balance Sheet**	
3		**As of September 30**	
4			
5		**ASSETS**	
6		Cash	$ 2,412,000
7		Accounts Receivable	328,000
8		Inventories	367,000
9		Property and Equipment	364,000
10		Other Assets	283,000
11		*Total Assets*	$3,754,000

Balance Sheet / Income Statement /

CHAPTER 2

Reporting and Interpreting Investing and Financing Results on the Balance Sheet

Understand what a balance sheet means to users.

LO1   Explain and select common balance sheet account titles.

Study how to analyze transactions.

LO2   Apply transaction analysis to business transactions.

Evaluate transactions using the debit/credit framework.

LO3   Use journal entries and T-accounts to show how business transactions affect the balance sheet.

LO4   Prepare an unadjusted trial balance and a balance sheet.

Reconsider the balance sheet concepts that users rely on.

LO5   Explain the concepts that determine whether an item is reported on the balance sheet and at what amount.

This chapter introduces the system of accounting, which gathers financial information and produces the balance sheet as well as the other financial statement reports. We focus on the investing and financing activities of First Choice Haircutters, Canada's dominant value-priced hair salon chain.

Do you spend hours looking for e-mail messages that you got just a couple of weeks ago? Have you ever found the perfect Web site, only to later misplace your bookmark to it? Does your directory of file folders contain meaningless labels like "stuff"? If so, you probably could use an organizing system that neatly sorts every e-mail, bookmark, and file into categories. With such a system, you might be able to quickly find that funny joke about the magician and the parrot, or the stats assignment that is due tomorrow.

Businesses also need systems for organizing information. Just think what could happen if a system didn't exist to track the millions of letters and packages handled by Canada Post every day, or the millions of phone calls at Bell Canada. Clearly, big companies need well-organized systems for tracking their business activities and financial results. But it's not just the big guys who need accounting systems. Small businesses, like your local **FIRST CHOICE HAIRCUTTERS (FCH)** salon, need them too. In this chapter, we'll focus on the decisions that business managers make when starting up a single FCH salon and how their accounting systems track the financial results of the salon's investing and financing activities. In later chapters, you'll see how things are basically the same, only bigger, at Regis Corporation—a public company that bought First Choice Haircutters in 2000 and now owns over 12,000 salons worldwide, making Regis eight times the size of its closest competitor.

You may remember our promise in Chapter 1 that you'd have time to learn the details about specific financial statement accounts in Chapters 2 through 4. That time has come: We begin this chapter with a look at the balance sheet and its accounts. This is a good place to start because the balance sheet is based on the basic accounting equation, which also happens to be the framework on which accounting systems are built. After you spend a bit of time becoming reacquainted with the balance sheet, you'll be all set to learn about the system of accounting—a topic that you'll be hearing lots about in this chapter and in Chapters 3 and 4. Although the accounting system tracks the results of all types of business activities, we focus on investing and financing in this chapter. (We'll spend Chapters 3 and 4 looking at how accounting systems track the results of operating activities, which affect both balance sheet and income statement accounts.) This chapter closes with a look at concepts that relate to the balance sheet. The goals that you should be trying to achieve when reading Chapter 2 are presented as Learning Objectives on the first page of this chapter.

UNDERSTAND _____
What a Balance Sheet Means to Users

BUSINESS ACTIVITIES AND COMMON BALANCE SHEET ACCOUNTS

To understand the items reported on the balance sheet of an FCH store, it's useful to first think about what's involved in getting a hair salon up and running. First, you will need to decide on a location. Because the idea behind FCH is to make hair care convenient for customers, you'll try to find space for your salon in a neighbourhood shopping mall, anchored by either a major grocery chain or mass merchandiser. This will ensure your salon attracts what are known as "destination shoppers." These are customers who avoid spending time driving from the grocery store to the video store to a hair salon. They want to do it all at one place, and your mall location makes this possible.

Okay, now that you've selected a location, you'll need to start investing in some assets. First, you'll need to renovate your salon space so that it presents an open and airy environment, consistent with the standard FCH design. Typically, these renovations take four to six weeks to complete and cost about $42,000. You'll also need to spend an additional $18,000 to buy furniture and equipment for the salon. This might seem like a lot of money, but, the next time you get your hair cut, just take a look around at all the different furnishings in a hair salon. You'll likely see a reception desk, lighting fixtures, styling chairs, shampoo stations, computer hardware (and software), mirrors, scissors, trimmers, razors, curlers, and dryers—and those fuzzy pink rollers.

But wait! You (and your parents) have got only $50,000 to contribute to starting up a company. To finance the cost of all those assets, you'll need to consider getting a loan from a bank. A $20,000 loan would give the company enough cash to pay for furniture and equipment and still leave some money to pay for operating supplies like shampoo and all that other hair gunk.

From the above description and what you remember from Chapter 1, try to think of the accounts that are likely to appear on the balance sheet of your FCH store. Really, cover up Exhibit 2.1 and take 10 seconds to picture what should be on the balance sheet of your business. When you're done, compare it with the balance sheet in Exhibit 2.1.

FCH salons operate in Canadian dollars. When a salon reports its results to Regis Corp., its parent company in the United States, it is important that the salon clearly states that the **unit of measure** used in its statements is millions of Canadian dollars so that Regis is not confused. All companies state the currency they use in their statements. For example, Sony reports in yen, Lego in Danish krone, and Adidas in euros.

So, how did you do? The most important thing at this stage is that you knew to think about assets, liabilities, and shareholders' equity accounts. To extend your thinking a bit, Exhibit 2.1 separately classifies some assets and liabilities as "current." This is called a **classified balance sheet.** We haven't created new accounts to do this. We've simply cut the assets and liabilities into current and long-term sections when reporting them in the

The **unit of measure assumption** states that results of business activities should be reported in an appropriate monetary unit.

A **classified balance sheet** is one that classifies assets and liabilities into current and other (long-term) categories.

exhibit 2.1 Sample Balance Sheet and Explanation of Items

FIRST CHOICE HAIRCUTTERS SALON **Balance Sheet** **At August 31, 2009** **(in Cdn. dollars)**		Who What When Unit of measure
Assets		
Current Assets		
Cash	$10,000	Cash in company's bank account
Supplies	630	Shampoo and other hair products to be used on customers
Total Current Assets	10,630	= 10,000 + 630
Furnishings and Equipment	60,000	Cost of store renovations, furniture, and equipment
Total Assets	$70,630	= 10,630 + 60,000
Liabilities		
Current Liabilities		
Accounts Payable	$ 630	Amount owed to supplier for purchases of supplies on account
Total Current Liabilities	630	
Notes Payable	20,000	Amount owed to bank for loan (under a formal agreement)
Total Liabilities	20,630	= 630 + 20,000
Shareholders' Equity		
Contributed Capital	50,000	Amount contributed by shareholders (you and your parents)
Retained Earnings	0	No operations yet, so no earnings to report as retained
Total Shareholders' Equity	50,000	= 50,000 + 0
Total Liabilities and Shareholders' Equity	$70,630	= 20,630 + 50,000

balance sheet, as suggested in Exhibit 2.2. **Current Assets** are the resources that your business owns because of a past transaction that will be used up or turned into cash within the next 12 months. Your business will spend the *Cash* and use the *Supplies* that are reported at August 31, 2009, during the next 12 months, so they are classified as current. On the other hand, the *Furnishings and Equipment* will last five to ten years, so they are reported outside of the current asset category to indicate that they are **long-term assets.** Notice that assets are listed in the order of how fast they will be used up or can be turned into cash. Note also that *all* assets share the key feature of having probable future economic benefits.

In the liabilities section of the balance sheet, back in Exhibit 2.1, you again see the "current" subheading. Go ahead, take a look. **Current Liabilities** are debts and other obligations that are to be paid or settled within the next 12 months. In our example, *Accounts Payable* is the only current liability. This line on the balance sheet shows the amounts still owed for things that were bought on credit and will be paid off within the next 12 months. Liabilities not included as current are considered **long-term liabilities.** In our example, *Notes Payable* represents amounts that your FCH salon owes to the bank. More than likely, your company has signed an agreement (or "note") to repay these amounts several years from now. Notice that *all* liabilities (whether current or long-term) require a future sacrifice of resources because of a past transaction—this is one of their key features.

The first account in the shareholders' equity section, *Contributed Capital,* includes the amount of financing contributed to the company by shareholders. The next account is *Retained Earnings.* In our FCH example, there is no amount reported for this account.

Current assets will be used up or converted into cash within the next 12 months.

Long-term assets include resources that will be used up or turned into cash more than 12 months after the balance sheet date.

Current liabilities are debts and obligations that will be paid or settled within the next 12 months.

Long-term liabilities are debts and obligations that will be paid or settled more than 12 months from the balance sheet date.

exhibit 2.2 Cutting Assets and Liabilities into Current and Long-Term

A classified balance sheet cuts assets and liabilities into current and long-term sections. Total assets (current and long-term) are equal to total liabilities (current and long-term) plus shareholders' equity.

This makes sense because your business isn't open to customers yet, so there can't be any earnings to report as having been retained by the company.

Don't be surprised if you used account names that differ from what we used in Exhibit 2.1. It's okay to use different account names as long as they have the same meaning as ours and are properly classified as assets, liabilities, or shareholders' equity. In the real world of financial reporting, even commonly used accounts are given different labels by different companies. Depending on the company, you may see a liability for a bank loan called a "note payable," "loan payable," or simply "long-term debt." When choosing names, most companies will attempt to use names that already exist, if appropriate, or come up with one that describes the underlying business activity. Once an account name is selected, it is given a reference number (for the accounting system to recognize), and this exact name and number are used for all business activities affecting that account.

A summary of account names and numbers, called the **chart of accounts,** is kept by each company and is used to ensure consistency in reporting its own financial results. Some common balance sheet accounts (without the numbers) from a typical chart of accounts are listed in Exhibit 2.3. The accounts in boldface appear in FCH's balance sheet in Exhibit 2.1, except that, for FCH, **Property, Plant, and Equipment** is **Furnishings and Equipment.** You'll come across the other accounts in later chapters.

The **chart of accounts** is a summary of all account names and corresponding account numbers used to record financial results in the accounting system.

STUDY _____
How to Analyze Transactions

TRANSACTION ANALYSIS

Transaction analysis is the process of studying a transaction to determine its economic effect on the business in terms of the accounting equation.

You may not have realized it, but in the previous section of this chapter you were already beginning to learn one of the key steps of accounting: analyzing business activities and determining their financial statement effects. Your instructor is likely to refer to this step as **transaction analysis.** Although a single phrase is used to describe this step, it actually has two parts: (1) analyzing business activities and (2) identifying transactions. The first part describes what you look at (business activities), and the second part describes what you look for (transactions). In other words, transaction analysis involves thinking about each business activity of your company with the goal of finding transactions that should

exhibit 2.3   Excerpt from Chart of Accounts (Balance Sheet Accounts Only)

Account Name	Description
ASSETS	
Cash	Includes cash in the bank and in the cash register
Accounts Receivable	Amounts owed to your business by customers for sales made on credit
Interest Receivable	Interest owed to your business by others
Inventories	Goods on hand that are being held for resale
Supplies	Items on hand that will be used to make goods or provide services
Prepaid Expenses	Rent, insurance, and other expenses paid for future services
Notes Receivable	Amounts lent to others under a formal agreement ("note")
Property, Plant, and Equipment	Cost of land, buildings, and equipment
Intangible Assets	Trademarks, brand names, other rights that lack a physical presence
Other Assets	A variety of assets with smaller balances
LIABILITIES	
Accounts Payable	Amounts owed to suppliers for goods or services bought on credit
Wages Payable	Amounts owed to employees for salaries, wages, and bonuses
Accrued Liabilities	Amounts owed to others for advertising, utilities, interest, etc.
Unearned Revenues	Amounts (customer deposits) received in advance of providing goods or services to customers
Notes Payable	Amounts borrowed from lenders; involves signing a promissory note
Bonds Payable	Amounts borrowed from lenders; involves issuance of bonds
Other Liabilities	A variety of liabilities with smaller balances
SHAREHOLDERS' EQUITY	
Contributed Capital	Amount of cash received for shares issued
Retained Earnings	Amount of accumulated earnings not distributed as dividends

COACH'S TIP

Read this chart of accounts but don't memorize it. Also, don't try to force this chart of accounts on all problems. When using account names in homework problems, follow a process similar to what companies do. Consider whether a common name already exists or is given in the problem. If there isn't one, make up a descriptive one. After you have chosen an account name, be sure to use it consistently throughout the problem.

be recorded in the accounting information system. To do this well, you first need to know what a transaction is.

An accounting **transaction** is an exchange or event that has a direct economic effect on the assets, liabilities, or shareholders' equity of a business. Most transactions are observable external events—exchanges involving assets, liabilities, and shareholders' equity—that you can see between the company and someone else. When Starbucks sells you one of its exclusive Frappucino® coffee-blended beverages, it is exchanging an icy taste of heaven for your cash. This is an external transaction that needs to be recorded in Starbucks' accounting system. These are the easiest transactions to understand, and we concentrate on these in Chapters 2 and 3.

Some transactions are trickier to identify because you can't really see them occur. An example of this type of transaction involves the interest cost that racks up on a bank loan as time passes. You don't see anything happen (other than the calendar page flipping

A **transaction** is an exchange or event that has a direct economic effect on the assets, liabilities, or shareholders' equity of a business.

over), but an event has occurred that has a direct economic effect on the business: It now has an obligation (liability) to pay the interest that the bank charges. We look at these in Chapter 4.

Although many business activities have direct economic effects on a company, some have only indirect effects, which are not recorded. For example, signing an agreement is not considered a transaction because it typically involves the exchange of only promises, not assets, liabilities, or shareholders' equity. If you were to sign an employment contract to hire a new stylist at your FCH store, no transaction occurs from an accounting point of view because no exchange of assets, liabilities, or shareholders' equity occurred when the contract was signed. The company merely agreed to pay the stylist, and she merely agreed to snip away at your customers' heads. This was only an exchange of promises. Sure, when she actually pulls out her scissors and leaves a mound of your professor's hair on the floor, your business will then be obligated to pay her for the services she has provided to your business, resulting in a transaction. However, until that time, there is only a promise of an exchange to occur at some time in the future. Of course, if you were actually to pay a cash bonus for her to sign the contract, like the $2.5 million Reebok reportedly paid to hockey phenom Sidney Crosby when he was 17 years old, then it would involve an exchange that is considered a transaction.[1]

THE IDEAS BEHIND TRANSACTION ANALYSIS

Two simple ideas are used when analyzing transactions:

1. *Duality of effects.* It's a fancy name, but the idea is simple. Every transaction has at least two effects on the basic accounting equation. To remember this, just think of expressions like "give and take" or "push and pull" or, if you're a closet scientist, Newton's Third Law of Motion. Just as every story has at least two sides and you never get something for nothing, every transaction affects at least two accounts.
2. $A = L + SE$. You know this already, right? You studied the basic accounting equation on page 5 in Chapter 1. Remember that assets *always* must equal liabilities plus shareholders' equity for every accounting transaction. If it doesn't, then you are missing something and you should go back to the first (duality of effects) idea.

Let's do a few examples to show how these ideas are used when analyzing transactions. Suppose that your FCH store paid cash to buy Tigi's Hard Head Hair Spray (supplies). This is a transaction because an exchange exists between your business and Tigi. Applying the duality of effects idea, look for the "give and take" in this transaction, where we have replaced "takes" with the more polite "receives":

Duality of Effects	Transaction	FCH Gives	FCH Receives
	Purchased hair spray supplies for cash	Cash	Supplies

Now, let's check to see whether the basic accounting equation still holds:

Accounting Equation	A	=	L	+	SE
	⇓ Cash				
	⇑ Supplies	=	No change	+	No change

As you can see, the decrease in one asset (cash) is offset by the increase in another asset (supplies), and there are no changes in liabilities or shareholders' equity. Consequently, the accounting equation remains in balance, as it should.

---

[1] "Big Market Means Big Dough for Crosby," *Edmonton Journal,* July 21, 2005.

In the above example, your FCH store paid cash to Tigi immediately upon receiving the supplies. When most companies buy goods or services from another company, they do so on credit with the promise to pay for it later. For the next example, let's assume that your store receives a case of Shine Junkie from Tigi and pays for this purchase at the end of the month. In this example, your FCH store has entered into *two* transactions: (1) the purchase of an asset on credit and (2) the eventual payment. In the first, your business "receives" supplies (an increase in an asset) and in return "gives" a promise to pay later, called accounts payable (an increase in a liability).

	Transaction	FCH Gives	FCH Receives
Duality of Effects	(1) Purchased hair supplies on credit	Accounts payable (promise to pay)	Supplies

COACH'S TIP

Any account name with the word "payable" is a liability.

Notice that A = L + SE for this transaction, as shown below.

	A	=	L	+	SE
Accounting Equation	(1) ⇑ Supplies	=	⇑ Accounts Payable	+	No change

In the second transaction, your store gives up cash (a decrease in an asset) to fulfill its promise to pay Tigi and, as a result, takes back its promise (a decrease in the liability called accounts payable). Think of this as taking back (receiving) an IOU you had previously given to someone. Once it is back in your hands, you no longer owe the money. Check the following table to see whether this analysis fits the duality of effects requirement described above.

	Transaction	FCH Gives	FCH Receives
Duality of Effects	(2) Paid the amount owed on account payable	Cash	Accounts payable (the promise has been fulfilled)

Now, let's make sure that the basic accounting equation is still in balance after we enter these effects:

	A	=	L	+	SE
Accounting Equation	(2) ⇓ Cash	=	⇓ Accounts Payable	+	No change

Note that the accounting equation remained in balance after each of the two transactions. In the first, the increase in an asset was accompanied by a corresponding increase in a liability, and, in the second, the decrease in an asset was accompanied by a corresponding decrease in a liability. Although you haven't seen it yet in this chapter, you also will run into transactions where a shareholders' equity account changes and is accompanied by a corresponding change in either an asset or liability account.

We should warn you that, when first learning transaction analysis, you might be tempted to rush to identifying what accounts are affected while accidentally skipping over the important task of determining whether a transaction even exists. Remember, for a transaction to exist, there must be some kind of exchange or event that has a direct economic effect on your company. If your store sent an order to Tigi for more slick-styling products and Tigi promised to send them next week, no transaction has taken place from an accounting point of view. Two promises have been exchanged; that's all. As soon as the goods are shipped to your FCH store, however, your business has *exchanged* a promise to pay for goods that you actually received, so a transaction has taken place, and the financial statements of your FCH store will be affected.

DECIDE: A SYSTEMATIC APPROACH TO TRANSACTION ANALYSIS

Use these steps when analyzing transactions, to **DECIDE** on the accounting effects:

1. **D**oes a transaction exist? Go to step 2 only if your answer is yes.
2. **E**xamine it for the accounts affected. Put names on what is given and what is received.
3. **C**lassify each account as asset (A), liability (L), or shareholders' equity (SE).
4. **ID**entify the direction and amount of the effects. By how much does each asset, liability, and shareholders' equity account increase or decrease?
5. **E**nsure that the basic accounting equation still balances.

COACH'S TIP

Don't skip this section! Most students say that, of all the topics in this course, transaction analysis is the one they wished they had spent more time on when first learning it.

Because the best way to learn how to account for business activities is to work through examples, let's analyze some typical financing and investing transactions, using this DECIDE approach. Assume the following events took place in August.

(*a*) **You incorporate First Choice Haircutters Salon on August 1. The company issues shares to you and your parents in exchange for $50,000, which is deposited in the company's bank account.**

1. **D**oes a transaction exist?

   Yes, because cash is received and shares are given

2. **E**xamine it for accounts affected.

   Cash and Contributed Capital.

3. **C**lassify each account affected.

   Cash is an asset (A), and Contributed Capital is shareholders' equity (SE).

4. **ID**entify direction and amount.

   Cash (A) +$50,000 and Contributed Capital (SE) +$50,000

5. **E**nsure the equation still balances.

   Yes, because Assets + $50,000 = Shareholders' Equity +$50,000 (see below)

	Assets	=	Liabilities	+	Shareholders' Equity
Ref.	Cash				Contributed Capital
(a)	+50,000	=			+50,000

Notice that, in the table above, we included a transaction reference (*a*) so that we can refer back to the original transaction description if needed. You, too, should use transaction letters (or numbers or dates) as references in your homework problems.

When first learning how to account for transactions, some people forget that they should examine them from the point of view of the company, not the company's owners. As you saw in Chapter 1, the separate entity concept states that personal transactions of the owners of a business are not to be mixed in with the results of the business itself. So if you thought transaction (*a*) involved an increase in an *asset* called "stock investment" (or something like that), you probably forgot to analyze the transaction from the company's point of view. For First Choice Haircutters Salon, the issuance of shares is a financing activity (not an investment), which was recorded as contributed capital in shareholders' equity.

(b) **A construction company renovates your store space at a cost of $42,000, which your company pays in cash.**

1. **D**oes a transaction exist?

Yes, because renovations have been received and cash is given

2. **E**xamine it for accounts affected.

Furnishings and Equipment and Cash

3. **C**lassify each account affected.

Furnishings and Equipment is an asset (A), and Cash is an asset (A).

4. **ID**entify direction and amount.

Furnishings and Equipment (A) +42,000 and Cash (A) −$42,000

5. **E**nsure the equation still balances.

Yes, because Assets +$42,000 − $42,000 = no change (see below)

Ref.	Assets		=	Liabilities	+	Shareholders' Equity
	Cash	Furnishings and Equipment				Contributed Capital
(a)	+ 50,000		=			+ 50,000
(b)	− 42,000	+ 42,000	=			No change

(c) **Your company installs $10,000 worth of equipment in the salon, paying $8,000 in cash and promising to pay the remaining $2,000 at the end of the month.**

1. **D**oes a transaction exist?

Yes, because equipment has been received, and cash and a promise to pay have been given

2. **E**xamine it for accounts affected.

Furnishings and Equipment, Cash, and Accounts Payable

3. **C**lassify each account affected.

Furnishings and Equipment is an asset (A), Cash is an asset (A), and Accounts Payable is a liability (L).

4. **ID**entify direction and amount.

Furnishings and Equipment (A) +10,000, Cash (A) −$8,000, and Accounts Payable (L) +$2,000

5. **E**nsure the equation still balances.

Yes, because Assets +$2,000 = Liabilities +$2,000 (see below)

Ref.	Assets		=	Liabilities	+	Shareholders' Equity
	Cash	Furnishings and Equipment		Accounts Payable		Contributed Capital
(a)	+ 50,000		=			+ 50,000
(b)	− 42,000	+ 42,000	=			
(c)	− 8,000	+ 10,000	=	+ 2,000		

If you ever run into a transaction that you have no idea how to analyze, simply break it down. Rather than trying to "solve" it all at once, begin by looking just for what is received. This **E**xamine step is crucial, and you may find that the reason you were having trouble is that there was more than one item received. After you find what is received, look just for what is given. Again, you may find that, as in event (c) here, more than one item is involved. After you **C**lassify and **ID**entify, **E**nsure the accounting equation remains in balance, because this may give you a clue about whether you've detected all the accounts affected.

(*d*) **Your company borrows $20,000 from a bank, depositing those funds in its bank account and signing a formal agreement to repay the loan in two years.**

1. **D**oes a transaction exist?

   Yes, because cash has been received and a formal promise to pay ("note") has been given

2. **E**xamine it for accounts affected.

   Cash and Notes Payable

3. **C**lassify each account affected.

   Cash is an asset (A) and Notes Payable is a liability (L).

4. **ID**entify direction and amount.

   Cash (A) +20,000 and Notes Payable (L) +$20,000

5. **E**nsure the equation still balances.

   Yes, because Assets +$20,000 = Liabilities +$20,000 (see below)

	Assets		=	Liabilities		+	Shareholders' Equity
Ref.	Cash	Furnishings and Equipment		Accounts Payable	Notes Payable		Contributed Capital
(a)	+ 50,000		=				+ 50,000
(b)	− 42,000	+ 42,000	=				
(c)	− 8,000	+ 10,000	=	+ 2,000			
(d)	+ 20,000		=		+ 20,000		

(*e*) **Your company orders $800 worth of shampoo and other operating supplies from Tigi. None have been received yet.**

1. **D**oes a transaction exist?

   No, because nothing has been received and only a promise has been given

Okay, it's time for you to start taking over. As you read transactions (*f*) to (*h*) below, use the five-step **DECIDE** approach and fill in the highlighted blanks in the self-study quiz. See (*h*) on the next page where you can summarize the effects of each transaction on the accounting equation at the end of the self-study quiz.

HOW'S IT GOING? A Self-Study Quiz

(*f*) **Your company buys $8,000 worth of furniture, paying the full amount in cash.**

1. **D**oes a transaction exist?

   Yes, because cash is given and furniture is received

2. **E**xamine it for accounts affected.

   Cash and Furnishings and Equipment

3. **C**lassify each account affected.

   Cash is an asset (A) and Furnishings and Equipment is ⬚ Asset ( )

4. **ID**entify direction and amount.

   Cash (A) −$8,000 and Furnishings and Equipment (+) $ ⬚

5. **E**nsure the equation still balances.

   Yes, because Assets +$8,000 − $8,000 = No change ⬚

(g) Your company pays the $2,000 owed to the equipment supplier in (c).

1. **D**oes a transaction exist?

   Yes, because [_____]

2. **E**xamine it for accounts affected.

   Cash and Accounts Payable

3. **C**lassify each account affected.

   Cash is an asset (A) and Accounts Payable is a liability (L).

4. **ID**entify direction and amount.

   Cash (A) −$2,000 and Accounts Payable (L) −$2,000

5. **E**nsure the equation still balances.

   Yes, because [_____].

   Note that (g) doesn't increase the *Furnishings and Equipment* asset again because the equipment was recorded in (c) at its full cost ($10,000) rather than at the amount of cash given when the equipment was received. This is an important concept (called the cost principle) that we will return to at the end of the chapter.

(h) Your company receives $630 worth of the supplies ordered in (e) and promises to pay for them next month.

1. **D**oes a transaction exist?

   Yes, because supplies are received and a promise to pay is given

2. **E**xamine it for accounts affected.

   Supplies and Accounts Payable

3. **C**lassify each account affected.

   Supplies is an asset (A) and Accounts Payable is a liability (L).

4. **ID**entify direction and amount.

   Supplies (A) [+ $ _____] *and Accounts Payable (L)* [+ $ _____]

5. **E**nsure the equation still balances.

   Yes, because assets and liabilities increase by the same amount

	Assets			=	Liabilities		+	Shareholders' Equity
Ref.	Cash	Supplies	Furnishings and Equipment		Accounts Payable	Notes Payable		Contributed Capital
(a)	+ 50,000			=				+ 50,000
(b)	− 42,000		+ 42,000	=				
(c)	− 8,000		+ 10,000	=	+ 2,000			
(d)	+ 20,000			=		+ 20,000		
(f)	− 8,000		[____]	=	[____]			
(g)	[____]			=	[____]			
(h)		[____]		=	[____]			
Total	10,000	630	60,000		630	20,000		50,000

After you have finished, check your answers with the solutions presented in the margin.

The self-study quiz that you just finished involved a company's first month of operations. As a result, the net changes during the month lead directly to the ending balances, which would be reported on a balance sheet. Notice that the totals in the self-study quiz correspond to the amounts shown in Exhibit 2.1 on page 43.

A **journal** is organized by date, and shows each day's transactions. A **ledger** is organized by account, and shows the effects of the day's transactions on the accounts. **Accounts** are those items a company wants to keep track of, such as its cash, its accounts payable, and its wages expense. The balances in the accounts provide the numbers that appear in the financial statements.

EVALUATE _____
Transactions Using the Debit/Credit Framework

It's possible to use a spreadsheet for entering the effects of transactions directly into the various accounts. By adding the increases, subtracting the decreases, and including the balances at the beginning of the month for each account, we could compute the ending balance in each account to be reported then on the balance sheet. Although this method would work, you can just imagine how impractical it would be in a company like Regis Corporation, which has transactions with about 12 million customers and 51,000 employees every month. Rather than create a spreadsheet as big as three football fields, a more sophisticated system is used to record and summarize transactions.

Fortunately, your experience as a student has made you familiar with a system of learning similar to the system used in accounting. Day after day, you go to class, take notes, go to class, take notes, repeat. The reason you take notes is to create a record of what happened in each class, kind of like an academic diary or journal. Then, when preparing for exams, you probably copy these notes to summary sheets to study from. These summary sheets make it easier to understand all those things you noted earlier in the month.

The system of accounting also uses this combination of note-taking and summarizing. First, a daily record of events (transactions) is noted in a journal. These journal entries are copied ("posted") to summary sheets that show, for each balance sheet account, the effects of the month's transactions. These summary sheets (which, as a group, are called a ledger) then become the basis for preparing financial statements. Exhibit 2.4 illustrates this process. Notice how the transaction on August 1 to issue shares, which increased the company's cash and contributed capital (as noted in the journal), can be seen in the *Cash* account in the ledger. The final step in the process, using the ledger to prepare the financial statements, is studied in Chapter 4.

Typically, when people are first shown an accounting **journal** and **ledger,** they have a tough time telling them apart. Take a quick look at Exhibit 2.4 again. Does it seem as though the journal and ledger pages look a lot alike? Both include dates, amounts, and lots of columns, so do they really differ from one another? Actually, yes. We will highlight their differences in the following sections by using simplified formats that strip away many of the lines (and some of the columns) that can make a journal and ledger

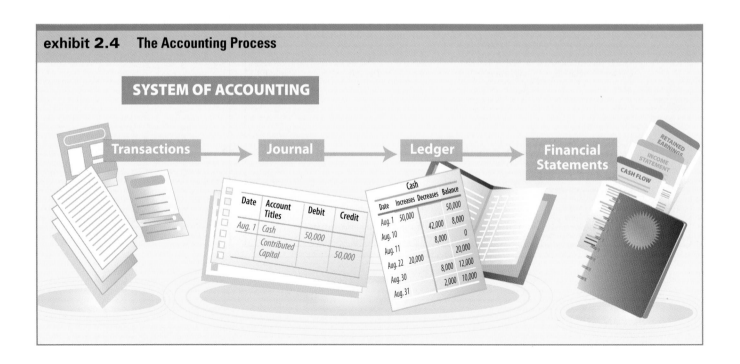

exhibit 2.4   The Accounting Process

look alike. These simplified formats should make it easier for you to distinguish the two types of accounting records and to focus on the main benefits of a journal (to take note of daily transactions) and a ledger (to summarize—for each **account**—the effects of those transactions). We'll start with the simplified version of a ledger account, which is called a **T-account.** One more glance at the ledger page in Exhibit 2.4 should reveal how a T-account gets its name. (Can you see the "T" in the ledger account for *Cash*?)

The **T-account** is a simplified version of an accounting ledger used in textbooks and classrooms for illustration purposes.

T-ACCOUNTS: SEPARATING INCREASES AND DECREASES IN THE BASIC ACCOUNTING EQUATION

Each item on the balance sheet has its own T-account, which separately summarizes the increases and decreases that occur during the accounting period. Because assets appear on the left-hand side of the basic accounting equation (A = L + SE), each asset T-account includes increases on the left side of the T (decreases go on the right side of the T). For liabilities and shareholders' equity, which appear on the right-hand side of the accounting equation, increases are included on the right side of the T (and decreases go on the left).

COACH'S TIP

Think of the accounting equation as a scale that tips at the equals sign. To keep the scale in balance, you need to put increases (and decreases) in assets on the opposite side used for increases (and decreases) in liabilities and shareholders' equity.

Assets		=	Liabilities		+	Shareholders' Equity	
+ Increases	Decreases −		− Decreases	Increases +		− Decreases	Increases +

Take a moment to see how the increase symbol + appears on the left side of the T for accounts on the left side of the accounting equation, and on the right side of the T for accounts on the right side of the equation. This same balancing logic applies to decreases, which are on the side of the T closest to the equals sign.

Now, just as boating enthusiasts use special terms like "port" and "starboard" to refer to different sides of a boat, accountants also use special terms to refer to different sides of an account.[2] The term *debit* refers to the left side and *credit* refers to the right, as Exhibit 2.5 shows. These terms (and their abbreviations *dr* and *cr*) are based on Latin

COACH'S TIP

Here's another way to picture how debits and credits affect accounts:

	dr	cr
Assets	↑	↓
Liabilities	↓	↑
Shareholders' **E**quity	↓	↑

exhibit 2.5   The Difference between Debits and Credits

---

[2] Thanks to Rita Cook for sharing this analogy.

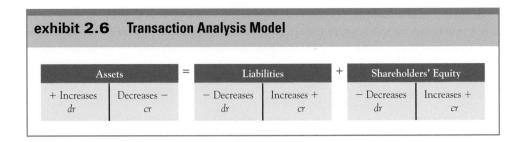

exhibit 2.6 **Transaction Analysis Model**

Assets		=	Liabilities		+	Shareholders' Equity	
+ Increases	Decreases −		− Decreases	Increases +		− Decreases	Increases +
dr	*cr*		*dr*	*cr*		*dr*	*cr*

words that had real meaning back in those days, but today they just mean "left" and "right." The journal columns in Exhibit 2.4 use the terms debit and credit.

To make this as easy for you as possible, we've combined these ideas in Exhibit 2.6, which we call the transaction analysis model. As you work on more transaction analysis exercises later in this chapter, you should refer to this model as often as you need to, until you can create it on your own without help.

You should note the following from the transaction analysis model in Exhibit 2.6:

- Asset accounts increase on the left (debit) side. Because they increase on the left, they almost always have debit balances at the end of a month. It would be highly unusual for an asset account, such as inventory, to have a negative (credit) balance.

- Liabilities and shareholders' equity accounts increase on the right (credit) side, and normally have credit balances. It's highly unusual for a liability or shareholders' equity account, such as contributed capital, to have a negative (debit) balance.

- In every transaction, the total dollar value of all debits equals the total dollar value of all credits. Later, we will add this equality check (Debits = Credits) to our DECIDE transaction analysis approach.

- After all transactions are posted, asset accounts normally have debit balances and liabilities and shareholders' equity accounts normally have credit balances.

Okay, now that you've seen how the T-account works as a simplified version of a ledger account, let's move on to the simplified format for noting each day's transactions in a journal.

JOURNAL ENTRIES

A debit-and-credit format is used when transactions are initially entered into the journal. Once transactions have been identified and analyzed, journalizing is the first step in the recording process. The formal format for these **journal entries,** as they are called, was shown in Exhibit 2.4. For purposes of this course, we will use the following simplified format:

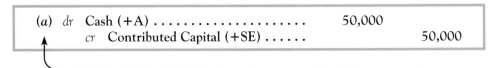

(*a*)	*dr*	Cash (+A)	50,000	
	cr	Contributed Capital (+SE)		50,000

Notice the following about the simplified journal entry format shown above:

- The source of the transaction is referenced using a number or letter, like the (*a*) given in our original description of the transaction.

- For each transaction, debits are written first (at the top) and credits are written below the debits. The account names and amounts to be credited are indented to the right. We recommend you also distinguish debits from credits by using *dr* and *cr* before the name of each account that is to be debited or credited.

- Total debits equal total credits ($50,000 = $50,000).

COACH'S TIP

Think of the accounting equation A = L + SE. Assets in this equation appear on the left-hand side or the debit side so an asset's normal balance is a debit. Liabilities and equity appear on the right-hand side or credit side of the equation so these accounts will normally have a credit balance.

Journal entries note the effects of each day's transactions on financial statement accounts.

While you are learning to perform transaction analysis, use the symbol A, L, or SE after each account name, as we did. By identifying accounts as assets (A), liabilities (L), or shareholders' equity (SE), you will become more familiar with the various types of accounts and you'll make it easier for others to interpret your journal entries. In the next few chapters, we include the direction of the effect before the symbol. For example, if the asset account *Cash* is to be increased (debited), we will show it as *dr* Cash (+A).

TRANSACTION ANALYSIS REVISITED

Now that you've been introduced to debits, credits, journal entries, and T-accounts, you are ready to revisit the five-step DECIDE approach used earlier to analyze transactions. To include these new concepts in the accounting process, we need to add two more steps, as highlighted in Exhibit 2.7.

exhibit 2.7   Transaction Analysis: The DECIDES Approach

1. **D**oes a transaction exist?
2. **E**xamine it for accounts affected.
3. **C**lassify each account affected.
4. **I**dentify direction and amount.
5. **D**ebit and credit the accounts affected.
6. **E**nsure the equation still balances and debits = credits.
7. **S**ummarize the transaction effects in T-accounts.

In the remainder of this section, we will work with you to use this transaction analysis approach to record the monthly transactions that were presented earlier in this chapter for your First Choice Haircutters Salon. Because we have completed steps 1 to 4 of the transaction analysis for these events already, we will not show them below, but you should understand that these steps *would* be performed had we not analyzed them earlier. The analysis below focuses on the results of steps 5 to 7, which involve the new concepts of debits, credits, journal entries, and T-accounts.

COACH'S TIP

Study all the material in this section carefully. This material is critical for understanding nearly all the remaining topics in this book. Spending time on this now will save you hours and hours of work and confusion later in the course.

(*a*) **You incorporate First Choice Haircutters Salon on August 1. The company issues shares to you and your parents in exchange for $50,000, which is deposited in the company's bank account.**

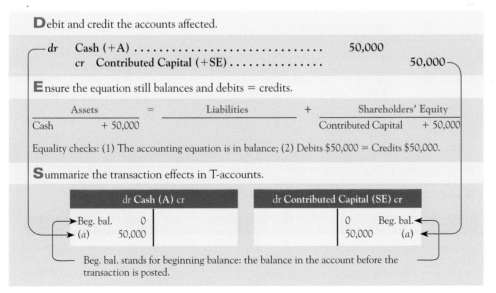

Debit and credit the accounts affected.

dr   Cash (+A) 50,000
        cr Contributed Capital (+SE) 50,000

Ensure the equation still balances and debits = credits.

Assets	=	Liabilities	+	Shareholders' Equity
Cash + 50,000				Contributed Capital + 50,000

Equality checks: (1) The accounting equation is in balance; (2) Debits $50,000 = Credits $50,000.

Summarize the transaction effects in T-accounts.

dr **Cash (A)** cr		dr **Contributed Capital (SE)** cr	
Beg. bal. 0			0 Beg. bal.
(*a*) 50,000			50,000 (*a*)

Beg. bal. stands for beginning balance: the balance in the account before the transaction is posted.

Your homework exercises will likely ask you to create a list of journal entries for *all* transactions before posting any of them to T-accounts. We show the journal entries and T-account postings together here, to show you how the posting to T-accounts simply involves copying the debit or credit amount from each line of the journal entry to the debit or credit side of the corresponding T-accounts.

(b) **A construction company renovates your store space at a cost of $42,000, which your company pays in cash.**

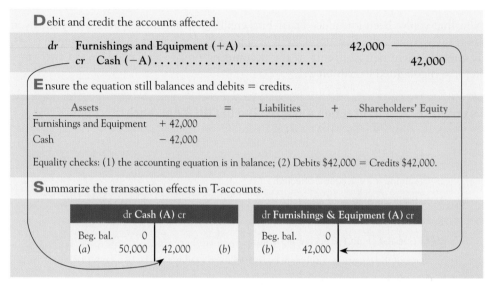

Notice above that the *Cash* T-account includes the postings for transactions (*a*) and (*b*). This accumulation of cash effects will continue until all of the month's transactions involving cash are included, at which time we will compute a total balance in the account by adding all the amounts in the debit column (increases) and subtracting all the amounts in the credit column (decreases). The excess of debits over credits will become the ending balance in this asset account, and it will carry over to become the beginning balance in the following month. But we've got a bunch more transactions in the month to **journalize** and post before we start totalling the T-accounts.

Journalize is the process of recording a transaction in the journal in the debits-equal-credits journal entry format.

(c) **Your company installs $10,000 worth of equipment in the salon, paying $8,000 in cash and promising to pay the remaining $2,000 at the end of the month.**

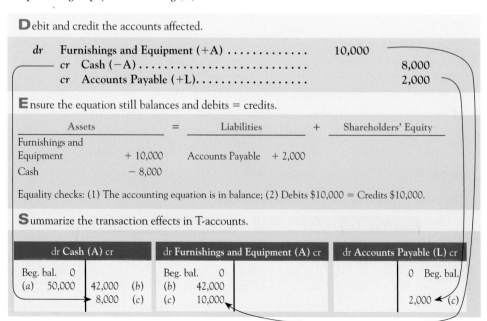

Let's briefly go over transaction (*c*), which affects three accounts: *Furnishings and Equipment, Cash,* and *Accounts Payable*. Because equipment was received, we need to record an increase in the asset account *Furnishings and Equipment*. The debit/credit rules indicate that asset increases are recorded on the left (debit) side of the T-account, so the journal entry includes a debit to Furnishings and Equipment for the $10,000 equipment cost. Because cash was given up, we need to record a decrease in the asset account *Cash*. The debit/credit rules indicate that asset decreases are recorded on the right (credit) side, so the journal entry includes a credit to Cash for the $8,000 given up. Because the company also gave a promise to pay the remaining $2,000, we need to record an increase in the liability *Accounts Payable*. The debit/credit rules indicate that liability increases are recorded on the right (credit) side of the T-account, so the journal entry includes a credit to Accounts Payable for $2,000. The net increase in assets of $2,000 ($10,000 − $8,000) is equal to the increase in liabilities of $2,000 (so the accounting equation is in balance), and the debit of $10,000 equals total credits of $10,000 ($8,000 + $2,000).

(*d*) **Your company borrows $20,000 from a bank, depositing those funds in its bank account and signing a formal agreement to repay the loan in two years.**

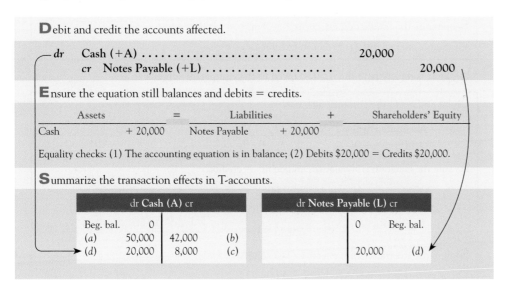

Debit and credit the accounts affected.

dr	Cash (+A)	20,000	
	cr Notes Payable (+L)		20,000

Ensure the equation still balances and debits = credits.

Assets		=	Liabilities		+	Shareholders' Equity
Cash	+ 20,000		Notes Payable	+ 20,000		

Equality checks: (1) The accounting equation is in balance; (2) Debits $20,000 = Credits $20,000.

Summarize the transaction effects in T-accounts.

dr **Cash (A)** cr			
Beg. bal.	0		
(*a*)	50,000	42,000	(*b*)
(*d*)	20,000	8,000	(*c*)

dr **Notes Payable (L)** cr		
	0	Beg. bal.
	20,000	(*d*)

Let's move on to event (*e*), which involved ordering (but not yet receiving) supplies from Tigi. Because this involved the exchange of only promises, it was not considered a transaction. For this reason, no journal entry is needed for event (*e*).

Are you getting the hang of it? The best way to know for sure is to try accounting for some transactions on your own. In the following self-study quiz, we will provide you with space to complete journal entries for three transactions. Complete each of the three journal entries first (as if you are recording transactions for a real company on a daily basis), and then summarize the effects in the corresponding T-accounts (as if you are posting the journal entries at the end of the month). The T-accounts are in Exhibit 2.8 on page 59.

HOW'S IT GOING?   A Self-Study Quiz

For events (*f*), (*g*), and (*h*) below, complete the journal entries and then post their effects to the T-accounts in Exhibit 2.8. Then check your answers with the solution at the end of the illustration.

(f) Your company buys $8,000 worth of furniture, paying the full amount in cash.

Debit and credit the accounts affected.

dr   Furniture (+A)   800
  cr   Cash (−A)   8,000

Ensure the equation still balances and debits = credits.

Assets	=	Liabilities	+	Shareholders' Equity
Furnishings and Equipment + 8,000				
Cash − 8,000				

Equality checks: (1) the accounting equation is in balance; (2) Debits $8,000 = Credits $8,000.

Summarize the transaction effects in T-accounts.

T-accounts are presented together in Exhibit 2.8.

(g) Your company pays the $2,000 owed to the equipment supplier in (c).

Debit and credit the accounts affected.

dr   Accounts Payable (−L)   2,000
  cr   Cash (−A)   2000

Ensure the equation still balances and debits = credits.

Assets	=	Liabilities	+	Shareholders' Equity
Cash − 2,000		Accounts Payable − 2,000		

Equality checks: (1) Does the accounting equation balance? ☐ (2) Debits $2,000 = Credits $2,000.

Summarize the transaction effects in T-accounts.

T-accounts are presented together in Exhibit 2.8.

(h) Your company receives $630 worth of the supplies ordered in (e) and promises to pay for them next month.

Debit and credit the accounts affected.

dr   Supplies (+A)   630
  cr   A.P. (+L)   630

Ensure the equation still balances and debits = credits.

Assets	=	Liabilities	+	Shareholders' Equity
Supplies + 630		Accounts Payable + 630		

Equality checks: (1) the accounting equation is in balance; (2) Debits $☐ = Credits $☐.

Summarize the transaction effects in T-accounts.

T-accounts are presented together in Exhibit 2.8.

COACH'S TIP

Try to fill in the missing line(s) of the journal entry, using only the description of the transaction. If you need some help, peek at the effects on the accounting equation.

Don't forget to post the journal entry effects to the T-accounts in Exhibit 2.8.

Quiz Answers

(*f*) Journal Entry
dr Furnishings and Equipment (+A)   8,000
  cr Cash (−A)   8,000

(*g*) Journal Entry
dr Accounts Payable (−L)   2,000
  cr Cash (−A)   2,000
Yes, the accounting equation is in balance.

(*h*) Journal Entry
dr Supplies (+A)   630
  cr Accounts Payable (+L)   630
Debits $630 = Credits $630

(All) Posting to T-Accounts
Verify that you properly posted the journal entries to the T-accounts by adding the increase side and subtracting the decrease side. The amount you get for each account should be the same as the double-underlined amount shown as the ending balance.

exhibit 2.8 T-Accounts Summarizing Transactions (*a*) to (*h*)

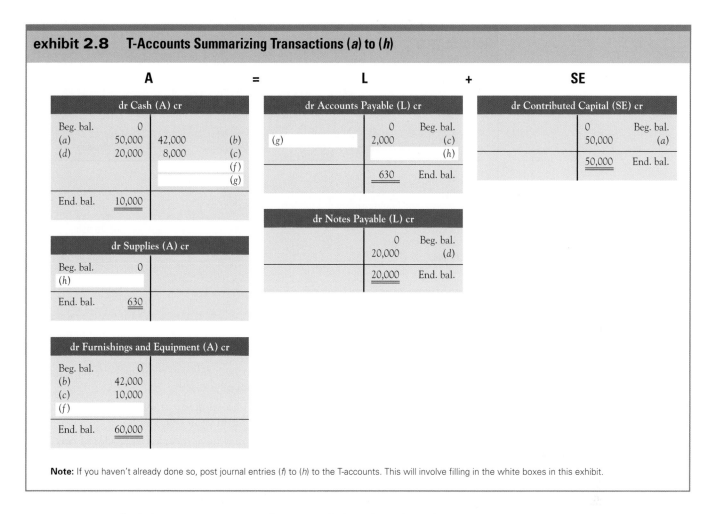

Note: If you haven't already done so, post journal entries (*f*) to (*h*) to the T-accounts. This will involve filling in the white boxes in this exhibit.

To compute the balance in T-accounts, draw a single line through each T-account below the amounts that you wish to total. Then calculate the ending balance by adding the increases to the beginning balance and deducting the decreases. For example, the equation for the ending balance in the Cash account is ($0 + 50,000 + 20,000 − 42,000 − 8,000 − 8,000 − 2,000 = $10,000).

Notice in Exhibit 2.8 that the ending balances are shown on the appropriate debit or credit side with a double underline.

UNADJUSTED TRIAL BALANCE

After posting journal entries to the various accounts, it's usually a good idea to check that the total recorded debits equal the total recorded credits. Unlike computerized accounting systems that prevent you from letting the accounting records get out of balance, it's easy to make mistakes when you're doing it by hand. Typical mistakes involve (*a*) posting a debit as a credit, (*b*) posting only part of a journal entry, (*c*) recording the wrong amount, or (*d*) miscalculating the ending balance.

The best way to ensure your accounts are "in balance" is to prepare a **trial balance.** The trial balance isn't part of the financial statements. It's actually an internal report used to determine whether total debits equal total credits. Exhibit 2.9 shows a trial balance, which lists all of the account names in one column (usually in financial statement order) and their ending balances (from Exhibit 2.8) in the appropriate debit or credit column.

Occasionally, you may find that your trial balance is out of balance. This only happens when you've made a mistake. Don't give up and hit Ctrl-Alt-Delete, because there are some shortcuts for finding the error. They all involve looking at the amount of the difference between total debits and total credits.

A **trial balance** is a list of all accounts and their balances, which is used to check on the equality of recorded debits and credits.

exhibit **2.9**	Sample Unadjusted Trial Balance		

FIRST CHOICE HAIRCUTTERS SALON
Unadjusted Trial Balance
As of September 30

Account Name	Debits	Credits
Cash	$ 10,000	
Supplies	630	
Furnishings and Equipment	60,000	
Accounts Payable		$ 630
Notes Payable		20,000
Contributed Capital		50,000
Totals	$70,630	$70,630

1. If the difference is *the same as* one of your account balances, you probably forgot to include the account in the trial balance.

2. If the difference is *twice* the amount of *an account balance*, you may have reported the account on the wrong side of the trial balance.

3. If the difference is *two times* the amount of *a particular transaction*, you may have posted a debit as a credit or a credit as a debit in your T-accounts.

4. If the difference is *evenly divisible by 9*, you may have reversed the order of two digits in a number or left a zero off the end of a number.

5. If the difference is *evenly divisible by 3*, you may have hit the key above or below the one you intended to hit (like a 9 instead of a 6) on your calculator or numeric keypad.

If you haven't already scanned the trial balance in Exhibit 2.9, take a moment to do it now. Notice that the title says *unadjusted* trial balance. It is called this because several adjustments will have to be made at the end of the accounting period to update the accounts. Don't worry about how to make the end-of-period adjustments yet. We'll spend all of Chapter 4 on that. For now, just realize that the accounts still have to be adjusted before we can prepare financial statements that follow generally accepted accounting principles.

PREPARING A BALANCE SHEET

It's easy to prepare a balance sheet from the trial balance. Just take the ending balances and group them as assets, liabilities, and shareholders' equity in proper balance sheet format. If you do this, you should end up with a balance sheet that looks like the one we presented back in Exhibit 2.1. We realize that the odds of your flipping all the way back to page 43 right now are slim, so we'll take this opportunity to show you a slightly different balance sheet format used by some companies. Exhibit 2.10 shows an alternative balance sheet layout called the account (side-by-side) format. Accountants can use either this format or the one shown in Exhibit 2.1, just as long as it balances (that is, total assets must equal the total of liabilities and shareholders' equity).

Now that you've seen how a balance sheet is created from the ending balances in ledger/T-accounts, which summarize journal entries that record each day's transactions, it's time to take a step back and think about what the balance sheet means for financial statement users.

COACH'S TIP

Even if total debits equal total credits, it's still possible that you've made an error. For example, if you accidentally debit an asset rather than an expense, total debits would still equal total credits. So, if they don't balance, you know you've made an error. If they do balance, it's still possible that a mistake has been made (and you just don't know it).

exhibit 2.10   Balance Sheet in Account Format

FIRST CHOICE HAIRCUTTERS SALON
Balance Sheet
At August 31, 2009
(in Cdn. dollars)

Assets		Liabilities	
Current Assets		Current Liabilities	
Cash	$10,000	Accounts Payable	$ 630
Supplies	630	Total Current Liabilities	630
Total Current Assets	10,630	Notes Payable	20,000
		Total Liabilities	20,630
		Shareholders' Equity	
		Contributed Capital	50,000
Furnishings and Equipment	60,000	Retained Earnings	0
		Total Shareholders' Equity	50,000
Total Assets	$70,630	Total Liabilities and Shareholders' Equity	$70,630

RECONSIDER _____
The Balance Sheet Concepts That Users Rely On

In Chapter 1, we introduced the term generally accepted accounting principles (GAAP). Everything you have learned so far about how financial statements are prepared and how business transactions are recorded complies with these principles. Since GAAP encompass a set of concepts as well as a set of applied techniques, it is important that we introduce you to the relevant concepts that underlie the techniques we study in each chapter of this text. Below we discuss the effects of focusing on transactions in accounting, and introduce you to two concepts related to this transaction focus: conservatism and the cost principle. Although both of these concepts make sense within our accounting framework, they also have their limitations, as we shall see below.

THE EFFECTS OF A TRANSACTION FOCUS

If you were interested in buying a company, you'd want to know what that company was worth. How would you figure that out? Could you find it out from the financial statements? Well, yes and no. There is a common misconception around this issue and that is why we look at it here.

If a company is public, there is an easy way to figure out its **market value.** You can calculate a public company's market value by looking at its share price. Let's assume that each of the company's 10,000 outstanding shares is selling for $25. This means that investors think the company is worth $250,000. But what if the company is not public? How do we know its worth then? Some people think that if you look at the balance sheet and see that the company's total shareholders' equity is $200,000, that is the company's market value. But that is not true. The $200,000 comes from the accounting records and is called the **book value** of the company, and this is not the same as the company's market value, for reasons that we will explain below. The only way to find out a private

Market value is what an item sells for in the marketplace.

Book value is the value an item is carried at in the accounting records (the books).

Business valuation is the process of analyzing a business to determine its worth.

company's value is to go through the complex calculations of a **business valuation,** which is beyond the scope of this text. What we will tell you is this. A company is worth more, and you'd be willing to pay more, if you think the company is going to be very profitable after you've bought the shares, because, as a shareholder, future profits will belong to you. So, the worth of a company is, to a great extent, driven by investors' expectations of future profits. How do investors predict future profits? One thing they will look at for sure is the financial statements. The income statement tells them if the company has made a profit in the past, and the balance sheet tells them what assets the company has on hand to help generate profits in the future.

Why is a company's market value different from its book value? The answer comes from understanding two things: accounting is primarily transaction-based, as we have seen throughout this chapter, and accountants are conservative. **Conservatism** is a concept that says that, when there is doubt about the amount at which assets and liabilities should be reported, the least optimistic measurements should be used. Accountants are conservative because they know the financial statements are going to be used by outsiders, such as bankers and investors, to make decisions, and they don't want to mislead them. If they paint too rosy a picture and, as a result, someone buys shares in a questionable company, investors may lose their money when things go wrong. This is a very important ethical issue to accountants. As a result, when faced with uncertainty about the numbers, accountants take a conservative approach.

Conservatism motivates accountants to use the least optimistic measures when uncertainty exists about the value of an asset or liability.

Transaction-based accounting and conservatism have three important implications for the balance sheet. They affect (1) what is (and is not) recorded, (2) how a transaction is recorded, and (3) the amounts assigned to recorded items. These three items cause a company's book value to be different from its market value.

1. *What is (and is not) recorded?* Because accounting is based on transactions, an item will be recorded only if it comes from an identifiable transaction. The asset *Furnishings and Equipment* on your First Choice Haircutters Salon balance sheet comes from having bought furniture and equipment. Other events that do *not* involve identifiable transactions are not entered into the accounting system and, therefore, do not make it to the balance sheet. For example, Regis Corporation will not report one of its most valuable assets (the name "Regis Salons") on its balance sheet because it wasn't acquired in an identifiable transaction. This doesn't mean that the name isn't valuable in attracting customers or isn't useful when estimating the value of Regis Corporation's business. It *is* valuable and useful. Rather, all it means is that it wasn't possible for Regis Corporation to point to a particular transaction and say, "There's where our name got its value." And, without an identifiable transaction, there is no recognition in the balance sheet (or in the other financial statements).

2. *How is it recorded?* Sometimes, when a company pays money for something, it is difficult to know if what it bought is an asset or an expense. Sure, the company hopes the item will generate future profits, but it can't be sure. You saw this in Chapter 1 when Mattel bought The Learning Company. Mattel thought TLC would bring them future profits, but that didn't happen. Conservatism requires that, if the company is not reasonably sure about the hoped-for future benefits, the debit side of the transaction should be recorded as an expense, not an asset, because this treatment will ensure that assets are not overstated.

The **cost principle** states that transactions should be recorded at their original cost to the company.

3. *Amounts assigned to recorded items.* Assets and liabilities are initially recorded at their original cost to the company. This **cost principle,** as it is called, is another of the principles of accounting. While cost measures value at the time a transaction is entered into, there is no guarantee that this amount will still represent the value of an asset or liability when the financial statements are prepared. It is possible that some assets and liabilities will change in value as time passes. However, increases in asset values (and decreases in liability values) are not recorded unless additional transactions have caused the change in value. So, although real estate values in Vancouver may have increased since the First Choice Haircutters locations were

opened there, this extra value would not be reported in the balance sheet because measurement (the dollar amount used to report transactions) is based on the original cost to the company. On the other hand, accountants do allow decreases in asset values to be recorded. In other words, accountants are willing to give up the cost figure to reflect decreases in value but not increases in value, which is consistent with conservatism.

We have introduced some pretty complex ideas here. We'll be talking more about them in future chapters, but let's recap. Because accounting is primarily transaction-based, and because of the conservatism principle, accounting is based on past transactions, and assets on the balance sheet are not carried at amounts greater than their original cost. Therefore, although the balance sheet can be used to value a business, it does not by itself measure the company's worth.

WHAT'S COMING UP

As you can see, you need to know quite a bit about the "how to" of accounting to be able to prepare financial statements. We will take a closer look at using the financial statements in decision-making in Chapter 5, but first you need to learn how the accounting system handles transactions related to the operating activities of a business and how it produces an income statement. That's the focus for Chapters 3 and 4. Before hitting those chapters, though, you should review and practise what we covered in this chapter.

_____ **FOR YOUR REVIEW**

DEMONSTRATION CASE

On April 1, 2009, three ambitious university students started Goodbye Grass Corporation (GGC). A summary of GGC's transactions completed through April 30, 2009, follows:

a. Issued shares to the three investors in exchange for cash totalling $9,000.
b. Acquired rakes and other hand tools (equipment) for $600, paying the hardware store $200 cash and signing a note for the balance, payable in three months.
c. Ordered three lawn mowers and two edgers costing $4,000 from XYZ Lawn Supply, Inc.
d. Purchased four hectares of land for the future site of a storage garage. Paid cash, $5,000.
e. Received the mowers and edgers that had been ordered, and signed a note to pay XYZ Lawn Supply in full in 60 days.
f. Sold for $1,250 one hectare of land to the city for a park. Accepted a six-month note from the city for payment.
g. One of the owners borrowed $3,000 from a local bank for personal use.

Required:

1. Analyze each transaction using the DECIDES approach outlined in this chapter. Show journal entries and equality checks for each transaction listed above.
2. Set up T-accounts for Cash, Notes Receivable (from the city), Equipment (hand tools and mowing equipment), Land, Notes Payable (to hardware store and equipment supply company), and Contributed Capital. Indicate the beginning balances of $0 in each T-account. Post all journal entries to the appropriate T-accounts. Identify each amount with its letter in the preceding list.
3. Use the amounts in the T-accounts, developed in requirement 2, to prepare a classified balance sheet for Goodbye Grass Corporation at April 30, 2009. Show the balances for all assets, liabilities, and shareholders' equity accounts.
4. As of April 30, 2009, has financing for GGC's assets come primarily from liabilities or shareholders' equity?

Check your answers with the solution in the following section.

Suggested Solution

1. Transaction analysis and journal entries:

(*a*) dr   Cash (+A)   9,000
      cr   Contributed Capital (+SE).   9,000

Assets	=	Liabilities	+	Shareholders' Equity
Cash + 9,000				Contributed Capital + 9,000

Equality checks: (1) The accounting equation is in balance; (2) Debits $9,000 = Credits $9,000.

(*b*) dr   Equipment (+A)   600
      cr   Cash (−A).   200
      cr   Notes Payable (+L).   400

Assets	=	Liabilities	+	Shareholders' Equity
Equipment + 600		Notes Payable + 400		
Cash − 200				

Equality checks: (1) The accounting equation is in balance; (2) Debits $600 = Credits $600.

(*c*) This is not an accounting transaction. No exchange has taken place. No accounts are affected.

(*d*) dr   Land (+A)   5,000
      cr   Cash (−A).   5,000

Assets	=	Liabilities	+	Shareholders' Equity
Land + 5,000				
Cash − 5,000				

Equality checks: (1) The accounting equation is in balance; (2) Debits $5,000 = Credits $5,000.

(*e*) dr   Equipment (+A)   4,000
      cr   Notes Payable (+L).   4,000

Assets	=	Liabilities	+	Shareholders' Equity
Equipment + 4,000		Notes Payable + 4,000		

Equality checks: (1) The accounting equation is in balance; (2) Debits $4,000 = Credits $4,000.

(*f*) dr   Notes Receivable (+A)   1,250
      cr   Land (−A).   1,250

Assets	=	Liabilities	+	Shareholders' Equity
Notes Receivable + 1,250				
Land − 1,250				

Equality checks: (1) The accounting equation is in balance; (2) Debits $1,250 = Credits $1,250.

(*g*) This is not a transaction of the company. The separate entity assumption states that transactions of the owners are separate from transactions of the business.

2. Posting journal entries to T-accounts:

dr Cash (A) cr			
Beg. bal. 0			
(a) 9,000	(b)		200
	(d)		5,000
End. bal. 3,800			

dr Equipment (A) cr	
Beg. bal. 0	
(b) 600	
(e) 4,000	
End. bal. 4,600	

dr Notes Payable (L) cr	
Beg. bal. 0	
	(b) 400
	(e) 4,000
End. bal. 4,400	

dr Notes Receivable (A) cr	
Beg. bal. 0	
(f) 1,250	
End. bal. 1,250	

dr Land (A) cr	
Beg. bal. 0	
(d) 5,000	(f) 1,250
End. bal. 3,750	

dr Contributed Capital (SE) cr	
Beg. bal. 0	
	(a) 9,000
End. bal. 9,000	

3. Preparing a balance sheet from the T-accounts:

GOODBYE GRASS CORPORATION
Balance Sheet
At April 30, 2009

Assets		Liabilities	
Current Assets		*Current Liabilities*	
Cash	$ 3,800	Notes Payable	$ 4,400
Notes Receivable	1,250		
Total Current Assets	5,050	**Shareholders' Equity**	
Equipment	4,600	Contributed Capital	9,000
Land	3,750	**Total Liabilities and**	
Total Assets	**$13,400**	**Shareholders' Equity**	**$13,400**

---

4. The primary source of financing for GGC's assets (totalling $13,400) has come from shareholders' equity ($9,000) rather than liabilities ($4,400).

CHAPTER SUMMARY

Explain and select common balance sheet account titles. p. 42   **LO1**

- A *classified balance sheet* separately classifies assets as current if they will be used up or converted into cash within one year. Liabilities are classified as current if they will be paid, settled, or fulfilled within one year.

- Typical balance sheet account titles include the following:

    Assets: Cash, Accounts Receivable, Inventories, Supplies, Property and Equipment

    Liabilities: Accounts Payable, Notes Payable, Bonds Payable

    Shareholders' Equity: Contributed Capital, Retained Earnings

Apply transaction analysis to business transactions. p. 44   **LO2**

- Transactions include observable external events and other events that are more difficult to identify.

- Transaction analysis is based on the duality of effects and the basic accounting equation. *Duality of effects* means that every transaction affects at least two accounts.

- Transaction analysis follows a systematic approach of determining whether a transaction exists; examining the transaction for the accounts affected; classifying the accounts as assets, liabilities, or shareholders' equity; identifying the direction and amount of the effects; and evaluating whether the accounting equation remains in balance.

LO3   **Use journal entries and T-accounts to show how business transactions affect the balance sheet. p. 52**

- Debit means left and credit means right.
- Debits increase assets and decrease liabilities and shareholders' equity.
- Credits decrease assets and increase liabilities and shareholders' equity.
- Journal entries express, in debit-equals-credit form, the effects of a transaction on various asset, liability, and shareholders' equity accounts. Journal entries are used to enter financial information into the accounting system, which is later summarized by account in the ledger (T-accounts).
- T-accounts are a simplified version of the ledger, which summarizes transaction effects for each account. T-accounts show increases on the left (debit) side for assets, which are on the left side of the accounting equation.
- T-accounts show increases on the right (credit) side for liabilities and shareholders' equity, which are on the right side of the accounting equation.

LO4   **Prepare an unadjusted trial balance and a balance sheet. p. 59**

- An unadjusted trial balance is an internal report that lists all accounts and their balances to check the equality of the recorded debits and credits.
- Classified balance sheets are structured with

    Assets categorized as "current assets" (those to be used up or turned into cash within the year), followed by all other (noncurrent) assets, such as property and equipment, and intangible assets.

    Liabilities categorized as "current liabilities" (those that will be paid with current assets), followed by all other (long-term) liabilities.

    Shareholders' equity accounts are listed as Contributed Capital first, followed by Retained Earnings.

LO5   **Explain the concepts that determine whether an item is reported on the balance sheet and at what amount. p. 61**

- Because accounting is transaction-based, the balance sheet does not necessarily represent the current value of a business.
- Some assets are not recorded because they do not arise from transactions or because their future benefits are so uncertain that they are recorded as expenses.
- The amounts recorded for assets and liabilities may not represent current values because under the cost principle they generally are recorded at cost, using the exchange amounts established at the time of the initial transaction.
- The concept of conservatism states that when uncertainty exists about the value of an asset or liability, care should be taken not to overstate the reported value of assets or understate the reported value of liabilities.

KEY TERMS TO KNOW

Accounts p. 52	Current Assets p. 43	Market Value p. 61
Book Value p. 61	Current Liabilities p. 43	T-account p. 53
Business Valuation p. 62	Journal p. 52	Transaction p. 45
Chart of Accounts p. 44	Journal Entry p. 54	Transaction Analysis p. 44
Classified Balance Sheet p. 42	Journalize p. 56	Trial Balance p. 59
Conservatism p. 62	Ledger p. 52	Unit of Measure Assumption p. 42
Cost Principle p. 62	Long-Term Assets p. 43	
	Long-Term Liabilities p. 43	

_____ **FOR YOUR PRACTICE**

QUESTIONS

1. Define the following:
   a. Asset
   b. Current asset
   c. Liability
   d. Current liability
   e. Contributed capital
   f. Retained earnings

2. Define a business transaction in the broad sense, and give an example of observable external, observable internal, and unobservable events.

3. For accounting purposes, what is an account? Explain why accounts are used in an accounting system.

4. What is the basic accounting equation?

5. Explain what *debit* and *credit* mean.

6. Briefly explain what is meant by *transaction analysis*. What are the two principles underlying transaction analysis? What are the steps of the DECIDES approach to transaction analysis?

7. What two different accounting equalities must be maintained in transaction analysis?

8. What is a *journal entry*? What is the typical format of a journal entry?

9. What is a *T-account*? What is its purpose?

10. What is the key feature that all assets possess? What is the key feature of all liabilities?

11. Explain what the following accounting terms mean:
    a. Cost principle
    b. Conservatism

12. What is the difference between a trial balance and a balance sheet?

MULTIPLE CHOICE

Select the one alternative that best answers the question or completes the sentence.

1. Which of the following is not an asset?
   a. Cash
   b. Land
   c. Equipment
   d. Contributed Capital

2. Which of the following statements describes transactions that would be recorded in the accounting system?
   (i) An exchange of one asset for another asset
   (ii) An exchange of a promise for an asset
   (iii) An exchange of a promise for another promise
   a. i
   b. i and ii
   c. i, ii, and iii
   d. None of the above

3. Total assets on a balance sheet prepared on any date must agree with which of the following?
   a. The sum of total liabilities and net income as shown on the income statement
   b. The sum of total liabilities and contributed capital
   c. The sum of total liabilities and retained earnings
   d. The sum of total liabilities and contributed capital and retained earnings

4. The "duality of effects" can best be described as follows:
   a. When one records a transaction in the accounting system, at least two effects on the basic accounting equation will result.
   b. When an exchange takes place between two parties, both parties must record the transaction.
   c. When a transaction is recorded, both the balance sheet and the income statement must be impacted.
   d. When a transaction is recorded, one account will always increase and one account will always decrease.

5. The T-account is used to summarize which of the following?
   a. Increases and decreases to a single account in the accounting system.
   b. Debits and credits to a single account in the accounting system.

    c.   Changes in specific account balances over a time period.

    d.   All of the above describe how T-accounts are used by accountants.

6. Which of the following describes how assets are listed on the balance sheet?

    a.   In alphabetical order

    b.   In order of magnitude, lowest value to highest value

    c.   From most current to least current

    d.   From least current to most current

7. How many of the following are true regarding *debits* and *credits?*

   • In any given transaction, the total dollar amount of the debits and the total dollar amount of the credits must be equal.

   • Debits decrease certain accounts and credits decrease certain accounts.

   • Liabilities and Shareholders' Equity accounts usually end in credit balances, while assets usually end in debit balances.

    a. None   *c.* Two

    b. One   *d.* Three

8. How many of the following statements are true regarding the Balance Sheet?

   • One cannot determine the true "current value" of a company by reviewing just its balance sheet.

   • Certain assets, which are not acquired through identifiable transactions, are not reported on a company's balance sheet.

   • A balance sheet shows only the ending balances, in a summarized format, of all "balance sheet accounts" in the accounting system as of a particular date.

    a. None   *c.* Two

    b. One   *d.* Three

9. Which of the following scenarios is possible when a transaction occurs?

    a.   Assets increase and liabilities decrease.

    b.   Liabilities increase and shareholders' equity increases.

    c.   Liabilities increase and shareholders' equity decreases.

    d.   Assets decrease and shareholders' equity increases.

10. A company was recently formed with $5,000 cash contributed to the company by shareholders. The company then borrowed $2,000 from a bank, and bought $1,000 worth of inventory on account. The company also purchased $5,000 worth of equipment by paying $2,000 in cash and issuing a note for the remainder. What is the amount of total assets to be reported on the balance sheet?

    a. $11,000   *c.* $9,000

    b. $10,000   *d.* None of the above

11. A company was recently formed with $5,000 cash contributed to the company by shareholders. The company then borrowed $2,000 from a bank, and bought $1,000 worth of inventory on account. The company also purchased $5,000 worth of equipment by paying $2,000 in cash and issuing a note for the remainder. What is the amount of cash to be reported on the balance sheet?

    a. $5,000   *c.* $7,000

    b. $4,000   *d.* None of the above

12. A company was recently formed with $5,000 cash contributed to the company by shareholders. The company then borrowed $2,000 from a bank, and bought $1,000 worth of inventory on account. The company also purchased $5,000 worth of equipment by paying $2,000 in cash and issuing a note for the remainder. What is the amount of total liabilities to be reported on the balance sheet?

    a. $8,000   *c.* $6,000

    b. $13,000   *d.* None of the above

Solutions to Multiple-Choice Questions

1.d 2.c 3.d 4.a 5.d 6.c 7.d 8.d 9.c 10.a 11.a 12.c

MINI-EXERCISES

M2-1 Identifying Increase and Decrease Effects on Balance Sheet Accounts   LO3

Complete the following table by entering either the word *increases* or *decreases* in each column.

	Debit	Credit
Assets	_____	_____
Liabilities	_____	_____
Shareholders' Equity	_____	_____

M2-2 Identifying Debit and Credit Effects on Balance Sheet Accounts   LO3

Complete the following table by entering either the word *debit* or *credit* in each column.

	Increase	Decrease
Assets	_____	_____
Liabilities	_____	_____
Shareholders' Equity	_____	_____

M2-3 Matching Terms with Definitions   LO2, LO3, LO5

Match each term with its related definition by entering the appropriate letter in the space provided. There should be only one definition per term (that is, there are more definitions than terms).

Term	Definition
____ 1. Journal entry	A. An exchange of more than promises between a business and other parties
____ 2. A = L + SE; Debits = Credits	B. Four periodic financial statements
____ 3. Transaction	C. The two equalities in accounting that aid in providing accuracy
____ 4. Liabilities	D. The results of transaction analysis in debit equals credit format
____ 5. Assets	E. The account that is debited when money is borrowed from a bank
____ 6. Income statement, balance sheet, statement of retained earnings, and statement of cash flows	F. Probable future economic benefits owned by a business
	G. Cumulative earnings of a company that are not distributed to the owners
	H. Every transaction has at least two effects.
	I. Debts or obligations to be paid with assets or fulfilled with services
	J. Assigning dollar amounts to transactions

M2-4 Classifying Accounts on a Balance Sheet   LO1, LO4

The following are a few of the accounts of Laurent-Matthieu Company:

L	1. Accounts Payable		L	9. Leasehold Improvements
A	2. Accounts Receivable		L	10. Notes Payable (due in three years)
A	3. Buildings		A	11. Notes Receivable (due in six months)
A	4. Cash		E	12. Prepaid Rent
SE	5. Contributed Capital		SE	13. Retained Earnings
A	6. Land		A	14. Supplies
A	7. Merchandise Inventory		E	15. Utilities Payable
E	8. Income Taxes Payable		E	16. Wages Payable

COACH'S TIP

For help, see the Chart of Accounts in Exhibit 2.3 on page 45.

In the space provided, classify each as it would be reported on a balance sheet. Use the following code:

CA = current asset   CL = current liability   SE = shareholders' equity

NCA = noncurrent asset   NCL = noncurrent liability

LO1, LO4   **M2-5   Identifying Accounts on a Classified Balance Sheet and Their Normal Debit or Credit Balances**

Mega Brands is headquartered in Montreal and sells its award-winning construction toys in more than 100 countries. Victor Bertrand, who founded the company in 1967, was inducted into the Canadian Toy Association Hall of Fame in 2001. The following are several of the accounts from a recent balance sheet.

1. Accounts Receivable
2. Current Portion of Long-Term Debt
3. Contributed Capital
4. Long-Term Debt
5. Prepaid Expenses
6. Property, Plant, and Equipment
7. Retained Earnings
8. Accounts Payable
9. Cash
10. Accrued Liabilities Payable
11. Inventories
12. Income Taxes Payable

Required:

Indicate how each account normally should be categorized on a classified balance sheet. Use CA for current asset, NCA for noncurrent asset, CL for current liability, NCL for noncurrent liability, and SE for shareholders' equity. Also indicate whether the account normally has a debit or credit balance.

LO1, LO4   **M2-6   Identifying Accounts on a Classified Balance Sheet and Their Normal Debit or Credit Balances**

Blockbuster, Inc., is the world's leading provider of rentable DVDs, videogames, and videocassettes, renting out more than 1 billion videos, DVDs, and video games each year. The following are several of the accounts included in a recent balance sheet:

1. Accounts Receivable
2. Movie Rental Library
3. Contributed Capital
4. Long-Term Debt
5. Prepaid Rent
6. Intangibles
7. Property and Equipment
8. Deficit
9. Accounts Payable
10. Cash
11. Accrued Liabilities Payable
12. Long-Term Liabilities
13. Merchandise Inventories
14. Income Taxes Payable

Required:

Indicate how each account normally should be categorized on a classified balance sheet. Use CA for current asset, NCA for noncurrent asset, CL for current liability, NCL for noncurrent liability, and SE for shareholders' equity. Also indicate whether the account normally has a debit or credit balance. [*Hint:* A deficit is the opposite of retained earnings. It means the company has accumulated net losses rather than net earnings since incorporation date.]

LO2   **M2-7   Identifying Events as Accounting Transactions**

Do the following events result in a recordable transaction for The Toro Company? Answer yes or no for each.

___ 1.   Toro purchased robotic manufacturing equipment that it paid for by signing a note payable.

___ 2.   Six investors in Toro sold their shares to another investor.

___ 3.   The company lent $150,000 to a member of the board of directors.

_____ 4.   The Toro Company ordered supplies from Office Max to be delivered next week.

_____ 5.   The president of The Toro Company purchased shares in another company.

_____ 6.   The company borrowed $1,000,000 from a local bank.

M2-8 Identifying Events as Accounting Transactions   LO2

Laura Secord is one of Canada's oldest and largest makers and retailers of boxed chocolates, candy, and ice cream. The company was founded in 1913 by Frank O'Conner, who named it after Laura Ingersoll Secord, the Canadian War of 1812 hero and patriot. Do the following events result in a recordable transaction for Laura Secord? Answer yes or no for each.

_____ 1.   Laura Secord bought an old warehouse in Prince George.

_____ 2.   The company issued shares to corporate officers.

_____ 3.   The company signed an agreement to rent store space in the Edmonton Mall.

_____ 4.   The company paid for renovations to prepare one of its Winnipeg stores for operations.

_____ 5.   The vice president of the company spoke at a literacy luncheon in Toronto, which contributed to building the company's reputation as a responsible company.

M2-9 Determining Financial Statement Effects of Several Transactions   LO2

For each of the following transactions of Nardozzi Inc. for the month of January 2010, indicate the accounts, amounts, and direction of the effects on the accounting equation. A sample is provided.

a.   (*Sample*) Borrowed $1,000 from a local bank on a note due in six months.
b.   Issued shares to investors for $3,000.
c.   Purchased $500 in equipment, paying $100 cash and promising the rest on a note due in one year.
d.   Paid $100 cash for supplies.
e.   Lent $200 to an employee who signed a note promising to repay the company in 60 days.

	Assets	=	Liabilities	+	Shareholders' Equity
a. Sample: Cash	+1,000	Notes Payable	+1,000		

M2-10 Preparing Journal Entries   LO2

For each of the transactions in M2-9 (including the sample), write the journal entry using the format shown in this chapter.

M2-11 Posting to T-Accounts   LO2

For each of the transactions in M2-9 (including the sample), post the effects to the appropriate T-accounts and determine ending account balances.

dr Cash (A) cr   dr Notes Receivable (A) cr   dr Equipment (A) cr

dr Supplies (A) cr   dr Notes Payable (L) cr   dr Contributed Capital (SE) cr

M2-12 Preparing an Unadjusted Trial Balance and a Classified Balance Sheet   LO4

Given the transactions in M2-9 (including the sample), prepare an unadjusted trial balance and a classified balance sheet for Nardozzi Inc. as of January 31, 2010.

EXERCISES

LO1, LO2, LO5

E2-1 Matching Terms with Definitions

Match each term with its related definition by entering the appropriate letter in the space provided. There should be only one definition per term (that is, there are more definitions than terms).

Term

____ 1.   Transaction   ____ 6.   Current assets
____ 2.   Separate entity concept   ____ 7.   Notes payable
____ 3.   Balance sheet   ____ 8.   Duality of effects
____ 4.   Liabilities   ____ 9.   Retained earnings
____ 5.   Assets = Liabilities + Shareholders' Equity   ____ 10. Debit

Definition

A.   Economic resources to be used or turned into cash within one year
B.   Reports assets, liabilities, and shareholders' equity.
C.   Decrease assets, increase liabilities and shareholders' equity.
D.   Increase assets, decrease liabilities and shareholders' equity.
E.   An exchange of more than promises between a business and other parties
F.   The assumption that businesses will operate into the foreseeable future
G.   Accounts for a business separate from its owners.
H.   The principle that assets should be recorded at their original cost to the company
I.   A standardized format used to accumulate data about each item reported on financial statements
J.   The basic accounting equation
K.   The two equalities in accounting that aid in providing accuracy
L.   The account that is credited when money is borrowed from a bank
M.   Cumulative earnings of a company that are not distributed to the owners
N.   Every transaction has at least two effects.
O.   Probable debts or obligations to be paid with assets or services

LO2, LO5

E2-2 Identifying Account Titles

The following are independent situations.

a.   A company orders and receives 10 personal computers for office use for which it signs a note promising to pay $25,000 within three months.
b.   A company purchases for $21,000 cash a new delivery truck that has a list, or sticker, price of $24,000.
c.   A women's clothing retailer orders 30 new display stands for $300 each for future delivery.
d.   A new company is formed and sells 100 shares for $12 per share to investors.
e.   A company purchases a piece of land for $50,000 cash. An appraiser for the buyer valued the land at $52,500.
f.   The owner of a local company buys a $10,000 car for personal use. Answer from the company's point of view.
g.   A company borrows $1,000 from a local bank and signs a six-month note for the loan.
h.   A company pays $1,500 owed on its note payable (ignore interest).

Required:

1.   Indicate titles of the appropriate accounts, if any, affected in each of the preceding events. Consider what the company gives and takes.
2.   At what amount would you record the delivery truck in b? The piece of land in e? What measurement principle are you applying?
3.   What reasoning did you apply in c? For f, what accounting concept did you apply?

E2-3 Classifying Accounts and Their Usual Balances

LO1, LO4

As described in a recent annual report, Digital Diversions, Inc. (DDI) designs, develops, and distributes videogames for computers and advanced game systems such as Paystation, Y-Box, Tamecube, and Gamegirl. DDI has been operating for only one full year.

Required:

For each of the following accounts from DDI's recent balance sheet, complete the following table. Indicate whether the account is classified as a current asset (CA), noncurrent asset (NCA), current liability (CL), noncurrent liability (NCL), or shareholders' equity (SE), and whether the account usually has a debit (*dr*) or credit (*cr*) balance.

Account	Balance Sheet Classification	Debit or Credit Balance
1. Land	_____	_____
2. Retained Earnings	_____	_____
3. Notes Payable (due in three years)	_____	_____
4. Accounts Receivable	_____	_____
5. Leasehold Improvements	_____	_____
6. Contributed Capital	_____	_____
7. Machinery and Equipment	_____	_____
8. Accounts Payable	_____	_____
9. Cash	_____	_____
10. Taxes Payable	_____	_____

COACH'S TIP

If an account has a balance, it almost always will be on the side that increases the account.

E2-4 Determining Financial Statement Effects of Several Transactions

LO2

The following events occurred for Favata Company:

a. Received $20,000 cash from organizers and issued shares to them.
b. Borrowed $6,000 cash from a bank.
c. Purchased land for $12,000; paid $1,000 in cash and signed a note for the balance.
d. Lent $300 to an employee who signed a note.
e. Purchased $8,000 worth of equipment, paying $1,000 in cash and signing a note for the rest.

Required:

For each of the events *a* through *e,* perform transaction analysis and indicate the account, amount, and direction of the effect (+ for increase and − for decrease) on the accounting equation. Check that the accounting equation remains in balance after each transaction. Use the following headings:

Event	Assets	=	Liabilities	+	Shareholders' Equity

E2-5 Determining Financial Statement Effects of Several Transactions

LO2

The Forzani Group is the largest and only national sporting goods retailer in Canada, operating stores under the names of Sport Chek, Sports Mart, Sports Experts, and Coast Mountain Sports. The firm was founded in 1974 by four football players from the Calgary Stampeders. The following activities occurred during a recent year. The amounts are presented in thousands of dollars.

a. Purchased property, plant, and equipment for $37,997; paid by signing a $7,429 long-term note and settling the rest with cash.
b. Issued $9,586 worth of additional shares for cash.
c. Several Forzani investors sold their shares to other investors on the stock exchange for $18.50 per share.

Required:

1. For each of these events, perform transaction analysis and indicate the account, amount (in thousands), and direction of the effect on the accounting equation. Check that the accounting equation remains in balance after each transaction. Use the following headings:

Event	Assets	=	Liabilities	+	Shareholders' Equity

2. Explain your response for transaction *c*.

LO3   **E2-6 Recording Investing and Financing Activities**
Refer to E2-4.

Required:

For each of the events in E2-4, open appropriate T-accounts and post the effects of these transactions in the T-accounts. Remember to check that debits equal credits for each transaction.

LO3   **E2-7 Recording Investing and Financing Activities**
Refer to E2-4.

Required:

For each of the events in E2-4, prepare journal entries, checking that debits equal credits.

LO3   **E2-8 Recording Investing and Financing Activities**
Refer to E2-5.

Required:

1. For each of the events in E2-5, open appropriate T-accounts and post the effects of these transactions in the T-accounts. Remember to check that debits equal credits for each transaction.
2. Explain your response for event *c*.

LO3   **E2-9 Recording Investing and Financing Activities**
Refer to E2-5.

Required:

1. For each of the events in E2-5, prepare journal entries, checking that debits equal credits.
2. Explain your response for event *c*.

LO2, LO3, LO5   **E2-10 Analyzing the Effects of Transactions in T-Accounts**
Mulkeen Service Company, Inc., was organized by Conor Mulkeen and five other investors. The following activities occurred during the year:

a. Received $60,000 total cash from the investors; each was issued 1,000 shares in the company.
b. Purchased equipment for use in the business at a cost of $12,000; one-fourth was paid in cash, and the company signed a note for the balance (due in six months).
c. Signed an agreement with a cleaning service to pay it $120 per week for cleaning the corporate offices, beginning next week.
d. Lent $2,000 to one of the investors, who signed a note due in six months.
e. Conor Mulkeen borrowed $10,000 for personal use from a local bank, signing a one-year note.

Required:

1. Create T-accounts for the following accounts: Cash, Notes Receivable, Equipment, Notes Payable, and Contributed Capital. Beginning balances are zero. For each of the above transactions, record its effects in the appropriate T-accounts. Include good referencing and totals for each T-account.

2. Using the balances in the T-accounts, fill in the following amounts for the accounting equation:

Assets $ _____ = Liabilities $ _____ + Shareholders' Equity $ _____

3. Explain your responses for events *c* and *e*.

E2-11 Inferring Investing and Financing Transactions and Preparing a Balance Sheet

LO2, LO4, LO5

During its first week of operations, January 1 to 7, 2010, Faith's Fine Furniture Corporation completed six transactions with the dollar effects indicated in the following schedule:

Accounts	\multicolumn{6}{c}{Dollar Effect of Each of the Six Transactions}	Ending Balance
	1	2	3	4	5	6	
Cash	$12,000	$50,000	$(4,000)	$4,000	$(7,000)		
Equipment					7,000		
Land			12,000			$3,000	
Long-term Debt		50,000	8,000	4,000		3,000	
Contributed Capital	12,000						

Required:

1. Write a brief explanation of transactions 1 through 6. Explain any assumptions that you made.
2. Compute the ending balance in each account, and prepare an unadjusted trial balance and a classified balance sheet for Faith's Fine Furniture Company on January 7, 2010.
3. As of January 7, 2010, has most of the financing for Faith's investment in assets come from liabilities or shareholders' equity?

E2-12 Inferring Investing and Financing Transactions and Preparing a Balance Sheet

LO2, LO4, LO5

During its first month of operations, March 2009, Faye's Fashions, Inc., completed four transactions with the dollar effects indicated in the following schedule:

Accounts	\multicolumn{4}{c}{Dollar Effect of Each of the Four Transactions}	Ending Balance
	1	2	3	4	
Cash	$50,000	$(4,000)	$5,000	$(4,000)	
Computer Equipment				4,000	
Delivery Truck		25,000			
Short-term Bank Loan			5,000		
Long-term Notes Payable		21,000			
Contributed Capital	50,000				

Required:

1. Write a brief explanation of transactions 1 through 4. Explain any assumptions that you made.
2. Compute the ending balance in each account, and prepare a classified balance sheet for Faye's Fashions, Inc., at the end of March 2009.
3. As of March 31, 2009, has most of the financing for Faye's investment in assets come from liabilities or shareholders' equity?

E2-13 Recording Journal Entries

LO1, LO3

Assume Down.com was organized on May 1, 2009, to compete with Despair.com—a company that sells demotivational posters and office products. The following events occurred during the first month of Down.com's operations.

   a.   Received $60,000 cash from the investors who organized Down.com Corporation.

   b.   Borrowed $20,000 cash and signed a note due in two years.

   c.   Ordered lighting fixtures costing $16,000.

   d.   Purchased $10,000 worth of equipment, paying $1,000 in cash and signing a six-month note for the balance.

   e.   Received and paid for the lighting fixtures ordered in *c*.

Required:

Prepare journal entries for each transaction. (Remember that debits go on the top and credits go on the bottom, indented.) Be sure to use good referencing, and categorize each account as an asset (A), liability (L), or shareholders' equity (SE). If a transaction does not require a journal entry, explain the reason.

LO2, LO4   **E2-14** **Analyzing the Effects of Transactions Using T-Accounts, Preparing and Interpreting a Balance Sheet**

Lee Delivery Company, Inc. (LDC), was organized in 2009. The following transactions occurred during that year:

   a.   Received $40,000 cash from organizers in exchange for shares in the new company.

   b.   Purchased land for $12,000, signing a two-year note (ignore interest).

   c.   Bought two used delivery trucks at the start of the year at a cost of $10,000 each; paid $2,000 cash and signed a note due in three years for the rest (ignore interest).

   d.   Sold one-fourth of the land for $3,000 to Birkins Moving, which signed a six-month note.

   e.   Paid $2,000 cash to a truck repair shop for a new motor for one of the trucks. [*Hint:* Increase the account you used to record the purchase of the trucks, since the productive life of the truck has been improved.]

   f.   Traded in the other truck and paid $6,000 cash for a new one.

   g.   Shareholder Jonah Lee paid $22,000 cash for land for his personal use.

Required:

1. Set up appropriate T-accounts with beginning balances of $0 for Cash, Notes Receivable, Land, Equipment, Notes Payable, and Contributed Capital. Using the T-accounts, record the effects of these transactions.

2. Prepare an unadjusted trial balance and a classified balance sheet for LDC at the end of 2009.

3. Using the balance sheet, indicate whether LDC's assets at the end of the year were financed primarily by liabilities or shareholders' equity.

LO2, LO3   **E2-15** **Explaining the Effects of Transactions on Balance Sheet Accounts Using T-Accounts**

Heavey and Lovas Furniture Repair Service, a company with two shareholders, began operations on June 1, 2009. The following T-accounts indicate the activities for the month of June.

Cash (A)				Notes Receivable (A)				Building (A)	
(a) 17,000	(b)	10,000	(c)	1,500			(b)	50,000	
	(c)	1,500							

Notes Payable (L)			Contributed Capital (SE)	
	(b)	40,000		(a) 17,000

Required:

Explain events *a* through *c* that resulted in the entries in the T-accounts. That is, for each account what transactions made it increase and/or decrease?

E2-16 Preparing a Classified Balance Sheet

LO4

The following accounts are taken from the December 31, 2006, financial statements of CanWest Global Communications, the largest media conglomerate in Canada and owner of the Global Television Network as well as the *National Post* newspaper. Numbers are in thousands of Canadian dollars.

Operating expenses	$1,551,852	General expenses	$ 817,424
Interest expense	194,216	Accounts payable	440,484
Other current liabilities	162,249	Revenue	2,878,625
Cash	283,104	Accounts receivable	454,452
Other current assets	261,339	Property and other assets	4,643,913
Long-term debt	3,668,960	Contributed capital	861,427
Other expenses	136,461	Retained earnings (end of 2006)	509,688

Required:

1. Prepare a classified balance sheet at December 31, 2006. [*Hint:* Some of the above accounts are not reported on the balance sheet.]
2. Using the balance sheet, indicate whether the assets of CanWest are financed primarily by liabilities or shareholders' equity.

COACHED PROBLEMS

CP2-1 Determining Financial Statement Effects of Various Transactions

LO1, LO2

Lester's Home Healthcare Services (LHHS) was organized on January 1, 2009, by four friends. Each organizer invested $10,000 in the company and, in turn, was issued 8,000 shares. To date, they are the only shareholders. During the first month (January 2009), the company had the following six events:

a. Collected a total of $40,000 from the organizers and, in turn, issued the shares.
b. Purchased a building for $65,000, equipment for $16,000, and three hectares of land for $12,000; paid $13,000 in cash and signed a note for the balance, which is due to be paid in 15 years.
c. One shareholder reported to the company that 500 of his Lester's shares had been sold and transferred to another shareholder for $5,000 cash.
d. Purchased supplies for $3,000 cash.
e. Sold one hectare of land for $4,000 cash to another company.
f. Lent one of the shareholders $5,000 for moving costs, receiving a signed six-month note from the shareholder.

COACH'S TIP

b. Five different accounts are affected.
c. Has this transaction caused LHHS to give or receive anything?
f. Remember to think about what LHHS has given up and what it has received.

Required:

1. Was Lester's Home Healthcare Services organized as a partnership or corporation? Explain the basis for your answer.
2. During the first month, the records of the company were inadequate. You were asked to prepare the summary of the preceding transactions. To develop a quick assessment of their economic effects on Lester's Home Healthcare Services, you have decided to complete the spreadsheet that follows and to use plus (+) for increases and minus (−) for decreases for each account. The first transaction is used as an example.

		Assets				= Liabilities +		Shareholders' Equity	
Cash	Supplies	Notes Receivable	Land	Building	Equipment	Notes Payable	Contributed Capital	Retained Earnings
(a) + 40,000						=	+ 40,000	

3. Did you include the transaction between the two shareholders—event *c*—in the spreadsheet? Why?

4. Based on only the completed spreadsheet, provide the following amounts (show computations):
   a. Total assets at the end of the month
   b. Total liabilities at the end of the month
   c. Total shareholders' equity at the end of the month
   d. Cash balance at the end of the month
   e. Total current assets at the end of the month

5. As of January 31, 2009, has the financing for LHHS's investment in assets come primarily from liabilities or from shareholders' equity?

LO1–LO5

CP2-2 Recording Transactions (in a Journal and T-Accounts), Preparing and Interpreting the Balance Sheet

Patrie Plastics Company (PPC) has been operating for three years. The December 31, 2009, account balances are:

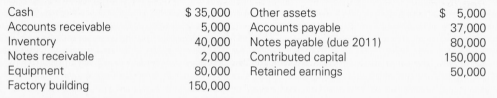

COACH'S TIP

You won't need to open any new accounts to record the transactions described here, so have a quick look at the ones listed before you start to answer this question

f. Three different accounts are affected.
g. Does PPC owe anything to its new president for the year ended December 31, 2010?
h. What does PPC give up and take back?

Cash	$ 35,000	Other assets	$ 5,000
Accounts receivable	5,000	Accounts payable	37,000
Inventory	40,000	Notes payable (due 2011)	80,000
Notes receivable	2,000	Contributed capital	150,000
Equipment	80,000	Retained earnings	50,000
Factory building	150,000		

During the year 2010, the company had the following summarized activities:

a. Purchased equipment that cost $30,000; paid $10,000 cash and signed a two-year note for the balance.
b. Issued an additional 2,000 shares for $20,000 cash.
c. Lent $12,000 to a supplier, who signed a six-month note.
d. Borrowed $20,000 cash from a local bank, payable June 30, 2011.
e. Purchased an "other asset" for $6,000 cash.
f. Built an addition to the factory for $42,000; paid $15,000 in cash and signed a three-year note for the balance.
g. Hired a new president on the last day of the year. The contract was for $85,000 for each full year worked.
h. Returned $2,000 worth of defective equipment to the manufacturer, receiving a cash refund.

Required:

1. Prepare journal entries to record transactions a to h.
2. Create T-accounts for each of the accounts on the balance sheet, and enter the balances at the end of 2009 as beginning balances on January 1, 2010.
3. Enter the effects of the transactions in T-accounts (including referencing) and determine the December 31, 2010, balances.
4. Explain your response to event g.
5. Prepare an unadjusted trial balance at December 31, 2010.
6. Prepare a classified balance sheet at December 31, 2010.
7. As of December 31, 2010, has the financing for PPC's investment in assets come primarily from liabilities or shareholders' equity?

GROUP A PROBLEMS

LO1, LO2, LO5

PA2-1 Determining Financial Statement Effects of Various Transactions

Mallard Incorporated (MI) is a small manufacturing company that makes model trains to sell to toy stores. It has a small service department that repairs customers' trains for a fee. The company has been in business for five years. At the end of the most recent full year, 2009, the accounting records reflected total assets of $500,000 and total liabilities of $200,000. During the current year, 2010, the following summarized events occurred:

a. Issued additional shares for $100,000 cash.
b. Borrowed $120,000 cash from the bank and signed a 10-year note.

c. Built an addition on the factory for $200,000 and paid cash to the contractor.
d. Purchased equipment for the new addition for $30,000, paying $3,000 in cash and signing a note due in six months for the balance.
e. Returned a $3,000 piece of equipment, from d, because it proved to be defective; received a reduction of the note payable.
f. Purchased a delivery truck (equipment) for $10,000; paid $5,000 cash and signed a nine-month note for the remainder.
g. At the end of 2010, lent $2,000 cash to the company president, Jennifer Mallard, who signed a note due in one year.
h. A shareholder sold $5,000 worth of his shares in Mallard Incorporated to his neighbour.

Required:

1. Complete the spreadsheet that follows, using plus (+) for increases and minus (−) for decreases for each account. The first transaction is used as an example.

	Assets			=	Liabilities	+	Shareholders' Equity	
Cash	Notes Receivable	Equipment	Building		Notes Payable		Contributed Capital	Retained Earnings
(a) + 100,000							+ 100,000	

2. Did you include event h in the spreadsheet? Why or why not?
3. Based on beginning balances plus the completed spreadsheet, provide the following amounts (show computations):
   a. Total assets at the end of the year
   b. Total liabilities at the end of the year
   c. Total shareholders' equity at the end of the year
4. As of December 31, 2010, has the financing for MI's investment in assets come primarily from liabilities or shareholders' equity?

PA2-2 Recording Transactions (in a Journal and T-Accounts), Preparing and Interpreting the Balance Sheet

LO1–LO5

Ethan Allen Interiors Inc. is a leading manufacturer and retailer of home furnishings in 315 retail stores worldwide. The following is adapted from a recent Ethan Allen balance sheet as of June 30. All amounts are in thousands.

Cash	$ 147,879	Other assets	$ 5,484
Accounts receivable	14,602	Accounts payable	26,650
Inventories	181,884	Wages and other expenses payable	35,243
Prepaid expenses		Other current liabilities	85,546
and other current assets	38,064	Long-term debt	202,868
Property, plant, and equipment	322,185	Other long-term liabilities	42,649
Intangibles	92,500	Contributed capital	330,742
		Retained earnings	78,900

Assume that the following events occurred in the quarter ended September 30:

a. Paid $3,400 cash for an additional "other asset."
b. Issued additional shares for $1,020 in cash.
c. Purchased property, plant, and equipment; paid $1,830 in cash and will pay the remaining $9,400 in two years.
d. Sold, at cost, other assets for $310 cash.
e. Conducted negotiations to purchase a sawmill, which is expected to cost $34,000.

Required:

1. Prepare journal entries to record transactions a to e.
2. Create T-accounts for each of the accounts on the balance sheet and enter the balances at the end of June as beginning balances for the July 1 to September 30 quarter.
3. Enter the effects of the transactions in T-accounts (including referencing) and determine the September 30 balances.

4. Explain your response to event *e*.
5. Prepare an unadjusted trial balance at September 30.
6. Prepare a classified balance sheet at September 30.
7. As of September 30, has the financing for Ethan Allen's investment in assets primarily come from liabilities or shareholders' equity?

GROUP B PROBLEMS

LO1, LO2, LO5   **PB2-1**   **Determining Financial Statement Effects of Various Transactions**

Swish Watch Corporation manufactures, sells, and services expensive, ugly watches. The company has been in business for three years. At the end of the most recent year, 2009, the accounting records reported total assets of $2,255,000 and total liabilities of $1,780,000. During the current year, 2010, the following summarized events occurred:

a. Issued additional shares for $109,000 cash.
b. Borrowed $186,000 cash from the bank and signed a 10-year note.
c. A shareholder sold $5,000 worth of his shares in Swish Watch Corporation to another investor.
d. Built an addition on the factory for $200,000 and paid cash to the construction company.
e. Purchased equipment for the new addition for $44,000, paying $12,000 in cash and signing a six-month note for the balance.
f. Returned a $4,000 piece of equipment, from *e*, because it proved to be defective; received a cash refund.
g. At the end of 2010, lent $2,000 cash to the company president, Thor Gunnarson, who signed a note with terms requiring repayment of the loan in one year.

Required:

1. Complete the spreadsheet that follows, using plus (+) for increases and minus (−) for decreases for each account. The first transaction is used as an example.

	Assets			=	Liabilities	+	Shareholders' Equity	
Cash	Notes Receivable	Equipment	Building		Notes Payable		Contributed Capital	Retained Earnings
(a) + 109,000				=			+ 109,000	

2. Did you include event *c* in the spreadsheet? Why?
3. Based on beginning balances plus the completed spreadsheet, provide the following amounts (show computations):
   a. Total assets at the end of the year
   b. Total liabilities at the end of the year
   c. Total shareholders' equity at the end of the year
4. As of December 31, 2010, has the financing for Swish Watch Corporation's investment in assets come primarily from liabilities or from shareholders' equity?

LO1–LO5   **PB2-2**   **Recording Transactions (in a Journal and T-Accounts), Preparing and Interpreting the Balance Sheet**

Starbucks is a coffee company—a big coffee company. During a 10-year period, the number of Starbucks locations grew from 165 to over 5,800 stores—an average increase of 43 per cent every year. The following is adapted from a recent Starbucks annual report as of October 1. All amounts are in thousands.

Cash	$ 312,606	Accounts payable	$ 778,778
Accounts receivable	224,271	Other current liabilities	1,156,842
Inventories	636,222	Long-term debt	1,958
Other current assets	356,689	Other long-term liabilities	262,857
Property, plant, and equipment	2,287,899	Contributed capital	40,149
Other long-term assets	611,254	Retained earnings	2,188,357

Assume that the following events occurred in the quarter which ended December 31:

a. Paid $10,400 cash for additional other long-term assets.
b. Issued additional shares for $5,300 in cash.

c. Purchased property, plant, and equipment; paid $11,800 in cash and signed additional long-term loans for $8,900.

d. Sold, at cost, other long-term assets for $3,000 cash.

e. Conducted negotiations to purchase a coffee farm, which is expected to cost $7,400.

Required:

1. Prepare journal entries to record transactions *a* to *e*.

2. Create T-accounts for each of the accounts on the balance sheet and enter the balances at the end of September as beginning balances for the October 1 to December 31 quarter.

3. Enter the effects of the transactions in T-accounts (including referencing) and determine the December 31 balances.

4. Explain your response for event *e*.

5. Prepare an unadjusted trial balance at December 31.

6. Prepare a classified balance sheet at December 31.

7. As of December 31, has the financing for the investment in assets made by Starbucks come primarily from liabilities or shareholders' equity?

SKILLS DEVELOPMENT CASES

S2-1 Finding Financial Information   LO1, LO5

Refer to the financial statements of High Liner in Appendix A at the end of this book, or download the annual report from the *Cases* section of the text's Web site at www.mcgrawhill.ca/college/phillips.

Required:

1. What is the company's fiscal year-end? Where did you find the exact date?

2. Use the company's balance sheet to determine the amounts in the accounting equation (A = L + SE).

3. On the balance sheet, the company reports inventories of $107,589,000. Does this amount represent the expected selling price? Why or why not?

4. What is the amount of the company's current liabilities?

5. Has financing for the company's investment in assets come primarily from liabilities or shareholders' equity?

S2-2 Comparing Financial Information   LO1, LO5

Refer to the financial statements of Sun-Rype by downloading the annual report from the *Cases* section of the text's Web site at www.mcgrawhill.ca/college/phillips.

Required:

1. Use the company's balance sheet to determine the amounts in the accounting equation (A = L + SE). Is Sun-Rype or High Liner larger in terms of total assets?

2. Does Sun-Rype have more or less inventories to sell than High Liner?

3. Does Sun-Rype have more or less current liabilities than High Liner?

4. Has financing for Sun-Rype investment in assets come primarily from liabilities or shareholders' equity? Thinking back to Chapter 1, what does this imply about the risk assumed by Sun-Rype's investors, relative to those investing in High Liner?

S2-3 Internet-Based Team Research: Examining the Balance Sheet   LO1, LO5

As a team, select an industry to analyze. Using your Web browser, each team member should acquire the financial reporting section of the annual report for one Canadian publicly traded company in the industry, with each member selecting a different company. (See S1-3 in Chapter 1 for a description of possible resources for these tasks.)

TEAM CASE

Required:

1. On an individual basis, each team member should write a short report that lists the following information.
   a. The date of the balance sheet
   b. The major noncurrent asset accounts and any significant changes in them
   c. The major noncurrent liability accounts and any significant changes in them
   d. Any significant changes in total shareholders' equity
   e. Whether financing for the investment in assets comes primarily from liabilities or shareholders' equity

2. Then, as a team, write a short report comparing and contrasting your companies using the above topics. Discuss any similarities across the companies that you as a team observe, and provide potential explanations for any differences discovered.

LO1, LO2, LO5

ETHICAL
ISSUES

S2-4 Ethical Decision Making: A Real-Life Example

In the world of financial fraud, a "Ponzi scheme" is famous. Here is the story behind how the scam got its name. Charles Ponzi started the Security Exchange Company in Boston on December 26, 1919. He thought he had discovered a way to purchase American stamps in a foreign country at significantly lower amounts than they were worth in the United States. He claimed his idea was so successful that anyone who gave money to his company would be repaid their original loan plus 50 per cent interest within 90 days. Friends and family quickly offered their money to Ponzi, and they were handsomely rewarded, being repaid their original loan and the 50 per cent interest within just 45 days. Thanks to an article in the *New York Times*, word spread quickly about Ponzi's business, attracting thousands of people seeking a similar payback. He might have had a successful business had his idea actually worked. The problem, however, was that it didn't. The 50 per cent interest paid to early investors did not come from the profits of a successful underlying business idea (which didn't even exist), but instead was obtained fraudulently from funds contributed by later lenders. This is a classic example of what is called borrowing from Peter to pay Paul. Eventually, the Ponzi scheme collapsed on August 10, 1920, after an auditor examined his accounting records.

1. Assume that on December 27, 1919, Ponzi's first three lenders provided his company with $5,000 each. Use the basic accounting equation to show the effects of these transactions on December 27, 1919.

2. If the first two lenders are repaid their original loan amounts plus the 50 per cent interest promised to them, how much cash is left in Ponzi's business to repay the third lender? Given what you discovered, how was it possible for Ponzi's company to remain in "business" for over eight months?

3. Who was harmed by Ponzi's scheme?

Epilogue: After taking in nearly $15 million from 40,000 people, Ponzi's company failed with just $1.5 million in total assets. Ponzi spent four years in prison before jumping bail, to become involved in fraudulently selling swampland in Florida. We're not kidding.

LO1, LO5

ETHICAL
ISSUES

S2-5 Ethical Decision Making: A Mini-Case

You work as an accountant for a small land development company that desperately needs additional financing to continue in business. The president of your company is meeting with the manager of a local bank at the end of the month to try to obtain this financing. The president has approached you with two ideas to improve the company's reported financial position. First, he claims that, because a big part of the company's value comes from its knowledgeable and dedicated employees, you should report their "Intellectual Abilities" as an asset on the balance sheet. Second, he claims that, although the local economy is doing poorly and almost no one is buying land or new houses, he is optimistic that eventually things will turn around. For this reason, he asks you to continue reporting the company's land on the balance sheet at its cost, rather than the much lower amount that real estate appraisers say it's really worth.

1. Thinking back to Chapter 1, why do you think the president is so concerned with the amount of assets reported on the balance sheet?

2. What accounting concept introduced in Chapter 2 relates to the president's first suggestion to report "Intellectual Abilities" as an asset?

3.   What accounting concept introduced in Chapter 2 relates to the president's second suggestion, to continue reporting land at its cost?

4.   Who might be hurt by the president's suggestions, if you were to do as he asks? What should you do?

S2-6 Critical Thinking: Evaluating the Reliability of a Balance Sheet   LO1, LO4, LO5

Betsy Jordan asked a local bank for a $50,000 loan to expand her small company. The bank asked Betsy to submit a financial statement of the business to supplement the loan application. Betsy prepared the following balance sheet.

Balance Sheet June 30, 2009	
Assets	
Cash	$ 9,000
Inventory	30,000
Equipment	46,000
Personal residence (monthly payments, $2,800)	300,000
Remaining assets	20,000
Total assets	**$405,000**
Liabilities	
Short-term debt to suppliers	$ 62,000
Long-term debt on equipment	38,000
Total debt	**100,000**
Shareholder's equity	**305,000**
Total liabilities and shareholder's equity	**$405,000**

Required:

The balance sheet has several flaws. However, there is at least one major deficiency. Identify it and explain its significance.

S2-7 Analyzing Transactions and Preparing a Balance Sheet   LO2

Assume you recently obtained a part-time accounting position at the corporate headquarters of Fairmont Hotels and Resorts in Toronto, the company that owns a number of prestigious hotels across Canada, including the Château Laurier in Ottawa and the Banff Springs Hotel in Banff. The following table summarizes accounts and their balances (in thousands) reported by Fairmont in a recent December 31 balance sheet.

eXcel

Cash	$ 279,200	Accounts Payable	$ 156,600
Accounts Receivable	91,700	Other Current Liabilities	64,900
Other Current Assets	28,300	Long-Term Debt	388,400
Property, Plant, and Equipment	1,409,000	Other Long-Term Liabilities	223,000
Other Noncurrent Assets	715,700	Contributed Capital	1,264,600
		Retained Earnings	426,400

Fairmont entered into the following transactions (amounts in thousands) during January:

Jan. 2   Purchase a new hotel at a cost of $17,000, by issuing a promissory note that becomes payable in three years.

Jan. 10   Use $4,000 cash to repay a short-term loan.

Jan. 21   Issue additional shares for $10,000 cash.

Jan. 28   Use cash to buy land for $5,000.

Required:

1. There are no inventories on Fairmont's list of accounts. Explain why not.
2. The controller at Fairmont has asked you to create a spreadsheet in which to display (a) the account balances at December 31, (b) the effects of the four January transactions, and (c) totals that combine the December 31 balances with the January transactions. You feel like you might be ready to tackle this assignment, but just to be sure you e-mail your friend Billy for advice. Here's his reply.

COACH'S TIP

See S1-7 for Billy's cell merge advice. For extra spreadsheet skills, you might also try creating a balance sheet with cells that are linked to the corresponding cells in the T-accounts. To do this, open a worksheet in the same file as the T-accounts. Then click on a cell in the balance sheet worksheet where you want to import a number from the T-accounts, then type =, then click on the tab for the T-account worksheet, click on the cell with the total to be transferred, and then press enter. This links the cells so that any changes to the T-accounts automatically update the balance sheet.

From: BillyTheTutor@yahoo.com
To: Overwhelmed@hotmail.com
Cc:
Subject: Excel Help

Wow, I can't believe you landed that great job at Fairmont.

1. My thinking is that you'll really impress your boss if you set up the spreadsheet to look like a bunch of T-accounts, one beside another. To do this, use the first column for date references, and then use the remaining columns for the balance sheet accounts. Use two columns for each balance sheet account (with the account name spanning the two columns) to make it look just like a T-account. You do remember how to use the cell merge command to make a header span two columns, right? If not, check the last e-mail I sent you. Here's a screenshot of how one part of the left-hand side of your worksheet might look just before you enter the September transactions.

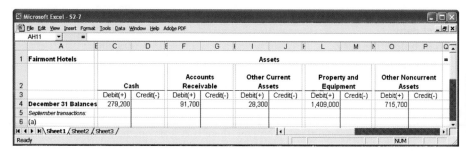

2. I guess the only thing that's left is to remind you that to compute the ending balances in each T-account you have to add the increases to the beginning balance and subtract the decreases. So, to compute the totals for a particular account, your formula might look like =(SUM(C4:C9)-SUM(D5:D9)).
3. Oh yeah, when you're all done, don't forget to save the file using a name that uniquely identifies you.

CHAPTER

3

Reporting and Interpreting Operating Results on the Income Statement

Understand what an income statement means to users.

LO1 Explain and select income statement account titles.

Study how to analyze operating transactions.

LO2 Apply transaction analysis to operating transactions.

Evaluate transactions using the debit/credit framework.

LO3 Use journal entries and T-accounts to show how operating transactions affect the balance sheet and income statement.

LO4 Prepare an unadjusted trial balance that includes balance sheet and income statement accounts.

Reconsider the income statement concepts that users rely on.

LO5 Explain the revenue and matching principles.

INSIDE LOOKING OUT

OUTSIDE LOOKING IN

This chapter continues our discussion of the accounting system, with an emphasis on how the financial results of operating activities are tracked inside the company, and how they are reported to outsiders using the income statement. We also continue to focus on First Choice Haircutters.

Aside from music, what do Toni Braxton and TLC have in common? Here's a hint. They're in the same club as Enron, Eaton's, Air Canada, and WorldCom (now called Verizon). That's right, they all have experienced bankruptcy. It may be difficult to believe that these big names could be involved in bankruptcy proceedings, with TLC having enjoyed six top-10 singles prior to the group's bankruptcy filing, and with Eaton's celebrating its 130-year anniversary as a retail giant in Canada before its bankruptcy filing. But it's true. Despite generating millions and millions of dollars in sales, these celebrities and huge corporations lived beyond their means—a problem that eventually led them to bankruptcy.

Toni Braxton's bankruptcy is an interesting tale that involves love, the law, and an income statement. Well, actually, it doesn't involve an income statement—that was part of the problem. Without an income statement to compare her revenues with her expenses, Toni had no way of seeing that she was headed for financial trouble. As it turns out, her personal revenues were "only" $400,000 a year—hardly enough to cover all the expenses that come from living a lavish celebrity lifestyle. She spent over $10,000 to attend a weekend runway show in New York, $15,000 to buy her Vera Wang wedding dress, and $1,200 to get hair extensions.[1] If only she had known that these and other costs totalled more than her personal revenues, perhaps she could have had her hair done at **FIRST CHOICE HAIRCUTTERS,** where the average customer pays a mere $13 for a cut.

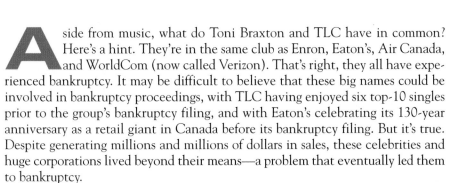

---

[1] "A Star Is Broke," *Entertainment Weekly*, February 20, 1998; www.chl.ca/JamMusicArtistsB/braxton_toni.html; and http://people.aol.com/people/news/now/0,10958,123191,00.html.

The first goal of this chapter is to help you see how an income statement indicates whether a business generated a profit or loss from the day-to-day business activities that occurred during the accounting period. Then we'll discuss various operating activities and show how the DECIDES transaction analysis approach from Chapter 2 can be used to analyze and record income statement transactions. Finally, at the close of the chapter, we will help you learn about the key accounting concepts that underlie income statement reporting. The most important things to get out of this chapter are presented as Learning Objectives on the first page of the chapter.

UNDERSTAND _____
What an Income Statement Means to Users

REVENUES AND EXPENSES

Just as it was useful in Chapter 2 to understand the balance sheet by thinking about the investing and financing activities needed to start up your First Choice Haircutters Salon, you will better understand the income statement if you spend a few minutes considering a salon's operating activities. Think back to the last time you got your hair cut. How does your salon generate revenues, and what expenses does it incur? For hair salons and most other businesses, **revenues** represent the amounts charged to customers. Specifically, revenues represent the increases in a company's resources that result from providing goods or services to customers. So, if your salon gives 1,560 haircuts in a month and charges customers $10 per cut, revenues would total $15,600. The amount of revenues earned during the period is reported in the top part of the body of the income statement.

The costs of operating the business are reported as **expenses** in the body of the income statement just underneath revenues. In general, expenses include any costs **incurred** to generate revenues in the period covered by the income statement. For hair salons, the big expenses relate to manager salaries and stylist wages, rent, advertising, insurance, and various utilities (telephone, fax, Internet, power, water). Our friends in the business tell us that a small salon that gives 1,500 haircuts in a month would typically incur operating expenses of $8,000 for salaries and wages, $2,400 for rent, $400 for advertising, $200 for insurance, and $700 for utilities. Big hair companies have similar expenses; for Regis Corporation, each expense is about 8,000 times bigger.

In addition to these typical operating activities, businesses often have other non-operating normal (but not central) transactions that result in revenues or expenses. For example, in addition to its core business of cutting hair, your First Choice Haircutters Salon might earn interest revenue from investing its cash in a certificate of deposit at the bank. Alternatively, it might have to pay interest expense on a bank loan. It might even generate a **gain** or **loss** from selling land that it owned. These items are not considered a central part of business operations because they have more to do with investing and financing than with how the business is run. To put it simply, hair salons are in business to generate a profit from selling haircuts, not from selling land or earning interest on their investments. Nonetheless, these non-operating transactions do affect net income, so these effects are included in the income statement, as shown in Exhibit 3.1. Because Canadian accounting rules do not clearly define the difference between the two, there is a lot of variation in income statement formats in practice.

Exhibit 3.1 introduces a subtotal called *Operating income*, which combines revenues and expenses from operating transactions only. This little subtotal can be quite a useful addition to the income statement. By excluding non-operating transactions, which are less likely to recur in the future, operating income can act as a starting point for forecasting how much profit will be generated in future accounting periods. That is, if hair keeps growing at 1.2 inches per month, as scientists say it will, the $3,900 of operating income shown in Exhibit 3.1 is likely to be earned in later months, too. Of course, operating

---

Revenues are increases in a company's resources created by providing goods or services to customers during the accounting period.

An **expense** is the cost that results when a company gives up its resources (by using up assets or incurring liabilities) to generate revenues during the accounting period.

When you purchase a good or a service and become obligated to pay for it, you may say that you have taken on a cost, or that you are responsible for a cost. Accountants say that you have **incurred** a cost.

A **gain** occurs when, as part of a non-operating transaction, a business sells something for an amount greater than what it's recorded at in the accounting records. A **loss** occurs when the business sells it for less than the amount recorded in the accounting records. Just like revenues, gains increase net income. Just like expenses, losses reduce net income.

COACH'S TIP

There is no rule about the order for reporting the various types of operating expenses. In many cases, operating expenses are listed from the largest to smallest amount.

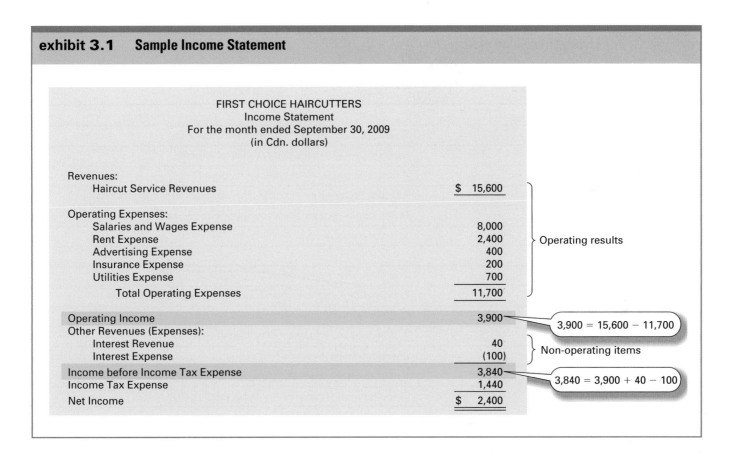

exhibit 3.1   Sample Income Statement

FIRST CHOICE HAIRCUTTERS
Income Statement
For the month ended September 30, 2009
(in Cdn. dollars)

Revenues:		
Haircut Service Revenues	$ 15,600	
Operating Expenses:		
Salaries and Wages Expense	8,000	
Rent Expense	2,400	Operating results
Advertising Expense	400	
Insurance Expense	200	
Utilities Expense	700	
Total Operating Expenses	11,700	
Operating Income	3,900	3,900 = 15,600 − 11,700
Other Revenues (Expenses):		
Interest Revenue	40	Non-operating items
Interest Expense	(100)	
Income before Income Tax Expense	3,840	3,840 = 3,900 + 40 − 100
Income Tax Expense	1,440	
Net Income	$ 2,400	

income isn't the final story on whether the business made a profit overall. To get to that "bottom line" net income number, we have to consider the results of non-operating transactions and income taxes charged on the company's profit.

You will also notice in Exhibit 3.1 that income tax expense is reported separately. Income tax is calculated on all the revenues and expenses of the company. For this reason, the company combines its revenues and expenses from operating and non-operating transactions in another subtotal called *Income before income tax expense*, as shown in Exhibit 3.1. *Income before income tax expense* is used to determine *Income tax expense*, which is then subtracted to arrive at *Net income*. (Although tax calculations can be very complex, for this course income tax expense will simply be a percentage of income before income tax expense. We will show this calculation in Chapter 4.) Exhibit 3.1 is a good example of how revenue and expense accounts can be arranged and reported on the income statement, but it presents only one format and includes only a handful of accounts. In Exhibit 3.2, we provide a more complete list of revenues, expenses, gains, and losses. The accounts in boldface appear in FCH's income statement in Exhibit 3.1. As we have already said, every company is different, and there is a lot of variety in practice. Exhibit 3.2 isn't intended to be all-inclusive. It's just supposed to give you ideas about possible account names for companies that aren't in the hair business.

Before you move on to the next section, we need to make sure you aren't confusing the terms "expenses" and "expenditures," which are used interchangeably in everyday life. In accounting, these terms have precise and different meanings. **Expenditures** are any outflows of cash for any purpose—whether to pay down a bank loan, buy land, or pay an employee. **Expenses,** on the other hand, are defined as the costs incurred to generate revenue. Expenses can be incurred by spending cash, using up another asset, or incurring a liability; they don't always involve an immediate outflow of cash.

Expenditures are any outflows of cash for any purpose.

exhibit 3.2   Excerpt from Chart of Accounts

Account Name	Description
REVENUES	
Sales Revenues	Sales of products in the ordinary course of business
Service Revenues	Sales of services in the ordinary course of business
Rental Revenues	Amounts earned by renting out company property
Interest Revenues	Amounts earned on savings accounts and certificates of deposit
Dividend Revenues	Dividends earned from investing in other companies
Other Revenues	Miscellaneous sources of revenues
EXPENSES	
Cost of Goods Sold	Cost of products sold in the ordinary course of business
Repairs and Maintenance	Cost of routine maintenance and upkeep of buildings/equipment
Advertising Expense	Cost of advertising services obtained during the period
Amortization Expense	Cost of plant and equipment or intangible assets used up
	or expired during the period
Insurance Expense	Cost of insurance coverage for the period
Salaries and Wages Expense	Cost of employees' salaries and wages for the period
Rent Expense	Cost of rent for the period
Supplies Expense	Cost of supplies used up during the period
Transportation Expense	Cost of freight to transport goods out to customers
Utilities Expense	Cost of power, light, heat, Internet, and telephone for the period
Interest Expense	Interest charged on outstanding debts owed
Income Tax Expense	Taxes charged on reported earnings
GAINS	
Gains on Asset Sales	Gains on asset sales (not central part of the business)
Gains on Sale of Investments	Gains from selling investments in other companies
LOSSES	
Losses on Asset Sales	Losses on asset sales (not central part of the business)
Losses on Sale of Investments	Losses from selling investments in other companies

STUDY _____

How to Analyze Operating Transactions

CASH-BASED MEASUREMENTS

Like most people, you probably look at the balance in your bank account to gauge your financial performance. If the overall balance increased this month, you'll likely take that as a sign that you've done a good job of managing your finances. If it has gone down, that's a clue that you need to tame yourself a little next month. The reason that the change in your bank balance tends to give a decent measure of financial performance is that your cash flows (in and out) occur close in time to the activities that cause those cash flows. For example, if you participate in a psychology experiment, you'll probably get paid on the spot, so the cash inflow is a good measure of how much your participation improved your financial situation. Similarly, if you pay cash for snacks, your declining

exhibit 3.3 Cash Basis Sometimes Provides a Decent Measure of Performance

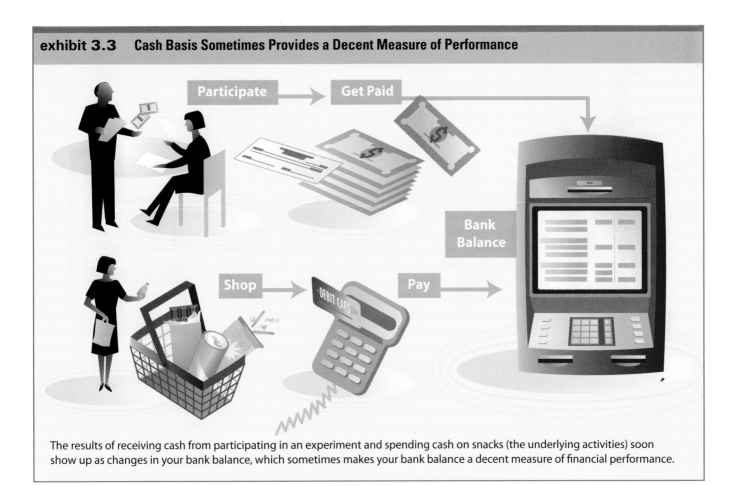

The results of receiving cash from participating in an experiment and spending cash on snacks (the underlying activities) soon show up as changes in your bank balance, which sometimes makes your bank balance a decent measure of financial performance.

cash balance will provide a timely measure of how much your snacking is costing you. Swiping your debit card to pay for your snacks takes money out of your bank account right away. As shown in Exhibit 3.3, when there is little delay between the underlying activities and the reporting of their effects on your bank balance, this **cash basis** of accounting is good enough.

Generally speaking, the cash basis of accounting doesn't measure financial performance very well when transactions are conducted using credit rather than cash. The problem is that credit often introduces a significant delay between the time an activity occurs and the time it impacts the bank account balance. You probably realize that, if you get a paycheque from your regular job only once a month, the results of your hard work don't show up until the end of the month. Similarly, if you go crazy with your credit card at the mall, these transactions won't affect your bank balance in the current month. This joyride only hits your cash balance the following month (or months) when you have to pay for what you bought. As shown in Exhibit 3.4, this delay in reporting the effects of the underlying activity makes the fluctuating bank balance a less useful measure of financial performance.

Because most businesses use credit for their transactions, the cash basis of accounting is not likely to correspond to the business activities that actually occurred during a given period of time. For this reason, generally accepted accounting principles do not allow cash basis accounting to be used for external reporting of income. Instead, generally accepted accounting principles require the **accrual basis** of accounting. The "rule of accrual" is that the financial effects of business activities are measured and reported when the activities actually occur, not when the cash related to them is received or paid. That is, *revenues are reported when they are* **earned** *and expenses are reported when they are* **incurred.**

Cash basis accounting records revenues when cash is received and expenses when cash is paid.

COACH'S TIP

Buying on credit means buying something now and promising to pay for it later. If you use a credit card to pay for your snacks, you are buying on credit rather than paying cash.

Accrual basis accounting records revenues when they are earned and expenses when they are incurred, regardless of the timing of cash receipts or payments. Revenues are **earned** when goods or services are provided to customers at a determined price and with reasonable assurance of collection. Expenses are **incurred** when the economic benefits of an item are used up in the current period, resulting in a decrease in the company's resources.

exhibit 3.4   Cash Basis Sometimes Provides a Poor Measure of Performance

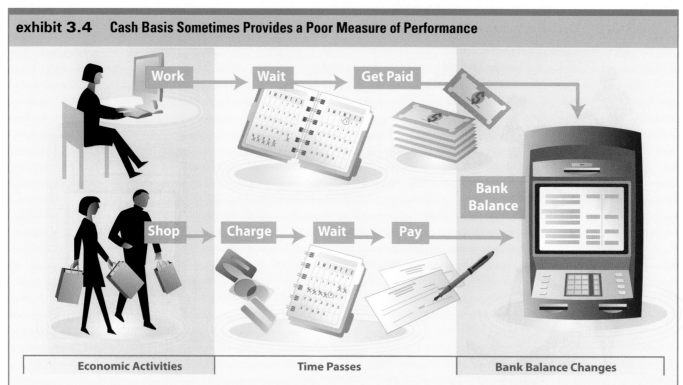

Economic Activities	Time Passes	Bank Balance Changes

The results of working and shopping (the underlying activities) eventually show up as changes in your bank account balance, but only after a significant delay. The delays between the underlying activities and their effects on the bank balance can cause your bank balance to be a poor measure of your financial performance.

ACCRUAL-BASED MEASUREMENT OF REVENUES

Do you know what it means to recognize revenues when they are *earned?* Quite simply, it means a company reports revenue *when it performs the acts promised to the customer.* These promised acts might involve providing services (like a haircut) or transferring to the customer ownership of goods (such as a tube of hair gel). Although the company expects to receive cash in exchange for providing goods and services, the timing of that cash receipt does not dictate when revenues are reported in the income statement. Instead, the key factor in determining when to report revenue is whether the company has done what it promised. This means that cash can be received (1) in the *same* period as the promised acts are performed, (2) in a period *before* the promised acts are performed, or (3) in a period *after* the promised acts are performed, as shown on the timeline in Exhibit 3.5. Let's see how to handle each of these cases.

1. **Cash is received in the *same* period as the promised acts are performed.** This is a common occurrence for First Choice Haircutters stores because customers pay within a few minutes of getting a haircut. In these cases, when cash is received in the same period as the promised acts are performed, the company reports an increase in its cash and a corresponding increase in revenues. Notice that this transaction affects both the balance sheet (*cash*) and the income statement (*revenues*).

2. **Cash is received in a period before the promised acts are performed.** This situation occurs, for example, when your First Choice Haircutters Salon receives cash for gift certificates that can be used to pay for *future* haircuts. You know that your First Choice Haircutters Salon has to record the cash received, but it hasn't done anything yet to earn the revenue—so how does it account for this other part of the transaction? When cash is received before promised acts are performed, the company receiving the cash will report an increase in cash and an increase in a liability, which represents the obligation to perform the acts in the future. The liability for these advances from

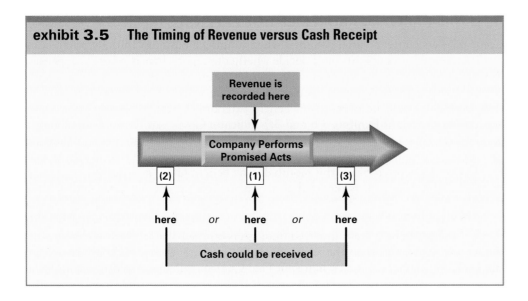

exhibit 3.5 The Timing of Revenue versus Cash Receipt

customers is called **unearned revenue.** There is no impact on the income statement at this time because the company has merely exchanged a promise for the customer's cash. When the company provides the promised goods or services to the customer, revenue will be reported on the income statement and the liability reduced.

Unearned revenue is a liability representing a company's obligation to provide goods or services to customers in the future.

3. *Cash is to be received in a period after the promised acts are performed.* This situation typically arises when a company sells to a customer on credit. In these cases, the company will record revenue when the promised act has been performed, and at that time also will record an asset called accounts receivable. When the company later collects cash from the customer, it will report an increase in cash and a corresponding reduction in accounts receivable. Again, notice that the income statement is affected in the period in which the promised acts are performed, not necessarily when cash is received.

It's worthwhile making sure you understand what sparks the recording of revenues because, later in this chapter, you'll see that this also triggers the recording of expenses. To ensure that you've got a handle on this, spend a couple of minutes on the Self-Study Quiz.

COACH'S TIP

When cash is received in the same period in which the company performs the promised acts, revenues determined using accrual accounting do not differ from cash basis revenues.

HOW'S IT GOING? A Self-Study Quiz

The following transactions are typical monthly operating activities for your First Choice Haircutters Salon. Indicate the amount of revenue, if any, that should be reported in September's income statement.

Operating Activity	Amount of Revenue in September (if any)
(a) Provided haircut services in September to customers for $15,000 cash.	
(b) Sold $300 worth of gift certificates at the beginning of September.	
(c) Customers used $100 worth of gift certificates to pay for haircuts in the third week of September.	
(d) Provided $500 worth of hair styling services to employees of a local TV station, which is billed every month.	
(e) The TV station paid $300 on its account.	

After you're finished, check your answers with the solutions in the margin.

Quiz Answers

(a) $15,000—This amount is earned when services are provided.

(b) $0—No amount has been earned because no services (or goods) have been provided to the customer. At the time of this transaction, your salon will record the increase in cash, along with a liability to provide future services.

(c) $100—Now that the haircut services have been provided, the revenue can be reported (and the gift certificate liability reduced).

(d) $500—This was earned when services were provided.

(e) $0—The revenue was earned and already recorded in (d).

ACCRUAL-BASED MEASUREMENT OF EXPENSES

The **cost** of an item is the amount of resources used to obtain it. A cost is said to be incurred when the company pays cash or uses credit to obtain the item.

Companies encounter a variety of **costs** when running a business. Initially, when costs are first incurred, accountants must decide whether to report them as assets or expenses. Remember that an asset is an item with probable future economic benefit. So, when a cost is incurred, the accounting decision depends on whether the costs lead to something with a probable future economic benefit extending beyond the end of the current accounting period, as Exhibits 3.6 and 3.7 indicate. Costs that do *not* benefit future periods are immediately reported as expenses on the income statement as they are incurred. For example, the cost of electrical services to power the hair dryers at your First Choice Haircutters Salon this month doesn't benefit future months (follow the top line in Exhibit 3.7), so it is reported as an expense on the income statement (called *Utilities Expense*).

A **capitalized** cost is a cost that is reported as an asset on the balance sheet.

In contrast, costs that have probable future economic benefits are **capitalized** initially as assets, and later are transferred from assets on the balance sheet to expenses on the income statement when the assets' future benefits are used up with the passage of time or through physical use. When your First Choice Haircutters salon pays for three months of rent in advance, the benefits from this cost extend over three months (see the downward sloping line in Exhibit 3.7), so this cost is initially reported as an asset (*Prepaid Rent*). Later, as each month passes, your salon will report *Rent Expense* equal to the amount of the prepaid rent benefit used up during that month (see the upward-sloping line in Exhibit 3.7).

When a company pays cash or uses credit to obtain something that doesn't benefit future periods, the transaction affects the balance sheet (reduced cash or increased liabilities) and the income statement (increased expenses). In other instances, where costs involve items that benefit future periods, such as those jars of Barbicide that you see in hair salons, the downward-sloping line in Exhibit 3.7 indicates that these costs initially affect only the balance sheet (e.g., the asset *Supplies* increases at the same time cash is paid or credit is used). Eventually, when some of the asset's economic benefits are used up, these costs will move from the asset account (*Supplies*) on the

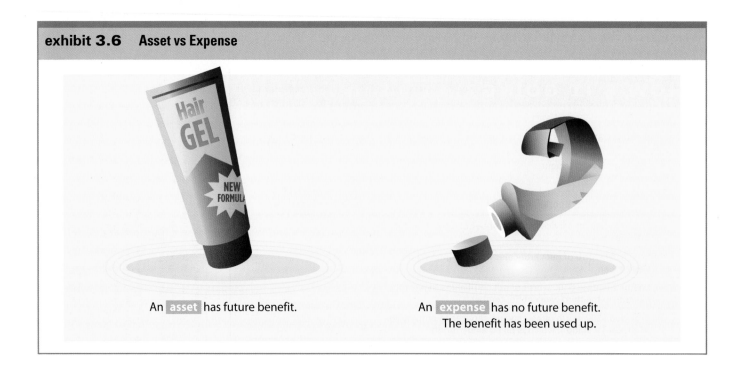

exhibit 3.6   Asset vs Expense

An asset has future benefit.

An expense has no future benefit.
The benefit has been used up.

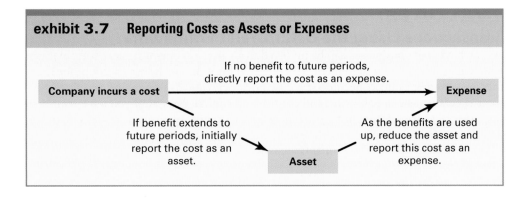

exhibit 3.7 Reporting Costs as Assets or Expenses

balance sheet to an expense account (*Supplies Expense*) on the income statement (the upward-sloping line). The point to take away from this discussion is that expenses are the decreases in a company's resources when the company either (*a*) incurs a cost that does not benefit future periods or (*b*) uses up the economic benefits of an existing asset.

You will remember from Chapter 2 that, when considerable uncertainty exists about whether or not a cost will have future benefits, conservatism dictates recording it as an expense. The following examples, however, do not contain this kind of uncertainty. It's time for you to practice determining which costs should be reported as expenses on an income statement prepared according to accrual basis accounting. As you work through the Self-Study Quiz below, feel free to glance at Exhibit 3.7 for help.

HOW'S IT GOING? A Self-Study Quiz

This self-study quiz continues our look at the typical monthly operating activities for your First Choice Haircutters Salon, focusing this time on costs incurred by your salon. Indicate the amount of expense, if any, that should be reported in September's income statement.

Operating Activity	Amount of Expense in September (if any)
(f) Paid stylists $8,000 for wages related to services they provided in September.	
(g) Paid September, October, and November rent in advance, at a total cost of $7,200.	
(h) Paid $2,400 for an insurance policy that covers the period from September 1 until August 31 of next year.	
(i) Received a bill for $400 for running a newspaper ad in September. The bill will be paid in October.	
(j) Paid utility bills totalling $700 for services received and billed in September.	

When you're finished, check your answers with the solutions in the margin.

Quiz Answers

(f) $8,000

(g) $2,400—The $7,200 provides mall space for three months, so only 1/3 of this cost is used up this month (1/3 × $7,200 = $2,400).

(h) $200—The $2,400 provides insurance coverage for a whole year, so only 1/12 of that has been used up this month ($2,400 × 1/12 = $200).

(i) $400—The newspaper ad ran in the current month.

(j) $700—The utilities services were received in the current month.

EVALUATE _____

Transactions Using the Debit/Credit Framework

As you have seen, businesses can be involved in a variety of operating activities, many of which affect the income statement. Chapter 2 did not discuss how to account for these income statement effects because it focused on investing and financing activities, and their effects on assets, liabilities, and contributed capital. Now that you have seen how operating activities can result in revenues and expenses, you need to know how the debit/credit framework works with revenues and expenses. We present these effects by adding a little jet fuel to the transaction analysis model from Chapter 2.

INCLUDING REVENUES AND EXPENSES IN THE TRANSACTION ANALYSIS MODEL

Let's start with the basic ingredients from Chapter 2—that is, assets equals liabilities plus shareholders' equity, or $A = L + SE$. For now, we're going to focus on the shareholders' equity category. As you already know from Chapters 1 and 2, shareholders' equity represents the shareholders' investment in the company, which comes from either (1) *capital contributed* to the company by the shareholders (in exchange for shares) or (2) *earnings* that are *retained* in the company (rather than being distributed to shareholders as dividends).

What's new in this chapter is that we've introduced revenue and expense accounts. (We've also introduced gains and losses, but rather than make things overly complicated, we'll just focus on revenues and expenses for now. As you will see later, gains are accounted for just like revenues, and losses are accounted for just like expenses.) In Chapter 1, we saw how net income (revenues less expenses) affects the retained earnings account on the balance sheet. But, when a transaction results in a revenue or expense, we don't make the entry directly into the retained earnings account. If we did that, we wouldn't have the detailed information on hand at the end of the year to prepare the income statement. Instead, we create separate accounts for every revenue and expense that we want to appear on the income statement. You can think of the revenue and expense accounts as subcategories within the retained earnings account. The effects of revenue and expense transactions *eventually* flow into retained earnings, as suggested in Exhibit 3.8, but they aren't initially recorded there.

Because revenue and expense accounts are subcategories of retained earnings, they are affected by debits and credits in the same way as all shareholders' equity accounts. You already know that increases in shareholders' equity are recorded on the right side of the Contributed Capital T-account. You also know that revenues increase net income, which increases the shareholders' equity account called retained earnings. So, putting these ideas together should lead to the conclusion that **revenues are recorded on the right (credit).** Here's the logic again: increases in shareholders' equity are on the right, revenues increase shareholders' equity, so revenues are recorded on the right. *Decreases* in shareholders' equity are recorded on the left side, so, since expenses decrease net income and retained earnings, **expenses are recorded on the left (debit).** Exhibit 3.8 summarizes these effects. The coach gives you another way of picturing how debits and credits affect the accounts.

USING THE DECIDES APPROACH WITH REVENUES AND EXPENSES

Okay, revenues are recorded with credits (on the right), and expenses are recorded with debits (on the left). Looks as though you're ready to practice analyzing some transactions using the DECIDES approach from Chapter 2. To avoid adding too many new things all at once, we'll analyze the same transactions that appeared in the self-study quizzes earlier in this chapter. Don't skip this part because, although you might understand *what* you're trying to do, the step of actually getting the accounting system to do what you want (using journal entries) requires practice, practice, and more practice.

COACH'S TIP

Here's another way to picture how debits and credits affect accounts:

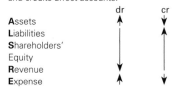

	dr	cr
Assets	↑	↓
Liabilities		
Shareholders' Equity		
Revenue		
Expense	↑	↓

exhibit 3.8   Expanded Transaction Analysis Model

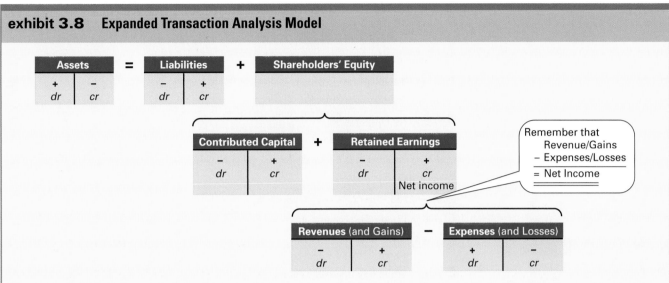

The expanded transaction analysis model shows that revenues and expenses are subcategories of retained earnings, which itself is a shareholders' equity account. All items that increase shareholders' equity (including revenues) are recorded with credits. All items that decrease shareholders' equity (including expenses) are recorded with debits. *Note:* Dividends declared (not shown here) also reduce retained earnings and are recorded with debits. Dividends will be discussed in a later chapter.

Revenues

(a) **Provided haircut services in September to customers for $15,000 cash.**

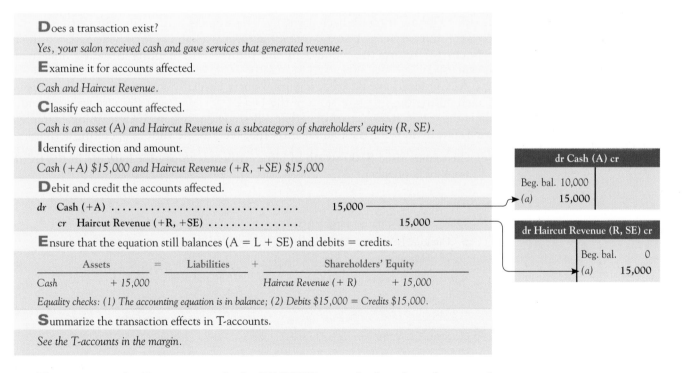

Does a transaction exist?

Yes, your salon received cash and gave services that generated revenue.

Examine it for accounts affected.

Cash and Haircut Revenue.

Classify each account affected.

Cash is an asset (A) and Haircut Revenue is a subcategory of shareholders' equity (R, SE).

Identify direction and amount.

Cash (+A) $15,000 and Haircut Revenue (+R, +SE) $15,000

Debit and credit the accounts affected.

dr   Cash (+A)   15,000
     cr   Haircut Revenue (+R, +SE)   15,000

Ensure that the equation still balances (A = L + SE) and debits = credits.

Assets		=	Liabilities	+	Shareholders' Equity	
Cash	+ 15,000				Haircut Revenue (+ R)	+ 15,000

Equality checks: (1) The accounting equation is in balance; (2) Debits $15,000 = Credits $15,000.

Summarize the transaction effects in T-accounts.

See the T-accounts in the margin.

The arrows in the T-accounts with the DECIDES example show how the journal entry is posted to the Cash and Haircut Revenue accounts. You've probably noticed that the Cash account has a beginning balance of $10,000. This is simply the balance from August 31 (in Chapter 2) that carries over to September 1 (in this chapter). The Haircut Revenue account has a balance of zero at the beginning of September because this is the first month of store operations.

(b) Sold $300 worth of gift certificates at the beginning of September.

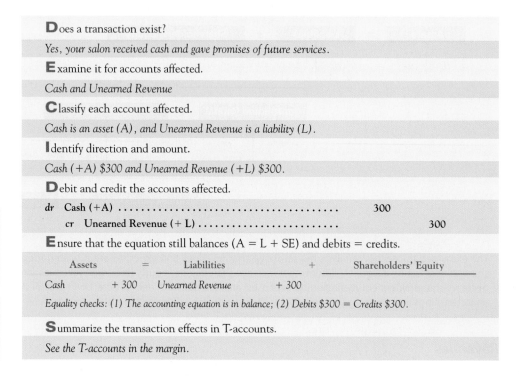

dr Cash (A) cr	
Beg. bal. 10,000	
(a) 15,000	
(b) 300	

dr Unearned Revenue (L) cr	
	Beg. bal. 0
	(b) 300

Does a transaction exist?

Yes, your salon received cash and gave promises of future services.

Examine it for accounts affected.

Cash and Unearned Revenue

Classify each account affected.

Cash is an asset (A), and Unearned Revenue is a liability (L).

Identify direction and amount.

Cash (+A) $300 and Unearned Revenue (+L) $300.

Debit and credit the accounts affected.

dr Cash (+A)   300
    cr   Unearned Revenue (+ L)   300

Ensure that the equation still balances (A = L + SE) and debits = credits.

Assets	=	Liabilities	+	Shareholders' Equity
Cash + 300		Unearned Revenue + 300		

Equality checks: (1) The accounting equation is in balance; (2) Debits $300 = Credits $300.

Summarize the transaction effects in T-accounts.

See the T-accounts in the margin.

In transaction *(b)*, the $300 cash received for gift certificates isn't recorded as revenue because it hasn't been earned yet (customers will use the gift certificates to pay for future services). Instead, your salon records a liability to provide $300 worth of services (or return the money) in the future. This liability is called unearned revenue.

As you may have noticed, a journal entry basically sums up the analyses completed during the first four steps of the DECIDES approach. Because we've already done these four steps as part of earlier self-study quizzes, in the remaining examples we'll start by showing the journal entry that records the various operating activities.

(c) Customers used $100 worth of gift certificates to pay for haircuts in the third week of September.

dr Unearned Revenue (L) cr	
	Beg. bal. 0
(c) 100	(b) 300

dr Haircut Revenue (R, SE) cr	
	Beg. bal. 0
	(a) 15,000
	(c) 100

Debit and credit the accounts affected.

dr Unearned Revenue (− L)   100
    cr   Haircut Revenue (+R, +SE)   100

Ensure that the equation still balances (A = L + SE) and debits = credits.

Assets	=	Liabilities	+	Shareholders' Equity
		Unearned Revenue − 100		Haircut Revenue (+R) + 100

Equality checks: (1) The accounting equation is in balance; (2) Debits $100 = Credits $100.

Summarize the transaction effects in T-accounts.

See the T-accounts in the margin.

In transaction *(c)*, your First Choice Haircutters Salon provided services worth $100, which need to be recorded as revenue. In return for these services, your salon took back $100 of gift certificates, which reduces its liability for honouring them in the future. To account for this, journal entry *(c)* reduces the liability Unearned Revenue and increases Haircut Revenue.

(d) **Provided $500 worth of hair styling services to employees of a local TV station, which is billed every month.**

Debit and credit the accounts affected.

dr   Accounts Receivable (+A)   500
      cr   Haircut Revenue (+R, +SE)   500

Ensure that the equation still balances (A = L + SE) and debits = credits.

Assets	=	Liabilities	+	Shareholders' Equity
Accounts Receivable + 500				Haircut Revenue (+R) +500

Equality checks: *(1) the accounting equation is in balance; (2) Debits $500 = Credits $500.*

Summarize the transaction effects in T-accounts.

See the T-accounts in the margin.

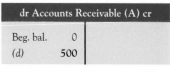

dr Accounts Receivable (A) cr	
Beg. bal. 0	
(d) 500	

dr Haircut Revenue (R, SE) cr	
	Beg. bal. 0
	(a) 15,000
	(c) 100
	(d) 500

Transaction *(d)* shows yet another instance where revenues are recorded based on whether services have been provided, not whether cash has been received. Because services have been provided, your salon has earned revenue and now has the right to collect $500 from the TV station. The right to collect money is an asset called Accounts Receivable.

(e) **The TV station paid $300 on its account.**

Debit and credit the accounts affected.

dr   Cash (+A)   300
      cr   Account Receivable (−A)   300

Ensure that the equation still balances (A = L + SE) and debits = credits.

Assets	=	Liabilities	+	Shareholders' Equity
Cash + 300				
Accounts Receivable − 300				

Equality checks: *(1) The accounting equation is in balance; (2) Debits $300 = Credits $300.*

Summarize the transaction effects in T-accounts.

See the T-accounts in the margin.

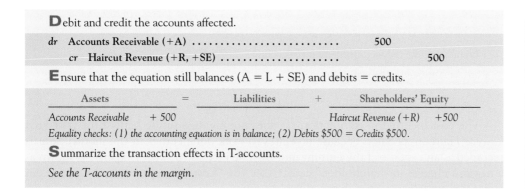

dr Cash (A) cr	
Beg. bal. 10,000	
(a) 15,000	
(b) 300	
(e) 300	

dr Accounts Receivable (A) cr	
Beg. Bal. 0	
(d) 500	*(e)* 300

In transaction *(e)*, cash increases and the receivable from the TV station decreases since it has now been partially paid.

Expenses

Okay, now it's time to switch to transactions involving expenses. Remember that expenses are decreases in a company's resources that arise when the company either incurs a cost that does not benefit future periods or uses up the economic benefits of an existing asset.

(f) **Paid stylists $8,000 for wages related to services they provided in September.**

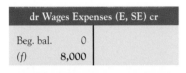

Debit and credit the accounts affected.

dr	Wages Expenses (+E, −SE).............................	8,000	
	cr Cash (− A).....................................		8,000

Ensure that the equation still balances (A = L + SE) and debits = credits.

Assets	=	Liabilities	+	Shareholders' Equity
Cash − 8,000				Wages Expenses (+E) −8,000

Equality checks: (1) The accounting equation is in balance; (2) Debits $ 8,000 = Credits $ 8,000

Summarize the transaction effects in T-accounts.

See the T-accounts in the margin.

The cost incurred in transaction *(f)* does not create a future benefit for your First Choice Haircutters Salon because it relates to work done earlier in the month, so it is recorded as an expense of the current month. The increase in wages expense is shown as a *negative* change in shareholders' equity (see the "**E**nsure" step) because increases in expenses cause decreases in shareholders' equity.

(g) **Paid September, October, and November rent in advance, at a total cost of $7,200.**

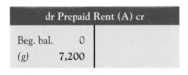

Debit and credit the accounts affected.

dr	Prepaid Rent (+A)	7,200	
	cr Cash (− A)		7,200

Ensure that the equation still balances (A = L + SE) and debits = credits.

Assets	=	Liabilities	+	Shareholders' Equity
Cash − 7,200				
Prepaid Rent + 7,200				

Equality checks: (1) The accounting equation is in balance; (2) Debits $ 7,200 = Credits $ 7,200.

Summarize the transaction effects in T-accounts.

See the T-accounts in the margin.

Notice that *not* every operating transaction immediately affects the income statement. Transaction *(g)* involves paying for the right to use the rented mall space for three months following the payment. At the time the payment is made, this cost provides a future economic benefit to your First Choice Haircutters Salon (mall space for three months), so it is reported as an asset called Prepaid Rent. Each month, after the rented space has been used, your salon will reduce the Prepaid Rent asset and show the amount used up as rent expense. The adjustment needed to report September's rent expense of $2,400 will be covered in Chapter 4.

(h) **Paid $2,400 for an insurance policy that covers the period from September 1 until August 31 of next year.**

Debit and credit the accounts affected.

dr	Prepaid insurance (+A).............................	2,400	
	cr Cash (−A)		2,400

Ensure that the equation still balances (A = L + SE) and debits = credits.

Assets	=	Liabilities	+	Shareholders' Equity
Cash − 2,400				
Prepaid Insurance + 2,400				

Equality checks: (1) The accounting equation is in balance; (2) Debits $2,400 = Credits $2,400

Summarize the transaction effects in T-accounts.

See the T-accounts in the margin.

dr Prepaid Insurance (A) cr	
Beg. bal. 0	
(h) 2,400	

dr Cash (A) cr			
Beg. bal. 10,000			
(a) 15,000		(f)	8,000
(b) 300		(g)	7,200
(e) 300		(h)	2,400

Transaction (h) provides another example of a prepayment that is initially recorded as an asset. The adjustment to record September's insurance expense of $200 will be covered in Chapter 4.

(i) **Received a bill for $400 for running a newspaper ad in September. The bill will be paid in October.**

Debit and credit the accounts affected.

dr Advertising Expense (+E, −SE) 400

   cr Accounts Payable (+L) 400

Ensure that the equation still balances (A = L + SE) and debits = credits.

Assets	=	Liabilities	+	Shareholders' Equity
		Accounts Payable + 400		Advertising Expense (+E) − 400

Equality checks: (1) The accounting equation is in balance; (2) Debits $400 = Credits $400.

Summarize the transaction effects in T-accounts.

See the T-accounts in the margin.

dr Advertising Expense (E, SE) cr	
Beg. bal. 0	
(i) 400	

dr Accounts Payable (L) cr		
	Beg. bal.	630
	(i)	400

Quiz Answer
(j) Journal Entry
dr Utilities Expense (+E, −SE) 700
  cr Cash (−A) 700

HOW'S IT GOING? A Self-Study Quiz

For transaction (j), complete the journal entry and then check your answer against the solution in the margin. If you need some help, take a look back at transaction (f).

(j) **Paid utility bills totalling $700 for services received and billed in September.**

Debit and credit the accounts affected.

dr [ ] .... [ ]

   cr [ ] .... [ ]

Ensure that the equation still balances (A = L + SE) and debits = credits.

Assets	=	Liabilities	+	Shareholders' Equity
Cash − 700				Utilities Expense (+E) − 700

Equality checks: (1) The accounting equation is in balance; (2) Debits $700 = Credits $700.

Summarize the transaction effects in T-accounts.

See the T-accounts in the margin.

dr Utilities Expense (E, SE) cr	
Beg. bal. 0	
(j) 700	

dr Cash (A) cr			
Beg. bal. 10,000			
(a) 15,000		(f)	8,000
(b) 300		(g)	7,200
(e) 300		(h)	2,400
		(j)	700

exhibit 3.9   First Choice Haircutters Salon T-Accounts (beginning balances are taken from Exhibit 2.9)

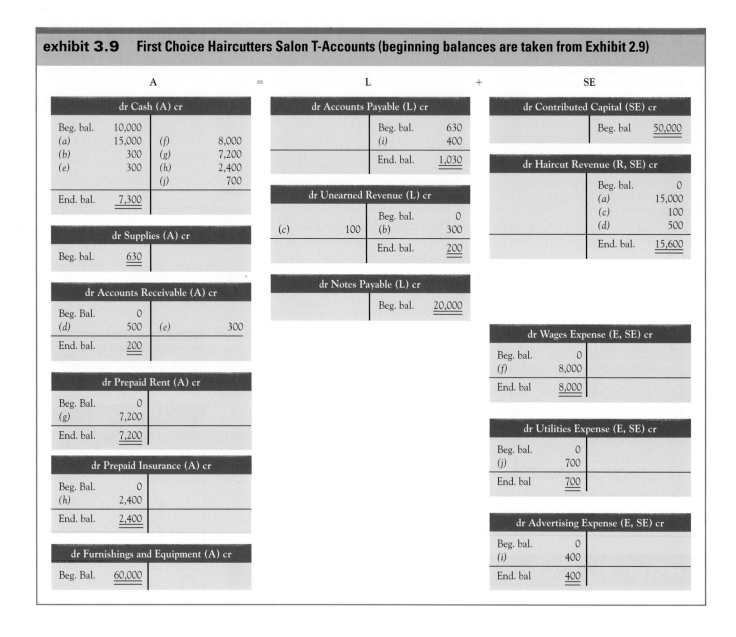

CALCULATING ACCOUNT BALANCES

Now that the effects of the journal entries have been entered into the T-accounts, it's time to calculate the ending account balances. In Exhibit 3.9, we have included all the T-accounts for your First Choice Haircutters Salon (from this chapter as well as Chapter 2). You've heard it before, but we'll just remind you that the ending balance in each account is determined by adding the amounts on one side and subtracting the amounts on the other side.

PREPARING THE UNADJUSTED TRIAL BALANCE

After posting the journal entries to the various accounts, let's prepare an unadjusted trial balance to check that the total recorded debits equal the total recorded credits. Exhibit 3.10 shows the trial balance, listing all the account names in one column (usually in financial statement order) and their ending balances (from Exhibit 3.9) in the appropriate debit or credit column.

exhibit 3.10 Sample Unadjusted Trial Balance

FIRST CHOICE HAIRCUTTERS SALON
Unadjusted Trial Balance
As of September 30

Account Name	Debits	Credits
Cash	$ 7,300	
Supplies	630	
Accounts Receivable	200	
Prepaid Rent	7,200	
Prepaid Insurance	2,400	
Furnishings and Equipment	60,000	
Accounts Payable		$ 1,030
Unearned Revenue		200
Notes Payable		20,000
Contributed Capital		50,000
Haircut Revenue		15,600
Wages Expense	8,000	
Utilities Expense	700	
Advertising Expense	400	
Totals	$86,830	$86,830

If your trial balance indicates that total debits don't equal total credits, remember not to panic or start randomly changing numbers. The first thing to do when you find yourself in a hole is stop digging. Calmly go back to your journal entries and T-account postings and find what you did wrong (using the hints on page 60).

Before financial statements are prepared for your First Choice Haircutters Salon, adjustments will have to be made to the numbers in the unadjusted trial balance to bring the accounts up to date. For example, some of the benefits of prepaid rent and prepaid insurance were used up in September, but this wasn't recorded yet. Also, income taxes haven't been calculated and recorded. These adjustments are part of the reporting phase of the accounting process and are studied in Chapter 4.

SUMMARIZING HOW TO ACCOUNT FOR REVENUES AND EXPENSES

To this point of the chapter, you've analyzed some transactions—10, actually—that involve operating activities. While this is a good introduction, it doesn't quite prepare you for the variety of operating activities that most companies engage in. What you really need is a general summary of everything you've learned about revenues, expenses, and journal entries, and then lots of practice applying it to a broad range of activities.

In the following sections, we summarize the basic structure of journal entries that are used to account for a variety of operating transactions. The exhibits in these sections can save time and make things clear for you, but only if you read them and understand them. So take the time now to read each exhibit and think about how the specific transactions that you saw earlier in this chapter fit with the summaries.

Accounting for Revenues: A Summary

Remember that revenues are recorded when the business fulfills its promise to provide goods or services to customers, which is not necessarily the same time that cash is received. Because of this, we look at three cases, where cash is received (1) at the *same* time as the promised acts are performed, (2) *before* the promised acts are performed, and (3) *after* the promised acts are performed. Start by reading the explanation at the end of Exhibit 3.11, and then read the middle, left, and right panels (in that order).

exhibit 3.11 A Summary of How Revenues Are Recorded

Accrual Basis Journal Entries for Revenues

(2) If cash is received **before** the company delivers goods/services, a liability (*Unearned Revenue*) is created because the company still owes goods/services. Later, when revenue is earned, this liability is reduced and *Revenue* is recorded.	(1) If cash is received in the **same** period in which the company delivers goods/services, only one journal entry is needed to record both *Cash* received and the type of *Revenue* earned.	(3) If cash is not received until **after** the company delivers goods/services, an asset account (*Accounts Receivable*) is created when the *Revenue* is recorded. Later, this asset is reduced when the customers pay *Cash* to the company for the amount the company is owed.

a) Cash received BEFORE revenue is earned

dr Cash (+A)   xx
   cr Unearned Revenue (+L)   xx

dr Unearned Revenue (–L)   xx
   cr _____Revenue (+R, +SE) xx

b) Cash at the SAME time as revenue

dr Cash (+A)   xx
   cr _____ Revenue (+R, +SE) xx

c) Cash received AFTER revenue is earned

dr Accounts Receivable (+A) xx
   cr _____ Revenue (+R, +SE) xx

dr Cash (+A)   xx
   cr Accounts Receivable (–A) xx

In the three different situations above, the red diamond (◆) indicates the point in time at which the company performs the promised act of delivering goods/services to the customer, and this is when the Revenue account is credited. The green dollar sign ($) indicates the point in time at which the company receives cash from the customer for the promised act, and this is when the Cash account is debited.

Did you notice how the panels in Exhibit 3.11 correspond to the revenue transactions for First Choice Haircutters Salon analyzed earlier in this chapter? If you didn't, see the coach for some hints. In Exhibit 3.11, we use a generic label " _____ Revenue" with the expectation that you will fill in the blank with whatever type of revenue you are recording. That is, when accounting for revenue from cutting hair, you should use an account name like Haircut Revenue. If it's revenue generated from sales of inflatable sumo costumes, you could call it Sales Revenue.

Accounting for Expenses: A Summary

Under accrual accounting, expenses are recorded when incurred (by acquiring items that do not have future economic benefits or by using up the economic benefits of assets that were acquired in previous periods). Expenses are not necessarily incurred at the same time that cash is paid. Because of this, we look at three cases, where cash is paid (1) at the *same* time the expense is incurred, (2) *before* the expense is incurred, and (3) *after* the expense is incurred. Start by reading the explanation at the bottom of Exhibit 3.12, and then read the middle, left, and right panels (in that order). Go ahead now and read the exhibit before continuing on below.

Did you notice which panels in Exhibit 3.12 correspond to the expense transactions for First Choice Haircutters Salon analyzed earlier in this chapter? If you didn't, see the coach for some help. In Exhibit 3.12, we use a generic label " _____ Expense" with the expectation that you will fill in the blank with whatever type of expense you are recording. Similarly, we use the generic asset name "Prepaid Expense" with the expectation that you will use more specific asset names, such as prepaid rent or supplies.

You've now seen how the operating activities of a business are analyzed to determine revenues, expenses, and net income for the period. In the final section of this chapter, we'll take a closer look at the accounting concepts that make this all possible.

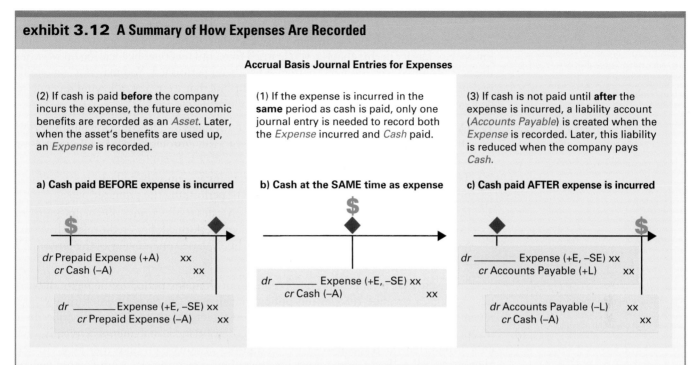

exhibit 3.12 A Summary of How Expenses Are Recorded

Accrual Basis Journal Entries for Expenses

(2) If cash is paid **before** the company incurs the expense, the future economic benefits are recorded as an *Asset*. Later, when the asset's benefits are used up, an *Expense* is recorded.

(1) If the expense is incurred in the **same** period as cash is paid, only one journal entry is needed to record both the *Expense* incurred and *Cash* paid.

(3) If cash is not paid until **after** the expense is incurred, a liability account (*Accounts Payable*) is created when the *Expense* is recorded. Later, this liability is reduced when the company pays *Cash*.

a) Cash paid BEFORE expense is incurred

dr Prepaid Expense (+A)   xx
  cr Cash (−A)   xx

dr _____ Expense (+E, −SE) xx
  cr Prepaid Expense (−A)   xx

b) Cash at the SAME time as expense

dr _____ Expense (+E, −SE) xx
  cr Cash (−A)   xx

c) Cash paid AFTER expense is incurred

dr _____ Expense (+E, −SE) xx
  cr Accounts Payable (+L)   xx

dr Accounts Payable (−L)   xx
  cr Cash (−A)   xx

In the three different situations above, the red diamond (◆) indicates the point in time at which the company incurs an expense, and this is when the Expense account is debited. The green dollar sign ($) indicates the point in time at which the company pays cash, and this is when the Cash account is credited.

RECONSIDER _____
The Income Statement Concepts That Users Rely On

The income statement is a key report. It tells shareholders whether management has been able to make a profit for them, which is the prime objective of a profit-oriented enterprise, but it also helps the following groups answer these important questions:

- Shareholders: Has management done a good job? Should we give them a bonus or replace them? Should we sell our shares or buy more?

- Bankers: How risky is the company? Should we lend money to the company? If we do, what interest rate should we charge?

- Employee unions: Can the company afford to give the employees a raise?

- Canada Revenue Agency: Has the company paid all the income taxes it should pay?

- Public interest groups: Is the company making a reasonable profit, or do consumers need price protection?

In addition, variations of the income statement, broken down by division and/or product, are used internally by management to answer such questions as: What products/divisions are successful? Which products should be eliminated? What divisions should be phased out or sold?

Some people mistakenly think that net income, as reported on the income statement, is money that can be paid out to shareholders. As you've learned in this chapter, net income is not the same thing as cash. Revenues and expenses are not recorded based on the timing of cash receipts and payments. Instead, they are reported using the accrual-based measurement of revenues and expenses, which is based on two key concepts: the *revenue principle* and the *matching principle*.

THE REVENUE PRINCIPLE

The **revenue principle** is a concept that requires that revenues be recorded when they are earned, rather than when cash is received for them.

The **revenue principle** defines when it is appropriate to record revenues in the accounting system. Earlier in this chapter, you learned to record revenues by focusing on whether the acts promised to customers (haircuts) had been performed. You may not have realized it, but there actually were two more conditions that were met, allowing revenue to be reported. The three conditions of the revenue principle are:

1. *Delivery has occurred or services have been rendered.* The company must perform all or substantially all of the acts promised to the customer (by providing goods or services).
2. *The price is fixed or determinable.* The company must be able to put a reliable number on the amount of revenue related to performing the promised acts.
3. *Collection is reasonably assured.* For cash sales, collection is never in question since cash is received when promised acts are performed. For credit sales, the company will judge whether cash collection is likely, based on a review of the customer's ability to pay.

A **revenue recognition policy** is a policy that defines when a company reports its revenue from operating activities.

To ensure that revenue reporting is consistent from one period to the next, all businesses adopt a **revenue recognition policy** that defines the time at which they report revenues from providing goods or services to customers. Most companies describe their revenue recognition policy in the first note to their financial statements. Typically, revenue is reported when the above three conditions are first met. Like your First Choice Haircutters Salon, Regis Corporation has the policy of recording its salon revenues when services are provided to customers. At this time, Regis has performed the promised act of cutting hair (Condition 1), and a determinable price (Condition 2) is paid by customers, so the probability of collecting cash is (more than) reasonably assured (Condition 3).

THE MATCHING PRINCIPLE

The **matching principle** is a concept that requires that expenses be recorded in the period in which they are incurred to generate revenue, rather than the period in which cash is paid for them.

The **matching principle** requires that all relevant expenses be recorded in the same period as the revenues that are generated from having incurred the expenses. By "matching" expenses to revenues recorded in the period, expenses can then be subtracted from revenues to produce a "bottom line" net income number that provides a reasonable measure of the company's financial performance for the period.

UNETHICAL VIOLATIONS OF THE REVENUE PRINCIPLE AND THE MATCHING PRINCIPLE

ETHICAL ISSUES

The revenue and matching principles might be easy to understand as concepts, but they are not easy to apply in practice. Accountants have to use judgment in deciding whether collection is reasonably assured, for example. Matching requires judgment as well. Sometimes the revenue numbers are known, but the invoices for the related expenses have not been received yet and it's the end of the accounting period. To achieve matching, the related expenses are estimated, and estimates are not always accurate. Accounting is not as black-and-white as a lot of people think. There is a lot of judgment involved. This is what makes accounting interesting, but, unfortunately, whenever judgment is used, it opens the door for poor judgments or deliberate misstatements to occur.

Fraud is the act of deliberately producing false information for your own financial benefit at the expense of others. It is different from making an honest error.

What happens to corporate executives who violate the revenue and matching principles? As a minimum, unethical behaviour leads to loss of reputation and puts your job and your company at risk. In addition, since producing **fraudulent** financial statements is not only unethical but also illegal, you will likely be prosecuted, and even incarcerated. Exhibit 3.13 shows a few recent, well-known cases where this has happened. Imagine being John Rigas, who, in 2005 at the age of 80, was sentenced to 15 years in prison for his tricks at Adelphia Communications. It's probably just as bad as having to face 25 years in jail when you're only 23. That's what happened to Barry Minkow in the 1980s when the company he was managing defrauded investors by recording revenue and accounts receivable that didn't even exist. Released in 1995, he is now helping government regulators, investigators, and prosecutors unravel the kinds of fraud that he once committed.

exhibit 3.13   Unethical Behaviour and Its Consequences

The CEO	The Fraud	Conviction/Plea	The Outcome
Conrad Black Hollinger International Inc.	Diverted corporate funds to personal accounts.	Convicted in 2007	Sentenced to 6½ years
Sanjay Kumar Computer Associates	Recorded sales in the wrong accounting period to boost earnings.	Pleaded guilty in 2006.	Sentenced to 12 years
Bernie Ebbers WorldCom Inc.	Among other tricks, capitalized expenses as assets to boost earnings.	Convicted in 2005	Sentenced to 25 years
John Rigas Adelphia Communications	Hid debt, thus defrauding investors.	Convicted in 2005	Sentenced to 15 years
Martin Grass Rite Aid Corp.	Booked rebates from companies before they were earned.	Pleaded guilty in 2003.	Sentenced to 8 years

WHAT'S COMING UP

In this chapter, we discussed how accountants analyze a company's operating activities as the starting point for determining net income for the period. We have now completed our study of the recording phase and are ready to turn our attention to the reporting phase of the accounting process. The next step will be to adjust fully the financial statements so that they are complete and up-to-date at the end of the accounting period. This adjustment process is the main topic for Chapter 4.

————— **FOR YOUR REVIEW**

DEMONSTRATION CASE

This case is a continuation of the Goodbye Grass Corporation case introduced in Chapter 2. The company was established, and property and equipment were purchased. The balance sheet at April 30, 2009, based on only the investing and financing activities (from Chapter 2), is as follows:

GOODBYE GRASS CORPORATION
Balance Sheet
At April 30, 2009

Assets		Liabilities	
Current Assets		*Current Liabilities*	
Cash	$ 3,800	Notes Payable	$ 4,400
Notes Receivable	1,250		
Total Current Assets	5,050	**Shareholders' Equity**	
Equipment	4,600	Contributed Capital	9,000
Land	3,750	**Total Liabilities and**	
Total Assets	**$13,400**	**Shareholders' Equity**	**$13,400**

The following activities also occurred during April 2009:

a. Purchased and used gasoline for mowers and edgers, paying $90 in cash at a local gas station.
b. In early April, received $1,600 cash from the city in advance for lawn maintenance service for April through July ($400 each month). The entire amount is to be recorded as Unearned Revenue.
c. In early April, purchased $300 worth of insurance covering six months, April through September. The entire payment is to be recorded as Prepaid Insurance.

d. Mowed lawns for residential customers, who are billed every two weeks. A total of $5,200 worth of service was billed in April.
e. Residential customers paid $3,500 on their accounts.
f. Paid wages every two weeks. Total cash paid in April was $3,900.
g. Received a bill for $320 from the local gas station for additional gasoline purchased on account and used in April.
h. Paid $40 interest on notes owed to XYZ Lawn Supply and the hardware store.
i. Paid $100 on accounts payable.

Required:

1. a. On a separate worksheet, set up T-accounts for Cash, Accounts Receivable, Notes Receivable, Prepaid Insurance, Equipment, Land, Accounts Payable, Unearned Revenue, Notes Payable, Contributed Capital, Retained Earnings, Mowing Revenue, Wages Expense, Fuel Expense, and Interest Expense. For the accounts shown on the balance sheet above, enter the balance as the opening balance in the corresponding T-accounts. For the remaining T-accounts, enter a beginning balance of $0.

   b. Analyze each transaction with the goal of preparing a separate worksheet that shows journal entries and indicates their effects on the basic accounting equation (Assets = Liabilities + Shareholders' Equity). Include the equality checks: (1) The accounting equation is in balance, and (2) Debits = Credits.

   c. Enter the effects of each transaction in the appropriate T-accounts. Identify each amount with its letter in the list of activities above.

   d. Compute balances in each of the T-accounts.

2. Use the amounts in the T-accounts to prepare an unadjusted trial balance for Goodbye Grass Corporation at April 30, 2009.

   After completing the above requirements, check your answers with the following suggested solution.

Suggested Solution

1. *Transaction analysis, journal entries, and T-accounts:*

(a)	dr	Fuel Expense (+E, −SE)	90	
	cr	Cash (−A).		90

Assets	=	Liabilities	+	Shareholders' Equity
Cash	− 90			Fuel Expense (+E) − 90

Equality checks: (1) The accounting equation is in balance; (2) Debits $90 = Credits $90.

(b)	dr	Cash (+A)	1,600	
	cr	Unearned Revenue (+L).		1,600

Assets	=	Liabilities	+	Shareholders' Equity
Cash	+ 1,600	Unearned Revenue + 1,600		

Equality checks: (1) the accounting equation is in balance; (2) Debits $1,600 = Credits $1,600

(c)	dr	Prepaid Insurance (+A).	300	
	cr	Cash (−A).		300

Assets	=	Liabilities	+	Shareholders' Equity
Cash	− 300			
Prepaid Insurance	+ 300			

Equality checks: (1) The accounting equation is in balance; (2) Debits $300 = Credits $300

(d) dr Accounts Receivable (+A)   5,200
    cr   Mowing Revenue (+R, +SE)   5,200

Assets	=	Liabilities	+	Shareholders' Equity

Accounts Receivable + 5,200   Mowing Revenue (+R) + 5,200

Equality checks: (1) The accounting equation is in balance; (2) Debits $5,200 = Credits $5,200

(e) dr Cash (+A)   3,500
    cr   Accounts Receivable (−A)   3,500

Assets	=	Liabilities	+	Shareholders' Equity

Cash   +   3,500
Accounts Receivable −   3,500

Equality checks: (1) The accounting equation is in balance; (2) Debits $3,500 = Credits $3,500.

(f) dr Wages Expense (+E, −SE)   3,900
    cr   Cash (−A)   3,900

Assets	=	Liabilities	+	Shareholders' Equity

Cash   − 3,900   Wages Expense (+E) − 3,900

Equality checks: (1) The accounting equation is in balance; (2) Debits $3,900 = Credits $3,900

(g) dr Fuel Expense (+E, −SE)   320
    cr   Accounts Payable (+L)   320

Assets	=	Liabilities	+	Shareholders' Equity

Accounts Payable + 320   Fuel Expense (+E)   − 320

Equality checks: (1) The accounting equation is in balance; (2) Debits $320 = Credits $320

(h) dr Interest Expense (+E, −SE)   40
    cr   Cash (−A)   40

Assets	=	Liabilities	+	Shareholders' Equity

Cash   − 40   Interest Expense (+E) − 40

Equality checks: (1) The accounting equation is in balance; (2) Debits $40 = Credits $40

(i) dr Accounts Payable (−L)   100
    cr   Cash (−A)   100

Assets	=	Liabilities	+	Shareholders' Equity

Cash   − 100   Accounts Payable − 100

Equality checks: (1) The accounting equation is in balance; (2) Debits $100 = Credits $100

T-accounts:

dr Cash (A) cr			
Bal. fwd.	3,800		
(b)	1,600	90	(a)
(e)	3,500	300	(c)
		3,900	(f)
		40	(h)
		100	(i)
End. bal.	4,470		

dr Accounts Receivable (A) cr			
Bal. fwd.	0		
(d)	5,200	3,500	(e)
End. bal.	1,700		

dr Notes Receivable (A) cr			
Bal. fwd.	1,250		
End. bal.	1,250		

dr Prepaid Insurance (A) cr			
Bal. fwd.	0		
(c)	300		
End. bal.	300		

dr Equipment (A) cr			
Bal. fwd.	4,600		
End. bal.	4,600		

dr Land (A) cr		
Bal. fwd.	3,750	
End. bal.	3,750	

dr Accounts Payable (L) cr			
		0	Bal. fwd.
(i)	100	320	(g)
		220	End. bal.

dr Unearned Revenue (L) cr			
		0	Bal. fwd.
		1,600	(b)
		1,600	End. bal.

dr Notes Payable (L) cr		
	4,400	Bal. fwd.
	4,400	End. bal.

dr Contributed Captial (SE) cr		
	9,000	Bal. fwd.
	9,000	End. bal.

dr Retained Earnings (SE) cr		
	0	Bal. fwd.
	0	End. bal.

dr Mowing Revenue (R) cr			
		0	Bal. fwd.
		5,200	(d)
		5,200	End. bal.

dr Wages Expense (E) cr		
Bal. fwd.	0	
(f)	3,900	
End. bal.	3,900	

dr Fuel Expense (E) cr		
Bal. fwd.	0	
(a)	90	
(g)	320	
End. bal.	410	

dr Interest Expense (E) cr		
Bal. fwd.	0	
(h)	40	
End. bal.	40	

COACH'S TIP

Balances carried forward from the previous month (Chapter 2) are indicated by the abbreviation Bal. fwd. You could also use Beg. bal. for Beginning balance.

2.   *Unadjusted trial balance:*

GOODBYE GRASS CORPORATION
Unadjusted Trial Balance
As of April 30, 2009

Account Name	Debits	Credits
Cash	$ 4,470	
Accounts Receivable	1,700	
Notes Receivable	1,250	
Prepaid Insurance	300	
Equipment	4,600	
Land	3,750	
Accounts Payable		$ 220
Unearned Revenue		1,600
Notes Payable		4,400
Contributed Capital		9,000
Retained Earnings		0
Mowing Revenue		5,200
Wages Expense	3,900	
Fuel Expense	410	
Interest Expense	40	
Totals	**$ 20,420**	**$ 20,420**

CHAPTER SUMMARY

Explain and select income statement account titles. p. 86   **LO1**

- The income statement reports net income, which is calculated by combining

    Revenues—increases in assets or settlements of liabilities from ongoing operations

    Expenses—decreases in assets or increases in liabilities from ongoing operations

    Gains—increases in assets or settlements of liabilities from non-operating activities

    Losses—decreases in assets or increases in liabilities from non-operating activities

- See Exhibit 3.2 on page 88 for a list of common account titles.

Apply transaction analysis to operating transactions. p. 88   **LO2**

- Revenues are recognized when earned, which is usually when the company performs the acts promised to customers. The timing of cash receipts does not dictate when revenues are recognized.

- Expenses are recognized when incurred, which happens when the economic benefits of an item are used up in the current period, resulting in a decrease in the company's resources. The timing of cash payments does not dictate when expenses are recognized.

Use journal entries and T-accounts to show how operating transactions affect the balance sheet   **LO3**
and income statement. p. 94

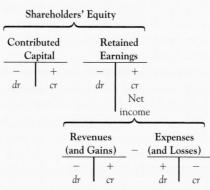

- The expanded transaction analysis model above includes revenues and expenses as subcategories of retained earnings.

- In journal entry format, increases in revenues are recorded with credits, and increases in expenses are recorded with debits.

Prepare an unadjusted trial balance that includes balance sheet income statement accounts.   **LO4**
p. 100

- The unadjusted trial balance is a list of all accounts and their unadjusted balances, and is used to check on the equality of recorded debits and credits.

Explain the revenue and matching principles. p. 103   **LO5**

- The two key concepts underlying the income statement are the following principles:

    Revenue principle—Recognize revenues when (1) delivery has occurred, (2) the price is fixed or determinable, and (3) collection is reasonably assured.

    Matching principle—Recognize expenses when they are incurred in generating revenue.

KEY TERMS TO KNOW

Accrual Basis Accounting
   p. 89
Capitalize p. 92
Cash Basis Accounting p. 89
Cost p. 92
Earned p. 89

Expenditures p. 87
Expense p. 86
Fraud p. 104
Gains p. 86
Incur red p. 86 and 89
Losses p. 86

Matching Principle p. 104
Revenues p. 86
Revenue Principle p. 104
Revenue Recognition Policy
   p. 104
Unearned Revenue p. 91

FOR YOUR PRACTICE _____

QUESTIONS

1. Indicate the income statement equation and define each element.
2. Explain the difference between
    a.   Revenues and gains
    b.   Expenses and losses
3. Define *accrual accounting* and contrast it with *cash basis accounting*.
4. What three conditions must normally be met for revenue to be recognized under accrual basis accounting?
5. Explain the matching principle.
6. Explain why shareholders' equity is increased by revenues and decreased by expenses.
7. Explain why revenues are recorded as credits and expenses as debits.
8. Complete the following table by entering either *debit* or *credit* in each cell:

COACH'S
TIP

Remember that gains are accounted for in the same way as revenues, and losses are accounted for just as expenses are.

Item	Increase	Decrease
Revenues		
Losses		
Gains		
Expense		

9. Complete the following table by entering either *increase* or *decrease* in each cell:

Item	Debit	Credit
Revenues		
Losses		
Gains		
Expense		

MULTIPLE CHOICE

Select the one alternative that best answers the question or completes the sentence.

1. Which of the following items is not a specific account in a company's chart of accounts?
    a.   Gain on sale of investments   *c.*   Revenue
    b.   Net income   *d.*   Unearned revenue
2. Which of the following is not one of the three conditions that normally must be met for revenue to be recognized according to the revenue principle for accrual basis accounting?

a. The price is fixed or determinable.
b. Services have been performed.
c. Cash already has been collected.
d. Reasonable assurance exists that the customer will pay.

3. The matching principle controls:
  a. Where on the income statement expenses should be presented
  b. How costs are allocated between Cost of Goods Sold (sometimes called Cost of Sales) and general and administrative expenses
  c. The ordering of current assets and current liabilities on the balance sheet
  d. When costs are recognized as expenses on the income statement

4. Which of the following would not be considered an operating item on the income statement?
  a. Administrative expenses
  b. Sales revenues
  c. Selling expenses
  d. Loss on disposal of a business division

5. If a company decides to record an expenditure as an asset rather than as an expense, how will this decision affect net income in the current period?
  a. Net income will be higher.
  b. Net income will be lower.
  c. Net income will not be affected by this decision.
  d. It's a mystery; nobody really knows.

6. When should a company report the cost of an insurance policy as an expense?
  a. When the company first signs the policy
  b. When the company pays for the policy
  c. When the company receives the benefits from the policy, over its period of coverage
  d. When the company receives payments from the insurance company for its insurance claims

7. When expenses exceed revenues in a given period (and there are no gains or losses):
  a. Shareholders' equity will not be impacted.
  b. Shareholders' equity will be increased.
  c. Shareholders' equity will be decreased.
  d. One cannot determine the impact on shareholders' equity without additional information.

8. Which account is *least* likely to be debited when revenue is recorded?
  a. Accounts payable   c. Cash
  b. Accounts receivable   d. Unearned revenue

9. Which of the following is the entry to be recorded by a law firm when it receives a retainer from a new client that will be earned when services are provided in the future?
  a. *Debit* to Accounts Receivable; *credit* to Legal Services Revenue
  b. *Debit* to Unearned Revenue; *credit* to Legal Services Revenue
  c. *Debit* to Cash; *credit* to Unearned Revenue
  d. *Debit* to Unearned Revenue; *credit* to Cash

10. Guessco reported the following amounts on its income statement: total revenues, $31,500; interest expense, $300; net income, $1,600; income tax expense, $900; and operating income, $2,800. What was the amount of Guessco's operating expenses?
  a. $1,200   c. $29,000
  b. $28,700   d. $29,900

11. Guessco reported the following amounts on its income statement: operating expenses, $16,500; interest expense, $1,000; net income, $2,100; income tax expense, $1,400; and operating income, $4,500. What was the amount of Guessco's total revenues?
  a. $39,900   c. $21,000
  b. $37,500   d. $23,400

12. Guessco reported the following amounts on its income statement: total revenues, $14,700; interest income, $800; operating expenses, $10,200; and income tax expense, $1,100. What was the amount of Guessco's net income?
  a. $4,200   c. $3,400
  b. $2,600   d. $3,500

MINI-EXERCISES

LO1, LO2

M3-1 Reporting Cash Basis versus Accrual Basis Income

Mostert Music Company had the following transactions in March:

a. Sold instruments to customers for $10,000; received $6,000 in cash and the rest on account. The cost of the instruments was $7,000.
b. Purchased $4,000 of new instruments inventory; paid $1,000 in cash and owed the rest on account.
c. Paid $600 in wages for the month.
d. Received a $200 bill for utilities that will be paid in April.
e. Received $1,000 from customers as deposits on orders for new instruments to be sold to the customers in April.

Complete the following statements:

Cash Basis Income Statement		**Accrual Basis Income Statement**	
Revenues:		Revenues:	
Cash sales	$	Sales to customers	$
Customer deposits			
Expenses:		Expenses:	
Inventory purchases		Cost of sales	
Wages paid		Wages expense	
		Utilities expense	
Cash income	$	Net income	$

LO2

M3-2 Identifying Revenues

The following transactions are July 2009 activities of Bob's Bowling, Inc., which operates several bowling centres. If revenue is to be recognized in July, indicate the amount. If revenue is not to be recognized in July, explain why.

Activity	Amount or Explanation
a. Bob's collected $10,000 from customers for games played in July.	
b. Bob's billed a customer for $200 for a party held at the centre on the last day of July. The bill is to be paid in August.	
c. Bob's received $1,000 from credit sales made to customers last month (in June).	
d. The men's and women's bowling leagues gave Bob's advance payments totalling $1,500 for the fall season that starts in September.	

LO2

M3-3 Identifying Expenses

The following transactions are July 2009 activities of Bob's Bowling, Inc., which operates several bowling centres. If an expense is to be recognized in July, indicate the amount. If an expense is not to be recognized in July, explain why.

Activity	Amount or Explanation
a. Bob's paid $1,000 to plumbers for repairing a broken pipe in the restrooms.	
b. Bob's paid $2,000 for the June electricity bill and received the July bill for $2,200, which will be paid in August.	
c. Bob's paid $4,000 to employees for work in July.	

M3-4 Recording Revenues   LO3

For each of the transactions in M3-2:

1. Write the journal entry using the format shown in the chapter.
2. Open an appropriate set of T-accounts and post the entries to the T-accounts.

M3-5 Recording Expenses   LO3

For each of the transactions in M3-3:

1. Write the journal entry using the format shown in the chapter.
2. Open an appropriate set of T-accounts and post the entries to the T-accounts.

M3-6 Determining the Financial Statement Effects of Operating Activities Involving   LO2
Revenues

The following transactions are July 2009 activities of Bob's Bowling, Inc., which operates several bowling centres. For each of the following transactions, complete the spreadsheet, indicating the amount and effect (+ for increase and − for decrease) of each transaction. Write NE if there is no effect. The first transaction is provided as an example. (*Hint:* Remember that revenues and expenses affect the balance sheet because they are subcategories of retained earnings.)

	Balance Sheet			Income Statement		
Transaction	**Assets**	**Liabilities**	**Shareholders' Equity**	**Revenues**	**Expenses**	**Net Income**
a. Bob's collected $10,000 from customers for games played in July.	+ 10,000	NE	+ 10,000	+ 10,000	NE	+ 10,000
b. Bob's billed a customer for $200 for a party held at the centre on the last day of July. The bill is to be paid in August.						
c. Bob's received $1,000 from credit sales made to customers last month (in June).						
d. The men's and women's bowling leagues gave Bob's advance payments totalling $1,500 for the fall season that starts in September.						

M3-7 Determining the Financial Statement Effects of Operating Activities Involving   LO2
Expenses

The following transactions are July 2009 activities of Bob's Bowling, Inc., which operates several bowling centres. For each of the following transactions, complete the spreadsheet, indicating the amount and effect (+ for increase and − for decrease) of each transaction. Write NE if there is no effect. The first transaction is provided as an example.

	Balance Sheet			Income Statement		
Transaction	**Assets**	**Liabilities**	**Shareholders' Equity**	**Revenues**	**Expenses**	**Net Income**
e. Bob's paid $1,000 to plumbers for repairing a broken pipe in the restrooms.	− 1,000	NE	− 1,000	NE	+ 1,000	− 1,000
f. Bob's paid $2,000 for the June electricity bill and received the July bill for $2,200, which will be paid in August.						
g. Bob's paid $4,000 to employees for work in July.						

LO4 **M3-8 Preparing an Income Statement**

Given the transactions in M3-6 and M3-7 (including the examples), prepare an income statement for Bob's Bowling, Inc., for the month of July 2009.

EXERCISES

LO1, LO5 **E3-1 Matching Definitions with Terms**

Match each definition with its related term by entering the appropriate letter in the space provided.

Term	Definition
____ 1. Expenses	A. Record expenses when incurred in earning revenue.
____ 2. Matching principle	B. A liability account used to record the obligation to provide future services or return cash that has been received before revenues have been earned.
____ 3. Revenue principle	
____ 4. Cash basis accounting	
____ 5. Unearned revenue	C. Costs that result when a company gives up resources to generate revenues.
____ 6. Accrual basis accounting	
____ 7. Prepaid expenses	D. Record revenues when certain criteria are met (delivery of goods or services has occurred, the price is fixed or determinable, and collection is reasonably assured).
	E. Record revenues when received and expenses when paid.
	F. An asset account used to record the benefits obtained when cash is paid before expenses are incurred.
	G. Record revenues when earned and expenses when incurred.

LO1, LO2 **E3-2 Identifying Revenues**

Revenues are normally recognized when the delivery of goods or services has occurred, the price is fixed or determinable, and collection is reasonably assured. The amount recorded is the sales price. The following transactions occurred in September:

a. A customer orders and receives 10 personal computers from Gateway.com. The customer promises to pay $25,000 within three months. Answer from Gateway's standpoint.
b. For $21,000 cash, Sam Goh Dodge sells a truck with a list, or "sticker," price of $24,000.
c. The Bay orders 1,000 men's shirts from Arrow Shirt Company for $18 each for future delivery. The terms require payment in full within 30 days of delivery. Answer from Arrow's standpoint.
d. Arrow Shirt Company completes production of the shirts described in c and delivers the order. Answer from Arrow's standpoint.
e. Arrow receives payment from The Bay for the order described in c. Answer from Arrow's standpoint.
f. A customer purchases a ticket from Westjet in September for $500 cash to travel in December. Answer from Westjet's standpoint.

Required:

For each of the transactions, if revenue is to be recognized in September, indicate the amount. If revenue is not to be recognized in September, explain why.

LO1, LO2 **E3-3 Identifying Revenues**

Revenues are normally recognized when the delivery of goods or services has occurred, the price is fixed or determinable, and collection is reasonably assured. The amount recorded is the sales price. The following transactions occurred in September:

a. General Motors of Canada issues $26 million in new common shares.
b. The Ottawa Senators Hockey Club receives $20,000,000 cash for season tickets. None of the 40 games in the 2009–2010 season have been played yet.
c. The Senators play the first hockey game referred to in b.

d. Hall Construction Company signs a contract with a customer for the construction of a new $500,000 warehouse. At the signing, Hall receives a cheque for $50,000 as a deposit to be applied against amounts earned during the first phase of construction. Answer from Hall's standpoint.

e. A popular snowboarding-magazine company receives a total of $1,800 today from subscribers. The subscriptions begin in the next fiscal year. Answer from the magazine company's standpoint.

f. Sears sells a $100 minifridge to a customer who charges the sale on his store credit card. Answer from the standpoint of Sears.

Required:

For each of the transactions, if revenue is to be recognized in September, indicate the amount. If revenue is not to be recognized in September, explain why.

E3-4 Identifying Expenses

LO1, LO2

Expenses are decreases in a company's resources that occur when the company either (1) incurs a cost that does not benefit future periods, or (2) uses up the economic benefits of existing assets. Assume the following transactions occurred in January:

a. Gateway pays its computer service technicians $90,000 in salary for the two weeks ended January 7. Answer from Gateway's standpoint.

b. At the beginning of January, Turner Construction Company pays $4,500 in worker's compensation insurance for the first three months of the year.

c. McGraw-Hill Ryerson—publisher of this textbook—uses $1,000 worth of electricity and natural gas in January for which it has not yet been billed.

d. Pooler Company receives and pays in January a $1,500 invoice from a consulting firm for services received in January.

e. The campus bookstore receives 500 accounting texts at a cost of $50 each. The terms indicate that payment is due within 30 days of delivery.

f. Schergevitch Incorporated has its delivery van repaired in January for $280 and charges the amount on account.

Required:

For each of the transactions, if an expense is to be recognized in January, indicate the amount. If an expense is not to be recognized in January, indicate why.

E3-5 Identifying Expenses

LO1, LO2

Expenses are decreases in a company's resources that occur when the company either (1) incurs a cost that does not benefit future periods, or (2) uses up the economic benefits of existing assets. The following transactions occurred in January:

a. Sam Goh Dodge pays its salespersons $3,500 in commissions related to December automobile sales. Answer from Sam Goh Dodge's standpoint.

b. On January 31, Sam Goh Dodge determines that it will pay its salespersons $4,200 in commissions related to January sales. The payment will be made in early February. Answer from Sam Goh Dodge's standpoint.

c. A new grill is purchased and installed at a McDonald's restaurant at the end of the day on January 31. A $12,000 cash payment is made on that day.

d. The University of Toronto orders 6,000 season football tickets from its printer, and pays $600 in advance for the custom printing. The first game will be played in September. Answer from the university's standpoint.

e. A Waterloo community college employee works eight hours, at $15 per hour, on January 31; however, payday is not until February 3. Answer from the college's point of view.

f. Wang Company paid $3,600 for a fire insurance policy on January 1. The policy covers 12 months beginning on January 1. Answer from Wang's point of view.

g. Ziegler Company, a farm equipment company, receives its telephone bill at the end of January for $230 for January calls. The bill has not been paid to date.

Required:

For each of the transactions, if an expense is to be recognized in January, indicate the amount. If an expense is not to be recognized in January, indicate why.

LO2

E3-6 Determining Financial Statement Effects of Various Transactions

The following transactions occurred during a recent year:

a. Issued shares to owners for cash (example).
b. Borrowed cash from local bank.
c. Purchased equipment on credit.
d. Earned revenue, collected cash.
e. Incurred expenses, on credit.
f. Earned revenue, on credit.
g. Paid cash on account.
h. Incurred expenses, paid cash.
i. Earned revenue, collected half in cash, balance on credit.
j. Collected cash from customers on account.
k. Incurred expenses, paid half in cash, balance on credit.
l. Paid income tax expense for the period.

Required:

For each of the transactions, complete the table below, indicating the effect (+ for increase and − for decrease) of each transaction. Write NE if there is no effect. The first transaction is provided as an example. For a hint, see M3-6.

	Balance Sheet			Income Statement		
Transaction	**Assets**	**Liabilities**	**Shareholders' Equity**	**Revenues**	**Expenses**	**Net Income**
(a) (example)	+	NE	+	NE	NE	NE

LO2

E3-7 Determining Financial Statement Effects of Various Transactions

Wolverine World Wide, Inc., manufactures military, work, sport, and casual footwear and leather accessories under a variety of brand names, such as Caterpillar, Hush Puppies, Wolverine, and Steve Madden. Assume that the following transactions occurred during a recent year. Dollars are in thousands.

a. Issued common shares to investors for $49,000 cash (example).
b. Purchased $300,000 worth of additional supplies on account.
c. Borrowed $58,000 on long-term notes.
d. Purchased $18,600 worth of additional property, plant, and equipment.
e. Incurred $87,000 in selling expenses, paying two-thirds in cash and owing the rest on account.
f. Incurred $4,700 in interest expense.

Required:

For each of the transactions, complete the table below, indicating the effect (+ for increase and − for decrease) and amount of each transaction. Write NE if there is no effect. The first transaction is provided as an example. For a hint, see M3-6.

	Balance Sheet			Income Statement		
Transaction	**Assets**	**Liabilities**	**Shareholders' Equity**	**Revenues**	**Expenses**	**Net Income**
(a) (example)	+ 49,000	NE	+ 49,000	NE	NE	NE

LO2, LO3

E3-8 Recording Journal Entries

Cara Operations is one of the largest Canadian food-service and restaurant operators, running airport concessions, flight kitchens, and restaurants such as Harvey's, Swiss Chalet, and Montana's Cookhouse. The following transactions are typical of those that occurred in a recent year. (All amounts are rounded to the nearest thousand.)

a.   Borrowed $80,000 from a bank, signing a short-term note payable.
b.   Provided $10,000 worth of service to customers, with $9,500 on account and the rest received in cash.
c.   Purchased building and equipment for $130,000 in cash.
d.   Purchased $8,000 worth of inventory on account.
e.   Paid employee wages of $1,000.
f.   Received $410 on account from a customer.
g.   Purchased and used fuel worth $400,000 in delivery vehicles during the year (paid for in cash).
h.   Paid $8,200 cash on accounts payable.
i.   Incurred $20,000 in utility expenses during the year, of which $15,000 was paid in cash and the rest owed on account.

Required:

For each of the transactions:

1.   Write the journal entry, using the format shown in this chapter. Determine whether the accounting equation remains in balance, and debits equal credits after each entry.
2.   Open an appropriate set of T-accounts and post the entries to the T-accounts.

E3-9 Recording Journal Entries   LO2, LO3

Twin Peaks Incorporated is a ski resort in Québec's Gatineau Hills. The company sells lift tickets, ski lessons, and ski equipment. It operates several restaurants and rents townhouses to vacationing skiers. The following hypothetical December transactions are typical of those that occur at the resort.

a.   Borrowed $500,000 from the bank on December 1, signing a note payable, due in six months.
b.   Purchased a new snowplow for $20,000 cash on December 31.
c.   Purchased ski accessories for $10,000 on account to sell in the ski shop.
d.   Incurred $22,000 in routine maintenance expenses for the chairlifts; paid cash.
e.   Sold $72,000 worth of partial-season passes (beginning in the new year) and received cash.
f.   Daily lift passes were sold this month for a total of $76,000 cash.
g.   Received a $320 deposit on a townhouse to be rented for five days in January.
h.   Paid half the charges incurred on account in c.
i.   Paid $18,000 in wages to employees for the month of December.

Required:

1.   Prepare journal entries for each transaction. Be sure to categorize each account as an asset (A), liability (L), shareholders' equity (SE), revenue (R), or expense (E), and check that debits equal credits for each journal entry.
2.   Open an appropriate set of T-accounts and post the entries to the T-accounts.

E3-10 Recording Journal Entries   LO2, LO3

Rowland & Sons Air Transport Service, Inc., has been in operation for three years. The following transactions occurred in February:

Feb. 1   Paid $200 for rent of hangar space in February.
Feb. 2   Purchased fuel supplies costing $450, on account, for the next flight to Dallas.
Feb. 4   Received customer payment of $800 to ship several items to Calgary next month.
Feb. 7   Flew cargo from Vancouver to Kelowna; the customer paid $900 for the air transport.
Feb. 10   Paid pilot $1,200 in wages for flying in January.
Feb. 14   Paid $60 for an advertisement run in the local paper on February 14.
Feb. 18   Flew cargo for two customers from Halifax to Montreal for $1,700; one customer paid $500 cash, and the other asked to be billed.
Feb. 25   Purchased, on account, $1,350 worth of spare parts for the planes.

Required:

1.   Prepare journal entries for each transaction. Be sure to categorize each account as an asset (A), liability (L), shareholders' equity (SE), revenue (R), or expense (E).
2.   Open an appropriate set of T-accounts and post the entries to the T-accounts.

LO2, LO3, LO5   **E3-11 Recording Journal Entries and Posting to T-Accounts**

Hurst's Piano Rebuilding Company has been operating for one year (2009). At the beginning of 2010, its income statement accounts had zero balances, and its balance sheet account balances were as follows:

Cash	$ 6,000	Accounts payable	$ 8,000
Accounts receivable	25,000	Unearned revenue (deposits)	3,200
Supplies	1,200	Notes payable	40,000
Equipment	8,000	Contributed capital	8,000
Land	6,000	Retained earnings	9,000
Building	22,000		

Required:

1. Create T-accounts for the balance sheet accounts and for these additional accounts: Piano Rebuilding Revenue, Rent Revenue, Wages Expense, and Utilities Expense. Enter the beginning balances.

2. Prepare journal entries for the following January 2010 transactions, using the letter of each transaction as a reference:
   a. Received a $500 deposit from a customer who wanted her piano rebuilt.
   b. Rented a part of the building to a bicycle repair shop for $300 rent, received in January.
   c. Delivered five rebuilt pianos to customers, who paid $14,500 in cash.
   d. Delivered two rebuilt pianos to customers for $7,000, charged on account.
   e. Received $6,000 from customers as payment on their accounts.
   f. Received an electric and gas utility bill for $350 for January services, to be paid in February.
   g. Ordered $800 worth of supplies.
   h. Paid $1,700 on account in January.
   i. Paid $10,000 in wages to employees in January for work done this month.
   j. Received and paid cash for the supplies in g.

3. Post the journal entries to the T-accounts. Show the unadjusted ending balances in the T-accounts.

LO4   **E3-12 Preparing an Unadjusted Trial Balance**

Refer to E3-11.

Required:

Use the balances in the completed T-accounts in E3-11 to prepare an unadjusted trial balance at the end of January 2010.

LO2, LO3, LO4   **E3-13 Inferring Operating Transactions and Preparing an Unadjusted Trial Balance**

ElectroGolf Corporation operates indoor golf simulators that allow individual customers and golf club members to experience courses like Pebble Beach in California without leaving their own neighbourhood. Its stores are located in rented space in malls and shopping centres. During its first month of business, ended April 30, 2010, ElectroGolf Corporation completed eight transactions, with the dollar effects indicated in the following schedule:

	Dollar Effect of Each of the Eight Transactions								
Accounts	**a**	**b**	**c**	**d**	**e**	**f**	**g**	**h**	**Ending Balance**
Cash	$100,000	$(30,000)	$ (200)	$ 9,000	$(2,000)	$(1,000)	$2,000		
Accounts receivable				1,000					
Supplies			1,000						
Prepaid expenses					2,000				
Equipment		30,000							

continued

Accounts	Dollar Effect of Each of the Eight Transactions *(continued)*								Ending Balance
	a	*b*	*c*	*d*	*e*	*f*	*g*	*h*	
Accounts payable			800					1,200	
Unearned revenue							2,000		
Contributed capital	100,000								
Sales revenue				10,000					
Wages expense						1,000			
Utilities expense								1,200	

Required:

1. Write a brief explanation of transactions *a* through *h*. Include any assumptions that you made.
2. Compute the ending balance in each account, and prepare an unadjusted trial balance for ElectroGolf Corporation on April 30, 2010.

E3-14 Inferring Transactions and Computing Effects Using T-Accounts   LO1, LO2, LO3

A recent annual report of Dow Jones & Company, the world leader in business and financial news and information (and publisher of *The Wall Street Journal*), included the following accounts. Dollars are in millions.

dr Accounts Receivable (A) cr			dr Prepaid Expenses(A) cr			dr Unearned Revenue(L) cr		
1/1	313		1/1.	25			240	1/1
	2,573	?		43	?	?	328	
12/31	295		12/31	26			253	12/31

Required:

1. For each T-account, describe the typical transactions that cause it to increase and decrease.
2. Express each T-account in equation format, and then solve for the missing amounts (in millions). For example, the Accounts Receivable T-account can be expressed as: $313 + 2,573 - ? = 295$. By rearranging the equation, you can solve for $313 + 2,573 - 295 = ?$

E3-15 Finding Financial Information as an Investor   LO1, LO2

You are evaluating your current portfolio of investments to determine those that are not performing to your expectations. You have all the companies' most recent annual reports.

Required:

For each of the following, indicate where you would locate the information in an annual report.

1. The total cost incurred for repairs and maintenance during the year
2. Accounts receivable
3. Description of a company's revenue recognition policy
4. The cost of wages incurred during the year

E3-16 Comprehensive Exercise   LO2, LO3, LO4

Sony Online Entertainment (SOE) is the division of Sony that is best known for creating "massively multiplayer online" (MMO) games. The company sells subscriptions to its games online. For the sake of this exercise, assume that SOE has been selling subscriptions for its games for one full year (2008) at $15 per month. At the beginning of 2009, its income statement accounts had zero balances, and its balance sheet account balances were as follows:

Cash	$ 1,500,000	Accounts payable	$ 108,000
Accounts receivable	150,000	Unearned revenue	73,500
Supplies	14,700	Long-term notes payable	60,000
Equipment	874,500	Contributed capital	2,500,000
Land	1,200,000	Retained earnings	1,419,700
Building	422,000		

In addition to the above accounts, SOE's chart of accounts includes the following: Subscription revenue, Licensing revenue, Wages expense, Advertising expense, and Utilities expense.

Required:

1. Analyze the effect of the January 2009 transactions (shown below) on the accounting equation, using the format shown in the demonstration case on page 106.
    a. Received $50,000 cash from customers for subscriptions, earned in 2008.
    b. Received $25,000 cash from Electronic Arts, Inc., for licensing revenue earned in the month of January 2009.
    c. Purchased 10 new computer servers for $33,500; paid $10,000 cash and signed a note for the remainder owed.
    d. Paid $10,000 for an Internet advertisement run on Yahoo! in January 2009.
    e. Sold 15,000 monthly subscriptions at $15 each for services provided in the month of January 2009. Half was collected in cash, and half was sold on account.
    f. Received an electricity and gas utility bill for $5,350 for January 2009 utility services. The bill will be paid in February.
    g. Paid $378,000 in wages to employees for work done in January 2009.
    h. Purchased $3,000 worth of supplies on account.
    i. Paid $3,000 cash to the supplier in (h).

2. Prepare journal entries for the January 2009 transactions listed in requirement 1, using the letter of each transaction as a reference.

3. Create T-accounts, enter the beginning balances shown above, post the journal entries to the T-accounts, and show the unadjusted ending balances in the T-accounts.

4. Prepare an unadjusted trial balance as of January 31, 2009.

5. Prepare an income statement for the month ended January 31, 2009, using unadjusted balances from requirement 4.

6. Prepare a statement of retained earnings for the months ended January 31, 2009, using the beginning balance given above and the net income from requirement 5. Assume SOE has no dividends.

7. Prepare a classified balance sheet at January 31, 2009, using your response to requirement 6.

COACHED PROBLEMS

LO1, LO2, LO3   ### CP3-1 Recording Non-quantitative Journal Entries

The following list includes a series of accounts for B-ball Corporation, which has been operating for three years. These accounts are listed alphabetically and numbered for identification. Following the accounts is a series of transactions. For each transaction, indicate the account(s) that should be debited and credited by entering the appropriate account number(s) to the right of each transaction. If no journal entry is needed, write *none* after the transaction. The first transaction is used as an example.

Account No.	Account Title	Account No.	Account Title
1	Accounts payable	8	Income taxes payable
2	Accounts receivable	9	Note payable
3	Cash	10	Prepaid insurance
4	Contributed capital	11	Service revenue
5	Equipment	12	Supplies expense
6	Rent expense	13	Supplies
7	Income tax expense	14	Wages expense
		15	Wages payable

Transactions	Debit	Credit
a. Example: Purchased equipment for use in the business; paid one-third cash and signed a note payable for the balance.	5	3, 9
b. Issued shares to new investors.	_____	_____
c. Paid cash for rent this period.	_____	_____
d. Collected cash for services performed this period.	_____	_____
e. Collected cash on accounts receivable for services performed last period.	_____	_____
f. Performed services this period on credit.	_____	_____
g. Paid cash on accounts payable for expenses incurred last period.	_____	_____
h. Employees worked this period but won't be paid until next period.	_____	_____
i. Purchased supplies to be used later; paid cash.	_____	_____
j. Used some of the supplies for operations.	_____	_____
k. Paid three-fourths of the income tax expense for the year; the balance will be paid next year.	_____	_____
l. On the last day of the current period, paid cash for an insurance policy covering the next two years.	_____	_____

COACH'S TIP

h. Remember what the matching principle says.
k. You can think of this as two transactions: (1) incur expense and liability, and (2) pay part of the liability.

CP3-2 Recording Journal Entries

LO2, LO3

Ryan Olson organized a new company, MeToo, Inc. The company provides online networking management services on MySpace, Facebook, and other electronic social networks. Ryan believes that his target market is college, university, and high school students. You have been hired to record the transactions occurring in the first two weeks of operations.

a. May 1:   Issued 1,000 shares to investors for $30 per share.
b. May 1:   Borrowed $50,000 from the bank to provide additional funding to begin operations; the note due in two years.
c. May 1:   Paid $2,400 for a one-year fire insurance policy (recorded as prepaid insurance).
d. May 3:   Purchased furniture and fixtures for the office for $15,000 on account. The amount is due within 30 days.
e. May 5:   Placed advertisements in local college and university newspapers for a total of $250 cash.
f. May 9:   Sold services for $400 cash.
g. May 14: Made full payment for the furniture and fixtures purchased on account on May 3.

COACH'S TIP

c. For convenience, simply record the full amount of the payment as an asset (called prepaid insurance). At the end of the month, this account will be adjusted to its proper balance. We will study this adjustment process in Chapter 4, so just leave it as prepaid insurance for now.

Required:

1. For each of the transactions, prepare journal entries. Be sure to categorize each account as an asset (A), liability (L), shareholders' equity (SE), revenue (R), or expense (E).
2. Open appropriate T-accounts, and post the transactions to the T-accounts.

CP3-3 Analyzing the Effects of Transactions Using T-Accounts and Preparing an Unadjusted Trial Balance

LO1, LO2, LO3, LO4

Barbara Jones, a textbook editor, opened Barb's Book Fixing on February 1, 2009. The company specializes in editing accounting textbooks. You have been hired as manager. Your duties include maintaining the business's financial records. The following transactions occurred in February 2009, the first month of operations.

a. Received four shareholders' contributions, totalling $16,000 cash, to form the corporation; issued shares.
b. Paid three months' rent for the office premises at $800 per month (recorded as prepaid rent).
c. Purchased supplies for $300 cash.
d. Negotiated a two-year loan at the bank, depositing $10,000 in the company's bank account.
e. Used the money from *d* to purchase a computer for $2,500, and the balance for furniture and fixtures for the office.
f. Placed an advertisement in the local paper for $425 cash.
g. Made sales totalling $1,800; $1,525 was in cash and the rest on accounts receivable.

b. For convenience, simply record the full amount of the payment as an asset (called prepaid rent). At the end of the month, this account will be adjusted to its proper balance. We will study this adjustment process in Chapter 4, so just leave it as prepaid rent for now.

j. Most repairs involve costs that do not provide extra future economic benefits. Repairs merely maintain an asset's existing benefits.

1. When preparing the T-accounts, you might find it useful to group them by type: assets, liabilities, shareholders' equity, revenues, and expenses.

h. Incurred and paid employee wages of $420.

i. Collected accounts receivable of $50 from customers.

j. Made a repair to one of the computers for $120 cash.

Required:

1. Set up appropriate T-accounts for Cash, Accounts Receivable, Supplies, Prepaid Rent, Equipment, Furniture and Fixtures, Notes Payable, Contributed Capital, Sales Revenue, Advertising Expense, Wages Expense, and Repair Expense. All accounts begin with zero balances.

2. Record in the T-accounts the effects of each transaction for Barb's Book Fixing in February, referencing each transaction in the accounts with the transaction letter. Show the unadjusted ending balances in the T-accounts.

3. Prepare an unadjusted trial balance at the end of February.

4. Refer to the revenues and expenses shown on the unadjusted trial balance. Based on this information, write a short memo to Barbara, offering your opinion on the results of operations during the first month of business.

GROUP A PROBLEMS

LO1, LO2, LO3

PA3-1 Recording Non-quantitative Journal Entries

The following is a series of accounts for Dewan & Allard, Incorporated, which has been operating for two years. The accounts are listed alphabetically and are numbered for identification. Following the accounts is a series of transactions. For each transaction, indicate the account(s) that should be debited and credited by entering the appropriate account number(s) to the right of each transaction. If no journal entry is needed, write *none* after the transaction. The first transaction is given as an example.

Account No.	Account Title	Account No.	Account Title
1	Accounts payable	9	Land
2	Accounts receivable	10	Note payable
3	Advertising expense	11	Prepaid insurance
4	Buildings	12	Service revenue
5	Cash	13	Supplies expense
6	Contributed capital	14	Supplies
7	Income tax expense	15	Wages expense
8	Income taxes payable	16	Wages payable

Transactions		Debit	Credit
a.	Issued shares to new investors.	5	6
b.	Performed services for customers this period on credit.	___	___
c.	Purchased supplies on credit but did not use them this period.	___	___
d.	Prepaid a fire insurance policy this period to cover the next 12 months.	___	___
e.	Purchased a building this period by making a 20 per cent cash down payment and signing a note payable for the balance.	___	___
f.	Collected cash this year for services that had been provided and recorded in the prior year.	___	___
g.	Paid cash this period for wages that had been earned and recorded last period.	___	___
h.	Paid cash for supplies that had been purchased on accounts payable in the prior period.	___	___
i.	Paid cash for advertising expense incurred in the current period.	___	___
j.	Incurred advertising expenses on credit to be paid next period, but recorded this period.	___	___
k.	Collected cash for services rendered this period.	___	___
l.	Used supplies on hand to clean the offices.	___	___

m. Recorded income taxes for this period to be paid at the
beginning of the next period.   _____ _____

n. In this period a shareholder sold some shares to another person
for an amount above the original issuance price.   _____ _____

PA3-2 Recording Journal Entries

LO2, LO3

Diana Mark is the president of ServicePro, Inc., a company that provides temporary employees for not-for-profit companies. ServicePro has been operating for five years; its revenues are increasing with each passing year. You have been hired to help Diana in analyzing the following transactions for the first two weeks of April:

April 2	Purchased office supplies for $500 on account.
April 5	Billed the local United Way office $1,950 for temporary services provided.
April 8	Paid $250 for supplies purchased and recorded on account last period.
April 8	Placed an advertisement in the local paper for $400 cash.
April 9	Purchased a new computer for the office costing $2,300 cash.
April 10	Paid employee wages of $1,200. Of this amount, $200 had been earned by employees in the prior period and already recorded in the Wages Payable account.
April 11	Received $1,000 on account from the local United Way office billed on April 5.
April 12	Purchased land as the site of a future office for $10,000. Paid $2,000 down and signed a note payable for the balance.
April 13	Issued 2,000 additional shares of stock for $40 per share in anticipation of building a new office.
April 14	Billed Family and Children's Services $2,000 for services rendered this month.
April 15	Received the April telephone bill for $245 to be paid next month.

Required:

1. For each of the transactions, prepare journal entries. Be sure to categorize each account as an asset (A), liability (L), shareholders' equity (SE), revenue (R), or expense (E).
2. Open appropriate T-accounts, and post the entries to the T-accounts.

PA3-3 Analyzing the Effects of Transactions Using T-Accounts, and Preparing an Unadjusted Trial Balance

LO1, LO2, LO3, LO4

Spicewood Stables, Inc., was established in Red Deer, Alberta, on April 1, 2009. The company provides stables, care for animals, and grounds for riding and showing horses. You have been hired as the new Assistant Controller. The following transactions for April 2009 are provided for your review.

a. Received contributions of $200,000 in cash from five investors ($40,000 each).
b. Built a barn for $142,000. The company paid half the amount in cash on April 1, 2009, and signed a three-year note payable for the balance.
c. Provided $15,260 in animal care services for customers, all on credit.
d. Rented stables to customers who cared for their own animals; received cash of $13,200.
e. Received from a customer $1,500 to board her horse in May, June, and July (record as unearned revenue).
f. Purchased hay and feed supplies on account for $3,210.
g. Paid $840 in cash for water utilities incurred in the month.
h. Paid $1,700 on accounts payable for previous purchases.
i. Received $1,000 from customers on accounts receivable.
j. Paid $4,000 in wages to employees who worked during the month.
k. At the end of the month, prepaid a two-year insurance policy for $3,600.
l. Received an electricity utility bill for $1,200 for usage in April; the bill will be paid next month.

Required:

1. Set up appropriate T-accounts. All accounts begin with zero balances.
2. Record in the T-accounts the effects of each transaction for Spicewood Stables in April, referencing each transaction in the accounts with the transaction letter. Show the unadjusted ending balances in the T-accounts.

3. Prepare an unadjusted trial balance as of April 30, 2009.

4. Refer to the revenues and expenses shown on the unadjusted trial balance. Based on this information, write a short memo to the five owners, offering your opinion on the results of operations during the first month of business.

GROUP B PROBLEMS

LO1, LO2, LO3

PB3-1 Recording Non-quantitative Journal Entries

Roots Canada is a specialty retailer of casual apparel. Founded in 1973 as a footwear store in Toronto, today it is Canada's leading lifestyle brand known around the world for its quality leather goods, clothing, and accessories. The following is a series of typical accounts for Roots. The accounts are listed alphabetically and are numbered for identification. Following the accounts is a series of transactions. For each transaction, indicate the account(s) that should be debited and credited by entering the appropriate account number(s) to the right of each transaction. If no journal entry is needed, write *none* after the transaction. The first transaction is given as an example.

Account No.	Account Title	Account No.	Account Title
1	Accounts payable	8	Rent expense
2	Accounts receivable	9	Supplies expense
3	Cash	10	Supplies
4	Contributed capital	11	Unearned revenue
5	Equipment	12	Wages expense
6	Interest revenue	13	Wages payable
7	Prepaid rent		

	Transactions	Debit	Credit
a.	Example: Incurred wages expense; paid cash.	12	3
b.	Collected cash on account.		
c.	Used up supplies (cash register tapes, etc.) this period.		
d.	Sold gift certificates to customers; none redeemed this period.		
e.	Purchased equipment, paying part in cash and charging the balance on account.		
f.	Paid cash to suppliers on account.		
g.	Issued additional shares for cash.		
h.	Paid rent to landlords for next month's use of mall space.		
i.	Earned and received cash for interest on investments.		

LO2, LO3

PB3-2 Recording Journal Entries

Robin Harrington established Time Definite Delivery on January 1. The following transactions occurred during the company's most recent quarter.

a. Issued shares for $80,000.

b. Provided delivery service to customers, receiving $72,000 in accounts receivable and $16,000 in cash.

c. Purchased equipment costing $82,000 and signed a long-term note for the full amount.

d. Incurred repair costs of $3,000 on account.

e. Collected $65,000 from customers on account.

f. Borrowed $90,000 by signing a long-term note.

g. Prepaid $74,400 cash to rent equipment and aircraft next quarter.

h. Paid employees $38,000 for work done during the quarter.

i. Purchased (with cash) and used $49,000 worth of fuel for delivery equipment.

j. Paid $2,000 on accounts payable.

k. Ordered, but haven't yet received, $700 in supplies.

Required:

1. For each of the transactions, prepare journal entries. Be sure to categorize each account as an asset (A), liability (L), shareholders' equity (SE), revenue (R), or expense (E).
2. Open appropriate T-accounts and post the entries to the T-accounts.

PB3-3 Analyzing the Effects of Transactions Using T-Accounts, and Preparing an Unadjusted Trial Balance

LO1, LO2, LO3, LO4

Jessica Pothier opened FunFlatables on June 1, 2009. The company rents out moon walks and inflatable slides for parties and corporate events. The company also has obtained the use of an abandoned ice rink located in a local shopping mall, where its rental products are displayed and available for casual hourly rental by mall patrons. The following transactions occurred during the first month of operations.

a. Jessica contributed $50,000 cash to the company in exchange for its shares.
b. Purchased inflatable rides and inflation equipment, paying $20,000 cash.
c. Received $5,000 cash from casual hourly rentals at the mall.
d. Rented rides and equipment to customers for $10,000. Received cash of $2,000, and the rest is due from customers.
e. Received $2,500 from a large corporate customer as a deposit on a party booking for July 4.
f. Began to prepare for the July 4th party by purchasing various party supplies on account for $600.
g. Paid $6,000 in cash for renting the mall space this month.
h. Prepaid next month's mall space rental charge of $6,000.
i. Received $1,000 from customers on accounts receivable.
j. Paid $4,000 in wages to employees for work done during the month.
k. Paid $1,000 for running a television ad this month.

Required:

1. Set up appropriate T-accounts. All accounts begin with zero balances.
2. Record, in T-accounts, the effects of each transaction for FunFlatables in June, referencing each transaction in the accounts with the transaction letter. Show the unadjusted ending balances in the T-accounts.
3. Prepare an unadjusted trial balance for the end of June 2009.
4. Jessica has become alarmed at how quickly the company's cash balance has fallen. Refer to the revenues and expenses shown on the unadjusted trial balance and write a short memo to Jessica, offering your opinion on the results of operations during the first month of business.

SKILLS DEVELOPMENT CASES

S3-1 Finding Financial Information

LO1

Refer to the financial statements of High Liner in Appendix A at the end of this book, or download the annual report from the *Cases* section of the text's Web site at www.mcgrawhill.ca/college/phillips.

Required:

1. Have High Liner's total revenues increased or decreased in the most recent year? By how much? Calculate this change as a percentage of the previous year's total revenues by dividing the amount of the change by the previous year's revenues and multiplying by 100 per cent.
2. State the amount of the largest expense on the most recent income statement, and describe the transaction represented by the expense. Did this expense increase or decrease from the previous year, and by what percentage?
3. Did High Liner report any non-operating items in its most recent income statement? What percentage of revenues did these items represent? What percentage of net income did these items represent?

LO1

S3-2 Comparing Financial Information

Refer to the financial statements of Sun-Rype by downloading the annual report from the *Cases* section of the text's Web site at www.mcgrawhill.ca/college/phillips.

Required:

1. Have Sun-Rype's total revenues increased or decreased in the most recent year? By how much? Calculate this change as a percentage of the previous year's total revenues. Is the trend in Sun-Rype's revenues more or less favourable than High Liner's?

2. State the amount of the largest expense on the most recent income statement and describe the transaction represented by the expense. Did this expense increase or decrease, and by what percentage, as compared with the previous year? Is the trend in Sun-Rype's largest expense more or less favourable than the trend for High Liner's largest expense?

3. Did Sun-Rype report any non-operating items in its most recent income statement? What percentage of revenues did these items represent? What percentage of net income did these items represent? Do non-operating items have a greater influence on the net income of Sun-Rype or High Liner?

LO1, LO5

TEAM CASE

S3-3 Internet-Based Team Research: Examining the Income Statement

As a team, select an industry to analyze. Using your Web browser, each team member should acquire the financial reporting section of the annual report for one Canadian publicly traded company in the industry, with each member selecting a different company. (See S1-3 in Chapter 1 for a description of possible resources for these tasks.)

Required:

1. On an individual basis, each team member should write a short report that lists the following information:
   a. The major revenue and expense accounts on the most recent income statement
   b. Description of how the company has followed the conditions of the revenue principle
   c. The percentage of revenues that go to covering expenses, and that are in excess of expenses (in other words, the percentage that remains as net income)

2. Then, as a team, write a short report comparing and contrasting your companies using these attributes. Discuss any patterns across the companies that you, as a team, observe. Provide potential explanations for any differences discovered.

LO1, LO5

POINT OF INTEREST

Forbes magazine listed the Toronto Maple Leafs as the league's best financial performer, with a U.S.$14.1 million operating profit for the 2002–2003 season.

S3-4 Using Financial Information in Collective Bargaining

The National Hockey League cancelled its 2004–2005 season when the players and owners could not reach an agreement. Although 11 of the league's teams were showing profits, 19 others were operating at a loss, and the league as a whole felt that players' salaries were costing them too much. Because the teams are privately-owned, individual team data are not readily available, but the NHL provided this summary data for the league at the time of the strike.

NATIONAL HOCKEY LEAGUE **Partial Income Statement** **For the 2002–2003 Season** **(in millions of U.S. dollars)**	
Combined revenues	$1,996
Player costs (salaries and bonuses)	(1,494)
Other operating costs	(775)
Operating loss (before amortization, interest, and taxes)	($273)

Source: www.NHLCBANEWS.com

Required:

1. What percentage of league revenues are the player costs in this example? How does this percentage compare with the salary data presented for First Choice Haircutters in Exhibit 3.1 on page 87?

2. When an organization is showing a loss, briefly explain what it can do to return to a more profitable situation.

3. Why might some teams be making a profit and others recording losses?

4. The disagreement was settled in 2005, with player costs being held at a maximum of 54 per cent of total league-wide revenues. Assuming that revenues and other operating costs stay the same, prepare the expected income statement for the league's 2005–2006 season. Did it then look as though the league would be profitable under the new contract?

S3-5 Ethical Decision Making: A Real-Life Example

Read the following excerpt from a September 2, 2002, article in *Fortune* magazine and answer the questions that appear below.

Forget about fraud. Companies don't need to lie, cheat, and steal to fool investors. Clever managers have always had, and continue to have, access to perfectly legal tricks to help make their balance sheets and income statements look better than they really are—tricks that *even today* won't jeopardize their ability to swear to the [securities legislators] that their books are on the up and up. . . . One of the most controversial of all number games—the one that got WorldCom in trouble—is to capitalize expenses. That can have a tremendous impact on the bottom line.

1. In this chapter, you learned that, when a company incurs a cost, its accountants have to decide whether to record the cost as an asset or expense. This builds on Chapter 2, where you learned that it was appropriate to capitalize costs as assets, provided they possess certain characteristics. What are those characteristics?

2. The author of the article argues that, even with clear rules like those referenced in question 1 above, accounting still allows managers to use "tricks" like *capitalizing expenses*. What do you suppose the author means by the expression *capitalizing expenses*?

3. Suppose that, in the current year, a company inappropriately records a cost as an asset when it should be recorded as an expense. What is the effect of this accounting decision on the current year's net income? What is the effect of this accounting decision on the following year's net income?

4. Later in the article (not shown) the author says that the video game industry is one where companies frequently capitalize software development costs as assets. These costs include wages paid to programmers, fees paid to graphic designers, and amounts paid to game testers. Evaluate whether software development costs are likely to possess the main characteristics possessed by all assets. Can you think of a situation where software development costs might not possess these main characteristics?

5. Do you think it is always easy and straightforward to determine whether costs should be capitalized or expensed? Do you think it is always easy and straightforward to determine whether a manager is acting ethically or unethically? Give examples to illustrate your views.

S3-6 Ethical Decision Making: A Mini-Case

Mike Lynch is the manager of a regional office for an insurance company. As the regional manager, his pay package includes a base salary, commissions, and a bonus when the region sells new policies in excess of its quota. Mike has been under enormous pressure lately, stemming largely from two factors. First, he is experiencing a mounting personal debt caused by a family member's illness. Second, compounding his worries, the region's sales of new insurance policies have dipped below the normal quota for the first time in years.

You have been working for Mike for two years, and, like everyone else in the office, you consider yourself lucky to work for such a supportive boss. You also feel great sympathy for his personal problems over the last few months. In your position as accountant for the regional office, you are only too aware of the drop in new policy sales and the impact this will have on the manager's bonus. While you are working on the year-end financial statements, Mike stops by your office.

Mike asks you to change the manner in which you have accounted for a new property insurance policy for a large local business. A cheque for the premium, substantial in amount, came in the mail on December 31, the last day of the reporting year. The premium covers a period beginning on January 5. You deposited the cheque and correctly debited cash and credited an *unearned revenue* account. Mike says, "Hey, we have the money this year, so why not count the revenue this year? I never did understand why you accountants are so picky about these things anyway. I'd like you to change the way you've recorded the transaction. I want you to credit a *revenue* account. And anyway, I've done favours for you in the past, and I am asking for such a small thing in return." With that, he leaves your office.

Required:

How should you handle this situation? What are the ethical implications of Mike's request? Who are the parties who would be helped or harmed if you went along with the request? If you fail to comply with his request, how will you explain your position to him?

LO1, LO2, LO4   **S3-7 Critical Thinking: Analyzing Changes in Accounts and Preparing a Trial Balance**

Hordichuk Painting Service Company was organized on January 20, 2010, by three individuals, each receiving 5,000 shares from the new company. The following is a schedule of the cumulative account balances immediately after each of the first 10 transactions ending on January 31, 2010.

Accounts	Cumulative Balances								
	a	*b*	*c*	*d*	*e*	*f*	*g*	*h*	*i*
Cash	$75,000	$70,000	$85,000	$71,000	$61,000	$61,000	$46,000	$44,000	$60,000
Accounts receivable			12,000	12,000	12,000	26,000	26,000	26,000	10,000
Supplies					5,000	5,000	4,000	4,000	4,000
Office fixtures		20,000	20,000	20,000	20,000	20,000	20,000	20,000	20,000
Land				18,000	18,000	18,000	18,000	18,000	18,000
Accounts payable					3,000	3,000	3,000	1,000	1,000
Notes payable		15,000	15,000	19,000	19,000	19,000	19,000	19,000	19,000
Contributed capital	75,000	75,000	75,000	75,000	75,000	75,000	75,000	75,000	75,000
Paint revenue			27,000	27,000	27,000	41,000	41,000	41,000	41,000
Supplies expense							1,000	1,000	1,000
Wages expense					8,000	8,000	23,000	23,000	23,000

Required:

1. Analyze the changes in this schedule for each transaction; then explain the transaction. Transactions *a* and *b* are examples:
    a. Cash increased $75,000, and Contributed Capital (shareholders' equity) increased $75,000. Therefore, transaction *a* was an issuance of the capital shares of the corporation for $75,000 cash.
    b. Cash decreased $5,000, office fixtures (an asset) increased $20,000, and notes payable (a liability) increased $15,000. Therefore, transaction *b* was a purchase of office fixtures that cost $20,000. Payment was made as follows: cash, $5,000; notes payable, $15,000.
2. Based only on the preceding schedule after transaction *i*, prepare an unadjusted trial balance.

LO2, LO3, LO4   **S3-8 Analyzing Transactions and Preparing an Unadjusted Trial Balance**

Assume you recently started up a new company that rents machines for making frozen drinks like smoothies, frozen juices, tea slush, and iced cappuccinos. For $100, your business will deliver a machine, provide supplies (straws, paper cups), set up the machine, and pick up the machine the next morning. Drink mix and other supplies are sold by other businesses in your city. Being a one person operation, you are responsible for everything from purchasing to marketing to operations to accounting.

You've decided that you'll just write notes about what happens during the month, and then do the accounting at the end of the month. You figure this will be more efficient. Plus, by waiting until the end of the month to do the accounting, you'll be less likely to make a mistake because by that time you'll be way past the accounting cycle chapters. Your notes said the following about your first month of operations:

Oct.2	Incorporated Slusher Gusher Inc. and contributed $10,000 for shares in the company.
Oct.12	Paid cash to buy three frozen drink machines on eBay at a total cost of $1,500. What a deal!
Oct.13	Paid cash to buy $70 worth of supplies. The store was packed.
Oct.16	Received $500 cash for this past week's rentals. I'm rich!
Oct.17	Determined that $45 worth of supplies had been used up. Hmm, looks like I'll need some more.
Oct.20	Bought $100 worth of supplies on account. I can't believe the party store gave me credit like that.
Oct.23	Feeling tired after a busy week (six rentals this time). Received $400 cash and expect to receive $200 more sometime this week.
Oct.25	Received $100 cash from one of the customers who hadn't paid up yet. Called the other customer to remind him I'm waiting.
Oct.26	Ran an ad in the local paper today for $25 cash. Maybe that'll drum up some business.
Oct.27	Received $150 cash for a two-machine office party to be held on November 15. It's a good thing I got this money because no other bookings are in sight for the rest of the month.

Required:

Create a spreadsheet in which to record the effects of the October transactions, and calculate end-of-month totals. Using the spreadsheet, prepare a trial balance that checks whether debits = credits. Because you're dealing with your own business this time, you want to be extra sure that you do this just right, so you e-mail your friend Billy for advice. Here's his reply:

From: BillyTheTutor@yahoo.com
To: Overwhelmed@hotmail.com
Cc:
Subject: Excel Help

Wow, you're a CEO already? I always thought you were a mover and a shaker! So you want my advice on how to set up your spreadsheet? My advice is *read the last e-mail I sent*. The main thing that's new here is you'll need to include some columns for revenue and expenses under the shareholders' equity heading. Here's a screenshot of how the right-hand side of your worksheet might look just before you enter the October transactions. Notice that, because shareholders' equity is decreased by expenses, the debit side is used to record expenses.

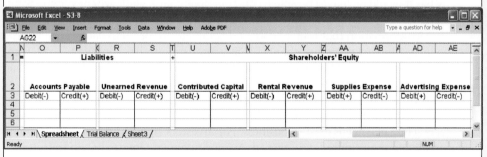

To prepare the trial balance, create three columns. In the first, copy and paste the account names (one per row). In the second column, link in each debit balance by entering = in a cell and then clicking on the debit total from the T-account. Repeat this with all the accounts. Then do the same with the credit balances. At the bottom of the trial balance, use the SUM function to compute totals.

Don't forget to save the file using a name that uniquely identifies you (as my true hero).

Adjustments, Financial Statements, and the Quality of Financial Reporting

INSIDE LOOKING OUT

OUTSIDE LOOKING IN

This chapter continues our discussion of the accounting system, focusing specifically on the adjustments that are needed under accrual basis accounting. We continue to focus on First Choice Haircutters.

Understand why adjustments are needed.
> **LO1** Explain the goals accomplished by recording adjustments.

Study how adjustments are made.
> **LO2** Prepare adjustments needed at the end of the period.

Evaluate the quality of adjusted financial statements.
> **LO3** Explain how adjustments affect information quality.

Reconsider the accounting process.
> **LO4** Prepare an adjusted trial balance.
> **LO5** Prepare adjusted financial statements.
> **LO6** Explain the closing process.

If you've ever used an on-line course management system, like Blackboard or WebCT, you'll know how great it is to be able to check your course standing at any given time. Even if you haven't used a system like this, just imagine what it would be like to be able to find out your course grade whenever you want. The key for making this kind of system work effectively is ensuring that it uses grade information that is up to date and complete. To be up to date, it needs to be adjusted for any test-score changes that your instructor has approved. To be complete, it needs to include the results of all assignments and tests that you've had graded. With up-to-date and complete information like this, you can know exactly where you stand in the course and you can make better-informed decisions about where to devote your limited study time during the upcoming week.

The same needs exist in business. For investors and creditors to decide where to devote their limited resources, they need financial reports that contain up-to-date and complete information. To ensure that this kind of information is available, accountants adjust their company's accounting records before financial statements are prepared and released to users. These adjustments are used to update amounts already recorded in the accounting records, and to include events that have occurred but haven't yet been recorded as transactions. For **FIRST CHOICE HAIRCUTTERS,** this includes updating the supplies account for shampoo used during the month, and including the interest that mounted on debt owed by the company. These kinds of adjustments are needed to ensure that the financial statements include the financial results of *all* the company's activities for the period. They're also a key part of generally accepted accounting principles.

In the next section of this chapter, we'll help you to understand why adjustments are a necessary part of accrual basis accounting. Once you understand the purpose of adjustments, you'll be in a better position to learn about the process involved in figuring out what adjustments are needed, and how they are recorded, using journal entries, which is the focus for the second part of this chapter. In the third section, we consider how adjustments can affect external financial statement users. The final section reconsiders the complete process involved in preparing financial statements. The goals that you should be trying to achieve when reading Chapter 4 are presented as Learning Objectives on the first page of this chapter.

UNDERSTAND _____
Why Adjustments Are Needed

Accounting systems have two parts: the recording phase and the reporting phase. Chapters 2 and 3 reviewed the recording phase, the part of the process that is ongoing. Day after day, as the business is operating, the accounting system is tracking the activities so that those that meet the definition of a transaction are identified, analyzed, and recorded in the journal and posted to the ledger. At some point, the company asks, "How are we doing?" This question is answered by using the information in the general ledger to prepare financial statements. This reporting phase is the focus of this chapter.

Accounting systems are designed to record most recurring daily transactions, particularly any involving cash. This focus on cash is okay, particularly if cash receipts and payments occur in the same accounting period as the related activities. The top timeline in Exhibit 4.1 shows a situation in which cash receipts and payments occur in the same accounting period as the related activities; **adjustments** are not needed to record revenues and expenses in the proper period. In contrast, the bottom line in Exhibit 4.1 shows a situation where the activities that lead to the revenues and expenses occur in the current accounting period, but their related cash receipts and payments occur in other periods. To record the revenue and expenses from transactions like these in the proper period, adjustments will have to be made to the accounting records before financial statements are prepared.

Making adjustments is consistent with the principles of accrual accounting and matching. Accrual accounting requires that all revenues be recorded in the period in which they are earned and all expenses be recorded in the period in which they are incurred, regardless of when the cash changes hands. The matching principle requires that all expenses be recorded in the same period as the revenues to which they relate. After making the necessary adjustments, the accounting system will include all the revenues and expenses of the period, which ensures that the income statement provides a meaningful measure of business success. These adjustments also ensure that the related

> **Adjustments** are journal entries made at the end of every accounting period to ensure that revenues and expenses are recorded in the proper period.

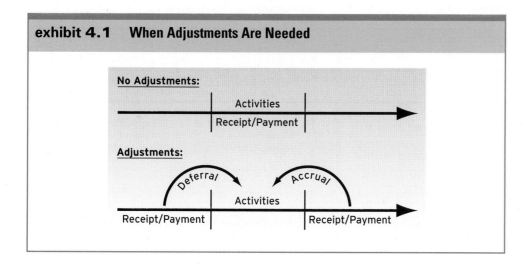

exhibit 4.1   When Adjustments Are Needed

No Adjustments:

Activities
Receipt/Payment

Adjustments:

Deferral
Accrual
Activities
Receipt/Payment   Receipt/Payment

accounts on the balance sheet are (1) up to date and (2) complete. Two types of adjustments are recorded to accomplish these goals: deferral adjustments and accrual adjustments.

1. DEFERRAL ADJUSTMENTS

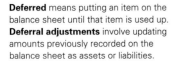

Deferred means putting an item on the balance sheet until that item is used up. **Deferral adjustments** involve updating amounts previously recorded on the balance sheet as assets or liabilities.

Deferral adjustments are used for updating accounts involving previously recorded transactions. If cash is exchanged before the related revenue or expense is recorded, deferral adjustments may be needed at the end of the accounting period to bring the accounting records **up to date.** In particular, **deferral adjustments** are needed in either of the following situations:

a. Some or all of an asset's future benefits have expired or been used up in the current period (but these expenses haven't been recorded as of the end of the period).

b. The company provides goods or services in the current period to satisfy an existing liability (but these revenues haven't been recorded as of the end of the period).

Many of the accounts that are affected by deferral adjustments are summarized in the middle column in Exhibit 4.2. The lines in the exhibit indicate that deferral adjustments affect assets and their related expenses, or liabilities and their related revenues.

2. ACCRUAL ADJUSTMENTS

COACH'S TIP

Accrual adjustments involve the inclusion ("accrual") of new amounts in balance sheet and income statement accounts.

Accrual adjustments are used for including transactions not previously recorded. If cash is not exchanged until after the related revenue is earned or expense is incurred, an accrual adjustment may be needed to make the accounting records *complete* at the end of the period. In particular, accrual adjustments are needed in either of the following situations:

a. Assets and revenues are generated in the current period but haven't been recorded as of the end of the period (perhaps because cash hasn't been received yet).

b. Liabilities and expenses are incurred in the current period but haven't been recorded as of the end of the period (perhaps because cash hasn't been paid yet).

---

exhibit 4.2   Types of Adjustments

	Deferral Adjustments		*Accrual Adjustments*	
a. What we want to accomplish	Report **up-to-date** information.		Report **complete** information.	
b. How do we accomplish it?	Update what's already recorded.		Include what's not yet recorded.	
c. What accounts are affected?	**Assets** — Balance Sheet: Inventories, Supplies, Prepaid Rent — Income Statement: Cost of Goods Sold, Supplies Expense, Rent Expense (**Expenses**)		**Assets** — Balance Sheet: Interest Receivable, Rent Receivable — Income Statement: Interest Revenue, Rent Revenue (**Revenues**)	
	Liabilities — Balance Sheet: Unearned Ticket Revenue, Subscriptions Paid in Advance — Income Statement: Ticket Sales Revenue, Subscriptions Revenue (**Revenues**)		**Liabilities** — Balance Sheet: Income Taxes Payable, Wages Payable, Interest Payable — Income Statement: Income Tax Expense, Wages Expense, Interest Expense (**Expenses**)	

Deferral adjustments are used to ensure that the information reported in financial statements is updated to the financial statement date. Each deferral adjustment affects an asset account and an expense account, or a liability account and a revenue account. *Accrual adjustments* are used to ensure that the information reported in financial statements is complete. Unlike deferral adjustments, each accrual adjustment affects an asset account and a revenue account, or a liability account and an expense account.

Many of the accounts that are affected by accrual adjustments are summarized in the right-hand column of Exhibit 4.2. Notice that accrual adjustments create corresponding adjustments to assets and revenues, or liabilities and their related expenses.

If you didn't already read the explanation in Exhibit 4.2, read it now. Notice that every adjustment involves a pair of balance sheet and income statement accounts. The best way to determine what specific adjustments are needed is to scan the unadjusted trial balance, while thinking about each different transaction the company enters into, and considering whether the pair of accounts affected by these transactions are up to date and complete as of the financial statement date. Has the company earned revenues or incurred expenses in this period but not yet recorded them? If so, the accounting records need to be adjusted before financial statements are prepared.

STUDY_____

How Adjustments Are Made

To make each necessary adjustment, apply the following steps:

1. Obtain the current unadjusted balances in the pair of accounts to be adjusted.
2. Calculate the amount of the adjustment needed.
3. Prepare a journal entry to make the adjustment (called an adjusting journal entry).

Adjusting journal entries are used at the end of each accounting period to update the records and include all revenues and expenses of that period.

Step 1: is easy. Look in the accounting records (T-accounts or unadjusted trial balance) for the balances in the pair of balance sheet and income statement accounts that you will be adjusting. Sometimes it's enough to know the unadjusted balance in either the balance sheet or income statement account, but, where possible, you should always try to identify the balances in both of the related accounts.

Step 2: is more challenging. To calculate the adjustment needed, you will use information gathered in Step 1, along with facts about the transactions that affect each pair of accounts to be adjusted. When calculating the amount of revenues or expenses that relate to the current period, it's useful to draw pictures or timelines, as we do in later examples.

Step 3: involves converting the calculations from Step 2 into journal-entry format. This step is made easier by using T-accounts to picture what you're trying to accomplish.

EXAMPLES OF DEFERRAL ADJUSTMENTS

Let's begin by looking at common examples of deferral adjustments, which, again, are adjustments used to make the accounting records up to date—in this case, at the end of September.

Supplies Used during Period

(a) In August 2009, your salon received its first shipment of hair supplies, which was recorded in Chapter 2 with the following journal entry:

dr	Supplies (+A)	630	
	cr Accounts Payable (+L)		630

Supplies were used during September, but their use wasn't recorded because it simply wasn't efficient to record a journal entry each day that the supplies were used. Instead, it's easier to make an end-of-period adjustment, determined as follows.

Step 1: The unadjusted trial balance at September 30 (in Exhibit 3.10 on page 101) shows that the unadjusted balance for *Supplies* is $630. *Supplies Expense* does not appear in the unadjusted trial balance because no adjusting entries have yet been made and, therefore, the balance in the *Supplies Expense* account is $0.

Step 2: At the end of September 2009, by counting the bottles of shampoo and tubes of gel on hand, your salon manager determined that $400 worth of supplies were left. If only $400 worth of supplies are left from the $630 on hand at the start of the month, the $230 difference must be the cost of supplies used this month. The matching principle says this cost should be expensed in September.

Step 3: The *Supplies* T-account shown below (on the left) currently has an unadjusted balance of $630, but, as we just calculated in Step 2, the desired adjusted balance is $400. To go from $630 to $400, we need an adjustment to decrease (credit) this asset by $230.

The *Supplies Expense* T-account (on the right) currently has an unadjusted balance of $0, but the balance should be the cost of supplies used up so far this year, which means the desired adjusted balance is $230. To go from $0 to $230, we need an adjustment to increase (debit) the expense by $230.

dr Supplies (A) cr		
Unadjusted bal. 630		
	230	Adjustment
Desired adj. bal. 400		

dr Supplies Expense (E) cr		
Unadjusted bal. 0		
Adjustment 230		
Desired adj. bal. 230		

Taken together, this analysis indicates that our adjusting journal entry should debit *Supplies Expense* and credit *Supplies* by $230, shown as follows:

dr	Supplies Expense (+ E, − SE) 230	
	cr Supplies (−A)	230

When posted to the accounts, the above adjusting journal entry will reduce the asset *Supplies* and increase *Supplies Expense*, as shown in the T-accounts above. The effects of this adjusting journal entry on the accounting equation are shown below, and the financial statement effects are pictured in Exhibit 4.3.

Assets	=	Liabilities	+	Shareholders' Equity
Supplies − 230				Supplies Expense (+E) − 230

Rent and Insurance Benefits Expired during Period

Back in Chapter 3, your First Choice Haircutters Salon had prepaid its rent and insurance. Now that some of the benefits of these prepayments have been used up as of the end of September, the salon needs to adjust the accounts related to these prepaid expenses. We will show how to make the adjustment for prepaid rent in part **(b)**, and then give you some practice with a Self-Study Quiz to adjust prepaid insurance in **(c)**.

(b) In September 2009, your salon paid $7,200 rent for September, October, and November. This $7,200 prepayment was recorded in Chapter 3 as an asset (*Prepaid Rent*).

Step 1: The account balances (obtained from the unadjusted trial balance) include $7,200 for *Prepaid Rent*. There is a $0 balance so far for *Rent Expense* since the adjusting entries have not yet been made.

Step 2: The timeline in Exhibit 4.4 shows that the September prepayment of $7,200 represented three equal components of $2,400. The benefits of the first component (pictured in red) have now expired, so only two of the three months (2/3) remain prepaid at September 30. Thus, the $7,200 that was prepaid on September 1 needs to be adjusted on September 30 to $4,800 (= 2/3 × $7,200), which is the cost of the two remaining months of prepaid rent (pictured in blue).

exhibit 4.3   Transferring the Cost of an Asset to an Expense Account

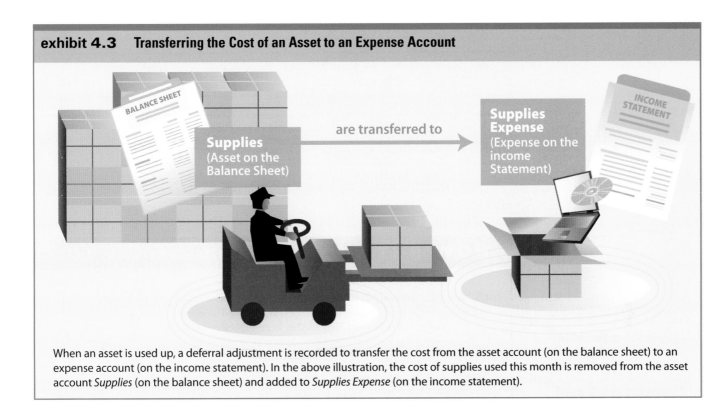

When an asset is used up, a deferral adjustment is recorded to transfer the cost from the asset account (on the balance sheet) to an expense account (on the income statement). In the above illustration, the cost of supplies used this month is removed from the asset account *Supplies* (on the balance sheet) and added to *Supplies Expense* (on the income statement).

Step 3: As shown in the following T-accounts, *Prepaid Rent* currently has an unadjusted balance of $7,200, but the desired adjusted balance is $4,800 (as calculated in Step 2), so we require an adjustment to decrease (credit) the asset by $2,400. *Rent Expense* has an unadjusted balance of $0 but (as calculated in Step 2) the desired adjusted balance is $2,400, so we require an adjustment to increase (debit) the expense by $2,400.

dr Prepaid Rent (A) cr	
Unadjusted bal. 7,200	
	2,400 Adjustment
Desired adj. bal. 4,800	

dr Rent Expense (E) cr	
Unadjusted bal. 0	
Adjustment 2,400	
Desired adj. bal. 2,400	

exhibit 4.4   Using a Timeline to Calculate Adjustments

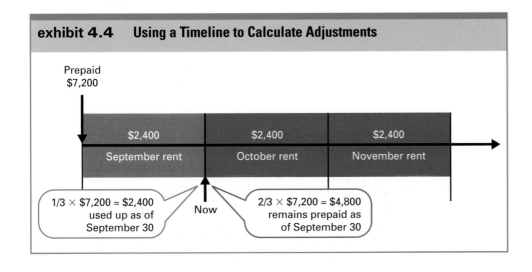

Prepaid $7,200

$2,400	$2,400	$2,400
September rent	October rent	November rent

1/3 × $7,200 = $2,400 used up as of September 30

Now

2/3 × $7,200 = $4,800 remains prepaid as of September 30

In journal entry format, the required adjustment is

dr	Rent Expense (+ E, − SE)	2,400	
	cr Prepaid Rent (− A)		2,400

Assets		=	Liabilities		+	Shareholders' Equity	
Prepaid Rent	− 2,400					Rent Expense (+E)	− 2,400

For *(c)*, in the self-study quiz that follows, fill in the missing information and complete the adjusting journal entry.

HOW'S IT GOING? A Self-Study Quiz

(c) Your salon prepaid $2,400 for an insurance policy that covers the period from September 1 until August 31 of next year. The full amount was recorded as *Prepaid Insurance*. No *Insurance Expense* has been reported.

Step 1: The unadjusted balances are $ [____] for *Prepaid Insurance* and $ [____] for *Insurance Expense*.

Step 2: The benefits from the $2,400 payment relate to 12 months (September 1 through August 31). As of September 30, one month of these benefits (1/12) has been used up and 11/12 of them remain. To reflect this, the balance in *Prepaid Insurance* should be adjusted to $2,200 (= 11/12 × $2,400). *Insurance Expense* should be adjusted to $ [____] (= 1/12 × $2,400).

Step 3:

dr Prepaid Insurance (A) cr	
Unadjusted bal. 2,400	
	[____] Adjustment
Desired adj. bal. 2,200	

dr Insurance Expense (E) cr	
Unadjusted bal. 0	
Adjustment [____]	
Desired adj. bal. 200	

September 30 adjusting journal entry:

dr	Insurance Expense (+ E, −SE)	[____]
	cr Prepaid Insurance (− A)	[____]

Assets		=	Liabilities		+	Shareholders' Equity	
Prepaid Insurance	− 200					Insurance Expense (+E)	− 200

When you're finished, check your answers with the solution in the margin.

Notice that, for events *(a)*, *(b)*, and *(c)*, the deferral adjustments have two effects: (1) they reduce the **carrying value** of assets on the balance sheet, and (2) they transfer the amount of the reductions to related expense accounts. This happens whether we're recording the use of supplies, prepaid expenses, or even long-term assets like property and equipment. When accounting for the use of property and equipment, there is one slight difference in how the carrying value is reduced, as we'll explain next.

Amortization Recorded for Use of Property and Equipment

The matching principle implies that, when buildings and equipment are used to generate revenues in the current period, part of their cost should be transferred to an expense account in that period. This process is referred to as **amortization,** so an account named *Amortization Expense* is used to report the cost of these assets used up during the period.

Carrying value simply means the amount an asset or liability is reported at ("carried at") in the financial statements. It is also known as "net book value" or simply "book value."

Amortization is the process of allocating the cost of property and equipment to the accounting periods in which they are used. The term depreciation is used sometimes instead of amortization.

exhibit 4.5   Recording Amortization Expense and Accumulated Amortization

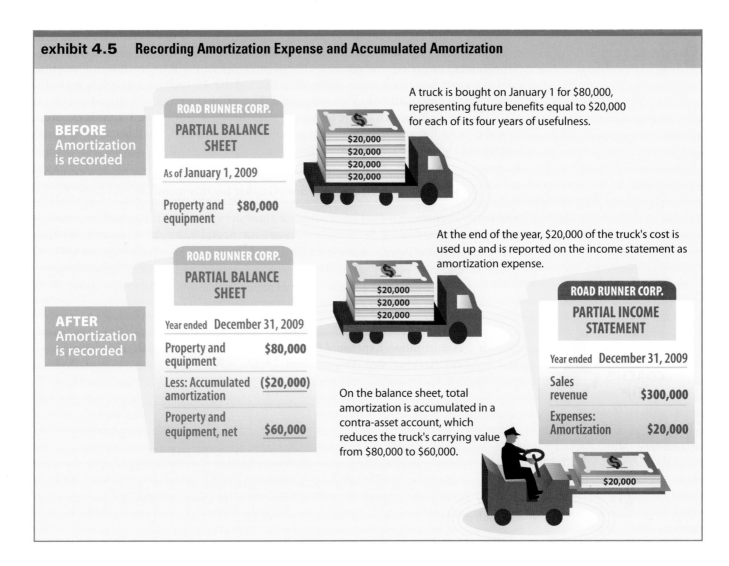

A truck is bought on January 1 for $80,000, representing future benefits equal to $20,000 for each of its four years of usefulness.

BEFORE Amortization is recorded

ROAD RUNNER CORP.
PARTIAL BALANCE SHEET
As of **January 1, 2009**

Property and equipment   **$80,000**

At the end of the year, $20,000 of the truck's cost is used up and is reported on the income statement as amortization expense.

AFTER Amortization is recorded

ROAD RUNNER CORP.
PARTIAL BALANCE SHEET
Year ended **December 31, 2009**

Property and equipment   **$80,000**

Less: Accumulated amortization   **($20,000)**

Property and equipment, net   **$60,000**

ROAD RUNNER CORP.
PARTIAL INCOME STATEMENT
Year ended **December 31, 2009**

Sales revenue   **$300,000**

Expenses: Amortization   **$20,000**

On the balance sheet, total amortization is accumulated in a contra-asset account, which reduces the truck's carrying value from $80,000 to $60,000.

The use of an expense account to record the part of the assets used up is not new to you. What is new, however, is that, rather than take the amount of amortization directly out of the asset accounts, a **contra-account** is created to keep track of all the amortization that is recorded against the property and equipment. As shown in Exhibit 4.5, this contra-account, named *Accumulated Amortization*, is reported in the assets section of the balance sheet and is subtracted from the *Property and Equipment* account.

> A **contra-account** is an account that is an offset to, or reduction of, another account.

By recording amortization in *Accumulated Amortization* separate from *Property and Equipment*, it's possible to report both the original cost of the property and equipment and the amount that has already been amortized. This gives users a rough idea of how much of the asset's original cost (and original usefulness) has been used up as of the balance sheet date and how much remains to be amortized (and used) in the future.

Before showing how amortization is recorded for your First Choice Haircutters Salon, we need to ensure you don't misunderstand what it is. Some people mistakenly think that amortization reflects an asset's decline in market value. This is more likely to happen when the term depreciation is used, since people often say that a new car "depreciates" when it is driven off the lot because it has become a "used" car. From an accounting standpoint, a car is not amortized until it actually is used to generate revenues. And that's because amortization is used in accounting to match part of an asset's original cost to the revenues generated in the periods in which the asset is used. In accounting, amortization is never intended to show a reduction in market value. In some cases, amortization might appear to mirror a decline in market value, but that's just a fluke.

COACH'S TIP

Unlike amortization expense, which relates only to the current period's amortization, accumulated amortization is a running total of amortization. Each year's amortization is added to the total from previous years. In this way, accumulated amortization does actually **accumulate** all the amortization that has been recorded since the underlying asset was originally acquired.

One of the challenges in accounting for amortization is figuring out how much to record. Unlike prepaid rent or prepaid insurance, there's no written agreement that states the number of periods for which buildings or equipment will be used, so it's tough to know exactly how much amortization to report. Exhibit 4.5 shows one simple way (called the straight-line method). The total $80,000 cost of the truck is charged evenly at $20,000 per year to each of the four years that the truck will be used. In this chapter's examples, we'll simply tell you the amount to use. In Chapter 9, you'll learn the methods commonly used for estimating amortization.

(d) In Chapter 2, your salon had bought furnishings and equipment costing $60,000. Your salon manager figures that amortization for this month should be $1,000.

Step 1: No entries have yet been made for amortization, so the unadjusted account balances are $0 for *Accumulated Amortization* and $0 for *Amortization Expense*.

Step 2: Only one month of amortization ($1,000) needs to be recorded for September.

Step 3: We don't need T-accounts to figure out what's needed. To go from the unadjusted balances of $0 to the desired adjusted balances of $1,000, we increase the expense and contra-account balances as follows:

dr Amortization Expense (+ E, − SE)	1,000	
cr Accumulated Amortization (+xA, −A)		1,000

Assets	=	Liabilities	+	Shareholders' Equity
Accumulated Amort.(+xA) − 1,000				Amortization Expense (+E) − 1,000

COACH'S TIP

The notation for a contra-account is a small "x." So "xA" indicates a contra-account for an asset. An increase in this contra account (+ xA) decreases the carrying value of the underlying asset (−A).

Note that a contra-account always is recorded in a way that opposes the account that it offsets. For example, in *(d)*, the increase in *Accumulated Amortization* was recorded with a credit because this account reduces the carrying value of an underlying asset, *Furnishings and Equipment*, which was recorded as a debit.

Gift Cards Redeemed for Service

Just as deferral adjustments are used to record expenses incurred when assets are used up, they also can be used to record the revenues earned when a company fulfills its obligation to provide goods or services to customers—an example we look at in adjustment *(e)*.

(e) On the last day of September, one of the stylists had $75 in gift certificates at her station that customers had given her as payment for haircuts done that day. These had not yet been reported as sales.

Step 1: The unadjusted trial balance in Exhibit 3.10 includes $15,600 of *Haircut Revenue* and $200 of *Unearned Revenue* recorded earlier in September (in Chapter 3). The unearned revenue balance of $200 represents the $300 of gift certificates that were sold in early September less the $100 of gift certificates that were redeemed and recorded in the third week of September.

Step 2: Because these gift certificates of $75 relate to haircuts provided on the last day of September, these revenues have been earned and should be recorded in September, to bring total revenue to $15,675. Also, by taking in $75 of additional gift certificates, the salon's liability for honouring gift certificates in the future should be reduced by $75 (from $200 to $125).

Step 3: The analysis in Step 2 indicates that an adjustment is needed to record a $75 increase in haircut revenue and a $75 decrease in unearned revenue. Let's double-check to see if this will bring the T-accounts to the desired balances:

dr Unearned Revenue (L) cr		dr Haircut Revenue (R) cr	
	Unadjusted bal. 200		Unadjusted bal. 15,600
Adjustment 75			Adjustment 75
	Desired adj. bal. 125		Desired adj. bal. 15,675

That'll do the trick. Here's the adjusting journal entry to make it happen (along with a check to see that the accounting equation remains in balance).

dr Unearned Revenue (− L)	75	
cr Haircut Revenue (+ R, + SE)		75

Assets	=	Liabilities	+	Shareholders' Equity	
		Unearned Revenue − 75		Haircut Revenue (+R)	+ 75

EXAMPLES OF ACCRUAL ADJUSTMENTS

Let's now look at common examples of accrual adjustments, which are adjustments that make the accounting records complete by including transactions that have not been previously recorded—in this case, by the end of September.

Interest Revenue Earned but Not Yet Recorded

(f) On September 1, your salon moved some cash into a certificate of deposit (CD) at the bank. A CD is a special type of bank account that pays a higher interest rate than a regular savings account, but it pays this interest only after a specified period of time. The CD that your salon acquired will pay $120 interest on November 30.

Step 1: No amounts have been recorded for interest earned.

Step 2: The timeline shown in Exhibit 4.6 indicates that the $120 interest that will be received on November 30 actually is *earned* over the three previous months. The revenue principle says that interest earned in September should be recorded in September.

Step 3: The adjusting journal entry to record the interest earned and receivable as of September 30 is

dr Interest Receivable (+ A)	40	
cr Interest Revenue (+ R, + SE)		40

Assets	=	Liabilities	+	Shareholders' Equity	
Interest Receivable + 40				Interest Revenue (+R)	+ 40

Interest Expense Incurred but Not Yet Recorded

(g) Your salon has not paid or recorded the $100 interest that it owes this month on its note payable to the bank. (The note payable was issued in Chapter 2.)

Step 1: No amounts have been recorded for interest incurred.

Step 2: Because interest is incurred in September, a liability and expense need to be recorded, increasing the balances from $0 to $100.

Step 3: The adjusting journal entry needed to record the interest incurred and owed as of September 30 is

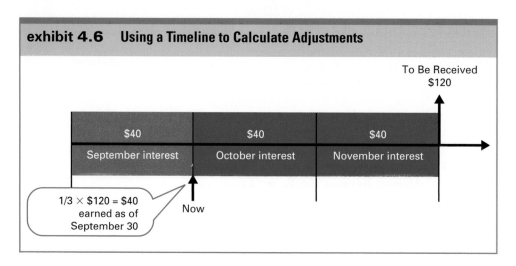

exhibit 4.6   Using a Timeline to Calculate Adjustments

| dr | Interest Expense (+ E, − SE) . . . . | 100 | |
| | cr   Interest Payable (+ L) . . . . | | 100 |

| Assets | = | Liabilities | | + | Shareholders' Equity | |
| | | Interest Payable | + 100 | | Interest Expense (+E) | − 100 |

Wages Expense Incurred but Not Yet Recorded

If you have ever had a part-time job, you know that you don't usually get paid at the end of every day for the hours you worked that day. As such, adjustments for wages are also common.

(h) Assume that First Choice Haircutters pays its employees every second Friday, and the last pay day was Friday, September 23. The salon's employee time sheets for the last days of September show that the haircutters are owed $960 for hours they worked up to and including September 30, which they will receive on Friday, October 7.

Step 1: The unadjusted trial balance in Exhibit 3.10 includes $8,000 for Wages Expense. This includes wages incurred up to the last pay day, which have been paid, so there is no balance for Wages Payable.

Step 2: Because additional wages are incurred in September and are not recorded by month-end, a liability and an expense need to be recorded, increasing the balances from $8,000 and $0 to $8,960 and $960.

Step 3: The adjusting journal entry to record the wages incurred and owed as of September 30 is

---

| dr | Wages Expense (+ E, − SE) . . . . | 960 | |
| | cr   Wages Payable (+ L) . . . . | | 960 |

| Assets | = | Liabilities | | + | Shareholders' Equity | |
| | | Wages Payable | + 960 | | Wages Expense (+E) | − 960 |

Accrual adjustments also may be required for items such as utilities and property taxes that are incurred and owed during the current period (but not yet recorded). The adjusting journal entry required for each of these items would be identical to the ones shown in *(g)* and *(h),* except that the words "interest" and "wages" would be replaced with the particular type of cost incurred, and the appropriate amounts would be used. For purposes of your First Choice Haircutters Salon example, we'll assume that the only remaining expense to record is the accrual of income taxes that are incurred this month but won't be paid until a later accounting period.

Income Taxes Expense Incurred but Not Yet Recorded

Just like you, a corporation is responsible for income tax when it generates income in the current period. It is calculated by multiplying (1) the company's (adjusted) income before income taxes by (2) the company's tax rate. Let's calculate the first part (adjusted income before income taxes) by starting with the unadjusted revenue and expense numbers for your First Choice Haircutters Salon, which were included in the unadjusted trial balance (in Exhibit 3.10). Then we'll update these numbers for the adjustments made in this chapter.

COACH'S TIP

Always calculate income tax expense after adjusting all other revenue and expense accounts. This way, you'll have the adjusted *Income before income taxes* number available for calculating the amount of income taxes.

	Revenues (and Gains)	Expenses (and Losses)	
Unadjusted totals	$15,600	$ 9,100	← From Exhibit 3.10
Adjustments:			
(a)		230	
(b)		2,400	
(c)		200	
(d)		1,000	
(e)	75		
(f)	40		
(g)		100	
(h)		960	
Adjusted totals	$15,715	− $13,990	=$1,725 ← Adjusted income before income tax

(i) **Your First Choice Haircutters Salon pays income tax at an average rate equal to 40 per cent of the salon's income before taxes. No income tax has been recorded for September.**

Step 1: No amounts have been recorded for income taxes.

Step 2: Because income was earned in September, the matching principle requires that we record an expense in September. Because these taxes haven't been paid yet, a liability also is recorded. The amount of tax is $690, which is calculated as $1,725 (income before income tax) × 40% (tax rate).

Step 3: Nothing has been recorded for income taxes, so the adjusting journal entry needed to record income taxes incurred and owed as of September 30 is

dr	Income Tax Expense (+ E, − SE)......	690	
cr	Income Tax Payable (+ L).........		690

Assets	=	Liabilities	+	Shareholders' Equity
		Income Tax Payable + 690		Income Tax Expense (+E) − 690

Dividends Declared

Now that your First Choice Haircutters Salon has generated a profit, it's time shareholders got a return for having invested in the business. This comes in the form of a dividend that will be paid to shareholders in cash. This decision to pay a dividend is made by a board of directors, which is a group of people who represent and act on behalf of the shareholders. The declaration of a dividend isn't taken lightly. According to law, an obligation is created the moment a dividend is declared.

(j) **Your First Choice Haircutters Salon declared a dividend on September 30. The dividend (totalling $500) will be paid in cash to shareholders in early October.**

Step 1: No amounts have been recorded for the dividend declared on September 30.

Step 2: An adjustment is needed to record a liability for the legal obligation to pay the dividend. The adjustment also must record the dividend as a reduction in shareholders' equity. Because it is declared only after the company generates profits and it is declared on behalf of the shareholders, **a dividend is *not* considered an expense of the business,** so it is recorded in its own special account (which is not included in the income statement but instead appears on the statement of retained earnings).

Step 3: The adjusting journal entry needed to record the dividend declared on September 30 is

dr	Dividends Declared (+ D, − SE)........	500	
	cr Dividends Payable (+ L)...........		500

Assets	=	Liabilities	+	Shareholders' Equity
		Dividends Payable　+ 500		Dividends Declared (+D)　− 500

Final Notes

There are two last things to understand before leaving this section. One, notice that none of the adjusting journal entries affected the *Cash* account. **Adjusting journal entries never involve cash.** The regular recording part of the accounting process picks up cash transactions. So, as you are doing the problems assigned for this chapter, if you think that one side of an adjusting journal entry should be to the cash account, think again!

Two, in our examples, the First Choice Haircutters Salon made its adjusting journal entries at the end of the month. Some companies only prepare adjusting entries at the end of the quarter or at the end of the year. The frequency depends on how often the company prepares financial statements, since statements prepared for outside use must be complete and accurate. As an example, let's look at First Choice Haircutters $100 accrual for interest expense made on September 30. A similar adjustment would also be made at the end of October, November, and December if First Choice Haircutters prepares monthly statements. But, if First Choice Haircutters prepares only December 31 year-end statements, rather than month-end statements, all of its adjusting journal entries would be made on December 31, and the entry for accrued interest expense on its note payable would be for $400 (four months interest from the time First Choice Haircutters borrowed the money on August 31 to its year-end on December 31), when the books need to be brought up to date. As you are working on the problems assigned for this chapter, make sure you understand the timeline in the problem.

EVALUATE _____

The Quality of Adjusted Financial Statements

ADJUSTMENTS FOR GOOD, NOT EVIL

There are lots of reasons why managers care about accounting numbers and lots of research that shows how management behaviour and accounting numbers are linked. Managers may be motivated to manipulate the numbers, for example, if they get a bonus based on net income or if shareholders have made it clear the manager's job is on the line if profits and share prices don't meet certain targets.

You may have read articles or heard stories about how managers have encouraged their accountants to use adjusting journal entries to understate expenses or overstate revenues. There's something about this topic that fascinates people, so it's always in the news. The problem with all this hype is that it gives the impression that *all* managers and accountants report assets and revenues that don't exist, or they fail to report liabilities and expenses that do exist. And, while you hear lots about the damage done by a few high-profile cases of fraud each year, you don't hear about all the other instances where deferral and accrual adjustments have helped financial statement users to judge better how well a company is performing.

The reason for adjustments is to make the information more complete and accurate and therefore useful. But, because adjustments involve making judgments, there is always the possibility that people will make poor judgments, or even be deliberately dishonest. So are adjustments good or evil? Many accounting research studies have looked into the question of whether accrual and deferral adjustments make financial statements more or less informative. They've found that, while some managers may have used adjustments to mislead, overall, adjustments significantly improve the quality of financial statements. By ensuring that revenues are recognized when they are earned and expenses are recorded when incurred to generate those revenues, these adjustments help financial statement users to better evaluate past decisions and predict future financial results.[1]

POINT OF INTEREST

If a company bases its adjustments on honest but optimistic estimates that lead to a higher net income, most people will refer to the company as "aggressive" and its earnings as "lower quality."

RECONSIDER _____
The Accounting Process

You're now through the hardest part of the accounting process. Exhibit 4.7 shows the complete process from start to finish. The steps in purple are in the recording phase and are done on an ongoing basis during the accounting period. The blue boxes show the

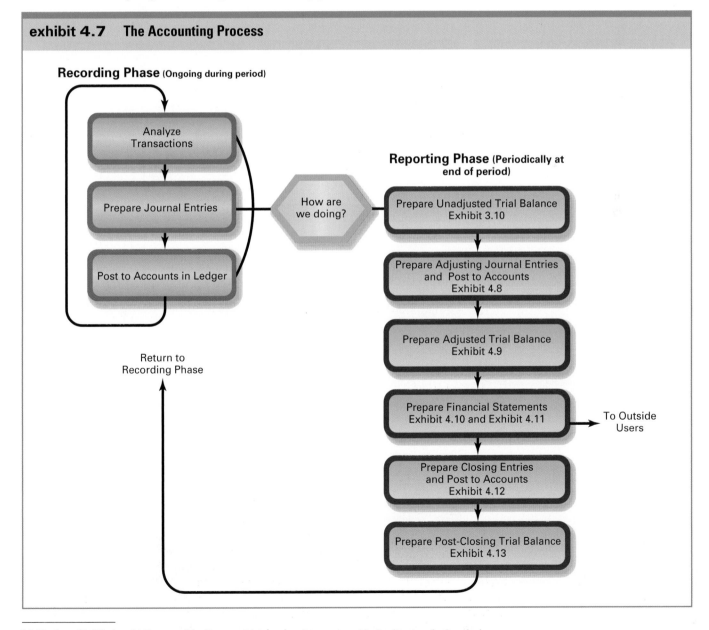

exhibit 4.7   The Accounting Process

Recording Phase (Ongoing during period)

- Analyze Transactions
- Prepare Journal Entries
- Post to Accounts in Ledger

How are we doing?

Reporting Phase (Periodically at end of period)

- Prepare Unadjusted Trial Balance Exhibit 3.10
- Prepare Adjusting Journal Entries and Post to Accounts Exhibit 4.8
- Prepare Adjusted Trial Balance Exhibit 4.9
- Prepare Financial Statements Exhibit 4.10 and Exhibit 4.11 → To Outside Users
- Prepare Closing Entries and Post to Accounts Exhibit 4.12
- Prepare Post-Closing Trial Balance Exhibit 4.13

Return to Recording Phase

---

[1] P. Healy and J. Whalen, "A Review of the Earnings Management Literature and Its Implications for Standard Setting," *Accounting Horizons* 13, no. 4 (December 1999).

steps in the reporting phase, steps that are done at the end of each reporting period. At this point in the chapter, we're ready to post our adjusting journal entries to the accounts, so let's get on with it.

To make life easier for you, we've posted all but one of this chapter's adjusting journal entries (AJEs) to the T-accounts (summarized in Exhibit 4.8). Just so you don't forget how it's done, we've left AJE (a) for you to post to Exhibit 4.8. AJE (a) was

dr Supplies Expenses (+ E, – SE)	230	
cr Supplies (– A).		230

After you post this adjusting journal entry to the T-accounts, we'll check to see that the accounts are still in balance, and then we'll prepare the financial statements.

exhibit 4.8   First Choice Haircutters Salon T-Accounts (unadjusted balances come from Exhibit 3.10)

A   =   L   +   SE

dr Cash (A) cr

Unadj. bal.	7,300	

dr Supplies (A) cr

Unadj. bal.	630	
		AJE (a)
Adj. bal.	400	

dr Accounts Receivable (A) cr

Unadj. bal.	200	

dr Interest Receivable (A) cr

Unadj. bal.	0	
AJE (f)	40	
Adj. bal.	40	

dr Prepaid Rent (A) cr

Unadj. bal.	7,200	
		AJE (b) 2,400
Adj. bal.	4,800	

dr Prepaid Insurance (A) cr

Unadj. bal.	2,400	
		AJE (c) 200
Adj. bal.	2,200	

dr Furnishings and Equipment (A) cr

Unadj. bal.	60,000	

dr Accounts Payable (L) cr

	Unadj. bal.	1,030

dr Unearned Revenue (L) cr

	Unadj. bal.	200
AJE (e) 75		
	Adj. bal.	125

dr Interest Payable (L) cr

	Unadj. bal.	0
	AJE (g)	100
	Adj. bal.	100

dr Wages Payable (L) cr

	Unadj. bal.	0
	AJE (h)	960
	Adj. bal.	960

dr Income Taxes Payable (L) cr

	Unadj. bal.	0
	AJE (i)	690
	Adj. bal.	690

dr Dividends Payable (L) cr

	Unadj. bal.	0
	AJE (j)	500
	Adj. bal.	500

dr Contributed Capital (SE) cr

	Unadj. bal.	50,000

dr Dividends Declared (D, SE) cr

Unadj. bal.	0	
AJE (j)	500	
Adj. bal.	500	

dr Haircut Revenue (R, SE) cr

	Unadj. bal.	15,600
	AJE (e)	75
	Adj. bal.	15,675

dr Interest Revenue (R, SE) cr

	Unadj. bal.	0
	AJE (f)	40
	Adj. bal.	40

dr Wages Expense (E, SE) cr

Unadj. bal.	8,000	
AJE (h)	960	
Adj. bal.	8960	

dr Utilities Expense (E, SE) cr

Unadj. bal.	700	

dr Advertising Expense (E, SE) cr

Unadj. bal.	400	

continued

exhibit 4.8   First Choice Haircutters Salon T-Accounts (unadjusted balances come from Exhibit 3.10)

| A | = | L | + | SE |

dr Accumulated Amortization (xA) cr

Unadj. bal.	0
AJE *(d)*	1,000
Adj. bal	1,000

dr Notes Payable (L) cr

| Unadj. bal. | 20,000 |

dr Supplies Expense (E, SE) cr

Unadj. bal.	0
AJE *(a)*	
Adj. bal.	230

dr Rent Expense (E, SE) cr

Unadj. bal.	0
AJE *(b)*	2,400
Adj. bal.	2,400

dr Insurance Expense (E, SE) cr

Unadj. bal.	0
AJE *(c)*	200
Adj. bal.	200

dr Amortization Expense (E, SE) cr

Unadj. bal.	0
AJE *(d)*	1,000
Adj. bal.	1,000

dr Interest Expense (E, SE) cr

Unadj. bal.	0
AJE *(g)*	100
Adj. bal.	100

dr Income Tax Expense (E, SE) cr

Unadj. bal.	0
AJE *(i)*	690
Adj. bal.	690

PREPARING THE ADJUSTED TRIAL BALANCE

Just like the *unadjusted* trial balance in Chapter 2, an **adjusted trial balance** is prepared to check that the accounts are still in balance after the adjustments have been posted. Exhibit 4.9 presents an adjusted trial balance, which involves simply copying and adding up the ending balances from the T-accounts shown in Exhibit 4.9.

    Now that we know the accounts are complete, accurate, and in balance, financial statements can be prepared. Typically, the income statement is prepared first because the net income number from it flows into the statement of retained earnings, and then the retained earnings number from the statement of retained earnings flows into the balance sheet. As you will see in later chapters of this book, the statement of cash flows and notes to the financial statements are prepared last because they include information

An **adjusted trial balance** is a list of all accounts and their balances to check on the equality of recorded debits and credits after adjustments have been made.

exhibit 4.9 Sample Adjusted Trial Balance

FIRST CHOICE HAIRCUTTERS SALON
Adjusted Trial Balance
As of September 30

Account Name	Debits	Credits
Cash	$ 7,300	
Supplies	400	
Accounts Receivable	200	
Interest Receivable	40	
Prepaid Rent	4,800	
Prepaid Insurance	2,200	
Furnishings and Equipment	60,000	
Accumulated Amortization		$ 1,000
Accounts Payable		1,030
Unearned Revenue		125
Interest Payable		100
Wages Payable		960
Income Taxes Payable		690
Dividends Payable		500
Notes Payable		20,000
Contributed Capital		50,000
Retained Earnings		0
Dividends Declared	500	
Haircut Revenue		15,675
Interest Revenue		40
Wages Expense	8,960	
Utilities Expense	700	
Advertising Expense	400	
Supplies Expense	230	
Rent Expense	2,400	
Insurance Expense	200	
Amortization Expense	1,000	
Interest Expense	100	
Income Tax Expense	690	
Totals	$90,120	$90,120

COACH'S TIP

Accounts are combined ("aggregated") to avoid cluttering up the financial statements with too much detail.

obtained from the income statement, statement of retained earnings, and balance sheet (plus other sources).

PREPARING THE INCOME STATEMENT AND STATEMENT OF RETAINED EARNINGS

To prepare the income statement, just copy (from the adjusted trial balance) the names and amounts for any revenues, expenses, gains, and losses, as shown in Exhibit 4.10.[2] Make sure your income statement includes the subtotals discussed in Chapter 3 (and shown in Exhibit 4.10). Also, it's common for companies to combine together similar accounts into a single amount, as we do in Exhibit 4.10 by combining five expense accounts into a single line-item called "General and Administrative Expenses."

Exhibit 4.10 shows that preparation of the statement of retained earnings also involves copying account balances. Notice, however, that the amount coming from the adjusted trial balance is the beginning-of-year balance for *Retained Earnings*. This account balance doesn't yet include revenues, expenses, and dividends declared for the current year, because they've been recorded in their own separate accounts. Eventually we will transfer ("close") those accounts into *Retained Earnings*, but that's only done at the end of the year. For now, the retained earnings account on the adjusted trial balance

---

[2] Thanks to Philip Fink for suggesting this format.

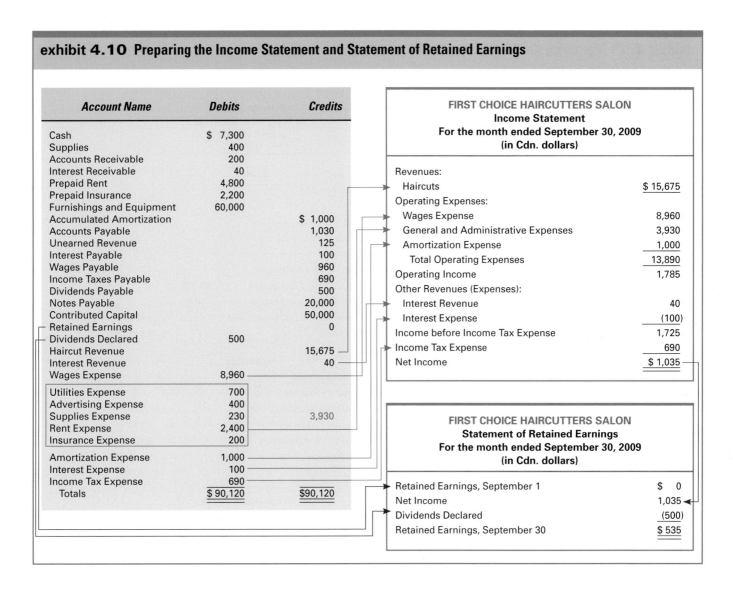

exhibit 4.10 Preparing the Income Statement and Statement of Retained Earnings

Account Name	Debits	Credits
Cash	$ 7,300	
Supplies	400	
Accounts Receivable	200	
Interest Receivable	40	
Prepaid Rent	4,800	
Prepaid Insurance	2,200	
Furnishings and Equipment	60,000	
Accumulated Amortization		$ 1,000
Accounts Payable		1,030
Unearned Revenue		125
Interest Payable		100
Wages Payable		960
Income Taxes Payable		690
Dividends Payable		500
Notes Payable		20,000
Contributed Capital		50,000
Retained Earnings		0
Dividends Declared	500	
Haircut Revenue		15,675
Interest Revenue		40
Wages Expense	8,960	
Utilities Expense	700	
Advertising Expense	400	
Supplies Expense	230	3,930
Rent Expense	2,400	
Insurance Expense	200	
Amortization Expense	1,000	
Interest Expense	100	
Income Tax Expense	690	
Totals	$ 90,120	$90,120

FIRST CHOICE HAIRCUTTERS SALON
Income Statement
For the month ended September 30, 2009
(in Cdn. dollars)

Revenues:	
Haircuts	$ 15,675
Operating Expenses:	
Wages Expense	8,960
General and Administrative Expenses	3,930
Amortization Expense	1,000
Total Operating Expenses	13,890
Operating Income	1,785
Other Revenues (Expenses):	
Interest Revenue	40
Interest Expense	(100)
Income before Income Tax Expense	1,725
Income Tax Expense	690
Net Income	$ 1,035

FIRST CHOICE HAIRCUTTERS SALON
Statement of Retained Earnings
For the month ended September 30, 2009
(in Cdn. dollars)

Retained Earnings, September 1	$ 0
Net Income	1,035
Dividends Declared	(500)
Retained Earnings, September 30	$ 535

provides the opening amount on the statement of retained earnings. You can get the net income number for the statement of retained earnings from the income statement, and the dividends declared number from the adjusted trial balance.

PREPARING THE BALANCE SHEET

To prepare the balance sheet, copy the balance sheet account names and amounts from the adjusted trial balance, combining any similar accounts into a single amount, as shown in Exhibit 4.11. When preparing the balance sheet, watch out for two things. First, remember that *Accumulated Amortization* is subtracted from *Furnishings and Equipment*. Second, get the retained earnings balance from the statement of retained earnings, not from the adjusted trial balance. (The retained earnings account on the adjusted trial balance still contains only this period's opening balance.)

PREPARING THE STATEMENT OF CASH FLOWS AND NOTES TO THE FINANCIAL STATEMENTS

If you didn't look so tired, we'd spend another hour here talking about how the statement of cash flows (SCF) and notes to the financial statements are prepared. But it looks as though you'll be ready for a break soon, so we'll leave the SCF for Chapter 12, and we'll slide information about financial statement notes into each of the remaining chapters.

exhibit 4.11 Preparing the Balance Sheet

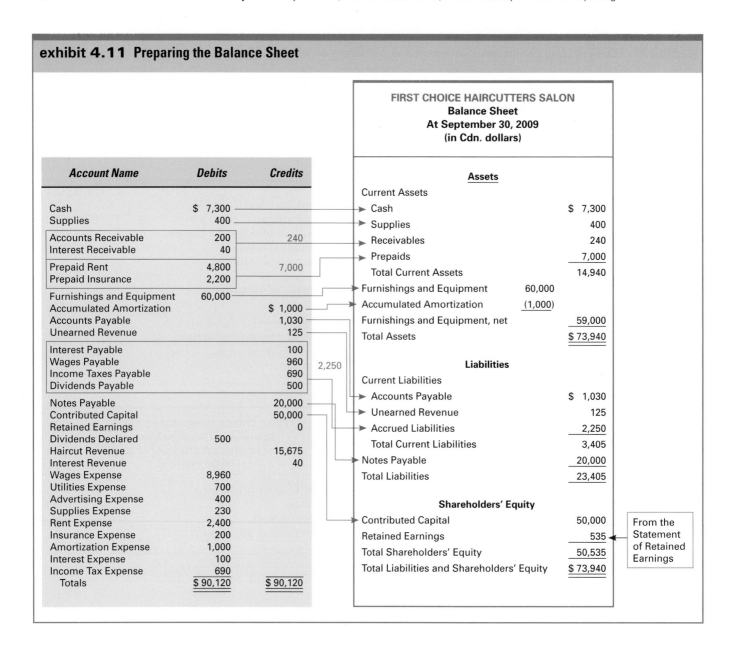

Account Name	Debits	Credits
Cash	$ 7,300	
Supplies	400	
Accounts Receivable	200	240
Interest Receivable	40	
Prepaid Rent	4,800	7,000
Prepaid Insurance	2,200	
Furnishings and Equipment	60,000	
Accumulated Amortization		$ 1,000
Accounts Payable		1,030
Unearned Revenue		125
Interest Payable		100
Wages Payable		960
Income Taxes Payable		690
Dividends Payable		500
Notes Payable		20,000
Contributed Capital		50,000
Retained Earnings		0
Dividends Declared	500	
Haircut Revenue		15,675
Interest Revenue		40
Wages Expense	8,960	
Utilities Expense	700	
Advertising Expense	400	
Supplies Expense	230	
Rent Expense	2,400	
Insurance Expense	200	
Amortization Expense	1,000	
Interest Expense	100	
Income Tax Expense	690	
Totals	$ 90,120	$ 90,120

FIRST CHOICE HAIRCUTTERS SALON
Balance Sheet
At September 30, 2009
(in Cdn. dollars)

Assets

Current Assets		
Cash		$ 7,300
Supplies		400
Receivables		240
Prepaids		7,000
Total Current Assets		14,940
Furnishings and Equipment	60,000	
Accumulated Amortization	(1,000)	
Furnishings and Equipment, net		59,000
Total Assets		$ 73,940

Liabilities

Current Liabilities		
Accounts Payable		$ 1,030
Unearned Revenue		125
Accrued Liabilities		2,250
Total Current Liabilities		3,405
Notes Payable		20,000
Total Liabilities		23,405

Shareholders' Equity

Contributed Capital		50,000
Retained Earnings		535
Total Shareholders' Equity		50,535
Total Liabilities and Shareholders' Equity		$ 73,940

From the Statement of Retained Earnings

2,250

Before we move on, it might be a good idea for you to go back for a moment to Exhibit 1.9 on page 15 to review how the statements we have just prepared fit together. Remember that the balance sheet reports a snapshot of the company at a certain date. The income statement, statement of retained earnings, and statement of cash flows all cover a period of time and explain what happened from the last balance sheet date to the current balance sheet date.

The last two topics that we cover in this chapter relate to cleaning up the accounting records at the end of each year, to get them ready to begin tracking the results in the following year. Take a quick glance at Exhibit 4.7 on page 143 to see where we are in the accounting process.

CLOSING THE INCOME STATEMENT AND DIVIDEND ACCOUNTS

Temporary accounts track financial results for a limited period of time by having their balances zeroed out at the end of each accounting year. All income statement and dividends-declared accounts are temporary accounts.

In Chapter 3, you learned to think of revenue and expense (and gain and loss) accounts as subcategories of *Retained Earnings,* which are used to track earnings-related transactions of the current year. Earlier in this chapter, you saw that a dividends-declared account is similarly used to track dividends declared during the current year. All revenue, expense, gain, loss, and dividends-declared accounts are known as **temporary accounts** because they are used to track only the current year's results. At the end of each year, after all the year's transactions and adjustments are recorded, closing journal entries are recorded to move the balances from the temporary accounts to where they belong—in *Retained Earnings*. The retained earnings account, like all other balance sheet accounts, is a **permanent account** because its ending balance from one year becomes its beginning balance for the following year.

Closing journal entries serve two purposes:

1. *They transfer net income (or loss) and dividends to Retained Earnings:* After the closing journal entries are prepared and posted, the balance in the *Retained Earnings* account will agree with the statement of retained earnings and the balance sheet.
2. *To establish zero balances in all income statement and dividend accounts:* After the closing journal entries are prepared and posted, the balances in the temporary accounts are reset to zero to start accumulating next year's results.

Closing journal entries follow the usual debits-equal-credits format used for the transaction journal entries (in Chapters 2 and 3) and adjusting journal entries (shown earlier in this chapter). Because they're the last thing done during the year, they're posted immediately to the accounts. (Some computerized systems even prepare and post closing journal entries automatically.) Three closing journal entries are needed:[3]

1. Debit each revenue and each gain account for the balance in the account. The other side of this compound journal entry is a credit to *Retained Earnings* for the total of the revenue and gain accounts. This effectively closes all revenues and gains to *Retained Earnings*.
2. Credit each expense and each loss account for the balance in the account. The other side of this compound journal entry is a debit to *Retained Earnings* for the total of the expense and loss accounts. This effectively closes all expenses and losses to *Retained Earnings*.

    The effect of steps 1 and 2 is that *Retained Earnings* goes up by an amount equal to net income. (If the company has a net loss, these steps will cause *Retained Earnings* to go down.)
3. Credit the dividends-declared account for the amount of its debit balance, and debit *Retained Earnings* for the same amount. This effectively closes the dividends-declared account to *Retained Earnings*.

Exhibit 4.12 shows the closing process for your First Choice Haircutters Salon (if it were to close its books on the last day of September). The top part shows the closing journal entries, and the bottom part shows the accounts after these entries are posted.

POST-CLOSING TRIAL BALANCE

After the closing journal entries are posted, all temporary accounts should have zero balances. These accounts will be ready for recording transactions in the new accounting period. The ending balance in **Retained Earnings** is now up to date (it matches the year-end amount on the statement of retained earnings and balance sheet) and is carried forward as the beginning balance for the next period. As the last step of the accounting process, you should prepare a **post-closing trial balance** (as shown in Exhibit 4.13). In this context, *post* means "after," so a post-closing trial balance is an "after-closing" trial balance that is prepared as a final check that total debits still equal total credits and that all temporary accounts have been closed.

> **Permanent accounts** track financial results from year to year by carrying their ending balances into the next year. All balance sheet accounts are permanent accounts.

> **COACH'S TIP**
>
> Closing journal entries are recorded only at the end of each accounting year. Until that time, the **Retained Earnings** balance in the accounting system will not equal the ending amount reported on the statement of retained earnings.

> **A post-closing trial balance** is prepared as the last step in the accounting cycle to check that debits equal credits and all temporary accounts have been closed.

---

[3]Some companies use a four-step process, by closing (1) revenue and (2) expense accounts to a special summary account, called Income Summary, (3) which then is closed to Retained Earnings, (4) along with dividends declared.

exhibit 4.12 Preparing and Posting the Closing Journal Entries

Preparing the Closing Journal Entries (CJEs)

1. Close revenue accounts to Retained Earnings:

   dr Haircut Revenue (− R) 15,675

   dr Interest Revenue (− R) 40

      cr Retained Earnings (+SE)... **15,715**

2. Close expense accounts to Retained Earnings:

   dr Retained Earnings (− SE).................................... **14,680**

      cr Wages Expense (− E) 8,960

      cr Utilities Expense (− E).. 700

      cr Advertising Expense (− E)............................... 400

      cr Supplies Expense (− E) 230

      cr Rent Expense (− E)... 2,400

      cr Insurance Expense (− E) 200

      cr Amortization Expense (− E)........................... 1,000

      cr Interest Expense (− E) 100

      cr Income Tax Expense (− E)................................ 690

3. Close the dividends declared account to the
   Retained Earnings account:

   dr Retained Earnings (− SE) **500**

      cr Dividends Declared (− D) 500

COACH'S TIP

If you've prepared the first two closing journal entries correctly, the net credit to **Retained Earnings** should equal the year's net income. [$15,715 − $14,680 = $1,035] A net loss for the year, where expenses exceed revenues, would result in a net debit to Retained Earnings. Remember, you are not closing the **Retained Earnings** account. You are closing the temporary accounts **to** the Retained Earnings account.

Posting the Closing Journal Entries (CJEs)

dr Retained Earnings (SE) cr			
CJE (2)	14,680	Adj. Bal.	0
CJE (3)	500	CJE (1)	15,715
		Closed bal.	535

dr Utilities Expense (E, SE) cr			
Adj. Bal.	700		
		CJE (2)	700
Closed bal.	0		

dr Amortization Expense (E, SE) cr			
Adj. Bal.	1,000		
		CJE (2)	1000
Closed bal.	0		

dr Dividends Declared (D, SE) cr			
Adj. Bal.	500		
		CJE (3)	500
Closed bal.	0		

dr Advertising Expense (E, SE) cr			
Adj. Bal.	400		
		CJE (2)	400
Closed bal.	0		

dr Interest Expense (E, SE) cr			
Adj. Bal.	100		
		CJE (2)	100
Closed bal.	0		

dr Haircut Revenue (R, SE) cr			
		Adj. Bal.	15,675
CJE (1)	15,675		
		Closed bal.	0

dr Supplies Expense (E, SE) cr			
Adj. Bal.	230		
		CJE (2)	230
Closed bal.	0		

dr Income Tax Expense (E, SE) cr			
Adj. Bal.	690		
		CJE (2)	690
Closed bal.	0		

dr Interest Revenue (E, SE) cr			
		Adj. Bal.	40
CJE (1)	40		
		Closed bal.	0

dr Rent Expense (E, SE) cr			
Adj. Bal.	2,400		
		CJE (2)	2,400
Closed bal.	0		

dr Wages Expense (E, SE) cr			
Adj. Bal.	8,960		
		CJE (2)	8,960
Closed bal.	0		

dr Insurance Expense (E, SE) cr			
Adj. Bal.	200		
		CJE (2)	200
Closed bal.	0		

exhibit 4.13 Sample Post-Closing Trial Balance

FIRST CHOICE HAIRCUTTERS SALON
Post-Closing Trial Balance
As of September 30

Account Name	Debits	Credits
Cash	$ 7,300	
Supplies	400	
Accounts Receivable	200	
Interest Receivable	40	
Prepaid Rent	4,800	
Prepaid Insurance	2,200	
Furnishings and Equipment	60,000	
Accumulated Amortization		1,000
Accounts Payable		1,030
Unearned Revenue		125
Interest Payable		100
Wages Payable		960
Income Taxes Payable		690
Dividends Payable		500
Notes Payable		20,000
Contributed Capital		50,000
Retained Earnings		535
Dividends Declared	0	
Haircut Revenue		0
Interest Revenue		0
Wages Expense	0	
Utilities Expense	0	
Advertising Expense	0	
Supplies Expense	0	
Rent Expense	0	
Insurance Expense	0	
Amortization Expense	0	
Interest Expense	0	
Income Tax Expense	0	
Totals	$74,940	$74,940

COACH'S TIP

Total debits on the post-closing trial balance don't equal the total assets on the balance sheet because accumulated amortization (a credit balance on the trial balance) is subtracted from assets on the balance sheet.

WHAT'S COMING UP

This chapter discussed the final steps of the internal accounting process. This end to the internal part of the accounting process, however, is just the beginning of the process of communicating accounting information to external financial statement users. In the next chapter, we take a closer look at the process by which financial information is made available to external users. In that chapter, you'll also learn more about what they do when analyzing and interpreting information in the financial statements.

FOR YOUR REVIEW _____

DEMONSTRATION CASE

We take our final look at the accounting activities of Goodbye Grass Corporation by illustrating the activities at the end of the accounting cycle: the adjustment process, financial statement preparation, and the closing process. No adjustments had been made to the accounts yet to reflect all revenues earned and expenses incurred in April. Your starting point will be the following unadjusted trial balance as of April 30, 2009:

GOODBYE GRASS CORPORATION
Unadjusted Trial Balance
As of April 30, 2009

Account Name	Debits	Credits
Cash	$4,470	
Accounts Receivable	1,700	
Interest Receivable	0	
Notes Receivable	1,250	
Prepaid Insurance	300	
Equipment	4,600	
Accumulated Amortization		$ 0
Land	3,750	
Accounts Payable		220
Unearned Revenue		1,600
Wages Payable		0
Income Taxes Payable		0
Notes Payable		4,400
Contributed Capital		9,000
Retained Earnings		0
Mowing Revenue		5,200
Interest Revenue		0
Wages Expense	3,900	
Fuel Expense	410	
Insurance Expense	0	
Amortization Expense	0	
Interest Expense	40	
Income Tax Expense	0	
Totals	$20,420	$20,420

In reviewing the trial balance, three deferred accounts (Prepaid Insurance, Equipment, and Unearned Revenue) may need to be adjusted, and additional accruals may be necessary related to wages, income taxes, and interest earned on Notes Receivable. The following information is determined at the end of the accounting cycle:

Deferral Adjustments

a. One-fourth of the $1,600 cash received from the city at the beginning of April for future mowing service has been earned in April. The $1,600 in Unearned Revenue represents four months of service (April through July).

b. Insurance purchased at the beginning of April for $300 provides coverage for six months (April through September). The insurance coverage for April has now been used.

c. Mowers, edgers, rakes, and hand tools (equipment) have been used in April to generate revenues. The company estimates $300 in amortization each year.

Accrual Adjustments

d. Interest earned and receivable on Goodbye Grass Corporation's outstanding note receivable from the city is $25 for the month of April.

e. Wages have been paid through April 28. Employees worked the last two days of April and will be paid in May. Wages amount to $200 per day.

f. The estimated income tax rate for Goodbye Grass Corporation is 35 per cent.

Required:

1. Using the process outlined in this chapter, determine the adjusting journal entries required at the end of April.

2. Set up T-accounts for each account affected by the adjusting journal entries in 1. Enter the amounts from the unadjusted trial balance as beginning balances, post the adjusting journal entries from 1 into the accounts, and calculate April 30 balances.

3. Prepare an adjusted trial balance to ensure debit and credit balances are equal, remembering to include all accounts in the trial balance (and not just the ones affected by the adjusting journal entries).

4. Prepare an income statement, statement of retained earnings, and balance sheet from the amounts in the adjusted trial balance. Don't worry about combining ("aggregating") similar accounts.

5. Prepare the closing journal entries that would be required if Goodbye Grass Corporation's fiscal year ended April 30, 2009.

    After completing requirements 1 to 5, check your answers with the following solution.

Suggested Solution

1. **Adjusting journal entries required:**

    a. ***Unearned Revenue—Mowing Revenue***

    Step 1: The unadjusted balances are $1,600 for Unearned Revenue and $5,200 for Mowing Revenue.

    Step 2: One-fourth of the $1,600 has been earned in April ($400 = 1/4 × $1,600) bringing total mowing revenues for the month to $5,600 (= $5,200 + $400). Three-fourths of the $1,600 remains unearned at the end of April ($1,200 = 3/4 × $1,600).

    Step 3: The T-accounts below show that, to reach the desired balances, we need an adjustment that decreases Unearned Revenue by $400 and increases Mowing Revenue by $400.

dr Unearned Revenue (L) cr		dr Mowing Revenue (R) cr	
	Unadjusted bal. 1,600		Unadjusted bal. 5,200
Adjustment 400			Adjustment 400
	Desired adj. bal. 1,200		Desired adj. bal. 5,600

The adjusting journal entry needed to accomplish this is

dr Unearned Revenue (−L)	400	
cr Mowing Revenue (+R, +SE)		400

Assets	=	Liabilities	+	Shareholders' Equity
		Unearned Revenue − 400		Mowing Revenue (+R) + 400

b.   *Prepaid Insurance—Insurance Expense*

Step 1: The unadjusted balance for Prepaid Insurance is $300, but the Insurance Expense account has not yet been set up.

Step 2: One-sixth of the $300 has expired in April, resulting in an insurance expense for the month of $50 (= 1/6 × $300). Five of the six months of insurance coverage remain unused at the end of April ($250 = 5/6 × $300).

Step 3: The T-accounts below show that, to reach the desired balances, we need an adjustment that decreases Prepaid Insurance by $50 and increases Insurance Expense by $50.

dr Prepaid Insurance (A) cr				dr Insurance Expense (E) cr		
Unadjusted bal.	300			Unadjusted bal.	0	
		Adjustment	50	Adjustment	50	
Desired adj. bal.	250			Desired adj. bal.	50	

The adjusting journal entry needed to accomplish this is

dr	Insurance Expense (+E, −SE).....................	50	
	cr Prepaid Insurance (−A)........................		50

Assets	=	Liabilities	+	Shareholders' Equity
Prepaid Insurance − 50				Insurance Expense (+E) − 50

c.   *Equipment (Accumulated Amortization)—Amortization Expense*

Step 1: No entries have yet been made for amortization, so the unadjusted balances are $0 for Accumulated Amortization and $0 for Amortization Expense.

Step 2: Yearly amortization of $300 equals just $25 for one month (= $300 × 1/12).

Step 3: To go from the unadjusted balances of $0 to the desired adjusted balances of $25, we increase the expense and contra-account balances as follows.

dr Accumulated Amortization (xA) cr			dr Amortization Expense (E) cr		
	Unadjusted bal.	0	Unadjusted bal.	0	
	Adjustment	25	Adjustment	25	
	Desired adj. bal.	25	Desired adj. bal.	25	

The adjusting journal entry needed to accomplish this is

dr	Amortization Expense (+E, −SE)...................	25	
	cr Accumulated Amortization (+xA, −A)..........		25

Assets	=	Liabilities	+	Shareholders' Equity
Accumulated Amortization (+xA) − 25				Accumulated Expense (+E) − 25

d.   *Interest Receivable—Interest Revenue*

Step 1: The unadjusted balances are $0 for Interest Receivable and $0 for Interest Revenue.

Step 2: Interest earned and receivable was $25 for the month of April.

Step 3: The following adjusting journal entry is needed to increase Interest Receivable and Interest Revenue from $0 to $25:

dr	Interest Receivable (+A)..........................	25	
	cr Interest Revenue (+R, +SE)....................		25

Assets	=	Liabilities	+	Shareholders' Equity
Interest Receivable + 25				Interest Revenue (+R) + 25

e. *Wages Payable—Wages Expense*

Step 1: The unadjusted balances are $0 for Wages Payable and $3,900 for Wages Expense.

Step 2: Because the final two days of work done in April are unpaid, we need to record a liability for $400 (= 2 × $200). Total wages expense for the month should include the $3,900 paid for work from April 1 to 28 plus the $400 not yet paid for work on April 29 and 30.

Step 3: The T-accounts below show that to reach the desired balances, we need an adjustment increasing Wages Payable by $400 and Wages Expense by $400.

dr Wages Payable (L) cr		dr Wages Expense (E) cr	
Unadjusted bal.	0	Unadjusted bal. 3,900	
Adjustment	**400**	**Adjustment** 400	
Desired adj. bal.	400	Desired adj. bal. 4,300	

The adjusting journal entry needed to accomplish this is

dr Wages Expenses (+E, −SE).	400	
cr Wages Payable (+L).		400

Assets	=	Liabilities	+	Shareholders' Equity
		Wages Payable + 400		Wages Expense (+E) − 400

f. *Income Taxes Payable—Income Tax Expense*

Step 1: The unadjusted balances are $0 for Income Taxes Payable and $0 for Income Tax Expense.

Step 2: Information given for Goodbye Grass Corporation indicates that income taxes are calculated as 35 per cent of adjusted income before tax for the month, which is calculated as follows:

	Revenues and Gains	Expenses and Losses	
Unadjusted totals	$5,200	$4,350	←— From unadjusted trial balance
Adjustments: **(a)**	400		
(b)		50	
(c)		25	
(d)	25		
(e)		400	
Adjusted totals	$5,625	$4,825	

	Revenues and Gains		Expenses and Losses		
Adjusted totals	$5,625	−	$4,825	= $800	Adjusted income before income tax
				× 35%	Tax rate
				$280	Income tax

Step 3: The following adjusting journal entry will increase Income Taxes Payable and Income Tax Expense from $0 to $280.

dr Income Tax Expense (+E, −SE)	280	
cr Income Tax Payable (+L)		280

Assets	=	Liabilities	+	Shareholders' Equity
		Income Tax Payable + 280		Income Tax Expense (+E) − 280

2. T-accounts (for adjusted accounts only):

dr Prepaid Insurance (A) cr			
Bal. fwd.	300		
		50	*(b)*
End. bal.	250		

dr Wages Payable (L) cr			
	0	Bal. fwd.	
	400	*(e)*	
	400	End. bal.	

dr Insurance Expense (E) cr		
Bal. fwd.	0	
(b)	50	
End. bal.	50	

dr Interest Receivable (A) cr			
Bal. fwd.	0		
(d)	25		
End. bal.	25		

dr Income Taxes Payable (L) cr		
	0	Bal. fwd.
	280	*(f)*
	280	End. bal.

dr Amortization Expense (E) cr		
Bal. fwd.	0	
(c)	25	
End. bal.	25	

dr Accumulated Amortization (xA) cr		
	0	Bal. fwd.
	25	*(c)*
	25	End. bal.

dr Mowing Revenue (R) cr		
5,200	Bal. fwd.
400	*(a)*
5,600	End. bal.

dr Wages Expense (E) cr		
Bal. fwd.	3,900	
(e)	400	
End. bal.	4,300	

dr Unearned Revenue (L) cr		
	1,600	Bal. fwd.
(a)	400	
	1,200	End. bal.

dr Interest Revenue (R) cr		
	0	Bal. fwd.
	25	*(d)*
	25	End. bal.

dr Income Tax Expense (E) cr		
Bal. fwd.	0	
(f)	280	
End. bal.	280	

3. Adjusted trial balance:

GOODBYE GRASS CORPORATION
Adjusted Trial Balance
As of April 30, 2009

Account Name	Debits	Credits
Cash	$4,470	
Accounts Receivable	1,700	
Interest Receivable	25	
Notes Receivable	1,250	
Prepaid Insurance	250	
Equipment	4,600	
Accumulated Amortization		$ 25
Land	3,750	
Accounts Payable		220
Unearned Revenue		1,200
Wages Payable		400
Income Taxes Payable		280
Notes Payable		4,400
Contributed Capital		9,000
Retained Earnings		0
Mowing Revenue		5,600
Interest Revenue		25
Wages Expense	4,300	
Fuel Expense	410	

Insurance Expense	50	
Amortization Expense	25	
Interest Expense	40	
Income Tax Expense	280	
Totals	$21,150	$21,150

4. Income statement, statement of retained earnings, and balance sheet:

GOODBYE GRASS CORPORATION
Income Statement
For the Month Ended April 30, 2009

Operating Revenues:	
Mowing Revenue	$5,600
	5,600
Operating Expenses:	
Wages Expense	4,300
Fuel Expense	410
Insurance Expense	50
Amortization Expense	25
	4,785
Operating Income	815
Other Items:	
Interest Revenue	25
Interest Expense	(40)
Income before Income Taxes	800
Income Tax Expense	280
Net Income	**$ 520**

GOODBYE GRASS CORPORATION
Statement of Retained Earnings
For the Month Ended April 30, 2009

Balance, April 1, 2009	$ 0
Net Income	520
Dividends Declared	0
Balance, April 30, 2009	$ 520

GOODBYE GRASS CORPORATION
Balance Sheet
April 30, 2009

Assets		**Liabilities**	
Current Assets:		Current Liabilities:	
Cash	$ 4,470	Accounts Payable	$ 220
Accounts Receivable	1,700	Unearned Revenues	1,200
Interest Receivable	25	Wages Payable	400
Notes Receivable	1,250	Income Tax Payable	280
Prepaid Insurance	250	Notes Payable	4,400
Total Current Assets	7,695	Total Current Liabilities	6,500
Land	3,750		
Equipment	4,600	**Shareholders' Equity**	
Less: Accumulated Amortization	(25)	Contributed Capital	9,000
		Retained Earnings	520
Total Assets	**$16,020**	**Total Liabilities and Shareholders' Equity**	**$ 16,020**

5. **Closing journal entries:**

If Goodbye Grass Corporation had adopted an April 30 year-end, the company would require journal entries to close its revenue and expense accounts into retained earnings. Because the company has not declared a dividend, there is no dividends declared account to close into retained earnings. The closing journal entries needed to close revenues and expenses into retained earnings is

dr	Mowing Revenue (− R)	5,600
dr	Interest Revenue (− R)...........................	25
cr	Retained Earnings (+SE)........................	5,625
dr	Retained Earnings (−SE)	5,105
cr	Wages Expense (− E)...........................	4,300
cr	Fuel Expense (− E)	410
cr	Insurance Expense (− E)........................	50
cr	Amortization Expense (− E).....................	25
cr	Interest Expense (− E)...........................	40
cr	Income Tax Expense (− E)	280

Since the net credit to **Retained Earnings** ($520 = $5,625 − $5,105) is equal to **Net Income** ($520), we have confidence that we have closed all the income statement accounts.

CHAPTER SUMMARY

LO1 **Explain the goals accomplished by recording adjustments. p. 131**

Adjustments are recorded for two primary reasons:

- Make the financial statements **up to date** by updating previously recorded ("deferred") assets and liabilities, along with their corresponding expense and revenue accounts.
- Make the financial statements **complete** by including ("accruing") assets and liabilities not previously recorded, along with their corresponding revenue and expense accounts.

LO2 **Prepare adjustments needed at the end of the period. p. 133**

- The three-step process for preparing adjustments includes:
  1. Identify the unadjusted balances in the pair of balance sheet and income statement accounts to be adjusted.
  2. Calculate the amount of the adjustment needed, using a timeline where appropriate.
  3. Prepare an adjusting journal entry to make the adjustment.
- Adjusting journal entries never affect the Cash account.

LO3 **Explain how adjustments affect information quality. p. 142**

Research shows that, overall, adjustments significantly improve the quality of financial statements, allowing financial statement users to better evaluate past decisions and predict future financial results.

LO4 **Prepare an adjusted trial balance. p. 145**

An adjusted trial balance is a list of all accounts, with their adjusted debit or credit balances indicated in the appropriate column to provide a check on the equality of the debits and credits.

LO5 **Prepare adjusted financial statements. p. 146**

Adjusted account balances are used in preparing the following financial statements:

- Income Statement: Revenues − Expenses = Net Income
- Statement of Retained Earnings: Beginning Retained Earnings + Net Income − Dividends Declared = Ending Retained Earnings
- Balance Sheet: Assets = Liabilities + Shareholders' Equity

The statement of cash flows and notes to the financial statements are important components of adjusted financial statements, but they will be studied in later chapters.

Explain the closing process. p. 148   **LO6**

* Closing journal entries are required to *(a)* transfer net income (or loss) and dividends declared into retained earnings, and *(b)* prepare all temporary accounts (revenues, gains, expenses, losses, dividends) for the following year by establishing zero balances in these accounts.

* Three closing journal entries are needed:

    1. Debit each revenue and gain account and credit retained earnings for the total.

    2. Credit each expense and loss account and debit retained earnings for the total.

    3. Credit the dividends declared account for the amount of its balance, and debit retained earnings for the same amount.

KEY TERMS TO KNOW

Adjusted Trial Balance p. 145

Adjusting Journal Entries p. 133

Adjustments p. 131

Amortization p. 136

Carrying Value (Net Book Value, Book Value) p. 136

Contra-Account p. 137

Deferred p. 132

Deferral Adjustments p. 132

Permanent Accounts p. 149

Post-Closing Trial Balance p. 149

Temporary Accounts p. 148

———— **FOR YOUR PRACTICE**

QUESTIONS

1. Briefly explain the purpose of adjustments. List the two types of adjustments, and give an example of an adjustment affecting revenues and expenses for each type.

2. Explain the effect of adjusting journal entries on cash.

3. Explain the relationships between adjustments and the following Chapter 3 concepts: (a) the time period assumption, (b) the revenue principle, and (c) the matching principle.

4. What is a contra-asset? Give an example of one.

5. What is an adjusted trial balance? What is its purpose?

6. What is the equation for each of the following statements: (*a*) income statement, (*b*) balance sheet, and (*c*) statement of retained earnings?

7. Explain how the financial statements in question 6 relate to each other.

8. What is the purpose of closing journal entries?

9. How do permanent accounts differ from temporary accounts?

10. Why are the income statement accounts closed but the balance sheet accounts are not?

11. Is Dividends Declared considered an asset, liability, or shareholders' equity account? Is it a permanent or temporary account? Does it normally have a debit or a credit balance?

12. What is a post-closing trial balance? Is it a useful part of the accounting cycle? Explain.

MULTIPLE CHOICE

Select the one alternative that best answers the question or completes the sentence.

1. Which of the following accounts would not appear in a closing journal entry?
    a. Interest revenue
    b. Accumulated amortization
    c. Retained earnings
    d. Salary expense

2. Which account is least likely to appear in an adjusting journal entry?
   a. Cash
   b. Interest receivable
   c. Income tax expense
   d. Salaries payable

3. When a concert promotions company collects cash for ticket sales two months in advance of the show date, which of the following accounts is recorded?
   a. Accrued liability
   b. Accounts receivable
   c. Prepaid expense
   d. Unearned revenue

4. On December 31, an adjustment is made to reduce unearned revenue and report (earned) revenue. How many accounts will be included in this adjusting journal entry?
   a. None
   b. One
   c. Two
   d. Three

5. An adjusting journal entry to recognize accrued salaries payable would cause which of the following?
   a. A decrease in assets and shareholders' equity
   b. A decrease in assets and liabilities
   c. An increase in expenses, liabilities, and shareholders' equity
   d. An increase in expenses and liabilities and a decrease in shareholders' equity

6. An adjusted trial balance:
   a. Shows the ending balances in a "debit" and "credit" format before posting the adjusting journal entries.
   b. Is prepared after closing entries have been posted.
   c. Is a tool used by financial analysts to review the performance of publicly traded companies.
   d. Shows the ending balances resulting from the adjusting journal entries in a "debit" and "credit" format.

7. Company A owns a building. Which of the following statements regarding amortization is false from an accounting perspective?
   a. As the value of the building decreases over time, we amortize it.
   b. Amortization is an estimated expense to be recorded each period during the building's life.
   c. As amortization is recorded, shareholders' equity is reduced.
   d. As amortization is recorded, total assets are reduced.

8. Which of the following trial balances are used as a source for preparing the income statement?
   a. Unadjusted trial balance
   b. Pre-adjusted trial balance
   c. Adjusted trial balance
   d. Post-closing trial balance

9. Assume the balance in Prepaid Insurance is $2,500 but it should be $1,500. The adjusting journal entry should include which of the following?
   a. Debit to Prepaid Insurance for $1,000
   b. Credit to Insurance Expense for $1,000
   c. Debit to Insurance Expense for $1,000
   d. Debit to Insurance Expense for $1,500

10. Assume a company receives a bill for $10,000 for advertising done during the current year. If this bill is not yet recorded at the end of the year, what will the adjusting journal entry include?
    a. Debit to Advertising Expense of $10,000
    b. Credit to Advertising Expense of $10,000
    c. Debit to Accrued Liabilities of $10,000
    d. Need more information to determine.

Solutions to Multiple-Choice Questions

1.b 2.a 3.d 4.c 5.d 6.d 7.a 8.c 9.c 10.a

MINI-EXERCISES

M4-1 Preparing an Adjusted Trial Balance

LO4

DeVita Company has the following adjusted accounts and balances at year-end (June 30, 2009):

Accounts payable	$200	Cash	$120	Land	$ 200
Accounts receivable	350	Contributed capital	300	Long-term debt	1,300
Accrued liabilities	150	Cost of goods sold	820	Prepaid expenses	40
Accumulated		Income taxes expense	110	Salaries expense	660
amortization	250	Income taxes payable	30	Sales revenue	2,400
Amortization expense	110	Interest expense	80	Rent expense	400
Buildings and		Interest revenue	50	Retained earnings	120
equipment	1,400	Inventories	610	Unearned revenue	100

Required:

Prepare an adjusted trial balance for DeVita Company at June 30, 2009.

M4-2 Recording Closing Journal Entries

LO6

Refer to the adjusted accounts in M4-1. Prepare closing journal entries on June 30, 2009.

M4-3 Matching Transactions with Type of Adjustment

LO1, LO2

Match each transaction with the type of adjustment that will be required, by entering the appropriate letter in the space provided.

Transaction		Type of Adjustment
____ 1.	Revenue has been collected in advance and will be earned later.	A. Accrual adjustment
____ 2.	Office supplies on hand will be used in the next accounting period.	
____ 3.	Rent has not yet been collected, but is already earned.	B. Deferral adjustment
____ 4.	An expense has been incurred, but not yet paid or recorded.	
____ 5.	An expense has not yet been incurred, but has been paid in advance.	

M4-4 Matching Transactions with Type of Adjustment

LO1, LO2

Match each transaction with the type of adjustment that will be required, by entering the appropriate letter in the space provided.

Transaction		Type of Adjustment
____ 1.	At year-end, wages payable of $3,600 had not been recorded or paid.	A. Accrual adjustment
____ 2.	Supplies for office use were purchased during the year for $500, and $100 of the office supplies remained on hand (unused) at year-end.	B. Deferral adjustment
____ 3.	Interest of $250 on a note receivable was earned at year-end, although collection of the interest is not due until the following year.	
____ 4.	At year-end, service revenue of $2,000 was collected in cash but was only partly earned.	

M4-5 Recording Adjusting Journal Entries (Deferral Accounts)

LO2

For each of the following transactions for SkyZaa Company, give the adjusting journal entry required at the end of the month on December 31, 2009:

a. Collected $900 rent for the period December 1, 2009, to February 28, 2010, which was credited to Unearned Rent Revenue on December 1, 2009.

b.   Paid $2,400 for a two-year insurance premium on December 1, 2009; debited Prepaid Insurance for that amount.

c.   Used a machine purchased on December 1, 2009. The company estimates *annual* amortization of $3,600.

LO2, LO5   **M4-6 Determining Financial Statement Effects of Adjusting Journal Entries (Deferral Accounts)**

For each of the transactions in M4-5, indicate the amounts and direction of effects of the adjusting journal entry on the elements of the balance sheet and income statement. Using the following format, indicate + for increase, − for decrease, and NE for no effect.

	Balance Sheet			Income Statement		
Transaction	Assets	Liabilities	Shareholders' Equity	Revenues	Expenses	Net Income
a						
b						
c						

LO2   **M4-7 Recording Adjusting Journal Entries (Accrual Accounts)**

For each of the following transactions for SkyZaa Company, give the adjusting journal entry required at the end of the month on December 31, 2009:

a.   Received a $220 utility bill for electricity usage in December, to be paid in January 2010.

b.   Owed wages to 10 employees who worked three days at $120 each per day at the end of December. The company will pay employees at the end of the first week of January 2010.

c.   On December 1, 2009, lent money to an executive who agreed to repay the loan in one year along with one full year of interest equal to $360.

LO2, LO5   **M4-8 Determining Financial Statement Effects of Adjusting Journal Entries (Accrual Accounts)**

For each of the transactions in M4-7, indicate the amounts and direction of effects of the adjusting journal entry on the elements of the balance sheet and income statement. Using the following format, indicate + for increase, − for decrease, and NE for no effect.

	Balance Sheet			Income Statement		
Transaction	Assets	Liabilities	Shareholders' Equity	Revenues	Expenses	Net Income
a						
b						
c						

LO5   **M4-9 Reporting an Income Statement**

SkyZaa Company has the following adjusted trial balance at December 31, 2009. No dividends were declared.

	Debit	Credit
Cash	$ 1,500	
Accounts receivable	2,000	
Interest receivable	30	
Prepaid insurance	2,300	
Notes receivable	3,000	
Equipment	12,000	
Accumulated amortization		$ 300
Accounts payable		1,600
Accrued expenses payable		3,820
Income taxes payable		2,900
Unearned rent revenue		600
Contributed capital		2,400
Retained earnings		1,000
Sales revenue		42,000
Interest revenue		30
Rent revenue		300
Wages expense	21,600	
Amortization expense	300	
Utilities expense	220	
Insurance expense	100	
Rent expense	9,000	
Income tax expense	2,900	
Total	$54,950	$ 54,950

Prepare an income statement for 2009. SkyZaa's core operations relate to computer technology services. How much net income did SkyZaa Company generate during 2009?

M4-10 Reporting a Statement of Retained Earnings   LO5
Refer to M4-9. Prepare a statement of retained earnings for 2009.

M4-11 Reporting a Balance Sheet   LO5
Refer to M4-7, M4-9, and M4-10. Prepare a classified balance sheet at December 31, 2009. Are SkyZaa Company's assets financed primarily by debt or equity?

M4-12 Recording Closing Journal Entries   LO6
Refer to the adjusted trial balance in M4-9. Prepare the closing journal entries on December 31, 2009.

M4-13 Preparing and Posting Adjusting Journal Entries   LO2
At December 31, the unadjusted trial balance of H&R Tacks reports Supplies Inventory of $8,400 and Supplies Expense of $0. On December 31, supplies costing $1,300 are on hand. Prepare the adjusting journal entry on December 31. In separate T-accounts for each account, enter the unadjusted balances, post the adjusting journal entry, and report the adjusted balance.

LO2 **M4-14** **Preparing and Posting Adjusting Journal Entries**

At December 31, the unadjusted trial balance of H&R Tacks reports Equipment of $28,000 and zero balances in Accumulated Amortization and Amortization Expense. Amortization for the period is estimated to be $5,400. Prepare the adjusting journal entry on December 31. In separate T-accounts for each account, enter the unadjusted balances, post the adjusting journal entry, and report the adjusted balance.

LO2 **M4-15** **Preparing and Posting Adjusting Journal Entries**

At December 31, the unadjusted trial balance of H&R Tacks reports Prepaid Insurance of $4,800 and Insurance Expense of $0. The insurance was purchased on July 1 and provides coverage for 12 months. No adjusting journal entries were made during the year. Prepare the adjusting journal entry on December 31. In separate T-accounts for each account, enter the unadjusted balances, post the adjusting journal entry, and report the adjusted balance.

LO2 **M4-16** **Preparing and Posting Adjusting Journal Entries**

At December 31, the unadjusted trial balance of H&R Tacks reports Unearned Revenue of $3,000 and Sales and Service Revenues of $31,800. One-half of the unearned revenues have been earned as of December 31. Prepare the adjusting journal entry on December 31. In separate T-accounts for each account, enter the unadjusted balances, post the adjusting journal entry, and report the adjusted balance.

LO2 **M4-17** **Preparing and Posting Adjusting Journal Entries**

At December 31, the unadjusted trial balance of H&R Tacks reports Wages Payable of $0 and Wages Expense of $17,000. Employees have been paid for work done up to December 27, but the $900 they have earned for December 28 to 31 has not yet been paid or recorded. Prepare the adjusting journal entry on December 31. In separate T-accounts for each account, enter the unadjusted balances, post the adjusting journal entry, and report the adjusted balance.

LO2 **M4-18** **Preparing and Posting Adjusting Journal Entries**

At December 31, the unadjusted trial balance of H&R Tacks reports Interest Payable of $0 and Interest Expense of $0. Interest incurred and owed in December totals $200. Prepare the adjusting journal entry on December 31. In separate T-accounts for each account, enter the unadjusted balances, post the adjusting journal entry, and report the adjusted balance.

LO2 **M4-19** **Preparing and Posting Adjusting Journal Entries**

At December 31, the unadjusted trial balance of H&R Tacks reports Dividends Declared of $0 and Dividends Payable of $0. A $500 dividend was declared on December 27, with payment in cash to occur three weeks later, and has not yet been recorded. Prepare the adjusting journal entry on December 31. In separate T-accounts for each account, enter the unadjusted balances, post the adjusting journal entry, and report the adjusted balance.

LO4 **M4-20** **Preparing an Adjusted Trial Balance**

The unadjusted trial balance for H&R Tacks reported the following account balances: Cash $3,000; Accounts Receivable $500; Supplies Inventory $8,400; Prepaid Insurance $4,800; Equipment $28,000; Accounts Payable $1,200; Unearned Revenue $3,000; Notes Payable $5,000; Contributed Capital $15,000; Retained Earnings $5,700; Sales and Service Revenue $31,800; and Wages Expense $17,000. Prepare an adjusted trial balance as of December 31 that includes the adjustments required in M4-13 through M4-19.

LO2, LO4–LO6 **M4-21** **Organizing the Steps in the Accounting Process**

The following eight steps are included in the accounting process. In one column write the numbers 1 through 8. Beside each number, indicate the steps in their proper order: (a) prepare financial statements, (b) analyze transactions, (c) prepare a post-closing trial balance, (d) prepare an adjusted trial balance, (e) prepare journal entries and post to accounts, (f) prepare closing journal entries and post to accounts, (g) prepare adjusting journal entries and post to accounts, and (h) prepare an unadjusted trial balance.

EXERCISES

E4-1 Preparing an Adjusted Trial Balance from Adjusted Account Balances

LO4

Goodison Consultants, Inc., provides marketing research for clients in the retail industry. The company had the following unadjusted balances at September 30, 2010:

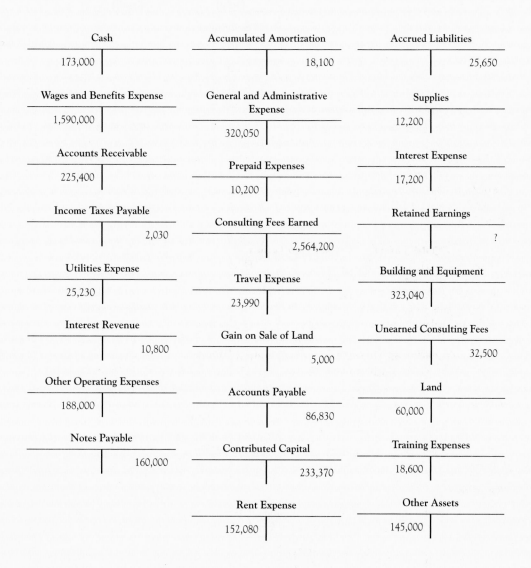

Cash			Accumulated Amortization			Accrued Liabilities	
173,000				18,100			25,650

Wages and Benefits Expense			General and Administrative Expense			Supplies	
1,590,000			320,050			12,200	

Accounts Receivable			Prepaid Expenses			Interest Expense	
225,400			10,200			17,200	

Income Taxes Payable			Consulting Fees Earned			Retained Earnings	
	2,030			2,564,200			?

Utilities Expense			Travel Expense			Building and Equipment	
25,230			23,990			323,040	

Interest Revenue			Gain on Sale of Land			Unearned Consulting Fees	
	10,800			5,000			32,500

Other Operating Expenses			Accounts Payable			Land	
188,000				86,830		60,000	

Notes Payable			Contributed Capital			Training Expenses	
	160,000			233,370		18,600	

			Rent Expense			Other Assets	
			152,080			145,000	

Required:

Prepare an adjusted trial balance for Goodison Consultants, Inc., at September 30, 2010. Solve for the "?" in retained earnings.

E4-2 Identifying Adjustments by Scanning a Trial Balance

LO1

Coach, Inc.—the maker of handbags and other women's and men's accessories—was previously owned by Sara Lee Corporation until April 2001, when Coach was spun off as a separate company. The following adjusted balances were used to prepare Coach's June 30, 2007, year-end financial statements.

COACH INCORPORATED
Adjusted Trial Balance
At June 30, 2007
(thousands of dollars)

	Debit	Credit
Cash	$ 556,956	
Accounts receivable	107,814	
Inventories	291,192	
Prepaid expenses	87,069	
Property and equipment	581,752	
Accumulated amortization		$ 213,291
Other assets	1,038,020	
Accounts payable		109,309
Accrued liabilities		298,452
Income taxes payable		36,448
Notes payable		2,865
Other liabilities		92,084
Contributed capital		982,389
Retained earnings		264,300
Sales revenue		2,612,456
Cost of sales	589,470	
Selling, general, and administrative expenses	1,029,589	
Interest revenue		41,273
Other income		27,136
Income tax expense	398,141	
	$ 4,680,003	$ 4,680,003

Required:

1. Based on the information in the trial balance, list two pairs of balance sheet and income statement accounts that likely required *deferral adjustments* as of June 30 (no computations are necessary).

2. Based on the information in the trial balance, list two pairs of balance sheet and income statement accounts that likely required *accrual adjustments* as of June 30 (no computations are necessary).

LO1, LO2 **E4-3 Recording Adjusting Journal Entries**

Cell Yell Company completed its first year of operations on December 31, 2009. All of the 2009 entries have been recorded, except the following:

a. At year-end, employees had earned wages of $6,000, which will be paid on the next payroll date, January 6, 2010.
b. At year-end, the company had earned interest revenue of $3,000. It will be collected March 1, 2010.

Required:

1. What is the annual reporting period for this company?
2. Identify whether each required adjustment is a deferral or an accrual.
3. Using the format shown in the Demonstration Case, show the accounting equation effects of each required adjustment.
4. Why are these adjustments needed?

E4-4 Recording Adjusting Journal Entries   LO1, LO2

Refer to E4-3.

Required:

Record the required adjusting journal entry for transactions *a* and *b*.

E4-5 Recording Adjusting Journal Entries and Reporting Balances in Financial   LO1, LO2
Statements

Fes Company is making adjusting journal entries for the year ended December 31, 2010. In developing information for the adjusting journal entries, you learned the following:

a. A two-year insurance premium of $7,200 was paid on January 1, 2010, for coverage beginning on that date. As of December 31, 2010, the unadjusted balances were $7,200 for Prepaid Insurance and $0 for Insurance Expense.
b. At December 31, 2010, you obtained the following data relating to shipping supplies.

Unadjusted balance in Shipping Supplies on December 31, 2010	$15,000
Unadjusted balance in Shipping Supplies Expense on December 31, 2010	72,000
Shipping supplies on hand, counted on December 31, 2010	11,000

Required:

1. Of the $7,200 paid for insurance, what amount should be reported on the 2010 income statement as Insurance Expense? What amount should be reported on the December 31, 2010, balance sheet as Prepaid Insurance?
2. What amount should be reported on the 2010 income statement as Shipping Supplies Expense? What amount should be reported on the December 31, 2010, balance sheet as Shipping Supplies?
3. Using the format shown in the demonstration case, indicate the accounting equation effects of the adjustment required for (a) insurance and (b) shipping supplies at December 31, 2010.

E4-6 Recording Adjusting Journal Entries   LO1, LO2

Refer to E4-5.

Required:

Using the process illustrated in the chapter, prepare adjusting journal entries for (a) insurance and (b) shipping supplies at December 31, 2010.

E4-7 Determining Financial Statement Effects of Adjusting Journal Entries   LO2, LO5

Refer to E4-3 and E4-5.

Required:

For each of the transactions in E4-3 and E4-5, indicate the amount and direction of effects of each adjusting journal entry on the elements of the balance sheet and income statement. Using the following format, indicate + for increase, − for decrease, and NE for no effect.

	Balance Sheet			Income Statement		
Transaction	*Assets*	*Liabilities*	*Shareholders' Equity*	*Revenues*	*Expenses*	*Net Income*
E4-3 *a*						
E4-3 *b*						
E4-5 *a*						
E4-5 *b*						

LO1, LO2

E4-8   Recording Seven Typical Adjusting Journal Entries

Bauer's Board Store is completing the accounting process for its first year, ended December 31, 2009. The transactions during 2009 have been journalized and posted, but no adjustments have been made so far. The following data are available to determine adjusting journal entries at year-end:

a.   The unadjusted balance in Office Supplies at December 31, 2009, was $850. A year-end count showed $300 worth of supplies on hand.

b.   Wages earned by employees during December 2009, unpaid and unrecorded at December 31, 2009, amounted to $2,700. The last paycheques were issued December 28; the next payments will be made on January 6, 2010.

c.   A portion of the store's basement is rented for $1,100 per month to N. Myers. On November 1, 2009, the store collected six months' rent in the amount of $6,600, in advance, from Myers. It was credited in full to Unearned Rent Revenue when collected.

d.   The remaining basement space is rented to Kim's Specialty Shop for $520 per month, payable monthly. On December 31, 2009, the rent for November and December 2009 had not been collected or recorded. Collection is expected January 10, 2010.

e.   The store purchased delivery equipment at the beginning of the year. The estimated amortization for 2009 is $3,000, although none has been recorded yet.

f.   On December 31, 2009, the unadjusted balance in Prepaid Insurance was $3,600. This was the amount paid in the middle of the year for a two-year insurance policy with coverage beginning on July 1, 2009. The unadjusted balance in Insurance Expense was $800, which was the cost of insurance from January 1 to June 30, 2009.

g.   Bauer's operates a repair shop, doing some work for Myers. At the end of December 31, 2009, Myers had not paid for work completed amounting to $750. This amount has not yet been recorded as Repair Shop Revenue in Bauer's records. Collection is expected during January 2010.

Required:

1.   For each of the items listed above, identify whether an accrual adjustment, a deferral adjustment, or no adjustment is required.

2.   Using the process illustrated in this chapter, prepare for each situation the adjusting journal entry that should be recorded for Bauer's at December 31, 2009.

LO2, LO5

E4-9   Determining Financial Statement Effects of Seven Typical Adjusting Journal Entries

Refer to E4-8.

Required:

For each of the transactions in E4-8, indicate the amount and direction of effects of the adjusting journal entry on the elements of the balance sheet and income statement. Using the following format, indicate + for increase, − for decrease, and NE for no effect.

	Balance Sheet			Income Statement		
Transaction	**Assets**	**Liabilities**	**Shareholders' Equity**	**Revenues**	**Expenses**	**Net Income**
a						
b						
c						
etc.						

E4-10 Recording Transactions, Including Adjusting and Closing Journal Entries

The following accounts are used by Mouse Potato, Inc., a computer-game maker.

Codes	Accounts	Codes	Accounts
A	Cash	K	Contributed capital
B	Office supplies	L	Retained earnings
C	Accounts receivable	M	Dividends declared
D	Office equipment	N	Service revenue
E	Accumulated amortization	O	Interest revenue
F	Note payable	P	Wage expense
G	Wages payable	Q	Amortization expense
H	Interest payable	R	Interest expense
I	Dividends payable	S	Supplies expense
J	Unearned service revenue	T	None of the above

Required:

For each of the following independent situations, give the journal entry by entering the appropriate code(s) and amount(s). We've done the first one for you as an example.

	Debit		Credit	
Independent Situations	**Code**	**Amount**	**Code**	**Amount**
a. Accrued wages, unrecorded and unpaid at year-end, $400 (example)	P	400	G	400
b. Service revenue collected in advance, $800				
c. Dividends declared during year but not yet paid, $900				
d. Amortization expense for year, $1,000				
e. Service revenue earned but not yet collected at year-end, $600				
f. Balance in office supplies account, $400; supplies on hand at year-end, $150				
g. At year-end, interest on note payable not yet recorded or paid, $220				
h. Balance at year-end in Service Revenue account, $62,000 Give the journal entry to close this one account at year-end.				
i. Balance at year-end in Interest Expense account, $420 Give the journal entry to close this one account at year-end.				

E4-11 Inferring Transactions from Accrual Accounts

Deere & Company was incorporated in 1868 and today is the world's leading producer of agricultural equipment. Oddly enough, the company also provides credit, managed health care plans, and insurance products for businesses and the general public. The following information is taken from a recent annual report (in millions of dollars):

Income Tax Payable		Dividends Payable		Interest Payable	
	Beg. bal. 87		Beg. bal. 53		Beg. bal. 65
84	(a) ?	(b) ?	211	544	(c) ?
	End. bal. 227		End. bal. 53		End. bal. 79

Required:

1. For each accrued liability account, describe the typical transactions that cause it to increase and decrease.

2. Express each T-account in equation format, and then solve for the missing amounts for **(a), (b),** and **(c)** (in millions). For example, the Interest Payable T-account can be expressed as: 65 + ? − 544 = 79. By rearranging the equation, you can solve for ? = 79 + 544 − 65.

LO2, LO5   **E4-12 Analyzing the Effects of Adjusting Journal Entries on the Income Statement and Balance Sheet**

On December 31, 2009, Alan and Company prepared an income statement and balance sheet, but they failed to take into account four adjusting journal entries. The income statement, prepared on this incorrect basis, reported income before income taxes of $30,000. The balance sheet (before the effect of income taxes) reflected total assets, $90,000; total liabilities, $40,000; and shareholders' equity, $50,000. The data for the four adjusting journal entries follow:

a. Amortization of $8,000 for the year, on equipment, was not recorded.
b. Wages amounting to $17,000 for the last three days of December 2009 were not paid and not recorded (the next payroll will be on January 10, 2010).
c. Rent revenue of $4,800 was collected on December 1, 2009, for office space for the three-month period December 1, 2009, to February 28, 2010. The $4,800 was credited in full to Unearned Rent Revenue when collected.
d. Income taxes for the year were not recorded. The income tax rate for the company is 30 per cent.

Required:

Complete the following table to show the effects of the four adjusting journal entries (indicate deductions with parentheses):

Items	Net Income	Total Assets	Total Liabilities	Shareholders' Equity
Amounts reported	$30,000	$90,000	$40,000	$50,000
Effect of amortization	____	____	____	____
Effect of wages	____	____	____	____
Effect of rent revenue	____	____	____	____
Adjusted balances	6,600	82,000	55,400	26,600
Effect of income taxes	____	____	____	____
Correct amounts	____	____	____	____

LO2, LO5   **E4-13 Preparing Adjusting Journal Entries and Indicating Their Effects on the Income Statement and Balance Sheet**

On December 31, 2009, the bookkeeper for Tait Company prepared the income statement and balance sheet summarized on page 171, but neglected to consider three adjusting journal entries.

	As Prepared	Effects of Adjusting Journal Entries	Adjusted Amounts
Income Statement			
Revenues	$98,000	_____	_____
Expenses	(72,000)	_____	_____
Income tax expense	_____	_____	_____
Net income	$26,000		
Balance Sheet			
Assets			
Cash	$20,000	_____	_____
Accounts receivable	22,000	_____	_____
Rent receivable		_____	_____
Equipment	50,000	_____	_____
Accumulated amortization	(10,000)	_____	_____
	$82,000		
Liabilities			
Accounts payable	$10,000	_____	_____
Income taxes payable		_____	_____
Shareholders' Equity			
Contributed capital	40,000	_____	_____
Retained earnings	32,000	_____	_____
	$82,000		

Data on the three adjusting journal entries follow.

a. Amortization of $5,000 on the equipment for 2009 was not recorded.
b. Rent revenue of $2,000, earned during December 2009, was neither collected nor recorded.
c. Income tax expense of $6,900 for 2009 was neither paid nor recorded.

Required:

1. Prepare the three adjusting journal entries that were omitted. Use the account titles shown in the income statement and balance sheet above.
2. Complete the two columns to the right in the above table to show the correct amounts on the income statement and balance sheet.

E4-14 Reporting an Adjusted Income Statement

LO2, LO5

Dyer, Inc., completed its first year of operations on December 31, 2009. Because this is the end of the annual accounting period, the company bookkeeper prepared the following tentative income statement:

Income Statement, 2009		
Rental revenue		$114,000
Expenses:		
Salaries and wages expense	$28,500	
Maintenance expense	12,000	
Rent expense	9,000	
Utilities expense	4,000	
Gas and oil expense	3,000	
Other expenses	1,000	
Total expenses		57,500
Net Income		$ 56,500

You are an independent accountant hired by the company to audit the company's accounting systems and financial statements. In your audit, you developed additional data as follows:

a. Wages for the last three days of December amounting to $310 were not recorded or paid.
b. The $400 telephone bill for December 2009 has not been recorded or paid.
c. Amortization on rental autos, amounting to $23,000 for 2009, was not recorded.
d. Interest of $500 on the note payable by Dyer, Inc., was not recorded.
e. The Unearned Rental Revenue account includes $4,000 revenue to be earned in January 2010.
f. Maintenance expense does not include the cost of maintenance supplies used during 2009, which amounts to $600.
g. The income tax expense for 2009 is $7,000, but it won't actually be paid until 2010.

Required:

1. What adjusting journal entry for each item *a* through *g* should be recorded at December 31, 2009? If none is required, explain why.
2. Prepare an adjusted income statement for 2009.

LO2, LO5   **E4-15   Recording Adjustments and Preparing an Adjusted Trial Balance**

Ninja Sockeye Star prepared the following unadjusted trial balance at the end of its second year of operations, December 31, 2009.

Account Titles	Debit	Credit
Cash	$ 12,000	
Accounts receivable	6,000	
Prepaid rent	2,400	
Machinery	21,000	
Accumulated amortization		$ 1,000
Accounts payable		1,000
Utilities payable		0
Income taxes payable		0
Contributed capital		29,800
Retained earnings		2,100
Sales revenue		45,000
Cost of goods sold expense	25,000	
Utilities expense	12,500	
Rent expense	0	
Amortization expense	0	
Income tax expense	0	
Total	$ 78,900	$ 78,900

Other data not yet recorded at December 31, 2009:

a. Rent incurred during 2009, $1,200
b. Amortization expense for 2009, $1,000
c. Utilities payable, $9,000
d. Income tax expense, $800

Required:

1. Using the format shown in the demonstration case, indicate the accounting equation effects of each required adjustment.

2. Prepare the adjusting journal entries required at December 31, 2009.
3. Summarize the adjusting journal entries in T-accounts. After entering the beginning balances and computing the adjusting ending balances, prepare an adjusted trial balance as of December 31, 2009.

E4-16 Adjusting Unearned Subscriptions

LO2, LO5

You are the regional sales manager for Abruzzo News Company. Abruzzo is making adjusting journal entries for the year ended March 31, 2010. On September 1, 2009, $18,000 cash was received from customers in your region for three-year magazine subscriptions beginning on that date. The magazines are published and mailed to customers every month. These were the only subscription sales in your region during the year.

Required:

1. What amount should be reported on the 2009-2010 income statement for subscriptions revenue?
2. What amount should be reported on the March 31, 2010, balance sheet for unearned subscriptions revenue?
3. Give the adjusting journal entry at March 31, 2010, assuming that the subscriptions received on September 1, 2009, were recorded for the full amount in Unearned Subscriptions Revenue.

E4-17 Recording Four Adjusting Journal Entries and Preparing an Adjusted Trial Balance

LO2, LO4

Seneca Company prepared the following unadjusted trial balance at the end of its second year of operations, ending December 31, 2009. To simplify this exercise, the amounts given are in thousands of dollars.

Account Titles	Debit	Credit
Cash	38	
Accounts receivable	9	
Prepaid insurance	6	
Machinery	80	
Accumulated amortization		
Accounts payable		9
Wages payable		
Income taxes payable		
Contributed capital		76
Retained earnings		4
Sales revenue		80
Cost of goods sold expense	26	
Wages expense	10	
Total	169	169

Other data (in thousands of dollars) not yet recorded at December 31, 2009:
a. Insurance expired during 2009, $5
b. Amortization expense for 2009, $4
c. Wages payable, $7
d. Income tax expense, $9

Required:

1. Prepare the adjusting journal entries for 2009.
2. Using T-accounts, determine the adjusted balances in each account, and prepare an adjusted trial balance as of December 31, 2009.

LO5   **E4-18   Reporting an Income Statement, Statement of Retained Earnings, and Balance Sheet**
Refer to E4-17.

Required:

Using the adjusted balances in E4-17, prepare an income statement, statement of retained earnings, and balance sheet for 2009.

LO6   **E4-19   Recording Closing Entries**
Refer to E4-17.

Required:

Using the adjusted balances in E4-17, give the closing journal entries for 2009. What is the purpose of "closing the books" at the end of the accounting period?

LO6   **E4-20   Making Closing Journal Entries**
Bob's Bowling recorded its first ever net loss in 2009, primarily because of a labour strike, which lasted two months. Below is the income statement for the year (here called a statement of net loss). Bob's Bowling declared a $10,000 dividend in 2009.

BOB'S BOWLING, INC. Statement of Net Loss For the year ended December 31, 2009	
Revenues:	
Bowling revenues	$ 88,000
Interest revenue	2,000
Total revenues	90,000
Expenses:	
Selling, general, and administrative expenses	82,200
Amortization expense	24,000
Total expenses	106,200
Net loss	$ 16,200

Required:

Make the closing journal entry or entries for the year ending December 31, 2009.

COACHED PROBLEMS

LO4, LO6   **CP4-1   Preparing an Adjusted Trial Balance, Closing Journal Entries, and Post-Closing Trial Balance**
Sobeys is a direct competitor of Loblaws. Sobeys runs the largest number of grocery stores in Canada (over 1,300). It operates under the Sobeys, IGA, and Price Chopper banners. The following is a list of accounts and amounts (in millions) reported for the year ended May 6, 2006, just before Sobeys went private. The accounts have normal debit or credit balances, and the dollars are rounded to the nearest million.

Accounts payable	$1,158	Inventories	627
Accounts receivable	208	Long-term debt	465
Accrued liabilities	71	Other assets	892
Accumulated amortization	1,444	Other current assets	22
Amortization expense	197	Other long-term liabilities	209
Cash	332	Prepaid expenses	46
Contributed capital	906	Property, plant, and equipment	3,057
Cost of goods sold	10,203	Retained earnings (opening)	780
Dividends declared	41	Sales revenue	12,853
Other expenses	7	Selling, general, and	
Income tax expense	100	administrative expenses	2,119
Interest expense	35		

Required:

1. Prepare an adjusted trial balance at May 6, 2006. Is the Retained Earnings balance of $780 the amount that would be reported on the balance sheet as of May 6, 2006?
2. Prepare the closing entry(ies) required at May 6, 2006.
3. Prepare a post-closing trial balance at May 6, 2006.
4. Compare Loblaws and Sobeys (see S4-7). Which company has the largest revenues? Assets? Net income?

CP4-2 Recording Adjusting Journal Entries

McCall Company's annual accounting year ends on December 31, and no adjustments are made during the year. It is now December 31, 2009, and all of the 2009 entries have been made except for entries necessary to adjust for the following:

a. On September 1, 2009, McCall collected $4,800 covering six months' rent on storage space. At that date, McCall debited Cash and credited Unearned Rent Revenue for $4,800.
b. The company earned service revenue of $3,000 on a special job that was completed December 29, 2009. Collection will be made during January 2010. No entry has been recorded.
c. On November 1, 2009, McCall paid a one-year premium for property insurance, $4,200, for coverage starting on that date. Cash was credited and Prepaid Insurance was debited for this amount.
d. At December 31, 2009, wages earned by employees totalled $1,100. The employees will be paid on the next payroll date, January 15, 2010.
e. Amortization of $1,000, on a service truck purchased this year, must be recognized.
f. On December 27, 2009, the company received a tax bill of $400, from the city, for 2009 property taxes on land. The tax bill is payable during January 2010.
g. The company owes three months interest ($400) on a bank loan taken out on October 1, 2009. The interest will be paid when the loan is repaid on September 30, 2010.
h. The income before any of the adjustments or income taxes was $27,400. The company's income tax rate is 30 per cent. Compute adjusted income based on a through g to determine and record income tax expense.

Required:

1. Indicate whether each transaction relates to a deferral or an accrual.
2. Give the adjusting journal entry required for each item in a to h at December 31, 2009.

LO1, LO2

COACH'S TIP

a. $4,800 for six months equals $800 per month. This means $3,200 is earned during the four months from September 1 to December 31, and $1,600 remains unearned at December 31.
c. $4,200 for 12 months equals $350 per month.
h. Adjusted income based on **a** through **g** is $30,000.

COACH'S TIP

Remember that A = L + SE; Revenues − Expenses = Net Income; and Net Income accounts are closed to Retained Earnings, a part of Shareholders' Equity.

LO2, LO5

CP4-3 Determining Financial Statement Effects of Adjusting Journal Entries
Refer to CP4-2.

Required:

Using the following headings, indicate the effect of each adjusting journal entry and the amount of the effect. Use + for increase, − for decrease, and NE for no effect.

	Balance Sheet			Income Statement		
Transaction	Assets	Liabilities	Shareholders' Equity	Revenues	Expenses	Net Income
a						
b						
c						
etc.						

LO2, LO5

CP4-4 Analyzing a Student's Business, and Preparing an Adjusted Income Statement

During the summer between her third and fourth years at university, Susan Irwin needed to earn enough money for the coming academic year. Unable to obtain a job with a reasonable salary, she decided to try the lawn care business for three months. After a survey of the market potential, Susan bought a used pickup truck on June 1 for $1,500. On each door she painted "Susan's Lawn Service, Phone 555-4487." She also spent $900 for mowers, trimmers, and tools. To acquire these items, she borrowed $2,500 cash by signing a note payable, promising to pay the $2,500 plus interest of $75 at the end of the three months (ending August 31).

At the end of the summer, Susan realized that she had done a lot of work, and her bank account looked good. This fact made her think about how much profit the business had earned.

A review of the cheque stubs showed the following: Bank deposits of collections from customers totalled $12,600. The following cheques had been written: gas, oil, and lubrication, $920; pickup repairs, $210; mower repair, $75; miscellaneous supplies used, $80; helpers, $4,500; payroll taxes, $175; payment for assistance in preparing payroll tax forms, $25; insurance, $125; telephone, $110; and $2,575 to pay off the note, including interest (on August 31). A notebook kept in the pickup, plus some unpaid bills, reflected that customers still owed her $800 for lawn services provided, and that she owed $200 for gas and oil (credit card charges). She estimated that the amortization on the truck and the other equipment amounted to $500 for three months.

COACH'S TIP

Remember that, when using accrual basis accounting, revenues will include amounts received in cash as well as amounts charged on credit.

Notice that, while interest on the note payable is an expense, the repayment of the note's original amount is not (it is a reduction in a liability).

Required:

1. Prepare an accrual basis income statement for Susan's Lawn Service covering the quarter from June 1 to August 31. Assume that the business is not subject to income tax.
2. Assuming Susan's Lawn Service remains in business, do you see a need for one or more additional financial reports for this company for this summer and thereafter? Explain.

LO1, LO2, LO4–LO6

CP4-5 Comprehensive Review Problem: From Recording Transactions (including Adjusting Journal Entries) to Preparing Financial Statements and Closing Journal Entries (Chapters 2, 3, and 4)

Brothers Harry and Herman Hausyerday began operations of their machine shop (H & H Tool, Inc.) on January 1, 2007. The annual reporting period ends December 31. The trial balance on January 1, 2009, follows (the amounts are rounded to thousands of dollars to simplify):

Account Titles	Debit	Credit
Cash	3	
Accounts receivable	5	
Supplies	12	
Land		
Equipment	60	
Accumulated amortization (on equipment)		6
Other assets	4	
Accounts payable		5
Notes payable		
Wages payable		
Interest payable		
Income taxes payable		
Dividends payable		
Contributed capital		65
Retained earnings		8
Dividends declared		
Service revenue		
Amortization expense		
Income tax expense		
Interest expense		
Supplies and other operating expenses		
Totals	84	84

COACH'S TIP

e. When credit is used for operating costs, Accounts Payable, typically, is used rather than Accrued Liabilities. The account Accrued Liabilities typically is used only for accrual adjustments made at the end of the period.

k. When a dividend is declared, the company establishes a liability and records the dividend itself in a temporary account.

l. Payment of the dividend in cash reduces the dividend liability.

m. What was the unadjusted balance in the supplies account at the end of the year?

Transactions during 2009 (summarized in thousands of dollars) follow:

a. Borrowed $10 cash on a short-term note payable dated March 1, 2009.
b. Purchased land for future building site; paid cash, $9.
c. Earned revenues for 2009, $160, including $40 on credit and $120 collected in cash.
d. Issued additional shares for $3.
e. Recognized operating expenses for 2009, $85, including $15 on credit and $70 paid in cash.
f. Collected accounts receivable, $24.
g. Purchased other assets, $10 cash.
h. Paid accounts payable, $13.
i. Purchased supplies on account for future use, $18.
j. Signed a $25 service contract to start February 1, 2010.
k. Declared a dividend, $17.
l. Paid the $17 dividend in cash.

Data for adjusting journal entries:

m. Supplies counted on December 31, 2009, $14
n. Amortization for the year on the equipment, $6
o. Accrued interest on notes payable of $1
p. Wages earned since the December 24 payroll not yet paid, $12
q. Income tax for the year was $8. It will be paid in 2010.

Required:

1. Set up T-accounts for the accounts on the trial balance and enter beginning balances.
2. Record journal entries for transactions *a* through *l* and post them to the T-accounts.
3. Prepare an unadjusted trial balance.
4. Record and post the adjusting journal entries *m* through *q*.
5. Prepare an adjusted trial balance.

6. Prepare an income statement, statement of retained earnings, and balance sheet.

7. Prepare and post the closing journal entries.

8. Prepare a post-closing trial balance.

9. How much net income did H & H Tool, Inc., generate during 2009? Is the company financed primarily by debt or equity?

GROUP A PROBLEMS

LO4, LO6

PA4-1 Preparing a Trial Balance, Closing Journal Entry, and Post-Closing Trial Balance

Starbucks Corporation purchases and roasts high-quality whole-bean coffees and sells them along with fresh-brewed coffees, its exclusive line of Frappucino® blended beverages, Italian-style espresso beverages, and premium teas, all in a variety of pompously named sizes. In addition to sales through its company-operated retail stores, Starbucks also sells coffee and tea products through other channels of distribution. The following is a simplified list of accounts, and amounts reported in recent financial statements. The accounts have normal debit or credit balances and the dollars are rounded to the nearest million. Assume the year ended on September 30, 2009.

Accounts payable	$ 56	Interest revenue	$ 9
Accounts receivable	48	Inventories	181
Accrued liabilities	131	Long-term debt	40
Accumulated amortization	321	Other current assets	72
Amortization expense	98	Other long-term assets	106
Cash	66	Other operating expenses	51
Contributed capital	647	Prepaid expenses	19
Cost of goods sold	741	Property, plant, and equipment	1,081
General and administrative		Retained earnings	212
expenses	90	Service revenues	1,680
Income tax expense	62	Short-term bank debt	64
Interest expense	1	Store operating expenses	544

Required:

1. Prepare an adjusted trial balance at September 30, 2009. Is the Retained Earnings balance of $212 the amount that would be reported on the balance sheet as of September 30, 2009?

2. Prepare the closing entries required at September 30, 2009.

3. Prepare a post-closing trial balance at September 30, 2009.

LO1, LO2

PA4-2 Recording Adjusting Journal Entries

Big Towing Company is at the end of its accounting year, December 31, 2009. The following data that must be considered were developed from the company's records and related documents:

a. On July 1, 2009, a three-year insurance premium on equipment in the amount of $1,200 was paid and debited in full to Prepaid Insurance on that date. Coverage began on July 1.

b. At the end of 2009, the unadjusted balance in the office supplies account was $1,000. A physical count of supplies on December 31, 2009, indicated supplies costing $300 were still on hand.

c. On December 31, 2009, YY's Garage completed repairs on one of the company's trucks at a cost of $800. The amount is not yet recorded. It will be paid during January 2010.

d. In December, the 2009 property tax bill for $1,600 was received from the city. The taxes, which have not been recorded, will be paid on February 15, 2010.

e. On December 31, 2009, the company completed work for a company and billed them $8,000, payable by the customer within 30 days. No cash has been collected, and no journal entry has been made for this transaction.

f. On July 1, 2009, the company purchased a new hauling van. Amortization for July to December 2009, estimated to total $2,750, has not been recorded.

g. The company owes three months interest of $500 on a bank loan taken out on October 1, 2009. The interest will be paid when the loan is repaid on September 30, 2010.

h. The income before any of the adjustments or income taxes was $30,000. The company's federal income tax rate is 30 per cent. Compute adjusted income based on all of the preceding information, and then determine and record income tax expense.

Required:

1. Indicate whether each transaction relates to a deferral or an accrual.
2. Give the adjusting journal entry required for each transaction at December 31, 2009. No adjustments have been made during the year.

PA4-3 Determining Financial Statement Effects of Adjusting Journal Entries   LO2, LO5
Refer to PA4-2.

	Balance Sheet			Income Statement		
Transaction	Assets	Liabilities	Shareholders' Equity	Revenues	Expenses	Net Income
a						
b						
c						
etc.						

Required:

Using a table like the one above, indicate the effect of each adjusting journal entry and the amount of each. Use + for increase, − for decrease, and NE for no effect.

PA4-4 Analyzing a Business and Preparing an Adjusted Income Statement   LO2, LO5

Upon graduation from high school, John Abel immediately accepted a job as an electrician's apprentice for a large local electrical repair company. After many years of hard work, and having finally fulfilled all the requirements, John received an electrician's licence and decided to start his own business. He had saved $12,000, which he invested in the business. First, he transferred this amount from his savings account to a business bank account for Abel Electric Repair Company, Incorporated. His lawyer had advised him to start as a corporation. He then purchased a used panel truck for $9,000 cash and second-hand tools for $1,500; rented space in a small building; inserted an ad in the local paper; and opened the doors on October 1, 2009. Immediately, John was very busy; after one month, he employed an assistant.

Although John knew practically nothing about the financial side of the business, he realized that a number of reports were required and that costs and collections had to be controlled carefully. At the end of the year, prompted in part by concern about his income tax situation (previously he had to report only salary), John recognized the need for financial statements. On December 31, 2009, John's wife, Jane, gathered the following data for the three months just ended. Bank account deposits of collections for electrical repair services totalled $32,000. The following cheques had been written: electrician's assistant, $8,500; payroll taxes, $175; supplies purchased and used on jobs, $9,500; oil, gas, and maintenance on truck, $1,200; insurance, $700; rent, $500; utilities and telephone, $825; and miscellaneous expenses (including advertising), $600. Also, uncollected bills to customers for electrical repair services amounted to $3,000. The $200 rent for December had not been paid. John estimated that the amortization on the truck and tools during the three months was $1,200. Income taxes for the three-month period were $3,480.

Required:

1. John knows that you're good with numbers, so he has asked you to prepare a quarterly income statement for Abel Electric Repair for the three months October through December 31, 2009. Do it.

2. Do you think that John may have a need for one or more additional financial reports for 2009 and thereafter? Explain.

LO1, LO2, LO4–LO6

PA4-5 Comprehensive Review Problem: From Recording Transactions (including Adjusting Journal Entries) to Preparing Financial Statements and Closing Journal Entries (Chapters 2, 3, and 4)

Drs. Glenn Feltham and Gary Entwistle began operations of their physical therapy clinic called Northland Physical Therapy on January 1, 2008. The annual reporting period ends December 31. The trial balance on January 1, 2009, was as follows (the amounts are rounded to thousands of dollars to simplify):

Account Titles	Debit	Credit
Cash	7	
Accounts receivable	3	
Supplies	3	
Equipment	6	
Accumulated amortization (on equipment)		1
Other assets	6	
Accounts payable		5
Notes payable		
Wages payable		
Interest payable		
Income taxes payable		
Unearned revenue		
Dividends payable		
Contributed capital		15
Retained earnings		4
Dividends declared		
Service revenue		
Amortization expense		
Income tax expense		
Interest expense		
Supplies and other operating expenses		
Totals	25	25

Transactions during 2009 (summarized in thousands of dollars) follow:

a. Borrowed $22 cash on July 1, 2009, signing a short-term note payable.
b. Purchased equipment for $20 cash on July 1, 2009.
c. Issued additional shares for $5.
d. Earned revenues for 2009, $55, including $8 on credit and $47 received in cash.
e. Recognized operating expenses for 2009, $30, including $5 on credit and $25 in cash.
f. Purchased other assets, $3 cash.
g. Collected accounts receivable, $9.
h. Paid accounts payable, $7.
i. Purchased, on account, supplies for future use, $8.
j. Received a $3 deposit from a hospital for a contract to start January 5, 2010.
k. Declared a dividend, $4.
l. Paid the $4 dividend in cash.

Data for adjusting journal entries:

m. Supplies of $4 were counted on December 31, 2009.
n. Amortization for 2009, $5.
o. Accrued interest on notes payable of $1.
p. Wages earned since the December 27 payroll not yet paid, $2.
q. Income tax for 2009 was $4, and will be paid in 2010.

Required:

1. Set up T-accounts for the accounts on the trial balance and enter beginning balances.
2. Record journal entries for transactions *a* through *l* and post them to the T-accounts.
3. Prepare an unadjusted trial balance.
4. Record and post the adjusting journal entries *m* through *q.*
5. Prepare an adjusted trial balance.
6. Prepare an income statement, statement of retained earnings, and balance sheet.
7. Prepare and post the closing journal entries.
8. Prepare a post-closing trial balance.
9. How much net income did the physical therapy clinic generate during 2009? Is the business financed primarily by debt or equity?

GROUP B PROBLEMS

PB4-1 Preparing a Trial Balance, Closing Journal Entry, and Post-Closing Trial Balance

LO4, LO6

Reitmans is a well-known retailer of women's wear in Canada, operating under the banners of Reitmans, Addition-Elle, Smart Set, Penningtons, RW & Co, and Thyme Maternity. Herman and Sarah Reitman opened the first Reitmans, a general store in Montreal, in 1926. The following is a simplified list of accounts and amounts reported in the company's financial statements for the year ended February 3, 2007 (in thousands).

Accounts payable and		Income taxes payable	$ 40,289
Accrued liabilities	$ 85,317	Interest expense	1,056
Accounts receivable	3,439	Inventories	61,834
Accumulated amortization	143,426	Investment income	12,556
Amortization expense	44,946	Long-term liabilities	37,362
Cash	188,491	Net sales	1,042,509
Contributed capital	24,906	Other long-term assets	98,508
Cost of goods sold and		Prepaid expenses	21,405
Selling, general, and		Property, plant, and equipment	370,160
administrative expenses	855,697	Retained earnings (opening)	328,744
Income tax expense	70,897	Short-term loans payable	1,324

Required:

1. Prepare an adjusted trial balance at February 3, 2007. Is the Retained Earnings balance of $328,744 the amount that would be reported on the balance sheet as of February 3, 2007?
2. Prepare the closing entries required at February 3, 2007.
3. Prepare a post-closing trial balance at February 3, 2007.

PB4-2 Recording Adjusting Journal Entries

LO1, LO2

Brandon Company's annual accounting year ends on June 30 and adjustments are made only at the end of the fiscal year. It is June 30, 2009, and all of the 2009 entries except the following adjusting journal entries have been made:

a. On March 30, 2009, Brandon paid a six-month premium for property insurance, $3,200, for coverage starting on that date. Cash was credited and Prepaid Insurance was debited for this amount.

b. At June 30, 2009, wages of $900 were earned by employees but not yet paid. The employees will be paid on the next payroll date, July 15, 2009.

c. On June 1, 2009, Brandon collected two months' maintenance revenue of $450. At that date, Brandon debited Cash and credited Unearned Maintenance Revenue for $450.

d. Amortization of $1,500 must be recognized on a service truck purchased on July 1, 2008.

e. Cash of $4,200 was collected on May 1, 2009, for services to be rendered evenly over the next year beginning on May 1. Unearned Service Revenue was credited when the cash was received.

f. The company owes five months interest of $600 on a bank loan taken out on February 1, 2009. The interest will be paid when the loan is repaid on January 31, 2010.

g. The company earned service revenue of $2,000 on a special job that was completed June 29, 2009. Collection will be made during July 2009; no entry has been recorded.

h. The income before any of the adjustments or income taxes was $31,675. The company's income tax rate is 30 per cent. Compute adjusted income based on all of the preceding information, and then determine and record income tax expense.

Required:

1. Indicate whether each transaction relates to a deferral or accrual.
2. Give the adjusting journal entry required for each transaction at June 30, 2009.

LO2, LO5 **PB4-3** **Determining Financial Statement Effects of Adjusting Journal Entries**
Refer to PB4-2.

Required:

Using a table like the following, indicate the effect of each adjusting journal entry and the amount of the effect. Use + for increase, − for decrease, and NE for no effect.

	Balance Sheet			Income Statement		
Transaction	**Assets**	**Liabilities**	**Shareholders' Equity**	**Revenues**	**Expenses**	**Net Income**
a						
b						
c						
etc.						

LO2, LO5 **PB4-4** **Analyzing a Student's Business, and Preparing an Adjusted Income Statement**
Before she could start university in the fall, Kelly Gordon needed to make some money. She was a pro at using presentation software and had a good handle of other cutting-edge graphics software, so she thought the best way to make some money would be to develop some fun applications that her high-school teachers could use in their classes. Based on the advice from a friend of her family, she created a corporation called Gordon's Flash. On July 1, 2010, Kelly began her business by investing $1,000 of her own money in the company, and by having her mother invest an additional $3,000 in it. She immediately used some of this money to buy some computer hardware and software, at a total cost of $3,000. She then rented space in a small building; sent a flyer to her former teachers; and got to work creating a Web site and some sample applications. In no time, several of her teachers contacted her and agreed to purchase her services.

After a couple of months of working like mad, Kelly's business teacher asked her how things were going. She told him that she had enough work to keep busy every single minute of her life, but her company's bank account didn't seem to be reflecting that. Her teacher suggested that she prepare an income statement to get a better idea of whether her business was profitable. With his help, she gathered the following data for the three months ended September 30, 2010. The company's bank account showed deposits totalling $3,000 that Kelly had collected for preparing computer-based presentations. The following cheques had been written: assistant's pay, $1,800; payroll taxes, $60; computer supplies purchased and used on jobs, $200; insurance, $165; rent, $400; utilities, telephone, and cable modem, $325; and miscellaneous expenses (including advertising), $300. Also, uncollected bills to customers for software programming services amounted to $3,400. The $200 rent for September had not been paid. Kelly estimated that amortization on the computer hardware and software during the three months was $450. Income taxes for the three-month period were $500.

Required:

1. Prepare a quarterly income statement for Gordon's Flash for the three months July through September 2010.
2. Do you think that Kelly may have a need for one or more additional financial reports for 2010 and thereafter? Explain.

PB4-5 Comprehensive Review Problem: From Recording Transactions (including Adjusting Journal Entries) to Preparing Financial Statements and Closing Journal Entries (Chapters 2, 3, and 4)

LO1, LO2, LO4–LO6

Alison and Chuck Renny began operations of their furniture repair shop (Lazy Sofa Furniture, Inc.) on January 1, 2008. The annual reporting period ends December 31. The trial balance on January 1, 2009, was as follows (the amounts are rounded to thousands of dollars to simplify):

Account Titles	Debit	Credit
Cash	5	
Accounts receivable	4	
Supplies	2	
Small tools	6	
Equipment		
Accumulated amortization (on equipment)		
Other assets	9	
Accounts payable		7
Notes payable		
Wages payable		
Interest payable		
Income taxes payable		
Unearned revenue		
Dividends payable		
Contributed capital		15
Retained earnings		4
Dividends declared		
Service revenue		
Amortization expense		
Income tax expense		
Interest expense		
Supplies and other operating expenses	—	—
Totals	26	26

Transactions during 2009 (summarized in thousands of dollars) follow:

a. Borrowed $20 cash on July 1, 2009, signing a short-term note payable.
b. Purchased equipment for $18 cash on July 1, 2009.
c. Issued additional shares for $5.
d. Earned revenues for 2009, $65, including $9 on credit and $56 received in cash.
e. Recognized operating expenses for 2009, $35, including $7 on credit and $28 in cash.
f. Purchased additional small tools, $3 cash.
g. Collected accounts receivable, $8.
h. Paid accounts payable, $11.
i. Purchased, on account, supplies for future use, $10.
j. Received a $3 deposit on work to start January 15, 2010.
k. Declared a dividend, $10.
l. Paid the $10 dividend in cash.

Data for adjusting journal entries:

m.   Supplies of $4 were counted on December 31, 2009.
n.   Amortization for 2009, $2
o.   Accrued interest on notes payable of $1
p.   Wages earned since the December 24 payroll not yet paid, $3
q.   Income tax for 2009 was $4, and will be paid in 2010.

Required:

1.   Set up T-accounts for the accounts on the trial balance and enter beginning balances.
2.   Record journal entries for transactions *a* through *l* and post them to the T-accounts.
3.   Prepare an unadjusted trial balance.
4.   Record and post the adjusting journal entries *m* through *q.*
5.   Prepare an adjusted trial balance.
6.   Prepare an income statement, statement of retained earnings, and balance sheet.
7.   Prepare and post the closing journal entries.
8.   Prepare a post-closing trial balance.
9.   How much net income did Lazy Sofa Furniture, Inc., generate during 2009? Is the company financed primarily by debt or equity?

SKILLS DEVELOPMENT CASES

LO1, LO5   ### S4-1   Finding Financial Information

Refer to the financial statements of High Liner in Appendix A at the end of this book, or download the annual report from the Cases section of the text's Web site at www.mcgrawhill.ca/college/phillips.

Required:

1.   What is the amount of Prepaid Expenses as of the end of 2007?
2.   Refer to the notes to the financial statements to determine what interest rate High Liner is paying on its bank loans in 2007.
3.   Refer to the notes to see what types of inventories High Liner has.
4.   In which line of the income statement does High Liner likely include the expense for advertising?

LO1-LO5   ### S4-2   Comparing Financial Information

Refer to the financial statements of Sun-Rype by downloading the annual report from the **Cases** section of the text's Web site at www.mcgrawhill.ca/college/phillips.

Required:

1.   Does Sun-Rype report more or less for Prepaid Expenses than High Liner? What might be included in Sun-Rype's prepaid expenses?
2.   What interest rate is Sun-Rype paying on its promissory note in 2007? Is this more or less than High Liner is paying on its bank loans?
3.   Does Sun-Rype have the same kinds of inventories that High Liner has?
4.   Can you determine from the income statement whether Sun-Rype or High Liner incurs the largest advertising expense?

LO1-LO5   ### S4-3   Internet-Based Team Research: Examining Deferrals and Accruals

As a team, select an industry to analyze. Using your Web browser, each team member should acquire the financial reporting section of the annual report for one Canadian publicly traded company in the industry, with each member selecting a different company. (See S1-3 in Chapter 1 for a description of possible resources for these tasks.)

Required:

1. On an individual basis, each team member should write a short report listing the following:
   a. The company's total assets and total liabilities at the end of each year.
   b. The company's prepaid expenses and accrued liabilities at the end of each year.
   c. The percentage that prepaid expenses are of total assets, and the percentage that accrued liabilities are of total liabilities.
   d. Describe and explain the types of accrued liabilities reported in the notes to the financial statements.
2. Discuss any patterns that you, as a team, observe. Then, as a team, write a short report comparing and contrasting your companies according to the preceding attributes. Provide potential explanations for any differences discovered.

S4-4 Ethical Decision Making: A Real-Life Example

L01, L03, L05

Atlas Cold Storage offers temperature-controlled warehousing and distribution services to chilled-food processors and retailers. Atlas, based in Toronto, is North America's second largest cold storage company, operating over 50 warehouses in Canada and the United States. In August 2003, Atlas announced that it had to adjust its previously reported numbers for 2001 and 2002 to the tune of almost $5 million. Part of the problem was that $3.6 million of expenditures had been capitalized in 2001 and 2002 when they should have been expensed. A second issue related to $950,000 of expenses that should have been accrued in 2001 but were recorded when paid in 2002 instead. A third error was the treatment given to a refund of $600,000 received by Atlas on assets bought in 2002; it had been recorded as a reduction in expenses rather than as a reduction of the asset's cost.

An investigation into how all of this had happened revealed that the accounting department had been instructed by the Chief Executive Officer (CEO) to record the items inappropriately so that the earnings targets would be met and bonuses would be paid to the Atlas executives. This finding led to the firing of the CFO, the VP Finance, and the auditors, and to the resignation of the CEO and most of the board of directors. Atlas's stock price fell from $13 in August 2003 to $5 in the fall of 2004.

Required:

1. Discuss whether large adjustments, such as those made by Atlas, necessarily indicate improper accounting procedures.
2. What does it mean to say that the company *capitalized* certain operating expenses? For a distinction between capitalize and expense, refer to Exhibit 3.7 (on page 93). Drawing on concepts presented in Chapters 2 and 3, explain why it is improper to capitalize expenses that aren't really assets.
3. Assume that $3 million in bonuses were recorded in the last quarter of 2002. What journal entry would have been used to record this accrual? What journal entry would have been used to record the $3 million in bonuses paid in the first quarter of 2003?
4. What accounting concept is violated by recording an expense for 2001 when it is paid in 2002?
5. Make the adjusting journal entry in 2002 to correct the improper treatment of the $600,000 refund.

S4-5 Ethical Decision Making: A Mini-Case

L01, L03, L05

Assume you work as an assistant accountant in the head office of a national video rental store. With the increasing popularity of online movie rental operations, your company has struggled to meet its earnings targets for the year. It's important for the company to meet its earnings targets this year because the company is renegotiating a bank loan next month, and the terms of that loan are likely to depend on the company's reported financial success. Also, the company plans to issue more shares to the public in the upcoming year, to obtain funds for establishing its own presence in the online movie rental business. The chief financial officer (CFO) has approached you with a solution to the earnings dilemma. She proposes that the amortization period for the reusable DVDs on hand be extended from 3 months to 15 months. She explains that by lengthening the amortization period, a smaller amount of amortization expense will be recorded in the current year, resulting in a higher net income. She claims that generally accepted accounting principles require estimates like this, so it wouldn't involve doing anything wrong.

Required:

Discuss the CFO's proposed solution. In your discussion, consider the following questions. Will the change in amortization affect net income in the current year in the way that the CFO described? How will it affect net income in the following year? Is the CFO correct when she claims that the change in estimated amortization is allowed by GAAP? Who relies on the video company's financial statements when making decisions? Why might their decisions be affected by the CFO's proposed solution? Is it possible that their decisions would not be affected? What should you do?

LO1, LO2, LO5   **S4-6 Critical Thinking: Adjusting an Income Statement and a Balance Sheet for Deferrals and Accruals**

Masterful Moving Corporation has been in operation since January 1, 2009. It is now December 31, 2009, the end of the annual accounting period. The company does not have much cash at the end of the first year, although revenue has been fairly good. Three shareholders manage the company, but they have not given much attention to record-keeping. In view of a serious cash shortage, they have applied to your bank for a $20,000 loan. As a loan officer, you requested a complete set of financial statements. The following 2009 annual financial statements were prepared by the company's office staff.

After briefly reviewing the statements and "looking into the situation," you requested that the statements be redone (with some expert help) to "incorporate amortization, accruals, supply counts, income taxes, and so on." As a result of a review of the records and supporting documents, the following additional information was developed:

a.   The amount of $6,000 for supplies shown on the balance sheet has not been adjusted for supplies used during 2009. A count of the supplies on hand on December 31, 2009, showed $1,800.

b.   The insurance premium paid in 2009 was for years 2009 and 2010. The total insurance premium was debited in full to Prepaid Insurance when paid in 2009, and no adjustment has been made.

c.   The equipment cost $40,000 when purchased January 1, 2009. It had an estimated annual amortization of $8,000. No amortization has been recorded for 2009.

d.   Unpaid (and unrecorded) salaries at December 31, 2009, amounted to $2,200.

e.   At December 31, 2009, transportation revenue collected in advance amounted to $7,000. This amount was credited in full to Transportation Revenue when the cash was collected earlier during 2009.

f.   Income taxes for the year are calculated as 25 per cent of income before tax.

MASTERFUL MOVING CORPORATION

Income Statement For the Period Ended December 31, 2009		Balance Sheet At December 31, 2009	
Transportation revenue	$85,000	**Assets**	
Expenses:		Cash	$ 2,000
Salaries expense	17,000	Receivables	3,000
Supplies expense	12,000	Supplies	6,000
Other expenses	18,000	Equipment	40,000
Total expenses	47,000	Prepaid insurance	4,000
Net income	$38,000	Other assets	27,000
		Total assets	$82,000
		Liabilities	
		Accounts payable	$ 9,000
		Shareholders' Equity	
		Contributed capital	35,000
		Retained earnings	38,000
		Total liabilities and Shareholders' equity	$82,000

Required:

1. Prepare the adjusting journal entries required on December 31, 2009, based on the preceding additional information. You may need to create new accounts not yet included in the income statement or balance sheet.

2. Redo the preceding statements after taking into account the adjusting journal entries. One way to organize your response follows:

Items	Amounts Reported	Changes		Corrected Amounts
		Plus	Minus	
(List here each item from the two statements)				

3. The effects of recording the adjusting journal entries were to:
   a. *Increase* or *decrease* (select one) Net income by $_____ .
   b. *Increase* or *decrease* (select one) Total assets by $_____ .

4. Write a letter to the company explaining the results of the adjustments and your preliminary analysis.

S4-7 Aggregating Accounts on an Adjusted Trial Balance to Prepare an Income Statement, Statement of Retained Earnings, and Balance Sheet

LO4, LO5

Assume you recently were hired for a job at the head office of Loblaw Companies Limited. Loblaws, with more than 1,000 stores, has the largest market share in the Canadian supermarket business. Its banners include Atlantic SaveEasy, No Frills, Provigo, Your Independent Grocer, and Zehrs Market, to name a few. Its President's Choice brand features financial services as well as traditional and organic groceries. Your first assignment is to review the company's lengthy adjusted trial balance to determine the accounts that can be combined ("aggregated") into single line-items that will be reported on the financial statements. Assume that, by querying the accounting system, you were able to obtain the following alphabetical list of accounts and their adjusted balances as of December 31 (in millions).

Accounts payable	$ 2,158	Goodwill	$ 794	Prepaid insurance	$ 19
Accounts receivable	714	Income tax expense	248	Prepaid rent	20
Accrued interest payable	42	Income tax payable	109	Properties under	
Accrued wages payable	238	Insurance expense	61	development	726
Accrued utilities payable	51	Interest expense	259	Rent expense	36
Accumulated amortization	3,853	Interest receivable	14	Retained earnings	
Amortization expense	590	Inventory of other products	427	(opening balance)	4,694
Cash	549	Inventory of supplies		Salaries expense	6,211
Cash equivalents	120	and materials	183	Sales of food products	17,002
Contributed capital	1,196	Land	1,699	Sales of other products	7,219
Cost of goods sold—		Long-term contracts payable	234	Shipping expenses	784
food products	16,945	Long-term notes payable	4,212	Store buildings	3,386
Cost of goods sold—		Notes payable (current)	675	Transport equipment	1,215
other products	3,210	Office buildings	670	Utilities expense	504
Dividends declared	230	Office supplies expense	11	Warehouse buildings	899
Equipment and fixtures—		Other long-term assets	689		
offices	598	Other current assets	475		
Equipment and fixtures—		Other long-term liabilities	326		
stores	2,715				

Required:

With the above account names and balances, prepare an adjusted trial balance using a spreadsheet. Also prepare an income statement, statement of retained earnings, and balance sheet that import their numbers from the adjusted trial balance or from the other statements where appropriate. If similar accounts can be aggregated into a single line-item for each financial statement, use a formula to compute the aggregated amount. Using the format shown in Exhibits 4.9 and 4.10 (pages 146 and 147) for First Choice Haircutters' income statement and balance sheet as a guide, prepare statements that combine accounts as much as possible. To be sure that you understand how to import numbers from other parts of a spreadsheet, you e-mail your friend Billy for advice. Here's his reply.

From: BillyTheTutor@yahoo.com
To: Overwhelmed@hotmail.com
Cc:
Subject: Excel Help

Hey pal. You're bouncing from job to job like one of those ping-pong balls that your company sells. Okay, to import a number from another spreadsheet, you first click on the cell where you want the number to appear. For example, if you want to enter the Cash balance in the balance sheet, click on the cell in the balance sheet where the cash number is supposed to appear. Enter the equals sign (=) and then click on the tab that takes you to the worksheet containing the adjusted trial balance. In that worksheet, click on the cell that contains the amount you want to import into the balance sheet and then press enter. This will create a link from the adjusted trial balance cell to the balance sheet cell. At the end of this message, I've pasted a screen shot showing the formula I would enter on the balance sheet to import the total of three related inventory accounts from the adjusted trial balance. Don't forget to save the file using a name that indicates who you are.

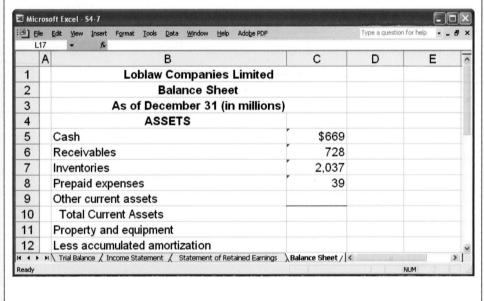

CHAPTER 5

Understanding Financial Statements and the Financial Reporting Environment

Understand the financial reporting environment.

LO1 Describe the main financial statement users and the key qualities of useful information that are of interest to them.

LO2 Explain why managers might misrepresent their financial results and what helps to prevent this from occurring.

Study common approaches to analyzing financial statements.

LO3 Calculate and interpret the debt-to-assets, asset-turnover, and net-profit-margin ratios.

Evaluate sources of information other than annual financial statements.

LO4 Describe the information found in press releases and stock-exchange filings.

Reconsider the financial reporting environment.

LO5 Describe what investors can do to protect themselves.

OUTSIDE LOOKING IN

INSIDE LOOKING OUT

This chapter focuses on how financial statement users analyze financial statements to get information to use in their decision making. We focus on Reitmans (Canada) Limited, a Canadian success story that recently celebrated its eightieth anniversary.

A friend asks you to look at how his favourite basketball team did last season and to advise him on who's likely to win this season. While it's tempting to just look in the newspaper to see who won last year, or to recommend the tallest team for this year, you know you'll have to drill down deeper than that. There's no guarantee that last year's champ will do well this year, because not all the players will be returning, and who knows how good the new recruits will be? Also, the tallest team isn't always the best. Some teams make more out of their talents than others. Plus, you need to know what's happening with other teams in the league to do a good job of interpreting what it all means for the future.

You'll face the same issues when predicting how your friend's favourite company will do this year. If you're evaluating **REITMANS (CANADA) LIMITED**—Canada's largest and most profitable ladies wear retailer, operating under the banners of Reitmans, Smart Set, RW & Co., Thyme Maternity, Penningtons, and Addition Elle—you might be tempted to look just at how many stores it operates, but you really should analyze its published financial reports. Start by looking at the sales levels and then drill down further, considering such things as the income generated from those sales and the investment in assets needed to generate those sales. To predict future results, you'll need to consider whether the $60 million Reitmans paid on new and renovated stores and offices in 2006 will pay off for them. You'll also consider the state of consumer spending in Canada, as well as key changes in the industry, such as the new European apparel

The term **stakeholders** is used to describe the numerous groups with an interest (a stake) in a particular company.

competitors entering the Canadian market. After gathering all this information, you'll have to pull it together somehow to figure out what it implies about the company's past and future financial performance. In this chapter, we'll guide you through this with a simple framework for financial statement analysis.

Now that you've seen the basic steps in accounting for business activities, it's time to take a step back and have a better look at how accounting information is used. The first part of this chapter focuses on the financial reporting environment. In the second section, you'll be introduced to some techniques for analyzing financial statements that can help you evaluate how well a company is being run. Finally, you'll see how all of this will help you make informed investment decisions. These are your Learning Objectives, as summarized on the front page of this chapter.

UNDERSTAND

The Financial Reporting Environment

WHO ARE THE MAIN USERS AND WHAT DO THEY NEED?

Chapter 1 provided a quick look at the many people who use financial statements, loosely called **stakeholders,** including employees, tax and other regulatory authorities, lobby groups, and the community at large. A more detailed analysis is presented in Exhibit 5.1 for the two prime user groups, investors and creditors, plus another key group, directors. As you can see, each group needs accounting information for different purposes. Managers are not included in the exhibit, since they are internal users of accounting information and have access to detailed information that they use to make decisions about how the business should be run. When accounting information is used in this way, to make business decisions, it is being used to fulfill a *management accounting*, rather than a financial accounting, function.

exhibit **5.1** Key Users and Uses of Accounting Information		
Accounting information is used by . . .	**to . . .**	**This is called . . .**
Directors	Oversee the business	Governance
Creditors	Administer business contracts	Contracting
Investors	Value the business	Valuation

Shareholders

↓ elect

Directors

↓ oversee

Managers

Directors

"Directors" is the short title often used to describe members of the board of directors. As the shareholders' own elected representatives, directors ensure that managers make decisions that benefit shareholders. Just as air traffic controllers use radar to keep flights on course, directors use accounting information to oversee management of the business, hopefully avoiding financial turbulence. When accounting information is used in this way, to oversee the business and evaluate the performance of managers, it is being used in a *governance* role.

Creditors

Creditors use accounting information in several ways. Suppliers, for example, use it to decide whether it is the kind of company they want to enter into contracts with. Bankers often use it to limit a company's activities, by requiring the company to satisfy certain financial targets, such as minimum levels of assets or shareholders' equity. These **loan covenants,** as they are called, help to ensure the company will have money to repay the loan to the bank when it comes due. When accounting information is used in these ways, to administer contracts, it is being used in a *contracting* role.

Loan covenants are terms of a loan agreement which, if broken, entitle the lender to demand immediate repayment or renegotiation of the loan.

Investors

Investors (and their advisers) look to accounting information, in combination with other information, to help evaluate the financial strength of a business and, ultimately, to estimate its value. When accounting information is used to assess share prices, it is being used in a *valuation* role. In late summer of 2007, Reitmans shares plummeted 22 per cent from a high of $27, because investors sold off their shares when the company reported poorer-than-expected operating results. By the end of 2007, however, investment advisers were issuing a Strong Buy recommendation for Reitmans shares. The Canadian loonie was at an all-time high, and Reitmans was well-positioned to benefit because of its extensive United States imports. Reitmans' solid financial position, combined with a strong Canadian dollar, a positive outlook for consumer spending in general, and share prices at a 52-week low of $17.69, made Reitmans shares a good deal for investors looking to buy.

POINT OF INTEREST

Share prices can react quickly to news about a company. The price of shares in Hudson's Bay Company, Canada's oldest corporation, rose 21.5 per cent in one day in 2005 when an American investor made a bid of $1 billion for HBC.

WHAT DO USERS GET?

Although directors have the right to access all the information they need directly from the company's records, creditors and investors are external to the company and usually must rely on the accounting information reported in the financial statements. For this reason, *the primary objective of external financial reporting is to provide economic information that is useful to creditors and investors.*

Okay, so what exactly makes information "useful"? To be useful, financial statement information must possess four main characteristics: (1) **reliability,** (2) **relevance,** (3) **consistency,** and (4) **comparability.** At this point in the course, we're not going to get into a detailed discussion of these characteristics—you'll get that in Chapter 13. For now, we just want you to be aware of these characteristics so you can begin to understand why accounting is done the way it is. Let's briefly look at each of the four characteristics and help you to see how they relate back to some of the topics in Chapters 1 to 4.

Information is **reliable** if it is accurate, unbiased, and verifiable. It is **relevant** if it can affect a decision. Information is **consistent** if it can be compared over time, and it is **comparable** if it allows comparisons across companies.

Reliability

Is the information accurate? The two equality checks that you have used throughout the recording of every transaction (A = L + SE *and* Debits = Credits) help to prevent errors from occurring, leading to more accurate information, which enhances its reliability.[1]

Relevance

Does the information help in making decisions? The adjustments made under accrual basis accounting help to ensure that the financial statements are complete and up to date, thereby enhancing their relevance.

Consistency

Does the company handle similar events in the same way from one period to the next? The chart of accounts ensures that transactions in the current month are recorded in the same accounts as similar transactions in previous months, thereby enhancing consistency. From a broader perspective, companies are required to use the rules of GAAP consistently from period to period. Consistent rules result in consistent information.

COACH'S TIP

To better understand these characteristics, think about your academic life. Your transcript provides *reliable* information because the grade on your transcript is the grade you received, no doubt about it. Most employers consider your grades to be *relevant* for deciding whom to hire because better performing students tend to be better employees. Grades are measured with *consistency*, from one year to the next, possibly on a scale of 0 to 100 per cent or a 4.0 grade-point scale. Finally, grades provide *comparable* information because they allow someone to compare you with other students.

---

[1] As Canada makes the transition to IFRS, the CICA has proposed that the term *faithful representation* be used instead of *reliability* to describe the idea that information should be accurate and neutral, but this proposal has not yet been approved.

Comparability

Do different companies handle similar events in the same way? The rules of GAAP must be followed by all companies that prepare financial statements for external reporting, which enhances the comparability of different companies' financial statements. Some choices do exist within GAAP, however, so it is important to read the notes to companies' financial statements so that you know whether the companies you are comparing have used the same accounting methods. Otherwise, you may be comparing apples with oranges!

These four characteristics underlie many other aspects of accounting, but this is enough for now. As you learn additional accounting rules in Chapters 6 to 13, think about how those rules ensure that financial statements are reliable, relevant, consistent, and comparable.

WHY WOULD MANAGEMENT MISREPRESENT THE FINANCIAL RESULTS?

In Chapter 4, you learned that it was possible for management to dilute the quality of financial reporting by misrepresenting the company's financial results. In the early part of this decade, the accounting world was rocked by many cases of scandal and fraud and, as a result, accounting fraud and how to reduce it are hot topics these days.

Three things have to exist for an accounting fraud to occur. First, there must be an incentive for someone to commit the fraud. Second, an opportunity must exist to commit the fraud. Third, the person committing the fraud must possess personal characteristics that allow the fraud to be rationalized and concealed.

Incentive to Commit Fraud

Financial misrepresentation is both unethical and illegal, so there must be some strong incentives driving some managers to act so despicably. These incentives fit into two categories: (1) creating business opportunities and (2) satisfying personal greed.

1. Creating business opportunities   Management is under constant pressure to produce pleasing financial results for at least three business reasons:

a. Satisfy loan covenants.   As you learned earlier in this chapter, lenders rely on financial statements to determine whether a company has violated its loan covenants by failing to meet certain financial targets. If managers overstate their company's financial condition, they can avoid violating loan covenants which otherwise could require the company to pay a higher interest rate, repay its loan balance right away, or be forced to put up extra collateral to secure the loan.

b. Increase equity financing.   The amount of money obtained from issuing shares depends, in part, on the price of the shares when they are issued. An issuance of 100,000 shares will yield double the money if the price is $20 per share rather than $10 per share. Managers can lead investors to pay more than a company is really worth, if they overstate the company's reported financial performance.

c. Attract business partners.   By making the business appear more stable or more profitable than it actually is, management can mislead suppliers and other companies into wanting to pursue a business relationship with the company.

2. Satisfying personal greed   By producing pleasing financial results, members of top management can benefit personally in three ways:

a. Enhance job security.   The financial statements are a report card on both the company and the company's management. If top management reports strong financial results, shareholders are more likely to think management is doing a good job.

ETHICAL ISSUES

POINT OF INTEREST

The documentary movie *Enron: The Smartest Guys in the Room,* which tells the story behind the infamous scandal, was nominated for an Academy Award in 2006, but lost to *March of the Penguins.*

---

exhibit 5.2   Possible Incentives for Misrepresenting Financial Results

Creating Business Opportunities	*Satisfying Personal Greed*
a. Satisfy loan covenants.	*a.* Enhance job security.
b. Increase equity financing.	*b.* Increase personal wealth.
c. Attract business partners.	*c.* Obtain a bigger paycheque.

---

b. Increase personal wealth. Members of top management often own shares in the company, so their personal shareholdings will be worth more (and their personal wealth will increase) if their company reports financial results that send its share price skyward.

c. Obtain a bigger paycheque. Managers often receive cash bonuses based on the strength of their company's reported financial performance. Better reported results mean larger bonuses.

Exhibit 5.2 summarizes the above reasons.

Opportunity to Commit Fraud

As you saw in Chapters 2 to 4, financial statements are produced by an accounting system that involves analyzing, recording, and summarizing the results of business activities. Weaknesses in this system create an opportunity for fraudulent information to be entered into it, which increases the risk that the financial statements will be fraudulently misreported. To reduce this risk, certain procedures and policies can be put in place to help ensure that information entered into the accounting system and reported in the financial statements is accurate and complete. These internal controls, as they are called, can't completely eliminate the opportunity for fraud, but they can limit it if they operate effectively. You will learn more about specific internal controls in Chapter 6.

Character to Rationalize and Commit Fraud

For people to commit fraud and keep it secret, they have to feel "okay" with their actions. Most fraudsters achieve this through a sense of personal entitlement, which outweighs other moral principles, such as fairness, honesty, and concern for others. Many are said to be egotistical and possess an ability to lie or pressure others to look the other way.[2] It's not easy to counteract these undesirable traits, but recent changes in the financial reporting environment are beginning to do so, as we discuss in the next section.

WHY WOULD MANAGEMENT NOT MISREPRESENT THE FINANCIAL RESULTS?

Now that we've shown several reasons why a manager might behave dishonestly, we should point out many good reasons for managers to report honestly. First, there's the personal satisfaction and pride that comes from doing the right thing. The **full disclosure principle** of accounting makes it clear that the right thing is to reliably report all information that is relevant to financial statement users. A second reason is that managers can develop reputations for honest reporting, which leads investors to place more trust in them and their financial reports. For most people, these reasons are more than enough to encourage them to report honestly. However, for the few morally bankrupt people, there's a third reason to report honestly: new corporate fraud laws in the United States and Canada include harsh penalties for managers who knowingly report fraudulent financial results.

These new laws were introduced in response to the many financial frauds and accounting scandals ocurring in the late 1990s and early 2000s. Confidence in the stock markets had been shaken by the high-profile frauds involving Enron (now bankrupt), WorldCom (now part of Verizon), and others, so the United States Congress stepped in to create the Sarbanes-Oxley Act of 2002 (SOX) in an attempt to improve the financial reporting environment and restore investor confidence. SOX is the most significant change to the financial reporting environment in the United States since the Securities Acts were introduced in the 1930s, and it has had a huge impact, not just on managers and auditors of public companies, but on everyone in the business world. Among other things, the act requires that top managers sign a report certifying their responsibility for the financial statements, maintain an audited system of internal controls to ensure accuracy in accounting reports, and maintain an independent committee to ensure managers co-operate with auditors. As a result of SOX, corporate executives now face severe consequences—up to 20 years in prison and $5 million in fines—if they are found guilty of committing accounting fraud. Employees may also have to repay any bonuses they received or profits from stock sales obtained as a result of questionable accounting. In Canada, the Canadian Securities Administrators (CSA) have introduced a series of national instruments and policies that, to a great extent, closely follow SOX, but strive to accommodate the unique nature of the Canadian financial market.

THE ROLE OF AUDITORS, DIRECTORS, AND ANALYSTS

Apart from personal ethics and legislative controls, there are a number of groups that also help to counteract the possibility that financial data may be misstated, either through honest error or deliberate fraud. As we saw in Chapter 1, securities legislation requires publicly traded companies to have their financial statements audited by public accountants. Many privately owned companies also have their financial statements audited, often at the request of lenders or private investors who want to be sure the financial statements possess the four characteristics described earlier. The auditors, who are experts in financial reporting, issue a one-page report that states whether the company's financial statements appear to have been prepared using GAAP. We say "appear to" because auditors can't check every single business transaction to ensure it was accurately reported, so they can't be 100 per cent sure that the financial statements *exactly* follow GAAP. But they do check enough to be "reasonably" sure the financial statements are "fair"—which is what their audit report says. If the audit report is **unqualified,** the company can point to it as further evidence that the financial statements are useful and that creditors and investors can trust what is reported. For an example of an unqualified audit report, see the annual report for High Liner Foods in Appendix A at the back of this book.

The **full disclosure principle** states that relevant information should be disclosed in either the main financial statements or the notes.

POINT OF INTEREST

In 2005, 12 of Nortel's most senior executives agreed to return $8.6 million in bonuses they received in years when the financial results were apparently overstated. At the same time, Nortel took legal action in Ontario to recover another $13 million from three other executives who had been fired when the irregularities became known.

Being unqualified for a job is a bad thing. Getting an **unqualified audit report** (also called a *clean* audit report) is a good thing. Auditors give an *adverse* audit report when the financial statements are not prepared in accordance with GAAP and are not fairly presented.

---

[2] David T. Wolfe and Dana R. Hermanson, "The Fraud Diamond: Considering the Four Elements of Fraud," CPA Journal, December 2004.

After the financial statements are prepared, they are presented to the board of directors, who have the opportunity to question management about anything that looks unusual in the statements.

A whole industry of stock and credit analysts has developed to help investors and creditors make their investment and credit decisions, and they also play a role in monitoring management's reporting practices. Stock analysts actively seek out information about a company and produce multi-page reports that evaluate an individual company's past performance, make predictions about its future earnings, and conclude with a recommendation about whether investors should buy, hold, or sell shares in the company. To make these evaluations, **earnings forecasts,** and stock recommendations, analysts rely heavily on insights they gain from following developments occurring in the company, its industry, and the economy, and by analyzing the company's financial statements. Credit analysts also evaluate a company's past performance, but, rather than to make stock recommendations, their goal is to assess the risk that the company will be unable to pay its liabilities. Good analysts often raise red flags about information that they find suspect.

In this section, we have described the main players in the financial reporting environment and their roles in the quest for high quality information. In the next section of this chapter, we present a simple business and financial analysis model that is useful in analyzing corporate performance.

An **earnings forecast** is a prediction of the amount of earnings expected for future accounting periods.

STUDY _____
How to Analyze Financial Statements

A MODEL OF REITMANS' BUSINESS

Before evaluating or predicting Reitmans' financial performance, it is useful first to get an idea of what's involved in running a retail company. If you are more of a bookworm than a shopaholic, think about a book publisher instead—the two businesses are very similar. In both, you have to have a product that people want to buy, and you have to sell your product for more than you pay for it in order to make a profit. There are four parts to the business:

1. *Obtain financing* from lenders and investors, which is used to invest in assets.
2. *Invest in assets,* which are used to generate revenues.
3. *Generate revenues,* which lead to net income.
4. *Produce net income,* which is needed to satisfy investors, to comfort lenders, and to provide resources for future expansion.

Based on this description of Reitmans' business, a skeleton of a business model can be developed, as shown in Exhibit 5.3.

Now it's time to pack some muscle onto the skeleton business model in Exhibit 5.3, with numbers from the financial statements. Information about Reitmans' debt and equity financing (in box 1 of Exhibit 5.3) is indicated by the liabilities and shareholders' equity sections of the balance sheet in Exhibit 5.4. There we see that the company relies quite a bit on debt (total liabilities = $126 million), but depends on investors for most of its financing (total shareholders' equity = $495 million). By reducing its reliance on debt financing, Reitmans can avoid the interest costs that lenders charge. Also, because shareholders' equity doesn't have to be repaid (like liabilities do), this is considered a less risky financing strategy. Notice that the balance sheet presents two years worth of data, which enhances the comparability and therefore the usefulness of the numbers.

Reitmans' balance sheet also helps us to understand the company's investment in assets (box 2 of Exhibit 5.3). As of February 2, 2008, Reitmans held lots of cash and short-term investments (over $214 million). For most companies, it's rare for cash and short-term investments to make up a significant portion of the total assets. Rather than have cash just sitting in the bank earning a tiny bit of interest, most companies use these funds to buy additional inventory or property and equipment, which helps them make

exhibit 5.3   A Simple Business Model

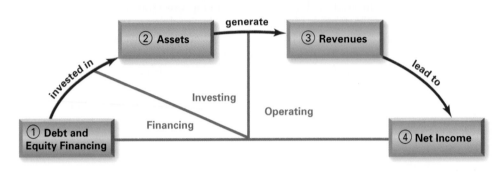

This exhibit shows a simple business model that connects significant financing, investing, and operating activities, and relates them to items reported on the financial statements.

exhibit 5.4   Comparative Balance Sheet (modified)

REITMANS (CANADA) LIMITED
Balance Sheet
(in thousands of Cdn. dollars)

	February 2, 2008	February 3, 2007
Assets		
Current Assets:		
Cash and Short-Term Investments	$214,301	$ 188,491
Accounts Receivable	3,546	3,439
Inventories	52,441	61,834
Other Current Assets	54,672	21,405
Total Current Assets	324,960	275,169
Property and Equipment, Net	247,963	226,734
Goodwill	42,426	42,426
Other Assets	5,611	56,082
Total Assets	$620,960	$600,411
Liabilities and Shareholders' Equity		
Current Liabilities:		
Accounts Payable and Accrued Liabilities	$69,189	$ 85,317
Other Current Liabilities	18,453	41,613
Total Current Liabilities	87,642	126,930
Long-Term Debt	38,199	37,362
Total Liabilities	125,841	164,292
Shareholders' Equity:		
Contributed Capital	27,778	24,906
Retained Earnings	467,341	411,213
Total Shareholders' Equity	495,119	436,119
Total Liabilities and Shareholders' Equity	$620,960	$600,411

---

exhibit 5.5   Income Statement (modified)

REITMANS (CANADA) LIMITED
Income Statement
(in thousands of Cdn. dollars)

| | Year ended February 2 and 3, | |
	2008	2007
Sales	$1,057,720	$1,042,509
Total Operating Expenses	908,642	900,643
Operating Income	149,078	141,866
Interest Income, Net	10,138	11,500
Income before Income Tax Expense	159,216	153,366
Income Tax Expense	44,314	70,897
Net Income	$114,902	$82,469

---

and sell more products and generate greater profits. This appears to be what Reitmans has done, as Reitmans has invested $52 million in inventory and another $248 million in property and equipment. Property and equipment is the largest asset on Reitmans balance sheet, even though it rents almost all of its store space.

For information on revenues and net income (boxes 3 and 4 in the business model in Exhibit 5.3 on page 196), we look at the income statement in Exhibit 5.5, where we also present two years of data. There we see that revenues for the year ended February 2, 2008, were $1 billion, which produced net income of $115 million.

COMPARING RESULTS WITH BENCHMARKS

If you're like most people, you probably find it hard to know whether $115 million in net income and $1 billion in revenues are decent levels for these items. To interpret amounts like these, it's useful to have points of comparison, or "benchmarks." Two commonly used benchmarks are:

1. *Prior periods.* By comparing Reitmans' current period results with its own results in prior periods, we can gain a sense of how the company's performance is changing over time. The trend is your friend. In Wall Street language, this comparison of the same company over a *series* of prior *time* periods is called **time-series analysis.**

2. *Competitors.* Although an analysis focused on one company is useful, it doesn't show what's happening in the industry. It's possible that Reitmans is improving (good), but still hasn't caught up to others in the same industry (not so good). Or it could be that Reitmans' performance is declining (bad), but it hasn't yet experienced the financial problems others face (not so bad). To get this industry-wide perspective, most analysts will compare competitors within a particular industry. The name for comparing *across* companies that compete in the same *section* of an industry is **cross-sectional analysis.**

In Exhibit 5.6, we present a time-series chart that compares Reitmans with itself on each of the dimensions of our business model (which was pictured in Exhibit 5.3 on page 196). From this chart, we can see that Reitmans' financial profile changed very little from 2006 to 2007. For ease of analysis, results for Reitmans' 12 months ending February 2, 2008, are labelled as results for the 2007 fiscal year in the following discussion. In comparison with Reitmans' 2006 year-end balance, $38 million less debt was outstanding at the end of 2007. This decrease in liabilities was accompanied by a 13 per cent increase in shareholders' equity, suggesting that Reitmans' financing strategy shifted

POINT OF INTEREST

Wall Street is the main financial centre of the United States, housing the New York Stock Exchange and the headquarters of the largest banks and investment houses. The comparable spot in Canada is Bay Street in Toronto.

A **time-series analysis** compares a company's results for one period with its own results over a series of time periods.

Cross-sectional analysis compares the results of one company with those of others in the same industry.

exhibit 5.6   Chart of Reitmans' Time-Series Analysis

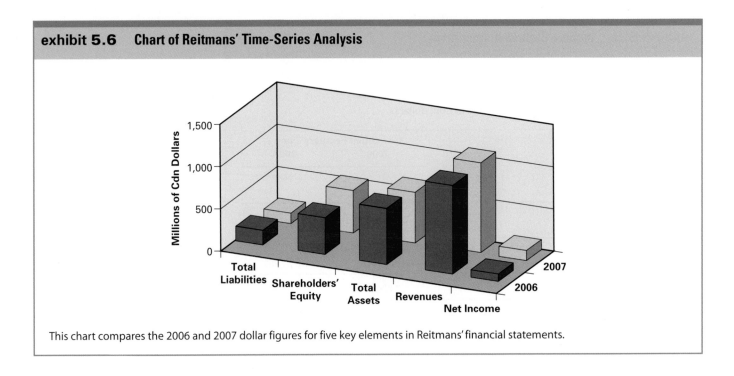

This chart compares the 2006 and 2007 dollar figures for five key elements in Reitmans' financial statements.

a bit during the year. We also see from Exhibit 5.6 that Reitmans grew over that period, with total assets, revenues, and net income all larger in 2007 than in 2006.

In Exhibit 5.7, we present a cross-sectional chart that compares Reitmans with two other Canadian companies in the specialty clothing industry—Le Château and Danier Leather—based on financial statement data for the 2007 fiscal year. Le Château's year-end is January 31, 2008, which is essentially the same as Reitmans, while Danier ends its fiscal year on June 30, 2007. All three year-ends are labelled as 2007 in the following discussion.

From Exhibit 5.7, we learn that Reitmans is much larger than both Le Château and Danier, as indicated by their greater bar heights across the various financial measures. In fact, Reitmans is more than twice the size of Le Château and Danier *combined* in every category except debt. Given these differences in size, should we simply conclude that Reitmans is the winner and give them our pocketful of investment tokens? In a word, no. All that this means is that Reitmans is a bigger company. It says nothing about whether it's best at using the resources provided to it. This kind of conclusion usually requires some *fraction action*, a process business professionals refer to more formally as financial statement ratio analyses.

FINANCIAL STATEMENT RATIO ANALYSIS

The goal of ratio analysis is to get to the heart of how well each company performed, given the resources it had available. Huge companies with vast sources of financing should be expected to invest in more assets, which generate greater revenues, which produce larger profits. The real question is, given the financing available, how well did the company perform? To answer this question, we add three ratios to our business model in Exhibit 5.3 to create the version in Exhibit 5.8.

Rather than examine the levels of financial statement accounts in dollars at each stage of the business model, ratio analyses focus on *relationships* between stages. Although it is possible to consider relationships that cut across the stages, say between *Assets* (box 2) and *Net Income* (box 4), this chapter focuses on only the links between neighbouring stages. Also, because this chapter is your first look at financial statement ratio analyses, we discuss only one ratio per link—ratios that use totals in the financial statements. In

exhibit 5.7   Cross-Sectional Analysis of Specialty Clothing Companies for the 2007 Fiscal Year

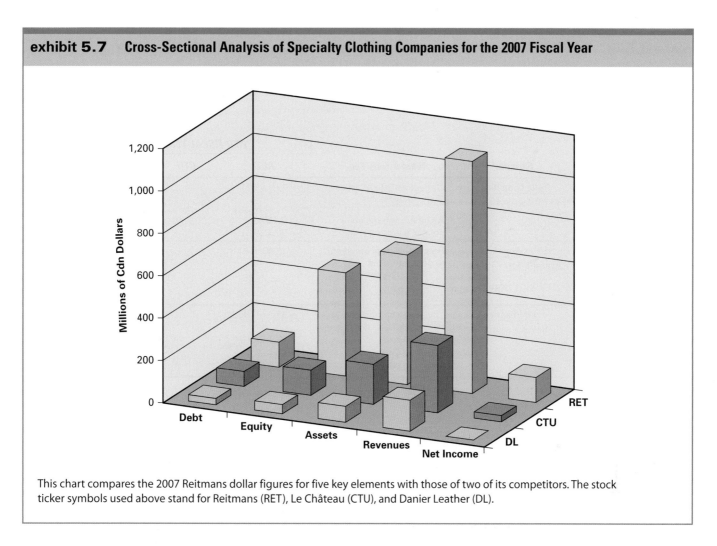

This chart compares the 2007 Reitmans dollar figures for five key elements with those of two of its competitors. The stock ticker symbols used above stand for Reitmans (RET), Le Château (CTU), and Danier Leather (DL).

later chapters, we will analyze links that cut across the stages, and we will introduce additional ratios that replace totals with data from specific accounts (e.g., inventories, cost of goods sold).

The formula for each ratio named in Exhibit 5.8 and an example of its calculation (using numbers reported in Reitmans' 2007 year-end financial statements) are presented in Exhibit 5.9. We also have presented the corresponding ratios for Le Château and Danier Leather for their 2007 fiscal year-ends for comparison and, for practice, a final column that you can complete as part of an upcoming self-study quiz. Before you do the

exhibit 5.8   A Framework for Financial Statement Ratio Analyses

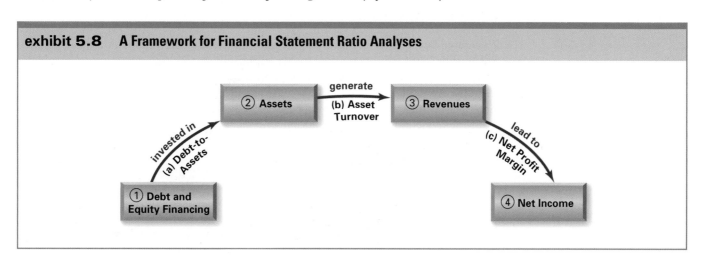

exhibit 5.9   Summary of Financial Statement Ratio Analyses

Name of Measure	Formula	What It Tells You	2007 FISCAL YEAR RET	CTU	DL	SELF-STUDY QUIZ 2006 RET
a. Debt-to-assets ratio	Total Liabilities / Total Assets	• The percentage of assets financed by debt	= 126 ÷ 621			
		• A higher ratio means greater financing risk.	= 0.203 or 20.3%	35.5%	40.4%	☐
b. Asset-turnover ratio	Sales Revenue / Average Total Assets	• How well assets are used to generate sales	= 1,058 ÷ 611			
		• A higher ratio means greater efficiency.	= 1.73	1.72	1.93	☐
c. Net-profit-margin ratio	Net Income / Sales Revenue	• The ability to generate sales while controlling expenses	= 115 ÷ 1,058			
		• A higher ratio means better performance.	= 0.1087 or 10.9%	1.0%	1.0%	☐

This table uses 2007 financial statement data for Reitmans, Le Château, and Danier Leather to calculate the ratios pictured in Exhibit 5.8

COACH'S TIP

To understand why ratio calculations differ, think about whether the pieces of data for each ratio came from the same basic financial statement.

quiz, we first need to explain why some ratios are reported as percentages but others aren't, and why averages are used in some ratios but not others. By looking at Exhibits 5.8 and 5.9, can you detect why ratio *b* isn't shown as a percentage like ratios *a* and *c?* Also, can you discover why we use an average in ratio *b* but not in ratios *a* and *c?* If you want help, see what the coach has to say.

Did you discover that ratio *b* takes information from both the balance sheet and income statement, whereas *a* and *c* use information from only one statement? This explains why asset turnover, ratio *b*, isn't reported as a percentage like the debt-to-assets and net-profit-margin ratios. When a ratio combines information from two separate statements, it typically is not reported as a percentage. Only those ratios that combine information from the same statement are reported using percentages. A percentage is calculated by multiplying the ratio by 100 per cent, as in 0.203 × 100 per cent = 20.3 per cent.

The key to understanding why averages are included in some ratios but not others is to remember that the balance sheet reports the results at a single *point* in time, whereas the income statement reports the results of managing those balance sheet accounts to generate profits *for the period* from one balance sheet date to the next. Some ratios are calculated by combining information from both the income statement and the balance sheet. The asset-turnover ratio, for example, takes sales revenues from the income statement for the top part of the ratio, and total assets from the balance sheet for the bottom. We need to calculate the average of the beginning *and* ending balance sheet amounts to include in the bottom part of the ratio, as shown in Exhibit 5.10, so that both the numerator and denominator are *for the period*.

Vertical Analysis

Vertical analysis (also called common-size analysis) involves showing (a) each item on a balance sheet as a percentage of total assets, or (b) each item on an income statement as a percentage of total revenues.

The debt-to-assets ratio divides total liabilities by total assets to determine the percentage of assets financed by debt. This same type of analysis can be conducted to determine how significant each individual type of asset is by dividing the amount shown for each asset by the total assets. This kind of analysis, which compares each individual line item on a financial statement with a total on that statement, is often called a **vertical,** or common-size, **analysis.** Vertical analysis can be applied to the income statement as well, to determine

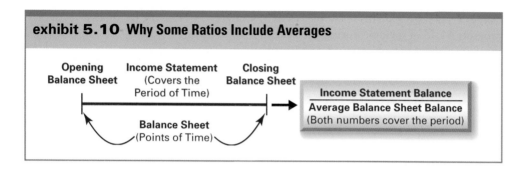

exhibit 5.10 Why Some Ratios Include Averages

Opening Balance Sheet — Income Statement (Covers the Period of Time) — Closing Balance Sheet

Balance Sheet (Points of Time)

$$\frac{\text{Income Statement Balance}}{\text{Average Balance Sheet Balance}}$$
(Both numbers cover the period)

HOW'S IT GOING? A Self-Study Quiz

Compute the ratios for the final column in Exhibit 5.9, using financial statement information in Exhibits 5.4 and 5.5, as well as the following information obtained from Reitmans' January 28, 2006, balance sheet. As of January 28, 2006, Reitmans reported (in thousands of dollars) assets totalling $523,233. When you're finished, check your answers with the solutions in the margin.

what percentage of total revenues each individual expense represents. It is easier for investors to see relationships among the numbers on the financial statements if the dollar figures have been converted to percentages by means of vertical analysis.

Interpreting the Ratios

Most newcomers to ratio analyses want to be told rules of thumb that indicate "good" or "bad" levels for each ratio. The truth is ratios vary so much from industry to industry that rules of thumb aren't that useful. It's more informative to compare over time or across competitors, as we do here.

a. Debt-to-Assets Ratio. This ratio indicates the proportion of total assets that are financed by debt. It's important to know how much debt is used to finance assets, because debt has to be repaid whether or not a company is doing well financially. If assets are financed primarily by debt, rather than equity, this ratio will be high, which would suggest that the company has adopted a risky financing strategy. Ultimately, a company would be forced into bankruptcy if it took on more debt than it could ever repay.

Exhibit 5.9 (and the numbers below) indicate that all three companies have debt-to-assets ratios between 20 and 40 per cent, with Reitmans having the lowest percentage of debt financing at 20.3 per cent. Reitmans' ratio is down slightly from 27.3 per cent in 2006.

	RET	CTU	DL
Debt-to-Assets (2007 Fiscal Year)	20.3%	35.5%	40.4%

b. Asset-Turnover Ratio. The asset-turnover ratio represents sales revenue per dollar invested in the assets of the business. So, the higher this ratio is, the more efficiently the business is utilizing its assets. An efficiently run business produces lots of sales for each dollar invested in assets. On the other hand, an inefficiently run business will tend to have assets sitting around idle and not generating sales, which results in a lower asset-turnover ratio.

Exhibit 5.9 on page 200, and the numbers below, indicate that Reitmans' asset-turnover-ratio of 1.73 was a bit better than Le Château's ratio of 1.72 but not as good as

COACH'S TIP

If you're having trouble understanding how sales per asset dollar measures efficiency, try thinking about a car's fuel efficiency. Just as kilometres are the output from using a litre of gas, sales are the output from using a dollar of assets.

Danier's ratio of 1.93. This result means that, for every $1 of assets, Reitmans was able to generate $1.73 of revenue during the year.

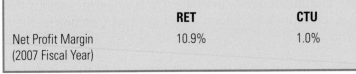

	RET	CTU	DL
Asset-Turnover Ratios (2007 Fiscal Year)	1.73	1.72	1.93

c. **Net-Profit-Margin Ratio.**   This ratio measures the amount of net income ("profit") generated from each dollar of sales. This is a key ratio, because it indicates how well executives manage the tricky balancing act between generating more sales and controlling expenses. What's so tricky about increasing sales and reducing expenses? Well, retailers may have found that consumers won't spend more than $100 for new jeans, so they can't jack up the price to increase total sales revenues. Instead, they try to increase sales levels by making and selling cool new clothes. The problem is that this strategy may require lots of advertising and promotion, which increases the company's expenses. The trick is to find the right balance between generating new sales and controlling the expenses needed to generate those new sales. A company generating tons of sales will go bankrupt if its expenses are out of control, and a company that tightly controls its expenses will fail if it doesn't generate enough sales. Net profit margin takes this trade-off into account, and indicates the company's ability to generate sales while controlling expenses.

Exhibit 5.9 on page 200, and the numbers below, indicate that Reitmans' profit margin, at 10.9 per cent, is ten times better than both Le Château's and Danier's ratios. In its annual report, Reitmans management explains that, despite the very competitive retail environment, the strength of the Canadian dollar, combined with significant United States imports, had a favourable impact on earnings.

	RET	CTU	DL
Net Profit Margin (2007 Fiscal Year)	10.9%	1.0%	1.0%

COACH'S TIP

The basic accounting equation (A = L + SE) implies that, as the ratio of debt-to-assets gets bigger, the ratio of shareholders' equity-to-assets gets smaller.

Assume that you are a financial analyst for the retail sector. Based on the levels and ratio analyses that we've just conducted in this chapter, who do you think wins gold, silver, and bronze in 2007? While there's no single correct answer for this, you might consider the graphic summary of financial statement ratios in Exhibit 5.11.

Exhibit 5.11 (ratio *a*) suggests that Danier Leather was financed with the largest proportion of debt. As the coach explains, this also implies that the company was financed with the smallest proportion of shareholders' equity, and means that the company is riskier than the others. We also know, from ratios *b* and *c*, that Danier Leather had the largest asset turnover, while Reitmans earned a higher net profit margin than the others. This implies that Danier was more efficient than Reitmans at using its shareholders' investments to generate revenues, but that Reitmans was better able to earn profit from those revenues in 2007.

Taken together, these three ratios usually illustrate the classic relationship between risk and return. A company with the least risk normally has the least profit. The conventional wisdom is that a company may be willing to take on more risk if it expects to make more profit from this risky behaviour. Is the risk worth it? Since nobody can predict the future, you have to wait and see. When a company takes a risk, investors will decide whether they believe the risk will pay off and whether they are comfortable with holding a risky investment. If not, they will sell their shares. Remember that risk tolerance varies from person to person. In our example, Reitmans has less risk than the other companies and the most profit. No wonder the investment community was listing Reitmans as a good buy.

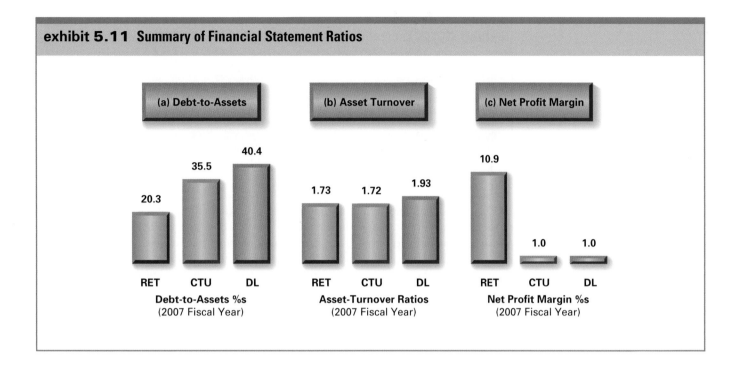

exhibit 5.11 Summary of Financial Statement Ratios

(a) Debt-to-Assets

	40.4
35.5	
20.3	
RET	CTU	DL

Debt-to-Assets %s
(2007 Fiscal Year)

(b) Asset Turnover

1.73 1.72 1.93

RET   CTU   DL

Asset-Turnover Ratios
(2007 Fiscal Year)

(c) Net Profit Margin

10.9

1.0   1.0

RET   CTU   DL

Net Profit Margin %s
(2007 Fiscal Year)

EVALUATE

Sources of Information Other Than Annual Financial Statements

Although our discussion in this chapter has focused on annual financial statements, we don't want you to get the impression that this is the only source of information about a company's financial performance. As an outsider looking in, there are lots of other places you can go to learn more—some of them useful and others not so useful. In this section, you'll learn about which sources are likely to provide information that sheds light on the company's results, and which are dark alleys.

FINANCIAL NEWS

The financial news that appears in newspapers and magazines, as well as in radio and television broadcasts, is a rich source of information about companies. Business reporters and newscasters are adept at digging up information that is newsworthy and useful. In addition to news items that are initiated and written by the communications industry, companies notify the major agencies when they have news they want to share with the public, such as announcements about dividends, changes in management, the status of a labour strike, or plans for the future.

To provide timely information for all external users, Reitmans and almost all other public companies announce quarterly and annual earnings through a press release. This press release isn't issued until three or four weeks after the accounting period ends, because it takes time to identify and compute all the necessary adjusting journal entries that you learned about in Chapter 4. The press release typically includes key figures, management's discussion of the results, and attachments containing a condensed income statement and balance sheet. The information in a press release is fairly reliable, because it's not released until the numbers in it have been checked by management (and by auditors, in the case of *annual* earnings releases). Exhibit 5.12 shows an excerpt from a typical quarterly press release for Reitmans. Notice that it took four weeks from the end of the company's quarter to prepare, check, and release this information.

POINT OF INTEREST

Not every press release is trustworthy. A 23-year-old student was sentenced to 44 months in federal prison in the United States for sending out his own phony press release about Emulex Corporation, which allegedly defrauded investors of $241,814.

---

exhibit **5.12** Excerpt from Earnings Press Release for Reitmans

REITMANS (CANADA) LIMITED RESULTS FOR THE SIX MONTHS ENDED AUGUST 4, 2007

MONTREAL, Sept. 5   Sales for the six months ended August 4, 2007, increased 4.2% to $522,637,000 as compared with $501,797,000 for the six months ended July 29, 2006. The increase in sales is attributed to the net addition of 45 stores year over year. Same store sales for the comparable 26 weeks decreased 1.2%. Operating earnings before depreciation and amortization (EBITDA) decreased 5.9% to $94,691,000 as compared with $100,672,000 last year.

Pro forma numbers show what a company's results would have been had certain events not occurred.

You should realize that management often is motivated to emphasize positive aspects of their financial performance in the press release. A common tactic for emphasizing the positive is to make up "what-if" or **pro forma** numbers that suggest how the company's results would have looked had certain events not occurred during the period. These pro forma numbers typically present a company in a more favourable light than the full set of GAAP numbers reported in the financial statements. Recent studies found that about 85 per cent of American companies and 42 per cent of Canadian companies report pro forma numbers.[3] We provide an example of pro forma reporting in Exhibit 5.13. Since the pro forma earnings for this company were $1.7 billion, and the net income according to GAAP was only $390.9 million, you probably can understand from this example why some analysts refer to pro forma earnings numbers as "earnings before bad stuff."

Many companies follow their press releases with a conference call broadcast on the Internet that allows analysts to grill the company's senior executives with questions about the financial results. By listening to these calls, you can learn a lot about a company's business strategy, its expectations for the future, and the key factors that analysts consider when they evaluate a company. You can check out this useful source of information by visiting each company's own Web site or the archive of conference calls at biz.yahoo.com/cc.

ANNUAL AND QUARTERLY REPORTS

Companies issue a formal quarterly or annual report several weeks after the press release. They aren't issued at the same time as the press release, because it takes some time to gather and report all the detailed information that goes into the financial statement notes.

---

exhibit **5.13** Excerpts from Earnings Press Release

- Income climbs 17% to $1.7 billion, before special items, income taxes, and goodwill amortization
- Net income for the year amounts to $390.9 million

BODY OF RELEASE
Income before special items, income taxes, and goodwill amortization for the year increased 17% to $1.7 billion, compared with $1.4 billion **on the same basis** for the preceding year. Earnings per share before special items and goodwill amortization rose to $0.81, a 16% increase compared with $0.70 on the same basis for the previous year. After the net effect for the special items and goodwill amortization, **net income for the year reached $390.9 million,** or $0.27 per share, against a net income of $975.4 million, or $0.70 per share last year.

Source: "Informative or Misleading?" *CAmagazine,* November 2004. Reproduced with permission from *CAmagazine,* published by the Canadian Institute of Chartered Accountants, Toronto, Canada.

---

[3] Barbara Lougee and Carol Marquardt, "Earnings Informativeness and Strategic Disclosure: An Empirical Examination of 'Pro Forma' Earnings," *The Accounting Review,* July 2004; Entwistle, Feltham, and Mbagwu, "Informative or Misleading?" *CAmagazine,* November 2004.

The annual reports of many publicly traded companies are a thing of beauty. The first half of the report usually begins with a friendly letter to investors from the company's top executives. This is followed by glossy pictures of the company's products and glowing commentaries about the company's brilliant positioning to expand, improve, or even take over its industry. Having developed the right mood with these jazzy marketing tactics in the first half of the report, the annual report then presents the real core: the financial section. This section contains (not necessarily in this order):

1. *Summarized financial data*—key figures covering a period of 5 or 10 years.
2. *Management's discussion and analysis (MD&A)*—an honest and detailed analysis of the company's financial condition and operating results.
3. *Management's statement of responsibility*—describes the steps taken by management to ensure the statements are accurate.
4. *Auditor's report*—the auditor's conclusion about whether GAAP was followed. The warning alarms should go off if this report is qualified in any way.
5. *Financial statements*—the four basic statements that provide the data for the financial analyses you just learned about in this chapter.
6. *Notes*—further information about the financial statements. As you will learn in later chapters, this part is crucial to understanding the financial statement data.
7. *Recent stock price data*—brief summary of highs and lows during the year.
8. *Unaudited quarterly data*—condensed summary of each quarter's results.
9. *Directors and officers*—a list of who's overseeing and running the company.

The MD&A is a must-read for any serious financial statement user.

Now that you've got a handle on what's in an annual report, it'll be easy for you to understand what's in a quarterly report because it's merely a supercondensed version of an annual report. Quarterly reports normally begin with a short letter to shareholders. This is followed by a condensed income statement for the quarter, which often shows less detail than the annual income statement, a condensed balance sheet dated at the end of the quarter, and a condensed statement of cash flows. These condensed financial statements are not audited, so they are labelled as unaudited. Quarterly reports often omit the statement of retained earnings and many notes to the financial statements which are repetitive with those in the company's annual report. Obviously, with all these limitations, the quarterly reports aren't quite as informative as the annual reports, but they have the benefit of being released on a timelier basis (every three months rather than every year).

CANADIAN SECURITIES ADMINISTRATORS (CSA) FILINGS

All Canadian public companies are required to file documents electronically with the stock exchanges where their shares trade and with the Canadian Securities Administrators. These filings are available to the public through the System for Electronic Document Analysis and Retrieval (SEDAR) system, found at www.sedar.com. The most common filings include audited annual financial statements and unaudited interim (quarterly) financial statements, which are similar to the printed reports published for investors, except they don't have the glossy pictures and hype. Companies also file general news releases and material change reports for things like a change in year-end or a change in auditor. The management's discussion and analysis (MD&A) section of the annual report provides some very useful information. For example, Reitmans' MD&A includes 13 pages of information about the operating results and outlook for each of its business segments, as well as a discussion of the risks the company faces and how the company plans to handle those risks.

INVESTOR INFORMATION WEB SITES

In addition to companies' own Web sites, Hoovers.com, fin-info.com, and Yahoo!Finance are three of the thousands of investor information Web sites that contain information about Canadian and American public companies. There is also a lot

of useful information to be found in the business section of the Statistics Canada Web site. Some sections of investor information Web sites provide useful information for evaluating and predicting a company's financial performance, whereas others do not. For example, at Yahoo!CanadaFinance, you can obtain valuable financial information about a company and its industry sector, including financial ratios similar to those you've read about earlier in this chapter. However, at messages.yahoo.com, you also can chat it up with someone using the alias plum_cray_z.

The obvious problem with many of these sites is that it's difficult to sort out what's good versus bad information. Another problem, particularly in the case of financial ratios, is that you're rarely told whether the underlying information is audited or unaudited. As a consequence, it's tough to know whether the analyses are as reliable as they might seem. An additional problem is that many Web sites do not show the formulas used to calculate ratios. That can be a big deal, because *ratios with similar sounding names might be calculated differently.* For example, a few Web sites use long-term debt, rather than total liabilities, to calculate the debt-to-assets ratio. This could cause the ratio to be reported as 6 per cent when it's actually 20 per cent using the ratio shown in this chapter. As with most things in life, be sure you understand and trust it before using it.

RECONSIDER _____
The Financial Reporting Environment

INVESTOR BEWARE

As a financial statement user, you'll have to be on your toes to make sure you don't become the next victim of faulty analysis or management misrepresentation. A good understanding of the financial reporting environment and its potential pitfalls will help keep you on track. Exhibit 5.14 summarizes the financial reporting environment described in this chapter. As the figure suggests, management can get away with misrepresentation only if the company's directors, auditors, analysts, investors, and creditors are

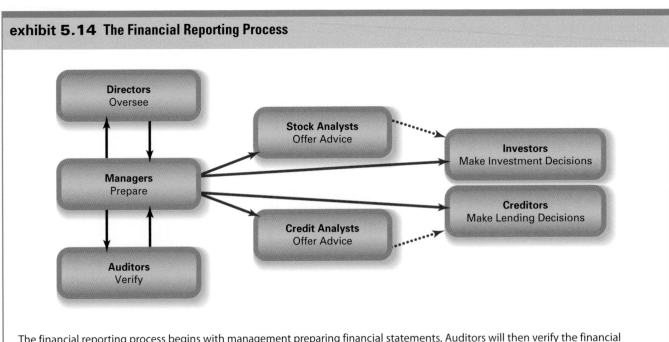

exhibit 5.14 **The Financial Reporting Process**

The financial reporting process begins with management preparing financial statements. Auditors will then verify the financial statements (if annual) and issue an audit report. Directors and legislators provide oversight of the process. The audited financial statements are then distributed to analysts, investors, and creditors as indicated by the solid lines. Dotted lines indicate that analyst reports, which are based in part on a company's financial statements, are provided to investors and creditors.

---

exhibit 5.15 How to Avoid Becoming a Victim of Financial Reporting Fraud

Investor Alert: Stock Market Fraud "Survivor" Checklist
- **Be skeptical.** When you see an offer on the Internet, consider it a scam until you can prove it's legitimate through your own independent research.
- **Consider the source.** Remember that people touting a stock may be company insiders or paid promoters who stand to profit at your expense.
- **Independently verify claims.** Don't rely solely on claims by companies or promoters about new product developments, lucrative contracts, or the company's financial health.
- **Beware of High Pressure Pitches.** Watch out for promoters who pressure you to buy before you have an opportunity to fully research an offer.
- **Research the company.** Always ask for, and carefully read, the company's current financial statements.

Source: Retrieved November 15, 2007, from SEC Web site, www.sec.gov/investor/pubs/fraudsurvivor.htm.

ETHICAL ISSUES

tricked or coerced into going along with the misrepresented results. Although it's difficult to imagine that management could dupe all of these groups, it has happened in the past.

Some investment advisers have claimed that management is able to mislead investors and the other user groups in Exhibit 5.14 only if these users are lax in evaluating a company and its reported results. If you want to avoid becoming the next "point of interest" in a future edition of this book, you should ensure you understand a company's business and its financial statements before investing in it. This sounds a lot like some advice both the CSA and the SEC (the United States' Securities and Exchange Commission) offer to financial statement users on how to avoid becoming a victim of financial reporting fraud. Excerpts of the SEC's advice appear in Exhibit 5.15.

Whereas it might be a while before you can use this advice in your daily life, we can offer a suggestion that will help you right now, right here in this course. As you read the remaining chapters in this book, keep your eyes open for places where accounting numbers are based on estimates or where management can choose from alternative accounting rules. Historically, these are two places where management has made accounting decisions that deceived all but the wisest of financial statement users. And keep adding more ratios to your bag of analytical tools. They will help you understand what's really going on in a business and make you less vulnerable to poor investing decisions.

POINT OF INTEREST

To educate investors about the risk of relying on false information, the SEC in the United States has created a false investment opportunity that promises huge returns to investors. To see this site, go to www.mcwhortle.com.

FOR YOUR REVIEW

DEMONSTRATION CASE

Earlier in this chapter, we said the retail business was similar to the book publishing business. In this demonstration case, we'll take a look at just how similar they are in terms of financial results by analyzing the financial statements of the company that published this textbook. Shortened versions of McGraw-Hill Ryerson's (MHR) financial statements are shown on page 208:

MCGRAW-HILL RYERSON LIMITED
Income Statement (modified)
(Cdn dollars in thousands)
For the Years Ended December 31

	2006	2005
Sales and Other Revenue	$92,878	$87,707
Operating Expenses	41,285	39,496
Editorial, Selling, General and Administrative Expenses	33,546	31,296
Other Expenses	6,915	7,698
Income before Taxes	11,132	9,217
Income Tax Expense	4,126	3,388
Net Income	$ 7,006	$ 5,829

MCGRAW-HILL RYERSON LIMITED
Balance Sheet (modified)
(Cdn. dollars in thousands)
December 31

Assets

	2006	2005
Current Assets	$64,157	$58,485
Other Assets	31,054	29,199
Total Assets	$95,211	$87,684

Liabilities and Shareholders' Equity

	2006	2005
Current Liabilities	$18,499	$16,147
Other Liabilities	214	398
Total Liabilities	18,713	16,545
Shareholders' Equity	76,498	71,139
Total Liabilities and Shareholders' Equity	$95,211	$87,684

Required:

1. Compute MHR's debt-to-assets ratio at the end of the 2006 and 2005 fiscal years. How has MHR changed its financing strategy from 2005 to 2006? Is this likely to be considered a riskier or safer strategy? How similar is the proportion of debt financing used by the book publisher to that used by the retail companies analyzed in Exhibit 5.9?

2. Compute MHR's asset-turnover ratio for 2006 and for 2005. (In thousands, MHR's total assets at December 31, 2004, were $87,372.) Between 2005 and 2006, was there a change in MHR's efficiency in using its assets to generate revenues? Does the book publisher generate more or less sales from each dollar invested in assets than the retail companies analyzed in Exhibit 5.9?

3. Compute MHR's net-profit-margin ratios for the 2006 and 2005 fiscal years. How has this aspect of MHR's financial performance changed? Does the book publisher make more or less profit from each dollar of sales than the retail companies analyzed in Exhibit 5.9?

After completing requirements 1 to 3, check your answers with the following solution.

Suggested Solution

1. **Debt-to-Assets Ratio = Total Liabilities ÷ Total Assets**

	2006	*2005*
$\dfrac{\text{Total Liabilities}}{\text{Total Assets}}$	$\dfrac{\$18,713}{\$95,211} = 0.1965$ or 19.7%	$\dfrac{\$16,545}{\$87,684} = 0.1887$ or 18.9%

MHR has moved toward a slightly riskier financing strategy in 2006, by relying more on debt (up from 18.9 per cent in 2005 to 19.7 per cent in 2006). However, MHR relies much less on debt than the specialty clothing companies in Exhibit 5.9, which financed between 20 and 40 per cent of their total assets using debt.

2. **Asset-Turnover Ratio = Sales Revenue ÷ Average Total Assets**

	2006	*2005*
$\dfrac{\text{Sales Revenue}}{\text{Average Total Assets}}$	$\dfrac{\$92,878}{(\$95,211 + \$87,684)/2} = 1.02$	$\dfrac{\$87,707}{(\$87,684 + \$87,372)/2} = 1.00$

MHR generated slightly more sales per dollar invested in assets in 2006 (1.02) than in 2005 (1.00). In comparison with the specialty cothing companies in Exhibit 5.9, it appears that MHR's assets are not generating sales with nearly the same efficiency. The clothing company that was least efficient at using assets to generate sales (with an asset-turnover ratio of 1.72) was still better than MHR.

3. **Net-Profit-Margin Ratio = Net Income ÷ Sales Revenue**

	2006	*2005*
$\dfrac{\text{Net Income}}{\text{Sales Revenue}}$	$\dfrac{\$7,006}{\$92,878} = 0.0754$ or 7.5%	$\dfrac{\$5,829}{\$87,707} = 0.0665$ or 6.7%

MHR has improved its net profit margin from 6.7 per cent in 2005 to 7.5 per cent in 2006. This means that, in 2006, MHR made almost 8 cents of profit for each dollar of sales. These ratios are much higher than those of Le Château and Danier Leather, but less than Reitmans' 10.9 per cent.

CHAPTER SUMMARY

Describe the main financial statement users and the key qualities of useful information that are of interest to them. p. 190   **LO1**

- The four main financial statement users are:

    Managers, who use accounting information to run the business

    Directors, who use accounting information to oversee the business

    Creditors, who use accounting information to administer business contracts

    Investors, who use accounting information to value the business

- The key qualities of useful information are (1) reliability, (2) relevance, (3) consistency, and (4) comparability.

Explain why managers might misrepresent their financial results, and what helps to prevent this from occurring. p. 192   **LO2**

- Managers can be motivated to misrepresent financial results to create business opportunities (by satisfying loan covenants, increasing equity financing, and attracting business partners) and to satisfy personal greed (enhancing job security, increasing personal wealth, and obtaining a bigger paycheque).

- Managers are deterred from misrepresenting their financial results because doing so is unethical and illegal, and it can result in significant financial and legal penalties. Also, honest managers can develop a reputation for honest reporting, which leads investors to place more trust in them and their financial reports.

- Auditors, directors, and analysts also play a role in reducing the risk of management misrepresentation.

LO3   **Calculate and interpret the debt-to-assets, asset-turnover, and net-profit-margin ratios. p. 195**

- Two commonly used benchmarks for analyzing a company's performance are comparing company results with results in prior periods (time-series analysis) and with competitors' results (cross-sectional analysis).

- The debt-to-assets ratio is calculated by dividing total liabilities by total assets. It indicates the percentage of assets financed by debt, with a higher ratio indicating a riskier financing strategy.

- The asset-turnover ratio is calculated by dividing sales revenue for the period by average total assets held during the period. Average total assets usually is calculated by adding the beginning and ending total assets together and dividing by two. The asset-turnover ratio indicates how well assets are used to generate sales, with a higher ratio indicating greater efficiency.

- The net-profit-margin ratio is calculated by dividing net income by sales revenue. It indicates the ability to generate sales while controlling expenses, with a higher ratio indicating better performance.

LO4   **Describe the information in press releases and stock exchange filings. p. 203**

- News releases typically include key figures (sales revenues, net income), management's discussion of the results, and attachments containing a condensed income statement and balance sheet.

- The annual report includes the annual financial statements, statement of management's responsibility, auditor's report, management's discussion and analysis, stock price data, and other financial schedules.

- Interim financial reports include the quarterly financial statements.

- Material change reports are forms that companies use to report significant current events, such as changes in auditors, and acquisitions of other companies.

LO5   **Describe what investors can do to protect themselves. p. 206**

- Investors cannot afford to be lax in evaluating a company and its reported results. They must ensure that they understand a company's business and its financial statements before investing in it.

FINANCIAL STATEMENT ANALYSIS TIPS

To determine the percentage of assets financed by debt—as a sign of the company's financing risk—calculate the debt-to-assets ratio:

$$\text{Debt-to-Assets Ratio} = \text{Total Liabilities} / \text{Total Assets}$$

To determine how well assets are used to generate sales, calculate the asset-turnover ratio:

$$\text{Asset-Turnover Ratio} = \frac{\text{Sales Revenue}}{\text{Average Total Assets}}$$

To determine a company's ability to generate sales while controlling expenses, calculate the net-profit-margin ratio:

$$\text{Net-Profit-Margin Ratio} = \frac{\text{Net Income}}{\text{Sales Revenue}}$$

KEY TERMS TO KNOW

Comparable
  Information p. 191
Consistent
  Information p. 191
Cross-Sectional
  Analysis p. 197
Earnings Forecast p. 195

Full Disclosure
  Principle p. 194
Loan Covenants p. 191
Pro Forma p. 204
Relevant Information p. 191
Reliable Information p. 191
Stakeholders p. 190

Time-Series Analysis p. 197
Unqualified Audit
  Report p. 194
Vertical (Common-Size)
  Analysis p. 200

_____ **FOR YOUR PRACTICE**

QUESTIONS

1. Describe one decision that each of the four main financial statement user groups makes with financial statement information.

2. What are the four characteristics of *useful* information? Briefly describe each.

3. What three conditions have to be met in order for accounting fraud to occur?

4. In what ways are accounting fraud and academic dishonesty (e.g., cheating) similar? Consider the three conditions necessary for fraud to occur.

5. Why would managers misrepresent the financial results of their companies? What are the incentives for doing this? What are the reasons for not misrepresenting financial results?

6. What role do auditors play in the financial reporting process?

7. Explain the simple business model that starts with obtaining financing and then proceeds through other investing and operating decisions.

8. What two benchmarks are commonly used to interpret and evaluate amounts reported for specific financial statement items?

9. Why are some ratios expressed as percentages whereas others are not?

10. Why do some ratios use just the ending balance sheet amounts, whereas others use averages of the beginning and ending balances?

11. What are the key business activities that the debt-to-assets, asset-turnover, and net-profit-margin ratios assess?

12. What are two potential problems with relying on investor information Web sites for financial statement ratio analyses?

MULTIPLE CHOICE

Select the one alternative that best answers the question or completes the sentence.

1. If total assets increase but total liabilities remain the same, what is the impact on the debt-to-assets ratio?

   a. Increases
   b. Decreases
   c. Remains the same
   d. Cannot be determined without additional information

2. Costco and Sam's Club are two companies that offer low prices for items packaged in bulk. This strategy increases total sales volume, but generates less profit for each dollar of sales. Which of the following ratios is improved by this strategy?

   a. Net-profit-margin
   b. Asset-turnover
   c. Debt-to-assets
   d. All of the above

3. Which of the following would increase the net-profit-margin ratio in the current period?

   a. Increase the amount of research and development in the last month of the year.
   b. Decrease the amount of sales in the last month of the year.
   c. Postpone routine maintenance checks that were to be done this year.
   d. All of the above

4. The asset turnover ratio is directly affected by which of the following categories of business decisions?

   a. Operating and investing decisions
   b. Operating and financing decisions
   c. Investing and financing decisions
   d. Operating, investing, and financing decisions

5. Which of the following reports is not filed annually with the CSA?

   a. Annual financial statements
   c. Comparability report
   b. Interim financial statements
   d. News release

6. Which of the following describes a cross-sectional analysis of your academic performance?

   a. Counting the number of As on your transcript
   b. Comparing the number of As you received this year with the number you received last year
   c. Comparing the number of As you received this year with the number your friend received
   d. Counting the total number of As given out to your class as a whole

7. Which of the following is not a normal function of a financial analyst?

   a. Make predictions about a company's future earnings.
   b. Examine the records underlying the financial statements to verify the use of GAAP.
   c. Make buy, hold, and sell recommendations on a company's shares.
   d. Evaluate a company's past performance.

8. Which of the following is always included in an annual report but never in a quarterly report?

   a. Balance sheet
   c. Management's discussion and analysis
   b. Income statement
   d. Auditor's report

9. Which of the following transactions will increase the debt-to-assets ratio?

   a. The company issues shares to investors.
   b. The company uses cash to buy land.
   c. The company issues a note payable to buy machinery.
   d. None of the above

10. What type of audit report does a company hope to include with its annual report?

    a. Conservative report
    c. Comparable report
    b. Qualified report
    d. Unqualified report

Solutions to Multiple-Choice Questions

1. b   2. b   3. c   4. a   5. c   6. c   7. b   8. d   9. c   10. d

MINI-EXERCISES

L01

M5-1 Matching Players in the Financial Reporting Process with Their Definitions

Match each player with the related definition by entering the appropriate letter in the space provided.

Players		Definitions	
____ 1.	Directors	A.	Advisers who analyze financial and other economic information to form forecasts and stock recommendations
____ 2.	Independent auditors	B.	Investors and creditors (among others)
____ 3.	External users	C.	People who are elected by shareholders to oversee a company's management
____ 4.	Financial analysts	D.	Public accountants who examine financial statements and attest to their fairness

M5-2 Determining the Effects of Transactions on the Balance Sheet   **LO3**
and Income Statement

Complete the following table, indicating the sign and amount of the effect (+ for increase, − for decrease, and NE for no effect) of each transaction. Consider each item independently.

a. Recorded services provided on account for $100.
b. Recorded advertising expense of $10 incurred but not paid for.

	Balance Sheet			Income Statement		
Transaction	**Assets**	**Liabilities**	**Shareholders' Equity**	**Revenues**	**Expenses**	**Net Income**
a						
b						

M5-3 Determining the Effects of Transactions on Debt-to-Assets, Asset-Turnover,   **LO3**
and Net-Profit-Margin

Using the transactions in M5-2, complete the following table by indicating the sign of the effect (+ for increase, − for decrease, NE for no effect, and CD for cannot determine) of each transaction. Consider each item independently.

Transaction	**Debt-to-Assets**	**Asset-Turnover**	**Net-Profit-Margin**
a			
b			

M5-4 Determining the Effects of Transactions on the Balance Sheet and Income   **LO3**
Statement

Complete the following table, indicating the sign and amount of the effect (+ for increase, − for decrease, and NE for no effect) of each transaction. Consider each item independently.

a. Equipment costing $4,000 was purchased by issuing a note payable.
b. Issued 10,000 shares for $90,000 cash.
c. Recorded amortization of $1,000 on the equipment.

	Balance Sheet			Income Statement		
Transaction	**Assets**	**Liabilities**	**Shareholders' Equity**	**Revenues**	**Expenses**	**Net Income**
a						
b						
c						

LO3   M5-5 Determining the Effects of Transactions on Debt-to-Assets, Asset-Turnover, and Net-Profit-Margin

Using the transactions in M5-4, complete the following table by indicating the sign of the effect (+ for increase, − for decrease, NE for no effect, and CD for cannot determine) of each transaction. Consider each item independently.

Transaction	Debt-to-Assets	Asset-Turnover	Net-Profit-Margin
a			
b			
c			

LO3   M5-6 Computing and Interpreting the Net-Profit-Margin Ratio

Gilmore Golf Corporation recently reported the following December 31 amounts in its financial statements (in thousands):

	Current Year	Prior Year
Operating income	$ 170	$140
Net income	85	70
Total assets	1,000	900
Total shareholders' equity	800	750
Sales revenue	900	700

Compute the net profit margin ratio for the current and prior years. What do these analyses indicate?

LO3   M5-7 Computing and Interpreting the Debt-to-Assets Ratio

Using the data in M5-6, compute the debt-to-assets ratio for the current and prior years. What do these analyses indicate?

LO3   M5-8 Computing and Interpreting the Asset-Turnover Ratio

Using the data in M5-6, compute the asset-turnover ratio for the current year. Assuming the asset-turnover ratio in the prior year was 85.2 per cent (0.852), what does your analysis indicate?

LO3   M5-9 Computing and Interpreting Financial Ratios

Key financial data for Columbia Sportwear and Levi Strauss follow. Using two ratios included in this chapter, compare their relative abilities to generate (a) sales from assets and (b) net income from sales. Which company appears more successful on each of these measures?

	Columbia	Levi Strauss
Sales	$1,156	$4,125
Net income	131	156
Total assets, end of year	971	2,814
Total assets, beginning of year	949	2,886

EXERCISES

E5-1 Matching Components of the Financial Reporting Process with Their Definitions   LO1, LO2

Match each component with the related definition by entering the appropriate letter in the space provided.

Components	Definitions
____ 1. CSA	A. Adviser who analyzes financial and other economic information to form forecasts and stock recommendations
____ 2. External auditor	
____ 3. Investor	B. Financial institution or supplier that lends money to the company
____ 4. CEO and CFO	
____ 5. Creditor	C. Chief executive officer and chief financial officer, who have primary responsibility for the information presented in financial statements
____ 6. Financial analyst	
____ 7. Investor information Web site	D. Independent accountant who examines financial statements and attests to their fairness
	E. Canadian Securities Administrators, which regulates financial disclosure requirements
	F. Gathers, combines, and transmits financial and related information from various sources
	G. Individual who purchases shares in companies for personal ownership or for pension funds or mutual funds

E5-2 Matching Definitions with Information Releases Made by Public Companies   LO4

Following are the titles of various information releases. Match each definition with the related release by entering the appropriate letter in the space provided.

Information Release	Definitions
____ 1. Annual report	A. A company-prepared news announcement that is normally distributed to major news agencies
____ 2. Press release	
____ 3. Audited financial statements	B. Annual report filed by public companies with the CSA that contains detailed financial information
____ 4. Interim report	C. Quarterly report filed by public companies with the CSA that contains unaudited financial information
____ 5. MD&A	D. Comprehensive printed report containing the four basic financial statements and related notes, statements by management and auditors, and other descriptions of the company's activities
	E. Detailed description of the company's business risks and strategies

E5-3 Understanding the Financial Reporting Process   LO4

During the first half of 2008, the following information about an interactive computer-game company became available to the public. Match each date in the table below with the related report by entering the appropriate letter in the space provided.

Date Filed/Issued	Report
____ 1. February 24, 2008	A. Annual report mailed to shareholders
____ 2. February 25, 2008	B. Earnings information published in local newspapers around the country
____ 3. March 10, 2008	C. Annual earnings news release
____ 4. June 1, 2008	D. Annual financial statements filed with SEDAR

LO1   **E5-4 Understanding Concepts**

For each of the following practices, give one number from the list that best illustrates the accounting concept that makes the practice useful:

_____ 1. Relevance

_____ 2. Reliability

_____ 3. Consistency

_____ 4. Comparability

_____ 5. Separate entity

_____ 6. Unit of measure

_____ 7. Cost principle

_____ 8. Revenue principle

_____ 9. Matching principle

_____ 10. Full disclosure principle

_____ 11. Conservatism

A. Some costs are expensed when the uncertainty associated with possible future benefits is too great for the cost to qualify as an asset.

B. Revenue is recorded in the income statement only when it has been earned.

C. A note describing the company's accounting policies is included with the financial statements.

D. All the companies in the industry use the same accounting policies.

E. The cost of an asset can be checked for accuracy by looking at the original invoice.

F. The personal assets of the owner are excluded from the balance sheet of the owner's business.

G. The costs of running a business must appear in the income statement at the same time as the revenues they help to generate.

H. A company tries to release its annual earnings information as soon after year-end as possible.

LO1   **E5-5 Matching Events with Concepts**

Following are the concepts of accounting covered in Chapters 2 through 5. Match each event with its related concept by entering the appropriate letter in the space provided. Use one letter for each blank.

Concepts	Events
_____ 1. Users of financial statements	A. Counted unsold items of inventory at the end of the period and valued them in Canadian dollars.
_____ 2. Objective of financial statements	B Reported the amount of amortization expense because it likely will affect important decisions of statement users.
_____ 3. Relevance	C. Maintained a list of all parties who requested a copy of the financial statements.
_____ 4. Reliability	
_____ 5. Consistency	D. Engaged an outside independent accountant to audit the financial statements.
_____ 6. Comparability	
_____ 7. Separate entity	E. Established an accounting policy that sales revenue shall be recognized only when ownership of the goods sold passes to the customer.
_____ 8. Unit of measure	
_____ 9. Cost principle	F. Prepared and distributed financial statements that provide useful economic information.
_____ 10. Revenue principle	
_____ 11. Matching principle	G. Established a policy not to include in the financial statements the personal financial affairs of the owners of the business.
_____ 12. Full disclosure principle	
_____ 13. Conservatism	H. Changed the company's year-end to correspond with that used by others in the industry.
	I. Valued an asset, such as land, at less than its purchase cost because its value had declined permanently.
	J. Disclosed all relevant financial information about the business in the financial statements (including the notes to the financial statements).
	K. Established a policy to report the company's recurring business activities in the same way from year to year.

    L. Adjusted the rent accounts to show the cost of rent relating to the current period.

    M. Acquired a vehicle for use in the business, reporting it at the agreed-upon purchase price rather than its higher sticker price.

E5-6 Understanding the Characteristics of Useful Financial Information and the Financial Reporting Process

LO1, LO4

Your parents would never have imagined that you could make money from video games, but some game developers turned $250 and a good game idea into a $28-million enterprise.[4] The new idea was a game called Pong, and the enterprise was Atari Incorporated. Over the years, Atari has been owned by a variety of companies, including Time-Warner, Hasbro, and, most recently, Infogrames (a public company in France). Infogrames made the following announcement in 2003:

> On March 28, 2003, the Company announced that it has changed its fiscal year-end from June 30 to March 31. As a result of this change, the Company's fiscal year 2003 was a nine-month period. The Company believes that the March 31 year-end is consistent with more of its peers in the video game industry, allowing for more meaningful analysis and comparisons within the sector.

Required:

1. To which of the four characteristics of useful information is the company referring? (*Hint:* Rather than look for key words in the announcement, read it for meaning.)
2. On what type of form would the change in year-end be reported?
3. Since the 2003 fiscal period includes only nine months, will the debt-to-assets, asset-turnover, and net-profit-margin ratios be meaningful in 2003? Explain your reasoning.

E5-7 Computing and Interpreting the Net-Profit-Margin Ratio

LO3

Cascade Corporation manufactures all kinds of lumber and paper products, and sells office supplies through its Office Max division. On January 22, the company issued a press release that reported the following amounts (in thousands) for the year just ended on December 31:

	Current Year	Prior Year
Sales revenue	$8,245	$7,412
Operating income	148	118
Net income	8	11

Required:

Compute the net-profit-margin ratio for the current and prior years. What do these analyses indicate?

E5-8 Understanding the Financial Reporting Process

LO4

1. The information in E5-7 indicated that the Cascade press release was issued on January 22, yet the company's year-end was three weeks earlier on December 31. Why did the company wait so long to issue the press release? Why weren't the financial results announced on January 1?
2. The press release stated that the annual financial statements would be filed sometime in March. Why would the company wait so long to file the statements? Why wouldn't they file them at the same time the press release was issued?
3. Is the company's glossy annual report likely to be issued before or after the electronic filing of the annual financial statements?

---

[4] "Game Boy," *Fortune*, July 8, 2002, p. 122, and retrieved March 12, 2004, from www.thecpl.com.

LO3   **E5-9**   **Analyzing and Interpreting Asset-Turnover and Net-Profit-Margin**

Papa John's is one of the fastest-growing pizza delivery and carry-out restaurant chains in the United States. Presented here are selected income statement and balance sheet amounts (in millions of U.S. dollars).

	Current Year	Prior Year
Total revenue	$1,002	$969
Net income	63	46
Average total assets	365	363

Required:

1. Compute the asset-turnover and net-profit-margin ratios for the current and prior years.
2. Would security analysts more likely increase or decrease their estimates of share value on the basis of these changes? Explain by interpreting what the changes in these two ratios mean.

LO3   **E5-10**   **Analyzing and Interpreting Asset-Turnover and Net-Profit-Margin**

RadioShack Corporation (now part of The Source By Circuit City) has populated the world with its stores—not bad for a company that originally started business as American Hide & Leather Company. Presented here are selected amounts (in millions of U.S. dollars) reported in RadioShack's income statement and balance sheet.

	2006	2005	2004
Net sales	$4,778	$5,082	$4,841
Net income	73	270	337
Total assets	2,070	2,205	2,517
Total liabilities	1,416	1,616	1,595

Required:

1. Compute the asset-turnover and net-profit-margin ratios for 2006 and 2005.
2. Would investment analysts be more likely to increase or decrease their estimates of share value on the basis of these changes? Explain what the changes in these two ratios mean.
3. Compute the debt-to-assets ratio for 2006 and 2005.
4. Would credit analysts be more likely to increase or decrease their estimates of RadioShack's ability to repay lenders on the basis of this change? Explain by interpreting what the change in this ratio means.

LO3   **E5-11**   **Determining the Effects of Transactions on the Balance Sheet and Income Statement**

Gildan Activewear, founded in Montreal in 1984, makes blank T-shirts and other activewear for private label use, and now holds over 40 per cent of the industry market share in the United States. Listed here are selected aggregate transactions from a recent year (in millions). Complete the following table, indicating the sign (+ for increase, − for decrease, and NE for no effect) and amount of the effect of each transaction. Consider each item independently.

a.   Recorded collections of cash from customers of $732.
b.   Repaid $24 of long-term debt.

	Balance Sheet			Income Statement		
Transaction	Assets	Liabilities	Shareholders' Equity	Revenues	Expenses	Net Income
a						
b						

E5-12 Determining the Effects of Transactions on Debt-to-Assets, Asset-Turnover, and Net-Profit-Margin Ratios

LO3

Using the transactions in E5-11, complete the following table by indicating the sign of the effect (+ for increase, − for decrease, NE for no effect, and CD for cannot determine) of each transaction. Consider each item independently.

Transaction	Debt-to-Assets	Asset Turnover	Net Profit Margin
a			
b			

COACHED PROBLEMS

CP5-1 Determining the Effects of Transactions on the Balance Sheet and Income Statement

LO3

Yahoo! Inc. is a leading provider of Internet products and services. (Like you needed to be told that.) Listed here are selected aggregate transactions from 2006 (in millions). Complete the following table, indicating the sign (+ for increase, − for decrease, and NE for no effect) and amount of the effect of each transaction. Consider each item independently.

a. Recorded marketing revenues on account of $4,594.
b. Raised $747 cash by issuing shares.
c. Incurred product development expense of $547, which was paid in cash.
d. Acquired, but haven't yet paid for, equipment for $160.

	Balance Sheet			Income Statement		
Transaction	Assets	Liabilities	Shareholders' Equity	Revenues	Expenses	Net Income
a						
b						
c						
d						

CP5-2 Determining the Effects of Transactions on Debt-to-Assets, Asset Turnover, and Net Profit Margin

LO3

Using the transactions in CP5-1, complete the following table by indicating the sign of the effect (+ for increase, − for decrease, NE for no effect, and CD for cannot determine) of each transaction. Consider each item independently.

Transaction	Debt-to-Assets	Asset Turnover	Net Profit Margin
a			
b			
c			
d			

COACH'S TIP

CP-5-2
a. For a review of how transactions affect ratios, refer to the Chapter 5 Supplement A in the Online Learning Centre.
b. A = L + SE implies that total assets are always greater than total liabilities. This means that, if assets and liabilities change by the same dollar amount, the impact on liabilities will be proportionally bigger than the impact on assets.

CP5-3 Relating Debt-to-Assets Ratio to Vertical Analysis

LO3, LO4

Below, we present a condensed balance sheet for Hudson's Bay Company (HBC) and a partially completed vertical analysis. HBC was founded in 1670 as a fur-trading enterprise and is Canada's oldest corporation as well as its largest department store chain, operating under the banners of The Bay, Zellers, Fields, and Home Outfitters. The numbers presented are as at January 31, 2005, before it was bought and taken private by an American investment firm that paid almost $1 billion.

HUDSON'S BAY COMPANY Balance Sheet (summarized) (in millions of Cdn. dollars) January 31, 2005					
Cash and short-term					
investments	$262	7%	Short-term borrowings	$226	6%
Accounts receivable	547	14	Accounts payable and		
Inventories	1,412	(a)	accrued liabilities	873	(d)
Other current assets	65	2	Long-term debt	709	18
Property and equipment	1,050	(b)	Total Liabilities	1,808	(e)
Goodwill	529	(c)	Contributed capital	1,483	37
Other assets	144	4	Retained earnings	718	18
			Total Shareholders' Equity	2,201	55
			Total Liabilities and		
Total assets	$4,009	100%	Shareholders' Equity	$4,009	100%

Required:

1. Complete the vertical analysis by computing each line-item (*a*) to (*e*) as a percentage of total assets.

2. What were the two largest assets on HBC's balance sheet? What reasons can you think of that would explain this relative emphasis?

3. Does the (rounded) percentage that you calculated in 1 (*e*) correspond to the debt-to-assets ratio reported in Exhibit 5.9?

4. In October 2005, HBC decided to sell its credit card division. Should this decision have been reported to the public? What accounting principle is at risk if a company decides not to report this type of information? How would a decision like this normally be reported to the public? Do some research of your own to see if HBC reported this decision.

COACH'S TIP

1. Cash was 7 per cent of total assets, computed as ($262 ÷ $4,009) × 100.

LO3, LO4

CP5-4 Relating Net-Profit-Margin Ratio to Vertical Analysis

Below, we present a condensed income statement for Wal-Mart, the world's largest retailer, along with a partially completed vertical analysis.

POINT OF INTEREST

Reitmans does not disclose its cost of sales, so we cannot compare Wal-Mart's markup with Reitmans'. At this time, Canadian GAAP encourages but does not require companies to disclose this figure.

WAL-MART STORES INC. Income Statement (summarized) (in billions of U.S. dollars) For the Year Ended January 31					
		2007		**2006**	
Net revenues	$349	100%		$312	100%
Cost of sales	264	(a)		238	76
General, administrative,					
sales, and marketing expenses	64	(b)		55	18
Operating income	21	6		19	6
Other gains (losses)	(4)	(1)		(2)	(1)
Income before income taxes	17	5		17	5
Income tax expense	6	(c)		6	2
Net income	$11	(d)%		$11	3%

Required:

1. Complete the vertical analysis by computing each line-item (*a*) to (*d*) as a percentage of net revenues.
2. Does Wal-Mart's 2007 cost of sales, as a percentage of revenues, represent better or worse performance as compared with 2006?

COACH'S TIP

1. Cost of sales was 76 per cent of net revenues in 2006, which was computed as ($238 ÷ $312) × 100.

GROUP A PROBLEMS

PA5-1 Determining the Effects of Transactions on the Balance Sheet and Income Statement

Listed here are transactions that typically occur each year (in millions). Complete the following table, indicating the sign (+ for increase, − for decrease, and NE for no effect) and amount of the effect of each transaction. Consider each item independently.

a. Recorded revenues of $10 on account.
b. Paid cash to purchase property and equipment costing $4.
c. Purchased additional property and equipment costing $3, by issuing a note payable.
d. Repaid bank loan payable of $10.

LO3

eXcel

	Balance Sheet			Income Statement		
Transaction	Assets	Liabilities	Shareholders' Equity	Revenues	Expenses	Net Income
a						
b						
c						
d						

PA5-2 Determining the Effects of Transactions on Debt-to-Assets, Asset Turnover, and Net Profit Margin

Using the transactions in PA5-1, complete the following table by indicating the sign of the effect (+ for increase, − for decrease, NE for no effect, and CD for cannot determine) of each transaction. Consider each item independently.

LO3

eXcel

Transaction	Debt-to-Assets	Asset Turnover	Net Profit Margin
a			
b			
c			
b			

PA5-3 Relating Debt-to-Assets Ratio to Vertical Analysis

On page 222, we present a condensed balance sheet for Porsche AG, the German luxury car maker, and a partially completed vertical analysis.

LO3

eXcel

PORSCHE AS
Balance Sheet (summarized)
July 31, 2006

(in millions of Euros)					
Cash and short-term			Current liabilities	€4,199	29%
investments	€1,989	14%	Long-term liabilities	5,054	35
Accounts receivable	203	1	Total Liabilities	9,253	(b)
Inventories	594	4	Total Shareholders'		
Other current assets	3,884	(a)	Equity	5,376	(c)
Property and			Total Liabilities and		
equipment	1,178	8	Shareholders'		
Other assets	6,781	46	Equity	€14,629	100%
Total Assets	€14,629	100%			

Required:

1. Complete the vertical analysis by computing each line-item (*a*) to (*c*) as a percentage of total assets.

2. What percentages of Porsche's assets relate to inventories versus property and equipment? What does this tell you about the relative significance of these two assets to Porsche's business?

3. What percentage of Porsche's assets is financed by total shareholders' equity? By total liabilities?

LO3

PA5-4 Relating Net-Profit-Margin Ratio to Vertical Analysis

Below, we present a condensed income statement for Porsche AG, the German luxury car maker, along with a partially completed vertical analysis.

PORSCHE AS
Income Statement (summarized)
For the Year Ended July 31

(in millions of Euros)	2006		2005	
Sales revenues	€7,123	100%	€6,256	100%
Cost of products sold	3,274	46	2,748	(d)
Selling, general, and				
administrative expenses	1,526	(a)	1,403	22
Other operating expenses	664	9	971	16
Non-operating income	451	(b)	104	2
Income before income taxes	2,110	30	1,238	(e)
Income tax expense	717	10	459	7
Net income	€1,393	(c)%	€779	(f)%

Required:

1. Complete the vertical analysis by computing each line-item (*a*) to (*f*) as a percentage of sales revenues.

2. Does Porsche's cost of products sold for the year ended July 31, 2006, as a percentage of revenues, represent better or worse performance as compared with that for the year ended July 31, 2005?

3. Use the percentages that you calculated in 1(*c*) and (*f*) to comment on whether Porsche's net profit margin has improved or deteriorated over the two years?

PA5-5 Calculating Ratios and Performing Ratio Analysis   LO3

Below you will find key figures for three Canadian companies in the beverage industry: a winery, a brewery, and a producer of carbonated soft drinks.

(in thousands)	Andrés Wines Ltd.	Big Rock Brewery	Cott Corporation
Total Assets	$ 162,819	$ 40,928	$ 1,022,000
Average Total Assets	$ 154,896.5	$ 40,869.5	$ 965,400
Total Liabilities	$ 75,651	$ 11,408	$ 540,900
Sales Revenue	$ 167,634	$ 38,790	$ 1,646,300
Net Income	$ 8,538	$ 6,767	$ 78,300

Required:

1. Calculate (*a*) the debt-to-assets ratio, (*b*) the asset-turnover ratio, and (*c*) the net-profit-margin ratios for the three companies.
2. Which company is the most heavily financed by debt? Does this make the company more or less risky than the others?
3. Comment on the profitability of the three companies.
4. List two questions you would want to ask about the above numbers that might impact on how confident you are in your analysis.

GROUP B PROBLEMS

PB5-1 Determining the Effects of Transactions on the Balance Sheet and Income   LO3
Statement

Bombardier, founded in Québec in 1942 and still controlled by the Bombardier family, is a world leader in making civil aircraft, business jets, and railway equipment. It recently sold its recreational business, which produced the legendary Ski-Doo® and Sea-Doo®, as well as ATVs. Listed here are transactions that occurred in a recent year (in millions). Complete the following table, indicating the sign (+ for increase, − for decrease, and NE for no effect) and amount of the effect of each transaction. Consider each item independently.

a. Recorded manufacturing revenues of $14,816.
b. Paid cash to purchase property and equipment costing $308.
c. Declared and paid cash dividend totalling $28.
d. Recorded amortization on property and equipment totalling $518.

	Balance Sheet			Income Statement		
Transaction	Assets	Liabilities	Shareholders' Equity	Revenues	Expenses	Net Income
a						
b						
c						
d						

PB5-2 Determining the Effects of Transactions on Debt-to-Assets, Asset Turnover, and   LO3
Net Profit Margin

Using the transactions in PB5-1, complete the following table by indicating the sign of the effect (+ for increase, − for decrease, NE for no effect, and CD for cannot determine) of each transaction. Consider each item independently.

Transaction	Debt-to-Assets	Asset Turnover	Net Profit Margin
a			
b			
c			
d			

LO3   PB5-3 Relating Debt-to-Assets Ratio to Vertical Analysis

Below, we present a condensed balance sheet and a partially completed vertical analysis for Intrawest, the Canadian company that owns ski and all-season luxury resorts, such as Whistler Blackcomb Ski Resort in British Columbia and Sandestin Golf and Beach Resort in Florida. The figures are for July 30, 2006, before Intrawest was taken private by an international investment firm that bought it for $2.8 billion.

INTRAWEST CORPORATION
Balance Sheet (summarized)
(in thousands of U.S. dollars)   July 30, 2006

Cash	$ 120,374	5%	Current liabilities	$ 534,079	20%
Accounts receivable	200,648	8%	Long-term liabilities	1,132,511	(b)
Other current assets	561,178	21%	Total Liabilities	1,666,590	62%
Resort and travel properties	1,444,638	(a)	Contributed capital	491,095	18%
Other assets	340,244	13%	Retained earnings	509,397	19%
			Total Shareholders' Equity	1,000,492	(c)
			Total Liabilities and Shareholders' Equity		
Total Assets	$2,667,082	100%	Equity	$2,667,082	100%

Required:

1. Complete the vertical analysis by computing each line-item (a) to (c) as a percentage of total assets.
2. What percentage of Intrawest's assets relates to resort and travel properties? What does this tell you about the relative significance of this asset to Intrawest's business?
3. What percentage of Intrawest's assets is financed by total shareholders' equity? By total liabilities?

LO3   PB5-4 Relating Net-Profit-Margin Ratio to Vertical Analysis

Below, we present a condensed income statement for Intrawest, along with a partially completed vertical analysis.

INTRAWEST CORPORATION
Income Statement (adapted)
(in thousands of U.S. dollars)   For the Year Ending June 30

	2006		2005	
Sales revenues—resort, travel, and management operations	$1,108,656	69%	$983,240	61%
Sales revenues—real estate development	488,610	31%	627,515	(d)
Total sales revenues	1,597,266	100%	1,610,755	100%
Operating expenses	1,376,411	(a)	1,486,822	92%

(Continued)

INTRAWEST CORPORATION Income Statement (adapted) (in thousands of U.S. dollars) For the Year Ending June 30				
	2006		**2005**	
General and administrative expenses	33,405	2%	21,271	1%
Amortization expense	104,409	7%	71,837	5%
Other gains	40,289	3%	1,990	0%
Income before income taxes	123,330	8%	32,815	2%
Income tax expense	8,120	(b)	0	0%
Net income	$115,210	(c)	$32,815	(e)

Required:

1. Complete the vertical analysis by computing each line-item (*a*) to (*e*) as a percentage of sales revenues.
2. What part of Intrawest's operations did they seem to concentrate on in 2006 as compared with 2005?
3. Intrawest's sales were lower in 2006 compared with 2005, yet their net income in 2006 was more than triple what it was in 2005. Can you explain why this happened?

PB5-5 Calculating Ratios and Performing Ratio Analysis   LO3

Below you will find key figures for three Canadian companies in the oil and gas industry, taken from recent financial statements.

(in thousands)	Canadian Oil Sands	Pan-Ocean Energy	Primewest Energy
Total Assets	$ 5,067,700	$ 137,506	$ 2,240,900
Average Total Assets	$ 4,663,900	$ 115,879.5	$ 1,965,700
Total Liabilities	$ 2,431,800	$ 45,719	$ 1,046,00
Sales Revenue	$ 1,352,000	$ 87,416	$ 521,900
Net Income	$ 509,200	$ 6,279	$ 103,400

Required:

1. Calculate (*a*) the debt-to-assets ratio, (*b*) the asset-turnover ratio, and (*c*) the net-profit-margin ratios for the three companies.
2. Which company is the most heavily financed by debt? Does this make the company more or less risky than the others?
3. Comment on the profitability of the three companies.
4. List two questions you would want to ask about the above numbers that might impact on how confident you are in your analysis.

SKILLS DEVELOPMENT CASES

S5-1 Finding Financial Information   LO4

Refer to the financial statements of High Liner's financing in Appendix A at the end of this book, or download the annual report from the *Cases* section of the text's Web site at www.mcgrawhill .ca/college/phillips.

Required:

1. Calculate the debt-to-assets ratio for 2007 and 2006. Based on these calculations, has High Liner's financing become more or less risky in 2007 compared with 2006?

2.   Calculate the asset-turnover ratio for 2007 and 2006. (Total assets at December 31, 2005, were $127,253,000.) Based on these calculations, has High Liner used its assets more or less efficiently in 2007 than in 2006?

3.   Calculate the net-profit-margin ratio for 2007 and 2006. Based on these calculations, has High Liner generated more or less profit per dollar of sales in 2007 than in 2006?

LO4

S5-2   Comparing Financial Information

Refer to the financial statements of Sun-Rype by downloading the annual report from the *Cases* section of the text's Web site at www.mcgrawhill.ca/college/phillips.

Required:

1.   Calculate the debt-to-assets ratio for 2007. Based on this calculation, was Sun-Rype's financing more or less risky than High Liner's in 2007?

2.   Calculate the asset-turnover ratio for 2007. Based on this calculation, did Sun-Rype use its assets more or less efficiently than High Liner in 2007?

3.   Calculate the net-profit-margin ratio for 2007. Based on this calculation, did Sun-Rype generate more or less profit per dollar of sales than High Liner in 2007?

LO3

TEAM
CASE

S5-3   Internet-Based Team Research: Examining an Annual Report

As a team, select an industry to analyze. Using your Web browser, each team member should acquire the audited annual financial statements for one Canadian publicly traded company in the industry, with each member selecting a different company. (See S1-3 in Chapter 1 for a description of possible resources for these tasks.)

Required:

1.   On an individual basis, each team member should write a short report that incorporates the following:
     a.   Calculate the debt-to-assets ratio at the end of the current and prior year, and explain any change between the two years.
     b.   Calculate the asset-turnover ratio at the end of the current and prior year, and explain any change between the two years. (To calculate average assets for the prior year, you will need the total assets number for the beginning of the prior year. If this isn't reported in the summarized financial data section in the current annual report, you will need to get it from the prior annual report.)
     c.   Calculate the net-profit-margin ratio at the end of the current and prior years, and explain any change between the two years.

2.   Then, as a team, write a short report comparing and contrasting your companies using these attributes. Discuss any patterns across the companies that you, as a team, observe. Provide potential explanations for any differences discovered.

LO1–LO5

ETHICAL
ISSUES

S5-4   Ethical Decision Making: A Real-Life Example

On February 18, 2000, the board of directors of Aurora Foods Inc.—the maker of Duncan Hines® and Mrs. Butterworth's® products—issued a press release announcing that a special committee had been formed to conduct an investigation into the company's accounting practices. During the financial statement audit for the year ended December 31, 1999, Aurora's auditors had discovered documents that raised questions about how the company accounted for marketing costs incurred to entice grocery stores to promote Aurora's products. The company's stock price fell by 50 per cent in the week following this announcement.

After nearly a year of investigation, Aurora filed revised quarterly reports with the Securities and Exchange Commission (SEC) in the United States, showing that the company had not accrued adequately for liabilities and expenses that had been incurred during the third and fourth quarter of 1998 and during the first three quarters of 1999. Key financial figures for these quarters, as initially reported and as later restated, are shown on page 227.

| | 1998 Q3 | | 1998 Q4 | | 1999 Q1 | | 1999 Q2 | | 1999 Q3 | |
| | (September 30) | | (December 31) | | (March 31) | | (June 30) | | (September 30) | |
(in millions of U.S. dollars)	Initial Report	Restated Report	Initial Report	Restated Report	Initial Report	Restated Report	Initial Report	Restated Report	Initial Report	Restated Report
Assets	$1,457	$1,455	$1,434	$1,448	$1,474	$1,463	$1,558	$1,521	$1,614	$1,553
Liabilities	869	879	830	868	862	882	937	944	983	972
Revenues	220	219	280	277	261	254	222	214	238	231
Net income (loss)	1	(12)	16	5	8	0	8	(4)	11	4

The SEC also investigated and filed a legal claim alleging that Aurora's 36-year-old chief financial officer (CFO) had violated federal securities laws by instructing accounting staff to make false journal entries and prepare two sets of records—one for the company's internal use and another to be provided to the auditors. The SEC alleged that her actions allowed Aurora to meet the net income targets set by Wall Street analysts and the expectations of Aurora investors, and to obtain loans from Chase Manhattan Bank and other lenders. The CFO pled guilty to the charges, was sentenced to 57 months in prison, was barred for life from ever serving as an executive of a public company, and had to return to the company the stock and bonuses that had been awarded to her on the basis of Aurora's false and substantially inflated financial results.

Epilogue: On December 8, 2003, Aurora Foods filed for bankruptcy protection after violating several of its lenders' loan covenants. On March 19, 2004, Aurora emerged from bankruptcy and has since merged with Pinnacle Foods, the maker of Vlasic pickles and Swanson TV dinners.

Required:

1. Using the initially reported numbers, calculate the debt-to-assets ratio (reported as a percentage) at the end of each quarter.

2. Using the restated numbers, calculate the debt-to-assets ratio (reported as a percentage) at the end of each quarter.

3. On an overall basis, did the initially reported numbers suggest more or less financing risk than the restated numbers? Of the key financial statement users mentioned earlier in this chapter in Exhibit 5.1, which would be most influenced by this impact on the debt-to-assets ratio?

4. Using the initially reported numbers, calculate the asset-turnover ratio for the last quarter of 1998 and the first three quarters of 1999. (Note that the asset-turnover ratio will be substantially less than the examples shown earlier in this chapter because they use only three months of revenues. Do not attempt to convert them to annual amounts.)

5. Using the restated numbers, calculate the asset-turnover ratio for the last quarter of 1998 and the first three quarters of 1999.

6. On an overall basis, did the initially reported numbers or the restated numbers present Aurora in a better light? Of the key financial statement users mentioned earlier in this chapter in Exhibit 5.1, which would be most influenced by this impact on the asset-turnover ratio?

7. Using the initially reported numbers, calculate the net-profit-margin ratio (reported as a percentage) at the end of each quarter.

8. Using the restated numbers, calculate the net-profit-margin ratio (reported as a percentage) at the end of each quarter.

9. On an overall basis, did the initially reported numbers or the restated numbers present Aurora in a better light? Of the key financial statement users mentioned earlier in this chapter in Exhibit 5.1, which would be most influenced by this impact on the net-profit-margin ratio?

10. What important role(s) did Aurora's auditors play in this case?

11. Based on specific information in the case, identify the incentives or goals that might have led the CFO to misreport Aurora's financial results. Looking back at the consequences of her dishonest actions, did she fulfill those goals?

LO1–LO5

S5-5 Ethical Decision Making: A Mini-Case

ETHICAL ISSUES

Assume you've been hired to replace an accounting clerk for a small public company. After your second month on the job, the chief financial officer (CFO) approached you directly with a "special project." The company had just finished installing a new production line earlier in the year, and the CFO wanted you to go through all the company's expense accounts with the goal of finding any costs that might be related to the machinery's installation or to "tinkering with it" to get the line working just right. He said that the previous accounting clerk, whom you had replaced, didn't understand that these costs should have been recorded as part of the production line (an asset) rather than as expenses of the period. The CFO indicated that there was some urgency, as the company had to finalize its quarterly financial statements so that they could be filed with the CSA. Also, the company was close to violating its loan covenants, and it needed a few extra dollars of profit this quarter to ensure that the bank didn't demand immediate repayment of the loan. As you thought about this situation, you tried to remember what Chapter 2 in your accounting textbook said regarding the key characteristics of assets.

Required:

1. Which of the three ratios discussed in this chapter (debt-to-assets, asset-turnover, and net-profit-margin) are affected by the decision to record costs as an asset rather than an expense? Indicate whether each ratio will be higher or lower if costs are recorded as an asset rather than an expense.
2. Is there anything in the case that makes you uncomfortable with the work that you've been asked to do?
3. What should you do?

LO2, LO3

S5-6 Critical Thinking: Analyzing Income Statement-Based Executive Bonuses

Callaway Golf believes in tying executives' compensation to the company's performance as measured by accounting numbers. Suppose, in a recent year, Callaway had agreed to pay its executive officers bonuses of up to 60 per cent of base salary, provided that (a) *asset turnover* meets or exceeds 0.8 and (b) *net profit margin* meets or exceeds 5.0 per cent. Callaway's income statement for 2005 is presented here.

CALLAWAY GOLF COMPANY	
Income Statement (adapted)	
Year Ended December 31, 2005	
(in thousands of U.S. dollars)	
Net sales	$ 998,093
Cost of goods sold	583,679
Selling expenses	290,074
General and administrative expenses	80,145
Research and development costs	26,989
Total operating expenses	980,887
Income from operations	17,206
Interest expense	2,279
Other expenses	390
Income before income taxes	14,537
Income tax expense	1,253
Net income	$ 13,284

Callaway executives receive bonuses if *asset turnover* meets (or exceeds) 0.8 or *net profit margin* meets (or exceeds) 5.0 per cent. Their bonuses are even larger if asset turnover meets (or exceeds) 1.6 and net profit margin meets (or exceeds) 7.0 per cent. Total assets were $735,737 (thousand) and $764,498 (thousand) at December 31, 2004 and 2005 respectively.

Required:

1. Use the preceding information to determine whether Callaway executives met the two bonus targets for 2005.

2. Explain why the bonus arrangement might be based on both *asset-turnover* and *net-profit-margin* ratios, rather than just one of these two ratios.

S5-7 Understanding Concepts

LO1

For each of the following cases, discuss the accounting concepts involved, and recommend what should be done.

Case A

Didier Construction purchased a truck with a sticker price of $10,000. They got a great deal, paying only $8,400. The accountant made the following journal entry:

dr	Machinery 10,000		
	cr	Cash	8,400
	cr	Miscellaneous revenue	1,600

Case B

Can-Pacific Airlines offers frequent flyer points to customers. When the points are redeemed, the company gives the customer a free trip. At the end of the year, there are many million points outstanding in the hands of customers. If these points are all redeemed next year, Can-Pacific will have to give thousands of free trips to these frequent flyers. Can-Pacific does not record the cost of free trips, nor does it disclose details of the frequent flyer program in the notes to its financial statements.

S5-8 Computing, Charting, and Interpreting Time-Series and Cross-Sectional Analyses

LO3

Assume that *Candy Industry Magazine* has contracted you to write an article discussing the financial status of Hershey Foods Corporation over the last few years. The editor suggests that your article should also compare Hershey's recent financial performance with the performance of their competitors, like Tootsie Roll Industries and gum-maker Wm. Wrigley Jr. You gather the following information from the three companies' Web sites (all have December 31 year-ends).

e**X**cel

(in millions of U.S. dollars)	Hershey Foods Corporation			Tootsie Roll Industries	Wm. Wrigley Jr. Company
	2004	2005	2006	2006	2006
Total Liabilities	$2,676	$3,246	$3,474	$161	$2,274
Total Assets	$3,813	$4,263	$4,158	$792	$4,662
Sales Revenues	$4,416	$4,820	$4,944	$496	$4,686
Net Income	$ 574	$ 489	$ 559	$ 66	$ 529

Required:

LO2

Enter the above information into a spreadsheet and perform the following analyses:

1. **Time-series analysis:** Demonstrate the changes in Hershey's size over the last three years by charting its total liabilities, total assets, sales revenues, and net income.

2. **Cross-sectional analysis:** Demonstrate the size of Hershey relative to Tootsie Roll and Wm. Wrigley Jr. by charting the three companies' total liabilities, total assets, sales revenues, and net income for 2006.

3. **Ratio analysis:** Compare the performance of Hershey relative to Tootsie Roll and Wm. Wrigley Jr. by computing the debt-to-assets and net-profit-margin ratios for 2006.

Although you're confident you can use a spreadsheet to complete the ratio analyses, you realize you'll need Billy's help with the charting to be done in the time-series and cross-sectional analyses. Here's his reply.

From: BillyTheTutor@yahoo.com
To: Overwhelmed@hotmail.com
Cc:
Subject: Excel Help

I can imagine that the readers of *Candy Industry Magazine* are on a constant sugar rush, so that's a great idea to present the time-series and cross-sectional analyses in easily digested charts. Using the charting function in Excel isn't too difficult. The first thing to do is enter the data into a spreadsheet exactly as it appears in the table. Next, display the chart toolbar by clicking on View/Toolbar/Chart.

   To produce the time-series chart, click on the cell containing Hershey's 2006 total liabilities and drag to the cell containing Hershey's 2004 net income. With these cells selected, click on the 3D column chart icon to chart the data. You can change the layout by clicking on the chart and then Chart/Source Data in the pull-down menu. Click on the Data Range tab to indicate whether the data are presented as columns or rows in your spreadsheet (select Columns). To add labels, click on the Series tab, select each series one at a time, and enter a name for each (Series 1 should be named 2006). Before you close the box, click on the icon beside the "Category (X) axis labels:" which will take you back to your spreadsheet. Once there, select the financial statement category names by clicking on the name "total liabilities" and dragging to "net income." After selecting these cells, hit enter on the keyboard. If you followed these directions exactly, you should have a decent-looking time-series chart. Play around with the appearance by selecting 3-D View . . . from the Chart pull-down menu. Follow these same basic steps to produce the cross-sectional chart.

CHAPTER

6

Financial Reporting Controls for Merchandising Operations

Understand internal control.
LO1 Describe the purpose of internal controls.

Study financial reporting controls related to cash, inventory, purchases, and sales.
LO2 Perform a key cash control by reconciling to bank statements.

LO3 Describe an operating cycle, and explain the use of a perpetual inventory system as a control in a merchandising operation.

LO4 Account for and analyze purchase and sales transactions under a perpetual inventory system.

LO5 (Supplement A) Account for inventory under a periodic inventory system.

Evaluate the operating results of merchandisers.
LO6 Analyze a merchandiser's multi-step income statement.

Reconsider the impact of operating cycles on financial results.
LO7 Explain factors to consider when comparing across industries.

INSIDE LOOKING OUT

OUTSIDE LOOKING IN

This chapter focuses on how merchandisers track and report operating activities related to cash, product purchases, and sales. We focus on Shoppers Drug Mart Corporation, Canada's only nationwide, as well as its largest, drugstore chain.

During a long night of studying, there's nothing like a revitalizing snack to perk you up, right? Imagine your disappointment if you went to snack on a stack of Pringles™ chips but discovered the container was empty. How could this have happened? Did you forget that you already ate them, or did that sneaky roommate of yours pilfer them? Oh well, there's always the yogurt you've got in the fridge. Oh, wait, it's mouldy. Looks like you'll have to go to the ATM so you can buy more goodies at a nearby convenience store. But what if you found that someone had emptied almost all of your bank account last month? What an unpleasant surprise that would be! All of these problems could have been avoided had you exercised tighter control over your day-to-day activities.

Good controls are needed, not only by individuals, but also by every business, ranging from small convenience stores to massive box supercentres. At a very basic level, these businesses face many of the same potential problems as you did in our opening example. They need to ensure that they have inventory on hand to meet their customers' needs, but they don't want too much inventory hanging around because it can become spoiled, stale, damaged, obsolete, or stolen before it is sold to customers. To combat these potential problems, most businesses, including **SHOPPERS DRUG MART**, use special accounting systems to track and control inventory purchases and sales. These companies also implement strict controls to monitor their cash levels because, like many inventory items, cash is easy to carry and ready to use—two features that make it attractive to thieves. We'll discuss some common controls in this chapter, which will help you to gain a better understanding of how business operations are managed. It also should give you some useful ideas on how to ensure that your own snacks and cash don't unknowingly disappear.

This company was only founded in 1962, but what was once a small pharmacy in Toronto has grown into an organization of over 1,000 stores from coast to coast, with thousands of products and almost $8 billion in sales annually. Shoppers needs state-of-the-art accounting systems to track its inventory purchases and sales and to ensure that the cash related to these activities is properly recorded in its accounts. In this chapter, you will learn about unique aspects of operating a merchandising company like Shoppers, and systems that control operating activities. You'll also learn what to look for in a merchandiser's financial statements, and how this differs from analyzing the financial statements of other types of companies. The Learning Objectives, found on the first page of this chapter, provide the specifics about where you should focus in this chapter.

UNDERSTAND _____
Financial Reporting Controls

Internal controls are the methods that a company uses to protect against theft of assets, to enhance the reliability of accounting information, to promote efficient and effective operations, and to ensure compliance with applicable laws and regulations.

Internal control has been important to companies for decades. However, with the business failures and accounting scandals involving Enron and numerous other companies in the early 2000s, a lot more attention has been placed recently on controls, particularly those relating specifically to financial reporting. The new SOX rules and their Canadian equivalents, mentioned in Chapter 5, have led companies to strengthen their internal controls and better inform users about how effective their accounting systems are in producing accurate financial statements. Effective internal controls play an essential role in creating an ethical environment, and ultimately in improving financial performance. As explained in earlier chapters, every public company's annual report must include a report from management on the company's internal control over financial reporting. The goal of this rule is to tell financial statement users whether the company's controls give reasonable assurance that its assets are safeguarded from material loss and inappropriate use, and that transactions are authorized and recorded accurately. For an example of a Statement of Management's Responsibility, see page 618 for the annual report of High Liner Foods in Appendix A at the back of this book.

The increased use of computers and other electronic devices in business over the last few decades has both helped and hindered the control process. On the plus side, computerized accounting systems are a lot more accurate than manual systems, and devices such as electronic sensors on valuable merchandise have reduced theft for stores like Reitmans and Danier Leather. On the other hand, computer systems also provide unique ways for errors to occur and for employees and outsiders to commit fraud. For example, when companies transact online, as Shoppers does, security issues are key. Companies must protect themselves against unauthorized access as well as against system failures.

Internal control is a broad concept that includes much more than accounting. It includes instilling ethical principles, setting strategic objectives for the company, identifying risks facing the company, hiring good employees, motivating them to achieve the company's objectives, and providing the resources and information they need to fulfill those objectives. Rather than overload you with a list of all the control principles that senior executives must think about, we're going to focus on just five basic principles that relate to financial reporting, the main topic in this textbook, and that you're likely to see as an employee working in a company. Then we'll introduce you to a few specific examples, focusing on cash, and purchases and sales of merchandise inventory. When you encounter controls during your career, you should be able to appreciate why they exist and ensure that others respect them.

PRINCIPLES OF INTERNAL CONTROL

Exhibit 6.1 presents five principles of internal control that are used to design accounting systems. These principles are applied to all aspects of a company's business activities, such as human resource management, finance, and marketing, but our focus here is on those that relate to merchandising operations. We should mention that other control principles and many, many examples exist. We can't possibly cover them all, so in this chapter, we give a few examples to show how merchandisers apply the basic principles to activities involving cash, purchases, and sales of inventory. Other internal controls will be discussed in later chapters and in advanced courses in accounting and management.

1. Establish Responsibility.   Assign each task to only one employee because it allows you to determine who caused any errors or thefts that occur. That's the reason Shoppers assigns a separate cash register drawer to each employee at the beginning of a shift. If two cashiers were to use the same drawer, it would be impossible to know which cashier caused the drawer to be short on cash. With only one person responsible for putting money in and taking money out of the drawer, there's no doubt about who is responsible for a cash shortage.

2. Segregate Duties.   Segregation of duties involves assigning responsibilities so that one employee can't make a mistake or commit a dishonest act without someone else knowing it. That's why cashiers at Shoppers need a manager to approve price changes at the checkout. Without this control, cashiers could ring up a sale, collect cash from the customer, and later reduce the amount of the sale and pocket the excess cash without anyone knowing. Segregation of duties is most effective when responsibilities for related activities are assigned to two or more people and when responsibilities for record-keeping are assigned to people who do not also handle the assets that they are accounting for. One employee should not initiate, approve, record, and have access to the items involved in a transaction.

> **Segregation of duties** is an internal control that is designed into the accounting system. It involves separating employees' duties so that the work of one person can be used to check the work of another person.

To segregate duties in an effective way, a company should:

1. Never have one individual responsible for initiating, approving, and recording any given transaction, and
2. Separate the responsibility of physically handling assets from the process of recording transactions related to those assets.

exhibit 6.1   Common Principles of Internal Control

Principle	Explanation	Examples	
1. Establish responsibility	Assign each task to only one employee.	Each Shoppers cashier uses a different cash drawer.	
2. Segregate duties	Do not make one employee responsible for all parts of a transaction.	Shoppers cashiers, who ring up sales, do not also approve price changes.	
3. Restrict access	Do not provide access to assets or information unless it is needed to fulfill assigned responsibilities.	Shoppers secures video games, cash, and its own computer systems (passwords, firewalls).	
4. Document procedures	Prepare documents to show activities that have occurred.	Shoppers pays suppliers using pre-numbered cheques.	
5. Independently verify	Check others' work.	Shoppers compares cash balances in its accounting records to the cash balances reported by its bank, and accounts for any differences.	

3. Restrict Access.   Some controls involve rather obvious steps like physically locking up valuable assets (such as Shoppers' inventory of video games) and electronically securing access to other assets and information (such as requiring a password to open a cash register or installing a firewall on the computer system). Access should be provided on an as-needed basis. If it's not needed to fulfill your assigned responsibilities, you should be denied access to it.

4. Document Procedures.   Documents are such a common part of business that you might not realize they actually represent an internal control. By documenting each business activity, a company creates a record of whether goods have been shipped, customers billed, cash received, and so on. Without documents, a company wouldn't know what transactions have already been or still need to be entered into its accounting system. To enhance this control further, most companies assign a sequential number to each document and then check at the end of every accounting period that each document number corresponds to one, and only one, entry in the accounting system. So the next time you get a movie ticket from your local AMC Theater, a bill for cable services from Rogers, or an electronic receipt from PayPal, you should realize that these represent important internal controls.

5. Independently Verify.   Independent verification can occur in various ways. The most obvious is to hire someone (an internal auditor) to check that the work done by others within the company is appropriate and supported by documentation. Independent verification also can be made part of a person's job. For example, before Shoppers issues a cheque to pay the bill for a truckload of merchandise, a clerk first verifies that the bill relates to goods actually received and is calculated correctly. A final form of independent verification involves comparing the company's accounting information with information kept by an independent third party. This commonly occurs when the company's cash records are compared with a statement of account issued by a bank. This procedure, called a *bank reconciliation*, is demonstrated in the next section.

Limitations of Internal Control

One thing to be aware of is that internal control systems have their limitations. For example, it may not be practical for a small business to segregate duties adequately. One employee may have access to the whole system and, in this case, it is even more important than usual to hire a competent and trustworthy individual. Secondly, no system, no matter how well designed, can entirely eliminate errors or the potential for fraud. Even good employees get tired or rushed sometimes and will make mistakes or cut corners. If an employee is really out to beat the system, he or she will find a way to do it. People can work together (collude) to get around particular controls, or even disarm (override) controls. Third, control systems cost money and, taken to the extreme, can overload a business with excessive procedures and policies. For example, you could probably design a system that would eliminate merchandise theft entirely, but it might cost many times more than the theft itself. As with any investment, management has to decide whether the benefits exceed the costs.

STUDY _____
Control and Accounting for Cash, Purchases, and Sales

CASH CONTROL AND REPORTING

Cash is money or any instrument that banks will accept for deposit and immediate credit to a company's account, such as a cheque, money order, or bank draft.

Every type of company—service, merchandising, and manufacturing—keeps tight control over its **cash**. You probably use some of the same controls as many companies, without even knowing it. Go ahead, fill in the following checklist, and we'll tell you how you're doing.

Do you ...		Yes	No
...	**keep a limited supply of cash on hand?**	☐	☐
...	**prevent others from writing cheques against your bank account?**	☐	☐
...	**regularly account for differences between the balance in your chequebook and the balance on your bank statement?**	☐	☐

If you answered yes to the first question, you clearly understand that it is safer not to carry around a huge wad of cash. You probably make use of direct deposit for the salary you get from your part-time job, and pay for your purchases with debit or credit cards, pre-authorized payments, or cheques. The term *petty cash* refers to the small amount of cash that is kept on hand by a business to deal with small necessary cash purchases, such as COD courier charges and taxis for staff. A number of control procedures are put in place for petty cash, such as keeping the amount small, keeping it in a locked box accessible by only one person who is held accountable for it, and having a separate person review the receipts before the fund is replenished.

If you're like most people, you probably answered yes to the first two questions, and no to the third. Unfortunately, this is one instance where two out of three is bad. The process of accounting for differences between your cash records and your bank's records is called "reconciling," and it is one of the most important of all cash controls. By preparing a **bank reconciliation**, you can identify differences that exist between your records and those kept by someone independent of you, which essentially means it's a way to double-check the accuracy of what you've recorded. Businesses consider bank reconciliations so important that they prepare a new one every month. You should, too. In the remainder of this section, we'll show you how.

> A **bank reconciliation** is an internal report prepared to verify the accuracy of both the bank statement and the cash accounts of a business or individual.

Need for Reconciliation

A bank reconciliation involves comparing your own cash records with the cash balance reported in your bank's statement of account to see whether the records are in agreement. Your records can differ from your bank's records for two basic reasons: (1) you've recorded some items in your records that the bank doesn't know about at the time it prepares your statement of account, or (2) the bank recorded some items in its records that you don't know about until you read your bank statement. Examples of these differences are summarized in Exhibit 6.2 and are discussed below.

1. Bank errors. Bank errors happen in real life just as they do in Monopoly®. If you discover a bank error, you'll need to ask the bank to correct its records, but you needn't change yours.

2. Time lags. Time lags are very common, even when you use electronic banking. A time lag occurs, for example, when you make a deposit after the bank's normal business hours. *You* know you've made the deposit, but your bank doesn't know until it processes the deposit the next day. Time lags involving deposits are called *deposits in transit*. Another common time lag is an *outstanding cheque*. This occurs when you write and mail a cheque, say, to your cable company, but your bank doesn't find out about it until the cable company deposits the cheque in its own bank, which then notifies your bank. Online banking transactions are often processed on the next business day. As you will see later, deposits in transit and outstanding cheques are a significant part of a bank reconciliation, but they do not require any further action on your part.

exhibit 6.2   Possible Differences between What You and Your Bank Know

Your bank may not know about . . .	You may not know about . . .
1. Errors made by the bank	3. Interest the bank has put into your account
2. Time lags	4. Electronic funds transfers (ETF)
a. Deposits that you made recently	5. Service charges taken out of your account
b. Cheques that you wrote recently	6. Customer cheques you deposited but that bounced
	7. Errors made by you

3. Interest deposited.   You may know that your bank pays interest to you, but you probably don't know exactly how much interest you'll get because it varies, depending on the average balance in your account during that month. When you read your bank statement, you'll learn how much interest you need to add to your records.

4. Electronic funds transfers (ETF).   It doesn't happen every day, but occasionally funds may be transferred into or out of your account without your knowing about it. If you discover these electronic transfers on your bank statement, you'll need to record them in your accounts.

5. Service charges.   These are amounts the bank charges you for processing your transactions. Rather than send a bill to you and wait for you to pay it, the bank just takes the amount directly out of your account. You'll need to reduce your book balance to reflect these charges.

6. Bounced cheques.   These are cheques that you have previously deposited in your bank account but are later rejected by your bank because the cheque writer did **not** have **sufficient funds** to cover the cheque. Because the bank increased your account when you first deposited the cheque, the bank will decrease your account when it discovers it was not a valid deposit. You will need to reduce the cash balance in your records for these bounced cheques, and you'll have to try once again to collect the amount still owed to you by the cheque writer.

7. Your errors.   These are mistakes that you've made or amounts that you haven't yet recorded in your cheque book, such as those ATM slips that you didn't get around to recording before they went through the wash. You'll now have to adjust your records for these items.

The Bank Statement

Before we get into the nitty gritty of how you can prepare a bank reconciliation, let's have a quick look at what a typical bank statement reports. Exhibit 6.3 presents a typical bank statement for Wonderful Merchandise and Things (WMT).

Reconciling the Accounting Records and Bank Statement

Usually, the ending cash balance as shown on the bank statement does not agree with the ending cash balance shown by the related *Cash* account on the books of the company. For example, the *Cash* account of WMT at the end of June might contain the information shown in the T-account below the bank statement.

exhibit 6.3 Example of a Bank Statement

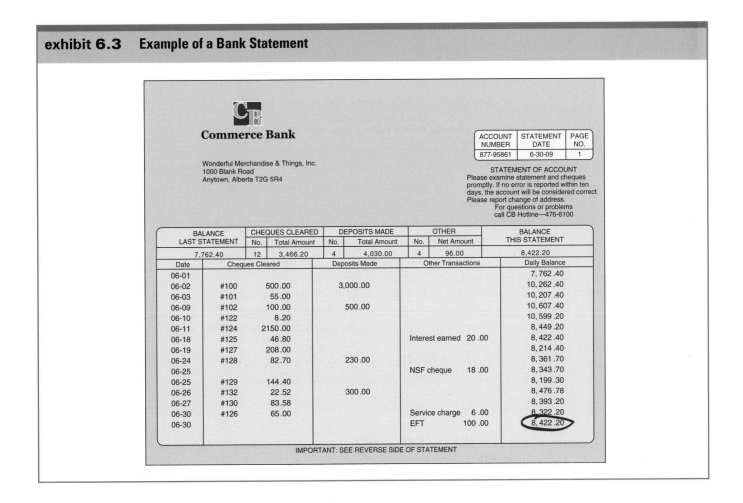

Commerce Bank

ACCOUNT NUMBER	STATEMENT DATE	PAGE NO.
877-95861	6-30-09	1

Wonderful Merchandise & Things, Inc.
1000 Blank Road
Anytown, Alberta T2G 5R4

STATEMENT OF ACCOUNT
Please examine statement and cheques promptly. If no error is reported within ten days, the account will be considered correct. Please report change of address.
For questions or problems call CB Hotline—476-6100

BALANCE LAST STATEMENT	CHEQUES CLEARED		DEPOSITS MADE		OTHER		BALANCE THIS STATEMENT
	No.	Total Amount	No.	Total Amount	No.	Net Amount	
7,762.40	12	3,466.20	4	4,030.00	4	96.00	8,422.20

Date	Cheques Cleared		Deposits Made	Other Transactions		Daily Balance
06-01						7,762.40
06-02	#100	500.00	3,000.00			10,262.40
06-03	#101	55.00				10,207.40
06-09	#102	100.00	500.00			10,607.40
06-10	#122	8.20				10,599.20
06-11	#124	2150.00				8,449.20
06-18	#125	46.80		Interest earned	20.00	8,422.40
06-19	#127	208.00				8,214.40
06-24	#128	82.70	230.00			8,361.70
06-25				NSF cheque	18.00	8,343.70
06-25	#129	144.40				8,199.30
06-26	#132	22.52	300.00			8,476.78
06-27	#130	83.58				8,393.20
06-30	#126	65.00		Service charge	6.00	8,322.20
06-30				EFT	100.00	8,422.20

IMPORTANT: SEE REVERSE SIDE OF STATEMENT

dr Cash (A) cr			
June 1 balance	6,971.40		
June deposits	5,830.00	June cheques written	3,743.40
Ending balance	9,058.00		

COACH'S TIP

This T-account shows only the total deposits and total cheques written during June. Details for each deposit and each cheque are available in the company's daily deposit and cheque records.

The $8,422.20 ending cash balance shown on the bank statement (Exhibit 6.3) differs from WMT's ending cash balance of $9,058.00. To determine the appropriate cash balance, these balances need to be reconciled. Exhibit 6.4 shows the bank reconciliation prepared by WMT for the month of June. The completed reconciliation finds that the up-to-date cash balance is $9,145.00, an amount that differs from both the bank's statement and WMT's accounting records. This balance is the amount that WMT will report on its balance sheet after adjusting its *Cash* balance with the adjusting journal entries presented below—after we describe the steps WMT uses to prepare the bank reconciliation.

WMT followed these steps in preparing the bank reconciliation in Exhibit 6.4:

1. Identify the deposits in transit.   A comparison of WMT's recorded deposits with those listed on the bank statement revealed that WMT made a deposit of $1,800 on June 30 that was not listed on the bank statement. More than likely, the bank won't process this deposit until the first business day after the July 1 holiday. Because this amount was

exhibit 6.4   Bank Reconciliation Illustrated

WONDERFUL MERCHANDISE AND THINGS, INC.
Bank Reconciliation
For the Month Ending June 30, 2008

Bank Statement		Company's Books	
Ending cash balance per bank statement	$ 8,422.20	Ending cash balance per books	$9,058.00
Additions		Additions	
(1) Deposit in transit	1,800.00	(3a) Interest received from the bank	20.00
	10,222.20	(3b) ETF received from customer	100.00
			9,178.00
Deductions		Deductions	
(2) Outstanding cheques	1,077.20	(3c) NSF cheque of R. Smith	18.00
		(3d) Bank service charges	6.00
		(4) Error in recording cheque no. 126	9.00
Up-to-date ending cash balance	$ 9,145.00	Up-to-date ending cash balance	$9,145.00

in WMT's books on June 30, it is entered on the reconciliation as an addition to update the bank's records.

2. Identify the outstanding cheques.   A comparison of the cheques listed on the bank statement with the company's record of written cheques showed the following were still outstanding (had not been processed by the bank) at the end of June:

Cheque No.	Amount
103	$ 145.00
123	815.00
131	117.20
Total	$1,077.20

This total was entered on the reconciliation (in Exhibit 6.4) as a deduction from the bank account because the bank will eventually deduct these cheques when they clear the bank. (They've already been deducted from the company's cash records.)

3. Record other transactions on the bank statement.

a. *Interest received* from the bank, $20—entered on the bank reconciliation as an addition to the book balance because it's included in the bank balance but not yet in the company's books.

b. *Electronic funds transfer* received from customer, $100—entered on the bank reconciliation as an addition to the book balance because it's included in the bank balance but not yet in the company's books.

c. *NSF cheque* of R. Smith, $18—entered on the bank reconciliation as a deduction from the book balance because it was deducted from the bank statement balance but not yet deducted from the company's cash records.

d. *Service charges*, $6—entered on the bank reconciliation as a deduction from the book balance because it has been deducted from the bank balance but not yet removed from the *Cash* account in the company's books.

4. Determine the impact of errors. After performing the three steps listed above, WMT found that the reconciliation was out of balance by $9. Upon checking the journal entries made during the month, WMT found that cheque no. 126 was recorded in the company's accounts as $56 when, in fact, the cheque had been filled out for $65 (in payment of an account payable). As Exhibit 6.3 shows on page 237, the bank correctly processed the cheque (on June 30) as $65. To correct its own error, WMT must deduct $9 (= $65 − $56) from the company's books side of the bank reconciliation.

There is one other step in the reconciliation process that is not part of our example. If there were outstanding cheques or deposits on last month's bank reconciliation, make sure that they cleared the bank this month. If not, they must appear as reconciling items on this month's reconciliation as well.

Now that we know the up-to-date cash balance is $9,145.00, we need to prepare and record adjusting journal entries that will bring the *Cash* account to that balance. Remember that the entries on the *Bank Statement* side of the bank reconciliation do not need to be adjusted by WMT because they will work out automatically when the bank processes them next month. Only the items on the company's books side of the bank reconciliation need to be adjusted in the company's records, using the following entries:

This example involves the company's error in recording the amount of the cheque. In other cases, the bank errs if it processes the cheque at the wrong amount. In all instances, the amount written on the cheque is the correct amount at which the transaction should be recorded.

Interest Received:

3.	(a)	dr	Cash (+A)	20	
		cr	Interest Revenue (+R, +SE)		20

To record interest received from the a customer

ETF Received:

3.	(b)	dr	Cash (+A)	100	
		cr	Accounts Receivable (−A)		100

To record ETF received from a customer

NSF Cheque:

3.	(c)	dr	Accounts Receivable (+A)	18	
		cr	Cash (−A)		18

To record amount rejected by bank and still owed by customer

Service Charges:

3.	(d)	dr	Bank Fee Expense (+E, −SE).	6	
		cr	Cash (−A)		6

To record service charge deducted by bank

Companies that record bank charges in an account called "other expenses" lose the opportunity to monitor and control these charges effectively, and, if you have a bank account, you know how quickly they can add up. Keeping them in their own account allows for better control, and that is what we have done here.

Company Error:

4.		dr	Accounts Payable (−L).	9	
		cr	Cash (−A)		9

To correct error made in recording a cheque paid to a creditor

Assets	=	Liabilities	+	Shareholders' Equity
Cash $(+20 +100 - 18 - 6 - 9) +87$		Accounts Payable -9		Interest Revenue $(+R) +20$
Accounts Receivable $(100 - 18) - 82$				Bank Fee Expense $(+E) -6$

In addition to preparing a monthly bank reconciliation, other common cash controls include reconciling cash receipts with bank deposit slips and matching purchase orders with supplier invoices before authorizing payments to suppliers. Speaking of suppliers, we'll now take a look at how merchandising companies control and account for purchases of inventory from suppliers. But before we do that, we should define merchandising companies and explain how they differ from other types of businesses.

HOW'S IT GOING? A Self-Study Quiz

Indicate which of the following items discovered when preparing a company's bank reconciliation will require an adjustment to the *Cash* balance on the company's books.

1. Outstanding cheques

2. Deposits in transit

3. Bank service charges

4. NSF cheques that were deposited

After you have finished, check your answers with the solutions presented in the margin.

Quiz Answers

Only 3 and 4 require adjustment.

3. Bank service charges are deducted from the company's account, so, cash must be reduced and an expense must be recorded.

4. All cheques are recorded on the books as increases in the cash account when they are deposited. So, when the bank later rejects an NSF cheque, cash must be decreased and the related account receivable increased.

OPERATING CYCLES

Operating Activities and Cycles

A **service company** sells services rather than physical goods. A **merchandising company** sells goods that have been obtained from a supplier. A **manufacturing company** sells goods that it has made itself.

An **operating cycle** is the series of activities that a company undertakes to generate sales and, ultimately, cash.

Based on their operating activities, businesses can be classified into three types: (1) **service companies**, (2) **merchandising companies**, and (3) **manufacturing companies**. As Exhibit 6.5 shows, these business types involve slightly different operating cycles. Service companies sell services, ranging from fitness training to Internet access to hairstyling, which you learned about through studying First Choice Haircutters in Chapters 2 to 4. The **operating cycle** for service companies is simple: use cash to provide services that are sold to customers, and then collect cash from those customers. The operating cycle for merchandising companies like Shoppers Drug Mart has an additional step: use cash to buy physical goods (called inventory); then sell the inventory to customers and collect cash from those customers. Manufacturing companies, like Mattel in Chapter 1, also sell physical products, but rather than acquire these in a ready-to-sell format, manufacturing companies make their own products from raw materials that they buy from suppliers.

This chapter focuses on merchandising companies. When talking about merchandising companies, most business people refer to two specific subcategories: *retail* merchandising companies that sell directly to consumers, as Shoppers does, and *wholesale* merchandising companies, like Oakley, that sell to retailers rather than to end consumers. The discussion in this chapter applies equally to retail and wholesale merchandisers.

Despite the differences in operating activities shown in Exhibit 6.5, all types of companies share one thing in common: to be successful, they must be able to achieve what they want and avoid problems and surprises along the way. To achieve this, they will implement the principles of good internal control that we discussed earlier, including doing bank

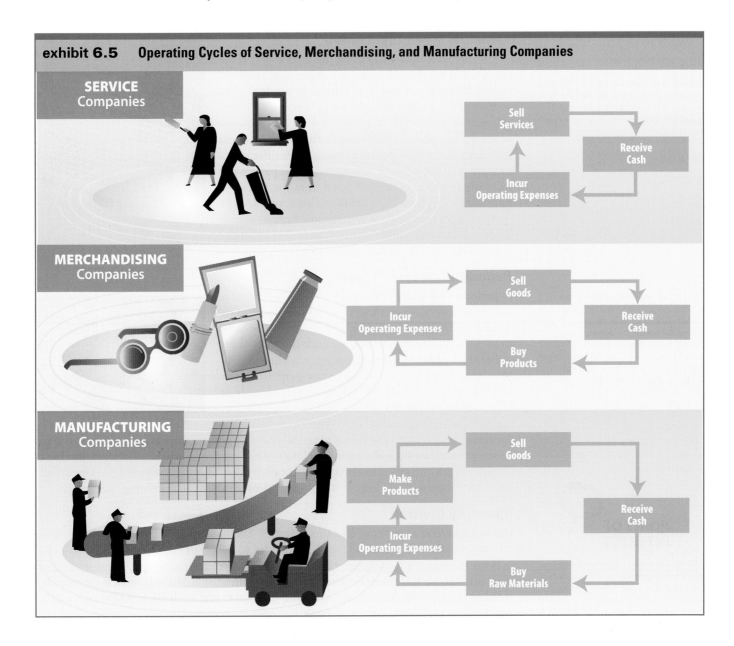

exhibit 6.5   Operating Cycles of Service, Merchandising, and Manufacturing Companies

reconciliations on a regular basis. In this section, we focus specifically on financial reporting controls and procedures relating to purchases and sales of merchandise inventory.

INVENTORY CONTROLS AND TRACKING SYSTEMS

Merchandising companies spend a great deal of time and money tracking their inventory transactions because, after all, inventory management is vital in their business. A strong accounting system plays three roles in the inventory management process. First, it must provide up-to-date information on inventory quantities and costs, so that managers can make informed decisions. Second, it has to provide accurate information for preparing financial statements. Inventory is reported as an asset on the balance sheet until it is sold, at which time it is removed from the balance sheet and reported on the income statement as an expense called cost of goods sold. The third role for an inventory system is to provide information that controls inventory and helps protect it from theft. Companies use one of two types of inventory accounting systems: *perpetual* or *periodic*.

COACH'S TIP

In addition to showing the various types of operating cycles, Exhibit 6.5 also reinforces two additional concepts. First, the arrows indicate that operating activities involve both inflows and outflows of cash. Second, by lining up sales of services/products with operating expenses, it suggests that operating performance should be measured using accrual basis accounting, where expenses are matched with sales revenues.

In a **perpetual inventory system,** the inventory records are updated "perpetually," that is, every time inventory is bought, sold, or returned. Perpetual systems often are combined with bar codes and optical scanners (as shown at the right).

In a **periodic inventory system,** the inventory records are updated "periodically," that is, at the end of the accounting period. To determine how much merchandise has been sold, periodic systems require that inventory be physically counted at the end of the period (as shown at the right).

POINT OF INTEREST

Until 2002, Nordstrom department stores in the United States relied on a periodic system, using loose-leaf binders to track inventory levels.
Source: Business Week, July 30, 2001, p. 9.

Perpetual Inventory System

In a **perpetual inventory system,** the inventory records are updated every time an item is bought, sold, or returned. You may not realize it, but the bar-code readers at Shoppers' checkouts serve two purposes: (1) they calculate and record the sales revenue for each product you're buying, and (2) they remove the product and its cost from Shoppers' inventory records. Similar scanners are used back in the "employees only" part of the store where products are unloaded from the trucks or returned to suppliers. As a result of this continuous or "perpetual" updating on a transaction-by-transaction basis, the *Inventory* and *Cost of Goods Sold* accounts always contain updated balances.

Periodic Inventory System

A **periodic inventory system** differs from a perpetual system in several ways, most of which we describe in detail later in this chapter. For now, however, the most important difference for you to understand is that, rather than update the inventory records immediately after each purchase and sale (that is, perpetually), a periodic system updates the inventory records only *at the end of the accounting period* (periodically). Consequently, an accurate record of inventory on hand and inventory sold is not available during the period. To determine these amounts, the inventory has to be physically counted. This is what's going on when you see a store that is closed "for inventory." This inventory count is then used to compute the correct balances for *Inventory* and *Cost of Goods Sold* and adjust them at the end of the period.

Inventory Control

Perpetual inventory systems, like those used by Shoppers, provide more timely information than periodic systems, allowing companies to keep just the right quantity of products on the shelves for the right amount of time. When inventory systems were done manually, which was time-consuming and labour-intensive, periodic systems were common. In the last few decades, as affordable computers and tools such as optical scanners appeared on the scene, perpetual inventory systems became the norm, creating tremendous efficiencies for companies like Shoppers. One study has found that Wal-Mart's perpetual inventory system accounted for over half of the productivity gains in general merchandise sales in the United States economy during 1995 to 1999.[1] Improved performance due to inventory controls and systems are likely to continue into the future, as merchandise companies experiment with new microchip technologies that use radio waves to transmit data automatically from every inventory item that enters, moves within, exits, and later re-enters its stores. With this technology, it might even be possible for stores to identify shoppers who bought their goods at one of its stores.

Another benefit of a perpetual inventory system is that it allows managers to estimate "shrinkage," which is the politically correct term for loss of inventory from theft, fraud, and error. When it comes to shrinkage, it is important to pay attention. A recent study suggests that over $37 billion went missing at United States retailers in 2005[2], and, contrary to what you might think, most companies believe their own employees, not their customers, are their biggest source of inventory losses.

---

[1] "Retail: The Wal-Mart Effect," The McKinsey Quarterly, no. 1 (2002).

[2] "2005 National Retail Security Survey," Professor Richard Hollinger, University of Florida (2005).

You might wonder how companies can estimate how much of their inventory has gone missing, because isn't it, by definition, *missing*? Here's how they do it, and how you can use a similar process to figure out if your roommate is swiping your stuff. It relies on knowing the kinds of transactions that are recorded in the inventory account.

1. **Determine what's on hand at the beginning of the period.**
2. **Monitor every piece of inventory entering and exiting your stock during the period.**
   a. **Add purchases.**
   b. **Subtract goods sold.**

By perpetually tracking every movement, your inventory records should match exactly the amount of inventory on hand—unless items have been wrongfully removed.

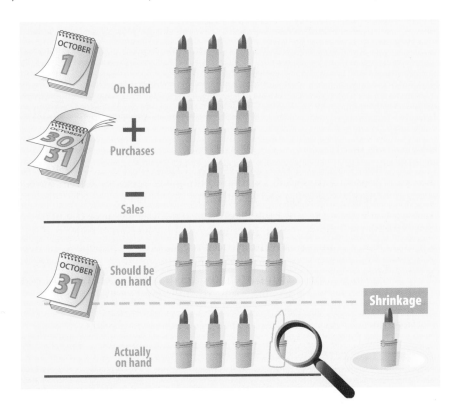

3. **Count the inventory to determine what's actually there.** If your records say that you have more on hand than what you counted, it's likely that the difference is the amount of inventory that has been removed without your permission ("shrinkage"). In plain English, you've been robbed.

Notice that you can't do this kind of detective work with a periodic inventory system because it doesn't provide an up-to-date record of the inventory that *should* be on hand when you count it. Also note that, even if you're using a perpetual inventory system, you still need to count the inventory occasionally (at least yearly) to ensure that the accounting records are accurate and that any shrinkage is detected.

It's difficult for a merchandiser to survive in business today without using a perpetual system. To ensure that you learn the latest in inventory accounting, the next section of this chapter focuses on the accounting process used in perpetual systems. It's possible that you could encounter a periodic system, particularly in smaller companies or large ones that have been slow to switch, so we do discuss the accounting process for periodic systems in Supplement A on page 257. You should find out from your instructor (or course outline) whether you are responsible for it.

COACH'S TIP

The process for determining shrinkage is based on the following relationship:

Beginning Inventory
+ Purchases
− Goods Sold
= Ending Inventory

The chapter supplement on page 257 shows how the above relationship can be used to estimate the cost of goods sold.

PURCHASES, PURCHASE RETURNS AND ALLOWANCES, AND PURCHASE DISCOUNTS

Purchases

In a perpetual system, all purchases of merchandise inventory are recorded directly into the *Inventory* account. As you learned in earlier chapters, most companies use credit rather than cash to purchase goods, so *Accounts Payable* usually is the other account used in the journal entry to record these purchases. For example, if Shoppers purchased some Revlon products on account for $5,000, the journal entry and accounting equation effects would be as follows:

dr	**Inventory (+A)**	5,000	
	cr **Accounts Payable (+L)**		5,000

Assets	=	Liabilities	+	Shareholders' Equity
Inventory + 5,000		Accounts Payable + 5,000		

Transportation Cost

The inventory that Shoppers purchases doesn't just magically appear in its stockroom. It has to be shipped from the supplier's location to Shoppers' premises. Often, the supplier will pay the cost of transportation and recover it by charging more for the inventory. In this situation, transportation cost is built into the purchaser's cost of the inventory, so there are no additional costs to record. In other cases, however, an outside trucking company might be hired to transport inventory from the supplier to Shoppers. To illustrate, assume Shoppers pays $300 cash to a trucker who delivers goods to Shoppers. In this situation, the additional cost of transporting the goods to Shoppers (called freight-in) would be added to the *Inventory* account, using the following journal entry:

dr	**Inventory (+A)**	300	
	cr **Cash (−A)**		300

Assets	=	Liabilities	+	Shareholders' Equity
Cash − 300				
Inventory + 300				

Purchase Returns and Allowances

When goods purchased from a supplier do not meet specifications or arrive in damaged condition, the buyer can either return them for a full refund or keep them and ask for a cost reduction (called an "allowance"). These **purchase returns and allowances** are accounted for by reducing the cost of the inventory and recording the cash refund or the reduction in the liability owed to the supplier. For example, assume that Shoppers returned to its supplier some broken bottles of nail polish and received a $400 reduction in the balance it owed. This transaction would be recorded as follows:

dr	**Accounts Payable (−L)**	400	
	cr **Inventory (−A)**		400

Assets	=	Liabilities	+	Shareholders' Equity
Inventory − 400		Accounts Payable − 400		

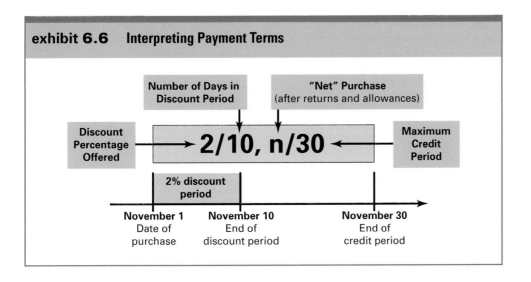

exhibit 6.6 Interpreting Payment Terms

Purchase Discounts

When merchandise is bought on credit, terms such as 2/10, n/30 are sometimes specified. The 2/10 part means that if the purchaser pays within 10 days of the date of purchase, a 2 per cent **purchase discount** is applied to the purchaser's cost. Although 2 per cent might seem small, if taken consistently on all purchases made throughout the year, it can add up to substantial savings. The n/30 part implies that if payment is not made within the 10-day discount period, the full amount is due 30 days after the purchase. If a purchaser fails to pay by the end of this credit period, interest will be charged, further credit can be denied, and nice or not-so-nice people from a collection agency may contact the purchaser to collect the amount owed. Exhibit 6.6 illustrates a 2/10, n/30 purchase occurring on November 1.

When a purchase discount is offered, the purchaser accounts for it in two stages. Initially, the purchase is accounted for at its full cost because, at the time a company purchases goods, it's not clear whether it will take advantage of the purchase discount. Later, *if payment is made within the discount period,* the purchaser will reduce the *Inventory* account for the purchase discount because this discount, in effect, reduces the cost of the inventory. Let's work through an example of this. You do the first part—the initial purchase of the inventory—and then we'll show the journal entry for recording the purchase discount, assuming the purchaser pays within the discount period.

A **purchase discount** is a cash discount received for prompt payment of a purchase on account.

Quiz Answers

dr Inventory (+A) 1,000
  cr Accounts Payable (+L) 1,000

Assets	=	Liabilities	+	Shareholders' Equity
Inventory + 1,000		Accounts Payable + 1,000		

HOW'S IT GOING? A Self-Study Quiz

Assume Shoppers receives a crate of vitamins that it bought from Jamieson Laboratories. The invoice shows a price of $1,000 and terms of 2/10, n/30. Prepare the journal entry and show the accounting equation effects for this purchase transaction.

dr ꞮꞰⱽ

cr

Assets	=	Liabilities	+	Shareholders' Equity

After you have finished, check your answers with the solutions presented in the margin.

If Shoppers takes advantage of the 2/10, n/30 purchase discount by paying within the 10-day discount period, it would record the following journal entry:

dr	Accounts Payable (−L)	1,000	
	cr Cash (−A)		980
	cr Inventory (−A)		20

Assets		=	Liabilities		+	Shareholders' Equity
Cash	− 980		Accounts Payable	− 1,000		
Inventory	− 20					

If Shoppers decided *not* to take advantage of the purchase discount, it would pay the full $1,000 owed, recording a debit to *Accounts Payable* and a credit to *Cash* for $1,000.[3]

Summary of Purchase-Related Transactions

Perpetual inventory systems provide better control over inventory than do periodic systems, which is why we study them in this chapter. Another feature of a good internal control system is accurate records, which is why we've covered accounting for several types of purchase-related transactions here. By applying these accounting methods, management has accurate numbers for the net cost of its inventory on hand, and can make better decisions regarding how to manage and sell these goods. Before you learn how to account for sales of this merchandise, make sure you understand how these purchase-related transactions affect *Inventory*, as summarized in the T-account in Exhibit 6.7.

exhibit 6.7   Effects of Purchase-Related Transactions

dr **Inventory (A)** cr			
Bal. Fwd.	1,290,000		
Purchases (of cosmetics)	5,000		
Transportation	300	Purchase Returns and Allowances	400
Purchases (of vitamins)	1,000	Purchase Discounts	20
Cost of Goods Available for Sale	1,295,880		

SALES, SALES RETURNS AND ALLOWANCES, AND SALES DISCOUNTS

Sales

For all merchandisers, inventory is considered "sold" when ownership of the goods transfers to the customer. For a retail merchandiser like Shoppers, this transfer occurs when a customer takes the goods to the checkout and agrees to pay for them, using cash or a credit card. For a wholesale merchandiser, this transfer of ownership occurs at a time stated in a written sales agreement between the seller and the customer. Most sales agreements use one of two possible times: (1) when the goods leave the *shipping* department at the seller's premises, or (2) when the goods reach their *destination* at the customer's premises.[4] For the examples in this textbook, we assume that ownership transfers when the goods leave the seller's premises.

---

[3]An alternative approach to accounting for purchase discounts (called the net method) exists, but we leave that topic for discussion in intermediate accounting textbooks.

[4]These two possible arrangements often are referred to as FOB (free on board) shipping point and FOB destination, but in most instances these are not the correct labels (FOB refers only to shipments by sea or inland waterway). The International Chamber of Commerce Web site (www.iccwbo.org/index_incoterms.asp) precisely defines FOB and other trade terms.

In a perpetual system, two journal entries are made when inventory is sold:

1. Record the increase in *Sales Revenue* and a corresponding increase in either *Cash* (if it is a cash sale) or *Accounts Receivable* (if the sale is made on credit).
2. Record a reduction in *Inventory* and a corresponding increase in *Cost of Goods Sold* (also called *Cost of Sales*).

For example, assume Shoppers sells you a Philips sonicare toothbrush for $175 cash when the cost of the toothbrush to Shoppers was $125. The two journal entries and their effects on the accounting equation are as follows:

dr	Cash (+A)	175	
	cr Sales Revenue (+R, +SE).		175
dr	Cost of Goods Sold (+E, −SE)	125	
	cr Inventory (−A)		125

Assets		=	Liabilities	+	Shareholders' Equity	
Cash	+ 175				Sales Revenue (+R)	+ 175
Inventory	− 125				Cost of Goods Sold (+E)	− 125

Holding everything else equal, management wants to maximize its sales revenue. Once goods are sold for a given price, however, sales revenue could be reduced after the fact if the company allows sales returns and allowances and sales discounts. A good internal control system will allow management to monitor and control these costs, and therefore we study these topics in this chapter.

Sales Returns and Allowances

Sales returns and allowances are the same thing as purchase returns and allowances except that, instead of looking at them from the purchaser's perspective, we're now seeing them from the seller's side. For example, suppose that, after you bought the toothbrush from Shoppers, you changed your mind and returned it to Shoppers. Assuming that it is still in its original packaging, you can expect Shoppers to refund $175 to you, take back the toothbrush, and act as if the sale had never been made in the first place.

To allow its accounting records to reflect this, Shoppers will record two journal entries that are basically the opposite of what this stellar seller recorded above when the toothbrush was initially sold. We say "basically" because there is one catch: Shoppers will not directly reduce its *Sales Revenue* account. Instead, for control purposes, Shoppers will track the amount of sales returns and allowances in a contra-revenue account, which is deducted from total sales revenue. By using a contra-revenue account, rather than directly reducing the *Sales* account, Shoppers can quickly determine the amount of goods that customers return, which can provide clues about whether Shoppers' customers are happy with the quality and price of its products.[5] This is an example where accounting information functions as an internal control that serves to promote efficient and effective operations. Here are the journal entries and their effects:

Sales returns and allowances are reductions given to customers after goods have been sold and found unsatisfactory.

dr	Sales Returns and Allowances (+xR, −SE)	175	
	cr Cash (−A)		175
dr	Inventory (+A)	125	
	cr Cost of Goods Sold (−E, +SE)		125

---

[5] We have assumed that the return occurs in the same period as the sale. When significant returns are likely to occur after the period of sale, the seller records an estimate of those expected returns, using methods described in Chapter 7.

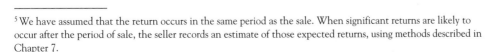

	Assets		=	Liabilities	+	Shareholders' Equity	
Cash		− 175				Sales Returns and Allowances (+xR)	− 175
Inventory		+ 125				Cost of Goods Sold (−E)	+ 125

Sales Discounts

You already know that buyers are sometimes given purchase discounts to encourage them to pay promptly for purchases they've made on account. From the seller's point of view, these discounts are called **sales discounts.** Just like purchase discounts, sales discounts involve two parts: (1) the initial sale, and (2) the discount given for prompt payment.

Let's split up and use this as another chance for you to practise the part that you've already seen—recording the initial sale using a perpetual inventory system. We'll then show you the journal entry needed when the discount is taken.

A **sales discount** is given to customers for prompt payment of an account receivable.

HOW'S IT GOING?   A Self-Study Quiz

Assume that Shoppers' specialty store (called Home HealthCare) sells two wheelchairs to a seniors' residence on account for $1,000, with payment terms of 2/10, n/30. The wheelchairs had cost Shoppers $670. Prepare the journal entries Shoppers will record in its perpetual inventory system and show their effects on the accounting equation.

dr ~~Cash~~ A/R 1000
  cr ~~A/R~~ Rev 1000
dr COGS 670
  cr Inv 670

Assets	=	Liabilities	+	Shareholders' Equity

After you have finished, check your answers with the solutions presented in the margin.

Quiz Answers

dr Accounts Receivable (+A)......... 1,000
  cr Sales Revenue (+R, +SE)....   1,000
dr Cost of Goods Sold (+E, −SE)..   670
  cr Inventory (−A)............   670

Assets	=	Liabilities	+	Shareholders' Equity
Accts. Rec. + 1,000				Sales Revenue (+R) + 1,000
Inventory − 670				Cost of Goods Sold (+E) − 670

If Shoppers receives the customer's payment within the 10-day discount period, it would record the following journal entry:

dr	Cash (+A)	980	
dr	Sales Discounts (+xR, −SE)...........	20	
	cr Accounts Receivable (−A)		1,000

	Assets	=	Liabilities	+	Shareholders' Equity	
Cash	+ 980				Sales Discounts (+xR)	− 20
Accts. Receiv.	− 1,000					

If the seniors' residence pays the full amount to Shoppers *after* the discount period, Shoppers would record a debit to *Cash* and a credit to *Accounts Receivable* for $1,000. What if a customer doesn't pay? We discuss that important issue in detail in Chapter 7.

Before leaving the topic of sales discounts, we need to clear up a common misconception. Sales discounts differ from the "discount" that you get as a consumer buying clearance items at a reduced selling price. The sales discounts discussed in this section are given in business-to-business (B2B) transactions for prompt payment. As a consumer, you're not likely to be offered this kind of discount.

Summary of Sales-Related Transactions

The sales-related transactions introduced in this section were recorded using contra-revenue accounts. Their effects on sales reporting are summarized in Exhibit 6.8.

As we have discussed, contra-revenue accounts are used as an internal control to allow managers to separately monitor and control how sales discounts and sales returns affect the company's revenues. The numbers in Exhibit 6.8 show that, of the $4,175 sold during the period, customers returned 4.2 per cent of these goods ($175 ÷ 4,175 × 100). We cannot conclude whether this is good or bad without more information, but keeping track of this information is part of a good internal control system. For example, if customers are frequently returning a product for being defective, it would show up as an increase in the *Sales Returns and Allowances* account. Upon seeing the increase, Shoppers' managers could decide to discontinue selling the product or find a new supplier for it. This kind of detailed information is a key part of a merchandiser's business strategy, so, to avoid revealing these secrets to competitors, most companies allow only *internal* financial statement users to see the balances in these contra-revenue accounts. For external reporting purposes, contra-revenue accounts are subtracted from total *Sales Revenue*, as shown in Exhibit 6.8, but this calculation is made "behind the scenes." Rather than show all of these accounts, externally reported income statements usually just begin with *Net Sales*. Despite this secrecy, external financial statement users can still conduct useful financial statement analyses, as we'll see in the next section.

---

exhibit 6.8   Effects of Sales-Related Transactions

Sales Revenue		$4,175
Less:	**Sales Returns and Allowances**	175
	Sales Discounts	20
Net Sales		$3,980

The contra-revenue accounts are subtracted from *Sales Revenue* to compute *Net Sales*. For reasons discussed in the text, most companies report only *Net Sales* in their externally reported income statements. The detailed breakdown shown above is available only to internal financial statement users.

A FINAL WORD ON INTERNAL CONTROL

We have only shown you a small number of internal control procedures: bank reconciliations, perpetual inventory systems, and the use of contra accounts for sales returns and allowances and sales discounts. A well-managed company will have control procedures in place for all aspects of its business. You'll study the topic of internal control in much greater detail in advanced controllership and auditing courses.

EVALUATE _____
The Operating Results of Merchandisers

DRILLING DOWN IN A MULTI-STEP INCOME STATEMENT

One of the basic facts of merchandising is that goods have to be sold at a profit for a merchandiser to survive. Sure, cash has to be controlled, but the fact remains that there won't be much cash to control unless goods are sold at a profit. That's the only way companies like Shoppers can generate enough money to cover their operating expenses. To make it easy for financial statement users to see how much is earned from product sales, without being clouded by other operating costs, merchandise companies often present their income statement using a multi-step format. A multi-step income statement is similar to what you've seen in earlier chapters, with expenses being subtracted from revenues to arrive at net income. The key difference for financial statement users is that a multi-step format separates *Cost of Goods Sold* from other expenses. As shown in Exhibit 6.9, this extra step produces a subtotal called **gross profit,** which is the amount the company earned from selling goods, over and above the cost of the goods. If you buy something for $70 and sell it for $100, you'll have a gross profit of $30. Shoppers, like many Canadian companies, does not disclose its cost of goods sold, so Exhibit 6.9 shows data for both Shoppers and one of its competitors, the Jean Coutu Group. The Jean Coutu Group is headquartered in Québec and operates in New Brunswick, Québec, and Ontario, as well as in the United States under the Eckerd name.

> **Gross profit** (also called gross margin or simply margin) is net sales minus cost of goods sold. It is a subtotal, not an account.

Notice in Exhibit 6.9 that, after the gross profit line, the multi-step income statement presents other items in a similar format to what you saw for a service company in Chapter 3 (Exhibit 3.1). The category called Selling, General, and Administrative Expenses includes a variety of operating expenses, including wages, utilities, advertising, and rent. These expenses are subtracted from Gross Profit to yield Operating Income, which is a measure of the company's income from regular operating activities, before considering the effects of interest, income taxes, and any non-operating items. Under the Shoppers columns, total operating expenses are combined into one number for each year, and no separate numbers are disclosed for either cost of goods sold or gross profit.

exhibit 6.9   Sample Multi-step Income Statement

| | THE JEAN COUTU GROUP (PJC) LTD. | | SHOPPERS DRUG MART CORPORATION | |
| | (in millions of U.S. dollars) | | (in millions of Cdn. dollars) | |
	Year ending June 4, 2007	Year ending May 27, 2006	Year ending December 29, 2007	Year ending December 30, 2006
Net Sales	$11,676	$11,143	$8,478	$7,786
Cost of Goods Sold	8,837	8,401		
Gross Profit	2,839	2,742	7,688*	7,103*
Selling, General, and Administrative Expenses (net)	2,460	2,477		
Operating Income	379	265	790	683
Financing Expenses	216	205	53	50
Income before Income Taxes	163	60	737	633
Income Taxes (recovery)	22	(44)	243	211
Net Income	$141	$104	$494	$422

*Shoppers discloses Total Cost of Goods Sold and General, Selling, and Administrative Expenses as one number ($7,688 and $ 7,103) and does not disclose its gross profit.

GROSS PROFIT PERCENTAGE

Let's focus again on the gross profit line on the income statement in Exhibit 6.9. Although the dollar amount of gross profit can be interesting, this number is difficult to interpret by itself. In Exhibit 6.9, we see that Jean Coutu's gross profit increased from 2006 to 2007. The problem is that Jean Coutu also increased its sales over these years, so we don't know whether the increase in gross profit dollars arises because Jean Coutu increased its sales volume or whether it is generating more profit per sale. To determine the amount of gross profit included in each dollar of sales, analysts typically evaluate **gross profit percentage,** which is calculated as follows:

> **Gross profit percentage** indicates how much above cost a company sells its products.

$$\text{Gross Profit Percentage} = \frac{\text{Gross Profit}}{\text{Net Sales}} \times 100\% = \frac{(\text{Net Sales} - \text{Cost of Goods Sold})}{\text{Net Sales}} \times 100\%$$

The gross profit percentage measures how much above cost a company sells its products. As discussed below, this ratio is used to (1) analyze changes in the company's operations over time, (2) compare one company with another, and (3) determine whether a company is earning enough on each sale to cover its operating expenses. A higher gross profit percentage means that, all else being equal, a company will have more resources to cover operating expenses, leading to greater net income.

Because gross profit percentage is a useful ratio, and it cannot be calculated without knowing cost of goods sold, you might wonder why Canadian accounting rules don't require the cost of goods sold figure to be disclosed in the financial statements. The answer might be that, on this issue, the rule-makers have sided with the companies that believe this information is proprietary. Some companies don't want their customers or their competitors to know the markup on their products.

As we can see in the graphic at the right, Jean Coutu's gross profit percentage decreased 0.3 per cent in 2007. Each dollar of sales in 2006 included 24.6 cents of gross profit, whereas in 2007 each dollar of sales included only 24.3 cents. So, although Jean Coutu sold more in 2007 than in 2006, it generated slightly less profit per sale. How is this possible? To find out, we read the Management's Discussion and Analysis section of Jean Coutu's annual report. There we found out that about 80 per cent of Jean Coutu's sales are generated in the United States by the Eckerd drugstore chain. We further found out that drugstores in the United States have an average gross profit percentage of more than 24 per cent, whereas, in Canada, the average gross profit percentage is just over 9 per cent. But, unfortunately, in 2007, more of Jean Coutu's growth came from the smaller-profit Canadian market. So, in 2007, Jean Coutu had more of the lower yielding locations, which decreased its overall gross profit percentage. You might wonder whether it's even worth talking about changes of three-tenths of a percentage point, but just remember that a small change in the gross profit percentage can lead to a big change in net income. If these were Wal-Mart's numbers, for example, because the company has such a huge volume of sales, a decrease in gross profit of just one percentage point in 2007 would translate into about $3.6 billion. Yes, that's billion with a "b."

As we saw in this chapter, managing inventory is a key function in a merchandising company, but it is only one part of the business. By looking at the net-profit-margin ratio (one of the ratios studied in Chapter 5), in addition to the gross margin percentage, we can see how a company managed the business as a whole. Specifically, we can see whether Jean Coutu's improvement in gross profit dollars followed through to its bottom line. Exhibit 6.10 looks at Jean Coutu's net profit margin and compares it with Shoppers Drug Mart's ratio. We see that, consistent with the increase in Jean Coutu's gross profit in 2007, its net profit margin also increased from 0.9 per cent to 1.2 per cent that year. However, its net profit margin in both years was much less than that of Shoppers Drug Mart.

24.3% 24.6%

2007 2006

Gross Profit Percentage

exhibit 6.10   Net-Profit-Margin Ratio

	THE JEAN COUTU GROUP (PJC) LTD.		SHOPPERS DRUG MART CORPORATION	
	June 4, 2007	May 27, 2006	December 29, 2007	December 30, 2006
$\dfrac{\text{Net income}}{\text{Net sales}}$	1.2%	0.9%	5.8%	5.4%

exhibit 6.11   A Framework for Financial Statement Ratio Analyses

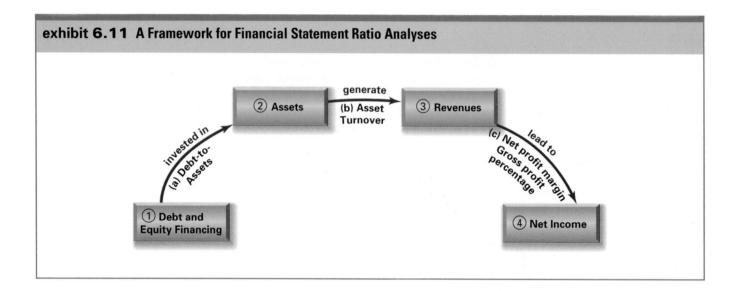

Turning revenues into gross profit is one way to increase bottom-line net income, and this ratio belongs alongside the net profit margin in our framework for financial statement analysis, as shown in Exhibit 6.11.

RECONSIDER _____
The Impact of Operating Cycles on Financial Results

The gross profit percentage is particularly useful when analyzing merchandising and manufacturing companies because it shows how much profit is included in the selling price of an average product. Although it's less obvious to think of service companies, like hotels, movie theatres, and restaurants, as selling a product, some service-oriented companies report gross profit. For service companies, gross profit represents the amount of profit earned over and above the cost of each customer transaction, without considering general and administrative costs like advertising and corporate salaries.

COMPARING OPERATING RESULTS ACROSS COMPANIES AND INDUSTRIES

Be aware that gross profit percentages can vary greatly between companies. For example, pharmaceutical companies recently reported an average gross profit percentage of 74 per cent compared with only 15 per cent reported by automakers. Of course, these

COACH'S TIP

A product is considered "high-margin" if the gross profit percentage from it is greater than the average gross profit percentage from other products.

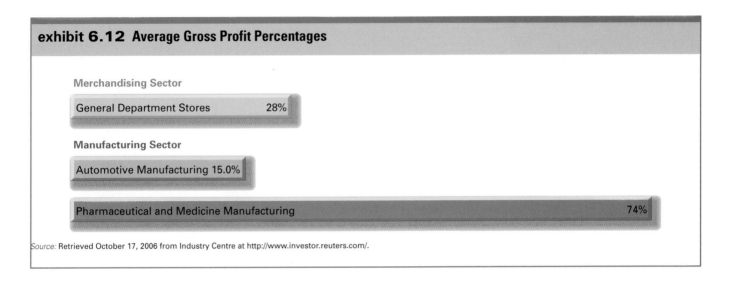

exhibit 6.12 Average Gross Profit Percentages

Merchandising Sector

General Department Stores   28%

Manufacturing Sector

Automotive Manufacturing 15.0%

Pharmaceutical and Medicine Manufacturing   74%

Source: Retrieved October 17, 2006 from Industry Centre at http://www.investor.reuters.com/.

across-industry differences are expected. Drug companies, for example, need a higher gross profit percentage than car-makers because they have more research and development expenses to cover.

Even within a single industry sector, however, gross profit percentages are likely to vary from company to company, depending on business strategies and the nature of their products. A high-end department store like Saks in the United States enjoys a 37.5 per cent gross profit percentage, whereas Wal-Mart's 22 per cent is characteristic of its business strategy, which is true to its slogan of selling at "Low Prices, Always." Saks may charge an extra 15.5 cents on every dollar of sales, but, fortunately for Wal-Mart, its low-price strategy attracts herds of customers who buy lots of merchandise. This enhanced sales volume counteracts the lower gross profit percentage, which allowed Wal-Mart to gross a hefty $81 billion in 2007, compared with Saks' $54 million.

BE ON THE ALERT

Because gross profit percentages vary so much depending on the nature of a company's products, strategy, and operating cycle, they are more useful in comparing one company with itself over time than in comparing across companies. Even when comparing across years, though, you shouldn't jump to the conclusion that a change in gross profit percentage in one year will continue in the following years. To truly know whether changes represent one-time blips or a sustained effect, you must understand the sources of the change. For example, an increase in the gross profit percentage resulting from selling more high-margin winter clothing during a hard winter is likely to be a one-hit wonder, whereas an increase that comes from selling an entirely new line of products is likely to continue in future periods.

WHAT'S COMING UP

Throughout our discussions in this chapter, we quietly assumed that all sales ultimately are collected as cash. Unfortunately, this isn't always the case in the real world—companies aren't always successful in collecting every account receivable that is created by sales on account. In Chapter 7, you'll learn how companies account for the situation where they sell on account to customers, some of whom won't end up paying all that they owe. But, before we start looking down the road to the collection of credit sales, you first need to review and practise the material covered in this chapter.

FOR YOUR REVIEW _____

DEMONSTRATION CASE A

Kat Bardash, a student at a small university, has just received her chequing account statement, for the month ended September 30. This was her first chance to attempt a bank reconciliation. The bank's statement of account showed the following:

Bank balance, September 1	$1,150
Deposits made during September	650
Cheques cleared during September	900
Bank service charge	25
Interest earned	5
Bank balance, September 30	880

Kat was surprised that her bank had not yet reported the deposit of $50 she made on September 29 and was pleased that her rent cheque of $200 had not cleared her account. Her September 30 cheque book balance was $750.

Required:

1. Complete Kat's bank reconciliation. What adjustments, if any, does she need to make in her chequebook?
2. Why is it important for individuals and businesses to do a bank reconciliation each month?

Suggested Solution

1.

KAT BARDASH
Bank Reconciliation (Chequing Account)
For the Month Ending September 30

Bank Statement		Kat's Books	
September 30 cash balance	$880	September 30 cash balance	$750
Additions		Additions	
Deposit in transit	50	Interest earned	5
Deductions		Deductions	
Outstanding cheque	(200)	Bank service charge	(25)
Up-to-date cash balance	$730	Up-to-date cash balance	$730

    Kat should increase her cheque book balance by $5 for the cash given by the bank for interest, and reduce her chequebook balance by $25 for the cash given to the bank for service charges.

2. Bank statements, whether personal or business, should be reconciled each month to help ensure that a correct balance is reflected in the depositor's books. Failure to reconcile a bank statement increases the chance that an error will not be discovered and may result in bad cheques being written. Businesses reconcile their bank statements for an additional reason: The up-to-date balance that is calculated during reconciliation is reported on the balance sheet.

DEMONSTRATION CASE B

Assume Oakley Incorporated—the maker of stylish sunglasses, goggles, and many other leading products—made merchandise costing $137,200 and sold it on credit to Sunglass Hut for $405,000 with terms 2/10, n/30. Some of the merchandise differed from what Sunglass Hut had ordered, so Oakley agreed to give an allowance of $5,000. Sunglass Hut satisfied the remaining balance (of $400,000) by paying within the discount period.

Required:

1. Assuming that both companies use perpetual inventory systems, prepare the journal entries that both Oakley and Sunglass Hut would use to record the following transactions:
   a. Sale from Oakley to Sunglass Hut
   b. Allowance granted by Oakley
   c. Payment made by Sunglass Hut to Oakley
2. Compute Oakley's net sales, assuming that sales returns and allowances and sales discounts are treated as contra-revenues.
3. Compute Oakley's gross profit and gross profit percentage on the sale. Compare this ratio with the 72.0 per cent gross profit percentage recently reported by the Luxottica Group—the Italian company that makes Killer Loop® and Ray-Ban® sunglasses, which are sold through its Sunglass Hut stores. What does it imply about the two companies?

COACH'S TIP

Transaction *b* depicts an allowance but no return of goods. Had goods been returned, Oakley also would increase its inventory and decrease its cost of goods sold.

Suggested Solution

1. Journal entries:

   a. Sale from Oakley to Sunglass Hut

Oakley	Sunglass Hut

dr Accounts Receivable (+A)............ 405,000
    cr Sales Revenue (+R, +SE)   405,000
 dr Cost of Goods Sold (+E, −SE)...... 137,200
    cr Inventory (−A)   137,200
	dr Inventory (+A)............................. 405,000
	    cr Accounts Payable (L) 405,000

   b. Allowance granted by Oakley

Oakley	Sunglass Hut

dr Sales Returns and
      Allowances (+xR, −SE)............... 5,000
    cr Accounts Receivable (−A)....   5,000
	dr Accounts Payable (−L)................ 5,000
	    cr Inventory (−A) 5,000

   c. Payment made by Sunglass Hut to Oakley

Oakley	Sunglass Hut

dr Cash (+A)....................................... 392,000
 dr Sales Discounts (+xR, −SE)   8,000
    cr Accounts Receivable (−A)....   400,000
 	
 ($8,000 = $400,000 × 2%)
	dr Accounts Payable (−L)................. 400,000
	    cr Cash (−A)............................. 392,000
	    cr Inventory (−A) 8,000

2. Sales returns and allowances and sales discounts should be subtracted from sales revenue to compute net sales:

Sales Revenue	$405,000
Less: Sales Returns and Allowances	5,000
Sales Discounts [0.02 × (405,000 − 5,000)]	8,000
Net Sales	$392,000

3. Gross profit and gross profit percentage are calculated as follows:

	In Dollars	Percentage of Net Sales
Net Sales (calculated in 2)	$392,000	100.0%
Less: Cost of Goods Sold	137,200	35.0
Gross Profit	$254,800	65.0%

The 65 per cent gross profit percentage indicates that Oakley generates 7 cents less gross profit on each dollar of sales than Luxottica ($7.0 = 72.0 - 65.0$). This difference implies that Luxottica is including a higher markup in its selling prices.

CHAPTER SUMMARY

LO1   **Describe the purpose of internal controls. p. 232**

- Internal controls are used to protect against theft and fraudulent financial reporting, and to serve the organization by promoting efficient and effective operations and by alerting company officials to possible violations of laws and regulations.

LO2   **Perform a key cash control by reconciling to bank statements. p. 234**

- The bank reconciliation requires determining two categories of items: (1) those that have been recorded in the company's books but not in the bank's statement of account, and (2) those that have been reported in the bank's statement of account but not in the company's books. The second category of items provides the data needed to adjust the Cash records to the balance reported on the balance sheet.

LO3   **Describe an operating cycle, and explain the use of a perpetual inventory system as a control in a merchandising operation. p.240**

- Service companies sell services rather than physical goods; consequently, their income statements show cost of services rather than cost of goods sold.
- Merchandise companies sell goods that have been obtained from a supplier. Retail merchandise companies sell direct to consumers, whereas wholesale merchandise companies sell to retail companies.
- Manufacturing companies sell goods that they have made themselves.
- Perpetual inventory systems protect against undetectable theft because they provide an up-to-date record of inventory that should be on hand at any given time, which can be compared with a count of the physical quantity that actually is on hand.
- Perpetual inventory systems serve to promote efficient and effective operations because they are updated every time inventory is purchased, sold, or returned.

LO4   **Account for purchase and sales transactions under a perpetual inventory system. p. 244**

- In a perpetual inventory system, the *Inventory* account is increased every time inventory is purchased. The account should include any costs, such as transportation-in, that are needed to get the inventory into a condition and location ready for sale.
- In a perpetual inventory system, the purchaser's *Inventory* account is decreased whenever the purchaser returns goods to the supplier or is given a discount for prompt payment.
- In a perpetual inventory system, two entries are made every time inventory is sold: one entry records the sale (and corresponding debit to cash or accounts receivable) and the other entry records the cost of the goods sold (and corresponding credit to inventory).
- By recording *sales discounts* and *sales returns* and *allowances* in contra accounts, management is better able to control these activities and promote efficient and effective operations.

LO5   **(Supplement A) Account for inventory under a periodic inventory system. p. 257**

- A periodic inventory system does not track cost of goods sold during the accounting period, but rather calculates it using a four-step process at the end of the accounting period.

LO6   **Analyze a merchandiser's multi-step income statement. p.250**

- One of the key items in a merchandiser's multi-step income statement is Gross Profit, which is a subtotal calculated by subtracting *Cost of Goods Sold* from *Net Sales.* The gross profit percentage can be calculated by dividing Gross Profit by Net Sales. This measure indicates the amount of gross profit that is included in each dollar of sales.

Explain factors to consider when comparing across industries. p. 252

L07

- As with other measures of operating performance, the gross profit percentage varies between companies, depending on the nature of the operating cycle (e.g., service, merchandising, manufacturing), business strategy, and product mix.

FINANCIAL STATEMENT ANALYSIS TIP

To determine the amount of gross profit included in every dollar of sales, calculate the gross profit percentage:

$$\text{Gross Profit Percentage} = \frac{\text{Gross Profit}}{\text{Net Sales}} \times 100\% = \frac{(\text{Net Sales} - \text{Cost of Goods Sold})}{\text{Net Sales}} \times 100\%$$

KEY TERMS TO KNOW

Bank Reconciliation p. 235

Cash p. 234

Cost of Goods Sold Equation p. 258

Gross Profit (or Gross Margin) p. 250

Gross Profit Percentage p. 251

Internal Controls p. 232

Manufacturing Company p. 240

Merchandising Company p. 240

NSF (Not Sufficient Funds) Cheque p. 236

Operating cycle p. 240

Periodic Inventory System p. 242

Perpetual Inventory System p. 242

Purchase Discounts p. 245

Purchase Returns and Allowances p. 244

Sales Discount p. 248

Sales Returns and Allowances p. 247

Segregation of Duties p. 233

Service Company p. 240

SUPPLEMENT A: PERIODIC INVENTORY SYSTEMS

As described in the body of this chapter, a *periodic* inventory system updates the inventory records only *at the end of the accounting period*. Unlike the perpetual inventory system, a periodic system does not track the cost of goods sold during the accounting period. Instead, this information is determined by following a four-step process:

1. *Determine beginning inventory.* You get this simply by looking in the T-account or balance sheet for last period's ending inventory balance.
2. *Track this period's purchases.* The purchases account would include the total cost of all purchases (invoice costs, duty, taxes, freight-in, etc). The cost of all transactions related to inventory is recorded in separate accounts called *Purchases*[7], *Purchase Discounts*, and *Purchase Returns and Allowances*.
3. *Determine ending inventory.* The number of units of inventory on hand at the end of the period is determined through an inventory count. These quantities are then multiplied by the cost of each unit to determine the cost of ending inventory.
4. *Calculate the cost of goods sold.* This step combines data from the first three steps to "force out" the cost of goods sold. You start with the cost of beginning inventory and add the cost of every piece of inventory that you bought during the period (net of any purchase discounts or purchase returns and allowances). The result is the cost of all of the goods that *could* have been sold during the period. If you sold everything, this would be the cost of goods sold. But you know that some of the goods weren't sold because you counted a bunch of items during the inventory count. So the cost of what you did sell is equal to the difference between what you could have sold and what you didn't sell. In other words, the **cost of goods sold equation** is:

[7] The *Purchases* account would include the total cost of all *purchases* (invoice costs, duty, taxes, freight-in, etc.).

The **cost of goods sold equation** is:

Beginning Inventory
+ Purchases
− Purchase Discounts
− Purchase Returns and
  Allowances
────────────────────
Cost of Goods Available for Sale
− Ending Inventory (counted)
────────────────────
Cost of Goods Sold

$$\text{Cost of Goods Sold} = \text{Beginning Inventory} + \text{Net Purchases} - \text{Ending Inventory}$$

where Net Purchases = Purchases − Purchase Discounts − Purchase Returns and Allowances.

Comparison of the Accounting Processes Used in Periodic and Perpetual Systems

The typical journal entries recorded in a periodic inventory system are presented below and contrasted with the entries that would be recorded in a perpetual inventory system. The effects of these journal entries on the accounting equation are then summarized. Note that the total effects are identical, and only the timing and nature of recording differs.

Assume, for this illustration only, that Shoppers stocks and sells only one item, the Obusforme backrest, and that only the following events occurred in 2008:

Jan.	1	Beginning inventory: 800 units, at unit cost of $50
Apr.	14	Purchased: 1,100 additional units on account, at unit cost of $50
Nov.	30	Sold: 1,300 units on account, at unit sales price of $83
Dec.	31	Counted: 600 units, at unit cost of $50

Periodic Records	*Perpetual Records*
A. Record purchases April 14, 2008:	**A. Record purchases** April 14, 2008:

dr Purchases (+A) (1,100 units at $50) 55,000
   cr Accounts Payable (+L)................. 55,000
	dr Inventory (+A) (1,100 units at $50) 55,000
	   cr Accounts Payable (+L)................. 55,000

B. Record sales (but not cost of goods sold) November 30, 2008:	**B. Record sales and cost of goods sold** November 30, 2008:

dr Accounts Receivable (+A)................. 107,900
   cr Sales Revenue (+R, +SE)
   (1,300 units at $83) 107,900
 	
No cost of goods sold entry
	dr Accounts Receivable (+A)................. 107,900
	   cr Sales Revenue (+R, +SE)
	   (1,300 units at $83) 107,900
	dr Cost of Goods Sold (+E, −SE).............. 65,000
	   cr Inventory (−A) (1,300 units at $50) 65,000

C. Record end-of-period adjustments At the end of the period, compute cost of goods sold using the four-step process and adjust the inventory accounts.	**C. Record end-of-period adjustments** At the end of the accounting period, the balance in the *Cost of Goods Sold* account is reported on the income statement. It is not necessary to compute cost of goods sold because the *Cost of Goods Sold* account is up to date. Also, the *Inventory* account shows the ending inventory amount reported on the balance sheet. A physical inventory count is still necessary to assess the accuracy of the perpetual records and identify theft and other forms of shrinkage. Any shrinkage would be recorded by reducing the *Inventory* account and increasing an expense account (such as *Inventory Shrinkage* or *Cost of Goods Sold*). This illustration assumes no shrinkage is detected.

1. Beginning inventory (last period's ending) $40,000
2. Add net purchases   55,000
   Cost of goods available for sale   95,000
3. Deduct ending inventory
   (physical count—600 units at $50)   30,000
4. Cost of goods sold $65,000	

December 31, 2008: **Transfer beginning inventory and net purchases to cost of goods sold:** (act *as* if *all* goods were sold)	

dr Cost of Goods Sold (+E, −SE).............. 95,000
   cr Inventory (−A) (beginning)............. 40,000
   cr Purchases (−A) 55,000
	No entry

Adjust the cost of goods sold by subtracting the amount of ending inventory still on hand: (recognize that not all goods were sold)

dr Inventory (+A) (ending)   30,000
   cr Cost of Goods Sold (−E, +SE)   30,000

Assets		=	Liabilities		+	Shareholders' Equity	
Purchases	+55,000		Accounts Payable	+55,000			
Accts. Rec.	+107,900					Sales Revenue	+107,900
Inventory	−40,000					Cost of Goods Sold (+E)	−95,000
Purchases	−55,000						
Inventory	+30,000					Cost of Goods Sold (−E)	+30,000
Totals	+97,900			+55,000			+42,900

Assets		=	Liabilities		+	Shareholders' Equity	
Inventory	+55,000		Accounts Payable	+55,000			
Accts. Rec.	+107,900					Sales Revenue	+107,900
Inventory	−65,000					Cost of Goods Sold (+E)	−65,000
Totals	+97,900			+55,000			+42,900

_____ **FOR YOUR PRACTICE**

QUESTIONS

1. From an organizational perspective, what is included in an internal control system?
2. What are five common internal control principles?
3. Why is it a good idea to assign each task to only one employee?
4. Why should responsibilities for certain duties, like cash handling and cash recording, be separated? What types of responsibilities should be separated?
5. What are some of the methods for restricting access?
6. In what ways does documentation act as a control?
7. In what ways can independent verification occur?
8. What are the major limitations of internal control?
9. Define *cash* and indicate the types of items that should be reported as cash.
10. What are the purposes of a bank reconciliation? What balances are reconciled?
11. What is the distinction between service and merchandising companies? What is the distinction between merchandising and manufacturing companies? What is the distinction between retail and wholesale merchandising companies?
12. What is the main distinction between perpetual and periodic inventory systems? Which type of system provides better internal control over inventory? Explain why.
13. Why is a physical count of inventory necessary in a periodic inventory system? Why is it still necessary in a perpetual system?
14. Describe how transportation costs to obtain inventory (freight-in) are accounted for by a merchandising company using a perpetual inventory system. Explain the reasoning behind this accounting treatment.
15. What is the distinction between *purchase returns and allowances* and *purchase discounts?*
16. What is a purchase discount? Use 1/10, n/30 in your explanation.
17. Describe in words the journal entries that are made in a perpetual inventory system when inventory is sold on credit.
18. Explain the difference between sales revenue and net sales.
19. Why are contra-revenue accounts used rather than directly deducting from the sales account (recording a debit to sales)?

20. What is gross profit? How is the gross profit percentage computed? Illustrate its calculation and interpretation, assuming net sales revenue is $100,000 and cost of goods sold is $60,000.

MULTIPLE CHOICE

Select the one alternative that best answers the question or completes the sentence.

1. Mountain Gear, Inc., buys bikes, tents, and climbing supplies from Rugged Rock Corporation for sale to consumers. What type of company is Mountain Gear, Inc.?
   - *a.* Service
   - *b.* Retail merchandiser
   - *c.* Wholesale merchandiser
   - *d.* Manufacturer

2. Which of the following does not enhance internal control?
   - *a.* Ensuring that transactions are authorized and properly recorded
   - *b.* Ensuring that adequate records are maintained
   - *c.* Hiring good employees
   - *d.* None of the above—All enhance internal control.

3. Upon review of your bank statement, you discover that you recently deposited a cheque from a customer that was rejected by your bank as NSF. Which of the following describes the actions to be taken when preparing your bank reconciliation?

	Balance per Bank	Balance per Books
a.	Decrease	No change
b.	Increase	Decrease
c.	No change	Decrease
d.	Decrease	Increase

4. Upon review of the most recent bank statement, you discover that a cheque was made out to your supplier for $76 but was recorded in your *Cash* and *Accounts payable* accounts as $67. Which of the following describes the actions to be taken when preparing your bank reconciliation?

	Balance per Bank	Balance per Books
a.	Decrease	No change
b.	Increase	Decrease
c.	No change	Decrease
d.	Decrease	Increase

5. Which of the following is false regarding a perpetual inventory system?
   - *a.* Physical counts are never needed, since records are maintained on a transaction-by-transaction basis.
   - *b.* The balance in the inventory account is updated with each inventory purchase and sale transaction.
   - *c.* Cost of goods sold is increased as sales are recorded.
   - *d.* The account *Purchases* is not used as inventory is acquired.

6. Purchase discounts with terms 2/10, n/30 means:
   - *a.* 10 per cent discount for payment within 30 days
   - *b.* 2 per cent discount for payment within 10 days, or the full amount (less returns) is due within 30 days
   - *c.* Two-tenths of a per cent discount for payment within 30 days
   - *d.* None of the above

7. Which of the following describes how payments to suppliers, made within the purchase discount period, are recorded in a perpetual inventory system (using the method shown in the chapter)?
   - *a.* Reduce cash, reduce accounts payable.
   - *b.* Reduce cash, reduce accounts payable, reduce inventory.
   - *c.* Reduce cash, reduce accounts payable, increase purchase discounts.
   - *d.* Reduce cash, reduce accounts payable, decrease purchase discounts.

8. Which of the following is not a component of net sales?
   a. Sales returns and allowances
   b. Sales discounts
   c. Cost of goods sold
   d. Gross sales

9. Earlier this year, your company negotiated larger purchase discounts when paying for its merchandise inventory, which it has consistently taken throughout the year. What effect will this factor have on the company's gross profit percentage this year, in comparison with last year?
   a. The ratio will not change.
   b. The ratio will increase.
   c. The ratio will decrease.
   d. Either b or c

10. The main reason why sales discounts are recorded to a contra-revenue account is:
   a. to allow management to monitor and control discounts.
   b. to allow management to eliminate sales discounts.
   c. because they are credits and must be accounted for that way.
   d. sales discounts are not recorded to a contra-revenue account.

MINI-EXERCISES

M6-1 Identifying Internal Controls over Financial Reporting

LO1

Fox Erasing has a system of internal control with the following procedures. Match the procedure to the corresponding financial reporting control objective.

Procedure	Financial Reporting Control Objective
____ 1. Only the treasurer may sign cheques.	A. Ensure that adequate records are maintained.
____ 2. The treasurer is not allowed to make bank deposits.	B. Ensure that transactions are authorized and properly recorded.
____ 3. The company's cheques are prenumbered.	C. Prevent or detect unauthorized activities involving the company's assets.

M6-2 Identifying Internal Control Principles

LO1

Identify the internal control principle represented by each of the following points.

1. One office employee places all merchandise orders.
2. Goods are received only by warehouse employees.
3. The warehouse is locked and activities are electronically monitored.
4. Merchandise orders are recorded on a purchase order form.
5. Receiving reports are completed to indicate goods received.
6. Goods billed by suppliers are compared with purchase orders and receiving reports before they are paid.

M6-3 Organizing Items on the Bank Reconciliation

LO2

Indicate whether the following items would be added ($+$) or subtracted ($-$) from the company's books or the bank statement side of a bank reconciliation.

Reconciling Item	Bank Statement	Company's Books
a. Outstanding cheques of $12,000		
b. Bank service charge of $15		
c. Deposit in transit of $2,300		
d. Interest earned of $5		

LO2   **M6-4 Preparing Journal Entries after a Bank Reconciliation**

Using the information in M6-3, prepare any journal entries needed to adjust the company's books.

LO3   **M6-5 Distinguishing among Operating Cycles**

Identify the type of business as service (S), retail merchandiser (RM), wholesale merchandiser (WM), or manufacturer (M) for each of the following.

_____ 1. The company reports no inventory on its balance sheet.

_____ 2. The company's customers have been slow in paying their accounts because their own customers have been slow in paying.

_____ 3. Approximately one-third of the company's inventory requires further work before it will be ready for sale.

_____ 4. The company rarely extends credit to its customers when selling goods.

LO3   **M6-6 Choosing between a Perpetual and Periodic Inventory System**

Nordstrom, Inc., started in business in 1901. It only took 100 years, but eventually the company changed from a periodic inventory system to a perpetual inventory system (in 2002). Write a brief report describing how this change is likely to improve the company's inventory control.

LO3   **M6-7 Calculating Shrinkage in a Perpetual Inventory System**

Koonce's Campus Store has $25,000 worth of inventory on hand at the beginning of the month. During the month, the company buys $4,000 worth of merchandise and sells merchandise that had cost $15,000. At the end of the month, $13,000 worth of inventory is on hand. How much "shrinkage" occurred during the month?

LO4   **M6-8 Determining Inventory Cost in a Perpetual System**

Assume Anderson's General Store in Kapuskasing bought, on credit, a truckload of merchandise costing $23,000. If the company was charged $650 in transportation cost, immediately returned goods costing $1,200, and then took advantage of a 2/10, n/30 purchase discount, how much should Anderson's report as the cost of inventory?

LO4   **M6-9 Preparing Journal Entries for Purchases, Purchase Discounts, and Purchase Returns, Using a Perpetual System**

Using the information in M6-8, prepare journal entries to record the inventory transactions, assuming that Anderson's uses a perpetual inventory system.

LO3, LO4   **M6-10 Recording Journal Entries for Purchases and Sales, Using a Perpetual Inventory System**

Inventory at the beginning of the year cost $13,400. During the year, the company purchased (on account) inventory costing $54,000, and inventory, which had cost $60,000, was sold on account for $75,000. At the end of the year, inventory was counted, and its cost was determined to be $7,400. Prepare journal entries to record these transactions, assuming that a perpetual inventory system is used.

LO4   **M6-11 Reporting Net Sales and Gross Profit with Sales Discounts**

Merchandise costing $1,500 is sold for $2,000 on terms 2/10, n/30. If the buyer pays within the discount period, what amounts will be reported on the income statement as net sales and as gross profit?

LO4   **M6-12 Recording Journal Entries for Sales and Sales Discounts**

Using the information in M6-11, prepare the journal entries needed at the time of sale and collection, assuming the company uses a perpetual inventory system.

M6-13 Journal Entries to Record Sales Discounts

LO4

Inventory that cost $500 is sold for $700, with terms of 2/10, n/30. Give the journal entries to record (a) the sale of merchandise and (b) collection of the accounts receivable, assuming that it occurs during the discount period. (Use the method shown in this chapter for recording sales discounts.)

M6-14 Reporting Net Sales with Sales Discounts and Sales Returns

LO4

Total sales for the period include the following:

Sales paid for with cash	$8,000
Sales made on account (terms 2/15, n/60)	$9,500

Sales returns relating to sales on account were $500. All returns were made by customers before they paid their account balances. One-half of the sales amount on account (net of returns) was paid within the discount period. The company records all discounts and returns as contra-revenues. What amount will be reported on the income statement as net sales?

M6-15 Preparing a Multi-step Income Statement

LO6

Sellall Department Stores reported the following amounts in its adjusted trial balance prepared as of its December 31, 2008, fiscal year-end: Administrative expenses, $2,300; Cost of goods sold, $12,300; Gain on sale of equipment, $500; General expenses, $6,700; Income tax expense, $2,400; Interest expense, $1,300; Sales revenue, $36,000; Sales discounts $2,400; Sales returns and allowances, $920; and Delivery (freight-out) expense $2,500. Prepare a multi-step income statement for distribution to external financial statement users, using the format shown in Exhibit 6.9.

M6-16 Computing and Interpreting the Gross Profit Percentage

LO6, LO7

Using the information in M6-15, calculate the gross profit percentage for 2008. Evaluate the company's performance using Exhibit 6.12 as a benchmark.

M6-17 Computing and Interpreting the Gross Profit Percentage

LO6, LO7

Ziehart Pharmaceuticals reported net sales of $178,000 and cost of goods sold of $58,000. Candy Electronics Corp. reported net sales of $36,000 and cost of goods sold of $26,200. Calculate the gross profit percentage for each company. From these calculations, can you determine which company is more successful? Explain.

EXERCISES

E6-1 Identifying Internal Control Procedure and Financial Reporting Control Objective

LO1

At most movie theatres, one employee sells tickets and another employee collects them. One night, when you're at the movies, your friend comments that this is a waste of the theatre's money.

Required:

1. Identify the name of the control procedure and control objective to which this situation relates.
2. Explain to your friend what could happen if the same person did both jobs.

E6-2 Identifying Financial Reporting Control Objectives

LO1

Your student club recently volunteered to go door-to-door collecting cash donations on behalf of a local charity. The charity's accountant went absolutely berserk when you happened to say you bothered to write receipts only for donors who asked for one.

Required:

Identify the control objective or objectives that you violated, and explain why the accountant reacted so strongly. What controls might be appropriate to use in the future?

LO2   **E6-3 Preparing a Bank Reconciliation and Journal Entries, and Reporting Cash**

Jones Company's June 30, 2008, bank statement and the June ledger account for cash are summarized here:

Bank Statement

	Cheques	Deposits	Other	Balance
Balance, June 1, 2008				$ 7,200
Deposits during June		$17,000		24,200
Cheques cleared during June	$18,100			6,100
Bank service charges			$50	6,050
Balance, June 30, 2008				6,050

dr Cash (A) cr

June 1	Balance	6,800	June	Cheques written	18,400
June	Deposits	19,000			

Required:

1. Prepare a bank reconciliation. A comparison of the cheques written with the cheques that have cleared the bank shows outstanding cheques of $700. Some of the cheques that cleared in June were written prior to June. No deposits in transit were noted in May, but a deposit is in transit at the end of June.
2. Give any journal entries that should be made as a result of the bank reconciliation.
3. What is the balance in the *Cash* account after the reconciliation entries?
4. In addition to the balance in its bank account, Jones Company also has $300 cash on hand. This amount is recorded in a separate T-account called *Cash on Hand*. What is the total amount of cash that should be reported on the balance sheet at June 30?

LO2   **E6-4 Preparing a Bank Reconciliation and Journal Entries, and Reporting Cash**

The September 30, 2008, bank statement for Cadieux Company and the September ledger account for cash are summarized here:

Bank Statement

	Cheques	Deposits	Other	Balance
Balance, September 1, 2008				$ 6,300
Deposits recorded during September		$27,000		33,300
Cheques cleared during September	$28,500			4,800
NSF cheques—Betty Brown			$150	4,650
Bank service charges			50	4,600
Balance, September 30, 2008				4,600

dr Cash (A) cr

Sept. 1	Balance	6,300	June	Cheques written	28,600
Sept	Deposits	28,000			

No outstanding cheques and no deposits in transit were noted in August. However, there are deposits in transit and cheques outstanding at the end of September.

Required:

1. Prepare a bank reconciliation.
2. Give any journal entries that should be made as a result of the bank reconciliation.
3. What should the balance in the *Cash* account be after recording the journal entries in requirement 2?

4. If the company also has $400 in cash on hand (recorded in a separate account), what total amount of cash should the company report on the September 30 balance sheet?

E6-5 Inferring Shrinkage, Using a Perpetual Inventory System

LO3

Calculate the amount of shrinkage for each of the following independent cases:

Cases	Beginning Inventory	Purchases	Cost of Goods Sold	Ending Inventory (as counted)	Shrinkage
A	$100	$700	$300	$420	$?
B	200	800	850	150	?
C	150	500	200	440	?
D	260	600	650	200	?

E6-6 Inferring Shrinkage, Using a Perpetual Inventory System

LO3

JCPenney Company, Inc., is a major United Srates retailer with department stores in all 50 states. The main part of the company's business consists of providing merchandise and services to consumers through department stores. In a recent annual report, JCPenney reported cost of goods sold of $10,969 million, ending inventory for the current year of $3,058 million, and ending inventory for the previous year of $2,969 million.

Required:

If you knew that the cost of inventory purchases was $11,060 million, could you estimate the cost of shrinkage during the year? If so, prepare the estimate, and, if not, explain why.

E6-7 Recording the Cost of Purchases for a Merchandiser

LO4

Apparel.com purchased 80 new shirts and recorded a total cost of $3,015, determined as follows:

Invoice cost	$2,600
Transportation cost (freight-in)	165
Estimated cost of shipping to customers	250
	$3,015

Required:

Calculate the correct inventory cost, and give the journal entry or entries to record the above purchase information in the correct amount, assuming a perpetual inventory system. Show computations.

E6-8 Reporting Purchases and Purchase Discounts, Using a Perpetual Inventory System

LO4

During the months of January and February, Axe Corporation purchased goods from three suppliers. The sequence of events was as follows:

Jan.	6	Purchased goods for $1,000 from Green with terms 2/10, n/30
	6	Purchased goods from Munoz for $800 with terms 2/10, n/30
	14	Paid Green in full
Feb.	2	Paid Munoz in full
	28	Purchased goods for $500 from Reynolds with terms 2/10, n/45

Required:

Assume that Axe uses a perpetual inventory system, the company had no inventory on hand at the beginning of January, and no sales were made during January and February. Calculate the cost of inventory as of February 28. Did Axe take advantage of all purchase discounts available to it?

LO4   **E6-9   Recording Journal Entries for Purchases and Purchase Discounts, Using a Perpetual Inventory System**

Using the information in E6-8, prepare journal entries to record the transactions, assuming Axe uses a perpetual inventory system.

LO4   **E6-10   Reporting Purchases, Purchase Discounts, and Purchase Returns, Using a Perpetual Inventory System**

During the month of June, Ace Incorporated purchased goods from two suppliers. The sequence of events was as follows:

June	3	Purchased goods for $2,200 from Zip Inc. with terms 2/10, n/30.
	5	Returned goods costing $1,200 to Zip Inc. for full credit.
	6	Purchased goods from Nadda Corp. for $2,000 with terms 2/10, n/30.
	11	Paid the balance owed to Zip.
	22	Paid Nadda in full.

Required:

Assume that Ace uses a perpetual inventory system, and that the company had no inventory on hand at the beginning of the month. Calculate the cost of inventory as of June 30. Did Ace take advantage of all purchase discounts available to it?

LO4   **E6-11   Recording Journal Entries for Purchases, Purchase Discounts, and Purchase Returns, Using a Perpetual Inventory System**

Using the information in E6-10, prepare journal entries to record the transactions, assuming Ace uses a perpetual inventory system.

LO4   **E6-12   Reporting Net Sales with Credit Sales and Sales Discounts**

During the months of January and February, Zax Corporation sold goods to three customers. The sequence of events was as follows:

Jan.	6	Sold goods for $1,000 to Blue Inc. with terms 2/10, n/30. The goods cost Zax $700.
	6	Sold goods to VeraCorp for $800 with terms 2/10, n/30. The goods cost Zax $600.
	14	Collected cash due from Blue Inc.
Feb.	2	Collected cash due from Vera Corp.
	28	Sold goods for $500 to Wrapp, with terms 2/10, n/45. The goods cost Zax $300.

Required:

Assuming that sales discounts are reported as contra-revenue, compute net sales for the two months ended February 28.

LO4   **E6-13   Recording Journal Entries for Net Sales with Credit Sales and Sales Discounts**

Using the information in E6-12, prepare journal entries to record the transactions, assuming Zax uses a perpetual inventory system.

LO4   **E6-14   Reporting Net Sales with Credit Sales and Sales Discounts**

The following transactions were selected from the records of Evergreen Company:

July	12	Sold merchandise to Wally Butler for $980 cash. The goods cost Evergreen Company $600.
	15	Sold merchandise to Claudio's Chair Company at a selling price of $5,000, on terms 3/10, n/30. The goods cost Evergreen Company $3,500.

	20	Sold merchandise to Otto's Ottomans at a selling price of $3,000, on terms 3/10, n/30. The goods cost Evergreen Company $1,900.
	23	Collected payment from Claudio's Chair Company from July 15 sale.
Aug.	25	Collected payment from Otto's Ottomans from July 20 sale.

Required:

Assuming that sales discounts are reported as contra-revenue, compute net sales for the two months ended August 31.

E6-15 Recording Journal Entries for Net Sales with Credit Sales and Sales Discounts   LO4

Using the information in E6-14, prepare journal entries to record the transactions, assuming Evergreen Company uses a perpetual inventory system.

E6-16 Reporting Net Sales with Credit Sales, Sales Discounts, and Sales Returns   LO4

The following transactions were selected from among those completed by Bear's Retail Store in 2008:

Nov.	20	Sold two items of merchandise to Cheryl Jahn for $392 cash. The goods cost Bear's $300.
	25	Sold 20 items of merchandise to Vasko Athletics at a selling price of $4,000 (total); terms 3/10, n/30. The goods cost Bear's $2,500.
	28	Sold 10 identical items of merchandise to Nancy's Gym at a selling price of $6,000 (total); terms 3/10, n/30. The goods cost Bear's $4,000.
	29	Nancy's Gym returned one of the items purchased on the 28th. The item was defective, and credit was given to the customer.
Dec.	6	Nancy's Gym paid the account balance in full.
	30	Vasko Athletics paid in full for the invoice of November 25, 2008.

Required:

Assuming that sales returns and sales discounts are reported as contra-revenues, compute net sales for the two months ended December 31, 2008. Assuming that returns normally average 5 per cent of sales, were Bear's returns more or less than average for the two months ended December 31?

E6-17 Recording Journal Entries for Net Sales with Credit Sales, Sales Discounts, and Sales Returns   LO4

Using the information in E6-16, prepare journal entries to record the transactions, assuming Bear's Retail Store uses a perpetual inventory system.

E6-18 Determining the Effects of Credit Sales, Sales Discounts, and Sales Returns and Allowances on Income Statement Categories

Rockland Shoe Company records sales returns and allowances and sales discounts as contra-revenues. Complete the following table, indicating the amount and direction of effect (+ for increase, − for decrease, and NE for no effect) of each transaction on Rockland.

COACH'S TIP

For E6-17, note that defective items are not returned to inventory. Assume they remain as an expense.

LO4

July	12	Rockland sold merchandise to Kristina Zee at its factory store for $300 cash.
July	15	Sold merchandise to Shoe Express at a selling price of $5,000, with terms 3/10, n/30.
July	20	Collected cash due from Shoe Express.
July	21	Sold merchandise to Fleet Foot Co. at a selling price of $2,000, with terms 2/10, n/30.
July	23	Fleet Foot Co. returned $1,000 worth of shoes, and promised to pay for the remaining goods in August.

Transaction	Sales Revenue	Sales Returns and Allowances	Sales Discounts	Net Sales
July 12				
July 15				
July 20				
July 21				
July 23				

LO4   **E6-19 Recording Sales and Purchases with Discounts**

Cycle Wholesaling sells merchandise on credit terms of 2/10, n/30. A sale invoiced at $800 (cost of goods sold of $500) was made to Sarah's Cycles on February 1, 2008. On March 4, 2008, Cycle Wholesaling purchased bicycles and accessories from a supplier on credit, invoiced at $8,000 with terms 1/15, n/30. Assume Cycle Wholesaling uses a perpetual inventory system.

Required:

Sales Transactions

1. Give the journal entry Cycle Wholesaling would make to record the sale to Sarah's Cycles.
2. Give the journal entry to record the collection of the account, assuming it was collected in full on February 9, 2008.
3. Give the journal entry, assuming, instead, that the account was collected in full on March 2, 2008.

Purchase Transactions

4. Give the journal entry to record the purchase on credit.
5. Give the journal entry to record the payment of Cycle Wholesaling's account, assuming it was paid in full on March 12, 2008.
6. Give the journal entry, assuming, instead, that the account was paid in full on March 28, 2008.

LO4   **E6-20 Recording Purchases, Purchase Returns, and Sales**

The records for Hamil Company at December 31, 2008, show the following:

	Units	Unit Price
Cash sales during period	10,000	$10 (selling price)
Inventory at beginning of year	2,000	6 (at cost)
Cash purchases during the year	16,000	6
Purchased units returned during the year for cash	100	6
Inventory at end of the year	?	6

Required:

1. Prepare journal entries to record the purchases, purchase returns, sales, and cost of goods sold in 2008.
2. Calculate the number of units that should be on hand at year-end.
3. Assume that Hamil counts 7,500 units on hand at December 31. If there is a difference between this number and the one you calculated in requirement 2 above, how might the difference be explained?

LO6   **E6-21 Inferring Missing Amounts Based on Income Statement Relationships**

Supply the missing dollar amounts for the 2008 income statement of Williamson Company for each of the following independent cases:

	Case A	Case B	Case C
Sales revenue	$8,000	$6,000	$?
Sales returns and allowances	150	?	275
Net sales revenue	?	?	5,920
Cost of goods sold	5,750	4,050	5,400
Gross profit	?	1,450	?

E6-22 Inferring Missing Amounts Based on Income Statement Relationships

LO6

Supply the missing dollar amounts for the 2008 income statement of Lewis Retailers for each of the following independent cases:

Cases	Sales Revenue	Beginning Inventory	Purchases	Cost of Goods Sold	Cost of Ending Inventory	Gross Profit
A	$ 650	$100	$700	$300	?	$?
B	900	200	800	?	150	?
C	?	150	?	200	300	400
D	800	?	600	650	250	?
E	1,000	50	900	?	?	500

E6-23 Analyzing Gross Profit Percentage on the Basis of a Multi-step Income Statement

LO6

The following summarized data were provided by the records of Mystery Incorporated for the year ended December 31, 2008:

Sales of merchandise for cash	$220,000
Sales of merchandise on credit	32,000
Cost of goods sold	147,000
Selling expense	40,200
Administrative expense	19,000
Sales returns and allowances	7,000
Income tax expense	11,600

Required:

1. Based on these data, prepare a multi-step income statement (showing both gross profit and operating income).
2. What was the amount of gross profit? What was the gross profit percentage? Explain what these two amounts mean.

E6-24 Analyzing Gross Profit Percentage on the Basis of an Income Statement

LO6, LO7

Wolverine World Wide Inc. prides itself as being the "world's leading marketer of United States branded non-athletic footwear." The following data were taken from its recent annual report (in thousands):

Sales of merchandise	$1,141,887
Income taxes	38,645
Cash dividends paid	16,079
Selling and administrative expense	318,243
Cost of products sold	700,349
Interest income	202
Other expenses	1,205

Required:

1. Based on these data, prepare a multi-step income statement.
2. How much was the gross profit? What was the gross profit percentage (rounded to the nearest tenth of a per cent)? Explain what these two amounts mean.
3. Compare Wolverine's gross profit percentage to Wal-Mart's average gross profit percentage of 22 per cent. From this information, can you determine which company is more successful? Why or why not?

LO6, LO7   **E6-25 Analyzing Gross Profit Percentage on the Basis of an Income Statement**

Sleeman Breweries prides itself on its heritage, having produced beer in Canada for five generations. The following data were taken from its recent annual report (in thousands):

Sales of merchandise	$206,674
Income taxes	4,697
Selling and administrative expense	77,017
Cost of goods sold	100,565
Interest expense	7,837
Amortization expense	8,461

Required:

1. Based on these data, prepare a multi-step income statement.
2. How much was the gross profit? What was the gross profit percentage (rounded to the nearest tenth of a per cent)? Explain what these two amounts mean.
3. Compare Sleeman's gross profit percentage with the 64.7 gross profit percentage of Calgary-based Big Rock Breweries. From this information, can you determine which company is more successful? Why or why not?
4. Find the sales and cost of goods sold figures for one other Canadian brewery or wine producer and compare this gross profit percentage with Sleeman's and Big Rock's. (See S1-3 in Chapter 1 for a discussion of possible resources for this data.)

LO6   **E6-26 Comparing Multi-step Income Statements**

Abbreviated and adapted income statements for Best Buy and Circuit City are shown below for the year ended February, 2007.

	Best Buy	*Circuit City*
Net sales	$35,934	$12,430
Cost of goods sold	27,165	9,502
Gross profit	8,769	2,928
Operating expenses	6,770	2,842
Income from operations	1,999	86
Other income	130	73
Income before income taxes	2,129	159
Income tax expense	752	31
Net income	$1,377	$128

Required:

1. Which company generated more net income and gross profit during the year?
2. Which company generated a greater gross profit percentage? Show calculations.
3. Interpret your findings from 1 and 2.

E6-27 (Supplement A) Recording Purchases and Sales Using Perpetual and Periodic Inventory Systems

LO4, LO5

Kangaroo Jim Company reported beginning inventory of 100 units at a unit cost of $25. It had the following purchase and sales transactions during 2008:

Jan. 14   Sold 25 units at unit sales price of $45 on account.

Apr.   9   Purchased 15 additional units at unit cost of $25 on account.

Sep.   2   Sold 50 units at sales price of $50 on account.

Dec. 31   Counted inventory and determined 40 units were still on hand.

Required:

Record each transaction, assuming that Kangaroo Jim Company uses (a) a perpetual inventory system and (b) a periodic inventory system.

E6-28 (Supplement A) Recording Purchases, Sales, and Cost of Sales

LO5

The records for Counter Company at December 31, 2008, show the following:

	Units	Unit Price
Cash sales during period	10,000	$10 (selling price)
Inventory at beginning of year	2,000	6 (at cost)
Cash purchases during the year	16,000	6
Inventory counted at end of year	7,500	6

Required:

Prepare journal entries to record the purchases, sales, and cost of sales in 2008, assuming that Counter uses a periodic inventory system. Determine if there is a shortage.

COACHED PROBLEMS

CP6-1 Preparing a Bank Reconciliation and Journal Entries, and Reporting Cash

LO2

The bookkeeper at Hopkins Company has not reconciled the bank statement with the *Cash* account, saying, "I don't have time." You have been asked to prepare a bank reconciliation and review the procedures with the bookkeeper.

The April 30, 2008, bank statement and the April T-account for cash showed the following (summarized):

Bank Statement

	Cheques	Deposits	Other	Balance
Balance, April 1, 2008				$25,850
Deposits during April		$37,050		62,900
Interest earned			$20	62,920
Cheques cleared during April	$44,200			18,720
NSF cheques—A. B. Wright			140	18,580
Bank service charges			50	18,530
Balance, April 30, 2008				18,530

COACH'S TIP

1. Think of the following relationship to determine outstanding cheques:
   Outstanding cheques last month
   + Cheques written this month
   − Cheques cleared this month
   = Outstanding cheques this month

2. Journal entries are needed only for reconciling items on the company's books side of the bank reconciliation.

	dr Cash (A) cr		
Apr. 1 Balance	23,250	Apr. Cheques written	43,800
Apr. Deposits	42,000		

Hopkins Company's bank reconciliation at the end of March 2008 showed outstanding cheques of $2,600. No deposits were in transit at the end of March, but a deposit was in transit at the end of April.

Required:

1. Prepare a bank reconciliation for April.
2. Prepare any journal entries required as a result of the bank reconciliation. Why are they necessary?
3. After the reconciliation journal entries are posted, what balance will be reflected in the *Cash* account in the ledger?
4. If the company also has $100 on hand, which is recorded in a different account called *Cash on Hand*, what total amount of cash should be reported on the balance sheet at the end of April?

LO2   **CP6-2 Identifying Outstanding Cheques and Deposits in Transit, and Preparing a Bank Reconciliation and Journal Entries**

The August 2008 bank statement for Martha Company and the cash T-account for August 2008 follow:

Bank Statement

Date	Cheques	Deposits	Other		Balance
Aug.1					$17,470
2	$ 300				17,170
3		$12,000			29,170
4	400				28,770
5	250				28,520
9	890				27,630
10	310				27,320
15		4,000			31,320
21	400				30,920
24	21,000				9,920
25		7,000			16,920
30	800				16,120
30			Interest earned	$20	16,140
31			Service charge	10	16,130

COACH'S TIP

Put a check mark beside each item that appears in both the bank statement and what's already recorded in the accounting records (either in the T-account this month or the outstanding items from last month). Any item in the accounting records without check marks should appear on the bank statement side of the bank reconciliation. Any items in the bank statement without check marks should appear on the company's books side of the bank reconciliation.

dr Cash (A) cr

Aug. 1 Balance	16,520	Cheques written	
Deposits		Aug. 2	310
Aug. 2	12,000	4	890
12	4,000	15	290
24	7,000	17	550
31	5,000	18	800
		18	400
		23	21,000

Outstanding cheques at the end of July were for $250, $400, and $300. No deposits were in transit at the end of July.

Required:

1. Identify and list the deposits in transit at the end of August.
2. Identify and list the outstanding cheques at the end of August.
3. Prepare a bank reconciliation for August.
4. Give any journal entries that the company should make as a result of the bank reconciliation. Why are they necessary?
5. After the reconciliation journal entries are posted, what balance will be reflected in the *Cash* account in the ledger?
6. If the company also has $100 on hand, which is recorded in a different account called *Cash on Hand*, what total amount of cash should be reported on the August 31, 2008, balance sheet?

CP6-3 Preparing a Multi-step Income Statement with Sales Discounts and Sales Returns and Allowances, and Computing the Gross Profit Percentage

LO4, LO5

Psymon Company, Inc., sells heavy construction equipment. The annual fiscal period ends on December 31. The following adjusted trial balance was created from the general ledger accounts on December 31, 2008:

Account Titles	Debit	Credit
Cash	$ 42,000	
Accounts receivable	18,000	
Inventory	65,000	
Property and equipment	50,000	
Accumulated amortization		$ 21,000
Liabilities		30,000
Contributed capital		90,000
Retained earnings, January 1, 2008		11,600
Sales revenue		182,000
Sales returns and allowances	7,000	
Sales discounts	8,000	
Cost of goods sold	98,000	
Selling expense	17,000	
Administrative expense	18,000	
General expenses	2,000	
Income tax expense	9,600	
Totals	$334,600	$334,600

Required:

1. Prepare a multi-step income statement that would be used for internal reporting purposes. Treat sales returns and allowances and sales discounts as contra-revenue accounts.
2. Prepare a multi-step income statement that would be used for external reporting purposes, beginning with the amount for *net sales*.
3. Assuming that in previous years the returns and allowances averaged 5 per cent of sales, comment on Psymon's returns and allowances for the year ended December 31, 2008.
4. Compute the gross profit percentage and explain its meaning.

COACH'S TIP

Remember that contra-revenue accounts are rarely reported in financial statements used for external reporting.

CP6-4 Recording Sales and Purchases with Discounts and Returns

LO4

Campus Stop, Incorporated, is a student co-op. Campus Stop uses a perpetual inventory system. The following transactions (summarized) have been selected from 2008:

a.	Sold merchandise for cash (cost of merchandise $137,500).	$275,000
b.	Received merchandise returned by customers as unsatisfactory, for cash refund (original cost of merchandise $800).	1,600
	Purchased items from suppliers on credit:	
c.	Purchased merchandise from Super Supply Company, with terms 3/10, n/30.	5,000
d.	Purchased merchandise from other suppliers, with terms 3/10, n/30.	120,000
e.	Purchased equipment for use in store; paid cash.	2,200
f.	Purchased office supplies for future use in the store; paid cash.	700
g.	Freight on merchandise purchased; paid cash.	400
	Paid accounts payable in full during the period as follows:	
h.	Paid Super Supply Company after the discount period.	5,000
i.	Paid other suppliers within the 3 per cent discount period.	116,400

COACH'S TIP

Inventory includes only merchandise purchased for sale. Other purchases, such as supplies for internal use, are recorded in separate accounts.

Required:

Prepare journal entries for each of the preceding transactions.

LO4, LO5

CP6-5 Reporting Sales and Purchase Transactions between Wholesale and Retail Merchandisers, with Sales/Purchase Allowances and Sales/Purchase Discounts, Using Perpetual Inventory Systems

The transactions listed below are typical of those involving Ghostmaker Garments and First Fashions. Ghostmaker is a wholesale merchandiser, and First Fashions is a retail merchandiser. Assume that the following transactions between the two companies occurred in the order listed, during the year ended December 31, 2008. Assume that all sales of merchandise from Ghostmaker to First Fashions are made with terms 2/10, n/30, and that the two companies use perpetual inventory systems.

Transactions during 2008:

a. Ghostmaker sold merchandise to First Fashions at a selling price of $230,000. The merchandise had cost Ghostmaker $175,000.
b. Two days later, First Fashions complained to Ghostmaker that some of the merchandise differed from what First Fashions had ordered. Ghostmaker agreed to give an allowance of $5,000 to First Fashions.
c. Just three days later, First Fashions paid Ghostmaker, which settled all amounts owed.

COACH'S TIP

1a. Gross profit is a subtotal which is affected when a company records sales and cost of goods sold.
1b. When an allowance is granted and no inventory is returned, the seller records only one journal entry.

Required:

1. For each of the events a through c, indicate the amount and direction of the effect (+ for increase, − for decrease, and NE for no effect) on Ghostmaker Garments in terms of the following items.

Sales Revenues	Sales Returns and Allowances	Sales Discounts	Net Sales	Cost of Goods Sold	Gross Profit

2. Which of the above items are likely to be reported on Ghostmaker's external financial statements, and which items will be combined "behind the scenes."
3. Indicate the effect (direction and amount) of each transaction on the balance in First Fashions' inventory account.

LO4

CP6-6 Journalizing Sales and Purchase Transactions between Wholesale and Retail Merchandisers, with Sales/Purchase Allowances and Sales/Purchase Discounts, Using Perpetual Inventory Systems

Use the information presented in CP6-5 to complete the following requirements.

Required:

1. Prepare the journal entries that Ghostmaker Garments would record, and show any computations.
2. Prepare the journal entries that First Fashions would record, and show any computations.

COACH'S TIP

When using a perpetual inventory system, the seller always makes two journal entries when goods are sold.

LO5

CP6-7 (Supplement A) Journalizing Sales and Purchase Transactions between Wholesale and Retail Merchandisers, with Sales/Purchase Allowances and Sales/Purchase Discounts, Using Periodic Inventory Systems

Use the information presented in CP6-5 and transaction a (only) to complete the following requirements, except assume that both companies use periodic inventory systems.

Required:

1. Prepare the journal entry (or entries) that Ghostmaker Garments would record for transaction a only.
2. Prepare the journal entry (or entries) that First Fashions would record for transaction a only.
3. Assume that, during the year, First Fashions sold merchandise on credit for $160,000. Prepare the journal entry (or entries) that First Fashions would record.
4. Assume that, at the end of the year, First Fashions counted the inventory on hand that had been purchased from Ghostmaker Garments and determined that its cost was $80,000. Prepare any journal entries that First Fashions would record, and show any computations.

COACH'S TIP

When using a periodic inventory system, the seller makes only one journal entry when goods are sold.

GROUP A PROBLEMS

LO2

PA6-1 Preparing a Bank Reconciliation and Journal Entries, and Reporting Cash

The bookkeeper at Martin Company has asked you to prepare a bank reconciliation as of May 31, 2008. The May 31, 2008, bank statement and the May T-account for cash showed the following (summarized):

Bank Statement

	Cheques	Deposits	Other	Balance
Balance, May 1, 2008				$11,500
Deposits during May		$18,000		29,500
Interest earned			$120	29,620
Cheques cleared during May	$22,100			7,520
NSF cheques—B. A. Dugry				
(customer)			280	7,240
Bank service charges			60	7,180
Balance, May 31, 2008				7,180

dr Cash (A) cr

May 1	Balance	8,800	May	Cheques written	23,400
May	Deposits	22,000			

Martin Company's bank reconciliation at the end of April 2008 showed outstanding cheques of $2,700. No deposits were in transit at the end of April, but a deposit was in transit at the end of May.

Required:

1. Prepare a bank reconciliation for May.

2. Prepare any journal entries required as a result of the bank reconciliation. Why are they necessary?

3. After the reconciliation journal entries are posted, what balance will be reflected in the *Cash* account in the ledger?

4. If the company also has $50 on hand, which is recorded in a different account called *Cash on Hand*, what total amount of cash should be reported on the balance sheet at the end of May?

LO2

PA6-2 Identifying Outstanding Cheques and Deposits in Transit, and Preparing a Bank Reconciliation and Journal Entries

The December 2008 bank statement for Stewart Company and the cash T-account for December 2008 follow:

Bank Statement

Date	Cheques	Deposits	Other		Balance
Dec.1					$48,000
2	$400; 300	$17,000			64,300
4	7,000; 90				57,210
6	120; 180; 1,600				55,310
11	500; 1,200; 70	28,000			81,540
13	480; 700; 1,900				78,460
17	12,000; 8,000				58,460
23	60; 23,500	36,000			70,900
26	900; 2,650				67,350
28	2,200; 5,200				59,950
30	17,000; 1,890	19,000	NSF*	$300	59,760
31	1,650; 1,350		Interest earned	50	
			Service charge	150	56,660

*NSF cheque from J. Left, a customer.

dr Cash (A) cr				
Dec 1 Balance	64,100	Cheques written during December:		
Deposits		60	5,000	2,650
Dec. 11	28,000	17,000	5,200	1,650
23	36,000	700	1,890	2,200
30	19,000	3,300	1,600	7,000
31	13,000	1,350	120	300
		180	90	480
		12,000	23,500	8,000
		70	500	1,900
		900	1,200	

The November 2008 bank reconciliation showed the following: up-to-date cash balance at November 30, $64,100; deposits in transit on November 30, $17,000; and outstanding cheques on November 30, $400 + $500 = $900.

Required:

1. Identify and list the deposits in transit at the end of December.
2. Identify and list the outstanding cheques at the end of December.
3. Prepare a bank reconciliation for December.
4. Give any journal entries that the company should make as a result of the bank reconciliation. Why are they necessary?
5. After the reconciliation journal entries are posted, what balance will be reflected in the *Cash* account in the ledger?
6. If the company also has $300 on hand, which is recorded in a different account called *Cash on Hand*, what total amount of cash should be reported on the December 31, 2008, balance sheet?

LO6, LO7   **PA6-3 Preparing a Multi-step Income Statement with Sales Discounts and Sales Returns and Allowances, and Computing the Gross Profit Percentage**

Big Tommy Corporation is a local grocery store organized seven years ago as a corporation. The store is in an excellent location, and sales have increased each year. At the end of 2008, the bookkeeper prepared the following statement (assume that all amounts are correct, but note the incorrect terminology and format):

BIG TOMMY CORPORATION Profit and Loss December 31, 2008		
	Debit	**Credit**
Sales		$420,000
Cost of goods sold	$279,000	
Sales returns and allowances	10,000	
Sales discounts	6,000	
Selling expense	58,000	
Administrative expense	16,000	
General expenses	1,000	
Income tax expense	15,000	
Net profit	35,000	
Totals	$420,000	$420,000

Required:

1. Prepare a multi-step income statement that would be used for internal reporting purposes. Treat sales returns and allowances and sales discounts as contra-revenue accounts.

2. Prepare a multi-step income statement that would be used for external reporting purposes, beginning with the amount for *net sales*.

3. Assuming that in previous years the returns and allowances averaged 1 per cent of sales, comment on Big Tommy's returns and allowances for the year ended December 31, 2008.

4. Compute the gross profit percentage and explain its meaning.

PA6-4 Recording Sales and Purchases with Discounts and Returns

LO4

Hair World Inc. is a wholesaler of hair supplies. Hair World uses a perpetual inventory system. The following transactions (summarized) have been selected from 2008:

a.	Sold merchandise for cash (cost of merchandise $30,600).	$51,200
b.	Received merchandise returned by customers as unsatisfactory, for cash refund (original cost of merchandise $360).	600
	Purchased items from suppliers on credit:	
c.	Purchased merchandise from Cari's Comb Company with terms 3/10, n/30.	1,000
d.	Purchased merchandise from other suppliers with terms 3/10, n/30.	24,000
e.	Purchased equipment for use in store; paid cash.	400
f.	Purchased office supplies for future use in the store; paid cash.	140
g.	Freight on merchandise purchased; paid cash.	100
	Paid accounts payable in full during the period as follows:	
h.	Paid Cari's Comb Company after the discount period.	1,000
i.	Paid other suppliers within the 3 per cent discount period.	23,280

Required:

Prepare journal entries for each of the preceding transactions.

PA6-5 Reporting Sales and Purchase Transactions between Wholesale and Retail Merchandisers, with Sales/Purchase Allowances and Sales/Purchase Discounts, Using Perpetual Inventory Systems

LO4

The transactions listed below are typical of those involving New Books Inc. and Readers' Corner. New Books is a wholesale merchandiser, and Readers' Corner is a retail merchandiser. Assume that the following transactions between the two companies occurred in the order listed during the year ended August 31, 2008. Assume that all sales of merchandise from New Books to Readers' Corner are made with terms 2/10, n/30, and that the two companies use perpetual inventory systems.

Transactions during the year ended August 31, 2008:

a. New Books sold merchandise to Readers' Corner at a selling price of $550,000. The merchandise had cost New Books $415,000.

b. Two days later, Readers' Corner complained to New Books that some of the merchandise differed from what Readers' Corner had ordered. New Books agreed to give an allowance of $10,000 to Readers' Corner.

c. Just three days later, Readers' Corner paid New Books, which settled all amounts owed.

Required:

1. For each of the events *a* through *c*, indicate the amount and direction of the effect (+ for increase, − for decrease, and NE for no effect) on New Books in terms of the following items.

Sales Revenues	Sales Returns and Allowances	Sales Discounts	Net Sales	Cost of Goods Sold	Gross Profit

2. Which of the above items are likely to be reported on New Books' external financial statements, and which items will be combined "behind the scenes"?

3. Indicate the effect (direction and amount) of each transaction on the balance in Readers' Corner's inventory account.

LO4   **PA6-6** **Journalizing Sales and Purchase Transactions between Wholesale and Retail Merchandisers, with Sales/Purchase Allowances and Sales/Purchase Discounts, Using Perpetual Inventory Systems**

Use the information presented in PA6-5 to complete the following requirements.

Required:

1. Prepare the journal entries that New Books would record, and show any computations.
2. Prepare the journal entries that Readers' Corner would record, and show any computations.

LO5   **PA6-7** **(Supplement A) Journalizing Sales and Purchase Transactions between Wholesale and Retail Merchandisers, with Sales/Purchase Allowances and Sales/Purchase Discounts, Using Periodic Inventory Systems**

Use the information presented in PA6-5 and transaction *a* (only) to complete the following requirements, except assume that both companies use periodic inventory systems.

Required:

1. Prepare the journal entries that New Books would record for transaction *a* only.
2. Prepare the journal entries that Readers' Corner would record for transaction *a* only.
3. Assume that, during the year, Readers' Corner sold merchandise on credit for $250,000. Prepare the journal entries that Readers' Corner would record.
4. Assume that, at the end of the year, Readers' Corner counted the inventory it had purchased from New Books and determined that its cost was $135,000. Prepare any journal entries that Readers' Corner would record, and show any computations.

GROUP B PROBLEMS

LO2   **PB6-1** **Preparing a Bank Reconciliation and Journal Entries, and Reporting Cash**

The bookkeeper at Tony Company has asked you to prepare a bank reconciliation as of February 28, 2008. The February 28, 2008, bank statement and the February T-account for cash showed the following (summarized):

Bank Statement

	Cheques	*Deposits*	*Other*	*Balance*
Balance, February 1, 2008				$52,600
Deposits during February		$30,650		83,250
Interest earned			$150	83,400
Cheques cleared during May	$49,200			34,200
NSF cheques—S. H. Schaffer			320	33,880
Bank service charges			40	33,840
Balance, February 28, 2008				33,840

dr Cash (A) cr			
Feb 1. Balance	49,400	Feb Cheques written	50,400
Feb. Deposits	38,450		

Tony Company's bank reconciliation at the end of January 2008 showed outstanding cheques of $3,200. No deposits were in transit at the end of January, but a deposit was in transit at the end of February.

Required:

1. Prepare a bank reconciliation for February.
2. Prepare any journal entries required as a result of the bank reconciliation. Why are they necessary?
3. After the reconciliation journal entries are posted, what balance will be reflected in the *Cash* account in the ledger?

4. If the company also has $50 on hand, which is recorded in a different account called *Cash on Hand*, what total amount of cash should be reported on the balance sheet at the end of February?

PB6-2 Identifying Outstanding Cheques and Deposits in Transit, and Preparing a Bank Reconciliation and Journal Entries

LO2

The September 2008 bank statement for Terrick Company and the cash T-account for September 2008 follow:

Bank Statement

Date	Cheques	Deposits	Other		Balance
Sept.1					$75,900
2	$620; 550	$25,000			99,730
4	2,000; 200				97,530
6	1,500; 870; 21,000				74,160
11	300; 1,500; 600	14,000			85,760
13	650; 600; 6,550				77,960
17	10,000; 9,000				58,960
23	90; 500	27,000			85,370
26	700; 3,220				81,450
28	8,000; 8,200				65,250
29	730; 3,200	17,000	NSF*	$500	77,820
30	400; 4,400		Interest earned	60	
			Service charge	40	73,040

*NSF cheque from B. Frank, a customer.

dr Cash (A) cr				
Sept. 1 Balance	98,780	Cheques written during September:		
Deposits		730	8,000	3,220
Sept. 11	14,000	21,000	200	550
23	27,000	600	3,680	4,400
29	17,000	700	650	9,000
30	21,000	6,550	3,200	600
		560	500	840
		2,000	8,200	10,000
		90	300	400
		870	1,500	

The August 2008 bank reconciliation showed the following: up-to-date cash balance at August 30, $98,780; deposits in transit on August 31, $25,000; and outstanding cheques on August 31, $620 + $1,500 = $2,120.

Required:

1. Identify and list the deposits in transit at the end of September.
2. Identify and list the outstanding cheques at the end of September.
3. Prepare a bank reconciliation for September.
4. Give any journal entries that the company should make as a result of the bank reconciliation. Why are they necessary?
5. After the reconciliation journal entries are posted, what balance will be reflected in the *Cash* account in the ledger?
6. If the company also has $200 on hand, which is recorded in a different account called *Cash on Hand*, what total amount of cash should be reported on the September 30, 2008, balance sheet?

PB6-3 Preparing a Multi-step Income Statement with Sales Discounts and Sales Returns and Allowances, and Computing the Gross Profit Percentage

LO4, LO6

Emily's Greenhouse Corporation is a local greenhouse organized 10 years ago as a corporation. The greenhouse is in an excellent location, and sales have increased each year. At the end of

2008, the bookkeeper prepared the following statement (assume that all amounts are correct, but note the incorrect terminology and format):

EMILY'S GREENHOUSE CORPORATION
Profit and Loss
December 31, 2008

	Debit	Credit
Sales		$504,000
Cost of goods sold	$311,000	
Sales returns and allowances	11,000	
Sales discounts	8,000	
Selling expense	61,000	
Administrative expense	13,000	
General expenses	3,000	
Income tax expense	18,000	
Net profit	79,000	
Totals	$504,000	$504,000

Required:

1. Prepare a multi-step income statement that would be used for internal reporting purposes. Treat sales returns and allowances and sales discounts as contra-revenue accounts.
2. Prepare a multi-step income statement that would be used for external reporting purposes, beginning with the amount for *net sales*.
3. Assuming that in previous years the returns and allowances averaged 2.5 per cent of sales, comment on Emily's returns and allowances for the year ended December 31, 2008.
4. Compute the gross profit percentage and explain its meaning.

LO4   **PB6-4   Recording Sales and Purchases with Discounts and Returns**

Larry's Hardware, Incorporated, is a locally owned and operated hardware store. Larry's Hardware uses a perpetual inventory system.

The following transactions (summarized) have been selected from 2008:

a.	Sold merchandise for cash (cost of merchandise $325,000).	$500,000
b.	Received merchandise returned by customers as unsatisfactory, for cash refunds (original cost of merchandise $1,900).	3,000
	Purchased items from suppliers on credit:	
c.	Purchased merchandise from Do It Yourself Company with terms 3/10, n/30.	27,000
d.	Purchased merchandise from other suppliers with terms 3/10, n/30.	237,000
e.	Purchased equipment for use in store; paid cash.	5,000
f.	Purchased office supplies for future use in the store; paid cash.	400
g.	Freight on merchandise purchased; paid cash.	350
	Paid accounts payable in full during the period as follows:	
h.	Paid Do It Yourself Company after the discount period.	27,000
i.	Paid other suppliers within the 3 per cent discount period.	229,890

Required:

Prepare journal entries for each of the preceding transactions.

PB6-5 Reporting Sales and Purchase Transactions between Wholesale and Retail Merchandisers, with Sales/Purchase Allowances and Sales/Purchase Discounts, Using Perpetual Inventory Systems

LO4

The transactions listed below are typical of those involving The Hockey Company (THC) and Canadian Tire. THC is a wholesale merchandiser selling CCM and KOHO equipment, and Canadian Tire is a retail merchandiser. Assume the following transactions between the two companies occurred in the order listed during the year ended December 31, 2008. Assume all sales of merchandise from THC to Canadian Tire are made with terms 2/10, n/30, and that the two companies use perpetual inventory systems.

Transactions during 2008:

a. THC sold merchandise to Canadian Tire at a selling price of $125,000. The merchandise had cost THC $94,000.
b. Two days later, Canadian Tire complained to THC that some of the merchandise differed from what Canadian Tire had ordered. THC agreed to give an allowance of $3,000 to Canadian Tire.
c. Just three days later Canadian Tire paid THC, which settled all amounts owed.

Required:

1. For each of the events a through c, indicate the amount and direction of the effect (+ for increase, − for decrease, and NE for no effect) on THC in terms of the following items.

Sales Revenues	Sales Returns and Allowances	Sales Discounts	Net Sales	Cost of Goods Sold	Gross Profit

2. Which of the above items are likely to be reported on THC's external financial statements, and which items will be combined "behind the scenes"?
3. Indicate the effect (direction and amount) of each transaction on the balance in Canadian Tire's inventory account.

PB6-6 Journalizing Sales and Purchase Transactions between Wholesale and Retail Merchandisers, with Sales/Purchase Allowances and Sales/Purchase Discounts, Using Perpetual Inventory Systems

LO4

Use the information presented in PB6-5 to complete the following requirements.

Required:

1. Prepare the journal entries that THC would record, and show any computations.
2. Prepare the journal entries that Canadian Tire would record, and show any computations.

PB6-7 (Supplement A) Journalizing Sales and Purchase Transactions between Wholesale and Retail Merchandisers, with Sales/Purchase Allowances and Sales/Purchase Discounts, Using Periodic Inventory Systems

LO5

Use the information presented in PB6-5 and transaction a (only) to complete the following requirements, except assume that both companies use periodic inventory systems.

Required:

1. Prepare the journal entries that THC would record for transaction a only.
2. Prepare the journal entries that Canadian Tire would record for transaction a only.
3. Assume that, during the year, Canadian Tire sold merchandise on credit for $97,000. Prepare the journal entries that Canadian Tire would record.
4. Assume that, at the end of the year, Canadian Tire counted the inventory it had purchased from THC and determined that its cost was $43,000. Prepare any journal entries that Canadian Tire would record, and show any computations.

SKILLS DEVELOPMENT CASES

LO2, LO3, LO6

S6-1 Finding Financial Information

Refer to the financial statements of High Liner in Appendix A at the end of this book, or download the annual report from the *Cases* section of the text's Web site at www.mcgrawhill.ca/college/phillips.

Required:

1. How much cash (including cash equivalents) does the company report at the end of the most recent year?
2. Compute the company's gross profit percentage for the most recent two years. Has it risen or fallen? Explain the meaning of the change.
3. Assume that High Liner experienced no shrinkage in the most recent year. Using the balance sheet and income statement, estimate the amount of purchases in the most recent year.

LO2, LO3, LO6

S6-2 Comparing Financial Information

Refer to the financial statements of Sun-Rype by downloading the annual report from the *Cases* section of the text's Web site at www.mcgrawhill.ca/college/phillips.

Required:

1. Does Sun-Rype report more or less cash (including cash equivalents) than High Liner at the end of the most recent year?
2. Compute the company's gross profit percentage for the most recent two years. Is it greater or less than High Liner's? Explain the meaning of the comparison.
3. Assume that Sun-Rype experienced no shrinkage in the most recent year. Using the balance sheet and income statement, estimate the amount of purchases in the most recent year. How much greater (or less) were Sun-Rype's purchases than High Liner's for the most recent year?

LO1, LO6, LO7

S6-3 Internet-Based Team Research: Examining an Annual Report

TEAM CASE

As a team, select an industry to analyze. Using your Web browser, each team member should acquire the audited annual financial statements for one Canadian publicly traded company in the industry, with each member selecting a different company. (See S1-3 in Chapter 1 for a description of possible resources for these tasks.) Make sure you find a company that discloses its cost of goods sold figure.

Required:

1. On an individual basis, each team member should write a short report that incorporates the following:

    a. Describe the company's business in sufficient detail to be able to classify it as a service, merchandising, or manufacturing company. What products or services does the company provide?

    b. Calculate the gross profit percentage at the end of the current and prior years, and explain any change between the two years.

2. Then, as a team, write a short report comparing and contrasting your companies using these attributes. Discuss any patterns across the companies that you as a team observe. Provide potential explanations for any differences discovered.

LO1, LO3

S6-4 Ethical Decision Making: A Real-Life Example

ETHICAL ISSUES

When some people think about inventory theft, they imagine a shoplifter running out of a store with goods stuffed inside a jacket or bag. But that's not what the managers thought at the Famous Footwear store on Chicago's Madison Street. No, they suspected their own employees were the main cause of their unusually high shrinkage. One scam involved dishonest cashiers who would let their friends take a pair of Skechers without paying for them. To make it look as though the shoes had been bought, cashiers would ring up a sale, but instead of charging $50 for shoes, they would charge only $2 for a bottle of shoe polish. That's when the company's managers decided to put its accounting system to work. In just two years, the company cut its Madison Street inventory losses in half. Here's how a newspaper described the store's improvements:

Retailers Crack Down on Employee Theft
South Coast Today, **September 10, 2000, Chicago**
By Calmetta Coleman, *Wall Street Journal Staff Writer*

. . . Famous Footwear installed a chainwide register-monitoring system to sniff out suspicious transactions, such as unusually large numbers of refunds or voids, or repeated sales of cheap goods.

. . . [B]efore an employee can issue a cash refund, a second worker must be present to see the customer and inspect the merchandise.

. . . [T]he chain has set up a toll-free hotline for employees to use to report suspicions about co-workers.

These improvements in inventory control came as welcome news for investors and creditors of Brown Shoe Company, the company that owns Famous Footwear. Despite these improvements at the Chicago store, Brown Shoe has been forced to shut down operations in other United States cities.

Required:

1. Explain how the register-monitoring system would allow Famous Footwear to cut down on employee theft.
2. What is the name of the control, and of the financial reporting control objective, that is addressed by Famous Footwear's new cash refund procedure?
3. If Famous Footwear used a periodic inventory system, rather than a perpetual inventory system, how would the company detect shrinkage?
4. Think of and describe at least four different parties that are harmed by the type of inventory theft described in this case.

S6-5 Ethical Decision Making: A Mini-Case

LO4, LO6

Assume you work as an accountant in the merchandising division of a large public company that makes and sells athletic clothing. To encourage the merchandising division to earn as much profit on each individual sale as possible, the division manager's pay is based, in part, on the division's gross profit percentage. To encourage control over the division's operating expenses, the manager's pay also is based on the division's net income.

You are currently preparing the division's financial statements. The division had a good year, with sales of $100,000, cost of goods sold of $50,000, sales returns and allowances of $5,000, sales discounts of $5,000, and other selling expenses of $30,000. (Assume the division does not report income taxes.) The division manager stresses that *"it would be in your personal interest"* to classify sales returns and allowances and sales discounts as selling expenses rather than as contra-revenues on the division's income statement. He justifies this "friendly advice" by saying that he's not asking you to fake the numbers—he just believes that those items are more accurately reported as expenses. Plus, he claims, being a division of a larger company, you don't have to follow GAAP.

Required:

1. Prepare an income statement for the division, using the classifications shown in this chapter. Using this income statement, calculate the division's gross profit percentage.
2. Prepare an income statement for the division using the classifications advised by the manager. Using this income statement, calculate the division's gross profit percentage.
3. What reason (other than reporting "more accurately") do you think is motivating the manager's advice to you?
4. Do you agree with the manager's statement that "he's not asking you to fake the numbers"?
5. Do you agree with the manager's statement about not having to follow GAAP?
6. How should you respond to the division manager's "friendly advice"?

LO1, LO2   **S6-6 Critical Thinking: Analyzing**

Cripple Creek Company has one trusted employee who, as the owner said, "handles all of the bookkeeping and paperwork for the company." This employee is responsible for counting, verifying, and recording cash receipts and payments, making the weekly bank deposit, preparing cheques for major expenditures (signed by the owner), making small expenditures from the cash register for daily expenses, and collecting accounts receivable. The owners asked the local bank for a $20,000 loan. The bank asked that an audit be performed covering the year just ended. The independent auditor (a local CA), in a private conference with the owner, presented some evidence of the following activities of the trusted employee during the past year:

a.   Cash sales sometimes were not entered in the cash register, and the trusted employee pocketed approximately $50 per month.

b.   Cash taken from the cash register (and pocketed by the trusted employee) was replaced with expense memos with fictitious signatures (approximately $12 per day).

c. $300 collected on an account receivable from a valued out-of-town customer was pocketed by the trusted employee and was covered by making a $300 entry as a debit to *Sales Returns* and a credit to *Accounts Receivable*.

d. $800 collected on an account receivable from a local customer was pocketed by the trusted employee and was covered by making an $800 entry as a debit to *Sales Discounts* and a credit to *Accounts Receivable*.

Required:

1.   What was the approximate amount stolen during the past year?
2.   What would be your recommendations to the owner?

LO1   **S6-7 Critical Thinking: Evaluating Internal Controls**

Shari Hill has worked for Dr. Mario Bartucci as a receptionist in his dental office for several years and is an extremely loyal employee. One of Shari's primary duties is to open the mail and list the cheques received from patients. She also takes cash from patients at the cashier window as patients leave. At times, it is so hectic that Shari doesn't bother with giving each patient a receipt for the cash paid on their accounts. She assures them she will see that they receive the proper credit. Shari deposits the cash in the bank every two weeks. When the traffic is slow in the office, Shari offers to help Mary post the payments to the patients' accounts receivable. Mary is always happy to receive Shari's help, because she is a very conscientious worker.

Required:

List three possible weaknesses in internal control that you detect in the above situation.

LO6   **S6-8 Preparing Multi-step Income Statements and Calculating Gross Profit Percentage**

Assume that you have been hired by Big Sky Corporation as a summer student. The company is in the process of preparing their annual financial statements. To help in the process, you are asked to prepare an income statement for internal reporting purposes and an income statement for external reporting purposes. Your boss has also requested that you determine the company's gross profit percentage based on the statements that you are to prepare. The following adjusted trial balance was created from the general ledger accounts on May 31, 2008.

Account Titles	Debit	Credit
Cash	$ 57,000	
Accounts receivable	67,000	
Inventory	103,000	
Property and equipment	252,000	
Accumulated amortization		$ 103,000
Liabilities		75,000
Contributed capital		120,000
Retained earnings, January 1, 2007		145,900
Sales revenue		369,000

Account Titles	Debit	Credit
Sales returns and allowances	10,500	
Sales discounts	13,000	
Cost of goods sold	248,000	
Selling expense	19,000	
Administrative expense	23,000	
General expenses	5,000	
Income tax expense	15,400	
Totals	$812,900	$812,900

Your boss wants you to create the spreadsheet in a way that automatically recalculates net sales and any other related amounts whenever changes are made to the contra-revenue accounts. To do this, you know that you'll have to use formulas throughout the worksheets, and even import or link cells from one worksheet to another. Once again, your friend Billy is willing to help.

From: BillyTheTutor@yahoo.com
To: Overwhelmed@hotmail.com
Cc:
Subject: Excel Help

Sounds like you are going to get some great experience this summer. Okay, to import a number from another spreadsheet, you first click on the cell where you want the number to appear. For example, if you want to enter the Net sales balance in the external income statement, click on the cell in the external income statement where the net sales number is supposed to appear. Enter the equals sign (=) and then click on the tab that takes you to the worksheet containing the internal income statement. In that worksheet, click on the cell that contains the amount you want to import into the external income statement and then press enter. This will create a link from the internal income statement cell to the external income statement cell. Here's a screen shot showing the formula that will appear after you import the number.

Don't forget to save the file using a name that indicates who you are.

Required:

Enter the trial balance information into a spreadsheet and complete the following:

1. Prepare a multi-step income statement that would be used for internal reporting purposes. Classify sales returns and allowances and sales discounts as contra-revenue accounts.

2. Prepare a multi-step income statement that would be used for external reporting purposes, beginning with the amount for *net sales*.

3. Compute the gross profit percentage.

7 Reporting and Interpreting Receivables

Understand key receivables management decisions.

LO1 Describe the trade-offs involved in extending credit to customers.

Study how to account for receivables.

LO2 Estimate and report the effects of uncollectible accounts.

LO3 Report notes receivable and compute interest.

Evaluate receivables management practices.

LO4 (Supplement A) Report uncollectible accounts using the direct write-off method.

LO5 Understand how management can speed up the collection process.

LO6 Compute and interpret the receivables-turnover ratio.

Reconsider how receivables reporting affects analyses.

LO7 Explain how estimates of uncollectible accounts affect evaluations of receivables management practices.

INSIDE LOOKING OUT

OUTSIDE LOOKING IN

This chapter focuses on how to account for receivables and the cost of bad debts. We focus on Sony Corporation, maker of the highly profitable PlayStation home video game system and one of the world's top consumer electronics firms.

One of the most challenging parts of your academic and professional careers will involve managing things that you can't completely control. For example, think about a group project that you have to complete this term. You might believe that, in theory, the work should take only six days from start to finish. But you know from experience that someone in your group is likely to be late with the assigned work or may not complete his or her task at all. The problem is you don't know for sure which particular group member will be late, nor do you know how late that person will be—these matters are largely beyond your control. To allow for the possibility that someone will be late, you might set a shorter time period (say four days) for group members to finish their work. By subtracting this two-day allowance, you'll have a realistic basis for planning and successfully completing the group project.

This situation is similar to a problem faced by many companies, including **SONY,** the well-known Japanese company that sells to Future Shop and thousands of other companies around the world. When Sony sells to a company on account, it's not clear whether that customer will actually pay on time and, more important, it's not clear whether the customer will even pay at all. Sony's managers know from experience that some customers won't end up paying what they owe. The problem is that, at the time a sale is made, it's not possible to identify who these "bad" customers are. In the rest of this chapter you'll learn about a method

of accounting for these uncertainties that is similar to the allowance approach described above for your group project. This method allows Sony's managers to report in a timely manner how much money their company is likely to collect from customers, which gives financial statement users a realistic basis for making decisions.

The most important topics in this chapter are summarized in the Learning Objectives, found on the first page of the chapter. You'll learn about key trade-offs managers consider when they decide whether to allow sales on account, how the business decision to extend credit affects accounting methods, the analyses that financial statement users rely on to evaluate **accounts receivable** management practices, and how these analyses can be affected by decisions made when accounting for accounts receivable.

Accounts receivable (also called trade receivables or simply receivables) are amounts owed to a business by its customers.

UNDERSTAND _____
Key Receivables Management Decisions

CASH MANAGEMENT

Exhibit 6.5 on page 241 illustrated the operating activities of service, merchandising, and manufacturing companies, showing them as loops, or cycles. On the next page, in Exhibit 7.1, we reproduce the **operating cycle** of a manufacturing company like Sony. Sony pays cash to buy raw materials, spends more cash to operate the manufacturing, sales, and collection processes, and finally gets cash back from the sale. Holding everything else constant, a company wants to shorten its operating cycle, the time it takes to go from point (2) to point (6) in the cycle. There are three ways to do this: lengthen the time it takes to pay bills (studied in Chapter 10), shorten the time it takes to make and sell products (studied in Chapter 8), and shorten the time it takes to collect receivables (studied in this chapter). We start by looking at why companies extend credit to customers.

A company's **operating cycle** is its cash to cash cycle: the time it takes to go from paying cash for inventory to receiving cash from a sale.

EXTENDING CREDIT TO CUSTOMERS

Although Sony operates a few stores at which it sells directly to consumers, most of its sales are made to other companies. A key issue for Sony's managers is to decide whether to extend credit to these companies. If Sony decides not to allow sales on account, these companies are likely to buy instead from Sony's competitors. To be in the running to get business from these companies, Sony will need to consider extending credit to them. When making this decision, Sony's managers realize that, by extending credit, the company will incur the following additional costs:

1. *Increased wage costs.* Sony will need employees to (*a*) evaluate whether each customer is creditworthy, (*b*) track how much each customer owes, and (*c*) follow up to ensure they collect the receivable from each customer.
2. *Bad debt costs.* Inevitably, some customers dispute what they owe and pay only a portion of the total amount that they've been charged. In extreme circumstances (such as a retailer's bankruptcy), Sony may never collect the amount that is receivable from the customer. These "bad debts," as they are called, can be a significant additional cost of extending credit.
3. *Delayed receipt of cash.* Even if Sony were to collect in full from customers, it would likely have to wait 30 to 60 days before receiving the cash. During this period of time, it's possible that Sony would have to take out a short-term bank loan to obtain cash for other business activities. The interest on such a loan would be another cost of extending credit to customers.

Most managers find that the sales revenue (or, more accurately, the gross profit) to be gained from selling on account is greater than the additional costs listed above. They attempt to control these costs by using accounting records, which we discuss in the next section, to carefully screen and monitor customers.

---

exhibit 7.1 Operating Cycle of a Manufacturing Company

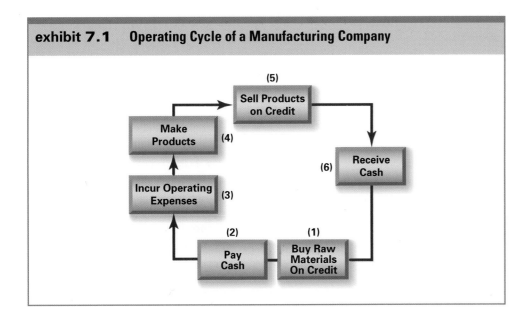

In cases where a customer is having difficulty paying its balance, Sony could establish a formal repayment schedule for the customer, which essentially converts the account receivable into a "note receivable." A **note receivable** is a formal contract stating (1) specified payments to be received at definite future dates and (2) a specified rate of interest, which is charged on the outstanding balance. By converting from an account receivable to a note receivable, Sony establishes in writing its legal right to collect the original amount owed plus any additional interest charged by Sony. In our examples below, we show how interest is charged and recorded on unpaid notes receivable. (We'll save you the trouble of learning how to record interest on unpaid accounts receivable by simply telling you it's basically the same as for notes receivable.)

A **note receivable** is a formal written promise that requires another party to pay the business according to a written agreement (like an IOU).

STUDY _____

How to Account for Receivables

In Chapter 6, we studied how to account for cash sales, credit sales, sales discounts, and sales returns and allowances in connection with our discussion of internal control. Here we look at how the receivables that result from credit sales are presented on the balance sheet, and how we account for the fact that not all receivables are ultimately collected.

In this section, we describe how to account for Accounts Receivable and Notes Receivable. Exhibit 7.2 shows how Sony reports these two accounts in its financial statements for the year ended March 31, 2007.

As you can see in the balance sheet excerpt in Exhibit 7.2, Sony reported almost ¥1.5 billion in *Trade Accounts and Notes Receivable* at March 31, 2007. Notice that these items are classified as current assets, indicating that they are expected to be collected in cash sometime in the 2008 fiscal year.

THE ALLOWANCE METHOD OF ACCOUNTING FOR ACCOUNTS RECEIVABLE AND BAD DEBTS

Notice in Exhibit 7.2 that trade accounts receivable were reported "less allowances." In this section, we explain what these allowances are and where they come from.

When Sony extends credit to retail stores, it knows that some of these customers are not likely to pay their debts. It's just like that friend of yours who says he'll pay you later, but, for one reason or another, never gets around to it. Two key accounting concepts come into play in accounting for receivables. Consistent with conservatism, accounting rules require that Sony report accounts receivable at the amount it actually expects to collect rather than the total that it would collect if everyone paid. At the

POINT OF INTEREST

Before cash was invented, business transactions involved trading assets or services. The term "trade" is still used today by some companies to describe receivables that arise in the ordinary course of business.

exhibit 7.2   Balance Sheet Disclosure of Receivables

SONY CORPORATION
(Partial) Balance Sheet
March 31, 2007 and 2006
(in millions of yen)

Current Assets	2007	2006
Cash and Cash Equivalents	¥799,899	¥703,098
Marketable Securities	493,315	536,968
Trade Accounts and Notes Receivable	1,490,452	1,075,071
Less Allowances	(120,675)	(89,563)
Inventories	940,875	804,724
Prepaid Expenses and Other Current Assets	942,857	739,226
Total Current Assets	**¥4,546,723**	**¥3,769,524**

same time, the matching principle requires that all expenses, including the cost of bad debts, be recorded in the accounting period in which the related credit sales are made. These two points lead to the same solution: reduce both accounts receivable and net income by the amount of credit sales included this period in receivables and net income that are unlikely ever to be collected as cash.

The only problem with this solution is that, just as it takes you a while to find out which friends you can't trust, some time will pass before Sony discovers which particular credit sales and customer balances aren't going to be paid. More than likely, it will be discovered in an accounting period following the sale, rather than in the same period as the sale. As Exhibit 7.3 shows, if you record sales in one period when they occur and bad debts in a different period when they are discovered, you will violate the matching principle. This failure to match bad debt expense with sales revenue in the same period will lead to distorted views of net income in the period of the sale as well as in the period when the bad debt is discovered. To see how this could be a problem, take a moment to read Exhibit 7.3 right now.

Clearly, we need to record bad debts in the same period as the sale. The only way to do this is to estimate the amount of bad debts when the sale is recorded. Later, the accounting records will be adjusted when uncollectible accounts become known with certainty. This approach is called the **allowance method,** and it follows a two-step process, which we walk through with you below.

The **allowance method** is a method of accounting that reduces accounts receivable (as well as net income) for an estimate of uncollectible accounts (bad debts).

1. *Record an estimated bad debt expense in the period in which the sale took place* by making an adjusting journal entry at the end of that period.

2. *Remove ("Write off") specific customer balances in the period in which they are determined to be uncollectible.*

exhibit 7.3   Distortion Occurs If Bad Debts Are Not Matched to Sales

YEAR 1 (CREDIT SALE OCCURS)		YEAR 2 (BAD DEBT DISCOVERED)	
Sales revenues	$10,000	Sales revenues	$ 0
Cost of goods sold	6,000	Cost of goods sold	0
Bad debt expense	0	Bad debt expense	1,000
Net income	$ 4,000	Net income (loss)	$ (1,000)

1. Record Estimated Bad Debt Expense

Bad debt expense (also called doubtful accounts expense or uncollectible accounts expense) is an estimate of this period's credit sales that the company won't collect from customers. As you know from Chapter 6, credit sales, when first recorded, increase Accounts Receivable and Sales Revenue. Most of the receivables will eventually be collected but, to account for those that won't, we use the allowance method, which reduces Accounts Receivable by means of a contra-asset account (Allowance for Doubtful Accounts) and reduces net income with an expense account (Bad Debt Expense). To illustrate, assume that Sony estimated bad debt expense for the year ended March 31, 2007, to be ¥71,592 (all numbers in millions of yen).[1] The following adjusting journal entry would have been used to record this estimate at the end of the accounting period:

dr	Bad Debt Expense (+E, −SE)	71,592
cr	Allowance for Doubtful Accounts (+xA, −A)	71,592

Assets	=	Liabilities	+	Shareholders' Equity
Allowance for Doubtful Accounts (+xA) − 71,592				Bad Debt Expense (+E) − 71,592

The credit in the journal entry could not be recorded to *Accounts Receivable* because, at the time the journal entry is prepared, there is no way to know which customers' accounts receivable will go bad. If Sony were to remove the customer accounts believed to be uncollectible, it would lose track of which customers owed money, and thus the opportunity to continue to pursue the customers for payment. So the credit is made, instead, to a contra-asset account called **Allowance for doubtful accounts** (also called allowance for bad debts, allowance for uncollectible accounts, reserve for bad debts, or simply allowance). As a contra-asset, the balance in *Allowance for Doubtful Accounts* is subtracted from the balance of the asset *Accounts Receivable*, thereby reducing the reported accounts receivable without directly reducing a particular customer balance in that account. To make it clear which account we're talking about, we'll refer to the total amount receivable as Gross Accounts Receivable, and we'll use the name Net Accounts Receivable to refer to the amount receivable after subtracting the allowance for doubtful accounts. The top part of Exhibit 7.4 shows this relationship using the amounts reported

Bad debt expense (doubtful accounts expense or uncollectible accounts expense) is an estimate of this period's credit sales that customers will fail to pay.

Allowance for doubtful accounts (allowance, allowance for bad debts, allowance for uncollectible accounts, reserve for bad debts) is a contra-asset account containing the estimated dollar value of the accounts receivable that will not be collected.

exhibit 7.4 Interpreting Gross and Net Receivables

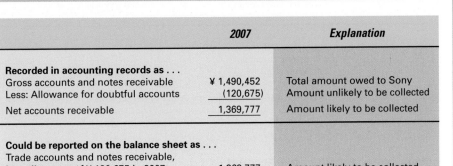

	2007	Explanation
Recorded in accounting records as . . .		
Gross accounts and notes receivable	¥ 1,490,452	Total amount owed to Sony
Less: Allowance for doubtful accounts	(120,675)	Amount unlikely to be collected
Net accounts receivable	1,369,777	Amount likely to be collected
Could be reported on the balance sheet as . . .		
Trade accounts and notes receivable, less allowance of ¥ 120,675 in 2007	1,369,777	Amount likely to be collected

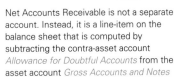

COACH'S TIP

Net Accounts Receivable is not a separate account. Instead, it is a line-item on the balance sheet that is computed by subtracting the contra-asset account *Allowance for Doubtful Accounts* from the asset account *Gross Accounts and Notes Receivable*.

[1]Sony does not disclose its bad debt expense, and so the amount is assumed. In this estimate, Sony would also include estimated future sales returns and allowances. For ease of understanding, we refer to only the estimated bad debts. Accounting for estimated future sales returns and allowances is done in the same manner as for estimated bad debts.

by Sony at March 31, 2007. The bottom part shows how most companies report these amounts in the balance sheet.

2. Remove (Write Off) Specific Customer Balances

When it becomes clear that a particular customer will not pay its balance, Sony will record a journal entry to remove the account receivable from its accounting records. With the receivable removed, there's no longer a need to include an allowance for it, so the corresponding amount also is removed from the allowance for doubtful accounts. This act of removing the uncollectible account and its corresponding allowance is called a **write-off.** Assume that in March 2007 it gave up all hopes of collecting customer accounts totalling ¥96,557. The journal entry to summarize Sony's write-offs of these previously allowed for doubtful accounts is:

> **Write off** describes the act of removing an uncollectible account and its corresponding allowance from the accounting records.

COACH'S TIP

The main purpose for writing off an uncollectible account is to clean up the accounting records. It's just like throwing away an old piece of mouldy bread. You figured out a while ago that you weren't going to eat it, so there's no point in keeping it around any longer.

dr	Allowance for Doubtful Accounts (−xA, +A)	96,557	
	cr Accounts Receivable (−A)		96,557

Assets	=	Liabilities	+	Shareholders' Equity
Accounts Receivable	− 96,557			
Allowance for Doubtful Accounts (−xA)	+ 96,557			

Notice in the above journal entry that the write-off did not affect income statement accounts. The estimated bad debt expense relating to these uncollectible accounts was already recorded with an adjusting journal entry in the period the sale was recorded, so there is no additional expense when the account is written off. Also, notice that the journal entry does not change the amount reported as Net accounts receivable because the decrease in Gross accounts and notes receivable is offset by the decrease in the Allowance for doubtful accounts.

Summary of the Allowance Method   To make it easy for you to review the two main steps of the allowance method, here's a quick summary:

Step	Timing	Journal Entry	Financial Statement Effects		
1. Record adjustment for estimated bad debts	End of the period in which sales are made	*dr* Bad Debt Expense (+E, −SE) *cr* Allowance for Doubtful Accounts (+xA, −A)	**Balance Sheet** Gross accounts and notes receivable — no effect Less: Allowance ↑ Net accounts receivable ↓	**Income Statement** Revenues — no effect Expenses Bad Debt Expense ↑ Net Income ↓	
2. Identify and write off actual bad debts	As accounts are determined uncollectible	*dr* Allowance for Doubtful Accounts (−xA, +A) *cr* Accounts Receivable (−A)	**Balance Sheet** Gross accounts and notes receivable ↓ Less: Allowance ↓ Net accounts receivable — no effect	**Income Statement** Revenues — no effect Expenses Bad Debt Expense — no effect Net Income — no effect	

Recovery of an Uncollectible Account   In the same way that someone you've written off as a friend might do something to win you back, a customer might pay an account balance that was previously written off. Collection of a previously written off account is called a recovery, and it is accounted for in two parts. First, put the receivable back on the books by recording a journal entry opposite to what was recorded to write off the account in the first place. Second, record the collection of the account. To illustrate, let's assume that in 2008 Sony collects ¥350 on an account that had been written off in 2007. This recovery would be recorded using the following journal entries:

(1)	*dr*	Accounts Receivable (+A)	350	
	cr	Allowance for Doubtful		
		Accounts (+xA, −A)		350
(2)	*dr*	Cash (+A)	350	
	cr	Accounts Receivable (−A)		350

Assets	=	Liabilities	+	Shareholders' Equity
Cash + 350				
Accounts Receivable +350−350 = no change				
Allowance for Doubtful Accounts (+xA) −350				

Look closely at the journal entries used for a recovery and you'll see that Accounts Receivable is debited and then credited for ¥350. Because of this, you might be tempted to make just one journal entry, a debit to Cash and a credit to Allowance for Doubtful Accounts, but don't do it, because that would create an inaccurate credit history for the customer. It would look as though the customer never paid you, but that isn't the case. It's more accurate to set the receivable up again with the first entry, and then record the payment with the second entry.

Estimating Bad Debts

In our earlier example, we simply gave you the amount of the estimated bad debt expense to be recorded. In the real world, the amount of bad debt expense is estimated based on either (1) total credit sales for the period or (2) an aging of accounts receivable. Both methods are acceptable under GAAP and are widely used in practice.

Percentage of Credit Sales Methods Many companies come up with bad debt estimates using the **percentage of credit sales method,** which bases bad debt expense on the historical percentage of credit sales that result in bad debts. Because of its focus on income statement accounts (sales and bad debt expense), this method is also known as the income statement method. The estimated bad debt expense is estimated by multiplying the current year's credit sales by the average percentage of credit sales that in prior years resulted in bad debts. For example, if Sony has credit sales in the current year of ¥7,159,166, and it had experienced bad debt losses of 0.1 per cent of credit sales in prior years, Sony could estimate the current year's bad debt expense as:

Credit sales this year	¥ 7,159,166
× Bad debt loss rate (0.1%)	× .001
Bad debt expense this year	¥ 71,592

This amount would be recorded using the following journal entry, which you saw earlier in this chapter.

dr	Bad Debt Expense (+E, −SE)	71,592	
	cr	Allowance for Doubtful Accounts		
		(+xA, −A)		71,592

The **percentage of credit sales method** bases bad debt expense on the percentage of credit sales of prior years that weren't collected.

COACH'S TIP

The percentage of credit sales method focuses on computing bad debt expense. Because bad debt expense is a temporary account, which is closed each year to retained earnings, it does not have an opening balance, so the calculated amount is directly entered into the accounts.

The effects of this journal entry on the account balances are shown in the T-accounts below:

dr Allowance for Doubtful Accounts (xA) cr			
		112,674	Beginning balance
Write-offs	96,557	71,592	% of sales adjustment
		87,709	Ending balance

dr Bad debt expense (E) cr		
% of sales adjustment	71,592	
Ending balance	71,592	

Aging of Accounts Receivable Method

As an alternative to the percentage of credit sales method, many companies use the **aging of accounts receivable method.** This method relies on the fact that, as accounts receivable become older and more overdue, it is less likely that they will prove to be collectible. For example, a receivable that was due in 30 days but remains unpaid after 120 days is less likely to be collected, on average, than a similar receivable that has been unpaid for just 45 days. Based on prior experience, the company can estimate the proportion of receivables of different ages that will not be collected. Because of its focus on balance sheet accounts (accounts receivable and allowance for doubtful accounts), this method is also known as the balance sheet method.

To see how this method works, assume that Sony prepared the aged listing of accounts receivable shown in Exhibit 7.5.[2] This listing separates the total amount owed by each customer into aging categories that represent how many days have passed since uncollected amounts were first recorded in the customer's account. The total receivable for each aging category on this listing is multiplied by *estimated* bad debt loss rates for each category to estimate the amount of allowance needed to cover bad debts in each category. The total of the estimated uncollectible amounts across all the aging categories represents the balance that should be in the Allowance for Doubtful Accounts at the end of the period. In our example in Exhibit 7.5, this estimated uncollectible balance is ¥88,915 (6,216 + 12,262 + 28,228 + 42,209).

The aging method records the estimated bad debt expense by debiting and crediting the same accounts as the percentage of credit sales method, but the method for computing the amount of the journal entry differs. When we used the percentage of credit sales method earlier, we simply calculated the amount to be recorded as *Bad Debt Expense* on

COACH'S TIP

exhibit 7.5   Aged Listing of Accounts Receivable

Customer	Total	NUMBER OF DAYS UNPAID			
		0–30	31–60	61–90	Over 90
Adam's Computer Shop	¥ 6,599	¥ 4,590	¥ 1,980	¥ 29	—
Backyard Game Company	23,459	—	—	—	23,459
. . .	. . .	. . .	. . .	. . .	. . .
Zero Fear Inc.	121,142	77,444	23,657	12,300	7,741
Total Receivables	¥ 1,189,887	¥ 621,600	¥ 306,550	¥ 141,140	¥ 120,597
× Estimated bad debt rates		1%	4%	20%	35%
= **Estimated uncollectible**	¥ 88,915	¥ 6,216	¥ 12,262	¥ 28,228	¥ 42,209

[2]In addition to being used to estimate bad debt expense, an aging schedule also helps to identify customers that haven't paid on time and that need to be reminded by the company to pay what is owed.

the income statement and added that same amount to the *Allowance for Doubtful Accounts*. **The aging method requires two steps: (1) compute the** *final ending balance* **that we expect to have in the** *Allowance for Doubtful Accounts* **after we make the adjusting entry for bad debt expense, and (2) calculate the amount of the adjustment needed to reach that balance.** As shown below, the difference between the unadjusted balance and the estimated uncollectible balance is recorded as the adjusting entry for bad debt expense for the period:

dr Allowance for Doubtful Accounts (xA) cr	
Write-off 96,557	Beginning balance 112,674
	Unadjusted balance 16,117
	Bad debt expense adjustment ?
	Final ending balance 88,915

Step 2. Calculate Amount of Adjustment
(= ¥88,915 − 16,117 = ¥72,798)

Step 1. Compute Estimated Uncollectible
(see Exhibit 7.5 calculation)

The adjustment of ¥72,798 would be recorded using the following journal entry, which would affect the account balances in the manner shown in the T-accounts below:

dr **Bad Debt Expense (+E, −SE)**   72,798
    cr **Allowance for Doubtful Accounts**
        (+xA, −A)   72,798

dr Allowance for Doubtful Accounts (xA) cr		
	112,674	Beginning balance
Write-offs 96,557	72,798	Aging adjustment
	88,915	Ending balance

dr Bad debt expense (E) cr	
Aging adjustment 72,798	
Ending balance 72,798	

COACH'S TIP

The aging of accounts receivable method focuses on computing the allowance for doubtful accounts. Because this is a permanent account, which is not closed at the end of the year, it typically has an existing balance that needs to be considered when determining the amount of adjustment to make to the account.

Notice that the amount of the journal entry and, therefore, the account balances differ under the percentage of credit sales and the aging of accounts receivable methods. As we've explained before, accounting policy choices affect accounting numbers. Although it is rare for different methods to lead to exactly the same numbers, they generally lead to similar estimates, as they do here (the difference is only ¥1,206 [¥72,798 − ¥71,592]).

Actual Write-Offs Compared with Estimates

The amount of uncollectible accounts actually written off seldom equals the estimated amount previously recorded. This situation is resolved when the adjusting entry is made at the end of the next accounting period: A higher or lower amount is recorded to make up for the previous period's error in estimate. *When estimates are found to be incorrect, financial statement values for prior annual accounting periods are not corrected.*

Reporting Accounts Receivable and Bad Debts

Bad debt expense typically isn't reported separately in the income statement. Instead, it usually is combined with other selling expenses in an appropriately named line-item like "Selling expenses." Similarly, accounts receivable write-offs are not reported separately in the financial statements. Although they are not usually reported separately, these numbers are potentially informative because, for example, changes in the level of bad debt expense from one period to another suggest whether the company is extending credit to riskier customers. So, if the information is useful, why is it not reported? Well, one reason is that it is not required by Canadian or by international GAAP. In contrast, the SEC in the United States recently ruled that bad debt expense and accounts receivable write-offs must be disclosed by public companies in SEC filings if the amounts are significant. As the world moves towards harmonization of accounting standards, it will be interesting to see how this discrepancy will be resolved.

Quiz Answers

1. *dr* Bad debt expense (+E, −SE)............ 88,000
   cr Allowance for doubtful accounts (+xA, −A)   88,000

2.

dr Allowance for Doubtful Accounts (xA) cr	
	Beg. bal. 100,000
Write-offs 92,000	Bad debt expense (solve) 88,000
	End. bal. 96,000

Beginning + Bad debt expense − Write-offs = Ending
100,000 + x − 92,000 = 96,000; x = 88,000

HOW'S IT GOING?   A Self-Study Quiz

1. Assuming that Sony estimated that 1.1 per cent of credit sales would prove uncollectible for the year, what adjusting journal entry would be needed to record bad debts at the end of a year in which credit sales were ¥8,000,000 (in millions of yen)?

2. In an earlier year, Sony reported beginning and ending balances in the Allowance for Doubtful Accounts of ¥100,000 and ¥96,000, respectively. It also reported that write-offs of bad accounts amounted to ¥92,000 (all numbers in millions of yen). Assuming that no previously written-off accounts had been collected (there were no recoveries), what amount did Sony record as bad debt expense for the period? Use the Allowance for Doubtful Accounts T-account to solve for the missing value.

dr Allowance for Doubtful Accounts (xA) cr	

After you're finished, check your answers with the solution in the margin.

OTHER METHODS OF ACCOUNTING FOR ACCOUNTS RECEIVABLE AND BAD DEBTS

In the previous section, you learned how to use the allowance method to account for bad debts arising from sales to customers on credit. This method requires that either the percentage of credit sales method or aging of accounts receivable method be used to estimate future bad debts so that they can be recorded in the period in which sales are made. You should be aware that some small companies use an alternative method called the direct write-off method. This alternative method violates conservatism and the matching principle, so it is not considered a generally accepted accounting method. The Canada Revenue Agency (CRA), however, does use this method for tax purposes. Because of this potential use, we demonstrate it in Supplement A on page 308. Check with your instructor (or your course outline) to see whether you are responsible for this supplement.

ACCOUNTING FOR NOTES RECEIVABLE

Receivables don't come only from sales. The receivables on Sony's balance sheet, for example, include notes receivable. This type of receivable represents amounts that are owed to Sony under formal written contracts (called "notes").

Most notes receivable arise when a company lends money to another business or individual, such as when Sony lends money to its executives and key employees for various reasons (such as financing their relocation to a different city). Because notes receivable provide a stronger legal claim than accounts receivable, notes may also be used for big-dollar sales transactions. Regardless of the reason for the note, each note typically outlines the amount owed (called the *principal*), the date by which it is to be repaid to the company (called the *maturity date*), and the interest rate charged while the note remains unpaid. Most interest charged on these arrangements is simple (not compound) interest. Let's begin by looking at how this simple interest is calculated.

To calculate interest, three variables must be considered: (1) the principal, which is simply the amount of cash that is owed, (2) the interest rate, which always is given in annual terms, and (3) the time period covered in the interest calculation. Because interest rates are stated in terms of a full year, the "time" variable is used when interest is calculated for a period shorter than a year. It indicates how many months out of 12 the

POINT OF INTEREST

The former CEO of Tyco International—Dennis Kozlowski—was accused of lending over $100 million to employees who used the money to buy outrageous items, such as a $6,000 shower curtain. It was alleged that these loans were written off later without collecting a penny.
Source: *BusinessWeek*, December 23, 2002, p.64.

interest period covers. The following **interest formula** shows that, to calculate interest, the three variables are multiplied together:

The **interest formula** is:

$$I = P \times R \times T$$

where I = interest calculated, P = principal, R = annual interest rate, and T = time period covered in the interest calculation (number of months out of 12).

$$\text{Interest} = \text{Principal} \times \text{Interest Rate} \times \text{Time}$$

To illustrate, assume that, on February 1, 2008, Sony lends ¥100,000 cash to an inventor who is developing a new video game. The loan agreement says that Sony will be paid 12 per cent interest on the note. The interest is split into two instalments, payable on July 31, 2008, and January 31, 2009. Sony is to receive the ¥100,000 principal when the final interest payment is made on the maturity date of January 31, 2009. Here's a timeline that shows what the promissory note says.

Record Note Receivable	Accrue Interest		Record Interest Received		Record Interest and Principal Received
	2 months		4 months	6 months	
Establish Note 2/1/08	Year End 3/31/08		1st Interest Payment 7/31/08		Note Matures 1/31/09

Establishing a Note Receivable

To record the ¥100,000 note receivable established by lending cash to the inventor on February 1, 2008, Sony would use the following journal entry:

dr	Note Receivable (+A).	100,000
cr	Cash (−A)	100,000

Assets	=	Liabilities	+	Shareholders' Equity
Note Receivable + 100,000				
Cash − 100,000				

COACH'S TIP

If interest is calculated for a full year, the time variable is 12 months out of 12. Because 12/12 equals 1, this is a case in which the time variable has no effect on the interest calculation.

Recording Interest Earned

Under accrual basis accounting, and consistent with the revenue recognition principle, interest revenue is recorded when it is earned rather than when the interest payment is actually received in cash. Sony earned *two* months of interest revenue in the year ended March 31, 2008, because its note receivable was outstanding for all of February and March 2008. As you learned in Chapter 4, when interest is earned in the current period, but not received until a later period, an adjusting journal entry is used at the end of the current period to accrue the interest earned. Assuming that Sony makes adjusting journal entries at the end of its fiscal year, not monthly, the amount of interest to be recorded for the two months of 2008 is computed as follows:

Interest	=	Principal	×	Interest Rate	×	Time
¥2,000	=	¥100,000	×	12%	×	$^2\!/_{12}$

The adjusting journal entry to record the ¥2,000 of interest revenue that is receivable on March 31, 2008, is

| dr | Interest Receivable (+A) . . . . | 2,000 | |
| | cr   Interest Revenue (+R, +SE) . . . . | | 2,000 |

Assets	=	Liabilities	+	Shareholders' Equity
Interest Receivable + 2,000				Interest Revenue (+R) + 2,000

Recording Interest Received

On July 31, 2008, Sony receives the first interest payment of ¥6,000, which was calculated as ¥100,000 × 12% × 6/12. This receipt of cash includes the ¥2,000 of interest that was receivable at March 31, 2008, plus ¥4,000 of interest that has been earned during the next four months of 2008 (from April 1 to July 31). To record the collection of this interest, Sony would make the following journal entry:

dr	Cash (+A)	6,000	
	cr Interest Receivable (−A)		2,000
	cr Interest Revenue (+R, −SE)		4,000

Assets	=	Liabilities	+	Shareholders' Equity
Cash + 6,000				
Interest Receivable − 2,000				Interest Revenue (+R) + 4,000

Recording Receipt of Interest and Principal at Maturity

Let's assume Sony does not make any more entries for the note until it comes due on January 31, 2009. On that date, Sony will receive the second interest payment of ¥6,000 plus the principal of ¥100,000. Let's record this in two parts. First, the receipt of ¥6,000 cash for interest would be recorded using the following journal entry:

| dr | Cash (+A) . . . . | 6,000 | |
| | cr   Interest Revenue (+R, +SE) . . . . | | 6,000 |

Assets	=	Liabilities	+	Shareholders' Equity
Cash + 6, 000				Interest Revenue (+R) + 6,000

A second journal entry is needed to record the collection of the ¥100,000 principal owed on the note receivable. For our example, this journal entry would be:

| dr | Cash (+A) . . . . | 100,000 | |
| | cr   Note Receivable (−A). . . . . | | 100,000 |

Assets	=	Liabilities	+	Shareholders' Equity
Cash + 100,000				
Note Receivable − 100,000				

Accounting for Uncollectible and Defaulted Notes

Just as a customer might fail to pay its accounts receivable balance, some companies also might fail to pay the principal (and interest) that they owe on a note receivable. When the collectibility of notes receivable is in doubt, a company should record an allowance for doubtful accounts against the notes receivable, just as it records an allowance for doubtful accounts against accounts receivable. If a company defaults on a note (fails to pay it when due), the holder of the note may decide to write off the note and any unpaid accrued interest, in the same way that it writes off regular accounts receivable.

EVALUATE _____
Receivables Management Practices

SPEEDING UP THE COLLECTION PROCESS

To generate the cash needed to pay for a company's business activities, managers must ensure that receivables are collected on a timely basis. You might wonder what managers can do to speed up sluggish receivables collections. One obvious tactic is to start hounding customers for payment. This brute force approach has at least two drawbacks: (1) it is time-consuming and costly, and (2) it can annoy customers and cause them to take their business elsewhere. In Chapter 6, we looked at a more reasonable strategy: offering discounts to customers that pay within a specified period of time. Selling with payment terms of 2/10, n/30 encourages customers to pay quickly, but this strategy comes at a hefty cost. Let's say the customer would pay in 40 days if you didn't offer a discount, but pays in 10 days when you offer it. This means that it costs the company 2 per cent to receive the cash one month early, which equates to a very pricey 24 per cent annual financing arrangement.

An alternative approach, and one that is generally cheaper than offering discounts directly to customers, is to sell outstanding accounts receivable to another company (called a factor). The way this **factoring** arrangement works is that your company receives cash for the receivables it sells to the factor (minus a factoring fee), and the factor then has the right to collect the outstanding amounts owed by your customers. In the same way that you can get cash immediately at a local Money Mart store for any cheque, factoring is a fast and easy way for your company to get cash for its receivables. Although companies of all types can make use of factoring, one of the most common forms of factoring takes place when companies allow their customers to pay with credit cards. In effect, these companies are selling their receivables to the credit card company and getting the cash almost immediately.

> **Factoring** is an arrangement where receivables are sold to another company (called a factor) for immediate cash (minus a factoring fee).

Credit Card Sales

Most retail merchandise companies allow their customers to pay for goods using credit cards like Visa or MasterCard. This practice helps to increase sales, speed up cash collections (because the company is able to deposit credit card receipts directly into its bank account as if it's actually cash), and reduce losses from customers writing bad cheques. But these benefits come at a cost: the credit card company charges a fee (called a **credit card discount**) for the service it provides. When customers use their credit cards to buy from the online Sony store, and Sony deposits its credit card receipts in the bank, it might receive credit for only 97 per cent of the sales price. If we assume Sony made credit card sales of ¥3,000 and incurred a 3 per cent fee, the ¥90 credit card discount (¥3,000 × 3%) would be recorded using the journal entry shown below.

> A **credit card discount** is a fee charged by a credit card company for its services.

dr	Cash (+A)	2,910
dr	Credit Card Discounts (+xR, −SE)	90
	cr Sales Revenue (+R)	3,000

Assets	=	Liabilities	+	Shareholders' Equity	
Cash + 2,910				Sales Revenue (+R)	+ 3,000
				Credit Card Discounts (+xR)	− 90

POINT OF INTEREST

You can read more about how credit card sales are processed by going to www.usa.visa.com and reading the search results for "visa transaction."

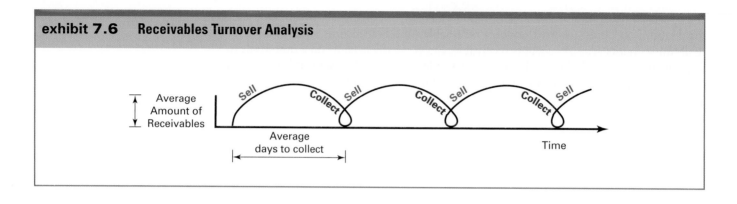

exhibit 7.6   Receivables Turnover Analysis

If Sony were using a perpetual inventory system, it would also record a reduction in *Inventory* and an increase in *Cost of Goods Sold* at the time of sale for the cost of these goods, as we saw in Chapter 6. The credit card discount expense, like any expense, is reported on Sony's income statement. For a company that regularly sells its receivables, the cost of factoring is included with selling expenses. If a company factors infrequently, the fee is considered an "other" expense.

RECEIVABLES TURNOVER ANALYSIS

Managers, directors, investors, and creditors evaluate the effectiveness of a company's credit-granting and collection activities by conducting a receivables turnover analysis. The idea behind a receivables turnover analysis is shown in Exhibit 7.6. As a company sells goods or services on credit, its receivables balance goes up, and, as it collects from these customers, the receivables balance goes down. At the same time, the old receivables are being replaced with new receivables as the company continues to sell more goods on credit. This process of selling and collecting is called **receivables turnover,** because it is repeated over and over during each accounting period, for each customer.

To assess how many times, on average, this process of selling and collecting is repeated over and over during the period, financial statement users calculate the receivables-turnover ratio:

Receivables turnover is the process of selling and collecting on account. The receivables-turnover ratio determines how many times this process occurs during the period on average.

COACH'S TIP

The average receivables balance outstanding over the entire year is used in the bottom of the ratio to correspond with the top part of the ratio, which also represents the year's results. Ideally, the ratio would use net credit sales, but that is not reported separately, so analysts typically use net sales instead.

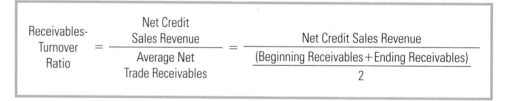

$$\text{Receivables-Turnover Ratio} = \frac{\text{Net Credit Sales Revenue}}{\text{Average Net Trade Receivables}} = \frac{\text{Net Credit Sales Revenue}}{\dfrac{(\text{Beginning Receivables} + \text{Ending Receivables})}{2}}$$

The higher the ratio, the faster will be the collection of receivables. And the faster the collection of receivables, the more cash your company will have available. That's a good thing. A lower ratio is a warning sign, suggesting that the company is offering a longer time for customers to pay. As you learned earlier in this chapter, the longer an account goes without being collected, the bigger is the risk that it will never be collected. Analysts watch for changes in the receivables-turnover ratio, because a sudden decline may mean that a company is recording sales that customers are likely to return later, or is allowing them a longer-than-normal period of time to pay their accounts to entice them to buy as much as possible—a practice known in business as "stuffing the channel."

Rather than evaluate the number of times accounts receivable turn over during a year, some people find it easier to think in terms of the amount of time (in days) it takes to collect accounts receivable. It's easy to convert a year's receivables-turnover ratio into the average days to collect. Simply calculate 365 ÷ receivables-turnover ratio and you'll have the average **days to collect**:

$$\text{Days to Collect} = \frac{365}{\text{Receivables-Turnover Ratio}}$$

This measure doesn't say anything different about the company's ability to collect receivables—it's just a little easier to interpret. In terms of Exhibit 7.6, the receivables turnover-ratio counts the number of loops in a given period of time, whereas the days to collect tells you the average number of days between loops.

It might be helpful to think of the turnover ratio as an efficiency measure, indicating how well the company manages its receivables and the days to collect as a liquidity measure, indicating how close the receivables are to cash and telling us about the composition of the company's assets. With these two interpretations in mind, we show the turnover ratio in the (b) section in our framework for financial statement analysis, and the days to collect in the (a) section, as shown in Exhibit 7.7 below.

Be on the Alert

Receivables-turnover ratios and the number of days to collect can vary across industries. Exhibit 7.8 shows Sony's receivables-turnover ratio, as well as the ratios for two companies in different industries: Canadian National Railway (CNR), Canada's largest railway, and the Forzani Group, the largest and only national sporting goods retailer in Canada, operating under a number of banners, including Sport Chek and Sport Mart. Of the three companies, Forzani has the highest turnover ratio of 18.8 times, which means a fast collection period of about 19 days. CNR is more sluggish, as indicated by its receivables-turnover ratio of 11.7 times. This is about 31 days to collect. Sony was the worst performer. It turned over its receivables only 6.4 times during 2007, which is once every 57 days. With this big a range in ratios among industries, you should compare a company's turnover only with its figures from prior periods or with figures for other companies in the same industry. For practice at computing and comparing with prior periods, try the following Self-Study Quiz, which asks you to calculate Sony's receivables-turnover ratio and days to collect in 2006.

> **Days to collect** is a measure of the average number of days from the time a sale is made on account to the time it is collected. Calculate it by dividing 365 by the year-long receivables-turnover ratio. Other names for days to collect are the number of days' sales in receivables or the average days' sales uncollected.

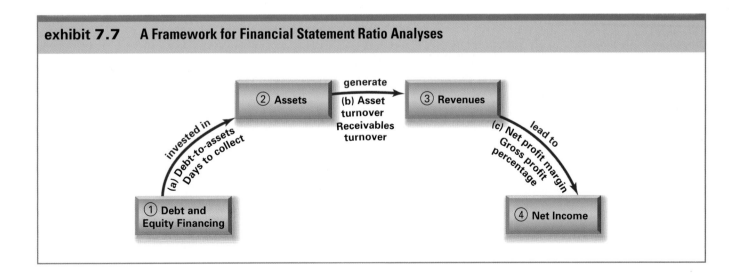

exhibit 7.7   A Framework for Financial Statement Ratio Analyses

---

exhibit 7.8   Summary of Receivables Ratio Analyses

Name of Measure	Formula	What It Tells You	Forzani Group	CNR	2007 Sony	SELF-STUDY QUIZ 2006 Sony
a. Receivables-turnover ratio	$\dfrac{\text{Net Sales Revenue}}{\text{Average Net Trade Receivables}}$	• The number of times receivables turn over • A higher ratio means faster turnover.	18.8 times	11.7 times	$\dfrac{7,567,359}{(1,369,777 + 985,528)/2}$ $= 6.4$ times	
b. Days to collect	$\dfrac{365}{\text{Receivables Turnover}}$	• Average number of days from sale on account to collection • A higher number means a longer time to collect.	19 days	31 days	$\dfrac{365}{6.4}$ $= 57$ days	

Quiz Answers

a. $\dfrac{6,692,776}{(985,528 + 1,025,362)/2} = 6.7$ times

b. $365 \div 6.7 = 54.5$ days

Sony's receivables turnover declined in 2007.

HOW'S IT GOING?   A Self-Study Quiz

Compute the ratios for the final column in Exhibit 7.8, using financial statement information in Exhibit 7.2, as well as the following information. Sony reported net sales revenues of ¥6,692,776 in 2006 and net trade receivables of ¥1,025,362 at March 31, 2005 (in millions of yen). Did Sony's receivables turnover improve or decline in 2007, as compared with 2006?

After you're finished, check your answers with the solutions in the margin.

RECONSIDER _____
How Receivables Reporting Affects Analyses

THE IMPACT OF ESTIMATION

As we have noted throughout this chapter, the Allowance for Doubtful Accounts and Bad Debt Expense accounts are based on estimates of future events. Although these estimates might be accurate forecasts of what will happen in the future, they can be a source of misstatement. In some cases, managers have been unintentionally biased by their natural managerial optimism, estimating greater collections on account than what actually turned out to be true. In other cases, they have acted dishonestly to understate Bad Debt Expense to boost net income, and to overstate Net accounts receivable to make the balance sheet appear stronger. Either way, overly optimistic estimates can mislead financial statement users.

Financial statement users also can be misguided by overly pessimistic bad debt estimates. Some managers have made unethical accounting decisions by overestimating bad debts in years of strong sales and high gross profits to build up a cushion in the Allowance for Doubtful Accounts. The extra bad debt expense recorded in those years is more than offset by extra sales and gross profits, so financial statement users do not react adversely to the increase in bad debt expense. The extra cushion in the Allowance for Doubtful Accounts allows managers to reduce the amount of bad debt expense that is added to it in a later year, while still ensuring an adequate ending balance in the Allowance for Doubtful Accounts. The result is that the net income in the current year is understated (the good year does not appear quite so good) and the net income in the later year is overstated (the bad year does not appear quite so bad). This dishonest behaviour is known as **income smoothing.** An example of income smoothing can be found in Chapter 7 Supplement B in the Online Learning Centre.

Financial statement auditors devote extra attention to detecting bad debt estimates that are overly optimistic or overly pessimistic. These efforts are designed to catch unscrupulous managers who blatantly misreport these estimates. So, as a financial statement user, you shouldn't have to worry that you're being duped. However, when evaluating a company's results or comparing two companies, you will want to be aware of the degree of optimism or pessimism in their bad debt estimates. Here are some steps that you can take when evaluating them:

1. *Assess the consistency of estimates.* In normal circumstances, the allowance for doubtful accounts should be a fairly consistent percentage of gross accounts receivable. Also, the bad debt expense should be a consistent percentage of net sales. If you notice any unexplained fluctuations, it might be cause for concern.

2. *Don't rely on just one number.* In our example, by focusing on net income, users would have overlooked other clues that bad debts were misestimated. An overly optimistic estimate about the collectibility of accounts receivable has the effect of decreasing bad debt expense, which increases net income, but it has the opposite effect on the receivables-turnover ratio—turnover will appear to have slowed. On the other hand, if the company records too much bad debt expense in the current period, its receivables turnover will appear to have picked up, but its net income will have dropped. This is one of the good features about double-entry accounting and financial statement reporting: It's difficult to misstate them in a way that doesn't raise *some* questions or "red flags."

3. *Understand how management develops estimates.* In addition to evaluating the estimates themselves, assess the process used to generate the estimates. You wouldn't go on a blind date without knowing how your friend picked "the one for you," so don't just accept the estimated bad debt expense and allowance for doubtful accounts numbers without knowing how they're estimated. Companies describe their methods in the Summary of Significant Accounting Policies note to their financial statements. They may also explain them in greater detail in the annual report section called Management's Discussion and Analysis, but often these descriptions are scanty, especially in countries where detailed disclosure is not required. We'll close this chapter with Exhibit 7.9, which shows what three different companies from three different countries say about their approaches for managing and estimating bad debts. The first company is Sony (Japan), the second is Microsoft (the United States), maker of PlayStation's competitor XBox, and the third is Mega Brands, a Canadian toy company that is second in the world in construction toys. Notice that Microsoft provides more detailed disclosures on its policy for doubtful accounts than the others do, which is what we would expect, given that the United States GAAP requirements in this area are more extensive.

ETHICAL ISSUES

Income smoothing is the dishonest practice of manipulating accounting estimates to keep net income levels stable or "smooth" over a series of periods.

COACH'S TIP

Calculate the allowance as a percentage of gross accounts receivable as follows:

$$\frac{\text{Allowance}}{\text{Gross accounts receivable}} \times 100\%$$

| **exhibit 7.9**   **Excerpts of Receivables Policy Notes** |

Sony (Japan)
General administrative expenses include operating items such as . . . , a provision for doubtful accounts, ...

Microsoft (United States)
The allowance for doubtful accounts reflects our best estimate of probable losses inherent in the accounts receivable balance. We determine the allowance based on known troubled accounts, historical experience, and other currently available evidence. Activity in the allowance for doubtful accounts was as follows: (details provided) . . . .

Mega Brands (Canada)
The most significant areas requiring the use of management estimates relate to: . . . . , valuation of year-end provision on accounts receivable, ...

Source: **Annual Reports.**

WHAT'S COMING UP

We'll continue our journey down the assets side of the balance sheet in Chapter 8 by focusing on inventory and the related income statement account called *Cost of Goods Sold.* Just as you saw in this chapter for receivables, inventory reporting also involves choosing among alternative accounting methods and considering estimates of future value when reporting current balances. So be sure you get a good handle on how to account for receivables in the following review and practice problems—it only makes things easier as you progress through the next chapters.

FOR YOUR REVIEW _____

DEMONSTRATION CASE

Shooby Dooby Shoe (SDS) sold $950,000 in merchandise on credit during 2008. Also during 2008, SDS determined that it would not be able to collect a $500 account balance that was owed by a deceased customer (Captain Cutler).

Required:

1. Prepare a journal entry to write off the account receivable from Captain Cutler, and show its effects on the accounting equation.
2. Assume that SDS uses the percentage of credit sales method for estimating bad debt expense, and that it estimates that 1 per cent of credit sales will result in bad debts. Prepare a journal entry to record bad debt expense for 2008, and show its effects on the accounting equation.
3. Assume instead that SDS uses the aging of accounts receivable method and that it estimates that $11,000 of its year-end accounts receivable is uncollectible. As of December 31, 2008, the Allowance for Doubtful Accounts had an unadjusted credit balance of $3,000. Prepare a

journal entry to record bad debt expense for 2008, and show its effects on the accounting equation.

4. Assume that SDS reported net accounts receivable of $160,000 at December 31, 2008, and $150,000 at December 31, 2007. Calculate the receivables-turnover ratio for 2008.

5. If the receivables-turnover ratio was 6.4 in 2007, what was the number of days to collect in 2007? Given your calculations in 4, conclude whether SDS collections are faster or slower in 2008 than in 2007.

6. Assume that, on October 1, 2008, SDS signed a $5,000 note receivable from an employee. The note states an annual interest rate of 8 per cent, with the first payment to be made on March 31, 2008. Prepare journal entries to record the issuance of the note on October 1 and any interest revenue earned in 2008.

Take 10 minutes to attempt the requirements, and then check your answers with the following solution.

Suggested Solution

1. The journal entry to write off this account is

dr	Allowance for Doubtful Accounts (−xA, +A)..........	500
	cr Accounts Receivable (−A)......................	500

Assets	=	Liabilities	+	Shareholders' Equity
Accounts Receivable − 500				
Allowance for Doubtful Accounts (−xA) + 500				

2. The percentage of credit sales method directly estimates the amount of bad debt expense to record.

dr	Bad Debt Expense (+E, −SE) (0.01 × $950,000)	9,500
	cr Allowance for Doubtful Accounts (+xA, −A)......	9,500

Assets	=	Liabilities	+	Shareholders' Equity
Allowance for Doubtful Accounts (+xA) − 9,500				Bad Debt Expense (+E) − 9,500

3. Under the aging of accounts receivable method, we determine the estimated balance for the allowance for doubtful accounts, and then subtract its unadjusted balance to determine the amount of the adjustment.

dr	Bad Debt Expense (+E, −SE)	8,000
	cr Allowance for Doubtful Accounts (+xA, −A)	
	($11,000 − 3,000)	8,000

Assets	=	Liabilities	+	Shareholders' Equity
Allowance for Doubtful Accounts (+xA) − 8,000				Bad Debt Expense (+E) − 8,000

4. Receivables-turnover ratio is calculated as Net sales ÷ Average accounts receivable. The average accounts receivable in 2008 was $155,000 (= [$160,000 + 150,000]/2), so the receivables-turnover ratio for 2008 was 6.13 (= $950,000 ÷ 155,000).

5. Days to collect is calculated as 365 ÷ receivables-turnover ratio. The 6.4 turnover in 2007 equates to 57 days (and the 6.13 turnover in 2008 equates to 60 days). Collections are slower in 2008 than in 2007.

6.   The entry to record the issuance of the note on October 1, 2008 is:

dr	Note Receivable (+A)	5,000	
	cr Cash (−A)		5,000

Assets	=	Liabilities	+	Shareholders' Equity
Note Receivable + 5,000				
Cash − 5,000				

Interest revenue is earned when the note is outstanding during the accounting period, not when the interest payment is received. During 2008, the loan has been outstanding for October, November, and December, which equals 3 months (out of 12). The adjusting journal entry to accrue this is:

dr	Interest Receivable (+A) (5,000 × 8% × 3/12)	100	
	cr Interest Revenue (+R, +SE)		100

Assets	=	Liabilities	+	Shareholders' Equity
Interest Receivable + 100				Interest Revenue (+R) + 100

CHAPTER SUMMARY

LO1   **Describe the trade-offs involved in extending credit to customers. p. 288**

- By extending credit to customers, a company is likely to attract a greater number of customers willing to buy from it.

- The additional costs of extending credit include increased employee costs, bad debt costs, and delayed receipt of cash.

LO2   **Estimate and report the effects of uncollectible accounts. p. 289**

- When bad debts are material, the company must use the allowance method to account for uncollectibles. This method involves the following steps:

  1. Estimate and record uncollectibles with an end-of-period adjusting journal entry to bad debt expense and the allowance for doubtful accounts.

  2. Identify and write off specific customer balances in the period when they are determined to be uncollectible.

- The adjusting entry reduces net income as well as net accounts receivable. The write-off affects neither.

LO3   **Report notes receivable and compute interest. p. 296**

- A note receivable specifies the amount lent, when it is to be repaid, and the interest rate associated with the note receivable. As time passes and interest is earned on the note, accountants must record an adjusting journal entry that accrues the interest revenue that is receivable on the note.

LO4   **(Supplement A) Report uncollectible accounts using the direct write-off method. p. 308**

- Under the direct write-off method, an allowance for doubtful accounts is not used. Receivables are written off directly to bad debt expense when they are deemed uncollectible. This method violates both conservatism and the matching principle, but can be used for tax purposes or when uncollectible accounts are immaterial.

LO5   **Understand how management can speed up the collection process. p. 299**

- Management can accelerate the cash collection process by offering discounts for early payment, by allowing customers to pay with a credit card, or by selling receivables through other factoring arrangements.

Compute and interpret the receivables-turnover ratio. p. 300

LO6

- The receivables-turnover ratio measures the effectiveness of credit-granting and collection activities. It reflects how many times average trade receivables were recorded and collected during the period.

- Analysts and creditors watch this ratio because a sudden decline in it may mean that a company is extending payment deadlines in an attempt to prop up lagging sales, or is even recording sales that later will be returned by customers.

Explain how estimates of uncollectible accounts affect evaluations of receivables management practices. p. 302

LO7

- Receivables are reported net of estimated uncollectible accounts. If these estimates are overly optimistic, net receivables will be too high and bad debt expense will be too low (which causes net income to be too high). To guard against overly optimistic or overly pessimistic estimates, analysts should: assess the consistency of the estimates, rely on more than one single estimate or number, and consider the process management uses to develop the estimates.

FINANCIAL STATEMENT ANALYSIS TIPS

To determine the average number of times that accounts receivable are recorded and collected during the period, calculate the receivables-turnover ratio:

$$\text{Receivables-Turnover Ratio} = \frac{\text{Net Credit Sales Revenue}}{\text{Average Net Trade Receivables}} = \frac{\text{Net Credit Sales Revenue}}{\dfrac{(\text{Beginning receivables} + \text{Ending Receivables})}{2}}$$

Calculate the following to express the annual receivables-turnover ratio in terms of number of days to collect:

$$\text{Days to Collect} = \frac{365}{\text{Receivables-Turnover Ratio}}$$

KEY TERMS TO KNOW

Accounts Receivable p. 288

Aging of Accounts Receivable Method p. 294

Allowance for Doubtful Accounts p. 291

Allowance Method p. 290

Bad Debt Expense p. 291

Credit Card Discount p. 299

Days to Collect p. 301

Factoring p. 299

Income Smoothing p. 303

Interest Formula p. 297

Notes Receivable p. 289

Operating Cycle p. 288

Percentage of Credit Sales Method p. 293

Receivables Turnover p. 300

Write Off p. 292

SUPPLEMENT A: DIRECT WRITE-OFF METHOD

As described in the body of this chapter, an alternative method exists to account for uncollectible accounts. This alternative approach, called the direct write-off method, is okay for tax purposes, but it is not acceptable under generally accepted accounting principles. Consequently, it isn't used very often for external financial reporting, but may be used by small companies that don't need GAAP financial statements.

The reason the direct write-off method isn't considered a GAAP method is that it ignores the conservatism concept and the matching principle. It breaks the conservatism concept by reporting accounts receivable at the total amount owed by customers (an overly optimistic point of view) rather than what is estimated actually to be collectible (a more realistic viewpoint). Under the direct write-off method, an allowance for doubtful accounts is not used. The direct write-off method breaks the matching principle by recording bad debt expense in the period in which customer accounts are determined to be bad, rather than matching the expense to the revenues reported in the period when the credit sales are actually made. The journal entry used by the direct write-off method to record $1,000 of bad debt expense is:

dr	Bad Debt Expense (+E,−SE)	1,000	
	cr Accounts Receivable (−A)		1,000

It's easy to see why this method is defective if you imagine a case where a company provides services to customers on account for $1,000 in year 1, but then discovers in year 2 that none of the amounts will be collected. Under the direct write-off method, the company would report sales of $1,000 and no bad debt expense in year 1, but in year 2 would then report no sales and bad debt expense of $1,000. By failing to match expenses to revenues, the direct write-off method doesn't provide useful information for evaluating the company's financial performance.

FOR YOUR PRACTICE_____

QUESTIONS

1. What are the advantages and disadvantages of extending credit to customers?
2. What's the difference between accounts receivable and notes receivable?
3. Which basic accounting principles does the allowance method of accounting for bad debts satisfy?
4. Using the allowance method, is bad debt expense recognized in the period in which (*a*) sales related to the uncollectible account were made or (*b*) the seller learns that the customer is unable to pay?
5. What is the effect of the write-off of bad debts (using the allowance method) on (*a*) net income and (*b*) net accounts receivable?
6. What are the three components of the interest formula? Explain how this formula adjusts for interest periods that are less than a full year.
7. Are interest revenues recognized in the period in which (*a*) a note receivable has remained unpaid or (*b*) the company receives a cash payment for the interest?
8. Does an increase in the receivables-turnover ratio generally indicate faster or slower collection of receivables? Explain.
9. What two approaches can managers take to speed up sluggish collections of receivables? List one advantage and one disadvantage for each approach.
10. Define income smoothing and explain how it can potentially mislead financial statement users.
11. (Supplement A) Describe how (and when) the direct write-off method accounts for uncollectible accounts. What are the disadvantages of this method?
12. What is a credit card discount? How does it affect amounts reported on the income statement?

MULTIPLE CHOICE

Select the one alternative that best answers the question or completes the sentence.

1. When a company using the allowance method writes off a specific customer's account receivable from the accounting system, how many of the following are true?
   - Total shareholders' equity remains the same.
   - Total assets remain the same.
   - Total expenses remain the same.

   a. None
   b. One
   c. Two
   d. Three

2. When using the allowance method, as bad debt expense is recorded:
   a. Total assets remain the same and shareholders' equity remains the same.
   b. Total assets decrease and shareholders' equity decreases.
   c. Total assets increase and shareholders' equity decreases.
   d. Total liabilities increase and shareholders' equity decreases.

3. You have determined that Carefree Company estimates bad debt expense using the aging of accounts receivable method. Assuming Carefree has no write-offs or recoveries, its estimate of uncollectible receivables resulting from the aging analysis equals:
   a. Bad debt expense for the current period
   b. The ending balance in the allowance for doubtful accounts for the period
   c. The change in the allowance for doubtful accounts for the period
   d. Both a and c

4. If the allowance for doubtful accounts opened with a $10,000 balance, ended with an adjusted balance of $20,000, and included write-offs of $5,000 (with no recoveries) during the period, what was the amount of bad debt expense?
   a. $5,000
   b. $10,000
   c. $15,000
   d. Cannot determine without knowing whether percentage of credit sales or aging of accounts receivable method was used.

5. When an accounts receivable is "recovered":
   a. Total assets increase.
   b. Total assets decrease.
   c. Shareholders' equity increases.
   d. None of the above.

6. If a 10 per cent note receivable for $10,000 is created on January 1, 2007, and it has a maturity date of December 31, 2011,
   a. No interest revenue will be recorded in 2007.
   b. The note receivable will be classified as a current asset.
   c. Interest revenue of $1,000 will be recorded in 2007.
   d. None of the above

7. If the receivables-turnover ratio decreased during the year,
   a. The days to collect also decreased.
   b. Receivables collections slowed down.
   c. Sales revenues increased at a faster rate than receivables increased.
   d. None of the above

8. What is the best description of a *credit card discount?*
   a. The discount offered by a seller to a consumer for using a national credit card like Visa
   b. The fee charged by a seller to a consumer for the right to use a credit card, calculated as a percentage of total revenue for the sale
   c. The discount offered by a seller to a customer for early payment of an account receivable
   d. The percentage fee charged by a credit card company to a seller

9. All else being equal, if Sony incurs a 3 per cent fee to factor $10,000 of its accounts receivable, its net income will
   a. Increase by $10,000.
   b. Increase by $9,700.
   c. Increase by $300.
   d. Decrease by $300.

10. Which of the following steps can financial statement users take to evaluate the degree of optimism in management's bad debt estimates?
    a. Assess the consistency of estimates.
    b. Don't rely on just one number like net income.
    c. Understand how management develops its estimates.
    d. All of the above.

MINI-EXERCISES

LO1   **M7-1 Evaluating the Decision to Extend Credit**

Nutware Productions Inc. generated sales of $30,000 and gross profit of $10,000 last year, without extending credit to any of its customers. The company estimates that it would have generated sales of $60,000 had it extended credit, but there would be additional costs for associated wages and bad debts totalling $25,000 if they did so. Should the company extend credit?

LO2   **M7-2 Reporting Accounts Receivable and Recording Write-Offs Using the Allowance Method**

At the end of 2008, Bully's Full Fitness has adjusted balances of $600,000 in gross accounts receivable and $44,000 in allowance for doubtful accounts. On January 2, 2009, the company learns that certain customer accounts are not collectible, so management authorizes a write-off of these accounts, totalling $8,000.

a. Show how the company would have reported its receivable accounts on December 31, 2008. As of that date, what amount did Bully's Full Fitness expect to collect?
b. Prepare the journal entry to write off the accounts on January 2, 2009.
c. Assuming no other transactions occurred between December 31, 2008, and January 3, 2009, show how Bully's Full Fitness would have reported its receivable accounts on January 3, 2009. As of that date, what amount did Bully's Full Fitness expect to collect? Has this changed from December 31, 2008? Explain why or why not.

LO2   **M7-3 Recording Recoveries Using the Allowance Method**

Let's go a bit further with the example from M7-2. Assume that on February 2, 2009, Bully's Full Fitness received a payment of $500 from one of the customers whose balance had been written off. Prepare the journal entries to record this transaction.

LO2   **M7-4 Recording Write-Offs and Bad Debt Expense Using the Allowance Method**

Prepare journal entries for each transaction listed.

a. During the period, customer balances are written off in the amount of $17,000.
b. At the end of the period, bad debt expense is estimated to be $14,000.

LO2   **M7-5 Determining Financial Statement Effects of Write-Offs and Bad Debt Expense Using the Allowance Method**

Using the following categories, indicate the effects of the following transactions. Use + for increase and − for decrease, and indicate the accounts affected and the amounts.

a. During the period, customer balances are written off in the amount of $8,000.
b. At the end of the period, bad debt expense is estimated to be $10,000.

Assets	=	Liabilities	+	Shareholders' Equity

LO3   **M7-6 Using the Interest Formula to Compute Interest**

Complete the following table by computing the missing amounts (?) for the following independent cases.

Principal Amount on Note Receivable	Annual Interest Rate	Time Period	Interest Earned
a. $100,000	10%	6 months	?
b. ?	10%	12 months	$4,000
c. $ 50,000	?	9 months	$3,000

M7-7 Recording Note Receivable Transactions
LO3

Scotia Corporation hired a new corporate controller and agreed to provide her a $20,000 relocation loan on a six-month, 7 per cent note. Prepare journal entries to record the following transactions for Scotia Corporation. Rather than using letters to reference each transaction, use the date of the transaction.

a. The company lends the money on January 1, 2008.
b. The new employee pays Scotia the full principal and interest on its maturity date.

M7-8 Recording Note Receivable Transactions
LO3

RecRoom Equipment Company received an $8,000, six-month, 10 per cent note to settle an unpaid balance owed by a customer. Prepare journal entries to record the following transactions for RecRoom. Rather than using letters to reference each transaction, use the date of the transaction.

a. The note is accepted by RecRoom on November 1, 2008, causing the company to increase its notes receivable and decrease its accounts receivable.
b. RecRoom adjusts its records for interest earned to December 31, 2008.
c. RecRoom receives the principal and interest on the note's maturity date.

M7-9 Evaluating the Decision to Extend Credit
LO5

On December 22, 2009, Belly Total Fitness issued a press release announcing that it had sold a significant portion of its accounts receivable. The CEO justified the decision by stating "we focused on simplifying the business." Explain how Belly's decision will simplify its business.

M7-10 Recording Credit Card Discounts
LO5

Donalda Ladies Wear had sales of $6,400 on December 31, 2009. Of this, $1,600 was paid for with cash and the balance was paid by credit card. All credit card receipts are deposited in the bank at the end of the day. Donalda pays a 3 per cent fee to all credit card companies. The goods cost Donalda $5,000, and Donalda uses a perpetual inventory system. Make the journal entries to record sales for that day.

M7-11 Determining the Effects of Credit Policy Changes on Receivables-Turnover Ratio and Days to Collect
LO6

Indicate the most likely effect of the following changes in credit policy on the receivables-turnover ratio and days to collect (+ for increase, − for decrease, and NE for no effect).

a. Granted credit with shorter payment deadlines.
b. Increased effectiveness of collection methods.
c. Granted credit to less creditworthy customers.

M7-12 Evaluating the Effect of Factoring on the Receivables-Turnover Ratio, and Computing the Cost of Factoring
LO6

After noting that its receivables-turnover ratio had declined, Imperative Company decided to sell $500,000 of receivables to a factoring company. The factor charges a factoring fee of 3 per cent of the receivables sold. All else being equal, how will this affect Imperative's receivables-turnover ratio in the future? How much cash does Imperative receive on the sale? Calculate the factoring fee, and describe how it is reported by Imperative Company.

M7-13 (Supplement A) Recording Write-Offs and Reporting Accounts Receivable Using the Direct Write-Off Method
LO4

Complete all the requirements of M7-2, except assume that Bully's Full Fitness uses the direct write-off method. Note that this means Bully's does not have an allowance for doubtful accounts balance.

EXERCISES

LO2   **E7-1   Recording Bad Debt Expense Estimates and Write-Offs Using the Percentage of Credit Sales Method**

During 2009, Kimberly Productions, Inc., recorded credit sales of $650,000. Based on prior experience, the company estimates a 1.5 per cent bad debt rate on credit sales.

Required:

Prepare journal entries for each transaction.

a.   The appropriate bad debt expense adjustment was recorded for the year 2009.
b.   On December 31, 2009, an account receivable for $1,000 from March 2009 was determined to be uncollectible and was written off.

LO2   **E7-2   Determining Financial Statement Effects of Bad Debt Expense Estimates and Write-Offs**

Using the following categories, indicate the effects of the transactions listed in E7-1. Use + for increase and − for decrease and indicate the accounts affected and the amounts.

Assets	=	Liabilities	+	Shareholders' Equity

LO2   **E7-3   Recording Write-Offs, Recoveries, and Bad Debt Expense Estimates Using the Percentage of Credit Sales Method**

During 2009, Huang Electronics, Incorporated, recorded credit sales of $720,000. Based on prior experience, it estimates a 0.5 per cent bad debt rate on credit sales.

Required:

Prepare journal entries for each transaction.

a.   On August 31, 2009, a customer balance of $300 from a prior year was determined to be uncollectible and was written off.
b.   On December 15, 2009, the customer balance of $300 written off on August 31, 2009, was collected in full.
c.   On December 31, 2009, the appropriate bad debt expense adjustment was recorded for the year 2009.

LO2   **E7-4   Determining Financial Statement Effects of Write-Offs, Recoveries, and Bad Debt Expense Estimates**

Using the following categories, indicate the effects of the transactions listed in E7-3. Use + for increase and − for decrease, and indicate the accounts affected and the amounts.

Assets	=	Liabilities	+	Shareholders' Equity

LO2   **E7-5   Recording and Determining the Effects of Write-Offs, Recoveries, and Bad Debt Expense Estimates on the Balance Sheet and Income Statement**

Copy Catchers Corporation operates a plagiarism detection service for universities and community colleges. While most of its customers reliably pay amounts owed, the company has historically experienced a 2 per cent rate of bad debts on credit sales. The company estimates bad debts with the percentage of credit sales method.

Required:

1.   Prepare journal entries for each transaction below.

a.   On March 31, 2009, ten customers were billed for detection services, totalling $50,000.
b.   On October 31, 2009, a customer balance for $1,600 from a prior year was determined to be uncollectible and was written off.
c.   On December 15, 2009, a customer paid an old balance of $600, which had been written off in a prior year.
d.   On December 31, 2009, the appropriate bad debt expense adjustment was recorded for the year 2007.

2. Complete the following table, indicating the amount and effect (+ for increase, − for decrease, and NE for no effect) of each transaction.

Transaction	Net Receivables	Net Sales	Income from Operations
a			
b			
c			
d			

E7-6 Computing Bad Debt Expense Using Aging of Accounts Receivable Method

LO2

Brown Cow Dairy uses the aging approach to estimate bad debt expense. The balance of each account receivable is aged on the basis of three time periods as follows: (1) 1 to 30 days old, $12,000, (2) 31 to 90 days old, $5,000, and (3) more than 90 days old, $3,000. Experience has shown that, for each age group, the average loss rate on the amount of the receivable due to uncollectibility is (1) 2 per cent, (2) 10 per cent, and (3) 30 per cent, respectively. At December 31, 2009 (end of the current year), the Allowance for Doubtful Accounts balance was $300 (credit) before the end-of-period adjusting entry is made.

Required:

1. What amount should be recorded as Bad Debt Expense for the current year?
2. If the unadjusted balance in the Allowance for Doubtful Accounts was a $600 debit balance, what would be the amount of bad debt expense in 2009?

E7-7 Recording and Reporting Allowance for Doubtful Accounts Using Aging of Accounts Receivable Method

LO2

Arias Company uses the aging approach to estimate bad debt expense. The balance of each account receivable is aged on the basis of three time periods, as follows: (1) 1 to 30 days old, $65,000, (2) 31 to 90 days old, $10,000, and (3) more than 90 days old, $4,000. Experience has shown that, for each age group, the average loss rate on the amount of the receivable due to uncollectibility is (1) 1 per cent, (2) 15 per cent, and (3) 40 per cent, respectively. At December 31, 2009 (end of the current year), the Allowance for Doubtful Accounts balance was $100 (credit) before the end-of-period adjusting entry is made.

Required:

1. Prepare the appropriate bad debt expense adjusting entry for the year 2009.
2. Show how the various accounts related to accounts receivable should be shown on the December 31, 2009, balance sheet.

E7-8 Recording, Reporting, and Evaluating a Bad Debt Estimate

LO2

During the year ended December 31, 2009, Kelly's Camera Shop had sales revenue of $170,000, of which $85,000 was on credit. At the beginning of 2009, Accounts Receivable showed a $10,000 debit balance, and the Allowance for Doubtful Accounts showed an $800 credit balance. Collections of accounts receivable during 2009 amounted to $68,000.

Data during 2009 follows:

a. On December 10, 2009, a customer balance of $1,500 from a prior year was determined to be uncollectible, so it was written off. This was the only write-off in 2009.
b. On December 31, 2009, a decision was made to continue the accounting policy of basing estimated bad debt losses on 2 per cent of credit sales for the year.

Required:

1. Give the required journal entries for the two events in December 2009.
2. Show how the amounts related to Accounts Receivable and Bad Debt Expense would be reported on the income statement and balance sheet for 2009.
3. On the basis of the data available, does the 2 per cent rate appear to be reasonable? Explain.

LO3   **E7-9 Recording Note Receivable Transactions, Including Accrual Adjustment for Interest**

The following transactions took place for Big Whiskers Grooming Service.

2008	July 1	Lent $10,000 to the president of the company and received from the president a one-year 10 per cent note.
	Dec. 31	Accrued interest on the note.
2009	July 1	Received principal and interest on the note. (No interest has been accrued since December 31.)

Required:

Prepare the journal entries that Big Whiskers would record for the above transactions.

LO3   **E7-10 Recording Note Receivable Transactions, Including Accrual Adjustment for Interest**

To attract retailers to its shopping centre, the Marketplace Mall will lend money to tenants under formal contracts, provided that they use it to renovate their store space. On November 1, 2008, the company lent $10,000 to a new tenant on a one-year note with a stated annual interest rate of 6 per cent. Interest is to be received by Marketplace Mall on April 30, 2009, and at maturity on October 31, 2009.

Required:

Prepare journal entries that Marketplace Mall would record related to this note on the following dates: (*a*) November 1, 2008; (*b*) December 31, 2008 (Marketplace Mall's fiscal year-end); (*c*) April 30, 2009; and (*d*) October 31, 2009.

LO2, LO6   **E7-11 Using Financial Statement Disclosures to Infer Write-Offs and Bad Debt Expense and to Calculate the Receivables-Turnover Ratio**

Microsoft develops, produces, and markets a wide range of computer software, including the Windows operating system. For a recent year, Microsoft reported the following information (in millions) about net sales revenue and accounts receivable.

	Current Year	*Prior Year*
Accounts receivable, net of allowances of $117 and $142	$ 11,338	$ 9,316
Net revenues	51,122	44,282

According to its annual report, Microsoft recorded bad debt expense of $64 and did not recover any previously written-off accounts during the current year.

Required:

1. What amount of bad debts was written off during the current year?
2. Assuming that Microsoft uses the percentage of sales method to estimate bad debt expense, solve for the percentage the company used in estimating bad debt expense for the current year.
3. What was Microsoft's receivables-turnover ratio in the current year?

LO2   **E7-12 Using Financial Statement Disclosures to Infer Bad Debt Expense**

A recent annual report for Sears contained the following information at the end of its fiscal year:

	Year 1	*Year 2*
Accounts receivable	$7,022,075,000	$7,336,308,000
Allowance for doubtful accounts	(86,605,000)	(96,989,000)
	$6,935,470,000	$7,239,319,000

A footnote to the financial statements disclosed that accounts receivable write-offs amounted to $55,000,000 during year 1 and $69,000,000 during year 2. Assume that Sears did not record any recoveries.

Required:

Determine the bad debt expense for year 2 based on the above facts.

E7-13 Determining the Effects of Uncollectible Accounts on the Receivables-Turnover Ratio

LO2, LO6

Refer to the information about Sears given in E7-12.

Required:

Complete the following table, indicating the direction of the effect (+ for increase, − for decrease, and NE for no effect) of each transaction during year 2:

Transaction	Net Credit Sales	Average Net Accounts Receivable	Receivables-Turnover Ratio
a. Write-off of $69,000,000 in uncollectible accounts			
b. Recording bad debt expense			

E7-14 Analyzing and Interpreting Receivables-Turnover Ratio and Days to Collect

LO6

A recent annual report for Federal Express contained the following data (in thousands):

	Current Year	Previous Year
Accounts receivable	$1,034,608	$805,495
Less: Allowance for doubtful accounts	36,800	38,225
Net accounts receivable	$ 997,808	$767,270
Net sales (assume all on credit)	$7,015,069	

Required:

1. Determine the accounts receivable-turnover ratio and days to collect for the current year.
2. Explain the meaning of each number.

E7-15 Determining the Effects of Bad Debts on Receivables-Turnover Ratio

LO2, LO6

During 2009, Jesse Enterprises Corporation recorded credit sales of $650,000. Based on prior experience, the company estimates a 1 per cent bad debt rate on credit sales. At the beginning of the year, the balance in Net trade accounts receivable was $50,000. At the end of the year, but *before* the bad debt expense adjustment was recorded and *before* any bad debts had been written off, the balance in Net trade accounts receivable was $55,500.

Required:

1. Assume that, on December 31, 2009, the appropriate bad debt expense adjustment was recorded for the year 2009, and accounts receivable totalling $6,000 for the year were determined to be uncollectible and were written off. What was the receivables-turnover ratio for 2009?
2. Assume instead that, on December 31, 2009, the appropriate bad debt expense adjustment was recorded for the year 2009, and $7,000 of accounts receivable was determined to be uncollectible and was written off. What was the receivables-turnover ratio for 2009?
3. Explain why the answers to requirements 1 and 2 differ or do not differ.

E7-16 (Supplement A) Recording Write-Offs and Reporting Accounts Receivable, Using the Direct Write-Off Method

LO4

Trevorson Electronics is a small company privately owned by Jon Trevorson, an electrician who installs wiring in new homes. Because the company's financial statements are prepared only for tax purposes, Jon uses the direct write-off method. During 2008, its first year of operations,

Trevorson Electronics sold $30,000 worth of services on account. The company collected $26,000 of these receivables during the year, and Jon believed that the remaining $4,000 was fully collectible. In 2009, Jon discovered that none of the $4,000 would be collected, so he wrote off the entire amount. To make matters worse, Jon sold only $5,000 worth of services during the year.

Required:

1. Prepare journal entries to record the transactions in 2008 and 2009.
2. Using only the information provided (ignore other operating expenses), prepare comparative income statements for 2008 and 2009. Was 2008 really as profitable as indicated by its income statement? Was 2009 quite as bad as indicated by its income statement? What should Jon do if he wants better information for assessing his company's ability to generate profit?

COACHED PROBLEMS

LO2

CP7-1   Recording Accounts Receivable Transactions Using the Allowance Method

Intrawest is a well-known Canadian company that operates ski, beach, and golf resorts. In 2006, Intrawest was bought for $2.8 billion and taken private by a foreign investment group. Assume that the company recently reported the following amounts in its unadjusted trial balance as of June 30, 2008 (all amounts in millions):

	Debits	*Credits*
Accounts receivable	$155	
Allowance for doubtful accounts		$ 13
Sales		1,843

Required:

COACH'S TIP

1. Remember that the percentage of credit sales method (also known as the income statement method) focuses mainly on calculating bad debt expense.
2. Remember that the aging of accounts receivable method (also known as the balance sheet method) focuses on calculating what the adjusted allowance for doubtful accounts balance should be.

1. Assume Intrawest uses 1/2 of 1 per cent of sales to estimate its bad debt expense for the year. If you also assume that no bad debt expense has been recorded for 2008, what adjusting journal entry would be required at June 30, 2008, for bad debt expense?
2. Assume Intrawest uses the aging of accounts receivable method and estimates that $23 of accounts receivable will be uncollectible. Prepare the adjusting journal entry required at June 30, 2008, for recording bad debt expense.
3. Repeat requirement 2, except this time assume the unadjusted balance in Intrawest's allowance for doubtful accounts at June 30, 2008, was a debit balance of $10.
4. If one of Intrawest 's main customers declared bankruptcy in 2009, what journal entry would be used to write off its $8 balance?

LO2

CP7-2   Interpreting Disclosure of Allowance for Doubtful Accounts

Saucony, Inc., designs, develops, and markets performance-oriented athletic footwear, athletic apparel, and casual leather footwear. It recently disclosed the following information concerning the allowance for doubtful accounts in its annual report submitted to the Securities and Exchange Commission in the United States.

SCHEDULE II **Valuation and Qualifying Accounts** **(dollars in thousands)**				
Allowance for Doubtful Accounts	**Balance at Beginning of Year**	**Additions Charged to Bad Debt Expense**	**Deductions from Allowance**	**Balance at End of Year**
Yr 3	$1,108	$6,014	$5,941	$1,181
Yr 2	2,406	?	5,751	1,108
Yr 1	2,457	4,752	?	2,406

Required:

1. Create a T-account for the allowance for doubtful accounts and enter into it the Year 3 amounts from the above schedule. Then write the T-account in equation format to prove that the above items account for the changes in the account.
2. Record summary journal entries for Year 3 related to (*a*) estimating bad debt expense and (*b*) writing off specific balances.
3. Supply the missing dollar amounts noted by ? for Year 2 and Year 1.
4. If Saucony had written off an additional $200 of accounts receivable during Year 3, how would net receivables have been affected? How would net income have been affected? Explain why.

COACH'S TIP

1. Because the allowance for doubtful accounts is a contra-asset account, increases are reported on the credit (right) side and decreases are on the debit (left) side.

CP7-3 Recording Notes Receivable Transactions

Jung & Newbicalm Advertising (JNA) recently hired a new creative director, Howard Rachell, for its Toronto office. To persuade Howard to move from New York, JNA agreed to advance him $100,000 on April 30, 2009, on a one-year, 2 per cent note, with interest payments required on October 31, 2009, and April 30, 2010. JNA issues quarterly financial statements on March 31, June 30, September 30, and December 31.

LO3

Required:

1. Prepare the journal entry that JNA will make to record the promissory note created on April 30, 2009.
2. Prepare the journal entries that JNA will make to record the interest accruals at each quarter-end and interest payments at each payment date.
3. Prepare the journal entry that JNA will make to record the principal payment at the maturity date.

COACH'S TIP

In requirement 2 of CP7-3, interest receivable will be accrued at the end of each quarter, and then will be reduced when each payment is received.

CP7-4 Recording and Reporting Accounts Receivable and Notes Receivable Transactions

Sports Canada Corp. distributes athletic gear to sporting goods stores throughout the country. Most of its sales are made on account, but some particularly large items (such as sport court systems) are sold in exchange for notes receivable. Sports Canada reported the following balances in its December 31, 2008, unadjusted trial balance:

LO2, LO3

	Debit	Credit
Accounts receivable	$1,110,000	
Allowance for doubtful accounts		$ 5,000
Bad debt expense	0	
Interest receivable	0	
Interest revenue		0
Notes receivable	25,200	
Sales made on account		5,600,000
Sales in exchange for notes		25,200

Notes receivable consists of principal owed by a customer on a two-year, 5 per cent note accepted on November 1, 2008. The note requires the customer to make annual interest payments on October 31, 2009 and 2010. Sports Canada has no concerns about the collectibility of this note. Sports Canada does estimate, however, that 1 per cent of its sales made on account will be uncollectible.

COACH'S TIP

1. The note receivable has been outstanding for two months in 2008, so the company has earned two months of interest. Also, notice that sales made on account are recorded in a different account than sales made in exchange for notes.

2. Current assets include assets that will be used up or converted to cash during 2009.

Required:

1. Prepare the December 31, 2008, adjusting journal entries related to accounts receivable and notes receivable.
2. Show how the adjusted balances for the above balance sheet accounts will be reported on Sports Canada's classified balance sheet as of December 31, 2008.

LO6

CP7-5 Analyzing Allowance for Doubtful Accounts, Receivables-Turnover Ratio, and Days to Collect

Mattel and Hasbro are two of the largest and most successful toymakers in the world, in terms of the products they sell and their receivables management practices. To evaluate their ability to collect on credit sales, consider the following information reported in their 2006 and 2005 annual reports (amounts in millions).

	Mattel			Hasbro		
Fiscal Year Ended:	*2006*	*2005*	*2004*	*2006*	*2005*	*2004*
Net sales	$5,650	$5,179	$5,103	$3,151	$3,088	$2,998
Gross accounts receivable	963	785	792	584	553	616
Allowance for doubtful accounts	19	25	33	28	30	37
Net accounts receivable	944	760	759	556	523	579

Required:

1. Calculate the receivables-turnover ratios and days to collect for Mattel and Hasbro for 2006 and 2005. (Round to one decimal place.) Which of the companies is quicker to convert its receivables into cash?

2. Comment on the trend in each company's allowance for doubtful accounts over the three years. Is each company growing more or less optimistic about its ability to collect its accounts receivable? Consider the dollar amount of the allowance for doubtful accounts, as well as its percentage of gross accounts receivable.

3. In its 2006 annual report, Mattel states that it sold $412 million of receivables in 2006 and $443 in 2005 to a number of factoring organizations. Given this additional information, recalculate what the receivables-turnover ratio and days to collect would have been in 2006 if Mattel had not factored its receivables. Does this help to explain the apparent differences determined in requirement 1 above?

COACH'S TIP

1. Use average net accounts receivable in your calculations.
2. To calculate the percentage, divide the allowance by gross accounts receivable and multiply by 100.
3. To remove the effect of factoring, add the amount factored to net accounts receivable for each of the two years and recalculate the average net receivable balance to use in your computations.

GROUP A PROBLEMS

LO2

PA7-1 Recording Accounts Receivable Transactions Using the Allowance Method

Maple Leaf Foods is a leading meat and bread producer in Canada. Assume that the company recently reported the following amounts in its unadjusted trial balance as of December 31, 2008 (all amounts in thousands):

	Debits	*Credits*
Accounts receivable	$316,000	
Allowance for doubtful accounts		$ 15,800
Sales		6,863,200

Required:

1. Assume Maple Leaf uses ½ of 1 per cent of sales to estimate its bad debt expense for the year. If you also assume that no bad debt expense has been recorded for 2008, what adjusting journal entry would be required at December 31, 2008, for bad debt expense?

2. Assume Maple Leaf uses the aging of accounts receivable method and estimates that $53,000 of accounts receivable will be uncollectible. Prepare the adjusting journal entry required at December 31, 2008, for recording bad debt expense.

3. Repeat requirement 2, except this time assume the unadjusted balance in Maple Leaf's allowance for doubtful accounts at December 31, 2008, was a debit balance of $10,000.

4. If one of Maple Leaf's main customers declared bankruptcy in 2009, what journal entry would be used to write off its $100 balance?

PA7-2 Interpreting Disclosure of Allowance for Doubtful Accounts

Rocky Mountain Chocolate Factory (RMCF) manufactures and sells chocolates. The majority of RMCF's sales are made on credit to other companies that operate Rocky Mountain stores. In addition to these accounts receivable, RMCF also has long-term notes receivable arising from the sale of 28 of its stores to other companies. In Schedule II of its recent annual report, RMCF reported the following changes in its allowance for doubtful accounts, which relates to both its accounts receivable and its notes receivable:

Balance at Beginning of Period	Charged to Costs and Expenses	Amounts Written Off	Balance at End of Period
$298,959	$1,754,524	$1,938,920	$114,563

Required:

1. Create a T-account for the allowance for doubtful accounts and enter into it the amounts from the above schedule. Then write the T-account in equation format to prove that the above items account for the changes in the account.
2. Record summary journal entries related to (*a*) estimating bad debt expense and (*b*) writing off specific balances during the year. (*Note:* Use the generic account name "receivables" to refer to the combined accounts receivable and notes receivable.)
3. If RMCF had written off an additional $20,000 of accounts receivable during the period, how would net accounts and notes receivable have been affected? How would net income have been affected? Explain why.

PA7-3 Recording Notes Receivable Transactions

C&S Marketing (CSM) recently hired a new marketing director, Jeff Otos, for its downtown Winnipeg office. As part of the arrangement, CSM agreed on February 28, 2009, to advance Jeff $50,000 on a one-year, 8 per cent note, with interest payments required on August 31, 2009, and February 28, 2010. CSM issues quarterly financial statements on March 31, June 30, September 30, and December 31.

Required:

1. Prepare the journal entry that CSM will make to record the execution of the note.
2. Prepare the journal entries that CSM will make to record the interest accruals at each quarter-end and interest payments at each payment date.
3. Prepare the journal entry that CSM will make to record the principal payment at the maturity date.

PA7-4 Recording and Reporting Accounts Receivable and Notes Receivable Transactions

Merle Adventures, Inc., is a distributor of kayaks, kayaking equipment, and kayaking accessories. The company ships mainly to retail stores in Québec and Ontario. Most of its sales are made on account, but some particularly large orders are sold in exchange for notes receivable. Merle Adventures reported the following balances in its December 31, 2008, unadjusted trial balance:

	Debit	Credit
Accounts receivable	$2,500,000	
Allowance for doubtful accounts		$ 10,000
Bad debt expense	0	
Interest receivable	0	
Interest revenue		0
Notes receivable	120,000	
Sales on account		10,225,000
Sales in exchange for notes		120,000

Notes receivable consists of principal owed by a customer on a two-year, 6 per cent note accepted on November 1, 2008. The note requires the customer to make annual interest payments on

October 31, 2009 and 2010. Merle Adventures has no concerns about the collectibility of this note. Merle Adventures does estimate, however, that 1 per cent of its sales made on account will be uncollectible.

Required:

1. Prepare the December 31, 2008, adjusting journal entries related to accounts receivable and notes receivable.
2. Show how the adjusted balances for the above balance sheet accounts will be reported on Merle Adventures' classified balance sheet as of December 31, 2008.

LO6

PA7-5 Analyzing Allowance for Doubtful Accounts, Receivables-Turnover Ratio, and Days to Collect

Coca-Cola and PepsiCo are two of the largest and most successful beverage companies in the world in terms of the products that they sell and in terms of their receivables management practices. To evaluate their ability to collect on credit sales, consider the following information reported in their recent annual reports (amounts in millions).

Fiscal Year Ended:	Coca-Cola			PepsiCo		
	2006	**2005**	**2004**	**2006**	**2005**	**2004**
Net sales	$24,088	$23,104	$21,742	$35,137	$32,562	$29,261
Gross accounts receivable	2,650	2,353	2,313	3,789	3,261	2,999
Allowance for doubtful accounts	63	72	69	64	105	116
Net accounts receivable	2,587	2,281	2,244	3,725	3,156	2,883

Required:

1. Calculate the receivables-turnover ratios and days to collect for Coca-Cola and PepsiCo for 2006 and 2005. (Round to one decimal place.) Which of the companies is quicker to convert its receivables into cash?
2. Comment on the trend in each company's allowance for doubtful accounts over the three years. Is each company growing more or less optimistic about its ability to collect its accounts receivable? Consider the dollar amount of the allowance for doubtful accounts as well as the percentage of gross accounts receivable that the allowance represents.

LO6

PA7-6 Receivables-Turnover Ratio and Days to Collect

Gildan Activewear and West49 are both well-known Canadian companies. Gildan is a world leader in manufacturing T-shirts, sweatshirts, and other athletic wear, and selling them to wholesalers. West49 is a specialty retailer of youth apparel and action sports gear. To evaluate their ability to collect on credit sales, consider the following information reported in their recent annual reports (amounts in thousands). (West49's results for its fiscal year ending January 26, 2008, are presented here as 2007 results.)

Fiscal Year Ended:	Gildan			West49		
	2007	**2006**	**2005**	**2007**	**2006**	**2005**
Net sales	$964,429	$773,190	$653,851	$204,894	$195,268	$135,128
Net accounts receivable	206,088	165,870	108,646	1,537	3,007	3,987

Required:

Calculate the receivables-turnover ratios and days to collect for Gildan and West49 for 2007 and 2006. (Round to one decimal place.) Which of the companies is quicker to convert its receivables into cash? If there is a difference, what do you think might be a reasonable explanation?

PA7-7 Recording Sales and Accounts Receivable Transactions

LO2, LO6

Chester Company had the following accounts in its unadjusted trial balance at November 30, 2009:

Accounts receivable	$95,000	
Allowance for doubtful accounts		$3,420

During December, the company had the following activity:

a. Cash sales $60,000; credit sales to corporate customers $532,000 on terms of 2/10, n/30
b. Wrote off a customer's account, $1,200.
c. Collected $200,000 of receivables within the discount period; collected another $365,000 of receivables past the discount date.
d. On the basis of aging the December 31 receivables, decided that an allowance of $5,000 was needed for the December 31, 2009, year-end statements.

Required:

1. Prepare journal entries to record the above data for December.
2. Show the amounts that would appear for Accounts Receivable and Allowance for Doubtful Accounts in the December 31, 2009, balance sheet.
3. Calculate Chester's receivables-turnover ratio and days to collect for the month of December.
4. What effect does offering a discount for early payment have on the receivables-turnover ratio?

GROUP B PROBLEMS

PB7-1 Recording Accounts Receivable Transactions Using the Allowance Method

LO2

Research in Motion (RIM) is the Canadian company that produces the hand-held wireless computer known as a BlackBerry. Assume the company recently reported the following amounts in its unadjusted trial balance as March 3, 2007 (all amounts in thousands):

	Debits	Credits
Trade receivables	$578,044	
Allowance for doubtful accounts		$ 5,407
Sales		3,037,103

Required:

1. Assume RIM uses ½ of 1 per cent of sales to estimate its bad debt expense for the year. If you also assume that no bad debt expense has been recorded for 2007, what adjusting journal entry would be required at March 3, 2007, for bad debt expense?
2. Assume RIM uses the aging of accounts receivable method and estimates that $20,000 of accounts receivable will be uncollectible. Prepare the adjusting journal entry required at March 3, 2007, for recording bad debt expense.
3. Repeat requirement 2, except this time assume the unadjusted balance in RIM's allowance for doubtful accounts at March 3, 2007, was a debit balance of $5,000.
4. If one of RIM's main customers declared bankruptcy in 2008, what journal entry would be used to write off its $150 balance?

PB7-2 Interpreting Disclosure of Allowance for Doubtful Accounts

LO2

Xerox Corporation is the company that made the photocopier popular, although it now describes itself as a technology and services enterprise that helps businesses deploy document management strategies and improve productivity. Wow, how impressive is that? It recently disclosed the following information concerning the allowance for doubtful accounts in its annual report.

SCHEDULE II **Valuation and Qualifying Accounts** **(dollars in millions)**				
Allowance for Doubtful Accounts	**Balance at Beginning of Year**	**Additions Charged to Bad Debt Expense**	**Deductions from Allowance**	**Balance at End of Year**
2005	$459	$72	$166	$365
2004	533	?	184	459
2003	606	224	?	533

Required:

1. Create a T-account for the allowance for doubtful accounts and enter into it the 2005 amounts from the above schedule. Then, write the T-account in equation format to prove that the above items account for the changes in the account.
2. Record summary journal entries for 2005 related to (*a*) estimating bad debt expense and (*b*) writing off specific balances.
3. Supply the missing dollar amounts noted by *?* for 2004 and 2003.
4. If Xerox had written off an additional $20 million of accounts receivable during 2005, how would net accounts receivable have been affected? How would net income have been affected? Explain why.

LO3   **PB7-3 Recording Notes Receivable Transactions**

Stinson Company recently agreed to lend its CEO $100,000 for the purchase of a new house. The loan was executed on May 31, 2009, and is a one-year, 7 per cent note, with interest payments required on November 30, 2009, and May 31, 2010. Stinson Co. issues quarterly financial statements on March 31, June 30, September 30, and December 31.

Required:

1. Prepare the journal entry that Stinson Co. will make to record the execution of the note.
2. Prepare the journal entries that Stinson Co. will make to record the interest accruals at each quarter-end and interest payments at each payment date.
3. Prepare the journal entry that Stinson Co. will make to record the principal payment at the maturity date.

LO2, LO3   **PB7-4 Recording and Reporting Accounts Receivable and Notes Receivable Transactions**

Tractors-R-Us is a supplier of garden tractors. Most of its sales are made on account, but some particularly large orders are sold in exchange for notes receivable. Tractors-R-Us reported the following balances in its December 31, 2008, unadjusted trial balance:

	Debits	Credits
Accounts receivable	$1,650,000	
Allowance for doubtful accounts		$ 15,000
Bad debt expense	0	
Interest receivable	0	
Interest revenue		0
Notes receivable	105,000	
Sales on account		8,250,000
Sales in exchange for notes		105,000

Notes receivable consists of principal owed by a customer on a two-year, 5 per cent note accepted on July 1, 2008. The note requires the customer to make annual interest payments on June 30, 2009 and 2010. Tractors-R-Us has no concerns about the collectibility of this note. Tractors-R-Us does estimate, however, that 1 per cent of its sales made on account will be uncollectible.

Required:

1. Prepare the December 31, 2008, adjusting journal entries related to accounts receivable and notes receivable.
2. Show how the adjusted balances for the above balance sheet accounts will be reported on Tractors-R-Us's classified balance sheet as of December 31, 2008.

PB7-5 Analyzing Allowance for Doubtful Accounts, Receivables-Turnover Ratio, and Days to Collect

LO6

Wal-Mart and Target are two of the largest and most successful retail chains in the world. To evaluate their ability to collect on credit sales, consider the following information reported in their 2006 and 2005 annual reports (amounts in millions).

	Wal-Mart			**Target**		
Fiscal Year Ended:	**2006**	**2005**	**2004**	**2006**	**2005**	**2004**
Net sales	$285,222	$312,427	$285,222	$59,878	$52,620	$46,839
Net accounts receivable	2,840	2,476	1,586	6,194	5,666	5,069

Required:

Calculate the receivables-turnover ratios and days to collect for Wal-Mart and Target for 2006 and 2005. (Round to one decimal place.) Which of the companies is quicker to convert its receivables into cash?

PB7-6 Analyzing Receivables-Turnover Ratio and Days to Collect

LO6

Royal Dutch Shell and Petro-Canada are two successful companies in the oil and gas industry. To evaluate their ability to collect on credit sales, consider the following information reported in their recent annual reports (amounts in millions).

	Shell			**Petro-Canada**		
Fiscal Year Ended:	**2007**	**2006**	**2005**	**2007**	**2006**	**2005**
Net sales	$355,782	$318,845	$306,731	$21,710	$18,911	$17,585
Net accounts receivable	74,238	59,668	66,386	1,973	1,600	1,617

Required:

Calculate the receivables-turnover ratios and days to collect for Shell and Petro-Canada for 2007 and 2006. (Round to one decimal place.) Which of the companies is quicker to convert its receivables into cash?

PB7-7 Recording Sales and Accounts Receivable Transactions

LO2, LO3, LO6

Dionne Company had the following accounts in its unadjusted trial balance at November 30, 2009:

Accounts receivable	$160,000	
Allowance for doubtful accounts		$10,000

During December, the company had the following activity:

    a. $10,000 loan made to the president for personal reasons on December 1; the president signed a note promising to repay the loan with 6 per cent interest on December 1, 2010.

    b.   Cash sales $20,000; credit card sales to retail customers $185,000; credit sales to corporate customers $675,000 on terms of 2/10, n/30. The credit card companies charge a 3 per cent fee.

    c.   Collected $2,000 on a receivable that had been written off in 2008.

    d.   Collected $275,000 of receivables within the discount period; collected another $460,000 of receivables past the discount date.

    e.   On the basis of aging the December 31 receivables, decided that an allowance of $15,000 was needed for the December 31, 2009, year-end statements.

Required:

1. Prepare journal entries to account for the above data.
2. Show the amounts that would appear for receivables in the December 31, 2009, balance sheet.
3. Calculate Dionne's accounts receivables-turnover ratio and days to collect for the month of December.

SKILLS DEVELOPMENT CASES

LO2, LO6   ### S7-1 Finding Financial Information

Refer to the financial statements of High Liner in Appendix A at the end of this book, or download the annual report from the *Cases* section of the text's Web site at www.mcgrawhill.ca/college/phillips.

Required:

1. Does the company report an allowance for doubtful accounts on the balance sheet or in the notes? Explain why it does or does not.
2. Compute the company's receivables-turnover ratio and days to collect for the most recent year. Are these comparable to the examples shown in Exhibit 7.8?

LO2, LO6   ### S7-2 Comparing Financial Information

Refer to the financial statements of Sun-Rype by downloading the annual report from the *Cases* section of the text's Web site at www.mcgrawhill.ca/college/phillips.

Required:

1. Does the company report an allowance for doubtful accounts in its financial statements? Does Sun-Rype have more or less accounts receivables on its balance sheet than High Liner does?
2. Compute the company's receivables-turnover ratio and days to collect for the most recent year. Which company collects its receivables faster—High Liner or Sun-Rype?
3. Calculating the receivables-turnover ratio is not considered useful for companies that sell almost exclusively on a cash basis. Can you think of a type of business that would not normally have trade receivables?

LO1, LO2, LO6   ### S7-3 Internet-Based Team Research: Examining an Annual Report

As a team, select an industry to analyze. Using your Web browser, each team member should acquire the annual report for one Canadian or American publicly traded company in the industry, with each member selecting a different company. (See S1-3 in Chapter 1 for a description of possible resources for these tasks.)

Required:

TEAM CASE

1. On an individual basis, each team member should write a short report that incorporates the following:
   a. Calculate the receivables-turnover ratio for the current and prior year, and explain any change between the two years. (To obtain the beginning accounts receivable number for the prior year, you will need the prior year's annual report.)
   b. If you used an American company, look in the 10-K on www.sec.gov/edgar.shtml for the Schedule II analysis of "Valuation and Qualifying Accounts," which provides additional disclosures concerning the allowance for doubtful accounts. From this schedule, determine the level of bad debt expense, as a percentage of sales, for the current and prior year.
2. Then, as a team, write a short report comparing and contrasting your companies using these attributes. Discuss any patterns across the companies that you as a team observe. Provide potential explanations for any differences discovered.

LO6   ### S7-4 Analyzing Receivables

Nortel Networks of Brampton, Ontario, is a telecom giant that provides large-scale communication systems and infrastructures to companies around the world. During the technology boom of the 1990s,

Nortel's growth was impressive. Total assets almost tripled from U.S.$6.8 billion in 1990 to U.S.$19.7 billion in 1998. During this boom, Nortel extended significant financing to its customers, many of which were start-up companies, to help them finance their large investments in the latest Nortel technology. As long as the companies succeeded, Nortel would eventually get paid. Unfortunately for Nortel and many of its customers, the technology sector was in serious trouble by the year 2000.[3] Below are Nortel's sales and receivables figures (in millions of U.S. dollars) for selected years.

	1999	2000	2001	2002	2003
Accounts receivable	$ 6,806	$ 7,647	$ 3,585	$ 2,731	$ 2,698
Allowance for doubtful accounts	328	363	659	502	194
Net receivables	6,478	7,284	2,926	2,229	2,504
Sales	$20,558	$27,966	$18,912	$11,022	$10,193

Required:

1. Calculate the receivables-turnover ratios and days to collect for Nortel for the years 1999 to 2003. Round to one decimal place. Comment on the changes over time. (1998 net receivables were $5,214.)

2. Comment on the trend in Nortel's allowance for doubtful accounts over the five years. Consider the dollar amount of the allowance for doubtful accounts, as well as the percentage of gross accounts receivable that the allowance represents.

3. Is the technology sector risky? Are new companies riskier than established companies? What do you think of the wisdom of Nortel's decision to grant large amounts of credit to start-up companies in the tech sector?

S7-5 Ethical Decision Making: A Real-Life Example

LO2, LO3, LO7

ETHICAL ISSUES

As an auditor for a large international accounting firm, you have been assigned the job of evaluating whether your client's allowance for doubtful accounts balance is a fair estimate of its uncollectible accounts. You've obtained an aged listing of the company's customer account balances for each month of the year to see if any particular customer accounts appear uncollectible. As you scan the listings, you notice something odd. An account receivable from a customer named CT&T first appeared early in the year. This customer's account balance continued to grow and age with each passing month, because the customer wasn't paying the balance it owed to your client. CT&T owed $30 million to your client by the middle of the year, and $100 million just one month before your client's year-end. Then, in the final month of the year, CT&T's balance disappeared. Upon looking more closely at the aged listings, you notice a similar pattern for a customer called Telemedia. Its balance had grown to $2 million before disappearing in the final month of the year. You ask the accounts receivable manager, Walter Pavlo, what happened. He said the two customers "obtained some financing . . . I guess out of nowhere" and then paid off their accounts receivable balances. As strange as this seemed, you decided that these customer accounts no longer existed, so they weren't your concern.

To estimate what your client's allowance for doubtful accounts balance should be, you combine the year-end aged listing of accounts receivable balances with an analysis of your client's historical bad debt loss rates. You calculated an estimate that was significantly higher than what your client had recorded in the allowance for doubtful accounts. Walter had left for the day, so you asked his assistant why the recorded amount wasn't higher. The staff member replied, "The $35 million owed to us by Hi-Rim, which is included in the over 120 days category, doesn't require an allowance because Hi-Rim will pay it off as soon as Walter advances funds to Hi-Rim as part of the promissory note that we're arranging with Hi-Rim."

Required:

1. Discuss whether it makes sense to exclude a particular customer account from an aged listing of accounts receivable when using historical bad debt loss rates to estimate uncollectible accounts.

2. Given what you learned about Hi-Rim, what do you think may have happened with the accounts receivable from CT&T and Telemedia? Should you investigate this matter further? Explain why or why not.

---

[3]For a good review of Nortel's fall from grace, read "An Anniversary for Nortel," *CAmagazine*, October 2005, p. 8.

Epilogue: The events described above are based on an article in the June 10, 2002, issue of *Forbes* magazine that describes how, in the mid-1990s, Walter Pavlo was pressured to commit accounting fraud at MCI, a company later taken over by WorldCom. WorldCom went on to commit an $11-billion fraud, the largest ever at the time.

LO2, LO7   **S7-6 Ethical Decision Making: A Mini-Case**

Having just graduated with a business degree, you're excited to begin working as a junior accountant at Clear Optics, Inc. The company supplies lenses, frames, and sunglasses to opticians and retailers throughout the country. Clear Optics is currently in the process of finalizing its third quarter (Q3) operating results. All Q3 adjusting entries have been made, except for bad debt expense. The preliminary income statement for Q3 is shown below, along with reported results for Q2 and Q1.

ETHICAL ISSUES

	Q3 (preliminary)	Q2 (as reported)	Q1 (as reported)
Net sales	$135,800	$135,460	$130,100
Cost of goods sold	58,400	58,250	55,990
Gross profit	77,400	77,210	74,110
Selling, general, and administrative expenses	56,560	53,975	53,690
Bad debt expense	—	6,050	4,200
Income before income taxes	20,840	17,185	16,220
Income tax expense	5,620	5,155	5,020
Net income	$ 15,220	$ 12,030	$ 11,200

CLEAR OPTICS, INC.
Quarterly Income Statements
(amounts in thousands of Cdn. dollars)

The corporate controller has asked you to examine the allowance for doubtful accounts and use the aged listing of accounts receivable to determine the adjustment needed to record estimated bad debts for the quarter. The controller states that, "Although our customers are somewhat slower in paying this quarter, we can't afford to increase the allowance for doubtful accounts. If anything, we need to decrease it—an adjusted balance of about $8,000 is what I'd like to see. Play around with our estimated bad debt loss rates until you get it to work."

You were somewhat confused by what the controller had told you, but you chalked it up to your lack of experience and decided to analyze the allowance for doubtful accounts. You summarized the transactions recorded in the allowance for doubtful accounts using the T-account below:

dr Allowance for Doubtful Accounts cr			
		7,900	January 1 bal. fwd.
Q1 Write-offs	4,110	4,200	Q1 Bad debts estimate
		7,990	March 31 adjusted
Q2 Write-offs	4,120	6,050	Q2 Bad debts estimate
		9,920	June 30 adjusted
Q3 Write-offs	4,030	—	
		5,890	September 30 unadjusted

Required:

1. What bad debts estimate for Q3 will produce the $8,000 balance that the controller would like to see?

2. Prepare the adjusting journal entry that would be required to record this estimate.

3. If the entry in requirement 2 is made, what does it do to the Q3 income and the trend in earnings? (Assume that income tax expense does not change.)

4. Reconsider the statement the controller made to you. Is his suggestion a logical way to use the aging method to estimate bad debts?

5. What would be the Q3 net income if the bad debt expense estimate was the average of bad debt expense in Q2 and Q1? What would this do to the trend in net income across the three quarters? (Assume that income tax expense does not change.)

6. Is there any evidence of unethical behaviour in this case? Explain your answer.

S7-7 Critical Thinking: Analyzing

LO1, LO6

Problem Solved Company has been operating for five years as a software consulting firm. During this period, it has experienced rapid growth in sales revenue and in accounts receivable. To solve its growing receivables problem, the company hired you as its first corporate controller. You have put into place more stringent credit-granting and collection procedures that you expect will reduce receivables by approximately one-third by year-end. You have gathered the following data related to the changes (in thousands):

	Beginning of Year	End of Year (projected)
Accounts receivable	$1,000,608	$ 660,495
Less: Allowance for doubtful accounts	36,800	10,225
Net accounts receivable	$ 963,808	$ 650,270

	Prior Year	Current Year (projected)
Net sales (assume all on credit)	$7,515,444	$7,015,069

Required:

1. Compute the accounts receivable-turnover ratio based on three different assumptions:

   a. The stringent credit policies reduce the balance in Net accounts receivable and decrease Net sales as projected in the tables above.

   b. The stringent credit policies reduce the balance in Net accounts receivable as projected in the tables above but do not decrease Net sales from the prior year.

   c. The stringent credit policies are not implemented, resulting in no change from the beginning of the year accounts receivable balance and no change in Net sales from the prior year.

2. On the basis of your findings in requirement 1, write a brief memo explaining the potential benefits and drawbacks of more stringent credit policies and how they are likely to affect the accounts receivables-turnover ratio.

S7-8 Using an Aging Schedule to Estimate Bad Debts and Improve Collections from Customers

LO2

Assume you were recently hired by Caffe D'Amore, the company that formulated the world's first flavoured instant cappuccino and now manufactures several lines of coffee flavoured cappuccino mixes. The company recently has experienced tremendous growth in its sales to retailers, given that there are now an estimated 8 million weekly drinkers of iced cappuccino nationwide. Given its tremendous sales growth, Caffe D'Amore's receivables also have grown. Your job is to evaluate and improve collections of the company's receivables.

By analyzing collections of accounts receivable over the past five years, you were able to estimate bad debt loss rates for balances of varying ages. To estimate this year's uncollectible accounts, you jotted down the historical loss rates on the last page of a recent aged listing of outstanding customer balances (see next page).

Customer	Total	Number of Days Unpaid				
		1–30	31–60	61–90	91–120	Over 120
Subtotal from previous page	$280,000	$150,000	$60,000	$40,000	$20,000	$10,000
Jumpy Jim's Coffee	1,000					1,000
Surrey Coffee Company	24,500	14,500	8,000	2,000		
Phillips Blender House	17,000	12,000	4,000		1,000	
Pugsly's Trading Post	26,600	19,600	7,000			
Q-Coffee	12,400	8,400	3,000	1,000		
Special Sips	10,000	6,000	4,000			
Uneasy Isaac's	3,500	500				3,000
Total accounts receivable	375,000	211,000	86,000	43,000	21,000	14,000
Bad debt loss rates		1%	5%	8%	12%	20%

Required:

1. With a spreadsheet, use the above information to calculate the total estimated uncollectible accounts.

2. Prepare the year-end adjusting journal entry to adjust the allowance for doubtful accounts to the balance you calculated above. Assume the allowance account has an unadjusted credit balance of $10,000.

3. Of the customer account balances shown above on the last page of the aged listing, which should be your highest priority for contacting and pursuing collection?

4. Assume Jumpy Jim's Coffee account is determined to be uncollectible. Prepare the journal entry to write off the entire account balance.

CHAPTER

8

Reporting and Interpreting Inventories

Understand key inventory management decisions.
LO1 Describe inventory management goals.

Study inventory costing and reporting decisions.
LO2 Describe the different types of inventory.
LO3 Compute costs using four inventory costing methods.
LO4 (Supplement A) Compute costs using a perpetual inventory system.
LO5 Explain why inventory is reported at the lower of cost or market.

Evaluate inventory management practices.
LO6 Compute and interpret the inventory-turnover ratio.

Reconsider how inventory reporting decisions affect analyses.
LO7 Explain how accounting methods affect evaluations of inventory management.
LO8 Compute the effects of inventory errors.

This chapter focuses on how the costs of inventories on hand and goods sold are reported in financial statements. We focus on Oakley Inc., a company that sells goggles, sunglasses, watches, and other apparel and that was bought out by the Italian eyewear giant Luxxotica in 2007.

You are near the middle of the term, so it's time to ask yourself how you're doing. Suppose you've taken three tests and scored 30 per cent on the first, 60 per cent on the second, and 90 per cent on the third. Does this mean you're doing well, terribly, or average? It could be any of these three interpretations, depending on whether you focus on the first test, the last test, or the average of all three. Wouldn't this be a lot easier to figure out if there were rules describing how to interpret your test scores?

The same issue exists when companies report the cost of their inventories. Inflation can cause these costs to increase over time, while technological innovation can cause them to decrease. Either way, inventory is likely to be made up of some items acquired at lower unit costs and others at higher costs. Suppose **OAKLEY,** the sunglass maker for Annika Sorenstam, produces three pairs of its Half Jacket® sunglasses, at costs of $30, $60, and $90 each. Do these numbers suggest that their cost is low, moderate, or high? As with your test scores, it could mean any of the three, depending on how you look at it. Fortunately, in accounting, certain rules are used when determining the cost of inventory on hand and the cost of inventory sold. The tricky part is that these rules allow accountants to use one of several possible methods when determining the costs of inventories and goods sold, with each method leading to a different number. This flexibility of choice can be a good thing because it allows managers to use the method that best fits their business environment. This flexibility makes it essential, however, that you know which methods are being used and how they work. That's what we'll be reflecting on in this chapter.

Do you know what managers worry about when making inventory decisions, how the results of their decisions are reported, and how you can use the reported results to evaluate the quality of their inventory decisions? If any of your answers are NO, then you're doing exactly what you should be doing—reading this chapter. In it, we address these questions, which cover the specific Learning Objectives shown on the first page of the chapter.

UNDERSTAND
Key Inventory Management Decisions

What have you learned about inventory so far? In Chapter 5, you learned that it is not unusual for inventory to be one of the largest assets on a company's balance sheet, as it was for Reitmans. In Chapter 6's discussion of internal control, you studied how to account for purchases and sales using a perpetual inventory system for a merchandising company (the periodic system was reviewed in the Supplement). In this chapter, we expand our discussion into other key areas of inventory management.

THE BUSINESS OF INVENTORY MANAGEMENT

You may not make or sell inventory, but you buy it all the time. The things that concern you as a consumer are the same issues that concern managers who make inventory decisions. The primary goals of inventory managers are (1) to ensure sufficient quantities of inventory are available to meet customers' needs and (2) to ensure inventory quality meets customers' expectations and company standards. At the same time, they try (3) to minimize the costs of acquiring and carrying inventory (including costs related to purchasing, production, storage, spoilage, theft, obsolescence, and financing). Purchasing or producing too few units of a hot-selling item causes stock-outs that mean lost sales revenue and decreases in customer satisfaction. Conversely, purchasing too many units of a slow-selling item increases storage costs, as well as interest costs on short-term borrowings that finance the purchases. It may even lead to losses if the merchandise becomes outdated and cannot be sold at regular prices.

For many managers, there's a fourth factor that drives their inventory decisions: product innovation. Oakley believes so strongly in product innovation that it once described itself as "a technology company, in business to seek out problems with existing consumer products and solve them in ways that redefine product categories." These four factors are tricky to manage because, as one of them changes (e.g., quality), so, too, do the others (e.g., cost). Ultimately, inventory management often comes down to purchasing goods that can be sold soon after they are purchased.

STUDY
Inventory Costing and Reporting Decisions

TYPES OF INVENTORY

Inventory is tangible ("touchable") property held for sale in the normal course of business or used in producing goods for sale.

Inventory includes goods that are (1) held for sale in the normal course of business or (2) used to produce goods for sale. Inventory is reported on the balance sheet as a current asset because it is used or converted into cash within a company's operating cycle, which is normally less than one year. Goods in inventory are initially recorded at cost, which is the amount given up to acquire the asset and bring it into a condition and location ready for sale. The general name "inventory" can include several specific types of inventory, which usually differ between merchandisers and manufacturers. Since Oakley is both a merchandiser and a manufacturer, let's briefly describe how its various types of inventory differ:

- **Merchandisers** hold *merchandise inventory*, which usually is acquired in a finished condition and is ready for sale without further processing.

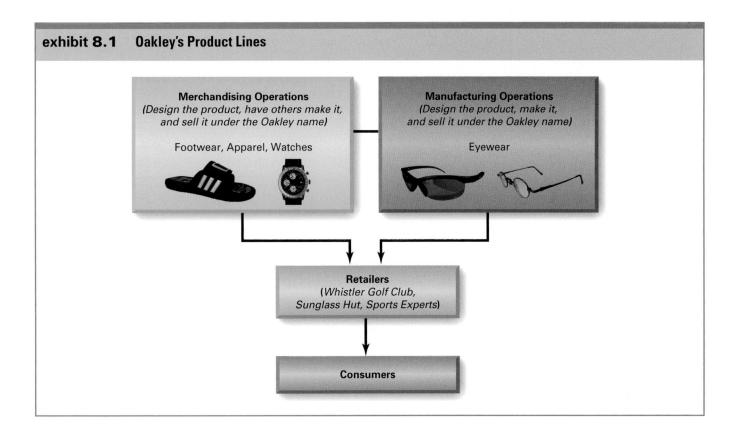

exhibit 8.1 Oakley's Product Lines

■ **Manufacturers** often hold three types of inventory, with each representing a different stage in the manufacturing process:

1. *Raw materials inventory* includes materials that eventually are processed further to produce finished goods. Oakley owns lots of different raw materials, including a stock of titanium that gives the same lightweight strength to sunglasses that it gives to jet engines. Items are included in raw materials inventory until they enter the production process, at which time they become part of work in process inventory.

2. *Work in process inventory* includes goods that are in the process of being manufactured, but are not yet complete. When completed, work in process inventory becomes finished goods inventory.

3. *Finished goods inventory* includes manufactured goods that are complete and ready for sale. At this stage, finished goods are treated just like merchandise inventory.

Excerpts from Oakley's balance sheet and financial statement notes are shown in Exhibit 8.2. The balance sheet reports the total of the inventories on hand and refers to Note 3, which provides details about the various types of inventory included in the total.

Notice that Note 3 includes only two categories of inventories: raw materials and finished goods. As with many companies that have both merchandising and manufacturing operations, Oakley combines *merchandise inventory* with manufactured *finished goods inventory* because both categories relate to goods that are ready to sell. You'll also notice that Oakley did not report any *work in process inventory*. Although it's possible that Oakley did not have any semi-completed goods in production at year-end, the more likely explanation is that Oakley had an insignificant amount of them, so their costs are included with either raw materials or finished goods inventories. This illustrates an accounting concept called **materiality,** which states that relatively small amounts not likely to influence decisions may be recorded and reported in the most cost-beneficial way. Based on this concept, Oakley separately reports only those amounts that are large enough to influence a user's decision.

Materiality is a concept stating that relatively small amounts not likely to influence decisions may be recorded and reported in the most cost-beneficial way. No one knows with certainty the amount that will influence a user's decision, so this assessment is subjective.

exhibit 8.2	Inventory Reporting Sample

OAKLEY, INC.
Consolidated Balance Sheet
(in thousands)

December 31	2006	2005	2004
Assets			
Current Assets			
Cash and Cash Equivalents	$ 31,313	$ 82,157	$ 51,738
Accounts Receivable, net	109,168	99,430	102,817
Inventories (Note 3)	155,377	119,035	115,061
Prepaid Income Taxes and Other Expenses	38,255	33,554	27,274
Total Current Assets	334,113	334,176	296,890

OAKLEY, INC.
Notes to the Consolidated Financial Statements
(in thousands)

Note 3—Inventories

Inventories at December 31 consist of the following:	2006	2005	2004
Raw Materials	$ 24,223	$ 28,776	$ 29,219
Finished Goods	131,154	90,259	85,842
	155,377	119,035	115,061

For simplicity, we'll focus on merchandise inventories in the balance of this chapter, but be aware that the concepts we cover apply equally to manufacturers' inventory.

Two other terms may be used in accounting to describe inventory. **Consignment inventory** refers to goods a company is holding on behalf of the goods' owner. Typically, this arises when a company is willing to sell the goods for the owner (for a fee), but does not want to take ownership of the goods in case the goods are difficult to sell. Consignment inventory is reported on the balance sheet of the owner, not the company holding the inventory. **Goods in transit** are inventory being transported. This type of inventory is reported on the balance sheet of the owner, not the company transporting it. In Chapter 6, you learned that ownership of inventory in transit is determined by the terms of the sales agreement. If a sale is made **FOB destination,** the goods belong to the seller until they are delivered to the customer. If the sale is made **FOB shipping point,** inventory belongs to the customer the moment it leaves the seller's premises.

Consignment inventory refers to goods held on behalf of the goods' owner.

Goods in transit include inventory being transported.

FOB destination and **FOB shipping point** are terms of sale that tell you whether the ownership of the goods is transferred to the buyer when the goods arrive at their destination or when they leave their shipping point.

INVENTORY COST

Exhibit 8.2 reports that the cost of Oakley's inventory on hand at December 31, 2006, was $155,377. As we saw in Chapter 6, merchandise inventory cost includes not just the purchase price of acquiring the goods, but any additional costs of acquiring and getting the goods ready for sale, such as the costs of freight-in, customs, duty, and packaging. If any purchase discounts have been taken, they are recorded as deductions in the cost of inventory.

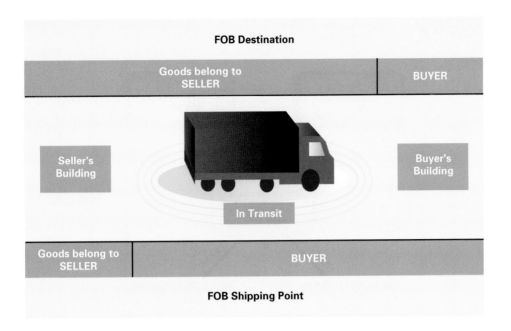

COST OF GOODS SOLD

As seen in Chapter 6, when goods are sold by a company using a perpetual system, two journal entries are made: one to record the sale (and the resulting increase in cash or receivables) and one to record the cost of the goods sold (and the resulting decrease in inventory on hand). As shown in Exhibit 8.3, the Cost of Goods Sold figure (CGS) is shown on the income statement directly below the figure for Sales. Sales revenue for an accounting period is the number of units sold multiplied by the sales price. The calculation for cost of goods sold uses the same number of units used to calculate sales revenue, except it is multiplied by the unit *cost* of the items sold. The difference between these two line-items is a subtotal called gross profit.

Now let's examine the relationship between cost of goods sold on the income statement and inventory on the balance sheet. Oakley starts each accounting period with a stock of inventory called *beginning inventory* (BI). During the accounting period, new *purchases* (P) are added to inventory. As shown in Exhibit 8.4, the sum of these two amounts is the **goods available for sale** during that period. What remains unsold at the end of the period is reported as *ending inventory* (EI) on the balance sheet. The portion of goods available for sale that is sold becomes *cost of goods sold* on the income statement. The ending inventory for one accounting period then becomes the beginning inventory for the next period. The relationships between these various inventory amounts are brought together in the **cost of goods sold (CGS) equation,** $BI + P - EI = CGS.$

Goods available for sale refers to the sum of beginning inventory and purchases for the period.

The **cost of goods sold (CGS) equation** is

$$BI + P - EI = CGS$$

exhibit 8.3	Sample Income Statement

OAKLEY, INC.
Consolidated Income Statements
(in thousands)

For the Years Ended December 31	2006	2005	2004
Net Sales	$761,865	$648,131	$585,468
Cost of Goods Sold	349,114	277,230	262,483
Gross Profit	412,751	370,901	322,985

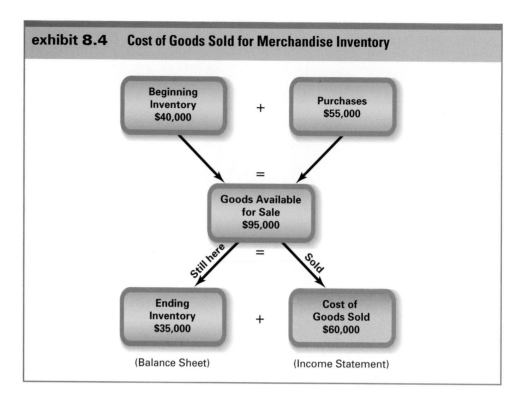

exhibit 8.4   Cost of Goods Sold for Merchandise Inventory

To illustrate the CGS equation, assume that Oakley began the period with $40,000 of Detonator™ watches in beginning inventory, purchased additional merchandise during the period for $55,000, and had $35,000 left in inventory at the end of the period. These amounts can be combined as follows to compute cost of goods sold of $60,000:

Beginning inventory	$40,000
+ Purchases of merchandise during the year	+ 55,000
= Goods available for sale	= 95,000
− Ending inventory	− 35,000
= Cost of goods sold	= $60,000

These same relationships can be represented in the merchandise inventory T-account as follows:

dr Merchandise Inventory (A) cr			
Beginning inventory	40,000		
Purchases of inventory	55,000	Cost of goods sold	60,000
Ending inventory	35,000		

If three of these four values are known, either the cost of goods sold equation or the inventory T-account can be used to solve for the fourth value. You get a chance to practise this in the Self-Study Quiz on page 335.

INVENTORY COSTING METHODS

In the Overdrive golf shoes example presented in the Self-Study Quiz, the cost of all units of the shoes was the same—$75. If inventory costs normally stayed constant like this, we'd be finished right now. But just as you don't always get 90 per cent on every test, the cost of goods doesn't stay constant forever. In recent years, the costs of many manufactured items, such as automobiles, have risen moderately. In some industries, such

HOW'S IT GOING? A Self-Study Quiz

Assume the following facts for Oakley's Overdrive™ golf shoe product line for the year 2007:

    Beginning inventory 500 units at unit cost of $75

    Purchases of inventory 1,200 units at unit cost of $75.

    Sales of 1,100 units at a sales price of $100 (cost per unit $75).

1. Using the cost of goods sold equation or the T-account, compute the dollar amount of Overdrive golf shoes in inventory at the end of the period.

		dr Merchandise Inventory (A) cr		
Beginning inventory	$ _____			
+ Purchases of merchandise during the year	_____	BI _____		
− Ending inventory	_____	P _____	_____ CGS	
= Cost of goods sold	$ _____	EI _____		

2. Prepare the first three lines of the income statement (showing computation of gross profit) for the Overdrive golf shoe line for the year 2007.

After you have finished, check your answers with the solutions in the margin.

Quiz Answers

1. BI = 500 × $75 = $37,500   BI + P − EI = CGS
   P = 1,200 × $75 = $90,000   37,500 + 90,000 − EI = 82,500
   CGS = 1,100 × $75 = $82,500   37,500 + 90,000 − 82,500 = EI
                                    45,000 = EI

2. Net sales $110,000
   Cost of goods sold   82,500
   Gross profit $ 27,500

as the computer and other electronics industries, costs of production have dropped dramatically.

When inventory costs change, how inventory items are treated (as sold or as remaining in inventory) can turn profits into losses and cause companies to pay or save hundreds of millions of dollars in taxes. A simple example will illustrate these dramatic effects.

Assume that one of Oakley's retailers experienced the following:

Jan.	1	Beginning inventory: Two units of Wisdom™ snow goggles at $70 each
March 12		Purchased four units of Wisdom snow goggles at $80 each.
June	9	Purchased one unit of Wisdom snow goggles at $100.
Nov.	5	Sold four units for $180 each.

Note that cost of the goggles *rose* rapidly between January and June. On November 5, four units are sold for $180 each, so revenues of $720 are recorded. What amount is recorded as cost of goods sold? The answer depends on which goggles we assume were sold. Four inventory costing methods have developed over the years for determining this:

1. **Specific identification**
2. **First-in, first-out (FIFO)**
3. **Last-in, first-out (LIFO)**
4. **Weighted average**

The different inventory costing methods are alternative ways to split the total dollar amount of goods available for sale between (1) ending inventory and (2) cost of goods sold. The first method specifically identifies which items remain in inventory and which are sold. The remaining methods *assume* inventory costs flow in a certain way from *Inventory* on the balance sheet to *Cost of Goods Sold* on the income statement. Notice that the two purchases above were made before the retailer sold any of the goggles. This is important because it means that the calculations in the following pages are the same regardless of whether the company uses a perpetual or a periodic inventory system.

Of the four methods, LIFO has been the method least commonly used in Canada, and, in fact, the CICA removed it as an acceptable costing method in 2008, to conform to international financial reporting standards (IFRS). LIFO continues to be a popular method in the United States, however. Because of this, and because seeing all four methods helps in understanding how different accounting methods affect net income and balance sheet accounts, we continue to illustrate it in this chapter.

Specific Identification Method

Specific identification method is the inventory costing method that identifies the cost of the specific item that was sold.

When the **specific identification method** is used, the cost of each item sold is individually identified and recorded as cost of goods sold. This method requires keeping track of the purchase cost of each item. This is done by either (1) coding the purchase cost on each unit before placing it in stock, or (2) keeping a separate record of the unit and identifying it with a serial number. In the snow goggles example, any four of the items could have been sold. If the coding systems tells us that one of the $70 items, two of the $80 items, and the one $100 item have been sold, the cost of those items ($70 + $80 + $80 + $100) would become cost of goods sold ($330). The cost of the remaining items ($70 + $80 + $80) would be included in ending inventory ($230) on the balance sheet.

The specific identification method is impractical when large quantities of similar items are stocked. On the other hand, when dealing with expensive and unique items, such as houses or fine jewellery, this method is appropriate. A drawback of this method is that it can allow for the unethical manipulation of financial results when the units are identical, because it's possible to alter the cost of goods sold and ending inventory accounts by picking and choosing the items to sell from among the different unit costs.

To prevent accounting manipulations that can occur using the specific identification method, inventory often is accounted for using one of three cost flow assumptions. Under these cost flow assumptions, *inventory costs are not based on the actual physical flow of goods* on and off the shelves. Rather, they are based on an assumed flow of costs from the balance sheet to the income statement. This is why they are called cost flow *assumptions.* A useful tool for imagining inventory cost flow assumptions is a bin, or container, as shown below. Try picturing the following inventory costing methods as flows of inventory costs in and out of the bin.

Although the actual physical flow of goods can differ from the cost flow assumption used, it's useful to picture in your mind how the costs flow from the balance sheet to the income statement.

First-In, First-Out (FIFO) Method

The **first-in, first-out (FIFO)** method assumes that the costs of the first goods purchased (first in) are the costs of the first goods sold (first out).

No, it's not the name of a dog. The **first-in, first-out method,** usually called **FIFO,** is a method for computing inventory costs. It assumes that the costs for the oldest goods (the first ones in) are used first to calculate cost of goods sold, and the newer costs are left to calculate ending inventory. It's as if costs flow in and out of the inventory bin as shown in Exhibit 8.5, corresponding to the following two-step process.

Step 1: Each purchase is treated as if it were deposited in the bin from the top in sequence. In our example, the costs for the oldest units (two units in beginning inventory at $70) are first in, followed by the next oldest (four units at $80), and finally the most recent purchase (one unit at $100). In total, these costs result in goods available for sale that cost $560.

Step 2: The cost of each unit sold is then removed from the bottom in sequence, as if the bottom of the bin swung open and the *first* costs *in* are the *first* costs *out.* In our example, four units are sold, so the cost of goods sold is calculated as the cost of the first two units in at $70 and two more units from the next layer at $80 each. These costs totalling $300 are reported as the cost of goods sold (CGS).

The costs of any remaining units (two units at $80 and one at $100 = $260) are reported as ending inventory. FIFO allocates the *oldest* unit costs to *cost of goods sold* and the *newest* unit costs to *ending inventory.*

Last-In, First-Out (LIFO) Method

The **last-in, first-out method,** usually called **LIFO,** assumes that the costs of the newest goods (the last ones in) are sold first, and the oldest costs are left in ending inventory. Picture this kind of cost flow as picking the goggles to be sold from the top of the bin. Go ahead, flip ahead to Exhibit 8.6, take a look, and then come right back here.

The **last-in, first-out (LIFO)** method assumes that the costs of the last goods purchased (last in) are the costs of the first goods sold (first out).

Step 1: As in FIFO, each purchase is treated as if it were deposited from the top (two units at $70 followed by four units at $80, and one unit at $100), resulting in the goods available for sale of $560.

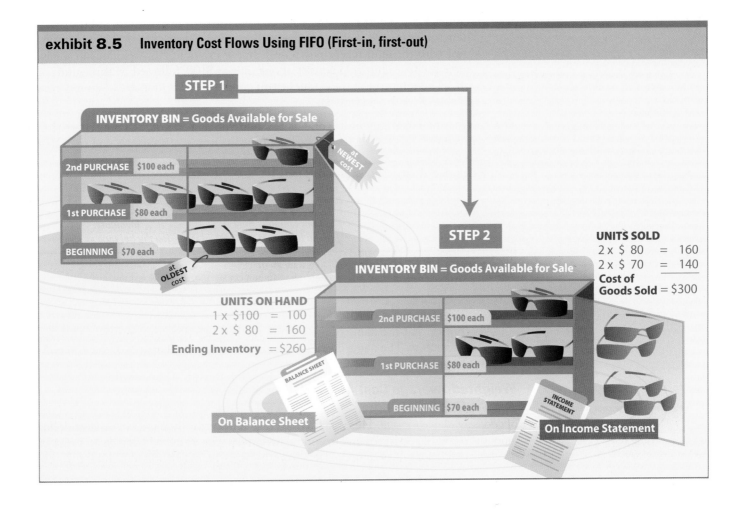

exhibit 8.5   Inventory Cost Flows Using FIFO (First-in, first-out)

exhibit 8.6   Inventory Cost Flows Using LIFO (Last-in, first-out)

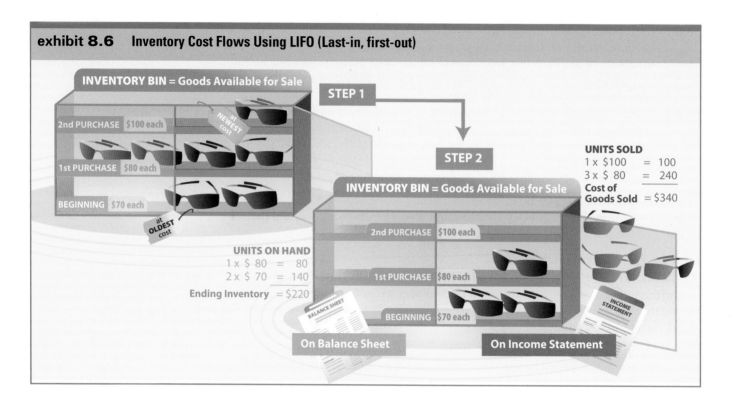

Step 2: Unlike FIFO, where costs are removed from the bottom of the bin, in LIFO each item sold is treated as if its cost were removed in sequence from the top (beginning with the most recent purchases). In our example, this would mean we assume the four units sold consist of one unit at $100, followed by three units at $80. The total cost of these four *last-in* goods ($340) is ***first out*** when reported as cost of goods sold (CGS).

The costs of the remaining units (one at $80 and two at $70 = $220) are reported as ending inventory. LIFO allocates the *newest* unit costs to *cost of goods sold* and the *oldest* unit costs to *ending inventory*.

Notice that the cost flows assumed for LIFO are the exact opposite of FIFO.

	Cost of Goods Sold *(on the income statement)*	Inventory *(on the balance sheet)*
FIFO	First-in (oldest) unit costs	Newest unit costs
LIFO	Last-in (newest) unit costs	Oldest unit costs

Also notice that the name of the costing method describes the unit costs that are *first out* of inventory. The name doesn't mention the unit costs that are still here in ending inventory.

Weighted-Average Cost Method

The **weighted-average cost method** uses the weighted-average unit cost of the goods available for sale for calculations of both cost of goods sold and ending inventory.

The **weighted-average cost method** requires calculating the weighted-average unit cost of goods available for sale. This weighted-average unit cost is then used to assign a dollar amount to cost of goods sold and to ending inventory. The weighted-average unit cost of goods available for sale is computed as shown in Steps 1*a* and 1*b* and in Exhibit 8.7.

Step 1a. Determine the number of units and the cost of goods available for sale. Using our example, these would be calculated as follows:

Number of Units	×	Unit Cost	=	Total Cost
2	×	$ 70	=	$140
4	×	$ 80	=	320
1	×	$100	=	100
7		Available for Sale		$560

Step 1b. Calculate the weighted-average cost per unit, as follows:

This step has the effect of mixing all the unit costs together in the bin as if it were Kool-Aid in a jug. For our example as shown in Exhibit 8.7, this would be calculated as follows:

$$\text{Weighted Average Cost} = \frac{\$560}{7 \text{ Units}} = \$80 \text{ per unit}$$

Step 2. Assign the same weighted-average unit cost to cost of goods sold and ending inventory. In our example, this would be calculated as follows:

$$\text{Cost of Goods Sold} = 4 \text{ units} \times \$80 = \$320$$
$$\text{Ending Inventory} = 3 \text{ units} \times \$80 = \$240$$

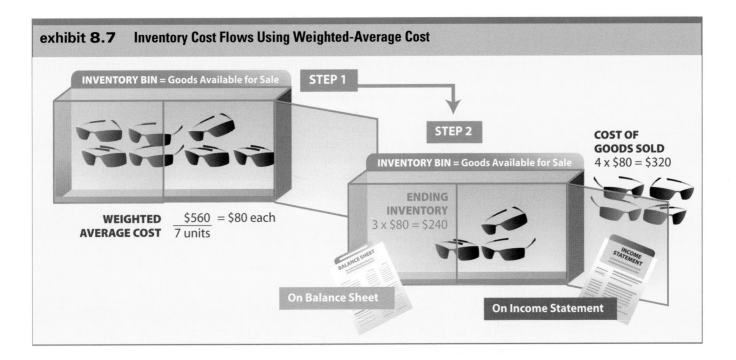

exhibit 8.7   Inventory Cost Flows Using Weighted-Average Cost

Perpetual and Periodic Inventory Systems

In Chapter 6, you learned that most companies use a perpetual inventory system because it provides better control. Calculating cost of goods sold was easy in Chapter 6, because all the goods available for sale cost the same amount. In this chapter, we show you the more realistic situation where the goods available for sale are purchased at different amounts, forcing the company to choose a cost flow assumption. The different costing methods work the same way regardless of whether the company uses a periodic or a perpetual inventory system. The only difference is how often the calculation is made. When a perpetual system is used, the company calculates and records the cost of goods sold every time it makes a sale, which could be many times a day. When a periodic system is used, the company calculates and records cost of goods sold every time it wants to prepare financial statements, which could be only once a year. Imagine making the calculations you just studied every day by hand, which is what companies using perpetual systems did before computers came along, and you can easily understand why periodic systems were so common 25 years ago.

The Oakley example used in this chapter had two purchases during the year, in March and in June, and then one sale, in November. Because no sales were made until all the goods acquired during the year were on hand, our calculations for ending inventory and cost of goods sold are consistent with both a perpetual and a periodic system. This would not be the case if, for example, the company sold the four units sometime between the first and second purchase. Why not? A periodic system calculates cost of goods sold and ending inventory *as if* all sales occurred at the end of the period, even if, in reality, they were dispersed throughout the period. A perpetual system, on the other hand, requires that the cost of goods sold be calculated and recorded every time there is a sale, using the cost of goods available for sale *at that date*. The mechanics of using the different costing methods in a perpetual system are reviewed in the Supplement to this chapter (page 352). You should find out from your instructor (or course outline) whether you are responsible for inventory costing using perpetual systems.

There is another key difference between perpetual and periodic systems, and it relates to the form of the journal entries that are made when goods are purchased and sold. We presented these journal entries in Chapter 6 and, if you've forgotten them, you may want to review the Supplement to that chapter on page 257. Because entries that update *Inventory* and *Cost of Goods Sold* are made on an ongoing basis when a perpetual system is used, the books are always up to date and reflect the results of all transactions. If you want to know the value of inventory on hand, you look at the *Inventory* account in the ledger. Similarly, if you want to know the company's gross profit, you look at the difference between the *Sales* and the *Cost of Goods Sold* accounts. On the other hand, the ledger accounts of companies that use perpetual systems are not up to date. They do not calculate cost of goods sold every time there is a sale. When they sell goods, they make one entry only, the one that records the sale. No entry is made to record the cost of those sales and the corresponding reduction in the Inventory account as a result of those sales. Because of this, the balance in the *Inventory* account is the opening balance for the period, and there is a zero balance in the *Cost of Goods Sold* account. If you want to know the up-to-date values for these accounts, you have to calculate them by determining the number of inventory units on hand, costing them by using one of the cost flow assumptions, and then calculating the cost of goods sold by deducting the cost of inventory on hand from the cost of goods available for sale.

Financial Statement Effects of Inventory Costing Methods

Exhibit 8.8 summarizes the financial statement effects of the FIFO, LIFO, and weighted-average methods in our example. When faced with increasing costs per unit, as in our example, a company that uses FIFO will have the highest income before income taxes ($140) and the highest inventory on the balance sheet ($260). A company that uses LIFO will have the lowest income before income taxes ($100) and the lowest inventory on the balance sheet ($220). Not surprisingly, the weighted-average method, because it is an average, produces a result somewhere between the two: income before income taxes

	FIFO	LIFO	Weighted Average
exhibit 8.8 **Financial Statement Effects of Inventory Costing Methods**			

Cost of Goods Sold Calculation

	FIFO	LIFO	Weighted Average
Beginning inventory	$140	$140	$140
Add: Purchases	420	420	420
Goods available for sale	560	560	560
Subtract: Ending inventory (to balance sheet)	260	220	240
Cost of goods sold (to income statement)	$300	$340	$320
Effect on the Income Statement			
Sales	$720	$720	$720
Cost of goods sold	300	340	320
Gross profit	420	380	400
Other expenses	280	280	280
Income before income taxes	140	100	120
Effect on the Balance Sheet			
Inventory	$260	$220	$240

of $120 and inventory of $240. Remember that these differences are not "real" economic effects, meaning they have no direct effect on cash flow. The cash outflow for purchases is the same, regardless of the method used to split the costs of goods available for sale between the balance sheet and the income statement. However, since income tax is based on the reported income statement figure, there is a secondary cash flow effect when different methods are used.

If a company can choose any of the four inventory costing methods, how does management choose? LIFO gives the lowest income before income taxes, and, for this reason, about 30 per cent of companies in the United States use it, since it results in the lowest income taxes and it is permitted there. However, in Canada, the LIFO method is not permitted for calculating income taxes, and, effective in 2008, is not permitted for accounting purposes either. The FIFO method gives the highest income before income taxes, and managers who are paid a bonus based on reported profits might prefer this method. However, a manager who selects an accounting method that is not optimal for the company, solely to increase his or her own pay, is engaging in questionable behaviour.

ETHICAL ISSUES

It should also be noted that the results presented in Exhibit 8.8 hold only because prices in our example rose during the period. If prices dropped instead, the results would be the reverse. LIFO would give the highest net income and year-end inventory, and FIFO the lowest. Weighted average would still be somewhere in the middle. Given this, a company cannot hope to pick one method and get a constant result over time, so it hardly makes sense to choose a method to try to manipulate the numbers. The bottom line is that a company should choose the method that best portrays its economic performance. In Canada, FIFO and weighted average are both widely used. A recent report showed that 59 per cent of companies used average cost and 36 per cent used FIFO[1].

A common question people ask is: Can a manager choose weighted average one period, FIFO the next, and then back to weighted average, depending on whether unit costs are rising or declining during the period? Because this would make it difficult to

---

[1]*Financial Reporting in Canada, 32nd Edition*, by Byrd, Chen, and Smith, published by the Canadian Institute of Chartered Accountants, Toronto, Canada, 2007.

compare financial results across periods, accounting rules (and tax rules) prevent it. A change in method is allowed only if it will improve the accuracy with which financial results and financial position are measured, and that's likely to happen only once during a company's life. It may be permissible, however, for companies to use different inventory methods for different product lines included in inventory, as long as the methods are used consistently over time.

ADDITIONAL INVENTORY COST FLOW COMPUTATIONS

Now that you've seen how these cost flow assumptions work and that they actually make a difference in the reported results, you could probably use some practice with a more complex example. In the following problem, we will show you how to calculate the cost of ending inventory using the FIFO cost flow assumption, and then how to "force out" the cost of goods sold using the CGS equation. Pay close attention to this example, because you'll be using the same numbers in LIFO computations in the Self-Study Quiz that follows it.

Assume Oakley started buying and selling a new line of products during the year and had the following transactions, which resulted in a total cost of goods available for sale of $5,350. Based on a year-end inventory count, Oakley determined that 200 units were still on hand. The cost of ending inventory is calculated using the first-in, first-out (FIFO) cost flow assumption, and the remainder of the cost of goods available for sale is the cost of goods sold (as indicated by the CGS equation).

COACH'S TIP

Under FIFO, newest costs are assigned to ending inventory (last-in, still here). Because the number of units in ending inventory (200) is greater than the 150 units bought on August 11, we go to the next most recent purchases for unit costs. That is, we assume that 50 of the 150 units bought on June 15 remain in ending inventory.

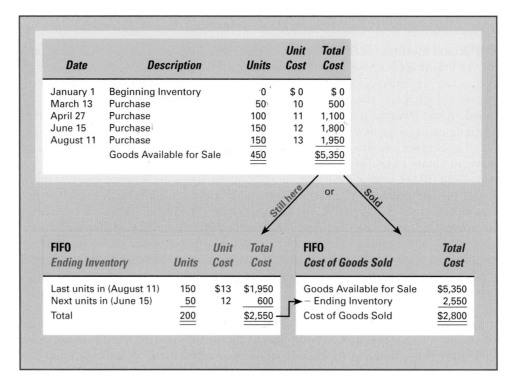

Date	Description	Units	Unit Cost	Total Cost
January 1	Beginning Inventory	0	$ 0	$ 0
March 13	Purchase	50	10	500
April 27	Purchase	100	11	1,100
June 15	Purchase	150	12	1,800
August 11	Purchase	150	13	1,950
	Goods Available for Sale	450		$5,350

Still here   or   Sold

FIFO Ending Inventory	Units	Unit Cost	Total Cost
Last units in (August 11)	150	$13	$1,950
Next units in (June 15)	50	12	600
Total	200		$2,550

FIFO Cost of Goods Sold	Total Cost
Goods Available for Sale	$5,350
– Ending Inventory	2,550
Cost of Goods Sold	$2,800

In the above example, we used the CGS equation to force out the cost of goods sold. This approach will always produce the correct cost of goods sold if the cost of goods available for sale and cost of ending inventory are calculated correctly. There's always the risk, however, that you made a mistake when calculating them. To double-check your calculations, you can calculate the cost of goods sold directly by applying the FIFO cost flow assumption to the 250 units sold, as shown on the next page. Notice that we assume that only 100 units from the June 15 purchase are sold, which complements our earlier assumption that 50 units from this purchase are still sitting in ending inventory.

FIFO Cost of Goods Sold	*Units*	*Unit Cost*	*Total Cost*
First units in (March 13)	50	$10	$ 500
Next units in (April 27)	100	11	1,100
Next units in (June 15)	100	12	1,200
Total	250		$2,800

COACH'S TIP

This direct calculation of cost of goods sold is a great way to prove that the number forced out of the CGS equation is correct.

HOW'S IT GOING? A Self-Study Quiz

Using the information provided on the previous page, compute (1) the LIFO cost of ending inventory and (2) the LIFO cost of goods sold (using the CGS equation).

LIFO Ending Inventory	Units	Unit Cost	Total Cost	LIFO Cost of Goods Sold	Total Cost
First units in				Goods Available for Sale	
Next units in				− Ending Inventory	
Next units in				Cost of Goods Sold	
Total					

After you have finished, check your answers with the solutions in the margin.

REPORTING INVENTORY AT THE LOWER OF COST OR MARKET

You've spent a lot of time learning how to calculate inventory costs using different methods. And it's been time well spent because most of the time inventories are reported at cost, just like the cost principle says. However, you're not quite finished yet, because you need to know what happens when inventory value falls below its recorded cost. The value of inventory can fall below its recorded cost for two reasons: (1) it's easily replaced by identical goods at a lower cost, or (2) it's become outdated or damaged. The first case typically involves high-tech goods like cell phones or Oakley's Plutonite® lenses, which become cheaper to make when companies become more efficient at making them. The second case commonly occurs with fad or seasonal goods, like Oakley's board shorts, when their value drops at the end of the season. In either instance, when the value of inventory falls below its recorded cost, the amount recorded for *Inventory* is written down to its lower market value. This rule is known as reporting inventories at the **lower of cost or market (LCM),** which ensures inventory assets are not reported at more than they're worth. Let's look at how the inventory writedown is determined and recorded.

Although there are different ways that market value can be defined, net realizable value (what the item can be sold for less costs to sell) has recently become the recommended definition in Canada. Assume Oakley's ending inventory includes two items where their net realizable values have recently fallen as a result of lower demand in the market. Each item's net realizable value is used as an estimate of market value, which is then compared with the recorded cost per unit. The lower of these two amounts is called

Lower of cost or market (LCM) is a valuation rule that requires the inventory account to be reduced when the value of the inventory falls to an amount less than its cost.

Item	Quantity	Cost per Item	Net Realizable Value (Market) per Item	LCM per Item	Total Lower of Cost or Market
Plutonite lenses	1,000	$165	$150	$150	1,000 × $150 = $150,000
Unobtainium inlays	400	20	25	20	400 × $20 = 8,000

the lower of cost or market, and it is multiplied by the number of units on hand to calculate the amount that this inventory should be reported at after all adjustments have been made.

Because the market value of the 1,000 Plutonite lenses ($150) is *lower* than the recorded cost ($165), the amount recorded for ending inventory needs to be written down by $15 per unit ($165 − $150), using the following journal entry:

COACH'S TIP

Loss in inventory value is typically combined with selling expenses or cost of goods sold for purposes of external reporting.

dr **Loss in Inventory Value (+E, − SE)**		
[1,000 × ($165 − 150)]	15,000	
cr **Inventory (− A)**		15,000

Assets	=	Liabilities	+	Shareholders' Equity
Inventory −15,000				Loss in Inventory Value (+E) −15,000

Because the net realizable value of the inlays ($25) is still higher than the original cost ($20), no writedown is necessary. The inlays remain on the books at their cost of $20 per unit ($8,000 in total). They are not *increased* in value to the higher net realizable value because GAAP requires that they be reported at the *lower* of cost or market, an example of the conservatism principle.

Most companies explain the use of inventory costing methods and the LCM rule for inventory in Note 1 in their financial statement footnotes. Oakley's is shown in Exhibit 8.9.

The failure to estimate the market value of inventory appropriately is one of the most common types of financial statement errors. You will learn more about how these and other inventory errors can affect the financial statements at the end of this chapter.

---

exhibit 8.9   Sample Inventory Accounting Policy Note

OAKLEY, INC.
Notes to the Consolidated Financial Statements

Note 1—Significant Accounting Policies
Inventories—Inventories are stated at the lower of cost or market. Cost is determined using a first-in, first-out or moving average cost method; market is based upon net realizable value. The Company regularly reviews inventory quantities on hand and writes down any excess or obsolete inventories to net realizable value.

EVALUATE _____
Inventory Management Practices

INTERPRETING CHANGES IN INVENTORY LEVELS

If you see a company's inventory balance increase from $120,000 in one period to $150,000 in the next, is it good news or bad news? It could be good news, if it occurs because management is building up stock in anticipation of increasing sales in the near future. On the other hand, it could be bad news if the buildup is a result of having bought or made a bunch of crusty old inventory that nobody wants. If you work inside the company, it's easy to determine whether the reason for a change in inventory levels is good or bad news: you just talk to the sales managers. But, if you're a typical financial statement user on the outside, how can you tell? The method used by most analysts is called an **inventory turnover** analysis. Does this sound familiar? Yes, it's similar to the total asset turnover and the receivables turnover that you studied in Chapters 5 and 7 respectively, except that this time we're dealing with inventory and cost of goods sold.

Inventory Turnover Analysis

The idea behind an inventory turnover analysis is shown in Exhibit 8.10. As a company buys goods, its inventory balance goes up, and, as it sells these goods, the inventory balance goes down. At the same time, the old inventory is being replaced with new inventory as the company continues buying goods. This process of buying and selling is called inventory turnover, because it is repeated over and over during each accounting period, for each line of products.

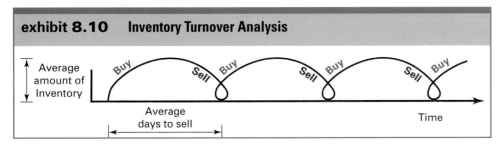

exhibit 8.10   Inventory Turnover Analysis

Analysts assess how many times average inventory has been bought (or made) and sold during the period by calculating the inventory-turnover ratio:

$$\text{Inventory-Turnover Ratio} = \frac{\text{Cost of Goods Sold}}{\text{Average Inventory}} = \frac{\text{Cost of Goods Sold}}{\dfrac{(\text{Beginning Inventory} + \text{Ending Inventory})}{2}}$$

A higher ratio indicates that inventory moves more quickly from purchase (or production) to the ultimate customer, reducing storage and obsolescence costs. Because less money is tied up in inventory, the excess can be invested to earn interest income or reduce borrowing, which reduces interest expense. More efficient purchasing and production techniques, as well as high product demand, cause this ratio to be high. Analysts compare the inventory-turnover ratio from period to period because a sudden decline may mean that a company is facing an unexpected drop in demand for its products or is becoming sloppy in its inventory management.

Some people find it easier to think in terms of the amount of time it takes to sell inventory, rather than the number of times inventory is turned over during a particular year. It's easy to convert the inventory-turnover ratio into the average days to sell. Simply calculate 365 ÷ inventory-turnover ratio and you'll have the average **days to sell:**

$$\text{Days to Sell} = \frac{365}{\text{Inventory-Turnover Ratio}}$$

This measure doesn't say anything different about the company's ability to buy and sell inventory. In terms of Exhibit 8.10, the inventory-turnover ratio counts the number of loops in a given period of time, whereas the days-to-sell ratio tells you the average number of days between loops.

The turnover ratio can be viewed as an efficiency measure, indicating how well the company manages its inventories, and the days to sell as a liquidity measure, indicating how close the inventories are to cash and telling us about the composition of the company's assets. With these two interpretations in mind, we show the turnover ratio in the (b) section in our framework for financial statement analysis, and the days to sell in the (a) section as shown in Exhibit 8.11 on the next page.

Inventory turnover is the process of buying and selling inventory.

COACH'S TIP

Notice three things: (1) The top number in this ratio is Cost of Goods Sold (not sales revenue). This makes the top part of the ratio comparable to the bottom part, which also is based on costs. (2) We use average inventory so that both the numerator and the denominator cover the same period. (3) Beginning inventory for the current year is the same as ending inventory for the prior year.

Days to sell is a measure of the average number of days from the time inventory is bought to the time it is sold. It is calculated by dividing the year-long inventory-turnover ratio into 365. Other names for days to sell are days in inventory and days' sales in inventory.

exhibit 8.11 A Framework for Financial Statement Ratio Analyses

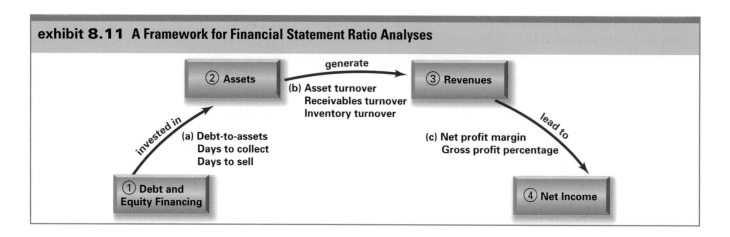

Be on the Alert

Inventory-turnover ratios and the number of days to sell vary by type of company. For merchandisers, inventory turnover refers to the time between buying and selling goods. For manufacturers, it refers to the time required to produce and deliver inventory to customers. Turnover also varies by industry, as shown in Exhibit 8.12, with McDonald's having a turnover ratio of 36.5, which means it takes about ten days to sell its entire food inventory (including the stuff in its freezers). The motorcycles at Harley-Davidson hog more time, as indicated by its inventory-turnover ratio of 14.0, which equates to about 26 days to produce and sell. Oakley's inventory turned over only 2.5 times during the year, which is just once every 146 days. With differences this big, you should compare a company's inventory turnover only with its figures from prior periods or with figures for other companies in the same industry. For practice at calculating and comparing with prior years, calculate Oakley's 2005 turnover and days to sell in the following Self-Study Quiz.

exhibit 8.12 Summary of Inventory Ratio Analyses

Name of Measure	Formula	What It Tells You	McDonald's	Harley-Davidson	OAKLEY	SELF-STUDY QUIZ 2005 OAKLEY
				2006 FISCAL YEAR		
a. Inventory turnover	$\dfrac{\text{Cost of Goods Sold}}{\text{Average Inventory}}$	• The number of times inventory turns over	36.5 times	14.0 times	$\dfrac{349{,}114}{(155{,}377 + 119{,}035)/2}$ = 2.5 times	
		• A higher ratio means faster turnover.				
b. Days to collect	$\dfrac{365}{\text{Inventory Turnover}}$	• Average number of days from purchase to sale	10 days	26 days	$\dfrac{365}{2.5}$ = 146 days	
		• A higher number means a longer time in stock.				

HOW'S IT GOING? A Self-Study Quiz

Compute the ratios for the final column in Exhibit 8.12, using financial statement information in Exhibits 8.2 and 8.3. Did Oakley's inventory turnover improve or decline in 2006, as compared with 2005? When you're finished, check your answers with the solutions in the margin.

RECONSIDER _____
How Inventory Numbers Affect Analyses

THE IMPACT OF INVENTORY COSTING METHODS

As you saw earlier in Exhibit 8.8, the use of different inventory cost flow assumptions can lead to different amounts being reported for inventory and cost of goods sold, *even when the underlying business transactions are identical*. Because inventory and cost of goods sold numbers are the main inputs into the inventory-turnover ratio and average days to sell calculations, these two measures of turnover will be affected by the cost flow assumption used. This is a bit of a problem for you, as a financial statement user, because not all companies use the same cost flow assumption.

As you might expect, the accounting rule makers who develop GAAP knew that, by allowing companies to choose alternative cost flow assumptions, they would run the risk that financial statements wouldn't be comparable across companies. To alert readers to this possibility, the company must state in the notes to its financial statements the method it has used. In the United States, where LIFO is commonly used, accounting rules require that any company that chooses to use LIFO must report in its notes what its inventory balance would have been had it used FIFO, because the differences between LIFO and FIFO can be large, particularly if the company has been around for a long time. These differences can have similarly large effects when inventory numbers are used in analyses, such as the inventory-turnover ratio. The lesson here for now is that the onus is on users to read the notes and, when analyzing a company's inventory or cost of goods sold numbers, you should compare that company only with its own results in prior periods or with another company that uses the same cost flow assumption.

THE IMPACT OF ERRORS IN ENDING INVENTORY

You saw earlier in this chapter that the failure to apply the LCM rule correctly to ending inventory is considered an error. Other errors can occur when inappropriate quantities or unit costs are used in calculating inventory cost. Regardless of the reason, errors in inventory can significantly affect both the balance sheet and the income statement. As the cost of goods sold equation indicates, a direct relationship exists between ending inventory and cost of goods sold because items not in the ending inventory are assumed to have been sold. Thus, any errors in ending inventory will affect the balance sheet (current assets) and the income statement (cost of goods sold, gross profit, and net income). The effects of inventory errors are felt in more than one year because the ending inventory for one year becomes the beginning inventory for the next year. To determine the effects of inventory errors on the financial statements in both the current year and the following year, use the cost of goods sold equation. For example, let's assume that ending inventory was overstated by $10,000 because of an error that was not discovered until the following year. This would have the following effects in the current year:

Current Year	
Beginning inventory	**Accurate**
+ Purchases of merchandise during the year	**Accurate**
− Ending inventory	**Overstated $10,000**
= Cost of goods sold	**Understated $10,000**

POINT OF INTEREST

Deere Company, the American maker of John Deere farm, lawn, and manufacturing equipment, had a difference of over U.S.$1 billion between FIFO and LIFO cost of its 2005 inventory. Inventory valued at FIFO was more than 1.5 times what it was using LIFO.

POINT OF INTEREST

Greeting card maker Gibson Greetings overstated its net income one year by 20 per cent because one of its divisions had overstated its ending inventory for the year.

Because cost of goods sold was understated, gross profit and income before income taxes would be overstated by $10,000 in the current year. (Net income would be overstated as well, although the effects would be offset somewhat by overstated income tax expense.)

The current year's ending inventory becomes next year's beginning inventory, so the error above would have the following effects next year (assuming that ending inventory is calculated correctly that year):

Next Year	
Beginning inventory	**Overstated $10,000**
+ Purchases of merchandise during the year	**Accurate**
− Ending inventory	**Accurate**
= Cost of goods sold	**Overstated $10,000**

Because cost of goods sold is overstated, gross profit and income before income taxes would be understated by the same amount in the next year. (Net income would be understated as well, although the effects would be offset somewhat by understated income tax expense.)

Ignoring income taxes, the effects of these errors on net income in each of the two years is shown in Exhibit 8.13. Notice that the cost of goods sold is overstated in the first year and understated in the second year. Over the two years, these errors offset one another. Inventory errors will "self-correct" like this only if ending inventory is accurately calculated at the end of the following year and adjusted to that correct balance.

WHAT'S COMING UP

This chapter completes our look at current assets. Chapter 9 will focus on long-lived assets, which are the assets that allow companies to produce and sell inventory and provide services. You'll see yet again that different accounting methods are allowed—this time when accounting for long-lived assets. So, before you move on to learn about new accounting methods, make sure you review and practice the material covered in this chapter.

exhibit 8.13 Two-Year Income Effects of Inventory Error

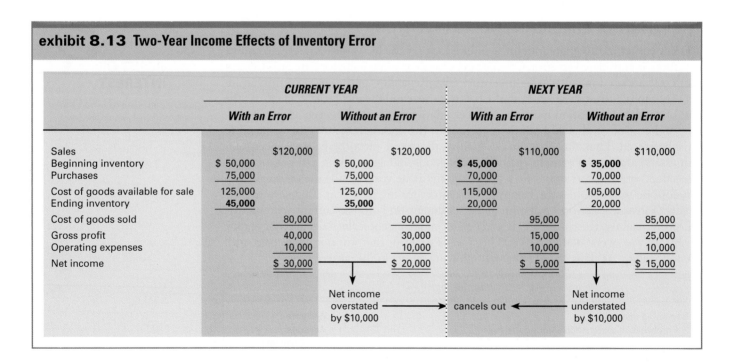

	CURRENT YEAR		NEXT YEAR	
	With an Error	**Without an Error**	**With an Error**	**Without an Error**
Sales	$120,000	$120,000	$110,000	$110,000
Beginning inventory	$ 50,000	$ 50,000	$ 45,000	$ 35,000
Purchases	75,000	75,000	70,000	70,000
Cost of goods available for sale	125,000	125,000	115,000	105,000
Ending inventory	45,000	35,000	20,000	20,000
Cost of goods sold	80,000	90,000	95,000	85,000
Gross profit	40,000	30,000	15,000	25,000
Operating expenses	10,000	10,000	10,000	10,000
Net income	$ 30,000	$ 20,000	$ 5,000	$ 15,000
	Net income overstated by $10,000 →		cancels out ←	Net income understated by $10,000

DEMONSTRATION CASE

Ebert Electronics distributes a number of consumer electronics goods. One product, DVD recorders, has been selected for purposes of this case. Assume that the following summarized transactions were completed during the year ended December 31, 2009, in the order given (assume that all transactions are cash):

	Units	Unit Cost
a. Beginning inventory (January 1)	11	$200
b. New inventory purchases (March 15)	5	209
c. New inventory purchases (July 21)	9	220
d. Sales (selling price, $420)	12	

Required:

1. Compute the following amounts, assuming the application of the FIFO, LIFO, and weighted-average inventory costing methods:

	Ending Inventory		Cost of Goods Sold	
	Units	Dollars	Units	Dollars
FIFO				
LIFO				
Weighted average				

2. Assuming that inventory cost was expected to follow current trends and that Ebert wants to maximize its net income, which method would you suggest that Ebert select to account for these inventory items? Explain your answer.

3. Assuming that other operating expenses were $500 and the income tax rate is 25 per cent, prepare the income statement for the period using the method selected in requirement 2.

4. Compute and interpret the inventory-turnover ratio for the current period using the selected method.

Suggested Solution

1.

	Ending Inventory		Cost of Goods Sold	
	Units	Dollars	Units	Dollars
FIFO	13	$2,816	12	$2,409
LIFO	13	2,618	12	2,607
Weighted average	13	2,717	12	2,508

Computations

Description	Units	Unit Cost	Total Cost
Beginning Inventory	11	$200	$ 2,200
Purchase	5	209	1,045
Purchase	9	220	1,980
Goods Available for Sale	25		$5,225

Still here   or   *Sold*

FIFO Ending Inventory	Units	Unit Cost	Total Cost
Last units in (July 21)	9	$ 220	$1,980
Next units in (March 15)	4	209	836
Total	13		$ 2,816

FIFO Cost of Goods Sold		Total Cost
Goods Available for Sale		$ 5,225
— Ending Inventory		2,816
Cost of Goods Sold		$2,409

Direct CGS Calculations

FIFO:

11 units × $200	=	$2,200
1 unit × $209	=	209
12 units		$2,409

LIFO:

9 units × $220	=	$1,980
3 units × $209	=	627
12 units		$2,607

LIFO Ending Inventory	Units	Unit Cost	Total Cost
First units in (January 1)	11	$200	$2,200
Next units in (March 15)	2	209	418
Total	13		$2,618

LIFO Cost of Goods Sold	Total Cost
Goods Available for Sale	$5,225
— Ending Inventory	2,618
Cost of Goods Sold	$2,607

Weighted Average Computations

$$\text{Average Cost} = \frac{\$5,225}{25 \text{ Units}} = \$209 \text{ per unit}$$

Ending Inventory = 13 units × $209 = $2,717
Cost of Goods Sold = 12 units × $209 = $2,508

2. FIFO should be selected. Because costs are rising, FIFO produces the lowest cost of goods sold, which means the highest net income. Unfortunately, it also means they will pay the highest income taxes.

3.

EBERT ELECTRONICS **Statement of Income** **Year Ended December 31, 2009**	
Sales (12 × $420)	$5,040
Cost of goods sold	2,409
Gross profit	2,631
Other expenses	500
Income before income taxes	2,131
Income tax expense (25%)	533
Net income	$1,598

4. Inventory-turnover ratio = Cost of Goods Sold ÷ Average Inventory
= $2,409 ÷ [($2,200 + $2,816) ÷ 2 = $2,508]
= .96

The inventory-turnover ratio reflects how many times average inventory was bought and sold during the period. Based on our calculations, Ebert Electronics bought and sold its average inventory a little less than once during the year, meaning its days to sell was 380 days (365 ÷ .96). (This seems pitiful, when you think Best Buy turns over its inventory of electronics, on average, in just 46 days.)

CHAPTER SUMMARY

LO1 **Describe inventory management goals. p. 330**

- Make or buy a sufficient *quantity,* of *quality* and *innovative* products, at the lowest possible *cost.*
- Minimize the costs of obtaining and carrying inventory (purchasing, production, storage, spoilage, theft, obsolescence, and financing), while avoiding stock-outs that mean lost sales revenue and decreases in customer satisfaction.

LO2 **Describe the different types of inventory. p. 330**

- Inventory is initially recorded at cost, which includes all amounts given up to acquire the asset and bring it into a condition and location ready for sale.

- When *raw materials* enter the production process, they become *work in process* inventory, which is further transformed into *finished goods* that are ultimately sold to customers. *Merchandise inventory* is bought in a ready to sell format.

Compute costs using four inventory costing methods. p. 334   LO3

- Four methods have developed over the years to allocate the cost of inventory available for sale between goods that are sold and goods that remain on hand at the end of the accounting period.

- Specific identification assigns costs to ending inventory and cost of goods sold by tracking and identifying each specific item of inventory.

- Under FIFO, the costs first in are assigned to cost of goods sold, and the costs last in (most recent) are assigned to the inventory that is still on hand in ending inventory.

- Under LIFO, the costs last in are assigned to cost of goods sold, and the costs first in (oldest) are assigned to the inventory that is still on hand in ending inventory.

- Under weighted-average cost, the weighted-average cost per unit of inventory is assigned equally to goods sold and those still on hand in ending inventory.

(Supplement A) Compute costs using a perpetual inventory system. p. 352   LO4

- A company using a perpetual inventory system calculates its cost of goods sold every time goods are sold, based on the costs of the goods available for sale on that day.

Explain why inventory is reported at the lower of cost or market. p. 343   LO5

- The accounting concept of conservatism requires that, when the value of an asset like inventory is uncertain, it should be reported at the lowest value expected to be recovered.

Compute and interpret the inventory-turnover ratio. p. 344   LO6

- The inventory-turnover ratio measures the efficiency of inventory management. It shows how many times average inventory was produced and sold during the period. The inventory-turnover ratio is calculated by dividing Cost of Goods Sold by Average Inventory. It can be divided into 365 to determine the average number of days to sell inventory.

Explain how accounting methods affect evaluations of inventory management. p. 347   LO7

- To help financial statement users compare the inventory levels and ratios of companies that use different inventory cost flow assumptions, accounting rules require that a company disclose which method it uses in the notes to its financial statements.

Compute the effects of inventory errors. p. 348   LO8

- Errors in ending inventory affect the balance sheet (current assets) and the income statement (cost of goods sold, gross profit, and net income).

- The effects of inventory errors are felt in more than one year because the ending inventory for one year becomes the beginning inventory for the next year.

FINANCIAL STATEMENT ANALYSIS TIPS

To determine how frequently inventory turns over during the period, calculate the inventory-turnover ratio:

$$\text{Inventory-Turnover Ratio} = \frac{\text{Cost of Goods Sold}}{\text{Average Inventory}} = \frac{\text{Cost of Goods Sold}}{\frac{(\text{Beginning Inventory} + \text{Ending Inventory})}{2}}$$

Calculate the following to express the annual inventory-turnover ratio in terms of number of days to sell:

$$\text{Days to Sell} = \frac{365}{\text{Inventory-Turnover Ratio}}$$

KEY TERMS TO KNOW

Consignment Inventory
  p. 332
Cost of Goods Sold (CGS)
  Equation p. 333
Days to Sell p. 345
First-In, First-Out (FIFO)
  p. 336
FOB destination p. 332
FOB shipping point p. 332

Goods Available for Sale
  p. 333
Goods in Transit
  p. 332
Inventory p. 330
Inventory Turnover p. 345
Last-In, First-Out (LIFO)
  p. 337

Lower of Cost or Market
  (LCM) p. 343
Materiality p. 331
Specific Identification
  Method p. 336
Weighted-Average
  Cost Method p. 338

SUPPLEMENT A: APPLYING FIFO, LIFO, AND WEIGHTED-AVERAGE IN A PERPETUAL INVENTORY SYSTEM

In this supplement, we show how to apply FIFO, LIFO, and weighted-average cost methods to calculate cost of goods sold and cost of ending inventory on a perpetual basis. You will see that this can be a daunting task. The good news is that, in the real world, these detailed calculations are done by computers, not manually. The mechanics are presented here so that you understand what the computers are doing and why the costing methods applied to perpetual systems result in different numbers than when they are applied to periodic systems.

Assume that one of Oakley's retailers experienced the following:

Jan.	1	Beginning inventory: Two units of Wisdom snow goggles at $70 each
March 12		Purchased four units of Wisdom snow goggles at $80 each.
April 27		Sold four units of Wisdom snow goggles for $180 each.
June 9		Purchased one unit of Wisdom snow goggles at $100.

Note that this example is identical to the one presented in the body of this chapter, except for one important difference. The example in the chapter assumes that the four units are sold on November 5 after all purchases have been made. In the current example, the units are sold (and must be recorded under the perpetual system) on April 27 before the June 9 purchase is made and recorded. This small difference changes the cost of goods sold and ending inventory calculations because, at the time of the sale, the goggles last in were acquired on March 12 at $80 each, which excludes the unit purchased on June 9 at $100. Because this purchase occurs after the cost of goods sold is recorded in the perpetual system, it is included in the cost of inventory still on hand at the end of the period. These perpetual cost flows are illustrated in Exhibit 8A.1.

Remember that, if this company were using the periodic system, we would assume that the sales took place at the end of the period, even though they actually took place in April. We would end up with exactly the same numbers as we did in the body of the chapter; therefore, the resulting numbers from the chapter have been added to the bottom of the Exhibit to represent the results of using the periodic system. This will allow you to compare these periodic results with the results of using the perpetual system in the upper part of the Exhibit.

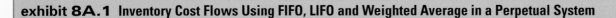

exhibit 8A.1 **Inventory Cost Flows Using FIFO, LIFO and Weighted Average in a Perpetual System**

		FIFO		LIFO		Weighted Average	
		CGS	End. Inv.	CGS	End. Inv.	CGS.	End. Inv.
Beginning Inventory	$2 \times 70 = 140$	$2 \times 70 = 140$			$2 \times 70 = 140$		
+ March 12 Purchase	$4 \times 80 = 320$	$2 \times 80 = 160$	$2 \times 80 = 160$	$4 \times 80 = 320$			
= Goods Available for Sale 6	460						
– April 27 Sale	(4)?					$4 \times \left(\dfrac{460}{6}\right) = 307$	$2 \times \left(\dfrac{460}{6}\right) = 153$
+ June 9 Purchase	$1 \times 100 = 100$		$1 \times 100 = 100$		$1 \times 100 = 100$		$1 \times 100 = 100$
= Ending Inventory 3	?						
Perpetual system:							
Cost of Goods Sold		$300		$320		$307	
Ending Inventory			$260		$240		$253
Periodic system (From body of chapter):							
Cost of Goods Sold		$300		$340		$320	
Ending Inventory			$260		$220		$240

*These numbers result from using the periodic system, regardless of when the sales take place during the year, as well as from using the perpetual system if all the sales were made after June 9.

Look over Exhibit 8A.1 carefully. Pay attention not only to the mechanics of the calculations, but also to how the different methods affect the balance sheet and the income statement numbers. In particular, you should note the following:

- There is no difference between the supplement (perpetual) and the chapter (periodic) numbers for cost of goods sold and ending inventory under the FIFO method. This will always hold true.
- For both the LIFO and weighted-average methods, there are differences between the supplement (perpetual) and chapter (periodic) numbers. The perpetual cost of goods sold is lower than the periodic cost of goods sold. This will always hold true when prices are rising, as they are in this example.
- FIFO has the lowest cost of goods sold and the highest ending inventory; LIFO has the highest cost of goods sold and the lowest ending inventory; and the weighted-average numbers are somewhere in the middle. This is true for both the periodic and perpetual systems, but the differences are larger with the periodic system. This will hold true as long as prices rise steadily throughout the year.

Three other points that are not obvious from Exhibit 8A.1 are:

- The ending inventory calculated on June 9 becomes the beginning inventory for the next round of costing that takes place.
- The faster the inventory turns over (the less it sits on the shelf), the more often the perpetual calculations will be made, and the larger the differences will be between the periodic and perpetual numbers.
- The faster the inventory turns over, the more often the perpetual calculations will be made and the smaller the differences will be across the three costing methods.

_____ **FOR YOUR PRACTICE**

QUESTIONS

1. What are four goals of inventory management?
2. Describe the specific types of inventory reported by merchandisers and manufacturers.
3. Explain how the concept of materiality is applied to inventory reporting.
4. If a Regina-based company ships goods on September 30 to a customer in Australia with sales terms FOB destination, does the Regina-based company include the inventory or the sale in its September financial statements?

5. Define *goods available for sale*. How does it differ from cost of goods sold?

6. Define *beginning inventory* and *ending inventory*.

7. This chapter discussed four inventory costing methods. List the four methods and briefly explain each.

8. Explain how income can be manipulated when the specific identification inventory costing method is used for identical units of inventory.

9. Contrast the effects of LIFO versus FIFO on ending inventory when (*a*) costs are rising and (*b*) costs are falling.

10. Contrast the income statement effect of LIFO versus FIFO (on cost of goods sold and gross profit) when (*a*) costs are rising and (*b*) costs are falling.

11. Explain briefly the application of the LCM concept to ending inventory. Describe its effect on the balance sheet and income statement when market is lower than cost.

12. (Supplement A) Distinguish perpetual inventory systems from periodic inventory systems by describing when and how cost of goods sold is calculated.

13. Explain why an error in ending inventory in one period affects the following period.

MULTIPLE CHOICE

Select the one alternative that best answers the question or completes the sentence.

1. How many of the following statements are true regarding *Cost of Goods Sold?*
   - Cost of goods sold represents the cost that a company incurred to purchase or produce inventory in the current period.
   - Cost of goods sold is an expense on the income statement.
   - Cost of goods sold is affected by the inventory method selected by a company (FIFO, LIFO, etc.).

   a. None   *c.* Two
   b. One   *d.* Three

2. The inventory costing method selected by a company can affect:
   a. The balance sheet
   b. The income statement
   c. The statement of retained earnings
   d. All of the above

3. Which of the following is not a name for a specific type of inventory?
   a. Finished goods
   b. Merchandise inventory
   c. Raw materials
   d. Goods available for sale

4. Each period, the cost of goods available for sale is allocated between:
   a. Assets and liabilities
   b. Assets and expenses
   c. Assets and revenues
   d. Expenses and liabilities

5. A Montreal bridal dress designer that makes high-end custom wedding dresses and needs to know the exact cost of each dress most likely uses which inventory costing method?
   a. FIFO   *c.* Weighted average
   b. LIFO   *d.* Specific identification

6. If costs are rising, which of the following will be true?
   a. The cost of goods sold will be greater if LIFO is used rather than weighted average.
   b. The cost of ending inventory will be greater if FIFO is used rather than LIFO.
   c. The gross profit will be greater if FIFO is used rather than LIFO.
   d. All of the above are true.

7. Which inventory method provides a better matching of current costs with sales revenue on the income statement but also results in older values being reported for inventory on the balance sheet?
   a. FIFO   *c.* LIFO
   b. Weighted average   *d.* Specific identification

8. How many of the following regarding the *lower of cost or market* rule for inventory are true?
   - The lower of cost or market rule is an example of the historical cost principle.
   - When the market value of inventory drops below the cost shown in the financial records, net income is reduced.

- • When the market value of inventory drops below the cost shown in the financial
    records, total assets are reduced.
    a. None   c. Two
    b. One   d. Three

9. An increasing inventory-turnover ratio:
    a. Indicates a longer time span between the ordering and receiving of inventory
    b. Indicates a shorter time span between the ordering and receiving of inventory
    c. Indicates a shorter time span between the purchase and sale of inventory
    d. Indicates a longer time span between the purchase and sale of inventory

10. Which of the following is true regarding American companies that report their inventories
    on a LIFO basis?
    a. They will always have a higher income tax expense.
    b. They also must report the cost of ending inventory on a FIFO basis.
    c. Both of the above
    d. None of the above

11. Assume the folowing for a company that uses FIFO costing: opening inventory—24 units at
    $10 each; purchase #1—15 units at $11 each; purchase #2—20 units at $12 each. If 35 units
    were sold during the period, what would be the company's cost of goods sold for the period?
    a. $350
    b. $361
    c. $405
    d. None of the above

12. Which of the following is true for a company that overstates its ending inventory in 2007?
    a. 2007 net income is overstated.
    b. 2006 net income is understated.
    c. 2008 net income is overstated.
    d. 2006 net income is overstated.

MINI-EXERCISES

M8-1 Items Included in Inventory   LO2

Explain whether the following items should be included in the inventory of The Knot, a company
that arranges and supplies wedding services for couples and wedding consultants.

    a. Goods are being held by The Knot on consignment from The Bridal Shoppe.
    b. Goods in transit to Wildwood Bridal Consultants, sold by The Knot FOB shipping
        point
    c. Goods in transit to The Knot, purchased by The Knot FOB shipping point

M8-2 Matching Inventory Items to Type of Business   LO2

Match the type of inventory with the type of business by placing check marks in the applicable
columns:

	Type of Business	
Type of Inventory	**Merchandising**	**Manufacturing**
Merchandise Finished goods Work in process Raw materials		

M8-3 Inferring Purchases Using the Cost of Goods Sold Equation   LO2

LensCrafters pioneered one-stop shopping for vision care and eyewear in 1983. It now has almost
900 locations across Canada, the United States, and Puerto Rico. It was acquired by the Italian
eyewear giant Luxottica in 1995, the same company that bought Oakley in 2007. In its annual
report for the year ended December 31, 2006, Luxottica reported cost of goods sold of € 1,426
million, ending inventory for the current year of € 401 million, and ending inventory for the
previous year of € 370 million. Is it possible to develop a reasonable estimate of the merchandise
purchases for the year? If so, prepare the estimate. If not, explain why.

LO3   **M8-4 Matching Financial Statement Effects to Inventory Costing Methods**

Complete the following table by indicating which inventory costing method (FIFO or LIFO) would lead to the effects noted in the rows, for each of the circumstances described in the columns.

	1. Rising Costs	*2. Declining Costs*
a. Highest net income		
b. Highest ending inventory		

LO3   **M8-5 Matching Inventory Costing Method Choices to Company Circumstances**

Indicate whether a company interested in minimizing its income before income taxes should choose the FIFO or LIFO inventory costing method under each of the following circumstances.

a.   Rising costs   _____
b.   Declining costs   _____

LO3   **M8-6 Calculating Cost of Goods Sold and Ending Inventory under Periodic FIFO, LIFO, and Weighted Average**

Using the following information, calculate sales, cost of goods sold, and gross profit under the (*a*) FIFO, (*b*) LIFO, and (*c*) weighted-average cost flow assumptions. Assume that a periodic inventory system is used.

July   1   Beginning inventory: 100 units at $10 each

July 13   Purchase: 500 units at $13 each

July 25   Sold 200 units for $15 each.

July 31   Ending inventory 400 units.

LO3   **M8-7 Calculating Cost of Goods Sold and Ending Inventory under Periodic FIFO, LIFO, and Weighted Average**

Using the following information, calculate cost of goods sold and ending inventory under the (*a*) FIFO, (*b*) LIFO, and (*c*) weighted-average cost flow assumptions. Assume that a periodic inventory system is used.

July   1   Beginning inventory: 2,000 units at $20 each

July   5   Sold 1,000 units.

July 13   Purchased 6,000 units at $22 each.

July 17   Sold 3,000 units.

July 25   Purchased 8,000 units at $25 each.

July 27   Sold 5,000 units.

COACH'S TIP

When fewer units are sold than are in ending inventory, it's faster to calculate the cost of goods sold directly, and use the CGS equation to force out the cost of ending inventory.

LO3   **M8-8 Calculating Cost of Goods Sold and Ending Inventory under Periodic FIFO, LIFO, and Weighted Average**

In its first month of operations, Reading for Seniors opened a new bookstore and bought merchandise in the following order: (1) 200 units at $6 on January 1, (2) 300 units at $7 on January 8, and (3) 500 units at $8 on January 29. Assuming 600 units are on hand at the end of the month, calculate the cost of goods sold and ending inventory on January 31 under the (*a*) FIFO, (*b*) LIFO, and (*c*) weighted-average cost flow assumptions. Assume a periodic inventory system is used.

LO5   **M8-9 Reporting Inventory under Lower of Cost or Market**

The Jewel Fool had the following inventory items on hand at the end of the year.

	Quantity	*Cost per Item*	*Market Value per Item*
Necklaces	50	$75	$70
Bracelets	25	60	50

Determine the lower of cost or market per unit, and the total amount that should be reported on the balance sheet for each item of inventory.

M8-10 Determining the Effects of Inventory Management Changes on the Inventory-Turnover Ratio

LO6

Indicate the most likely effect of the following changes in inventory management on the inventory-turnover ratio (+ for increase, − for decrease, and NE for no effect).

___ a. Inventory delivered by suppliers daily (small amounts) instead of weekly (larger amounts).

___ b. Shorten production process from 10 days to 8 days.

___ c. Extend payments for inventory purchases from 15 days to 30 days.

M8-11 Calculating the Inventory-Turnover Ratio and Days to Sell

LO6

Using the data in M8-3, calculate the inventory-turnover ratio and days to sell for Luxxotica. In a recent year, 1-800 Contacts Inc., an American company that sells contact lenses exclusively by phone or via the Internet, reported an inventory-turnover ratio of 63.0. Which company's inventory turnover is faster?

M8-12 Reporting FIFO Ending Inventory in the Financial Statement Notes

LO7

Koss Corporation is an American public company with 95 employees involved exclusively in making and selling stereo headphones. Koss reported ending inventory at June 30, 2007, of $9,923,544 under the LIFO costing method. In Note 1 to its financial statements, Koss reported that its FIFO inventory cost was $1,258,954 higher than LIFO at June 30, 2007. According to accounting rules in the United States, show how Koss would report this in its financial statement notes.

M8-13 (Supplement A) Calculating Cost of Goods Sold and Ending Inventory under Perpetual FIFO and LIFO

LO4

Repeat M8-8 (parts a and b only), except assume Reading for Seniors uses a perpetual inventory system and it sold 400 units between January 9 and January 28.

M8-14 Determining the Financial Statement Effects of Inventory Errors

LO8

Assume the 2009 ending inventory of Shea's Shrimp Shack was understated by $10,000. Explain how this error would affect the amounts reported for cost of goods sold and gross profit for 2009 and 2010.

M8-15 Determining the Financial Statement Effects of Inventory Errors

LO8

Repeat M8-14, except assume that the 2009 ending inventory was *over*stated by $100,000.

EXERCISES

E8-1 Inferring Missing Amounts Based on Income Statement Relationships

LO3

Supply the missing dollar amounts for the 2009 income statement of Lewis Retailers for each of the following independent cases:

Cases	Sales Revenue	Beginning Inventory	Purchases	Total Available	Ending Inventory	Cost of Goods Sold	Gross Profit	Operating Expenses	Operating Income or (Loss)
A	$ 650	$100	$700	$?	$500	$?	$?	$200	$?
B	900	200	800	?	?	?	?	150	0
C	?	150	?	?	300	200	400	100	?
D	800	?	600	?	250	?	?	250	100
E	1,000	?	900	1,100	?	?	500	?	(50)

E8-2 Inferring Merchandise Purchases

LO3

The Hockey Company is the exclusive equipment supplier to the National Hockey League. Assume that you are employed as a stock analyst and your boss has just completed a review of the Hockey Company's annual report. She provided you with her notes, but they are missing some information that you need. Her notes show that the ending inventory for The Hockey Company in the current year was $49,500, and in the previous year was $44,400. Net sales for the current year were $239,900. Gross profit was $107,700, and net income was $17,000 (all numbers in thousands). For your analysis, you determine that you need to know the amount of purchases for the year and cost of goods sold.

Required:

Do you need to ask your boss for her copy of the annual report, or can you develop the information from her notes? Explain and show calculations.

LO3   **E8-3 Calculating Cost of Ending Inventory and Cost of Goods Sold under Periodic FIFO, LIFO, and Weighted Average**

Assume Oahu Kiki's uses a periodic inventory system, which shows the following for the month of January, when it sold 120 units.

	Date	Units	Unit Cost	Total Cost
Beginning Inventory	January 1	60	$8	$ 480
Purchase	January 15	190	9	1,710
Purchase	January 24	100	11	1,100
Total				$3,290

Required:

1. Calculate the cost of ending inventory, using the (*a*) FIFO, (*b*) LIFO, and (*c*) weighted-average cost methods.
2. Given your answer to requirement 1, use the cost of goods sold equation to force out the cost of goods sold under (*a*) FIFO, (*b*) LIFO, and (*c*) weighted-average cost methods.
3. Double-check your answers to requirement 2 by directly calculating the cost of the 120 units sold under the (*a*) FIFO, (*b*) LIFO, and (*c*) weighted-average cost methods.

LO3   **E8-4 Analyzing and Interpreting the Financial Statement Effects of FIFO, LIFO, and Weighted Average**

Lunar Company is a Canadian company using a periodic inventory system. At the end of the annual accounting period, December 31, 2009, the accounting records provided the following information:

Transactions	Units	Unit Cost
a. Inventory, December 31, 2008	3,000	$12
For the year 2009:		
b. Purchase, April 11	9,000	10
c. Purchase, June 1	8,000	13
d. Sale, May 1 (sold for $40 per unit)	5,000	
e. Sale, July 3 (sold for $40 per unit)	6,000	
f. Operating expenses (excluding income tax expense), $195,000		

Required:

1. Compute the cost of goods sold under (*a*) FIFO, (*b*) LIFO, and (*c*) weighted average.
2. Prepare an income statement that shows 2009 amounts for the FIFO method in one column, the LIFO method in another column, and the weighted average method in a final column. Include the following line-items in the income statement: sales, cost of goods sold, gross profit, operating expenses, and operating income.
3. Compare the operating income and the ending inventory amounts that would be reported under the three methods. Explain the similarities and differences.
4. Should Lunar choose LIFO inventory costing to reduce their income taxes? Explain.

LO3   **E8-5 Analyzing and Interpreting the Financial Statement Effects of FIFO, LIFO, and Weighted Average**

Scoresby Inc. uses a periodic inventory system. At the end of the annual accounting period, December 31, 2009, the accounting records provided the following information:

Transactions	Units	Unit Cost
a. Inventory, December 31, 2008	6,000	$8
For the year 2009:		
b. Purchase, March 5	19,000	9
c. Purchase, September 19	10,000	11
d. Sale, April 15 (sold for $29 per unit)	8,000	
e. Sale, October 31 (sold for $31 per unit)	16,000	
f. Operating expenses (excluding income tax expense), $500,000		

Required:

1. Compute the cost of goods sold under (*a*) FIFO, (*b*) LIFO, and (*c*) weighted average.
2. Prepare an income statement that shows 2009 amounts for the FIFO method in one column, the LIFO method in another column, and the weighted-average method in a final column. Include the following line-items in the income statement: sales, cost of goods sold, gross profit, operating expenses, and operating income.
3. Compare the operating income and the ending inventory amounts that would be reported under the two methods. Explain the similarities and differences.
4. Which inventory costing method may be preferred by Scoresby if management receives a bonus based on profit? Explain.

E8-6 Evaluating the Effects of Inventory Methods on Operating Income, Income Taxes, and Net Income

Courtney Company uses a periodic inventory system. Data for 2009: beginning merchandise inventory (December 31, 2008), 2,000 units at $35; purchases, 8,000 units at $38; operating expenses (excluding income taxes), $142,000; ending inventory per physical count at December 31, 2009, 1,800 units; sales price per unit, $70; and average income tax rate, 30 per cent.

Required:

1. Prepare income statements under the FIFO, LIFO, and weighted-average costing methods. Use the format below.
2. Between FIFO and weighted average, which method is preferable in terms of (*a*) maximizing operating income or (*b*) minimizing income taxes? Explain.
3. What would be your answer to requirement 2 if costs were falling? Explain.

| | | Inventory Costing Method | | |
Income Statement	Units	FIFO	LIFO	Weighted Average
Sales revenue	___	$___	$___	$___
Cost of goods sold				
Beginning inventory	___	___	___	___
Purchases	___	___	___	___
Goods available for sale	___	___	___	___
Ending inventory	___	___	___	___
Cost of goods sold	___	___	___	___
Gross profit		___	___	___
Operating expenses		___	___	___
Operating income		___	___	___
Income tax expense		___	___	___
Net income		___	___	___

E8-7 Evaluating the Effects of Inventory Methods on Operating Income, Income Taxes, and Net Income

Following is partial information for the income statement of Timber Company under three different inventory costing methods, assuming the use of a periodic inventory system:

	FIFO	LIFO	Weighted Average
Sales ($50 per unit)			
Cost of goods sold			
Beginning inventory (330 units)	$11,220	$11,220	$11,220
Purchases (475 units)	17,100	17,100	17,100
Goods available for sale			
Ending inventory (510 units)			
Cost of goods sold			
Expenses	1,600	1,600	1,600
Income before income taxes			

Required:

1. Compute cost of goods sold under the FIFO, LIFO, and weighted-average inventory costing methods.

2. Prepare an income statement (up to income before income taxes) that compares the three methods.

3. Rank the three methods in order of (a) highest income before income taxes and (b) highest total assets.

LO3

E8-8 Choosing LIFO versus FIFO When Costs Are Rising and Falling

Use the following information to complete this exercise: sales, 500 units for $12,500; beginning inventory, 300 units; purchases, 400 units; ending inventory, 200 units; and operating expenses, $4,000. Begin by setting up the following table, and then complete the requirements that follow.

	Costs Rising		Costs Falling	
	Situation A	Situation B	Situation C	Situation D
Income Statement	**FIFO**	**LIFO**	**FIFO**	**LIFO**
Sales revenue	$12,500	$12,500	$12,500	$12,500
Beginning inventory	3,600			
Purchases	5,200			
Goods available for sale	8,800			
Ending inventory	2,600	____	____	____
Cost of goods sold	6,200	____	____	____
Gross profit	6,300			
Operating expenses	4,000	4,000	4,000	4,000
Operating income	$ 2,300			

Required:

1. Complete the table for each situation. In Situations A and B (costs rising), assume the following: beginning inventory, 300 units at $12 = $3,600; purchases, 400 units at $13 = $5,200. In Situations C and D (costs falling), assume the opposite; that is, beginning inventory, 300 units at $13 = $3,900; purchases, 400 units at $12 = $4,800. Use periodic inventory procedures.

2. Describe the relative effects on operating income as demonstrated by requirement 1 when costs are rising and when costs are falling.

3. Would you recommend FIFO or LIFO, assuming that both are permissible? Explain.

LO5

E8-9 Reporting Inventory at Lower of Cost or Market

Peterson Furniture Designs is preparing the annual financial statements dated December 31, 2009. Ending inventory information about the five major items stocked for regular sale follows:

	Ending Inventory, 2009		
Item	**Quantity on Hand**	**Unit Cost When Acquired (FIFO)**	**Net Realizable Value (Market) at Year-End**
Alligator Armoires	50	$15	$13
Bear Bureaus	75	40	40
Cougar Beds	10	50	52
Dingo Cribs	30	30	30
Elephant Dressers	400	8	6

COACH'S TIP

To apply the LCM rule, set up a table similar to the one shown in this chapter (page 343), with columns for Item, Quantity, Cost per Item, Market per Item, LCM per Item, and Total LCM.

Required:

Compute the amount that should be reported for the 2009 ending inventory, using the LCM rule applied to each item.

LO5

E8-10 Reporting Inventory at Lower of Cost or Market

Sandals Company was formed on January 1, 2009, and is preparing the annual financial statements dated December 31, 2009. Ending inventory information about the four major items stocked for regular sale follows:

	Ending Inventory, 2009		
Product Line	**Quantity on Hand**	**Unit Cost When Acquired (FIFO)**	**Net Realizable Value (Market) at Year-End**
Air Flow	20	$12	$13
Blister Buster	75	40	38
Coolonite	35	55	52
Dudesly	10	30	35

COACH'S TIP

1. See the advice for E8-9.
2. Calculate the writedown by determining the total cost of ending inventory, and comparing it with the LCM calculated in requirement 1.

Required:

1. Compute the amount that should be reported for the 2009 ending inventory using the LCM rule applied to each item.
2. How will the writedown of inventory to lower of cost or market affect the amount of cost of goods sold (or selling expenses) reported for the year ended December 31, 2009?

E8-11 Preparing the Journal Entry to Record Lower of Cost or Market (LCM) Adjustments

LO5

In 2007, TiVo Inc, the California company that sells digital video recorders and had over 4.4 million subscribers at that time, reported that it wrote down excess and slow-moving inventory by approximately $11.2 million, leading to a $17.7 million net loss for its second quarter. The write-down was necessary because of the rapid shift by retailers to newer, high-definition recorders. Show the journal entry that the company would have made to record this adjustment, as well as its effects on the accounting equation.

E8-12 Analyzing and Interpreting the Inventory-Turnover Ratio

LO6

Mega Brands is a major toy manufacturer in Canada. It reported the following amounts in its financial statements (in thousands):

	2006	*2005*	*2004*
Net sales revenue	$547,347	$384,863	$234,581
Cost of sales	328,822	214,668	128,659
Average inventory	111,455	54,203	25,283

Required:

1. Determine the inventory-turnover ratio and average days to sell inventory for 2006, 2005, and 2004.
2. Comment on any trends, and compare the effectiveness of inventory managers at Mega Blocks with inventory managers at its Danish competitor, Lego, where inventory turns over 3.5 times per year (104 days to sell). Both companies use the same inventory costing method (FIFO).

E8-13 Analyzing and Interpreting the Effects of the LIFO/FIFO Choice on Inventory-Turnover Ratio

LO3, LO6

Simple Plan Enterprises uses a periodic inventory system. Its records at the end of January 2009 showed the following:

Inventory, December 31, 2008, using FIFO → 19 Units @ $14 = $266

Inventory, December 31, 2008, using LIFO → 19 Units @ $10 = $190

Transactions	**Units**	**Unit Cost**	**Total Cost**
Purchase, January 9, 2009	25	$15	$375
Purchase, January 20, 2009	50	16	800
Sale, January 11, 2009 (at $38 per unit)	40		
Sale, January 27, 2009 (at $39 per unit)	28		

Required:

Compute the inventory-turnover ratio under the FIFO and LIFO inventory costing methods (show computations).

LO7   **E8-14**   **Analyzing Notes to Adjust Inventory from LIFO to FIFO, and Calculating the Effects on the Inventory-Turnover Ratio and Days to Sell**

The Ford Motor Company uses the LIFO method to determine the cost of most of its inventories, which were reported at a recent year-end as follows:

	Inventory (in $ millions)	
	Current Year	*Previous Year*
Total	$10,271	$10,766

If FIFO were used by the company, inventories would have been $1,009 million higher than reported at the current year-end, and $1,001 million higher than reported the previous year.

Required:

1. Determine whether costs were rising or falling during the year for Ford.
2. Determine the amount that would have been reported for ending inventory in the current year if Ford had used only FIFO.
3. The cost of goods sold reported by Ford for the current year was $144,944 million using LIFO. If Ford had used FIFO, its cost of goods sold would have been $144,952 instead. Calculate the inventory-turnover ratio and days to sell for the current year under LIFO and FIFO, and comment on the significance of the inventory costing methods to these analyses of Ford's inventory.

LO5   **E8-15**   **Reporting Inventory at Lower of Cost or Market**

Hudson's Bay Company (HBC) is Canada's largest department store chain and its oldest corporation. When Martha Stewart, the homemaking diva, was indicted on criminal charges of securities fraud, HBC decided to discontinue the Martha Stewart product line at its Zellers stores, and it wrote down inventory by approximately $7.3 million as a result. Show the journal entry that HBC would have made to record this adjustment, as well as its effects on the accounting equation.

LO4   **E8-16**   **(Supplement A) Calculating Cost of Ending Inventory and Cost of Goods Sold under Perpetual FIFO, LIFO, and Weighted-Average Methods**

Refer to the information in E8-3. Assume Oahu Kiki uses a perpetual inventory system and that its 120 units were sold between January 16 and 23. Calculate the cost of ending inventory and cost of goods sold for the end of January, using the FIFO, LIFO, and weighted-average methods.

LO4   **E8-17**   **(Supplement A) Calculating Cost of Ending Inventory and Cost of Goods Sold under Perpetual FIFO, LIFO, and Weighted-Average Methods**

Refer to the information in E8-4. Assume Lunar uses a perpetual inventory system. Calculate the cost of ending inventory and cost of goods sold for 2009, using the FIFO, LIFO, and weighted-average methods.

LO4   **E8-18**   **(Supplement A) Calculating Cost of Ending Inventory and Cost of Goods Sold under Perpetual FIFO, LIFO, and Weighted-Average Methods**

Refer to the information in E8-5. Assume Scoresby uses a perpetual inventory system. Calculate the cost of ending inventory and cost of goods sold for 2009, using the FIFO, LIFO, and weighted-average methods.

LO8   **E8-19**   **Analyzing and Interpreting the Impact of an Inventory Error**

Demers Corporation prepared the following two income statements (in millions):

	First Quarter 2009		Second Quarter 2009	
Sales revenue		$15,000		$18,000
Cost of goods sold				
Beginning inventory	$ 3,000		$ 4,000	
Purchases	7,000		12,000	
Goods available for sale	10,000		16,000	
Ending inventory	4,000		9,000	
Cost of goods sold		6,000		7,000
Gross profit		9,000		11,000
Operating expenses		5,000		6,000
Operating income		$ 4,000		$ 5,000

During the third quarter, the company's internal auditors discovered that the ending inventory for the first quarter should have been $4,400. The ending inventory for the second quarter was correct.

Required:

1. What effect would the error have on the total operating income for the two quarters combined? Explain.
2. What effect would the error have on the operating income for each of the two quarters? Explain.
3. Prepare a corrected income statement for each quarter.

COACHED PROBLEMS

CP8-1 Analyzing the Effects of Four Alternative Inventory Methods in a Periodic Inventory System

LO3

Scrappers Supplies uses a periodic inventory system. At the end of the annual accounting period, December 31, 2009, the inventory records showed the following:

Transactions	Units	Unit Cost
Beginning inventory, January 1, 2009	400	$30
Transactions during 2009:		
a. Purchase, March 2	600	32
b. Sale, April 1 ($46 each)	(700)	
c. Purchase, June 30	500	36
d. Sale, August 1 ($46 each)	(100)	

COACH'S TIP

Although the purchases and sales are listed in chronological order, in a periodic inventory system the cost of goods sold is determined after all of the purchases have occurred.

Required:

1. Compute the cost of goods available for sale, cost of ending inventory, and cost of goods sold at December 31, 2009, under each of the following inventory costing methods:
   a. Last-in, first-out
   b. Weighted-average cost
   c. First-in, first-out
   d. Specific identification, assuming that the April 1, 2009, sale was selected one-fifth from the beginning inventory and four-fifths from the purchase of March 2, 2009. Assume that the sale of August 1, 2009, was selected from the purchase of June 30, 2009.
2. Of the four methods, which will result in the highest gross profit? Which will result in the lowest inventory on the year-end balance sheet?

LO5

CP8-2 Evaluating the Income Statement and Income Tax Effects of Lower of Cost or Market

Smart Company prepared its annual financial statements dated December 31, 2009. The company used the FIFO inventory costing method, but it failed to apply LCM to the ending inventory. The preliminary 2009 income statement follows:

Sales revenue		$280,000
Cost of goods sold		
Beginning inventory	$ 30,000	
Purchases	182,000	
Goods available for sale	212,000	
Ending inventory (FIFO cost)	44,000	
Cost of goods sold		168,000
Gross profit		112,000
Operating expenses		61,000
Operating income		51,000
Income tax expense (30%)		15,300
Net income		$ 35,700

COACH'S TIP

Inventory writedowns do not affect the cost of goods available for sale. Instead, the effect of the writedown is to reduce ending inventory, which increases cost of goods sold, and then affects other amounts reported lower in the income statement.

Assume that you have been asked to restate the 2009 financial statements to incorporate LCM. You have developed the following data relating to the 2009 ending inventory:

Item	Quantity	Acquisition Cost Per Unit	Acquisition Cost Total	Net Realizable Value (Market)
A	3,000	$3	$ 9,000	$4
B	1,500	4	6,000	2
C	7,000	2	14,000	4
D	3,000	5	15,000	3
			$44,000	

Required:

1. Restate the income statement to reflect LCM valuation of the 2009 ending inventory. Apply LCM on an item-by-item basis and show computations.
2. Compare and explain the LCM effect on each amount that was changed in requirement 1.
3. What is the conceptual basis for applying LCM to merchandise inventories?

LO6

CP8-3 Calculating and Interpreting the Inventory-Turnover Ratio and Days to Sell

Circuit City is a leading retailer of brand-name consumer electronics, personal computers, and entertainment software. The company reported the following amounts in its financial statements (in millions).

	2006	2005
Net sales revenue	$11,598	$10,470
Cost of sales	8,767	7,901
Beginning inventory	1,455	1,517
Ending inventory	1,698	1,455

COACH'S TIP

For requirement 3, set up a table like this:

	FIFO	WA
CGS	H L	H L
Avg. Inv.	H L	H L

For each part of the ratio, circle whether it will be higher (H) or lower (L) in amount under that method. The larger ratio will be the one with H on top and L on the bottom.

Required:

1. Determine the inventory-turnover ratio and average days to sell inventory for 2006 and 2005.
2. Comment on any changes in these measures, and compare the effectiveness of inventory managers at Circuit City with that of inventory managers at Best Buy, where inventory turns over 7.9 times per year (46 days to sell).
3. Circuit City uses the weighted-average cost method to determine the cost of goods sold and ending inventory. In contrast, Best Buy uses the FIFO method. If the cost of electronics merchandise is falling, which of these two costing methods will produce the higher cost of

goods sold? Will this method produce a higher or lower ending inventory cost than the other method? Taken together, which method will suggest a faster inventory turnover?

CP8-4 (Supplement A) Analyzing the Effects of the LIFO Inventory Method in a Perpetual Inventory System

LO4

Using the information in CP8-1, calculate the cost of goods sold and ending inventory for Scrappers Supplies, assuming it uses the LIFO cost method in combination with a perpetual inventory system. Compare these amounts to the periodic LIFO calculations in requirement 1*a* of CP8-1. Does the use of a perpetual inventory system result in a higher or lower cost of goods sold when costs are rising?

COACH'S TIP

In CP8-4, the sale of 700 units on April 1 is assumed, under LIFO, to consist of the 600 units purchased March 2 and 100 units from beginning inventory.

CP8-5 (Supplement A) Analyzing the Effects of the Weighted-Average Inventory Method in a Perpetual Inventory System

LO4

Using the information in CP8-1, calculate the cost of goods sold and ending inventory for Scrappers Supplies, assuming it uses the weighted-average cost method in combination with a perpetual inventory system. Compare these amounts with the periodic weighted-average calculations in requirement 1*b* of CP8-1. Does the use of a perpetual inventory system result in a higher or lower cost of goods sold when costs are rising?

CP8-6 (Supplement A) Analyzing the Effects of the FIFO Inventory Method in a Perpetual Inventory System

LO4

Using the information in CP8-1, calculate the cost of goods sold and ending inventory for Scrappers Supplies, assuming it uses the FIFO cost method in combination with a perpetual inventory system. Compare these amounts with the periodic FIFO calculations in requirement 1*c* of CP8-1. Does the use of a perpetual inventory system result in a higher or lower cost of goods sold when costs are rising?

CP8-7 Analyzing and Interpreting the Effects of Inventory Errors

LO8

Partial income statements for Murphy & Murphy (M & M) reported the following summarized amounts:

	2006	2007	2008	2009
Sales revenue	$50,000	$49,000	$71,000	$58,000
Cost of goods sold	32,500	35,000	43,000	37,000
Gross profit	$17,500	$14,000	$28,000	$21,000

After these amounts were reported, M & M's accountant determined that the inventory on December 31, 2007, was understated by $3,000. The inventory balance on December 31, 2008, was accurately stated.

COACH'S TIP

2. Gross profit percentage is calculated as:
$$\frac{\text{Gross profit}}{\text{Sales revenue}} \times 100\%$$

Required:

1. Restate the income statements to reflect the correct amounts, after fixing the inventory error.
2. Compute the gross profit per centage for each year (*a*) before the correction and (*b*) after the correction. Do the results lend confidence to your corrected amounts? Explain.

CP8-8 Analyzing and Interpreting the Effects of Inventory Errors

LO6, LO8

The following numbers were reported in the financial statements of Cheung Automotive Limited for the years indicated:

	2007	2008	2009
Cost of goods sold	$64,500	$72,000	$68,000
Inventory	17,500	20,000	13,000

After the 2009 audit was completed, Cheung's accountant realized that the inventory on December 31, 2008, was overstated by $3,000. The inventory balance on December 31, 2009, was correctly stated.

COACH'S TIP

1. Don't forget to think about how one number affects subtotals and totals in the financial statement, as well as income taxes, and list these, too.

Required:

1. What numbers on the 2007 to 2009 balance sheets and income statements would be incorrect as a result of this error?

2. Restate the incorrect numbers to reflect the correct amounts.

3. Compute the inventory-turnover ratio and days to sell for 2008 and 2009 (*a*) before the correction and (*b*) after the correction. Do the results lend confidence to your corrected amounts? Explain.

GROUP A PROBLEMS

L03   **PA8-1** **Analyzing the Effects of Four Alternative Inventory Methods in a Periodic Inventory System**

Gladstone Company uses a periodic inventory system. At the end of the annual accounting period, December 31, 2009, the accounting records for the most popular item in inventory showed the following:

Transactions	Units	Unit Cost
Beginning inventory, January 1, 2009	1,800	$2.50
Transactions during 2009:		
a. Purchase, January 30	2,500	3.10
b. Sale, March 14 ($5 each)	(1,450)	
c. Purchase, May 1	1,200	4.00
d. Sale, August 31 ($5 each)	(1,900)	

Required:

1. Compute the amount of goods available for sale, ending inventory, and cost of goods sold at December 31, 2009, under each of the following inventory costing methods:
   a. Last-in, first-out
   b. Weighted-average cost
   c. First-in, first-out
   d. Specific identification, assuming that the March 14, 2009, sale was selected two-fifths from the beginning inventory and three-fifths from the purchase of January 30, 2009. Assume that the sale of August 31, 2009, was selected from the remainder of the beginning inventory, with the balance from the purchase of May 1, 2009.

2. Of the four methods, which will result in the highest gross profit? Which will result in the lowest inventory on the year-end balance sheet?

L05   **PA8-2** **Evaluating the Income Statement and Income Tax Effects of Lower of Cost or Market**

Springer Anderson Gymnastics prepared its annual financial statements dated December 31, 2009. The company used the FIFO inventory costing method, but it failed to apply LCM to the ending inventory. The preliminary 2009 income statement follows:

Sales revenue		$140,000
Cost of goods sold		
Beginning inventory	$ 15,000	
Purchases	91,000	
Goods available for sale	106,000	
Ending inventory (FIFO cost)	22,000	
Cost of goods sold		84,000
Gross profit		56,000
Operating expenses		31,000
Operating income		25,000
Income tax expense (30%)		7,500
Net income		$ 17,500

Assume that you have been asked to restate the 2009 financial statements to incorporate LCM. You have developed the following data relating to the 2009 ending inventory:

| | | Acquisition Cost | | Net Realizable |
Item	Quantity	Per Unit	Total	Value *(Market)*
A	1,500	$3	$ 4,500	$4
B	750	4	3,000	2
C	3,500	2	7,000	4
D	1,500	5	7,500	3
			$22,000	

Required:

1. Restate the income statement to reflect LCM valuation of the 2009 ending inventory. Apply LCM on an item-by-item basis and show computations.
2. Compare and explain the LCM effect on each amount that was changed in requirement 1.
3. What is the conceptual basis for applying LCM to merchandise inventories?

PA8-3 Calculating and Interpreting the Inventory-Turnover Ratio and Days to Sell

LO6

Harman International Industries is a world leading producer of loudspeakers and other electronics products, which are sold under brand names like JBL, Infinity, and Harman/Kardon. The company reported the following amounts in its financial statements (in millions):

	2006	2005
Net sales revenue	$3,248	$3,031
Cost of sales	2,095	1,999
Beginning inventory	312	292
Ending inventory	345	312

Required:

1. Determine the inventory-turnover ratio and average days to sell inventory for 2006 and 2005.
2. Comment on any changes in these measures, and compare the effectiveness of inventory managers at Harman with inventory managers at Boston Acoustics, where inventory turns over 3.7 times per year (99 days to sell). Both companies use the same inventory costing method (FIFO).

PA8-4 Calculating and Interpreting the Inventory-Turnover Ratio and Days to Sell

LO6

The Brazilian company AmBev merged in 2004 with Interbrew to create InBev, the largest brewer in the world. InBev has a collection of more than 200 global beer brands, including Stella Artois, Miller, and Labatt's. The company reported the following amounts in its financial statements (in millions of euros):

	2006	2005
Net sales revenue	€13,308	€11,656
Cost of sales	5,477	5,082
Beginning inventory	929	847
Ending inventory	1,017	929

Required:

1. Determine the inventory-turnover ratio and average days to sell inventory for 2006 and 2005.
2. Comment on any changes in these measures, and compare the effectiveness of inventory managers at InBev to inventory managers at Sleeman, the much smaller Canadian brewer, where inventory turns over 3.0 times per year (121.6 days to sell). (Both InBev and Sleeman use average costing.)

LO4   **PA8-5   (Supplement A) Analyzing the Effects of the LIFO Inventory Method in a Perpetual Inventory System**

Using the information in PA8-1, calculate the cost of goods sold and ending inventory for Gladstone Company, assuming it uses the LIFO cost method in combination with a perpetual inventory system. Compare these amounts with the periodic LIFO calculations in requirement 1*a* of PA8-1. Does the use of a perpetual inventory system result in a higher or lower cost of goods sold when costs are rising?

LO4   **PA8-6   (Supplement A) Analyzing the Effects of the Weighted-Average Inventory Method in a Perpetual Inventory System**

Using the information in PA8-1, calculate the cost of goods sold and ending inventory for Gladstone Company, assuming it uses the weighted-average cost method in combination with a perpetual inventory system. Compare these amounts with the periodic weighted-average calculations in requirement 1*b* of PA8-1. Does the use of a perpetual inventory system result in a higher or lower cost of goods sold when costs are rising?

LO4   **PA8-7   (Supplement A) Analyzing the Effects of the FIFO Inventory Method in a Perpetual Inventory System**

Using the information in PA8-1, calculate the cost of goods sold and ending inventory for Gladstone Company, assuming it uses the FIFO cost method in combination with a perpetual inventory system. Compare these amounts with the periodic FIFO calculations in requirement 1*c* of PA8-1. Does the use of a perpetual inventory system result in a higher or lower cost of goods sold when costs are rising?

LO3, LO4   **PA8-8   (Supplement A) Analyzing the Effects of the Weighted-Average and FIFO Inventory Methods in a Perpetual and a Periodic System**

At the end of 2009, the inventory records for Ito Machinery Limited showed the following annual information for an item that sold at $14 per unit:

Transactions	Units	Unit Cost
Beginning inventory	1,800	$3.00
Purchase, January 30	2,500	4.00
Sale, March 14	(1,450)	
Purchase, May 1	1,200	4.50
Sale, August 31	(1,900)	

Required:

1. Calculate cost of goods sold and ending inventory for this item in 2009, assuming that the company uses:
   a.   Weighted average and a periodic system
   b.   FIFO and a periodic system
   c.   Weighted average and a perpetual system
   d.   FIFO and a perpetual system
2. Of the four methods, which will result in the highest inventory on the year-end balance sheet? Which will result in the lowest net income for the year?

LO8   **PA8-9   Analyzing and Interpreting the Effects of Inventory Errors**

The income statement for Sherwood Company, summarized for a four-year period, shows the following:

	2006	2007	2008	2009
Sales revenue	$2,000,000	$2,400,000	$2,500,000	$3,000,000
Cost of goods sold	1,400,000	1,660,000	1,770,000	2,100,000
Gross profit	$ 600,000	$ 740,000	$ 730,000	$ 900,000

An audit revealed that, in determining these amounts, the ending inventory for 2007 was overstated by $20,000. The inventory balance on December 31, 2008, was accurately stated. The company uses a periodic inventory system.

Required:

1. Restate the income statements to reflect the correct amounts, after fixing the inventory error.

2. Compute the gross profit percentage for each year (*a*) before the correction and (*b*) after the correction. Do the results lend confidence to your corrected amounts? Explain.

PA8-10 Analyzing and Interpreting the Effects of Inventory Errors

LO6, LO8

The following numbers were reported in the financial statements of Desroches Foods Limited for the years indicated:

	2007	2008	2009
Cost of goods sold	$202,000	$196,500	$210,000
Inventory	37,500	28,000	56,000

After the 2009 audit is completed, Desroches's accountant realized that the inventory on December 31, 2008, was understated by $10,000. The inventory balance on December 31, 2009, was correctly stated.

Required:

1. What numbers on the 2007 to 2009 balance sheets and income statements would be incorrect as a result of this error?

2. Restate the incorrect numbers to reflect the correct amounts.

3. Compute the inventory-turnover ratio and days to sell for 2008 and 2009 (*a*) before the correction and (*b*) after the correction. Do the results lend confidence to your corrected amounts? Explain.

GROUP B PROBLEMS

PB8-1 Analyzing the Effects of Four Alternative Inventory Methods in a Periodic Inventory System

LO3

Mojo Industries uses a periodic inventory system. At the end of the annual accounting period, January 31, 2009, the inventory records showed the following for an item that sold at $18 per unit:

Transactions	Units	Total Cost
Inventory, January 1, 2009	500	$2,500
Sale, January 10	(400)	
Purchase, January 12	600	3,600
Sale, January 17	(300)	
Purchase, January 26	160	1,280

Required:

1. Compute the amount of goods available for sale, ending inventory, and cost of goods sold at January 31, 2009, under each of the following inventory costing methods:

   a. Weighted-average cost
   b. First-in, first-out
   c. Last-in, first-out
   d. Specific identification, assuming that the January 10 sale was from the beginning inventory and the January 17 sale was from the January 12 purchase

2. Of the four methods, which will result in the highest gross profit? Which will result in the lowest inventory on the year-end balance sheet?

LO5   **PB8-2 Evaluating the Income Statement and Income Tax Effects of Lower of Cost or Market**

Mondetta Clothing prepared its annual financial statements, dated December 31, 2009. The company used the FIFO inventory costing method, but it failed to apply LCM to the ending inventory. The preliminary 2009 income statement follows:

Sales revenue		$420,000
Cost of goods sold		
Beginning inventory	$45,000	
Purchases	273,000	
Goods available for sale	318,000	
Ending inventory (FIFO cost)	66,000	
Cost of goods sold		252,000
Gross profit		168,000
Operating expenses		93,000
Operating income		75,000
Income tax expense (30%)		22,500
Net income		$ 52,500

Assume that you have been asked to restate the 2009 financial statements to incorporate LCM. You have developed the following data relating to the 2009 ending inventory:

Item	Quantity	Acquisition Cost Per Unit	Acquisition Cost Total	Net Realizable Value (Market)
A	3,000	$4.50	$13,500	$6.00
B	1,500	6.00	9,000	4.00
C	7,000	3.00	21,000	6.00
D	3,000	7.50	22,500	4.50
			$ 66,000	

Required:

1. Restate the income statement to reflect LCM valuation of the 2009 ending inventory. Apply LCM on an item-by-item basis and show computations.
2. Compare and explain the LCM effect on each amount that was changed in requirement 1.
3. What is the conceptual basis for applying LCM to merchandise inventories?

LO6   **PB8-3 Calculating and Interpreting the Inventory-Turnover Ratio and Days to Sell**

Amazon.com reported the following amounts in its financial statements (in millions):

	2006	2005
Net sales revenue	$10,711	$8,490
Cost of sales	8,255	6,451
Beginning inventory	566	480
Ending inventory	877	566

Required:

1. Determine the inventory-turnover ratio and average days to sell inventory for 2006 and 2005.
2. Comment on any changes in these measures, and compare the inventory turnover at Amazon. com with inventory turnover at Borders, where inventory turns over 2.2 times (166 days to sell). Based on your own experience, what's the key difference between Amazon.com and Borders that leads one company's results to be the picture of über-efficiency and the other to seem like a library?

PB8-4 Calculating and Interpreting the Inventory-Turnover Ratio and Days to Sell

LO7

Humpty Dumpty Snack Foods was the leading maker of potato chips in Canada until Frito-Lay expanded its operations here. Humpty Dumpty reported the following amounts in its financial statements (in thousands) just before it went bankrupt :

	Most recent year	Prior year
Net sales revenue	$160,789	$157,869
Cost of sales	106,146	105,971
Beginning inventory	9,015	7,302
Ending inventory	7,697	9,015

Required:

1. Determine the inventory-turnover ratio and average days to sell inventory for both years.
2. Comment on any changes in these measures, and compare the effectiveness of inventory managers at Humpty Dumpty to inventory managers at Sun-Rype, where its inventory of healthy snack foods turns over 5.5 times per year (66 days to sell). (Both companies use the weighted-average cost method to determine the cost of goods sold and ending inventory.)

PB8-5 (Supplement A) Analyzing the Effects of the LIFO Inventory Method in a Perpetual Inventory System

LO4

Using the information in PB8-1, calculate the cost of goods sold and ending inventory for Mojo Industries, assuming it uses the LIFO cost method in combination with a perpetual inventory system. Compare these amounts with the periodic LIFO calculations in requirement 1c of PB8-1. Does the use of a perpetual inventory system result in a higher or lower cost of goods sold when costs are rising?

PB8-6 (Supplement A) Analyzing the Effects of the Weighted-Average Inventory Method in a Perpetual Inventory System

LO4

Using the information in PB8-1, calculate the cost of goods sold and ending inventory for Mojo Industries assuming it uses the weighted-average cost method in combination with a perpetual inventory system. Compare these amounts with the periodic weighted-average calculations in requirement 1a of PB8-1. Does the use of a perpetual inventory system result in a higher or lower cost of goods sold when costs are rising?

PB8-7 (Supplement A) Analyzing the Effects of the FIFO Inventory Method in a Perpetual Inventory System

LO4

Using the information in PB8-1, calculate the cost of goods sold and ending inventory for Mojo Industries assuming it uses the FIFO cost method in combination with a perpetual inventory system. Compare these amounts with the periodic FIFO calculations in requirement 1b of PB8-1. Does the use of a perpetual inventory system result in a higher or lower cost of goods sold when costs are rising?

PB8-8 (Supplement A) Analyzing the Effects of the Weighted-Average and FIFO Inventory Methods in a Perpetual and a Periodic System

LO3, LO4

At the end of 2009, Mojito Beverages Inc.'s inventory records showed the following yearly information for an item that sold at $20 per unit:

Transactions	Units	Total Cost
Beginning inventory	500	$3,000
Sale, January 27	(400)	
Purchase, May 16	600	4,200
Sale, October 20	(300)	
Purchase, December 27	160	1,280

Required:

1. Calculate cost of goods sold and ending inventory for this item in 2009, assuming that the company uses:

    a. Weighted average and a periodic system
    b. FIFO and a periodic system
    c. Weighted average and a perpetual system
    d. FIFO and a perpetual system

2. Of the four methods, which will result in the highest inventory on the year-end balance sheet? Which will result in the lowest net income for the year?

LO8   **PB8-9** **Analyzing and Interpreting the Effects of Inventory Errors**

"Oops" was the song being sung by the accountants at Spears & Cantrell when they announced inventory had been overstated by $30 (million) at the end of the second quarter. The error wasn't discovered and corrected in the company's periodic inventory system until after the end of the third quarter. The following table shows the amounts (in millions) that were originally reported by the company.

	Q1	Q2	Q3
Sales revenue	$3,000	$3,600	$3,750
Cost of goods sold	2,100	2,490	2,655
Gross profit	$ 900	$1,110	$1,095

Required:

1. Restate the income statements to reflect the correct amounts, after fixing the inventory error.

2. Compute the gross profit percentage for each quarter (*a*) before the correction and (*b*) after the correction. Do the results lend confidence to your corrected amounts? Explain.

LO8   **PB8-10** **Analyzing and Interpreting the Effects of Inventory Errors**

The following numbers were reported in the financial statements of Country Comforts Furniture for the years indicated:

	2007	2008	2009
Cost of goods sold	$56,500	$44,500	63,000
Inventory	7,500	6,000	9,500

After the 2009 audit was completed, the accountant realized that the inventory on December 31, 2008, was overstated by $2,500. The inventory balance on December 31, 2009, was correctly stated.

Required:

1. What numbers on the 2007, 2008, and 2009 balance sheets and income statements would be incorrect as a result of this error?
2. Restate the incorrect numbers to reflect the correct amounts.
3. Compute the inventory-turnover ratio and days to sell for 2008 and 2009 (*a*) before the correction and (*b*) after the correction. Do the results lend confidence to your corrected amounts? Explain.

SKILLS DEVELOPMENT CASES

LO2, LO3, LO6, LO7   **S8-1** **Finding Financial Information**

Refer to the financial statements of High Liner in Appendix A at the end of this book, or download the annual report from the *Cases* section of the text's Web site at www.mcgrawhill.ca/college/phillips.

Required:

1. How much inventory does the company hold at the end of the most recent year? Does this represent an increase or decrease in comparison with the prior year?
2. What method(s) does the company use to determine the cost of its inventory? Describe where you found this information.
3. Compute the company's inventory-turnover ratio and days to sell for the most recent year. Are these comparable to McDonald's numbers shown in Exhibit 8.12? What does this analysis suggest to you?

S8-2 Comparing Financial Information

LO2, LO3, LO6, LO7

Refer to the financial statements of Sun-Rype by downloading the annual report from the *Cases* section of the text's Web site at www.mcgrawhill.ca/college/phillips.

Required:

1. Does Sun-Rype hold more or less inventory than High Liner at the end of the most recent year?
2. What method does Sun-Rype use to determine the cost of its inventory? Comment on how this affects comparisons you might make between Sun-Rype's and High Liner's inventory-turnover ratios.
3. Compute Sun-Rype's inventory-turnover ratio for the most recent year, and compare it with High Liner's. What does this analysis suggest to you?

S8-3 Internet-Based Team Research: Examining an Annual Report

LO2–LO7

As a team, select an industry to analyze. Using your Web browser, each team member should acquire the annual report for one publicly traded company in the industry, with each member selecting a different company. (See S1-3 in Chapter 1 for a description of possible resources for these tasks.)

Required:

1. On an individual basis, each team member should write a short report that incorporates the following:
   - *a.* Describe the types of inventory held by the company. Does the company indicate its inventory management goals anywhere in its annual report?
   - *b.* Describe the inventory costing method that is used. Why do you think the company chose this method rather than the other acceptable methods? Do you think its inventory costs are rising or falling?
   - *c.* Calculate the inventory-turnover ratio for the current and prior years, and explain any change between the two years. Since not all Canadian companies disclose this information, make sure you select one that does. (To obtain the beginning inventory number for the prior year, you will need the prior year's annual report.)
   - *d.* Search the annual report for information about the company's approach for applying the LCM rule to inventory. Did the company report the amount of inventory written down during the year?
2. Then, as a team, write a short report comparing and contrasting your companies, using these attributes. Discuss any patterns across the companies that you, as a team, observe. Provide possible explanations for any differences discovered.

TEAM CASE

S8-4 Analyzing Financial Information

LO6

Nortel Networks of Brampton, Ontario, is a telecom giant that provides large-scale communication systems and infrastructures to companies around the world. During the technology boom of the 1990s, Nortel's growth was impressive. Total assets almost tripled from U.S.\$6.8 billion in 1990 to U.S.\$19.7 billion in 1998. Unfortunately for Nortel and many of its customers, the technology sector was in serious trouble by the year 2000. Below are the figures for Nortel's sales, cost of sales, and average inventory (in millions of U.S. dollars) for selected years.

	1998	1999	2000	2001	2002	2003
Sales	17,575	20,558	27,966	18,912	11,022	10,193
Cost of sales	10,050	11,315	15,124	14,616	7,112	5,851
Average inventory	1,726	2,242	3,313	2,708	1,547	1,349

Required:

1. Do the sales figures for Nortel over the period reflect what was happening in the technology sector at that time?

2. Calculate the inventory-turnover ratios and average days to sell inventory for Nortel for the years 1998 to 2003. (Round to one decimal place.)

3. Comment on the trend in these ratios. Do they reflect what was happening in the market for Nortel's products during that period?

4. When a company's customers are in financial difficulty, what inventory valuation issue (other than inventory costing) does the accountant have to think about at year-end?

LO3, LO5   ### S8-5 Ethical Decision Making: A Real-Life Example

Assume that you are on a jury hearing a trial involving a large national drugstore company. Your immediate task is to identify suspicious events in the following evidence that suggest financial fraud may have occurred.

In just seven years, the company grew from 15 to 310 stores, reporting sales of more than $3 billion. Some retail experts believed the company was going to be the next Wal-Mart. The apparent secret to the company's success was its ability to attract customers to its stores by selling items below cost. Then the company would make it easy for customers to buy other items, particularly pharmaceuticals, which earned a high gross profit. This strategy appeared to be working, so the company's top executives built up massive pharmaceutical inventories at its stores, causing total inventory to increase from $11 million to $36 million to $153 million in the last three years. The company hadn't installed a perpetual inventory system, so inventory had to be physically counted at each store to determine the cost of goods sold. To help its auditors verify the accuracy of these inventory counts, top management agreed to close selected stores on the day inventory was counted. All they asked was that they be given advance notice of which stores' inventory counts the auditors were planning to attend, so that the temporary closures could be conveyed to employees and customers at those stores. The external auditors selected four stores to test each year and informed the company several weeks in advance. To further assist the auditors with counting the inventory, top management reduced the inventory levels at the selected stores by shipping some of their goods to other stores that the auditors weren't attending.

After the inventory was counted and its cost was calculated, the company applied the LCM test. On a store-by-store basis, top management compared the unit cost and market value of inventory items, and then prepared journal entries to write down the inventory. Some of the journal entries were large in amount and involved debiting an account called "cookies" and crediting the inventory account. Management reported that the cookies account was used to accumulate the required writedowns for all the company's stores. Just before the financial statements were finalized, the cookies account was emptied by allocating it back to each of the stores. In one instance, $9,999,999.99 was allocated from cookies to a store's account called "accrued inventory."

ETHICAL ISSUES

Required:

Prepare a list that summarizes the pieces of evidence that indicate that fraud might have occurred and, for each item on the list, explain why it contributes to your suspicion.

Epilogue: This case is based on a fraud involving Phar Mor, as described by David Cottrell and Steven Glover in the July 1997 issue of the *CPA Journal*. Phar Mor's management was collectively fined over $1 million, and two top managers received prison sentences ranging from 33 months to 5 years. The company's auditors paid over $300 million in civil judgments for failing to uncover the fraud.

LO3   ### S8-6 Ethical Decision Making: A Mini-Case

David Exler is the CEO of AquaGear Enterprises, an American company that has been making boats in Wellfleet, Massachusetts, for seven years. After many long months of debate with the company's board of directors, David obtained the board's approval to expand into water ski sales. David firmly believed that AquaGear could generate significant profits in this market, despite recent increases in the cost of skis. A board meeting will be held later this month for David to present the financial results for the first quarter of ski sales. As AquaGear's corporate comptroller, you reported to David that the results weren't great. Although sales were better than expected at $330,000 (3,000 units at $110 per unit), the cost of goods sold was $295,000. This left a gross profit of $35,000. David knew this amount wouldn't please the board. Desperate to save the ski division, David asks you to "take another look at the cost calculations to see if there's any way to reduce the cost of goods sold. I know you accountants have different methods for figuring things out, so maybe you can do your magic now when I need it most." You dig out your summary of inventory purchases for the quarter to recheck your calculations, using the LIFO method that has always been used for the company's inventory of boats.

	Date	Units	Unit Cost	Total Cost
Beginning inventory of water skis	January 1	0	—	—
Purchases	January 15	1,500	$ 60	$ 90,000
Purchases	February 18	2,000	90	180,000
Purchases	March 29	2,500	100	250,000

ETHICAL ISSUES

Required:

1. Calculate cost of goods sold using the LIFO method. Does this confirm the statement you made to David about the gross profit earned on water ski sales in the first quarter?

2. Without doing any calculations, is it likely that any alternative inventory costing method will produce a lower cost of goods sold?

3. Calculate cost of goods sold using the FIFO method. Would use of this method solve David's current dilemma?

4. Is it acceptable within GAAP to report the water skis using one inventory costing method and the boats using a different method?

5. Do you see any problems with using the FIFO numbers for purposes of David's meeting with the board?

S8-7 Critical Thinking: Income Manipulation under the LIFO Inventory Method

L03

Mandalay Industries is an international company operating in a country that permits LIFO costing. During the year 2009, the inventory records reflected the following:

	Units	Unit Cost	Total Cost
Beginning inventory	15	$12,000	$180,000
Purchases	40	10,000	400,000
Sales (45 units at $25,000 each)			

Inventory is valued at cost using the LIFO inventory method. On December 28, 2009, the unit cost of the test equipment declined to $8,000. The cost is expected to fall again during the first quarter of next year, but then increase later in the year.

Required:

1. Complete the following income statement summary, assuming LIFO is applied with a periodic inventory system (show computations):

2. Although costs are likely to fall again early next year, Mandalay's management is considering buying 20 additional units on December 31, 2009, at $8,000 each. Redo the income statement (and ending inventory), assuming that this purchase is made on December 31, 2009.

3. How much did operating income change because of the decision to purchase additional units on December 31, 2009? Is there any evidence of deliberate income manipulation? Explain.

Sales revenue	$ _____
Cost of goods sold	_____
Gross profit	_____
Operating expenses	300,000
Operating income	$ _____
Ending inventory	$ _____

S8-8 Calculating and Recording the Effects of Lower of Cost or Market (LCM) on Ending Inventory

L05

Assume that you recently obtained a job in the head office of Perfumania, the specialty retailer of discounted fragrances. Your job is to estimate the amount of writedown required to value inventory at the lower of cost or market. The cost of inventory is calculated using the weighted-average cost method and, at approximately $70 million, it represents the company's biggest and most important asset. Assume that the corporate comptroller asked you to prepare a spreadsheet that can be used to determine the amount of LCM writedown for the current year. The comptroller provides the following hypothetical numbers for you to use in the spreadsheet.

Product Line	Quantity on Hand	Weighted-Average Unit Cost	Replacement Cost (Market) at Year-End
Alfred Sung Shi	80	$22	$20
Animale	75	15	16
Azzaro	50	10	10
Mambo	30	16	17
OP Juice	400	8	7

You realize that you'll need to multiply the quantity of each item by the lower of cost or market per unit, but you can't figure out how to get the spreadsheet to choose the lower number. You e-mailed your friend Billy for help, and here's his reply.

From: BillyTheTutor@yahoo.com
To: Overwhelmed@hotmail.com
Cc:
Subject: Excel Help

So you don't have a sniff about how to pick the lower of cost or market? You can do this several different ways, but the easiest is to use the MIN command. Set up your spreadsheet similar to the table you sent me, and then add two new columns. In the first new column, enter the command "_MIN(costcell, marketcell)" where costcell is the cell containing the cost per unit and marketcell is the cell containing the market value per unit. Next, in the second new column, multiply the quantity by the LCM per unit. Here's a screenshot of what this will probably look like in your spreadsheet.

Be sure to enter a formula to sum down the Total LCM column for all the products so that this grand total can be subtracted from the cost presently recorded in the inventory accounting records to determine the write-down.

COACH'S TIP

To determine the amount of the journal entry in requirement 2, subtract the total LCM from the total cost of the five products (which you'll calculate using data on quantities and unit costs for each product).

	Microsoft Excel - S8-8							
	File Edit View Insert Format Tools Data Window Help Adobe PDF						Type a question for help	
	G5		*fx* =MIN(E5,F5)					
	A	B	C	D	E	F	G	H
1								
2				**Perfumania LCM Spreadsheet**				
3								
4		**Product**		**Quantity**	**Cost**	**Market**	**LCM**	**Total LCM**
5		Alfred Sung Shi		80	$22	$20	$20	
6		Animale		75	15	16		
7		Azzaro		50	10	10		
8		Mambo		30	16	17		
9		OP Juice		400	8	7		
10		TOTAL						

LCM / Sheet2 / Sheet3 /
Ready   NUM

Required:

1. Prepare a spreadsheet that calculates total LCM for inventory, applied on an item-by-item basis.
2. Prepare a journal entry to record the writedown needed for the five products in this problem.

CHAPTER

Reporting and Interpreting Long-Lived Tangible and Intangible Assets

Understand the types of long-lived assets used in business.

LO1 Define, classify, and explain the nature of long-lived assets.

Study how to account for long-lived assets.

LO2 Apply the cost principle to the acquisition of long-lived assets.

LO3 Apply various amortization methods as future economic benefits are used up over time.

LO4 Explain the effect of asset impairment on the financial statements.

LO5 Analyze the disposal of long-lived tangible assets.

LO6 Analyze the acquisition, use, and disposal of long-lived intangible assets.

LO7 (Supplement A) Analyze changes in amortization estimates.

Evaluate the effectiveness of long-lived asset management decisions.

LO8 Interpret the fixed-asset-turnover ratio.

Reconsider how reporting decisions affect analyses.

LO9 Describe factors to consider when comparing across companies.

This chapter focuses on how long-lived tangible and intangible assets and their amortization (or depreciation) are reported in financial statements. We focus on Club-Link Corporation, which owns 38 golf courses and several golf resorts in Ontario and Québec.

If you're an average North American, you gobble about three pounds of peanut butter per year, which equals 1,500 peanut butter sandwiches eaten before your high school graduation.[1] That makes you an expert at knowing how much peanut butter to spread on sandwiches. It also prepares you for learning how to report amortization on long-lived assets. Really. Reporting amortization is a lot like spreading peanut butter on sandwiches. The amount of peanut butter to spread on each sandwich is just like the amount of amortization to spread over each accounting period. It depends on the amount that you begin with in the jar (or the cost you begin with in the account) and the number of sandwiches (or accounting periods) that you'll be spreading it over. Just like peanut butter on a sandwich, there'll be a little bit on each sandwich if it's spread over many years or lots if it's spread over fewer years.

For the rest of this chapter, we're going to focus on **CLUBLINK**—Canada's largest owner and operator of golf courses, including the Glen Abbey Golf Course, Canada's #1 public course, where Tiger Woods hit the "Shot of 2000" and won his Triple Crown.[2] As of December 31, 2007, its land, clubhouses, golf carts, and

---

[1]Retrieved January 8, 2008, from www.peanutbutter.com/funfacts.asp.
[2]Tiger's six-iron 218-yard shot from a fairway bunker on the 18th hole clinched the Bell Canadian Championship for him.

other long-lived assets accounted for over 96 per cent of its total assets, so it's the perfect setting for you to learn how these assets are reported and the analyses you can conduct to determine how well they're managed.

The main topics of this chapter are presented as Learning Objectives on the first page of the chapter. When you begin the next section, focus on understanding what long-lived assets are, and why they're important to many business decisions. In the second section, you'll study the accounting methods and procedures used inside the business to track these assets from the time they are first acquired, to when they are used, to when they are discarded. In the last parts of the chapter, you'll see how analysts outside the organization evaluate how effectively these assets have been used, and then you'll pull it all together by considering how different accounting methods and procedures for these long-lived assets can affect analyses of reported financial results.

UNDERSTAND _____

The Types of Long-Lived Assets Used in Business

DEFINING AND CLASSIFYING LONG-LIVED ASSETS

Long-lived (also called long-term) **assets** are any assets that will not be used up within the next year. For most companies, these assets are the heart of their businesses. Without them, Mattel wouldn't have the robotics that make toys, First Choice Haircutters wouldn't have the salons for providing hair care services, Shoppers Drug Mart wouldn't have the stores for selling its products, and Oakley wouldn't have the legal rights for protecting its sunglasses from counterfeiting and piracy. So when you hear the label "long-lived assets," don't just think of rusty old equipment, because this class of assets is much broader than that. Long-lived assets include the following:

1. *Tangible assets.* These are long-lived assets that have physical substance, which simply means that you can see, touch, or kick them. The most prominent examples of tangible assets are land, buildings, factories, machinery, and office equipment, which are typically grouped into a single line-item on the balance sheet called property, plant, and equipment. This category includes the 8,170 acres of skiable mountain at Whistler/Blackcomb, the Mighty Canadian Minebuster roller coaster at Paramount Canada's Wonderland, and the thousands of golf carts that criss-cross the ClubLink courses.

2. *Intangible assets.* These long-lived assets have special rights, but no physical substance. Most intangible assets are evidenced only by legal documents. Unlike with the various tangible assets, like the store buildings and cash registers that you see in your daily life, you probably have less familiarity with intangible assets. For this reason, we'll spend time later in this chapter describing the various types of intangibles. For now it is enough that you know it includes things like patents, trademarks, and copyrights.

Exhibit 9.1 indicates just how important long-lived assets are to ClubLink, by showing the complete assets section of its balance sheet at December 31, 2007 and 2006.

With 96 per cent of its total assets invested in property and equipment, ClubLink is a good example of what is called a **capital-intensive** business. Other examples of capital-intensive businesses in Canada follow:

Long-lived (or long-term) assets are the resources owned by a business that will provide economic benefits beyond the upcoming fiscal year. We use the term long-lived in this chapter because that is the term used by Canadian GAAP.

COACH'S TIP

Long-lived assets are known by other names as well. Tangible long-lived assets are sometimes called fixed assets, because they are fixed in place. Tangible and intangible long-lived assets (excluding goodwill) can be combined under the heading capital assets.

A **capital-intensive** business is one with a high percentage of total assets invested in property, plant, and equipment.

	Total Assets (in millions)	Percentage of Total Assets in Property and Equipment
Canadian National Railway	$24,004	88%
Petro-Canada	22,646	82%
Hydro One	12,234	86%
WestJet Airlines	2,727	79%
Tim Hortons	1,745	67%

exhibit **9.1**	ClubLink's Assets		
December 31		2007	2006
(in thousands)			
Assets			
Current Assets		$ 11,087	$ 19,999
Property and Equipment			
Land		329,793	326,082
Buildings		150,720	144,113
Roads, Cart Paths, and Irrigation		79,932	72,903
Golf Carts		16,446	14,671
Maintenance, Clubhouse, and Office Equipment		70,565	63,413
		647,456	621,182
Less Accumulated Amortization		106,712	91,504
		540,744	529,678
Other Assets		11,328	13,186
Total Assets		$ 563,159	$ 562,863

COACH'S TIP

1. In Exhibit 9.1, we combined ClubLink's three types of land into one line for simplicity. ClubLink has (1) golf course lands (owned and operating golf courses), (2) lands under development (owned land that is still under development), and (3) leased lands (golf courses on land that is leased by ClubLink for an extended period of time, usually from the local municipality).
2. Accumulated amortization is reported here as a total for the entire tangible assets category. Alternatively, it can be reported separately for each type of tangible asset.

STUDY
How to Account for Long-Lived Assets

In this section, you will study the accounting decisions that relate to long-lived assets. The concepts of accrual accounting have an impact on these decisions, so let's refresh our memories. In Chapter 3, you learned that, when costs are incurred, accountants decide whether to report them as assets or expenses, depending on whether or not the costs will lead to probable future economic benefits. If they do, the costs will be capitalized as assets on the balance sheet, and then transferred to expenses on the income statement as the assets' future benefits are used up. If they aren't likely to result in future benefits, the costs are treated as an expense right away.

We'll start our discussion with *tangible* long-lived assets and consider key accounting decisions related to their (1) acquisition, (2) use, and (3) disposal. Accounting for *intangible assets* will be the focus of the last part of this section.

ACQUISITION OF TANGIBLE ASSETS

The general rule for tangible assets, under the cost principle, is that all reasonable and necessary costs of acquiring and preparing an asset for use should be recorded as a cost of the asset. The act of recording costs as assets (rather than as expenses) is what accountants and analysts call capitalizing the costs.

For tangible assets, it's not always obvious whether a cost is reasonable and necessary for acquiring or preparing them for use, so the decision to capitalize versus expense a cost is one that can involve lots of judgment. Laying a proper foundation for heavy machinery seems a necessary cost, but paying to have the machinery painted to match the prevailing colour scheme in the factory probably isn't. If costs that are really expenses are capitalized, the result is a balance sheet that appears stronger (larger assets) and an income statement that appears more profitable (lower expenses) than if these costs had been expensed. One of the cases at the end of this chapter (S9-5) shows a well-known real-world example of this. For now, as you read the next couple of pages, focus on learning what kinds of costs should be capitalized and what kinds should be expensed.

Costs Incurred at the Time of Acquiring Tangible Assets

To help you understand the types of costs that should be capitalized when a tangible asset is acquired, we list several costs below that are considered necessary for acquiring and preparing tangible assets for use. Notice that the costs to be capitalized are not just the amounts paid to purchase or construct the assets themselves. For example, the land account at Club-Link would include legal fees incurred to purchase land, fees to hire land surveyors, and commissions paid to real estate brokers. Take a moment right now to read the other similar types of costs that are capitalized when acquiring buildings and equipment.

COACH'S TIP

If a company buys land, a building, or a piece of used equipment and incurs demolition, renovation, or repair costs *before* it can be used, these additional costs would be capitalized as a cost of the land, building, or equipment.

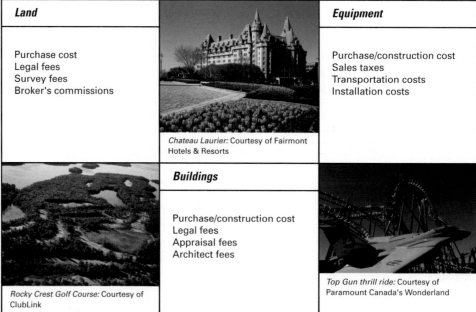

Land		Equipment
Purchase cost Legal fees Survey fees Broker's commissions		Purchase/construction cost Sales taxes Transportation costs Installation costs

Chateau Laurier: Courtesy of Fairmont Hotels & Resorts

	Buildings	
	Purchase/construction cost Legal fees Appraisal fees Architect fees	

Rocky Crest Golf Course: Courtesy of ClubLink

Top Gun thrill ride: Courtesy of Paramount Canada's Wonderland

In some instances, land, buildings, and equipment will be purchased as a group, as they were when ClubLink bought the Green Hills Golf and Country Club in London, Ontario. When this kind of "basket purchase" occurs, the total cost is broken up and allocated to each asset in proportion to the market value of the assets as a whole. This allocation of the total purchase price among individual assets is necessary because the cost of each different type of asset will be spread over different periods of time.

To illustrate how a basket purchase is recorded, let's assume that ClubLink purchased an existing golf course just outside Montreal for $15 million. An appraisal was done on the property at that time to estimate what percentage of the price should be allocated to the various components of the purchase. ClubLink then spent an additional $3 million renovating the clubhouse, and $2 million on course improvements, specifically repaving the cart paths and improving the drainage. ClubLink would calculate the costs to be capitalized as follows:

	Relative Value Per Appraisal	Purchase Price	Additional Costs	Total Costs
Golf course lands	60%	9,000,000		9,000,000
Buildings	20%	3,000,000	3,000,000	6,000,000
Roads, cart paths, and irrigation	10%	1,500,000	2,000,000	3,500,000
Golf carts	5%	750,000		750,000
Maintenance, clubhouse, and office equipment	5%	750,000		750,000
	100%	$15,000,000	$5,000,000	$20,000,000

The journal entry required to record this asset depends on whether the purchase is paid for in cash or financed using credit.

Cash Purchase. Assuming that ClubLink paid cash for the golf course and related improvements, the transaction is recorded as follows:

dr	Golf course lands (+A)	9,000,000	
	Buildings (+A)	6,000,000	
	Roads, cart paths, and irrigation (+A) ...	3,500,000	
	Golf carts (+A)	750,000	
	Maintenance, clubhouse, and office equipment (+A)............	750,000	
cr	Cash (−A).....................		20,000,000

Assets		=	Liabilities	+	Shareholders' Equity
Cash	−20,000,00				
Golf course lands	+9,000,000				
Buildings	+6,000,000				
Roads, cart paths, and irrigation	+3,500,000				
Golf carts	+750,000				
Maintenance, clubhouse, and office equipment	+750,000				

You might find it hard to believe that ClubLink would pay cash for assets that cost $20 million, but this really isn't unusual. Companies often use cash that has been generated from operations or that has been borrowed recently. It's also possible for the seller to extend credit to the buyer, a situation that we examine next.

Credit Purchase. Let's assume that ClubLink bought 161 hectares (400 acres) of prime land on Lake Muskoka north of Toronto for $10 million, with plans to develop a 36-hole golf course and resort there by the year 2015. ClubLink signed a note payable for the land and paid $5,000 cash for the legal fees associated with the purchase. ClubLink would record the following journal entry:

dr	Land under development (+A).........	10,005,000	
cr	Cash (−A).....................		5,000
cr	Note Payable (+L)...............		10,000,000

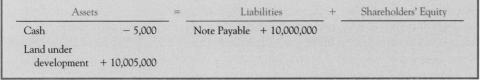

Assets		=	Liabilities	+	Shareholders' Equity
Cash	− 5,000		Note Payable + 10,000,000		
Land under development	+ 10,005,000				

COACH'S TIP

Notice that the amount capitalized to the tangible asset account is unaffected by the method of payment or financing.

Self-Constructed Tangible Assets. In some cases, a company may construct a tangible asset for its own use instead of buying it from a manufacturer. When a company does this, the cost of the asset should include all the necessary costs associated with construction, such as labour, materials, and, in some situations, a portion of the interest incurred during the construction period, called **capitalized interest.** The amount of interest to be capitalized is a complex computation discussed in other accounting courses.

Before we leave this section, we should mention that not all long-lived asset costs are capitalized. The cost of some long-lived assets, like staplers for instance, is such a small amount that it's not worth the trouble of recording them as assets. Instead, these costs are expensed as incurred. Such policies are considered acceptable under GAAP because immaterial (relatively small dollar) amounts will not affect users' decisions when analyzing financial statements.

Capitalized interest represents interest expenditures included in the cost of a self-constructed asset.

Quiz Answers

1. $21,000,000 + $800,000 + $70,000 + $50,000 = $21,920,000

2.

Assets	=	Liabilities	+	Shareholders' Equity
a. PPE + 21,920,000				
Cash − 21,920,000				
b. PPE + 21,920,000		Note Payable + 15,344,000		
Cash − 6,576,000				

HOW'S IT GOING?   A Self-Study Quiz

In a recent year, the New Bakery Company of Manitoba opened a new computer-integrated baking plant priced at $21 million. The plant can make 3,420 buns per minute, which are enough buns for 1.2 billion sandwiches a year. Assume that the company paid $800,000 for sales taxes on the plant; $70,000 for transportation costs; and $50,000 for installation and preparation of the assets before use.

1. Compute the acquisition cost to be recorded as property, plant, and equipment (PPE).

2. Under the following assumptions, indicate the effects of the acquisition on the accounting equation. Use + for increase and − for decrease, and indicate the accounts and amounts.

Assets	=	Liabilities	+	Shareholders' Equity

a. Paid all in cash.

b. Paid 30 per cent in cash and the rest by signing a note payable.

After you're finished, check your answers with the solutions in the margin.

USE OF TANGIBLE ASSETS

Maintenance Costs Incurred during Time of Use

Most tangible assets require substantial expenditures over the course of their lives to maintain or enhance their ability to operate. Maintenance is a big deal in the golf course business, where it's important to have carpet-smooth greens, pristine bunkers, and well-groomed fairways. Frequent use and Canada's harsh natural elements make grounds maintenance a critical part of ClubLink's success. When there's a $5-million purse on the line, the players on the PGA tour expect the course to be in the kind of shape that will allow them to play their best. You would probably feel the same way if you paid $235 to play 18 holes at Glen Abbey. This level of grooming comes from spending lots of money on two types of maintenance during an asset's period of use.

1. Ordinary repairs and maintenance.   Ordinary repairs and maintenance are expenditures for routine maintenance and upkeep of long-lived assets. Just like an oil change for your car, these expenditures are recurring in nature, involve relatively small amounts of money at each occurrence, and do not directly lengthen the useful life of the asset. Because these expenditures occur frequently and maintain the productive capacity of the asset for a short period of time, they do not meet the definition of an asset and are therefore recorded as *expenses* in the current period.

In the case of ClubLink, examples of ordinary repairs and maintenance include cutting the fairways and greens, cleaning the clubhouse, and replacing the lights in the parking lots.

2. Extraordinary repairs, replacements, and additions.   Extraordinary repairs are expenditures that occur infrequently, involve large amounts, and increase an asset's economic usefulness in the future through increased efficiency, increased capacity, or longer life. Examples include additions, major overhauls, complete reconditioning, and major replacements and improvements (often called betterments), such as replacing the sand in the bunkers, expanding the locker rooms, and renovating the pro shop. Because these costs increase the usefulness of tangible assets beyond their original condition, they do meet the definition of an asset and are added to the appropriate *asset* accounts. For

Ordinary repairs and maintenance are expenditures for routine operating upkeep of long-lived assets, and are recorded as expenses.

Extraordinary repairs are expenditures that increase a tangible asset's economic usefulness in the future, and are recorded as increases in asset accounts, not as expenses. In contrast to ordinary repairs, extraordinary repairs are done less frequently and yield longer-lasting benefits.

example, if an existing storage shed is expanded at a cost of $18,000, the entry to record this would be:

dr	Storage shed (+A)..................	18,000	
cr	Cash (−A)		18,000

How to account for extraordinary repairs and improvements is further addressed in the supplement to this chapter.

HOW'S IT GOING? A Self-Study Quiz

As you know from living in an apartment, dorm, or house, buildings require continuous maintenance and repair. For each of the following expenditures, indicate whether it should be expensed in the current period or capitalized as part of the cost of the building.

	Expense or Capitalize?
1. Replacing electrical wiring throughout the building *Extended* Cap	
2. Repairing the hinge on the front door of the building Exp.	
3. Yearly cleaning of the building's air conditioning filters Exp	
4. Repairing major structural damage from a rare flood Cap.	

After you're finished, check your answers with the solutions in the margin.

Amortization Expense

Even if companies regularly spend money to maintain and upgrade their assets, these assets don't usually last forever. To reflect the fact that they have a limited life, another expense, other than repairs and maintenance, is reported every period that a tangible asset is used. This expense, called **amortization** (or **depreciation**), does not involve new costs arising from using the asset. Instead, amortization expense is the *allocation of existing costs* that have been recorded as a long-lived asset. The idea is that the cost of a long-lived asset is essentially a prepaid cost representing future benefits. These benefits are used up when the asset is used, so a portion of its cost is allocated to the period of its use and is reported as an expense. You should recognize that this corresponds to the *matching principle* in accrual accounting, which requires expenses to be reported in the same period as the revenues they generate. For ClubLink, revenues are earned when its golf courses, dining room, golf school, and pro shop are open to customers, so amortization expense also is recorded during that period to show the allocated cost of the tangible assets that are used to generate those revenues.

In Chapter 4, you learned the adjusting journal entry that is needed at the end of each period to reflect the use of property and equipment for the period:

dr	Amortization Expense (+E, −SE)	xxxxx
cr	Accumulated Amortization (+xA, −A)	xxxxx

The amount of amortization recorded during each period is reported on the income statement as *Amortization Expense*. The amount of amortization expense accumulated since the acquisition date is reported on the balance sheet as a contra-account, *Accumulated Amortization*, and deducted from the related asset's cost. The net amounts on the balance sheet are called book values or carrying values. The **book (or carrying) value** of a long-lived asset is its acquisition cost less the accumulated amortization from acquisition date to the balance sheet date. If you're not crystal clear on how these things are reported, take a quick look at Exhibit 9.1 on page 379. You should see that, at the end of

---

Amortization (also called **depreciation**) is the allocation of the cost of long-lived tangible assets over their productive lives using a systematic and rational method.

COACH'S TIP

Because amortization involves allocating the *cost* of tangible assets, rather than determining their current values, the amounts reported on a balance sheet for long-lived tangible assets are likely to differ from their current market values.

Book (or carrying) value is the acquisition cost of an asset less accumulated amortization.

2007, ClubLink's total cost of property and equipment (in thousands) was $647,456, accumulated amortization was $106,712, and the book (or carrying) value was $540,744 ($647,456 − $106,712). Amortization expense (of $16,941) is included in ClubLink's 2007 income statement. Canadian GAAP requires that amortization expense be disclosed in the income statement.[3]

To calculate amortization expense, you need three amounts:

1. **Asset cost.** This includes all the costs capitalized for the asset. You saw earlier in this chapter that this cost can include purchase cost, sales tax, legal fees, and other related costs.

2. **Residual value.** Residual value is an estimate of the amount that the company will get when it disposes of the asset. ClubLink will recover some of the initial cost of its golf carts when it disposes of them either by selling them "as is" to other golf courses or by dismantling them and selling their components to parts dealers or scrap metal companies.

3. *Useful life.* **Useful life** is an estimate of the asset's useful economic life *to the company* (rather than its economic life to all potential users). Economic life may be expressed in terms of years or units of asset capacity, such as the number of units it can produce or the number of kilometres it will travel. **Land is the only tangible asset that's assumed to have an unlimited (indefinite) useful life. Because of this, land is not amortized.**

The basic idea of amortization is to allocate the amount of the asset that will be used up (asset cost minus residual value) over the periods it will be used to generate revenue (useful life). Just as you might plan to leave some peanut butter in the jar for your roommate when you've finished making your sandwich, you plan to leave a little of the asset's cost in the accounts when you're finished amortizing it. You do this because, when you dispose of the asset, you're likely to get back some of what you initially paid for it. So, ultimately, the "true" net cost of the asset is what you paid minus what you get back (asset cost minus residual value). This amount is often called the **amortizable cost.** The total amortization expense that accumulates over an asset's useful life should not exceed amortizable cost, which also means that an asset's end-of-life book value should equal its estimated residual value.

If every company used the same techniques for calculating amortization, we could stop right here. However, because companies own different assets and use them differently, accountants have not been able to agree on a single best method of amortization. As a result, managers are allowed to choose from several different acceptable amortization methods, basing their decision on how they believe their assets will generate revenues over time. These alternative amortization methods produce different amortization numbers, so you need to understand how the alternative methods work to interpret differences in amortization.

Alternative Amortization Methods

We will discuss the three most common amortization methods:

- Straight-line
- Units-of-production
- Declining-balance

To show how each method works, let's assume that ClubLink acquired a new turf mower on January 1, 2009. The relevant information is shown in Exhibit 9.2.

Residual value is the estimated amount to be recovered at the end of the company's estimated useful life of an asset. It is also sometimes called salvage value.

Useful life is the expected service life of an asset to the present owner.

POINT OF INTEREST

Useful lives can be as short as three years for assets like computer equipment, and as long as 100 years for large structures like hydroelectric dams.

Amortizable cost is the portion of the asset's cost that will be used in generating revenue. It is calculated as asset cost minus residual value, and it is allocated to amortization expense throughout the asset's life.

---

[3]For internal reporting purposes, companies keep track of the amortization expense and accumulated amortization related to each building and class of equipment. However, for financial reporting purposes, they generally report only the total for their capital assets as a whole. For simplicity, our journal entries will assume the company keeps only one account for amortization expense and one for accumulated amortization.

---

exhibit 9.2 Information Used to Show Amortization Computations under Alternative Methods

CLUBLINK—ACQUISITION OF A NEW TURF MOWER

Cost, purchased on January 1, 2009	$62,500		
Estimated residual value	$2,500		
Estimated useful life	3 years	**OR**	100,000 kilometres
Actual kilometres driven in: 2009			30,000 kilometres
2010			50,000 kilometres
2011			20,000 kilometres

Straight-Line Method. Under the **straight-line method,** an equal portion of an asset's amortizable cost is allocated to each accounting period over its estimated useful life. The formula to estimate annual amortization expense is

Straight-line is an amortization method that allocates the cost of an asset in equal periodic amounts over its useful life.

Straight-Line (SL) Formula:

$$(\text{Cost} - \text{Residual Value}) \times \frac{1}{\text{Useful Life}} = \text{Amortization Expense}$$

$$(\$62,500 - \$2,500) \times \frac{1}{3\text{ years}} = \$20,000 \text{ per year}$$

COACH'S TIP

The SLN worksheet function in Microsoft Excel computes amortization expense using the straight-line formula shown in this text.

In the straight-line formula, "Cost minus Residual Value" is the total amount to be amortized (the amortizable cost). "1 ÷ Useful Life" is the straight-line rate. Using the information in Exhibit 9.2, the amortization expense for ClubLink's new mower would be $20,000 per year. An amortization schedule for the entire useful life of the mower follows:

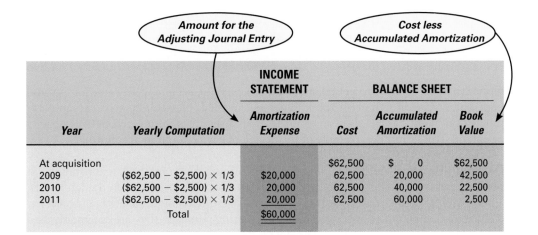

Amount for the Adjusting Journal Entry

Cost less Accumulated Amortization

		INCOME STATEMENT	BALANCE SHEET		
Year	**Yearly Computation**	**Amortization Expense**	**Cost**	**Accumulated Amortization**	**Book Value**
At acquisition			$62,500	$ 0	$62,500
2009	($62,500 − $2,500) × 1/3	$20,000	62,500	20,000	42,500
2010	($62,500 − $2,500) × 1/3	20,000	62,500	40,000	22,500
2011	($62,500 − $2,500) × 1/3	20,000	62,500	60,000	2,500
	Total	$60,000			

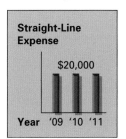

Straight-Line Expense

$20,000

Year '09 '10 '11

Notice that, as the name "straight-line" suggests,

1. Amortization expense is a *constant* amount each year.
2. Accumulated amortization increases by an *equal* amount each year.
3. Book value decreases by the same *equal* amount each year.

Notice also that the straight-line method relies on estimates of an asset's useful life and its residual value at the end of that life. These are difficult things to estimate with precision, so accountants are encouraged to update amortization calculations regularly for new estimates of useful lives and residual values, as discussed in the Supplement at the end of the chapter.

Units-of-Production Method.

The **units-of-production method** allocates the cost of an asset over its useful life, based on the relationship of its periodic output to its total estimated output. This method is also sometimes called units-of-output.

Units-of-Production Method.   Like the straight-line method, the **units-of-production method** allocates each asset's amortizable cost over its useful life—only there's one key difference. Whereas straight-line defines useful life by number of years, units-of-production defines it by production. Specifically, the units-of-production method relates amortizable cost to the total number of estimated units of output. This output could be in terms of kilometres, units produced, or machine hours operated. The formula to estimate amortization expense under the units-of-production method is as follows:

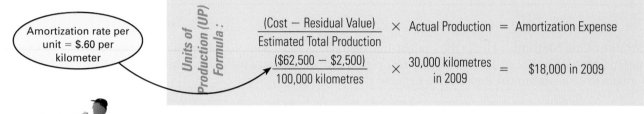

Amortization rate per unit = \$.60 per kilometer

$$\text{Units of Production (UP) Formula:} \quad \frac{(\text{Cost} - \text{Residual Value})}{\text{Estimated Total Production}} \times \text{Actual Production} = \text{Amortization Expense}$$

$$\frac{(\$62{,}500 - \$2{,}500)}{100{,}000 \text{ kilometres}} \times \begin{array}{c} 30{,}000 \text{ kilometres} \\ \text{in } 2009 \end{array} = \$18{,}000 \text{ in } 2009$$

COACH'S TIP

Think of the units-of-production formula as consisting of two steps: (1) calculating the amortization rate per unit, and (2) applying the rate to the actual output.

Dividing the amortizable cost by the estimated total production yields the amortization rate per unit of production, which is then multiplied by the actual production for the period to determine amortization expense. In our illustration, for every kilometre that the mower travels, ClubLink would record amortization expense of \$0.60. The amortization schedule for the mower under the units-of-production method would appear as follows:

Units-of-Production Expense

\$30,000
\$18,000
\$12,000

Year   '09   '10   '11

		INCOME STATEMENT	BALANCE SHEET		
Year	**Yearly Computation**	**Amortization Expense**	**Cost**	**Accumulated Amortization**	**Book Value**
At acquisition			\$62,500	\$ 0	\$62,500
2009	\$.60 rate × 30,000 kilometres	\$18,000	62,500	18,000	44,500
2010	\$.60 rate × 50,000 kilometres	30,000	62,500	48,000	14,500
2011	\$.60 rate × 20,000 kilometres	12,000	62,500	60,000	2,500
	Total	\$60,000			

Notice that, from period to period, amortization expense, accumulated amortization, and book value vary directly with the kilometers travelled. Notice also that the units-of-production method is based on an estimate of an asset's total future productive capacity or output. This is another example of the degree of wiggle room in accounting.

Declining-Balance Method.

The **declining-balance** method is a method that allocates the cost of an asset over its useful life, based on a multiple of the straight-line rate (often two times).

Declining-Balance Method.   Under the **declining-balance method,** amortization expense amounts are higher in the early years of an asset's life and lower in the later years. This is why it is sometimes called an *accelerated amortization* method. Although accelerated methods aren't often used for financial reporting purposes, they are commonly used in tax reporting (a point we discuss in greater detail later).

Declining-balance amortization is based on applying an amortization rate to the book value of the asset at the beginning of the accounting period. The rate can be any rate that management thinks is meaningful. A common approach is to take double (two times) the straight-line rate and, when this approach is used, it is termed the *double-declining-balance rate*. For example, if the straight-line rate is 20 per cent (1 ÷ 5 years) for a five-year estimated useful life, then the double-declining-balance rate is 40 per cent (2 × the straight-line rate). Because double-declining is the rate adopted most frequently by companies that choose an accelerated method, we will use it in our illustration.

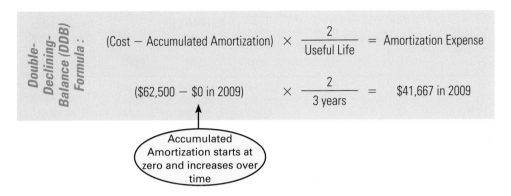

Double-Declining-Balance (DDB) Formula:

$$(\text{Cost} - \text{Accumulated Amortization}) \times \frac{2}{\text{Useful Life}} = \text{Amortization Expense}$$

$$(\$62{,}500 - \$0 \text{ in } 2009) \times \frac{2}{3 \text{ years}} = \$41{,}667 \text{ in } 2009$$

Accumulated Amortization starts at zero and increases over time

Notice in our example that we use the beginning-of-year accumulated amortization balance. Also note that *residual value is not included in the formula for computing amortization expense,* so you have to take extra care to ensure an asset's book value is not being amortized below its residual value. If the normal amortization calculated for the year reduces book value below residual value, a lower amount of amortization must be recorded, so that book value equals residual value. Let's show you what we mean by computing amortization for each of the three years of our example:

Year	Yearly Computation	INCOME STATEMENT Amortization Expense	Cost	BALANCE SHEET Accumulated Amortization	Book Value
At acquisition			$62,500	$ 0	$62,500
2009	($62,500 − $0) × 2/3	$41,667	62,500	41,667	20,833
2010	($62,500 − $41,667) × 2/3	13,889	62,500	55,556	6,944
2011	($62,500 − $55,556) × 2/3	~~4,629~~	62,500	~~60,185~~	~~2,315~~
		4,444	62,500	60,000	2,500
	Total	$60,000			

Computed amount is too large

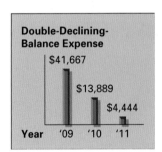

Double-Declining-Balance Expense

$41,667

$13,889

$4,444

Year   '09   '10   '11

If the calculated amortization expense for 2011 ($4,629) were recorded, the asset's book value would fall below its residual value. This isn't allowed, so in the final year of the asset's life, just enough amortization is recorded ($4,444) to make the book value of the asset equal to its residual value of $2,500.

Partial Years.   When a company buys or sells an asset during the year, it has to decide how it wants to handle amortization for this partial year. Calculating amortization to the closest month-end is considered acceptable, and this is what you should do in all problems unless told otherwise. Some companies adopt policies that trade off some accuracy for simplicity, such as charging a half year in the year of acquisition and a half-year in the year of disposal, or charging a full year of amortization in the year of acquisition and none in the year of disposal, regardless of the actual purchase and sale dates. These policies are acceptable as long as they do not materially misstate the financial statements.

Summary.   The following table summarizes the three amortization methods and computations. The graph shows the differences in amortization expense patterns over the asset's useful life for each method.

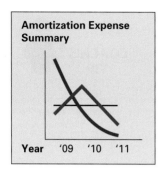

Amortization Expense Summary

Year   '09 '10 '11

Method	Computation	Amortization Expense			Accumulated Amortization
		2009	**2010**	**2011**	**End of 2011**
SL	(C – RV)/UL	$20,000	$20,000	$20,000	$60,000
UP	(C – RV)/ (Act Prod/Est Prod)	18,000	30,000	12,000	60,000
DDB	(C – AA) × (2/UL)	41,667	13,889	4,444	60,000

SL = straight-line; UP = units-of-production; DDB = double-declining-balance;

C = cost; RV = residual value; UL = useful life; Act Prod = actual production;

Est Prod = estimated total production; AA = accumulated amortization

Managers and accountants are allowed to choose any rational and systematic amortization methods, provided that they describe them in their financial statement notes (in keeping with the full disclosure principle discussed in Chapter 5). Also, because not every tangible asset is identical, different amortization methods can be used for different classes of assets, provided the methods are used consistently over time so that financial statement users can easily compare across time periods. So what methods do companies use? In a recent survey, straight-line was used by 87 per cent of companies, units-of-production by 11 per cent, and declining-balance by 3 per cent.[4] Straight-line is the preferred choice because it's the easiest to use and understand, plus it does a good job of matching amortization expense to revenues when assets are used evenly over their useful lives. Units-of-production typically is used only when asset use fluctuates significantly from period to period. Declining-balance methods apply best to assets that are most productive when they are new, and quickly lose their usefulness as they get older.

HOW'S IT GOING?   A Self-Study Quiz

Assume that ClubLink has acquired new computer equipment at a cost of $240,000. The equipment has an estimated life of six years, an estimated operating life of 50,000 hours, and an estimated residual value of $30,000. Determine amortization expense for the first full year under each of the following methods:

1. Straight-line method

2. Double-declining-balance method

3. Units-of-production method (assume the equipment ran for 8,000 hours in the first year)

After you're finished, check your answers with the solutions in the margin.

Quiz Answers

1. ($240,000 − $30,000) × 1/6 = $35,000

2. ($240,000 − 0) × 2/6 = $80,000

3. [($240,000 − $30,000) ÷ 50,000] × 8,000 = $33,600

Amortization and Income Tax.   Before we leave the topic of amortization methods, we should note that most public companies use one method of amortization for reporting to shareholders and a different method for determining income taxes. Essentially, these companies keep two sets of accounting records. This is not because they are trying to cheat on their taxes. It is because the objectives of GAAP and those of the Canada Revenue Agency (CRA) differ.

The CRA has its own way of recording amortization, called **capital cost allowance** (CCA), and it is the only method permitted for calculating taxable income and income taxes owed to the government. CCA is similar, but not identical, to the declining-balance

Capital cost allowance is the amortization process required by the Canada Revenue Agency for calculating taxable income and income taxes.

---

[4]*Financial Reporting in Canada, 32nd Edition*, by Byrd, Chen, and Smith, published by the Canadian Institute of Chartered Accountants, Toronto, Canada, 2007.

Financial Reporting (GAAP)	*Tax Reporting (Income Tax Act)*
The objective of financial reporting is to provide economic information about a business that is useful in projecting future cash flows of the business. Financial reporting rules follow generally accepted accounting principles.	The objective of the Canada Revenue Agency (CRA) is to raise sufficient revenues to pay for the expenditures of the federal government. Many tax provisions are designed to encourage certain behaviours that are thought to benefit society (e.g., contributions to charities are made tax deductible to encourage people to support worthy programs).

method illustrated in this chapter. But, because CCA doesn't usually do a good job of matching costs and revenues, few companies use it for financial reporting. For example, in order to encourage spending on technology, the government might set the CCA rate at 100 per cent for a certain piece of medical equipment, which allows a company to write off the whole asset in the year of acquisition. That is great for saving taxes, but, if that equipment were used for 10 years, it would violate the matching principle to expense the whole asset in the first year for financial reporting purposes.

We already saw that 87 per cent of Canadian companies use straight-line amortization for financial reporting purposes. It follows that most companies keep two sets of records: one for reporting to shareholders and one for reporting to the CRA. We will leave further discussion of this topic to more advanced accounting courses.

ASSET IMPAIRMENT LOSSES

Because the goal of amortization is to allocate costs, rather than to value assets, it's possible that the carrying value of property, plant, and equipment could exceed the value of their future benefits—particularly if the assets become impaired. An **impairment** loss is recorded when events or changed circumstances cause both the estimated future cash flows (from using the asset) and the estimated fair value (from selling the asset) to fall below the book value, with the difference between book value and fair value reported as an impairment loss. Impairment losses typically are included with other expenses reported below "operating income" in the bottom part of the income statement.

Intrawest, the Canadian company that owns ski and golf resorts, including Whistler/Blackcomb and Mont Tremblant, wrote down the value of its five stand-alone golf courses in 2005 and reported an impairment loss in its income statement that year. To see how this decision would be accounted for, let's assume that the book value of Intrawest's golf properties was $50 million, and that both the future cash flows and the fair value of the golf courses were below that number. If the fair value was estimated at $32.4 million, the impairment loss is calculated as $17.6 million ($50 − $32.4). To record this impairment loss, a write-down of $17.6 million is needed, as shown in the following journal entry:

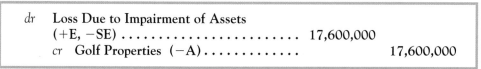

dr **Loss Due to Impairment of Assets** (+E, −SE)	17,600,000	
cr **Golf Properties** (−A)		17,600,000

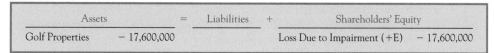

Assets	=	Liabilities	+	Shareholders' Equity
Golf Properties − 17,600,000				Loss Due to Impairment (+E) − 17,600,000

When Intrawest reported this loss on its income statement, it caused a huge drop in net income. Because the loss was so large and unusual in nature, it was reported as a separate line-item. Intrawest also described the impairment loss and asset write-down in the financial statement notes, as shown in Exhibit 9.3.

| **exhibit 9.3** | **Excerpt from Financial Statement Note Describing Write-Down of Golf Properties** |

7. Resort and Travel Operations:

· · · · ·

During the year ended June 30, 2005, the Company determined that its stand-alone golf courses (located outside of its resorts) were no longer core assets and therefore it would offer them for sale. In preparation for sale, the golf course assets were independently appraised and a write-down of $17,568,000 was recorded. The company remains committed to the golf business at its resorts.

DISPOSAL OF TANGIBLE ASSETS

In some cases, a business may *voluntarily* decide not to hold a long-term asset for its entire life. For example, your local gym might decide to replace its treadmills with elliptical trainers, or a company may drop a product from its line and no longer need the equipment that was used to produce its product. To get rid of used assets, companies do just what you do. They trade them in on a new asset, sell them on eBay, or "retire" them to a junkyard. Sometimes, assets are damaged or destroyed in storms, fires, or accidents, creating what are politely called *involuntary disposals*.

Disposals of long-term assets seldom occur on the last day of the accounting period. Therefore, amortization must be recorded to the date of disposal, in accordance with the company's policy for partial-year amortization. The disposal of an amortizable asset usually requires journal entries to:

1. *Update the amortization expense and accumulated amortization accounts.*
2. *Record the disposal.* The cost of the asset and any accumulated amortization at the date of disposal must be removed from the accounts. The difference between any resources received on disposal of an asset and its book value at the date of disposal is treated as a gain or loss on the disposal of the asset, which is reported on the income statement. It's not really operating revenue (or an operating expense) because it arises from non-operating activities, so it's usually shown below operating income in the bottom half of the income statement.

Assume that in the middle of year 17, ClubLink sold one of its resort hotels for $5 million cash. The original cost of the hotel of $20 million had been amortized using the straight-line method over 20 years with no residual value ($1 million amortization expense per year). The last accounting for amortization was at the end of year 16, and the company's policy is to calculate amortization to the nearest month-end in the year of acquisition and disposal, so amortization expense must be recorded for the first half of year 17 [$1,000,000 × ½ = $500,000]. Journal entry (1) to update amortization expense for the first half of year 17 is:

dr	**Amortization Expense (+E, −SE)**	500,000
	cr **Accumulated Amortization**	
	(+xA, − A)	500,000

The gain or loss on disposal is calculated as follows:

Cash received		$5,000,000
Original cost of hotel	$20,000,000	
Less: Accumulated amortization ($1,000,000 × 16.5 years)	16,500,000	
Book value at date of sale		3,500,000
Gain on sale of hotel		$1,500,000

Journal entry (2) to record the sale of the hotel and the resulting gain is

dr	Cash (+A)......................	5,000,000	
dr	Accumulated Amortization		
	(−xA, +A).......................	16,500,000	
	cr Buildings (−A)		20,000,000
	cr Gain on Sale of Hotel Building		
	(+R, +SE)		1,500,000

COACH'S TIP

Although gains on disposal work the same as revenues (recorded with a credit and causing an increase in net income), they are not reported with sales revenues because they arise from non-operating activities rather than normal operations. Instead, they are reported below operating income in the bottom half of the income statement.

The accounting equation effects of the two entries (to update amortization and record the gain on asset sale) are:

Assets	=	Liabilities	+	Shareholders' Equity
1. Accumulated				
Amortization (+xA) − 500,000				Amortization Expense (+E) − 500,000
2. Buildings − 20,000,000				Gain on Sale of Asset (+R) + 1,500,000
Accumulated				
Amortization (−xA) + 16,500,000				
Cash + 5,000,000				

HOW'S IT GOING?   A Self-Study Quiz

Now let's assume the same facts as above except that the asset was sold for $2,500,000 cash. Prepare the two entries on the date of the sale.

1. Update amortization expense for the first half of year 17.

2. Record the sale:

Assets	=	Liabilities	+	Shareholders' Equity
1. Accumulated				
Amortization (+xA) −500,000				Amortization Expense (+E) −500,000
2. Buildings −20,000,000				Loss on Sale of Asset (+E) −1,000,000
Accumulated				
Amortization (−xA) +16,500,000				
Cash +2,500,000				

After you're finished, check your answers with the solutions in the margin.

Quiz Answers
1. dr Amortization expense (+E) 500,000
   cr Accumulated amortization (+xA, − A)   500,000
2. dr Cash (+A)   2,500,000
   dr Accumulated amortization (−xA, +A)...... 16,500,000
   dr Loss on sale of hotel (+E, − SE)......   1,000,000
   cr Buildings (−A)   20,000,000

It's time now to move on to accounting for intangibles, which are long-lived assets that lack physical substance and, instead, are evidenced by legal documents.

TYPES OF INTANGIBLE ASSETS

There are many types of intangibles that you might see in the real world, each one giving some kind of exclusive right or benefit to the owner. Here we discuss six of the most common.

Patents.   A **patent** is an exclusive right granted by the federal government for a period of 20 years, typically to whoever invents a new product or discovers a new process. The patent enables the owner to be the only one who can use, manufacture, or sell the patented item. This protection is intended to encourage people to be inventive, because it prevents others from simply copying innovations until after the inventor has had time to earn some money from the new product or process.

A **patent** is a right to exclude others from making, using, selling, or importing an invention.

A **trademark** or trade name is a special name, image, or slogan identified with a product or company.

A **copyright** is a form of protection provided to the original authors of literary, musical, artistic, dramatic, and other works of authorship.

A **licensing right** is the limited permission to use property according to specific terms and conditions set out in a contract.

A **franchise** is a contractual right to sell certain products or services, use certain trademarks, or perform activities in a certain geographical region.

Goodwill is the premium a company pays to obtain the favourable reputation and other intangible strengths associated with another company.

Research and development costs are expenditures that may someday lead to patents, copyrights, or other intangible assets, but uncertainty about their future benefits means that they are expensed.

Trademarks and Trade Names.   A **trademark** or a trade name is a special name, image, or slogan identified with a product or a company, like the name Kleenex or the image of McDonald's golden arches. Once a trademark or trade name is registered with the appropriate government agency (in Canada, it's the Canadian Intellectual Property Office), its use is restricted, and anyone who uses it without permission can be prosecuted. Since registration can be renewed every 15 years, trademarks and trade names are considered to have indefinite lives.

Copyrights.   A **copyright** gives the owner the exclusive right to publish, use, and sell a literary, musical, artistic, or dramatic work for a period not exceeding 50 years after the author's death. The book you are reading is copyrighted, which makes it illegal, for example, for an instructor to copy several chapters from this book and hand them out in class without first obtaining permission from the copyright owner.

Licensing Rights.   **Licensing rights** are limited permissions to use something according to specific terms and conditions. Your university likely has obtained the licensing right to make computer programs available for use on your campus network. A licensing right also is what allows Paramount Canada's Wonderland to use SpongeBob SquarePants in its 3D motion simulator movie ride.

Franchises.   A **franchise** is a contractual right to sell certain products or services, use certain trademarks, or perform activities in a geographical region. McDonald's is probably the best-known franchise in the world. First Choice Haircutters, our focus company in earlier chapters, also operates as a franchise operation, and Tim Hortons is another of our homegrown favourites. Tim Hortons typically grants these rights in exchange for an upfront fee ranging from $430,000 to $480,000 per store plus ongoing fees based on a percentage of store sales.[5]

Goodwill.   **Goodwill** tops the charts as the most frequently reported intangible asset. It is the asset that captures all the intangible competitive advantages of a company. Goodwill results from all kinds of good things, like a favourable location, a loyal customer base, a great reputation, great employee morale, and superior management. Although many companies have probably built up their own goodwill, GAAP doesn't allow it to be reported as an intangible asset on the balance sheet unless it has been purchased from another company. To understand the reasons behind this, keep reading. We explain them in the next section.

ACQUISITION, USE, AND DISPOSAL OF INTANGIBLE ASSETS

Just as there are two ways to acquire tangible assets (self-construct or buy), there are two ways to acquire intangible assets: develop them yourself or buy them from someone else that has developed them. However, self-developed intangibles are accounted for differently from self-constructed tangibles. If a company pays $500,000 to build a parking garage, for example, the garage meets the definition of an asset and the cost will be capitalized. But, if the same company spends $500,000 on research that it hopes will eventually lead to a patentable product or process, it will expense those costs because the future benefits are too uncertain.

Therefore, aside from being invisible, one of the biggest things distinguishing intangibles from long-lived tangible assets is that *almost all intangible assets are recorded as assets only if they have been purchased.* The costs of almost all *self-constructed or self-developed intangibles are reported as expenses,* often as **research and development costs.** We say "almost all" because there are exceptions. Canadian accounting rules allow development costs to be capitalized once it is clear that an asset with enough future benefits to recover the costs has been created. Following our patent example, initial research costs would be expensed, but once a viable product is developed, further costs, such as testing prototypes and registering the patent, will be capitalized in the patent account. Another common example is the capitalization of computer software and Web site development costs into

---

[5]www.timhortons.com/en/franchise

a technology intangible account. Sometimes capitalized development costs are disclosed under the general heading of **deferred charges** on the balance sheet.

The primary reason that most self-developed intangibles are not reported as assets is that it's easy for Joe Schmo to claim that he's developed a valuable (but invisible) intangible asset. But to believe what Joe is saying, you really need to see some evidence that it's worth what Joe says it's worth. In other words, an intangible asset is not reported as an asset until there's reasonable certainty that it exists. That certainty definitely exists when someone gives up their hard-earned cash to buy it. At that time, the *purchaser* can always record the intangible asset *at its acquisition cost*.

Some people describe goodwill as the value paid for unidentifiable net assets. Huh? Did you read that right—"the value paid for unidentifiable net assets"? How can you put a value on something you can't identify? Actually, it is possible. When one company buys another business, the purchase price often is greater than the value of all of the **net assets** of the business. Why would a company pay more for a business as a whole than it would pay if it bought the assets individually? The answer is to obtain its goodwill. You could easily buy equipment to produce and sell a bunch of generic chocolate-wafer cookies, but this strategy likely wouldn't be as successful as acquiring the goodwill associated with the Oreo business. That's the reason Kraft Foods paid $40 billion more than the value of Nabisco's identifiable assets—to acquire the goodwill associated with Nabisco's Oreo and Ritz snacks business.

For accounting purposes, goodwill (also called "cost in excess of net assets acquired") is defined as the difference between the purchase price of a company as a whole and the fair market value of its net assets:

> Purchase price
> − Fair market value of identifiable assets, net of liabilities
> = Goodwill to be reported

Both parties to the sale estimate an acceptable amount for the goodwill of the business and add it to the appraised fair value of the business's net assets. Then the sales price of the business is negotiated. In conformity with the *cost principle*, the resulting goodwill is recorded as an intangible asset only when it is actually purchased at a measurable cost.

Okay, that's enough on the acquisition of intangible assets. Let's talk about what happens to the cost of intangible assets after they have been purchased. The accounting rules here depend on whether the intangible asset has a limited or unlimited life.

■ **Limited life.** The cost of an intangible asset with a limited life, such as a patent or copyright, is amortized, usually on a straight-line basis, over each period of its useful life. Most companies do not estimate a residual value for their intangible assets because, unlike tangible assets that can be sold as scrap, intangibles have no value at the end of their useful lives. Amortization expense is included on the income statement each period, and the intangible assets are reported on the balance sheet at cost net of accumulated amortization. In contrast to tangible assets, however, a separate accumulated amortization account is seldom used for intangibles. The asset account is usually credited directly, as shown below.

Let's assume a company purchases the patent for a jet-propelled surfboard for $800,000 and intends to use it for 20 years. The adjusting entry each year to record $40,000 in patent amortization expense ($800,000 ÷ 20 years) is as follows:

dr **Patent Amortization Expense** (+E, −SE) 40,000
  cr **Patent** (−A). 40,000

	Assets	=	Liabilities	+	Shareholders' Equity	
Patent	− 40,000				Patent Amortization Expense (+E)	− 40,000

Deferred charges are costs that have been capitalized on the balance sheet as long-lived assets because management believes they will generate future revenues. You can think of them as long-term prepaid expenses.

Net assets is the shorthand term used to refer to assets minus liabilities.

POINT OF INTEREST

There are significant differences in the way research and development (R&D) costs are accounted for around the globe. In the United States and Germany, all R & D costs must be expensed. Great Britain, Japan, and Korea, like Canada, permit some development costs to be capitalized, while other countries, like Italy and Sweden, permit full capitalization of R & D.

POINT OF INTEREST

To find information about intellectual property in Canada, search the government's Web site at strategis.ic.gc.ca/scmrksv/cipo.

exhibit 9.4 Accounting Rules for Long-Lived Tangible and Intangible Assets

Stage	Subject	Tangible Assets	Intangible Assets
Acquire	**Purchased asset**	Capitalize all related costs.	Capitalize all related costs.
Acquire	**Self-constructed asset**	Capitalize all related costs.	Expense related costs, unless future benefits clearly exist.
Use	**Repairs/maintenance** Ordinary	Expense related costs.	Expense related costs if applicable.
Use	Extraordinary **Amortization** Limited life	Capitalize related costs. One of several methods: • Straight-line • Units-of-production • Declining-balance	Capitalize related costs if applicable. Typically, use only the straight-line method (others permitted).
Use	Unlimited life **Impairment test**	Do not amortize (e.g., land). Write down if necessary.	Do not amortize (e.g., goodwill). Write down if necessary.
Dispose	**Report gain (loss) when . . .**	Receive more (less) on disposal than book value.	Receive more (less) on disposal than book value.

- *Unlimited life.* Intangibles with potentially unlimited (or indefinite) lives, such as goodwill and trademarks, are not amortized, but are subject to impairment tests.

There are few maintenance costs connected with intangibles, but the same principles as we saw for tangibles would apply: expense ordinary costs and capitalize extraordinary ones. An extraordinary maintenance cost that would be capitalized to the patent account, for example, would be the legal costs of winning a patent infringement lawsuit. In addition, just as with long-lived tangible assets, each intangible is tested for possible impairment, and the asset's book value is written down (decreased) to its fair value if impaired. Similarly, disposals of intangible assets result in gains (or losses) if the amounts received on disposal are greater than (less than) their book values.

The accounting rules for long-lived tangible and intangible assets are summarized and compared in Exhibit 9.4.

BRICKS AND CLICKS

Just as we saw that some companies are capital-intensive (have lots of property, plant, and equipment), other companies are primarily technology or knowledge-based and have lots of intangibles. Shaw Communications Inc., the cable TV provider, had 59 per cent of its total assets ($4.8 billion) invested in broadcast licences at the end of 2006. Nortel, the communications giant, increased its goodwill account by $18.5 billion to 41 per cent of its total assets in the year 2000, after going on an acquisition binge.

One of the problems in evaluating companies that are primarily technology, computer, or knowledge-based (called a "click" company, as opposed to a "brick" company with assets like buildings) is that many knowledge assets are not recorded under current accounting rules. If valuable assets do not appear on balance sheets, investors may have a more difficult time understanding and analyzing the company. As technology and competitive advantages become even more important aspects of doing business everywhere, the significance of intangibles to all types of companies is likely to grow.

NATURAL RESOURCES

Before we move on to the next section, let's take a minute to talk a bit about accounting for natural resources, since this sector plays a large role in the Canadian economy. Accounting in this industry can be complex, so we'll only cover two basic issues here. The first issue a natural resource company faces is what costs can be capitalized. The underlying principle that we have used so far to answer this question applies to natural resource companies as well—all costs that create assets should be capitalized—but there is one unique feature of how the principle is applied in this industry. If an oil company drills 10 wells and only one is successful, the company can (but is not required to) capitalize the costs of drilling all 10 wells, even the unsuccessful ones, using the argument that it is necessary to drill 10 wells to find one successful well. Some people argue that this is inconsistent with the fact that research costs in other industries, like biotechnology, have to be expensed. There are significant differences between Canadian and international accounting practices in this area, and we can expect to see accounting practices evolve as we move towards adoption of International Financial Reporting Standards in 2011.

Once costs are capitalized, the second problem involves amortization, called **depletion** in this industry. The units-of-production method makes sense for depletion of natural assets, but estimating the barrels of oil in a well or the ounces of gold in a mine is usually much more difficult than estimating the kilometres that a golf cart can be driven.

Depletion is the process of amortizing the capitalized costs of natural resources.

EVALUATE _____
The Effectiveness of Long-Lived Asset Management Decisions

WHAT'S AN OPTIMAL LEVEL OF INVESTMENT?

One of the major challenges business managers face is forecasting the right amount to invest in tangible and intangible assets. If they underestimate the amount needed to produce goods or provide services for customers, they will miss an opportunity to earn revenue. On the other hand, if they overestimate the amount needed, their companies will incur excessive costs that will reduce profitability.

If you've ever played golf, you know the business provides an outstanding example of the difficulties involved in these long-lived asset decisions. If the company builds more golf courses than it needs to satisfy golfers, the courses will be empty. The company will still incur all of the costs to operate the courses and facilities, but it will generate only a fraction of the possible revenue. Unlike merchandise companies, a golf course cannot build up an "inventory" of unused tee-off times to be sold in the future. On the other hand, a golf course also can run into trouble if it overcrowds its courses and other facilities. Just think how you felt the last time you had to wait behind eight people on the first tee, or you had to set your alarm so you could call in early enough to get the tee-off time you wanted. To keep its members happy, and stay profitable at the same time, ClubLink has to decide how many courses to buy or develop and how many memberships to sell. They have to be sensitive to that delicate balance between supply and demand. Since it costs a lot of money to get up and running, ClubLink's research about demand in an area had better be right. Just like you, they have to do their homework.

TO LEASE OR BUY?

In this chapter, we focused our discussion on companies that acquire their assets by buying or constructing them. But they could decide instead to lease their buildings and equipment. There are many advantages to leasing, and it is a common practice in Canada and elsewhere. If the lease is an ordinary rental agreement, called an **operating lease,** the leased assets (and the future rental payments) do not appear on the balance sheet. For example, Kimberly-Clark—the Kleenex and Huggies company—admits in its annual report that it "acquires the use of automobiles, fork lifts, office equipment, warehouses, and some manufacturing equipment" through short-term rental agreements, whereby "no asset . . . is recorded on the Corporation's balance sheet." Under another type of

An **operating lease** is an arrangement where a company rents fixed assets from other companies, but does not record them on its balance sheet.

A **capital lease** is a long-term agreement between two companies that is accounted for like a credit purchase.

lease, called a **capital lease,** the company records the lease as a credit purchase, and both a long-lived tangible asset and a long-term liability appear on its books. More advanced accounting courses discuss lease accounting in more detail.

EVALUATING THE USE OF LONG-LIVED TANGIBLE ASSETS

Just as managers carefully plan what to invest in long-lived tangible and intangible assets, financial analysts closely evaluate how well management uses these assets to generate revenues. In previous chapters, we used turnover ratios to evaluate the use of total assets (Chapter 5), receivables (Chapter 7), and inventories (Chapter 8). Here we use the fixed-asset-turnover ratio to study the use of property, plant, and equipment.

COACH'S TIP

1. A ratio is considered "high" or "low" depending on whether it is above or below the industry average.
2. Remember that "fixed assets" is another term for property, plant, and equipment.

$$\text{Fixed-Asset-Turnover Ratio} = \frac{\text{Net Sales Revenue}}{\text{Average Net Fixed Assets}} = \frac{\text{Net Sales Revenue}}{\left(\dfrac{\text{Beginning Net Fixed Assets} + \text{Ending Net Fixed Assets}}{2}\right)}$$

The fixed-asset-turnover ratio measures the sales dollars generated by each dollar invested in fixed assets. Just as kpl (kilometers per litre) provides a measure of a car's fuel efficiency, the fixed-asset-turnover ratio provides a measure of fixed asset operating efficiency. Generally speaking, a high or increasing turnover ratio suggests better use of fixed assets, whereas a low or declining ratio usually means the opposite. As an efficiency ratio, we show the fixed-asset-turnover ratio in the (b) section in our framework for financial statement analysis, as shown in Exhibit 9.5.

Be on the Alert

A low or declining ratio doesn't *always* mean bad news. A declining ratio, for example, could be caused by a company's acquiring additional assets during the current period in anticipation of higher sales in future periods, which is usually a good thing. Similarly, a high or increasing fixed-asset-turnover ratio doesn't *always* mean good news. It could be caused by renting rather than buying fixed assets. Renting by means of operating leases allows a company to generate revenues by using assets that are not reported in the property, plant, and equipment accounts, which has the effect of increasing the fixed-asset-turnover ratio.

Note that fixed asset turnover ratios can vary between industries. A company like Yahoo!, for example, needs fewer tangible assets to generate revenues, so it is likely to have a high turnover ratio in comparison with companies like ClubLink and Canadian National Railway, which need to invest lots of money in tangible assets to attract customers. In Exhibit 9.6, we've shown the fixed-asset-turnover ratios for these three companies

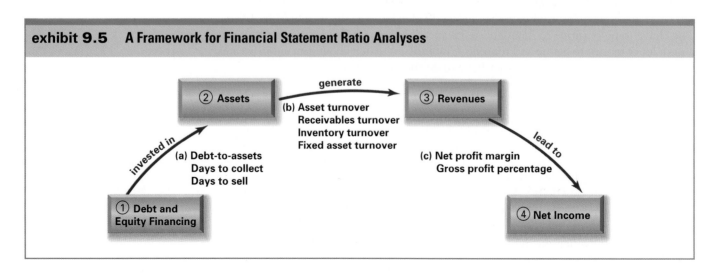

exhibit 9.5   A Framework for Financial Statement Ratio Analyses

| exhibit 9.6 | Summary of Fixed-Asset-Turnover Ratio Analyses | | | | | |

| | | | | 2007 FISCAL YEAR | | SELF-STUDY QUIZ 2006 |
Name of Measure	Formula	What It Tells You	Yahoo!	CN	ClubLink	ClubLink
Fixed-Asset-Turnover Ratio	$\dfrac{\text{Net Sales Revenue}}{\text{Average Net Fixed Assets}}$	• The efficiency with which fixed assets generate revenue • A higher ratio means greater efficiency.	4.31 times	0.38 times	$\dfrac{166{,}192}{(540{,}744 + 529{,}678)/2}$ $= 0.31$ times	

Note: Fixed assets include property, plant, and equipment.

in 2007. The details of the ClubLink calculations are shown, which divide the total net revenues of $166,192 (thousand) in 2007 by the average of the net fixed asset numbers reported in ClubLink's balance sheet in Exhibit 9.1. The Self-Study Quiz that follows gives you a chance to see whether you understand how to calculate this ratio.

HOW'S IT GOING? A Self-Study Quiz

Compute the ratio for the final column in Exhibit 9.6, using financial statement information in Exhibit 9.1, as well as the following information. ClubLink reported net revenues of $149,118 in 2006 and net fixed assets of $505,661 at December 31, 2005 (in thousands of dollars). Did the fixed-asset-turnover ratio improve, decline, or stay the same in 2007, as compared with 2006?

After you're finished, check your answers with the solutions in the margin.

Quiz Answers

$$\frac{149{,}118}{(529{,}678 + 505{,}661)/2} = 0.29 \text{ times}$$

The ratio increased slightly in 2007.

AMORTIZATION AND CASH FLOW

You should realize that amortization is an expense with no corresponding cash flow. Companies have cash outflows when they buy long-lived assets, and cash inflows when they sell them, but no cash flow when they amortize the assets. Keep this in mind when we turn our attention to the statement of cash flows in Chapter 12.

RECONSIDER _____
How Reporting Decisions Affect Analyses

THE IMPACT OF AMORTIZATION DIFFERENCES

As you've seen in the last section, differences in the nature of business operations affect financial analyses and the conclusions that you draw from them. The same is true for differences in amortization, whether they arise from using different amortization methods, different estimated useful lives, or different estimated residual values. In this section, we present a simple example to show how different amortization methods can affect analyses throughout the life of a long-lived asset. Don't let the simplicity of this example fool you. The differences in this example are identical to what often happens in the real world.

exhibit 9.7   Straight-Line and Double-Declining-Balance Amortization Schedules

CLUBLINK (STRAIGHT-LINE)			End of Year	INTRAWEST (DOUBLE-DECLINING-BALANCE)		
Amortization Expense	Accumulated Amortization	Book Value		Amortization Expense	Accumulated Amortization	Book Value
$124,000	$124,000	$526,000	1	$260,000	$260,000	$390,000
124,000	248,000	402,000	2	156,000	416,000	234,000
124,000	372,000	278,000	3	93,600	509,600	140,400
124,000	496,000	154,000	4	56,160	565,760	84,240
124,000	620,000	30,000	5	54,240	620,000	30,000

COACH'S TIP

For tips and practice involving the calculations in Exhibit 9.7, try S9-8 at the end of this chapter.

Assume that ClubLink and Intrawest each acquire 10 new turf mowers at the beginning of the year for $650,000, and estimate that the mowers will have residual values of $30,000 at the end of their five-year useful lives. Everything about the mowers is identical, except we'll assume ClubLink uses the straight-line amortization method and Intrawest uses the double-declining-balance method. Exhibit 9.7 shows the yearly amortization to be reported by the two companies. Notice that, early in the asset life, prior to year 2, the straight-line amortization expense reported by ClubLink is less than the declining-balance amortization expense reported by Intrawest. This means that, even if the two companies draw exactly the same number of customers, which lead to exactly the same total revenues, the reported net income will differ, just because the two companies use different (but equally acceptable) methods of amortization. This example shows why, as a user of financial statements, you need to understand what accounting methods are used by companies that you may be comparing.

The differences don't stop at amortization expense, however. Let's take the example one step further and assume that the two companies sell the mowers at the end of year 3 for $200,000. Since we've assumed the disposal occurs on the last day of the year, a full year of amortization will be recorded prior to the disposal. Thus, at the time of disposal, ClubLink's asset will have a book value of $278,000, whereas Intrawest's will have a book value of $140,400, as shown in the highlighted line in Exhibit 9.7 above. To account for the disposal at the end of year 3, the companies will record what they receive, remove what they give up (the book value of the asset), and recognize a gain or loss for the difference between what is received and given up. Exhibit 9.8 shows these calculations for the two companies.

Based on the information in Exhibit 9.8, which company appears better managed? Someone who doesn't understand accounting is likely to say Intrawest is better managed because it reports a gain on disposal, whereas ClubLink reports a loss. You know that this can't be right because both companies have experienced exactly the same business events. They bought the same assets at the same cost ($650,000) and sold them for the same amount of money ($200,000). The only difference between them is that ClubLink reported less amortization over the years leading up to the disposal, so its mower has a larger book value at the time of disposal. Intrawest reported more amortization in years 1

exhibit 9.8   Calculations of Gain/Loss on Disposal

	Cash Received	–	Net Book Value Given Up	=	Gain/Loss
ClubLink	$200,000	–	$278,000	=	Loss $78,000
Intrawest	$200,000	–	$140,400	=	Gain $59,600

to 3, so it has a smaller book value at the time of disposal. As a financial statement user, you should realize that any disposal gain or loss reported on the income statement tells you as much (and, in many cases, more) about the method previously used to amortize assets than about the apparent "wisdom" or management ability to negotiate the sale of long-lived assets.

Although our example used different amortization methods, the same effects can exist between two companies that use the same amortization methods but estimate different useful lives or different residual values for their long-lived assets. How big can these differences get? Well, even within the same industry, sizeable differences can exist. The financial statement notes of various companies in the airline industry, for example, reveal the following differences in estimated useful lives of their airplanes and other flight equipment:

Company	Estimated Life (in years)
Air Canada	Up to 30
Alaska Airlines	Up to 20
Singapore Airlines	Up to 15

COACH'S TIP

Useful lives vary for several reasons, including differences in (*a*) the type of equipment used by each company, (*b*) the frequency of repairs and maintenance, (*c*) the frequency and duration of use, and (*d*) the degree of conservatism in management's estimates.

Some analysts try to sidestep possible differences in amortization calculations by focusing on financial measures that exclude the effects of amortization. One popular measure is called **EBITA** (pronounced something like *ee bi tah*). This might seem like a goofy name, but it's actually the first letters of "earnings before interest, taxes, and amortization." Analysts calculate EBITA by starting with net income and adding back amortization expense (as well as non-operating expenses like interest and taxes). The idea is that this measure allows analysts to conduct financial analyses without having to think about possible differences in amortization.

The danger with using EBITA or any other non-GAAP measure of a company's performance is that it doesn't tell the whole story. As Exhibit 5.13 (page 204) on proforma measures warns, management may focus analysts' attention on the better looking subtotal rather than the bottom-line net income. ClubLink's partial income statement is illustrated below (in thousands). You will note that the EBITA subtotal is used, but an additional factor, called Other, is included. You will also note that ClubLink's EBITAO (in this case, we add the O for Other) is more than $47 million, but they ended up with a profit of less than $5 million after all items are included. Of course, informed readers of financial statements (such as you), are able to understand the subtleties of disclosures such as these and are not confused or misled by them.

EBITA is an abbreviation for "earnings before interest, taxes, and amortization," which is a measure of operating performance that some managers and analysts use in place of net income. You might also see **EBITDA** if the company uses both words, depreciation and amortization.

	2007	2006
Earnings before interest, taxes, amortization, and other	$47,419	$42,926
Amortization expense	16,941	18,479
Interest expense (net)	20,239	18,463
Other expenses	3,677	5,363
Income before income taxes	6,562	621
Income tax expense	1,685	205
Net Income	$ 4,877	$ 416

THE ROLE OF JUDGMENT

In this chapter, we have seen many instances where judgment is applied. A company has to decide whether a cost is reasonable and necessary for preparing a long-lived asset for use in order to know whether to capitalize it or not. It has to decide if development costs have probable future benefits. It has to decide how long an asset is likely to last, and what amortization method most fairly matches costs to revenues. It has to decide whether a long-lived asset has been impaired. Most companies make these decisions ethically and

ETHICAL ISSUES

responsibly, but, whenever judgments are made, there is potential for honest errors in judgment or outright misrepresentation of the data. When an estimate is changed or an error is found and corrected, the accounting can get complex. We cover changes in amortization estimates in the Supplement to this chapter. Other accounting changes are covered in more advanced accounting courses.

The decision to capitalize or expense costs is one that made the news in a spectacular fashion not too long ago. An $11-billion accounting fraud was committed at WorldCom (now called Verizon) in the early 2000s, in part by capitalizing costs that were a lot like rent and should have been expensed. This accounting decision led WorldCom to report huge increases in assets (rather than expenses) in the periods in which the costs were incurred. The CFO and four other employees in WorldCom's accounting group pleaded guilty to securities fraud and a variety of other charges. The CEO was charged with planning and executing the biggest fraud in the history of American business, and was sentenced to 25 years in prison.

WHAT'S COMING UP

This chapter concludes our look at the assets side of the balance sheet. In Chapter 10, we will study the liabilities that are needed to help finance asset purchases. For now, though, spend some time reviewing and practicing the material covered in this chapter.

FOR YOUR REVIEW _____

DEMONSTRATION CASE

Diversified Industries started as a house construction company. In recent years, it has expanded into heavy construction, ready-mix concrete, sand and gravel, construction supplies, and earthmoving services. The company completed the following transactions during 2009. Amounts have been simplified.

2009

Jan.   1   The management decided to buy a 10-year-old building for $175,000 and the land on which it was situated for $130,000. It paid $100,000 in cash and signed a note payable for the rest.

Jan.   3   Paid $38,000 in cash for renovations to the building prior to its use.

July   10   Paid $1,200 cash for ordinary repairs on the building.

Dec.   31   Considered the following information to determine year-end adjustments:

a.   The building will be amortized on a straight-line basis over an estimated useful life of 30 years. The estimated residual value is $33,000.

b   Diversified purchased another company several years ago at $100,000 more than the fair values of the net assets acquired. The goodwill has an unlimited life.

c.   At the beginning of the year, the company owned equipment with a cost of $650,000 and accumulated amortization of $150,000. The equipment is being amortized using the double-declining-balance method, with a useful life of 20 years and no residual value.

d.   At year-end, the company tested its long-lived assets for possible impairment of their value. Included in its equipment was a piece of old excavation equipment with a cost of $156,000 and book value of $120,000 (after making the adjustment for c). Because of its smaller size and lack of safety features, the old equipment has limited use. The future cash flows and fair value are expected to be $35,000. Goodwill was found not to be impaired.

December 31, 2009, is the end of the annual accounting period.

Required:

1. Indicate the accounts affected and the amount and direction (+ for increase and − for decrease) of the effect of each of the preceding events on the financial statement categories at the end of the year. Use the following headings:

Date	Assets	=	Liabilities	+	Shareholders' Equity

2. Prepare the journal entries to record each event that occurred during the year, and the adjusting journal entries required at December 31.
3. Show the December 31, 2009, balance sheet classification and amount for each of the following items:

    Property, plant, and equipment

    Intangible asset—goodwill
4. Assuming that the company had sales of $1,000,000 for the year and a book value of $500,000 for property, plant, and equipment at the beginning of the year, compute the fixed-asset-turnover ratio. Explain its meaning.

Suggested Solution

1. Effects of events (with computations in notes below the table):

(1) Capitalize the $38,000 expenditure because it is necessary to prepare the asset for use.

Date	Assets		=	Liabilities		+	Shareholders' Equity	
Jan. 1	Cash	−100,000		Note Payable	+205,000			
	Land	+130,000						
	Building	+175,000						
Jan. 3	Cash	−38,000						
(1)	Building	+38,000						
July 10	Cash	−1,200					Repairs Expense (+E)	−1,200
(2)								
Dec. 31 *a*	Accumulated Amortization (+xA)	−6,000					Amortization Expense (+E)	−6,000
(3)								
Dec. 31 *b*	No entry							
(4)								
Dec. 31 *c*	Accumulated Amortization	−50,000					Amortization Expense (+E)	−50,000
(5)								
Dec. 31 *d*	Equipment	−85,000					Loss Due to Asset Impairment (+E)	−85,000
(6)								

(2) This is an ordinary repair and should be expensed.

(3)
Cost of building		**Straight-line amortization**
Initial payment	$175,000	($213,000 cost − $33,000 residual value) × 1/30 years = *$6,000* annual amortization
Renovations prior to use	38,000	
Acquisition cost	$213,000	

(4) Goodwill has indefinite life and is therefore not amortized. Goodwill is tested for impairment but, as described later in the case, was found not to be impaired.

(5) **Double-declining-balance amortization**

($650,000 cost − $150,000 accumulated amortization) × 2/20 years = $50,000 annual amortization

(6)   **Asset impairment test**

The book value of old equipment ($120,000) exceeds expected future cash flows and fair value ($35,000). The asset has become impaired, so it needs to be written down to its fair value.

Impairment Loss:	
Book value	$120,000
Less: Fair value	−35,000
Loss due to impairment	$ 85,000

2.   **Journal entries for events during the year:**

January 1, 2009
dr	Land (+A)	130,000	
dr	Building (+A)	175,000	
	cr Cash (−A)		100,000
	cr Note Payable (+L)...........................		205,000

January 3, 2009
dr	Building (+A)	38,000	
	cr Cash (−A).................................		38,000

July 10, 2009
dr	Repairs Expense (+E, −SE)........................	1,200	
	cr Cash (−A)		1,200

Adjusting journal entries at December 31, 2009:

a.
dr	Amortization Expense (+E, −SE)...........	6,000	
	cr Accumulated Amortization (+xA, −A)...........		6,000

b.   No adjusting journal entry required because goodwill is assumed to have an unlimited (or indefinite) life.

c.
dr	Amortization Expense (+E, −SE).............	50,000	
	cr Accumulated Amortization (+xA, −A)...........		50,000

d.
dr	Loss Due to Asset Impairment (+E, −SE)	85,000	
	cr Equipment (−A)		85,000

3. **Partial balance sheet, December 31, 2009:**

Assets		
Property, plant, and equipment		
Land		$130,000
Building	$213,000	
Less: Accumulated amortization	6,000	207,000
Equipment ($650,000 − 85,000)	565,000	
Less: Accumulated amortization		
($150,000 + 50,000)	200,000	365,000
Total property, plant, and equipment		702,000
Intangible asset		
Goodwill		100,000

4. **Fixed-asset-turnover ratio:**

$$\frac{\text{Sales}}{(\text{Beginning Net Fixed Asset Balance} + \text{Ending Net Fixed Asset Balance}) \div 2} = \frac{\$1,000,000}{(\$500,000 + \$702,000) \div 2} = 1.66$$

This construction company is capital-intensive. The fixed asset turnover ratio measures the company's efficiency at using its investment in property, plant, and equipment to generate sales.

CHAPTER SUMMARY

Define, classify, and explain the nature of long-lived assets. p. 378 **LO1**

- Long-lived assets are those that a business retains for long periods of time for use in the course of normal operations rather than for sale. They may be divided into tangible assets (land, buildings, equipment) and intangible assets (including goodwill, patents, and franchises).

Apply the cost principle to the acquisition of long-lived assets. p. 379 **LO2**

- Acquisition cost of property, plant, and equipment is the cash-equivalent purchase price plus all reasonable and necessary expenditures made to acquire and prepare the asset for its intended use. These assets may be acquired using cash or debt, or through self-construction.

  Expenditures made after the asset is in use are either expensed or capitalized as a cost of the asset:

  a. Expenditures are *expensed* if they recur frequently, involve relatively small amounts, and do not directly lengthen the asset's useful life. These are considered ordinary repairs and maintenance expense.

  b. Expenditures are *capitalized as a cost of the asset* if they provide benefits for one or more accounting periods beyond the current period. This category includes extraordinary repairs, replacements, and additions.

Apply various amortization methods as future economic benefits are used up over time. p. 383 **LO3**

- In conformity with the matching principle, the cost of long-lived tangible assets (less any estimated residual value) is allocated to amortization expense over each period benefited by the assets.

- Because of amortization, the book value of an asset declines over time and net income is reduced by the amount of the expense.

- Common amortization methods include straight-line (a constant amount over time), units-of-production (a variable amount over time), and double-declining-balance (a decreasing amount over time).

Explain the effect of asset impairment on the financial statements. p. 389 **LO4**

- When events or changes in circumstances reduce the estimated future cash flows and fair value of a long-lived asset below its book value, the book value of the asset should be written down, with the amount of the write-down reported as an impairment loss.

Analyze the disposal of long-lived tangible assets. p. 390 **LO5**

When assets are disposed of through sale or abandonment,

- Record additional amortization arising since the last adjustment was made.
- Remove the cost of the old asset and its related accumulated amortization.
- Recognize the cash proceeds (if any).
- Recognize any gains or losses when the asset's book value is not equal to the cash received.

LO6   **Analyze the acquisition, use, and disposal of long-lived intangible assets. p. 391**

- Intangible assets are recorded at cost. The costs of most self-developed intangible assets are expensed, often as research and development, when incurred.

- Intangibles are reported at book value (cost less accumulated amortization) on the balance sheet.

- Amortization is calculated for intangibles with limited useful lives, usually using the straight-line method.

- Intangibles with unlimited useful lives, including goodwill, are not amortized, but are reviewed for impairment.

LO7   **(Supplement A) Analyze changes in amortization estimates. p. 405**

- When estimates of residual value or useful life change, or when an asset's capitalized cost changes during its life, the new unamortized asset balance less any revised residual value should be allocated over the revised estimated useful life.

LO8   **Interpret the fixed-asset-turnover ratio. p.395**

- The fixed-asset-turnover ratio measures the company's efficiency at using its investment in property, plant, and equipment to generate sales. Higher turnover ratios imply greater efficiency.

LO9   **Describe factors to consider when comparing across companies. p. 397**

- Companies in different industries require different levels of investment in long-lived assets. Beyond that, you should consider whether differences exist in amortization methods, estimated useful lives, and estimated residual values, which can affect the book value of long-lived assets as well as ratios calculated using these book values and any gains or losses reported at the time of asset disposal.

FINANCIAL STATEMENT ANALYSIS TIP

To determine the amount of sales generated by each dollar invested in property, plant, and equipment, calculate the fixed-asset-turnover ratio:

$$\text{Fixed-Asset-Turnover Ratio} = \frac{\text{Net Sales Revenue}}{\text{Average Net Fixed Assets}} = \frac{\text{Net Sales Revenue}}{\left(\dfrac{\text{Beginning Net Fixed Assets} + \text{Ending Net Fixed Assets}}{2}\right)}$$

KEY TERMS TO KNOW

Amortizable Cost p. 384

Amortization p. 383

Book (or Carrying) Value p. 383

Capital Cost Allowance p. 388

Capital-Intensive Business p. 378

Capital Lease p. 396

Capitalized Interest p. 381

Copyright p. 392

Declining-Balance Method p. 386

Deferred Charges p. 393

Depletion p. 395

Depreciation p. 383

EBITA p. 399

Extraordinary Repairs p. 382

Franchise p. 392

Goodwill p. 392

Impairment p. 389

Licensing Right p. 392

Long-Lived Assets p. 378

Net Assets p. 393

Operating Lease p. 395

Ordinary Repairs and Maintenance p. 382

Patent p. 391

Research and Development Costs p. 392

Residual (or Salvage) Value p. 384

Straight-Line Method p. 385

Trademark p. 392

Units-of-Production Method p. 386

Useful Life p. 384

SUPPLEMENT A: CHANGE IN AMORTIZATION ESTIMATES

Amortization is based on two estimates, useful life and residual value. These estimates are made at the time an amortizable asset is acquired. As you gain experience with the asset, one or both of these initial estimates may need to be revised. In addition, extraordinary repairs and additions may be added to the original acquisition cost at some time during the asset's use. When it is clear that either estimate should be revised to a significant degree or that the asset's cost has changed, the unamortized asset balance (less any residual value at that date) should be allocated over the remaining estimated life from the current year into the future.

To compute the new amortization expense necessitated by any of the above changes for any of the amortization methods described here, substitute the book value for the original acquisition cost, the new residual value for the original residual value, and the estimated remaining life for the original useful life. As an illustration, the formula using the straight-line method follows.

Original Straight-Line Formula Modified for a Change:

$$(\text{Cost} - \text{Residual Value}) \times \frac{1}{\text{Useful Life}} = \text{Amortization Expense}$$

$$(\text{Book Value} - \text{New Residual Value}) \times \frac{1}{\text{Remaining Life}} = \text{Amortization Expense}$$

Assume ClubLink built the largest and most luxurious clubhouse in the universe for $60,000,000, with an estimated useful life of 20 years and estimated residual value of $3,000,000. Shortly after the beginning of year 5, ClubLink changed the initial estimated life to 25 years and lowered the estimated residual value to $2,400,000. At the end of year 5, the computation of the new amount for amortization expense is as shown below.

Original amortization expense: ($60,000,000 − $3,000,000) × 1/20 = $ 2,850,000 per year

	× 4 years
Accumulated amortization at the end of year 4	$11,400,000

Book value at the end of year 4:

Acquisition cost	$60,000,000
Less: Accumulated amortization	11,400,000
Book value	$48,600,000

Amortization in years 5 through 25 based on changes in estimates:

(Book value − New residual value) × 1/remaining years = New amortization expense

($48,600,000 − $2,400,000) × 1/21 (25 − 4 years) = $2,200,000 per year

---

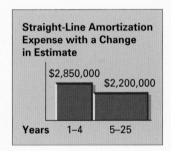

Straight-Line Amortization Expense with a Change in Estimate

$2,850,000 $2,200,000

Years 1–4 5–25

Companies may also change amortization methods (for example, from declining-balance to straight-line), although such a change requires significantly more disclosure, as described in intermediate accounting textbooks. Under GAAP, changes in accounting estimates and amortization methods should be made only when a new estimate or accounting method "better measures" the periodic income of the business.

HOW'S IT GOING? A Self-Study Quiz

Assume that ClubLink owned an irrigation system that originally cost $100,000. When purchased, the equipment had an estimated useful life of 10 years with no residual value. After operating the equipment for five years, ClubLink determined that the equipment had only two more years of remaining life. Based on this change in estimate, what amount of amortization should be recorded over the remaining life of the asset? ClubLink uses the straight-line method.

After you're finished, check your answer with the solution in the margin.

Quiz Answer

$50,000 (book value after five years)

÷ 2 years (remaining life)

= $25,000 Amortization expense per year.

FOR YOUR PRACTICE _____

QUESTIONS

1. Define *long-lived assets*. What are the two categories of long-lived assets? Describe each.
2. Under the cost principle, what amounts should be recorded as a cost of a long-lived asset?
3. What is it called when costs are recorded as assets rather than expenses?
4. Distinguish between ordinary repairs and extraordinary repairs. How is each accounted for?
5. Describe the relationship between the matching principle and accounting for long-lived assets.
6. In computing amortization, three values must be known or estimated. Identify and describe each.
7. What type of amortization expense pattern is used under each of the following methods, and when is its use appropriate?
   a.   The straight-line method
   b.   The units-of-production method
   c.   The double-declining-balance method
8. What is an *asset impairment*? How is it accounted for?
9. What is book value? When equipment is sold for more than book value, how is the transaction recorded? How is it recorded when the selling price is less than book value?
10. Distinguish between amortization and capital cost allowance.
11. Distinguish between amortization and depletion.
12. Why are intangible assets becoming more common and more significant on many companies' balance sheets?
13. Define *goodwill*. When is it appropriate to record goodwill as an intangible asset?
14. How is the fixed-asset-turnover ratio computed? Explain its meaning.
15. (Supplement A) Over what period should an addition to an existing long-lived asset be amortized? Explain.

MULTIPLE CHOICE

Select the one alternative that best answers the question or completes the sentence.

1. Which of the following should be capitalized when a piece of production equipment is acquired for a factory?
   a.   Sales taxes
   b.   Transportation costs
   c.   Installation costs
   d.   All of the above
2. When recording amortization, which of the following statements are true?
   a.   Total assets increase and shareholders' equity increases.
   b.   Total assets decrease and total liabilities increase.
   c.   Total assets decrease and shareholders' equity increases.
   d.   None of the above are true.
3. Under what amortization method(s) is an asset's book value used to calculate amortization each year?
   a.   Straight-line method
   b.   Units-of-production method
   c.   Declining-balance method
   d.   All of the above
4. A company wishes to report the highest earnings possible according to GAAP. Therefore, when calculating amortization for financial reporting purposes:
   a.   It will follow the CCA rates prescribed by the CRA.
   b.   It will select the shortest lives possible for its assets according to GAAP.

    c. It will select the longest lives possible for its assets according to GAAP.

    d. It will estimate lower residual values for its assets.

5. Barber, Inc., followed the practice of amortizing its building on a straight-line basis. A building was purchased on January 1, 2009, and it had an estimated useful life of 20 years and a residual value of $20,000. The company's amortization expense for 2009 was $20,000 on the building. What was the original cost of the building?

    a. $360,000

    b. $380,000

    c. $400,000

    d. $420,000

6. ACME, Inc., uses straight-line amortization for all of its amortizable assets. ACME sold a used piece of machinery on December 31, 2009, that it purchased on January 1, 2008, for $10,000. The asset had a five-year life, zero residual value, and accumulated amortization as of December 31, 2008, of $2,000. If the sale price of the used machine was $7,500, the resulting gain or loss on disposal was which of the following amounts?

    a. Loss of $3,500

    b. Gain of $3,500

    c. Loss of $1,500

    d. Gain of $1,500

7. What assets should be amortized using the straight-line method?

    a. Land

    b. Intangible assets with limited lives

    c. Intangible assets with unlimited lives

    d. All of the above

8. How many of the following statements regarding goodwill are true?

    • Goodwill is not reported unless purchased in an exchange.

    • Goodwill must be reviewed annually for possible impairment.

    • Impairment of goodwill results in a decrease in net income.

    a. None   *c.* Two

    b. One   *d.* Three

9. The Simon Company and the Allen Company each bought a new delivery truck on January 1, 2008. Both companies paid exactly the same cost, $30,000, for their respective vehicle. As of December 31, 2009, the book value of Simon's truck was less than the Allen Company's book value for the same type of vehicle. Which of the following are acceptable explanations for the difference in book value?

    a. Both companies elected straight-line amortization, but the Simon Company used a longer estimated life.

    b. The Simon Company estimated a lower residual value, but both estimated the same useful life and both elected straight-line amortization.

    c. Because GAAP specifies rigid guidelines regarding the calculation of amortization, this situation is not possible.

    d. None of the above explain the difference in book value.

10. (Supplement A) Thornton Industries purchased a machine for $45,000 and is amortizing it using the straight-line method over a life of 10 years, with a residual value of $3,000. At the beginning of the sixth year, a major overhaul was made costing $5,000, the estimated useful life was extended to 13 years, and no change was made to the estimated residual value. Amortization expense for year 6 is:

    a. $1,885

    b. $2,000

    c. $3,250

    d. $3,625

Solutions to Multiple-Choice Questions

1. d   2. d   3. c   4. c   5. d   6. d   7. b   8. d   9. b   10. c

MINI-EXERCISES

LO1, LO3, LO6   **M9-1 Classifying Long-Lived Assets, and Related Cost Allocation Concepts**

For each of the following long-lived assets, indicate its nature and related cost allocation concept. Use the abbreviations shown on the right:

Asset	Nature	Cost Allocation		Nature	
1. Operating licence	_____	_____	L	Land	
2. Property	_____	_____	B	Building	
3. New engine for old machine	_____	_____	E	Equipment	
4. Goodwill	_____	_____	I	Intangible	
5. Production plant	_____	_____	N	Natural Resources	
6. Warehouse	_____	_____		**Cost Allocation Concept**	
7. Oil wells	_____	_____	D	Depletion	
8. Trademark	_____	_____	A	Amortization	
9. Computers	_____	_____	NO	No cost allocation	

LO2, LO6   **M9-2 Identifying Capital and Revenue Expenditures**

American Golf Corporation operates over 170 golf courses throughout the United States. For each of the following items, enter the correct letter to the left to show whether the expenditure should be capitalized (C) or expensed (E).

Transactions

_____ 1. Purchased a golf course in Orange County, California.

_____ 2. Paid a landscaping company to clear 100 acres of land on which to build a new course.

_____ 3. Paid a landscaping company to apply fertilizer to the fairways on a golf course.

_____ 4. Paid a building maintenance company to build a 2,000 square foot addition on a clubhouse.

_____ 5. Paid a building maintenance company to replace the locks on a clubhouse and equipment shed.

_____ 6. Paid an advertising company to create a campaign to build goodwill.

LO2, LO6   **M9-3 Identifying Capital and Revenue Expenditures**

For each of the following items, enter the correct letter to the left to show whether the expenditure should be capitalized (C) or expensed (E).

Transactions

_____ 1. Paid $400 for ordinary repairs.

_____ 2. Paid $6,000 for extraordinary repairs.

_____ 3. Paid cash, $20,000, for addition to old building.

_____ 4. Paid for routine maintenance, $200, on credit.

_____ 5. Purchased a machine, $7,000; gave long-term note.

_____ 6. Purchased a patent, $4,300 cash.

_____ 7. Paid $10,000 for monthly salaries.

LO3   **M9-4 Computing Book Value (Straight-Line Amortization)**

Calculate the book value of a three-year-old machine that cost $21,500, has an estimated residual value of $1,500, and has an estimated useful life of four years. The company uses straight-line amortization.

M9-5 Computing Book Value (Units-of-Production Amortization)
LO3

Calculate the book value of a three-year-old machine that cost $21,500, has an estimated residual value of $1,500, and has an estimated useful life of 20,000 machine hours. The company uses units-of-production amortization and ran the machine 3,000 hours in year 1, 8,000 hours in year 2, and 7,000 hours in year 3.

M9-6 Computing Book Value (Double-Declining-Balance Amortization)
LO3

Calculate the book value of a three-year-old machine that cost $21,500, has an estimated residual value of $1,500, and has an estimated useful life of four years. The company uses double-declining-balance amortization. Round to the nearest dollar.

M9-7 Identifying Asset Impairment
LO4

For each of the following scenarios, indicate whether an asset has been impaired (Y for yes and N for no) and, if so, how much loss should be recorded.

	Book Value	Estimated Future Cash Flows	Fair Value	Is Asset Impaired?	If Yes, Amount of Loss
a. Machine	$ 16,000	$ 9,000	$ 9,000		
b. Copyright	40,000	37,000	39,000		
c. Factory building	50,000	52,000	48,000		
d. Building	230,000	212,000	210,000		

M9-8 Recording the Disposal of a Long-Lived Asset
LO5

Prepare journal entries to record these transactions: (a) Morrell Corporation disposed of two computers at the end of their useful lives. The computers had cost $3,800 and their accumulated amortization was $3,800. No residual value was received. (b) Assume the same information as (a), except that accumulated amortization, updated to the date of disposal, was $3,600.

M9-9 Recording the Disposal of a Long-Lived Asset (Straight-Line Amortization)
LO5

As part of a major renovation at the beginning of the year, Mullins' Pharmacy, Inc., sold shelving units (store fixtures) that were 10 years old for $1,400 cash. The shelves originally cost $6,200 and had been amortized on a straight-line basis over an estimated useful life of 12 years with an estimated residual value of $200. Assuming that amortization has been recorded to the date of sale, prepare the journal entry to record the sale of the shelving units.

M9-10 Capitalizing versus Expensing Intangible Asset Costs
LO6

Most highly visible companies spend significant amounts of money to protect their intellectual property, ensuring that no one uses this property without direct permission. For example, to include logos throughout this book, we had to obtain written permission from each company—a process that stretched over nearly a year and often resulted in requests being denied. Discuss whether companies should capitalize or expense the money paid to employees who evaluate requests for use of their logos and who search for instances where the companies' intellectual property has been used without permission. Draw an analogy to similar costs incurred for employees responsible for the use and upkeep of tangible assets.

M9-11 Computing Goodwill and Patents
LO6

Elizabeth Pie Company has been in business for 30 years and has developed a large group of loyal restaurant customers. Bonanza Foods made an offer to buy Elizabeth Pie Company for $5,000,000. The market value of Elizabeth Pie's recorded assets, net of liabilities, on the date of the offer is $4,600,000. Elizabeth Pie also holds a patent for a pie crust fluting machine that the company invented. (The patent, with a market value of $200,000, was never recorded by Elizabeth Pie because it was developed internally.) How much has Bonanza Foods included for intangibles in its offer of $5,000,000? Assuming Elizabeth Pie accepts this offer, which company will report goodwill on its balance sheet?

LO8   **M9-12 Computing and Evaluating the Fixed-Asset-Turnover Ratio**
The following information was reported by Amuse Yourself Theme Parks (AYTP) for 2009:

Net fixed assets (beginning of year)	$4,450,000
Net fixed assets (end of year)	4,250,000
Net sales for the year	3,250,000
Net income for the year	1,700,000

Compute the company's fixed-asset-turnover ratio for the year. What can you say about AYTP's fixed-asset-turnover ratio when compared with ClubLink's 2007 ratio in Exhibit 9.6?

LO8   **M9-13 Computing and Evaluating the Fixed-Asset-Turnover Ratio**
The following information was reported by Hydro One for 2007 (in millions):

Net fixed assets (beginning of year)	$10,526
Net fixed assets (end of year)	11,214
Net sales for the year	4,655
Net income for the year	399

Compute the company's fixed-asset-turnover ratio for the year. What can you say about Hydro One's fixed-asset-turnover ratio when compared with ClubLink's 2007 ratio in Exhibit 9.6?

EXERCISES

LO1   **E9-1 Preparing a Classified Balance Sheet**
The following is a list of account titles and amounts (in millions) reported by Canadian National Railway (CN). Canada's largest railway owns over 60,000 freight cars that run over more than 19,000 route miles in Canada and the United States.

Buildings	$1,915	Accumulated amortization	$6,448
Other current assets	714	Intangibles and other assets, net	929
Allowance for doubtful accounts	70	Locomotives and freight cars	4,059
Track, roadways, and land	16,105	Accounts receivable	863
Cash and cash equivalents	147	Other machinery and equipment	1,057

Required:

Prepare the asset section of a classified balance sheet for CN.

LO2, LO3   **E9-2 Computing and Recording a Basket Purchase and Straight-Line Amortization**
Sweet Company bought a building and the land on which it is located for $178,000 cash. The land is estimated to represent 60 per cent of the purchase price. The company also paid renovation costs on the building of $23,200.

Required:

1. Give the journal entry to record the purchase of the property, including all expenditures. Assume that all transactions were for cash and that all purchases occurred at the beginning of the year.
2. Compute straight-line amortization on the building at the end of one year, assuming an estimated 12-year useful life and a $14,000 estimated residual value.
3. What should be the book value of the land and building at the end of year 2?

LO2, LO3   **E9-3 Determining Financial Statement Effects of an Asset Acquisition and Straight-Line Amortization**
Conover Company ordered a machine on January 1, 2009, at a purchase price of $20,000. On date of delivery, January 2, 2009, the company paid $8,000 cash and signed a note payable for the balance. On January 3, 2009, it paid $250 for freight for delivery of the machine. On January 5, Conover paid installation costs relating to the machine amounting to $1,200. On December 31,

2009 (the end of the accounting period), Conover recorded amortization on the machine, using the straight-line method with an estimated useful life of 10 years and an estimated residual value of $3,450.

Required:

1. Indicate the effects (accounts, amounts, and + or −) of each transaction (on January 1, 2, 3, and 5) on the accounting equation. Use the following headings:

Date	Assets	=	Liabilities	+	Shareholders' Equity

2. Compute the acquisition cost of the machine.
3. Compute the amortization expense to be reported for 2009.
4. What should be the book value of the machine at the end of 2010?
5. What would be the amortization expense for 2009, and the book value at the end of 2010, if Conover bought and installed the machine on July 1, 2009, instead of in January, assuming that Conover calculates amortization to the closest month-end?

E9-4 Recording Straight-Line Amortization and Repairs

LO2, LO3

Wiater Company operates a small manufacturing facility. At the beginning of 2009, an asset account for the company showed the following balances:

Manufacturing equipment	$80,000
Accumulated amortization through 2008	55,000

During 2009, the following expenditures were incurred for repairs and maintenance:

Routine maintenance and repairs on the equipment	$ 850
Major overhaul of the equipment that improved efficiency	10,500

The equipment is being amortized on a straight-line basis over an estimated life of 15 years, with a $5,000 estimated residual value. The annual accounting period ends on December 31.

Required:

1. Give the adjusting journal entry that would have been made at the end of 2008 for amortization on the manufacturing equipment.
2. At the beginning of 2009, what is the remaining estimated life?
3. Give the journal entries to record the two expenditures for repairs and maintenance during 2009.

E9-5 Determining Financial Statement Effects of Straight-Line Amortization and Repairs

LO2, LO3

Refer to the information in E9-4.

Required:

Indicate the effects (accounts, amounts, and + or −) of the following two items on the accounting equation, using the headings shown below.

1. The adjustment for amortization at the end of 2008
2. The two expenditures for repairs and maintenance during 2009

Item	Assets	=	Liabilities	+	Shareholders' Equity

E9-6 Computing Amortization under Alternative Methods

LO3

Dorn Corporation bought a machine at the beginning of the year at a cost of $6,400. The estimated useful life was four years, and the residual value was $800. Assume that the estimated productive life of the machine is 80,000 units. Expected annual production is: year 1, 28,000 units; year 2, 22,000 units; year 3, 18,000 units; and year 4, 12,000 units.

Required:

1. Complete an amortization schedule for each of these alternative methods:

    a. Straight-line
    b. Units-of-production
    c. Double-declining-balance

		Income Statement		Balance Sheet		
Year	*Computation*	*Amortization Expense*	*Cost*	*Accumulated Amortization*	*Book Value*	
At acquisition						
1						
2						
3						
4						

2. Which method will result in the highest net income in year 2? Does this higher net income mean the machine was used more efficiently under this amortization method?

LO3   **E9-7 Computing Amortization under Alternative Methods**

Sonic Corporation purchased and installed electronic payment equipment at its drive-in restaurant at the beginning of the year at a cost of $27,000. The estimated useful life was three years, and the estimated residual value was $1,500. Per year, expected payment transactions are: year 1, 61,200 units; year 2, 140,250 units; and year 3, 53,550 units, for an expected total of 255,000 transactions.

Required:

1. Complete an amortization schedule for each of these alternative methods:

    a. Straight-line
    b. Units-of-production
    c. Double-declining-balance

		Income Statement		Balance Sheet		
Year	*Computation*	*Amortization Expense*	*Cost*	*Accumulated Amortization*	*Book Value*	
At acquisition						
1						
2						
3						

2. Which method will result in the highest net income in year 2? Does this higher net income mean the equipment was used more efficiently under this amortization method?

LO3   **E9-8 Computing Straight-Line Amortization for Partial Years**

Tao Corporation purchased equipment on May 1, 2009, at a cost of $16,000. The estimated useful life was three years, and the estimated residual value was $1,000. The company's year-end is December 31.

Required:

1. Calculate straight-line amortization on the equipment for years 2009 to 2012, assuming:

    a. the company has a policy of calculating amortization to the closest month-end.
    b. the company has a policy of charging a half-year's amortization in the year of acquisition and a half-year in the year of disposal.

    c. the company has a policy of charging a full-year's amortization in the year of acquisition and none in the year of disposal.

2. What is the total amortization that will be charged over the life of the equipment under the three alternatives?

E9-9 Interpreting Management's Choice of Different Amortization Methods for Tax and Financial Reporting   LO3

The annual report for Federal Supplies Corporation includes the following information:

> For financial reporting purposes, amortization of property and equipment is provided on a straight-line basis over the asset's service life. For income tax purposes, amortization is generally computed using accelerated methods.

Required:

Explain why Federal Supplies uses different methods of amortization for financial reporting and tax purposes.

E9-10 Inferring Asset Age and Recording Impairment on a Long-Lived Asset (Straight-Line Amortization)   LO3

On January 1, 2009, the records of Pastuf Corporation showed the following regarding production equipment:

Equipment (estimated residual value, $2,000)	$12,000
Accumulated amortization (straight-line, one year)	2,000

On December 31, 2009, management determined that the equipment was impaired because its future cash flows and fair value were only $6,800.

Required:

1. Based on the data given, compute the estimated useful life of the equipment.
2. Give all journal entries with respect to the equipment on December 31, 2009. Show computations.

E9-11 Demonstrating the Effect of Book Value on Recording an Asset Disposal   LO5

Purolator is Canada's leading express-distribution company with over 45,000 locations. In addition to its aircraft, the company has more than 5,000 ground vehicles that pick up and deliver packages at the rate of more than 1,000,000 packages a day. Assume that Purolator sold a small delivery truck for $5,000. Purolator had originally purchased the truck for $18,000, and had recorded amortization for three years.

Required:

1. Give the journal entry for the disposal of the truck, assuming that:
   a. The accumulated amortization was $13,000.
   b. The accumulated amortization was $12,400.
   c. The accumulated amortization was $13,400.

2. Based on the three preceding situations, explain how the amount of amortization recorded up to the time of disposal affects the amount of gain or loss on disposal.

E9-12 Determining Financial Statement Effects of the Disposal of an Asset   LO5

Refer to the information in E9-11.

Required:

Using the following structure, indicate the effects (accounts, amounts, and + or −) for the disposal of the truck assuming that:
   a. The accumulated amortization was $13,000.
   b. The accumulated amortization was $12,400.
   c. The accumulated amortization was $13,400.

LO6   **E9-13 Computing and Reporting the Acquisition and Amortization of Three Different Intangible Assets**

Kreiser Company had three intangible assets at the end of 2009 (end of the accounting year):

a. A patent purchased from J. Miller on January 1, 2009, for a cash cost of $5,640. Miller had registered the patent five years ago.

b. A self-developed trademark was registered with the federal government for $10,000. Management decided the trademark had an indefinite life.

c. Computer software and Web development technology was purchased on October 1, 2008, for $60,000. These assets were expected to have a four-year useful life to the company.

Required:

1. Compute the acquisition cost of each intangible asset.

2. Compute the amortization of each intangible for the year ended December 31, 2009. The company calculates amortization to the closest month-end.

3. Show how these assets and any related expenses should be reported on the balance sheet and income statement for 2009.

LO4, LO6   **E9-14 Recording the Purchase, Amortization, and Impairment of a Patent**

Nutek, Inc., holds a patent for the Full Service™ handi-plate, which the company's annual report describes as "a patented plastic buffet plate that allows the user to hold both a plate and cup in one hand" and that "has a multitude of uses including social gatherings such as backyard barbeques, buffets, picnics, tailgate and parties of any kind." (No, we're not making this up.) Recently, Nutek also purchased a patent for $1,000,000 for "a specialty line of patented switch plate covers and outlet plate covers specifically designed to light up automatically when the power fails." Assume the switch plate patent was purchased January 1, 2008, and it is being amortized over a period of 10 years.

Required:

1. Give the journal entries to record the purchase and the amortization of the switch plate patent in 2008.

2. After several months of unsuccessful attempts to manufacture the switch plate covers, Nutek determined that the patent was significantly impaired, and its book value on January 1, 2009, was written off. Give the journal entry to record the asset impairment.

3. Comment on Nutek's 2008 decision to invest in the patent.

LO8   **E9-15 Computing and Interpreting the Fixed-Asset-Turnover Ratio from a Financial Analyst's Perspective**

The following data were included in a recent Apple Computer annual report (in millions):

	2007	*2006*	*2005*	*2004*	*2003*	*2002*
Net sales	$24,006	$19,315	$13,931	$8,279	$6,207	$5,742
Net property, plant, and equipment	1,832	1,281	817	707	669	669

Required:

1. Compute Apple's fixed-asset-turnover ratio for 2003, 2005, and 2007 (the odd years). Round your answer to one decimal place.

2. If you were a financial analyst, what would you say about the results of your analyses?

E9-16 Computing Amortization and Book Value for Two Years, Using Alternative Amortization Methods and Interpreting the Impact on the Fixed-Asset-Turnover Ratio

LO3, LO8, LO9

Torge Company bought a machine for $65,000 cash. The estimated useful life was five years, and the estimated residual value was $5,000. Assume that the estimated useful life in productive units is 150,000. Units actually produced were 40,000 in year 1 and 45,000 in year 2.

Required:

1. Determine the appropriate amounts to complete the following schedule. Show computations.

Method of Amortization	Amortization Expense for		Book Value at the End of	
	Year 1	Year 2	Year 1	Year 2
Straight-line				
Units-of-production				
Double-declining-balance				

2. Which method would result in the lowest net income for year 1? For year 2?
3. Which method would result in the lowest fixed-asset-turnover ratio for year 1? Why?

E9-17 Evaluating the Impact of Capitalized Interest on Fixed Asset Turnover

LO2, LO8, LO9

You are a financial analyst charged with evaluating the asset efficiency of companies in the hotel industry. Fairmont Hotels and Resorts owns a number of luxury hotels in Canada, including the Banff Springs Hotel, Jasper Park Lodge, Château Lake Louise, and the Château Laurier in Ottawa. The financial statements for Fairmont include the following note:

Summary of Significant Accounting Policies

Property and Equipment
The Company's policy is to capitalize betterments and replacements and interest incurred during the construction period on new facilities and during the renovation period of major renovations to existing facilities.

Required:

1. Assume that Fairmont followed this policy for a major construction project this year. Would Fairmont's policy increase, decrease, or not affect the fixed-asset-turnover ratio in the current year?
2. Normally, if you saw a decrease in the fixed-asset-turnover ratio, what would you think about Fairmont's effectiveness in utilizing fixed assets?
3. If the fixed-asset-turnover ratio decreases because of interest capitalization, does this change indicate a real decrease in efficiency? Why or why not?

E9-18 Recording the Sale of a Long-Lived Tangible Asset

LO5

In a recent year, Fairmont Hotels and Resorts sold its Kea Lani Maui resort in Hawaii for cash proceeds of $355.4 million. Assume that this resort had a net book value of $246.6 million at that date, and that amortization of $28.4 had accumulated on the property. The original cost of the resort is in an asset account called Resort Properties.

Required:

Make the journal entry on Fairmont's books to record the sale.

E9-19 Finding Financial Information as a Potential Investor

LO1-LO6

You are considering investing the cash gifts you received for graduation in various companies. You have received several annual reports.

Required:

For each of the following, indicate where you would locate the information in an annual report:

1. The detail on major classifications of long-lived assets
2. The accounting method(s) used for financial reporting purposes

3. The amount of assets written off as impaired during the year
4. Net amount of property, plant, and equipment
5. Policies on amortizing intangibles
6. Amortization expense
7. Any significant gains or losses on disposals of fixed assets
8. Prior year's accumulated amortization

LO7   **E9-20 (Supplement A) Recording a Change in Estimate**
Refer to E9-4.

Required:

1. Give the adjusting entry that should be made at the end of 2009 for amortization of the manufacturing equipment, assuming no change in the original estimated total life or residual value. Show computations.
2. Give the adjusting entry that should be made at the end of 2009 for amortization of the manufacturing equipment, assuming the company now estimates that the asset will last until the end of 2014. Residual value is expected to stay the same. Show computations.

LO7   **E9-21 (Supplement A) Determining Financial Statement Effects of a Change in Estimate**
Refer to E9-4.

Required:

1. Using the following format, indicate the effects (accounts, amounts, and + or −) of the 2009 adjustment for amortization of the manufacturing equipment, assuming no change in the estimated life or residual value. Show computations.
2. Using the following format, indicate the effects (accounts, amounts, and + or −) of the 2009 adjustment for amortization of the manufacturing equipment, assuming the company now estimates that the asset will last until the end of 2014. Residual value is expected to stay the same. Show computations.

Date	Assets	=	Liabilities	+	Shareholders' Equity

COACHED PROBLEMS

LO2, LO3   **CP9-1 Computing Acquisition Cost and Recording Amortization under Three Alternative Methods**

At the beginning of the year, Montgomery Company bought three used machines from Hosey, Inc. The machines immediately were overhauled, installed, and started operating. Because the machines were different, each was recorded separately in the accounts.

	Machine A	Machine B	Machine C
Amount paid for asset	$7,600	$25,600	$6,800
Installation costs	300	500	200
Renovation costs prior to use	2,000	400	600
Repairs after production began	400	350	325

By the end of the first year, each machine had been operating 8,000 hours.

Required:

1. Compute the cost of each machine. Explain the rationale for capitalizing or expensing the various costs.

2. Give the journal entry to record amortization expense at the end of year 1, assuming the following:

| Machine | Estimates | | Amortization Method |
	Life	Residual Value	
A	5 years	$1,500	Straight-line
B	40,000 hours	900	Units-of-production
C	4 years	2,000	Double-declining-balance

CP9-2 Recording and Interpreting the Disposal of Long-Lived Assets

LO5

During 2009, Jensen Company disposed of two different assets. On January 1, 2009, prior to their disposal, the accounts reflected the following:

Asset	Original Cost	Residual Value	Estimated Life	Accumulated Amortization (straight-line)
Machine A	$20,000	$3,000	8 years	$12,750 (6 years)
Machine B	76,200	4,200	15 years	57,600 (12 years)

COACH'S TIP

When no cash is received on disposal, the loss on disposal will equal the book value of the asset at the time of disposal.

The machines were disposed of in the following ways:

a. Machine A: Sold on January 2, 2009, for $8,200 cash
b. Machine B: On January 2, 2009, this machine suffered irreparable damage from an accident and was removed immediately by a salvage company at no cost.

Required:

1. Give the journal entries related to the disposal of each machine at the beginning of 2009.
2. Explain the accounting rationale for the way that you recorded each disposal.

CP9-3 Determining Financial Statement Effects of Activities Related to Intangible Assets

LO6

During the 2009 annual accounting period, Chu Corporation completed the following transactions:

a. On January 1, 2009, purchased a licence for $7,200 cash (estimated useful life, three years).
b. On July 1, 2009, purchased another business for cash. The $120,000 purchase price included $115,000 for tangible assets of the business, and $24,000 for its liabilities, which were assumed by Chu. The remainder was goodwill with an indefinite life.
c. Expenditures during 2009 for research totalled $8,700.

COACH'S TIP

Goodwill is the amount paid over and above the value of net assets. Net assets are calculated as assets minus liabilities.

Required:

1. For each of these transactions, indicate the accounts, amounts and effects (+ for increase and − for decrease) on the accounting equation. Use the following structure:

Date	Assets	=	Liabilities	+	Shareholders' Equity

2. For each of the intangible assets, compute amortization for the year ended December 31, 2009.

CP9-4 (Supplement A) Analyzing and Recording Entries Related to a Change in Estimated Life and Residual Value

LO7

Petro-Canada is a major Canadian integrated oil and gas company with proven reserves of 1.2 billion barrels of oil equivalent. It operates primarily in western Canada, but also has interests off Canada's East Coast. Offshore drilling units and floating production and storage vessels (FPSO) cost many millions of dollars. Assume that Petro-Canada owns an FPSO acquired at an original

cost of $4,000,000. It is being amortized on a straight-line basis over a 20-year estimated useful life, and has a $500,000 estimated residual value. At the end of 2009, the FPSO had been amortized for a full eight years. In January 2010, a decision was made, on the basis of improved maintenance procedures, that a total estimated useful life of 25 years and a residual value of $730,000 would be more realistic. The accounting period ends December 31.

Required:

1. Compute (*a*) the amount of amortization expense recorded in 2009, and (*b*) the book value of the FPSO at the end of 2009.

2. Compute the amount of amortization that should be recorded in 2010. Show computations.

3. Give the adjusting entry for amortization at December 31, 2010.

LO8

CP9-5   Analyzing Investments in Capital and Intangible Assets

Shell and Petro-Canada are two capital-intensive companies in the oil and gas industry. To evaluate their investments in capital and intangible assets and their ability to manage their capital assets, consider the following information reported in their 2007 and 2006 annual reports (amounts in millions).

	Shell			Petro-Canada		
Fiscal Year Ended:	**2007**	**2006**	**2005**	**2007**	**2006**	**2005**
Net sales	$355,782	$318,845	$306,731	$21,710	$18,911	$17,585
Property, plant, and equipment	101,521	100,988	87,558	19,497	18,577	15,921
Intangible assets	5,366	4,808	4,350	731	801	737
Total assets	269,470	235,276	219,516	23,852	22,646	20,655

Required:

1. Based on 2007 numbers, which company is more capital-intensive, Shell or Petro-Canada?

2. Based on 2007 numbers, which company has more intangible assets as a percentage of their total assets? How does that compare with their investment in capital assets?

3. Calculate and compare each company's fixed-asset-turnover ratio for 2007 and 2006. Comment on the trend in each company's ratio over the two years.

GROUP A PROBLEMS

LO2, LO3

PA9-1   Computing Acquisition Cost and Recording Amortization under Three Alternative Methods

At the beginning of the year, Morgan Inc. bought three used machines from Abruzzo Corporation. The machines immediately were overhauled, installed, and started operating. Because the machines were different, each was recorded separately in the accounts.

	Machine A	*Machine B*	*Machine C*
Cost of the asset	$10,800	$32,500	$21,700
Installation costs	800	1,100	1,100
Renovation costs prior to use	600	1,400	1,600
Repairs after production began	200	300	300

By the end of the first year, each machine had been operating 7,000 hours.

Required:

1. Compute the cost of each machine. Explain the rationale for capitalizing or expensing the various costs.

2. Give the journal entry to record amortization expense at the end of year 1, assuming the following:

| | | Estimates | |
Machine	Life	Residual Value	Amortization Method
A	4 years	$1,000	Straight-line
B	33,000 hours	2,000	Units-of-production
C	5 years	1,400	Double-declining-balance

PA9-2 Recording and Interpreting the Disposal of Long-Lived Assets   LO5

During 2009, Kosik Company disposed of two different assets. On January 1, 2009, prior to their disposal, the accounts reflected the following:

Asset	Original Cost	Residual Value	Estimated Life	Accumulated Amortization (straight-line)
Machine A	$24,000	$2,000	5 years	$17,600 (4 years)
Machine B	59,200	3,200	14 years	48,000 (12 years)

The machines were disposed of in the following ways:

a. Machine A: Sold on January 1, 2009, for $5,750 cash
b. Machine B: On January 1, 2009, this machine suffered irreparable damage from an accident and was removed immediately by a salvage company at no cost.

Required:

1. Give the journal entries related to the disposal of each machine at the beginning of 2009.
2. Explain the accounting rationale for the way that you recorded each disposal.

PA9-3 Determining Financial Statement Effects of Activities Related to Intangible Assets   LO6

Norton (Canada) Pharmaceuticals entered into the following transactions that potentially affect intangible assets:

a. On January 1, 2009, the company spent $18,600 cash to buy a patent that expires in 15 years.
b. During 2009, the company spent $25,480 on a new drug that will be submitted to Health Canada for testing in 2009.
c. Norton Pharmaceuticals purchased another business in 2009 for a cash lump sum payment of $650,000. Included in the purchase price was "Goodwill, $75,000."

Required:

1. For each of these transactions, indicate the accounts, amounts, and effects (+ for increase and − for decrease) on the accounting equation. Use the following structure:

Item	Assets	=	Liabilities	+	Shareholders' Equity

2. For each of the intangible assets, compute amortization for the year ended December 31, 2009.

PA9-4 Recording Acquisitions, Amortization, and Disposal of Tangible and Intangible Assets   LO2, LO3, LO5, LO6

Surrey Saddle Co. purchased a machine for cash on January 1, 2009, paying $4,000 in shipping costs in addition to the invoice cost of $62,000. The machine has an $8,000 residual value and an eight-year useful life. On June 22, 2009, the company registered a patent for $2,000. On September 30, 2011, the machine was sold for $50,000. The company's fiscal year-end is December 31, and the company records amortization to the closest month-end.

Required:

1. Assuming the company uses the straight-line method of amortization, prepare journal entries to record the acquisitions, amortization expense for 2009, and the disposal of the machine in 2011.

2. Assuming the company uses the double-declining-balance method of amortization for machinery, prepare the journal entries to record amortization expense for 2009 and 2010.

LO8

PA9-5 Analyzing Fixed-Asset-Turnover Ratio

Air Canada and WestJet are two capital-intensive companies in the airline industry. To evaluate their investments in capital assets and their ability to manage these assets, consider the following information reported in their 2007 and 2006 annual reports (amounts in millions).

	Air Canada			WestJet		
Fiscal Year Ended:	**2007**	**2006**	**2005**	**2007**	**2006**	**2005**
Net sales	$10,599	$10,065	$9,458	$2,151	$1,765	$1,393
Property, plant, and equipment	7,919	5,946	5,451	2,213	2,159	1,803
Total assets	11,837	11,749	10,262	2,984	2,727	2,213

Required:

1. Based on 2007 numbers, which company is more capital-intensive, Air Canada or WestJet?

2. Calculate and compare each company's fixed-asset-turnover ratio for 2007 and 2006. Comment on the trend in each company's ratio over the two years.

GROUP B PROBLEMS

LO2, LO3

PB9-1 Computing Acquisition Cost and Recording Amortization under Three Alternative Methods

At the beginning of the year, Walters Company bought three used machines from Canadian Chopper, Inc. The machines immediately were overhauled, installed, and started operating. Because the machines were different, each was recorded separately in the accounts.

	Machine A	*Machine B*	*Machine C*
Amount paid for asset	$19,600	$10,100	$9,800
Installation costs	300	500	200
Renovation costs prior to use	100	300	600
Repairs after production began	220	900	480

By the end of the first year, each machine had been operating 4,000 hours.

Required:

1. Compute the cost of each machine. Explain the rationale for capitalizing or expensing the various costs.

2. Give the journal entry to record amortization expense at the end of year 1, assuming the following:

Machine	Estimates		Amortization Method
	Life	*Residual Value*	
A	7 years	$1,100	Straight-line
B	40,000 hours	900	Units-of-production
C	4 years	2,000	Double-declining-balance

PB9-2 Recording and Interpreting the Disposal of Long-Lived Assets

LO5

During 2009, Rayon Corporation disposed of two different assets. On January 1, 2009, prior to their disposal, the accounts reflected the following:

Asset	Original Cost	Residual Value	Estimated Life	Accumulated Amortization (straight-line)
Machine A	$60,000	$11,000	7 years	$28,000 (4 years)
Machine B	14,200	1,925	5 years	7,365 (3 years)

The machines were disposed of in the following ways:

a. Machine A: Sold on January 2, 2009, for $33,500 cash
b. Machine B: On January 2, 2009, this machine suffered irreparable damage from an accident and was removed immediately by a salvage company at no cost.

Required:

1. Give the journal entries related to the disposal of each machine at the beginning of 2009.
2. Explain the accounting rationale for the way that you recorded each disposal.

PB9-3 Determining Financial Statement Effects of Activities Related to Intangible Assets

LO6

Fearn Company entered into the following transactions that potentially affect intangible assets:

a. Soon after Fearn Company started business, in January 2007, it purchased another business for a cash lump sum payment of $400,000. Included in the purchase price was "Goodwill, $60,000." The account balance hasn't changed in three years.
b. The company purchased a patent at a cash cost of $54,600 on January 1, 2009. The patent has an estimated useful life of 13 years.
c. In 2009, Fearn hired a director of brand development to create a marketable identity for the company's products. The director devoted the entire year to this work, at a cost to the company of $125,000.

Required:

1. For each of these transactions, indicate the accounts, amounts, and effects (+ for increase and − for decrease) on the accounting equation in 2009. Use the following structure:

Item	Assets	=	Liabilities	+	Shareholders' Equity

2. For each of the intangible assets, compute amortization for the year ended December 31, 2009.

PB9-4 Recording Acquisitions, Amortization, and Disposal of Tangible and Intangible Assets

LO2, LO3, LO5, LO6

Kosmo Salad Company purchased a truck for cash on January 1, 2009, paying $4,000 for a new motor in addition to the invoice cost of $32,000. Kosmo expects to use the truck for 10 years and thinks it will have a residual value of $1,500 at the end of that time. On July 3, 2009, Kosmo pays $4,000 to have a company Web site developed. The developer expects the Web site to be usable for only three years before it will have to be scrapped and redone. On March 27, 2011, the truck is involved in an accident and is sold for $600 to a scrap dealer. The company's fiscal year-end is December 31, and the company records amortization to the closest month-end.

Required:

1. Assuming the company uses the straight-line method of amortization, prepare journal entries to record the acquisitions, amortization expense for 2009, and the disposal of the machine in 2011.
2. Assuming the company uses the double-declining-balance method of amortization for the truck, prepare the journal entries to record amortization expense for 2009 and 2010.

LO8

PB9-5 Analyzing Fixed-Asset-Turnover Ratio

Canadian National Railway (CN) and Amtrak are two capital-intensive companies in the railway industry. To evaluate their investments in capital assets and their ability to manage these assets, consider the following information reported in their 2007 and 2006 annual reports (amounts in millions).

	CN			Amtrak		
Fiscal Year Ended:	**2007**	**2006**	**2005**	**2007**	**2006**	**2005**
Net sales	$7,897	$7,929	$7,446	$2,152	$2,043	$1,886
Property, plant, and equipment (net)	20,413	21,053	20,078	8,306	8,200	8,075
Accumulated amortization	8,910	9,458	9,347	4,425	4,496	4,808
Total assets	23,460	24,004	22,188	10,165	9,919	9,747

Required:

1. Based on 2007 numbers, which company is more capital-intensive, CN or Amtrak?
2. Based on 2007 numbers, calculate the gross value of each company's property, plant, and equipment (before amortization), and the percentage that each company's accumulated amortization is of its gross investment in property, plant, and equipment. Is there anything this percentage tells you about the state of its capital assets?
3. Calculate and compare each company's fixed-asset-turnover ratio for 2007 and 2006. Comment on the trend in each company's ratio over the two years.

SKILLS DEVELOPMENT CASES

LO2, LO3, LO6, LO8

S9-1 Finding Financial Information

Refer to the financial statements of High Liner in Appendix A at the end of this book, or download the annual report from the *Cases* section of the text's Web site at www.mcgrawhill.ca/college/phillips.

Required:

1. What method of amortization does the company use?
2. What is the amount of accumulated amortization at the end of the current year? What percentage is this of the total cost of property and equipment?
3. For amortization purposes, what is the estimated useful life of buildings?
4. What amount of amortization expense was reported for the current year? What percentage of total revenues is it?
5. What amount did the company report for intangible assets in the current year? Are these assets amortized?
6. What is the fixed-asset-turnover ratio for the current year and the prior year?

LO2, LO3, LO6, LO8

S9-2 Comparing Financial Information

Refer to the financial statements of Sun-Rype by downloading the annual report from the *Cases* section of the text's Web site at www.mcgrawhill.ca/college/ phillips.

Required:

1. Does Sun-Rype use the same amortization method as High Liner?
2. What is the amount of accumulated amortization at the end of the current year? What percentage is this of the total cost of property and equipment? Is this a larger (or smaller) percentage of the total cost of property and equipment than for High Liner? What does it suggest to you about the length of time the assets have been amortized?

3. Compare the estimated useful lives of Sun-Rype's buildings with those of High Liner. If one company uses longer useful lives, how would that affect the fixed-asset-turnover ratios of the two companies?

4. What amount of amortization expense was reported for the current year? What percentage of total revenues is it? Compare this percentage with that of High Liner and describe what this implies about the two companies' operations.

5. What amount did the company report for intangible assets in the current year?

6. What is the fixed-asset-turnover ratio for the current year? Compare this ratio with that of High Liner and describe what it implies about the operations of the two companies.

S9-3 Internet-Based Team Research: Examining an Annual Report

LO1, LO3, LO6, LO8

TEAM CASE

As a team, select an industry to analyze. Using your Web browser, each team member should acquire the annual report for one publicly traded Canadian company in the industry, with each member selecting a different company. (See S1-3 in Chapter 1 for a description of possible resources for these tasks.)

Required:

1. On an individual basis, each team member should write a short report that incorporates the following:
    a. Describe the amortization methods used.
    b. Compute the percentage of fixed asset cost that has been amortized. What does this imply about the length of time the assets have been amortized?
    c. Compute the fixed-asset-turnover ratios for the current and prior years. What does this tell you about the efficiency of the company's asset use?
    d. Describe the kinds of intangible assets, if any, that the company reports on the balance sheet.

2. Then, as a team, write a short report comparing and contrasting your companies using these attributes. Discuss any patterns across the companies that you, as a team, observe. Provide potential explanations for any differences discovered.

S9-4 Analyzing Financial Information about Intangibles

LO6

Nortel Networks of Brampton, Ontario, is a telecom giant that provides large-scale communication systems and infrastructures to companies around the world. During the technology boom of the 1990s, Nortel's growth was impressive. Part of its growth was fueled by its strategy of acquiring other companies. In 2000, Nortel paid $20.4 billion to buy 11 companies, adding a whopping $18.5 billion to goodwill on its balance sheet. Unfortunately for Nortel, the technology sector was in serious trouble at that time. Below are selected figures for Nortel.

| | *(in millions)* | | | *2002* |
	1999	*2000*	*2001 **	*(as restated)*
Sales	$20,558	$27,966	$18,912	$11,022
Amortization of intangibles	2,046	6,321	4,664	162
Net income (loss)	(197)	(2,957)	(27,446)	(2,910)
Total property and equipment	2,458	3,421	2,573	1,692
Goodwill	3,274	17,354	1,933	1,291
Other intangibles	1,246	1,418	272	98
Total Assets	22,597	42,227	20,251	15,832

*These are the numbers released to the public in March 2002. Nortel released restated figures for 2001 in January 2005. The original numbers are used here because they shed light on the environment at that time.

Required:

1. What is goodwill? How does it get onto a company's balance sheet?

2. Calculate the percentage of Nortel's total assets represented by (a) plant and equipment, (b) goodwill, and (c) total intangibles for the years 1999 to 2002. (Round to one decimal place.)

3. In the 2001 fiscal year, Nortel recorded a $12.8-billion impairment loss on goodwill and other intangible assets. How much did this contribute to Nortel's net loss that year? Why do you think management decided it was appropriate to write down intangibles at that time?

4. In the light of the 2001 impairment loss, comment on Nortel's $20.4-billion investment decision in 2000.

5. In the notes to Nortel's 2000 financial statements, it states that "goodwill is being amortized over its estimated useful life of three to twenty years," which was consistent with Canadian GAAP at the time. Why did amortization of intangibles go down so much in Nortel's 2002 statements?

6. What happened to Nortel's share price on the Toronto Stock Exchange (TSE) over this period? Find prices for the following dates: December 31, 1999; April 30, 2000; December 31, 2000; December 31, 2001; and July 31, 2001. One place to find this data is by clicking "view historical stock prices" in the investor relations section of Nortel's Web site at www.nortel.com/corporate/investor/index.html.

LO2, LO3

S9-5 Ethical Decision Making: A Real-Life Example

ETHICAL ISSUES

Assume you work as a staff member in the accounting department of an Ontario-based company that owns theatres and produces live theatrical shows such as *Ragtime*, *The Phantom of the Opera*, and *Show Boat*. One morning, you are contacted by the assistant to the CFO and asked to come to the CFO's office. After a warm greeting, the CFO explains the reason for the visit. He hands you a list of journal entries he would like you to make before year-end, which is two weeks away, and explains the reasons for them as follows:

1. There are certain costs that were capitalized years ago into the account deferred pre-production costs that relate to shows no longer running. These costs are to be transferred to the buildings account.

2. There are other costs that have been capitalized to the show *Phantom*, which is currently running on Broadway, that have to be transferred to the show *Ragtime*, which is due to open in Toronto next year.

3. There are certain expenses and corresponding liabilities that have been accrued that should be reversed. They shouldn't be recorded yet since they apply to next year.

He wraps up the meeting by telling you that it is important that you not talk about the meeting or the adjusting entries to anyone. You assume he doesn't want the others to be jealous of your new important responsibility.

The company's amortization policy for capital costs is as follows:

1. Theatre buildings are amortized on a straight-line basis over 40 years.

2. The costs of producing a new show are capitalized as pre-production costs. Once the show is running, these costs are amortized on a straight-line basis over five years.

Once you've made the journal entries as requested by the CFO, you notice that the effect on the income statement is to change it by $18 million. You had no idea that the number would be so large, and now you feel a bit uncomfortable about what you've done. But you keep your promise to remain silent. Three weeks into the new fiscal year, after the earnings figures for the past year have been made public, the external accountant in charge of the audit stops by your office, accompanied by the head of your company's internal audit department, and questions you about "suspicious journal entries made by you that have not been substantiated by the appropriate supporting documentation." At the end of the meeting, you are advised to find yourself a lawyer.

Required:

1. Would the net income after the adjustments be more or less than it was before? Explain how each adjustment would change the net income figure. What do you think might have been the real reason for the adjustments?

2. What should have raised your suspicion about the real nature of your assigned task in this case?

3. Given your current circumstances, describe how you would have acted in the initial meeting with the CFO if you had been able to predict where it might lead you.

4. Eventually, after their investigation, the internal and external auditors realize what has happened. They are reluctant to make the situation public because it would be devastating for the company. They worry about whether their revelations would result in layoffs. Plus, they fear they would somehow end up being blamed for the mess. Beyond these personal consequences, describe other potential ways in which the findings would likely be devastating for the publicly traded company and those associated with it.

Epilogue: This case is based on Livent Inc., an Ontario theatre company that went public in 1993 and subsequently went bankrupt in 1998, after senior management concocted a massive scheme to fraudulently misrepresent the financial position of the company. The RCMP charged Garth Drabinsky, the CEO, and his partner, Myron Gottlieb, with fraud four years later, alleging that the accused defrauded creditors and private and public investors of approximately $500 million. Garth Drabinsky achieved great fame in Canada in the 1980s and 1990s as the colourful co-founder of the Cineplex Odeon theatre chain. Livent was the world's only publicly held company with live theatre production as its main business and, at its peak, it was the largest live theatre company in North America, with theatres in Toronto, Vancouver, Chicago, and New York. In July, 2007, an Ontario court ordered Drabinsky and Gottlieb to pay U.S.$36.6-million to U.S. investors who bought Livent's debt in the late 1990s. Drabinsky and Gottlieb were found guilty of fraud and forgery in March, 2009 and are currently awaiting sentencing.

S9-6 Ethical Decision Making: A Mini-Case

LO3, LO5

Assume that you are one of three members of the accounting staff working for a small, private company. At the beginning of this year, the company expanded into a new industry by acquiring equipment that will be used to make several new lines of products. The owner and general manager of the company has indicated that, as one of the conditions for providing financing for the new equipment, the company's bank will receive a copy of the company's annual financial statements. Another condition of the loan is that the company's total assets cannot fall below $250,000. Violation of this condition gives the bank the option to demand immediate repayment of the loan. Before making the adjustment for this year's amortization, the company's total assets are reported at $255,000. The owner has asked you to take a look at the facts regarding the new equipment and "work with the numbers to make sure everything stays onside with the bank."

ETHICAL ISSUES

An amortization method has not yet been adopted for the new equipment. Equipment used in other parts of the company is amortized using the double-declining-balance method. The cost of the new equipment was $35,000, and the manager estimates it will be worth "at least $7,000" at the end of its four-year useful life. Because the products made with the new equipment are only beginning to catch on with consumers, the company used the equipment to produce just 4,000 units this year. It is expected that, over all four years of its useful life, the new equipment will make a total of 28,000 units.

Required:

1. Calculate the amortization that would be reported this year under each of the three methods shown in this chapter. Which of the methods would meet the owner's objective?

2. Evaluate whether it is ethical to recommend that the company use the method identified in requirement 1. What two parties are most directly affected by this recommendation? How would each party be benefited or harmed by the recommendation? Does the recommendation violate any laws or applicable rules? Are there any other factors that you would consider before making a recommendation?

S9-7 Critical Thinking: Analyzing the Effects of Amortization Policies on Income

LO3, LO5, LO9

As an aspiring financial analyst, you have applied to a major investment services firm for a summer job. To screen potential applicants, the firm provides you with a short case study and asks you to evaluate the financial success of two hypothetical companies that started operations on January 1, 2009. Both companies operate in the same industry, use very similar assets, and have very similar customer bases. Among the additional information provided about the companies are the following comparative income statements.

	Fast Corporation		Slow Corporation	
	2010	*2009*	*2010*	*2009*
Net sales	$60,000	$60,000	$60,000	$60,000
Cost of goods sold	20,000	20,000	20,000	20,000
Gross profit	40,000	40,000	40,000	40,000
Selling, general, and administrative expenses	19,000	19,000	19,000	19,000
Amortization expense	3,555	10,667	5,000	5,000
Operating income	17,445	10,333	16,000	16,000
Other gains (losses)	2,222	—	(1,000)	—
Income before income taxes	$19,667	$10,333	$15,000	$16,000

Required:

Prepare an analysis of the two companies with the goal of determining which company is better managed. If you could request two additional pieces of information from these companies' financial statements, describe specifically what they would be and explain how they would help you to make a decision.

LO3

S9-8 Preparing Amortization Schedules for Straight-Line and Double-Declining-Balance

To make some extra money, you've started preparing templates of business forms and schedules for others to download from the Internet (for a small fee). After relevant information is entered into each template, it automatically performs calculations using formulas you have entered into the template. For the amortization template, you decide to produce two worksheets—one that calculates amortization and book value under the straight-line method, and another that calculates these amounts using the double-declining-balance method. The templates perform straightforward calculations of amortization and book value, when given the cost of an asset, its estimated useful life, and its estimated residual value. These particular templates won't handle disposals or changes in estimates—you plan to create a deluxe version for those functions. To illustrate that your templates actually work, you enter the information used to produce the amortization schedules shown in Exhibit 9.7, with ClubLink and Intrawest as examples.

Although you're confident you can use appropriate formulas in the spreadsheet to create a template for the straight-line method, you're a little uncertain about how to make the double-declining-balance method work. As usual, you e-mail your friend Billy for advice. Here's what he said:

From: BillyTheTutor@yahoo.com
To: Overwhelmed@hotmail.com
Cc:
Subject: Excel Help

I wish I'd thought of charging money for showing how to do ordinary accounting activities. You'd have made me rich by now. Here's how to set up your worksheets. Begin by creating an "input values" section. This section will allow someone to enter the asset cost, residual value, and estimated life in an area removed from the actual amortization schedule. You don't want someone accidentally entering amounts over formulas that you've entered into the schedule.

The cells from the input values section will be referenced by other cells in the amortization schedule. You will want to enter formulas in the cells for the first year row, and then copy and paste them to rows for the other years. When doing this, you will need to use what is called an "absolute reference," which means that the cell reference does not change when one row is copied and pasted to a different row. Unlike an ordinary cell reference that has a format of A1, an absolute reference has the format of A1, which prevents the spreadsheet from changing either the column

(A) or row (1) when copying the cell to other cells. You may find this useful when preparing both the straight-line and double-declining-balance schedules.

To create the amortization schedules, use five columns labelled: (1) year, (2) beginning of year accumulated amortization, (3) amortization, (4) end of year accumulated amortization, and (5) end of year book value.

The double-declining-balance template will be the trickiest to create because you need to be concerned that the book value is not amortized below the residual value in the last year of the asset's life. To force the template to automatically watch for this, you will need to use the IF function. Here's a screenshot of a template I created, using the IF function to properly calculate amortization for all years of the assets life. Notice the formula shown in the formula bar at the top.

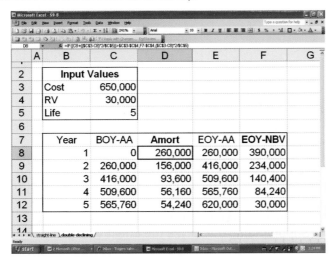

Required:

Create the spreadsheet templates to calculate amortization and book value using the straight-line and double-declining-balance methods. Demonstrate that the template works by reproducing the schedules in Exhibit 9.7.

CHAPTER 10

Reporting and Interpreting Liabilities

INSIDE LOOKING OUT

OUTSIDE LOOKING IN

This chapter focuses on reporting and interpreting the liabilities of Rogers Communications, owner of the Toronto Blue Jays and a major player in wireless, cable, and media communications.

Understand decisions that involve liabilities.

LO1   Explain how the reporting of liabilities assists decision-making.

Study how to account for and report liabilities.

LO2   Explain how to account for common types of current liabilities.

LO3   Analyze and record bond liability transactions.

LO4   (Supplement A) Analyze the effective-interest amortization method for discounts and premiums on bond liabilities.

Evaluate the likelihood that liabilities will be repaid in full.

LO5   Interpret the current ratio and times-interest-earned ratio.

Reconsider how liability decisions can be affected by unrecorded debt.

LO6   Describe the additional liabilities information reported in the notes to the financial statements.

They've turned in the reports, and they're just waiting to hear their letter grade. They're expecting an A and would be devastated if it's a B. Sounds like some high-achieving students, right? But can you give a grade to a dog, a berry, or a bird? Yes, you can. The Blackberry handheld, FIDO wireless plan, and the Toronto Blue Jays baseball team and their corporate bosses at **ROGERS COMMUNICATIONS** receive a letter grade just like you and your friends. Their grading process differs a bit from yours, because their grade is assigned by credit rating agencies like Standard & Poor's, Fitch, and Moody's, indicating the company's ability to pay its liabilities on a timely basis. Another difference is that their grades can range from AAA to D. The AAA rating is given to companies in rock-solid financial condition, and the D goes to those who have defaulted on their payments. In general, anything above BB is considered a good to high-quality credit rating, which is what Rogers typically earns.

In this chapter, you will learn about the accounting procedures and financial ratios used to report and interpret liabilities, and how they influence credit ratings. Although we focus on *corporate* reporting and analyses, this chapter also can help you to understand the kind of information others use to evaluate your own personal credit rating.

As you might suspect, liabilities are a key ingredient in credit ratings. So, that's where we'll start: helping you to understand what liabilities are and how they're accounted for. As the Learning Objectives found on the first page of this chapter show, you'll use this knowledge later in the chapter when learning about the financial analyses and other information used to evaluate whether a company is likely to meet its financial obligations.

UNDERSTAND _____
Decisions that Involve Liabilities

When a friend asks to borrow something and promises to pay you back later, you get to experience what it's like to be a credit manager for a company. Before lending something to a friend or extending credit to another company, two questions should quickly come to mind:

1. How much does the person or company owe to others? For what?
2. Can you expect the person or company to repay each of its debts? When?

Some of your friends might be offended if you came right out and asked these questions. Fortunately, if you're a credit manager, you can often find answers to these questions in a company's financial statements. Let's assume we are credit managers at Research in Motion (RIM), the Canadian company that makes Blackberry hand-held computers and supplies them to Rogers. Let's see if we can answer these questions by looking at the liabilities section of the Rogers balance sheet at the end of its 2007 fiscal year, which is shown, along with total assets and shareholders' equity, in Exhibit 10.1.

Starting with the first question, does Rogers owe anything to others? You bet! The liabilities section of the balance sheet, shown in Exhibit 10.1, indicates that Rogers owes over $10.7 billion at the end of 2007, and that 70 per cent of total assets have been financed by debt. If you knew nothing else about Rogers, you might feel uneasy about its creditworthiness because the company owes so much to others. Let's see if this feeling changes as we now move to the second question.

---

exhibit 10.1   Rogers' Communications Summarized Balance Sheets (in millions)

December 31	2007	2006
Total Assets	$15,325	$14,105
Current Liabilities		
Bank Loans	$ 61	$ 19
Accounts Payable and Accrued Liabilities	2,260	1,792
Current Portion of Long-Term Debt	196	458
Unearned Revenues	225	227
Total Current Liabilities	2,742	2,496
Long-Term Liabilities	7,959	7,409
Total Liabilities	10,701	9,905
Shareholders' Equity	4,624	4,200
Total Liabilities and Shareholders' Equity	$15,325	$14,105

CLASSIFICATION OF LIABILITIES

When can you expect Rogers to repay its debts? The balance sheet responds to this question by classifying some liabilities as current and others as long-term. **Current liabilities** are short-term obligations that will be paid with current assets within the current **operating cycle** of the business or within one year of the balance sheet date, whichever is longer. Because most companies have an operating cycle that is shorter than a year, the definition of current liabilities can be simplified as liabilities that are due within one year. This means that only $2.7 billion of the $10.7 billion of total liabilities shown in Exhibit 10.1 will be paid within one year. This should make you feel a little more comfortable, particularly if you require Rogers to pay your company in one year or less. The remaining $8 billion of liabilities are due more than a year from the balance sheet date, and they are referred to as noncurrent or long-term liabilities.

STUDY _____
How to Account for and Report Liabilities

A company must record a liability when a transaction or event obligates the company to give up assets or services in the future. In this section, we will discuss various types of obligations that are reported as liabilities. But, before we do that, let's make sure you clearly understand what the liability numbers on the balance sheet represent.

MEASUREMENT OF LIABILITIES

The dollar amount reported for liabilities is the result of three things:

1. *The initial amount of the liability.* A liability is initially recorded at its cash equivalent, which is the amount of cash that a creditor would accept to settle the liability immediately after the transaction or event occurred.

2. *Additional amounts owed to the creditor.* Liabilities are increased whenever additional obligations arise, including interest charges that arise as time passes.

3. *Payments or services provided to the creditor.* Liabilities are reduced whenever the company makes payments or provides services to the creditor.

Notice that a liability is first recorded at a cash-equivalent amount, which excludes any interest charge. This makes sense because, if you borrowed $10 from a friend and paid it back a split-second later, you wouldn't have to pay any interest. Interest arises only as time passes, so it is recorded as a liability only after time has passed.

CURRENT LIABILITIES

Rogers lists a number of typical items in its current liabilities section. We will discuss each item separately, starting with bank loans.

Bank Loans

Sometimes a company arranges for a short-term loan with its bank, and this type of borrowing is reported as a bank loan in its balance sheet. A common way of prearranging a loan is by asking for overdraft protection on your chequing account. That way, even when you have no money left in your account, you just keep writing cheques to pay your bills. Once your account balance goes into a negative balance (sometimes called being in the red), this **overdraft** is essentially a short-term loan, which has been approved by applying for a **line of credit** with your bank. Interest will be charged on the loan until you make a deposit and put your bank account back into a positive balance (in the black). Exhibit 10.1 on page 429 shows that Rogers had an overdraft balance of $1 million in 2007.

Accounts Payable

Most companies purchase goods and services from other companies on credit. Typically, these transactions involve three stages: (1) order the goods/services, (2) receive the goods/services, and (3) pay for the goods/services. Accountants record liabilities at the stage that "obligates the company to give up assets or services." When do *you* think Rogers becomes obligated to pay for the cell phones it buys to sell to you?

If the order is never filled, Rogers wouldn't be expected to pay for it. So the receipt of goods/services is the point at which a liability is created and recorded. Like Rogers, most companies call this liability "accounts payable." The great thing about using accounts payable to buy goods/services is that suppliers don't charge interest on unpaid balances unless they are overdue. According to Exhibit 10.1, Rogers owes about $2.3 billion in accounts payable and accrued liabilities at the end of 2007. We'll look at accrued liabilities next.

Accrued Liabilities

Often, a business incurs an expense in one accounting period and makes a cash payment in a later period. To account for these situations, an adjusting entry typically is made at the end of the first of these periods to record a liability. Chapter 4 called this an accrual adjustment, so it seems appropriate that the liability account is called **accrued liabilities.** Companies record **accrued liabilities** for various expenses, including electricity, salaries, taxes, and interest.

> **Accrued liabilities** report the liability for expenses that have been incurred but not paid at the end of the accounting period.

Rogers' accrued liabilities are included in the $2.3 billion shown as Accounts Payable and Accrued Liabilities in Exhibit 10.1. Rogers does not provide details of its accrued liabilities in its notes, so Exhibit 10.2 shows you the accrual details of another well-known company, Canadian National Railway. Of the $1.3 billion shown on CN's 2007 balance sheet in Accounts payable and accrued charges, only $457 million is for normal trade accounts payable. The other $.8 billion is for accruals, and most of the accruals are for payroll, taxes, and interest. Below we explain these common types of accrued liabilities.

Accrued Payroll. At the end of each accounting period, employees usually will have earned salaries that have not yet been paid, and these must be accrued to achieve matching, as we discussed in Chapter 4. In addition to unpaid salaries, companies must report the cost of employment benefits promised to and earned by employees but not yet paid. These benefits include retirement programs, vacation time, and health insurance.

---

exhibit 10.2   Canadian National Railway's Accounts Payable and Accrued Liabilities (in millions)

On Balance Sheet

Accounts payable and accrued charges (Note 8)	$1,282

In Notes to the Financial Statements

Note 8
Accounts payable and accrued charges

(in millions)	December 31, 2007
Trade accounts payable	$457
Income and other taxes	123
Accrued payroll	234
Accrued interest	118
Accrued general charges	146
Provisions and other	204
	$1,282

Payroll Deductions.   In addition to paying employees and providing vacation time, all businesses must calculate and withhold from employees a variety of payroll deductions, including federal and provincial income taxes, Canada Pension Plan (CPP), Employment Insurance (EI), and provincial health care insurance, such as Ontario's OHIP premiums. Other deductions can also be made for union dues, automatic savings plans, life insurance premiums, etc.

Employers also are required to make their own contributions to CPP, EI, and Workers' Compensation. The amounts withheld from employees, plus the required employer contributions, are recorded as accrued liabilities until the company forwards the amounts to the appropriate government agencies.

A company's compensation expense (also called salaries and wages expense) includes all amounts earned by its employees, along with any other compensation-related amounts paid by the company. To illustrate, let's assume Rogers accumulated the following simplified information in its payroll records for the first two weeks of June 2009:

Salaries and wages earned by employees	$1,800,000	
Less: Income taxes withheld from employees	275,000	} Owed to government agencies[1]
Less: CPP and EI contributions withheld from employees	105,000	
Net pay to employees	$1,420,000	⟶ Paid to employees

Assuming that the employer contributions to CPP and EI are $115,000[1], the journal entries to record the payroll follow:

dr	Compensation Expense (+E, −SE)	1,800,000	
	cr Liability for Income Taxes Withheld (+L)		275,000
	cr CPP and EI Contributions Payable (+L)		105,000
	cr Cash (−A)		1,420,000
dr	Compensation Expense (+E, −SE)	115,000	
	cr CPP and EI Contributions Payable (+L)		115,000

COACH'S TIP

Two journal entries are used, to make it easy to see that compensation expense and CPP and EI contributions payable include both employee CPP and EI contributions (in the top journal entry) and employer CPP and EI contributions (in the bottom).

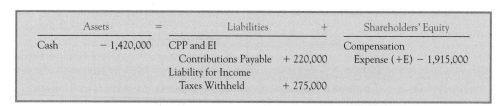

Assets	=	Liabilities	+	Shareholders' Equity
Cash − 1,420,000		CPP and EI		Compensation
		Contributions Payable + 220,000		Expense (+E) − 1,915,000
		Liability for Income		
		Taxes Withheld + 275,000		

The total compensation expense is $1,915,000. The biggest chunk of this is paid to employees ($1,420,000), with the remainder ($495,000) paid to the appropriate government agencies.

Accrued Taxes.   Corporations pay taxes on income they earn, just like you. Every year, a corporation must file a corporate tax return, called a T2 by CRA, which shows its taxable income, payments it made during the year, and the balance due. As we saw in Chapter 9 when we explained the difference between amortization expense and capital cost allowance, a company's taxable income is generally not the same as its income according to GAAP. The company uses the provisions in the Income Tax Act to calculate its taxable income, and that number is then multiplied by a tax rate, which for most large corporations is about 35 per cent. Rogers disclosed in Note 7 to its 2007 financial statements that its statutory income tax rate was 35.2 per cent. Corporate income taxes are due within three months after year-end, although most corporations are required to pay in instalments during the year.

---

[1] Rather than providing you with the detailed rules for calculating income taxes and CPP and EI contributions, which are taught in tax courses, here we simply provide reasonable numbers for these items.

PST and GST Payable.   In every province except Alberta, retail companies are required to charge a provincial sales tax (PST), which varies from province to province. In addition to PST, the federal government charges a goods and service tax (GST) of 5 per cent. Retailers collect sales tax from consumers at the time of sale and forward it to the provincial and federal governments. Just as with payroll taxes, the taxes collected by the company are reported as current liabilities until they are forwarded to the government. They are not an expense because the retailer simply collects and passes on the sales tax. So, if you bought a new Blackberry from Rogers in Manitoba for $500 cash plus taxes, the company would record the sale, 7 per cent PST, and 5 per cent GST using the following journal entry:

dr	Cash (+A)	560	
	cr PST Payable (+L)($500 × 7%)		35
	cr GST Payable (+L)($500 × 5%).....		25
	cr Sales Revenue (+R, +SE).........		500

Assets	=	Liabilities	+	Shareholders' Equity
Cash + 560		PST Payable + 35		Sales Revenue (+R) + 500
		GST Payable + 25		

When Rogers pays the taxes to the provincial and federal governments, the *PST Payable* and *GST Payable* accounts will be debited and *Cash* will be credited for the amount remitted. The HST (harmonized sales tax) is a combined PST and GST currently collected in New Brunswick, Nova Scotia, and Newfoundland and Labrador, and recently proposed in Ontario.

Interest Payable.   Interest due on late payments, loans, and bank overdrafts accrues with time and is included in accrued liabilities. The calculation of accrued interest is shown in the Notes Payable section later in the chapter.

Current Portion of Long-Term Debt

Remember when you were in grade 9 and it seemed as if it would be forever before you would graduate from high school? At that time, graduation was something that would happen in the long term. Later, however, when you made it to your senior year, high-school graduation had become a current event something that was less than a year away. We remind you of this to help you understand what happens with long-term debt.

If a company borrows money with the promise to repay it in two years, the amount of the loan is classified as long-term debt. Only the accrued interest on the loan is

---

HOW'S IT GOING?   A Self-Study Quiz

Assume that on December 1, 2009, your company borrowed $10,000, a portion of which is to be repaid each year on November 30. Specifically, your company will make the following principal payments: 2010, $1,000; 2011, $2,000; 2012, $3,000; and 2013, $4,000. Show how this loan will be reported in the December 31, 2010 and 2009, balance sheets, assuming that principal payments will be made when required.

	As of December 31	
	2010	**2009**
Current Liabilities:		
Current Portion of Long-Term Debt	$ ⎵⎵⎵	$ ⎵⎵⎵
Long-Term Debt	⎵⎵⎵	⎵⎵⎵
Total Liabilities	$9,000	$10,000

After you're finished, check your answers with the solution in the margin.

Quiz Answers

	As of December 31	
	2010	2009
Current Liabilities		
Current portion of long-term debt	$2,000	$ 1,000
Long-term debt	7,000	9,000
Total Liabilities	$9,000	$10,000

reported as a current liability in that year's balance sheet. After a year passes, however, the loan becomes a current liability, just as your graduation became a current event. When that happens, the loan needs to be reported in the current liabilities section of the balance sheet. Accountants don't actually create a different account for this—they just take the amount of principal to be repaid in the upcoming year out of the total long-term debt on the balance sheet and report it as a current liability called *Current Portion of Long-Term Debt*. Exhibit 10.1 on page 429 showed how Rogers did this in 2007 for $196 million of its long-term debt.

Unearned Revenue

Back in Chapter 4, you learned that some companies receive cash before they provide goods or services to customers. Exhibit 10.1 shows that Rogers had unearned revenues of $225 million on its 2007 balance sheet. Most of Rogers' unearned revenues stem from its media division. Rogers receives advertising revenue from selling radio and TV ads before the ads are aired. It also pre-sells tickets to the Toronto Blue Jays games, either as single-game tickets, flex-packs, or season tickets. In both cases, Rogers receives the cash before the revenue is earned. Rogers accounts for these transactions in two stages. (1) When the cash is received, Rogers records a liability for the future service. It is a liability at this point, because the customer paid Rogers in order to get something in return and, until Rogers provides that something, Rogers owes the customer. (2) When the service is provided, Rogers removes the liability and records the revenue that has been earned. According to Note 2(B) of its 2007 financial statements, Rogers records its advertising and ticket sales revenues as earned when the ads are aired and the baseball games are played.

This two-step process applies to all instances where cash is received before revenue is earned. As an example, let's look at the journal entries for the fee that Rogers collects for a 2009 Blue Jays season ticket. Assume that, in 2008, Rogers receives cash for your 2009 season ticket paid in advance that will allow you to see 80 home games at the Rogers Centre for $6,000. The company will account for this in two stages:

1. **Record cash received and liability created (in 2008):**

dr Cash (+A)	6,000	
cr Unearned Revenue (+L)		6,000

Assets	=	Liabilities	+	Shareholders' Equity
Cash + 6,000		Unearned Revenue + 6,000		

2. *Assuming that the Blue Jays play their first 20 games in April 2009,* reduce the liability as it is fulfilled and revenue is earned (on April 30, 2009):

dr Unearned Revenue (−L)	1,500	
cr Ticket Revenue (+R, +SE)		1,500
($6,000 × 20/80 = $1,500)		

Assets	=	Liabilities	+	Shareholders' Equity
		Unearned Revenue − 1,500		Ticket Revenue (+R) + 1,500

As each month passes, Rogers will make an adjusting journal entry to show that it has continued to fulfill its obligation and earn its ticket revenues, until all games have been played and all revenues have been earned.

Other Current Liabilities

Even though Rogers does not disclose any amounts under this heading, it is not unusual to see *Other Current Liabilities* listed in the current liability section of a balance sheet. Consistent with the matching principle, companies have to estimate liabilities for such things as warranties on their products. These estimated liabilities (sometimes called provisions) are often disclosed as other current liabilities. We'll now move on to another common current liability, *Notes Payable*, that Rogers does not list on its balance sheet.

Notes Payable

In Chapter 7, we described how a company accounts for promissory notes as *Notes Receivable* when it lends money to someone. In this section, you'll see how a company accounts for promissory notes as *Notes Payable* when they're used to borrow money.

For purposes of illustration, assume that, on November 1, 2009, Rogers negotiates with Scotiabank to borrow $100,000 cash on a *one-year* note. Scotiabank charges 6 per cent interest, which is the normal rate at the time. Interest payments are to be made in two cash instalments, on April 30 and October 31. The principal is to be repaid on the note's October 31, 2010, maturity date. These transactions can be summarized graphically as follows:

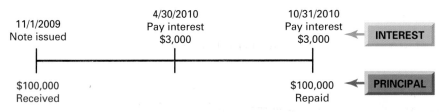

COACH'S TIP

Each interest payment of $3,000 is calculated as:

$100,000 \times 6\% \times 6/12.$

Over the life of this note, journal entries are needed for three things:

1. The initial recording of the note payable
2. Additional amounts owed
3. Payments made to the lender

1. Record the issuance of the note and receipt of cash. When Rogers receives $100,000 cash from Scotiabank on November 1, 2009, it has an obligation to repay that amount, which is recorded using the following journal entry:

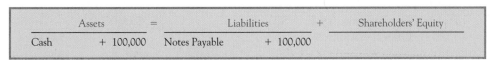

2. Record any interest owed by the end of the accounting period. Interest is rather like "rent" for using someone else's money over a period of time. Although interest becomes payable as each day passes, it is not paid nearly that often. Typically, interest is paid monthly or, in some cases, only once or twice per year. Rather than record the unpaid interest on each passing day, most companies record it at the end of the accounting period. These interest obligations are usually included in accrued liabilities on the balance sheet.

If Rogers were to prepare financial statements as of December 31, 2009, it would update its accounting records for any interest expense that has been incurred but not yet paid at that time. (See the graphic in the margin.)

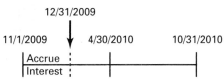

As you may recall from Chapter 7, interest is calculated using the formula:

$$\text{Interest} = \text{Principal Owed} \times \text{Interest Rate} \times \text{Time}$$

As of December 31, the note has been outstanding for only two months, so the unpaid interest is $1,000 = $100,000 \times 6\% \times 2/12$. Notice in these calculations that the "principal owed" is the amount owed at the beginning of the interest period, which is equal to the amount of the liability recorded in the *Notes Payable* account on November 1. "Time" is the fraction of the year for which interest is being accrued (2 months out of 12). Rather than prepare the journal entry for you, we'll give you a Self-Study Quiz that lets you practise what you learned back in Chapter 4 about accruing a liability for unpaid interest.

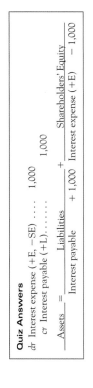

HOW'S IT GOING?   A Self-Study Quiz

Prepare the journal entry that Rogers would record on December 31 to accrue two months of interest on its promissory note. Show the effects on the accounting equation.

dr ☐☐   ☐

cr ☐☐   ☐

Assets	=	Liabilities	+	Shareholders' Equity

After you're finished, check your answers with the solution in the margin.

3. Record payments made to the lender. Rogers makes its first interest payment on April 30, 2010, which is six months after the note was signed. This payment totals $3,000 (= $100,000 \times 6\% \times 6/12$). The interest payment includes two months of interest expense accrued above for 2009 ($1,000) plus four additional months of interest expense incurred from January 1 to April 30, 2010 ($2,000 = $100,000 \times 6\% \times 4/12$). The journal entry to record the payment follows:

dr	**Interest Payable** (−L)..............	1,000	
dr	**Interest Expense** (+E, −SE)..........	2,000	
	cr **Cash** (−A).....................		3,000

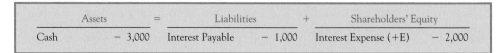

Assets	=	Liabilities	+	Shareholders' Equity
Cash − 3,000		Interest Payable − 1,000		Interest Expense (+E) − 2,000

What happens after April 30, 2010? Well, assuming Rogers hasn't made any other entries for the note until it matures on October 31, 2010, the following journal entries will be needed. First, to account for the payment of interest for the six months from April 30 to October 31 ($3,000 = $100,000 \times 6\% \times 6/12$), Rogers will record:

dr	**Interest Expense** (+E, −SE)...........	3,000	
	cr **Cash** (−A).....................		3,000

Quiz Answers

dr Interest expense (+E, −SE) 1,000
cr Interest payable (+L)......... 1,000

Assets	=	Liabilities	+	Shareholders' Equity
		Interest payable + 1,000		Interest expense (+E) − 1,000

Second, to account for the principal payment, Rogers will make the following entry:

dr	**Notes Payable** (−L)	100,000	
cr	**Cash** (−A)		100,000

The combined effect of these two entries on the accounting equation is

Assets	=	Liabilities	+	Shareholders' Equity	
Cash − 103,000		Interest Payable − 100,000		Interest Expense (+E)	− 3,000

After these entries are recorded, Rogers is finished accounting for the note payable. And so are we. Let's move on to long-term liabilities.

LONG-TERM LIABILITIES

Long-term liabilities include all obligations that are not classified as current liabilities. These obligations may be created by borrowing money, or they may result from other activities. In this section, we focus on long-term liabilities that are created by borrowing.

When a company like Rogers requires significant amounts of financing to expand its business, it will either borrow money through long-term loans (debt financing) or issue more shares (equity financing). We explain long-term debt financing in this section and equity financing in Chapter 11. We also discuss the pros and cons of these two types of financing in Chapter 11, after you've become a little more familiar with them.

Long-term debt financing is typically obtained in one of two ways: a private placement of a debt obligation or publicly issued debt certificates. In a private placement, the borrower identifies a potential lender, such as a bank, and negotiates terms for a loan

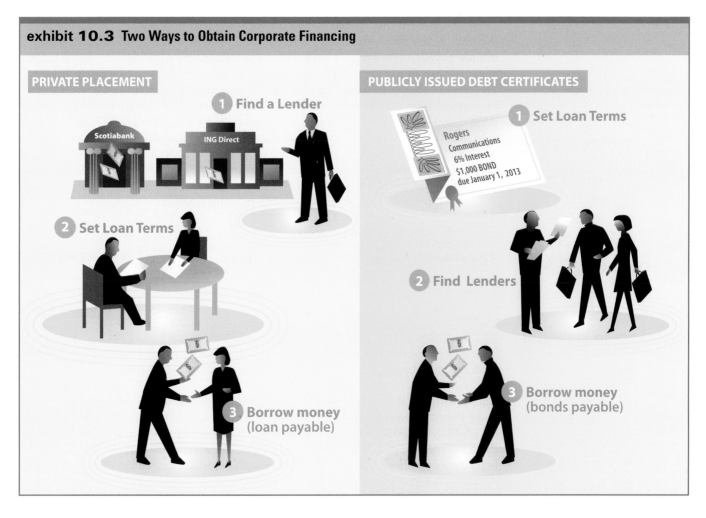

exhibit 10.3 Two Ways to Obtain Corporate Financing

PRIVATE PLACEMENT

1 Find a Lender

Scotiabank

ING Direct

2 Set Loan Terms

3 Borrow money (loan payable)

PUBLICLY ISSUED DEBT CERTIFICATES

1 Set Loan Terms

Rogers Communications 6% Interest $1,000 BOND due January 1, 2013

2 Find Lenders

3 Borrow money (bonds payable)

COACH'S TIP

The "lenders" involved in a bond issuance include companies and individuals who are interested in giving up money now in exchange for a series of fixed future payments of interest. This often appeals to retirees or their companies' pension funds.

with that lender. Accounting for a long-term loan is just like accounting for the notes payable that you studied in the previous section, except that this time it extends for more than one year. Publicly issued debt certificates, on the other hand, are used when a company needs more money than any single lender can provide. Because several hundred (or thousand) lenders might be involved in this financing, the company can't possibly negotiate different loan terms with each potential lender. Instead, the company begins by setting standard terms that will apply to all lenders. Then the company finds interested lenders. Notice in Exhibit 10.3 how the order of steps differs between a private placement and publicly issued debt certificates. This seemingly slight difference will become important later when we explain how publicly issued debt works.

Historically, the term *Notes Payable* was used when the company negotiated debt with one lender, usually for short-term purposes, and *Bonds Payable* was used when long-term debt was issued to the public. Over time, as the markets for debt instruments became more diverse and flexible, this distinction has disappeared and the terms are almost interchangeable. To avoid confusion in this text, we use the term notes payable for privately placed debt issued for one year or less, and the term bonds payable for publicly issued long-term debt instruments.

Since you've already learned how to account for notes payable and the interest that accrues on them, we'll focus this section on bonds payable. The terms of these bonds, such as the interest rate and maturity date, are detailed in a document called a bond certificate. An example of a bond certificate is shown on page 440. Interested lenders buy bonds on a bond market, which acts the same way as a stock market. The company receives cash in exchange for its promise to repay the lenders according to the terms stated on the bond certificate.

Bonds Payable

On the surface, a bond is a lot like your typical bank loan or promissory note. It states the interest payments, a maturity date, and the amount that is to be paid at maturity. Interest payments are typically made twice a year (semi-annually) or once a year (annually). To keep things manageable, we cover only annual interest payments in this text. The amount paid at maturity, which is called "face value," is often $1,000 per bond. To understand what the borrower will be required to pay to the lender from the day the bond is issued to the day it matures, you need to know three things—the interest rate, maturity date, and face value—all of which are stated on the bond certificate.

Let's look at an example. Assume that on January 1, 2009, Rogers receives $100,000 for bonds issued with a January 1, 2013, maturity date. The bonds pay $100,000 at maturity, and also state an interest rate of 6 per cent, which is paid each year on January 1. These bond payments can be summarized graphically as follows:

COACH'S TIP

Each interest payment of $6,000 is calculated as:

$100,000 × 6% × 12/12.

This looks a lot like the notes payable graphic shown on page 435, doesn't it? When lenders pay face value for the bonds, the accounting also is very similar.

Accounting for Bonds Issued at Face Value.   In accounting for bonds, accountants make journal entries (1) when the bonds are first issued, (2) when additional amounts are owed to lenders for interest, (3) when payments are made to lenders, and (4) when the bond liability is paid off. In this section, we discuss the first three points, using the bond described above as an example. The fourth point is discussed later in the chapter.

1. **Record the bond issue and receipt of cash.** The journal entry that the borrower, Rogers, uses to record the bond issuance on January 1, 2009, is

dr	Cash (+A)......................	100,000	
	cr	Bonds Payable (+L)...............		100,000

Assets	=	Liabilities	+	Shareholders' Equity
Cash + 100,000		Bonds Payable + 100,000		

2. **Record any interest owed by the end of the accounting period.** Interest expense on these bonds is calculated in the same way as it was for notes payable, as explained earlier in this chapter. If we assume Rogers hasn't made any entries for the bonds since January 1, it will record a liability for interest expense for the 12 months ended December 31, 2009. The amount of interest is \$6,000 (= \$100,000 × 6% × 12/12), and it is recorded with the following journal entry:

dr	Interest Expense (+E, −SE)...........	6,000	
	cr	Interest Payable (+L).............		6,000

Assets	=	Liabilities	+	Shareholders' Equity
		Interest Payable + 6,000		Interest Expense (+E) − 6,000

3. **Record payments made to lenders.** When Rogers pays the interest on January 1, 2010, the journal entry to record this payment would be

dr	Interest Payable (−L)...............	6,000	
	cr	Cash (−A).....................		6,000

Assets	=	Liabilities	+	Shareholders' Equity
Cash − 6,000		Interest Payable − 6,000		

COACH'S TIP

If the interest payment occurs on the same day that interest expense is recorded, entries 2 and 3 could be combined into one. It's best to show them separately to remind yourself that interest expense is recorded even if the interest payment hasn't yet been made.

As shown earlier in this chapter (for notes payable), the journal entries for interest expense and interest payments will continue until the bonds are fully repaid.

Bonds Issued below or above Face Value. If lenders always paid **face value** to acquire a bond, you'd have this topic aced already. However, sometimes the amount of money that lenders are willing to pay up front differs from what the borrower repays at maturity. Before getting into the mechanics of accounting for this, it's useful to understand why this might occur.

The key to understanding this is to remember that the borrower sets the terms of a bond before identifying its lenders. If the borrower sets a **stated interest rate** (6 per cent) that pays less than what lenders expect (say 8 per cent), lenders won't be attracted to the bond. It's just like asking you to give up \$1,000 for a stereo that doesn't have all the features you want. You aren't going to buy it unless (*a*) the necessary features are added, or (*b*) you're given a discount off the initial price. In the case of a bond, it's not practical to change its features because they're actually stated on the face of the bond. Instead, what happens is that lenders are required to pay less money up front to acquire the bond—they get a discount

Face value is the payment made when the bond matures.

The **stated interest rate** is the rate stated on the face of the bond, which is used to compute interest payments.

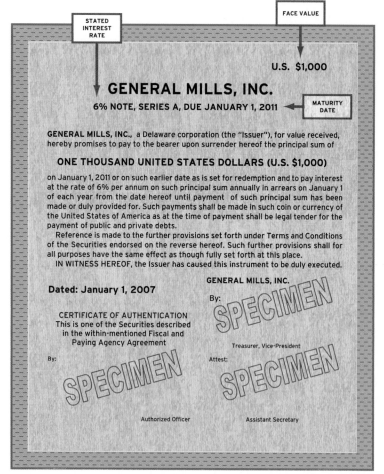

The opposite happens if bonds have features that make them attractive to lenders. Just as you might have to pay a premium to get tickets to popular concerts or sporting events, lenders have to give more money to acquire a bond that has popular features, such as an interest rate (6 per cent) that is higher than what similar bonds in the market pay (say 4 per cent). Lenders will be willing to pay a premium provided that they don't have to pay so much that they earn less than what they expect to earn from other similarly attractive bonds. The main point here is that bonds will be issued at amounts other than face value if their stated rate differs from the rate desired by lenders.

Before e-business became common, bond certificates that summarized the terms of the contract between the lender and the borrower were printed and physically held by the lenders as evidence of bond ownership, just as corporate shares were. But, these days, almost all stock and bond issues are kept track of electronically. Your parents may still have some Canada Savings Bonds in their safety deposit boxes but, in general, printed bond certificates are rare these days. Nevertheless, for learning purposes, it often helps to keep things visual, so here we present an actual bond certificate issued in 2007 by General Mills, the food company that supplies you with Trix cereal, Pillsbury crescent rolls, and Green Giant veggies.

Before we discuss how to account for bonds issued at amounts other than face value, let's summarize some important terms. First, let's start with the things you can see on a bond certificate. The value stated on the bond is called the face value. For clarity, we will always use this term when referring to it, but you probably should be aware that other people use alternative terms (such as par value). The interest rate stated on the bond is called the stated interest rate. Again, we will always use this term, but alternatives exist (such as coupon rate or contract rate).

Now, instead of talking about what's written on the face of the bond, let's turn to the terms that describe its true substance. The amount that the borrower actually receives when a bond is issued is called the **issue price.** The exact amount of the issue price is

The **issue price** is the amount of money that a lender pays (and the company receives) when a bond is issued.

determined by the lenders, who decide how much they're willing to give up to acquire the bond. Theoretically, this amount is based on a mathematical calculation called a **present value,** which is discussed in Appendix B at the end of this book. Bond dealers and news reports typically quote the bond issue price as a percentage of the face value of the bond (although they don't include the percentage symbol). So a $1,000 bond issued at a price of 95 means the bond was issued for 95 per cent of $1,000, or $950. The interest rate that lenders in the bond market demand from the bond (and use in their present value calculations to determine the bond issue price) is called the **market interest rate.** Some people also refer to this as the yield, discount rate, or effective-interest rate. Okay, now you're ready to pull together all these terms by considering how they relate to **premiums** and **discounts,** as shown here.

Present value is based on a mathematical calculation that determines the amount that one or more payments made in the future are worth today.

The market interest rate is the rate of interest that lenders demand from a bond.

A bond is issued at a **premium** when the issue price is greater than the face value. A bond is issued at a **discount** when the issue price is less than the face value.

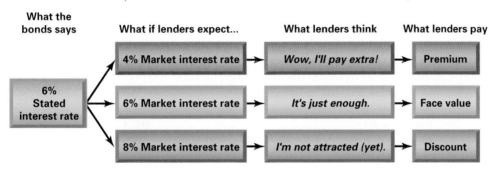

It's natural to feel a little overwhelmed by all of these new terms, so let's review two common questions at this point: "Why would the company sell bonds at a discount?" and "Why would lenders be willing to pay a premium?" The answer to both of these questions is the same. In general economic terms, the discount or premium is simply a price adjustment made by the marketplace in response to the laws of supply and demand. If the bonds are in demand, they'll sell at a premium. If not, they'll sell at a discount. It's the discount or premium that makes sure the bonds ultimately yield a fair (market-determined) rate—the rate that would emerge if the borrower and the lenders negotiated directly the terms of the bond.

Accountants use a little phrase when dealing with complex stuff like this that might help you here. The phrase is "substance over form," and what it means is that accountants try to account for the "true" substance of a transaction rather than what it suggests on the surface. In a way, you've already been exposed to this when you learned that expenses are accounted for using accrual rather than cash basis accounting. The same idea applies to bonds. Face value and stated interest rate reflect only the form of the bond. They merely describe the cash that the borrower repays to the lender. They do not reflect the substance of the bond or the real cost of borrowing, which instead is reflected in the bond's actual issue price (the starting point for the bond liabilities) and market interest rate (used to compute interest expense). These ideas are summarized in Exhibit 10.4.

Accounting for Bonds Issued at a Discount. When a company issues a bond at a discount, the borrower receives less money up front from the lenders, but repayment terms of the bond don't change. Borrowers still pay according to the terms stated on the face of the bond. Let's look at the case where a $100,000, four-year Rogers bond pays a stated interest rate of 6 per cent but lenders expect to earn the market interest rate of

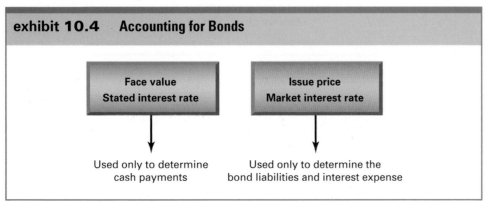

HOW'S IT GOING?   A Self-Study Quiz

For each of the following independent situations, indicate whether the bonds were issued at a premium (P), a discount (D), or at face value (FV).

Stated interest rate = 7% and market interest rate = 7%.

Stated interest rate = 5% and market interest rate = 6%.

Bond issue price = $10,100 and bond face value = $10,000.

When you're finished, check your answers with the solutions in the margin.

8 per cent. To get the 8 per cent that they expect, the lenders are willing to pay an issue price of only $93,376. That is, they've determined (by using present value calculations shown in Appendix B) that, if they pay $93,376 and receive back $6,000 interest every year plus $100,000 at maturity, in effect they will earn 8 per cent on the amount they've lent. The journal entry to record the issuance of the $100,000 bond, on January 1, 2009, at $93,376 (quoted as 93.376) is

dr	Cash (+A)........................	93,376	
dr	Discount on Bonds Payable (+xL, −L) ..	6,624	
	cr Bonds Payable (+L)..............		100,000

Assets	=	Liabilities	+	Shareholders' Equity
Cash + 93,376		Bonds Payable + 100,000 Discount on Bonds Payable (+xL) − 6,624		

The account *Discount on Bonds Payable* is a contra-liability account, which means it is deducted from the *Bonds Payable* account on the balance sheet. An example is shown in Exhibit 10.5. The *Bonds Payable* account reports the amount that Rogers will owe on the bond at maturity, whereas the line called *Bonds Payable, Net of Discount* (often called the "carrying value") reports the liability based on what Rogers owed when the bond was issued.

In our example, Rogers received only $93,376 when the bond was issued, but must pay back $100,000 when the bond matures. Rogers will pay back the extra cash as a way of adjusting the interest that lenders will earn. Remember that the terms of the bond were already set when the bond was issued, so the only way to adjust the lenders' interest was to discount the issue price for the bond. By paying less than face value for the bond, in effect lenders will earn the market interest rate they expect. From the perspective of

COACH'S TIP

Most companies simply report "Bonds payable, net of discount" on their balance sheets, and explain the discount in the notes to their financial statements (if it's a significant amount). This provides users with the necessary information, while avoiding too much clutter on the balance sheet.

---

exhibit 10.5   Sample Balance Sheet Reporting of Bond Discount

ROGERS COMMUNICATIONS, INC.
Balance Sheet (partial)
January 1, 2009

Long-Term Liabilities	
Bonds Payable	$100,000
Less: Discount on Bonds Payable	6,624
Bonds Payable, Net of Discount	93,376

Rogers, **the effect of a discount is to provide the borrower with less money than what is repaid at maturity, which increases the total cost of borrowing.** In effect, Rogers incurs interest equal to 8 per cent on the amount actually borrowed ($93,376), rather than the 6 per cent stated on the face of the bond.

To comply with the matching concept, this extra cost of borrowing must be matched to the periods in which the bond liability is owed. This is done each accounting period by taking an amount out of *Discount on Bonds Payable* and adding it to *Interest Expense* of that period. This process (called "amortizing" the discount) causes the *Discount on Bonds Payable* account to decline slowly to zero over the life of the bond, which causes the carrying value of the bond to increase until it reaches face value when the bond matures. This is shown in Exhibit 10.6.

Two different amortization methods exist to compute and record the amount to be taken out of *Discount on Bonds Payable* and added to *Interest Expense:* (1) straight-line, and (2) effective-interest. Generally accepted accounting principles require that the effective-interest method be used, and this method is covered in Supplement A beginning on page 455. Some people believe that straight-line is the easier method to understand, and companies might continue to use it if the straight-line method results in numbers that are not significantly ("materially") different from the effective-interest method. The straight-line method is covered in chapter 10 Supplement B (found in the Online Learning Centre (OLC) at www.mcgrawhill.ca/college/phillips), and a third approach, one that blends the simplicity of the straight-line method with the conceptual strengths of the effective-interest method is presented in the OLC as chapter 10 Supplement C. If you've been assigned any of these supplements, don't jump to them yet. We'll tell you later when it's best to read them.

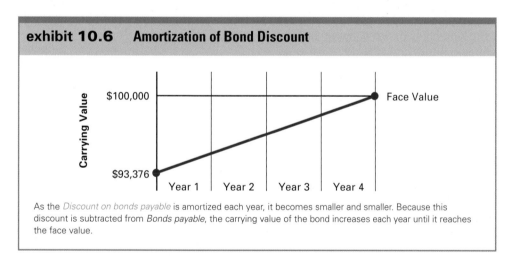

exhibit 10.6   Amortization of Bond Discount

As the *Discount on bonds payable* is amortized each year, it becomes smaller and smaller. Because this discount is subtracted from *Bonds payable,* the carrying value of the bond increases each year until it reaches the face value.

Accounting for Bonds Issued at a Premium.   When a bond is issued at a premium, *the borrower receives the face value of the bond plus the amount of the premium.* This means that, on the day of issue, the company owes more than just the face value of the bond. Let's look at the case where the market interest rate is 4 per cent yet the Rogers bond states an interest rate of 6 per cent. In this situation, lenders are willing to pay an issue price of $107,260 (which they've determined using present value calculations shown in Appendix B). The journal entry to record the issuance of the bond on January 1, 2009, for $107,260 is

dr	Cash (+A)	107,260	
cr	Bonds Payable (+L)		100,000
cr	Premium on Bonds Payable (+L)		7,260

exhibit **10.7**   Sample Balance Sheet Reporting of Bond Premium

ROGERS COMMUNICATIONS, INC.
Balance Sheet (excerpt)
January 1, 2007

Long-Term Liabilities	
Bonds Payable	$100,000
Add: Premium on Bonds Payable	7,260
Bonds Payable, Including Premium	107,260

Assets	=	Liabilities	+	Shareholders' Equity
Cash + 107,260		Bonds Payable + 100,000		
		Premium on Bonds		
		Payable + 7,260		

The carrying value of the bond is the total of the two accounts, *Bonds Payable* and *Premium on Bonds Payable,* as shown in Exhibit 10.7. Notice that the *Premium on Bonds Payable* account, called an adjunct-liability account rather than a contra-liability account, is *added* to the *Bonds Payable* account.

Rogers received $107,260 when the bond was issued, but repays only $100,000 when the bond matures. **The effect of the premium is to provide the borrower with more money than what is repaid at maturity, which reduces the total cost of borrowing.** As with a discount, the premium of $7,260 is allocated to each interest period. This amortization process reduces both *Premium on Bonds Payable* and *Interest Expense* in each period, causing the *Premium on Bonds Payable* account to decline to zero over the life of the bond. This also causes the carrying value of the bond to decrease until it reaches face value when the bond matures, as shown in Exhibit 10.8. Procedures that accomplish this are explained in chapter Supplements A, B, and C. (Supplements B and C are found on the Online Learning Centre at www.mcgrawhill.ca/college/phillips.) At this point, read any of the chapter supplements that you have been assigned; then come back here and continue with the remainder of this section. Supplement A begins on page 455.

Early Retirement of Debt.   Most bonds are retired (paid off) at maturity. There are some instances, however, where a company may decide to retire bonds before their maturity date. A company with lots of cash can retire debt early to reduce future interest expense, which increases net income in the future. Even companies that don't have extra cash might retire bonds early, particularly if interest rates have fallen since the

exhibit **10.8**   Amortization of Bond Premium

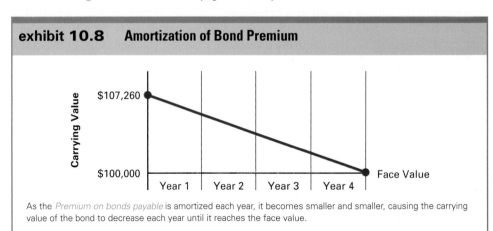

As the *Premium on bonds payable* is amortized each year, it becomes smaller and smaller, causing the carrying value of the bond to decrease each year until it reaches the face value.

original bonds were issued. By issuing new bonds at the lower interest rate and using the money received from this new bond issuance to retire the old bonds before their maturity date, companies can reduce their future interest expense (which increases future earnings).

When bonds are retired before maturity, the company's accountants do three things: (1) remove the bond balances from the accounting records, (2) record the cash paid, and (3) record a loss (if the company has to pay more cash than the carrying value of the bond liability) or a gain (if the cash paid to retire the bonds is less than their carrying value).

To illustrate, assume that, in 2000, Rogers issued $1 million worth of bonds at face value. Nine years later, in 2009, *The Globe and Mail* reports that the bonds are being retired at 103. Here's the journal entry to record the debt retirement with a cash payment of $1,030,000 ($1 million × 103%):

dr	Bonds Payable (−L)................. 1,000,000	
dr	Loss on Bonds Retired (+E, −SE) 30,000	
	cr Cash (−A).....................	1,030,000

COACH'S TIP

	Assets	=	Liabilities	+	Shareholders' Equity	
Cash	− 1,030,000	Bonds Payable	− 1,000,000		Loss on Bonds Retired (+E)	− 30,000

Notice that the journal entry does three things: (1) removes the bond balances (see the first line), (2) records the cash paid (third line), and (3) records the difference between the bond's carrying value and the cash paid as a gain or loss (middle line).

There are two things to note about the example above. First, the loss on bond retirement would be reported on the income statement with other gains and losses, somewhere between "operating income" and "income before income taxes." Second, the journal entry in our example doesn't remove a bond discount or bond premium account because we have assumed the bonds were issued at face value. If there was a premium or discount on the bonds, that balance would also be removed at the time of retirement and would affect the calculation of the gain or loss. Accounting for the retirement of bonds issued below or above face value is covered in detail in intermediate accounting courses.

FINANCIAL INSTRUMENTS

If you read financial newspapers or corporate reports, you have probably heard the term **financial instruments.** The most common financial instruments are cash, promises to pay or receive cash, and corporate shares. In this chapter, we have studied a number of financial (liability) instruments. In Chapter 11, we will cover financial (equity) instruments. There are many other financial instruments, like interest rate swaps and foreign exchange futures, which are too complex to be covered in this text. You should be aware that disclosure requirements for financial instruments are extensive, and that accounting for them continues to evolve as financial markets change.

Financial instruments are financial tools (like cash, loans, and shares) used to finance operating and investing activities.

Now that you know how liabilities are accounted for on the inside of a company, let's consider them again from the outside. How do users judge whether liabilities are likely to be repaid in full?

EVALUATE _____
The Likelihood That Liabilities Will Be Repaid in Full

When evaluating the ability of another person or company to pay you, a great place to start is with credit reports issued by credit rating agencies. However, credit raters don't report on everyone (particularly smaller companies). Even if they did, their reports might be too general and not address your specific concerns. So you really need to understand how to analyze a set of financial statements yourself in the same way a credit rater would. Essentially, you're going to assess whether the company has the assets available to pay what you're currently owed, and whether the company is likely to generate the resources needed to pay future amounts owed to you. Two financial ratios commonly used to make these assessments are the current ratio and the times-interest-earned ratio.

ANALYZING THE ABILITY TO PAY AMOUNTS CURRENTLY OWED

In Chapter 5, we learned that the debt-to-assets ratio measures the proportion of total assets that are financed by debt. This is a measure of a company's **solvency,** the ability to pay amounts in the long run. The current ratio is a complementary ratio that is commonly used to measure liquidity, which is the ability to pay liabilities as they become due in the short run.

> **Liquidity** is the ability to pay current obligations. It is commonly evaluated using the **current ratio,** which is the ratio of current assets to current liabilities.

$$\text{Current Ratio} = \frac{\text{Current Assets}}{\text{Current Liabilities}}$$

Specifically, the current ratio measures whether the company has enough current assets to pay its current liabilities. Generally speaking, a high ratio suggests good liquidity. An old rule of thumb was that companies should have a current ratio between 1 and 2. Today, many successful companies use sophisticated management techniques to minimize the funds invested in current assets and, as a result, have current ratios below 1.

Rogers is a company that minimizes what it holds in current assets. As shown in Exhibit 10.9, its total current assets are less than its total current liabilities, which makes its ratio less than 1 ($2,143 ÷ 2,742 = 0.78). For many companies, a ratio less than 1 can be a significant concern. It's not a big deal for Rogers, however, because the company has arranged a line of credit with banks that provides cash on an as-needed basis. Rather than hold extra cash to enhance its liquidity, Rogers can use its line of credit to borrow only when money is actually needed, avoiding significant interest expense. You can see that, in 2007, Rogers did not have any cash and cash equivalents on the asset side of its balance sheet. Instead, it had a $61-million bank loan on the liability side of its balance sheet, a fact we discussed earlier in the chapter.

exhibit 10.9   Roger's Current Assets and Current Liabilities (in millions)

Assets		
December 31	2007	2006
Current Assets		
Cash and Cash Equivalents	$ —	$ —
Receivables, Less Allowance for Doubtful Accounts	1,245	1,077
Inventories	—	—
Prepaid Expenses and Other Current Assets	898	657
Total Current Assets	2,143	1,734

Liabilities		
Bank Loan	$ 61	$ 19
Accounts Payable and Accrued Liabilities	2,260	1,792
Current Portion of Long-Term Debt	196	458
Unearned Revenues	225	227
Total Current Liabilities	2,742	2,496

exhibit 10.10 Summary of Current Ratio Analyses

Name of Measure	Formula	What It Tells You	2007 Telus	2007 BCE	2007 Rogers	SELF-STUDY QUIZ 2006 Rogers
Current ratio	$\dfrac{\text{Current Assets}}{\text{Current Liabilities}}$	• Whether current assets are sufficient to pay current liabilities • A higher ratio means greater ability to pay.	0.50	1.16	$= \dfrac{2{,}143}{2{,}742}$ $= 0.78$	

To better understand a company's current ratio, it's useful to compare it with the current ratios of other companies in the same industry. The 2007 current ratios for Telus, Bell Canada (BCE), and Rogers are presented in Exhibit 10.10. We've also included a column for you to practise calculating the current ratio yourself, as described in the Self-Study Quiz that follows. As you can see in Exhibit 10.10, only BCE has a ratio greater than 1.0. Both Rogers and Telus carry minimal levels of current assets relative to their current liabilities. They've been successfully managing their liquidity in this way for years.

Be on the Alert

The current ratio may be a misleading measure of liquidity if significant funds are tied up in assets that cannot be easily converted into cash. A company with a high current ratio might still have liquidity problems if the majority of its current assets are made up of slow-moving inventory. The current ratio also can be misleading because managers can manipulate it by entering into certain transactions just before the end of an accounting period. In most cases, for example, the current ratio can be improved by paying creditors just prior to the date of the financial statements. To watch out for this, it's useful to evaluate the current ratio at the end of each quarter and over several years and to look at other ratios as well.

COACH'S TIP

Some analysts calculate a "quick ratio," which divides total cash + receivables + short-term investments by current liabilities. A quick ratio greater than one means a company could cash in those assets, if needed, to instantly pay off its current liabilities.

HOW'S IT GOING? A Self-Study Quiz

Using financial statement information in Exhibit 10.9, compute the current ratio for Rogers in 2006 to complete the final column in Exhibit 10.10. Did the current ratio increase or decrease in 2007, as compared with 2006?

When you're finished, check your answers with the solutions in the margin.

Quiz Answers

1,734 ÷ 2,496 = 0.69 The current ratio improved slightly in 2007.

ANALYZING THE ABILITY TO GENERATE RESOURCES TO PAY FUTURE AMOUNTS OWED

By studying how (and when) accountants report interest owed on debt, you now know that liabilities do not include *all* of the future interest payments that will be made on existing liabilities. Liabilities include only the unpaid interest for periods ending before the balance sheet date. This means that the current ratio and any other ratios based on recorded liabilities don't tell you much about whether the company will be able to make future interest payments. One way to judge a company's future ability to pay interest is to analyze whether, in the past, it has generated enough income to cover its interest expense. Barring huge changes, the past can be a fair predictor of the future. The measure that most analysts use for this is the **times-interest-earned ratio:**

The **times-interest-earned ratio** divides net income before interest and taxes by interest expense to determine the extent to which earnings before taxes and financing costs are sufficient to cover interest incurred for debt.

$$\text{Times-Interest-Earned Ratio} = \frac{\text{Net Income} + \text{Interest Expense} + \text{Income Tax Expense}}{\text{Interest Expense}}$$

Notice that the times-interest-earned ratio adds interest and income tax expenses back into net income. The reason for this is fairly simple. We want to know whether the company generates enough income **before the costs of financing and taxes** to cover its interest expense. The way to achieve this is to add these expenses back into net income.

The times-interest-earned ratio shows the amount of resources generated for each dollar of interest expense. In general, a high ratio is viewed more favourably than a low ratio. A high ratio indicates an extra margin of protection in the event that future profitability declines.

Using information in Rogers' 2007 income statement (see the simplified version below), we have calculated and reported its times-interest-earned ratio in Exhibit 10.11. We've also included the ratios for Telus and BCE. Notice that the ratios show that all three companies are generating enough income to cover interest expense, but that Rogers, with a ratio of 2.53, falls short of the other two.

Every now and then you'll likely see a negative times-interest-earned ratio. **A negative ratio basically says that the company does *not* generate enough income to cover its interest expense.** This is a big problem. Most companies can survive for only a couple of years with negative times-interest-earned ratios before they have to declare bankruptcy.

ROGERS COMMUNICATIONS INC. Income Statement For the year ending December 31, 2007 (in millions)	
Net Sales	$10,123
Expenses:	
Cost of Sales	961
Selling, General, and Administrative	5,573
Interest, Net	579
Other Items, Net	2,124
Total Expenses	9,237
Income before Income Taxes	886
Income taxes	249
Net income	$ 637

---

exhibit 10.11   Summary of Times-Interest-Earned Ratio Analyses

Name of Measure	Formula	What It Tells You	2007 Telus	BCE	BBB
Times-Interest-Earned Ratio	$\frac{(\text{Net Income} + \text{Interest Expense} + \text{Income Tax Expense})}{\text{Interest Expense}}$	• Whether sufficient resources are generated to cover interest costs. • A higher ratio means greater coverage.	4.37	6.57	$\frac{637 + 579 + 249}{579}$ $= 2.53$
Standard + Poor's credit rating			BBB +	BB −	BBB −

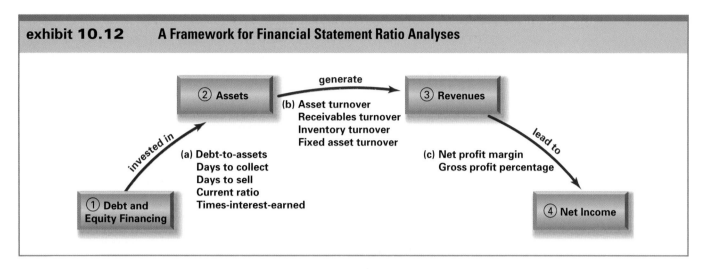

exhibit 10.12 **A Framework for Financial Statement Ratio Analyses**

Be on the Alert

The method of accounting for certain interest costs can make the times-interest-earned ratio potentially misleading. As you learned in Chapter 9, companies are allowed to capitalize interest that is incurred to self-construct property, plant, and equipment. If this occurs, the company's reported interest expense will be less than its actual interest costs, causing the times-interest-earned ratio to suggest greater interest coverage than what is actually the case. So don't jump to conclusions after calculating the times-interest-earned ratio. Read the financial statement notes to see whether any interest has been capitalized, because it might be distorting the ratio.

Since both the current and the times interest-earned-ratios tell us about the financial position of the company, we show both ratios in the (a) section in our framework for financial statement analysis, as shown in Exhibit 10.12.

UNDERSTANDING COMMON FEATURES OF DEBT

Convenient, attractive, wireless, coolest are adjectives that Rogers uses to describe its products or services. These adjectives are useful because they describe differences among the products, which help us to choose the products we want. In the same way, various adjectives are used to describe key terms in a debt agreement (e.g., secured, callable, convertible), which help creditors and borrowers choose the loan terms they want. We explain some of the more important ones below.

To reduce the risk of a loan, some lenders require borrowers to offer specific assets as "security" to creditors. This simply means that, if the borrower does not satisfy its liability, the creditor may take ownership of the assets used as security. A liability supported by this type of agreement is called a *secured debt*. Most car loans and house loans require you to offer your car or house as security for the loan. Some creditors are willing to lend money without security (called unsecured debt), but they typically demand a higher interest rate in return for taking on this extra risk. Another tactic that reduces risk is to allow lenders to demand immediate repayment of the loan if certain ratios, calculated using the borrower's financial statements, get out of whack. "Escape hatches" like these, which are common in many lending agreements, are called *loan covenants*. Borrowers report significant loan covenants in their financial statement notes. Exhibit 10.13 lists these and other common loan terms, along with explanations of them.

RECONSIDER _____
How Liability Decisions Can Be Affected by Unrecorded Debt

Hide and seek was a fun game to play as a kid. But when the executives at Enron used it as their guide to financial reporting, the fun ended. Investors, creditors, auditors, and practically everyone else in the business world has been affected by the Enron scandal that

ETHICAL ISSUES

exhibit 10.13   Explanations of Important Loan Terms

Loan Terms	What They Mean	Effects
Security	Security guarantees that the borrower's assets will be given to the creditor if the borrower doesn't pay	Reduces risk to creditors, making them willing to accept a lower interest rate
Loan Covenants	Allow the creditor to force immediate repayment of the loan if the borrower violates these terms	Reduces risk to creditors, making them willing to accept a lower interest rate
Seniority	Debt designated as "senior" is paid first in the event of bankruptcy, followed by "subordinated" debt	Reduces risk to senior creditors, making them willing to accept a lower interest rate
Convertibility	Gives the creditor an option to accept the borrower's shares as payment for the outstanding loan	Gives greater control to creditors, reducing their risk and making them willing to accept a lower interest rate
Callability	Gives the borrower control over the decision to fully repay the lender before the loan's maturity date	Gives greater control to borrowers, increasing creditors' risk and causing them to demand a higher interest rate

erupted in 2001. What exactly did Enron executives do wrong? Well, a lot of things. To understand precisely what they did, you'll need to take advanced courses in financial accounting. At a very simple level, however, one of their biggest offences was to "hide" debt owed by the company. In essence, the company didn't report all of its true liabilities.

UNRECORDED LIABILITIES

As a result of Enron, everyone in the business world has become much more sensitive to financial commitments that aren't reported on the balance sheet. As you will learn in this section, fraud isn't the only reason a company has unrecorded liabilities. In some cases, the accounting rules themselves actually require that certain liabilities *not* be reported on the balance sheet. We'll briefly introduce two topics where accounting rules can lead to unrecorded liabilities: leases and contingent liabilities. Both of these topics are covered in greater detail in intermediate accounting textbooks.

As you learned in Chapter 9, companies can use a lease to obtain the use of equipment and other property. In that chapter, we focused primarily on the *asset* obtained through the lease. Let's think now about the liabilities associated with leases. If a lease meets certain criteria, it is considered a *capital lease,* and a long-term liability is recorded for the present value of all future lease payments. That's basically the same way you account for a long-term note or bond payable. If the lease doesn't meet those criteria, it is considered an *operating lease,* and only the amounts past due are recorded as current liabilities on the balance sheet. If the company has kept up with all required payments, no liability is reported on the balance sheet for an operating lease. Thus, the classification of a lease as capital or operating can have a huge impact on total liabilities reported on the balance sheet. For example, even by conservative estimates, Rogers would have reported $500 million more liabilities had its operating leases been considered capital leases. The really interesting part of this is that it's sometimes a very fine line that distinguishes a capital lease from an operating lease, as you will learn in later accounting courses.

A **contingent liability** is a potential liability that arises as a result of past transactions or events, but the company is unable to determine whether it actually will be liable

A **contingent liability** is a potential liability that has arisen as a result of a past transaction or event. Its ultimate outcome will not be known until a future event occurs or fails to occur.

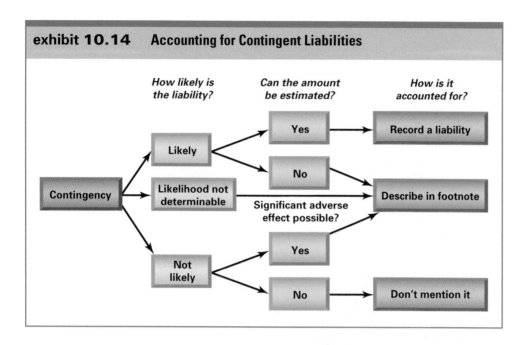

exhibit 10.14   Accounting for Contingent Liabilities

(or for what amount) until a future event occurs or fails to occur. The most common example of this is a lawsuit. Until it becomes clear that the company is liable and for what amount, the contingent liability is reported only in the company's notes to the financial statements. Once it is clear, the liability will be recorded. Sometimes the liability is accrued in stages, as information becomes more certain. Research in Motion (RIM) increased its accrued litigation liability every year from 2003 to 2006 as its legal battle over patent infringement rights associated with its Blackberry unfolded, until the suit was finally settled in March 2006 for U.S. $612.5 million. As you might expect, the actual accounting rules don't use loosey-goosey language like "until it becomes clear." Instead, they refer to the likelihood that the company will be found liable, whether it's possible to estimate the amount of liability, and whether significant adverse effects are possible from the lawsuit. The answers to these questions determine whether the contingent liability is recorded, described in a footnote, or not mentioned at all in the financial statements. Exhibit 10.14 tells you all you need to know for now about accounting for contingent liabilities. You will see from Exhibit 10.14 that a contingent liability is recorded only if the payment is likely and reasonably estimable.

In closing, we'll remind you that these unrecorded liabilities aren't illegal or unethical. In fact, good accounting requires that they remain unrecorded, at least until there's a reliable basis for recording them. Some companies are so upfront about potentially significant unrecorded liabilities that they even direct you to them by including a line-item in the balance sheet (following the liabilities section) called "commitments and contingencies," which references an explanatory note to the financial statements. Because these potential liabilities haven't been recorded in the accounting records, the line-item consists only of the name, without corresponding dollar amounts. This is what Altria Group, the largest tobacco company in the world and maker of Marlboro cigarettes, did in its 2006 annual report. In its balance sheet, it directs readers to Note 19, which describes in more than 8,000 words the billions in potential liabilities it faces for tobacco lawsuits. That's more than eight pages of single-spaced text. Having a line in the balance sheet with no number may look odd at first, but just think of it as a friendly reminder to consider potentially significant (but currently unrecorded) liabilities. Other companies alert readers to off-balance sheet items in less obvious ways. At the bottom of each financial statement, you often see the instruction "See notes to the financial statements." Rogers does this, but it also lists a number of specific notes to read, notably Commitments (note 23), Guarantees (note 24), and Contingent Liabilities (note 25).

WHAT'S COMING UP

This completes our in-depth coverage of liabilities. In Chapter 11, you will focus on the other section of the balance sheet related to a company's financing: shareholders' equity. You're likely to invest money in shares someday in the future, so it's important you learn about the various types of share transactions and how they are reported. But, before you move on to that, be sure to review and practise the material presented in this chapter.

FOR YOUR REVIEW _____

DEMONSTRATION CASE A (BONDS PAYABLE AND ACCRUED INTEREST)

At the end of October 2007, Hydro One, Ontario's electricity provider, issued $300 million in 5.18 per cent bonds payable, due to mature at the end of October 2017. Assume that the bonds pay semi-annual interest at the end of April and October, and that the annual rate of 5.18 per cent is comparable to other interest rates in the market at that time. Hydro One has a December 31 year-end and issues quarterly statements in March, June, and September before it issues its annual report. At the end of September 2007, assume that Hydro One had $946 million in current assets and $1,452 million in current liabilities.

Required:

1. Describe which sections of Hydro One's balance sheet are affected by the issuance of bonds.
2. Give the journal entry on October 31, 2007, to record the issuance of the bonds payable.
3. Give the journal entries at December 31, 2007, and March 31, 2008, to record interest expense.
4. Give the journal entry to record the first interest payment in April 2008.
5. Compute Hydro One's current ratio at the end of September 2007.
6. Assume that, as of December 31, 2007, the current assets and current liabilities of Hydro One had not changed since September except for the effect of the issuance of the notes in October. What is the effect, if any, of the bond issuance on the company's current ratio at the end of 2007?

Suggested Solution

1. The issuance of bonds increases Hydro One's cash (a current asset) and its bonds payable (a long-term liability) by $300 million. The bonds are issued at face value because the stated interest rate is a fair market rate.
2. October 31, 2007 (issuance date):

dr	Cash (+A)................................. 300,000,000	
	cr Bonds Payable (+L)	300,000,000

3. December 31, 2007 (accrual of interest expense for 2 months):

dr	Interest Expense (+E, −SE)	
	($300,000,000 × 5.18% × 2/12)................	2,590,000
	cr Interest Payable (+L)	2,590,000

March 31, 2008 (accrual of interest expense for 3 months):

> *dr* Interest expense (+E, −SE) 3,885,000
>   *cr* Interest payable (+L)
>   ($300,000,000 × 5.18% × 3/12)............ 3,885,000

4. April 30, 2008 (first interest payment date + accrual of interest for 1 month):

> *dr* Interest Expense (+E, −SE)
>   ($300,000,000 × 5.18% × 1/12)............... 1,295,000
> *dr* Interest Payable (−L)
>   (2,590,000 + 3,885,000) 6,475,000
>   *cr* Cash (−A)
>   ($300,000,000 × 5.18% × 6/12)............ 7,770,000

5. September 30, 2007, current ratio = Current assets ÷ Current liabilities
   = (946,000,000 ÷ 1,452,000,000) = 0.65

6. 2007 year-end current ratio = Current assets ÷ Current liabilities
   = (946,000,000 + 300,000,000) ÷ (1,452,000,000 +
   2,590,000)
   = 0.86

The issuance of the bonds increases the current ratio, because the cash from the bonds increases current assets by a sizeable amount, but the only increase in current liabilities is a relatively small amount of interest payable. The $300 million in bonds payable increases long-term liabilities.

DEMONSTRATION CASE B (BONDS PAYABLE)

To raise funds to build a new plant, Reed Company issued bonds with the following terms:

> Face value of the bonds: $100,000
> Dates: Issued February 1, 2009; due in 10 years on January 31, 2019
> Interest rate: 6 per cent per year, payable on January 31 each year

The bonds were issued on February 1, 2009, at 106. The annual accounting period for Reed Company ends on December 31.

Required:

1. How much cash did Reed Company receive from the sale of the bonds payable? Show computations.
2. What was the amount of premium on the bonds payable? Over how many months should it be amortized?
3. Give the journal entry on February 1, 2009, to record the sale and issuance of the bonds payable.

Suggested Solution

1. Sale price of the bonds: $100,000 × 106% = $106,000
2. Premium on the bonds payable: $106,000 − $100,000 = $6,000
   Months amortized: From date of issue, February 1, 2009, to maturity date, January 31, 2019
   = 10 years × 12 months per year = 120 months

3. February 1, 2009 (issuance date):

dr Cash (+A)................................	106,000	
cr Premium on Bonds Payable (+L)...........		6,000
cr Bonds Payable (+L)		100,000

CHAPTER SUMMARY

L01 **Explain how the reporting of liabilities assists decision-making. p. 429**

- Liabilities are any probable future sacrifices of economic benefits that arise from past transactions. Examples include accounts payable, accrued liabilities, notes payable, and bonds payable.

- Liabilities are classified as current if due to be paid with current assets within the current operating cycle of the business, or within one year of the balance sheet date (whichever is longer). All other liabilities are considered long-term.

L02 **Explain how to account for common types of current liabilities. p. 430**

- Liabilities are initially reported at their cash equivalent value, which is the amount of cash that a creditor would accept to settle the liability immediately after the transaction or event occurred.

- Liabilities are increased whenever additional obligations arise (including interest), and are reduced whenever the company makes payments or provides services to the creditor.

L03 **Analyze and record bond liability transactions. p. 437**

- For most public issuances of debt (bonds), the amount borrowed by the company does not equal the amount repaid at maturity. The effect of a bond discount is to provide the borrower with less money than the value stated on the face of the bond, which increases the cost of borrowing above the interest rate stated on the bond. The effect of a bond premium is to provide the borrower with more money than repaid at maturity, which decreases the cost of borrowing below the stated interest rate.

- Interest expense reports the true cost of borrowing, which equals the periodic interest payments plus (or minus) the amount of the bond discount (or premium) amortized in that interest period.

L04 **(Supplement A) Analyze the effective-interest amortization method for discounts and premiums on bond liabilities. p. 455**

- The effective-interest method, which is generally accepted and conceptually superior to the straight-line method, calculates interest expense by multiplying the true cost of borrowing times the carrying value of the bonds.

L05 **Interpret the current ratio and times-interest-earned ratio. p. 445**

- The current ratio measures liquidity, which is the company's ability to pay its current liabilities using its current assets.

- The times-interest-earned ratio measures a company's ability to meet its interest obligations with resources generated from its profit-making activities.

L06 **Describe the additional liabilities information reported in the notes to the financial statements. p. 449**

- The notes to the financial statements describe significant financial commitments, such as leases and contingencies.

- A contingent liability is a potential liability that has arisen as a result of a past transaction or event. Its ultimate outcome will not be known until a future event occurs or fails to occur.

FINANCIAL STATEMENT ANALYSIS TIPS

To determine how well a company is able to use its current assets to pay its current liabilities, calculate the current ratio:

$$\text{Current Ratio} = \frac{\text{Current Assets}}{\text{Current Liabilities}}$$

Calculate the following to determine the amount of income generated by the company (before interest and taxes) for each dollar of interest expense:

$$\text{Times-Interest-Earned Ratio} = \frac{\text{Net Income} + \text{Interest Expense} + \text{Income Tax Expense}}{\text{Interest Expense}}$$

KEY TERMS TO KNOW

Accrued Liabilities p. 431

Contingent Liability p. 450

Current Liabilities p. 430

Current Ratio p. 446

Discount p. 440

Effective-Interest Method of Amortization (Supplement A) p. 455

Face Value p. 439

Financial Instruments p. 445

Issue Price p. 440

Line of Credit p.430

Liquidity p. 446

Market Interest Rate p. 440

Overdraft p. 430

Premium p. 440

Present Value p. 440

Stated Interest Rate p. 439

Times-Interest-Earned Ratio p. 448

SUPPLEMENT A: EFFECTIVE-INTEREST AMORTIZATION OF BOND DISCOUNT AND PREMIUM

Earlier in the chapter, we described how, when a bond is issued at a discount, lenders provide the borrower with less money than what is repaid at maturity, which increases the cost of borrowing above the interest rate stated on the bond. For example, if a $100,000 bond is issued on January 1, 2009, for $93,376, the discount of $6,624 ($100,000 − 93,376) is an additional cost of borrowing, over and above the 6 per cent annual interest stated on the face of the bond. To comply with the matching concept, this extra cost of borrowing must be matched to the periods in which the bond liability is owed. This is done each accounting period by taking an amount out of *Discount on Bonds Payable* and adding it to *Interest Expense* of that period.

The **effective-interest method** is the generally accepted (and conceptually superior) method of amortizing bond discounts (and premiums) because it correctly calculates interest expense by multiplying the true cost of borrowing times the amount of money actually owed to lenders. The true cost of borrowing is the market interest rate that lenders used to determine the bond issue price. The actual amount owed to lenders is the carrying value of the bond, which equals the cash received when the bond was issued plus any interest costs that haven't been paid.

To clearly understand the effective-interest method, it helps to see how a bond's issue price depends on the market interest rate. As we mentioned in this chapter, lenders decide how much to pay for a bond by using a mathematical calculation called a present value. You can read instructions about how to calculate present values in Appendix B at the end of this book, but for now just focus on understanding what a present value is. Present value is the idea that something is worth more if you get it today than if you get it some time in the future. For example, if someone offered to pay you $100,000 today or $100,000 five years from now, you would be better off taking it today. You could invest the money and earn interest for five years, making it worth

> The **effective-interest method of amortization** reduces the bond discount (or premium) by the amount by which the borrower's interest payments are less (more) than the true cost of borrowing. The true cost of borrowing is calculated by multiplying the carrying value of the bond times the market interest rate that lenders used to determine the bond issue price.

exhibit 10A.1   Computing the Present Value of Bond Payments

	MARKET INTEREST RATES		
	4%	6%	8%
Present value of $100,000 (face value) paid four years from now	$ 85,480	$ 79,210	$73,503
Present value of $6,000 (interest) paid once a year for four years	21,780	20,790	19,873
Amount to pay	$107,260	$100,000	$93,376

way more than $100,000 five years from now. So if you won the lottery and got to choose between receiving $100,000 in five years or some smaller amount today (hey, it could happen), you can figure out how much to accept today by calculating the present value of $100,000. The only pieces of information you need for this calculation are (1) the amounts to be received in the future, (2) the number of months between now and then, and (3) the interest rate you expect to earn during that time.

In the bond context, lenders get some of this information from the face of the bond, and then they determine how much to pay for the bond by calculating the present value of the amounts paid periodically (as interest) and at maturity (as face value), using the interest rate that they want to earn. We have summarized this calculation in Exhibit 10A.1 for Rogers' 6 per cent, four-year bond described in the chapter. We show three different scenarios, with each one yielding different market interest rates that would be earned by lenders. The first column calculates the amount of money that lenders would be willing to give up if they needed to earn 4 per cent on the amount they pay for the bond. The second column calculates the amount lenders would pay if they wanted a bond returning an interest rate of 6 per cent. The third column calculates the amount that lenders would be willing to pay if they wanted to earn 8 per cent on the amount they pay for the bond. (For detailed calculations underlying the amounts in Exhibit 10A.1, see Appendix B at the end of the book.)

Notice that, when the bond pays interest at a rate that exactly matches the rate expected by lenders in the market (6 per cent), they are willing to pay face value for it. If the 6 per cent paid on the bond is more than lenders expect, they pay a premium for the bond (as shown in the first column). If the 6 per cent interest promised is less than the market interest rate, lenders pay less than face value for the bond, resulting in a discount as suggested in the third column. Let's now look at what happens to a bond discount and premium under the effective-interest amortization method.

Effective-Interest Amortization of a Bond Discount

When a company issues a bond at a discount, it receives less money up front than it repays at maturity. This creates a true cost of borrowing that is greater than the interest rate stated on the face of the bond. In other words, the true interest expense is greater than the interest paid. Under the effective-interest method, this unpaid interest is added to the true bond liability each period—a process known as amortizing the bond discount.

Let's continue the bond discount example presented earlier in the chapter. We had already recorded the issuance of bonds that stated a face value of $100,000 along with an annual interest rate of 6 per cent paid on January 1 each year. The bonds were issued for $93,376, which implied a discount of $6,624 and a market interest rate of 8 per cent.

Although the actual interest payment isn't made until January 1, the company has to record interest expense at the end of each year on December 31. Interest expense for the year is calculated by multiplying the amount actually borrowed by the market interest rate for the year ($93,376 × 8% × 12/12 = $7,470). The promised interest payment was indicated on the face of the bond as the face value times the stated interest rate for a full year ($100,000 × 6% × 12/12 = $6,000). The difference between the interest expense and the promised interest payment is the

COACH'S TIP

Because the promised interest payment is less than the interest expense, the bond liability increases (by reducing the contra-liability).

exhibit 10A.2   **Sample Balance Sheet Reporting of Bond Discount**

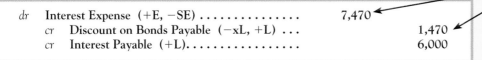

ROGERS COMMUNICATIONS INC.
Balance Sheet (partial)

Long-Term Liabilities	January 1, 2009	December 31, 2009
Bonds Payable	$100,000	$100,000
Less: Discount on Bonds Payable	6,624	5,154
Bonds Payable, Net of Discount	93,376	94,846

amount of discount that is amortized ($7,470 − 6,000 = $1,470). This is recorded with the following entry on December 31:

COACH'S TIP

Effective-interest amortization causes these amounts to change each period.

dr	Interest Expense (+E, −SE)	7,470	
cr	Discount on Bonds Payable (−xL, +L) ...		1,470
cr	Interest Payable (+L).................		6,000

Assets	=	Liabilities	+	Shareholders' Equity
		Discount on Bonds Payable (−xL) + 1,470		Interest Expense (+E) − 7,470
		Interest Payable + 6,000		

When the $6,000 interest payment is made on January 1, *Interest Payable* will be debited and *Cash* will be credited.

The T-account presented in the margin shows how the above journal entry reduces the balance of the *Discount on Bonds Payable* account. A reduction of this contra-liability account increases the carrying value of the long-term liability, as you can see by moving from left to right in Exhibit 10A.2.

Let's now consider the interest expense for 2010. As in 2009, the 2010 interest expense is calculated using the market interest rate. However, the amount of bonds payable actually owed at the end of 2009 increased, as shown in Exhibit 10A.2. Thus, interest expense also will increase, calculated as the unpaid balance on December 31, 2009, of $94,846 (see Exhibit 10A.2) times the market interest rate for the full year ($94,846 × 8% × 12/12 = $7,587rounded).

The difference between the 2010 interest expense ($7,587) and the promised cash payment ($6,000) is the amount of discount that is amortized ($1,587 = $7,587 − 6,000) in 2009. That is, because the true interest expense ($7,587) is greater than the promised payment ($6,000), the bond liability is increased (by reducing the contra-liability). This is recorded with the following entry on December 31:

dr Discount on Bonds Payable (xL) cr	
1/1/09 6,624	
	1,470 12/31/09
12/31/09 5,154	

dr	Interest Expense (+E, −SE)	7,587	
cr	Discount on Bonds Payable (−xL, +L) ...		1,587
cr	Interest Payable (+L).................		6,000

Assets	=	Liabilities	+	Shareholders' Equity
		Discount on Bonds payable (−xL) + 1,587		Interest Expense (+E) − 7,587
		Interest Payable + 6,000		

COACH'S TIP

The interest expense for 2010 is greater than that for 2009 because the carrying value of the bonds payable was greater in 2010 than in 2009.

Again, when the $6,000 interest payment is made on January 1, *Interest Payable* will be debited and *Cash* will be credited.

exhibit 10A.3   Bond Discount Amortization Schedule (Effective-Interest)

	CHANGES DURING THE PERIOD			ENDING BOND LIABILITY BALANCES		
Period Ended	(A) Interest Expense	(B) Interest Payable	(C) (= A − B) Amortization of Discount	(D) Bonds Payable	(E) Discount on Bonds Payable	(F) (= D − E) Bonds Payable, Net of Discount
01/01/09	—	—	—	100,000	6,624	93,376
12/31/09	7,470	6,000	1,470	100,000	5,154	94,846
12/31/10	7,587	6,000	1,587	100,000	3,567	96,433
12/31/11	7,715	6,000	1,715	100,000	1,852	98,148
12/31/12	7,852	6,000	1,852	100,000	0	100,000

Recorded each period with the following entry:

> *dr* Interest Expense (+ E, −SE) . . . .   (A)
>   *cr* Interest Payable (+ L) . . . .   (B)
>   *cr* Discount on Bonds Payable
>   (−xL,+L). . . . .   (C)

Reported at the end of each period on the balance sheet:

Liabilities:
Bonds payable $(D)
Less: Discount on bonds payable   (E)
Bonds payable, including premium   (F)

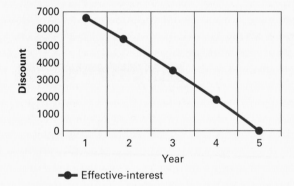

Effective-interest

COACH'S TIP

The interest expense for 12/31/10 is calculated as the carrying value at the beginning of the year (which is the $94,846 at 12/31/09) times the market interest rate (8%) for the full year (12/12). That is, $94,846 × 8% × 12/12 = $7,587 (rounded).

Some companies use a bond amortization schedule to summarize the detailed computations required under the effective-interest amortization method. A typical schedule is presented in Exhibit 10A.3. The following paragraph describes how to read the schedule.

The amortization schedule begins, in the first row, with the balance in *Bonds Payable* (column D, $100,000) and *Discount on Bonds Payable* (column E; $6,624) on the date of the bond issuance. The carrying value reported on the balance sheet as *Bonds Payable, Net of Discount* (column F, $93,376) is computed by subtracting the $6,624 discount from the $100,000 face value. This carrying value is then multiplied by the market interest rate for the full year ($93,376 × 8% × 12/12) to calculate interest expense for the first year (column A, $7,470). The interest to be paid (column B, $6,000) is computed by multiplying the face value of the bond by its stated interest rate for 12 months ($100,000 × 6% × 12/12). The amount of discount amortization (column C, $1,470) is computed by subtracting the promised interest payment of $6,000 (column B) from the interest expense of $7,470 (column A). The amount of discount amortization ($1,470) is subtracted from the previous balance in the *Discount on Bonds Payable* (column E; $6,624) to arrive at a new balance ($5,154), which is subtracted from the face value (column D, $100,000) to compute a new carrying value for the bonds (column D, $94,846). This new carrying value at the end of the first year (12/31/09) becomes the starting point for calculating interest expense in the following year. Take a moment right now to ensure you can calculate the amounts in Exhibit 10A.3 for the period ended 12/31/10. If you need help getting started, see the coach.

Effective-Interest Amortization of Bond Premium

The effective-interest method is applied in the same way for a premium as it was for a discount. Interest expense is computed by multiplying the current unpaid balance times the market interest rate for the length of the interest period. The amount of the bond premium to amortize is then calculated as the difference between interest expense and the cash interest payment promised on the bond. Let's use our earlier example of a bond premium to illustrate. The example involved 6 per cent bonds with a face value of $100,000 issued when the market interest rate was 4 per cent. The issue price of the bonds was $107,260, and the bond premium was $7,260.

The interest expense at the end of the year is calculated by multiplying the amount actually owed times the market interest rate for the full year ($107,260 × 4% × 12/12 = $4,290). The promised interest payment is calculated by multiplying the face value by the stated interest rate for the full year ($100,000 × 6% × 12/12 = $6,000). The difference between the interest expense and the promised interest payment is the amount of premium that is amortized ($6,000 − $4,290 = $1,710), as shown in the following journal entry.

dr	Interest Expense (+E, −SE)	4,290	
dr	Premium on Bonds Payable (−L)	1,710	
cr	Interest Payable (+L)		6,000

Assets	=	Liabilities	+	Shareholders' Equity
		Premium on Bonds Payable − 1,710		Interest Expense (+E) − 4,290
		Interest Payable + 6,000		

COACH'S TIP

Notice that, in each interest period, the borrower promises to pay more than its true cost of borrowing. The extra amount included in each payment goes to reducing the total bond liability (by reducing the premium).

When the $6,000 interest payment is made on January 1, *Interest Payable* will be debited and *Cash* will be credited. Notice in the journal entry above that the promised interest payment ($6,000) is greater than the true interest expense ($4,290), so the bond premium decreases. This illustrates the basic difference between effective-interest amortization of a bond premium versus a bond discount. Amortization of a premium reduces the carrying value of the liability, whereas the amortization of a discount increases it. An amortization schedule for our premium example is provided in Exhibit 10A.4. We completed the first two annual interest periods and left the last two for you to complete as part of the Self-Study Quiz that follows.

COACH'S TIP

Don't forget to read the rest of the chapter if you haven't already done so. It picks up on page 444.

---

exhibit 10A.4   Bond Premium Amortization Schedule (Effective-Interest)

	CHANGES DURING THE PERIOD			ENDING BOND LIABILITY BALANCES		
Period Ended	**(A) Interest Expense**	**(B) Interest Payable**	**(C) (= B − A) Amortization of Premium**	**(D) Bonds Payable**	**(E) Premium on Bonds Payable**	**(F) (= D + E) Bonds Payable, Net of Premium**
01/01/09	—	—	—	100,000	7,260	107,260
12/31/09	4,290	6,000	1,710	100,000	5,550	105,550
12/31/10	4,222	6,000	1,778	100,000	3,772	103,772
12/31/11	☐	☐	☐	☐	☐	☐
12/31/12	☐	☐	☐	☐	☐	☐

Recorded each period with the following entry:

dr	Interest Expense (+ E, −SE)	(A)
dr	Premium on Bonds Payable (−L)	(C)
cr	Interest Payable (+L)	(B)

Reported at the end of each period on the balance sheet:

Liabilities:
Bonds payable $(D)
Add: Premium on bonds payable   (E)
Bonds payable, including premium   (F)

HOW'S IT GOING?   A Self-Study Quiz

Complete the bond premium amortization schedule in Exhibit 10A.4 for the periods ended 12/31/11 and 12/31/12.

When you're finished, check your answers with the solutions in the margin.

Quiz Answers

From left to right in the table:

12/31/11: 4,151; 6,000; 1,849; 100,000; 1,923; 101,923

12/31/12: 4,077; 6,000; 1,923; 100,000; 0; 100,000

FOR YOUR PRACTICE _____

QUESTIONS

1. Define *liability*. What is the difference between a current liability and a long-term liability?
2. What three factors influence the dollar amount reported for liabilities?
3. Define *accrued liability*. Give an example of a typical accrued liability.
4. Why is *unearned revenue* considered a liability?
5. Why are *payroll deductions* considered liabilities?
6. If a company has a long-term loan that has only two years remaining until it matures, how is it reported on the balance sheet (*a*) this year, and (*b*) next year?
7. What are the reasons that some bonds are issued at a discount and others are issued at a premium?
8. Why are publicly issued debt certificates more likely to involve a discount or premium than a private placement of debt?
9. What is the difference between the stated interest rate and the market interest rate on a bond?
10. Will the stated interest rate be higher than the market interest rate, or will the market interest rate be higher than the stated interest rate, when a bond is issued (*a*) at face value, (*b*) at a discount, and (*c*) at a premium?
11. What is the carrying value of a bond payable?
12. What is the current ratio? How is it related to the classification of liabilities?
13. What is the difference between a secured and an unsecured loan? Which type carries more risk for the lender?
14. What amounts are reported as liabilities for *capital* versus *operating* leases?
15. What is a contingent liability? How is a contingent liability reported?
16. (Supplement A) How is interest expense calculated using the effective-interest method of amortization for a bond issued (*a*) at a discount and (*b*) at a premium?

MULTIPLE CHOICE

Select the one alternative that best answers the question or completes the sentence.

1. Which of the following best describes *accrued liabilities*?
   a. Long-term liabilities
   b. Current amounts owed to suppliers of inventory
   c. Expenses incurred, but not paid at the end of the accounting period
   d. Revenues that have been collected, but not earned
2. In 2006, Quebecor Inc., one of the world's top commercial printers, had 43,000 employees. Assume that, in the last pay period of the year, the company paid $8,000,000 to employees after deducting $2,000,000 for employee income taxes, and $612,000 for CPP and EI contributions. No payments have been made to the government relating to these taxes. Which of the following statements is true regarding this pay period?
   a. CPP and EI contributions payable is $612,000.
   b. CPP and EI contributions payable is more than $612,000.
   c. Compensation expense is $8,000,000.
   d. None of the above is true.
3. Assume that La Senza, one of Canada's best known lingerie chains, borrowed $100,000 from the bank to be repaid over the next five years, with principal payments beginning next month. Which of the following best describes the presentation of this debt in the balance sheet as of today (the date of borrowing)?
   a. $100,000 in the long-term liability section
   b. $100,000 *plus* the interest to be paid over the five-year period in the long-term liability section

c. A portion of the $100,000 in the current liability section, and the remainder of the principal in the long-term liability section

d. A portion of the $100,000 plus interest in the current liability section, and the remainder of the principal plus interest in the long-term liability section

4. Assume that Speedo International received $400,000 for long-term promissory notes that were issued on November 1. The notes pay interest on April 30 and October 31 at the annual rate of 6 per cent, which was comparable to other interest rates in the market at that time. Which of the following journal entries would be required at December 31?

a.	dr	Interest Expense...............	4,000	
		cr Interest Payable		4,000
b.	dr	Interest Expense...............	4,000	
		cr Cash......................		4,000
c.	dr	Interest Expense...............	4,000	
	dr	Interest Payable	8,000	
		cr Cash		12,000
d.	dr	Interest Expense...............	8,000	
	dr	Interest Payable	4,000	
		cr Cash		12,000

5. Which of the following does not have an impact on the calculation of the cash interest payments to be made to bondholders?
   a. Face value of the bond
   b. Stated interest rate
   c. Market interest rate
   d. The length of time between payments

6. Which of the following is false when a bond is issued at a premium?
   a. The bond will issue for an amount above its face value.
   b. Interest expense will exceed the cash interest payments.
   c. The market interest rate is lower than the stated interest rate.
   d. All of the above are true when a bond is issued at a premium.

7. When the company that borrows money by issuing a bond has the right to terminate a relationship with a lender early and repay the amount borrowed ahead of schedule, we say that the loan is
   a. Convertible   c. Amortizable
   b. Secured   d. Callable

8. To determine whether a bond will be issued at a premium, at a discount, or at face value, one must know which of the following pairs of information items?
   a. The face value and the stated interest rate on the date the bonds were issued
   b. The face value and the market interest rate on the date the bonds were issued
   c. The stated interest rate and the market interest rate on the date the bonds were issued
   d. You can't tell without having more information.

9. For the year ended December 31, 2009, Land O' Butter, Inc., reported operating income of $109,382, net income of $83,538, interest expense of $82,948, and income tax expense of $18,103. What was this dairy company's times-interest-earned ratio for the year?
   a. 0.76   c. 1.32
   b. 1.01   d. 2.23

10. Big Hitter Corp. is facing a class-action lawsuit in the upcoming year. It is possible, but not probable, that the company will have to pay a settlement of approximately $2,000,000. How would this fact be reported, if at all, in the financial statements to be issued at the end of the current month?
   a. Report $2,000,000 as a *current* liability.
   b. Report $2,000,000 as a *long-term* liability.
   c. Report the potential liability *in the notes* to the financial statements.
   d. Reporting is not required in this case.

Solutions to Multiple-Choice Questions

1. c 2. b 3. c 4. a 5. c 6. b 7. d 8. c 9. d 10. c

MINI-EXERCISES

LO2   M10-1 Recording Unearned Revenues

A local theatre company sells 500 season ticket packages at a price of $300 per package. The first show in the five-show season starts this week. Prepare the journal entries to record (a) the sale of the season tickets before the first show and (b) the revenue earned after putting on the first show.

LO2   M10-2 Recording Sales

Ahlers Clocks is a Brampton, Ontario, retailer of wall clocks. Assume that a customer bought a grandfather clock for $2,000 cash plus 5 per cent GST and 8 per cent PST. Prepare the journal entry Ahlers Clocks would use to record this transaction.

LO2   M10-3 Reporting Payroll Deductions

Lightning Electronics is a mid-sized manufacturer of lithium batteries. The company's payroll records for the November 1 to 14 pay period show that employees earned wages totalling $90,000, but that employee income taxes totalling $14,000 and CPP and EI contributions totalling $5,250 were withheld from this amount, leaving a net pay of $70,750, which was directly deposited into the employees' bank accounts. Prepare the journal entry or entries that Lightning would use to record the payroll. Include both employee and employer costs, assuming that the employer matches the employee contributions for CPP and EI.

LO2   M10-4 Reporting Current and Noncurrent Portions of Long-Term Debt

Assume that on December 1, 2009, your company borrowed $14,000, a portion of which is to be repaid each year on November 30. Specifically, your company will make the following principal payments: 2010, $2,000; 2011, $3,000; 2012, $4,000; and 2013, $5,000. Show how this loan will be reported in the December 31, 2010 and 2009, balance sheets, assuming that principal payments will be made when required.

LO2   M10-5 Recording a Note Payable

Farmer Corporation borrowed $100,000 on November 1, 2009. The note carried a 6 per cent interest rate, with the principal and interest payable on June 1, 2010. Prepare the journal entries to record (a) the note issued on November 1 and (b) the interest accrued on December 31, assuming that no adjusting entries have been made.

LO2   M10-6 Reporting Interest and Long-Term Debt, Including Current Portion

Barton Chocolates used a promissory note to borrow $1,000,000 on July 1, 2009, at an annual interest rate of 6 per cent. The note is to be repaid in yearly instalments of $200,000, plus accrued interest, on June 30th of every year until the note is paid in full (on June 30, 2014). Show how the results of this transaction would be reported in a classified balance sheet prepared as of December 31, 2009.

LO3   M10-7 Determining Bond Discount or Premium from Quoted Price

On January 10, 2008, biz.yahoo.com quoted a bond price of 102.0 for Ford Motor Company's 7.375 per cent bonds maturing on February 1, 2011. Were the bonds selling at a discount or premium? Does this mean the market interest rate was higher or lower than 7.375 per cent?

LO3   M10-8 Computing and Reporting a Bond Liability at an Issuance Price of 98

Coopers Company plans to issue $500,000 worth of 10-year, 4 per cent bonds. Interest is payable annually on December 31. All of the bonds will be issued on January 1, 2009. Show how the bonds would be reported on the January 2, 2009, balance sheet if they are issued at 98.

LO3   M10-9 Computing and Reporting a Bond Liability at an Issuance Price of 103

Repeat M10-8, assuming that the bonds are issued at 103.

LO3   M10-10 Recording Bonds Issued at Face Value

Schlitterbahn Waterslide Company issued 5,000 worth of 10-year, 6 per cent, $1,000 bonds on January 1, 2009, at face value. Interest is payable each January 1. Prepare journal entries to (*a*) record the issuance of these bonds on January 1, 2009, (*b*) accrue interest on December 31, 2009, and (*c*) record interest paid on January 1, 2010.

M10-11 Determining Financial Statement Effects of an Early Retirement of Debt   LO3

If the price of a bond increased after it was issued and the company decided to retire the debt early, would you expect the company to report a gain or a loss on debt retirement? Describe the financial statement effects of a debt retirement under these circumstances.

M10-12 Computing the Current Ratio and the Times-Interest-Earned Ratio   LO5

The balance sheet for Shaver Corporation reported the following: total assets, $250,000; noncurrent assets, $150,000; current liabilities, $40,000; total shareholders' equity, $90,000; net income, $3,320; interest expense, $4,400; income before income taxes, $5,280. Compute Shaver's current ratio and times-interest-earned ratio. Based on these ratios, does it appear that Shaver will be able to meet its obligations to pay current liabilities and future interest obligations as they become payable?

M10-13 Analyzing the Impact of Transactions on the Current Ratio   LO5

BSO, Inc., has a current ratio of 2.0. For each of the following transactions, determine whether the current ratio will increase, decrease, or remain the same.

a. Paid accounts payable in the amount of $50,000.

b. Recorded accrued salaries in the amount of $100,000.

c. Borrowed $250,000 from a local bank, to be repaid in 90 days.

d. Purchased $20,000 worth of new inventory on credit.

M10-14 Reporting a Contingent Liability   LO6

Buzz Coffee Shops is famous for its large servings of hot coffee. After reading about the famous case involving McDonald's, the lawyer for Buzz warned management (during 2008) that it could be sued if someone were to spill hot coffee and be burned. "With the temperature of your coffee, I can guarantee it's just a matter of time before you're sued for $1,000,000." Unfortunately, in 2009, the prediction came true when a customer filed suit. The case went to trial in 2010, and the jury awarded the customer $400,000 in damages, which the company immediately appealed. During 2011, the customer and the company settled their dispute for $150,000. What is the proper reporting of this liability in each year?

M10-15 (Supplement A) Recording Bond Issuance and Interest Payment (Effective-Interest Amortization)   LO4

Clem Company issued $800,000 worth of 10-year, 5 per cent bonds on January 1, 2009. The bonds sold for $741,000. Interest is payable annually on January 1. Using effective-interest amortization, prepare journal entries to record (*a*) the bond issuance on January 1, 2009, (*b*) the accrual of interest on December 31, 2009, and (*c*) the payment of interest on January 1, 2010. The market interest rate on the bonds is 6 per cent.

EXERCISES

E10-1 Recording a Note Payable through Its Time to Maturity with Discussion of Management Strategy   LO2

Many businesses borrow money during periods of increased business activity to finance inventory and accounts receivable. Sears is one of Canada's largest general merchandise retailers. Each Christmas, Sears builds up its inventory to meet the needs of Christmas shoppers. A portion of Christmas sales are on credit. As a result, Sears often collects cash from the sales several months after Christmas. Assume that on November 1, 2009, Sears borrowed $4.5 million cash from TD Canada Trust and signed a promissory note that matures in six months. The interest rate was 10 per cent payable at maturity. The accounting period ends December 31.

Required:

1. Give the journal entry to record the note on November 1.
2. Give any adjusting entry required at the end of the annual accounting period.

3. Give the journal entry to record payment of the note and interest on the maturity date, April 30, 2010.

4. If Sears needs extra cash during every Christmas season, should management borrow money on a long-term basis to avoid the necessity of negotiating a new short-term loan each year? Why or why not?

LO2

E10-2 Determining Financial Statement Effects of Transactions Involving Notes Payable

Use the information in E10-1 to complete the following requirements.

Required:

Indicate the accounts, amounts, and effects on the accounting equation (+ for increase, − for decrease, and NE for no effect) of (a) the issuance of the note on November 1, (b) the impact of the adjusting entry at the end of the accounting period, and (c) the payment of the note and interest on April 30, 2010. Use the following structure for your answer:

Date	Assets	=	Liabilities	+	Shareholders' Equity

LO2

E10-3 Recording Payroll Costs with Discussion

McLoyd Company completed the salary and wage payroll for March 2009. The payroll provided the following details:

Salaries and wages earned	$230,000
Employee income taxes withheld	46,000
Union dues withheld	3,000
Insurance premiums withheld	1,200
CPP and EI contributions withheld	16,445
Employer CPP and EI contributions	18,000

Required:

1. Prepare the journal entry to record the payroll for March, including employee deductions (but excluding employer CPP and EI contributions).

2. Prepare the journal entry to record the employer's CPP and EI contributions.

3. Assume the amounts owed to governmental agencies and other organizations are paid on April 4, 2009. Prepare the journal entry to record this payment.

4. What was the total labour cost for the company? Explain.

LO2, LO5

E10-4 Determining the Impact of Current Liability Transactions, Including Analysis of the Current Ratio

Bryant Company sells a wide range of inventories, which are purchased on accounts payable. Occasionally, a short-term note payable is used to obtain cash for current use. The following transactions were selected from those occurring during 2009:

a. On January 10, 2009, purchased merchandise on credit for $18,000. The company uses a perpetual inventory system.

b. On March 1, 2009, borrowed $40,000 cash from TD Canada Trust and gave an interest-bearing note payable: face amount, $40,000, due at the end of six months, with an annual interest rate of 8 per cent payable at maturity.

Required:

1. For each of the transactions, indicate the accounts, amounts, and effects on the accounting equation (+ for increase, − for decrease, and NE for no effect). Use the following structure:

Date	Assets	=	Liabilities	+	Shareholders' Equity

2. What amount of cash is paid on the maturity date of the note?

3. Discuss the impact of each transaction on the current ratio. (Assume Bryant Company's current assets have always been greater than its current liabilities.)

E10-5 Determining and Recording the Financial Statement Effects of Unearned Subscription Revenue

Reader's Digest Association is a publisher of magazines, books, and music collections. The following note is from a recent annual report:

> **Summary of Significant Accounting Policies—Revenues**
>
> Sales of our magazine subscriptions are deferred (as unearned revenue) and recognized as revenues proportionately over the subscription period.

Assume that Reader's Digest collected $10 million in 2009 for magazines that will be delivered in future years. During 2010, the company delivered $8 million worth of magazines on those subscriptions.

Required:

1. Using the information given above, indicate the accounts, amounts, and effects on the accounting equation (+ for increase, − for decrease, and NE for no effect). Use the following structure:

Date	Assets	=	Liabilities	+	Shareholders' Equity

2. Using the information given above, prepare the journal entries that would be recorded in each year.

E10-6 Preparing Journal Entries to Record Issuance of a Bond, Accrual of Interest, and Payment of Interest

On January 1, 2009, Applied Technologies Corporation (ATC) issued a $300,000 bond that matures in 10 years. The bond has a stated interest rate of 6 per cent. When the bond was issued, the market rate was 6 per cent. The bond pays interest once per year on January 1.

Required:

1. Determine the price at which the bond was issued, and the amount that ATC received at issuance.
2. Prepare the journal entry to record the bond issuance.
3. Prepare the journal entry to accrue interest on December 31, 2009.
4. Prepare the journal entry to record the interest payment on January 1, 2010.

E10-7 Preparing Journal Entries to Record Issuance of a Bond at Face Value, Accrual of Interest, Payment of Interest, and Early Retirement

On January 1, 2009, Innovative Solutions, Inc., issued a $200,000 bond at face value. The bond has a stated interest rate of 6 per cent. The bond matures in 10 years, and pays interest once per year on January 1.

Required:

1. Prepare the journal entry to record the bond issuance.
2. Prepare the journal entry to accrue interest on December 31, 2009.
3. Prepare the journal entry to record the interest payment on January 1, 2010.
4. Assume that the bond was retired immediately after the first interest payment on January 1, 2010, at a quoted price of 102. Prepare the journal entry to record the early retirement of the bond.

E10-8 Describing the Effects of a Premium Bond Issue and Interest Payment on the Financial Statements, Current Ratio, and Times-Interest-Earned Ratio

Grocery Corporation received $300,328 for $250,000, 11 per cent bonds issued on January 1, 2009, at a market interest rate of 8 per cent. The bonds stated that interest would be paid each January 1, and that they mature on January 1, 2019.

Required:

1. Describe how the bond issuance affects the financial statements, specifically identifying the account names and direction of effects (ignore amounts). Also, describe its impact on the current ratio and times-interest-earned ratios, if any.

2. Without doing calculations, describe how the financial statements are affected by the recording of interest on December 31, 2009. Also, describe the impact of the December 31 interest accrual, and of the January 1 interest payment on the current ratio and times-interest-earned ratio, if any.

LO5   **E10-9 Calculating the Current Ratio and Times-Interest-Earned Ratio**

According to its Web site, Kraft Foods Inc. sells enough Kool-Aid® mix to make 1,000 gallons of the nectar every minute during the summer, and over 560 million gallons each year. At a recent year-end, the company reported the following amounts (in millions) in its financial statements:

	Current Year	Prior Year
Total current assets	$8,153	$9,722
Total current liabilities	8,724	9,078
Interest and other debt expense	636	666
Income tax expense	1,209	1,274
Net income	2,632	2,665

Required:

1. Compute the current ratio and times-interest-earned ratio for the current and prior years.
2. Did Kraft appear to have increased or decreased its ability to pay current liabilities and future interest obligations as they become due?

LO4   **E10-10 (Supplement A) Recording the Effects of a Premium Bond Issue and First Interest Payment (Effective-Interest Amortization)**

Refer to the information in E10-8, and assume that Grocery Corporation uses the effective-interest method to amortize the bond premium.

Required:

1. Prepare the journal entry to record the bond issuance.
2. Prepare the journal entry to record the interest accrual on December 31, 2009.

LO4   **E10-11 (Supplement A) Recording the Effects of a Discount Bond Issue and First Interest Payment, and Preparing a Discount Amortization Schedule (Effective-Interest Amortization)**

On January 1, 2009, when the market interest rate was 9 per cent, Seton Corporation sold a $200,000, 8 per cent bond issue for $187,163. The bonds were dated January 1, 2009, pay interest each December 31, and mature 10 years from January 1, 2009. Seton amortizes the bond discount using the effective-interest method.

Required:

1. Prepare the journal entry to record the bond issuance.
2. Prepare the journal entry to record the interest payment on December 31, 2009.
3. Prepare a bond discount amortization schedule for these bonds, using the format shown in Exhibit 10A.3.

COACHED PROBLEMS

CP10-1 Recording and Reporting Current Liabilities with Evaluation of Effects on the Current Ratio

LO2, LO5

Curb Company completed the following transactions during 2009. The annual accounting period ends December 31, 2009.

Jan.	8	Purchased merchandise on account at a cost of $13,580. (Assume a perpetual inventory system.)
	17	Paid for the January 8 purchase.
Apr.	1	Received $40,000 from Bank of Montreal after signing a 12-month, 12 per cent interest-bearing note payable.
June	3	Purchased merchandise on account at a cost of $17,820.
July	5	Paid for the June 3 purchase.
Aug.	1	Rented out a small office in a building owned by Curb Company and collected six months' rent in advance, amounting to $5,100. (Use an account called Unearned Rent Revenue.)
Dec.	20	Received a $100 deposit from a customer as a guarantee to return a large trailer "borrowed" for 30 days.
	31	Determined wages of $6,500 were earned but not yet paid on December 31 (ignore payroll taxes).

COACH'S TIP

For the December 20 transaction, consider whether Curb Company has an obligation to return the money when the trailer is returned.

Required:

1. Prepare journal entries for each of the items listed above.
2. Prepare any adjusting entries required on December 31, 2009.
3. Show how all of the liabilities arising from these transactions are reported on the balance sheet at December 31, 2009.
4. For each transaction (including adjusting entries), state whether the current ratio is increased, decreased, or remains the same. (Assume Curb Company's current assets have always been greater than its current liabilities.)

CP10-2 Determining Financial Effects of Transactions Affecting Current Liabilities, with Evaluation of Effects on the Current Ratio

LO2, LO5

Using data from CP10-1, complete the following requirement.

e**X**cel

Required:

For each transaction (including adjusting entries) listed in CP10-1, indicate the accounts, amounts, and effects on the accounting equation (+ for increase, − for decrease, and NE for no effect), using the following schedule:

Date	Assets	=	Liabilities	+	Shareholders' Equity

CP10-3 Recording and Reporting Current Liabilities

LO2

During 2009, Riverside Company completed the following two transactions. The annual accounting period ends December 31.

a. Paid and recorded wages of $130,000 during 2009; however, at the end of December 2009, three days' wages are unpaid and unrecorded because the weekly payroll will not be paid until January 6, 2010. Wages for the three days total $3,600.

b. Collected rent revenue of $2,400 on December 10, 2009, for office space that Riverside rented to another business. The rent collected was for 30 days from December 11, 2009, to January 10, 2010, and was credited in full to Rent Revenue.

COACH'S TIP

Notice that the revenue recorded on December 31 includes revenue for 10 days (out of 30) that isn't earned until after December 31. This means the unadjusted rent revenue is too high.

Required:

1. Give the adjusting entry required on December 31, 2009, for unpaid wages from December 2009.

2. Give (*a*) the journal entry for the collection of rent on December 10, 2009, and (*b*) the adjusting journal entry on December 31, 2009.

3. Show how any liabilities related to these transactions should be reported on the company's balance sheet at December 31, 2009.

4. Explain why the accrual basis of accounting provides more relevant information to financial analysts than the cash basis.

LO3

CP10-4 Comparing Bonds Issued at Par, Discount, and Premium

Sikes Corporation, whose annual accounting period ends on December 31, issued the following bonds:

COACH'S TIP

See Exhibit 10.5 for an illustration distinguishing Bonds Payable from *Bonds Payable, Net.*

> Date of bonds: January 1, 2009
>
> Maturity amount and date: $100,000 due in 10 years (December 31, 2018)
>
> Interest: 10 per cent per year payable each December 31
>
> Date sold: January 1, 2009

Required:

1. Provide the following amounts to be reported on the January 1, 2009, financial statements immediately after the bonds are issued:

	Case A (issued at 100)	Case B (at 96)	Case C (at 102)
a. Bonds payable	$	$	$
b. Unamortized premium or discount			
c. Bonds payable, net			

2. Assume that you are an investment adviser and a retired person has written to you asking, "Why should I buy a bond at a premium when I can find one at a discount? Isn't that stupid? It's like paying list price for a car instead of negotiating a discount." Write a brief message in response to the question.

LO3

CP10-5 Comparing Carrying Value and Market Value and Recording Early Retirement of Debt

The name Hilton is well known for its hotels and notorious daughters. A recent Hilton annual report contained the following information concerning long-term debt:

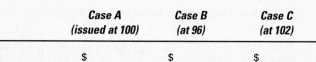

> **Long-Term Debt**
>
> The estimated current market value of long-term debt is based on the quoted market price for the same or similar issues. The current carrying value for long-term debt is $1,132.5 (million) and the current market value is $1,173.5 (million).

COACH'S TIP

For requirement 1, consider whether changes in the market interest rate affect carrying value and/or current market value of bonds.

Required:

1. Explain why there is a difference between the carrying value and the current market value of the long-term debt for Hilton.

2. Assume that Hilton retired all its long-term debt early (a very unlikely event) by buying the bonds in the bond market. This required a cash payment equal to the current market value. Prepare the journal entry to record the transaction.

LO6

CP10-6 Determining Financial Statement Reporting of Contingent Liabilities

Brunswick Corporation is a multinational company that manufactures and sells marine and recreational products. A recent annual report contained the following information:

Litigation

A jury awarded $44.4 million in damages in a suit brought by Independent Boat Builders, Inc., a buying group of boat manufacturers and its 22 members. Under the antitrust laws, the damage award has been tripled, and the plaintiffs will be entitled to their attorney's fees and interest. The Company has filed an appeal, contending the verdict was erroneous as a matter of law, both as to liability and damages.

COACH'S TIP

Required:

What are the alternative ways in which Brunswick could account for this litigation?

Consider the different possible outcomes that could arise from the appeal.

LO4

CP10-7 (Supplement A) Recording Bond Issuance and Interest Payments (Effective-Interest Amortization)

West Company issued bonds with the following details:

> Maturity value: $600,000
>
> Interest: 9 per cent per year payable each December 31
>
> Terms: Bonds dated January 1, 2009, due five years from that date

COACH'S TIP

The annual accounting period ends December 31. The bonds were issued at 104 on January 1, 2009, at an 8 per cent market interest rate. Assume the company uses effective-interest amortization.

Bonds pay face value at maturity.

Required:

1. Compute the issue (sale) price of the bonds (show computations).
2. Give the journal entry to record the issuance of the bonds.
3. Give the journal entries to record the payment of interest on December 31, 2009 and 2010.
4. How much interest expense would be reported on the income statements for 2009 and 2010? Show how the liability related to the bonds should be reported on the balance sheets at December 31, 2009 and 2010.

CP10-8 (Supplement A) Completing an Amortization Schedule (Effective-Interest Amortization)

LO4

Berkley Corporation issued bonds and received cash in full for the issue price. The bonds were dated and issued on January 1, 2008. The stated interest rate was payable at the end of each year. The bonds mature at the end of four years. The following schedule has been completed (amounts in thousands):

Date	Cash	Interest	Amortization	Balance
January 1, 2008				$6,101
End of year 2008	$450	$427	$23	6,078
End of year 2009	450	426	24	6,054
End of year 2010	450	?	?	?
End of year 2011	450	?	28	6,000

Required:

1. Complete the amortization schedule.
2. What was the maturity amount of the bonds?
3. How much cash was received at date of issuance (sale) of the bonds?
4. Was there a premium or a discount? If so, which, and how much was it?
5. How much cash will be paid for interest each period, and in total for the full life of the bond issue?
6. What is the stated interest rate?
7. What is the market interest rate?

COACH'S TIP

The stated interest rate can be calculated by comparing the cash payment with the face value of the bond (which is the balance paid at maturity).

8. What amount of interest expense should be reported on the income statement each year?

9. Show how the bonds should be reported on the balance sheet at the end of 2009 and 2010.

LO5

CP10-9 Analyzing the Ability of a Company to Pay Its Obligations

The Forzani Group is the largest and only national sporting goods retailer in Canada, operating under a number of banners including Sport Mart, SportChek, Coast Mountain Sports, and Nevada Bob's Golf. To evaluate Forzani's ability to repay its obligations, consider the following information reported in its most recent annual report (amounts in thousands).

COACH'S TIP

Notice that, for the debt-to-assets ratio, we use total liabilities and total assets, and the liabilities are the numerator, but, for the current ratio, we use only current assets and current liabilities, and the assets are the numerator.

Fiscal Year Ended	*2008*	*2007*
Net income	$ 47,451	$ 35,217
Income tax expense	24,390	21,279
Interest expense	5,797	7,354
Total liabilities	399,481	354,778
Current liabilities	331,773	232,140
Current assets	456,936	393,196
Total assets	754,964	682,591

Required:

1. Calculate and compare the percentage of the company's total assets that are financed by debt in 2008 and 2007 (the debt-to-assets ratio from Chapter 5). Comment on the company's solvency.

2. Calculate and compare the company's current ratios for 2008 and 2007. Comment on the company's liquidity.

3. Calculate and compare the company's times-interest-earned ratio for 2008 and 2007. Comment on the company's ability to generate the resources necessary to pay the interest on its long-term obligations.

GROUP A PROBLEMS

LO2, LO5

PA10-1 Recording and Reporting Current Liabilities, with Evaluation of Effects on the Current Ratio

Rocko Hammer Company completed the following transactions during 2009. The annual accounting period ends December 31, 2009.

Apr. 30   Received $550,000 from Royal Bank after signing a 12-month, 6 per cent interest-bearing note payable.

June 6   Purchased merchandise on account at a cost of $75,820.

July 15   Paid for the June 6 purchase.

Aug. 31   Signed contract to provide security service to a small apartment complex, and collected fees for six months in advance, amounting to $12,000. (Use an account called unearned service revenue.)

Dec. 31   Determined that salary and wages of $85,000 were earned but not yet paid December 31. (Ignore payroll taxes.)

Required:

1. Prepare journal entries for each of these transactions.

2. Prepare all adjusting entries required on December 31, 2009.

3. Show how all of the liabilities arising from these transactions are reported on the balance sheet at December 31, 2009.

4. For each transaction, state whether the current ratio is increased, decreased, or remains the same. (Assume that Rocko Hammer's current assets have always been greater than its current liabilities.)

PA10-2 Determining Financial Effects of Transactions Affecting Current Liabilities, with Evaluation of Effects on the Current Ratio

Using data from PA10-1, complete the following requirement.

Required:

For each transaction (including adjusting entries) listed in PA10-1, indicate the accounts, amounts, and effects on the accounting equation (+ for increase, − for decrease, and NE for no effect), using the following schedule:

Date	Assets	=	Liabilities	+	Shareholders' Equity

PA10-3 Recording and Reporting Current Liabilities

During 2009, Lakeside Company completed the following two transactions. The annual accounting period ends December 31.

a. Paid and recorded wages of $80,000 during 2009; however, at the end of December 2009, three days' wages are unpaid and unrecorded because the weekly payroll will not be paid until January 6, 2010. Wages for the three days total $1,600.

b. Collected rent revenue of $3,600 on December 10, 2009, for office space that Lakeside rented to another business. The rent collected was for 30 days from December 11, 2009, to January 10, 2010, and was credited in full to Rent Revenue.

Required:

1. Give the adjusting entry required on December 31, 2009, for unpaid wages from December 2009.

2. Give *(a)* the journal entry for the collection of rent on December 10, 2009, and *(b)* the adjusting journal entry on December 31, 2009.

3. Show how any liabilities related to these transactions should be reported on the company's balance sheet at December 31, 2009.

4. Explain why the accrual basis of accounting provides more relevant information to financial analysts than the cash basis.

PA10-4 Comparing Bonds Issued at Par, Discount, and Premium

Allfer One Corporation, whose annual accounting period ends on December 31, issued the following bonds:

Date of bonds: January 1, 2009

Maturity amount and date: $100,000 due in 10 years (December 31, 2018)

Interest: 10 per cent per year, payable each December 31

Date sold: January 1, 2009

Required:

1. Provide the following amounts to be reported on the January 1, 2009, financial statements immediately after the bonds were issued:

	Case A (issued at 100)	Case B (at 97)	Case C (at 101)
a. Bonds payable	$	$	$
b. Unamortized premium or discount			
c. Bonds payable, net			

2. Assume that you are an investment adviser and that a retired person has written to you asking, "Why should I buy a bond at a premium when I can find one at a discount? Isn't that stupid? It's like paying list price for a car instead of negotiating a discount." Write a brief message in response to the question.

LO3

PA10-5 Comparing Carrying Value and Market Value, and Recording Early Retirement of Debt

Quaker Oats is a well-known name at most breakfast tables. Before it was acquired by PepsiCo, Quaker Oats reported the following information about its long-term debt in its annual report:

> ### Long-Term Debt
>
> The fair value of long-term debt was $779.7 million at the end of the current fiscal year, which was based on market prices for the same or similar issues, or on the current rates offered to the Company for similar debt of the same maturities. The carrying value of long-term debt as of the same date was $759.5 million.

Required:

1. Explain what is meant by "fair value." Explain why there is a difference between the carrying value and the fair value of the long-term debt for Quaker Oats.
2. Assume that Quaker Oats retired all of its long-term debt early (a very unlikely event) by buying the bonds in the bond market. This required a cash payment equal to the current market value. Prepare the journal entry to record the transaction.

LO6

PA10-6 Determining Financial Statement Reporting of Contingent Liabilities

CIBC is one of Canada's largest banks. After the collapse of Enron in the United States, CIBC was named in a number of lawsuits alleging that they had, along with other banks, aided and abetted the Enron fraud.[2] CIBC described the legal proceedings in the notes to its 2004 financial statements as follows:

> ### Contingent liabilities
>
> CIBC is a party to a number of legal proceedings, including regulatory investigations, in the ordinary course of business. In certain of these matters, claims for substantial monetary damages are asserted against CIBC and its subsidiaries. There exists an inherent difficulty in predicting the outcome of such matters, but, based on current knowledge and consultation with legal counsel, we do not expect the outcome of any of these matters, individually or in aggregate, to have a material adverse effect on our consolidated financial position. However, the outcome of any particular matter may be material to our operating results for a particular year. We regularly assess the adequacy of CIBC's contingent liabilities accrual, including the adequacy of the accrual for Enron-related matters.

Required:

1. Does it appear from the wording of the note that CIBC's 2004 liabilities included an amount related to these lawsuits? If so, does it disclose the amount of the accrual?
2. In August 2005, CIBC reported that it would pay $2.674 billion in out-of-court settlements related to the Enron lawsuits, the largest one-time hit in Canadian banking history. The payout is more than a year's profit for CIBC, accounts for 20 per cent of its entire shareholders' equity, and is apparently eight times what CIBC had previously accrued. Why would CIBC not have accrued the full amount of its contingent liability by the end of 2004?

LO5

PA10-7 Analyzing the Ability of a Company to Pay Its Obligations

Canadian Tire is one of Canada's best-known and most successful retailers, with more than 455 stores from coast to coast. To evaluate Canadian Tire's ability to repay its obligations, consider the following information reported in its most recent annual report (amounts in millions).

---

[2]*The Ottawa Citizen*, August 6, 2005, p. D1.

Fiscal Year Ended	2007	2008
Net income	$ 417.6	$ 354.6
Income tax expense	202.5	200.8
Interest expense	78.4	75.7
Total liabilities	3,648.8	3,019.4
Current liabilities	2,109.6	1,663.6
Current assets	3,116.1	2,541.0
Total assets	6,742.7	5,804.6

Required:

1. Calculate and compare the percentage of the company's total assets that are financed by debt in 2007 and 2008 (the debt-to-assets ratio from Chapter 5). Comment on the company's solvency.
2. Calculate and compare the company's current ratio for 2007 and 2006. Comment on the company's liquidity.
3. Calculate and compare the company's times-interest-earned ratio for 2007 and 2006. Comment on the company's ability to generate the resources necessary to pay the interest on its long-term obligations.

GROUP B PROBLEMS

PB10-1 Recording and Reporting Current Liabilities, with Evaluation of Effects on the Current Ratio

LO2, LO5

Little Rock Company completed the following transactions during 2009. The annual accounting period ends December 31, 2009.

Jan.	3	Purchased merchandise on account at a cost of $23,660. (Assume a perpetual inventory system.)
	27	Paid for the January 3 purchase.
Apr.	1	Received $80,000 from Canadian Western Bank after signing a 12-month, 8 per cent interest-bearing note payable.
June	13	Purchased merchandise on account at a cost of $7,910.
July	25	Paid for the June 13 purchase.
Aug.	1	Rented out a small office in a building owned by Little Rock Company and collected rent for eight months in advance, amounting to $8,000. (Use an account called unearned rent revenue.)
Dec.	31	Determined that wages of $12,000 were earned but not yet paid on December 31. (Ignore payroll taxes.)

Required:

1. Prepare journal entries for each of the items listed above.
2. Prepare any adjusting entries required on December 31, 2009.
3. Show how all of the liabilities arising from these transactions are reported on the balance sheet at December 31, 2009.
4. For each transaction (including adjusting entries), state whether the current ratio is increased, decreased, or remains the same. (Assume Little Rock Company's current assets have always been greater than its current liabilities.)

PB10-2 Determining Financial Effects of Transactions Affecting Current Liabilities, with Evaluation of Effects on the Current Ratio

LO2, LO5

Using data from PB10-1, complete the following requirement.

Required:

For each transaction (including adjusting entries) listed in PB10-1, indicate the accounts, amounts, and effects on the accounting equation (+ for increase, − for decrease, and NE for no effect), using the following schedule:

Date	Assets	=	Liabilities	+	Shareholders' Equity

LO2   **PB10-3** **Recording and Reporting Current Liabilities**

During 2009, Colorade Company completed the following two transactions. The annual accounting period ends December 31.

a. Paid and recorded wages of $240,000 during 2009; however, at the end of December 2009, wages for two days are unpaid and unrecorded because the weekly payroll will not be paid until January 5, 2010. Wages for the two days total $2,000.

b. Collected rent revenue of $1,500 on December 10, 2009, for office space that Colorade rented to another business. The rent was collected for 60 days from December 11, 2009, to February 10, 2010, and was credited in full to Rent Revenue.

Required:

1. Give the adjusting entry required on December 31, 2009, for unpaid wages from December 2009. (Ignore payroll deductions.)

2. Give (a) the journal entry for the collection of rent on December 10, 2009, and (b) the adjusting journal entry on December 31, 2009.

3. Show how any liabilities related to these transactions should be reported on the company's balance sheet at December 31, 2009.

4. Explain why the accrual basis of accounting provides more relevant information to financial analysts than the cash basis.

LO3   **PB10-4** **Completing Schedule Comparing Bonds Issued at Par, Discount, and Premium**

Quartz Corporation sold a $500,000, 7 per cent bond issue on January 1, 2009. The bonds pay interest each December 31 and mature 10 years from January 1, 2009.

Required:

1. Provide the following amounts to be reported on the January 1, 2009, financial statements immediately after the bonds were issued:

	Case A (issued at 100)	Case B (at 98)	Case C (at 102)
a. Bonds payable	$	$	$
b. Unamortized premium or discount			
c. Bonds payable, net			

2. Assume that you are an investment adviser and that a retired person has written to you asking, "Why should I buy a bond at a premium when I can find one at a discount? Isn't that stupid? It's like paying list price for a car instead of negotiating a discount." Write a brief message in response to the question.

LO3   **PB10-5** **Understanding the Early Retirement of Debt**

On August 12, 2009, the OBC Entertainment Company sold $11\frac{7}{8}$ per cent bonds in the amount of $52,720,000, and used the $52,720,000 cash proceeds to retire bonds with a coupon rate of 13.6 per cent. At that time, the 13.6 per cent bonds had a book value of $50,000,000.

Required:

1. Prepare the journal entries to record the issuance of the new bonds and the early retirement of the old bonds.
2. How should OBC report any gain or loss on this transaction?
3. Why might the company have issued new bonds to retire the old bonds?

PB10-6 Determining Financial Statement Reporting of Contingent Liabilities

LO6

On August 4, 2005, an Air France Airbus A340 skidded off a runway at Toronto's Pearson Airport and burst into flames. All of the 340 people on board survived, but 43 people suffered minor injuries.[3] The next day, a $75 million class action lawsuit was filed against Air France, the Greater Toronto Airport Authority (GTAA), and Nav Canada.

Required:

How should the GTAA account for this lawsuit in its 2005 financial statements? What information would you like to have to assist you in making this decision?

PB10-7 Analyzing the Ability of a Company to Pay Its Obligations

LO5

Tim Hortons is one of Canada's best-known and most successful chains, with more than 2,800 outlets in Canada alone. To evaluate Tim Hortons' ability to repay its obligations, consider the following information reported in its most recent annual report (amounts in thousands).

Fiscal Year Ended	2007	2006
Net income	$ 269,551	$ 259,596
Income tax expense	138,851	101,162
Interest expense	24,118	22,253
Total liabilities	795,048	726,583
Current liabilities	327,298	275,189
Current assets	402,818	386,894
Total assets	1,797,131	1,744,987

*e**X**cel*

Required:

1. Calculate and compare the percentage of the company's total assets that are financed by debt in 2007 and 2006 (the debt-to-assets ratios from Chapter 5). Comment on the company's solvency.
2. Calculate and compare the company's current ratios for 2007 and 2006. Comment on the company's liquidity.
3. Calculate and compare the company's times-interest-earned ratio for 2007 and 2006. Comment on the company's ability to generate the resources necessary to pay the interest on its long-term obligations.

SKILLS DEVELOPMENT CASES

S10-1 Finding Financial Information

LO5

Refer to the financial statements of High Liner in Appendix A at the end of this book, or download the annual report from the *Cases* section of the text's Web site at www.mcgrawhill.ca/college/phillips.

Required:

1. Calculate the company's current ratio at the most recent year-end. Does this ratio cause you any concern about the company's ability to pay its current liabilities? As part of your answer, consider the financing that is available under the existing credit facilities (discussed in Note 6).

---

[3]*The Ottawa Citizen*, August 6, 2005, p. A5.

2. Calculate the company's times-interest-earned ratio for the most recent year. Does this ratio cause you any concern about the company's ability to meet future interest obligations as they become payable?

LO5

S10-2 Comparing Financial Information

Refer to the financial statements of Sun-Rype by downloading the annual report from the *Cases* section of the text's Web site at www.mcgrawhill.ca/college/phillips.

Required:

1. Calculate the company's current ratio at the most recent year-end. Does this ratio cause you any concern about the company's ability to pay its current liabilities? As part of your answer, consider the financing that is available under the credit facility (discussed in Note 3). Based on your analyses of the current ratio and financing available, does High Liner or Sun-Rype appear to be better able to pay its current liabilities?

2. Calculate the company's times-interest-earned ratio for the most recent year. Does it appear that High Liner or Sun-Rype will be better able to meet future interest obligations as they become payable?

LO1–LO5

S10-3 Internet-Based Team Research: Examining an Annual Report

As a team, select an industry to analyze. Using your Web browser, each team member should acquire the annual report for one publicly traded Canadian company in the industry, with each member selecting a different company. (See S1-3 in Chapter 1 for a description of possible resources for these tasks.)

TEAM CASE

Required:

1. On an individual basis, each team member should write a short report that incorporates the following:
   a. What are the most significant types of current liabilities owed by the company?
   b. Read the company's financial statement note regarding long-term debt and commitments and contingencies. Does the company have any significant amounts coming due in the next five years?
   c. Compute and analyze the current ratio and times-interest-earned ratio.

2. Then, as a team, write a short report comparing and contrasting your companies using these attributes. Discuss any patterns across the companies that you as a team observe. Provide potential explanations for any differences discovered.

LO3

S10-4 Ethical Decision Making: A Real-Life Example

Many retired people invest a significant portion of their money in bonds of corporations because of their relatively low level of risk. During the 1980s, significant inflation caused some interest rates to rise to as high as 20 per cent. Many retired people who had bought bonds years before that paid only 8 per cent continued to earn at the lower rate. During the 1990s, inflation subsided and interest rates declined. Many corporations took advantage of the callability feature of bonds that had been issued at higher rates and retired the bonds early. Many of these early retirements of high interest rate bonds were replaced with low interest rate bonds.

ETHICAL ISSUES

Required:

In your judgment, is it ethical for corporations to continue paying low interest rates when rates increase, but to call bonds when rates decrease? Why or why not?

LO3

S10-5 Ethical Decision Making: A Mini-Case

Assume that you are a portfolio manager for a large insurance company. The majority of the money you manage is from retired school teachers who depend on the income you earn on their investments. You have invested a significant amount of money in the bonds of a large corporation and have just received a call from the company's president explaining that it is unable to meet its current interest obligations because of deteriorating business operations related to increased international competition. The president has a recovery plan that will take at least two years.

ETHICAL ISSUES

During that time, the company will not be able to pay interest on the bonds and, she admits, if the plan does not work, bondholders will probably lose more than half of their money. As a creditor, you can force the company into immediate bankruptcy and probably get back at least 90 per cent of the bondholders' money. You also know that your decision will cause at least 10,000 people to lose their jobs if the company ceases operations.

Required:

Given only these two options, what should you do? Consider who would be helped or harmed by the two options, taking into consideration to whom you, as the portfolio manager, are responsible.

S10-6 Critical Thinking: Evaluating Effects on Current Ratio   LO5

Assume that you work as an assistant to the chief financial officer (CFO) of Fashions First, Inc. The CFO reminds you that the fiscal year-end is only two weeks away and that he is looking to you to ensure that the company stays in compliance with its loan covenant to maintain a current ratio of 1.25 or higher. A review of the general ledger indicates that current assets total $690,000 and current liabilities are $570,000. Your company has an excess of cash ($300,000) and an equally large balance in accounts payable ($270,000), although none of its accounts payable are due until next month.

Required:

1. Determine whether the company is currently in compliance with its loan covenant.
2. Assuming the level of current assets and current liabilities remains unchanged until the last day of the fiscal year, evaluate whether Fashions First should pay down $90,000 of its accounts payable on the last day of the year, before the accounts payable become due.

S10-7 Critical Thinking: Evaluating Lease Alternatives   LO5

As the new vice-president for consumer products at Acme Manufacturing, you are attending a meeting to discuss a serious problem associated with delivering merchandise to customers. Bob Smith, director of logistics, summarized the problem: "It's easy to understand; we just don't have enough delivery trucks given our recent growth." Barb Bader, from the accounting department, responded: "Maybe it's easy to understand, but it's impossible to do anything. Because of Bay Street's concern about the amount of debt on our balance sheet, we're under a freeze and cannot borrow money to acquire new assets. There's nothing we can do."

On the way back to your office after the meeting, your assistant offers a suggestion: "Why don't we just lease the trucks we need? That way we can get the assets we want without having to record a liability on the balance sheet."

Required:

How would you respond to this suggestion?

S10-8 Analyzing Financial Condition for a Loan Renewal   LO5

Roundabout Tourist Adventures (RTA) applied for and was granted a $100,000, 6 per cent, one-year bank loan on April 1, 2009, on the strength of its financial statements for the year ending December 31, 2008. It is now March 25, 2010. The loan is due soon and, rather than repay it, RTA has applied for renewal of the loan. Below are excerpts from RTA's financial statements.

	2009	*2008*
Current assets	$ 526,000	$ 472,500
Current liabilities	386,765	210,000
Total liabilities	750,000	610,000
Interest expense	18,000	8,500
Income tax expense	33,400	28,250
Net income	113,400	89,250

Required:

1. Calculate RTA's current and times-interest-earned ratios for both 2008 and 2009.
2. On the basis of the ratios, would you recommend renewing the loan? Would you consider changing the terms of the loan? If so, specify how.

LO4

S10-9 (Supplement A) Preparing a Bond Amortization Schedule (Effective-Interest Amortization)

Assume that the authors of a popular introductory accounting text have hired you to create spreadsheets that will calculate bond discount amortization schedules like those shown in Exhibits 10A.3. As usual, you e-mail your friend Billy for some guidance. Much to your disappointment, you receive an auto-reply message from Billy indicating that he's gone skiing in Chile. After a bit of panicking, you realize you can refer to Billy's previous e-mail messages for spreadsheet advice that will help you complete this task. From his advice for Chapter 9, you decide to create a data input section for the stated interest rate, market interest rate, face value, issue price, and years to maturity. The spreadsheet file also will have a separate amortization schedule worksheet that contains only formulas, references to the cells in the data input section, and references to other cells in the amortization schedule. All amounts will be rounded to the nearest dollar (using the Round function in Excel), which means the discount amortization in the final year might be off a few dollars (unless you use the If function in Excel to eliminate any remaining discount in the final year of the bond's life, in the same way that Billy showed in Chapter 9 for declining-balance amortization).

Required:

Prepare a worksheet that reproduces the effective-interest bond discount amortization schedule shown in Exhibit 10A.3. Display both the completed spreadsheet and a "formulas revealed" (Ctrl ~) version of it.

CHAPTER

11

Reporting and Interpreting Shareholders' Equity

Understand the characteristics of corporate equity.

LO1   Explain the role of shares in financing a corporation.

Study how to account for equity transactions.

LO2   Explain and analyze common share transactions.

LO3   Explain and analyze cash dividends, stock dividends, and stock split transactions.

LO4   Describe the characteristics of preferred shares, and analyze transactions affecting preferred shares.

LO5   (Supplement A) Analyze the equity transactions in sole proprietorships and partnerships.

Evaluate the return to shareholders.

LO6   Analyze the earnings-per-share (EPS) and return-on-equity (ROE) ratios.

Reconsider decisions that affect measures of shareholder returns.

LO7   Explain how share transactions affect ROE and EPS.

INSIDE LOOKING OUT

OUTSIDE LOOKING IN

This chapter focuses on reporting and interpreting the shareholders' equity of Toronto-based Danier Leather Inc., one of the world's largest specialty retailers of leather apparel.

Suppose you buy a DVD containing all the episodes of your favourite TV show from last season. Are you likely to watch one episode every few days, or will you save the DVD until you have free time for all of it? If you start into it now, you'll get some immediate enjoyment. But if you save it until you have an entire weekend free, it might be more fun, because then you'll be able to become totally engrossed in it. It's really a question of how you want to balance smaller immediate rewards with potentially greater long-term returns.

As an investor, you'll face a similar question. Do you want an immediate return on your shares (through dividends), or do you seek long-term returns (through higher stock prices)? Similarly, the directors at **DANIER LEATHER** have to decide whether the company should pay dividends to shareholders or reinvest those funds in the company. By paying dividends in the current period, the company provides an immediate return on shareholders' investments, but, by reinvesting its funds, Danier can potentially create even greater long-run returns for shareholders. Again, it's a question of balancing immediate and long-term returns. This chapter focuses on issues like these, which involve shareholders' equity.

To make operations more efficient, companies like Danier assign names to their various departments. We've done the same thing for the main sections of this chapter. Take a moment to read the Learning Objectives on the first page of this chapter to see what you'll be learning about. It'll make your reading more efficient.

UNDERSTAND _____
Forms of Business Organization

If you plan start a business, one of the first decisions you'll have to make is what form you'll want your business to take. The three most common choices are sole proprietorship, partnership, or corporation. If you want to keep things simple, can finance the business on your own, and want to control the decisions yourself, you will probably decide on a sole proprietorship, which is an unincorporated business owned by one person. A partnership is an unincorporated business owned by more than one person. The advantages of going this route are that your partners can contribute money and expertise to the business that you may be lacking, and also share the risk with you. On the downside, your partners will also share the decision-making, and you will have the administrative task of preparing a partnership agreement that lays out each partner's rights and responsibilities.

A distinctive feature of an unincorporated business is that, even though you may keep the accounting records for the business separate from your personal accounts, there is no legal distinction between a sole proprietorship or a partnership and its owners. This leads to two further disadvantages of these business forms. First, all owners of an unincorporated business share joint and several liability, which means that, if the business defaults on its debts, the creditor can sue any one or all of the business owners, taking both business and personal assets. Second, an owner's share of the business profits is taken onto the individual's income tax return and is taxed at personal tax rates, which are often higher than the tax rates available to incorporated businesses. One way to avoid these two disadvantages is to incorporate the business.[1]

The Characteristics of Corporate Equity

UNDERSTANDING CORPORATIONS

The corporation is a very common form of doing business, particularly for large entities. If you were to write the names of 50 familiar businesses on a piece of paper, most of them would likely be corporations.

You probably remember from Chapter 1 that the act of creating a corporation is costly, and its operations are subject to significant regulation, so why is the corporate form so popular? One critical advantage over sole proprietorships and partnerships is the one we mentioned above: Shareholders are not liable for the corporation's debts. Creditors have no legal claim on the personal assets of shareholders as they do on the personal assets belonging to owners of sole proprietorships and partnerships. So, if you owned shares in the old Eaton's department store, which went bankrupt and was liquidated in 1999, you would lose what you paid to buy the shares, but you wouldn't have to pay the millions that the company owed but couldn't pay.

A second distinctive characteristic of a corporation is that it pays taxes as a corporation, and is often taxed at lower rates than individuals are. However, the downside to this aspect of a corporation is that individual shareholders are taxed when they receive dividends from these corporations or if they make a profit on the sale of the corporation's shares.

A common misconception is that every corporation is a public company. As you learned in Chapter 1, this isn't so. Many private corporations are able to obtain adequate financing from private owners (as equity) and banks (as debt). There are a lot more private businesses in Canada than there are public companies, and even private companies can be large. McCain Foods, based in New Brunswick and the largest French fry maker in the world, with sales of over $4 billion a year, is still privately owned by the McCain

---

[1]Other forms of business organization exist. For example, income trusts and limited liability partnerships (LLPs) are becoming common in Canada, but they are not covered in this text.

exhibit 11.1	Excerpt from the Consolidated Balance Sheets of Danier Leather Inc

DANIER LEATHER INC.
Summarized Balance Sheets
(in thousands)

	June 30, 2007	June 24, 2006
Total Assets	$81,746	$82,210
Total Liabilities	$33,037	$34,254
Shareholders' Equity		
Contributed Capital	22,475	22,973
Retained Earnings	26,234	24,983
Total Shareholders' Equity	48,709	47,956
Total Liabilities and Shareholders' Equity	$81,746	$82,210

family. Unfortunately, unless companies are public, we don't have easy access to information about them, so it's the public corporations that get most of the attention.

The key advantage to going public is that public companies can raise large amounts of money because both large and small investors can easily participate in a corporation's ownership. This ease of participation is related to two factors.

- **Shares can be purchased in small amounts.** According to finance.yahoo.com, as of January 22, 2008, you could have become one of Danier's owners by buying a single company share for just $8.76.

- **Ownership interests are transferable.** The shares of public companies are regularly bought and sold on established markets, such as the Toronto or New York Stock Exchange. So if you decide to sell your shares in Danier, or buy more, it's quick and easy to do. Danier is traded on the TSE under the ticker symbol DL-SV.

About half of Canadians own shares, either directly or indirectly through a mutual fund or pension program. Stock ownership offers them the opportunity to earn higher returns than the interest paid on bank accounts. Because stock ownership in corporations is so prevalent today, this chapter focuses on *corporate* equity. The unique features of accounting for sole proprietorships and partnerships are covered in Supplement A to this chapter, beginning on page 500.

Exhibit 11.1 presents the shareholders' equity of Danier Leather Inc. at June 30, 2007, as well as Danier's total assets and total liabilities. Danier's assets are financed 60 per cent by shareholders ($48,709 as a percentage of $81,746). Of the total $48,709 in shareholders' equity, $22,475 comes from *Contributed Capital* and $26,234 comes from *Retained Earnings*. *Contributed Capital* represents the amount of money that shareholders have contributed by purchasing shares from the company. This amount is broken down into its components later in the chapter. Also in Exhibit 11.1, you can see the amount that the company itself has contributed through its profit-making activities. That is, the *Retained Earnings* account reports the cumulative amount of net income earned less the cumulative amount of dividends declared since the corporation was first organized.

COACH'S TIP

When we discuss the equity of a corporation, the terms shares and stock can be used interchangeably.

OWNERSHIP OF A CORPORATION

The law recognizes a corporation as a separate legal entity. It may own assets, incur liabilities, expand and contract in size, sue others, be sued, and enter into contracts independently of its shareholders. A corporation exists separate and apart from its owners, which means it doesn't die when its owners die. John H. Sleeman started brewing beer in Guelph, Ontario, in 1846. He is no longer around, but his company continues in existence today.

To protect everyone's rights, the creation and oversight of corporations are tightly regulated by law. Corporations are created by submitting an application to the government (federal or provincial). On approval of the application, the government issues a charter, usually called the articles of incorporation. Federally incorporated companies are regulated by the Canada Business Corporations Act (CBCA), while provincially incorporated businesses are regulated by the legislation in effect for the particular province. For example, Danier, formerly Royal Leather Goods Limited, was incorporated under the Business Corporations Act (Ontario) in 1972.

Benefits of Share Ownership

When you invest in a corporation, you are known as a shareholder (or stockholder). As a shareholder, you receive shares that you later can sell. Owners of shares receive a number of benefits:

- **Dividends.** You receive a share of the profits when distributed as dividends.
- **Residual claim.** Should the company cease operations, creditors would be paid first and you would share in any remaining assets.
- **Voting.** You get to vote on major issues, such as who will serve on the board of directors and which accounting firm will be appointed as external auditors.

As a shareholder, you have the ultimate authority in a corporation. You're the boss. The board of directors, the CEO, the external auditors, and, indirectly, all the employees are accountable to the shareholders.

Authorized, Issued, and Outstanding Shares

Okay, so as a shareholder in Danier, you can be the company's ultimate authority—well, you and a whole bunch of other investors. To be the ultimate authority, you need to own a lot of shares. The financial statements report information concerning the **authorized number of shares** (the maximum number of shares that can be sold) and the **issued shares** (number that have been sold to date). Let's look at the share information reported by Danier in the notes to its 2007 financial statements and summarized in Exhibit 11.2 on page 483.

In addition to setting out the number of authorized shares, a company's articles of incorporation also lay out the types (called classes) of shares it will be authorized to issue. At least one of these classes will be voting shares. From Exhibit 11.2, we note the following details of Danier's shares:

- Danier authorized four different classes of shares, including two classes of voting shares.
- Danier authorized 1,224,329 Special Voting Shares. As of June 30, 2007, Danier had issued all of the authorized shares in this class for a total consideration of less than $1,000.
- Danier authorized an unlimited number of Regular Voting Shares: As of June 30, 2007, Danier had issued 5,209,425 shares in this class for a total consideration of $22,475,000.
- Danier authorized an unlimited number of Class A and Class B preferred shares, but none of these have been issued to date. The rights and privileges of preferred shares will be discussed later in this chapter.

The notes explain that the two classes of voting shares are identical except that the special shares entitle the holder (Mr. Wortzman, Danier's president and CEO) to 10 votes per share and the regular shares (the ones trading on the TSE) entitle the holder to one vote per share.

For a number of reasons, a company might want to buy back shares that have already been sold to the public. After buying back its shares, the company can hold onto them or cancel them. If the company holds onto its own shares, these shares are called

The **authorized number of shares** is the maximum number of shares of a corporation that can be issued, as specified in the charter.

Issued shares indicates the total number of shares that have been sold.

exhibit 11.2   Danier Leather Inc. Authorized and Issued Shares

(a) Authorized:

1,224,329 Special Voting Shares
Unlimited Regular Voting Shares
Unlimited Class A and B Preferred Shares

(b) Issued:	Number	June 30, 2007 (in thousands)
Special Voting Shares	1,224,329	$ —
Regular Voting Shares:		
Balance, June 24, 2006	5,328,925	$22,973
Issued during the year	4,000	24
Repurchased and cancelled	(123,500)	(522)
Balance, June 30, 2007	5,209,425	$22,475

exhibit 11.3   Authorized, Issued, and Outstanding Shares

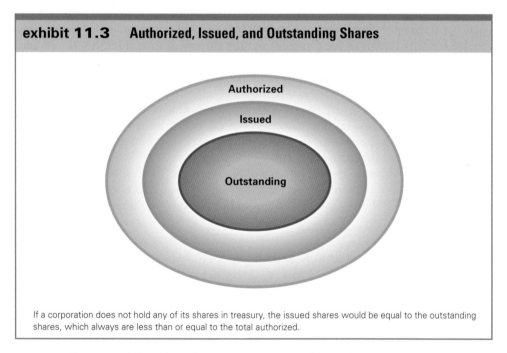

If a corporation does not hold any of its shares in treasury, the issued shares would be equal to the outstanding shares, which always are less than or equal to the total authorized.

treasury shares, and they don't have voting, dividend, or other shareholder rights. Because a company can't own or invest in itself, treasury shares reduce the number of shares that are considered **outstanding** with investors. If the company cancels these shares later, they are removed from treasury shares, and from the number of shares considered issued. The relationship between authorized, issued, and outstanding shares is shown in Exhibit 11.3.

Notice in Exhibit 11.2 that Danier repurchased 123,500 common shares during the year ending June 30, 2007, and cancelled them. This information implies that Danier held no treasury shares at the balance sheet date.

Treasury shares consist of issued shares that have been bought back by the company and not cancelled.

Outstanding shares consist of issued shares that are currently held by shareholders other than the corporation itself.

STUDY _____

How to Account for Equity Transactions

We should mention right at the start that all transactions between a company and its shareholders affect only balance sheet accounts. None of the transactions covered in this chapter affect the income statement. Nevertheless, knowing how these transactions are reported is crucial when evaluating how a company has performed for its shareholders, as you will see later in the chapter.

COMMON SHARE TRANSACTIONS

Common shares are the basic voting shares issued by a corporation to shareholders.

All corporations must have at least one type of shares, called **common shares.** Because common shareholders have the right to vote on important decisions of the corporation and to share in its profitability, common shareholders are the ultimate owners of a corporation. Sharing of the company's profits is done through dividends, which are determined by the shareholders' representatives—the board of directors of the corporation. As mentioned earlier, corporations also have the option to issue other types of shares, but for now let's focus on common shares.

Issuance of Shares

Two names are used for transactions involving the initial sale of a company's shares to the public. An *initial public offering,* or IPO, involves the very first sale of a company's shares to the public. This is what most people are referring to when they say a private company is "going public," as Danier did in 1998. After a company's shares have been traded on established markets, additional issuances of new shares by the company are called *seasoned new issues.* Whether shares are issued as part of an IPO or as a seasoned new issue, a company accounts for it in the same way. Note that a company does not account for the sale of shares from one shareholder to another because these transactions involve only the owners of the company and not the corporation itself. It's like an auto dealer who records the initial sale of a car to a customer, but doesn't later record another sale when the customer sells the car to someone else.

So far, we have used the account *Contributed Capital* to keep track of all share transactions. But, when a company issues different classes of shares, it opens a separate account for each and provides information about each class in its financial statements, either on the face of the balance sheet or in the notes. Below we use the account *Common Shares* to record the share issue.

Most sales of shares to the public are cash transactions. To illustrate the accounting for an initial issuance of shares, assume that, during the fiscal year ended June 24, 2009, Danier sold 100,000 shares for $10 per share. The company would record the following journal entry:

dr	Cash (+A) (100,000 × $10).........	1,000,000
cr	Common Shares (+SE)...........	1,000,000

Assets		=	Liabilities	+	Shareholders' Equity	
Cash	+ 1,000,000				Common Shares	+ 1,000,000

Par value is an insignificant value per share specified in the charter.

Notice that the common share account is credited for the number of shares sold times the issue price per share. In some jurisdictions, companies assign to their shares an arbitrary stated value, called a **par value.** Since par value has nothing to do with the market value or issue price of the shares, par value shares tend to confuse people, and the practice has fallen out of favour. The CBCA prohibits use of par values, but they are still seen in some provinces and are common in the United States.

Repurchase of Shares

In order to protect shareholders, there are strict rules about how actively a company can buy and sell its own shares. But, as long as it follows the rules, a company can repurchase some of its own issued shares from existing shareholders. This might be done for a number of reasons: (1) to reduce the number of shares outstanding in the market, (2) to send a signal to investors that the company itself believes its own shares are undervalued in the market, and are therefore worth purchasing, (3) to obtain shares that can be reissued as payment for purchases of other companies, and (4) to obtain shares to reissue to employees as part of employee stock option plans that provide workers with shares of the company as part of their pay. Because of regulations concerning newly issued shares, it might be less costly for companies to give employees repurchased shares than to issue new ones. If a company repurchases its shares for reasons (2), (3), or (4), it will hold them in the company treasury for a period of time until they are reissued. The CBCA requires that all repurchased shares be cancelled. As a result, treasury shares are rare in Canada, and, for this reason, accounting for treasury shares is not covered here.

If a company wants to reduce the number of its shares outstanding in the market (reason [1] above), it will repurchase and cancel the shares. To illustrate accounting for the repurchase and cancellation of shares, let's look at how Danier accounted for the 123,500 shares it repurchased for $8.745 each in fiscal year 2007. Danier first had to calculate the carrying (book) value of the outstanding shares at the time of repurchase. Exhibit 11.2 shows that at June 24, 2006, Danier had a total of 5,328,925 common shares outstanding for a total consideration of $22,973,000, or an average issue price of $4.31 per share. Danier therefore paid $8.745 per share to repurchase shares that had (on average) originally been issued for $4.31. Therefore, you could say that Danier lost money on this transaction. But accounting rules prohibit gains and losses on share transactions from going through the income statement, primarily because the standard-setters don't want to encourage companies to trade in their own shares to manipulate earnings. Instead, such "losses" are debited directly to *Retained Earnings*, as shown below. Danier accounted for this transaction as follows:

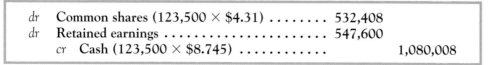

dr	**Common shares (123,500 × $4.31)**	532,408	
dr	**Retained earnings**	547,600	
	cr **Cash (123,500 × $8.745)**		1,080,008

If Danier had repurchased the shares for $4 instead of for $8.745, creating a "gain" instead of a "loss," the credit needed to balance the journal entry would have been made to a *Contributed Capital* account called *Contributed Surplus*, as follows:

dr	**Common shares (123,500 × $4.31)**	532,408	
	cr **Cash (123,500 × $4)**		494,000
	cr **Contributed Surplus**		38,408

DIVIDENDS ON COMMON SHARES

Investors buy common shares because they expect a return on their investment. This return can come in two forms: dividends and increases in stock price. Some investors prefer to buy shares that pay little or no dividends (called a "growth" investment), because companies that reinvest the majority of their earnings tend to increase their future earnings potential, along with their share price. Dell Corporation, the world's #1 direct-sale computer vendor, has never paid a dividend, yet, if your parents had bought 100 Dell shares when they were first issued on June 22, 1988, for $850, the investment would be worth over $200,000 at the time this chapter was being written. Rather than wait for growth in share value, other investors, such as retired people who need a steady income, might prefer to receive their return in the form of dividends. These people often seek shares that consistently pay dividends (called an "income" investment), such as Coca-Cola, which has paid cash dividends each year since 1893.

A corporation does not have a legal obligation to pay dividends. It is a decision made annually or quarterly by the board of directors. Once the board of directors formally declares a dividend, a liability is created. In its 2007 fiscal year, Danier did not declare any dividends, but it did in 2006. Below is a press release announcing a 2006 dividend declaration for Danier:

Danier Leather Inc. Board Declares Quarterly Dividend of 6 Cents per Share

Jan 19, 2006 – 14:11 ET

TORONTO, ONTARIO—Danier Leather Inc. (TSX:DL.SV) announced today that its Board of Directors has declared a quarterly cash dividend of 6 cents per share on the outstanding subordinate voting shares and multiple voting shares of the Corporation. The dividend is payable March 1, 2006, to shareholders of record at the close of business on February 16, 2006.

Notice that this announcement contains three important dates: (1) the declaration date (January 19), (2) the date of record (February 16), and (3) the date of payment (March 1).

<table>
<tr><td>The **declaration date** is the date on which the board of directors officially approves a dividend.</td><td>

1. **Declaration date—January 19, 2006.** The **declaration date** is the date on which the board of directors officially approves the dividend. As you learned in Chapter 4, as soon as the board makes the declaration, the company records a dividend liability. Assuming 5,300,000 shares are outstanding, the dividend of $318,000 ($0.06 × 5,300,000) would be recorded as
</td></tr>
</table>

dr	Dividends Declared (+D, −SE). 318,000	
	cr Dividends Payable (+L)	318,000

Assets	=	Liabilities	+	Shareholders' Equity	
		Dividends Payable	+ 318,000	Dividends Declared (+D)	− 318,000

The **record date** is the date on which the corporation prepares the list of current shareholders as shown on its records; dividends can be paid only to the shareholders who own shares on that date.

2. **Date of record—February 16, 2006.** The **record date** follows the declaration. It is the date on which the corporation prepares the list of current shareholders, based on its records. The dividend is payable only to those names listed on the record date. No journal entry is made on this date. Setting the date of record some time after the declaration date gives the stock market time to properly reflect the dividend. The share price should decline after the date of record, since the people buying the shares after that date will not receive the dividend.

The **payment date** is the date on which a cash dividend is paid to the shareholders of record.

3. **Date of payment—March 1, 2006.** The **payment date** is the date on which the cash is disbursed to pay the dividend liability. It follows the date of record, as described in the dividend announcement. Continuing our example above, when the dividend is paid and the liability satisfied on March 1, the following journal entry is recorded:

dr	Dividends Payable (−L) 318,000	
	cr Cash (−A)	318,000

Assets		=	Liabilities		+	Shareholders' Equity
Cash	− 318,000		Dividends Payable	− 318,000		

Notice that the declaration of a cash dividend increases the temporary account *Dividends Declared*, which will reduce *Retained Earnings* when it is closed at the end of each fiscal year. Also notice that the payment of a cash dividend reduces *Cash* by the same amount. These two observations explain the two fundamental requirements for payment of a cash dividend:

1. **Sufficient retained earnings.** The corporation must have accumulated a sufficient amount of retained earnings to cover the amount of the dividend. Incorporation laws often limit cash dividends to the balance in the *Retained Earnings* account.

2. **Sufficient cash.** The corporation must have sufficient cash to pay the dividend and meet the operating needs of the business. The cash generated in the past by earnings represented in the *Retained Earnings* account may already have been spent before the dividend was declared. In the case of Danier, this money may have been used to design and manufacture a new line of inventory, or to decorate some new retail outlets. So, the mere fact that the *Retained Earnings* account has a large credit balance does not mean that there is sufficient cash to pay a dividend. Remember, retained earnings is not cash.

HOW'S IT GOING?   A Self-Study Quiz

Answer the following questions concerning dividends:

1. On which dividend date is a liability created?

2. A cash outflow occurs on which dividend date?

3. What are the two fundamental requirements for the payment of a dividend?

After you're finished, check your answers with the solutions in the margin.

Quiz Answers
1. Declaration date
2. Date of payment
3. Dividends can be paid only if sufficient retained earnings and sufficient cash are both available.

STOCK DIVIDENDS AND STOCK SPLITS

Stock Dividends

The term *dividend*, when used alone with no adjectives, implies a cash dividend. However, there are some dividends that are not paid with cash, but instead involve existing shareholders receiving additional shares. These dividends, called **stock dividends,** are distributions of additional shares to its shareholders on a pro rata basis at no cost to the shareholder. The phrase "pro rata basis" means that each shareholder receives additional shares equal to the percentage of shares held. A shareholder with 10 per cent of the outstanding shares would receive 10 per cent of any additional shares issued as a stock dividend.

> A **stock dividend** is a distribution of additional shares of a corporation to existing shareholders.

The value of a stock dividend is the subject of much debate. In reality, a stock dividend by itself has no economic value. All shareholders receive a pro rata distribution of shares, which means that each shareholder owns exactly the same proportion of the company as before. If you get change for a dollar, you do not have more wealth because you hold four quarters instead of only one dollar coin. Similarly, if you own 10 per cent of a company, you are not wealthier simply because the company declares a stock dividend, fires up a laser printer, and gives you (and all other shareholders) more shares.

So **why do corporations issue stock dividends?** Academics and financial executives offer three main reasons: (1) it reminds shareholders of their accumulating wealth in the company; (2) it reduces the market price per share; and (3) it permanently reinvests a portion of retained earnings in the business, so that it is not available for future dividends. Regardless of the reason, accounting for the stock dividend is the same. The CBCA requires that stock dividends be valued at the current market price of the shares. For example, the following journal entry would be made if Danier had 5.3 million common shares outstanding and it issued a 5 per cent stock dividend when the share price was $8.50 per share:

> | | | | |
> |---|---|---|---|
> | *dr* | **Stock Dividends Declared (+D, −SE)** | | |
> | | ($8.50 × 5,300,000 × 5% dividend) . . . . . | 2,252,500 | |
> | *cr* | **Stock Dividend Distributable (+SE)** . . . | | 2,252,500 |

After the date of record, when the shares are issued, the entry would be:

> *dr*   **Stock Dividend Distributable (−SE)** **2,252,500**
>   *cr*   **Common Shares (+SE) (265,000 shares)**   **2,252,500**

Just as with cash dividends, the *Stock Dividends Declared* account will be closed to *Retained Earnings* at the end of the year. But, unlike with *Dividends Payable*, the *Stock Dividend Distributable* account is an equity, not a liability, account, since it will be honoured by issuing shares, not by paying cash. As we see below, the net effect of a stock dividend is that *Retained Earnings* is decreased and *Common Shares* is increased by the value of the shares.

Assets	=	Liabilities	+	Shareholders' Equity	
				Retained Earnings	− 2,252,500
				Common Shares	+ 2,252,500

Notice that this journal entry to record a stock dividend changes some of the shareholders' equity account balances, but it doesn't change total shareholders' equity.

Stock Splits

A **stock split** is an increase in the total number of authorized shares by a specified ratio. It does not decrease retained earnings.

Stock splits are not dividends. While they are similar to a stock dividend, they are quite different in terms of their impact on the shareholders' equity accounts. In a **stock split,** the total number of authorized shares is increased by a specified amount, such as 2-for-1. In this instance, each share held is called in and two new shares are issued in its place. Cash is not affected when the company splits its stock, so the total resources of the company do not change. It's just like taking a four-piece pizza and cutting each piece into two smaller pieces.

Typically, a stock split involves reducing the carrying value of all authorized shares, so that the total carrying value of the shares is unchanged. For instance, if Danier executes a 2-for-1 stock split when it has 5,300,000 shares outstanding with a total issue price of $21,200,000, it reduces the per share book value of its shares and doubles the number of shares outstanding. The decrease in book value per share offsets the increase in the number of shares, so that no journal entry is needed, as shown below.

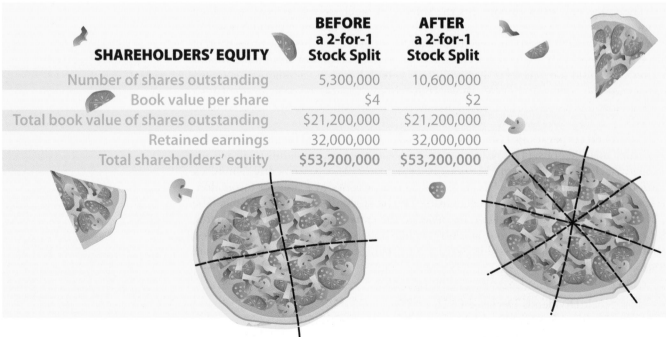

SHAREHOLDERS' EQUITY	BEFORE a 2-for-1 Stock Split	AFTER a 2-for-1 Stock Split
Number of shares outstanding	5,300,000	10,600,000
Book value per share	$4	$2
Total book value of shares outstanding	$21,200,000	$21,200,000
Retained earnings	32,000,000	32,000,000
Total shareholders' equity	$53,200,000	$53,200,000

Stock splits and stock dividends are similar in a number of ways.

1. They both result in an increase in the number of shares issued.
2. They both result in an increase in the number of shares owned by any one shareholder.
3. There is no change in the assets, liabilities, or total shareholders' equity accounts of the company.
4. There is no change in the percentage ownership in the company by any one shareholder. If you owned 10 per cent of the company before the stock dividend or stock split, you'd still own 10 per cent of the company afterwards.

The key difference between a stock dividend and a stock split is that a stock dividend changes the dollar figures that appear on the balance sheet for *Common Shares* and *Retained Earnings*, whereas a stock split does not. When a stock dividend is declared, a portion of *Retained Earnings* is transferred to *Common Shares*. Remember that a company needs to have an adequate balance in retained earnings to declare cash dividends. Stock dividends therefore permanently reduce the ability of a company to issue cash dividends in the future, and, for this reason, you would think they are not very popular. But, in fact, they are quite common. How can we explain this? One explanation is that companies use stock dividends to signal to financial statement users that the company expects strong financial performance in the near future. In other words, they don't care that retained earnings is reduced by a stock dividend because they fully expect future earnings to build up retained earnings enough to allow cash dividends to be issued.

HOW'S IT GOING? A Self-Study Quiz

Joey & Chandler's Dollar Stores wanted to reduce the market price of its shares, so it issued 10,000 new common shares in a 10 per cent stock dividend when there were 100,000 shares outstanding and the market value was $30 per share.

1. Prepare the journal entry that J&C Dollar Stores would use to record this transaction. Theoretically, what would be the new stock price after the split?

2. What journal entry would be required if the transaction instead involved a 2-for-1 stock split? Theoretically, what would be the new stock price after the split?

After you're finished, check your answers with the solutions in the margin.

Quiz Answers

1. *dr* Retained earnings (−SE)
  ($100,000 × 10% × $30)   300,000
    cr Common shares (+SE)   300,000
  The new price should drop to $27.27 ($30 ÷ 1.1).

2. No journal entry is required in the case of a stock split. Theoretically, the new price would be one-half of what it was before the split ($30 × 1/2 = $15).

PREFERRED SHARES

In addition to common shares, some corporations issue **preferred shares.** Preferred shares differ from common shares based a number of rights granted to the shareholders. The most significant differences are:

■ ***Preferred shares generally do not grant voting rights.*** As a result, preferred shares do not appeal to investors who want some control over the operations of a company. Existing common shareholders may like to see preferred shares issued because preferred shares allow a company to raise funds without reducing their own control.

■ ***Preferred shares are less risky.*** Generally, preferred shares are less risky than common shares because preferred shareholders are paid dividends before common shareholders. Also, if the corporation goes out of business, creditors are paid first, followed by preferred shareholders. Common shareholders are paid last, using whatever assets remain after having paid preferred shareholders.

■ ***Preferred shares typically have a fixed dividend rate.*** For example, a "$0.60 preferred share" pays a dividend each year of $0.60 per share. The fixed dividend is attractive to certain investors who want a stable income from their investments.

In addition to these differences, preferred shares can be issued with special features that are similar to some of the debt features we saw in Exhibit 10.13 on page 450. Just like

Preferred shares are shares that have specified rights over common shares.

debt instruments, preferred shares can be convertible into common shares at the option of the holder, or callable (can be bought back) at the option of the issuer.

Danier has authorized two classes of preferred shares but has not issued any of them. To illustrate the accounting for an initial issuance of preferred shares, assume that during the fiscal year ended June 27, 2009, Danier issued 100,000 preferred shares for $5 per share. The company would record the following journal entry:

> *dr*   **Cash (+A)(100,000 × $5)**   500,000
>   *cr*   **Preferred Shares (+SE)**   500,000

Assets	=	Liabilities	+	Shareholders' Equity
Cash + 500,000				Preferred Shares + 500,000

Dividends on Preferred Shares

Because investors who purchase preferred shares give up voting rights that are available to investors in common shares, preferred shares offer dividend preferences. The two most common dividend preferences are current and cumulative, both of which are explained below.

Current Dividend Preference.   This preference requires that the current preferred dividend be paid before any dividends are paid to holders of common shares. After the **current dividend preference** has been met and if no other preference exists, dividends can be paid to the common shareholders.

Let's look at an example, assuming that Danier's 100,000 shares had a $.50 dividend rate. This means that preferred shareholders will be paid the first $50,000 of any dividends declared for the year ($50,000 = 100,000 shares outstanding × $.50 dividend rate). Any additional dividends would go entirely to common shareholders. If the declared dividends were less than this amount, no dividends would be paid to common shareholders and preferred shareholders would not get their full dividend that year. The preferred shareholders would lose their rights to this unpaid portion, unless the preferred shares also have what is called a "cumulative dividend preference." Let's see what that means.

Cumulative Dividend Preference.   This preference states that if all or a part of the current dividend is not paid in full, the cumulative unpaid amount, known as **dividends in arrears,** must be paid before any future common dividends can be paid. To illustrate the **cumulative dividend preference,** let's assume that no dividends were declared by Danier in the year ended June 28, 2008, and that the Danier preferred shares carried a cumulative dividend preference. This means that, as of June 28, 2008, the dividends on Danier's preferred shares were $50,000 in arrears. Let's now assume that Danier declared total dividends of $400,000 during the year ended June 27, 2009. This dividend would be distributed to shareholders as follows:

Current dividend preference is the feature of preferred shares that grants priority on preferred dividends over common dividends.

Cumulative dividend preference is the preferred share feature that requires specified current dividends not paid in full to accumulate for every year in which they are not paid. These cumulative unpaid amounts (called **dividends in arrears**) must be paid before any common dividends can be paid.

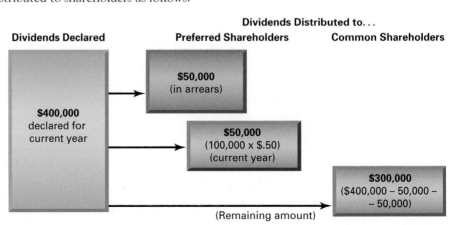

Dividends Declared	Dividends Distributed to...	
	Preferred Shareholders	**Common Shareholders**

$400,000 declared for current year

$50,000 (in arrears)

$50,000 (100,000 x $.50) (current year)

$300,000 ($400,000 − 50,000 − − 50,000)

(Remaining amount)

Because dividends are not an actual liability until the board of directors declares them, dividends in arrears are not reported on the balance sheet. Instead, they are disclosed in the notes to the statements. The following note from American Skiing—the company that operates ski, snowboard, and golf resorts throughout the United States, including Colorado's Steamboat and Vermont's Killington—is typical:

As of July 31, 2005, cumulative dividends in arrears totalled approximately $23.7 million and $109.3 million, for the Series C-1 Preferred Stock and Series C-2 Preferred Stock, respectively.

RETAINED EARNINGS

As its name suggests, Retained Earnings represents the company's total earnings that have been retained in the business (rather than being distributed to shareholders). The balance in this account increases each year that the company reports net income on the income statement, and it decreases each year that the company reports a net loss (expenses greater than revenues) or declares cash or stock dividends to shareholders. Think of retained earnings as the amount of equity that the company itself has generated for shareholders (through profitable operations) but not yet distributed to them.

Should a company ever accumulate more net losses than net income over its life, it will report a negative (debit) balance in the Retained Earnings account. This amount is (a) shown in parentheses in the shareholders' equity section of the balance sheet, (b) deducted when computing total shareholders' equity, and (c) typically called an Accumulated Deficit rather than Retained Earnings. Exhibit 11.4 provides a recent example courtesy of the digital music pioneer Napster, Inc.

exhibit 11.4 **Reporting Negative Retained Earnings (Accumulated Deficit)**

NAPSTER, INC.
Balance Sheet (Partial)
December 31, 2006
(in thousands of dollars)

Shareholders' equity:	
Contributed capital	$ 260,233
Accumulated deficit	(169,698)
Total shareholders' equity	90,535

Okay, now that you know how dividends and other shareholders' equity transactions are accounted for inside a company, it's time to evaluate things from the outside. In the next section, you will learn to evaluate how well a company is using its capital to generate returns for the company and, ultimately, for its shareholders.

EVALUATE _____
The Return to Shareholders

EARNINGS PER SHARE (EPS)

The most famous of all ratios, earnings-per-share (EPS), reports how much profit is earned for each common share outstanding. The calculation of EPS can involve many details and intricacies, especially when there are many classes of shares and/or there have been share transactions during the year, but, in its basic form, it is computed as

$$\text{Earnings per share} = \frac{\text{Net Income Belonging to Common Shareholders}}{\text{Weighted Average Number of Common Shares Outstanding}}$$

When a company has only one class of shares (common shares), which is what we will assume in the rest of this discussion, all of its net income belongs to the common share-holders, and the numerator becomes net income. Most companies calculate EPS at the end of each quarter and year, and report it either on the income statement immediately below *Net income* or in the notes to the financial statements.[2]

You might be wondering why *earnings* per share is so popular when dividends and stock prices ultimately determine the return to shareholders. The reason is that current earnings can predict future dividends and stock prices. If a company generates increased earnings in the current year, it will be able to pay higher dividends in future years. In other words, current EPS influences expectations about future dividends, which investors factor into the stock price.

Another reason that EPS is so popular is that it allows you to make comparisons easily over time. When a company's net income increases during the year, it seems like good news, but it is hard to know whether it's a good thing for each shareholder, because it's possible that the number of shares increased at a faster pace than net income. For example, assume a company has net income that grows by $50,000 a year from 2007 to 2010. That sounds good, but take a look at the numbers below. The number of common shares increased each year, as well, so is that good or bad for each shareholder? The EPS tells the story: EPS rose in 2008 but declined in both 2009 and 2010.

	2007	2008	2009	2010
Net income	$100,000	$150,000	$200,000	$250,000
Weighted Average Number of Common Shares	50,000	67,500	95,000	120,000
EPS	$2.00	$2.22	$2.10	$2.08

By considering earnings on a per share basis, we adjust for the effect of additional shares issued, resulting in a clearer picture of what profit increases mean for each investor.

Be on the Alert

While EPS is an effective and widely used measure for comparing a company with itself over time, it is not appropriate for comparing across companies. As you have seen in earlier chapters, net income can be affected by differences in estimates of bad debts (Chapter 7), methods of inventory costing (Chapter 8), estimated useful lives of long-lived tangible assets (Chapter 9), and estimates of losses from contingent liabilities (Chapter 10). But, even if companies use identical accounting methods, EPS will be misleading if the dollar amounts for the shares being compared differ significantly. Two companies reporting $2 EPS might appear comparable, but, if shares in one company cost $10 while shares of the other cost $150, they are not. You spend a lot less for shares in one company than you do for the other. Thus, when evaluating return to shareholders, it's important to consider not just the number of shares but also how much they cost.

---

[2] Although companies report their annual EPS numbers only at the end of their fiscal years, most analysts find it useful to update annual EPS as each quarter's results are reported. To do this, analysts will compute their own "trailing 12 months" EPS measure by summing the most recent four quarters of EPS. This way, they can get a timely measure of year-long EPS, without having to wait until the end of the fiscal year.

RETURN ON EQUITY (ROE)

EPS may be the most famous of all ratios, but ROE is considered by many to be the most important overall performance ratio. The ROE ratio tells you how much profit the company makes on every dollar invested by shareholders. What makes this ratio so useful is that it allows shareholders to see how well investing in this company pays off compared with other investment opportunities, such as putting the money in the bank or investing in real estate.

As was the case with EPS, ROE calculations can get complicated but, in its simplest form, ROE is computed as follows:

$$\text{Return on Equity} = \frac{\text{Net Income}}{\text{Average Shareholders' Equity}}$$

COACH'S TIP

The bottom number in the return-on-equity ratio is calculated by summing the beginning and ending total shareholders' equity balances and dividing by 2.

Just as EPS is useful in understanding a company's stock price, so is ROE. In the long run, companies with higher ROE are likely to have higher stock prices than companies with lower ROE.

According to Yahoo! Finance, the average ROE in the apparel industry is approximately 20 per cent. Exhibit 11.5 shows a recent year's ROE calculations for Danier and two other Canadian companies in the industry, Le Château and Reitmans. Reitmans and Le Château had ROEs just around the industry average of 20 per cent, while Danier's ROE was a lot lower at only 3.4 per cent. The Self-Study Quiz that follows gives you a chance to see whether you understand how to calculate this ratio, using the numbers for Le Château in 2006 (since Danier had a loss that year).

exhibit 11.5 Summary of Return on Equity (ROE) Ratio Analyses

| Name of Measure | Formula | What It Tells You | 2007 | | | SELF-STUDY QUIZ 2006 |
			Reitman's	Le Château	Danier Leather	Le Château
Return-on-Equity Ratio	$\dfrac{\text{Net Income}}{\text{Average Shareholder's Equity}}$	• The amount earned for each dollar invested by shareholders • A higher ratio means shareholders are likely to enjoy greater returns.	20.0%	23.2%	$\dfrac{1,653}{(48,709 + 47,956)/2}$ $= 0.034,$ or 3.4%	

HOW'S IT GOING? A Self-Study Quiz

Compute the ratio for the final column in Exhibit 11.5 using the following information. In its financial statements for the year ended January 31, 2006, Le Château reported net income of $23,513 and beginning and ending total shareholders' equity of $85,244 and $105,245 respectively (in thousands). Did the return-on-equity ratio improve or decline in 2007 as compared with 2006?

When you're finished, check your answers with the solutions in the margin.

Quiz Answers

$$\frac{23,513}{(85,244 + 105,245)/2} = 0.247 \text{ or } 24.7\%$$

The 23.2 per cent ratio in 2007 represented a slight decline from the 24.7 per cent in 2006.

Since both EPS and ROE are profitability ratios, we show them in the (c) section in our framework for financial statement analysis, as shown in Exhibit 11.6 below.

exhibit 11.6   Framework for Financial Statement Ratio Analyses

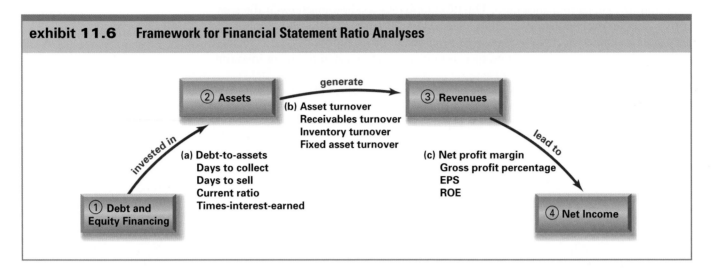

COACH'S TIP

If a company has preferred shares outstanding, the ROE ratio can be adjusted to focus on the common shareholders' perspective. Simply deduct any preferred dividends from net income, and exclude any preferred share accounts from the calculation of average shareholders' equity.

Be on the Alert

Because ROE, like EPS, uses net income in its numerator, we have the same reservations about how different estimates and accounting policies affect our ability to compare ratios across companies. You should also note that ROE is calculated by using the total dollar amount contributed to or reinvested in the company. This amount does not necessarily reflect what each individual investor pays to acquire the company's share, nor does it represent the current value of all outstanding shares, which could be much more than what's reported on the balance sheet for shareholders' equity. Remember, these accounts are not updated for changes in share value. Because of this, the ROE ratio does not equal the return that each individual shareholder will enjoy on his or her own investment in that company, but rather what all shareholders earn as a group.

RECONSIDER _____
Decisions that Affect Measures of Shareholder Returns

In addition to evaluating the historical relationship between a company's earnings and shareholders' equity levels, investors also should keep their eyes open for events that might have an impact on shareholders' equity in the future. Here we look at three of these: debt versus equity financing, dividend restrictions, and employee stock options.

EQUITY VERSUS DEBT

Whenever a company needs a large amount of long-term financing, its executives will have to decide whether to obtain it through equity (issue shares) or debt (borrow money). Equity has certain advantages over debt, but it also has disadvantages. Exhibit 11.7 summarizes some of these pros and cons.

Financial leverage, also called "trading on the equity," is the practice of borrowing money from creditors and using it to generate profits for shareholders.

One additional issue should be considered when choosing between equity and debt financing. The concept of **financial leverage** can seem quite complex, but here we'll try to keep the explanation simple. Imagine that you are considering investing in a $10,000 project and that you expect to make a profit of 15 per cent ($1,500) on this project. Should you use your own money or borrow it from a bank? The quick answer is that, if you can borrow money and pay less than 15 per cent interest, you will be better off borrowing. That sounds like a no-brainer, but is there any downside to this strategy? Yes, there is, because, if you are wrong in your estimate of the profit and the project doesn't make you enough money to repay the principal and the interest on the debt, you are in big trouble. The lender can put you into bankruptcy, because debt is a legal liability and *must* be repaid. Chapter 11 Supplement B in the Online Learning Centre

---

 exhibit 11.7 **Advantages and Disadvantages of Equity Financing (Relative to Debt)**

Advantages of Equity Financing

1. **Equity does not have to be repaid.**
   Debt must be repaid or refinanced.

2. **Dividends are optional.**
   Interest must be paid on debt.

Disadvantages of Equity Financing

1. **Change in shareholder control**
   New shareholders get to vote and share in the earnings, diluting existing shareholders co ntrol.

2. **Dividends are not tax deductible.**
   Interest on debt is tax deductible.

---

that accompanies this text contains some numerical examples of financial leverage, so you'll want to find out from your instructor whether you are responsible for this topic.

In the above example, you expected to make $1,500 on a $10,000 investment. This is a ratio we call the **return-on-asset (ROA)** ratio, which can be used to measure the return on any particular asset or project that the company is evaluating.

The **return-on-asset (ROA)** ratio measures the return on any particular asset or project that the company is evaluating.

$$\text{Return on Asset} = \frac{\text{Net Income from Project}}{\text{Amount Invested in Project}}$$

We include ROA here because it is a useful and common ratio, but we do not include the ROA in our framework because it is not used for financial statement analysis, but rather for internal project analysis.

RETAINED EARNINGS RESTRICTIONS

Several types of business transactions may place restrictions on retained earnings that limit a company's ability to pay dividends in the future. The most typical example involves borrowing money from a bank. To reduce its risk, a bank might include a clause in its lending agreement that limits the amount of dividends a corporation can pay. If this loan covenant is violated, the bank can demand immediate repayment of the debt. It is important for shareholders to be aware of any dividend restrictions that may exist, and they will find this information in the notes to the financial statements.

COACH'S TIP

The bank imposes dividend restrictions because it doesn't want to lend money to a corporation and then have the corporation pay it out in dividends to shareholders.

STOCK OPTIONS AND DILUTED EARNINGS PER SHARE

Most publicly traded companies, including Danier, grant stock options to their employees. The accounting rules for stock options are complex, so they're covered in detail in intermediate accounting courses. However, because stock options are so common, we should tell you in simple terms what they are and how they potentially affect financial statement users. Stock options are agreements that give employees the option to buy the company's shares at a fixed price in the future, say at $7 per share. If employees work hard to improve the company and increase its share price to say $10, they can "exercise the option" to buy shares from the company for $7 per share. The result is a $3 per share benefit for employees, kind of like a bonus tied to the company's stock price.

For investors, employee stock option plans can be both good news and bad news. The good news is that they potentially motivate employees to improve the company's financial performance, which can increase the share price, leading to an increase in investors' personal wealth. The bad news is that, when stock options are exercised by employees, the company issues more common shares, which, all else being equal, reduces or "dilutes" the existing shareholders' control of the company as well as their claims on the company's future earnings. For example, if a company has 40 shares outstanding and you own 4 of them, you'd be considered a 10 per cent owner (4 ÷ 40 = 10%). If the company then issued 10 additional shares to employees when they exercise their stock options, the total number of shares outstanding would increase to 50, causing your ownership percentage to fall to 8 per cent (4 ÷ 50 = 8%). In other words, you'd have less control of the company, and, when the company's earnings are distributed as dividends, you would share them with more shareholders.

To advise financial statement users of these potential effects, accounting rules require companies to report two versions of the earnings per share (EPS) number. The first version, called basic EPS (shown earlier in this chapter), indicates what the current period's earnings are for each existing share. The second version, called diluted EPS, shows what the current earnings would have been for each share if the company had issued additional shares for unexercised stock options (and any other existing agreements that would require the company to issue additional shares).

BE ON THE ALERT FOR STOCK REPURCHASES

Before closing this chapter, we need to remind you to interpret changes in EPS and ROE in the light of your new knowledge about accounting for stock repurchases. As you know from the previous section in this chapter, stock repurchases cause a decrease in the number of outstanding shares as well as a decrease in total shareholders' equity. Because of these effects, stock repurchases generally lead to increases in EPS and ROE.[3] Some people jump to the conclusion that increases in EPS and ROE mean the company has become more profitable in the current year. This is not necessarily true, because a company with the same $1 million of net income in two consecutive years can still report an increase in EPS and ROE if it repurchases its shares during the second year. So, beware; changes in EPS and ROE can be caused by reductions in the denominator of the ratios (number of shares and average shareholders' equity) rather than improvements in the numerator (net income).

WHAT'S COMING UP

This completes our in-depth coverage of the balance sheet accounts. Chapter 12 returns to one of the four basic accounting reports introduced in Chapter 1: the statement of cash flows. Following that, Chapter 13 pulls everything together by demonstrating the analyses that can be conducted using a full set of financial statements, and by reviewing the concepts that underlie financial accounting. But don't get ahead of yourself yet. Be sure to review and practise testing your understanding of what you've read in this chapter.

FOR YOUR REVIEW _____

DEMONSTRATION CASE A (STOCK ISSUANCE AND REPURCHASES)

This case focuses on selected transactions from the first year of operations of Zoogle Corporation, which became a public company on January 1, 2009, for the purpose of operating a lost-pet search business. The charter authorized the following classes of shares:

> Common: 20,000 shares
> $5 Preferred: noncumulative, 5,000 shares

The following summarized transactions, selected from 2009, were completed on the dates indicated:

a.   Jan.   1   Issued a total of 8,000 common shares for cash at $50 per share.

b.   Feb.   1   Sold 2,000 preferred shares at $102 per share; cash collected in full.

c.   July   1   Purchased 400 common shares that had been issued earlier. Zoogle Corporation paid the shareholder $54 per share and cancelled the shares.

d.   Dec. 31   The board decided not to declare any dividends for the current year.

---

[3] We say *generally* because it is possible for stock repurchases to have an indirect effect on net income as well, as they would, for example, if the company sold a money-making division to get the funds to repurchase the shares. In that case, EPS and ROE could rise or fall.

Required:

1. Give the appropriate journal entries, and show calculations for each transaction.
2. Prepare the shareholders' equity section of the balance sheet for Zoogle Corporation at December 31, 2009. Assume retained earnings is $31,000 before these transactions are accounted for.

Suggested Solution

1. **Journal entries:**

   a. Jan. 1, 2009

dr	Cash (+A) ($50 × 8,000 shares)	400,000	
	cr Common Shares (+SE)		400,000

   b. Feb. 1, 2009

dr	Cash (+A) ($102 × 2,000 shares)	204,000	
	cr Preferred Shares (+SE)		204,000

   c. July 1, 2009

dr	Common shares ($50 × 400) (−SE)	20,000	
dr	Retained earnings (−SE)	1,600	
	cr Cash (−A) ($54 × 400 shares)		21,600

   d. Dec. 31, 2009   No journal entry is required.

2. **Shareholders' equity section of the balance sheet:**

ZOOGLE CORPORATION		
Partial Balance Sheet		
At December 31, 2009		
Shareholders' Equity		
Contributed capital		
$5 Preferred shares, 5,000 authorized,		
2,000 issued and outstanding shares	$204,000	
Common shares, authorized 20,000,		
7,600 issued and outstanding	380,000	
Total contributed capital		$584,000
Retained earnings		29,400
Total shareholders' equity		$613,400

DEMONSTRATION CASE B (CASH DIVIDENDS AND STOCK DIVIDENDS)

This case extends Demonstration Case A by focusing on dividend transactions occurring during Zoogle Corporation's second year. The following summarized transactions, selected from 2010, were completed on the dates indicated:

a. Nov. 1 To remind common shareholders of their accumulating wealth, the board declared and issued a 10 per cent stock dividend on the outstanding common shares. The share price at that time on the open market was $49.80.

b. Dec. 1 The board declared a cash dividend on the preferred shares, payable on December 22, 2010, to shareholders of record as of December 15, 2010.

c. Dec. 31 The temporary dividends declared account was closed.

Required:

Give the appropriate journal entries, and show calculations for each transaction.

Suggested Solution

a.   Nov. 1, 2010

dr	Retained Earnings (−SE).....................	378,480	
	cr Common Shares (+SE)..................		378,480
	[(7,600 common shares issued and outstanding) × $49.80]		

b.   Dec. 1, 2010

dr	Dividends Declared (+D, −SE)	10,000	
	cr Dividends Payable (+L)		10,000
	(2,000 preferred shares × $5 dividend rate)		

Dec. 15, 2010 No journal entry is required.
Dec. 22, 2010

dr	Dividends Payable (−L).....................	10,000	
	cr Cash (−A)...............................		10,000

c.   Dec. 31, 2010

dr	Retained Earnings (−SE)	10,000	
	cr Dividends Declared (−D, +SE)		10,000

CHAPTER SUMMARY

LO1   **Explain the role of shares in financing a corporation. p. 480**

- The law recognizes corporations as separate legal entities. Owners invest in a corporation and receive capital shares that can be bought from and sold to other investors. Shares provide a number of rights, including the rights to vote, to receive dividends, and to share in residual assets at liquidation.

LO2   **Explain and analyze common share transactions. p. 483**

- A number of key transactions involve common shares: (1) initial issuance of shares, (2) repurchase of shares into treasury, and (3) either cancellation of the shares or reissuance of the treasury shares.

LO3   **Explain and analyze cash dividends, stock dividends, and stock split transactions. p. 485**

- Cash dividends reduce shareholders' equity (retained earnings) and create a liability (dividends payable) when they are declared by the board of directors (on the date of declaration). The liability is reduced when the dividends are paid (on the date of payment).
- Stock dividends are pro rata distributions of a company's shares to existing owners. The transaction typically is accounted for by transferring an amount out of retained earnings and into common share accounts.
- A stock split also involves the distribution of additional shares to owners but no additional amount is transferred into the common share account. Instead, the carrying value of each share is reduced.

LO4   **Describe the characteristics of preferred shares and analyze transactions affecting preferred shares. p. 489**

- Preferred shares provide investors with certain advantages, including current dividend preferences and a preference on asset distributions in the event the corporation is liquidated.

- If preferred shares carry cumulative dividend rights, any part of a current dividend that is not paid (called dividends in arrears) must be paid in full before any additional dividends can be paid.

(Supplement A) Analyze the equity transactions in sole proprietorships and partnerships. p. 500   LO5

- The equity section of sole proprietorships and partnerships is different from that of an incorporated company. Instead of Contributed Capital and Retained Earnings accounts, there are Capital accounts that show how much equity each owner has in the business.

Analyze the earnings-per-share (EPS) and return-on-equity (ROE) ratios. p. 491   LO6

- The earnings-per-share (EPS) ratio makes it easy to compare a company's earnings over time. Although EPS adjusts for differences in the number of shares outstanding, it does not take into account possible differences in the price of shares, making it a poor measure for comparing across companies.
- The return-on-equity ratio relates earnings to each dollar contributed to and retained by the company.

Explain how share transactions affect ROE and EPS. p. 494   LO7

- Accounting rules require companies to report a "diluted EPS" number, which indicates how employee stock options (and other commitments potentially to issue additional shares in the future) would have affected existing shareholders' claims to a company's earnings had additional shares been issued to fulfill these commitments.
- Stock repurchases reduce the number of and dollar amount reported for outstanding common shares, causing increases in EPS and ROE (assuming all else is equal).

FINANCIAL STATEMENT ANALYSIS TIPS

To determine the amount of income generated for each common share, calculate the earnings-per-share (EPS) ratio:

$$\text{Earnings per share} = \frac{\text{Net Income}}{\text{Weighted Average Number of Common Shares Outstanding}}$$

$$\text{Return on Equity} = \frac{\text{Net Income}}{\text{Average Shareholders' Equity}}$$

KEY TERMS TO KNOW

Authorized Number of
    Shares p. 482
Common Shares p. 484
Cumulative Dividend
    Preference p. 490
Current Dividend
    Preference p. 490
Declaration Date p. 486

Dividends in Arrears p. 490
Financial Leverage p. 495
Issued Shares p. 482
Outstanding Shares p. 483
Par Value p. 484
Payment Date p. 486
Preferred Shares p. 489

Record Date p. 486
Return on Asset (ROA)
    p. 495
Stock Dividend p. 487
Stock Split p. 488
Treasury Shares p. 483

SUPPLEMENT A: ACCOUNTING FOR EQUITY IN SOLE PROPRIETORSHIPS AND PARTNERSHIPS

Owner's Equity for a Sole Proprietorship

A sole proprietorship is an unincorporated business owned by one person. Only two owner's equity accounts are needed: (1) a capital account for the proprietor (H. Simpson, Capital) and (2) a drawing (or withdrawal) account for the proprietor (H. Simpson, Drawings).

The capital account of a sole proprietorship serves two purposes: to record investments by the owner and to accumulate periodic income or loss. The drawing account is used to record the owner's withdrawals of cash or other assets from the business, similar to recording dividends declared by corporations. The drawing account is closed to the capital account at the end of each accounting period. Thus, after the drawing account is closed, the capital account reflects the cumulative total of all investments by the owner and all earnings of the entity less all withdrawals from the entity by the owner.

In most respects, the accounting for a sole proprietorship is the same as for a corporation. Exhibit 11A.1 presents the recording of selected transactions of a new sole proprietor, and the owner's equity section of the balance sheet.

Because a sole proprietorship does not file a separate tax return, its financial statements do not reflect income tax expense or income taxes payable. Instead, the net income of a sole proprietorship is taxed by including it on the owner's personal income tax return. Likewise, the owner's salary is not recognized as an expense in a sole proprietorship because an employer/employee contractual relationship cannot exist with only one party involved. The owner's salary is therefore accounted for as a distribution of profits—a withdrawal—instead of salary expense, as it would be in a corporation.

Accounting for Partnership Equity

A partnership is "an association of two or more persons to carry on as co-owners of a business for profit." Small businesses and professionals such as accountants, doctors, and lawyers often use the partnership form of business.

A partnership is formed by two or more persons reaching mutual agreement about the terms of the relationship. The agreement between the partners constitutes a partnership contract. This agreement should specify details of matters like division of income, management responsibilities, transfer or sale of partnership interests, disposition of assets upon liquidation, and procedures to be followed in case of the death of a partner.

In comparison with a corporation, the primary advantages of a partnership are (1) ease of formation, (2) complete control by the partners, and (3) lack of income taxes on the business itself. The primary disadvantage is the unlimited liability of each partner for the partnership's debts. If the partnership does not have sufficient assets to satisfy outstanding debt, creditors of the partnership can seize each partner's personal assets. In some cases, this can even result in one partner being held responsible for another partner's share of the partnership's debt.

As with a sole proprietorship, accounting for a partnership follows the same underlying principles as any other form of business organization, except for those entries that directly affect owners' equity. Accounting for partners' equity follows the same pattern as for a sole proprietorship, except that separate capital and drawings accounts must be established for each partner. Investments by each partner are credited to that partner's capital account, and withdrawals are debited to their respective drawings accounts. The net income of a partnership is divided among the partners in accordance with the partnership agreement, and credited to

exhibit 11A.1 Accounting for Owner's Equity for a Sole Proprietorship

Selected Entries during 2009

January 1, 2009

Homer Simpson started a retail store by investing $150,000 of personal savings. The journal entry follows:

> dr   Cash (+A) 150,000
>   cr   H. Simpson, Capital (+OE)   150,000

Assets	=	Liabilities	+	Shareholders' Equity
Cash +150,000				H. Simpson, Capital + 150,000

During 2009

Each month during the year, Homer withdrew $1,000 cash from the business for personal living costs. Accordingly, each month the following journal entry was made:

> dr   H. Simpson, Drawings (+D, −OE) 1,000
>   cr   Cash (−A)..........................   1,000

Assets	=	Liabilities	+	Shareholders' Equity
Cash − 1,000				H. Simpson, Capital − 1,000

Note: At December 31, 2009, after the last of 12 withdrawals, the drawings account reflected a debit balance of $12,000.

December 31, 2009

The usual journal entries for the year, including adjusting and closing entries for the revenue and expense accounts, resulted in an $18,000 net income, and the journal entries were closed to the capital account as follows:

> dr   Individual Revenue and Expense Accounts
>   (−R&E) 18,000
>   cr   H. Simpson, (+OE)   18,000

Assets	=	Liabilities	+	Shareholders' Equity
				Revenues and Expenses − 18,000
				H. Simpson, Capital + 18,000

December 31, 2009

The drawings account was closed as follows:

> dr   H. Simpson, Capital (−OE) 12,000
>   cr   H. Simpson, Drawings (−D, +OE)   12,000

Assets	=	Liabilities	+	Shareholders' Equity
				H. Simpson, Capital − 12,000
				H. Simpson, Drawings + 12,000

exhibit 11A.1   (Concluded)

Balance Sheet, December 31, 2009 (partial)

Owner's equity	
H. Simpson, capital, January 1, 2009	$150,000
Add: Net income for 2009	18,000
Total	$168,000
Less: Withdrawals for 2009	(12,000)
H. Simpson, capital, December 31, 2009	$156,000

each account. The respective drawings accounts are closed to the partner capital accounts. After the closing process, each partner's capital account reflects the cumulative total of all that partner's investments plus that partner's share of the partnership earnings less all that partner's withdrawals.

Exhibit 11A.2 presents selected journal entries and partial financial statements for AB Partnership to illustrate the accounting for the distribution of income and partners' equity.

exhibit 11A.2   Accounting for Partners' Equity

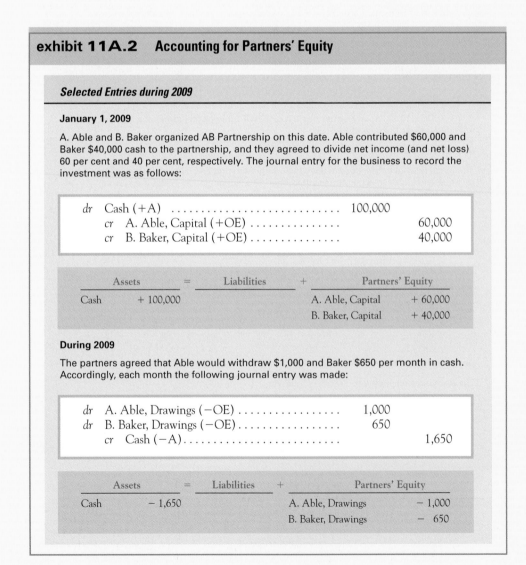

Selected Entries during 2009

January 1, 2009

A. Able and B. Baker organized AB Partnership on this date. Able contributed $60,000 and Baker $40,000 cash to the partnership, and they agreed to divide net income (and net loss) 60 per cent and 40 per cent, respectively. The journal entry for the business to record the investment was as follows:

dr	Cash (+A)	100,000	
	cr A. Able, Capital (+OE)		60,000
	cr B. Baker, Capital (+OE)		40,000

Assets	=	Liabilities	+	Partners' Equity	
Cash + 100,000				A. Able, Capital	+ 60,000
				B. Baker, Capital	+ 40,000

During 2009

The partners agreed that Able would withdraw $1,000 and Baker $650 per month in cash. Accordingly, each month the following journal entry was made:

dr	A. Able, Drawings (−OE)	1,000	
dr	B. Baker, Drawings (−OE)	650	
	cr Cash (−A).........................		1,650

Assets	=	Liabilities	+	Partners' Equity	
Cash − 1,650				A. Able, Drawings	− 1,000
				B. Baker, Drawings	− 650

exhibit 11A.2 (Concluded)

December 31, 2009

Assume that the normal closing entries for the revenue and expense accounts resulted in a net income of $30,000. The partnership agreement specified Able would receive 60 per cent of earnings and Baker would get 40 per cent. The closing entry was as follows:

> *dr* Individual Revenue and Expense Accounts
>   (−R&E) 30,000
>   *cr* A. Able, Capital (+OE) (60% × $30,000)   18,000
>   *cr* B. Baker, Capital (+OE) (40% × $30,000)   12,000

Assets	=	Liabilities	+	Partners' Equity	
				Revenues and Expenses	− 30,000
				A. Able, Capital	+ 18,000
				B. Baker, Capital	+ 12,000

December 31, 2009

The journal entry required to close the drawings accounts follows:

> *dr* A. Able, Capital (−OE) 12,000
> *dr* B. Baker, Capital (−OE) 7,800
>   *cr* A. Able, Drawings (+OE) 12,000
>   *cr* B. Baker, Drawings (+OE) 7,800

Assets	=	Liabilities	+	Partners' Equity	
				A. Able, Capital	− 12,000
				B. Baker, Capital	− 7,800
				A. Able, Drawings	+ 12,000
				B. Baker, Drawings	+ 7,800

A separate statement of partners' capital, similar to the following, is customarily prepared to supplement the balance sheet:

AB PARTNERSHIP
Statement of Partners' Equity
For the Year Ended December 31, 2009

	A. Able	B. Baker	Total
Investment, January 1, 2009	$60,000	$40,000	$100,000
Add: Additional investments			
during the year	0	0	0
Net income for the year	18,000	12,000	30,000
Totals	78,000	52,000	130,000
Less: Drawings during the year	(12,000)	(7,800)	(19,800)
Partners' equity, December 31, 2009	$66,000	$44,200	$110,200

FOR YOUR PRACTICE _____

QUESTIONS

1. Identify the primary advantages of the corporate form of business.
2. Explain each of the following terms: (a) authorized common shares, (b) issued common shares, and (c) outstanding common shares.
3. What are the differences between common shares and preferred shares?
4. What are the usual characteristics of preferred shares?
5. What are the two basic sources of shareholders' equity? Explain each.
6. Why do corporations repurchase their own shares?
7. What are the two basic requirements to support the declaration of a cash dividend? What are the effects of a cash dividend on assets and shareholders' equity?
8. What is the difference between cumulative and noncumulative preferred shares?
9. What is a stock dividend? How does a stock dividend differ from a cash dividend?
10. What are the primary reasons for issuing a stock dividend?
11. Identify and explain the three important dates with respect to dividends.
12. Why is the EPS number so popular? What are its limitations?
13. What are the advantages and disadvantages of equity financing (relative to debt financing)?
14. How do stock repurchases affect the EPS and ROE ratios?
15. Explain the concept of financial leverage.

MULTIPLE CHOICE

Select the one alternative that best answers the question or completes the sentence.

1. Which feature is not applicable to common share ownership?
   a.   Right to receive dividends before preferred shareholders
   b.   Right to vote on appointment of external auditor
   c.   Right to receive residual assets of the company should it cease operations
   d.   All of the above are applicable to common share ownership.
2. Which statement regarding treasury shares is false?
   a.   Treasury shares are considered to be issued but not outstanding.
   b.   Treasury shares have no voting, dividend, or liquidation rights.
   c.   Treasury shares carry voting rights but no dividend rights.
   d.   None of the above is false.
3. Which of the following statements about stock dividends is true?
   a.   Stock dividends are reported on the income statement.
   b.   Stock dividends increase the number of shares held by each shareholder.
   c.   Stock dividends increase total shareholders' equity.
   d.   Stock dividends decrease total shareholders' equity.
4. Which of the following is ordered from the largest number of shares to the smallest number of shares?
   a.   Shares authorized, shares issued, shares outstanding
   b.   Shares issued, shares outstanding, shares authorized
   c.   Shares outstanding, shares issued, shares authorized
   d.   Shares in treasury, shares outstanding, shares issued
5. Which of the following statements about the relative advantages and disadvantages of equity and debt financing is false?
   a.   An advantage of equity financing is that it does not have to be repaid.
   b.   An advantage of equity financing is that dividends are optional.
   c.   A disadvantage of equity financing is that new shareholders get to vote and share in the earnings of the company.

   d.   A disadvantage of equity financing is that it always leads to a smaller return on shareholders' equity.

6. With regard to dividends, a journal entry is not recorded on what date?

   a.   Date of declaration

   b.   Date of record

   c.   Date of payment

   d.   A journal entry is recorded on all of the above dates.

7. Which of the following transactions will increase the return on equity?

   a.   Declare and issue a stock dividend.

   b.   Split the stock 2-for-1.

   c.   Repurchase the company's shares.

   d.   None of the above

8. Which statement regarding dividends is false?

   a.   Dividends represent a sharing of corporate profits with owners.

   b.   Both stock and cash dividends reduce retained earnings.

   c.   Cash dividends paid to shareholders reduce net income.

   d.   None of the above statements is false.

9. When treasury shares are purchased with cash and cancelled, what is the impact on the balance sheet equation?

   a.   No change—the reduction of the asset "Cash" is offset by the addition of the asset "Treasury Shares."

   b.   Assets decrease and Shareholders' Equity increases.

   c.   Assets increase and Shareholders' Equity decreases.

   d.   Assets decrease and Shareholders' Equity decreases.

10. In what situation does an investor's personal wealth increase immediately?

   a.   When receiving a cash dividend

   b.   When receiving a stock dividend

   c.   When a stock split is announced

   d.   An investor's wealth is increased instantly in all of the above situations.

MINI-EXERCISES

M11-1 Evaluating Shareholders' Rights   LO1
Name three rights of shareholders. Which of these is most important in your mind? Why?

M11-2 Computing the Number of Unissued Shares   LO1
The balance sheet for Crutcher Corporation reported 147,000 shares outstanding, 200,000 shares authorized, and 10,000 shares in the treasury. Compute the maximum number of new shares that Crutcher could issue.

M11-3 Recording the Sale of Common Shares   LO2
To expand operations, Aragon Consulting issued 100,000 previously unissued common shares. The selling price for the shares was $75 per share. Record the sale of these shares.

M11-4 Comparing Common Shares and Preferred Shares   LO2, LO4
Your parents have just retired and have asked you for some financial advice. They have decided to invest $100,000 in a company very similar to Danier Leather. The company has issued both common and preferred shares. Which type of shares would you recommend? What factors would you consider in giving them advice?

M11-5 Determining the Amount of a Dividend   LO3
Jacobs Company has 300,000 common shares authorized, 270,000 shares issued, and 50,000 shares in the treasury. The company's board of directors declares a dividend of 50 cents per share. What is the total amount of the dividend that will be paid?

LO3   ### M11-6 Recording Dividends

On April 15, 2009, the board of directors for Auction.com declared a cash dividend of 20 cents per share payable to shareholders of record on May 20. The dividends will be paid on June 14. The company has 500,000 shares outstanding. Prepare any necessary journal entries for each date.

LO3   ### M11-7 Determining the Impact of a Stock Dividend

Armstrong Tools Inc. announced a 10 per cent stock dividend. Determine the impact (increase, decrease, no change) of this dividend on the following:

1. Total assets
2. Total liabilities
3. Common shares (dollar value)
4. Total shareholders' equity
5. Market value per common share

LO3   ### M11-8 Determining the Impact of a Stock Split

Complete the requirements of M11-7 assuming that the company announced a 2-for-1 stock split.

LO3   ### M11-9 Recording a Stock Dividend

To reduce its share price, Shriver Food Systems, Inc., declared and issued a 5 per cent stock dividend. The company has 800,000 shares authorized and 200,000 shares outstanding. The book value is $75 per share, and the market value is $100 per share. Prepare the journal entry to record this stock dividend.

LO4   ### M11-10 Determining the Amount of a Preferred Dividend

Colliers Inc. has 200,000 shares of cumulative preferred shares outstanding. The preferred shares pay dividends in the amount of $2 per share, but, because of cash flow problems, the company did not pay any dividends last year. The board of directors plans to pay dividends in the amount of $1 million this year. What amount will go to preferred shareholders?

LO6   ### M11-11 Calculating and Interpreting Earnings per Share (EPS) and Return on Equity (ROE)

Toonce's Driving School reported the following amount in its financial statements:

	2009	2008
Number of common shares	11,500	11,500
Net income	$ 23,000	$ 18,000
Cash dividends paid on common shares	$ 3,000	$ 3,000
Total shareholders' equity	$240,000	$220,000

Calculate 2009 EPS and ROE. Another driving school in the same city reported a higher net income ($45,000) in 2009, yet its EPS and ROE ratios were lower than those for Toonce's Driving School. Explain how this apparent inconsistency could occur.

LO7   ### M11-12 Determining the Impact of Transactions on Earnings per Share (EPS) and Return on Equity (ROE)

Indicate the direction of effect (+ for increase, − for decrease, or NE for no effect) of each of the following transactions on EPS and ROE.

	EPS	ROE
a. Sold and issued 6,000 common shares for cash.	_____	_____
b. Purchased 50 shares and cancelled them.	_____	_____
c. Declared and paid a cash dividend.	_____	_____
d. Declared and issued a stock dividend.	_____	_____

M11-13 (Supplement A) Comparing Shareholder's Equity to Owner's Equity   LO5

James Riggins contributed $20,000 to start his business. At the end of the year, the business had generated $30,000 in sales revenues, incurred $18,000 in operating expenses, and distributed $5,000 for James to pay some personal expenses. Prepare the section of the balance sheet showing (*a*) his shareholder's equity, assuming this is a corporation, or (*b*) his owner's equity, assuming this is a sole proprietorship.

EXERCISES

E11-1 Computing Shares Outstanding   LO1

A recent annual report for Big Dog Sportswear disclosed that 30 million common shares have been authorized. At the end of Year 1, 9,698,284 shares had been issued and the number of shares in the treasury was 1,455,152. During Year 2, no additional common shares were issued, but additional shares were purchased for the treasury and shares were sold from the treasury. The net change was a decrease of 149,516 treasury shares.

Required:

Determine the number of shares outstanding at the end of Year 2.

E11-2 Reporting Shareholders' Equity and Determining Dividend Policy   LO2, LO3

Sampson Corporation was organized in 2009 to operate a financial consulting business. The charter authorized the following: common shares, 12,000 shares. During the first year, the following selected transactions were completed:

a. Sold and issued 6,000 common shares for cash at $20 per share.
b. Sold and issued 2,000 common shares for cash at $23 per share.

Required:

1. Give the journal entry required for each of these transactions.
2. Prepare the shareholders' equity section as it should be reported on the 2009 year-end balance sheet. At year-end, the accounts reflected net income of $100.
3. Sampson has $30,000 in the company's bank account. Can the company declare cash dividends at this time? Explain.

E11-3 Preparing the Shareholders' Equity Section of the Balance Sheet   LO2, LO4

Skyhawk Corporation received its charter during January 2009. The charter authorized the following:

$.80 Preferred shares: authorized 20,000

Common shares: authorized 50,000 shares

During 2009, the following transactions occurred in the order given:

a. Issued a total of 40,000 common shares to the four organizers at $11 per share.
b. Sold 5,000 preferred shares at $18 per share.
c. Sold 3,000 common shares at $14 per share and 1,000 preferred shares at $28.
d. Net income for the year was $48,000.

Required:

Prepare the shareholders' equity section of the balance sheet at December 31, 2009.

E11-4 Reporting a Statement of Shareholders' Equity   LO2–LO4

Shelby Corporation was organized in January 2009 by 10 shareholders to operate an air conditioning sales and service business. The articles of incorporation authorized the following capital shares:

Common: 200,000 shares

$.60 Preferred: 50,000 shares

During January and February 2009, the following share transactions were completed:

a.   Collected $40,000 cash from each of the 10 organizers, and issued 2,000 common shares to each of them.

b.   Sold 15,000 preferred shares at $25 per share; collected the cash and immediately issued the shares. Net income for 2009 was $40,000; cash dividends declared and paid at year-end were $10,000.

Required:

Prepare a statement of shareholders' equity for the year ended December 31, 2009.

LO2–LO4   E11-5   Determining the Effects of the Issuance of Common and Preferred Shares

Kelly, Incorporated, was issued a charter on January 15, 2009, that authorized the following capital:

Common: 100,000 shares.

$.70 Preferred: 5,000 shares.

During 2009, the following selected transactions were completed in the order given:

a.   Sold and issued 20,000 common shares at $18 cash per share.
b.   Sold and issued 3,000 preferred shares at $22 cash per share.
c.   At the end of 2009, the accounts showed net income of $38,000.

Required:

1.   Prepare the shareholders' equity section of the balance sheet at December 31, 2009.
2.   Assume that you are a common shareholder. If Kelly needed additional capital, would you prefer to have it issue additional common shares or addiional preferred shares? Explain.

LO2–LO4   E11-6   Recording and Reporting Shareholders' Equity Transactions

Teacher Corporation obtained a charter at the beginning of 2009 that authorized 50,000 common shares and 20,000 preferred shares. During 2009, the following selected transactions occurred:

a.   Collected $40 cash per share from four individuals and issued 4,000 common shares to each.
b.   Sold and issued 6,000 common shares to an outside investor at $40 cash per share.
c.   Sold and issued 8,000 preferred shares at $20 cash per share.

Required:

1.   Give the journal entries indicated for each of these transactions.
2.   Prepare the shareholders' equity section of the balance sheet at December 31, 2009. At the end of 2009, the accounts reflected net income of $36,000.

LO2–LO4   E11-7   Finding Amounts Missing from the Shareholders' Equity Section

The shareholders' equity section on the December 31, 2009, balance sheet of Chemfast Corporation follows:

Shareholders' Equity	
Contributed capital	
Preferred shares (authorized 10,000 shares,	
? issued at $20 each)	$104,000
Common shares (authorized 20,000 shares,	
issued and outstanding 8,000 shares)	600,000
Contributed surplus, preferred	14,300
Retained earnings	30,000

Required:

Complete the following statements and show your computations.

1.   The number of preferred shares issued was _____.
2.   The number of preferred shares outstanding was _____.

3. The average issue price of the common shares was $ _____.
4. What might have caused the Contributed Surplus account?
5. Total shareholders' equity is $ _____.

E11-8 Recording Shareholders' Equity Transactions

LO2, LO3

The annual report for Haliburton Corporation reported the following transactions affecting shareholders' equity:

a. Purchased for cancellation common shares for $3.5 million that had been issued for $2.7 million.
b. Declared and paid cash dividends in the amount of $254.2 million.
c. Issued a 10 per cent common stock dividend on 222.5 million shares when the shares had a book value of $10 per share and a market value of $15 per share.

Required:

Prepare journal entries to record each of these transactions.

E11-9 Computing Dividends on Preferred Shares and Analyzing Differences

LO3, LO4

The records of Hoffman Company reflected the following balances in the shareholders' equity accounts at December 31, 2009:

Common shares, 40,000 shares outstanding

$.80 Preferred shares, 6,000 shares outstanding

Retained earnings, $220,000

On December 31, 2009, the board of directors was considering the distribution of a $62,000 cash dividend. No dividends were paid during 2007 and 2008.

Required:

1. Determine the total and per share amounts that would be paid to the common shareholders and to the preferred shareholders under two independent assumptions:

   a. The preferred shares are noncumulative.
   b. The preferred shares are cumulative.

2. Briefly explain why the common dividends per share were less for the second assumption.
3. What factors would cause a more favourable dividend for the common shareholders?

E11-10 Recording the Payment of Dividends

LO3

A recent annual report for Snears disclosed that the company paid preferred dividends in the amount of $119.9 million. It declared and paid dividends on common shares in the amount of $2 per share. During the year, Snears had 1,000,000,000 common shares authorized; 387,514,300 shares had been issued; 41,670,000 shares were in the treasury. Assume that the dividend transaction occurred on July 15.

Required:

Prepare journal entries to record the declaration and payment of common and preferred dividends.

E11-11 Analyzing Stock Dividends

LO3

On December 31, 2009, the shareholders' equity section of the balance sheet of R & B Corporation reflected the following:

Common shares (authorized 60,000 shares, outstanding 25,000 shares)	$250,000
Retained earnings	75,000

On February 1, 2010, the board of directors declared a 12 per cent stock dividend to be issued April 30, 2010. The market value of the shares on February 1, 2010, was $18 per share.

Required:

1. For comparative purposes, prepare the shareholders' equity section of the balance sheet (*a*) immediately before the stock dividend and (*b*) immediately after the stock dividend. (*Hint:* Use two columns for the amounts in this requirement.)
2. Explain the effects of this stock dividend on the assets, liabilities, and shareholders' equity.

LO3   **E11-12   Recording Cash Dividends**

Le Château is a leading Canadian specialty retailer offering fashion-forward apparel, accessories, and footwear to style-conscious women and men. A press release on November 30, 2006, contained the following announcement:

> Montreal, November 30, 2006 — Le Château Inc. (TSX: CTU.A) said today it has declared two dividends to the holders of Class A Subordinate Voting Shares and Class B Voting Shares. The Board of Directors has increased the regular quarterly dividend by 50 per cent to $0.375 per share and has declared a one-time dividend of $3.00 per share. Both dividends are payable on February 13, 2007, to shareholders of record on January 30, 2007.

At the time of the press release, Le Château had an unlimited number of Class A and B shares authorized, and 6,220,000 shares issued and outstanding.

Required:

Prepare journal entries as appropriate for each of the three dates mentioned above.

LO3   **E11-13   Recording Stock Dividends**

Le Château is a leading Canadian specialty retailer offering fashion-forward apparel, accessories, and footwear to style-conscious women and men. A press release on June 27, 2007 contained the following announcement:

> Montreal, June 27, 2007 — Le Château Inc. (TSX: CTU.A) announced that, at its annual shareholder meeting held earlier today, the shareholders approved the split of the Class A subordinate voting shares and Class B voting shares on a four-for-one basis. The record date for the split will be July 18, 2007.

At the time of the press release, Le Château had an unlimited number of Class A and B shares authorized and 6,227,941 shares issued and outstanding for a total dollar value of $30,367,000.

Required:

1. Prepare journal entries as appropriate to record the stock split.
2. Show the details of Le Château's share capital before and after the stock split (number of shares, total value in common share account, and carrying value per share).
3. Before the stock split, Le Château's Class A shares were trading at $64.50. What would you expect happened to the share price after the split? Explain your reasoning.

LO3   **E11-14   Comparing Stock Dividends and Splits**

On July 1, 2009, Jones Corporation had the following capital structure:

Common shares (200,000 authorized, 150,000 issued)	$250,000
Retained earnings	172,000

Required:

Complete the following table based on two independent cases involving share transactions:

Case 1: The board of directors declared and issued a 20 per cent stock dividend when the shares were selling at $4 per share.

Case 2: The board of directors voted a 2-for-1 stock split. The market price prior to the split was $4 per share.

	Before Stock Transactions	Case 1 After 20 per cent Stock Dividend	Case 2 After Stock Split
Items			
Number of shares outstanding	_____	_____	_____
Book value per share	$_____	$_____	$_____
Common share account	$_____	$_____	$_____
Retained earnings	$ 172,000	_____	_____
Total shareholders' equity	$_____	$_____	$_____

E11-15 Analyzing Dividends in Arrears

LO4

Mission Critical Software, Inc., was a leading provider of systems management software for Windows NT network and Internet infrastructure. Like many start-up companies, Mission Critical struggled with cash flows as it developed new business opportunities. A student found a financial statement for Mission Critical that stated that the increase in dividends in arrears on preferred shares this year was $264,000.

The student who read the note suggested that the Mission Critical preferred shares would be a good investment because of the large amount of dividend income that would be earned when the company started paying dividends again: "As the owner of the shares, I'll get dividends for the period I hold the shares, plus some previous periods when I didn't even own them." Do you agree? Explain.

E11-16 Recording Share Transactions and Dividends

LO2, LO3

Magna Company had the following shareholders' equity accounts at December 31, 2009.

Common shares : (2,000,000 authorized, 1,056,000 issued)	$1,584,000
Retained earnings	2,565,000

In 2010, the following transactions occurred related to Magna shares:

- *a.* Issued 200,000 common shares at $1.75 each.
- *b.* Issued a 10 per cent stock dividend when the shares were trading at $2.
- *c.* Repurchased 20,000 of the outstanding shares for $2.10.
- *d.* Declared and paid a cash dividend of $0.10 on the outstanding shares.

Required:

1. Prepare journal entries to record the above transactions.
2. Prepare the shareholders' equity section of Magna's balance sheet at December 31, 2010, assuming that Magna had net income of $567,000 in 2010.

E11-17 Determining the Financial Statement Effects of Cash and Stock Dividends

LO3, LO4

Lynn Company has outstanding 60,000 common shares and 25,000 $1.60 preferred shares. On December 1, 2008, the board of directors voted a cash dividend on the preferred shares and a 10 per cent stock dividend on the common shares. At the date of declaration, the common shares were selling at $35 and the preferred at $20 per share. The dividends are to be paid, or issued, on February 15, 2009. The annual accounting period ends December 31.

Required:

Compare the effects of the two dividends on the assets, liabilities, and shareholders' equity *(a)* through December 31, 2008, *(b)* on February 15, 2009, and *(c)* the overall effects from

December 1, 2008, through February 15, 2009. A schedule using the following structure might be helpful:

	Comparative Effects Explained	
Item	**Cash Dividend on Preferred**	**Stock Dividend on Common**

a) Through December 31, 2008:
    Effect on Assets
    Effect on Liabilities
    Effect on Shareholders' Equity		

LO3, LO6

E11-18   Preparing a Statement of Shareholders' Equity and Evaluating Dividend Policy

The following account balances were selected from the records of clothing retailer Blake Corporation at December 31, 2009, after all adjusting entries were completed:

Common shares (authorized 100,000 shares, issued 35,000 shares)	$525,000
Contributed surplus	180,000
Dividends declared and paid in 2009	18,000
Retained earnings, January 1, 2009	76,000

Net income for the year was $28,000.

Required:

1. Prepare the shareholders' equity section of the balance sheet at December 31, 2009.
2. Compute the ROE ratio, assuming total shareholders' equity was $629,000 on December 31, 2008. How does it compare with the ratios of companies shown in Exhibit 11.5?

LO3, LO7

E11-19   Analyzing Stock Repurchases and Stock Dividends

Reitmans (Canada) Limited operates more than 800 stores across Canada, under the banners of Reitmans, Additional-Elle, Smart Set/Dalmys, Penningtons, RW & Co., and Thyme Maternity. A November 22, 2007, press release contained the following information:

> Montreal, Nov. 22 /CNW Telbec/ – Reitmans (Canada) Limited ("the Corporation") announced today that it has received approval from the Toronto Stock Exchange to proceed with a normal-course issuer bid. Under the bid, the Corporation may purchase up to 2,870,615 Class A non-voting shares of the Corporation (the "Shares"), representing 5 per cent of the issued and outstanding Class A non-voting shares as at November 9, 2007. . . . The bid will commence on November 28, 2007, and may continue to November 27, 2008.

Required:

1. Determine the impact of this share buyback on the financial statements.
2. Why do you think the board decided to repurchase the shares?
3. What impact will this purchase have on Reitmans' future dividend obligations?
4. On April 18, 2005, the company issued a 100 per cent stock dividend. Why would Reitmans choose such a large stock dividend rather than an actual stock split?
5. What impact would this stock dividend have had on Reitmans' financial statements? What impact would it have had on the EPS and ROE ratios?

LO5

E11-20   (Supplement A) Comparing Shareholders' Equity Sections for Alternative Forms of Organization

Assume for each of the following independent cases that the annual accounting period ends on December 31, 2009, and that the total of all revenue accounts was $150,000 and the total of all expense accounts was $130,000.

Case A: Assume that the company is a *sole proprietorship* owned by Proprietor A. Prior to the closing entries, the capital account reflected a credit balance of $50,000, and the drawings account a balance of $8,000.

Case B: Assume that the company is a *partnership* owned by Partner A and Partner B. Prior to the closing entries, the owners' equity accounts reflected the following balances: A, Capital, $40,000; B, Capital, $38,000; A, Drawings, $5,000, and B, Drawings, $9,000. Profits and losses are divided equally.

Case C: Assume that the company is a *corporation*. Prior to the closing entries, the shareholders' equity accounts showed the following: Common Shares $150,000 (authorized 30,000 shares, outstanding 15,000 shares); Contributed Surplus, $5,000; Retained Earnings, $65,000.

Required:

1. Give all the closing entries required at December 31, 2009, for each of the separate cases.
2. Show how the equity section of the balance sheet would appear at December 31, 2009, for each case.

COACHED PROBLEMS

CP11-1 Preparing the Shareholders' Equity Section of a Balance Sheet after Selected Transactions

LO2

Worldwide Company obtained a charter from the federal government in January 2009, which authorized 200,000 common shares. The shareholders were 30 local citizens. During the first year, the company earned $38,200, and the following selected transactions occurred in the order given:

a. Sold 60,000 common shares at $12 per share.
b. Purchased 2,000 shares at $15 cash per share from one of the 30 shareholders who needed cash and wanted to sell the shares back to the company. Cancelled these shares.
c. Declared a $.20 dividend to be paid after the year-end.

COACH'S TIP

Dividends are issued on outstanding shares.

Required:

1. Prepare journal entries for the above transactions.
2. Prepare the shareholders' equity section of the balance sheet at December 31, 2009.

CP11-2 Finding Missing Amounts

LO2–LO6

At December 31, 2009, the records of Nortech Corporation provided the following selected and incomplete data:

Common shares (no changes during 2009)

Shares authorized, 200,000

Shares issued, __?__; issue price $17 per share

Common share account, $2,125,000

Net income for 2009, $118,000

Dividends declared and paid during 2009, $75,000

Retained earnings balance, January 1, 2009, $155,000

COACH'S TIP

To determine the number of shares issued, divide the balance in the common share account by the book value per share

Required:

1. Complete the following:

   Shares authorized _____

   Shares issued _____

   Shares outstanding _____
2. Earnings per share is $_____.
3. Common dividends paid per share is $_____.

4. Assume that the board of directors approved a 2-for-1 stock split. After the stock split, the book value per share will be $_____, and the number of outstanding shares will be _____.
5. Disregard the stock split (assumed above). Assume instead that a 10 per cent stock dividend was declared and issued when the market price of the common shares was $21. Give any journal entry that should be made.

LO2–LO4

CP11-3 Comparing Stock and Cash Dividends

Water Tower Company had the following shares outstanding and retained earnings at December 31, 2009:

Common shares (30,000 outstanding)	$240,000
$.70 Preferred shares (6,000 outstanding)	60,000
Retained earnings	280,000

COACH'S TIP

Preferred shareholders with cumulative dividends are paid dividends for any prior years (in arrears) and for the current year before common shareholders are paid

The board of directors is considering the distribution of a cash dividend to the common and preferred shareholders. No dividends were declared during 2007 or 2008. Three independent cases are assumed:

Case A: The preferred shares are noncumulative; the total amount of dividends is $30,000.
Case B: The preferred shares are cumulative; the total amount of dividends is $12,600.
Case C: Same as Case B, except the amount is $66,000.

Required:

1. Compute the amount of dividends, in total and per share, that would be payable to each class of shareholders for each case. Show computations.
2. Assume that, to remind shareholders of their accumulating wealth in the company, a 10 per cent common stock dividend was issued when the market value per share was $24. Complete the following schedule.

COACH'S TIP

Remember that the denominator of the ROE ratio uses the average shareholders' equity.

	Amount of Dollar Increase (Decrease)	
Item	Cash Dividend, Case C	Stock Dividend
Assets	$	$
Liabilities	$	$
Shareholders' equity	$	$

LO6–LO7

CP11-4 Computing and Interpreting Return-on-Equity (ROE)

Two publicly traded rental companies reported the following in their 2009 financial statements (in thousands):

	Baron Rents, Inc.		Rent-an-Office, Inc.	
	2009	*2008*	*2009*	*2008*
Net income	$ 36,426	$ 27,440	$181,496	$172,173
Total shareholders' equity	320,186	280,545	794,830	842,400

Required:

1. Compute the 2009 ROE for each company. Which company appears to generate greater returns on shareholders' equity in 2009?
2. Rent-an-Office repurchased 2,544 (thousand) common shares in June and July 2009 at $73 per share. Recalculate the company's ROE for 2009, assuming that this stock repurchase did not occur. Does this change your interpretation of the ROE ratios calculated in requirement 1?

GROUP A PROBLEMS

PA11-1 Preparing the Shareholders' Equity Section of a Balance Sheet after Selected Transactions

LO2

Global Marine obtained a charter from the federal government in January 2009, which authorized 1,000,000 common shares. During the first year, the company earned $429,000, and the following selected transactions occurred in the order given:

a. Sold 700,000 common shares at $54 per share. Collected the cash and issued the shares.
b. Purchased 25,000 shares at $50 cash per share and cancelled them.
c. Issued and paid a $.25 dividend.

Required:

1. Prepare journal entries for the above transactions.
2. Prepare the shareholders' equity section of the balance sheet at December 31, 2009.

PA11-2 Finding Missing Amounts

LO2–LO4, LO6

At December 31, 2009, the records of Kozmetsky Corporation provided the following selected and incomplete data:

Common shares (no changes during 2009)

Shares authorized, 5,000,000

Shares issued, ___?___ ; issue price $80 per share

Net income for 2009, $4,800,000

Common share account, $120,000,000

Dividends declared and paid during 2009, $2 per share

Retained earnings balance, January 1, 2009, $82,900,000

Required:

1. Complete the following:

    Shares issued _____

    Shares outstanding _____
2. Earnings per share is $_____.
3. Total dividends paid on common shares during 2009 is $_____.
4. Assume that the board of directors voted a 2-for-1 stock split. After the stock split, the book value per share will be $_____, and the number of outstanding shares will be _____.
5. Disregard the stock split (assumed above). Assume instead that a 10 per cent stock dividend was declared and issued when the market price of the common shares was $21. Explain how shareholders' equity will change.

PA11-3 Comparing Stock and Cash Dividends

LO2–LO4

Ritz Company had the following shares outstanding and retained earnings at December 31, 2009:

Common shares (500,000 outstanding)	$500,000
$.80 Preferred shares (21,000 outstanding)	210,000
Retained earnings	900,000

The board of directors is considering the distribution of a cash dividend to the common and preferred shareholders. No dividends were declared during 2007 or 2008. Three independent cases are assumed:

Case A: The preferred shares are noncumulative; the total amount of dividends is $25,000.
Case B: The preferred shares are cumulative; the total amount of dividends is $25,000.
Case C: Same as Case B, except the amount is $75,000.

Required:

1. Compute the amount of dividends, in total and per share, payable to each class of shareholders for each case. Show computations.

2. Assume that the company issued a 15 per cent stock dividend on the outstanding common shares when the market value per share was $50. Complete the following schedule, which compares the effects of the two dividends on assets, liabilities, and shareholders' equity.

	Amount of Dollar Increase (Decrease)	
Item	Cash Dividend, Case C	Stock Dividend
Assets	$	$
Liabilities	$	$
Shareholders' equity	$	$

LO6, LO7

PA11-4 Computing and Interpreting Return on Equity (ROE)

Two magazine companies reported the following in their 2008 financial statements (in thousands):

	Business World		Fun and Games	
	2009	2008	2009	2008
Net income	$ 55,000	$ 54,302	$ 91,420	$172,173
Total shareholders' equity	587,186	512,814	894,302	934,098

Required:

1. Compute the 2009 ROE for each company. Which company appears to generate greater returns on shareholders' equity in 2009?

2. Fun and Games repurchased 32,804 (thousand) common shares in 2009 at $4 per share. Recalculate the company's ROE for 2009, assuming that this stock repurchase did not occur. Does this change your interpretation of the ROE ratios calculated in requirement 1?

LO6, LO7

PA11-5 Computing and Interpreting Return on Equity (ROE)

Two publicly traded Canadian companies in the telecommunications sector reported the following in their 2007 financial statements (in millions):

	Research in Motion		Telus	
	2006	2007	2006	2007
Net income	$ 631.6	$1,293.9	$ 967.2	$1,062.9
Total shareholders' equity	2,483.5	3,933.6	6,409.4	6,009.5

Required:

Compute the 2007 ROE for each company. Which company generated greater returns on shareholders' equity in 2007?

LO2–LO4

PA11-6 Journalizing Share Transactions

Goya Corporation had the following share transactions during its fiscal year (in this order):

a. 20,000 common shares were issued for cash at $10 per share.
b. 2,000 $.60 preferred shares were issued for cash at $20 per share.
c. Cash dividends of $10,000 were declared and paid. Indicate the split between common and preferred dividends.
d. 2,000 common shares were repurchased for $9 each and cancelled.
e. A 10 per cent stock dividend was declared and issued on the outstanding common shares when the shares had a value of $9 each.

Required:

Make all necessary journal entries for the year to record the above transactions.

PA11-7 (Supplement A) Recording Transactions for a Partnership

LO5

The partnership of Susan Wong and Gary Chan had the following transactions during its first fiscal year:

a. Susan and Gary both put $15,000 cash into the partnership.
b. The partnership earned $25,000, which Susan and Gary split 60:40.
c. Gary took out $2,000 cash at the end of the year.

Required:

1. Make all necessary journal entries for the year to record the above transactions.
2. What is the balance in each partner's capital account at the end of the year?

GROUP B PROBLEMS

PB11-1 Preparing the Shareholders' Equity Section of a Balance Sheet after Selected Transactions

LO2

Whyville Corporation obtained its charter from the federal government in January 2009, which authorized 500,000 common shares. During the first year, the company earned $58,000, and the following selected transactions occurred in the order given:

a. Sold 200,000 common shares at $23 per share. Collected the cash and issued the shares.
b. Purchased 5,000 shares at $24 cash per share and cancelled them.

Required:

1. Prepare journal entries for the above transactions.
2. Prepare the shareholders' equity section of the balance sheet at December 31, 2009.

PB11-2 Finding Missing Amounts

LO2–LO4, LO6

At December 31, 2009, the records of Seacrest Enterprises provided the following selected and incomplete data:

Common shares (no changes during 2009)

Shares authorized, 10,000,000

Shares issued, ___?___ ; issue price $10 per share

Net income for 2009, $2,400,000

Common share account $15,000,000

Dividends declared and paid during 2009, $1 per share
Retained earnings balance, January 1, 2009, $36,400,000

Required:

1. Complete the following:
   Shares issued _____
2. Earnings per share is $ _____ .
3. Total dividends paid on common shares during 2009 is $ _____ .
4. Assume that the board of directors voted a 2-for-1 share split. After the share split, the book value per share will be $ _____ , and the number of outstanding shares will be _____ .
5. Disregard the share split (assumed above). Assume instead that a 10 per cent share dividend was declared and issued, when the market price of the common shares was $21. Explain how shareholders' equity will change.

LO2–LO4   **PB11-3   Comparing Stock and Cash Dividends**

Reuben Company had the following shares outstanding and retained earnings at December 31, 2009:

Common shares (490,000 outstanding)	$490,000
$.80 Preferred shares (19,000 outstanding)	190,000
Retained earnings	966,000

The board of directors is considering the distribution of a cash dividend to the common and preferred shareholders. No dividends were declared during 2007 or 2008. Three independent cases are assumed:

> **Case A:** The preferred shares are noncumulative; the total amount of dividends is $24,000.
> **Case B:** The preferred shares are cumulative; the total amount of dividends is $24,000.
> **Case C:** Same as Case B, except the amount is $67,000

Required:

1. Compute the amount of dividends, in total and per share, payable to each class of shareholders for each case. Show computations.
2. Assume that the company issued a 10 per cent stock dividend on the outstanding common shares when the market value per share was $45. Complete the following comparative schedule, including explanation of the comparative differences.

	Amount of Dollar Increase (Decrease)	
Item	**Cash Dividend, Case C**	**Stock Dividend**
Assets	$	$
Liabilities	$	$
Shareholders' equity	$	$

LO6, LO7   **PB11-4   Computing and Interpreting Return on Equity (ROE)**

Two music companies reported the following in their 2009 financial statements (in thousands):

	Urban Youth		Sound Jonx	
	2009	**2008**	**2009**	**2008**
Net income	$ 27,500	$ 24,302	$ 41,500	$ 36,739
Total shareholders' equity	387,101	300,399	516,302	521,198

Required:

1. Compute the 2009 ROE for each company. Which company appears to generate greater returns on shareholders' equity in 2009?
2. Sound Jonx repurchased 5,000 (thousand) common shares in 2009 at $13 per share. Recalculate the company's ROE for 2009, assuming that this stock repurchase did not occur. Does this change your interpretation of the ROE ratios calculated in requirement 1?

LO6, LO7   **PB11-5   Computing and Interpreting Return on Equity (ROE)**

Two publicly traded Canadian companies in the resource sector reported the following in their 2007 financial statements (in millions):

	Barrick Gold		Suncor Energy	
	2006	**2007**	**2006**	**2007**
Net income	$ 1,506	$ 1,119	$2,971	$ 2,832
Total shareholders' equity	14,199	15,256	8,952	11,613

Required:

Compute the 2007 ROE for each company. Which company generated greater returns on shareholders' equity in 2007? Compare the ROE's for these resource companies with those in the retail sector presented in Exhibit 11.5.

PB11-6 Journalizing Share Transactions

LO2–LO4

Tandy Corporation had the following share transactions during its fiscal year (in this order):

a. 65,000 common shares were issued for cash at $5 per share.
b. 20,000 $.50 preferred shares were issued for cash at $25 per share.
c. Cash dividends were declared and paid on the preferred shares.
d. A 10 per cent stock dividend was declared and issued on the common shares, when the shares had a value of $6 each.
e. 5,000 preferred shares were repurchased for $30 each and cancelled.

Required:

Make all necessary journal entries for the year to record the above transactions.

PB11-7 (Supplement A) Recording Transactions for a Partnership

LO5

The partnership of Jerry Pound and Jeanne Lavoie had the following transactions during its first fiscal year:

a. Jeanne and Jerry both put $5,000 cash into the partnership.
b. The partnership earned $22,500, which Jeanne and Jerry split 50:50.
c. Jeanne took out $1,500 cash at the end of the year.

Required:

1. Make all necessary journal entries for the year to record the above transactions.
2. What is the balance in each partner's capital account at the end of the year?

SKILLS DEVELOPMENT CASES

S11-1 Finding Financial Information

LO1–LO3, LO6

Refer to the financial statements of High Liner in Appendix A at the end of this book, or download the annual report from the *Cases* section of the text's Web site at www.mcgrawhill.ca/college/phillips.

Required:

1. How many common shares are authorized? How many shares are issued at the most recent year-end? How many shares are outstanding? Are there any shares held in treasury?
2. According to the statement of retained earnings, how much did the company declare in dividends on common shares during the most recent year? Using your answer to requirement 1, calculate approximately how much this was per share.
3. Did High Liner issue or repurchase any shares during the year? Where did you look to answer this question?
4. How has High Liner's basic EPS changed in the past two years? Based on this trend, what do you predict will happen in the following year? Does High Liner maintain a stock option plan? How can you tell?
5. Calculate the ROE ratio for High Liner in the current and prior year. High Liner's shareholders' equity was $69,909 (thousands) at the end of 2005.

S11-2 Comparing Financial Information

LO1–LO3, LO6

Refer to the financial statements of Sun-Rype by downloading the annual report from the *Cases* section of the text's Web site at www.mcgrawhill.ca/college/phillips.

Required:

1. Did Sun-Rype have more or fewer authorized common shares than High Liner? What about issued common shares?

2. From the statement of retained earnings, does it appear that Sun-Rype declared dividends during the most recent year? Compared with High Liner's dividends policy, is Sun-Rype's policy on dividends better, worse, or just different?

3. Based on the note disclosures, how much did Sun-Rype pay to repurchase its shares during 2007?

4. How much has Sun-Rype's basic EPS changed in the past two years? How does this compare with High Liner's EPS data? Does Sun-Rype maintain a stock option plan? How can you tell?

5. Calculate the ROE ratio for Sun-Rype in the most recent and the prior year. Total shareholders' equity at the beginning of the prior year is $48,283 (thousands). How does Sun-Rype compare with High Liner on this ratio?

LO3, LO6

S11-3 Internet-Based Team Research: Examining an Annual Report

As a team, select an industry to analyze. Using your Web browser, each team member should acquire the annual report for one publicly traded Canadian company in the industry, with each member selecting a different company. (See S1-3 in Chapter 1 for a description of possible resources for these tasks.)

TEAM CASE

Required:

1. On an individual basis, each team member should write a short report that incorporates the following:
   a. Has the company declared cash or stock dividends during the past two years?
   b. What is the trend in the company's EPS over the past two years?
   c. Compute and analyze the return-on-equity ratio over the past two years.

2. Then, as a team, write a short report, comparing and contrasting your companies using these attributes. Discuss any patterns across the companies that you, as a team, observe. Provide potential explanations for any differences discovered.

LO1, LO3

S11-4 Ethical Decision Making: A Real-Life Example

Activision became a public company with an initial public offering of stock on June 9, 1983, at $12 per share. In June 2002, Activision issued 7.5 million additional shares to the public at approximately $33 per share in a seasoned new issue. In October 2002, when its stock was trading at about $22 per share, Activision executives announced that the company would spend up to $150 million to buy back shares from investors. On January 8, 2003, the *Wall Street Journal* reported that several analysts were criticizing Activision's executives because the company had sold the shares to the public at a high price ($33), and then were offering to buy them back at the going market price, which was considerably lower than the issue price in 2002.

ETHICAL ISSUES

Required:

1. Do you think it was inappropriate for Activision to offer to buy back the shares at a lower price in October 2002?

2. Would your answer to question 1 be different if Activision had not issued additional shares in June 2002?

3. The *Wall Street Journal* article also reported that, in December 2002, Activision executives had purchased over 530,000 shares in the company at the then-current price of $13.32 per share. If you were an investor, how would you feel about executives buying shares in their own company?

4. Would your answer to question 3 be different if you also learned that the executives had sold nearly 2.5 million shares of Activision shares earlier in the year, when the price was at least $26.08 per share?

S11-5 Ethical Decision Making: A Mini-Case

LO3

You are the president of a very successful Internet company that has had a remarkably profitable year. You have determined that the company has more than $10 million in cash generated by operating activities not needed in the business. You are thinking about paying it out to shareholders as a special dividend. You discuss the idea with your vice president, who reacts angrily to your suggestion:

> Our stock price has gone up by 200 per cent in the last year alone. What more do we have to do for the owners? The people who really earned that money are the employees who have been working 12 hours a day, six or seven days a week, to make the company successful. Most of them didn't even take vacations last year. I say we have to pay out bonuses and nothing extra for the shareholders.

As president, you know that you are hired by the board of directors, which is elected by the shareholders.

ETHICAL ISSUES

Required:

What is your responsibility to both groups? To which group would you give the $10 million? Why?

S11-6 Critical Thinking: Making a Decision as an Investor

LO3

You have retired after a long and successful career as a business executive, and now spend a good portion of your time managing your retirement portfolio. You are considering three basic investment alternatives. You can invest in (1) corporate bonds currently paying 7 per cent interest, (2) conservative stocks that pay substantial dividends (typically 5 per cent of the stock price every year), and (3) growth-oriented technology stocks that pay no dividends.

Required:

Analyze each of these alternatives and select one. Justify your selection.

S11-7 Charting Stock Price Movement around Important Announcement Dates

LO1

Using a Web search engine like Google, find either an earnings or dividend announcement for each of two different companies. Using a source such as bigcharts.com, or globeinvestor.com, determine the closing share price for each company for each day during the five business days before and after the announcement. Using a separate worksheet for each company, prepare a line chart of its share price movement.

Required:

Examine the chart for each company. Does the share price appear to change as a consequence of their announcements? Explain why or why not.

12

Reporting and Interpreting the Statement of Cash Flows

INSIDE LOOKING OUT

OUTSIDE LOOKING IN

This chapter focuses on reporting and interpreting the statement of cash flows of Magnotta Winery Corporation, a company that makes wine from grapes grown on its own vineyards in the Niagara Peninsula of Ontario.

Understand what a statement of cash flows reports.
    LO1 Classify cash flow statement items as part of net cash flows from operating, investing, and financing activities.

Study how to prepare a statement of cash flows.
    LO2 Report cash flows from operating activities.
    LO3 Report cash flows from investing activities.
    LO4 Report cash flows from financing activities.
    LO5 (Supplement A) Report cash flows from sales of property, plant, and equipment.

Evaluate financial results reported in a statement of cash flows.
    LO6 Interpret cash flows from operating, investing, and financing activities.
    LO7 Calculate and interpret the capital-acquisitions ratio.
    LO8 Calculate and interpret the cash-coverage ratio.

Reconsider financial performance in the light of cash flows.
    LO9 Calculate and interpret the quality-of-income ratio.

Have you ever closely analyzed your bank statements to see how much money you bring in and pay out during a typical month. According to one recent survey, an average college student earns $645 and spends about $1,080 each month. You don't have to be a financial genius to figure out that this means a net outflow of $435 cash each month. At this rate, your savings will quickly disappear, and you'll need to obtain a loan or other source of financing to see you through to graduation.

Managing cash inflows and outflows is just as important for a business as it is for an individual. In this chapter, we look at the cash flows of **MAGNOTTA WINERY**—maker of wines, premium beers, and juice for home-based wine production, with vineyards in Ontario and Chile. In 2007, Magnotta's operations generated $1.7 million in cash for the company. To control and report the causes of changes in its cash position, Magnotta prepares a statement of cash flows that tracks inflows and outflows of cash during the year, classifying them as operating, investing, and financing activities. As you will see later in this chapter, this statement can also help you, as a financial statement user, to understand better the company's financial performance.

The king is here! The king in financial reporting circles, according to some analysts, is the cash that's reported on the statement of cash flows. These analysts aren't dismissing the accrual basis of accounting. They just believe it's crucial to consider the cash flows of a business, too. A company must have cash or ready access to cash. Without it, the company may not be able to pay its debts as they become due, which will eventually lead to bankruptcy. In Chapter 7, you studied some important ways to manage cash effectively. In this chapter, you will study the statement that gives users specific information about how a company has used its cash.

Begin by reading the Learning Objectives on the first page of this chapter. Then, to help you truly understand what the items on this statement represent, you'll study how to create this statement yourself. The third section of the chapter will arm you with what you need to know as an outsider using the cash flow statement. We'll pull it all together in the final section, to show how you can use your knowledge about the statement of cash flows to evaluate the results reported in other financial statements.

UNDERSTAND _____
What a Statement of Cash Flows Reports

THE NEED FOR A STATEMENT OF CASH FLOWS

Companies haven't always been required to report a statement of cash flows. So why are they now? One of the reasons is that, before the statement of cash flows was required, some companies ran out of cash even when they were reporting profits, catching many financial statement users by surprise. Now, with the statement of cash flows to report all the cash receipts and cash payments of a business, it's much easier to detect cases where this might occur. Another benefit is that it's very difficult for dishonest managers to manipulate both a statement of cash flows and an accrual-based income statement at the same time.

POINT OF INTEREST

While the balance sheet has been around for thousands of years, and the income statement for 500, the cash flow is a baby by comparison. It was adopted in Canada only 20 years ago.

Clearly, net income is important, but seasonal fluctuations in sales, inventory purchases, and advertising expenditures can lead to odd combinations of income and cash flows. It's not unusual to have **high profits alongside net outflows of cash** in some quarters, and **losses combined with net cash inflows** in others. This occurs because, as we have seen in earlier chapters, the timing of revenues and expenses does not always line up with cash inflows and outflows. As a consequence, managers carefully monitor both cash flows and profits. For the same reasons, financial analysts consider the information in the statement of cash flows as well as the other financial statements.

The cash flow statement focuses attention on four things: (1) a company's ability to generate cash internally from its operating activities, (2) its management of current assets and current liabilities, (3) the amount spent on long-term assets, and (4) the amount received from external financing. It helps both managers and analysts answer important cash-related questions such as:

■ Will the company have enough cash to pay its short-term debts to suppliers and other creditors without additional borrowing?

■ Is the company adequately managing its accounts receivable and inventory?

■ Has the company purchased sufficient equipment and other long-term assets?

■ Did the company generate enough cash flow internally to finance these purchases, or did it rely on external financing?

■ Is the company changing the source of its external financing?

To understand how the statement of cash flows answers these questions, it's useful to see first how transactions are classified in the statement.

CLASSIFICATIONS IN THE STATEMENT OF CASH FLOWS

Basically, the statement of cash flows explains how the amount of cash on the balance sheet at the end of the previous period became the amount of cash at the end of the current period. For purposes of this statement, the definition of cash includes cash and cash equivalents, although that may change as Canada makes the transition to IFRS. **Cash equivalents** are short-term, highly liquid investments that are both

1. readily convertible to known amounts of cash, and
2. so near to maturity that there is little risk that their value will change.

For most companies, including Magnotta, cash and cash equivalents include cash on hand, cash deposited with banks, and highly liquid investments purchased within three months of maturity. In your personal life, cash equivalents could include cheques you've received but not yet deposited into your bank account, or Canada Savings Bonds that are about to mature.

So, if we want to explain how opening cash became closing cash, how do we go about it? Once way would be to look at every entry in the company's cash account for the year and summarize these transactions into the major types of cash inflows and out-flows. If the company is small, that might work, but it would be too time-consuming for most companies, with the thousands or millions of cash transactions they have in a year. So what you will learn here is another approach. We will use the information in the balance sheet and the income statement, which already contain summarized information, and, through analysis, figure out the cash flows for the year from these numbers. In order for this approach to make sense to you, you've really got to understand what you've learned so far in this course. We'll start by looking at the statement of cash flows, so you know where we want to end up. Then we'll explain how to get there.

Before we look at a sample statement, let's agree on two simplifications that'll allow you to read a little faster. First, rather than saying "cash and cash equivalents," let's just say "cash," with the understanding that it includes cash equivalents as well. Second, let's shorten statement of cash flows to SCF, which is what most accountants and analysts do in the real world. Okay, so let's look at the SCF. (See, you just saved two seconds.)

A condensed version of Magnotta's SCF is presented in Exhibit 12.1. We've con-densed the statement to show only the subtotals that report the net cash inflows (or outflows) from the three broad categories: (1) operating activities, (2) investing activi-ties, and (3) financing activities. We use different colours to highlight the sections so that you can easily match them to their specific components discussed later in the chap-ter. A complete version of Magnotta's SCF is presented in Exhibit 12.9 on page 540. For now, just focus on Exhibit 12.1 so that you can see how the net cash flows from each category combine to explain the total net increase (or decrease) in cash during the pe-riod. Operating activities are those that directly relate to earning income. Investing ac-tivities are those that relate to the acquisition or disposal of investments and long-lived assets. Financing activities relate to cash exchanges with shareholders or lenders.

Looking at the subtotals (which we've highlighted) in Exhibit 12.1, you can see that operating activities generated a net cash inflow of about $1.7 million cash during the year. Investing activities used $1.3 million, whereas financing activities required

COACH'S TIP

The operating (O) section is first, followed by the investing (I) and financing (F) sections. Try using the initialism OIF to remember the order in which the sections appear in the statement. Also note that net cash outflows are reported as negative cash flows (in parentheses).

exhibit **12.1** **Condensed Statement of Cash Flows (in thousands)***	
Cash Flows from Operating Activities	$1,723
Cash Flows from Investing Activities	(1,273)
Cash Flows from Financing Activities	(1,093)
Net increase (decrease) in cash and cash equivalents	(643)
Cash and cash equivalents, beginning of year	(4,757)
Cash and cash equivalents, end of year	$(5,400)

*Certain amounts have been adjusted to simplify the presentation and analysis.

Magnotta to use up another $1 million cash. Together, these three cash flow categories show a net decrease in cash of $.6 million (1.7 − 1.3 − 1). In the next section, we will begin to dissect the SCF a little further, by looking at what goes into each of the operating, investing, and financing activities.

The last two lines link the SCF to the balance sheet. The net increase (or decrease) in cash for the year is added to (or deducted from) the opening cash balance to calculate the closing cash balance, amounts that appear in the current asset section of the balance sheet. Some companies prefer to carry little or no cash and operate on lines of credit instead, as we saw in Chapter 10. This is not a problem, as long as the company is financially solid. Magnotta is one of these companies, showing a negative opening cash balance of $4,757 and a negative closing balance of $5,400. Negative cash is shown on the balance sheet as bank loans in the current liabilities section.

Cash Flows from Operating Activities

Cash flows from operating activities (or simply called cash flows from operations) are the cash inflows and outflows that relate directly to revenues and expenses reported on the income statement. Operating activities involve the day-to-day business activities with customers, suppliers, employees, landlords, and others. There are two alternative formats for presenting the operating activities section of the statement:

Cash flows from operating activities (cash flows from operations) are cash inflows and outflows directly related to components of net income.

1. The **direct method** reports the total cash inflow from each main operating activity that generates cash, as well as the total cash outflow for each main operating activity that uses cash. Typical operating inflows and outflows of cash are listed below.

The **direct method** of presenting the operating activities section of the cash flow statement reports the components of cash flows from operating activities as gross receipts and gross payments.

Inflows	*Outflows*
Cash provided by	**Cash used for**
Customers	Purchase of goods for resale and services (electricity, etc.)
Dividends and interest on investments	Salaries and wages
	Income taxes
	Interest on liabilities

POINT OF INTEREST

Why the indirect method continues to be so popular is not clear. The indirect method is a bit easier to prepare and has been around for longer. Maybe preparers prefer it for these reasons. Unless either users or accounting rules insist on the direct method, the indirect method will likely continue to be common.

The difference between these cash inflows and outflows is called *Net cash provided by (used for) operating activities*.

2. Although the direct method is considered to be more understandable and useful, it is rarely used. Instead, nearly 99 percent of large companies, including Magnotta, use the **indirect method,** which also is allowed by the CICA. The indirect method does not show actual cash inflows and outflows. Instead, it starts with net income from the income statement and then adjusts it by removing items that do not involve cash but were included in net income. By eliminating these "non-cash" items, we back into *Net cash provided by (used for) operating activities*.

The **indirect method** of presenting the operating activities section of the cash flow statement adjusts net income to compute cash flows from operating activities.

Net income
± Adjustments for non-cash items
= Net cash provided by (used for) operating activities

For now, the most important thing to remember about the two methods is that they are simply different ways to arrive at the same number. The total amount of *cash flows from operating activities is always the same regardless of whether it is computed using the direct or indirect method.* Management's choice of method for presenting its operating cash flows does not affect the other sections of the SCF.

Cash Flows from Investing Activities

Cash flows from investing activities are cash inflows and outflows related to the purchase and disposal of long-lived assets and short-term investments. Typical cash flows from investing activities are listed on page 526.

Cash flows from investing activities are cash inflows and outflows related to the purchase or sale of long-term assets and short-term investments.

Inflows	**Outflows**
Cash provided by Sale or disposal of property, plant, and equipment Sale or maturity of investments in securities	**Cash used for** Purchase of property, plant, and equipment Purchase of investments in securities

The difference between these cash inflows and outflows is called *Net cash provided by (used for) investing activities*.

Cash Flows from Financing Activities

Cash flows from financing activities are cash inflows and outflows related to financing sources that are external to the company (owners and lenders).

Cash flows from financing activities include exchanges of cash with shareholders and cash exchanges with lenders (related to principal of loans). Common cash flows from financing activities are listed below.

Inflows	**Outflows**
Cash provided by Borrowing from lenders through formal debt contracts Issuing shares to owners	**Cash used for** Repaying principal to lenders Repurchasing shares from owners Paying dividends to owners

The difference between these cash inflows and outflows is called *Net cash provided by (used for) financing activities*.

To check that you understand these classifications, try the following Self-Study Quiz.

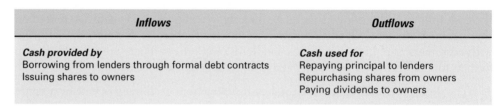

COACH'S TIP

Notice that dividends paid by the company, which do not affect its net income, are reported as a financing activity.

HOW'S IT GOING? A Self-Study Quiz

Vincor International—Canada's largest wine producer—makes and sells a number of brands, including Inniskillin. A listing of some of its cash flows follows. Indicate whether each item is disclosed in the operating activities (O), investing activities (I), or financing activities (F) section of the statement of cash flows.

☐	*a.* Shares issued to shareholders	☐	*d.* Purchase of plant and equipment
☐	*b.* Collections from customers	☐	*e.* Acquisition of investments
☐	*c.* Interest paid on debt	☐	*f.* Repaid long-term debt

After you're finished, check your answers with the solutions in the margin.

Quiz Answers

a. F, *b.* O, *c.* O, *d.* I, *e.* I, *f.* F

STUDY _____

How to Prepare a Statement of Cash Flows

RELATIONSHIPS TO THE BALANCE SHEET AND INCOME STATEMENT

Now that you've seen what an SCF looks like, let's study how you get there. As we explained earlier, the cash flow statement is prepared by analyzing the income statement and changes in balance sheet accounts, and relating these changes to the three sections of the cash flow statement. To prepare the SCF, you need the following:

1. **Comparative balance sheets,** used in calculating the cash flows from all activities (operating, investing, and financing)
2. **A complete income statement,** used primarily in calculating cash flows from operating activities
3. **Additional details** concerning selected accounts that increase and decrease as a result of investing and/or financing activities

Our approach to preparing the cash flow statement focuses on the changes in the balance sheet accounts. It relies on a simple manipulation of the balance sheet equation:

Assets = Liabilities + Shareholders' Equity
First, assets can be split into cash and all the other assets (that we'll call non-cash assets):
Cash + Non-cash assets = Liabilities + Shareholders' Equity
If we pick up the non-cash assets and move them to the right side of the equation, we get:
Cash = Liabilities + Shareholders' Equity – Non-cash Assets

Given this relationship, the changes (Δ) in cash between the beginning and end of the period must equal the changes (Δ) in the amounts on the right side of the equation between the beginning and end of the period:

$$\Delta \text{ Cash} = \Delta \text{ Liabilities} + \Delta \text{ Shareholders' Equity} - \Delta \text{ Non-cash Assets}$$

Thus, *any transaction that changes Cash must be accompanied by a change in Liabilities, Shareholders' Equity, or non-cash assets.* Exhibit 12.2 illustrates this concept for selected cash transactions.

---

exhibit 12.2   Selected Cash Transactions and Their Effects on Other Balance Sheet Accounts

Category	Transaction	Cash Effect	Other Account Affected
Operating	Collect accounts receivable.	+ Cash	− Accounts Receivable (A)
	Pay accounts payable.	− Cash	− Accounts Payable (L)
	Prepay rent.	− Cash	+ Prepaid Rent (A)
	Pay interest.	− Cash	− Retained Earnings (SE)
	Sell goods/services for cash.	+ Cash	+ Retained Earnings (SE)
Investing	Purchase equipment for cash.	− Cash	+ Equipment (A)
	Sell investment securities for cash.	+ Cash	− Investments (A)
Financing	Pay back debt to bank.	− Cash	− Bank Loan Payable (L)
	Issue shares for cash.	+ Cash	+ Contributed Capital (SE)

REPORTING CASH FLOWS FROM OPERATING ACTIVITIES

The operating section of an SCF achieves exactly the same end regardless of whether the indirect or direct method is used; it adjusts the income statement numbers to their cash flow equivalents. There are two differences between the methods: (1) the starting point for making the adjustments and (2) what shows up on the face of the SCF. The operating section may look very different under the two methods, but the logic behind the adjustments is exactly the same. We will start by explaining the logic that is common to both approaches. Then we will discuss how the indirect and direct methods differ.

Remember that:

1. Cash flow from operating activities is always the same, regardless of whether it is computed using the direct or indirect method.
2. The investing and financing sections are always presented in the same manner, regardless of the format of the operating section.

To prepare the operating section, we will follow the three steps shown in Exhibit 12.3 and explained in greater detail below. These steps draw extensively on the comparative balance sheet and the income statement for Magnotta, which are shown together in Exhibit 12.4. To get a glimpse of what we're trying to accomplish, take a peek right now at Exhibit 12.5 on page 531. Really. That's what we should end up with when we complete the three steps in Exhibit 12.3.

Step 1.   Mark an O beside the balance sheet accounts that relate to earning income (operating items). These accounts will include:

- **Most current assets.** Most current assets are used up or converted into cash through the company's regular operating activities. For example, when inventories are sold, they create accounts receivable, which are turned into cash when collected. When marking an O beside the current assets that relate to operating activities, exclude cash (because that's what we're trying to explain the change in) and exclude short-term investments (because this account relates to investing activities).

- **Most current liabilities.** Most current liabilities arise from buying goods or services that are used in a company's operations. Any amounts owed to owners and loans owed to banks and other financial institutions, however, should not be marked with an O because they relate to financing activities.

- **Accumulated amortization.** This contra-asset account increases each period by the amount of amortization expense. Because amortization expense affects net income, this account is related to operating activities.

- **Retained earnings.** This line-item includes activities related to both operating and financing. It increases each period by the amount of net income (which is the starting point for the operating section), and it decreases when dividends are paid (which is a financing activity). To show that the account relates to these two sections of the SCF, we mark it with O and F.

COACH'S TIP

Dividends payable is an example of a current liability owed to owners. It relates to financing, not operating, activities.

---

exhibit 12.3   Steps to Determine Operating Cash Flows

Step 1:	Identify balance sheet accounts related to operating activities.
Step 2:	Create a schedule of operating activities (like the one shown in Exhibit 12.5), which begins by assuming that the numbers on the income statement are cash flows.
Step 3:	Remove the effects of accrual adjustments included in the income statement numbers (Step 2), using changes in balance sheet accounts that relate to operations (Step 1).

exhibit 12.4   **Magnotta: Comparative Balance Sheet and Current Income Statement**

MAGNOTTA WINERY CORPORATION
Balance Sheet*
(in thousands)

Related Cash Flow Section		January 31, 2007	January 31, 2006	*Change*
	Assets			
	Current			
O	Accounts Receivable	$ 396	$ 347	+49
O	Inventories	22,761	20,506	+2,255
O	Prepaid Expenses	280	672	−392
	Total Current Assets	23,437	21,525	
I	Property, Plant, and Equipment	34,424	33,151	+1,273
O	Less: Accumulated Amortization	(12,655)	(11,320)	+1,335
I	Winery Licences	252	252	
	Total Assets	$45,458	$43,608	
	Liabilities and Shareholders' Equity			
	Current Liabilities			
Δ in Cash	Bank Indebtedness	$ 5,400	$ 4,757	+643
O	Accounts Payable	791	1,290	−499
O	Income Tax Payable	177	131	+46
F	Current Portion of Long-Term Debt	784	1,477	−693
	Total Current Liabilities	7,152	7,655	
F	Long-Term Debt	7,950	8,681	−731
O	Future Income Tax	966	1,048	−82
	Shareholders' Equity:			
F	Share Capital	6,497	6,166	+331
F	Contributed Surplus	210	210	
O, F[†]	Retained Earnings	22,683	19,848	+2,835
	Shareholders' Equity	29,390	26,224	
	Liabilities and Shareholders' Equity	$45,458	$43,608	

MAGNOTTA WINERY CORPORATION
Income Statement *
(in thousands)

	Year Ended January 31, 2007
Net Sales	$22,955
Cost of Goods Sold	12,027
Gross Profit	10,928
Operating Expenses:	
Selling, General, and Administrative Expenses	4,529
Amortization	1,335
Total Operating Expenses	5,864
Operating Income	5,064
Interest Expense	912
Net Income before Taxes	4,152
Income Tax Expense (current expense 1,399 less future recovery 82)	1,317
Net Income	$ 2,835

*Certain balances have been adjusted to simplify the presentation and analysis.

[†]This line-item includes transactions related to both operating and financing activities.

While you're at it, you might as well also mark whether the other balance sheet accounts relate to investing (I) or financing (F) activities. This will make it easier for you later when preparing the investing and financing sections of the SCF.

Step 2. Create a schedule of operating activities, which begins with the numbers as reported on the income statement. By starting with the income statement numbers, it's as though we assume all revenues resulted in cash inflows and all expenses resulted in cash outflows. There are lots of places where that isn't true, so the next step adjusts for this.

Step 3. Adjust the income statement numbers for the effects of items marked O that reflect differences in the timing of accrual basis net income and cash flows. The following adjustments are the ones most frequently encountered:

Operating Section Adjustments	Impact on the SCF
Income statement numbers	Starting point
Non-cash expenses (including amortization expense)	Added
Non-cash income (including future income tax recovery)	Subtracted
Decreases in current assets	Added
Increases in current liabilities	Added
Increases in current assets	Subtracted
Decreases in current liabilities	Subtracted

Use this table to remember how to adjust for changes in current assets and liabilities:

	Current Assets	Current Liabilities	
Increase	−	+	} SCF Adjustment
Decrease	+	−	

COACH'S TIP

To make it easy to "dial up" your memory, simplify this table even more:

	A	L
I	−	+
D	+	−

Step 3 is completed in two parts:

Step 3a. Adjust for non-cash items like amortization expense. Amortization is subtracted on the income statement to determine net income, but amortization does not affect cash. By adding amortization expense to our starting point on the SCF, we remove the effect of having deducted it in the income statement. It's like amortization expense digs a hole in the income statement and you need to fill the hole back in on the SCF by adding back the amount of amortization expense. In the Magnotta case, we remove the effect of amortization expense by adding back $1,335 (see Exhibit 12.5).[1]

Magnotta has one other non-cash item: a future income tax recovery ($82). Accounting for future income taxes is covered in more advanced accounting courses, so, for now, all you need to know is that, just like amortization, they do not affect cash. Magnotta's future income tax recovery has been added in arriving at the net income figure.[2] So this item must be taken out of net income (subtracted) to figure out cash from operating activities, as shown in Exhibit 12.5. Conversely, a future income tax expense would be deducted from net income, and added back to figure out cash from operating activities.

---

[1] Amortization expense for intangible assets (discussed in Chapter 9) is handled in exactly the same way as it is for tangible assets. Gains and losses on sales of equipment also are dealt with in a similar manner and are discussed in the chapter Supplement A. Other additions and subtractions for long-lived assets are discussed in more advanced accounting courses.

[2] The journal entry for the future portion of income tax is shown below for your information:

dr	Income tax recovery (future portion)	82	
cr	Future tax payable.		82

As you can see, this entry has no cash flow effect.

---

exhibit 12.5   **Magnotta: Schedule for Net Cash Flow from Operating Activities**

ADJUSTMENTS NEEDED TO CONVERT INCOME STATEMENT NUMBERS TO NET CASH FLOW FROM OPERATING ACTIVITIES

Adjustments	Amount (in thousands)	Explanation (see details below)
Add (subtract) to convert to cash basis:		
Amortization expense	+ 1,335	Add, because amortization expense does not affect cash but was subtracted on the income statement.
Other non-cash expenses (revenues)	−82	Deduct, because the future portion of income tax expense does not affect cash but was added on the income statement.
Accounts receivable increase	−49	Deduct, because the cash collected from customers is less than accrual basis revenues.
Inventory increase	−2,255	Deduct, because purchases are more than the cost of goods sold expense.
Prepaid expense increase	+ 392	Add, because cash prepayments for expenses are less than accrual basis expenses.
Accounts payable decrease	−499	Add, because amounts purchased on account (borrowed from suppliers) are more than cash payments to suppliers.
Income tax payable increase	+ 46	Add, because accrual basis expenses are more than the cash payments for expenses.

Step 3b.   Adjust for changes in current assets and current liabilities. Each *change* in current assets (other than cash and short-term investments) and current liabilities (other than amounts owed to owners and financial institutions) causes a difference between the income statement numbers and cash flow from operating activities. When converting the income statement numbers to cash flow from operating activities, apply the general rules you learned earlier in the table on page 530:

■   *Add the change when a current asset decreases or current liability increases.*

■   *Subtract the change when a current asset increases or current liability decreases.*

Understanding what makes these current assets and current liabilities increase and decrease is the key to understanding the logic of these additions and subtractions.

COACH'S TIP

The amortization add-back on the SCF is not intended to suggest that **amortization creates an increase in cash**. Rather, it's just showing that **amortization expense does not cause a decrease in cash**. This is a subtle, but very important, difference in interpretation.

Change in Accounts Receivable.   We will illustrate the logic behind Step 3b with the first operating item (O) listed on the Magnotta balance sheet in Exhibit 12.4, Accounts Receivable. The goal is to adjust the **sales** revenue included in net income to **cash** collected from customers. As shown in the equation below and in the T-account in the margin, sales revenues cause accounts receivable (A/R) to increase, and cash collected from customers causes accounts receivable to decrease:

+ Accounts Receivable (A) −	
Beginning balance	
Sales revenue	Cash collected
Ending balance	

If we move A/R (beginning) to the right-hand side of the equation, we get

This equation says that the difference between the sales revenue included in net income and the cash collected from customers is equal to the change in accounts receivable. In other words, to adjust from accrual-basis sales revenue to operating cash flows, we need to adjust for the change in accounts receivable. If we insert the numbers for Magnotta (from Exhibit 12.4) into the accounts receivable T-account and look at how the numbers work together, you can begin to understand why we *deduct* the change in accounts receivable when its balance increases:

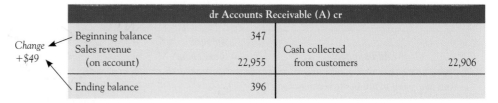

dr Accounts Receivable (A) cr			
Beginning balance	347		
Sales revenue (on account)	22,955	Cash collected from customers	22,906
Ending balance	396		

Change +$49 (arrows pointing to Beginning balance and Ending balance)

The cash collections were smaller than the sales included in net income, so the appropriate adjustment on the SCF is to deduct the amount by which cash collections are smaller than sales. (The opposite is true, as well. A decrease in accounts receivable would have been added.)

Take note that the adjustment on the SCF (see Exhibit 12.5) is not the total cash collections of $22,906. Because the income statement already includes sales of $22,955, the amount of the adjustment is the difference between $347 and $396, which can be easily determined by computing the change in accounts receivable:

Beginning balance	$ 347
− Ending balance	396
= Change	$ 49

This actually provides a shortcut for determining the SCF adjustment: Simply adjust for the change in the balance sheet account. One way to remember whether the adjustment on the SCF should be an increase or decrease is to think about the accounts receivable T-account (shown below). If the change in the account is explained by a debit (an increase), the SCF adjustment is reported just like a credit to cash (a decrease).

dr Accounts Receivable (A) cr		
Beginning balance	347	
Increase	49	
Ending balance	396	

Change in Inventory.   To convert CGS to cash paid to suppliers, we need to look at two adjustments, the change in inventory and the change in accounts payable, because (1) not all inventory that is purchased is sold, and (2) not all inventory purchases are for cash. We cover the change in accounts payable below, after the asset accounts have been dealt with. The income statement deducts the cost of goods sold when determining net income, yet we want the SCF to deduct the cash outflow for inventory purchases. As shown in the T-account on the left below, purchases of goods increase the balance in inventory, and recording the cost of goods sold decreases the balance in inventory. Using the beginning and ending inventory numbers (from Exhibit 12.4) in the T-account on the right, we see that inventory increased $2,255 during the year. This means that the company bought more merchandise than it sold or, in other words, more was spent on inventory than was expensed as cost of goods sold. So, to convert from CGS to the amount spent on inventory purchases, subtract the extra money spent on purchases, as shown in Exhibit 12.5. The extra money spent on purchases is the amount by which inventory increased. (If inventory had decreased, that amount would be added.)

dr Inventories (A) cr		
Beginning balance		
Purchases		Cost of goods sold
Ending balance		

dr Inventories (A) cr		
Beginning balance	20,506	
Increase	2,255	
Ending balance	22,761	

Change in Prepaid Expenses. The income statement reflects expenses of the period, but cash flow from operating activities must reflect the cash payments. Cash prepayments increase the balance in prepaid expenses, and the balance decreases when prepaid expenses are used up and expensed on the income statement.

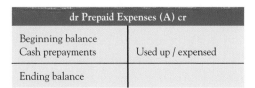

dr Prepaid Expenses (A) cr	
Beginning balance	
Cash prepayments	Used up / expensed
Ending balance	

dr Prepaid Expenses (A) cr		
Beginning balance 672		
	Decrease	392
Ending balance 280		

The Magnotta balance sheet (Exhibit 12.4) indicates a $392 decrease in prepaid expenses, which means that new cash prepayments were less than expenses. These extra cash prepayments must be *added* in Exhibit 12.5. (An increase is deducted.)

Change in Accounts Payable. Cash flow from operations must reflect cash purchases, but not all purchases are made using cash. As shown in the T-account below, purchases on account increase accounts payable, and cash paid to suppliers decreases accounts payable.

dr Accounts Payable (L) cr	
	Beginning balance
	Purchases on account
Cash payments	
	Ending balance

dr Accounts Payable (L) cr			
		Beginning balance	1,290
Decrease	499		
		Ending balance	791

Accounts payable *decreased* by $499 this period, which means that cash payments to suppliers were more than purchases on account. This increase must be *deducted* in Exhibit 12.5. (An increase is added.)

Change in Income Tax Payable. Magnotta has two accounts on its balance sheet related to income tax: income tax payable (a current liability, due within a year), and future income tax payable (a long-term liability, which may become payable at some point in the future). We already learned on page 530 that the increase in future income tax expenses and recoveries are non-cash items, so Magnotta's recovery of $82 is deducted in Exhibit 12.5, because it was added on the income statement but has no cash effect. Let's look at the income tax payable T-account:

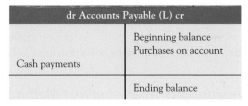

dr Income Tax Payable cr		
	Beginning balance	131
	Increase	46
	Ending balance	177

Cash flow from operations must reflect taxes paid, not tax expense. As with other liability accounts, the current portion of the tax expense increases income tax payable, and cash payments decrease income tax payable. When income tax payable increases during the year, it means the tax expense is more than the tax paid during the year, so the increase must be added in Exhibit 12.5. (A decrease is deducted.)

Now try the Self-Study Quiz on page 534.

Summary. The additions and subtractions to reconcile Magnotta's income statement numbers to its cash flows from operating activities are summarized in Exhibit 12.5. You may encounter other non-cash expenses and other current assets and liabilities besides the ones we have seen in our Magnotta example, so let's review the two general rules for the operating section: (1) Add back or deduct all non-cash items in the income statement. (2) Add and deduct all changes in current assets and liabilities, using the rules in

COACH'S TIP

When prepaids decrease during the period, it means, all else being equal, that the company bought less of these items, which is good news for the company's cash. So it makes sense that a decrease in prepaids is a positive adjustment in Exhibit 12.5. Conversely, an increase in prepaids means they bought more, which is bad news for cash. Thus, an increase in prepaids would be a negative adjustment.

COACH'S TIP

When payables decrease during the period, it means, all else being equal, that the company paid its suppliers more, which is bad news for the company's cash. So it makes sense that a decrease in payables is a negative adjustment in Exhibit 12.5. Conversely, an increase in payables means they paid their suppliers less, which is good news for cash. Thus, an increase in payables would be a positive adjustment.

COACH'S TIP

When taxes payable increase during the period, it means, all else being equal, that the company paid the government less, which is good news for the company's cash. So it makes sense that an increase in taxes payable is a positive adjustment in Exhibit 12.5. Conversely, a decrease in taxes payable means they paid more, which is bad news for cash. Thus, a decrease in taxes payable would be a negative adjustment.

HOW'S IT GOING?   A Self-Study Quiz

Indicate which of the following items taken from Vincor International's cash flow statement would be added (+), subtracted (−), or not included (0) in the conversion of the income statement numbers to cash flow from operations.

> *a.* Decrease in income tax payable

> *b.* Increase in accounts payable

> *c.* Amortization expense

> *d.* Increase in accounts receivable

> *e.* Increase in accrued liabilities

> *f.* Increase in prepaid expenses

After you're finished, check your answers with the solutions in the margin.

the table on page 530. Now we turn our attention to how these adjustments are used. Because they can be used to prepare the operating section in one of two formats, we will discuss them separately. Part A will describe the indirect method, and part B the direct method. Your instructor may choose to assign one, the other, or both. After you have completed the assigned part(s), you should move on to the discussion of Reporting Cash Flows from Investing Activities.

Part A: Reporting Cash Flows from Operating Activities—Indirect Method

To prepare the operating section using the indirect method, (1) use net income as your starting point, and (2) show the adjustments in the operating section of the SCF. By taking Magnotta's net income of $2,835 from Exhibit 12.4 and adjusting it by the items we listed in Exhibit 12.5, we calculate cash flow from operating activities as $1,723, which is what Magnotta shows in its SCF, as we will see in the top part of Exhibit 12.9 on page 540.

Cash Flows from Operating Activities:	
Net income	$2,835
Adjustments to reconcile net income to net cash provided by operating activities:	
Amortization	1,335
Other non-cash items	(82)
Changes in current assets and liabilities:	
Accounts receivable	(49)
Inventories	(2,255)
Prepaid expenses	392
Accounts payable	(499)
Income tax payable	46
Net cash provided by operating activities	$ 1,723

If your instructor has assigned only the indirect method, you should skip the next section and move on to the discussion of Reporting Cash Flows from Investing Activities (page 537).

Part B: Reporting Cash Flows from Operating Activities—Direct Method

To prepare the operating section using the direct method, (1) use the income statement as your starting point, adjusting *each line* accordingly, and (2) show the actual cash inflows and outflows in the operating section of the SCF. To illustrate, we start by putting the income statement from Exhibit 12.4 into the left-hand column below. Then we take each of the seven adjustments listed in Exhibit 12.5 and use them to adjust the individual line-items on the income statement.

	Accrual Basis	Adjustments		Cash Basis
Net sales	22,955	(a)	− 49	22,906
Cost of goods sold	− 12,027	(b)	− 2,255	
		(c)	− 499	− 14,781
Selling, general, and administrative	− 4,529	(d)	+ 392	− 4,137
Amortization	− 1,335	(e)	+ 1,335	0
Interest	− 912	(f)		− 912
Income tax expense—current	− 1,399	(g)	+ 46	− 1,353
—future	+ 82	(h)	− 82	0
Net income	= $2,835		− 1,112	
Net cash provided by operating activities				= $1,723

Let's briefly look at each of the adjustments to review how they relate to the individual lines.

(a) Receivables arise from credit sales, so changes in receivables go on the sales line to convert sales to cash collected from customers on the SCF. Deduct, because the cash collected from customers is less than accrual basis revenues, as explained on page 532.

(b) and (c) Cost of goods sold represents the cost of merchandise sold during the year. It may be more or less than the amount of cash paid to suppliers, which is what we want to show in the SCF. Changes in both inventories and accounts payable are necessary to convert cost of goods sold to cash paid to suppliers. Subtract the change in inventories, because purchases are more than the cost of goods sold expense, as explained on page 532. Deduct the change in accounts payable, because amounts purchased on account (borrowed from suppliers) are less than cash payments to suppliers, as explained on page 533.

(d) Prepaids arise on items like insurance and rent, expenses that appear in the selling, general, and administrative expenses. Add, because cash prepayments for expenses are less than accrual basis expenses, as explained on page 533.

(e) Add, because amortization expense does not affect cash but was subtracted when computing net income, as explained on page 530. Amortization does not appear anywhere in the SCF when the operation section is prepared using the direct method.

(f) There is no item on the balance sheet relating to interest, so there is no adjustment to be made. The expense must be equal to the cash paid for interest.

(g) We calculate income tax paid by adjusting the current portion of income tax expense by the change in the income tax payable. Add, because accrual basis tax expense is more than the cash payments for tax, as explained on page 533.

(h) Deduct, because the future portion of income tax does not affect cash but the recovery was added when computing net income, as explained on page 530. Like amortization, this non-cash item does not appear on the SCF when the operation section is prepared using the direct method.

The last column becomes the operating section of the SCF using the direct format. Notice that, with the direct method, we work directly with each revenue and expense listed on the income statement and ignore any totals or subtotals (including net income). If Magnotta were to report its SCF using the direct method, the information in Exhibit 12.6 would replace the operating activities section shown in Exhibit 12.9 on page 540.

exhibit 12.6   Magnotta: Schedule for Net Cash Flow from Operating Activities—Direct Method

(in thousands)

Cash Flows from Operating Activities:	
Cash collected from customers	$22,906
Cash payments to suppliers	(14,781)
Cash payments for operating expenses	(4,137)
Cash payments for interest	(912)
Cash payments for income taxes	(1,353)
Net cash inflow (outflow)	1,723

Income Statement Account	+/− Change in Balance Sheet Account(s)	= Operating Cash Flow
Sales Revenue	+ Decrease in Accounts Receivable (A) − Increase in Accounts Receivable (A)	= Collections from customers
Cost of Goods Sold	+ Increase in Inventory (A) − Decrease in Inventory (A) − Increase in Accounts Payable (L) + Decrease in Accounts Payable (L)	= Payments to suppliers of inventory
Other Expenses	+ Increase in Prepaid Expenses (A) − Decrease in Prepaid Expenses (A) − Increase in Accrued Expenses (L) + Decrease in Accrued Expenses (L)	= Payments to suppliers of services (e.g., rent, utilities, wages, interest)
Interest Expense	− Increase in Interest Payable (L) + Decrease in Interest Payable (L)	= Payments of interest
Income Tax Expense	+ Increase in Prepaid Income Taxes (Future Taxes) (A) − Decrease in Prepaid Income Taxes (Future Taxes) (A) − Increase in Income Taxes Payable (Future Taxes) (L) + Decrease in Income Taxes Payable (Future Taxes) (L)	= Payments of income taxes

Again, note that the net cash inflow or outflow is the same, regardless of whether the direct or indirect method of presentation is used (in this case, an inflow of $1,723). The two methods differ only in terms of the details reported on the statement.

To summarize, the adjustments in the table at the bottom of page 536 must commonly be made to convert the line-items in the income statement to the related operating cash flow amounts:

HOW'S IT GOING? A Self-Study Quiz

Indicate which of the following items taken from a cash flow statement would be added (+), subtracted (−), or not included (0) when calculating cash flow from operations using the direct method.

    ☐ *a.* Increase in inventories

    ☐ *b.* Payment of dividends to shareholders

    ☐ *c.* Cash collections from customers

    ☐ *d.* Purchase of plant and equipment for cash

    ☐ *e.* Payments of interest to lenders

    ☐ *f.* Payment of taxes to the government

After you're finished, check your answers with the solutions in the margin.

Quiz Answers
a. −, *b.* 0, *c.* +, *d.* 0, *e.* −, *f.* −

REPORTING CASH FLOWS FROM INVESTING ACTIVITIES

To prepare this section of the SCF, you must analyze accounts related to short-term investments and long-term asset accounts such as property, plant, and equipment and intangible assets.[3] The following relationships are the ones that you will encounter most frequently:

Related Balance Sheet Accounts	Investing Activity	Cash Flow Effect
Short-term investments	Purchase of investment securities for cash	Outflow
	Sale (maturity) of investment securities for cash	Inflow
Property, plant, and equipment	Purchase of property, plant, and equipment for cash	Outflow
	Sale of property, plant, and equipment for cash	Inflow
Intangible assets	Purchase of intangibles	Outflow
	Sale of intangibles	Inflow

COACH'S TIP

When analyzing investing activities, remember to include both of the following:

- Only purchases paid for with **cash** (or cash equivalents)
- The amount of **cash** received from the sale of these assets, regardless of whether the assets are sold at a gain or loss

In the case of Magnotta, the balance sheet (Exhibit 12.4) shows two investing assets (noted with an I), property, plant, and equipment (PPE) and winery licences (an intangible asset), but only PPE has changed during the year.

---

[3] Investing activities also include short-term and long-term investments (studied in Appendix C). Although not shown here, the cash flows for investments are similar to those for property, plant, and equipment. Cash received from the *sale* of investments is classified as an investing activity. In contrast, cash received from dividends and interest earned while the investments are owned is classified as an operating activity.

exhibit 12.7   Magnotta: Schedule for Net Cash Flow from Investing Activities

Items	Amount (in thousands)	Explanations
Purchase of property, plant, and equipment	(1,273)	Payment of cash for property, plant, and equipment
Net cash inflow (outflow)	(1,273)	Subtotal for the SCF

Property, Plant, and Equipment

To figure out the cause(s) for the change in the PPE number, accountants would examine the detailed accounting records for these accounts because there may have been both purchases and sales during the year, and these cash outflows and inflows should be shown separately on the SCF. In our example, Magnotta purchased equipment for $1,273 cash and did not sell any equipment during the year. The equipment purchase is a cash outflow, which we subtract in the schedule of investing activities in Exhibit 12.7. In our example, this purchase fully explains the increase in PPE of $1,273.

dr PPE (A) cr	
Beginning balance	33,151
Purchases	1,273
Ending balance	34,424

Intangible Assets

Magnotta's winery licences did not change during the year, so there are no cash inflows or outflows on the SCF for this asset. Just as with PPE, purchases and sales of intangible assets are investing activities. When intangible assets are amortized, the amortization expense is treated exactly as amortization on PPE.

REPORTING CASH FLOWS FROM FINANCING ACTIVITIES

This section of the cash flow statement includes changes in current liabilities owed to owners (dividends payable) and financial institutions (bank loans payable, short-term notes payable, current portion of long-term debt), as well as changes in long-term liabilities and shareholders' equity accounts. The following relationships are the ones that you will encounter most often:

Related Balance Sheet Accounts	Financing Activity	Cash Flow Effect
Short-term debt (notes payable)	Borrowing cash from bank or other financial institutions	Inflow
	Repayment of loan principal	Outflow
Long-term debt	Issuance of bonds for cash	Inflow
	Repayment of bond principal	Outflow
Contributed capital	Issuance of shares for cash	Inflow
	Repurchase of shares with cash	Outflow
Retained earnings	Payment of cash dividends	Outflow

To compute cash flows from financing activities, you should review changes in debt and shareholders' equity accounts. In the case of Magnotta, when we look at changes in the balance sheet (Exhibit 12.4), we find that long-term debt, share capital, and retained earnings changed during the period (noted with an F). If there was a change in contributed surplus during the year, we would have to find out why the account changed, and what effect, if any, the change had on cash. Changes in contributed surplus are financing activities.

Long-Term Debt

The change in long-term debt resulted from repaying $1,424 during the year, as shown in the T-account below (all figures in thousands). We'll include this cash outflow in a schedule of financing activities, shown in Exhibit 12.8. For this calculation, we add the current and long-term portions of long-term debt together.

dr Long-Term Debt (L) cr			
Repaid	1,424	Beginning balance	10,158 (1,477 + 8,681)
		Ending balance	8,734 (784 + 7,950)

Share Capital

The change in share capital resulted from the issuance of shares to employees for $331 in cash, which is a cash inflow. This accounts for the $331 increase in share capital, and is listed in the schedule of financing activities in Exhibit 12.8 (all figures in thousands).

dr Share Capital (SE) cr	
Beginning balance	6,166
Issue new shares	331
Ending balance	6,497

Retained Earnings

Changes in retained earnings result from two things: net income increases the account and dividends declared decreases it. Magnotta did not declare dividends during the year, so the total increase of $2,835 is due entirely to its net income, as shown below. The cash effects related to net income have been included in the operating activities section of the SCF, so there is nothing left to account for.

dr Retained Earnings (SE) cr			
Dividends declared	0	Beginning balance	19,848
		Net Income	2,835
		Ending balance	22,683

When dividends are declared and paid during the year, dividends paid will be shown on the SCF as a financing activity. But remember that dividends paid may be more or less than dividends declared, so you have to check the balance sheet to find the change in any dividends payable during the year.

exhibit 12.8   Magnotta: Schedule for Net Cash Flow from Financing Activities

Items	Amount (in thousands)	Explanations
Repaid long-term debt	(1,424)	Cash paid to reduce long-term debt
Proceeds from share issuance	331	Cash proceeds from issue of common shares
Net cash inflow (outflow)	(1,093)	Subtotal for the SCF

---

exhibit 12.9   Sample Statement of Cash Flows—Indirect Method

MAGNOTTA WINERY CORPORATION
Statement of Cash Flows *
Year Ended January 31, 2007
(in thousands)

Cash Flows from Operating Activities:	
Net income	$2,835
Adjustments to reconcile net income to net cash provided by operating activities:	
Amortization	1,335
Other non-cash items	(82)
Changes in current assets and liabilities:	
Accounts receivable	(49)
Inventories	(2,255)
Prepaid expenses	392
Accounts payable	(499)
Income tax payable	46
Net cash provided by operating activities	1,723
Cash Flows from Investing Activities:	
Purchases of property, plant, and equipment (net)	(1,273)
Net cash used by investing activities	(1,273)
Cash Flows from Financing Activities:	
Repaid long-term debt	(1,424)
Proceeds of share issuance	331
Net cash used in financing activities	(1,093)
Net decrease in cash and cash equivalents	(643)
Cash and cash equivalents, beginning of year	(4,757)
Cash and cash equivalents, end of year	$(5,400)

*Certain amounts have been adjusted to simplify the presentation and analysis.

FORMAT FOR THE STATEMENT OF CASH FLOWS

Now that you have determined the cash flows for the three main types of business activities in Exhibits 12.8, 12.7, and either 12.6 or 12.5, you can prepare the statement of cash flows in a proper format. Exhibit 12.9 shows the statement of cash flows for Magnotta, using the indirect method. The direct method would be identical except that the operating activities section would list the items in Exhibit 12.6. Under either method, the statement of cash flows combines cash flows from operating, investing, and financing activities to produce an overall net increase (or decrease) in cash. This net change is added to the beginning cash balance to arrive at the ending cash balance, which is the same cash balance as reported on the balance sheet. Negative cash balances are shown as current liabilities on the balance sheet; positive cash balances are shown as current assets.

ADDITIONAL SCF INFORMATION

Accounting rules require that the amount paid for interest and income taxes be shown in the SCF. If the operating section is prepared using the direct method, these amounts will show up automatically as individual line-items. If the operating section is prepared using the indirect method, these amounts will be disclosed as supplementary information in the SCF. Magnotta, which uses the indirect method, disclosed information about interest and income taxes paid at the bottom of its SCF.

In addition to their cash flows, all companies are required to report material investing and financing transactions that did not have cash flow effects (called "non-cash investing and financing activities"). For example, the purchase of a $10,000 piece of equipment with a $10,000 note payable to the supplier does not cause either an inflow or an outflow of cash. As a result, these activities are not listed in the three main sections of the SCF. This important information about investing and financing activities is normally presented for users in a supplementary schedule to the SCF or in the financial statement notes.

Before we move on, let's summarize the steps in preparing an SCF:

Step 1:   Identify balance sheet accounts related to operating activities.

Step 2:   Create a schedule of operating activities (like the one shown in Exhibit 12.5), which begins by assuming the numbers on the income statement are cash flows.

Step 3:   Remove the effects of accrual adjustments included in the income statement numbers (Step 2), using changes in balance sheet accounts that relate to operations (Step 1). These will include non-cash items like amortization expense and future income taxes, as well as changes in current assets and current liabilities.

Step 4:   Prepare the operating section of the SCF (using either the direct or indirect format), by applying the adjustments (Step 3) to net income.

Step 5:   Identify balance sheet accounts related to investing and financing activities, and prepare the investing and financing sections of the SCF.

Step 6:   Calculate the change in cash during the period (the total of the three types of activities on the SCF), and reconcile it to the opening and closing cash on the balance sheet.

Step 7:   Disclose any additional information required by GAAP.

EVALUATE

Financial Results Reported in a Statement of Cash Flows

When evaluating the SCF, a good way to start is by looking at the totals of each of the three main sections. A healthy company will show positive cash flows from operations that are sufficiently large to pay for replacing current property, plant, and equipment and to pay dividends to shareholders. Any additional cash (called "free cash flow") can (1) be used to expand the business through additional investing activities, (2) be used for other financing activities, or (3) simply build up the company's cash balance. After considering where the company stands, in relation to this big picture, you're ready to look at the details within each of the sections.

INTERPRETING CASH FLOWS FROM OPERATING ACTIVITIES

The operating activities section of the SCF indicates how well a company is able to generate cash internally through its operations and management of current assets and current liabilities. Most analysts believe that this is the most important section of the statement because, in the long run, operations are the only continuing source of cash. That is, investors will not invest in a company if they do not believe that cash generated from operations will be available to pay them dividends or expand the company. Similarly, creditors will not lend money if they do not believe that cash generated from operations will be sufficient to repay them. Many dot.com companies failed when investors stopped believing that Internet companies would turn business ideas into cash flows from operations.

When evaluating the operating activities section of the SCF, consider the absolute amount of cash flow (is it positive or negative?), keeping in mind that operating cash flows have to be positive over the long run for a company to be successful. Also, look for trends from one period to another. Most companies have ups and downs in operating cash flows, particularly if they are just starting out or if they operate a seasonal business. Magnotta, for example, experiences its strongest operating cash flows in the third quarter of the year. Of its 2007 $1.7 million operating cash inflow, fully $1.1 million of this occurred in the third quarter. Seasonality issues are usually discussed by management in the Management Discussion and Analysis section (MD&A) of the annual report. Exhibit 12.10 presents excerpts from the MD&A's of Magnotta, Sleeman Breweries, and

---

exhibit 12.10   Examples of MD&A Disclosures on Seasonality

Magnotta Winery
During a typical year, the Company experiences some seasonality in its sales. In fiscal 2007 and fiscal 2006, the Company experienced high demand during September to December when approximately 41.8 per cent and 41.4 per cent, respectively, of annual sales are usually generated.

Sleeman Breweries
The quarterly operating results of the Company vary considerably because of the seasonality of beer sales. The company historically realizes higher sales during summer months.

Intrawest
Resort and travel operations are highly seasonal. In fiscal 2005, approximately 55 per cent of our resort travel operations revenue was generated during the period from December to March, the prime ski season.

Intrawest that discuss seasonality in their respective industries. They talk about sales, and we can expect cash flows to lag a bit behind.

INTERPRETING CASH FLOWS FROM INVESTING ACTIVITIES

To maintain operating cash flows at their current levels, a company must replace existing equipment as it wears down. A good measure for determining whether the company is generating enough cash internally to purchase new long-term assets like equipment is the capital acquisitions ratio:

$$\text{Capital-Acquisitions Ratio} = \frac{\text{Net Cash Flow from Operating Activities}}{\text{Cash Paid for Property, Plant, and Equipment}}$$

The capital acquisitions ratio reflects the extent to which purchases of property, plant, and equipment are financed from operating activities (without the need for outside debt or equity financing or the sale of other investments or long-term assets). A ratio greater than 1.0 indicates that, all else being equal, outside financing was not needed to replace equipment in the current period. Generally speaking, the higher a company's capital acquisitions ratio, the less likely it is that external financing will be needed to fund future expansion.

Generally, the amount of cash paid for property, plant, and equipment (used in the bottom part of the ratio) is reported in the SCF's investing activities section in a line-item called something like "additions to property, plant, and equipment."

Because expenditures for property, plant, and equipment can vary greatly from year to year, the ratio often is calculated as an average over a longer time period. In Exhibit 12.11, we present the three-year average capital acquisitions ratio for Magnotta and one of its competitors, Andrew Peller Ltd. These ratios show that both Magnotta and Peller, with a ratio greater than one, were able to finance their purchases of property, plant, and equipment with cash generated from operating activities. As part of the self-study quiz that follows, you should complete the final column in the exhibit.

Be on the Alert

Because the needs for investment in plant and equipment differ dramatically across industries (for example, consider Magnotta versus First Choice Haircutters), a particular company's ratio should be compared only with its prior years' figures or with other

COACH'S TIP

The amount of cash paid for property, plant, and equipment can be found within the investing activities section of the SCF. Although it is shown as a negative number on the SCF (because it is an outflow of cash), treat it as a positive number in the capital acquisitions ratio.

---

exhibit 12.11   **Summary of Capital Acquisitions Ratio Analyses**

Name of Measure	Formula	What It Tells You	2005–2007 Peller	2005–2007 Magnotta	SELF-STUDY QUIZ 2002–2004 Magnotta
Capital Acquisitions Ratio	$\dfrac{\text{Net Cash from Operations}}{\text{Cash Paid for PPE}}$	• Whether operating cash flows are sufficient to pay for PPE purchases • A higher ratio means less need for external financing ☺.	1.25	1.46	☐

HOW'S IT GOING?   A Self-Study Quiz

Compute the ratio for the final column in Exhibit 12.11, using the cash flow from operations and cash paid for property, plant, and equipment shown in the table below. How did the ratio change between 2002 and 2004 and 2005 and 2007? Suggest a possible reason for this change.

(in thousands)	2004	2003	2002	Total
Cash flow from operating activities	2,777	1,809	572	5,158
Purchases of property, plant, and equipment	960	822	572	2,354

When you're finished, check your answers with the solutions in the margin.

companies in the same industry. Also, while a high ratio can indicate strong cash flows, it also might suggest a failure to update plant and equipment, which can limit a company's ability to compete in the future. The main point is that you have to interpret the ratio in relation to the company's activities and business strategy.

INTERPRETING CASH FLOWS FROM FINANCING ACTIVITIES

The long-term growth of a company can be financed from internally generated funds (cash from operating activities), the issuance of shares (equity financing), and money borrowed on a long-term basis (debt financing). Debt financing is the riskiest source of financing because (1) interest *must* be paid on debt (dividends do not have to be paid), and (2) debt *must* be repaid (shares do not). To determine possible changes in the risk related to a company's financing strategy, look within the financing activities section. All else being equal, a company that borrows additional money will be taking on greater risk than a company that pays down its debt.

In addition to considering changes in financing strategy, it also is useful to consider whether a company is generating sufficient cash flow to pay the interest it owes on debt. The times-interest-earned ratio (introduced in Chapter 10) is one way of assessing a company's ability to pay interest (by comparing net income before interest and taxes with the amount of interest expense). The problem with that ratio is that interest is paid with cash (not the net income used in that ratio). A more appropriate way to see whether a company has been able to pay its interest is to compare the cash flows generated from the company's operations with the cash paid for interest. The cash coverage ratio is used for this:

COACH'S TIP

The amounts of interest and income taxes paid usually are reported as supplementary cash flow information, either at the bottom of the SCF or in the notes to the financial statements.

$$\text{Cash-Coverage Ratio} = \frac{\text{Net Cash Flow from Operating Activities} + \text{Interest Paid} + \text{Income Taxes Paid}}{\text{Interest Paid}}$$

Interest and income taxes paid are added to net cash flow from operating activities because these outflows of cash were deducted in determining operating cash flows. By adding them back in, the cash-coverage ratio can determine whether the company generates enough cash before the costs of financing and taxes to cover its interest payments.

RECONSIDER _____
Financial Performance in the Light of Cash Flows

USING NET OPERATING CASH FLOWS TO EVALUATE NET INCOME

As you now know, both net operating cash flow and net income are important measures of a company's operating performance. Unlike net operating cash flow, which is based on actual cash inflows and outflows, net income *assumes* that all of the company's revenues eventually are realized as cash inflows, and that its expenses are associated with outflows of cash. These assumptions are necessary if net income is to provide a timely measure of operating performance. A useful ratio for checking the extent to which these assumptions affect a particular company (and, more generally, for evaluating whether net income is in sync with cash flows from operations) is the quality-of-income ratio:

$$\text{Quality-of-Income Ratio} = \frac{\text{Net Cash Flow from Operating Activities}}{\text{Net Income}}$$

The quality-of-income ratio measures the portion of income that was generated in cash. All other things being equal, a higher quality-of-income ratio indicates a higher likelihood that revenues are being realized in cash and that expenses are associated with cash outflows. This ratio is most useful when compared with industry competitors or with prior time periods. Any major deviations should be investigated. In some cases, a deviation may be nothing to worry about, but, in others, it could be the first sign of big problems to come. Four potential causes of deviations to consider include:

1. *Seasonality.* As in the Magnotta case, seasonal variations in sales and inventory production can cause the ratio to fluctuate. Usually, this isn't a cause for alarm. ☺

2. *The corporate life cycle (growth in sales).* New companies often experience rapid sales growth. When sales are increasing, accounts receivable and inventory normally increase faster than accounts payable. This often reduces operating cash flows below net income, which, in turn, reduces the ratio. This isn't a big deal, provided that the start-up company can get cash from financing activities until operating activities begin to stabilize. ☺

COACH'S TIP

Think of increases in accounts receivable and inventory as a sign that cash is "tied up" in these assets. Decreases in these assets indicate that the amount previously invested in them has now been released into cash.

exhibit **12.12** Summary of Quality-of-Income Ratios			
		2007	*2006*
	Peller	*Magnotta*	*Magnotta*
Quality-of-Income Ratio	0.79	.61	1.45

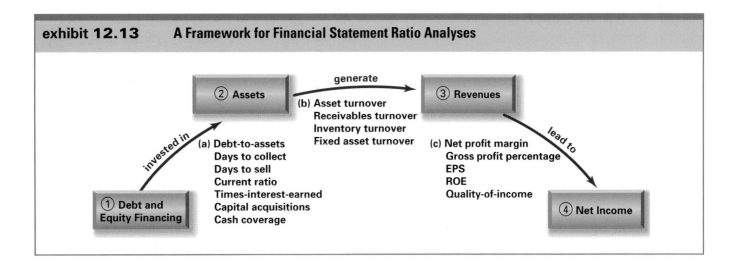

exhibit 12.13 A Framework for Financial Statement Ratio Analyses

3. *Changes in management of operating activities.* If a company's operating assets (like accounts receivable and inventories) are allowed to grow out of control, its operating cash flows and quality of income ratio will decrease. More efficient management will have the opposite effect. To investigate this potential cause more closely, use the accounts-receivable and inventory-turnover ratios covered in Chapters 7 and 8. ☹

4. *Changes in revenue and expense recognition.* Most cases of fraudulent financial reporting involve aggressive revenue recognition (recording revenues earlier than usual) or delayed expense recognition (deferring expenses longer than usual). Both of these tactics cause net income to increase in the current period, making it seem as though the company has improved its performance. Neither of these tactics, though, affects cash flows from operating activities. As a result, if a manager changes revenue and expense recognition policies to boost net income, the quality-of-income ratio will drop, providing one of the first clues that the financial statements might contain errors or fraud. ☹

Exhibit 12.12 shows the 2007 quality-of-income ratios for Andrew Peller and Magnotta, as well as Magnotta's 2006 ratio. Magnotta's ratio has dropped significantly from 2006, but is still not too far below its competitor's ratio. A quick look at the operating section of Magnotta's 2007 SCF shows that the drop in the 2007 ratio is due primarily to the large increase in inventories during 2007. Calculating the inventory-turnover ratio for Magnotta might provide some clues as to whether this increase is a cause for concern.

The quality-of-income ratio is a profitability ratio, and is shown in the (c) section in our framework for financial statement analysis in Exhibit 12.13. Since both the capital-acquisitions and the cash-coverage ratios tell us about the financial position of the company, both ratios have been added to the (a) section.

WHAT'S COMING UP

If you've been reading the chapters in the order presented, the next chapter will help you to pull together everything you've learned to this point in the course. If you've read this chapter just after completing the initial chapters that introduce the accounting cycle (Chapters 1 to 4), it's time to learn more about many of the decisions that are made when accounting for the variety of operating, investing, and financing transactions that a company enters into. Either way, ensure that you review and practice what was covered in this chapter before going on.

FOR YOUR REVIEW _____

DEMONSTRATION CASE A (INDIRECT METHOD)

During a recent quarter (ended March 31), Sleeman's Breweries reported net income of $1,610 (all numbers in thousands). The company reported the following activities:

a. Repaid $2,476 of long-term debt.
b. Accounts receivable decreased by $3,305.
c. Paid $1,229 in cash for purchase of property, plant, and equipment.
d. Recorded amortization expense of $1,955.
e. Prepaid expenses decreased by $664.
f. Inventories increased by $4,398.
g. Non-cash expenses (other than amortization) $257.
h. Accounts payable decreased by $121.
i. Issued shares to employees for $436 in cash.
j. Purchased intangible assets for $100.

Required:

Based on this information, prepare the cash flow statement using the indirect method up to the net change in cash and cash equivalents for the quarter. Evaluate the cash flows reported in the statement.

Suggested Solution

SLEEMAN BREWERIES LTD. Statement of Cash Flows For the Quarter Ended March 31 (in thousands)	
Cash Flows from Operating Activities	
Net Income	$ 1,610
Adjustments	
Amortization	1,955
Other non-cash expenses	257
Change in accounts receivable	3,305
Change in inventories	(4,398)
Change in prepaid expenses	664
Change in accounts payable	(121)
Net cash provided by (used for) operating activities	3,272
Cash Flows from Investing Activities	
Additions to property, plant, and equipment	(1,229)
Additions to intangibles	(100)
Net cash provided by (used for) investing activities	(1,329)
Cash Flows from Financing Activities	
Repayments of long-term debt	(2,476)
Proceeds from issuance of shares to employees	436
Net cash provided by (used for) financing activities	(2,040)
Increase (Decrease) in Cash and Cash Equivalents	$ (97)

Sleeman experienced a profit this quarter of $1,610, but its cash inflow from operating activities was twice that at $3,272, mainly because of the non-cash expenses, which totalled $2,212 (1,955 + 257). Management might want to look at why inventories have built up, since that puts a strain on cash, but, in this quarter, the decrease in receivables helped to ensure that Sleeman had enough cash to pay its accounts payable as they became due. Sleeman used its cash from operating activities to pay down $2,476 of its long-term debt and to buy $1,329 in productive long-term assets, actions which will likely pay off for Sleeman in the future.

DEMONSTRATION CASE B (DIRECT METHOD)

During the year ended December 31, 2006, Big Rock Brewery reported that its cash and cash equivalents had decreased from $5,722 in 2005 to $4,337 in 2006 (all amounts in thousands). The company also indicated the following:

a. Paid $14,361 to suppliers for inventory purchases.
b. Issued shares for $499 cash.
c. Paid $3,753 in cash for purchase of property, plant, and equipment.
d. Reported sales on account of $38,701. The company reported accounts receivable of $3,848 at the beginning of the year and $3,234 at the end.
e. Paid operating expenses totalling $14,152.
f. Cash payments for interest totalled $558.
g. Repaid debt, $470.
h. Paid $7,946 in dividends.
i. Collected $41 from the government for an overpayment of last year's taxes.

Required:

Based on this information, prepare the cash flow statement using the direct method. Evaluate the cash flows reported in the statement.

Suggested Solution

BIG ROCK BREWERY Statement of Cash Flows For the Year Ended December 31, 2006 (in thousands)	
Operating Activities	
Cash collected from customers ($38,701 + 3,848 − 3,234)	$39,315
Cash paid to suppliers	(14,361)
Cash paid for operating expenses	(14,152)
Cash paid for interest	(558)
Cash collected on income taxes	41
Net cash flow from operating activities	10,285
Investing Activities	
Additions to property, plant, and equipment	(3,753)
Net cash flow from (used for) investing activities	(3,753)
Financing Activities	
Share issuance	499
Debt repaid	(470)
Dividends paid	(7,946)
Net cash flow from (used for) financing activities	(7,917)
Increase (Decrease) in Cash and Cash Equivalents	(1,385)
Cash and cash equivalents, December 31, 2005	5,722
Cash and cash equivalents, December 31, 2006	$ 4,337

Big Rock had a good year. It was able to generate over $10 million in cash from operations. The other large inflow in 2006 was $.5 million received from the issue of new shares.[4] Big Rock used most of its cash inflows to make additions to its PPE ($3.8 million), pay down its debt ($.5 million) and pay dividends of $8 million. The net decrease in cash during 2006 was $1.4 million, which, when deducted from opening cash, still left Big Rock with over $4 million in cash going into 2007.

---

[4] Big Rock operates as an income trust. Income trusts call their shares units and call their dividends distributions. Here we use the more familiar terminology for simplicity.

CHAPTER SUMMARY

LO1   **Classify cash flow statement items as part of net cash flows from operating, investing, and financing activities. p. 523**

- The cash flow statement has three main sections: cash flows from operating activities, which are related to earning income from normal operations; cash flows from investing activities, which are related to the acquisition and sale of productive assets; and cash flows from financing activities, which are related to external financing of the enterprise.

- The net cash inflow or outflow for the period is the same amount as the increase or decrease in cash and cash equivalents for the period on the balance sheet. Cash equivalents are highly liquid investments with original maturities of less than three months.

LO2   **Report cash flows from operating activities. p. 528**

- Reporting cash flows from operating activities requires a conversion of the income statement numbers to net cash flow from operating activities. The conversion involves additions and subtractions for (1) non-cash expenses (such as amortization expense), and (2) changes in each of the individual current assets (other than cash and short-term investments) and current liabilities (other than short-term debt to financial institutions and current portion of long-term debt, which relate to financing), which reflect differences in the timing of accrual basis net income and cash flows.

- The indirect method for reporting cash flows from operating activities starts with net income and shows all the adjustments needed to convert this bottom-line number from an accrual basis to a cash basis. It shows this adjustment process on the face of the SCF.

- The direct method for reporting cash flows from operating activities adjusts each item on the income statement from an accrual basis to a cash basis. It reports all of the actual cash inflows and outflows from operating activities on the face of the SCF. The most common inflows are cash received from customers and dividends and interest on investments. The most common outflows are cash paid for purchases of services and goods for resale, salaries and wages, income taxes, and interest on liabilities.

LO3   **Report cash flows from investing activities. p. 537**

- Investing activities reported on the cash flow statement include cash payments to acquire fixed assets and short- and long-term investments and cash proceeds from the sale of fixed assets and short- and long-term investments.

LO4   **Report cash flows from financing activities. p. 538**

- Cash inflows from financing activities include cash proceeds from issuance of short- and long-term debt and company shares.

- Cash outflows include cash principal payments on short- and long-term debt, cash paid for the repurchase of the company's shares, and cash dividend payments.

- Cash payments associated with interest are a cash flow from operating activities.

LO5   **(Supplement A) Report cash flows from sales of property, plant, and equipment. p. 550**

- The cash inflow from the sale of PPE will be shown in the investing section of the SCF.

- Gains on sale must be deducted and losses must be added back in the operating section to adjust the income statement numbers to cash flow from operating activities.

LO6   **Interpret cash flows from operating, investing, and financing activities. p. 541**

- A healthy company will generate positive cash flows from operations, some of which will be used to pay for purchases of property, plant, and equipment. Any additional cash (called "free cash flow") can be used to further expand the business, used to pay down some of the company's debt, or returned to shareholders.

- A company is in trouble if it is unable to generate positive cash flows from operations in the long run because eventually creditors will stop lending to the company and shareholders will stop investing in it.

Calculate and interpret the capital-acquisitions ratio. p. 542   **LO7**

- The capital-acquisitions ratio (Cash Flow from Operating Activities ÷ Cash Paid for Property, Plant, and Equipment) reflects the portion of purchases of property, plant, and equipment financed from operating activities without the need for outside debt or equity financing or the sale of other investments or fixed assets.
- A high ratio indicates less need for outside financing when replacing current equipment and expanding in the future.

Calculate and interpret the cash-coverage ratio. p. 544   **LO8**

- The cash-coverage ratio [(Cash Flow from Operating Activities + Interest Paid + Income Taxes Paid) ÷ Interest Paid] indicates the amount of cash generated by the company for each dollar of interest paid.
- A ratio greater than 1 suggests a company is likely to make its interest payments, with a higher ratio indicating a higher likelihood.

Calculate and interpret the quality-of-income ratio. p. 544   **LO9**

- Quality-of-income ratio (Cash Flow from Operating Activities ÷ Net Income) measures the portion of income that was generated in cash.
- All other things being equal, a higher ratio also indicates a higher likelihood that revenues are being realized in cash and that expenses are associated with cash outflows.

FINANCIAL STATEMENT ANALYSIS TIPS

To determine a company's ability to finance purchases of property, plant, and equipment from operations, calculate the capital-acquisitions ratio:

$$\text{Capital-Acquisitions Ratio} = \frac{\text{Net Cash Flow from Operating Activities}}{\text{Cash Paid for Property, Plant, and Equipment}}$$

To determine whether a company has been able to pay the interest owed on debt, calculate the cash-coverage ratio:

$$\text{Cash-Coverage Ratio} = \frac{\text{Net Cash Flow from Operating Activities} + \text{Interest Paid} + \text{Income Taxes Paid}}{\text{Interest Paid}}$$

To determine the extent to which net income corresponds to actual operating cash flows, calculate the quality-of-income ratio:

$$\text{Quality-of-Income Ratio} = \frac{\text{Net Cash Flow from Operating Activities}}{\text{Net Income}}$$

KEY TERMS TO KNOW

Cash Equivalent p. 524

Cash Flows from Financing Activities p. 526

Cash Flows from Investing Activities p. 525

Cash Flows from Operating Activities (Cash Flows from Operations) p. 525

Direct Method p. 525

Indirect Method p. 525

SUPPLEMENT A: REPORTING SALES OF PROPERTY, PLANT, AND EQUIPMENT

Whenever a company sells a piece of property, plant, and equipment (PPE), it records three things: (1) a decrease in the PPE account for the book value of the asset sold, (2) an increase in the cash account for the cash received on disposal, and (3) a gain if the cash received is more than the book value of the asset sold (or a loss if the cash received is less than the book value of the asset sold). We can show this as:

$$\text{Cash received} = \text{Net book value} + \text{Gain on sale}$$

The only part of this transaction that qualifies for the SCF is the cash received on disposal (classified as an investing activity).

Okay, that seems straightforward, so why do we have a separate chapter supplement for this kind of transaction? Well, there is one complicating factor. As the above equation makes clear, the cash received includes the gain on sale, which is also included in the net income figure. To avoid double-counting, we have to make sure the gain is removed from the operating section of the SCF. This means that the list of adjustments (shown in Exhibit 12.5) needed to convert the income statement figures to cash flow from operating activities must include a deduction for any gains that have been included on the income statement. The flip side is also true. The list of adjustments must also include adding back any losses that have been included on the income statement, since cash received is equal to the net book value of the assets disposed of *less* the loss on sale. As we saw in the body of this chapter, these adjustments will be shown in the SCF if the indirect method is used. With the direct method, the gains and losses will be used as adjustments but will not appear on the SCF; this is similar to what happens with amortization expense. Let's look at one example.[5]

Assume that Magnotta sold a piece of its manufacturing equipment for $80,000. The equipment originally cost $100,000, and had $22,000 of accumulated amortization at the time of disposal. The journal entry to record the disposal was

dr	Cash (+A)	80,000	
dr	Accumulated Amortization (−xA, +A).	22,000	
	cr Property, Plant, and Equipment (−A)		100,000
	cr Gain on Disposal (+R, +SE).		2,000

Assets		=	Liabilities	+	Shareholders' Equity
Cash	+ 80,000				Gain on disposal (+R) + 2,000
Accumulated amortization (−xA)	+ 22,000				
Property, Plant, and Equipment	− 100,000				

The $80,000 inflow of cash is reported as an investing activity as shown in the bottom box of the partial SCF on the next page. In the top right-hand box, where we present the indirect method, because the $2,000 gain was included in net income, we must remove (subtract) it in the operating activities section of the statement. Thus, the disposal would show up in two parts of the SCF, if the indirect method is used. In the top left-hand box, where we present the direct method, the adjustment column removes the gain from the income statement figures, so that it does not appear at all in the operating section of the SCF.

A word of warning is warranted at this point. It is common for a company to report its property, plant, and equipment on its balance sheet net of accumulated amortization. Thus, any change in the asset account during the year can result from three things: purchases of new assets, disposals of old assets, and amortization of assets. Determining the cash effects of these changes requires a considerable amount of analysis, so don't forget to look for information about all three when you are tackling the problems at the end of this chapter.

---

[5] A second example with a loss on sale is shown in the Online Learning Centre.

OPERATING SECTION—DIRECT METHOD			
	Accrual Basis	*Adjustments*	*Cash Basis*
Net sales	. . . .	. . . .	. . . .
Cost of goods sold	. . . .	. . . .	. . . .
. . . .			
Gain on disposal	2,000	−2,000	0
. . . .	. . . .	. . . .	. . . .
Net income	. . . .		
Net cash provided by operating activities			. . . .

OR

OPERATING SECTION—INDIRECT METHOD	
Cash provided by operating activities	
Net income	$. . .
Adjustments to reconcile net income to net cash from operations:	
Amortization expense	. . .
Gain on disposal of property, plant, and equipment	(2,000)
. . .	. . .
Net cash provided by operating activities	. . .

INVESTING	
Cash provided by (used for) investing activities	
Additions to property, plant, and equipment	(. . .)
Cash received from sale of property, plant, and equipment	80,000
. . .	. . .
Net cash provided by investing activities	. . .

_____ **FOR YOUR PRACTICE**

QUESTIONS

1. Compare the purposes of the income statement, the balance sheet, and the statement of cash flows.

2. What information does the statement of cash flows report that is not reported on the other required financial statements?

3. What are cash equivalents? How are they reported on the statement of cash flows?

4. What are the major categories of business activities reported on the statement of cash flows? Define each of these activities.

5. What are the typical cash inflows from operating activities? What are the typical cash outflows from operating activities?

6. Why isn't net income equal to cash flows from operating activities?

7. Describe the types of items used to compute cash flows from operating activities under the two alternative methods of reporting.

8. On the statement of cash flows under the indirect method, amortization expense is added to net income to report cash flows from operating activities. Does amortization cause an inflow of cash?

9. Explain why cash outflows for purchases and salaries during the period are not specifically reported on a statement of cash flows prepared using the indirect method.

10. Explain why a $50,000 increase in inventory during the year must be included in computing cash flows from operating activities under both the direct and indirect methods.

11. What are the typical cash inflows from investing activities? What are the typical cash outflows from investing activities?

12. What are the typical cash inflows from financing activities? What are the typical cash outflows from financing activities?

13. What are non-cash investing and financing activities? Give one example. How are non-cash investing and financing activities reported on the statement of cash flows?

14. (Supplement A) How is the sale of equipment reported on the statement of cash flows using the indirect method?

MULTIPLE CHOICE

Select the one alternative that best answers the question or completes the sentence.

1. Where is the change in cash shown in the statement of cash flows?
   a. In the top part, before the operating activities section
   b. In one of the operating, investing, or financing activities sections
   c. In the bottom part, following the financing activities section
   d. None of the above

2. Which of the three sections of the statement of cash flows appears first when reading from top to bottom?
   a. Financing
   b. Investing
   c. Operating
   d. They can appear in any order.

3. Total cash inflow in the operating section of the statement of cash flows should include which of the following?
   a. Cash received from customers at the point of sale
   b. Cash collections from customer accounts receivable
   c. Cash received in advance of revenue recognition (unearned revenue)
   d. All of the above

4. If the balance in prepaid expenses increased during the year, what action should be taken on the statement of cash flows when following the indirect method, *and why?*
   a. The change in the account balance should be subtracted from net income, because the net increase in prepaid expenses did not impact net income but did reduce the cash balance.
   b. The change in the account balance should be added to net income, because the net increase in prepaid expenses did not impact net income but did increase the cash balance.
   c. The net change in prepaid expenses should be subtracted from net income, to reverse the income statement effect that had no impact on cash.
   d. The net change in prepaid expenses should be added to net income, to reverse the income statement effect that had no impact on cash.

5. Which of the following would not appear in the investing section of the statement of cash flows?
   a. Purchase of inventory
   b. Sale of short-term investments
   c. Purchase of land
   d. All of the above would appear in the investing section of the statement of cash flows.

6. Which of the following items would not appear in the financing section of the statement of cash flows?
   a. The issuance of the company's own shares
   b. The receipt of dividends

c.   The repayment of debt

d.   The payment of dividends

7. Which of the following is not added when computing cash flows from operations using the indirect method?

   a.   The net increase in accounts payable

   b.   The net decrease in accounts receivable

   c.   The net decrease in inventory

   d.   All of the above should be added.

8. Which of the following items does not appear in the operating section of a statement of cash flows using the indirect method?

   a.   Cash inflows from customers

   b.   Cash outflows for interest paid

   c.   Cash outflows for amortization

   d.   Cash inflows for interest received

9. The *total* change in cash as shown near the bottom of the statement of cash flows for the year should agree with which of the following?

   a.   The difference in retained earnings when reviewing the comparative balance sheet

   b.   Net income or net loss as found on the income statement

   c.   The difference in cash when reviewing the comparative balance sheet

   d.   None of the above

10. Which of the following is a ratio used to assess the extent to which operating cash flows are sufficient to cover replacement of property, plant, and equipment?

   a.   Free cash flow

   b.   Capital-acquisitions ratio

   c.   Cash-coverage ratio

   d.   Quality-of-income ratio

MINI-EXERCISES

M12-1 Identifying Companies from Cash Flow Patterns

LO1

Based on the cash flows shown, classify each of the following cases as a growing start-up company (S), a healthy established company (E), or an established company facing financial difficulties (F).

	Case A	Case B	Case C
Cash provided by (used for) operating activities	$(120,000)	$ 3,000	$80,000
Cash provided by (used for) investing activities	10,000	(70,000)	(40,000)
Cash provided by (used for) financing activities	75,000	75,000	(30,000)
Net change in cash	(35,000)	8,000	10,000
Cash position at beginning of year	40,000	2,000	30,000
Cash position at end of year	$ 5,000	$10,000	$40,000

M12-2 Matching Items Reported to Cash Flow Statement Categories (Indirect Method)

LO1

Humpty Dumpty Snack Foods was Canada's leader in snack foods before Frito-Lay's expansion. Some of the items included in its statement of cash flows, presented using the *indirect method,* are listed here. Indicate whether each item is disclosed in the operating activities (O), investing activities (I), or financing activities (F) section of the statement, or (NA) if the item does not appear on the statement.

_____ 1. Repayment of long-term debt
_____ 2. Purchase of property and equipment
_____ 3. Amortization expense
_____ 4. Accounts payable (increase)
_____ 5. Inventories (decrease)
_____ 6. Proceeds from share issuance

LO1   M12-3 Determining the Effects of Account Changes on Cash Flows from Operating Activities (Indirect Method)

Indicate whether each item would be added (+) or subtracted (−) in the computation of cash flow from operating activities using the indirect method.

_____ 1. Amortization expense
_____ 2. Inventories (increase)
_____ 3. Accounts payable (decrease)
_____ 4. Accounts receivable (decrease)
_____ 5. Accrued liabilities (increase)

LO1, LO2   M12-4 Matching Items Reported to Cash Flow Statement Categories (Direct Method)

Hassan Corporation reports the following items in its 2009 statement of cash flows, presented using the *direct method*. Indicate whether each item is disclosed in the operating activities (O), investing activities (I), or financing activities (F) section of the statement, or (NA) if the item does not appear on the statement.

_____ 1. Repayments of bank loan
_____ 2. Dividends paid
_____ 3. Proceeds from issuance of shares
_____ 4. Interest paid
_____ 5. Receipts from customers
_____ 6. Payment for equipment purchase

LO2   M12-5 Computing Cash Flows from Operating Activities (Indirect Method)

For each of the following independent cases, compute cash flows from operating activities. Assume the list below includes all balance sheet accounts related to operating activities.

	Case A	Case B	Case C
Net income	$ 25,000	$ 36,000	$ 2,000
Amortization expense	4,000	12,000	15,000
Accounts receivable increase (decrease)	10,000	(2,000)	20,000
Inventory increase (decrease)	(5,000)	5,000	(10,000)
Accounts payable increase (decrease)	(11,000)	7,000	12,000
Accrued liabilities increase (decrease)	6,000	(4,000)	(22,000)

LO2   M12-6 Computing Cash Flows from Operating Activities (Indirect Method)

For the following two independent cases, show the cash flows from operating activities section of the 2009 statement of cash flows using the indirect method.

	Case A		Case B	
	2009	**2008**	**2009**	**2008**
Sales revenue	$10,000	$9,000	$21,000	$18,000
Cost of goods sold	6,000	5,500	12,000	11,000
Gross profit	4,000	3,500	9,000	7,000
Amortization expense	1,000	1,000	2,000	1,500
Salaries expense	2,500	2,000	5,000	5,000
Net income	500	500	2,000	500
Accounts receivable	300	400	750	600
Inventories	600	500	790	800
Accounts payable	800	700	800	850
Salaries payable	1,000	1,200	200	250

M12-7 Computing Cash Flows from Operating Activities (Direct Method)   LO2

For each of the following independent cases, compute cash flows from operating activities. Assume the list below includes all items relevant to operating activities.

	Case A	*Case B*	*Case C*
Sales revenue	$75,000	$55,000	$95,000
Cost of goods sold	35,000	32,000	65,000
Amortization expense	10,000	2,000	10,000
Other operating expenses	5,000	13,000	8,000
Net income	25,000	8,000	12,000
Accounts receivable increase (decrease)	(1,000)	4,000	3,000
Inventory increase (decrease)	2,000	0	(4,000)
Accounts payable increase (decrease)	0	3,000	(2,000)
Accrued liabilities increase (decrease)	1,000	(1,000)	1,000

M12-8 Computing Cash Flows from Operating Activities (Direct Method)   LO2

Refer to the two cases presented in M12-6, and show the cash flow from operating activities section of the 2009 statement of cash flows using the direct method.

M12-9 Computing Cash Flows from Investing Activities   LO3

Based on the following information, compute cash flows from investing activities.

Cash collections from customers	$800
Purchase of used equipment	250
Amortization expense	100
Sale of short-term investments	300

M12-10 Computing Cash Flows from Financing Activities   LO4

Based on the following information, compute cash flows from financing activities.

Purchase of short-term investments	$ 250
Dividends paid	800
Interest paid	400
Additional short-term borrowing from bank	1,000

M12-11 Reporting Non-cash Investing and Financing Activities   LO3, LO4

Which of the following transactions would be considered non-cash investing and financing activities?

_____ 1. Purchase of equipment with short-term investments

_____ 2. Dividends paid in cash

_____ 3. Purchase of building with promissory note

_____ 4. Additional short-term borrowing from a bank

LO6

COACH'S
TIP

See the demonstration cases for
examples of evaluations of a statement
of cash flows.

M12-12 Interpreting Cash Flows from Operating, Investing, and Financing Activities

Quantum Dots, Inc., is a nanotechnology company that manufactures "quantum dots," which are tiny pieces of silicon consisting of 100 or more molecules. Quantum dots can be used to illuminate very small objects, enabling scientists to see the blood vessels beneath a mouse's skin ripple with each heartbeat, at the rate of 100 times per second. Evaluate this research-intensive company's cash flows, assuming the following information was reported in its statement of cash flows.

	Current Year	Previous Year
Cash Flows from Operating Activities		
Net cash provided by (used for) operating activities	$ (50,790)	$ (46,730)
Cash Flows from Investing Activities		
Purchases of research equipment	(250,770)	(480,145)
Proceeds from selling all short-term investments	35,000	–
Net cash provided by (used for) investing activities	(215,770)	(480,145)
Cash Flows from Financing Activities		
Additional long-term debt borrowed	100,000	200,000
Proceeds from share issue	140,000	200,000
Cash dividends paid	–	(10,000)
Net cash provided by (used for) financing activities	240,000	390,000
Net increase (decrease) in cash	(26,560)	(136,875)
Cash at beginning of period	29,025	165,900
Cash at end of period	$ 2,465	$ 29,025

LO7

M12-13 Calculating and Interpreting the Capital-Acquisitions Ratio

Airborne Kites Corporation reported the following information in its statement of cash flows:

	2009	2008	2007
Net cash flow from operating activities	$35,000	$32,000	$23,000
Interest paid	2,000	3,000	2,500
Income taxes paid	9,000	8,500	6,500
Purchases of property, plant, and equipment	31,818	22,857	20,325

Calculate the average capital-acquisitions ratio for the period covering 2007 to 2009, and the capital-acquisitions ratio for *each* year during this period. What does this analysis tell you about the company's need for using external financing to replace property, plant, and equipment?

LO8

M12-14 Calculating and Interpreting the Cash-Coverage Ratio

Using the information in M12-13, calculate the cash-coverage ratio for Airborne Kites for each of the three years. What do these ratios tell you about the company's ability to pay its interest costs?

LO9

M12-15 Calculating and Interpreting the Quality-of-Income Ratio

Sea Leather Products, Inc., reported net income of $80,000, amortization expense of $3,000, and cash flow from operations of $60,000. Compute the quality-of-income ratio. What does the ratio tell you about the company's accrual of revenues and/or deferral of expenses?

EXERCISES

LO1, LO2

E12-1 Matching Items Reported with Cash Flow Statement Categories (Indirect Method)

Adidas-Salomon, based in Germany, bought Reebok in 2005 and is now the world's second-largest sporting-goods company, behind Nike. Some of the items included in Adidas' recent statement of cash flows, presented using the *indirect method,* are listed here.

Indicate whether each item is disclosed in the operating activities (O), investing activities (I), or financing activities (F) section of the statement, or (NA) if the item does not appear on the statement.

_____ 1. Amortization expense
_____ 2. Purchase of property, plant, and equipment
_____ 3. Increase (decrease) in short-term borrowing
_____ 4. (Increase) decrease in other current assets
_____ 5. Disposal of property, plant, and equipment
_____ 6. Reductions in long-term borrowing
_____ 7. Issuance of bonds payable
_____ 8. (Increase) decrease in inventories
_____ 9. Net income
_____ 10. Dividends paid

E12-2 Comparing the Direct and Indirect Methods   LO2

To compare statements of cash flows reporting under the direct and indirect methods, enter check marks to indicate which line-items are reported on the statement of cash flows with each method.

Cash Flows (and Related Changes)	Statement of Cash Flows Method	
	Direct	**Indirect**
1. Receipts from customers		
2. Accounts receivable increase or decrease		
3. Payments to suppliers		
4. Inventory increase or decrease		
5. Accounts payable increase or decrease		
6. Payments to employees		
7. Wages payable, increase or decrease		
8. Amortization expense		
9. Net income		
10. Cash flows from operating activities		
11. Cash flows from investing activities		
12. Cash flows from financing activities		
13. Net increase or decrease in cash during the period		

E12-3 Reporting Cash Flows from Operating Activities (Indirect Method)   LO2

The following information pertains to Day Company:

Sales		$80,000
Expenses:		
Cost of goods sold	$50,000	
Amortization expense	6,000	
Salaries expense	12,000	68,000
Net income		$12,000
Accounts receivable increase	$ 5,000	
Merchandise inventory decrease	8,000	
Salaries payable increase	500	

Required:

Present the operating activities section of the statement of cash flows for Day Company using the indirect method.

E12-4 Reporting and Interpreting Cash Flows from Operating Activities from an   LO2, LO6
Analyst's Perspective (Indirect Method)

Kane Company completed its income statement and balance sheet for 2009 and provided the following information:

Service revenue		$50,000
Expenses:		
Salaries	$42,000	
Amortization	7,300	
Utilities	7,000	
Other expenses	1,700	58,000
Net loss		($ 8,000)
Decrease in accounts receivable	$12,000	
Bought a small service machine.	5,000	
Increase in salaries payable	9,000	
Decrease in other accrued liabilities	4,000	

Required:

1. Present the operating activities section of the statement of cash flows for Kane Company using the indirect method.

2. What were the major reasons that Kane was able to report a net loss but positive cash flow from operations?

3. Of the potential causes of differences between cash flow from operations and net income, which are the most important to financial analysts?

LO2, LO6   **E12-5 Reporting and Interpreting Cash Flows from Operating Activities, from an Analyst's Perspective (Indirect Method)**

Sizzler International, Inc., operates 700 family restaurants around the world. The company's annual report contained the following information (in thousands):

Operating Activities	
Net loss	$ (9,482)
Amortization expense	33,305
Increase in receivables	170
Decrease in inventories	643
Increase in prepaid expenses	664
Decrease in accounts payable	2,282
Decrease in accrued liabilities	719
Increase in income taxes payable	1,861
Reduction of long-term debt	12,691
Additions to equipment	29,073

Required:

1. Based on this information, compute cash flow from operating activities using the indirect method.

2. What were the major reasons that Sizzler was able to report a net loss but positive cash flow from operations?

3. Of the potential causes of differences between cash flow from operations and net income, which are the most important to financial analysts?

LO2   **E12-6 Inferring Balance Sheet Changes from the Cash Flow Statement (Indirect Method)**

CHC Helicopter, based in British Columbia, operates more than 300 helicopters worldwide, and is the largest provider of helicopter services to the global offshore oil and gas industry. Its statement of cash flows for a recent quarter reported the following information (in thousands):

Operating Activities	
Net income	$18,681
Amortization expense	8,617
Cash effect of changes in	
Accounts receivable	(16,863)
Inventories	12,622
Other current assets	(2,672)
Accounts payable	(45,657)
Other	15,454
Net cash used by operations	$ (9,818)

Required:

Based on the information reported in the operating activities section of the statement of cash flows for CHC, determine whether the following accounts increased or decreased during the period: Accounts Receivable, Inventories, Other Current Assets, and Accounts Payable.

E12-7 Inferring Balance Sheet Changes from the Cash Flow Statement (Indirect Method)   LO2

A recent statement of cash flows for Loblaw Companies Limited, Canada's largest grocery chain, contained the following information (in thousands):

Operating Activities (in millions)	
Net income	$968
Amortization expense	473
Changes in assets and liabilities	
Accounts receivable	(77)
Inventories	(75)
Other current assets	(7)
Accounts payable	116
Income taxes payable	(31)
Other adjustments	73
Net cash provided by operations	$1,440

Required:

For each of the asset and liability accounts listed in the operating activities section of the statement of cash flows, determine whether the account balances increased or decreased during the period.

E12-8 Reporting and Interpreting Cash Flows from Operating Activities, from an Analyst's Perspective (Direct Method)   LO2, LO6

Refer to the information for Kane Company in E12-4.

Required:

1. Present the operating activities section of the statement of cash flows for Kane Company, using the direct method. Assume that other accrued liabilities relate to other expenses on the income statement.
2. What were the major reasons that Kane was able to report a net loss but positive cash flow from operations?
3. Of the potential causes of differences between cash flow from operations and net income, which are the most important to financial analysts?

E12-9 Reporting and Interpreting Cash Flows from Operating Activities, from an Analyst's Perspective (Direct Method)   LO2, LO6

Refer back to the information given for E12-5, plus the following summarized income statement for Sizzler International, Inc.:

Revenues	$136,500
Cost of sales	45,500
Gross margin	91,000
Salary expense	56,835
Amortization expense	33,305
Other expenses	7,781
Net loss before income taxes	(6,921)
Income tax expense	2,561
Net loss	$ (9,482)

Required:

1. Based on this information, compute cash flow from operating activities using the direct method. Assume that prepaid expenses and accrued liabilities relate to other expenses.
2. What were the major reasons that Sizzler was able to report a net loss but positive cash flow from operations?

3. Of the potential causes of differences between cash flow from operations and net income, which are the most important to financial analysts?

LO2, LO9   **E12-10   Analyzing Cash Flows from Operating Activities (Indirect Method), and Calculating and Interpreting the Quality-of-Income Ratio**

A recent annual report for PepsiCo contained the following information for the period (in millions):

Net income	$4,078
Amortization expense	1,308
Increase in accounts receivable	272
Increase in inventory	132
Increase in prepaid expense	56
Increase in accounts payable	188
Increase in taxes payable	609
Decrease in other liabilities related to operations	791
Cash dividends paid	1,642

Required:

1. Compute cash flows from operating activities for PepsiCo, using the indirect method.
2. Compute the quality-of-income ratio.
3. What was the main reason that PepsiCo's quality-of-income ratio did not equal 1.0?

LO2   **E12-11   Calculating and Understanding Operating Cash Flows Relating to Inventory Purchases (Indirect Method)**

The following information was reported by three companies. When completing the requirements, assume that any and all purchases on account are for inventory.

	Aztec Corporation	Bikes Unlimited	Campus Cycles
Cost of goods sold	$175	$175	$350
Inventory purchases from suppliers made using cash	200	0	200
Inventory purchases from suppliers made on account	0	200	200
Cash payments to suppliers on account	0	160	160
Beginning inventory	100	100	200
Ending inventory	125	125	250
Beginning accounts payable	0	80	80
Ending accounts payable	0	120	120

Required:

1. What amount did each company deduct on the income statement related to inventory?
2. What total amount did each company pay out in cash during the period related to inventory purchased with cash and on account?
3. By what amount do your answers in 1 and 2 differ for each company?
4. By what amount did each company's inventory increase (decrease)? By what amount did each company's accounts payable increase (decrease)?
5. Using the indirect method of presentation, what amount(s) must each company add (deduct) from net income to convert from accrual to cash basis?
6. Describe any similarities between your answers to requirements 3 and 5. Are these answers the same? Why or why not?

LO3, LO4   **E12-12   Reporting Cash Flows from Investing and Financing Activities**

Rowe Furniture Corporation is a manufacturer of furniture. In a recent quarter, it reported the following activities:

Net income	$ 4,135
Purchase of property, plant, and equipment	871
Borrowings under line of credit (bank)	1,417
Proceeds from issuance of shares	11
Cash received from customers	29,164
Payments to reduce long-term debt	46
Proceeds from sale of short-term investments	134
Proceeds from sale of property and equipment	6,594
Dividends paid	277
Interest paid	90

Required:

Based on this information, present the cash flows from investing and financing activities sections of the cash flow statement.

E12-13 Reporting and Interpreting Cash Flows from Investing and Financing Activities with Discussion of Management Strategy   LO3–LO6

Gibraltar Corporation is a manufacturer of auto parts, based in Oshawa, Ontario. In a prior year, it reported the following activities:

Net income	$ 5,213
Purchase of property, plant, and equipment	10,468
Payments of notes payable (bank)	8,598
Net proceeds of share issuance	26,061
Amortization expense	3,399
Long-term debt reduction	17,832
Proceeds from sale of short-term investments	131
Proceeds from sale of property, plant, and equipment	1,817
Proceeds from long-term debt borrowed	10,242
Decrease in accounts receivable	1,137
Proceeds from notes payable (bank)	3,848

Required:

1. Based on this information, present the cash flows from investing and financing activities sections of the cash flow statement.
2. Referring to your response to requirement 1, comment on what you think Gibraltar's management plan was for the use of the cash generated by the share issuance.

E12-14 Analyzing and Interpreting the Capital-Acquisitions Ratio   LO7

A recent annual report for Sports-4-You Corporation contained the following data for the three most recent years (in thousands):

	2009	2008	2007
Cash flows from operating activities	$ 821	$ 1,460	$ 619
Cash flows from investing activities	(1,404)	(1,315)	(862)
Cash flows from financing activities	42,960	775	360

Assume that all investing activities involved acquisition of new plant and equipment.

Required:

1. Compute the capital-acquisitions ratio for the three-year period in total.
2. What portion of Sports-4-You investing activities was financed from cash flows from operating activities? What portion was financed from external sources or pre-existing cash balances during the three-year period?
3. What do you think is the likely explanation for the dramatic increase in cash flow from financing activities during the period?

E12-15 Calculating and Interpreting the Capital-Acquisitions Ratio   LO7

AMC Theatres® is one of the world's largest theatre chains. The following information was extracted from a recent set of financial statements.

	Year 3	Year 2	Year 1
Net income (loss)	(10,714)	(20,302)	(11,468)
Net cash provided by operating activities	183,278	128,747	101,091
Purchase of property and equipment	(110,823)	(107,984)	(106,501)
Cash paid for interest	78,479	78,677	59,824
Cash paid (refunded) for income taxes	3,880	(9,757)	(3,579)

Required:

1. Calculate the average-capital-acquisitions ratio for the three-year period.
2. Interpret the results of your calculations in requirement 1. What do they suggest about the company's need for external financing to acquire property and equipment?

LO8   **E12-16 Calculating and Interpreting the Cash-Coverage Ratio**

Refer to the information in E12-15.

Required:

1. Calculate the cash-coverage ratio for each year.
2. Interpret the results of your calculations in requirement 1. What do they suggest about the company's ability to pay interest on its debt financing?

LO9   **E12-17 Calculating and Interpreting the Quality-of-Income Ratio**

Refer to the information in E12-15.

Required:

1. Calculate the quality-of-income ratio for each year.
2. Interpret the results of your calculations in requirement 1. Given what you know about the movie theatre business from your own personal observations, provide one reason that could explain the sizeable difference between net income (loss) and net cash provided by operating activities.

LO5   **E12-18 (Supplement A) Determining Cash Flows from the Sale of Property**

Sobeys has about 1,300 grocery stores across Canada, operating under the Sobeys, IGA, and Price Chopper banners. In a recent year, the company sold property for $80.1 million cash and recorded a gain on sale of $14.6 million.

Required:

For the property sold by Sobeys, show how these amounts would be reported on its statement of cash flows, using the following format (which assumes the indirect method):

Cash flows from operating activities
Gain on sale of property
Cash flows from investing activities
Proceeds from disposition of property

LO5   **E12-19 (Supplement A) Determining Cash Flows from the Sale of Equipment**

During a recent period, English Company sold some excess equipment at a loss. The following information was collected from the company's accounting records:

From the Income Statement	
Amortization expense	$ 700
Loss on sale of equipment	3,000
From the Balance Sheet	
Beginning equipment	12,500
Ending equipment	8,000
Beginning accumulated amortization	2,000
Ending accumulated amortization	2,400

No new equipment was bought during the period.

Required:

For the equipment that was sold, determine its original cost, its accumulated amortization, and the cash received from the sale.

COACHED PROBLEMS

CP12-1 Determining Cash Flow Statement Effects of Transactions

Maple Leaf Foods is best known for its Maple Leaf, Hygrade, and Shopsy's brand foods. It also owns Canada Bread. For each of the following typical transactions for Maple Leaf, indicate whether operating (O), investing (I), or financing activities (F) are affected and whether the effect is a cash inflow (+) or outflow (−), or (NE) if the transaction has no effect on cash.

LO1

____ 1.   Recorded and paid income taxes to the federal government.

____ 2.   Repurchased shares for cash.

____ 3.   Prepaid rent for the following period.

____ 4.   Recorded an adjusting entry for expiration of a prepaid expense.

____ 5.   Paid cash to purchase new equipment.

____ 6.   Issued long-term debt for cash.

____ 7.   Collected payments on account from customers.

____ 8.   Recorded and paid salaries to employees.

____ 9.   Purchased new equipment by signing a promissory note.

COACH'S TIP

Think about the journal entry recorded for the transaction. The transaction affects net cash flows if and only if the account *Cash* is affected.

CP12-2 Computing Cash Flows from Operating Activities (Indirect Method)

Beta Company's accountants just completed the 2009 income statement and balance sheet for the year and have provided the following information (in thousands):

LO2

Income Statement

Sales revenue	$ 20,600
Expenses:	
Cost of goods sold	9,000
Amortization expense	2,000
Salaries expense	5,000
Rent expense	2,500
Insurance expense	800
Interest expense	600
Utilities expense	500
Net income	$ 200

Selected Balance Sheet Accounts

	2009	2008
Merchandise inventory	$ 82	$ 60
Accounts receivable	380	450
Accounts payable	240	210
Salaries payable	29	20
Utilities payable	20	60
Prepaid rent	2	7
Prepaid insurance	14	5

COACH'S TIP

Prepaid rent decreased in 2009 because the amount of rent expense taken out of prepaid rent was greater than the amount paid for rent during 2009. Under the indirect method, you need to add back the amount by which prepaid rent decreased.

Required:

Prepare the cash flows from operating activities section of the 2009 statement of cash flows using the indirect method.

CP12-3 Computing Cash Flows from Operating Activities (Direct Method)

Refer to the information in CP12-2.

LO2

COACH'S TIP

In CP12-3, convert the cost of goods sold to cash paid to suppliers by adding the increase in inventory and subtracting the increase in accounts payable.

Required:

Prepare the cash flows from operating activities section of the 2009 statement of cash flow using the direct method.

CP12-4 Preparing a Statement of Cash Flows (Indirect Method)

Hunter Company, a young winery in southern Ontario, is developing its annual financial statements at December 31, 2009. The statements are complete except for the statement of cash flows. The completed comparative balance sheets and income statement are summarized:

	2009	2008
Balance sheet at December 31		
Cash	$ 44,000	$ 18,000
Accounts receivable	27,000	29,000
Merchandise inventory	30,000	36,000
Property and equipment	111,000	102,000
Less: Accumulated amortization	(36,000)	(30,000)
	$176,000	$155,000
Accounts payable	$ 25,000	$ 22,000
Wages payable	800	1,000
Note payable, long-term	38,000	48,000
Contributed capital	80,000	60,000
Retained earnings	32,200	24,000
	$176,000	$155,000
Income statement for 2009		
Sales	$100,000	
Cost of goods sold	61,000	
Other expenses	27,000	
Net income	$ 12,000	

Additional Data:

a.   Bought equipment for cash, $9,000.
b.   Paid $10,000 on the long-term note payable.
c.   Issued new shares for $20,000 cash.
d.   Declared and paid a $3,800 cash dividend.
e.   Other expenses included amortization, $6,000; wages, $10,000; taxes, $3,000; other, $8,000.
f.   Accounts payable includes only inventory purchases made on credit. Because there are no liability accounts relating to taxes or other expenses, assume that these expenses were fully paid in cash.

Required:

1.   Prepare the statement of cash flows for the year ended December 31, 2009, using the indirect method.
2.   Use the statement of cash flows to evaluate Hunter's cash flows.
3.   Calculate Hunter's capital-acquisition and quality-of-income ratios. Compare Hunter's ratios to Magnotta's most recent ratios in the text.

GROUP A PROBLEMS

PA12-1 Determining Cash Flow Statement Effects of Transactions

Leon's Furniture Limited is an Ontario-based furniture chain. For each of the following typical transactions, indicate whether Leon's would designate these as operating (O), investing (I), or financing activities (F), and whether the effect is a cash inflow (+) or outflow (–), or (NE) if the transaction has no effect on cash.

____ 1.   Paid cash to purchase new equipment.
____ 2.   Declared and paid cash dividends to shareholders.
____ 3.   Collected payments on account from customers.
____ 4.   Recorded an adjusting entry to record accrued salaries expense.
____ 5.   Recorded and paid interest on debt to creditors.
____ 6.   Repaid principal on loan from bank.
____ 7.   Prepaid rent for the following period.
____ 8.   Bought used equipment for cash.
____ 9.   Made payment to suppliers on account.

COACH'S TIP

When evaluating the statement of cash flows in requirement 2, consider (a) are operating cash flows positive, (b) how much has the company spent on property and equipment, and (c) has the company had to take out new loans, issue more shares, or use up its cash, or has it been able to build up cash, pay down debt, or pay cash dividends? The demonstration cases provide good examples to follow.

PA12-2 Computing Cash Flows from Operating Activities (Indirect Method)

LO2

Gamma Company's accountants just completed the 2009 income statement and balance sheet for the year and have provided the following information (in thousands):

Income Statement

Sales revenue	$48,600
Expenses:	
Cost of goods sold	21,000
Amortization expense	6,000
Salaries expense	9,000
Rent expense	4,500
Insurance expense	1,900
Interest expense	1,800
Utilities expense	1,400
Net income	$ 3,000

Selected Balance Sheet Accounts

	2009	2008
Merchandise inventory	$ 99	$ 77
Accounts receivable	280	290
Accounts payable	220	230
Salaries payable	44	35
Utilities payable	11	8
Prepaid rent	11	9
Prepaid insurance	13	14

Required:

Prepare the cash flows from operating activities section of the 2009 statement of cash flows, using the indirect method.

PA12-3 Computing Cash Flows from Operating Activities (Direct Method)

LO2

Refer to the information in PA12-2.

Required:

Prepare the cash flows from operating activities section of the 2009 statement of cash flows, using the direct method.

PA12-4 Preparing a Statement of Cash Flows (Indirect Method)

LO2–LO4, LO6, LO7, LO9

XS Supply Company is developing its annual financial statements at December 31, 2009. The statements are complete except for the statement of cash flows. The completed comparative balance sheets and income statement are summarized here:

	2009	2008
Balance sheet at December 31		
Cash	$ 34,000	$ 29,000
Accounts receivable	35,000	28,000
Merchandise inventory	41,000	38,000
Property and equipment	121,000	100,000
Less: Accumulated amortization	(30,000)	(25,000)
	$201,000	$170,000
Accounts payable	$ 36,000	$ 27,000
Wages payable	1,200	1,400
Note payable, long-term	38,000	44,000
Contributed capital	88,600	72,600
Retained earnings	37,200	25,000
	$201,000	$170,000

Income statement for 2009

Sales	$120,000
Cost of goods sold	70,000
Other expenses	37,800
Net income	$ 12,200

Additional Data:

a. Bought equipment for cash, $21,000.
b. Paid $6,000 on the long-term note payable.
c. Issued new shares for $16,000 cash.
d. No dividends were declared or paid.
e. Other expenses included amortization, $5,000; wages, $20,000; taxes, $6,000; other, $6,800.
f. Accounts payable includes only inventory purchases made on credit. Because there are no liability accounts relating to taxes or other expenses, assume that these expenses were fully paid in cash.

Required:

1. Prepare the statement of cash flows for the year ended December 31, 2009, using the indirect method.
2. Use the statement of cash flows to evaluate XS Supply's cash flows.
3. Calculate XS Supply's capital-acquisition and quality-of-income ratios. Compare these ratios to Magnotta's most recent ratios in the text.

LO2 **PA12-5 Computing Cash Flows from Operating Activities (Direct Method)**
Refer to the information in PA12-4.

Required:

Prepare the cash flow from operating activities section of the 2009 statement of cash flows, using the direct method.

LO2–LO4, LO6, LO7, LO9 **PA12-6 Preparing a Statement of Cash Flows (Indirect Method)**
The following abbreviated balance sheets are for Mushrooms Ltd.

	2009	2008
Cash	$ 80,000	$ 70,000
Accounts receivable	120,000	140,000
Inventories	320,000	280,000
Property and equipment	575,000	520,000
Less: Accumulated amortization	(135,000)	(100,000)
Total Assets	$960,000	$910,000
Accounts payable	$ 90,000	$ 80,000
Salaries payable	20,000	15,000
Notes payable	350,000	400,000
Common shares	200,000	150,000
Retained earnings	300,000	265,000
Total Liabilities and Shareholders' Equity	$960,000	$910,000

Additional information: Mushrooms paid $12,000 cash dividends during the year.

Required:

1. Prepare the statement of cash flows for the year ended December 31, 2009, using the indirect method.
2. Use the statement of cash flows to evaluate Mushrooms Ltd.'s cash flows.
3. Calculate Mushrooms Ltd.'s capital acquisition and quality-of-income ratios. Compare these ratios to Magnotta's most recent ratios in the text.

PA12-7 Preparing a Statement of Cash Flows (Direct Method)

LO2

Refer to the information in PA12-6. Below is the income statement for Mushrooms Ltd. for the year ended December 31, 2009.

Sales	$450,000
Cost of goods sold	240,000
Supplies expense	15,000
Amortization expense	35,000
Wages and salaries expense	68,000
Interest expense	24,000
Income tax expense	21,000
Net income	$ 47,000

Required:

Prepare the operating section of the statement of cash flows, using the direct method, for the year ending December 31, 2009.

PA12-8 Preparing a Statement of Cash Flows (Indirect Method)

LO2–LO4, LO6, LO7, LO9

The amounts reported on the balance sheets (in thousands of dollars) are given below for Turcotte Brick Corporation.

	November 30	
	2010	**2009**
Cash	$ 35	$ 63
Accounts receivable	59	44
Inventory	120	107
Prepaid Insurance	27	33
Property, plant, and equipment	281	248
Accumulated amortization	(92)	(72)
Patent	9	12
	$439	$435
Accounts payable	$ 55	$ 52
Dividends payable	15	0
Interest payable	4	8
Income taxes payable	18	10
Long-term notes payable	92	100
Mortgage payable	48	57
Common shares	69	64
Retained earnings	138	144
	$439	$435

Below is Turcotte's Statement of Income and Retained Earnings for the year ended November 30, 2010 (in thousands of dollars):

Sales revenue		$925
Cost of goods sold	740	
Selling expenses	51	
Administrative expenses	85	
Interest expense	12	
Income taxes	18	906
Net income		19
Retained Earnings, beginning balance		144
Dividends declared		(25)
Retained Earnings, ending balance		$138

Additional Data:

a. There were no disposals of property, plant, and equipment or patents during the year.
b. Common shares were issued in exchange for some equipment during the year. No other shares were issued.
c. All amortization expense is included in administrative expenses.

Required:

1. Prepare the statement of cash flows for the year ended November 30, 2010, using the indirect method.
2. Use the statement of cash flows to evaluate Turcotte's cash flows.
3. Calculate Turcotte's capital-acquisition and quality-of-income ratios. Compare these ratios to Magnotta's most recent ratios in the text.

LO2   ### PA12-9 Preparing a Statement of Cash Flows (Direct Method)

Refer to the information in PA12-8.

Required:

Prepare the cash flow from operating activities section of the 2010 statement of cash flows, using the direct method.

GROUP B PROBLEMS

LO1   ### PB12-1 Determining Cash Flow Statement Effects of Transactions

Fantatech Inc. designs, develops, and produces high-tech entertainment products, including VirtuaSports, that allow novice players to experience hazardous and difficult real-life sports in virtual reality. The company also produces a 4-D theatre system that combines 3-D visual effects with special effects such as vibrating chairs, simulated drops, and scented air blasts. For each of the following transactions listed in a recent annual report, indicate whether operating (O), investing (I), or financing activities (F) are affected, and whether the effect is a cash inflow (+) or outflow (−), or (NE) if the transaction has no effect on cash.

_____ 1. Recorded and paid interest to debt holders.
_____ 2. Issued shares for cash.
_____ 3. Received deposits from customers for products to be delivered the following period.
_____ 4. Principal repayments on short-term loan.
_____ 5. Paid cash to purchase new equipment.
_____ 6. Received proceeds from short-term loan.
_____ 7. Collected payments on account from customers.
_____ 8. Recorded and paid salaries to employees.
_____ 9. Paid cash for building construction.

LO2   ### PB12-2 Computing Cash Flows from Operating Activities (Indirect Method)

Alpha Company's accountants just completed the 2009 income statement and balance sheet for the year and have provided the following information (in thousands):

Income Statement	
Sales revenue	$78,000
Expenses:	
Cost of goods sold	36,000
Amortization expense	16,000
Salaries expense	10,000
Rent expense	2,500
Insurance expense	1,300
Interest expense	1,200
Utilities expense	1,000
Net income	$10,000

Selected Balance Sheet Accounts

	2009	2008
Merchandise inventory	$ 43	$ 49
Accounts receivable	180	150
Accounts payable	120	130
Salaries payable	45	30
Utilities payable	10	0
Prepaid rent	5	10
Prepaid insurance	7	9

Required:

Prepare the cash flows from operating activities section of the 2009 statement of cash flows, using the indirect method.

PB12-3 Computing Cash Flows from Operating Activities (Direct Method)   LO2

Refer to the information in PB12-2.

Required:

Prepare the cash flows from operating activities section of the 2009 statement of cash flows, using the direct method.

PB12-4 Preparing a Statement of Cash Flows (Indirect Method)   LO2–LO4, LO6, LO7, LO9

Audio City, Inc., is developing its annual financial statements at December 31, 2009. The statements are complete except for the statement of cash flows. The completed comparative balance sheets and income statement are summarized here:

	2009	2008
Balance sheet at December 31		
Cash	$ 68,000	$ 65,000
Accounts receivable	15,000	20,000
Merchandise inventory	22,000	20,000
Property and equipment	210,000	150,000
Less: Accumulated amortization	(60,000)	(45,000)
Total Assets	$255,000	$210,000
Accounts payable	$ 8,000	$ 19,000
Wages payable	2,000	1,000
Note payable, long-term	60,000	75,000
Contributed capital	100,000	70,000
Retained earnings	85,000	45,000
Total Liabilities and Shareholders' Equity	$255,000	$210,000
Income statement for 2009		
Sales	$190,000	
Cost of goods sold	90,000	
Other expenses	60,000	
Net income	$ 40,000	

Additional Data:

a. Bought equipment for cash, $60,000.
b. Paid $15,000 on the long-term note payable.
c. Issued new shares for $30,000 cash.
d. No dividends were declared or paid.
e. Other expenses included amortization, $15,000; wages, $20,000; taxes, $25,000.
f. Accounts payable includes only inventory purchases made on credit. Because a liability relating to taxes does not exist, assume that they were fully paid in cash.

Required:

1. Prepare the statement of cash flows for the year ended December 31, 2009, using the indirect method.
2. Use the statement of cash flows to evaluate Audio's cash flows.
3. Calculate Audio's capital-acquisition and quality-of-income ratios. Compare these ratios with Magnotta's most recent ratios in the text.

LO2–LO4, LO6, LO7, LO9   **PB12-5   Computing Cash Flows from Operating Activities (Direct Method)**
Refer to the information in PB12-4.

Required:

Prepare the cash flow from operating activities section of the 2009 statement of cash flows, using the direct method.

LO2   **PB12-6   Preparing a Statement of Cash Flows (Indirect Method)**
The following abbreviated balance sheets are for BioTech Limited.

	2009	2008
Cash	$ 34,000	$ —
Accounts receivable	18,000	19,000
Inventories	25,000	20,000
Long-term investment	—	3,000
Property, plant, and equipment	93,000	60,000
Less: Accumulated amortization	(14,000)	(10,000)
Total Assets	$156,000	$92,000
Bank overdraft	$ —	$ 5,000
Accounts payable	12,000	6,000
Notes payable	40,000	23,000
Common shares	80,000	50,000
Retained earnings	24,000	8,000
Total Liabilities and Shareholders' Equity	$156,000	$92,000

Additional Data:

Sold the long-term investment at cost during the year.
Net income was $52,000 during the year.

Required:

1. Prepare the statement of cash flows for the year ended December 31, 2009, using the indirect method.
2. Use the statement of cash flows to evaluate Bio Tech's cash flows.
3. Calculate Bio-Tech's capital acquisition and quality-of-income ratios. Compare these ratios with Magnotta's most recent ratios in the text.

LO2   **PB12-7   Preparing a Statement of Cash Flows (Direct Method)**
Refer to the information in PA12-6. Below is the income statement for BioTech Limited for the year ended December 31, 2009.

Sales	$300,000
Cost of goods sold	180,000
Amortization expense	4,000
Other expenses	64,000
Net income	$52,000

Required:

Prepare the operating section of the statement of cash flows, using the direct method, for the year ending December 31, 2009.

PB12-8 (Supplement A) Preparing a Statement of Cash Flows (Indirect Method)   LO2–LO5, LO7, LO9

The following information is available for Buffalo Ltd. for the year ended 2010.

Buffalo Limited
Balance Sheet

	December 31	
	2010	**2009**
Cash	$ 10,000	$ 40,000
Accounts receivable	440,000	360,000
Marketable securities	380,000	460,000
Inventory	1,462,000	1,264,000
Land	660,000	820,000
Building, net	1,140,000	1,480,000
Machinery, net	1,722,000	1,326,000
Goodwill	220,000	220,000
Total assets	$6,034,000	$5,970,000
Current liabilities	$ 512,000	$ 662,000
Bonds payable	2,000,000	2,000,000
Preferred shares	2,096,000	1,686,000
Common shares	1,130,000	1,000,000
Retained Earnings	296,000	622,000
Total Liabilities and Shareholders' Equity	$6,034,000	$5,970,000

Buffalo Limited
Income Statement
For the Year Ended 31 December 2010

Sales	$ 3,368,000
Cost of sales	(2,206,000)
Gross profit	1,162,000
Amortization, building	220,000
Amortization, machinery	150,000
Interest	230,000
Other expenses	802,000
Gain on sale of land	(44,000)
Loss on sale of machinery	54,000
	1,412,000
Net income (loss) before income tax	(250,000)
Income tax	108,000
Net income (loss)	$ (142,000)

Additional Information:

a.   The building account is comprised of:

	December 31	
	2010	**2009**
Building, gross	2,080,000	2,240,000
Accumulated amortization	(940,000)	(760,000)

b. The machinery account is comprised of:

	December 31	
	2010	**2009**
Machinery, gross	2,160,000	1,750,000
Accumulated amortization	(438,000)	(424,000)

c. Marketable securities were sold during the year at their carrying value.

d. A partially amortized building was sold for an amount equal to its net book value.

e. Cash of $80,000 was received on the sale of machinery.

f. Preferred shares were issued for cash in March 2010.

g. Dividends of $100,000 were paid on the preferred shares.

h. In September 2010, 25,000 common shares were purchased and retired for $110,000, their original price.

i. In November 2010, 65,000 common shares were issued in exchange for machinery.

j. Because of its loss, the company received a refund of taxes paid in prior years of $108,000.

Required:

1. Prepare the statement of cash flows for the year ended December 31, 2009, using the indirect method.

2. Calculate Buffalo's capital acquisition and quality-of-income ratios. Compare these ratios to Magnotta's most recent ratios in the text.

LO2   **PB12-9 (Supplement A) Preparing a Statement of Cash Flows (Direct Method)**
Refer to the information in PB12-8.

Required:

Prepare the cash flow from operating activities section of the 2010 statement of cash flows, using the direct method.

SKILLS DEVELOPMENT CASES

LO1, LO8   ### S12-1 Finding Financial Information

Refer to the financial statements of High Liner in Appendix A at the end of this book, or download the annual report from the *Cases* section of the text's Web site at www.mcgrawhill.ca/college/phillips.

Required:

1. Which of the two basic reporting approaches for the cash flows from operating activities did High Liner use?

2. What amount of tax payments did High Liner make during the current year? Where did you find this information?

3. Ignoring acquisitions of other assets, what was the capital-acquisitions ratio averaged across the two years shown in High Liner's statement of cash flows?

4. How much cash did High Liner pay for interest during the current year? Using this information, calculate and interpret the cash-coverage ratio for the most recent year.

5. In the most recent year reported, High Liner generated $10.2 million from operating activities. Where did High Liner spend this money? List the two largest cash outflows.

LO1, LO8   ### S12-2 Comparing Financial Information

Refer to the financial statements of Sun-Rype by downloading the annual report from the *Cases* section of the text's Web site at www.mcgrawhill.ca/college/phillips.

Required:

1. Which of the two basic reporting approaches for the cash flows from operating activities did Sun-Rype use? Is this the same as the method High Liner used?

2. What net amount of tax payments did Sun-Rype make during the current year? Where did you find this information? Is this more or less than High Liner paid?

3. What was the capital-acquisitions ratio averaged across the two years shown in Sun-Rype's statement of cash flows? Do net operating cash flows pay for a greater or lesser proportion of Sun-Rype's capital acquisitions than High Liner's?

4. How much cash did Sun-Rype pay for interest during the current year? Using this information, calculate and interpret the cash-coverage ratio for Sun-Rype for the most recent year. Compare this with High Liner's ratio, and draw a conclusion about the companies' relative abilities to pay for interest.

5. In the most recent year reported, Sun-Rype generated $5,750,000 from operating activities. Where did Sun-Rype spend this money? List the two largest cash outflows. Do these uses differ significantly from High Liner's?

S12-3 Internet-Based Team Research: Examining an Annual Report

LO6–LO9

As a team, select an industry to analyze. Using your Web browser, each team member should acquire the annual report for one publicly traded Canadian company in the industry, with each member selecting a different company. (See S1-3 in Chapter 1 for a description of possible resources for these tasks.)

TEAM CASE

Required:

1. On an individual basis, each team member should write a short report that incorporates the following:
   a. Has the company generated positive or negative operating cash flows during the past three years?
   b. Has the company been expanding over the period? If so, what appears to have been the source of financing for this expansion (operating cash flow, additional borrowing, issuance of shares)?
   c. Compute and analyze the capital-acquisitions ratio averaged over the past three years.
   d. Compute and analyze the cash-coverage ratio in each of the past three years.
   e. Compute and analyze the quality-of-income ratio in each of the past three years.

2. Then, as a team, write a short report comparing and contrasting your companies using these attributes. Discuss any patterns across the companies that you, as a team, observe. Provide potential explanations for any differences discovered.

S12-4 Ethical Decision Making: A Real-Life Example

LO1, LO6

In a February 19, 2004, press release, the United States Securities and Exchange Commission described a number of fraudulent transactions that Enron executives concocted in an effort to meet the company's financial targets. One particularly well-known scheme is called the "Nigerian barge" transaction, which took place in the fourth quarter of 1999. According to court documents, Enron arranged to sell three electricity-generating power barges moored off the coast of Nigeria. The "buyer" was the investment banking firm of Merrill Lynch. Although Enron reported this transaction as a sale in its income statement, it turns out this was no ordinary sale. Merrill Lynch didn't really want the barges and had only agreed to buy them because Enron guaranteed, in a secret side-deal, that it would arrange for the barges to be bought back from Merrill Lynch within six months of the initial transaction. In addition, Enron promised to pay Merrill Lynch a hefty fee for doing the deal. In an interview on National Public Radio on August 17, 2002, Michigan Senator Carl Levin declared, "The case of the Nigerian barge transaction was, by any definition, a loan."

ETHICAL ISSUES

Required:

1. Discuss whether the Nigerian barge transaction should have been considered a loan rather than a sale. As part of your discussion, consider the following questions. Doesn't the Merrill Lynch payment to Enron at the time of the initial transaction automatically make it a sale, not a loan? What aspects of the transaction are similar to a loan? Which aspects suggest that the four criteria for revenue recognition (summarized on page 104 in Chapter 3) are not fulfilled?

2. The income statement effect of recording the transaction as a sale rather than a loan is fairly clear: Enron was able to boost its revenues and net income. What is somewhat less obvious,

but nearly as important, are the effects on the statement of cash flows. Describe how including the transaction with sales of other Enron products, rather than as a loan, would change the statement of cash flows.

3. How would the difference in the statement of cash flows (described in your response to requirement 2) affect financial statement users?

LO1, LO2, LO6

S12-5   Ethical Decision Making: A Mini-Case

ETHICAL ISSUES

Assume that you serve on the board of a local golf and country club. In preparation for renegotiating the club's bank loans, the president indicates that the club needs to increase its operating cash flows before the end of the current year. With a wink and sly smile, the club's treasurer reassures the president and other board members that he knows a couple of ways to boost the club's operating cash flows. First, he says, the club can sell some of its accounts receivable to a collections company that is willing to pay the club $97,000 up front for the right to collect $100,000 of the overdue accounts. That will immediately boost operating cash flows. Second, he indicates that the club paid about $200,000 last month to relocate the eighteenth fairway and green closer to the clubhouse. The treasurer indicates that, although these costs have been reported as expenses in the club's own monthly financial statements, he feels an argument can be made for reporting them as part of land and land improvements (a long-lived asset) in the year-end financial statements that would be provided to the bank. He explains that, by recording these payments as an addition to a long-lived asset, they will not be shown as a reduction in operating cash flows.

COACH'S TIP

Exhibit 3.7 illustrates the decision related to recording costs as an asset or expense.

Required:

1. Does the sale of accounts receivable to generate immediate cash harm or mislead anyone? Would you consider it an ethical business activity?

2. If cash is spent on long-lived assets, such as land improvements, how is it typically classified in the statement of cash flows? If cash is spent on expenses, such as costs for regular upkeep of the grounds, how is it typically classified in the statement of cash flows?

3. What facts are relevant to deciding whether the costs of the eighteenth hole relocation should be reported as an asset or as an expense? Is it appropriate to make this decision based on the impact it could have on operating cash flows?

4. As a member of the board, how would you ensure that an ethical decision is made?

LO2

S12-6   Critical Thinking: Interpreting Adjustments Reported on the Statement of Cash Flows from a Management Perspective (Indirect Method)

QuickServe, a chain of convenience stores, was experiencing some serious cash flow difficulties because of rapid growth. The company did not generate sufficient cash from operating activities to finance its new stores, and creditors were not willing to lend money because the company had not produced any income for the previous three years. The new controller for QuickServe proposed a reduction in the estimated life of store equipment to increase amortization expense; thus, "we can improve cash flows from operating activities because amortization expense is added back on the statement of cash flows." Other executives were not sure that this was a good idea, because the increase in amortization would make it more difficult to have positive earnings: "Without income, the bank will never lend us money."

Required:

What action would you recommend for QuickServe? Why?

LO2

S12-7   Using a Spreadsheet that Calculates Cash Flows from Operating Activities (Indirect Method)

eXcel

You've recently been hired by B2B Consultants to provide financial advisory services to small business managers. B2B's clients often need advice on how to improve their operating cash flows and, given your accounting background, you're frequently called upon to show them how operating cash flows would change if they were to speed up their sales of inventory and their collections of accounts receivable, or delay their payment of accounts payable. Each time you're asked to show the effects of these business decisions on the cash flows from operating activities, you get the uneasy feeling that you might inadvertently miscalculate their effects. To deal with this once and for all, you e-mail your friend Billy and ask him to prepare a template that automatically calculates the net operating cash flows from a simple comparative balance sheet. You received his reply today.

From: BillyTheTutor@yahoo.com
To: Overwhelmed@hotmail.com
Cc:
Subject: Excel Help

Hey, pal. I like your idea of working smarter, not harder. Too bad it involved my doing the thinking. Anyhow, I've created a spreadsheet file that contains four worksheets. The first two tabs (labelled BS and IS) are the input sheets where you would enter the numbers from each client's comparative balance sheet and income statement. Your clients are small, so this template allows for only the usual accounts. Also, I've assumed that amortization is the only reason for a change in accumulated amortization. If your clients' business activities differ from these, you'll need to contact me for more complex templates. The third worksheet calculates the operating cash flows using the indirect method, and the fourth does this calculation using the direct method. I'll attach the screenshots of each of the worksheets so you can create your own. To answer "what if" questions, all you'll need to do is change selected amounts in the balance sheet and income statement.

Microsoft Excel - S12-7

	B	C	D	E
4	ASSETS	Current Year	Prior Year	Change
5	Cash	$8,000	$12,000	(4,000)
6	Accounts receivable	16,900	8,500	8,400
7	Inventories	37,600	25,900	11,700
8	Total current assets	62,500	46,400	
9	Property, plant and equipment	105,000	105,000	0
10	Less: accumulated amortization	(20,000)	(10,000)	(10,000)
11	Total assets	$147,500	$141,400	
12	LIABILITIES			
13	Accounts payable	31,400	30,000	1,400
14	Income taxes payable	3,000	4,000	(1,000)
15	Interest payable	4,000	1,800	2,200
16	Other accrued liablities	11,000	14,000	(3,000)
17	Total current liabilities	49,400	49,800	
18	Long-term debt	40,000	40,000	0
19	Total liabilities	89,400	89,800	
20	SHAREHOLDERS' EQUITY			
21	Contributed capital	10,000	10,000	0
22	Retained earnings	48,100	41,600	6,500
23	Total Shareholders' Equity	58,100	51,600	
24	Total Liabilities and Shareholders' Equity	$147,500	$141,400	

BS / IS / Indirect / Direct /

Microsoft Excel - S12-7

	B	C
1	Small Business Client	
2	Income Statement	
3	For the Year Ended December 31	
4	Sales revenues	$102,000
5	Cost of goods sold	77,400
6	Amortization expense	10,000
7	Other operating expenses	1,800
8	Operating income	12,800
9	Interest expense	2,800
10	Income before income taxes	10,000
11	Income tax expense	3,500
12	Net income	$6,500

BS \ IS / Indirect / Direct /

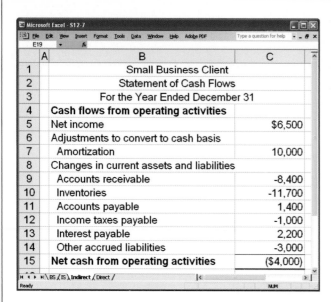

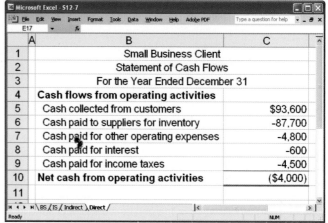

Required:

Copy the information from the worksheets for the balance sheet, income statement, and statement of cash flows (indirect method only) into a spreadsheet file. What was the net cash flow from operating activities?

LO2 **S12-8 Using a Spreadsheet that Calculates Cash Flows from Operating Activities (Direct Method)**

Refer to the information presented in S12-7.

Required:

Copy the information from the worksheets for the balance sheet, income statement, and statement of cash flows (direct method only) into a spreadsheet file. What was the net cash flow from operating activities?

LO6 **S12-9 Using a Spreadsheet to Answer "What If" Management Decisions (Indirect or Direct Method)**

Change the amounts for selected balance sheet accounts in the spreadsheets created for either S12-7 or S12-8 to calculate the cash flows from operating activities if, just before the current year-end, the company's management took the actions listed in the following requirements. Consider each question independently, unless indicated otherwise.

Required:

1. What if the company collected $10,000 of the accounts receivable?
2. What if the company had paid down its interest payable by an extra $2,000?
3. What if the company waited an additional month before paying $6,000 of its accounts payable?
4. What if the company had reported $5,000 more amortization expense?
5. What if all four of the above events had taken place?

CHAPTER 13

Measuring and Evaluating Financial Performance

Understand techniques used to evaluate financial performance.

LO1 Describe the purposes and uses of trend and ratio analyses.

Study how to evaluate financial performance (using High Liner Foods).

LO2 Perform trend analyses.

LO3 Categorize, calculate, and interpret key ratios relating to profitability, liquidity, and solvency.

LO4 (Supplement A) Study the treatment of non-recurring and other items.

Evaluate financial results in relation to stock price.

LO5 Calculate and interpret the price-earnings ratio.

Reconsider the conceptual framework for financial accounting.

LO6 Define the objective of financial reporting, and explain key accounting assumptions, principles, and constraints.

INSIDE LOOKING OUT

OUTSIDE LOOKING IN

This chapter reviews the measurement and analysis of financial performance, by focusing on High Liner Foods Incorporated. High Liner was founded in Lunenburg, Nova Scotia, in 1899 and is now one of North America's largest marketers of prepared frozen seafood, selling under the brand names High Liner® and Fisher Boy®.

The final chapter of this textbook considers all the different analysis techniques that could be used to assess a company's financial performance. **HIGH LINER FOODS** is the focus company for this chapter. In this chapter, you'll learn why High Liner is considered to be a strong, financially successful company.

Measuring and evaluating financial performance is like judging gymnastics or figure skating at the Olympics. You have to know three things: (1) the general categories to evaluate for each event, (2) the particular elements to consider within each category, and (3) how performance for each element is measured. You probably use a similar approach for judging your experience when eating High Liner fish products. General categories, like enjoyment and value, can be broken down into particular elements like convenience, flavour, price, and serving size. On the financial side, analysts consider general categories like profitability, liquidity, and solvency, which are broken down into particular elements like profit margin and asset turnover. For each of these elements, analysts measure performance using financial ratios, which themselves are based on information reported in the financial statements. By the time you finish reading this chapter, you'll understand how analysts use High Liner's financial results to help them understand their performance and, more generally, what you should look for when analyzing other companies' financial performance.

In this chapter, we describe techniques commonly used to evaluate financial performance, and then present a framework for organizing all the ratios you've learned throughout the previous chapters. Using the framework and ratios, we analyze the financial results of High Liner. Later sections discuss how financial results relate to stock prices, and then review key concepts that make financial accounting useful for evaluating a company and predicting its future.

UNDERSTAND _____

Techniques Used to Evaluate Financial Performance

A business evaluation includes a financial statement analysis and a market analysis (a study of the industry), as well as a forecast analysis (making predictions about the company's future), which are beyond the scope of this text. Here we'll focus on the two most common techniques used in financial statement analysis: (1) trend analysis and (2) ratio analysis, which we introduced in Chapter 5.[1] Trend analysis compares individual financial statement line-items over time with the general goal of identifying significant sustained changes ("trends") that exist. These changes are typically described in terms of dollar amounts, as well as year-over-year percentages. A year-over-year percentage simply expresses the change in the current year as a percentage of the prior year total, using the following calculation:

COACH'S TIP

Year-over-year comparisons are also called "time series analyses" because they compare across a series of time periods. They also are called "horizontal analyses" because they involve comparing financial statement amounts horizontally.

$$\text{Year-Over-Year Change (\%)} = \frac{\text{Change This Year}}{\text{Prior Year's Total}} \times 100\% = \frac{\text{Current Year's Total-Prior Year's Total}}{\text{Prior Year's Total}} \times 100\%$$

Let's use the following as an example.

	Current Year	Prior Year
Sales	$240	$200
Year-Over-Year Change	$= 20\% = \dfrac{(\$240 - 200)}{\$200} \times 100\%$	

The second technique that we will use is ratio analysis, which involves comparing an amount for one or more financial statement items with an amount for other items for the same year. Ratio analysis takes into account differences in the size of amounts being compared to allow you to evaluate how well a company has performed, *given the existing level of other company resources.* For example, it's one thing to know that current assets total $1 million, but it's much more informative if you also know that current liabilities are $4 million and that current assets are only 25 per cent (1/4) of the amount currently owed. A ratio this low suggests that the company won't have sufficient resources to pay its creditors on time.

As shown throughout other chapters in this book, a company's ratios can be calculated for each year, and then compared across years to identify additional trends not revealed in an analysis of individual financial statement line-items. Another possibility is to compare ratios from one company with those for close competitors, for other companies in the same industry even if they are not direct competitors, or for the industry as a whole. In a competitive economy, companies strive to outperform one another, so this type of analysis provides clues as to which companies are likely to survive and thrive in the long run.

For the purposes of our analyses, we favour comparisons with companies in the same industry. Rather than evaluate High Liner relative to all potential food processors, we want to understand how it's doing in relation to a small number of companies in the same industry. The firms we have chosen are listed on the next page. They are all food processors, but each produces a different product, is a different size, and is based in a different part of the country.

---

[1] Another type of analysis, called vertical analysis, expresses financial statements in percentages instead of absolute dollars. A vertical analysis of a balance sheet expresses each line-item as a percentage of total assets, while a vertical analysis of an income statement expresses each line-item as a percentage of total revenues. Vertical analysis is useful for understanding the relative importance of each line-item in a statement, such as when we say that ClubLink's property and equipment is 96 per cent of its total assets.

Name	Headquarters	Main Product	Number of Employees	Totals Assets
Focus company:				
High Liner Foods	Nova Scotia	Frozen fish	1,176	$ 300 million
Comparison companies:				
Sun-Rype Products	British Columbia	Fruit snacks and juices	400	$ 57 million
Saputo	Québec	Cheese	9,200	$2,733 million
Maple Leaf Foods	Ontario	Meat and bakery products	23,000	$2,998 million

Industry averages are reported in the *Annual Statement Studies,* which are published by the United States Risk Management Association. You can obtain industry averages also from marketguide.com or edgarscan.pwcglobal .com, both of which were available free of charge at the time this book was written.

One final point before we present our analyses. The goal for the next section is to show you an example of trend and ratio analyses. Rather than present every possible trend and ratio covering every year and every comparison company, we discuss the ones that do the best job of depicting High Liner's performance and financial position. We don't show how every single number in the ratios was calculated because previous chapters already have shown how to calculate and interpret financial ratios. If you feel a need to refresh your memory, just flip back to the corresponding chapters for each of the ratios, which are summarized in Exhibit 13.4. The USER framework in each chapter makes it easy to find the ratio discussion (in the "Evaluate" section). For extra practice with these calculations, make sure you attempt S13-7 at the end of this chapter, which asks you to calculate the ratios reported in this chapter. You can use these reported ratios as "check figures."

STUDY _____
How to Evaluate Financial Performance (Using High Liner)

The annual report of High Liner appears in Appendix A at the end of the book. To save you the trouble of flipping back and forth, we've presented a simplified summary of the balance sheets, income statements, and statements of cash flows from the three most recent years in Exhibits 13.1 to 13.3. High Liner defines its fiscal year as 52 weeks instead

exhibit 13.1   Summarized Balance Sheets

HIGH LINER FOODS INCORPORATED
Balance Sheets
(in thousands)

	Year Ended December 31		
	2007	**2006**	**2005**
Assets			
Current Assets			
Cash	$ 7,064	$ 240	$ 580
Accounts Receivable	68,662	31,221	28,095
Inventories	107,589	41,278	52,670
Other Current Assets	8,360	3,951	7,803
Total Current Assets	191,675	76,690	89,148
Property and Equipment	57,515	26,038	26,952
Intangible Assets and Goodwill	42,762	—	—
Other Assets	8,502	10,449	11,153
Total Assets	$ 300,454	$113,177	$127,253
Liabilities and Shareholders' Equity			
Current Liabilities	$ 113,388	$ 37,762	$ 54,900
Long-Term Liabilities	56,195	4,179	3,771
Total Liabilities	169,583	41,941	58,671
Shareholders' Equity	130,871	71,236	68,582
Total Liabilities and Shareholders' Equity	$ 300,454	$113,177	$127,253

exhibit 13.2   Summarized Income Statements

HIGH LINER FOODS INCORPORATED
Income Statements
(in thousands)

	Year Ended December 31		
	2007	2006	2005
Revenues	$ 275,391	$ 261,725	$ 250,203
Cost of Sales	221,202	212,414	201,966
Gross Profit	54,189	49,311	48,237
Operating and Other Expenses	43,226	38,984	40,876
Interest Expense	377	907	419
Income Tax Expense	3,669	4,297	3,088
Income from continuing operations	6,917	5,123	3,854
Gain (loss)	372	(793)	(44,323)
Net Income (loss)	$ 7,289	$ 4,330	$(40,469)
Earnings (loss) per Share	$ 0.58	$ .30	$(3.93)

exhibit 13.3   Summarized Statements of Cash Flows

HIGH LINER FOODS INCORPORATED
Statements of Cash Flows
(in thousands)

	Year Ended December 31		
	2007	2006	2005
Cash Flows from Operating Activities			
Income from continuing operations	$ 6,917	$ 5,123	$ 3,854
Adjustments to reconcile to cash flows from operations	3,253	15,218	(13,172)
Net cash provided by (used for) operating activities	10,170	20,341	(9,318)
Cash Flows from Investing Activities			
Purchases of property, plant, and equipment	(2,956)	(2,466)	(3,423)
Acquisition of FPI, including acquisition costs	(100,708)	—	—
Purchases and sales of other assets	(1,739)	172	3,282
Cash provided by (used for) investing activities	(105,925)	(2,294)	(141)
Cash Flows from Financing Activities			
Shares repurchased and cancelled	—	(73)	(5,545)
Issuance of long-term debt related to acquisition	53,625	—	—
Proceeds from issue of shares	419	192	1,025
Issuance (repayment) of debt	54,181	(14,693)	17,487
Dividends paid	(3,283)	(3,201)	(3,183)
Repayment of capital lease obligations	(418)	(444)	(473)
Cash provided by (used for) financing activities	104,524	(18,219)	9,311
Translation adjustment	(1,945)	(168)	222
Increase (decrease) in cash during the year	6,824	(340)	74
Cash, beginning of year	240	580	506
Cash, end of year	$ 7,064	240	$ 580
Supplemental Disclosure of Cash Flows			
Cash paid during the period for interest	$ 178	$ 994	$ 336
Cash paid during the period for income taxes	$ 491	$ 538	$ 262

of 365 days. For simplicity, we have assumed its year-end is December 31. Based on trends and ratios determined using these financial statements, we present a point-by-point analysis of High Liner's results below.

TREND ANALYSES OF HIGH LINER'S FINANCIAL STATEMENTS

Below is a trend analysis for selected data taken from Exhibits 13.1 to 13.3. For each line-item, we calculate the 2005-over-2007 change. As mentioned above, trend analysis can be performed on all financial statement line-items if desired.

	% Change from 2005 to 2007	
Total assets	↑136% =	($300 − 127) ÷ 127
Total property and equipment	↑115% =	($58 − 27) ÷ 27
Total liabilities	↑188% =	($170 − 59) ÷ 59
Total shareholders' equity	↑ 90% =	($131 − 69) ÷ 69
Revenues	↑ 10% =	($275.4 − 250.2) ÷ 250.2
Income from continuing operations	↑ 77% =	($6.9 − 3.9) ÷ 3.9
Cash flow from operations	↑209% =	($10.1 − (−9.3)) ÷ −9.3
Purchases of property and equipment	↓ 12% =	($3.0 − 3.4) ÷ 3.4

High Liner dramatically increased in size in 2007, with its balance sheets in Exhibit 13.1 showing a 136 per cent increase in total assets from $127 million in 2005 to $300 million in 2007. This increase was largely a result of the acquisition of FPI Limited, another seafood company based in the Maritimes, in December 2007. According to High Liner's annual report, "The 2007 acquisition of the FPI manufacturing and marketing assets has brought High Liner closer to achieving our vision to be the North American leader in frozen value-added seafood." High Liner's operations performed well during 2007. Including the post-acquisition sales of FPI, sales increased 10 per cent overall to $ 275.4 from $ 250.2 in 2005, and income from continuing operations rose 77 per cent to $6.9 million from $3.9 million in 2005. High Liner's total liabilities increased 188 per cent, while its shareholders' equity increased 90 per cent, from 2005 to 2007.

The purchase of FPI was completed December 21, 2007, and, as explained in note 2 to the financial statements, it was accounted for using the purchase method, which means the results of operations of FPI from December 21 to the end of the year are included in High Liner's income statement for the year ended December 31, 2007. The balance sheet, because it is at a point in time, includes the changes in assets, liabilities, and equity resulting from the purchase. For this reason, the ratios calculated using averages from the two years' balance sheets may be misleading. This will be discussed in evaluating the ratios.

The income statements in Exhibit 13.2 show that the company had a large loss from discontinued opeartions in 2005. This was the result of the sale of its Italian Foods operation, and included a write down of goodwill of $41 million. Excluding the impact of this item, trend analysis shows that income increased 77 per cent from 2005 to 2007, and cash from operating activities increased from an outflow of $9.3 million to an inflow of $10.2 million. Exhibit 13.3 shows that, other than the purchase of FPI, investment in property, plant, and equipment increased 12 per cent. The FPI acquisition was a major factor in investing and financing activities in 2007, resulting in an outflow of $105 million reported as investing activities and an inflow of $54 million in proceeds of related long-term debt under financing activities. The short story, based on this brief trend analysis, is that the company has been in transition, making changes to its asset base and capital structure so that it can focus on its core business in the future.

RATIO ANALYSES USING HIGH LINER'S FINANCIAL STATEMENTS

Throughout this text, we have been building a framework for financial statement analyses that will allow us to evaluate a company's performance. The framework appears in the top part of Exhibit 13.4, where it has been split into two sides:

1. The **efficiency** (turnover) ratios are shown on the right-hand side, combined with the other profitability ratios. **Profitability** ratios relate to performance in the current

Efficiency is the extent to which a company generates revenues, and is one aspect of profitability.

Profitability is the extent to which a company generates net income.

exhibit 13.4   A Framework for Financial Statement Ratio Analyses

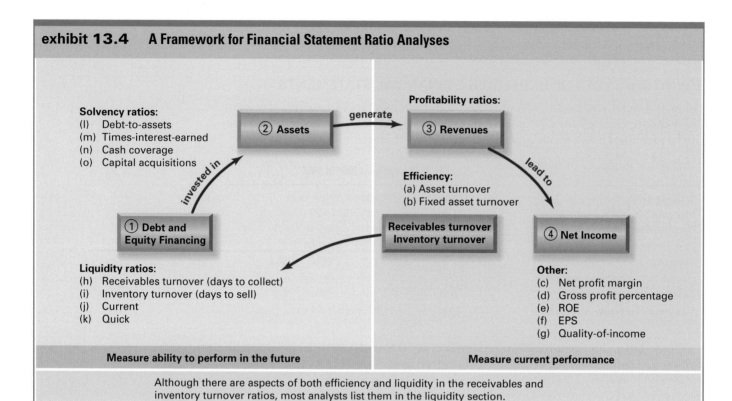

Solvency ratios:
(l) Debt-to-assets
(m) Times-interest-earned
(n) Cash coverage
(o) Capital acquisitions

② Assets

Profitability ratios:
③ Revenues

generate

Efficiency:
(a) Asset turnover
(b) Fixed asset turnover

invested in

① Debt and
Equity Financing

Receivables turnover
Inventory turnover

lead to

④ Net Income

Liquidity ratios:
(h) Receivables turnover (days to collect)
(i) Inventory turnover (days to sell)
(j) Current
(k) Quick

Other:
(c) Net profit margin
(d) Gross profit percentage
(e) ROE
(f) EPS
(g) Quality-of-income

Measure ability to perform in the future

Measure current performance

Although there are aspects of both efficiency and liquidity in the receivables and inventory turnover ratios, most analysts list them in the liquidity section.

Ratio	Basic Computation	Chapter/page
Tests of Profitability		
a. Asset turnover	$\dfrac{\text{Net sales revenue}}{\text{Average total assets}}$	5 (p. 210)
b. Fixed asset turnover	$\dfrac{\text{Net sales revenue}}{\text{Average net fixed assets}}$	9 (p. 396)
c. Net profit margin	$\dfrac{\text{Net income}}{\text{Net sales revenue}}$	5 (p. 210)
d. Gross profit percentage	$\dfrac{\text{Net sales revenue} - \text{Cost of goods sold}}{\text{Net sales revenue}}$	6 (p. 251)
e. Return on equity	$\dfrac{\text{Net income}}{\text{Average shareholder's equity}}$	11 (p. 493)
f. Earnings per share	$\dfrac{\text{Net income}}{\text{Weighted-average number of common shares outstanding}}$	11 (p. 492)
g. Quality-of-income	$\dfrac{\text{Net cash flows from operating activities}}{\text{Net income}}$	12 (p. 544)
Tests of Liquidity		
h. Receivables turnover	$\dfrac{\text{Net credit sales revenue}}{\text{Average Net receivables}}$	7 (p. 307)
• Days to collect	365/receivables turnover	

(continued)

i. Inventory turnover	$\dfrac{\text{Cost of goods sold}}{\text{Average inventory}}$	8 (p. 351)
• Days to sell	365/inventory turnover	
j. Current ratio	$\dfrac{\text{Current Assets}}{\text{Current liabilities}}$	10 (p. 446)
k. Quick ratio	$\dfrac{\text{Cash + short-term invesments + accounts receivable}}{\text{Current liabilities}}$	13 (p. 587)
Tests of Solvency		
l. Debt-to-assets	$\dfrac{\text{Total liabilities}}{\text{Total assets}}$	5 (p. 210)
m. Times-interest-earned	$\dfrac{\text{Net income + Interest expense + Income tax expense}}{\text{Interest expense}}$	10 (p. 448)
n. Cash coverage	$\dfrac{\text{Net cash flows from operating activities + Interest paid + Income tax paid}}{\text{Interest Paid}}$	12 (p. 544)
o. Capital acquisitions	$\dfrac{\text{Net cash flows from operating activities}}{\text{Cash paid for property, plant, and equipment}}$	12 (p. 542)

period. The focus is on the company's ability to generate net income during the period, and thus includes its ability to generate revenues from assets.

2. On the left-hand side are the ratios that relate to the company's ability to perform in the future. They have been split into two categories.

   a. **Liquidity,** which relates to the company's *short-term* survival. In particular, the focus is on the company's ability to use current assets to repay liabilities as they become due in the short term.

   b. **Solvency,** which relates to the company's *long-run* survival. In particular, the focus is on the company's ability to repay lenders when debt matures (and to make required interest payments prior to the date of maturity).

Liquidity is the extent to which a company is able to pay its currently maturing obligations.

Solvency is the ability to survive long enough to repay lenders when debt matures.

Exhibit 13.4 lists and defines the ratios from earlier chapters in terms of these categories, and adds one new ratio, the quick ratio, which is discussed later. The following analyses, focused on the food processing industry, show how these ratios can be used to interpret and evaluate a company's financial performance.

Profitability Ratios

The analyses in this section focus on how well the company did during the current period, in terms of its ability to generate profit.

COACH'S TIP

Remember from the discussions in prior chapters that calculated ratios often differ from one industry to the next.

a. ***Asset turnover.*** The asset-turnover ratio indicates the amount of sales generated for each dollar invested in assets. The ratios for the three years are:

Year Ended December 31	2007	2006	2005
Asset-turnover = $\dfrac{\text{Net sales revenue}}{\text{Average total assets}}$	1.3*	2.2	1.7

*1.33 = $275,391/([300,454 + 113,177]/2)

The asset-turnover analysis suggests that High Liner was less efficient at using assets to generate sales in 2007 than in prior years. The use of simple averages based on the two year-end values makes this result misleading. High Liner acquired FPI in mid-December 2007. By including the increase in assets using the simple average method, it appears that these assets were available for six months, when in fact they were owned for only approximately a half month. The net sales revenue includes the revenue from FPI for the period December 21 to the year-end. If we recalcualte the asset turnover using a weighted average, it results in a ratio of 2.3 for 2007 ($275,391 ÷ [$300,454 × 0.5 + $113,177 × 11.5] ÷ 12). It will be interesting to see the ratio for 2008 with a full year of operations for FPI.

To understand this ratio, it's useful to focus on key assets that are used to generate sales. For a company like High Liner, one key asset is its production facilities and equipment, which accounts for 19 per cent of High Liner's total assets. High Liner's ability to use these fixed assets to generate sales can be analyzed by using the fixed-asset ratio, which we look at next.

b. ***Fixed asset turnover.*** The fixed-asset-turnover ratio indicates how much the company generates in sales for each dollar invested in fixed assets like the production facilities and processing equipment. The ratios for three years are:

Year Ended December 31		*2007*	*2006*	*2005*
Fixed asset turnover = $\dfrac{\text{Net sales revenue}}{\text{Average net fixed assets}}$		6.6*	9.9	9.2

*6.6 = $275,391 ÷ ([57,515 + 26,038]/2)

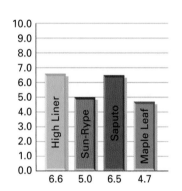

This analysis shows that High Liner has recently earned around $7 to $10 of sales for each dollar of fixed assets. Is this good? Well, yes, it appears so. This ratio for 2007 is lower than that for the previous years, but, as explained above, this is the result of the purchase of FPI late in 2007. High Liner's ratios are better than those of its competitors. When the ratios for Sun-Rype, Saputo, and Maple Leaf for 2007 are compared with High Liner's for 2007, High Liner's ratio is the highest at 6.6, and Maple's Leaf's is the lowest at 4.7. But we have to be careful making these comparisons. Because fixed assets last for many years, they don't have a huge impact on revenues in any one year. The more you invest in long-term assets, the more you can expect the fixed- and total-asset-turnover ratios to decline. Of the four companies, Sun-Rype had the highest percentage of total assets invested in fixed assets (49 per cent) in 2007, and High Liner the lowest (19 per cent), so differences in the fixed-asset ratios can be expected.

c. ***Net profit margin.*** Net profit margin represents the percentage of sales revenues that ultimately make it into net income, after deducting expenses. High Liner's net profit margins for each of the last three years are

Year Ended December 31		*2007*	*2006*	*2005*
Net profit margin = $\dfrac{\text{Net income}}{\text{Net sales revenue}}$		2.6%*	1.7%	−16.2%

*2.6% = 7,289 ÷ 275,391 × 100%

As you can see, High Liner's net profit margin has improved over the past three years. Even without the loss from discontinued operations in 2005, the ratio was 1.5 per cent. The 2.6 per cent earned in 2007 indicates that, for each dollar of sales, High Liner generated 2.6 cents of net income. High Liner's normal profit margin appears to be between 2 and 3 per cent. The increase from 1.5 per cent in 2005 to 2.6 per cent in 2007 might seem small to you, but, when considered in the light of High Liner's $275 million in sales, this increase of 1.1 per cent equates to

$3 million dollars of profit ($275 million × 1.1% = $3,025). To understand the net profit margin better, we need to look at the gross profit percentage.

d. Gross profit percentage. The gross profit percentage indicates how much profit is made after deducting the cost of goods sold. High Liner's gross profit percentages for three recent years are:

Year Ended December 31		2007	2006	2005
Gross profit percentage =	$\dfrac{\text{Net sales } - \text{ cost of goods sold}}{\text{Net sales}}$	19.7%*	18.8%	19.3%

*19.7% = (54,189) ÷ 275,391 × 100%

This analysis shows that, in 2007, after paying for the cost of making the food sold during the year, 19.7 per cent of each sales dollar was left over to cover other costs like employee wages, advertising, utilities, and other expenses. The 2007 gross profit percentage represents an increase of 0.4 per cent (19.7% − 19.3%) from 2005, which is slightly less than half the amount that net profit margin increased in that period. The remainder of the increase in net profit margin must have come from a reduction in other expenses (as a percentage of net revenue).

e. Return on equity (ROE). The return-on-equity ratio compares the amount of net income with average shareholders' equity. Like the interest rate on your savings account, ROE reports the net amount earned this period as a percentage of each dollar contributed (by shareholders) and retained in the business. The ROE ratios for the three years are:

Year Ended December 31		2007	2006	2005
Return on equity (ROE) =	$\dfrac{\text{Net income}}{\text{Average shareholder's equity}}$	7.2%*	6.2%	−43.0% 4.1% before discontinued operations

*7.2% = 7,289 ÷ ([130,871 ÷ 71,236]/2) × 100%

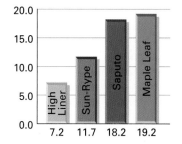

High Liner generated a return of 7.2 per cent, which is up from 2006. This is better than might be expected, given that average shareholders' equity increased significantly in 2007, a result of the purchase near year-end of FPI. Recalculating the ROE using a weighted average for shareholders' equity for 2007 results in an ROE of 9.9 per cent for 2007 ($7,289 ÷ [$130,871 × 0.5 + $71,236 × 11.5] ÷ 12). This level of ROE is still a bit below the returns generated by competitors, but the trend is quite encouraging. Sun-Rype had an ROE of 11.7 per cent, Saputo's ROE is 18.2 per cent, and Maple Leaf has the highest ROE of 19.2 per cent.

f. Earnings per share (EPS). Earnings per share indicates the amount of earnings generated for each common share. In Chapter 11, you saw that most companies report basic EPS and diluted EPS. For purposes of analyses in this course, we focus on basic EPS. (Diluted EPS is studied in greater detail in intermediate accounting courses.)

Year Ended December 31		2007	2006	2005
Earnings per share (EPS) =	$\dfrac{\text{Net income}}{\text{Weighted-average number of common shares}}$	$0.58*	$.30	−$3.93 $0.26 before discontinued operations

*Reported on the income statement

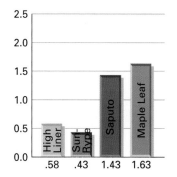

High Liner's earnings per share has increased from 26 cents in 2005 to 58 cents in 2007. This is higher than Sun-Rype's EPS of 43 cents but much lower than that of Saputo and Maple Leaf ($1.43 and $1.63 respectively).

g. *Quality-of-income.* The quality-of-income ratio relates operating cash flows (from the statement of cash flows) to net income, as follows:

Year Ended December 31	2007	2006	2005
Quality-of-income = $\dfrac{\text{Net cash flows from operating activities}}{\text{Net income}}$	1.4*	4.7	−2.4

*1.4 = $10,170 ÷ 7,289

The ratio of 1.4 in 2007 shown above indicates that High Liner generated $1.40 of operating cash flow for every dollar of net income This is a large increase from 2005, when High Liner was generating negative income, but High Liner's ratio has declined in 2007, compared with 2006. Whether this indicates a problem with cash flows will be examined more closely in the next section on liquidity ratios.

Let's pause to summarize what we've learned so far. The acquisition of FPI significantly increased the size of High Liner's operations in 2007. The year 2005 also saw a major event—the disposal of a significant portion of the company, Italian Foods. These events must be considered in interpreting the results of the ratios. Overall the ratios show that High Liner's profitability has improved in 2007 over the preceding two years.

Liquidity Ratios

The analyses in this section focus on the company's ability to survive in the short term, by generating cash that can be used to pay current liabilities as they come due.

h. *Receivables turnover.* Food processing companies sell their products to grocery chains like Loblaws and Sobey's on credit, so they have high levels of accounts receivable relative to sales revenues. Although the formula calls for net credit sales in the top of the ratio, companies never separately report credit sales and cash sales. Consequently, financial statement users use total sales revenue in the formula, resulting in a receivables-turnover ratio that does not measure exactly what we want to measure. For companies like High Liner, which sell mostly on credit, this is not a problem. On the other hand, for a company where the majority of sales are collected immediately as cash, such as restaurants, it would be more of a concern. We present the ratio below.

Year Ended December 31	2007	2006	2005
Receivables turnover = $\dfrac{\text{Net credit sales revenue}}{\text{Average net receivables}}$	5.5*	8.8	8.9

*5.5 = $275,391 ÷ (($68,662 + $31,221)/2).

The receivables-turnover ratio shows that High Liner's collection rate declined in 2007 to 5.5 from 8.8 in 2006. The number of days in receivables is 66 in 2007 (66 = 365 ÷ 5.5), and, since most companies offer 30 to 60 days for customers to pay their accounts, it appears as though High Liner collection efforts diminished in 2007, because the number of days in 2006 was only 41. As discussed in preceding sections, this result for 2007 can be misleading because of the impact of the purchase of FPI late in 2007. Estimating the impact of this purchase by using a weighted average results in a ratio of 8.4 for 2007 ($275,391 ÷ [$68,622 × 0.5 + $31,221 × 11.5 ÷ 12]). This result may also be incorrect, since it assumes that the 11.5 months preceding the purchase had a constant level of receivables. It is difficult to make a valid comparison of the ratio because of these factors.

i. *Inventory turnover.* As you probably know from personal experience, food can go bad quickly if it's left sitting out. The inventory-turnover ratio indicates how frequently raw materials are bought, converted into finished goods, and sold during the year, which is the efficiency aspect of this ratio.

Year Ended December 31		2007	2006	2005
Inventory turnover =	$\dfrac{\text{Cost of good sold}}{\text{Average inventory}}$	3.0*	4.5	4.1

*3.0 = $221,202 ÷ ([107,589 + 41,278]/2)

At first glance, you might be alarmed by High Liner's inventory-turnover ratio. A turnover of 3.0 suggests the company's inventory was on hand, on average, for 122 days (122 = 365 ÷ 3.0). That's a long time for seafood to sit out. But wait; if you do a little digging, you'll find a couple of reasons not to be too worried. First, High Liner's financial statement notes reveal that only one-quarter of High Liner's inventory consists of raw and semi-finished materials, the goods most prone to spoilage. Finished products are frozen and have a longer shelf life. Second, recent improvements in food preservation technology (such as cryogenic freezing) allow seafood to be "fresh frozen" and held in inventory for a long time, without harming flavour or freshness. And, as discussed under the receivables-turnover and earlier sections, the purchase of FPI near year-end had a negative impact on this ratio. Sun-Rype's finished goods are primarily dried fruit bars and fruit juices, and it carries inventory for an average of 66 days. Companies that sell fresh food, such as restaurants, should have higher turnover ratios than food processors. Outback Steakhouse, for example, brags about making everything fresh, and it sells its food every 17 days. The fast-food giant McDonald's beats that with a 10-day ratio. Because a lot of Canadian companies, including Maple Leaf and Saputo, do not disclose cost of goods sold in their income statements, this ratio cannot be calculated for every company.

j. Current ratio. The current ratio compares current assets with current liabilities, as follows:

Year Ended December 31		2007	2006	2005
Current ratio =	$\dfrac{\text{Current assets}}{\text{Current liabilities}}$	1.7*	2.0	1.6

*1.69 = $191,675 ÷ 113,388

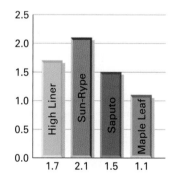

High Liner's current ratio indicates that the company's current assets are not twice its current liabilities. The higher the current ratio, the better. In 2006, High Liner's current assets were more than twice its current liabilities, which demonstrates a stronger working capital. Of the companies looked at, only Sun-Rype has a ratio greater than 2 to 1. The ratios of Saputo and Maple Leaf are lower than High Liner's at 1.5 and 1.1 respectively. Because some current assets are more liquid than others, another ratio, the quick ratio, is calculated to shed more light on liquidity.

k. Quick ratio. The quick ratio uses only the most liquid current assets in the numerator: cash, short-term investments, and receivables. This ratio is particularly useful if the inventory-turnover ratio suggests that inventory is becoming less saleable (which is not the case with High Liner).

Year Ended December 31		2007	2006	2005
Quick ratio =	$\dfrac{\text{Cash + Short-term investments +Accounts receivable}}{\text{Current liabilities}}$	0.7*	0.8	0.5

*0.67 = ($7,064 + 0 + 68,662) ÷ 113,388

With just the cash and receivables in the numerator, we see that, although High Liner does not have enough quick assets to pay off its entire current liabilities, 2006 was their best year.

High Liner could increase its current and quick ratios even more by deliberately keeping more cash and inventory on hand. Should they do this? Not necessarily. Nobody really wants a company to stockpile inventory, especially if it is food, or let its cash sit idle in the bank.

In summary, the liquidity ratios suggest that High Liner efficiently manages its short-term position. It collects its receivables every 66 days, and sells its inventories every 122 days. Since most suppliers expect to get paid within 30 to 60 days, High Liner appears to be in good shape. Another point worth noting is that the notes to the financial statements (note 6) tell us that High Liner has pre-arranged a short-term working capital loan of $120 million that it can access if needed.

Solvency Ratios

The analyses in this section focus on how well the company is positioned for long-term survival, in terms of its ability to repay debt when it matures, to pay interest until that time, and to finance the replacement and/or expansion of long-term assets.

l.   **Debt-to-assets.** The debt-to-assets ratio indicates the proportion of total assets that is financed by creditors. Remember, creditors *have to be paid* regardless of how tough a year a company might have had, so the higher the ratio, the riskier the financing strategy. The ratio is calculated as:

Year Ended December 31	2007	2006	2005
Debt-to-assets = $\dfrac{\text{Total liabilities}}{\text{Total assets}}$	0.6*	0.4	0.5

*0.6 = ($169,583) ÷ 300,454

High Liner's ratio of 0.6 at the end of 2007 indicates that creditors have contributed 60 per cent of the financing used by High Liner, which implies that shareholders' equity provides 40 per cent of the financing. We can see from the ratios above that the proportion of debt financing is up from 2005, which suggests High Liner has increased its level of financing risk. Relative to its competitors, High Liner now has 60 per cent debt financing, Maple Leaf is similar, with 61 per cent of its assets financed by debt. Saputo has 40 per cent of its operations financed by debt, while Sun-Rype has only 29 per cent debt financing. Because debt has to be paid back and equity does not, financing with debt is more risky. Since risk and return go hand-in-hand, lenders usually charge a higher interest rate on loans to riskier companies. Similarly, shareholders are happy with a high-debt strategy only if they get more return on their investment to compensate for the higher risk. Financing with debt to increase the return to shareholders is known as financial leverage, a concept studied in Chapter 11.

m.   **Times-interest-earned.** The times-interest-earned ratio indicates how many times interest is covered by operating results. This ratio is calculated using accrual-based interest expense and net income (before interest and taxes), as follows:

Year Ended December 31	2007	2006	2005
Times-interest-earned = $\dfrac{\text{Net income + Interest expense + Income tax expense}}{\text{Interest expense}}$	30.1*	10.5	−88.2

*30.1 = ($7,289 + 377 + 3,669) ÷ 377.

COACH'S TIP

Instead of the debt-to-assets ratio, analysts might use a debt-to-equity ratio, which gives the same basic information as debt-to-assets. Debt-to-equity typically is calculated as total liabilities ÷ total shareholders' equity. As with debt-to-assets, the higher the debt-to-equity ratio, the more the company relies on debt (rather than equity) financing.

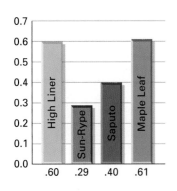

COACH'S TIP

If the company reports a net loss, rather than net income, include the loss as a negative number in the formula. A negative ratio indicates that the operating results (before the costs of financing and taxes) are less than the interest costs.

The message from the times-interest-earned ratio is that High Liner is generating more than enough profit from its business to cover its interest expense. Anything above 1.0 would indicate that net income (before the costs of financing and taxes) is sufficient to cover interest expense. Maple Leaf, financed with 61 per cent debt, has an interest-coverage ratio of 3.2, Saputo's ratio is 17.6, and Sun-Rype's is an amazing 46.7.

n. Cash coverage. Like the times-interest-earned ratio, the cash-coverage ratio indicates how many times interest is covered by operating results. Rather than use accrual-based numbers, however, the cash-coverage ratio compares the cash generated from the company's business operations (before interest and taxes) with its interest payments, as follows:

Year Ended December 31		2007	2006	2005
Cash coverage =	Net cash flows from operations + Interest paid + Income tax paid / Interest paid	60.9*	22.0	−26.0

*60.9 = ($10,170 + 178 + 491) ÷ 178

This analysis shows that, if the cash generated from operations wasn't spent on other financing or investing activities, High Liner could cover its interest payments many times over, with a high of 60.9 in 2007. Bankers and other long-term debt holders should sleep comfortably, knowing that they will be paid interest on time. This is a major improvement over 2005, when operations resulted in a net outflow of cash.

o. Capital acquisitions. The capital-acquisitions ratio compares cash flows from operations to cash paid for property and equipment, as follows:

Year Ended December 31		2007	2006	2005
Capital acquisitions =	Net cash flows from operations / Cash paid for PPE	3.4*	8.25	−2.7

*3.4 = $10,170 ÷ 2,956

The capital-acquisition ratios indicate that High Liner has, in 2006 and 2007, been able to pay for its new capital assets with cash from operating activities. It didn't have to borrow money from the bank or sell more shares to the public. It's a good sign when a company can finance its purchases of long-lived assets internally. This excludes the purchase of FPI in 2007. High Liner's 2007 ratio is much stronger that Sun-Rype's ratio of 1.2.

In summary, the solvency ratios depict a financially secure company. One story that emerges from these ratios is that internal operations are providing the funds needed to maintain operating capability.

OTHER CONSIDERATIONS

In the analyses just presented, we've considered High Liner's ratios for three years and made some comparisons with Sun-Rype, Saputo, and Maple Leaf. Where appropriate, we've discussed how differences in strategy (e.g., selling divisions) and business operations (e.g., selling fresh versus frozen foods) affect interpretations of the financial ratios. When comparing companies, you should consider two other matters: (1) are their accounting policies similar, and (2) are their results affected by non-recurring or other items? Let's look at item 1 below. The second item, non-recurring and other items, will be discussed in Supplement A starting on page 596.

Information about a company's accounting policies is presented in the notes to the financial statements. Exhibit 13.5 compares the policies used by the four companies

exhibit 13.5   Comparison of Accounting Methods

	High Liner	Sun-Rype	Saputo	Maple Leaf
Food inventory	FIFO and weighted-average	Weighted-average	FIFO and weighted-average	Weighted-average
Amortization	Straight-line Buildings: 20–40 years Equipment: 4–15 years	Straight-line Buildings: 15–20 years Equipment: 3–10 years	Straight-line Buildings: 2–40 years Equipment: 3–15 years	Straight-line Buildings: 17–40 years Equipment: 3–10 years

when accounting for inventory and amortization—the areas with the greatest impact on the results of these companies. As you can see, the four companies use similar, but not identical, policies. The inventory costing method varies, with High Liner and Saputo using both FIFO and weighted-average, and Maple Leaf and Sun-Rype using weighted-average costing. Although these different methods create somewhat different numbers, their overall impact on our ratios would depend on how much costs varied during the year.

The four companies calculate amortization using the straight-line method with similar ranges of estimated useful lives for buildings and equipment. Because inventories, buildings, and equipment make up a significant portion of each company's assets, these similarities go a long way toward making the financial results comparable across the companies. The conclusion from our analysis of Exhibit 13.5 is that, although some differences exist among the companies' accounting policies, they are unlikely (in this case) to have a major impact on our comparisons.

Remember that different stakeholder groups are interested in different aspects of a business, and each group may focus its analysis on certain selected ratios. For example, a banker wondering whether to approve a six-month loan would be interested primarily in the company's short-term liquidity ratios, while a holder of long-term bonds might look at the solvency ratios first. Shareholders might be interested primarily in the profitability ratios, since profits belong to them.

Let's turn now from the main accounting measures of performance to the main market measure of performance: the price of the company's shares. Whether Nasdaq is streaking them across its quarter-acre MarketSite Tower in Times Square, or your computer is streaming them onto your desktop, or a stock market analyst is going on about them on CTV, stock prices are everywhere. And if you pay attention to business news reports, you'll quickly see that stock prices depend a great deal on how well a company is doing.

POINT OF INTEREST

Nasdaq used to stand for the National Association of Securities Dealers Automated Quotations. Today, it is the name of the company that operates the world's largest electronic, screen-based stock market.

COACH'S TIP

Analysts typically use the most recent closing stock price as the top number, meaning that the P/E ratio will change every day that the stock price changes. For the bottom of the P/E ratio, analysts often use the most recent annual EPS figure, or the total of the four most recent quarterly EPS numbers. A common rule of thumb is that the P/E ratio should approximate the company's growth rate.

EVALUATE

Financial Results in Relation to Stock Price

THE RELATIONSHIP BETWEEN EARNINGS AND STOCK PRICES

Now that you know how to analyze a company's financial statements, does this mean that you're ready to tell people whether to buy shares in a company? No. The first thing to realize is that there's a difference between analyzing financial statements and predicting stock prices. When analyzing financial statements, you're trying to *evaluate* management's effectiveness. When predicting stock prices, you're trying to put a *value* on what the company is worth. To go from evaluation to valuation, you need additional tools and skills.

Sophisticated techniques to value a company are taught in advanced courses in corporate finance, but, for this course, let's focus on a simple tool. The **price/earnings ratio** is the most basic way to determine the value investors place on a company's common stock. The P/E ratio, as most people call it, measures how many times more than current year's earnings investors are willing to pay for a company's shares. The P/E ratio is calculated as:

$$\text{Price/Earnings Ratio} = \frac{\text{Stock Price (per Share)}}{\text{Earnings per Share (annual)}}$$

Generally, a relatively high P/E ratio means investors expect the company to do better in the future and increase profits, so they have factored the future earnings into the current stock price. A relatively low P/E ratio typically means that they don't expect strong future performance. P/E ratios can vary significantly across industries, so you'll find them most meaningful when comparing a company over time with itself or with competitors in the same industry.

Be on the Alert

Some people think a high P/E ratio means a stock is priced too high, or, conversely, the shares are cheap and therefore a good buy if the ratio is low. We caution against jumping to these conclusions. The P/E ratio differs from other ratios in that it uses information from a company's financial statements and information from the stock market. It combines factual information with information based on investor expectations as reflected in the share price. Therefore, interpretation of a high or low P/E ratio can be difficult. For example, a low P/E ratio may mean a company is headed for trouble, or a high P/E ratio may mean the company has made an important discovery or acquisition that hasn't yet affected EPS.

Over the five-year period from 2003 to 2008 High Liner's P/E ratio ranged from a low of 2 to a high of 37.5. For the same period the industry's P/E ranged from 6.2 to 36.6. High Liner's P/E ratio in November 2008 was 11.2, compared with an industry average of 3.7.

Stock prices rise on good news, since investors expect the good news to translate into higher profits for the company and ultimately for them in the future. Like most ratios, the P/E ratio does not tell you the whole story by itself. Instead, it's most useful in alerting you to the need to learn more about how the company is changing.

RECONSIDER _____
The Conceptual Framework for Financial Accounting

THE OBJECTIVE OF FINANCIAL REPORTING

It shouldn't come as a surprise to you that financial statements are useful for evaluating performance and predicting the future. After all, the accounting rule-makers at the CICA had these goals in mind when they developed the conceptual framework for financial accounting. We introduced you to concepts throughout this text when needed to clarify the topics under discussion. Here we organize the various components into a cohesive package. The conceptual framework, shown in Exhibit 13.6, begins at the top of the pyramid, with the primary objective of external financial reporting, and is developed further in the other layers of the pyramid. The primary objective is to provide useful economic information about a business to help external parties, primarily investors and creditors, make sound financial decisions. The first box in the middle layer of Exhibit 13.6 lists and defines the financial statement elements that are expected to convey this useful information.

The second box in the middle layer of Exhibit 13.6 summarizes the primary characteristics that make information "useful," including its **relevance, reliability, comparability and consistency,** and **understandability.** High Liner's financial statements

POINT OF INTEREST

High Liner's financial reporting is exemplary, as evidenced by the fact that it won the CICA's 2005 Corporate Reporting Award in its category.

provide relevant information because they give *feedback* on past results (how much property did the company acquire?); they are useful in *predicting* future results (the steady increase in EPS noted earlier suggests EPS will continue increasing in the future); and they are available on a *timely* basis (third-quarter results were released the following month). High Liner's results are *reliable* because they *faithfully represent* what really happened during the period, and because they are *neutral* (without bias) and *verifiable* by a third party (in 2007, the audit was done by Ernst & Young).[2]

As the bottom layer of Exhibit 13.6 indicates, financial accounting is based on four main assumptions. We've already discussed the separate entity and unit of measure assumptions in earlier chapters, so we won't take up your time repeating them here. If you need a refresher, read the definition in the exhibit, or flip back to the chapter where they were introduced (shown in brackets in Exhibit 13.6). The two assumptions that we haven't discussed yet are the time-period and going-concern assumptions. The **time-period assumption** is what allows High Liner's accountants to divide the company's long

The **time-period assumption** indicates that the long life of a company can be reported in shorter time periods.

---

exhibit 13.6   Conceptual Framework for Financial Accounting and Reporting

PRIMARY OBJECTIVE OF EXTERNAL FINANCIAL REPORTING
To provide useful economic information to external users (particularly investors and creditors) for decision making (assessing future cash flows) [Ch. 5]

ELEMENTS OF FINANCIAL STATEMENTS
Asset—economic resource with probable future benefits [Ch. 2]
Liability—probable future sacrifices of economic resources [Ch. 2]
Shareholders' Equity—financing provided by owners and operations (residual interest to owners) [Ch. 2]
Revenue—increase in assets or settlement of liabilities from ongoing operations [Ch. 3]
Expense—decrease in assets or increase in liabilities from ongoing operations [Ch. 3]
Gain—increase in assets or settlement of liabilities from peripheral activities [Ch. 3]
Loss—decrease in assets or increase in liabilities from peripheral activities [Ch. 3]

QUALITATIVE CHARACTERISTICS OF FINANCIAL INFORMATION
To be useful, information should possess:
Relevance—be capable of making a difference in decisions [Ch. 5]
- feedback value (assess prior expectations)
- predictive value (extrapolate into the future)
- timeliness (available to help with decisions)
Reliability—can be relied upon [Ch. 5]
- representational faithfulness (represents reality)
- verifiability (can be verified independently)
- neutrality (unbiased)
Comparability and consistency—information should be comparable across companies and consistent over time [Ch. 5]
Understandability—information should be understandable by readers if they have a reasonable grasp of business, economics, and accounting and they study the information with diligence [Ch. 13]

ASSUMPTIONS
Separate entity—activities of the business are separate from activities of the owners [Ch. 1]
Unit of measure—accounting measurements are in the national monetary unit [Ch. 2]
Time period—the long life of a company can be reported over a series of shorter time periods [Ch. 13]
Going concern (continuity)—entity will not go out of business in the near future [Ch. 13]

PRINCIPLES
Historical cost—cash equivalent price on the transaction date is used initially to measure elements [Ch. 2]
Revenue recognition—record revenue when earned, measurable, and realizable [Ch. 3]
Matching—record expenses in the same period as the revenues they help to generate [Ch. 3]
Full disclosure—provide all information sufficiently important to influence a decision [Ch. 5]

CONSTRAINTS
Conservatism—exercise care not to overstate assets and revenues or understate liabilities and expenses [Ch. 2]
Materiality—relatively small amounts not likely to influence decisions are to be recorded in the most cost-beneficial way [Ch. 8]
Cost-benefit—benefits to users should outweigh costs of providing information [Ch. 13]

---

[2] As Canada makes the transition to IFRS, the CICA has proposed that the term *reliability* be dropped and replaced with the term *faithful representation* when describing information that is complete, accurate and neutral, but this proposal has not yet been approved.

life into a series of shorter periods so that measures of its performance and financial position can be obtained on a timely basis. Given the time period assumption, accountants can divide a company's indefinite life into monthly, quarterly, or annual periods for financial reporting purposes. This is the main reason that adjusting journal entries are needed (as discussed in Chapter 4). The **going-concern assumption** (also called the **continuity** assumption) states that a business is assumed capable of continuing its operations long enough to meet its obligations. If a company runs into severe financial difficulty (such as bankruptcy), this assumption may no longer be appropriate, leading to what is called a "going-concern problem."[3]

The four main principles of accounting (summarized in the middle box in the bottom layer of Exhibit 13.6) have been introduced in earlier chapters. You also should be aware of the practical constraints listed in the bottom right of Exhibit 13.6, which may affect how things are reported in financial statements. In addition to issues like materiality and conservatism, which were discussed in earlier chapters, there is one additional constraint that we should discuss. The **cost-benefit constraint** recognizes that it is costly for companies to gather all the financial information that could possibly be reported. Accounting rules should be implemented only to the extent that the benefits outweigh the costs of doing so.

Before closing the book on this topic (and possibly this course), take a moment to attempt the following Self-Study Quiz. It'll give you a good idea of whether you should do a detailed review of the concepts introduced in earlier chapters, or whether you're ready to move on to review and practise the key aspects of this chapter.

The **going-concern (continuity) assumption** states that businesses are assumed to continue to operate into the foreseeable future.

The **cost-benefit constraint** advises that accounting rules should be followed to the extent that the benefits outweigh the costs of doing so.

HOW'S IT GOING? A Self-Study Quiz

Match each statement below with the characteristic, assumption, principle, or constraint to which it most closely relates.

1. I can use it, but only if I get it soon.
2. Don't let your hopes or wishes influence what you say.
3. Don't sweat it. It's not big enough to worry about.
4. Tell me like it is, based on what really happened.
5. I've told you everything you could possibly want to know.
6. When in doubt, don't be overly optimistic.
7. I know it's a long time, but let's look at it in stages.
8. You can reach a point where it's just not worth all the trouble.
9. At that rate, you may not survive past the end of the year.
10. Let's do it the way we always have.

(a) Neutrality
(b) Conservatism
(c) Going concern
(d) Timeliness
(e) Time period
(f) Cost-benefit
(g) Materiality
(h) Consistency
(i) Full disclosure
(j) Representational faithfulness

Quiz Answers
1. (d) 2. (a) 3. (g) 4. (j) 5. (i) 6. (b) 7. (e) 8. (f) 9. (c) 10. (h)

[3] When there is substantial doubt about the company's ability to continue as a going concern, this fact should be disclosed in the notes to the company's financial statements. If the auditor determines that the disclosure is not adequate, the auditor will draw attention to this issue in the auditor's report. When the going-concern (continuity) assumption is no longer appropriate for a company, all its assets and liabilities are measured at their liquidation values.

FOR YOUR REVIEW _____

DEMONSTRATION CASE

The following ratios for Sun-Rype were presented as benchmarks for interpreting High Liner's 2007 ratios:

Asset turnover = 1.33

Fixed asset turnover = 5.0

ROE = 11.7

Current ratio = 2.1

Debt-to-assets = 0.28

Capital-acquisitions ratio = 1.1 (two-year average)

Required:

With reference to the Sun-Rype annual report in the *Cases* section of the text's Web site at www.mcgrawhill.ca/college/phillips, demonstrate how the ratios listed above for 2007 were calculated.

Suggested Solution

Asset turnover	= Net sales revenue ÷ Average total sales
	= $135,134 ÷ [(56,884 + 59,447) / 2]
	= 1.33
Fixed asset turnover	= Net sales revenue ÷ Average net fixed assets
	= $135,134 ÷ [(27,867 + 25,947) / 2]
	= 5.0
Return on equity	= Net Income ÷ Average shareholders' equity
	= $4,636 ÷ [(41,023 + 38,008)/2]
	= 11.7
Current ratio	= Current assets ÷ Current liabilities
	= $29,017 ÷ 13,969
	= 2.1
Debt-to-assets	= Total liabilities ÷ Total assets
	= $15,861 ÷ 56,884
	= 0.28
Capital acquisitions	= Cash from operations (two years) ÷ Cash paid for PPE (two years)
	= (10,266 + 5,739) ÷ (7,358 + 6,639)
	= 1.1

CHAPTER SUMMARY

LO1   **Describe the purposes and uses of trend and ratio analyses. p. 578**

- Trend analyses compare financial statement items with comparable amounts in prior periods, with the goal of identifying sustained changes ("trends").

- Ratio analyses compare one or more financial statement items with an amount for other items for the same year. Ratios take into account differences in the sizes of amounts to allow for evaluations of performance, given existing levels of other company resources.

- When comparing over time and across companies, watch out for possible differences in business strategy, operations, accounting policies, and non-recurring events that can affect reported financial results.

LO2   **Perform trend analyses. p. 581**

- Calculate year-over-year percentage changes in key financial statement numbers to help assess company performance.

Categorize, calculate, and interpret key ratios relating to profitability, liquidity, and solvency. p. 591   **LO3**

- Profitability ratios focus on measuring the adequacy of net income by comparing it with other items reported on the financial statements.
- Liquidity ratios measure a company's ability to meet its current maturing debt.
- Solvency ratios measure a company's ability to meet its long-term obligations.
- Exhibit 13.4 lists these ratios and shows how to compute them.

(Supplement A) Study the treatment of non-recurring and other items. p. 596   **LO4**

- Discontinued operations and extraordinary items are non-recurring items that are shown separately in the income statement on a net-of-tax basis.
- Changes in accounting policies are treated retroactively in the financial statements.
- Accounting rules require that certain unrealized gains and losses be excluded from the calculation of net income. These special items are combined with net income on the income statement to arrive at comprehensive income.

Calculate and interpret the price-earnings ratio. p. 590   **LO5**

- The price/earnings (P/E) ratio measures the relationship between the current market price of a company's shares and its earnings per share. Typically, the ratio will be high for companies that are expected to produce higher future earnings, and low for companies that are expected to produce lower future earnings.

Define the objective of financial reporting, and explain key accounting assumptions, principles, and constraints. p. 591   **LO6**

- The primary objective of external financial reporting is to provide useful economic information about a business to help external parties, primarily investors and creditors, make sound financial decisions.
- Key accounting assumptions:
  - *a.* Separate-entity assumption—transactions of the business are accounted for separately from transactions of the owner(s).
  - *b.* Unit-of-measure assumption—financial information is reported in the national monetary unit.
  - *c.* Time-period assumption—the long life of a company can be reported over a series of shorter time periods.
  - *d.* Going-concern (continuity) assumption—it is assumed that a business will continue to operate into the foreseeable future.
- Key accounting principles:
  - *a.* Historical cost principle—financial statement elements should be recorded at the cash-equivalent cost on the date of the transaction.
  - *b.* Revenue recognition principle—record revenue when earned, measurable, and realizable.
  - *c.* Matching principle—record when expenses are incurred to generate revenues.
  - *d.* Full disclosure principle—provide information sufficiently important to influence a decision.
- Key accounting constraints:
  - *a.* Conservatism—exercise care not to overstate assets and revenues or understate liabilities and expenses.
  - *b.* Materiality—relatively small amounts not likely to influence decisions are to be recorded in the most cost-beneficial way.
  - *c.* Cost-benefit—benefits to users should outweigh costs of providing information.

FINANCIAL STATEMENT ANALYSIS TIPS

All ratios are summarized in Exhibit 13.4 on pages 582 and 583.

KEY TERMS TO KNOW

Cost-Benefit Constraint
p. 593
Discontinued Operations
p. 596
Efficiency p. 581

Extraordinary Items p. 596
Going-Concern (Continuity)
Assumption p. 593
Liquidity p. 583
Profitability p. 581

Retroactive p. 597
Solvency p. 583
Time-Period Assumption
p. 592

SUPPLEMENT A: NON-RECURRING AND OTHER ITEMS

Non-recurring Items

A company's income statement may include two types of non-recurring items: discontinued operations and extraordinary items. We discuss each of these below.

Discontinued Operations

> **Discontinued operations** result from the disposal of a major component of the business and are reported net of income tax effects.

Discontinued operations result from abandoning or selling a major business component. The discontinued operations line-item on the income statement includes any gain or loss on disposal of the discontinued operation, as well as any operating income generated during the current year prior to its disposal. Because gains or losses from discontinued operations appear below the income tax expense line on the income statement, any additional tax effects related to the gains or losses are included in their reported amounts.

High Liner reported a gain of $372,000 (net of taxes) from discontinued operations in its fiscal 2007 income statement and a loss of $793,000 in 2006, and restated its 2005 income statement numbers to show a loss of $44,323,000. You can read in Appendix A, Note 3, the details of the discontinued operations, including the sale of the Italian Foods division, and the sale of the Arnold Cove processing plant. Obviously, the sale of a particular business unit can happen only once, so these results are reported separately to inform users that they are not predictive of the company's future.

Extraordinary Items

> **Extraordinary items** are gains and losses that are both unusual in nature, and infrequent in occurrence, and are not the result of management decisions; they are reported net of tax on the income statement.

Extraordinary items are gains or losses that are considered both unusual in nature, infrequent in occurrence, and not the result of management decisions. Examples include losses suffered from natural disasters such as floods and hurricanes in parts of the world where such disasters are rare. Any items reported as extraordinary items must be explained in the notes to the financial statements. Clearly, transactions like these are not likely to recur in the future, so they are reported immediately following discontinued operations. Because they appear below income tax expense, extraordinary items are reported net of any taxes directly related to them. Extraordinary items are rare and the term is likely to disappear altogether in Canada as we transition to IFRS.

Special Items

POINT OF INTEREST

Because financial losses related to the September 11, 2001, attacks were so widespread, the FASB concluded that no single line-item could adequately capture them. As a result, the FASB ruled that the financial effects of these events should not be reported as extraordinary, even though we certainly think of them that way.

Starting in 2005, you may see that some companies include additional items on their income statement after the *Net Income* line. These items may be added to or subtracted from net income to arrive at something called *Comprehensive Income*. As you will learn in detail in intermediate courses in financial accounting, these items represent unrealized gains or losses relating to changes in the value of certain balance sheet accounts. While most gains and losses are included in the computation of net income, some (relating to changes in foreign currency exchange rates and the value of certain investments) are excluded from net income and included only when computing comprehensive income. The main reason for excluding these gains and losses from net income is that the changes in value that created them may very well disappear before they are ever realized (when the company gets rid of the assets or liabilities to which they relate). For this reason, most analysts will take a moment to consider the size of these special items in relation to net income, and, if they are not large, will exclude them from the profitability ratios presented earlier in this chapter.[4]

---

[4] Although comprehensive income has been around in the United States for years, it has only recently been adopted in Canada.

Changes in Accounting Methods

The final item that we must discuss reflects the income statement effects of any adjustment made to the accounts because of a change to a different acceptable accounting method. When a company changes accounting methods, GAAP often requires that we determine what the balance sheet and income statement amounts would be if the new accounting method had always been applied. These effects are shown **retroactively** in the financial statements, meaning that the balance sheet, income statement, and opening retained earnings figures reflect the new numbers. Retroactive adjustments are also made to any comparative figures for previous years, to maintain comparability across time. The cumulative effects for prior years are shown net-of-tax as an adjustment to opening retained earnings.

While most changes in accounting methods involve implementing new CICA rules, it is possible that managers will determine that a change to an alternative accounting method is necessary because of changes in business activities. For example, managers might switch from FIFO to weighted-average or from declining-balance to straight-line amortization. Any time an accounting method is changed, note disclosure explaining the change is required. Effective January 1, 2005, High Liner adopted a new accounting policy for stock options, as a result of a new accounting rule in Canada. High Liner appropriately treated this change retroactively, restating numbers back to 2002.

Retroactive treatment means that current and prior year financial statement numbers are restated to reflect the new accounting method.

———— **FOR YOUR PRACTICE**

QUESTIONS

1. What is the general goal of trend analysis?
2. How is a year-over-year percentage calculated?
3. What is ratio analysis? Why is it useful?
4. What benchmarks are commonly used for interpreting ratios?
5. Into what three categories of performance are most financial ratios split? To what in particular does each of these categories relate?
6. What ratios would a short-term lender be most interested in? A long-term lender? A shareholder?
7. What is one of the most basic ways to determine the value investors place on a company's shares?
8. Give two different interpretations of a high P/E ratio.
9. What is the primary objective of financial reporting?
10. Why is the time-period assumption necessary?
11. What is the going-concern assumption? What is a "going-concern problem"?
12. How does the cost-benefit constraint impact financial reporting?
13. (Supplement A) Name two types of non-recurring items, and explain where and how they are reported on the income statement.

MULTIPLE CHOICE

Select the one alternative that best answers the question or completes the sentence.

1. Which of the following ratios is *not* used to analyze profitability?
   a. Quality-of-income ratio
   b. Gross profit percentage
   c. Current ratio
   d. Return on equity
2. Which of the following would *not* change the receivables-turnover ratio for your company?
   a. Increases in the selling prices of your inventory
   b. A change in your credit policy
   c. Increases in the cost you incur to purchase inventory
   d. All of the above could change the receivables-turnover ratio.

3. Which of the following ratios is used to analyze liquidity?

    a. Earnings per share

    b. Debt-to-assets

    c. Current ratio

    d. Both *b* and *c*

4. Analysts use ratios to

    a. Compare different companies in the same industry.

    b. Track a company's performance over time.

    c. Compare a company's performance with industry averages.

    d. All of the above describe ways that analysts use ratios.

5. Which of the following ratios incorporates cash flows from operations?

    a. Inventory-turnover

    b. Earnings-per-share

    c. Quality-of-income

    d. All of the above

6. Given the following ratios for four companies (below), which company is least likely to experience problems paying its current liabilities promptly?

	Current Ratio	Receivables-Turnover Ratio
a.	1.2	7.0
b.	1.2	6.0
c.	1.0	6.0
d.	0.5	7.0

7. A decrease in selling and administrative expenses would impact what ratio?

    a. Fixed-asset-turnover ratio

    b. Times-interest-earned ratio

    c. Current ratio

    d. None of the above

8. A bank is least likely to use which of the following ratios when analyzing the likelihood that a borrower will pay all that it owes?

    a. Cash-coverage ratio

    b. Debt-to-assets ratio

    c. Times-interest-earned ratio

    d. Return-on-equity ratio

9. Which of the following accounting concepts requires accountants to use adjusting journal entries?

    a. Cost benefit

    b. Materiality

    c. Conservatism

    d. Time-period assumption

10. (Supplement A) Which of the following items is not reported net of related income taxes?

    a. Gain or loss from discontinued operations

    b. Gain or loss from extraordinary items

    c. Cumulative effect of accounting changes

    d. All of the above are reported net of related income taxes.

Solutions to Multiple-choice Questions
1. *c* 2. *c* 3. *c* 4. *d* 5. *c* 6. *a* 7. *b* 8. *d* 9. *d* 10. *d*

MINI-EXERCISES

COACH'S TIP

LO3

M13-1 Inferring Financial Information Using Gross Profit Percentage

Your campus computer store reported revenue of $1,680,000. The company's gross profit percentage was 60.0 per cent. What amount of cost of goods sold did the company report?

To calculate cost of goods sold in M13-1, work backwards from the gross profit percentage.

M13-2 Inferring Financial Information Using Gross Profit Percentage and Year-over-Year Comparisons **LO3**

A consumer products company reported a 25 per cent increase in sales from 2007 to 2008. Sales in 2007 were $20,000. In 2008, the company reported cost of goods sold in the amount of $15,000. What was the gross profit percentage in 2008?

M13-3 Computing the Return-on-Equity Ratio **LO3**

Compute the return-on-equity ratio for 2008 given the following data:

	2008	2007
Net income	$ 185,000	$ 160,000
Shareholders' equity	1,000,000	1,312,500
Total assets	2,400,000	2,600,000
Interest expense	40,000	30,000

M13-4 Analyzing the Inventory-Turnover Ratio **LO3**

A manufacturer reported an inventory-turnover ratio of 8.6 during 2007. During 2008, management introduced a new inventory control system that was expected to reduce average inventory levels by 25 per cent without affecting sales volume. Given these circumstances, would you expect the inventory-turnover ratio to increase or decrease during 2008? Explain.

M13-5 Inferring Financial Information Using the Current Ratio **LO3**

Scruggs Company reported total assets of $1,200,000 and noncurrent assets of $480,000. The company also reported a current ratio of 1.5. What amount of current liabilities did the company report?

M13-6 Analyzing the Impact of Accounting Alternatives **LO3**

Lexis Corporation operates in an industry where costs are rising. The company is considering changing its inventory method from FIFO to average cost and wants to determine the impact that the change would have on selected accounting ratios in future years. In general, what impact would you expect on the following ratios: net-profit-margin, fixed-asset-turnover, and current ratio?

M13-7 Inferring Financial Information Using the P/E Ratio **LO5**

In 2007, Drago Company reported earnings per share of $8.50 when its shares were selling for $212.50. In 2008, its earnings increased by 20 per cent. If all other relationships remain constant, what is the price of the shares in 2008? Explain.

M13-8 (Supplement A) Analyzing the Impact of Non-recurring Items **LO4**

Northern Drilling Corporation operates an oil exploration company in Nunavut. In March 2007, one of the company's drilling platforms was destroyed by a tornado, resulting in an uninsured equipment loss of $4 million. How would this event, which is highly unusual for Nunavut, affect the following ratios: net-profit-margin, fixed-asset-turnover, and current ratio?

EXERCISES

E13-1 Preparing a Schedule Using Year-over-Year Percentages **LO2**

Consumers have been hit hard at the pump in each of the last three years, with gas prices jumping 15 to 20 per cent per year. Let's see whether those changes were reflected in the income statements of Shell Canada for the years ended December 31, 2007, 2006, and 2005 (amounts in millions).

	2007	2006	2005	2004
Total revenues	$14,806	$14,394	$11,285	$9,117
Costs of crude oil and products	8,627	7,900	6,068	5,077
Other operating costs	3,944	3,727	3,337	2,832
Income before income tax expense	2,235	2,767	1,880	1,208
Income tax expense	497	766	597	398
Net income	$ 1,738	$ 2,001	$ 1,283	$ 810

Required:

Calculate the year-over-year changes for revenues, costs of crude oil and products, other operating costs, and net income. How did the changes in gas prices compare with these changes?

LO3   E13-2 Computing Profitability Ratios

Use the information in E13-1 to complete the following requirements.

Required:

1. Compute the gross profit percentage for each year. Assuming that the change from 2004 to 2007 is the beginning of a sustained trend, is Shell likely to earn more, less, or about the same gross profit from each dollar of sales in 2008?
2. Compute the net profit margin for each year. Given your calculations here and in requirement 1, explain whether Shell did a better or worse job of controlling expenses other than the costs of crude oil and products over the years.
3. Shell reported average net fixed assets of $11,368 million in 2007 and $8,550 million in 2006. Compute the fixed-asset-turnover ratios for both years. Did the company better utilize its investment in fixed assets to generate revenues in 2007 or 2006?
4. Shell reported average shareholders' equity of $8,890 million in 2007 and $7,372 million in 2006. Compute the return-on-equity ratios for both years. Did the company generate greater returns for shareholders in 2007 or 2006?

LO3   E13-3 Computing a Commonly Used Solvency Ratio

Use the information in E13-1 to complete the following requirement.

Required:

Interest expense in the amount of $42 million was included with "other operating costs" in 2007 ($12 million in 2006). Compute the times-interest-earned ratios for each year. In your opinion, does Shell generate sufficient net income (before taxes and interest) to cover the cost of debt financing?

LO3   E13-4 Matching Each Ratio with Its Computational Formula

Match each ratio or percentage with its formula by entering the appropriate letter for each numbered item.

Ratios or Percentages	Formula
_____ 1. Net profit margin	A. Net income ÷ Net sales revenue
_____ 2. Inventory-turnover ratio	B. (Net sales revenue − Cost of goods sold) ÷ Net sales revenue
_____ 3. Cash-coverage ratio	
_____ 4. Fixed-asset-turnover ratio	C. Current assets ÷ Current liabilities
_____ 5. Capital-acquisitions ratio	D. Cost of goods sold ÷ Average inventory
_____ 6. Return on equity	E. Net credit sales revenue ÷ Average net receivables
_____ 7. Current ratio	F. Net cash flows from operating activities ÷ Net income
_____ 8. Debt-to-assets ratio	
_____ 9. Price/earnings ratio	G. Net income ÷ Average number of common shares outstanding
_____ 10. Receivables-turnover ratio	H. Total liabilities ÷ Total assets
_____ 11. Earnings-per-share	I. (Net income + Interest expense + Income tax expense) ÷ Interest expense
_____ 12. Quality-of-income ratio	J. (Cash + Short-term investments + Accounts receivable) ÷ Current liabilities
_____ 13. Gross profit percentage	
_____ 14. Times-interest-earned ratio	K. Net cash flows from operating activities ÷ Cash paid for property, plant, and equipment
_____ 15. Quick ratio	L. Current market price per share ÷ Earnings per share
	M. Net income ÷ Average total shareholders' equity
	N. Net cash flows from operating activities (before interest and taxes) ÷ Interest paid
	O. Net sales revenue ÷ Average net fixed assets

E13-5 Computing Selected Liquidity Ratios

LO3

DuckWing Stores reported sales for the year of $600,000, of which one-half was on credit. The average gross profit percentage was 40 per cent on sales. Account balances follow:

	Beginning	Ending
Accounts receivable (net)	$40,000	$60,000
Inventory	70,000	30,000

Required:

1. Compute the turnover ratios for accounts receivable and inventory.
2. By dividing your ratios from requirement 1 into 365, calculate the average days to collect receivables and the average days to sell inventory.

E13-6 Computing Liquidity Ratios

LO3

Canadian Tire Corporation operates 400 stores across Canada that sell a lot more than tires. Selected information from the company's balance sheet follows. For 2007, the company reported sales revenue of $8,621 million.

	2007	2006
Balance Sheet (amounts in millions)		
Cash	$ 105.5	741.3
Accounts receivable	707.1	340.5
Inventories	756.7	667.3
Prepaid expenses and deposits	29.5	46.2
Accounts payable	1,847.8	1,579.5
Income taxes payable	59.0	81.1
Long-term debt due within one year	156.3	3.0

Required:

Compute the current ratio, quick ratio, and accounts-receivable-turnover ratio (assuming that 60 per cent of sales was on credit) for 2007. (Since Canadian Tire does not disclose its cost of sales, the inventory turnover cannot be calculated.)

E13-7 Analyzing the Impact of Selected Transactions on the Current Ratio

LO3

In its most recent annual report, Laurentian Beverages reported current assets of $54,000 and a current ratio of 1.8. Assume that the following transactions were completed: (1) purchased merchandise for $6,000 on account, and (2) purchased a delivery truck for $10,000, paying $1,000 cash and signing a two-year promissory note for the balance.

Required:

Compute the updated current ratio after each transaction.

E13-8 Analyzing the Impact of Selected Transactions on the Current Ratio

LO3

In its most recent annual report, Sunrise Enterprises reported current assets of $1,090,000 and current liabilities of $602,000.

Required:

Determine the impact of the following transactions on the current ratio for Sunrise: (1) sold long-term assets for cash, (2) accrued severance pay for terminated employees, (3) wrote down the carrying value of certain inventory items that were deemed to be obsolete, and (4) acquired new inventory by signing an 18-month promissory note (the supplier was not willing to provide normal credit terms).

LO3   **E13-9   Analyzing the Impact of Selected Transactions on the Current Ratio**

Forzani Group is the country's largest publicly traded full-line sporting goods retailer. Stores are operated under four corporate banners: Sport Chek, Sport Mart, National Sports, and Coast Mountain Sports. Assume one of the Forzani stores reported current assets of $88,000 and its current ratio was 1.75. Assume that the following transactions were completed: (1) paid $6,000 on accounts payable, (2) purchased a delivery truck for $10,000 cash, (3) wrote off a bad account receivable for $2,000, and (4) paid previously declared dividends in the amount of $25,000.

Required:

Compute the updated current ratio after each transaction.

LO3   **E13-10   Analyzing the Impact of Selected Transactions on the Current Ratio**

Current assets totalled $500,000, the current ratio was 2.0, and the Mountain Trail Company uses the perpetual inventory method. Assume that the following transactions were completed: (1) sold $12,000 in merchandise on short-term credit for $15,000, (2) declared but did not pay dividends of $50,000, (3) paid prepaid rent in the amount of $12,000, (4) paid previously declared dividends in the amount of $50,000, (5) collected an account receivable in the amount of $12,000, and (6) reclassified $40,000 of long-term debt as a current liability.

Required:

Compute the updated current ratio after each transaction.

LO3   **E13-11   Computing the Accounts-Receivable and Inventory-Turnover Ratios**

Gildan Activewear makes blank T-shirts and activewear for private label use and is headquartered in Montreal. Last year, sales for the company were $533,368 (all amounts in thousands). The annual report did not report the amount of credit sales, so we will assume that all sales were on credit. The average gross margin rate was 29 per cent on sales. Account balances follow:

	Beginning	**Ending**
Accounts receivable (net)	$ 64,260	$ 85,317
Inventory	103,503	116,615

Required:

1. Compute the turnover ratios for accounts receivable and inventory.
2. By dividing your ratios from requirement 1 into 365, calculate the average days to collect receivables and the average days to sell inventory.

COACH'S TIP

In E13-12, work backward from the fixed-asset-turnover and inventory-turnover ratios to compute the amounts needed for the gross profit percentage.

LO3   **E13-12   Inferring Financial Information from Profitability and Liquidity Ratios**

Humpty Dumpty makes branded and private label snack foods, and was once Canada's leading snack food brand. For the year ended September 30, 2004, the company reported average inventories of $6,856 (in thousands) and an inventory turnover of 15.48. Average total fixed assets were $38,674 (thousand), and the fixed-asset-turnover ratio was 4.16.

Required:

Rounded to one decimal place, calculate Humpty Dumpty's gross profit percentage for the year. What does this imply about the amount of gross profit made from each dollar of sales?

LO3   **E13-13   Using Financial Information to Identify Mystery Companies**

The following selected financial data pertain to four unidentified companies (balance sheet amounts reported in millions):

	Companies			
	1	**2**	**3**	**4**
Balance Sheet Data				
Cash	$ 5.1	$ 8.8	$ 6.3	$ 10.4
Accounts receivable	13.1	41.5	13.8	4.9
Inventory	4.6	3.6	65.1	35.8
Property and equipment	53.1	23.0	8.8	35.7
Selected Ratios				
Gross profit percentage	N/A*	N/A	45.2	22.5
Net profit margin	0.3	16.0	3.9	1.5
Current ratio	0.7	2.2	1.9	1.4
Inventory–turnover ratio	N/A	N/A	1.4	15.5
Debt-to-equity	2.5	0.9	1.7	2.3

*N/A Not applicable.

This financial information pertains to the following companies:

1. Cable TV company
2. Grocery store
3. Accounting firm
4. Retail jewellery store

Required:

Match each company with its financial information, and explain the basis for your answers.

E13-14 Analyzing the Impact of Alternative Inventory Methods on Selected Ratios   LO3

Company A uses the FIFO method to cost inventory, and Company B uses the weighted-average method. The two companies are exactly alike except for the difference in inventory costing methods. Costs of inventory items for both companies have been declining steadily in recent years, and each company has increased its inventory each year. Ignore income tax effects.

Required:

Identify which company will report the higher amount for each of the following ratios. If it is not possible to identify which will report the higher amount, explain why.

1. Current ratio
2. Debt-to-assets ratio
3. Earnings per share

COACHED PROBLEMS

CP13-1 Analyzing Comparative Financial Statements Using Year-over-Year Percentages   LO2

The comparative financial statements prepared at December 31, 2008, for Golden Corporation showed the following summarized data:

Calculate the increase (decrease) by subtracting 2007 from 2008. Calculate the percentage by dividing the amount of increase (decrease) by the 2008 balance.

	2008	2007	Increase (Decrease) 2008 over 2007	
			Amount	Percentage
Income Statement				
Sales revenue	$ 180,000*	$ 165,000		
Cost of goods sold	110,000	100,000		
Gross profit	70,000	65,000		
Operating expenses	53,300	50,400		
Interest expense	2,700	2,600		
Income before income taxes	14,000	12,000		
Income tax expense	4,000	3,000		
Net income	$ 10,000	$ 9,000		
Balance Sheet				
Cash	$ 4,000	$ 8,000		
Accounts receivable (net)	14,000	18,000		
Inventory	40,000	35,000		
Property and equipment (net)	45,000	38,000		
	$ 103,000	$ 99,000		
Current liabilities	$ 16,000	$ 19,000		
Long-term liabilities (6% interest)	45,000	45,000		
Common shares (6,000 issued)	30,000	30,000		
Retained earnings†	12,000	5,000		
	$ 103,000	$ 99,000		

*One-third of all sales are on account.
†During 2008, cash dividends amounting to $3,000 were declared and paid.

Required:

1. Complete the two final columns shown beside each item in Golden Corporation's comparative financial statements.
2. Does anything significant jump out at you from the year-over-year analyses?

LO3, LO5   **CP13-2** **Analyzing Comparative Financial Statements Using Selected Ratios**
Use the data given in CP13-1 for Golden Corporation.

Required:

1. Compute the gross profit percentages in 2008 and 2007. Is the trend going in the right direction?
2. Compute the net-profit-margin ratios in 2008 and 2007. Is the trend going in the right direction?
3. Compute the earnings per share for 2008 and 2007. Does the trend look good or bad? Explain.
4. Shareholders' equity totalled $30,000 at the end of 2006. Compute the return-on-equity ratios for 2008 and 2007. Is the trend going in the right direction?
5. Net property and equipment totalled $35,000 at the end of 2006. Compute the fixed-asset-turnover ratios for 2008 and 2007. Is the trend going in the right direction?
6. Compute the debt-to-assets ratios for 2008 and 2007. Is debt providing financing for a larger or smaller proportion of the company's asset growth? Explain.
7. Compute the times-interest-earned ratios for 2008 and 2007. Do they look good or bad? Explain.
8. After Golden released its 2008 financial statements, the company's shares were trading at $30. After the release of its 2007 financial statements, the company's stock price was $21 per share. Compute the P/E ratios for both years. Does it appear that investors have become more (or less) optimistic about Golden's future success?

CP13-3 Interpreting Profitability, Liquidity, Solvency, and P/E Ratios

LO3, LO5

Federated Department Stores (FDS) owns Macy's, the popular national retail department store in the United States. The company's total revenues in 2004 were $15 billion. Hudson's Bay Company (HBC), Canada's largest department store, is half that size with only $7 million in revenues, but we can compare the two by using ratio analysis.

Ratio	FDS*	HBC
Gross profit percentage	40.7 %	**
Net profit margin	9.4 %	0.08%
Return on equity	12.4 %	2.7%
EPS	$ 5.89	$ 0.86 %
Receivables-turnover ratio	4.71	12.3
Inventory-turnover ratio	2.89	**
Current ratio	1.19	2.08
Quick ratio	0.39	0.74
Debt-to-assets ratio	0.89	0.74
P/E ratio	11.01	17.50

* FDS ratios obtained from www.marketguide.com
** Cost of goods sold not available

Required:

1. Which company appears more profitable? Describe the ratio(s) that you used to reach this decision.
2. Which company appears more liquid? Describe the ratio(s) that you used to reach this decision.
3. Which company appears more solvent? Describe the ratio(s) that you used to reach this decision.
4. Are the conclusions from your analyses in requirements 1 to 3 consistent with the values of the two companies suggested by the P/E ratios of the two companies? If not, offer one explanation for any apparent inconsistency.

COACH'S TIP

When evaluating the P/E ratio in requirement 4, remember that the top number in the ratio represents investors' expectations about future financial performance, whereas the bottom number reports past financial performance.

CP13-4 Using Ratios to Compare Alternative Investment Opportunities

LO3, LO5

The 2008 financial statements for Benoit and Chapleau companies are summarized here:

	Benoit Company	Chapleau Company
Balance Sheet		
Cash	$ 35,000	$ 22,000
Accounts receivable (net)	40,000	30,000
Inventory	100,000	40,000
Property and equipment (net)	180,000	300,000
Other assets	45,000	408,000
Total assets	$ 400,000	$ 800,000
Current liabilities	$ 100,000	$ 50,000
Long-term debt	60,000	370,000
Total liabilities	160,000	420,000
Common shares	180,000	310,000
Retained earnings	60,000	70,000
Total liabilities and shareholders' equity	$ 400,000	$ 800,000
Income Statement		
Sales revenue (1/3 on credit)	$ 450,000	$ 810,000
Cost of goods sold	(245,000)	(405,000)
Expenses (including interest and income tax)	(160,000)	(315,000)
Net income	$ 45,000	$ 90,000
Selected Data from 2007 Statements		
Accounts receivable (net)	$ 20,000	$ 38,000
Inventory	92,000	45,000
Property and equipment (net)	170,000	290,000
Total assets	350,000	700,000
Long-term debt	60,000	70,000
Total shareholders' equity	231,000	440,000

(*Continued*)

	Benoit Company	**Chapleau Company**
Other Data		
Per share market price at end of 2008	$ 18	$ 27
Average income tax rate	30%	30%
Dividends declared and paid in 2008	$ 36,000	$ 150,000
Number of shares outstanding	15,000	20,000

The companies are in the same line of business and are direct competitors in a large metropolitan area. Both have been in business approximately 10 years, and each has had steady growth. The management of each has a viewpoint different in many respects from the viewpoint of the other. Chapleau is more conservative, and, as its president said, "We avoid what we consider to be undue risk." Neither company is publicly held. Chapleau Company has an annual audit by an independent accountant, but Benoit Company does not.

Required:

1. Complete a schedule similar to Exhibit 13.4 that reflects a ratio analysis of each company.
2. A client of yours has the opportunity to buy 10 per cent of the shares in one or the other company at the per share prices at the end of 2008, and has decided to invest in one of the companies. Based on the data given, prepare a comparative written evaluation of the ratio analyses (and any other available information) and give your recommended choice with the supporting explanation.

LO3, LO5

CP13-5 Analyzing an Investment by Comparing Selected Ratios

You have the opportunity to invest $10,000 in one of two companies from a single industry. The only information you have follows. The word *high* refers to the top third of the industry; *average* is the middle third; *low* is the bottom third.

Ratio	**Company A**	**Company B**
Current	High	Average
Inventory-turnover	Low	Average
Debt-to-assets	High	Average
Times-interest-earned	Low	Average
Price/earnings	Low	Average

COACH'S TIP

When interpreting ratios, think about how they are related to one another. For example, the current ratio and the inventory-turnover ratio both include the inventory balance. This means that the low inventory-turnover ratio can help you to interpret the high current ratio.

Required:

Which company would you select? Write a brief explanation for your recommendation.

GROUP A PROBLEMS

LO2

PA13-1 Analyzing Financial Statements Using Ratios and Percentage Changes

The comparative financial statements prepared at December 31, 2008, for Taber Company showed the following summarized data:

			Increase (Decrease)	
			2008 over 2007	
	2008	**2007**	**Amount**	**Percentage**
Income Statement				
Sales revenue*	$ 110,000	$ 99,000		
Cost of goods sold	52,000	48,000		
Gross profit	58,000	51,000		
Operating expenses	36,000	33,000		
Interest expense	4,000	4,000		
Income before Income taxes	18,000	14,000		
Income tax expense (30%)	5,400	4,200		
Net income	$ 12,600	$ 9,800		

(Continued)

			Increase (Decrease) 2008 over 2007	
	2008	*2007*	*Amount*	*Percentage*
Balance Sheet				
Cash	$ 49,500	$ 18,000		
Accounts receivable (net)	37,000	32,000		
Inventory	25,000	38,000		
Property and equipment (net)	95,000	105,000		
Total assets	$206,500	$193,000		
Accounts payable	$ 42,000	$ 35,000		
Income taxes payable	1,000	500		
Note payable, long-term	40,000	40,000		
Total liabilities	83,000	75,500		
Common shares (9,000 issued)	90,000	90,000		
Retained earnings†	33,500	27,500		
Total liabilities and shareholders' equity	$206,500	$193,000		

*One-half of all sales are on credit.
†During 2008, cash dividends amounting to $6,600 were declared and paid.

Required:

1. Complete the two final columns shown beside each item in Taber Company's comparative financial statements.

2. Does anything significant jump out at you from the year-over-year analyses?

PA13-2 Analyzing Comparative Financial Statements Using Selected Ratios   LO3, LO5
Use the data given in PA13-1 for Taber Company.

Required:

1. Compute the gross profit percentages in 2008 and 2007. Is the trend going in the right direction?

2. Compute the net-profit-margin ratios in 2008 and 2007. Is the trend going in the right direction?

3. Compute the earnings per share for 2008 and 2007. Does the trend look good or bad? Explain.

4. Shareholders' equity totalled $100,000 at the end of 2006. Compute the return-on-equity ratios for 2008 and 2007. Is the trend going in the right direction?

5. Net property and equipment totalled $110,000 at the end of 2006. Compute the fixed-asset-turnover ratios for 2008 and 2007. Is the trend going in the right direction?

6. Compute the debt-to-assets ratios for 2008 and 2007. Is debt providing financing for a larger or smaller proportion of the company's asset growth? Explain.

7. Compute the times-interest-earned ratios for 2008 and 2007. Do they look good or bad? Explain.

8. After Taber released its 2008 financial statements, the company's shares were trading at $18. After the release of its 2007 financial statements, the company's stock price was $15 per share. Compute the P/E ratios for both years. Does it appear that investors have become more (or less) optimistic about Taber's future success?

PA13-3 Interpreting Profitability, Liquidity, Solvency, and P/E Ratios   LO3, LO5
Coke and Pepsi are well-known international brands. Coca-Cola sells more than $13 billion worth of beverages each year, while annual sales of Pepsi products exceed $22 billion. Compare the two companies as a potential investment based on the following ratios:

Ratio	Coca-Cola	PepsiCo
Gross profit percentage	48.53 %	48.95 %
Net profit margin	2.63 %	4.14 %
Return on equity	66.19 %	23.27 %
EPS	$ 3.40	$ 1.54
Receivables-turnover ratio	11.49	9.82
Inventory-turnover ratio	15.06	12.76
Current ratio	1.47	1.40
Debt-to-assets ratio	0.94	0.72
P/E ratio	16.35	18.70

Required:

1. Which company appears more profitable? Describe the ratio(s) that you used to reach this decision.

2. Which company appears more liquid? Describe the ratio(s) that you used to reach this decision.

3. Which company appears more solvent? Describe the ratio(s) that you used to reach this decision.

4. Are the conclusions from your analyses in requirements 1 to 3 consistent with the values of the two companies suggested by the P/E ratios of the two companies? If not, offer one explanation for any apparent inconsistency.

LO3, LO5   **PA13-4 Using Ratios to Compare Loan Requests from Two Companies**

The 2008 financial statements for Rand and Tand companies are summarized here:

	Rand Company	Tand Company
Balance Sheet		
Cash	$ 25,000	$ 45,000
Accounts receivable (net)	55,000	5,000
Inventory	110,000	25,000
Property and equipment (net)	550,000	160,000
Other assets	140,000	57,000
Total assets	$880,000	$292,000
Current liabilities	$120,000	$ 15,000
Long-term debt	190,000	55,000
Common shares	530,000	214,000
Retained earnings	40,000	8,000
Total liabilities and shareholders' equity	$880,000	$292,000
Income Statement		
Sales revenue	$800,000	$280,000
Cost of goods sold	480,000	150,000
Expenses (including interest and income tax)	240,000	95,000
Net income	$ 80,000	$ 35,000
Selected Data from 2007 Statements		
Accounts receivable, net	$ 47,000	$ 11,000
Total assets	790,000	240,000
Long-term debt	190,000	55,000
Property and equipment, net	560,000	150,000
Inventory	95,000	38,000
Total shareholders' equity	580,000	202,000
Other Data		
Per share market price at end of 2008	$ 14.00	$ 11.00
Average income tax rate	30%	30%
Average number of shares outstanding	24,000	10,500

These two companies are in the same line of business, and in the same province but in different cities. One-half of Rand's sales are on credit, whereas one-quarter of Tand's sales are on credit. Each company has been in operation for about 10 years. Both companies received an unqualified audit opinion on the financial statements, which means the independent auditors found nothing wrong. Rand Company wants to borrow $75,000 cash, and Tand Company is asking for $30,000. The loans will be for a two-year period.

Required:

1. Complete a schedule that reflects a ratio analysis of each company. Compute the ratios discussed in the chapter.
2. Assume that you work in the loan department of a local bank. You have been asked to analyze the situation and recommend which loan is preferable. Based on the data given, your analysis prepared in requirement 1, and any other information, give your choice and the supported explanation.

PA13-5 Using Ratios to Compare Two Companies

LO3, LO5

Below are the 2008 financial statements for two companies that operate in the same industry.

	Remus Inc.	Romulus Ltd.
Balance Sheet		
Cash	$ 100,000	$ 50,000
Accounts receivable	300,000	400,000
Inventory	600,000	1,300,000
Property and equipment (net)	1,000,000	700,000
	$2,000,000	$2,450,000
Short-term bank loan	$ 200,000	$ 400,000
Accounts payable	100,000	600,000
Long-term liabilities	800,000	900,000
Contributed capital	10,000	100,000
Retained earnings	890,000	450,000
	$2,000,000	$2,450,000
Income Statement		
Sales	$2,400,000	$3,000,000
Cost of sales	1,400,000	1,200,000
Other expenses	820,000	1,520,000
Net income	$ 180,000	$ 280,000
Common Share Data		
Weighted-average number of shares outstanding during the year	10,000	5,000
Per share market price at end of 2008	$ 9	$ 125
Selected Information from End of 2007		
Accounts receivable	$ 260,000	$ 420,000
Total assets	1,800,000	2,100,000
Inventory	675,000	1,100,000
Property and equipment (net)	800,000	550,000
Shareholders' equity	775,000	450,000

Required:

1. Perform a ratio analysis of each company. Compute the ratios discussed in the chapter.
2. Assuming that both companies have applied for a two-year bank loan, which company would you recommend for the loan? Support your decision by referring to your ratio analysis and comment on other information you'd like to have in making this decision.
3. Assuming that your friend is considering buying shares in one of these companies, which company would you recommend? Support your decision by referring to your ratio analysis and comment on other information you'd like to have in making this decision.

LO3, LO5　**PA13-6**　**Analyzing an Investment by Comparing Selected Ratios**

You have the opportunity to invest $10,000 in one of two companies from a single industry. The only information you have is shown here. The word *high* refers to the top third of the industry; *average* is the middle third; *low* is the bottom third.

Ratio	Company A	Company B
Current	Low	High
Inventory-turnover	High	Low
Debt-to-assets	Low	Average
Times-interest-earned	High	Average
Price/earnings	High	Average

Required:

Which company would you select? Write a brief explanation for your recommendation.

LO3　**PA13-7**　**Using Ratios to Analyze Financial Performance**

Selected financial statement ratios are presented below for the Niagara Valley Fine Tools Company and for the industry that it operates in.

	Niagara			Industry
	2008	**2007**	**2006**	**Average**
Current ratio	2.36	2.01	1.98	2.25
Quick ratio	1.13	1.09	1.01	1.25
Inventory-turnover ratio	2.73	2.89	2.97	3.46
Return-on-equity ratio	0.18	0.12	0.13	0.11
Debt-to-assets ratio	0.76	0.67	0.60	0.51
Asset-turnover ratio	3.15	3.04	2.98	3.45
Profit margin	.08	.07	.07	.08
EPS	.51	.52	.49	1.56

Required:

1. Identify and comment on two ratios from the above list that would be of particular interest in making the following decisions.

   a. A bank is considering approving Niagara's request for a line of credit to provide cash for its daily needs. This line of credit will be secured by Niagara's inventory.

   b. A supplier is deciding whether to sell to Niagara on credit.

   c. An investment advisor is deciding whether to recommend Niagara's shares to his clients.

2. Comment on Niagara's overall performance.

GROUP B PROBLEMS

LO2　**PB13-1**　**Analyzing Financial Statements Using Ratios and Percentage Changes**

The comparative financial statements prepared at December 31, 2008, for Soon Company showed the following summarized data:

			Increase (Decrease) 2008 over 2007	
	2008	**2007**	**Amount**	**Percentage**
Income Statement				
Sales revenue*	$222,000	$185,000		
Cost of goods sold	127,650	111,000		
Gross profit	94,350	74,000		

(Continued)

	2008	2007	Increase (Decrease) 2008 over 2007	
			Amount	Percentage
Operating expenses	39,600	33,730		
Interest expense	4,000	3,270		
Income before income taxes	50,750	37,000		
Income tax expense (30%)	15,225	11,100		
Net income	$ 35,525	$ 25,900		
Balance Sheet				
Cash	$ 40,000	$ 38,000		
Accounts receivable (net)	18,500	16,000		
Inventory	25,000	22,000		
Property and equipment (net)	127,000	119,000		
Total assets	$210,500	$195,000		
Accounts payable	$ 27,000	$ 25,000		
Income taxes payable	3,000	2,800		
Note payable, long-term	75,500	92,200		
Total liabilities	105,500	120,000		
Common shares (25,000 issued)	25,000	25,000		
Retained earnings†	80,000	50,000		
Total liabilities and shareholders' equity	$210,500	$195,000		

*One-half of all sales are on credit.
†During 2008, cash dividends amounting to $5,525 were declared and paid.

Required:

1. Complete the two final columns shown beside each item in Soon Company's comparative financial statements.
2. Does anything significant jump out at you from the year-over-year analyses?

PB13-2 Analyzing Comparative Financial Statements Using Selected Ratios   LO3, LO5
Use the data given in PB13-1 for Soon Company.

Required:

1. Compute the gross profit percentages in 2008 and 2007. Is the trend going in the right direction?
2. Compute the net-profit-margin ratios in 2008 and 2007. Is the trend going in the right direction?
3. Compute the earnings per share for 2008 and 2007. Does the trend look good or bad? Explain.
4. Shareholders' equity totalled $65,000 at the end of 2006. Compute the return-on-equity ratios for 2008 and 2007. Is the trend going in the right direction?
5. Net property and equipment totalled $115,000 at the end of 2006. Compute the fixed-asset-turnover ratios for 2008 and 2007. Is the trend going in the right direction?
6. Compute the debt-to-assets ratios for 2008 and 2007. Is debt providing financing for a larger or smaller proportion of the company's asset growth? Explain.
7. Compute the times-interest-earned ratios for 2008 and 2007. Do they look good or bad? Explain.
8. After Soon released its 2008 financial statements, the company's shares were trading at $17. After the release of its 2007 financial statements, the company's stock price was $12 per share. Compute the P/E ratios for both years. Does it appear that investors have become more (or less) optimistic about Soon's future success?

LO3, LO5   **PB13-3 Interpreting Profitability, Liquidity, Solvency, and P/E Ratios**

Mattel is one of the biggest makers of games and toys in the world, selling nearly $5 billion worth of products each year. Mega Brands, the award-winning Canadian toy maker, is much smaller, with revenues of $235 million. Compare the two companies as a potential investment, based on the following ratios:

Ratio	Mattel	Mega Brands
Gross profit percentage	48.30%	45.15%
Net profit margin	10.28%	10.73%
Return on equity	23.63%	28.08%
EPS	$ 1.23	$ 0.93
Receivables-turnover ratio	7.17	2.24
Inventory-turnover ratio	5.50	9.28
Current ratio	1.86	3.10
Quick ratio	1.13	2.47
Debt-to-assets ratio	0.24	0.44
P/E ratio	15.18	20.43

Required:

1. Which company appears more profitable? Describe the ratio(s) that you used to reach this decision.
2. Which company appears more liquid? Describe the ratio(s) that you used to reach this decision.
3. Which company appears more solvent? Describe the ratio(s) that you used to reach this decision.
4. Are the conclusions from your analyses in requirements 1 to 3 consistent with the values of the companies suggested by the P/E ratios of the two companies? If not, offer one explanation for any apparent inconsistency.

LO3, LO5   **PB13-4 Using Ratios to Compare Loan Requests from Two Companies**

The 2008 financial statements for Thor and Gunnar Companies are summarized here:

	Thor Company	Gunnar Company
Balance Sheet		
Cash	$ 35,000	$ 54,000
Accounts receivable (net)	77,000	6,000
Inventory	154,000	30,000
Property and equipment (net)	770,000	192,000
Other assets	196,000	68,400
Total assets	$1,232,000	$ 350,400
Current liabilities	$ 168,000	$ 18,000
Long-term debt (12% interest rate)	266,000	66,000
Contributed capital	742,000	256,800
Retained earnings	56,000	9,600
Total liabilities and shareholders' equity	$1,232,000	$ 350,400
Income Statement		
Sales revenue	$1,120,000	$ 336,000
Cost of goods sold	672,000	180,000
Expenses (including interest and income tax)	336,000	114,000
Net income	$ 112,000	$ 42,000

(Continued)

	Thor Company	Gunnar Company
Selected Data from 2007 Statements		
Accounts receivable, net	$ 65,800	$ 13,200
Total assets	1,010,000	300,000
Inventory	133,000	45,600
Property and equipment, net	750,000	182,000
Long-term debt (12% interest rate)	276,000	276,400
Total shareholders' equity	798,000	266,400
Other Data		
Per share market price at end of 2008	$ 13.20	$ 19.60
Average income tax rate	30%	30%
Average number of shares outstanding	33,600	12,600

These two companies are in the same line of business, and in the same province but in different cities. One-half of Thor's sales are on credit, whereas one-quarter of Gunnar's sales are on credit. Each company has been in operation for about 10 years. Both companies received an unqualified audit opinion on the financial statements, which means the independent auditors found nothing wrong. Thor Company wants to borrow $105,000 cash, and Gunnar Company is asking for $36,000. The loans will be for a two-year period.

Required:

1. Complete a schedule that reflects a ratio analysis of each company. Compute the ratios discussed in the chapter.
2. Assume that you work in the loan department of a local bank. You have been asked to analyze the situation and recommend which loan is preferable. Based on the data given, your analysis prepared in requirement 1, and any other information, give your choice and the supported explanation.

PB13-5 Using Ratios to Analyze Company Performance   LO3

Below are the financial statements for Whistler Trading Company (in thousands).

	2008	2007
Balance Sheet		
Cash	$ 370	$ 194
Short-term investments	26	222
Accounts receivable	222	239
Inventory	155	131
Property and equipment (net)	727	547
Other assets	158	117
	$ 1,658	$ 1,450
Current liabilities	$ 221	$ 186
Long-term liabilities	155	124
Shareholders' equity	1,282	1,140
	$ 1,658	$ 1,450
Income Statement		
Sales revenue (90% on account)	$1,322	$ 1,210
Cost of sales	928	888
Other expenses	244	200
Net income	$ 150	$ 122
Selected Information from End of 2006		
Accounts receivable		250
Inventory		120
Property and equipment (net)		450
Shareholders' equity		1,000
Total assets		1,225

Selected Industry Data

Asset-turnover ratio	1.0	Receivables-turnover ratio	6.3	Inventory-turnover ratio	3.8
Debt-to-assets ratio	35%	Current ratio	2.0	Quick ratio	1.7
ROE	14%	Net profit margin	18%		

Required:

1. Perform a ratio analysis for the two years. Compute the ratios discussed in the chapter.
2. Based on your analysis in requirement 1 and the industry data provided, comment on the company's performance.

LO3, LO5   **PB13-6   Analyzing an Investment by Comparing Selected Ratios**

You have the opportunity to invest $10,000 in one of two companies from a single industry. The only information you have is shown here. The word *high* refers to the top third of the industry; *average* is the middle third; *low* is the bottom third.

Ratio	*Company A*	*Company B*
EPS	High	High
Return-on-equity	High	Average
Debt-to-assets	High	Low
Current	Low	Average
Price/earnings	Low	High

Required:

Which company would you select? Write a brief explanation for your recommendation.

SKILLS DEVEOPMENT CASES

LO3, LO5   **S13-1   Finding Financial Information**

Refer to the financial statements of Sun-Rype by downloading the annual report from the *Cases* section of the text's Web site at www.mcgrawhill.ca/college/phillips. Use the following balances from 2005 in calculating averages: Accounts Receivable $11,868, Inventory $13,321, Net Fixed assets $22,312, Total assets $68,253, and Shareholders' equity $48,283. From the list of ratios that were discussed in this chapter, select and compute the ratios that help you evaluate the company. Provide a written analysis that interprets your ratio computations.

LO3, LO5   **S13-2   Comparing Financial Information**

Download the financial statements of Saputo for its March 31, 2008 and 2007, year-ends from the company's Web site or the sources listed in S1-3 in Chapter 1. Use the following balances from 2006 in calculating averages: Accounts Receivable $302,112, Net Fixed assets $674,695, Total assets $2,253,933, and Shareholders' equity $1,402,543. From the list of ratios that were discussed in this chapter, select, compute, and interpret the ratios that help you compare Saputo with the 2007 and 2006 results for High Liner reported in this chapter. When comparing with High Liner's statements, assume that Saputo's financial statements for the year ended March 31, 2008, represent the results for 2007, and that the March 2007 financial statements represent results for 2006.

LO3, LO5   **S13-3   Internet-Based Team Research: Examining an Annual Report**

TEAM CASE

As a team, select an industry to analyze. Using your Web browser, each team member should acquire the annual report for one publicly traded Canadian company in the industry, with each member selecting a different company. (See S1-3 in Chapter 1 for a description of possible resources for these tasks.)

Required:

1. On an individual basis, each team member should write a short report that incorporates year-over-year percentage comparisons and as many of the ratios from the chapter as are applicable, given the nature of the selected company.

2. Then, as a team, write a short report comparing and contrasting your companies using these attributes. Discuss any patterns across the companies that you as a team observe. Provide potential explanations for any differences discovered.

S13-4 Ethical Decision Making: A Real-Life Example

LO3, LO5

During its deliberations on how to improve financial reporting after the Enron and Worldcom failures in the United States, the United States Senate considered numerous reports evaluating the quality of work done by external auditors. One study, by Weiss Ratings, Inc., focused on auditors' ability to predict bankruptcy. The study criticized auditors for failing to identify and report going-concern problems for audit clients that later went bankrupt. Based on a sample of 45 bankrupt companies, the Weiss study concluded that, had auditors noted unusual levels for just two of seven typical financial ratios, they would have identified 89 per cent of the sample companies that later went bankrupt. A follow-up to the Weiss study found that had the criteria in the Weiss study been applied to a larger sample of non-bankrupt companies, 46.9 per cent of non-bankrupt companies would have been predicted to go bankrupt.[*] In other words, the Weiss criteria would have incorrectly predicted bankruptcy for nearly half of the companies in the follow-up study and would have led the auditors to report that these clients had substantial going-concern problems when, in fact, they did not. Discuss the negative consequences that arise when auditors fail to predict companies that go bankrupt. Who is harmed by these failures? Discuss the negative consequences that arise when auditors incorrectly predict bankruptcy. Who is harmed by these errors? In your opinion, which of the potential consequences is worse?

[*]Michael D. Akers, Meredith A. Maher, and Don E. Giacomino, "Going-Concern Opinions: Broadening the Expectations Gap," CPA *Journal*, October 2003. Retrieved June 13, 2004, from www.nysscpa.org/cpajournal/2003/1003/features/f103803.htm.

S13-5 Ethical Decision Making: A Mini-Case

LO3

Almost Short Company requested a sizeable loan from Loaded Bank to acquire a large piece of land for future expansion. Almost Short reported current assets of $1,900,000 (including $430,000 in cash) and current liabilities of $1,075,000. Loaded Bank denied the loan request for a number of reasons, including the fact that the current ratio was below 2:1 and the quick ratio was below 1:1. When Almost Short was informed of the loan denial, the comptroller of the company immediately paid $420,000 that was owed to several trade creditors. The comptroller then asked Loaded Bank to reconsider the loan application. Based on these abbreviated facts, would you recommend that Loaded Bank approve the loan request? Why? Are the controller's actions ethical?

S13-6 Critical Thinking: Analyzing the Impact of Alternative Amortization Methods on Ratio Analysis

LO3

Speedy Company uses the double-declining-balance method to amortize its property, plant, and equipment, and Turtle Company uses the straight-line method. The two companies are exactly alike except for the difference in amortization methods.

Required:

1. Identify the financial ratios discussed in this chapter that are likely to be affected by the difference in amortization methods.
2. Which company will report the higher amount for each ratio that you have identified? If you cannot be certain, explain why.

S13-7 Using a Spreadsheet to Calculate Financial Statement Ratios

LO3

Enter the financial statement information from Exhibits 13.1, 13.2, and 13.3 into three separate worksheets in one spreadsheet file. Using the cell referencing instructions given in S6-8 for "importing" information from different worksheets, create a fourth worksheet that uses the formulas in Exhibit 13.4 to recalculate all the ratios for High Liner for 2007 and 2006. (For the EPS ratio, simply import the amount reported on the face of the income statement.)

High Liner Foods
Incorporated
2007 Annual Report

Embracing
Growth

Uncompromising
Quality

HIGH LINER FOODS
INCORPORATED

Owen Tilley
Corporate Chef

High Liner Foods Incorporated

Annual Report 2007

2007 Annual Report

TABLE OF CONTENTS

Highlights. . . . . see Online Learning Centre, www.mcgrawhill.ca/olc/phillips

Letter to Shareholders . . . . see Online Learning Centre

Building upon our capability to deliver. . . . . see Online Learning Centre

Driving growth...delivering value . . . . see Online Learning Centre

Corporate Governance . . . . see Online Learning Centre

Board of Directors . . . . see Online Learning Centre

MD&A. . . . . see Online Learning Centre

Auditors' report 618

Management's responsibility
     for financial reporting 618

Consolidated balance sheets. 619

Consolidated statements of income 620

Consolidated statement of comprehensive income 620

Consolidated statements of changes in shareholders' equity . . . . See Online Learning Centre

Consolidated statements of cash flows 621

Notes to consolidated financial statements 622–633

Ten-Year Financial Data . . . . see Online Learning Centre

Quarterly Financial Data . . . . see Online Learning Centre

Shareholder information . . . . see Online Learning Centre

Auditors' Report

To the Shareholders of High Liner Foods Incorporated

We have audited the consolidated balance sheets of **High Liner Foods Incorporated** as at December 29, 2007 and December 30, 2006 and the consolidated statements of income, shareholders' equity, cash flows and comprehensive income for the periods then ended. These financial statements are the responsibility of the Company's management. Our responsibility is to express an opinion on these financial statements based on our audits.

We conducted our audits in accordance with Canadian generally accepted auditing standards. Those standards require that we plan and perform an audit to obtain reasonable assurance whether the financial statements are free of material misstatement. An audit includes examining, on a test basis, evidence supporting the amounts and disclosures in the financial statements. An audit also includes assessing the accounting principles used and significant estimates made by management, as well as evaluating the overall financial statement presentation.

In our opinion, these consolidated financial statements present fairly, in all material respects, the financial position of the Company as at December 29, 2007 and December 30, 2006 and the results of its operations and its cash flows for the periods then ended in accordance with Canadian generally accepted accounting principles.

(Signed:)

Ernst & Young LLP
Chartered Accountants

Halifax, Canada

February 1, 2008

Management's Responsibility for Financial Reporting

The Management of High Liner Foods Incorporated includes corporate executives, operating and financial managers and other personnel working full-time on Company business. The statements have been prepared in accordance with generally accepted accounting principles consistently applied, using Management's best estimates and judgments, where appropriate. The financial information elsewhere in this report is consistent with the statements.

Management has established a system of internal control that it believes provides a reasonable assurance that, in all material respects, assets are maintained and accounted for in accordance with Management's authorization and transactions are recorded accurately on the Company's books and records. The Company's internal audit program is designed for constant evaluation of the adequacy and effectiveness of the internal controls. Audits measure adherence to established policies and procedures.

The Audit Committee of the Board of Directors is composed of five outside directors. The Committee meets periodically with management, the internal auditor and independent chartered accountants to review the work of each and to satisfy itself that the respective parties are properly discharging their responsibilities. The independent chartered accountants and the internal auditor have full and free access to the Audit Committee at any time. In addition, the Audit Committee reports its findings to the Board of Directors which reviews and approves the consolidated financial statements.

(Signed:)

K. L. Nelson, FCA
Vice President Corporate Services and Chief Financial Officer

Consolidated Financial Statements

Consolidated Balance Sheets

(in thousands of Canadian dollars)	Dec. 29, 2007	Dec. 30, 2006
Assets (notes 2, 6 and 7)		
Current:		
Cash	$ 7,064	$ 240
Accounts receivable (note 4)	68,662	31,221
Income tax receivable	2,414	161
Inventories (note 4)	107,589	41,278
Prepaid expenses	4,644	3,495
Future income taxes (note 11)	1,302	295
Total current assets	191,675	76,690
Property, plant and equipment (note 5)	57,515	26,038
Other:		
Future income taxes (note 11)	1,677	3,005
Other receivables and sundry investments	66	1,084
Employee future benefits (note 14)	6,759	6,360
Intangible assets and goodwill (note 2)	42,762	–
	51,264	10,449
	$ 300,454	$ 113,177
Liabilities and Shareholders' Equity (note 2)		
Current:		
Bank loans (note 6)	$ 61,280	$ 10,115
Accounts payable and accrued liabilities (note 6)	51,068	27,087
Income taxes payable	437	–
Current portion of capital lease obligations (note 7)	603	560
Total current liabilities	113,388	37,762
Long-term debt (note 7)	51,709	–
Long-term capital lease obligations (note 7)	259	477
Employee future benefits (note 14)	4,227	3,702
Shareholders' Equity (see Statement of Changes in Shareholders' Equity)		
Preference shares (note 8)	50,270	20,000
Common shares (note 8)	58,800	28,106
Contributed surplus	490	503
Retained earnings	40,112	36,204
Accumulated other comprehensive loss	(18,801)	(13,577)
	130,871	71,236
	$ 300,454	$ 113,177

Subsequent events (note 8)

See accompanying notes to the financial statements.

On behalf of the Board:

(Signed:)   (Signed:)

Henry E. Demone, Director   **David J. Hennigar,** Director

Consolidated Statements of Income

For the fifty-two weeks ended December 29, 2007 (with comparative figures for the fifty-two weeks ended December 30, 2006)

(in thousands of Canadian dollars, except per share information)	Fiscal 2007	Fiscal 2006
Sales	$ 275,391	$ 261,725
Cost of sales	221,202	212,414
Gross profit	54,189	49,311
Commission income	33	–
Selling, general and administrative expenses	(38,998)	(36,170)
Foreign exchange (loss) gain	(170)	427
Business acquisition transaction costs (note 2)	(1,286)	–
Depreciation and amortization	(3,087)	(3,017)
Interest expense:		
Short-term	(165)	(834)
Long-term	(212)	(73)
Other expense	(51)	(48)
Non-operating transactions (note 10)	333	(176)
Income before income taxes	10,586	9,420
Income taxes (note 11)		
Current	(2,505)	(2,482)
Future	(1,164)	(1,815)
Total income taxes	(3,669)	(4,297)
Income from continuing operations	6,917	5,123
Gain (loss) from discontinued operations; net of income tax (note 3)	372	(793)
Net income	$ 7,289	$ 4,330

Per share earnings

Earnings per common share (note 12)		
Basic from continuing operations	$ 0.55	$ 0.38
Basic from discontinued operations	0.03	(0.08)
Basic	$ 0.58	$ 0.30
Diluted from continuing operations	$ 0.54	$ 0.38
Diluted from discontinued operations	0.03	(0.08)
Diluted	$ 0.57	$ 0.30
Weighted average common shares outstanding (note 12)		
Basic	10,443,281	10,306,009
Diluted	10,591,693	10,370,974

See accompanying notes to the financial statements.

Consolidated Financial Statements

Consolidated Statement of Comprehensive Income

For the fifty-two weeks ended December 29, 2007

(in thousands of Canadian dollars)	Fiscal 2007
Net income for the period	$ 7,289
Other comprehensive income, net of future income taxes	
Unrealized foreign exchange losses on translation of self-sustaining foreign operations (net of nil income taxes)	(3,512)
Net loss on derivative financial instruments designated as cash flow hedges (net of $1.6 million income tax recovery)	(3,245)
Net loss on derivatives designated as cash flow hedges in prior periods transferred to net income in the current period (net of $0.6 million income tax recovery)	1,085
Change in gains and losses on derivatives designated as cash flow hedges	(2,160)
Other comprehensive income	(5,672)
Comprehensive income	$ 1,617

See accompanying notes to the financial statements.

Consolidated Financial Statements

Consolidated Statements of Cash Flows

For the fifty-two weeks ended December 29, 2007 (with comparative figures for the fifty-two weeks ended December 30, 2006)

(in thousands of Canadian dollars)	Fiscal 2007	Fiscal 2006
Cash provided by (used in) operations:		
Net income from continuing operations for the year	$ 6,917	$ 5,123
Charges (credits) to income not involving cash from operations:		
Depreciation and amortization	3,087	3,017
Stock compensation expense	135	33
Loss on asset disposals	85	259
Payments of employee future benefits in excess of expense	19	(463)
Future income taxes	1,164	1,815
Cash flow from continuing operations before changes in non-cash working capital:	11,407	9,784
Net change in non-cash working capital balances (note 15)	(1,612)	10,719
Cash flows from operating activities of discontinued operations	375	(162)
	10,170	20,341
Cash provided by (used in) financing activities:		
Change in current bank loans	54,181	(14,693)
Issuance of long term debt related to acquisition (notes 2 and 7)	53,625	–
Repayments of capital lease obligations	(418)	(444)
Dividends paid:		
Preference	(1,210)	(1,174)
Common	(2,073)	(2,027)
Repurchase of capital stock (note 8)	–	(73)
Issue of equity shares (note 8)	419	192
	104,524	(18,219)
Cash provided by (used in) investing activities:		
Purchase of property, plant and equipment	(2,956)	(2,466)
Net expenditures on disposal of assets	(49)	(1,740)
Use of investment tax credits	1,516	667
Acquisition of business (net of acquired cash of $1.0 million (note 2))	(100,479)	–
Business acquisition costs (note 2)	(4,229)	–
Decrease in other receivables	(61)	73
Investing activities of discontinued operations (note 15)	333	1,172
	(105,925)	(2,294)
Translation adjustment	(1,945)	(168)
Change in cash during the year	6,824	(340)
Cash, beginning of year	240	580
Cash, end of year	$ 7,064	$ 240

Supplemental cash flow information (note 15)

See accompanying notes to the financial statements.

Notes to Consolidated Financial Statements

December 29, 2007

1　Significant Accounting Policies

The accompanying consolidated financial statements have been prepared in accordance with Canadian generally accepted accounting principles.

1a) Basis of Presentation

Basis of Consolidation

The accompanying financial statements consolidate the accounts of the Company and all its subsidiary companies. All significant intercompany balances and transactions have been eliminated in consolidation.

Year End

The Company's fiscal year end is on the Saturday closest to December 31. This results in a 53-week fiscal year every five to seven years. However, both 2007 and 2006 fiscal years are 52 weeks.

Currency

Unless otherwise noted, all amounts in these financial statements are in Canadian dollars. The Company conducts its business in Canadian and US dollars. The average U.S. to Canadian dollar exchange rate throughout 2007 was 1.0747 (2006: 1.1342). The year-end exchange rate was 0.9785 (2006: 1.1653).

1b) Summary of Significant Accounting Policies

Cash and cash equivalents

Cash and cash equivalents are cash on hand, demand deposits or short-term, highly liquid investments that are readily convertible to known amounts of cash and which are subject to an insignificant risk of changes in value. Cash and cash equivalents do not include any restricted cash. As at the end of December 29, 2007 and December 30, 2006 cash and cash equivalents included cash on hand and that is what is used for purposes of the consolidated cash flow statement.

Inventory Valuation

Manufactured finished goods inventories are valued at the lower of cost (includes raw materials, direct labour and overhead) and net realizable value, with cost determined on a first-in, first-out basis. Procured finished goods inventory and unprocessed raw material inventory is valued at the lower of weighted average cost and net realizable value. Net realizable value is determined by reducing the most recent sales value by an estimate of the selling costs and the remaining production costs to bring products to saleable form.

Cost of inventories includes the transfer from accumulated other comprehensive income of gains and losses on qualifying cash flow hedges in respect of the purchases of procured raw materials and finished goods.

Foreign Currency

Assets and liabilities of the U.S. subsidiary operation, which is financially and operationally independent of the parent, are translated at exchange rates prevailing at the balance sheet date. The revenues and expenses are translated at average exchange rates prevailing during the year. The gains and losses on translation are deferred and recorded as accumulated other comprehensive income or loss until there is a realized reduction in the net investment of the U.S. subsidiary when an appropriate amount would be transferred to income.

Foreign currency denominated assets and liabilities of other operations are translated at exchange rates prevailing at the balance sheet date for monetary items and at exchange rates prevailing at the transaction date for non-monetary items as well as revenues and expenses. Gains or losses on translation are included in income.

Property, Plant and Equipment

Property, plant and equipment are carried at cost, net of accumulated depreciation. Depreciation is provided on the straight-line basis over the remaining useful lives or at the following rates per annum:

Buildings	Useful life
Burin, NL facility	Purchased in December 2007 and valued at cost, remaining estimated life to be determined as part of the final purchase price allocation in 2008 (note 2).
Danvers, MA facility	Purchased in December 2007 and valued at cost, remaining estimated life to be determined as part of the final purchase price allocation in 2008 (note 2).
Lunenburg, NS facility	Originally constructed in 1963, improvements since then have extended the useful life to 2024.
Portsmouth, NH facility	Originally constructed in 1967, improvements since then have extended the useful life to 2028.
Computers and electronic equipment	25%
Machinery and equipment, other	6 2/3%
Equipment under capital lease	Lease term

Long-Lived Asset Impairment

Long-lived assets, including property, plant and equipment and purchased intangible assets subject to amortization, are reviewed for impairment whenever events or changes in circumstances indicate that the carrying amount of an asset may not be recoverable. Recoverability of assets to be held and used is measured by a comparison of the carrying amount of an asset to estimated undiscounted future cash flows expected to be generated by the asset. If the carrying amount of an asset exceeds its estimated future cash flows, an impairment charge is recognized by the amount by which the carrying amount of the asset exceeds the fair value of the asset. Assets to be disposed of are separately presented in the balance sheet and reported at the lower of the carrying amount or fair value less costs to sell, and are no longer depreciated. The asset and liabilities of a disposed group held for sale are presented separately in the appropriate asset and liability sections of the balance sheet.

Investment Tax Credits

Investment tax credits (ITCs) earned as a result of purchasing capital assets are recorded as a reduction to property, plant and equipment. ITCs are amortized at the same rates as the related capital assets and the amortization of ITCs is recorded as a reduction of the amortization of the related capital assets.

Investment tax credits also arise as a result of the Company incurring eligible research and development expenses and these credits are recorded as a reduction to related expenses.

Stock-Based Compensation

The Company has a stock-based compensation plan, which is described in note 8 and recognizes compensation expense for option awards using the fair value method of accounting.

In January 2004, the Company amended its stock option plan to add tandem share appreciation rights (SARs) to option grants, which allow the employee to either exercise the stock option for shares, or to exercise the tandem SARs and thereby receive the value of the stock option in cash. The Company accrues compensation expense on a graded vesting basis in the amount by which the quoted market value of the common shares exceeds the option price. The counterpart of the expense relating to options is recorded as a liability. Changes, either increases or decreases, in the quoted market value of the common shares between the date of grant and the reporting period date result in a change in the measure of compensation expense for the option award.

When employees exercise their stock options for shares, thereby cancelling the tandem SARs, share capital is increased by the sum of the consideration paid by the employee and the liability reversed, with any difference being recorded in income.

Goodwill

Goodwill is the residual amount that results when the purchase price of an acquired business exceeds the sum of the amounts allocated to the assets acquired, less liabilities assumed, based on fair value. Goodwill is allocated, as of the date of the business combination, to the Company's reporting units that are expected to benefit from the synergies of the business combination.

Goodwill is not amortized and is tested for impairment annually, or when an event or circumstance occurs that more likely than not reduces the fair value of the reporting unit below its carrying amount. The impairment test is carried out in two steps. In the first step, the carrying amount of the reporting unit is compared with its fair value. When the fair value of a reporting unit exceeds its carrying amount, goodwill of the reporting unit is considered not to be impaired and the second step of the impairment test is unnecessary.

Notes to Consolidated Financial Statements

The second step is carried out when the carrying amount of a reporting unit exceeds its fair value, in which case, the implied fair value of the reporting unit's goodwill is compared with its carrying amount to measure the amount of the impairment loss, if any. The implied fair value of goodwill is determined in a similar manner as it would be determined in a business combination described above, using the fair value of the reporting unit as if it was the purchase price. When the carrying amount of reporting unit goodwill exceeds the implied fair value of the goodwill, an impairment loss is recognized in an amount equal to the excess and is presented as a separate line item in the consolidated statement of earnings before extraordinary items and discontinued operations. However, if assets other than goodwill valued as part of step two, have increased, a greater impairment loss of goodwill may result, and the increase in the value of the other assets are not recorded.

Intangible Assets
Intangible assets acquired separately are measured on initial recognition at cost. The cost of intangible assets acquired in a business combination is fair value as at the date of acquisition. Following initial recognition, intangible assets are carried at cost less any accumulated amortization and any accumulated impairment losses.

The useful life of an intangible asset is assessed to be either finite or indefinite. Intangible assets with finite lives are amortized over the useful economic life and assessed for impairment whenever there is an indication that the intangible asset may be impaired. The amortization period and the amortization method for an intangible asset with a finite useful life are reviewed at least at each financial year end. Changes in the expected useful life or the expected pattern of consumption of future economic benefits embodied in the asset are accounted for by changing the amortization period or method, as appropriate, and are treated as changes in accounting estimates. The amortization expense on intangible assets with finite lives is recognized in profit or loss in the expense category consistent with the function of the intangible asset.

Intangible assets with finite useful lives are amortized on a straight-line basis over their useful lives. As part of the purchase price equation (note 2), the Company will be determining the useful lives of the intangibles that arose on the 2007 acquisition of FPI Limited North American marketing and manufacturing business. Since the transaction closed near the end of the Company's fiscal year, the value currently recorded on the balance sheets as intangible assets and goodwill is preliminary and is likely to change when the Company completes its purchase price equation analysis in 2008.

Intangible assets with indefinite useful lives are tested for impairment annually either individually or at the cash generating unit level. Such intangibles are not amortized. The useful life of an intangible asset with an indefinite life is reviewed annually to determine whether indefinite life assessment continues to be supportable. If not, the change in the useful life assessment from indefinite to finite is made on a prospective basis.

Gains or losses arising from derecognition of an intangible asset are measured as the difference between the net disposal proceeds and the carrying amount of the asset and are recognized in earnings when the asset is derecognized.

Employee Benefit Plans
The Company accrues its obligations under employee benefit plans, net of plan assets. The cost of the Company's defined benefit pensions and other retirement benefits earned by employees is actuarially determined using the projected benefit method prorated on service and management's best estimate of expected plan investment performance, salary escalation and retirement ages of employees. For the purpose of calculating the expected return on plan assets, those assets are valued at fair value. Past service costs from plan amendments are amortized on a straight-line basis over the average remaining service period of employees active at the date of amendment. The excess of the net actuarial gain (loss) over 10% of the greater of the benefit obligation and the fair value of plan assets is amortized over the average remaining service period of the active employees. The average remaining service period of the active employees covered by the pension plan is 15.3 years. The average remaining service period of the active employees covered by the other benefits plan is 7 years. The cost of the Company's defined contribution plans is the amount of contributions the Company is required to pay for services rendered by its employees.

Financial Instruments
The Company, in accordance with a written policy to manage its foreign currency, commodity and interest rate exposures, utilizes derivative financial instruments. The policy prohibits the use of derivative financial instruments for trading or speculative purposes.

The Company formally documents all relationships between hedging instruments and hedged items, as well as its risk management objective and strategy for undertaking various hedge transactions. This process includes linking all derivatives to specific assets and liabilities on the balance sheet or to specific firm commitments or forecasted transactions. The Company also formally assesses, both at the hedge's inception and on an ongoing basis, whether the derivatives that are used in hedging transactions are effective in offsetting changes in fair values or cash flows of hedged items.

The Company uses hedge accounting for each type of derivative financial instrument used to manage its foreign exchange risk. Realized and unrealized gains or losses associated with derivative instruments which have been terminated or cease to be effective prior to maturity are recognized in income, in the same period as the corresponding gains/losses, revenues or expenses associated with the hedged items.

The Company systematically enters into foreign exchange forward contracts to hedge future cash flows. The contracts are valued at rates prevailing at the balance sheet date and gains and losses are recorded in other comprehensive income until they are realized when they are transferred to income.

Income Taxes
The Company follows the asset and liability method of accounting for income taxes, whereby future income tax assets and liabilities are determined based on the differences between the financial reporting and tax bases of assets and liabilities and are measured using enacted or substantively enacted tax rates and laws that are anticipated when these temporary differences are expected to reverse. The effect of a change in income tax rates on future income tax assets and liabilities is recognized in income in the period that includes the date of enactment or substantive enactment. Valuation allowances are also recorded to reduce income tax assets to amounts expected to be realized.

Use of Accounting Estimates and Measurement Uncertainty
The preparation of financial statements in conformity with Canadian Generally Accepted Accounting Principles requires management to make estimates and assumptions that affect the reported amounts of assets and liabilities and disclosure of contingent assets and liabilities at the date of the financial statements and the reported amounts of revenues and expenses during the reporting periods. Significant items requiring the use of management estimates include the carrying amount of property, plant and equipment, goodwill and intangibles, valuation allowances for receivables, inventories, future income tax assets, marketing accruals, fair values of financial instruments and depreciation of property, plant and equipment. Actual results could differ from those estimates.

Revenue Recognition
Sales are recognized in income when the related products have been shipped to customers using third party carriers, as this is when an invoice is issued at a fixed or determinable selling price. Based on experience, the Company is reasonably assured that the customer will accept the products. The Company experiences very few product returns and collectibility of its invoices is consistently high.

The Company offers various marketing programs to customers and consumers including volume rebates, cooperative advertising and various other trade marketing costs, and consumer discount coupons. Sales are recorded net of these estimated sales and marketing costs, which are recognized as incurred at the time of sale. Certain customers require the payment of one-time listing allowances (slotting fees) in order to obtain space for a new product on its shelves. These fees are recognized as reductions of revenue at the earlier of the date the fees are paid in cash or on which a liability to the customer is created (usually on shipment of the new product). Coupon redemption costs are also recognized when issued as reductions of sales.

1c) Changes in Accounting Policies During the Year:
Financial Instruments
The Company adopted the Canadian Institute of Chartered Accountants (CICA) Handbook Sections 1530 "Comprehensive Income", 3855 "Financial Instruments – Recognition and Measurement", 3861 Financial Instruments – Disclosure and Presentation", and 3865 "Hedges" on the first day of fiscal 2007. The adoption of these new standards resulted in changes in the accounting for financial instruments and hedges, as well as the recognition of certain transition adjustments, which have been recorded in opening accumulated comprehensive income and retained earnings as described below. These new standards have been adopted on a prospective basis with no restatement of prior period financial statements. The principal changes in the accounting for financial instruments and hedges due to the adoption of these accounting standards and the reclassification of translation losses on self-sustaining foreign operations are described on the following page.

Notes to Consolidated Financial Statements

Comprehensive Income

Comprehensive income includes the Company's net income and other comprehensive income. Other comprehensive income includes unrealized exchange gains and losses on translation of self-sustaining foreign operations and changes in the fair market value of derivative instruments designated as cash flow hedges, net of applicable income taxes. The components of comprehensive income are disclosed in the consolidated statement of comprehensive income and the consolidated statements of changes in equity.

Financial Assets and Financial Liabilities

Under the standards, all financial instruments are classified into one of the following five categories: held for trading, held-to-maturity investments, loans and receivables, available-for-sale financial assets or other financial liabilities. All financial instruments and derivatives are initially recorded in the balance sheet at fair value. In subsequent periods, loans and receivables, held-to-maturity investments and other financial liabilities are measured at amortized cost using the effective interest rate method; held-for-trading financial assets and liabilities are measured at fair value with changes recognized in net income, and available-for-sale financial instruments are measured at fair value with changes in fair value recorded in other comprehensive income until the instrument is derecognized or impaired.

As a result of the adoption of these standards, the Company has classified its cash as held-for-trading, accounts receivable are classified as loans and receivables, bank loans, accounts payable and accrued liabilities, long-term debt, and capital lease obligations have been classified as other financial liabilities, all of which are measured at amortized cost. The Company does not have any financial instruments that are classified as available-for-sale or held-to-maturity.

For financial assets or financial liabilities classified as held for trading, all transaction costs must be recognized in net income. For financial assets or financial liabilities not classified as held for trading, the Company has elected to add the transaction costs to the value of the associated financial asset or liability.

Upon adoption of this section, other assets of $0.1 million have been reclassified to retained earnings.

Derivatives and Hedge Accounting

Derivatives

All derivative instruments, including embedded derivatives, are recorded in the balance sheet at fair value unless exempted from derivative treatment as a normal purchase and sale. All changes in their fair value are recorded in income unless cash flow hedge accounting is used, in which case changes in fair value are recorded in other comprehensive income. The Company has chosen to apply this accounting treatment for all embedded derivatives in host contracts entered into on or after January 1, 2003. The impact of the change in the accounting policy related to embedded derivatives was not material.

Hedge Accounting

At the inception of a hedging relationship, the Company documents the relationship between the hedging instrument and the hedged item, as well as the risk management objectives and strategy for undertaking various hedge transactions. This process includes linking all derivatives to specific assets and liabilities on the consolidated balance sheets or to specific firm commitments or forecasted transactions. The Company also assesses, both at the inception of the hedge and on an ongoing basis, whether the derivatives that are used are effective in offsetting changes in fair values or cash flows of hedged items.

Under the previous standards, derivatives that met the requirements for hedge accounting were accounted for in accordance with AcG-13. Under the new standards, all derivatives are recorded at fair value.

All gains and losses from changes in the fair value of derivatives not designated as a part of a hedging relationship are recognized in the statement of income. These gains and losses are reported in other income (expense).

When derivatives are designated as hedges, the Company classifies them either as: (i) hedges in the change in fair value of recognized assets or liabilities or firm commitments (fair value hedges); (ii) hedges of the variability in highly probable future cash flows attributable to a recognized asset or liability, or a forecasted transaction (cash flow hedges); or (iii) hedges of net investments in a foreign operation (net investment hedges).

Cash Flow Hedges

The Company operates globally, which gives rise to the risk that its earnings and cash flows may be adversely affected by fluctuations in foreign exchange rates. The Company enters into foreign currency forward contracts and foreign currency option contracts to hedge foreign exchange exposures on anticipated purchases.

The effective portion of changes in the fair value of derivatives that are designated and qualify as cash flow hedges is recognized in other comprehensive income. Any gain or loss in fair value relating to the ineffective portion is recognized immediately in the statement of income in other income (expense).

Amounts accumulated in other comprehensive income are reclassified to the statement of income in the period in which the hedged item affects income. When a hedging instrument expires or is sold, or when a hedge no longer meets the criteria for hedge accounting, any cumulative gain or loss existing in other comprehensive income at that time remains in other comprehensive income as long as the forecasted transaction is still likely to occur and would be recognized in the statement of income in the period the hedged transaction impacts income. When a forecasted transaction is no longer expected to occur, the cumulative gain or loss that was reported in other comprehensive income is transferred to the statement of income. Upon adoption of the new standards, the Company recorded a net increase in derivative assets included on the balance sheet of $0.6 million designated as cash flow hedges, a decrease in future income tax assets of $0.2 million and an increase of $0.4 million after-tax in accumulated other comprehensive income.

Translation Losses on Self-Sustaining Foreign Operations

Recorded translation losses on the conversion of the Company's self-sustaining foreign operations, previously disclosed on the consolidated balance sheets as "foreign currency translation account", is now presented in accumulated other comprehensive income.

Future Changes in Accounting Policy

Standards issued but not yet effective.

Adoption of International Financial Reporting Standards

In January 2006 and confirmed in February 2008, the Accounting Standards Board announced its decision to require all Publicly Accountable Enterprises to report

under International Financial Reporting Standards (IFRS) for years beginning on or after January 1, 2011. This will include listed companies like High Liner Foods Incorporated. These changes reflect a global shift to IFRS and they are intended to facilitate capital flows and bring greater clarity and consistency to financial reporting in the global marketplace.

The Company is preparing a detailed plan in 2008, under the supervision of its Audit Committee, to manage the transition from Canadian Generally Accepted Accounting Principles to IFRS before the end of 2009 to ensure comparative information will be available for financing purposes in 2011.

A number of Canadian generally accepted accounting principles will converge with IFRS starting in 2008, such as the following provisions to be adopted by the Company for its interim financial statements for the first quarter of 2008.

Inventories

CICA Handbook Section 3031, Inventories, applies to interim and annual financial statements for fiscal years beginning on or after January 1, 2008. The major areas of change require that more guidance be provided with respect to the valuation of inventories, especially with respect to overhead costs, and more required disclosure. The Company is reviewing its methods of overhead application to inventory but expects only immaterial changes to inventory values as a result. The provisions can be applied retrospectively with or without restatement of prior periods. The changes to the Company's balance sheet and income statement are estimated by management to be immaterial. Additional disclosures and revised presentation will be required. The Company will adopt the provisions retrospectively without restatement of prior periods by adjusting opening inventory as at the beginning of the 2008 fiscal year and adjusting opening retained earnings.

Capital Management, Financial Instruments - Disclosure, Financial Instruments - Presentation

CICA Handbook Section 1535, 3862 and 3863 apply to interim and annual financial statements relating to fiscal years beginning on or after October 1, 2007. Early adoption is encouraged. This new standard requires disclosure of the Company's objectives, policies, and processes for managing capital; quantitative data about what the Company regards as capital; whether the Company has complied with and capital requirements; and, if the Company has not complied, the consequences of such non-compliance. The new accounting standard covers disclosure only and will have no effect on the financial results of the Company.

Financial Instruments – Disclosures, and Financial Instruments – Presentation

These new standards replace accounting standard 3861 Financial Instruments – Disclosure and Presentation. Presentation requirements have not changed. Enhanced disclosure is required to assist users of the financial statements in evaluating the significance of financial instruments on the Company's financial position and performance, including qualitative and quantitative information about the Company's exposure to risks arising from financial instruments. The new accounting standards cover disclosure only and will have no effect on the financial results of the Company.

Going Concern

Amendments to CICA Handbook Section 1400 apply to interim and annual financial statements relating to fiscal years beginning on or after January 1, 2008. The Company has reviewed these amended provisions and no changes in presentation or disclosure are required.

2 Business Acquisition

Effective December 21, 2007 the Company acquired the North American marketing and manufacturing business of FPI Limited. The total purchase price is estimated (subject to working capital and transaction cost adjustments) to be $162.7 million, including transaction costs. The consideration for the transaction consists of $98.7 million in cash, the issuance of 3 million common shares of the Company, and the issuance of 1.2 million Series A Preference shares. The Preference shares will be convertible to 3 million non-voting equity shares to be created at the Company's 2008 annual meeting. Transaction costs and transition severance and retention costs of $3.5 million are included in the purchase price. Other transition costs have been expensed and shown separately in the income statement in the amount of $1.3 million.

The Company accounted for this acquisition using the purchase method and the results of the acquired business have been consolidated with those of the Company from the date of acquisition.

The following table sets forth a preliminary allocation of the purchase cost to assets and liabilities acquired, based on preliminary estimates of fair value. Final valuations of goodwill, intangible assets, contingencies and future income tax assets/liabilities are not yet complete due to the inherent complexity associated with the valuations and the lateness in the year of the closing of the transaction. In addition, working capital estimates at closing will be adjusted for the actual working capital acquired based on the purchase and sale agreement for these assets. These allocations and adjustments will be completed in 2008. Consequently these adjustments may change the purchase price equation and result in different values for the acquired cash, accounts receivable, inventory, prepaids, property, plant and equipment, intangible assets, goodwill, accounts payable, employee future benefits and future income taxes. Therefore the purchase price allocation is preliminary and subject to adjustment over the course of 2008 on completion of the valuation process and analysis of resulting tax effects.

$000's

Preliminary purchase price allocation:

Cash	$ 1,030
Other working capital, net	84,404
Property, plant and equipment	33,639
Intangible assets and goodwill	43,842
Future employee benefits	(168)
Net assets acquired, at fair value	162,747

Consideration:

Cash	98,671
Common shares	30,270
Series A preference shares	30,270
Estimated transaction costs	3,536
Total consideration provided	162,747

The value of the common shares issued as consideration for the business acquisition was $10.09 per share, which was determined using the Company's average closing share price on the TSX over a reasonable period before and after the date on which the terms of the purchase consideration were agreed to and announced.

The value assigned to the Series A preference shares issued as consideration was deemed to be the same value assigned to the common shares as these new Series A shares are convertible into non-voting common shares.

Notes to Consolidated Financial Statements

3 Discontinued Operations

After several years of poor results, due in part to a reduction in market demand for pasta products in general, in 2005 the Company wrote down the assets related to its Italian Foods division, including goodwill, to net realizable value. On July 27, 2006 the Company sold this division for proceeds of $1.7 million ($1.1 million cash and $0.6 million note receivable). In addition, the Company collected $0.8 million of trade receivables and paid $1.2 million of accounts payable relating to the Italian Foods operations. Since the sale represented an exit from the Italian Foods category and cash flows from the business were eliminated from ongoing operations upon the sale, results for discontinued operations are presented separately and comparative figures have been restated. Prior to being reclassified as discontinued operations, the Italian Foods business operated as part of the Company's USA operating entity segment. The sale resulted in no gain or loss, as the assets of the operations were written down to fair market value in 2005.

Also in 2006, the Company reversed a payable relating to the disposal of its Arnold's Cove primary processing plant on October 8, 2004. The disposal was accounted for as discontinued operations and the payable reversal of pre-tax $0.4 million has been included in the non-operating transaction line along with other discontinued operations transactions for the period as noted below.

Information relating to the discontinued operations is summarized as follows:

Summary of Discontinued Operations

(in thousands of Canadian dollars)	Fiscal 2007	Fiscal 2006
Sales	$ 66	$ 4,296
Gain (loss) before the following:	68	(1,052)
Depreciation	-	(7)
Other income/ non-operating transactions	304	393
Discontinued operations before taxes	372	(666)
Income tax expense	-	(127)
Net income (loss) from discontinued operations	$ 372	$ (793)

4 Current Assets

4a) Accounts Receivable

Accounts receivable bear normal commercial credit terms, usually 30 days or less, and are non-interest bearing. Credit losses are minimal as the Company has done business with its customers for many years and closely follows their credit history. Amounts are net of an allowance for doubtful accounts of $1.4 million (2006; $0.5 million).

$000	Dec. 29, 2007	Dec. 30, 2006
Trade accounts receivable	$ 60,403	$ 27,648
Other accounts receivable	8,259	3,573
	$ 68,662	$ 31,221

Other receivables include $1.0 million in 2007 and 2006 (note 21) relating to the sale of the Company's Nova Scotia fishing assets in 2003. Arising out of this sale, the Company has sued the purchasers of the assets to recover $1.0 million of the purchase price withheld pending resolution of land title issues. As far as the Company's management is concerned, its obligations under the agreement have been met, and the Company intends to pursue the claim to a satisfactory end.

Inventories

$000	Dec. 29, 2007	Dec. 30, 2006
Finished goods	$ 74,482	$ 26,432
Raw and semi-finished material	26,681	11,029
Supplies, repair parts and other	6,426	3,817
	$ 107,589	$ 41,278

Notes to Consolidated Financial Statements

5   Property, Plant and Equipment

$000	Dec. 29, 2007	Dec. 30, 2006
Land	$ 2,193	$ 229
Buildings	38,471	23,923
Computers and electronic equipment	7,194	6,263
Machinery and equipment, other	55,073	41,714
Equipment under capital lease	2,542	2,595
	105,473	74,724
Less accumulated depreciation:		
Buildings	13,641	14,208
Computer and electronic equipment	4,620	4,677
Machinery and equipment, other	26,432	26,772
Equipment under capital lease	1,180	1,127
	45,873	46,784
Investment tax credits	(2,085)	(1,902)
	$ 57,515	$ 26,038

6   Current Liabilities

6a) Bank Loans

$000	Dec. 29, 2007	Dec. 30, 2006
Bank loans, denominated in Canadian dollars, interest rate currently not exceeding prime (average variable rate for amounts at 2007 year end was 6.933%)	$ 34,291	$ –
Bank loans, denominated in U.S. dollars, interest rate currently not exceeding U.S. base rate (average variable rate for amounts at 2007 year end was 7.37%; 6.10% for 2006 year end amounts) (2007; USD$28,461; 2006; USD$8,680)	27,849	10,115
Less financing costs	(860)	–
	$ 61,280	$ 10,115

On December 20, 2007, as part of the Business Acquisition (see note 2), the Company entered into a new three year committed $120 million revolving asset based working capital facility due for renewal in December 2010. The Company has pledged as collateral for this facility a general security agreement creating a first-ranking charge (subject to permitted encumbrances) over all of its personal property, including all of its intellectual property.

The new facility allows the Company to borrow Canadian dollar Prime Rate loans and U.S. Base Rate loans in US dollars at Prime or Base Rate plus 0.00% to 0.125%; Bankers' Acceptances (BA) loans at BA rates plus 1.00% to 1.375%; and LIBOR advances at LIBOR plus 1.00% to 1.375%. The Company will, to the extent feasible, borrow using the lowest cost instruments, typically LIBOR loans or BAs. The rate of interest charged on borrowings depends on a financial

leverage ratio. At this time, the Company borrows at the higher end of these ranges due to the recent Business Acquisition. Capital distributions, such as the payment of dividends or the repurchase of shares under a Normal Course Issuer Bid, are subject to a fixed charge coverage test. Other terms and conditions are typical to an asset-based financing structure.

The previous $40.0 million facility in place at the end of 2006, and replaced by the above facility, provided Canadian dollar Prime Rate loans and U.S. Base Rate loans in US dollars at Prime or Base Rate plus 0.00% to 0.25%; Bankers' Acceptances (BA) loans at BA rates plus 1.00% to 1.50%; and LIBOR advances at LIBOR plus 0.75% to 1.50%. The rate of interest charged on borrowings depended on a financial ratio. Prior to December 20, 2007, the Company borrowed at the lower of this range as determined by the ratio.

6b) Accounts Payable and Accrued Liabilities

$000	Dec. 29, 2007	Dec. 30, 2006
Trade accounts payable	$ 48,335	$ 26,601
Mark to market on cash flow hedged	2,643	
Other	90	486
	$ 51,068	$ 27,087

Accounts payable bear normal commercial credit terms, usually 30 days, and are non-interest bearing.

7   Long Term Debt and Capital Lease Obligations

Long Term Debt

$000	Dec. 29, 2007
Notes payable, due 2009 to 2012	
Series A at 6.31%	
Series B at 6.012% (USD$31,058)	$ 17,250
Series C at LIBOR plus 2.00% (USD$4,950)	30,390
Cross currency swap mark to market	4,843
	(112)
Less financing charges	(662)
	$ 51,709
Less current installments	–
	$ 51,709

Capital Lease Obligations

$000	Dec. 29, 2007	Dec. 30, 2006
Capital leases at 5.56% to 11.66% due 2008 to 2010	$ 862	$ 1,037
Less current installments	603	560
	$ 259	$ 477

As part of the Business Acquisition (see note 2), the Company entered into new long term funded debt of $52.5 million, as outlined above. All real property and equipment in its four production facilities and personal property including intellectual property are pledged as security. For the first 24 months of the term, only interest on the loans is payable. Repayments are based on a twelve-year amortization period, with the repaid balance due in full on December 20, 2012. The agreements include typical financial covenants for debt of this nature including debt coverage, defined cash flow to debt and debt to capitalization ratios. The Series C tranche of debt shown above will be repaid if the Company sells one of its US plants.

On December 20, 2007 the Company entered into a cross currency swap for the Series A note related to its U.S. operating entities to effectively convert both interest and principal payments to US dollars. The effective interest rate on the Series A loan after taking into account the swap was 6.26%. The Company is using hedge accounting for this swap.

The principal payments required, in Canadian dollars, on long-term debt and capital leases in each of the next five fiscal periods are as follows:

Cdn $000	Notes Payable	Capital Leases
2008	$ -	$ 603
2009	-	153
2010	4,378	106
2011	4,378	-
2012	43,727	-

 Share Capital

The share capital of the Company is as follows:

	Dec. 29, 2007	Dec. 30, 2006
Authorized		
Cumulative redeemable second preference shares of the par value of $100 each	200,000	200,000
Preference shares of the par value of $25 each, issuable in series	5,999,994	9,999,944
Series A preference shares of the par value of $25 each	4,000,000	-
Subordinated redeemable preference shares of the par value of $1 each, redeemable at par	1,025,542	1,025,542
Common shares, without par value	200,000,000	200,000,000

	December 29, 2007		December 30, 2006	
	Shares	($000)	Shares	($000)
Issued				
Preference				
Second preference shares	200,000	$ 20,000	200,000	$ 20,000
Series A preference shares	1,200,000	30,270	-	-
Common				
Common shares	13,380,709	$ 58,800	10,314,662	$ 28,106

Common shares issued are shown net of 1,047,118 shares (2006; 1,047,118 shares) in the amount of $11,121,920 (2006; $11,121,920), which are owned by a subsidiary company.

The Second Preference Shares are redeemable by the Company at their par value plus accrued and unpaid dividends. Cumulative dividends are payable quarterly at one-half a chartered bank's prime lending rate plus 3 percent.

Subsequent to year end the Company called all of its outstanding Second Preference Shares for mandatory redemption on February 20, 2008. The outstanding second preference shares will be redeemed at their Par Value plus any accrued and unpaid dividends to the redemption date.

The Company also announced that the majority of the holders of the Second Preference shares subscribed for 798,620 Series A Preference Shares, with a par value each of $25, from the Company's treasury for total proceeds of $19,965,500. Including the 1,200,000 Series A Preference shares issued in the Business Acquisition (note 2), there will be 1,998,620 Series A Preference shares outstanding for a total value of $50,235,500.

The Series A Preference shares are entitled to a quarterly per share dividend equal to 2.5 times dividends declared on the Company's common shares.

The Series A Preference Shares will be convertible into Non-Voting Common Shares at a rate of one Series A Preference Share for 2.5 Non-Voting Common Shares subsequent to the creation of the Non-Voting Common Shares at the Company's Annual Meeting in May 2008. The conversion would result in 4,996,550 Non-Voting Common shares outstanding. The Non-Voting shares are intended to be listed on the Toronto Stock Exchange shortly thereafter. If for some reason the Non-Voting Common Shares are not created and listed within 90 days of the 2008 Annual Meeting, the Series A Preference Shares will, at the Company's option, be either converted to Common Shares or redeemed for cash. The Series A Preference Shares cannot be redeemed for cash without the approval of the Company's lenders.

Common Share Transactions

In 2007, the Company did not purchase shares of the Company. In 2006, the Company purchased an aggregate of 8,000 shares at an average cost of $9.08 including commissions. The value of common shares increased in 2007 by $424,000 due to the exercise of stock options (2006; $216,000).

Share Option Plan

The Company has a common share option plan for designated directors, officers and certain managers of the Company and of subsidiary companies, with total options granted not to exceed 10 percent of the issued Common Shares. Stock options issued in 2004 and subsequent years were awarded with Tandem Stock Appreciation Rights ("SARs"). The SARs have the same vesting, expiry and exercise terms and conditions as the underlying options. The option holder has the choice to either exercise the option or forfeit the option and receive a cash payment equal to the difference between the market value of the shares on the date of exercise and the exercise price. The Company recognizes compensation expense for those options that have been awarded with Tandem SARs based on the excess of the market value at the balance sheet date over the exercise price.

Stock-based compensation cost charged against income in 2007 was $135,000 (2006; $33,000) with the offsetting amount recorded as a liability. Any consideration paid by employees on exercise of stock options is credited to share capital. All stock options exercised during the year that were originally credited to contributed surplus, are reclassified to capital stock.

Under the terms of the plan:

The Company's Human Resource and Corporate Governance Committee of the Board designates from time to time eligible participants to whom options will be granted, and the number of shares to be optioned to each:

a) Eligible participants are persons who are directors, members of management committee and senior managers of the Company and of subsidiary companies;

b) Shares to be optioned shall not exceed the aggregate number of 1,500,000; the number of Common Shares issuable to insiders, at any time, shall not exceed 10% of the issued and outstanding Common Shares; the number of Common Shares issued to insiders, within a one year period shall not exceed 10% of the issued and outstanding Common Shares;

c) The aggregate annual number of options granted to all Company directors in total cannot exceed 75,000. There are a remaining total of 1,081,662 common shares reserved for issuance under the plan;

d) The option price for the shares is determined by the Committee at the time of granting of the option but cannot be less than the fair market value of the shares at the time the option is granted;

e) The term during which any option granted may be exercised is determined by the Committee at the time the option is granted but may not exceed the maximum period permitted from time to time by The Toronto Stock Exchange;

f) The common share options vest after a one-year period;

g) The purchase price is payable in full at the time the option is exercised.

A summary of option activities is as follows:

	Fiscal 2007		Fiscal 2006	
	Options	Weighted Average Exercise Price	Options	Weighted Average Exercise Price
Beginning of year	561,025	$ 8.41	485,825	$ 8.19
Granted	75,500	9.64	171,625	8.65
Expired/cancelled	-	-	(3,150)	7.79
Forfeited	(10,775)	8.90	(54,350)	9.77
Exercised	(66,050)	6.35	(38,925)	4.92
End of year	559,700	$ 8.81	561,025	$ 8.41

All options outstanding were granted with the exercise price equaling the market price on the grant date. The following options were outstanding at year-end.

Exercise Price $	Contractual Life In Years	Expiry	December 29, 2007
4.75 – 5.15	0.25	2008	56,250
7.70	1.25	2009	69,025
7.75 – 8.25	0.25	2008	25,300
8.65	5.18	2012–2016	159,625
9.75	3.25	2011	85,500
10.99 – 11.10	2.25	2010	88,500
9.64	6.00	2013	75,500
			559,700

Included in the above figures are options of 135,500 at an average exercise price of $6.33 that were not exercisable on December 29, 2007, as they had not vested (December 30, 2006, 162,625 options at an average exercise price of $8.65). All other options outstanding on December 29, 2007 and December 30, 2006 were exercisable. Options with an expiry date of 2011 or later have Tandem Stock Appreciation Rights.

9   Accumulated Other Comprehensive Income

($000's)	December 29, 2007
Adjustments on adoption of financial instruments, net of future income taxes (note 1c)	
Unrealized foreign exchange losses on translation of self-sustaining foreign operations net of nil income tax	$ (13,577)
Unrealized net gains on derivative financial instruments designated as cash flow hedges, net of $0.2 million of future income taxes	448
	(13,129)
Unrealized foreign exchange losses on translation of self-sustaining foreign operations, net of nil future income taxes	(3,512)
Unrealized net losses on derivative financial instruments designated as cash flow hedges, net of $1.0 million of future income tax recovery	(2,160)
Total	$ (18,801)

Notes to Consolidated Financial Statements

10   Non-Operating Transactions

Non-operating transactions in 2007 and 2006 represent net costs/recoveries related to the disposal of the Company's Nova Scotia groundfish and scallop harvesting business.

11   Income Taxes

Temporary differences and loss carry forwards which give rise to future income tax assets and liabilities are as follows:

$000	Dec. 29, 2007	Dec. 30, 2006
Future income tax assets		
Property, plant and equipment	$ 2,778	$ 4,076
Tax loss carry forwards	13,506	16,462
Deferred charges and other	1,148	1,494
Unrealized foreign exchange losses	757	–
	18,189	22,032
Future income tax liabilities		
Property, plant and equipment	(5,945)	(1,209)
Goodwill	(354)	–
Investment tax credits	(205)	(382)
	(6,504)	(1,591)
Net tax assets before valuation allowance	11,685	20,441
Valuation allowance	(8,706)	(17,141)
Net future income tax assets	$ 2,979	$ 3,300
Less: current portion – asset	1,302	295
Less: long-term portion – asset	1,677	3,005
Long-term portion – liability	$ –	$ –

The Company has investment tax credit carry forwards recorded in the accounts of approximately $1.0 million (December 30, 2006; $2.4 million), available to reduce Canadian federal income taxes and expiring from 2008 through 2017. The Company also has unrecorded provincial investment tax credits carry forwards of approximately $0.5 million (December 30, 2006; $1.0 million). These are available to reduce provincial income tax, and expire from 2008 to 2010.

The Company has recorded future tax assets of $3.0 million after a valuation allowance of $8.7 million is taken into consideration. The valuation allowance is primarily for accumulated tax losses and the benefit of the write-down of goodwill in its U.S. subsidiary operation due to the uncertainty of fully utilizing these losses. Tax loss carry forwards for the U.S. subsidiary expire from 2008 to 2025.

In 2007, the Company recorded $0.4 million in investment tax credits ($0.5 million in 2006), as a reduction to property, plant and equipment. In 2006, the Company recorded $0.2 million as a reduction to expenses for investment tax credits earned on eligible research and development costs.

The Company's 2007 effective tax rate is lower than the statutory rate, as its US subsidiary's net future tax asset was fully allowed for and as a consequence no future income tax expense has been recorded against its current year's profits. In 2006, the Company's US subsidiary incurred a net loss, which due to the full valuation allowance, resulted in the Company's effective rate being higher than the statutory rate.

The reconciliation of the Company's effective income tax rate is as follows:

	Fiscal 2007 %	Fiscal 2006 %
Income tax statutory rate	35.7	35.8
Rate differences in foreign subsidiary	0.5	(0.6)
Adjustment on filing of tax return	–	2.1
Non taxable portion of capital (gains) losses	(0.5)	3.0
Non-deductible items	1.2	0.4
Valuation allowance	(3.4)	4.7
Other	1.2	0.2
	34.7	45.6

Notes to Consolidated Financial Statements

12 Per Share Earnings

The following is the reconciliation of the numerators and the denominators of basic and diluted earnings per share computations.

Based on Net Income

	Fiscal 2007			Fiscal 2006		
	Income ($000)	Shares (000)	Per Share Amount $	Income ($000)	Shares (000)	Per Share Amount $
Net income	7,289	-	-	4,330	-	-
Preference share dividends	(1,210)	-	-	(1,174)	-	-
Basic earnings per share:						
Income available to common shareholders	6,079	10,443	0.58	3,156	10,306	0.30
Diluted earnings per share:						
Effect of dilutive securities:						
Stock options	-	74	-	-	65	-
Series A preference shares	-	74	-	-	-	-
Income available to common shareholders and assumed conversions	6,079	10,591	0.57	3,156	10,371	0.30

Options to purchase 90,738 common shares at an average price of $11.06 per share (2006, 205,577 common shares at $10.40 per share) were outstanding and exercisable at year end but were not included in the compilation of diluted earnings per share because the options' exercise price was greater than the average market price of the common shares for the year.

As part of the Business Acquisition (note 2) the Company issued 1,200,000 Series A Preference Shares to the vendor. In connection with the redemption of the Second Preference Shares on February 20, 2008, the holders of substantially all of the shares subscribed for 798,620 Series A Preference Shares. Until these Series A Preference Shares are converted to Non Voting Common Shares (see note 8) they will receive a dividend equal to 2.5 times dividends on the common shares. No dividend entitlement was earned on these shares in 2007. Dividends on these shares, declared prior to their conversion to Non Voting Common Shares, will be deducted from income in calculating earnings per share.

13 Segmented Information

The Company operates in one dominant industry segment, the manufacturing and marketing of prepared and packaged frozen seafood. The Company evaluates performance of the reportable segments on a geographical basis using income before taxes from continuing operations. Operations and identifiable assets by reporting segment are as follows:

	Fiscal 2007			Fiscal 2006		
	Operating Entities			Operating Entities		
(All amounts in thousands)	Canada	USA	Total	Canada	USA	Total
Sales to geographic segments:						
Canada	$ 167,859	$ 1,514	$ 169,373	$ 154,421	$ 1,801	$ 156,222
Inter-segment (i)	-	(1,514)	(1,514)	-	(1,801)	(1,801)
	167,859	-	167,859	154,421	-	154,421
United States (i)	11,201	102,527	113,728	16,020	102,288	118,308
Inter-segment (i)	(9,994)	-	(9,994)	(14,382)	-	(14,382)
	1,207	102,527	103,734	1,638	102,288	103,926
Other	40	3,758	3,798	85	3,293	3,378
Net sales to external customers	$ 169,106	$ 106,285	$ 275,391	$ 156,144	$ 105,581	$ 261,725

(i) Inter-segment sales are at market.

Segment contribution to income before taxes from continuing operations:

	Fiscal 2007				Fiscal 2006			
	Canada	USA	Corporate	Total	Canada	USA	Corporate	Total
Income before the following:	$ 16,611	$ 2,520	$ (4,077)	$ 15,054	$ 14,779	$ 1,030	$ (2,241)	$ 13,568
Depreciation and amortization	(1,697)	(975)	(415)	(3,087)	(1,698)	(959)	(360)	(3,017)
Interest expense	-	-	(377)	(377)	-	-	(907)	(907)
Other (loss) income / non-operating transactions	-	-	(1,004)	(1,004)	-	-	(224)	(224)
Income from continuing operations before income tax	14,914	1,545	(5,873)	10,586	13,081	71	(3,732)	9,420
Capital Expenditures (ii)								
Gross capital expenditures	2,889	1,001	-	3,890	2,697	917	-	3,614
Investment tax credits	(431)	-	-	(431)	(520)	-	-	(520)
Net capital expenditures	$ 2,458	$ 1,001	$ -	$ 3,459	$ 2,177	$ 917	$ -	$ 3,094

(ii) Capital expenditures include additions financed through capital leases of $0.5 million in 2007 ($0.6 million in 2006).

Segmented Assets $000	Dec. 29, 2007	Dec. 30, 2006
Canada	$ 130,520	$ 73,003
USA	117,129	36,634
	247,649	109,637
Corporate	52,805	3,540
	$ 300,454	$ 113,177

Intangible assets and goodwill acquired (note 2) are included in corporate assets in the above table. Subsequent to the completion of the purchase price allocation these assets will be reallocated to the Company's two operating segments.

14 Employee Future Benefits

Description of Pension and Non-Pension Benefit Plans

In Canada, the Company maintains a number of defined contribution plans and defined benefit pension plans covering all Canadian employees. With respect to United States employees, the Company's subsidiary maintains two defined contribution plans (401k) that cover all U.S. employees. These U.S. plans will be merged in 2008.

The Company sponsors four funded and one non-funded defined benefit pension plans. The funded defined benefit plan for the Nova Scotia union employees is a flat-dollar plan with negotiated increases. The funded defined benefit plan for Canadian salaried employees is based on average career earnings. This plan is in the process of being wound up in 2008 and amounts will be either transferred to the Company's Defined Contribution Plan for salaried employees or annuities will be purchased for employees who do not elect a transfer. The Company has a senior officer retirement program (SORP) in the U.S. for selected employees. This plan ceased to accrue benefits to employees as of September 30, 2006. The non-funded supplemental executive retirement plan (SERP) and the funded defined benefit plan for management employees are both based on the employee's final average earnings. No Company pension plans provide indexation in retirement.

The Company sponsors a non-pension benefit plan for employees hired before May 19, 1993. This benefit is a paid-up life insurance policy or a lump sum payment based on the employee's final earnings at retirement.

Total Cash Payments for Pension Plans

The total cash payments for all defined benefit pension plans during 2007 by the Company was $0.4 million (2006; $1.3 million), which consisted of contributions, required to fund the defined benefit pension plans. The total cost for the Company's defined contribution pension plans was $0.6 million (2006; $0.6 million).

Measurement Dates

The Company measures the fair value of assets and the accrued benefit obligations as at December 29, 2007. The most recent accounting extrapolation on all pension and non-pension plans was completed as of December 29, 2007. The most recent funding valuations for the Company's defined benefit plans were completed as at May 31, 2006 for management and salaried employees, and December 31, 2004 for Nova Scotia union employees. A funding valuation for the SORP was in progress at December 29, 2007.

Notes to Consolidated Financial Statements

Reconciliation of the accrued benefit obligations and fair value of plan assets is below, segmented by plans with surplus and those with deficit:

$000	2007 Pension Benefit — Plans with Surplus	2007 Pension Benefit — Plans with Deficits	2007 Other Benefit Plan[(i)]	2006 Pension Benefit — Plans with Surplus	2006 Pension Benefit — Plans with Deficits	2006 Other Benefit Plan[(i)]
Accrued benefit obligation						
Balance at the beginning of the year	$ 21,756	$ 5,393	$ 516	$ 22,761	$ 5,385	$ 510
Current service cost (employer)	466	152	20	564	172	20
Interest cost	1,160	273	32	1,143	281	32
Exchange	-	(68)	-	-	-	-
Employee contributions	135	-	-	128	-	-
Benefits paid	(967)	(138)	(35)	(1,936)	(252)	(46)
Plan amendments	221	-	-	386	-	-
Actuarial (gain) loss	(329)	(109)	-	(1,290)	(193)	-
Obligations assumed (note 2)	-	340	-	-	-	-
Balance at end of year	22,442	5,843	533	21,756	5,393	516
Plan assets						
Fair value at the beginning of the year, estimated	25,514	1,440	-	24,307	1,444	-
Adjustment to actual assets at beginning of year	(49)	(34)	-	161	2	-
Actual return on plan assets	1,220	49	-	1,922	58	-
Employer contributions	228	54	-	1,073	144	-
Employees' contributions	135	-	-	128	-	-
Benefits paid	(967)	(99)	-	(1,936)	(211)	-
Fees and expenses	(157)	(17)	-	(141)	3	-
Assets assumed (note 2)	-	170	-	-	-	-
Fair value at end of year	25,924	1,563	-	25,514	1,440	-
Funded status – plans[(i)]	3,482	(4,280)	(533)	3,758	(3,953)	(516)
Unamortized net actuarial loss	2,313	566	-	2,490	22	-
Unamortized past service costs	964	20	-	112	745	-
Accrued benefit asset/ (liability)	6,759	(3,694)	(533)	6,360	(3,186)	(516)
Total accrued benefit assets	$ 6,759			$ 6,360		
Total accrued benefit liability[(i)]		$ (4,227)			$ (3,702)	

(i) The non-funded pension plans are a supplemental executive retirement plan (SERP), which accounts for $4.1 million (2006; $3.3 million) of the non-funded amount, and the Salaried Plan that accounts for the remainder. The Company has a letter of credit outstanding as at December 29, 2007 relating to the securitization of the Company's SERP benefit plan in the amount of $3.7 million.

(ii) The other benefit plan is non-funded.

Plan Assets consist of:

Breakdown of Plan Assets
Percentage of Plan Assets

	Dec. 29, 2007	Dec. 30, 2006
Equity securities – including income trusts [(iii)]	93%	91%
Debt securities	5%	9%
Cash and equivalents	2%	0%
Total	100%	100%

(iii) The plan assets include common shares in the Company at market value of $1.0 million (2006; $0.9 million).

Summary of the weighted average significant actuarial assumptions used in measuring the Company's accrued benefit obligations:

	Pension Benefit Plans 2007	Other Benefit Plans 2007	Pension Benefit Plans 2006	Other Benefit Plans 2006
Benefit cost for the year ended:				
Discount rate	5.19%	6.00%	4.97%	6.00%
Expected long-term rate on plan assets	7.37%	n/a	7.37%	n/a
Rate of compensation increase	2.86%	3.00%	2.85%	3.00%
Accrued benefit obligation as of year end:				
Discount rate	5.41%	6.00%	5.19%	6.00%
Rate of compensation increase	2.86%	3.00%	2.85%	3.00%

Components of defined costs recognized during the year:

$000	Pension Benefit Plans 2007	Other Benefit Plans 2007	Pension Benefit Plans 2006	Other Benefit Plans 2006
Current service cost	$ 618	$ 20	$ 736	$ 20
Interest cost	1,433	32	1,424	32
Actual return on plan assets	(1,047)	–	(2,007)	–
Plan amendments	221	–	386	–
Amortization of net actuarial (gain) loss	(447)	–	(1,483)	–
Costs arising in this period	778	52	(944)	52
Differences between costs arising in the period and costs recognized in the period in respect of:				
– Return on plan assets	(915)	–	141	–
– Actuarial gain	547	–	1,900	–
– Plan amendments	(126)	–	(308)	–
Defined benefit cost recognized	$ 284	$ 52	$ 789	$ 52

Notes to Consolidated Financial Statements

15 Supplemental Cash Flow Information

Cash interest and cash taxes paid in 2007 and 2006 are as follows:

$000	Fiscal 2007	Fiscal 2006
Interest	$ 178	$ 994
Income and capital taxes	$ 491	$ 538

Change in Non-Cash Working Capital Balances

$000	Fiscal 2007	Fiscal 2006
Receivables	$ (530)	$ (3,906)
Inventory	(2,467)	13,611
Prepaid expenses	753	(149)
Payables and accruals	632	(329)
	(1,612)	9,227
Tax recovery on the conversion of the U.S. subsidiary intercompany loans from debt to equity (note 9)	–	1,492
	$ (1,612)	10,719

16 Commitments

Operating lease commitments are less than $3.0 million for each of the next five years. They result principally from leases for office equipment, premises and production equipment. The Company has letters of credit outstanding as at December 29, 2007, relating to the procurement of inventories of $6.0 million (2006; $4.0 million) that are

denominated in U.S. dollars (translated at the balance sheet date rate). The Company also had a letter of credit outstanding as at December 29, 2007 relating to the securitization of the Company's SERP benefit plan (note 14) in the amount of $3.7 million (2006; $0.7 million).

Investing activities relating to discontinued operations in 2006 represent the cash proceeds on the sale of the Company's Italian Foods operations (note 3).

The Company has entered into non-monetary transactions with a media company whereby the Company receives advertising services from the media company in exchange for barter credits that it earned in previous years on the sale of inventory. The Company records such transactions at the fair value of the advertising credits received in prepaid expenses. The fair value of the exchange is $0.2 million (2006; $0.2 million).

Notes to Consolidated Financial Statements

17 Related Party Transactions

The Company has entered into certain transactions and agreements in the normal course of business with certain related parties. These transactions are measured at the exchange amount, which is the amount of consideration established and agreed to by the related parties.

During the year, the Company purchased $3.5 million (2006 - $3.6 million) of corrugated packaging from a related company at negotiated market prices. The Company uses corrugated packaging to ship its products to its customers. This related party is controlled by a company that owns a significant, non-controlling amount of the Company common stock.

As part of the Company's share repurchase plan, the Company paid immaterial commissions in 2006 to a company in which a director of the Company has an ownership interest.

At December 29, 2007, there were no material payables owed to related parties.

18 Financial Risk Management Objectives and Policies

The Company's principal financial liabilities, other than derivatives, comprise bank loans and overdrafts, letters of credit, notes payable, finance leases, and trade payables. The main purpose of these financial liabilities is to finance the Company's operations. The Company has various financial assets such as trade receivables, cash and short-term deposits, which arise directly from its operations. The Company also enters into derivative transactions, primarily interest rate swap and forward currency contracts. The purpose is to manage the interest rate and currency risks arising from the Company's operations and its sources of finance.

It is, and has been throughout 2007 and 2006, the Company's policy that no trading in derivatives shall be undertaken. The main risks arising from the Company's financial instruments are cash flow interest rate risk, liquidity risk, foreign currency risk and credit risk. The Audit Committee of the Board of Directors reviews and approves policies for managing each of these risks, which are summarized below.

Interest Rate Risk

The Company's exposure to the risk of changes in market interest rates arises out of the Company's short-term debt obligations with floating interest rates. The Company's policy is to manage its interest cost using a mix of fixed and variable rate debts. The Company's policy is to keep between 35% and 55% of its borrowings at fixed rates of interest. To manage this, the Company enters into interest rate swaps, in which the Company agrees to exchange, at specified intervals, the difference between fixed and variable rate interest amounts calculated by reference to an agreed upon notional principal amount. These swaps are designated to hedge underlying debt obligations.

Foreign Currency Risk

As a result of significant investment operations in the United States, the Company's balance sheet can be affected significantly by movements in the US$/C$ exchange rates. The Company seeks to mitigate the effect of its structural currency exposure by borrowing in US$. In January 2008, the Company designated $15.0 million of its US dollar denominated current bank debt in order to hedge 35% of this exposure.

The Company also has transactional currency exposures. Such exposure arises from sales or purchases by an operating unit in currencies other than the unit's functional currency. Taking into account the acquisition (note 2), approximately 40% of the Company's cost of sales are denominated in currencies other than the functional currency of the operating unit making the sale, whilst almost 100% of sales are denominated in the unit's functional currency.

The Company uses forward currency contracts to eliminate the currency exposures on any individual transactions in excess of US$100,000 for which payment is anticipated more than one month after the Company has entered into a firm commitment for a sale. The forward currency contracts must be in the same currency as the hedged item. The Company also hedges forecasted cash flows from the sale of products where the selling price is substantially known in advance. The policy dictates that cash flows out 15 months are hedged between a minimum and maximum percent that declines by quarter the further in the future the cash flows. The Company does not hedge cash flows related to true commodity products as their ultimate selling prices move depending in part on exchange rates. It is the Company's policy to negotiate the terms of the hedge derivatives to match the terms of the hedged item to maximize hedge effectiveness. The Company also has foreign exchange risk related to the input costs of commodities related to freight surcharges on transportation costs, paper products in packaging, grain products in its breading and batters, and cooking oils. The Company does not actively hedge these inputs relying instead on fixed price contracts with suppliers with terms from 3 to 12 months.

At December 29, 2007, the Company had hedged 66% of its targeted foreign currency purchases for its Canadian Operations, extending to December 2008. The Company does not include certain commodity products in its hedging program due to the commodity nature of the marketplace.

Credit Risk

The Company trades only with recognized, creditworthy third parties. It is the Company's policy that all customers who wish to trade on credit terms are subject to credit verification procedures. In addition, receivable balances are managed and monitored at the corporate level on an ongoing basis with the result that the Company's exposure to bad debts is not significant. The maximum exposure is the carrying amount as disclosed in note 4. The Company's top ten customers account for 54% of the trade receivables at year end with the largest customer accounting for 11%. Eight out of ten of the customers are investment grade with two being substantial private enterprises.

With respect to credit risk arising from the other financial assets of the Company, which comprise cash and cash equivalents and certain derivative instruments, the Company's exposure to credit risk arises from default of the counterparty, with a maximum exposure equal to the carrying amount of these instruments.

Liquidity Risk

The Company monitors its risk to a shortage of funds using a detailed budgeting process that identifies financing needs for the next 12 months. Working capital requirements are monitored daily and a sophisticated procurement system provides information on commitments. This process projects cash flows from operations. The Company's objective is to maintain a balance between continuity of funding and flexibility through the use of bank overdrafts, letters of credit, bank loans, notes payable, and finance leases.

19 Financial Instruments

Forward Range Contracts

At year-end, the Company had the following foreign exchange "average rate range forwards" purchase contracts outstanding, all with maturities of less than one year:

	December 29, 2007			December 30, 2007		
	Weighted Average Put Rate	Weighted Average Call Rate	Total USD Value	Weighted Average Put Rate	Weighted Average Call Rate	Total USD Value
Forward range contracts						
Average rate range	1.0048	1.0610	$ 50,449,500	1.0932	1.1497	$ 33,100,000

Average rate range forward purchase contracts

Where the average noon-day exchange rate during the contract term falls between the benefit and protection rates, no cash settlements are exchanged between the Company and the intermediary. If the average noon-day exchange rate during the contract term is less than the benefit rate, then on the contract settlement date, the Company would pay the intermediary the difference in the rate times the notional dollar value hedged. If the average noon-day exchange rate during the contract term is greater than the protection rate, then on the contract settlement date, the intermediary would pay the Company the difference in the rate times the notional dollar value hedged.

Fair value hedge

At December 29, 2007, the Company had an interest rate swap agreement in place with a notional amount of US$15,250,000 whereby it receives a US$ fixed rate of interest of 6.31% and pays a fixed C$ rate equal to 6.26% on the notional amount. This swap will convert principal payments from Canadian to US$ for a five-year period ending in 2012. The swap is being used to hedge the exposure to changes in the fair value of its 6.31% Series A note. The note and interest rate swap have the same critical terms. The swap is valued at rates prevailing at the balance sheet date. Gains and losses on the swap will be included in comprehensive income and will be transferred to income to offset gains and losses on the debt when realized. The offsetting entry is a reduction or increase in long term debt.

Other than described in the previous paragraph, the Company's net investment in its U.S. subsidiary was not hedged at December 29, 2007. The value of this net investment was US$43.1 million (December 30, 2006; US$16.8 million). Subsequent to year end the Company designated US$15.0 million of its US dollar debt as a hedge for the value of the net investment. Gains and losses on this debt will be recorded in other comprehensive income as an offset to changes in the value of the net investment.

Estimated fair value of financial instruments

The estimated fair value of financial instruments as at December 29, 2007 and December 30, 2006 are based on relevant market prices and information at that time. The fair-value estimate is not necessarily indicative of the amounts that the Company might receive or pay in actual market transactions. The total fair value of all of the foreign exchange future contracts as at December 29, 2007 was a net liability of $2.3 million (December 30, 2006; asset of $0.7 million). The fair value of the interest and principal cross currency swap was $0.1 million. The fair value of the foreign exchange contracts has been determined directly, by reference to published price quotations in an active market, and did not use a valuation technique.

The Company's remaining financial instruments consist of cash, receivables, current liabilities, long term debt and capital lease obligations. The difference between the carrying values and the fair market values of the primary financial instruments is not significant given the short-term maturities and, or the credit terms of those instruments and the fact that the long term debt was contracted shortly before period end.

Notes to Consolidated Financial Statements

 20   Contractual Agreements

As part of its Business Acquisition (note 2) the Company entered into an agreement with the Province of Newfoundland and Labrador (the Province) with respect to its operations in Burin, Newfoundland. The Company has agreed to maintain specified volumes of production in the plant until December 2012. Failure to maintain these volumes will result in a payment to the Province of $0.07 per lb for each lb of volume shortfall. In addition, over the period ending in December 2012 the Company has committed to spend $3 million, in product development activities in the Province and new equipment for Burin. Of these expenditures, 60% must be product development expenditures. As at December 29, 2007, the Company had spent $nil on these activities.

If the Company ceases permanent operation of the plant in Burin it must pay the Province $12,500 for each unionized worker that has been employed at Burin losing employment in the year of closure to be used as a worker transition fund by the Province. Based on current employment levels this would be approximately $2.3 million. The Company has current operating plans for Burin but may or may not maintain the agreed upon production levels in each year of the agreement.

The Company has also agreed not to sell its USA operations during the period ending 2012 without making a payment to the Province of $5 million.

 21   Contingencies

The Company may, from time to time, be involved in legal proceedings, claims and litigations that arise in the ordinary course of business which the Company believes would not reasonably be expected to have a material adverse effect on the financial statements of the Company.

22   Comparative Figures

Certain comparative financial information has been reclassified to conform to the presentation adopted in 2006 relating to discontinued operations and other balance sheet and cash flow reclassifications.

B

Present and Future Value Concepts

The concepts of present value (PV) and future value (FV) are based on the time value of money. The **time value of money** is the idea that, quite simply, money received today is worth more than money to be received one year from today (or at any other future date), because it can be used to earn interest. If you invest $1,000 today at 10 per cent, you will have $1,100 in one year. So $1,000 in one year is worth $100 less than $1,000 today because you lose the opportunity to earn the $100 in interest.

In some business situations, you will know the dollar amount of a cash flow that occurs in the future and will need to determine its value now. This type of situation is known as a **present value** problem. The opposite situation occurs when you know the dollar amount of a cash flow that occurs today and you need to determine its value at some point in the future. These situations are called **future value** problems. The value of money changes over time because money can earn interest. The following table illustrates the basic difference between present value and future value problems:

	Now	Future
Present value	?	$1,000
Future value	$1,000	?

Present and future value problems may involve two types of cash flow: a single payment or an annuity (which is the fancy word for a series of equal cash payments). Thus, you need to learn how to deal with four different situations related to the time value of money:

1. Future value of a single payment
2. Present value of a single payment
3. Future value of an annuity
4. Present value of an annuity

Most inexpensive hand-held calculators and any spreadsheet program can perform the detailed arithmetic computations required to solve future value and present value problems. In later courses and in all business situations, you will probably use a calculator or computer to solve these problems. At this stage, we encourage you to solve problems using Tables B.1 through B.4 on pages 644 to 647. We believe that using the tables will give you a better understanding of how and why present and future value concepts apply to business problems. The tables give the value of a $1 cash flow (single payment or annuity) for different periods (n) and at different interest rates (i). If a problem involves payments other than $1, it is necessary to multiply the value from the table by the amount of the payment.[1]

---

[1] Present value and future value problems involve cash flows. The basic concepts are the same for cash inflows (receipts) and cash outflows (payments). No fundamental differences exist between present value and future value calculations for cash payments versus cash receipts.

COMPUTING _____
Future and Present Values of a Single Amount

FUTURE VALUE OF A SINGLE AMOUNT

In problems about future value of a single amount, you will be asked to calculate how much money you will have in the future as the result of investing a certain amount in the present. If you were to receive a gift of $10,000, for instance, you might decide to put it in a savings account and use the money as a down payment on a house after you graduate. The future value computation would tell you how much money will be available when you graduate.

To solve a future value problem, you need to know three items:

1. Amount to be invested
2. Interest rate (i) the amount will earn
3. Number of periods (n) in which the amount will earn interest

The future value concept is based on compound interest, which simply means that interest is calculated on interest previously earned as well as on the principal amount. Thus, the amount of interest for each period is calculated using the principal plus any interest not paid out in prior periods. Graphically, the calculation of the future value of $1 for three periods at an interest rate of 10 per cent may be represented as follows:

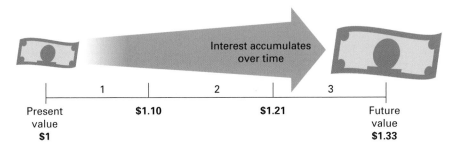

Assume that, on January 1, 2009, you deposit $1,000 in a savings account at 10 per cent annual interest, compounded annually. At the end of three years, the $1,000 will have increased to $1,331 as follows:

Year	Amount at Begining of Year	+	Interest During the Year	=	Amount at End of Year
1	$1,000	+	$1,000 × 10% = $100	=	$1,100
2	1,100	+	1,100 × 10% = 110	=	1,210
3	1,210	+	1,210 × 10% = 121	=	1,331

We can avoid the detailed arithmetic by referring to Table B.1, Future Value of $1, on page 644. For $i = 10\%$, $n = 3$, we find that the value of $1 is $1.3310. We then compute the balance at the end of year 3 as follows:

> From Table B.1, Interest rate = 10%, $n = 3$

$$\$1,000 \times 1.3310 = \$1,331$$

Note that the increase of $331 is due to the time value of money. It is interest revenue to the owner of the savings account and interest expense to the bank.

PRESENT VALUE OF A SINGLE AMOUNT

The present value of a single amount is the worth to you today of receiving that amount some time in the future. For instance, you might be offered an opportunity to invest in a financial instrument that would pay you $10,000 in 10 years. Before you decided whether to invest, you would want to determine the present value of the instrument.

To compute the present value of an amount to be received in the future, we must discount (a procedure that is the opposite of compounding) at *i* interest rate for *n* periods. In discounting, the interest is subtracted rather than added, as it is in compounding. Graphically, the present value of $1 due at the end of the third period with an interest rate of 10 per cent can be represented as follows:

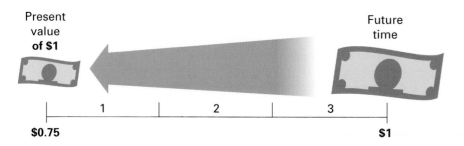

Assume that today is January 1, 2009, and you have the opportunity to receive $1,000 cash on December 31, 2011. At an interest rate of 10 per cent per year, how much is the $1,000 payment worth to you on January 1, 2009? You could discount the amount year by year,[2] but it is easier to use Table B.2, Present Value of $1, on page 645. For *i* = 10%, *n* = 3, we find that the present value of $1 is 0.7513. The present value of $1,000 to be received at the end of three years can be computed as follows:

From Table B.2,
Interest rate = 10%,
n = 3

$1,000 × 0.7513 = $751.30

It's important to learn not only how to compute a present value but also to understand what it means. The $751.30 is the amount you would pay now to have the right to receive $1,000 at the end of three years, assuming an interest rate of 10 per cent. Conceptually, you should be indifferent between having $751.30 today and receiving $1,000 in three years. If you had $751.30 today but preferred $1,000 in three years, you could simply deposit the money in a savings account that pays 10 per cent interest and it would grow to $1,000 in three years. Alternatively, if you had a contract that promised you $1,000 in three years, you could sell it to an investor for $751.30 in cash today because it would permit the investor to earn the difference in interest.

What if you could earn only 6 per cent during the three-year period from January 1, 2009, to December 31, 2011? What would be the present value on January 1, 2009, of receiving $1,000 on December 31, 2011? To answer this we would take the same approach, using Table B.2, except that the interest rate would change to *i* = 6%. Referring to Table B.2, we see the present value factor for *i* = 6%, *n* = 3, is 0.8396. Thus, the present value of $1,000 to be received at the end of three years, assuming a 6 per cent interest rate, would be computed as $1,000 × 0.8396 = $839.60. Notice that, when we assume a 6 per cent interest rate, the present value is greater than when we assumed a 10 per cent

---

[2]The detailed discounting is as follows:

Periods	Interest for the Year	Present Value*
1	$1,000 − ($1,000 × 1/1.10) = $90.91	$1,000 − $90.91 = $909.09
2	$909.09 − ($909.09 × 1/1.10) = $82.65	$909.09 − $82.65 = $826.44
3	$826.44 − ($826.44 × 1/1.10) = $75.14[†]	$826.44 − $75.14 = $751.30

*Verifiable in Table B.2.

[†]Adjusted for rounding.

HOW'S IT GOING? A Self-Study Quiz

1. If the interest rate in a present value problem increases from 8 per cent to 10 per cent, will the present value increase or decrease?
2. What is the present value of $10,000 to be received 10 years from now if the interest rate is 5 per cent, compounded annually?
3. If $10,000 is deposited in a savings account that earns 5 per cent interest compounded annually, how much will it be worth 10 years from now?

After you're finished, check your answers with the solution in the margin.

---

interest rate above. The reason for this difference is that, to reach $1,000 three years from now, you'd need to deposit more money in a savings account now if it earns 6 per cent interest than if it earns 10 per cent interest.

COMPUTING _____
Future and Present Values of an Annuity

Instead of a single payment, many business problems involve multiple cash payments over a number of periods. An **annuity** is a series of consecutive payments characterized by:

1. An equal dollar amount each interest period
2. Interest periods of equal length (year, half a year, quarter, or month)
3. An equal interest rate each interest period

Examples of annuities include monthly payments on a car or house, yearly contributions to a savings account, and monthly pension benefits.

An **annuity** is a series of periodic cash receipts or payments that are equal in amount each interest period.

FUTURE VALUE OF AN ANNUITY

If you are saving money for some purpose, such as a new car or a trip to Europe, you might decide to deposit a fixed amount of money in a savings account each month, which meets the definition of an annuity. The future value of an annuity computation will tell you how much money will be in your savings account at some point in the future.

The future value of an annuity includes compound interest on each payment from the date of the payment to the end of the term of the annuity. Each new payment accumulates less interest than prior payments, only because the number of periods remaining in which to accumulate interest decreases.

When using the annuity tables in B.3 and B.4, it is important to understand the timelines involved, because these tables are used only for **ordinary annuities**. Assume that the beginning of our timeline is January 1, 2009, and the first payment is made at December 31, 2009. This annuity is an ordinary annuity, which means we are standing at January 1, 2009, and calculating how much money we will have at the end of 3 full years (at December 31, 2011). In this case, we use Table B.3 and set $n = 3$. If, however, we define the beginning of our timeline as December 31, 2009, and the first cash payment is on that date, we are describing an **annuity due**. There are tables for annuities due as well, but we do not provide them in this text. Therefore, it is important that you set up your timelines as ordinary annuities if you plan to use the tables provided in this text.

An **ordinary annuity** is one where the payments are made at the end of each period. Tables B.3 and B.4 provide the factors for ordinary annuities.

An **annuity due** is one where the payments are made at the beginning of each period. This text does not provide tables for annuities due.

The future value of this ordinary annuity of $1 for three periods at 10 per cent may be represented graphically as:

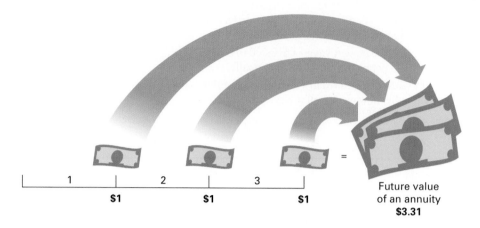

1		2		3	
$1		$1		$1	

Future value
of an annuity
$3.31

Assume that each year, for three years, you deposit $1,000 cash in a savings account at 10 per cent interest per year. You make the first $1,000 deposit on December 31, 2009, the second one on December 31, 2010, and the third and last one on December 31, 2011. The first $1,000 deposit earns compound interest for two years (for a total principal and interest of $1,210); the second deposit earns interest for one year (for a total principal and interest of $1,100). The third deposit earns no interest because it was made on the day that the balance is computed. Thus, the total amount in the savings account at the end of three years is $3,310 ($1,210 + $1,100 + $1,000).

To calculate the future value of this annuity, we could compute the interest on each deposit, similarly to what's described above. However, a faster way is to refer to Table B.3 on page 646, Future Value of an Annuity of $1 for $i = 10\%$, $n = 3$ to find the value 3.3100. The future value of your three deposits of $1,000 each can be computed as follows:

From Table B.3,
Interest rate = 10%,
$n = 3$

$1,000 × 3.3100 = $3,310

The Power of Compounding

Compound interest is a remarkably powerful economic force. In fact, the ability to earn interest on interest is the key to building economic wealth. If you save $1,000 per year for the first 10 years of your career, you will have more money when you retire than you would if you had saved $15,000 per year for the last 10 years of your career. This surprising outcome occurs because the money you save early in your career will earn more interest than the money you save at the end of your career. If you start saving money now, the majority of your wealth will not be the money you saved but the interest your money was able to earn.

The graph in the margin illustrates the power of compounding over a brief 10-year period. If you deposit $1 each year in an account earning 10 per cent interest, at the end of just 10 years only 63 per cent of your balance will be made up of money you have saved. The rest will be interest you have earned. After 20 years, only 35 per cent of your balance will be from saved money. The lesson associated with compound interest is that even though saving money is hard, you should start now.

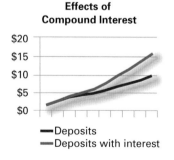

**Effects of
Compound Interest**

$20
$15
$10
$5
$0

— Deposits
— Deposits with interest

PRESENT VALUE OF AN ANNUITY

The present value of an annuity is the value now of a series of equal amounts to be received (or paid out) for some specified number of periods in the future. It is computed by discounting each of the equal periodic amounts. A good example of this type of problem is a retirement program that offers employees a monthly income after retirement. The present value of an annuity of $1 for three periods at 10 per cent may be represented graphically as:

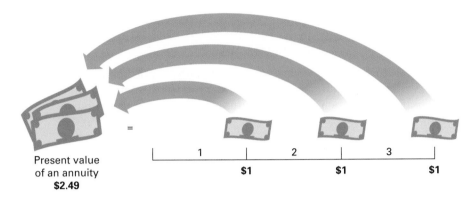

Present value
of an annuity
$2.49

1   **$1**   2   **$1**   3   **$1**

Assume you are to receive $1,000 cash on each December 31, in 2009, 2010, and 2011. How much would the sum of these three $1,000 future amounts be worth on January 1, 2009, assuming an interest rate of 10 per cent per year? One way to determine this is to use Table B.2 to calculate the present value of each single amount, as follows:

Year	Amount		Factor from Table B.2 $i = 10\%$		Present Value
1	$1,000	×	0.9091 (n = 1)	=	$ 909.10
2	1,000	×	0.8264 (n = 2)	=	826.40
3	1,000	×	0.7513 (n = 3)	=	751.30
			Total present value	=	$2,486.80

Alternatively, we can compute the present value of this annuity more easily by using Table B.4 on page 647, as follows:

> $1,000 × 2.4869 = $2,487 (rounded)

From Table B.4,
Interest rate = 10%,
$n = 3$

INTEREST RATES AND INTEREST PERIODS

The preceding illustrations assumed annual periods for compounding and discounting. Although interest rates are almost always quoted on an annual basis, many compounding periods encountered in business are less than one year. When interest periods are less than a year, the values of n and i must be restated to be consistent with the length of the interest period.

To illustrate, 12 per cent interest compounded annually for five years requires the use of $n = 5$ and $i = 12\%$. If compounding is quarterly, however, the interest period is one quarter of a year (four periods per year), and the quarterly interest rate is one quarter of the annual rate (3 per cent per quarter). Therefore, 12 per cent interest compounded quarterly for five years requires use of $n = 20$ and $i = 3\%$.

COACH'S TIP

The help function in Excel describes how to calculate the present value of an annuity using its PV worksheet function.

ACCOUNTING _____

Applications of Present Values

Many business transactions require the use of future and present value concepts. In finance classes, you will see how to apply future value concepts. In this section, we apply present value concepts to three common accounting cases.

CASE A—PRESENT VALUE OF A SINGLE AMOUNT

On January 1, 2009, General Mills bought some new delivery trucks. The company signed a note and agreed to pay $200,000 on December 31, 2010, an amount representing the cash equivalent price of the trucks plus interest for two years. The market interest rate for this note was 12 per cent.

1. How should the accountant record the purchase?

Answer: This case requires the computation of the present value of a single amount. In conformity with the cost principle, the cost of the trucks is their current cash equivalent price, which is the present value of the future payment. The problem can be shown graphically as follows:

```
1/1/2009                        12/31/2009                    12/31/2010
   |◄──────────────────────────────|────────────────────────────|
   ?                                                        $200,000
```

The present value of the $200,000 is computed as follows:

$$\$200,000 \times 0.7972 = \$159,440$$

From Table B.2, Interest rate = 12%, n = 2

Therefore, the journal entry to record the purchase of the trucks is:

dr	Delivery Trucks (+A) 159,440	
	cr Note Payable (+L)	159,440

Assets	=	Liabilities	+	Shareholders' Equity
Delivery Trucks + 159,440		Note Payable + 159,440		

2. What journal entry should be made at the end of 2009 and 2010 to record interest expense?

Answer: Each year's interest expense is recorded in an adjusting entry as follows:

December 31, 2009

dr	Interest Expense (+E, −SE) 19,132*	
	cr Note Payable (+L)	19,132

*$159,440 × 12% × 12/12 = $19,132 (rounded).

Assets	=	Liabilities	+	Shareholders' Equity
		Note Payable + 19,132		Interest expense (+E) − 19,132

December 31, 2010

dr	Interest Expense (+E, −SE) 21,428*	
	cr Note Payable (+L)	21,428

*($159,440 + $19,132) × 12% × 12/12 = 21,428 (rounded).

Assets	=	Liabilities	+	Shareholders' Equity
		Note Payable + 21,428		Interest Expense (+E) − 21,428

3. What journal entry should be made on December 31, 2010, to record payment of the debt?

Answer: At this date the amount to be paid is the balance in *Note Payable*, after it has been updated for interest pertaining to 2010, as shown in the T-account in the margin. Notice that, just prior to its repayment, the balance for the note on December 31, 2010, is the same as the maturity amount on the due date.

The journal entry to record full payment of the debt follows:

dr	**Note Payable (−L)**	200,000
cr	**Cash (−A)**	200,000

	dr Note Payable (L) cr	
	159,440	Jan. 1, 2009
	19,132	Interest 2009
	21,428	Interest 2010
	200,000	Dec. 31, 2010

Assets	=	Liabilities	+	Shareholders' Equity
Cash − 200,000		Note Payable − 200,000		

CASE B—PRESENT VALUE OF AN ANNUITY

On January 1, 2009, General Mills bought new milling equipment. The company elected to finance the purchase with a note payable to be paid off in three years in annual instalments of $163,686. Each instalment includes principal plus interest on the unpaid balance at 11 per cent per year. The annual instalments are due on December 31, 2009, 2010, and 2011. This problem can be shown graphically as follows:

1/1/2009	12/31/2009	12/31/2010	12/31/2011
?	$163,686	$163,686	$163,686

1. What is the amount of the note?

Answer: The note is the present value of each instalment payment, $i = 11\%$ and $n = 3$. This is an annuity because the note repayment is made in three equal instalments. The amount of the note is computed as follows:

From Table B.4, Interest rate = 11%, $n = 3$

$$\$163,686 \times 2.4437 = \$400,000$$

The acquisition on January 1, 2009, is recorded as follows:

dr	**Milling Equipment (+A)**	400,000
cr	**Note Payable (+L)**	400,000

Assets	=	Liabilities	+	Shareholders' Equity
Milling Equipment + 400,000		Note Payable + 400,000		

2. What journal entries should be made at the end of each year to record the payments on this note?

Answer:

December 31, 2009
dr   **Interest Expense (+E, −SE)**
     ($400,000 × 11% × 12/12)   44,000
dr   **Note Payable (−L)** ($163,686 − $44,000). . . .   119,686
   cr   **Cash (−A)**   163,686

Assets		=	Liabilities		+	Shareholders' Equity	
Cash	− 163,686		Note Payable	− 119,686		Interest Expense (+E)	− 44,000

December 31, 2010
dr   **Interest Expense (+E, −SE)** 30,835*
dr   **Note Payable (−L)** ($163,686 − $30,835). . . .   132,851
   cr   **Cash (−A)**   163,686

*Interest: [($400,000 − $119,686) × 11% × 12/12 = $30,835].

Assets		=	Liabilities		+	Shareholders' Equity	
Cash	− 163,686		Note Payable	− 132,851		Interest Expense (+E)	− 30,835

---

dr Note Payable (L) cr		
	400,000	Jan 1, 2009
Dec. 31, 2009 119,686		
Dec. 31, 2010 132,851		
Dec. 31, 2011 147,463		
	0	Dec. 31, 2011

December 31, 2011
dr   **Interest Expense (+E, −SE)** 16,223*
dr   **Note Payable (−L)** ($163,686 − $16,223). . . .   147,463
   cr   **Cash (−A)**   163,686

*Interest: [($400,000 − $119,686 − $132,851) × 11% × 12/12 = $16,223 (adjusted to accommodate rounding errors)].

Assets		=	Liabilities		+	Shareholders' Equity	
Cash	− 163,686		Note Payable	− 147,463		Interest Expense (+E)	− 16,223

COACH'S TIP

Each interest payment of $6,000 is calculated as:
$100,000 × 6% × 12/12.

CASE C—PRESENT VALUE OF A SINGLE AMOUNT AND AN ANNUITY

On January 1, 2009, General Mills issued a four-year, $100,000 bond. The bond pays interest annually at a rate of 6 per cent of face value. What would investors be willing to pay for the bond if they require an annual return of (*a*) 4 per cent, (*b*) 6 per cent, or (*c*) 8 per cent? *Answer:* This case requires the computation of the present value of a single amount (for the $100,000 face value paid at maturity) plus the present value of an annuity (for annual interest payments of $6,000). The problem can be shown graphically as follows:

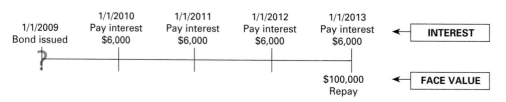

a.   4 Per Cent Market Interest Rate

The present value of the $100,000 face value is computed as follows:

$$\$100,000 \times 0.8548 = \$85,480$$

From Table B.2,
Interest rate = 4%,
n = 4

The present value of the $6,000 annuity is computed as follows:

$$\$6,000 \times 3.6299 = \$21,780^*$$

From Table B.4,
Interest rate = 4%,
n = 4

*Adjusted to accommodate rounding in the present value factor

The present value of the total bond payments, computed using the discount rate of 4%, is:

$$\$107,260 \,(= \$85,480 + \$21,780)$$

b.   6 Per Cent Market Interest Rate

The present value of the $100,000 face value is computed as follows:

$$\$100,000 \times 0.7921 = \$79,210$$

From Table B.2,
Interest rate = 6%,
n = 4

The present value of the $6,000 annuity is computed as follows:

$$\$6,000 \times 3.4651 = \$20,790^*$$

From Table B.4,
Interest rate = 6%,
n = 4

*Adjusted to accommodate rounding in the present value factor

The present value of the total bond payments, computed using the discount rate of 6%, is:

$$\$100,000 \,(= \$79,210 + \$20,790)$$

c.   8 Per Cent Market Interest Rate

The present value of the $100,000 face value is computed as follows:

$$\$100,000 \times 0.7350 = \$73,500$$

From Table B.2,
Interest rate = 8%,
n = 4

The present value of the $6,000 annuity is computed as follows:

$$\$6,000 \times 3.3121 = \$19,876^*$$

From Table B.4,
Interest rate = 8%,
n = 4

*Adjusted to accommodate rounding in the present value factor

The present value of the total bond payments, computed using the discount rate of 8%, is

$$\$93,376 \,(= \$73,500 + \$19,876)$$

COACH'S TIP

The present values in *a, b,* and *c* demonstrate the calculation of the bond issue prices used in Chapter 10.

Of course, these calculations are just the starting point for understanding how bond liabilities are determined and reported. Chapter 10 describes the journal entries that would be used to enter this information into the accounting system.

TABLE B.1

Future Value of $1

Periods	2%	3%	4%	5%	6%	7%	8%
0	1.	1.	1.	1.	1.	1.	1.
1	1.02	1.03	1.04	1.05	1.06	1.07	1.08
2	1.0404	1.0609	1.0816	1.1025	1.1236	1.1449	1.1664
3	1.0612	1.0927	1.1249	1.1576	1.1910	1.2250	1.2597
4	1.0824	1.1255	1.1699	1.2155	1.2625	1.3108	1.3605
5	1.1041	1.1593	1.2167	1.2763	1.3382	1.4026	1.4693
6	1.1262	1.1941	1.2653	1.3401	1.4185	1.5007	1.5869
7	1.1487	1.2299	1.3159	1.4071	1.5036	1.6058	1.7138
8	1.1717	1.2668	1.3686	1.4775	1.5938	1.7182	1.8509
9	1.1951	1.3048	1.4233	1.5513	1.6895	1.8385	1.9990
10	1.2190	1.3439	1.4802	1.6289	1.7908	1.9672	2.1589
11	1.2434	1.3842	1.5395	1.7103	1.8983	2.1049	2.3316
12	1.2682	1.4258	1.6010	1.7959	2.0122	2.2522	2.5182
13	1.2936	1.4685	1.6651	1.8857	2.1329	2.4099	2.7196
14	1.3195	1.5126	1.7317	1.9799	2.2609	2.5785	2.9372
15	1.3459	1.5580	1.8009	2.0789	2.3966	2.7590	3.1722
16	1.3728	1.6047	1.8730	2.1829	2.5404	2.9522	3.4259
17	1.4002	1.6529	1.9479	2.2920	2.6928	3.1588	3.7000
18	1.4283	1.7024	2.0258	2.4066	2.8543	3.3799	3.9960
19	1.4568	1.7535	2.1069	2.5270	3.0256	3.6165	4.3157
20	1.4859	1.8061	2.1911	2.6533	3.2071	3.8697	4.6610

Periods	9%	10%	11%	12%	13%	14%	15%
0	1.	1.	1.	1.	1.	1.	1.
1	1.09	1.10	1.11	1.12	1.13	1.14	1.15
2	1.1881	1.2100	1.2321	1.2544	1.2769	1.2996	1.3225
3	1.2950	1.3310	1.3676	1.4049	1.4429	1.4815	1.5209
4	1.4116	1.4641	1.5181	1.5735	1.6305	1.6890	1.7490
5	1.5386	1.6105	1.6851	1.7623	1.8424	1.9254	2.0114
6	1.6771	1.7716	1.8704	1.9738	2.0820	2.1950	2.3131
7	1.8280	1.9487	2.0762	2.2107	2.3526	2.5023	2.6600
8	1.9926	2.1436	2.3045	2.4760	2.6584	2.8526	3.0590
9	2.1719	2.3579	2.5580	2.7731	3.0040	3.2519	3.5179
10	2.3674	2.5937	2.8394	3.1058	3.3946	3.7072	4.0456
11	2.5804	2.8531	3.1518	3.4786	3.8359	4.2262	4.65240
12	2.8127	3.1384	3.4985	3.8960	4.3345	4.8180	5.35030
13	3.0658	3.4523	3.8833	4.3635	4.8980	5.4924	6.15280
14	3.3417	3.7975	4.3104	4.8871	5.5348	6.2613	7.07580
15	3.6425	4.1773	4.7846	5.4736	6.2543	7.1379	8.1371
16	3.9703	4.5950	5.3109	6.1304	7.0673	8.1372	9.3576
17	4.3276	5.0545	5.8951	6.8660	7.9861	9.2765	10.7613
18	4.7171	5.5599	6.5436	7.6900	9.0243	10.5752	12.3755
19	5.1417	6.1159	7.2633	8.6128	10.1974	12.0557	14.2318
20	5.6044	6.7275	8.0623	9.6463	11.5231	13.7435	16.3665

TABLE B.2

Present Value of $1

Periods	2%	3%	4%	5%	6%	7%	8%
1	0.9804	0.9709	0.9615	0.9524	0.9434	0.9346	0.9259
2	0.9612	0.9426	0.9246	0.9070	0.8900	0.8734	0.8573
3	0.9423	0.9151	0.8890	0.8638	0.8396	0.8163	0.7938
4	0.9238	0.8885	0.8548	0.8227	0.7921	0.7629	0.7350
5	0.9057	0.8626	0.8219	0.7835	0.7473	0.7130	0.6806
6	0.8880	0.8375	0.7903	0.7462	0.7050	0.6663	0.6302
7	0.8706	0.8131	0.7599	0.7107	0.6651	0.6227	0.5835
8	0.8535	0.7894	0.7307	0.6768	0.6274	0.5820	0.5403
9	0.8368	0.7664	0.7026	0.6446	0.5919	0.5439	0.5002
10	0.8203	0.7441	0.6756	0.6139	0.5584	0.5083	0.4632
11	0.8043	0.7224	0.6496	0.5847	0.5268	0.4751	0.4289
12	0.7885	0.7014	0.6246	0.5568	0.4970	0.4440	0.3971
13	0.7730	0.6809	0.6006	0.5303	0.4688	0.4150	0.3677
14	0.7579	0.6611	0.5775	0.5051	0.4423	0.3878	0.3405
15	0.7430	0.6419	0.5553	0.4810	0.4173	0.3625	0.3152
16	0.7285	0.6232	0.5339	0.4581	0.3937	0.3387	0.2920
17	0.7142	0.6050	0.5134	0.4363	0.3714	0.3166	0.2703
18	0.7002	0.5874	0.4936	0.4155	0.3503	0.2959	0.2503
19	0.6864	0.5703	0.4746	0.3957	0.3305	0.2765	0.2317
20	0.6730	0.5537	0.4564	0.3769	0.3118	0.2584	0.2145

Periods	9%	10%	11%	12%	13%	14%	15%
1	0.9174	0.9091	0.9009	0.8929	0.8850	0.8772	0.8696
2	0.8417	0.8264	0.8116	0.7972	0.7831	0.7695	0.7561
3	0.7722	0.7513	0.7312	0.7118	0.6931	0.6750	0.6575
4	0.7084	0.6830	0.6587	0.6355	0.6133	0.5921	0.5718
5	0.6499	0.6209	0.5935	0.5674	0.5428	0.5194	0.4972
6	0.5963	0.5645	0.5346	0.5066	0.4803	0.4556	0.4323
7	0.5470	0.5132	0.4817	0.4523	0.4251	0.3996	0.3759
8	0.5019	0.4665	0.4339	0.4039	0.3762	0.3506	0.3269
9	0.4604	0.4241	0.3909	0.3606	0.3329	0.3075	0.2843
10	0.4224	0.3855	0.3522	0.3220	0.2946	0.2697	0.2472
11	0.3875	0.3505	0.3173	0.2875	0.2607	0.2366	0.2149
12	0.3555	0.3186	0.2858	0.2567	0.2307	0.2076	0.1869
13	0.3262	0.2897	0.2575	0.2292	0.2042	0.1821	0.1625
14	0.2993	0.2633	0.2320	0.2046	0.1807	0.1597	0.1413
15	0.2745	0.2394	0.2090	0.1827	0.1599	0.1401	0.1229
16	0.2519	0.2176	0.1883	0.1631	0.1415	0.1229	0.1069
17	0.2311	0.1978	0.1696	0.1456	0.1252	0.1078	0.0929
18	0.2120	0.1799	0.1528	0.1300	0.1108	0.0946	0.0808
19	0.1945	0.1635	0.1377	0.1161	0.0981	0.0830	0.0703
20	0.1784	0.1486	0.1240	0.1037	0.0868	0.0728	0.0611

TABLE B.3

Future Value of Annuity of $1

Periods*	2%	3%	4%	5%	6%	7%	8%
1	1.	1.	1.	1.	1.	1.	1.
2	2.02	2.03	2.04	2.05	2.06	2.07	2.08
3	3.0604	3.0909	3.1216	3.1525	3.1836	3.2149	3.2464
4	4.1216	4.1836	4.2465	4.3101	4.3746	4.4399	4.5061
5	5.2040	5.3091	5.4163	5.5256	5.6371	5.7507	5.8666
6	6.3081	6.4684	6.6330	6.8019	6.9753	7.1533	7.3359
7	7.4343	7.6625	7.8983	8.1420	8.3938	8.6540	8.9228
8	8.5830	8.8923	9.2142	9.5491	9.8975	10.2598	10.6366
9	9.7546	10.1591	10.5828	11.0266	11.4913	11.9780	12.4876
10	10.9497	11.4639	12.0061	12.5779	13.1808	13.8164	14.4866
11	12.1687	12.8078	13.4864	14.2068	14.9716	15.7836	16.6455
12	13.4121	14.1920	15.0258	15.9171	16.8699	17.8885	18.9771
13	14.6803	15.6178	16.6268	17.7130	18.8821	20.1406	21.4953
14	15.9739	17.0863	18.2919	19.5986	21.0151	22.5505	24.2149
15	17.2934	18.5989	20.0236	21.5786	23.2760	25.1290	27.1521
16	18.6393	20.1569	21.8245	23.6575	25.6725	27.8881	30.3243
17	20.0121	21.7616	23.6975	25.8404	28.2129	30.8402	33.7502
18	21.4123	23.4144	25.6454	28.1324	30.9057	33.9990	37.4502
19	22.8406	25.1169	27.6712	30.5390	33.7600	37.3790	41.4463
20	24.2974	26.8704	29.7781	33.0660	36.7856	40.9955	45.7620

Periods*	9%	10%	11%	12%	13%	14%	15%
1	1.	1.	1.	1.	1.	1.	1.
2	2.09	2.10	2.11	2.12	2.13	2.14	2.15
3	3.2781	3.3100	3.3421	3.3744	3.4069	3.4396	3.4725
4	4.5731	4.6410	4.7097	4.7793	4.8498	4.9211	4.9934
5	5.9847	6.1051	6.2278	6.3528	6.4803	6.6101	6.7424
6	7.5233	7.7156	7.9129	8.1152	8.3227	8.5355	8.7537
7	9.2004	9.4872	9.7833	10.0890	10.4047	10.7305	11.0668
8	11.0285	11.4359	11.8594	12.2997	12.7573	13.2328	13.7268
9	13.0210	13.5975	14.1640	14.7757	15.4157	16.0853	16.7858
10	15.1929	15.9374	16.7220	17.5487	18.4197	19.3373	20.3037
11	17.5603	18.5312	19.5614	20.6546	21.8143	23.0445	24.3493
12	20.1407	21.3843	22.7132	24.1331	25.6502	27.2707	29.0017
13	22.9534	24.5227	26.2116	28.0291	29.9847	32.0887	34.3519
14	26.0192	27.9750	30.0949	32.3926	34.8827	37.5811	40.5047
15	29.3609	31.7725	34.4054	37.2797	40.4175	43.8424	47.5804
16	33.0034	35.9497	39.1900	42.7533	46.6717	50.9804	55.7175
17	36.9737	40.5447	44.5008	48.8837	53.7391	59.1176	65.0751
18	41.3013	45.5992	50.3959	55.7497	61.7251	68.3941	75.8364
19	46.0185	51.1591	56.9395	63.4397	70.7494	78.9692	88.2118
20	51.1601	57.2750	64.2028	72.0524	80.9468	91.0249	102.4436

*There is one payment each period.

TABLE B.4

Present Value of Annuity of $1

Periods*	2%	3%	4%	5%	6%	7%	8%
1	0.9804	0.9709	0.9615	0.9524	0.9434	0.9346	0.9259
2	1.9416	1.9135	1.8861	1.8594	1.8334	1.8080	1.7833
3	2.8839	2.8286	2.7751	2.7232	2.6730	2.6243	2.5771
4	3.8077	3.7171	3.6299	3.5460	3.4651	3.3872	3.3121
5	4.7135	4.5797	4.4518	4.3295	4.2124	4.1002	3.9927
6	5.6014	5.4172	5.2421	5.0757	4.9173	4.7665	4.6229
7	6.4720	6.2303	6.0021	5.7864	5.5824	5.3893	5.2064
8	7.3255	7.0197	6.7327	6.4632	6.2098	5.9713	5.7466
9	8.1622	7.7861	7.4353	7.1078	6.8017	6.5152	6.2469
10	8.9826	8.5302	8.1109	7.7217	7.3601	7.0236	6.7101
11	9.7869	9.2526	8.7605	8.3064	7.8869	7.4987	7.1390
12	10.5753	9.9540	9.3851	8.8633	8.3838	7.9427	7.5361
13	11.3484	10.6350	9.9857	9.3936	8.8527	8.3577	7.9038
14	12.1063	11.2961	10.5631	9.8986	9.2950	8.7455	8.2442
15	12.8493	11.9379	11.1184	10.3797	9.7123	9.1079	8.5595
16	13.5777	12.5611	11.6523	10.8378	10.1059	9.4467	8.8514
17	14.2919	13.1661	12.1657	11.2741	10.4773	9.7632	9.1216
18	14.9920	13.7535	12.6593	11.6896	10.8276	10.0591	9.3719
19	15.6785	14.3238	13.1339	12.0853	11.1581	10.3356	9.6036
20	16.3514	14.8775	13.5903	12.4622	11.4699	10.5940	9.8181

Periods*	9%	10%	11%	12%	13%	14%	15%
1	0.9174	0.9091	0.9009	0.8929	0.8550	0.8772	0.8696
2	1.7591	1.7355	1.7125	1.6901	1.6681	1.6467	1.6257
3	2.5313	2.4869	2.4437	2.4018	2.3612	2.3216	2.2832
4	3.2397	3.1699	3.1024	3.0373	2.9745	2.9137	2.8550
5	3.8897	3.7908	3.6959	3.6048	3.5172	3.4331	3.3522
6	4.4859	4.3553	4.2305	4.1114	3.9975	3.8887	3.7845
7	5.0330	4.8684	4.7122	4.5638	4.4226	4.2883	4.1604
8	5.5348	5.3349	5.1461	4.9676	4.7988	4.6389	4.4873
9	5.9952	5.7590	5.5370	5.3282	4.1317	4.9464	4.7716
10	6.4177	6.1446	5.8892	5.6502	5.4262	5.2161	5.0188
11	6.8052	6.4951	6.2065	5.9377	5.6869	5.4527	5.2337
12	7.1607	6.8137	6.4924	6.1944	5.9176	5.6603	5.4206
13	7.4869	7.1034	6.7499	6.4236	6.1218	5.8424	5.5832
14	7.7862	7.3667	6.9819	6.6282	6.3025	6.0021	5.7245
15	8.0607	7.6061	7.1909	6.8109	6.4624	6.1422	5.8474
16	8.3126	7.8237	7.3792	6.9740	6.6039	6.2651	5.9542
17	8.5436	8.0216	7.5488	7.1196	6.7291	6.3729	6.0472
18	8.7556	8.2014	7.7016	7.2497	6.8399	6.4674	6.1280
19	8.9501	8.3649	7.8393	7.3658	6.9380	6.5504	6.1982
20	9.1285	8.5136	7.9633	7.4694	7.0248	6.6231	6.2593

*There is one payment each period.

FOR YOUR REVIEW _____

KEY TERMS TO KNOW

Annuity p. 637   Future Value p. 634   Present Value p. 634

Annuity Due, p. 637   Ordinary Annuity, p. 637   Time Value of Money p. 634

FOR YOUR PRACTICE _____

QUESTIONS

1. Explain the concept of the time value of money.
2. Explain the basic difference between future value and present value.
3. If you deposited $10,000 in a savings account that earns 10 per cent, how much would you have at the end of 10 years? Use a convenient format to display your computations.
4. If you hold a valid contract that will pay you $8,000 cash 10 years from now and the going rate of interest is 10 per cent, what is its present value? Use a convenient format to display your computations.
5. What is an annuity?
6. Complete the following schedule:

	Table Values		
Concept	*i = 5%, n = 4*	*i = 10%, n = 7*	*i = 14%, n = 10*
FV of $1			
PV of $1			
FV of annuity of $1			
PV of annuity of $1			

7. If you deposit $1,000 at the end of each year for 10 years and you earn 8 per cent annual interest, how much would you have at the end of year 10? Use a convenient format to display your computations.

MULTIPLE CHOICE

Select the one alternative that best answers the question or completes the sentence.

1. You are saving up for a Porsche Carrera Cabriolet, which currently sells for nearly half a million dollars. Your plan is to deposit $15,000 at the end of each year for the next 10 years. You expect to earn 5 per cent each year. How much will you have saved after 10 years, rounded to the nearest 10 dollars?
   a. $150,000
   b. $188,670.
   c. $495,990
   d. None of the above

2. Which of the following is a characteristic of an annuity?
   a. An equal dollar amount paid each interest period
   b. Interest periods of equal length
   c. An equal interest rate earned each interest period
   d. All of the above are characteristics of an annuity.

3. Which of the following is most likely to be an annuity?
   a. Monthly payments on a credit card bill
   b. Monthly interest earned on a chequing account

    c.   Monthly payments on a home mortgage

    d.   Monthly utility bill payments

4. Assume you bought a plasma television set, with no payments to be made until two years from now, when you must pay $6,000. If the going rate of interest on most loans is 5 per cent, which table in this appendix would you use to calculate the television's equivalent cost if you were to pay for it today?

    a.   Table B.1 (Future Value of $1)

    b.   Table B.2 (Present Value of $1)

    c.   Table B.3 (Future Value of Annuity of $1)

    d.   Table B.4 (Present Value of Annuity of $1)

5. Assuming the facts in question 3, what is the television's equivalent cost if you were to pay for it today?

    a. $5,442

    b. $6,615

    c. $11,100

    d. $12,300

6. Assume you bought a car using a loan that requires payments of $3,000 to be made at the end of every year for the next three years. The loan agreement indicates the annual interest rate is 6 per cent. Which table in this appendix would you use to calculate the car's equivalent cost if you were to pay for it in full today?

    a.   Table B.1 (Future Value of $1)

    b.   Table B.2 (Present Value of $1)

    c.   Table B.3 (Future Value of Annuity of $1)

    d.   Table B.4 (Present Value of Annuity of $1)

7. Assuming the facts in question 6, what is the car's equivalent cost if you were to pay for it today? Round to the nearest hundred dollars.

    a. $2,600

    b. $3,600

    c. $8,000

    d. $9,600

8. Which of the following statements are true?

    a.   When the interest rate increases, the present value of a single amount decreases.

    b.   When the number of interest periods increases, the present value of a single amount increases.

    c.   When the interest rate increases, the present value of an annuity increases.

    d.   None of the above are true.

9. Which of the following describes how to calculate a bond's issue price?

	Face Value		Interest Payments
a.	Present value of single amount	+	Future value of annuity
b.	Future value of single amount	+	Present value of annuity
c.	Present value of single amount	+	Present value of annuity
d.	Future value of single amount	+	Future value of annuity

10. If interest is compounded quarterly, rather than yearly, how do you adjust the number of years and annual interest rate when using the present value tables?

	Number of Years	Annual Interest Rate
a.	Divide by 4	Divide by 4
b.	Divide by 4	Multiply by 4
c.	Multiply by 4	Divide by 4
d.	Multiply by 4	Multiply by 4

MINI-EXERCISES

MB-1   Computing the Present Value of a Single Payment
What is the present value of $500,000 to be paid in 10 years, with an interest rate of 8 per cent?

MB-2   Computing the Present Value of an Annuity
What is the present value of 10 equal payments of $15,000, with an interest rate of 10 per cent?

MB-3   Computing the Present Value of a Complex Contract
As a result of a slowdown in operations, Mercantile Stores is offering to employees who have been terminated a severance package of $100,000 cash; another $100,000 to be paid in one year; and an annuity of $30,000 to be paid each year for 20 years. What is the present value of the package, assuming an interest rate of 8 per cent?

MB-4   Computing the Future Value of an Annuity
You plan to retire in 20 years. Calculate whether it is better for you to save $25,000 a year for the last 10 years before retirement, or $15,000 for each of the 20 years. Assume you are able to earn 10 per cent interest on your investments.

EXERCISES

EB-1   Computing Growth in a Savings Account: A Single Amount
On January 1, 2009, you deposited $6,000 in a savings account. The account will earn 10 per cent annual compound interest, which will be added to the fund balance at the end of each year.

Required (round to the nearest dollar):

1. What will be the balance in the savings account at the end of 10 years?
2. What is the interest for the 10 years?
3. How much interest revenue did the fund earn in 2009? 2010?

EB-2   Computing Deposit Required and Accounting for a Single-Sum Savings Account
On January 1, 2009, Alan King decided to transfer an amount from his chequing account into a savings account that later will provide $80,000 to send his son to university (four years from now). The savings account will earn 8 per cent, which will be added to the fund each year-end.

Required (show computations and round to the nearest dollar):

1. How much must Alan deposit on January 1, 2009?
2. Give the journal entry that Alan should make on January 1, 2009, to record the transfer.
3. What is the interest for the four years?
4. Give the journal entry that Alan should make on (a) December 31, 2009, and (b) December 31, 2010.

EB-3   Recording Growth in a Savings Account with Equal Periodic Payments
On each December 31, you plan to transfer $2,000 from your chequing account into a savings account. The savings account will earn 9 per cent annual interest, which will be added to the savings account balance at each year-end. The first deposit will be made December 31, 2009 (at the end of the period).

Required (show computations and round to the nearest dollar):

1. Give the required journal entry on December 31, 2009.
2. What will be the balance in the savings account at the end of the 10th year (i.e., 10 deposits)?
3. What is the total amount of interest earned on the 10 deposits?
4. How much interest revenue did the fund earn in 2010? 2011?
5. Give all required journal entries at the end of 2010 and 2011.

EB-4 Computing Growth for a Savings Fund with Periodic Deposits

On January 1, 2009, you decide that, when you graduate four years from now, you will take a trip around the world. Your grandmother wants to deposit sufficient funds for this trip in a savings account for you. On the basis of a budget, you estimate that the trip currently would cost $15,000. Being the generous and sweet lady she is, your grandmother decided to deposit $3,500 in the fund at the end of each of the next four years, starting on December 31, 2009. The savings account will earn 6 per cent annual interest, which will be added to the savings account at each year-end.

Required (show computations and round to the nearest dollar):

1. How much money will you have for the trip at the end of year 4 (i.e., after four deposits)?
2. What is the total amount of interest earned over the four years?
3. How much interest revenue did the fund earn in 2009, 2010, 2011, and 2012?

EB-5 Computing Value of an Asset Based on Present Value

You have the chance to purchase an oil well. Your best estimate is that the oil well's net royalty income will average $25,000 per year for five years. There will be no residual value at the end of the five years. Assume that the cash inflow occurs at each year-end and that, considering the uncertainty in your estimates, you expect to earn 15 per cent per year on the investment. What should you be willing to pay for this investment right now?

COACHED PROBLEM

CPB-1 Comparing Options Using Present Value Concepts

After hearing a knock at your front door, you are surprised to see the Prize Patrol from a large, well-known magazine subscription company. It has arrived with the good news that you are the big winner, having won "$20 million." You discover that you have three options: (1) you can receive $1 million per year for the next 20 years, (2) you can have $8 million today, or (3) you can have $2 million today and receive $700,000 for each of the next 20 years. Your financial adviser tells you that it is reasonable to expect to earn 10 per cent on investments. Which option do you prefer? What factors influence your decision?

COACH'S TIP

All three scenarios require you to determine today's value of the various payment options. These are present value problems.

GROUP A PROBLEM

PAB-1 Comparing Options Using Present Value Concepts

After completing a long and successful career as senior vice-president for a large bank, you are preparing for retirement. After visiting the human resources office, you have found that you have several retirement options: (1) you can receive an immediate cash payment of $1 million, (2) you can receive $60,000 per year for life (your remaining life expectancy is 20 years), or (3) you can receive $50,000 per year for 10 years and then $70,000 per year for life (this option is intended to give you some protection against inflation). You have determined that you can earn 8 per cent on your investments. Which option do you prefer and why?

GROUP B PROBLEM

PBB-1 Comparing Options Using Present Value Concepts

After incurring a serious injury caused by a manufacturing defect, your friend has sued the manufacturer for damages. Your friend received three offers from the manufacturer to settle the lawsuit: (1) receive an immediate cash payment of $100,000, (2) receive $6,000 per year for life (your friend's remaining life expectancy is 20 years), or (3) receive $5,000 per year for 10 years and then $7,000 per year for life (this option is intended to compensate your friend for increased aggravation of the injury over time). Your friend can earn 8 per cent interest and has asked you for advice. Which option would you recommend and why?

APPENDIX

C Reporting and Interpreting Investments in Other Corporations

You're probably already thinking about how you're going to celebrate the end of the term with your friends. Perhaps you'll dine out, go to a nightclub, or just simply relax in front of the TV at somebody's place. While you can't always control what your friends decide to do, by being involved in the decision-making you can make sure they hear what you would like before a decision is made.

The managers at Motorola feel the same way—not about end-of-term celebrations but, instead, about business decisions that are made by other companies that supply services to or buy products from Motorola. To ensure that the impact on Motorola is considered in these decisions, Motorola might buy some of the shares issued by these other companies. As explained in Chapter 11, by becoming a common shareholder, Motorola gets one vote for each share it owns, to use when these other companies ask their shareholders to vote on important decisions. If Motorola buys enough common shares in other corporations, it could have a significant or possibly controlling influence over their decisions. In this appendix, you'll learn how Motorola accounts for the investments it makes in other corporations.

WHY _____
Does a Company Invest in Other Corporations?

A company can invest in either shares or bonds issued by another corporation. This appendix focuses on just share (equity) investments. In principle, bond investments are accounted for in a manner similar to what we describe below for certain equity investments, but there are several technical differences that we leave for intermediate accounting courses.

A company might invest in shares issued by other corporations for one of four reasons:

1. **To take control.** A company might want to expand into other industries or markets, and the fastest way to do this is to take over control of another corporation (typically by buying more than 50 per cent of its shares).

2. **To exert significant influence.** Instead of controlling the decisions of another corporation, the company might be satisfied with just having a significant influence on the decisions made by the other corporation. After buying 20 to 50 per cent of the common shares of a supplier or customer, a company usually will be able to exert this significant influence.[1]

3. **To passively invest in securities available for sale.** A company might have generated some extra cash from its operating activities, which it invests in another corporation's shares to earn dividends. The company doesn't become actively involved in the decisions made by the other companies. Rather, this is a passive form of investment

---

[1] In the United States, the 20 per cent cut-off for significant influence is a firm rule, whereas in Canada it is more of a guideline.

where the company just puts down some money and waits for the investment to pay off. Because these investments can be sold whenever the company is short of cash, they are called **securities available for sale.**

4. *Profit from buying and selling.* A company might actually be in the business of trading securities, which means trying to earn profits by buying securities at one price and selling them in the near future at a higher price. Investments made with this goal in mind are considered **trading securities.**

It's useful to understand these four reasons, not only to be a wiser business person, but also because they relate to how investments in other corporations are accounted for. As Exhibit C.1 indicates, the methods used to account for these investments depend on the company's level of involvement in the other corporation, and on the investing company's basic reason for investing in other corporations. As a guideline for determining the investor's level of involvement, the percentage of equity ownership is considered, using percentages shown in the first column of Exhibit C.1. So, for example, an investor owning more than 50 per cent of the shares of another corporation is presumed to control the other corporation. Other factors, like participation in setting operating and financing policies, also are considered. The following sections of this appendix discuss the different accounting methods listed in the third column of Exhibit C.1.

CONSOLIDATION METHOD FOR INVESTMENTS INVOLVING CONTROL

When a company controls the decisions of other companies, it is called the **parent.** The **subsidiary** is the company that the parent controls. Although we haven't made a big deal out of it, in earlier chapters you've studied many companies that were the parent of several subsidiaries. For example, Mattel is the parent of Fisher-Price and American Girl, and Regis Corporation is the parent of First Choice Haircutters and Supercuts. So how is it that you didn't know that these parent companies had invested in subsidiary companies until now? Why didn't they report an asset called investments? The answer is that the parent companies have accounted for their investments using the consolidation method.

Under the consolidation method, the parent company prepares a set of **consolidated financial statements** that combines the accounts of the parent company with the accounts of all its subsidiary companies. The parent doesn't report a separate investment

Securities available for sale are purchased with excess funds, with the intent of earning a return until the funds are needed for the company's operating or financing activities.

Trading securities are purchased with the intent of selling them in the near future at a profit.

COACH'S TIP

The fourth column in Exhibit C.1 will be most useful to you as a quick review of the different accounting methods. Don't spend time on it until after you read the following sections.

The **parent** company is the entity that controls another company. The **subsidiary** company is the entity that is controlled by the parent.

Consolidated financial statements combine the financial statements of parent and subsidiary companies into a single set of financial statements.

---

exhibit C.1 Accounting for Investments in Other Corporations' Stock

Level of Involvement in Decision Making (Percentage of Ownership)	Reason for the Investment	Method of Accounting	How It Works
Control (more than 50%)	To take over the company ⟶	Consolidation	Combine the financial statements of parent and subsidiaries.
Significant Influence (20–50%)	To Influence the company ⟶	Equity	Record investment at cost, add % share of net income, deduct % share of dividends.
Passive (less than 20%)	To Invest excess cash to earn greater return ⟶	Market Value for Securities Available for Sale	Record investment at cost but adjust to market value at period-end; report dividends and realized gains/losses as investment income on the income statement; report unrealized gains/losses in shareholders' equity.
Passive (less than 20%)	Securities trading ⟶	Market Value for Trading Securities	Record investment at cost but adjust to market value at period-end; report dividends and all gains/losses (either realized or unrealized) as investment income on the income statement.

exhibit C.2	Excerpt from Motorola's Consolidated Balance Sheet

MOTOROLA, INC. AND SUBSIDIARIES
Consolidated Balance Sheets (Partial)
(in millions)

	December 31	
	2007	**2006**
Assets		
Current Assets		
Cash	$ 2,752	$ 2,816
Accounts Receivable, Net	5,324	7,509
Inventories, Net	2,836	3,162
Other Current Assets	11,310	17,488
Total Current Assets	22,222	30,975
Property, Plant, and Equipment, Net	2,480	2,267
Investments	837	895
Other Assets	9,273	4,456
Total Assets	$ 34,812	$38,593

account on its balance sheet because it includes all of the accounts of the subsidiaries in its own consolidated financial statements. Basically, *the consolidation method can be thought of as adding together separate financial statements for two or more companies to make it appear as if a single company exists*. So, for example, the $2.7 billion of cash reported in the assets section of Motorola's balance sheet in Exhibit C.2 includes the cash in Motorola's bank accounts as well as the cash in its subsidiary companies' accounts. The same is true of the *Inventories* account, *Notes Payable* account, *Sales* account, and so on.

Motorola, Inc., is the parent of several subsidiaries. Although these subsidiaries exist as separate legal entities, their financial successes and failures ultimately belong to Motorola, so it makes sense for Motorola to report them as if they were Motorola's own financial results. To inform you that the financial statements include the parent and subsidiary companies, the first financial statement note proudly announces that the financial statements are prepared on a consolidated basis. Also, the heading of each financial statement is marked as *consolidated*, as shown in Motorola's balance sheet in Exhibit C.2.

You probably will notice that, in Exhibit C.2, Motorola reports *Investments* totalling $837 million at December 31, 2007. This particular line-item does *not* represent the amount Motorola has invested in subsidiaries because each account of each subsidiary already has been combined into the consolidated financial statements. Instead, the *Investments* account shown in Exhibit C.2 relates to investments where Motorola has either significant influence or passive interest in other corporations, as discussed in the following sections.

EQUITY METHOD FOR INVESTMENTS INVOLVING SIGNIFICANT INFLUENCE

The equity method is used when an investor can exert significant influence over an investee, which is normally presumed if the investor owns between 20 and 50 per cent of the investee's outstanding voting shares.[2] Because the investor does not actually control the investee's assets or its operating decisions, the accounts of the investee are not

COACH'S TIP

The account name *Investments in Associated Companies* is also used for investments accounted for using the equity method.

---

[2] Remember that the 20 per cent is only a guideline in Canada, and accountants must look at other factors that suggest influence is possible.

consolidated within each account of the investor. Instead, the investor records its investment in a single account called *Investments*. It's just as you would account for a building. Rather than record the stairs, doors, floors, and roofing in separate accounts, they're all included in a single account. Under the equity method, the investor initially records its investment at cost, and then, every year after that, records its share of the investee's net income and its share of dividends distributed by the investee for that year. These items affect the *Investments* account as follows:

■ **Net income of investee.** When the investee reports net income for the year, the investor increases (debits) its *Investments* account for its percentage share of the investee's net income. The investee's earnings represent a future benefit to the investor because they imply the investor can expect to enjoy greater dividends or increased investment value in the future. The credit portion of the journal entry is recorded as *Investment Income*, which is reported on the income statement along with other non-operating items like interest expense and other gains and losses. (If the investee reports a net loss for the year, the investor records a debit to *Investment Loss* for its share of the net loss along with a credit that reduces its *Investments* account.)

■ **Dividends received from investee.** If the investee pays dividends during the year, the investor increases the *Cash* account and reduces its *Investments* account when it receives its share of the dividends.

The investor records a reduction in its investment account when it receives dividends from the investee, because the investee's underlying assets are decreased by paying a dividend.

dr Investments (A) cr	
Beginning balance Initial investment (also credit to Cash) Company's percentage share of investee's net income (also credit to Investment Income)	Company's percentage share of investee's dividends declared for the period (also debit to Cash)
Ending balance	

Purchase of Shares

To illustrate the equity method of accounting, let's assume that, at the end of 2008, Motorola had no significant-influence investments. On January 1, 2009, Motorola bought 40,000 common shares of Personal Communications Corporation (PCC) for $300,000 cash. PCC had 100,000 common shares outstanding, so Motorola's purchase represented 40 per cent, and Motorola was able to exert significant influence over the investee (PCC). As a consequence, Motorola must use the equity method to account for this investment. The initial purchase of this investment is recorded at cost.

dr **Investments (+A)**...................... 300,000
  cr **Cash (−A)**......................   300,000

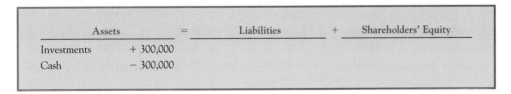

Assets		=	Liabilities	+	Shareholders' Equity
Investments	+ 300,000				
Cash	− 300,000				

Share of Net Income Earned

Because Motorola can influence PCC's processes for earning income, Motorola bases its investment income on PCC's earnings. During 2009, PCC reported net income of $250,000 for the year. Motorola's percentage share of PCC's income was $100,000 (40% × $250,000), which is recorded as follows:

COACH'S TIP

The investor's share of the investee's net income is also called "Equity in earnings of associated companies."

| dr | Investments (+A)...................... | 100,000 | |
| | cr Investment Income (+R, +SE).......... | | 100,000 |

Assets		=	Liabilities	+	Shareholders' Equity
Investments	+ 100,000				Investment Income (+R) + 100,000

If PCC were to report a net loss for the period, Motorola would have recorded its percentage share of the loss by decreasing the *Investments* account and recording an *Investment Loss*, which would be reported in the non-operating section of the income statement, with interest revenue, interest expense, and gains and losses on sales of assets.

Dividends Received

Because Motorola can exert significant influence over PCC's dividend policies, any dividends it receives from PCC should *not* be recorded as investment income. Instead, any dividends it receives will reduce its *Investments* account because dividends reduce the underlying assets of PCC. Assume that, at the end of 2009, PCC declared and paid a cash dividend of $2 per share to shareholders. Motorola received $80,000 in cash ($2 × 40,000 shares) from PCC, which the equity method accounts for as follows:

| dr | Cash (+A) .... | 80,000 | |
| | cr Investments (−A)..................... | | 80,000 |

Assets		=	Liabilities	+	Shareholders' Equity
Cash	+ 80,000			
Investments	− 80,000			

In summary, the effects for 2009 are reflected in the following T-accounts:

dr Investments (A) cr			
Beg. bal.	0		
Purchase	300,000		
Share of PCC's net income	100,000	80,000	Share of PCC's dividends
End. bal.	320,000		

dr Investment Income (R, SE) cr			
		0	Beg. bal.
		100,000	Share of PCC's net income
		100,000	End. bal.

HOW'S IT GOING?   A Self-Study Quiz

Assume that, on January 1, 2009, Motorola bought 30 per cent of the common shares of Intellicar Corporation (IC) for $120,000. IC reported net income of $100,000 for the year ended December 31, 2009. IC also declared and paid dividends totalling $50,000 for the year.

a.   At what amount should Motorola report its investment in IC at December 31, 2009?

b.   What amount should Motorola report as investment income?

When you're finished, check your answers with the solutions in the margin.

MARKET VALUE METHODS FOR PASSIVE INVESTMENTS

Before we discuss how the market value method is applied to Securities Available for Sale and to Trading Securities, let's consider the rationale for reporting these passive investments at market value. It's actually a rarity in accounting to report assets at market value, because it means that, in some instances, they'll be reported at an amount higher than historical cost. Let's take a closer look at this approach, which is dubbed "mark-to-market accounting."

1. *Why are passive investments reported at fair market value on the balance sheet?* Two primary factors determine the answer to this question:

   ■ ***Relevance.*** Analysts who study financial statements often attempt to forecast a company's future cash flows. They want to know how a company can generate cash for purposes such as expansion of the business, payment of dividends, or survival during a prolonged economic downturn. One source of cash is the sale of passive investments. The best estimate of the cash that could be generated by the sale of these securities is their current market value.

   ■ ***Measurability.*** Accountants record only those items that can be measured in dollar terms with a high degree of reliability. Determining the fair market value of most assets is very difficult because they are not actively traded. For example, although the New York Empire State Building is the most important asset owned by the Empire State Company, its balance sheet reports the building in terms of its cost, in part because of the difficulty in determining an objective value for it. Contrast the difficulty of determining the value of a building with the ease of determining the value of securities that Motorola owns. A quick look at stockcharts.com is all that is needed to determine the current price of IBM or BCE shares, because these securities are traded each day on established stock exchanges.

2. *When the investment account is adjusted to reflect changes in fair market value, what other account is affected when the asset account is increased or decreased?* Under the double-entry method of accounting, every journal entry affects at least two accounts. An asset valuation account is added to or subtracted from the investment account (maintained at cost) to produce the market value that is reported on the balance sheet. The second account affected is **Unrealized Holding Gains or Losses** that are recorded whenever the fair market value of investments changes. These are called *unrealized* because no actual sale has taken place. Simply by holding the security, the value has changed. If the value of the investments increases by $100,000 during the year, an adjusting journal entry records the increase in the asset valuation account and an unrealized holding gain for $100,000. If the value of the investments decreased by $75,000 during the year, an adjusting journal entry records the decrease in the asset valuation account and an unrealized holding loss of $75,000. The financial statement treatment of the unrealized holding gains or losses depends on whether the investment is classified as securities available for sale or trading securities.

> **Unrealized holding gains or losses** are amounts associated with price changes of securities that are currently held.

Securities Available for Sale

Exhibit C.3 displays information from Note 3 of Motorola's financial statements, which indicates that many of the investments reported on Motorola's balance sheet are securities available for sale (in millions, securities available for sale account for $333 out of $837). The details reported in Exhibit C.3 indicate that Motorola's securities available for sale (or SAS for short) initially cost $372 million, but were worth only $333 million at December 31, 2007.

To simplify our look at the accounting procedures that ultimately led to the amounts in Exhibit C.3, let's assume that Motorola had no passive investments at the end of 2006. The way in which the market value method is applied to securities available for sale is shown below Exhibit C.3.

exhibit **C.3**	**Motorola's Note Describing Securities Available for Sale (in millions)**

	December 31, 2007
Securities available for sale (SAS)	
Investment in SAS (at cost)	$ 372
Allowance to value SAS at market	(39)
Market value of securities available for sale	333
Equity method and other investments	504
Total investments	$837

Purchase of Shares.   At the beginning of 2007, Motorola purchases 10 million common shares of Wireless Networks Inc. (WNI) for $50 per share. There were 100 million outstanding shares, so Motorola owns 10 per cent of WNI ($10 \div 100$), which is considered a passive investment in securities available for sale. Such investments are recorded initially at cost:

dr	Investments in SAS (+A)	500	
	cr Cash (−A) (10 million shares × $50)		500

Assets		=	Liabilities	+	Shareholders' Equity
Investment in SAS	+ 500				
Cash	− 500				

After shares have been purchased, they can earn a return from two sources: (1) dividends, and (2) price increases. We will discuss price increases in a few moments, but for now let's focus on dividends.

Dividends Received.   Under the market value method, when dividends are received, the investor reports them as revenue on the income statement in an account called *Investment Income*. If Motorola receives a $1 per share cash dividend from WNI, which totals $10 million ($1 × 10 million shares), it would record the following journal entry:

dr	Cash (+A)	10	
	cr Investment Income (+R, +SE)		10

Assets		=	Liabilities	+	Shareholders' Equity	
Cash	+ 10				Investment Income (+R)	+ 10

COACH'S TIP

Unlike with the equity method, dividends received are reported under the market value method as investment income. Another difference from the equity method is that the investor's share of the investee's net income is not recorded under the market value method.

Price Increases.   *At the end of the accounting period, passive investments are reported on the balance sheet at fair market value.* Let's assume that WNI had a $293-per-share market value at the end of the year. That is, Motorola's investment had gained a whopping $243-per-share market value ($293 − 50 = $243) for the year. Since the investment has not been sold, this is only a holding gain, not a realized gain. The market value method for SAS investments requires that, unlike with dividends, all unrealized holding gains or losses should *not* be reported in the investor's net income. Because the investor expects to hold SAS investments into the future, it's likely that the value of the SAS investment will change again before any gain or loss is actually realized. Thus, unrealized gains or losses of this year might be recovered or become even larger next year. Either way, the unrealized gains and losses of this period are not likely to represent the true gains or losses that will be realized when the shares are ultimately sold, so they are not included in net income. Instead, they are recorded in a shareholders' equity account called *Other Comprehensive Income*. Only when the security is sold do the gains or losses become realized, at which time they are removed from shareholders' equity and included in net income.

In summary, reporting the SAS investment at market value requires adjusting it to market value at the end of each period, using the account *Allowance to Value SAS at Market* along with a corresponding entry to *Other Comprehensive Income*. If the ending balance in the *Allowance to Value SAS at Market* account is a debit, it is added to the *Investment in SAS* account when it is reported on the balance sheet. If it is a credit balance, it is subtracted. The *Other Comprehensive Income* account is reported in the shareholders' equity section of the balance sheet, either increasing shareholders' equity (if it represents an unrealized holding gain) or decreasing it (if it represents an unrealized holding loss).

The following chart is used to compute any unrealized gain or loss in securities available for sale:

POINT OF INTEREST

Within the last two months of 1999, Yahoo!'s stock price jumped from $181 per share to $404. At the time of writing, it was trading at $20 per share.

COACH'S TIP

Reporting the unrealized holding gain or loss in shareholders' equity has two purposes: (1) it reduces wild swings in net income, and (2) it informs users of the gains or losses that would occur if the securities were sold at market value.

Year	Market Value	−	Cost	=	Balance Needed in Valuation Allowance	−	Unadjusted Balance in Valuation Allowance	=	Amount for Adjusting Entry
2007	$2,930	−	$500	=	$2,430	−	$0	=	$2,430
	($293 × 10)		($50 × 10)				(We assumed there were no passive investments at the end of the prior year.)		An unrealized gain for the period

The adjusting entry at the end of 2007 is recorded as follows:

dr	Allowance to Value SAS at Market (+A)	2,430	
cr	Other Comprehensive Income (+SE)		2,430

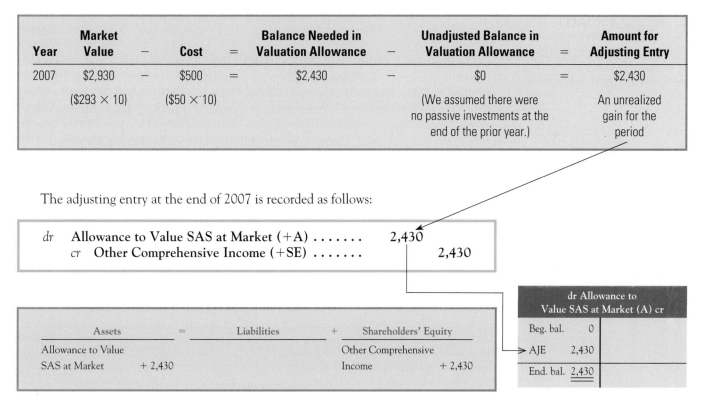

Assets	=	Liabilities	+	Shareholders' Equity
Allowance to Value SAS at Market + 2,430				Other Comprehensive Income + 2,430

dr Allowance to Value SAS at Market (A) cr	
Beg. bal. 0	
AJE 2,430	
End. bal. 2,430	

As Exhibit C.3 showed, the ending balance in *Allowance to Value SAS at Market* account is added to (or deducted from) the *Investment in SAS* account balance when determining the amount to report as *Investments* on the balance sheet. If management intends to sell these investments within a year, they would be classified as current. Given that all of Motorola's investments appear below the current assets subtotal in Exhibit C.2 (on page 654), we can assume that Motorola's management expects to keep

exhibit C.4	Balance Sheet Reporting of Unrealized Gains and Losses in Equity (in millions)

	December 31, 2007
Shareholders' Equity	
Common Shares	6,792
Additional Paid-In Capital	782
Retained Earnings	8,579
Other Comprehensive Income	2,430
Total Shareholders' Equity	$18,583

its SAS investments beyond the end of the upcoming year. The *Other Comprehensive Income* is reported in the shareholders' equity section, just like retained earnings. If the balance is a net unrealized loss, it would be reported as a negative amount. Assuming that Motorola has a $2,430 credit balance in its *Other Comprehensive Income* account at the end of 2007, its shareholders' equity would be reported as shown in Exhibit C.4.

Sale of Shares.   When SAS investments are sold, three accounts on the balance sheet (in addition to *Cash*) can be affected:

- Investment in SAS
- Allowance to Value SAS at Market
- Other Comprehensive Income

To illustrate, let's assume Motorola sold the WNI shares when the stock market reopened on January 2, 2008, after the New Year's holiday. If the share price was still $293 per share that day, Motorola would receive (in millions) $2,930 cash ($293 × 10 million shares) for shares that cost $500, resulting in a realized gain of $2,430, which would be reported as investment income. Two journal entries are needed to record this sale. In entry 1, the cash received, shares given up, and gain realized by the sale are recorded. In entry 2, the valuation allowance and the related *Other Comprehensive Income* account would be eliminated because the gain has now been realized.

1.	dr	Cash (+A)	2,930	
	cr	Investments in SAS (−A).............		500
	cr	Investment Income (+R, +SE)		2,430
2.	dr	Other Comprehensive Income (−SE)........	2,430	
	cr	Allowance to Value SAS at Market (−A)		2,430

Assets		=	Liabilities	+	Shareholders' Equity	
1. Cash	+ 2,930				Investment Income (+R)	+ 2,430
Investment in SAS	− 500					
2. Allowance to Value					Other Comprehensive	
SAS at market	− 2,430				Income	− 2,430

Trading Securities

Shares classified as trading securities are similar to securities available for sale in many ways. First, trading securities are considered passive investments because the investor does not acquire a sufficient quantity of shares to influence significantly the operating or financing decisions of the investee. Second, investments in trading securities are reported on the balance sheet at market value. Third, shares classified as trading securities also can earn a return from two sources: dividends and price increases.

Trading securities differ from securities available for sale in one small but very important way. Trading securities are purchased with the intent to profit *primarily* from price increases. *Buy low, sell high* is the motto of investors who invest in securities for trading purposes. This isn't the case with securities available for sale, where the investing company is likely to wait out periods of price changes because its goal is to safely "park" its excess cash in investments that generate a greater return than a bank's savings account.

Because trading securities are purchased with intent to profit from fluctuations in their stock prices, all gains and losses on trading securities are reported in the income statement, regardless of whether they are realized or unrealized. In terms of accounting procedures, this means that, rather than record unrealized gains and losses in a shareholders' equity account (as was done for securities available for sale), they are recorded in a temporary revenue or expense account, which is closed into retained earnings at the end of every year. If Motorola's investment in WNI shares had been considered an investment in trading securities (TS), the journal entry to adjust the *Investment in TS* to market value at the end of 2007 would have been:

COACH'S TIP

Notice that unrealized gains on trading securities are reported on the income statement as investment income, whereas, on SAS investments, they are reported on the balance sheet as shareholders' equity.

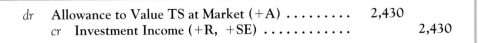

dr Allowance to Value TS at Market (+A)	2,430	
cr Investment Income (+R, +SE)		2,430

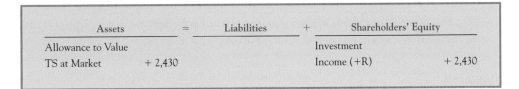

Assets	=	Liabilities	+	Shareholders' Equity	
Allowance to Value				Investment	
TS at Market	+ 2,430			Income (+R)	+ 2,430

The journal entries to record the purchase of shares and dividends received for trading securities are identical to the journal entries used for securities available for sale (except that references to SAS in the account names are replaced with TS). And, similarly to what you saw earlier for securities available for sale, the *Allowance to Value TS at Market* is combined with the *Investment in TS* account, with the total being reported on the balance sheet as *Investments*. Because investments in trading securities are intended to be sold in the near future, they are always classified as current assets.

Now that you've seen all four methods of accounting for investments in the shares of other corporations, return to Exhibit C.1 on page 653. Make sure you understand the final column that summarizes how the methods of accounting work for each type of investment.

_____ FOR YOUR REVIEW

DEMONSTRATION CASE A—EQUITY METHOD FOR SIGNIFICANT INFLUENCE INVESTMENTS

On January 1, 2009, Connaught Company purchased 40 per cent of the outstanding voting shares of London Company on the open market for $85,000 cash. London declared $10,000 in cash dividends and reported net income of $60,000 for the year.

Required:

1. Prepare the journal entries for 2009.
2. What accounts and amounts were reported on Connaught's balance sheet at the end of 2009? On Connaught's income statement for 2009?

Suggested Solution

1.

Jan. 1	dr	Investments (+A).....................	85,000	
	cr	Cash (−A)........................		85,000
Dividends	dr	Cash (+A) (40% × $10,000)...........	4,000	
	cr	Investments (+A).................		4,000
Dec. 31	dr	Investments (+A) (40% × $60,000).....	24,000	
	cr	Investment Income (+R, +SE)......		24,000

2.   On the Balance Sheet

Noncurrent Assets:

Investment $105,000
   ($85,000 − $4,000 + $24,000)

On the Income Statement

Other Items:

Investment income $24,000

DEMONSTRATION CASE B—MARKET VALUE METHOD FOR SECURITIES AVAILABLE FOR SALE

Howell Equipment Corporation sells and services a major line of farm equipment. Both sales and service operations have been profitable. The following transactions affected the company during 2009:

a.   Jan. 1   Purchased 2,000 common shares of Elk Company at $40 per share. This purchase represented 1 per cent of the shares outstanding. Based on management's intent, the Elk Company shares are considered securities available for sale.

b.   Dec. 28   Received $4,000 cash dividend on the Elk Company shares.

c.   Dec. 31   Determined that the current market price of the Elk shares was $41.

Required:

1.   Prepare the journal entry for each of these transactions.
2.   What accounts and amounts will be reported on the balance sheet at the end of 2009? On the income statement for 2009?

Suggested Solution

1.   *a.*

Jan. 1	dr	Investment in SAS (+A)..............	80,000	
	cr	Cash (−A)		80,000
		(2,000 shares × $40) per share.......		

b.

Dec. 28	dr	Cash (+A)	4,000	
	cr	Investment Income (+R, +SE)		4,000

c.

Dec. 31	dr	Allowance to Value SAS at Market (+A)....	2,000	
	cr	Other Comprehensive Income (+SE)...		2,000

Year	Market Value	−	Cost	=	Balance Needed in Valuation Allowance	−	Unadjusted Balance in Valuation Allowance	=	Adjustment to Valuation Allowance
2009	$82,000	−	$80,000	=	$2,000	−	$0	=	$2,000
	($41 × 2000 shares)								An unrealized gain for the period

2. On the Balance Sheet

Current or Noncurrent Assets:

Investment in SAS $82,000
    ($80,000 cost + $2,000 allowance)

Shareholders' Equity:

Other comprehensive income   2,000

On the Income Statement

Other Items:

Investment income $4,000

DEMONSTRATION CASE C—MARKET VALUE METHOD FOR TRADING SECURITIES

Assume the same facts as in Case B, except that the securities were purchased for the purpose of active trading.

Required:

1. Prepare the journal entry for each of these transactions.
2. What accounts and amounts will be reported on the balance sheet at the end of 2009? On the income statement for 2009?

Suggested Solution

1. *a.*

Jan. 1	dr	Investment in TS (+A)	80,000
	cr	Cash (−A)	
		(2,000 shares × $40) per share	80,000

b.

Dec. 28	dr	Cash (+A)	4,000
	cr	Investment Income (+R, +SE)	4,000

c.

Dec. 31	dr	Allowance to Value TS at Market (+A)	2,000
	cr	Investment Income (+R, +SE)	2,000

Year	Market Value	−	Cost	=	Balance Needed in Valuation Allowance	−	Unadjusted Balance in Valuation Allowance	=	Adjustment to Valuation Allowance
2009	$82,000	−	$80,000	=	$2,000	−	$0	=	$2,000
	($41 × 2000 shares)								An unrealized gain for the period

2. **On the Balance Sheet**   **On the Income Statement**
    Current Assets: *Other Nonoperating Items:*
    Investment in TS $82,000   Investment income $6,000
      ($80,000 cost + $2,000 allowance)   ($4,000 dividend + $2,000
                                                          unrealized gain)

KEY TERMS TO KNOW

Consolidated Financial   **Securities Available**   **Trading Securities** p. 653
  Statements p. 653   **for Sale** p. 653 **Unrealized Holding Gains or**
Parent Company p. 653   **Subsidiary Company** p. 653   **Losses** p. 657

FOR YOUR PRACTICE _____

QUESTIONS

1. When is it appropriate to use each of the (a) consolidation, (b) equity, and (c) market value methods for an investment in another corporation?
2. How do the accounting methods used for securities available for sale and trading securities differ?
3. How do the accounting methods used for passive investments and investments involving a significant influence differ?
4. How do the accounting methods used for investments involving a significant influence and investments involving control differ?
5. What are consolidated financial statements, and what do they attempt to accomplish?
6. Under the equity method, dividends received from the investee company are not recorded as revenue. To record dividends as revenue involves double counting. Explain.
7. What are the two sources of return for passive investments?
8. Where are unrealized gains and losses reported for securities available for sale? Where are unrealized gains and losses reported for trading securities? What's the reason for this reporting difference?

MULTIPLE CHOICE

Select the one alternative that best answers the question or completes the sentence.

1. Company A owns 40 per cent of Company B and exercises significant influence over the management of Company B. Therefore, Company A uses what accounting method for reporting its ownership of shares in Company B?
    a.   The consolidation method
    b.   The market value method for securities available for sale
    c.   The equity method
    d.   The market value method for trading securities
2. Company A purchases 10 per cent of Company X and intends to hold the shares for at least five years. At the end of the current year, how would Company A's investment in Company X be reported on Company A's December 31 (year-end) balance sheet?
    a.   At original cost, in the Current Assets section
    b.   At the December 31 market value, in the Current Assets section
    c.   At original cost, in the Noncurrent Assets section
    d.   At the December 31 market value, in the Noncurrent Assets section
3. Consolidated financial statements are required in which of the following situations?
    a.   Only when a company can exert significant influence over another company
    b.   Only when a company has a passive investment in another company
    c.   Only when a parent company can exercise control over its subsidiary
    d.   None of the above

4. When recording dividends received from an equity investment accounted for using the equity method, which of the following statements is true?

   a. Total assets are increased, and net income is increased.

   b. Total assets are increased, and total shareholders' equity is increased.

   c. Total assets are decreased, and total shareholders' equity is decreased.

   d. Total assets and total shareholders' equity do not change.

5. When using the equity method of accounting, when is revenue recorded on the books of the investor company?

   a. When the market value of the investee shares increases

   b. When a dividend is received from the investee

   c. When the investee company reports net income

   d. Both *b* and *c* above

6. Dividends received from shares that are reported as *Securities available for sale* in the balance sheet are reported as which of the following?

   a. An increase to cash and a decrease to the investment account

   b. An increase to cash and an unrealized gain on the balance sheet

   c. An increase to cash and an increase to investment income

   d. An increase to cash and an unrealized gain on the income statement

7. Realized gains and losses are recorded on the income statement for which of the following transactions in *Trading securities* and *Securities available for sale*?

   a. When adjusting *Trading securities* to market value

   b. When *Securities available for sale* to market value

   c. Only when recording the sale of *Trading securities*

   d. When recording the sale of *Trading securities* or *Securities available for sale*

8. Schlumber Corp. paid $200,000 to purchase 30 per cent of the shares of Schleep, Inc., this year. At the end of the year, Schleep reported net income of $50,000, and declared and paid dividends of $20,000. If Schlumber uses the equity method to account for its investment in Schleep, at what amount would the investment be reported at the end of the year?

   a. $200,000

   b. $209,000

   c. $215,000

   d. $221,000

9. During the current year, Winterpeg Enterprises purchased common shares of Lakeview Development Corp. (LDC) for $200,000, received a $2,000 dividend from LDC, and saw the market value of its investment in LDC increase by $4,000 by year-end. If Winterpeg considers its investment in LDC to be securities available for sale, what amount will Winterpeg report as investment income on its income statement this year?

   a. $2,000

   b. $4,000

   c. $6,000

   d. None of the above

10. Assume the same facts as described in 9 above, except that Winterpeg considers its investment in LDC to be trading securities. What amount will Winterpeg report as investment income on its income statement this year?

    a. $2,000

    b. $4,000

    c. $6,000

    d. None of the above

Answers to Multiple-Choice Questions

1. c 2. d 3. c 4. d 5. c 6. c 7. d 8. b 9. a 10. c

MINI-EXERCISES

MC-1 Recording Equity Method Securities Transactions

On January 2, 2009, Ubuy.com paid $100,000 to acquire 25 per cent (10,000 shares) of the common shares of E-Net Corporation. The accounting period for both companies ends

December 31. Give the journal entries for the purchase on January 2, and for each of the following transactions that occurred during 2009:

July   2   E-Net declared and paid a cash dividend of $3 per share.

Dec. 31   E-Net reported net income of $200,000.

MC-2 Determining Financial Statement Effects of Equity Method Securities

Using the following categories, indicate the effects (direction and amount) of the transactions listed in MC-1. Use + for increase and − for decrease.

	Balance Sheet			Income Statement		
Transaction	*Assets*	*Liabilities*	*Shareholders' Equity*	*Revenues*	*Expenses*	*Net Income*

MC-3 Recording Trading Securities Transactions

During 2009, Princeton Company acquired some of the 50,000 outstanding common shares of Cox Corporation as trading securities. The accounting period for both companies ends December 31. Give the journal entries for each of the following transactions that occurred during 2009:

July   2   Purchased 8,000 Cox common shares at $28 per share.

Dec. 15   Cox Corporation declared and paid a cash dividend of $2 per share.

31   Determined the current market price of Cox shares to be $29 per share.

MC-4 Determining Financial Statement Effects of Trading Securities Transactions

Using the following categories, indicate the effects (direction and amount) of the transactions listed in MC-3. Use + for increase and − for decrease.

	Balance Sheet			Income Statement		
Transaction	*Assets*	*Liabilities*	*Shareholders' Equity*	*Revenues*	*Expenses*	*Net Income*

MC-5 Recording Available for Sale Securities Transactions

Using the data in MC-3, assume that Princeton Company purchased the voting shares of Cox Corporation for its portfolio of securities available for sale instead of its trading securities portfolio. Give the journal entries for each of the transactions listed.

MC-6 Determining Financial Statement Effects of Securities Available for Sale Transactions

Using the following categories, indicate the effects (direction and amount) of the transactions referenced in MC-5. Use + for increase and − for decrease.

	Balance Sheet			Income Statement		
Transaction	*Assets*	*Liabilities*	*Shareholders' Equity*	*Revenues*	*Expenses*	*Net Income*

MC-7 Recording the Purchase and Sale of a Passive Investment

Rocktown Corporation bought 600 shares of General Electric on January 6, 2009, for its trading securities portfolio, at $35 per share. Rocktown sold the shares at $43 per share on March 20, 2009. Prepare the journal entries to record the transactions on each of these dates, assuming that the investment had not yet been adjusted to market value (that is, the investment was still recorded at cost at the time of sale).

EXERCISES

EC-1 Recording and Reporting an Equity Method Security

Felicia Company acquired 21,000 of the 60,000 shares of outstanding common shares of Nueces Corporation during 2009 as a long-term investment. The annual accounting period for both companies ends December 31. The following transactions occurred during 2009:

Jan. 10	Purchased 21,000 Nueces common shares at $12 per share.
Dec. 31	Nueces Corporation reported net income of $90,000.
Dec. 31	Nueces Corporation declared and paid a cash dividend of $0.60 per share.
Dec. 31	Determined the market price of Nueces shares to be $11 per share.

Required:

1. What accounting method should the company use? Why?
2. Give the journal entries for each of these transactions. If no entry is required, explain why.
3. Show how the long-term investment and the related revenue should be reported on the 2009 financial statements of Felicia Company, assuming the equity method is appropriate.

EC-2 Recording Holding Gains for Securities Available for Sale

On June 30, 2009, MacroMedia, Inc., purchased 10,000 Michek shares for $20 per share. The following information pertains to the price per share of Michek stock:

	Price
12/31/2009	$24
12/31/2010	31

Required:

Assume that management considers the shares to be securities available for sale. Prepare the journal entries required on each date given.

EC-3 Recording Holding Gains for Trading Securities

Refer to the data in EC-2.

Required:

Assume that MacroMedia management purchased the Michek shares as trading securities. Prepare the journal entries required on each date given.

EC-4 Reporting Holding Gains for Securities Available for Sale and Trading Securities

Refer to the data in EC-2.

Required:

1. Assume that management intends to hold the shares as securities available for sale for three years or more. Show how the equity investment and its holding gains would be reported at the end of 2010 and 2009 on the classified balance sheet and income statement.
2. Assume that management purchased the shares as trading securities. Show how the investment and holding gains would be reported at the end of 2010 and 2009 on the classified balance sheet and income statement.

EC-5 Recording Holding Losses for Securities Available for Sale

On March 10, 2009, Global Solutions, Inc., purchased 5,000 shares of Superior Technologies for $50 per share. The following information pertains to the price per share of Superior Technologies stock:

	Price
12/31/2009	$45
12/31/2010	42

Required:

Assume that management considers the shares to be securities available for sale. Prepare the journal entries required on each date given.

EC-6 Recording Holding Losses for Trading Securities

Refer to the data in EC-5.

Required:

Assume that Global Solutions purchased the Superior Technologies shares as trading securities. Prepare the journal entries required on each date given.

EC-7 Reporting Holding Gains for Securities Available for Sale and for Trading Securities

Refer to the data in EC-5.

Required:

1. Assume that management intends to hold the shares as securities available for sale for three years or more. Show how the equity investment and its holding gains would be reported at each year-end on the classified balance sheet and income statement.
2. Assume that management purchased the shares as trading securities. Show how the investment and holding gains would be reported at each year-end on the classified balance sheet and income statement.

COACHED PROBLEMS

CPC-1 Recording Passive Investments and Investments for Significant Influence

On August 4, 2008, Cappio Corporation purchased 1,000 shares of Maxwell Company for $45,000. The following information applies to the stock price of Maxwell Company:

	Price
12/31/2008	$52
12/31/2009	47
12/31/2010	38

Maxwell Company declares and pays cash dividends of $2 per share on June 1 of each year.

Required:

1. Prepare journal entries to record the facts in the case, assuming that Cappio considers the shares to be securities available for sale.
2. Prepare journal entries to record the facts in the case, assuming that Cappio considers the shares to be trading securities.
3. Prepare journal entries to record the facts in the case, assuming that Cappio uses the equity method to account for the investment. Cappio owns 30 per cent of Maxwell, and Maxwell reported $50,000 in income each year.

COACH'S TIP

In parts 1 and 2, the *Allowance to Value at Market* should change from a debit balance at the end of 2008 and 2009 to a credit balance at the end of 2010.

CPC-2 Comparing Methods to Account for Various Levels of Ownership of Voting Stock

Bart Company had outstanding 30,000 common shares. On January 1, 2009, Homer Company purchased some of these shares at $25 per share, with the intent of holding them for a long time. At the end of 2009, Bart Company reported the following: net income, $50,000, and cash dividends declared and paid during the year, $25,500. The market value of Bart Company shares at the end of 2009 was $22 per share.

For each case in CPC-2, divide the number of shares purchased by the number outstanding to determine the percentage of ownership. Then refer to Exhibit C.1 on page 653.

Required:

1. This problem involves two separate cases. For each case (shown in the table), identify the method of accounting that Homer Company should use. Explain why.

2. Give the journal entries for Homer Company at the dates indicated for each of the two independent cases. If no entry is required, explain why. Use the following format:

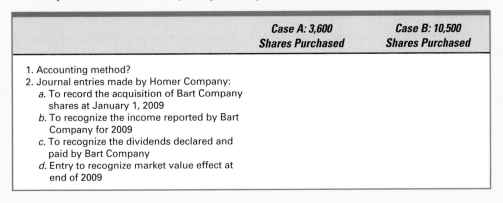

	Case A: 3,600 *Shares Purchased*	*Case B: 10,500* *Shares Purchased*
1. Accounting method?		
2. Journal entries made by Homer Company:		
a. To record the acquisition of Bart Company shares at January 1, 2009		
b. To recognize the income reported by Bart Company for 2009		
c. To recognize the dividends declared and paid by Bart Company		
d. Entry to recognize market value effect at end of 2009		

3. Complete the following schedule to show the separate amounts that should be reported on the 2009 financial statements of Homer Company:

	Dollar Amounts	
	Case A	*Case B*
Balance sheet		
Investments		
Shareholders' equity		
Income statement		
Investments income		

4. Explain why assets, shareholders' equity, and revenues for the two cases are different.

GROUP A PROBLEM

PAC-1 Recording Passive Investments and Investments for Significant Influence

On July 12, 2008, Rossow Corporation purchased 1,000 shares of Reimer Company for $30,000. The following information applies to the stock price of Reimer Company:

	Price
12/31/2008	$33
12/31/2009	28
12/31/2010	20

Reimer Company declares and pays cash dividends of $2 per share on May 1 of each year.

Required:

1. Prepare journal entries to record the facts in the case, assuming that Rossow considers the shares to be securities available for sale.

2. Prepare journal entries to record the facts in the case, assuming that Rossow considers the shares to be trading securities.

3. Prepare journal entries to record the facts in the case, assuming that Rossow uses the equity method to account for the investment. Rossow owns 30 per cent of Reimer, and Reimer reported $50,000 in income each year.

PAC-2   Comparing the Market Value and Equity Methods

Lisa Corporation had outstanding 100,000 common shares. On January 10, 2009, Marg Company purchased a block of these shares in the open market at $20 per share, with the intent of holding the shares for a long time. At the end of 2009, Lisa reported net income of $300,000 and cash dividends of $0.60 per share. At December 31, 2009, Lisa Corporation shares were selling at $18 per share.

Required:

1. This problem involves two separate cases. For each case (shown in the table), identify the method of accounting that Marg Company should use. Explain why.

2. Give the journal entries for Marg Company at the dates indicated for each of the two independent cases. If no entry is required, explain why. Use the following format:

	Case A: 10,000 Shares Purchased	Case B: 40,000 Shares Purchased
1. Accounting method?		
2. Journal entries made by Marg Company:		
a. To record the acquisition of Lisa Company shares at January 1, 2009		
b. To recognize the income reported by Lisa Company for 2009		
c. To recognize the dividends declared and paid by Lisa Company		
d. Entry to recognize market value effect at end of 2009		

3. Complete the following schedule to show the separate amounts that should be reported on the 2009 financial statements of Marg Company:

	Dollar Amounts	
	Case A	Case B
Balance sheet		
Investments		
Shareholders' equity		
Income statement		
Investments income		

4. Explain why assets, shareholders' equity, and revenues for the two cases are different.

Glossary

A

Accounts Records that summarize the items a company wants to keep track of, such as its cash, accounts payable, wages expense, and so on. The balances in the accounts provide the numbers that appear in the financial statements. (6, 52)

Accounting The process of capturing and reporting the results of a business's operating, investing, and financing activities. (3)

Accounts Receivable (Trade Receivables, Receivables) Amounts owed to a business by its customers. (288)

Accrual Adjustments Involve the inclusion ("accrual") of new amounts in balance sheet and income statement accounts.

Accrual Basis Accounting Records revenues when they are earned and expenses when they are incurred, regardless of the timing of cash receipts or payments. (89)

Accrued Liabilities Report the liability for expenses that have been incurred but not paid at the end of the accounting period. (431)

Adjusted Trial Balance A list of all accounts and their balances, to check on the equality of recorded debits and credits after adjustments have been made. (145)

Adjusting Journal Entries Are used at the end of each accounting period to update the records and include all revenues and expenses of that period. (133)

Adjustments Journal entries made at the end of every accounting period to ensure that revenues and expenses are recorded in the proper period. (131)

Aging of Accounts Receivable Method Estimates uncollectible accounts based on the age of each account receivable. (294)

Allowance for Doubtful Accounts (Allowance, Allowance for Bad Debts, Allowance for Uncollectible Accounts, Reserve for Bad Debts) A contra-asset account containing the estimated dollar value of the accounts receivable that will not be collected. (291)

Allowance Method A method of accounting that reduces accounts receivable (as well as net income) for an estimate of uncollectible accounts (bad debts). (290)

Amortizable Cost The portion of an asset's cost that will be used in generating revenue. It is calculated as asset cost minus residual value, and it is allocated to amortization expense throughout the asset's life. (384)

Amortization The allocation of the cost of long-lived tangible assets, such as property and equipment, to the accounting periods in which they are used over their productive lives, using a systematic and rational method. The term "depreciation" is sometimes used instead of amortization. (136, 383)

Annuity A series of periodic cash receipts or payments that are equal in amount each interest period. (637)

Annuity Due An annuity where the payments are made at the beginning of each period. (637)

Assets Resources (things of value) owned by a business. (5)

Auditors People who report on whether a public company's financial statements are, in fact, prepared following GAAP. (16)

Authorized Number of Shares Maximum number of shares of a corporation that can be issued, as specified in the charter. (482)

B

Bad Debt Expense (Doubtful Accounts Expenses, Uncollectible Accounts Expense, Provision for Uncollectible Accounts) An estimate of this period's credit sales that customers will fail to pay. (291)

Bank Reconciliation An internal report prepared to verify the accuracy of both the bank statement and the cash accounts of a business or an individual. (235)

Basic Accounting Equation (Balance Sheet Equation) $A = L + SE$, where A equals Assets; L equals Liabilities; and SE equals Shareholders' Equity. (5)

Book (or Carrying) Value The value an item is carried at in the accounting records (the books); the acquisition cost of an asset less accumulated amortization. (61, 383)

Business Valuation The process of analyzing a business to determine its worth. (62)

C

Capital-Intensive Business A business with a high percentage of total assets invested in property, plant, and equipment. (378)

Capitalized Cost A cost that is reported as an asset on the balance sheet rather than as an expense. (92)

Capitalized Interest Interest expenditures included in the cost of a self-constructed asset. (381)

Capital Lease A long-term agreement between two companies that is accounted for like a credit purchase. (396)

Capital Cost Allowance The amortization process required by the Canada Revenue Agency for calculating taxable income and income taxes. (388)

Carrying Value Amount an asset or liability is reported at ("carried at") in the financial statements; also known as "net book value" or "book value." (136, 383)

Cash Money or any instrument that banks will accept for deposit and immediate credit to a company's account, such as a cheque, money order, or bank draft. (234)

Cash Basis Accounting Records revenues when cash is received and expenses when cash is paid. (89)

Cash Equivalent Short-term, highly liquid investment that will mature in less than three months. (524)

Cash Flows from Financing Activities Cash inflows and outflows related to financing sources that are external to the company (owners and lenders). (526)

Cash Flows from Investing Activities Cash inflows and outflows related to the purchase or sale of long-term assets and short-term investments. (525)

Cash Flows from Operating Activities (Cash Flows from Operations) Cash inflows and outflows directly related to components of net income. (525)

Chart of Accounts A summary of all account names and corresponding account numbers used to record financial results in the accounting system. (44)

Classified Balance Sheet A balance sheet that classifies assets and liabilities into current and other (long-term) categories. (42)

Common Shares The basic voting shares issued by a corporation to shareholders. (484)

Comparable Information Allows comparisons across companies. (191)

Comparative Information Financial statements that report numbers for two or more periods to make it easy for users to compare account balances from one year to the next. (13, 191)

Conservatism The requirement to use the least optimistic measures when uncertainty exists about the value of an asset or liability. (62)

Consignment Inventory Goods held on behalf of the owner of the goods. (332)

Consistent Information Information that can be compared over time (because similar accounting methods have been applied). (191)

Consolidated Financial Statements Combine the financial statements of parent and subsidiary companies into a single set of financial statements. (653)

Contingent Liability Potential liability that has arisen as the result of a past transaction or event. Its ultimate outcome will not be known until a future event occurs or fails to occur. (450)

Contra-Account An account that is an offset to, or reduction of, another account. (137)

Copyright A form of protection provided to the original authors of literary, musical, artistic, dramatic, and other works of authorship. (392)

Corporations Operate as businesses separate from their owners. Owners of corporations (often called shareholders) are not personally responsible for debts of the corporation. (2)

Cost The amount of resources that a company uses to obtain goods or services, often said to be incurred when the company pays cash or uses credit to obtain them. (92)

Cost-Benefit Constraint Advises that accounting rules should be followed to the extent that the benefits outweigh the costs of doing so. (593)

Cost of Goods Sold (CGS) Equation BI + P − EI = CGS, i.e., beginning inventory plus purchases minus ending inventory. (258, 333)

Cost Principle States that transactions should be recorded at their original cost to the company. (62)

Creditor Any business or individual to whom the company owes money. (5)

Credit Card Discount A fee charged by a credit card company for its services. (299)

Cross-Sectional Analysis Compares the results of one company with those of another company in the same industry. (197)

Cumulative Dividend Preference Preferred share feature that requires specified current dividends not paid in full to accumulate for every year in which they are not paid. These cumulative unpaid amounts (called dividends in arrears) must be paid before any common dividends can be paid. (490)

Current Assets Assets that will be used up or converted into cash within 12 months. (43)

Current Dividend Preference The feature of preferred shares that grants priority on preferred dividends over common dividends. (490)

Current Liabilities Debts and liabilities that will be paid or settled within the next 12 months; short-term obligations that will be paid with current assets within the current operating cycle or one year, whichever is longer. (43, 430)

Current Ratio The ratio of current assets to current liabilities. (446)

D

Days to Collect A measure of the average number of days from the time a sale is made on account to the time it is collected. Calculate it by dividing 365 by the year-long receivables-turnover ratio. Other names for days to collect are "the number of days sales in receivables" or "the average days sales uncollected." (301)

Days to Sell A measure of the average number of days from the time inventory is bought to the time it is sold. It is calculated by dividing the year-long inventory-turnover ratio into 365. Other names for days to sell are "days in inventory" and "days sales in inventory." (345)

Declaration Date Date on which the board of directors officially approves a dividend. (486)

Declaration of Dividend When a company formally promises to pay out some of its resources to its owners. (10, 486)

Declining-Balance Method A method that allocates the cost of an asset over its useful life, based on a multiple of the straight-line rate (often two times). (386)

Deferral Adjustments Involve updating amounts previously recorded on the balance sheet as assets or liabilities. (132)

Deferred Putting an item on the balance sheet until that item is used up. (132)

Deferred Charges Costs that have been capitalized on the balance sheet as long-lived assets because management believes they will generate future revenues. You can think of them as long-term prepaid expenses. (393)

Depletion Process of amortizing the capitalized costs of natural resources. (395)

Depreciation The allocation of the cost of long-lived tangible assets over their productive lives, using a systematic and rational method. (383)

Discount A bond is issued at a discount when the issue price is less than the face value. (440)

Direct Method A method of presenting the operating activities section of the statement of cash flows in which the components of cash flows from operating activities are reported as gross receipts and gross payments. (525)

Discontinued Operations Result from the disposal of a major component of the business and are reported net of income tax effects. (596)

Dividends Payments a company periodically makes to its shareholders as a return on their investment. (7)

Dividends in Arrears Cumulative unpaid amounts of dividends on preferred shares. (490)

E

Earnings Forecast A prediction of the amount earnings expected for future accounting periods. (195)

Earned When goods or services are provided to customers at a determined price and with reasonable assurances of collection, revenues are earned. (89)

EBITA Abbreviation for "earnings before interest, taxes, and amortization," which is a measure of operating performance that some managers and analysts use in place of net income. You might also see **EBITDA** if the company uses both words, "depreciation" and "amortization." (399)

Effective-Interest Method Amortization Reduces the bond discount (or premium) by the amount by which the borrower's interest payments are less (or more) than the true cost of borrowing. The true cost of borrowing is calculated by multiplying the carrying value of the bond by the market interest rate that lenders used to determine the bond price. (455)

Efficiency Extent to which a company generates revenue, and one aspect of profitability. (581)

Expenditures Any outflows of cash for any purpose. (87)

Expense A cost that results when a company gives up its resources (by using up assets or incurring liabilities) to generate revenues during the accounting period. (8, 86)

Expenses The costs of running a business. (8)

Extraordinary Items Gains or losses that are both unusual in nature and infrequent in occurrence, and are not the result of management decisions; they are reported net of tax on the income statement. (596)

Extraordinary Repairs Expenditures that increase a tangible asset's economic usefulness in the future, and are recorded as increases in asset accounts, not as expenses. In contrast to ordinary repairs, extraordinary repairs are done less frequently and yield longer-lasting benefits. (382)

F

Face Value The payment made when a bond matures. (439)

Factoring An arrangement where receivables are sold to another company (called a factor) for immediate cash (minus a factoring fee). (299)

Financial Instruments Financial tools (like cash, loans, and shares) used to finance operating and investing activities. (445)

Financial Leverage The practice of borrowing money from creditors and using it to generate profits for shareholders; also called "trading on the equity." (495)

Financial Statements Reports that summarize the financial results of business activities. (2)

Financial Statement Users People who base their decisions, in part, on information reported in a company's financial statements. (2)

Financing Activities Involve raising money from lenders and owners or paying it back. (2)

First-In, First-Out (FIFO) Method Assumes that the costs of the first goods purchased (first in) are the costs of the first goods sold (first out). (336)

FOB Destination A term of a sale that indicates that the ownership of the goods is transferred to the buyer when the goods arrive at their destination. (332)

FOB Shipping Point A term of a sale that indicates that the ownership of the goods is transferred to the buyer when the goods leave their shipping point. (332)

Franchise A contractual right to sell certain products or services, use certain trademarks, or perform activities in a certain geographical region. (392)

Fraud The act of deliberately producing false information for your own financial benefit at the expense of others. It is different from making an honest error. (104)

Full Disclosure Principle States that relevant information should be disclosed in either the main financial statements or the notes to the financial statements. (194)

Future Value The amount to which a present amount will increase as the result of compound interest. (634)

G

Gain Occurs when, as part of a non-operating transaction, a business sells something for an amount greater than what it's recorded at in the accounting records. (86)

Generally Accepted Accounting Principles (GAAP) Rules for financial reporting. (16)

Generally Accepted Auditing Standards (GAAS) Rules used by auditors who report on whether a company's financial statements are, in fact, prepared following GAAP. (16)

Going-Concern (Continuity) Assumption States that businesses are assumed to continue to operate into the foreseeable future. (593)

Goods Available for Sale The sum of beginning inventory and purchases for the period. (333)

Goods in Transit Inventory being transported. (332)

Goodwill The premium a company pays to obtain the favourable reputation and other intangible strengths associated with another company. (392)

Gross Profit (Gross Margin) Net sales minus cost of goods sold. It is a subtotal, not an account. (250)

Gross Profit Percentage Indicates how much above cost a company sells its products; calculated as Gross Profit divided by Net Sales. (251)

I

Impairment Exists when the carrying amount of a long-lived asset exceeds its fair value. (389)

Income Smoothing The dishonest practice of manipulating accounting estimates to keep net income levels stable or "smooth" over a series of periods. (303)

Incur A cost is incurred when you purchase a good or a service and become obligated to pay for it. An expense is incurred when the economic benefits of an item are used up in the current period, resulting in a decrease in the company's resources. (86, 89)

Indirect Method A method of presenting the operating activities section of the statement of cash flows in which net income is adjusted to compute cash flows from operating activities. (525)

Interest Formula $I = P \times R \times T$, where I is interest calculated; P is principal; R is annual interest rate; and T is time period covered in the interest calculation (number of months out of 12). (297)

Internal Controls Methods that a company uses to protect itself against theft of assets, to enhance the reliability of accounting information, to promote efficient and effective operations, and to ensure compliance with applicable laws and regulations. (232)

Inventory Tangible (touchable) property held for sale in the normal course of business or used in producing goods for sale. (330)

Investing Activities Involve buying or selling long-lived items such as land, buildings, and equipment. (2)

Inventory Turnover The process of buying and selling inventory. (345)

Issue Price The amount of money that a lender pays (and the company receives) when a bond is issued. (440)

Issued Shares Total number of shares that have been sold; equals shares outstanding plus treasury shares held. (482)

J

Journal A record organized by date that shows each day's transactions. (52)

Journal Entries Note the effects of each day's transactions on financial statement accounts. (54)

Journalize The process of recording a transaction in the journal in the debits-equal-credits journal entry format. (56)

L

Last-In, First-Out (LIFO) Method Assumes that the costs of the last goods purchased (last in) are the costs of the first goods sold (first out). (337)

Ledger Organized by account, it shows the effects of the day's transactions on the accounts. (52)

Liabilities Amounts owed by a business. (5)

Licensing Right The limited permission to use property according to specific terms and conditions set out in a contract. (392)

Line of Credit A pre-arranged agreement that allows a company to borrow any amount of money at any time, up to a pre-arranged limit. (430)

Liquidity The ability to pay current obligations. It is commonly evaluated using the current ratio. (446, 583)

Loan Covenants Terms of a loan agreement which, if broken, entitle the lender to demand immediate repayment or renegotiation of the loan. (191)

Long-Lived Assets Resources owned by a business that will provide economic benefits beyond the upcoming fiscal year. (378)

Long-Term Assets Resources that will be used up or turned into cash more than 12 months after the balance sheet date. (43)

Long-Term Liabilities Debts and obligations that will be paid or settled more than 12 months from the balance sheet date. (43)

Loss Occurs when the business sells something for less than the amount recorded in the accounting records. (86)

Lower of Cost or Market (LCM) A valuation rule that requires the inventory account to be reduced when the value of the inventory falls to an amount less than its cost. (343)

M

Manufacturing Company A company that sells goods that it has made itself. (240)

Market Interest Rate The rate of interest that lenders demand from a bond. (440)

Market Value What an item sells for in the marketplace. (61)

Matching Principle A concept that requires expenses to be recorded in the period in which they are incurred to generate revenue, rather than in the period in which cash is paid for them. (104)

Materiality A concept stating that relatively small amounts not likely to influence decisions may be recorded and reported in the most cost-beneficial way. No one knows with certainty the amount that will influence a user's decision, so this assessment is subjective. (331)

Merchandising Company A company that sells goods that have been obtained from a supplier. (240)

N

Net Assets Shorthand term used to refer to assets minus liabilities. (393)

Net Income Is equal to revenues minus expenses. (8)

Notes (Footnotes) Provide additional information about the financial condition of a company, without which the financial statements cannot be fully understood. (14)

Notes Receivable A formally written promise that requires another party to pay the business according to a written agreement (like an IOU). (289)

NSF Cheque (Not Sufficient Funds) Occurs when the cheque writer (your customer) does not have sufficient funds in the bank account to cover the amount of a cheque. (236)

O

Operating Activities The day-to-day events involved in running a business. (2)

Operating Cycle (Cash-to-Cash Cycle) The series of activities that a company undertakes to generate sales and, ultimately, cash; the time it takes to go from paying cash for inventory to receiving cash from a sale; the time it takes to make sales to customers, collect from them, and pay suppliers. (240, 288, 430)

Operating Lease An arrangement where a company rents fixed assets from other companies, but does not record them on its balance sheet. (395)

Ordinary Annuity An annuity where the payments are made at the end of each period. (637)

Ordinary Repairs and Maintenance Expenditures for routine operating upkeep of long-lived assets, recorded as expenses. (382)

Outstanding Shares Issued shares that are currently held by shareholders other than the corporation itself. (483)

Overdraft A negative balance in a chequing account, which should be shown on the balance sheet as a short-term loan. (430)

P

Parent Company The entity that controls another company (the subsidiary). (653)

Partnerships Business organizations owned by two or more people. Each partner often is personally liable for debts that the partnership cannot pay. (2)

Par Value An insignificant value per share specified in the charter. (484)

Patent A right to exclude others from making, using, selling, or importing an invention. (391)

Payment Date The date on which a cash dividend is paid to the shareholders of record. (486)

Percentage of Credit Sales Method Bases bad debt expense on the percentage of credit sales of prior years that weren't collected. (293)

Periodic Inventory System Inventory records that are updated "periodically," that is, at the end of the accounting period. To determine how much merchandise has been sold, periodic systems require that inventory be physically counted at the end of the period. (242)

Permanent Accounts Accounts that track financial results from year to year by carrying their ending balances into the next year. All balance sheet accounts are permanent accounts. (149)

Perpetual Inventory System Inventory records are updated "perpetually," that is, every time inventory is bought, sold, or returned. Perpetual systems often are combined with bar codes and optical scanners. (242)

Post-Closing Trial Balance Prepared as the last step in the accounting cycle to check that debits equal credits and that all temporary accounts have been closed. (149)

Preferred Shares Shares that have specified rights over common shares. (489)

Premium A bond is issued at a premium when the issue price is greater than the face value. (440)

Present Value The current value of an amount to be received in the future, calculated by discounting a future amount for compound interest; based on a mathematical calculation that determines the amount that one or more payments made in the future are worth today. (441, 634)

Pro Forma A method of reporting what a company's results would have been had certain events not occurred. (204)

Profitability Extent to which a company generates income. (581)

Public Company A company that has its shares bought and sold on public stock exchanges. (Private companies' shares are bought and sold privately.) (3)

Purchase Discount Cash discount received for prompt payment of an account. (245)

Purchase Returns and Allowances Reductions in the cost of purchases associated with unsatisfactory goods. (244)

R

Receivables Turnover The process of selling and collecting on account. The receivables-turnover ratio determines how many times this process occurs during the period, on average. (300)

Record Date The date on which the corporation prepares the list of current shareholders as shown on its records. Dividends are paid only to the shareholders who own shares on that date. (486)

Relevant Information Information that can influence a decision. (It is timely and has predictive and/or feedback value.) (191)

Reliable Information Information that is accurate, unbiased, and verifiable. (191)

Research and Development Costs Expenditures that may someday lead to patents, copyrights, or other intangible assets, but uncertainty about their future benefits means that they are expensed. (392)

Residual Value The estimated amount to be recovered at the end of the company's estimated useful life of

an asset; it is also sometimes called salvage value. (384)

Retroactive A treatment that means that current and prior year financial statement numbers are restated to reflect a new accounting method. (597)

Return-on-Asset (ROA) A ratio that measures the return on any particular asset or project that the company is evaluating. (495)

Revenue The money earned from selling goods and services. (8)

Revenues Increases in a company's resources created by providing goods or services to customers during the accounting period. (86)

Revenue Principle A concept that requires that revenues be recorded when they are earned, rather than when cash is received for them. (104)

Revenue Recognition Policy A policy that defines when a company reports its revenues from operating activities. (104)

S

Sales Discount A discount given to customers for prompt payment of an account receivable. (248)

Sales Returns and Allowances Reductions given to customers after goods have been sold and found unsatisfactory. (247)

Securities Available for Sale Securities purchased with excess funds, with the intent of earning a return until the funds are needed for the company's operating or financing activities. (653)

Segregation of Duties An internal control that is designed into the accounting system. It involves separating employees' duties so that the work of one person can be used to check the work of another person. (233)

Separate-Entity Assumption States that the financial statements of a company are assumed to include the results of only that company's business activities. (5)

Service Company A company that sells services rather than physical goods. (240)

Shareholders' Equity The amount invested in the business by its owners. (5)

Sole Proprietorship A business organization owned by one person who is personally liable for the debts of the business. (2)

Solvency Ability to survive long enough to repay lenders when debt matures. (583)

Specific Identification Method An inventory costing method that identifies the cost of the specific item that was sold. (336)

Stakeholders Numerous groups with an interest (a stake) in a particular company. (190)

Stated Interest Rate The rate stated on the face of a bond, which is used to compute interest payments. (439)

Stock Dividend Distribution of additional shares of a corporation to existing shareholders. (487)

Stock Split An increase in the total number of authorized shares by a specified ratio; it does not decrease retained earnings. (488)

Straight-Line Amortization An amortiziation method that allocates the cost of an asset in equal periodic amounts over its useful life. (385)

Subsidiary Company An entity that is controlled by another company (the parent). (653)

T

T-Account A simplified version of a ledger account used in textbooks and classrooms for illustration purposes. (53)

Temporary Accounts Accounts that track financial results for a limited period of time by having their balances zeroed out at the end of each accounting year. All income statement accounts and dividends-declared accounts are temporary accounts. (148)

Time-Period Assumption The assumption that allows the long life of a company to be reported in shorter time periods. (592)

Times-Interest-Earned Ratio Divides net income before interest and taxes by interest expenses to determine the extent to which earnings before taxes and financing costs are sufficient to cover interest incurred for debt. (448)

Times-Series Analysis Compares a company's results for one period with its own results over a series of time periods. (197)

Time Value of Money The idea that money received today is worth more than the same amount received in the future because money received today can be invested to earn interest over time. (634)

Trademark (or Trade Name) A special name, image, or slogan identified with a product or company. (392)

Trading Securities Securities purchased with the intent of selling them in the near future for a profit. (653)

Transaction An exchange or event that has a direct economic effect on the assets, liabilities, or shareholders equity of a business. (45)

Transaction Analysis The process of studying a transaction to determine its economic effect on the business in terms of the accounting equation. (44)

Treasury Shares Issued shares that have been bought back by the company and not cancelled. (483)

Trial Balance A list of all accounts and their balances, which is used to check on the equality of recorded debits and credits. (59)

U

Unearned Revenue A liability representing a company's obligation to provide goods or services to customers in the future. (91)

Unit of Measure Assumption States that results of business activities should be reported in an appropriate monetary unit. (42)

Units-of-Production Method An amortization method that allocates the cost of an asset over its useful life based on the relationship of its periodic output to its total estimated output. This is sometimes called the units-of-output method. (386)

Unqualified Audit Report Auditor's statement that the financial statements are fair presentations in all material respects in conformity with GAAP. (194)

Unrealized Holding Gains or Losses Amounts associated with price changes of securities that are currently held. (657)

Useful Life The expected service life of an asset to the present owner. (384)

V

Vertical (Common-Size) Analysis Involves showing (a) each item on a balance sheet as a percentage of total assets, or (b) each item on an income statement as a percentage of total revenues. (200)

W

Weighted-Average Cost Method Uses the weighted-average unit cost of the goods available for sale for calculation of both cost of goods sold and ending inventory. (338)

Write Off The act of removing an uncollectible account and its corresponding allowance from the accounting records. (292)

Photo Credits

Name Index

A

Activision, 520
Addition-Elle, 181, 189
Adelphia Communications, 104, 105
Adidas, 42
Adidas-Salomon, 556
Ahlers Clocks, 462
Air Canada, 85, 399, 420
Air France, 475
Alaska Airlines, 399
Altria Group, 451
Amazon.ca, 370
AmBev, 367
AMC Theatres, 561–562
American Hide & Leather Company, 218
American Skiing, 491
Amtrak, 422
Andrew Peller Ltd., 542, 543
Apple Computer, 414
AquaGear Enterprises, 374–375
Atlas Cold Storage, 185
Aurora Foods Inc., 226–227

B

Bell Canada (BCE), 447
Best Buy, 270
Birkshire Hathaway, 489
Blockbuster, Inc., 8, 70
Bombardier, 223
Brunswick Corporation, 468–469

C

Calgary Stampeders, 73
Callaway Golf
  income statement, 228
Canadian National Railway (CNR), 301,
    378, 396, 410, 422, 431
Canadian Tire, 36, 281, 472–473, 601
CanWest Global, 38, 77
CHC Helicopters, 558
CIBC, 472
Cineplex Odeon, 425
Circuit City. See The Source By Circuit
    City
Clearly Canadian Beverage, 34
ClubLink, 395
  acquisition costs, 380
  amortization expense, 383–388
  business activities, 377
  cash purchase, 381
  change in amortization estimate, 405
  credit purchase, 381
  disposal of tangible assets, 390–391
  fixed-asset-turnover ratio, 396–397

gain/loss on disposals, 390–391
impact of amortization differences,
    398–399
long-lived asset management
    decisions, 395
long-lived assets of, 378, 379
maintenance costs, 382
revenues, 383
Coach Inc., 165
Coast Mountain Sports, 73
Coca-Cola, 320, 485, 607–608
Computer Associates, 105

D

Danier Leather, 198, 199, 200, 202, 232
  authorized shares, 482, 483
  common shares, 484
  cumulative dividend preference, 490
  current dividend preference, 490
  dividend decision, 479
  dividend declaration, 486
  issued shares, 482, 483
  return on equity, 493
  shareholders' equity, 481
  stock dividends, 487–488
  stock options, 495
  stock repurchase, 485
  stock split, 488–489
  treasury shares, 482–483
Dave & Buster's Inc., 30–31
Deere Company, 347
Deere & Company, 169
Dell Corporation, 485

E

Eaton's, 85, 480
Eckerd, 250
EDGAR, 38
Empire State Company, 657
Emulex Corporation, 203
Enron, 85, 192, 194, 573, 605
Ethan Allen Interiors Inc., 79

F

Fairmont Hotels and Resorts, 415
Famous Footwear, 281–282
Federal Department Stores (FDS), 605
Fields, 219
fin-info.com, 205
First Choice Haircutters, 392, 653
  accounting systems, 41
  accrual basis accounting, 89–93
  adjusted trial balance, 146
  amortization expense, 137–138

balance sheet, 43, 148
balance sheet accounts, 42–44
balance sheet preparation, 60– 61
cash received, 90–91
closing journal entries, 150
company background, 41
dividends payable, 142
expenses, 97–99
income statement, 87, 147
income taxes expense, 141
income tax expense, 141
interest expense, 140
post-closing trial balance, 151
prepaid rent and insurance, 134–136
recording revenues, 102
revenue and expenses, 86–87
revenue transactions, 95–97
statement of retained earnings, 147
supplies expense, 133–134
T-accounts, 100, 144–145
transaction focus, 61–63
transactions, 46, 47, 59, 95–97
types of adjustments, 132
unadjusted trial balance, 100–101
unearned revenue, 139–140
wages expense, 140–141
Fitch, 428
Ford Motor Company, 362, 462
Forzani Group, 73, 301, 470, 602
FPI Limited, 581
Frito-Lay, 553

G

General Mills, Inc., 440
Gibson Greetings, 347
Gildan Activewear, 218, 320, 602
Greater Toronto Airport Authority
    (GTAA), 475

H

Harley-Davidson, 346
Harman International, 367
Hasbro, 318
High Liner, 37, 81, 125, 184, 225, 232,
    282, 324, 372–373, 422 475, 519,
    572, 577, 604
  accounting methods, 589–590
  acquisition of business, 581
  balance sheet, 479
  capital-acquisitions ratio, 589
  cash coverage ratio, 589
  changes in accounting methods, 597
  competitors, 579
  current ratio, 587

debt-to-assets ratio, 588
discontinued operations, 581, 596
earnings per share, 585
evaluating performance, 577–578
financial reporting, 591–592
fixed-asset-turnover, 583
gross profit percentage, 585
income statement, 580
inventory turnover, 586–587
net profit margin, 584–585
price/earnings ratio, 590–591
quality of income, 586
receivables turnover, 586
return on equity, 585
statement of cash flows, 580
time period assumption, 592
times-interest-earned, 588
trend analysis, 581
Hilton Hotels Corp., 468
Hollinger International Inc, 38, 105
Home Outfitters, 219
Hoovers.com, 205
Hudson's Bay Company, 219, 362, 605
balance sheet, 220
share price, 191
year-end, 4
Humpty Dumpty Snack Foods, 371,
553, 602
Hydro One, 378

I

IGA, 174
InBev, 367
Interbrew, 367
Intrawest Corporation, 316, 389
balance sheet, 224
impact of amortization differences,
398–399
impairment losses, 389–390
income statement, 224, 225
seasonality disclosure, 542
write-down, 389–390
Italian Foods, 581, 586

J

JCPenney Company, Inc., 265
Jean Coutu Group, 250–252

K

Kimberley-Clark, 395
Koss Corporation, 357
Kraft, 393, 466

L

La Senza, 460
Laura Secord, 71
Le Château, 198, 199, 200, 201, 202,
493, 510
Lego, 42

LensCrafters, 355
Leon's Furniture, 31, 564
Livent Inc., 425
Loblaw Companies Limited, 559
Luxottica, 355

M

Macy's, 605
Magnotta Winery
accounts payable, 533
accounts receivable, 531–532
balance sheet changes, 537
capital-acquisitions-ratio analysis,
542–543
cash and cash equivalents, 525
company background, 522
comparative balance sheet, 528, 529
current income statement, 228, 529,
531
income statement, 529
income tax payable, 533
inventory, 532
investing activities, cash flows from,
537–538
net income, 530, 532
operating activities, cash flows from,
528–536
prepaid expenses, 533
property, plant and equipment, 538,
550–551
quality-of-income ratio, 544, 545
schedule for net cash flow from
operating activities, 531, 536
seasonality disclosure, 542
statement of cash flows, 524, 540
statement of operations, 540
Maple Leaf Foods, 27, 29, 318, 563,
579, 583, 587, 588
Mark's Work Warehouse, 36
Mattel, Inc., 318, 612
accounting policies, 14
accounts payable, 7
accounts receivable, 6
advertising and promotion expenses, 8
balance sheet, 5–7
beginning-of-year cash, 11
business activities, 3
cash assets, 6
cash flows from financing activities, 12
cash flows from investing activities,
12
cash flows from operating activities,
12
company background, 1, 2–3
comparative balance sheet, 14
contributed capital, 7
cost of goods sold expense, 8
end-of-year cash, 11
fraudulent financial reporting, 20

income statement, 8–10
inventories, 6
linked financial statements, 15
losses, 1
net cash flow, 11
net change in cash, 11
notes payable, 7
notes to financial statements, 14
other assets, 6, 14
property, plant and equipment, 6
retained earnings, 7, 10
revenues, 8
shareholders' equity, 7
statement of cash flows, 11–12, 19
statement of retained earnings,
10–11
stock price, 20
year-end, 4
McCain Foods, 27, 480–481
McDonald's, 346, 392, 587
McGraw-Hill Ryerson (MHR)
balance sheet, 208
income statement, 208
ratio analysis, 207–209
Mega Brands, 70, 304, 361
Merle Adventures, Inc., 319–320
Merrill Lynch, 573
Microsoft Corporation, 304, 314
moneycentral.msn.com, 198
Moody's, 428
Motorola, 654–661

N

Nabisco, 393
Napster, Inc., 491
Nasdaq, 590
National Hockey League, 126, 357
Nav Canada, 475
Nordstrom, 242
Nortel Networks, 194, 324–325,
373–374, 394, 423–424
Nutek, Inc., 414

O

Oakley, Inc., 28, 329–335, 340–344,
346, 355
beginning inventory, 334
consolidated balance sheet, 332
consolidated income statement, 333
inventory costs, 329, 330
inventory ratio analysis, 345
inventory turnover, 346
kinds of inventory, 330–332
lower-of-cost-or-market valuation,
343–344
notes to consolidated financial
statements, 344
product lines, 331
Outback Steakhouse, 587

P

Paramount Canada's Wonderland, 392
Penningtons, 181, 189
PepsiCo, 320, 472, 560, 607–608
Petro-Canada, 323, 378, 417–418
Phar Mor, 374
Pinnacle Foods, 227
Porsche AG
   balance sheet, 222
   income statement, 222
Price Chopper, 174
Purolator, 413

Q

Quaker Oats, 472
Quebecor Inc., 460

R

RadioShack Corporation, 218
Reader's Digest Association, 463465
Reebok, 46, 556
Regis Corporation, 41, 42, 62, 86, 653
Reitmans, 181, 189, 191, 195–204, 232
   asset-turnover ratio, 201–202
   business model, 195, 196
   comparative balance sheet, 196
   cross-sectional analysis, 197–198, 199
   debt-to-assets ratio, 201
   earnings press release, 203, 204
   financial statement ratio analysis, 198–202
   income statement, 197
   net-profit-margin ratio, 201–202
   return on equity, 493
   stock repurchase, 512
   time-series analysis, 197, 198
Research in Motion (RIM), 321, 429, 451
Risk Management Association, 198
Rita Aid Corp., 105
Rocky Mountain Chocolate Factory, 319
Rogers Communications, 428
   accounts payable, 429, 433
   accrued liabilities, 431–433
   accrued payroll, 431
   accrued taxes, 432
   bond discount, 442, 456–457
   bond premium, 443–444
   business background, 428
   and credit rating agencies, 428
   current liabilities, 430–431
   current portion of long-term debt, 433–434
   current ratio, 446
   early debt retirement, 444–445
   interest expense, 435, 439
   interest payment, 436, 439
   liabilities, 429–430
   notes payable, 435–437
   other current liabilities, 435
   payroll deductions, 432
   sales taxes payable, 433
   times-interest-earned ratio, 448
   unearned revenue, 434
   unrecorded liabilities, 450
Roots Canada, 124
Rowe Furniture Corporation, 560
Royal Dutch Shell, 323
Royal Leather Goods Limited, 482
RW & Co., 181, 189

S

Saks, 253
Saputo, 579, 585, 587, 588
Sara Lee Corporation, 165
Saucony, Inc., 316
Sears, 463
Shaw Communications, 394
Shell Canada, 28, 29, 418, 599–600
Sherwood Company, 368
Shoppers Drug Mart, 231–232, 233, 242, 250–253
   bar-code readers, 242
   independent verification, 234
   inventory control, 242
   multi-step income statement, 250
   operating cycle, 240
   purchase discounts, 246
   purchase returns and allowance, 244
   purchases, 244
   sales, 246–247
   sales discounts, 249
   sales returns and allowances, 247–248
   segregation of duties, 233
   transportation cost, 244
Singapore Airlines, 399
Sizzler International, Inc., 558, 559
Sleeman Breweries, 270, 542
Smart Set, 181, 189
Sobeys, 174, 562
Sony Corporation, 42 287–301
   accounts receivable policy, 289–290
   aging of accounts receivable, 294–295
   bad debt estimation, 293–294
   bad debt losses, 293
   balance sheet of receivables, 290
   credit card sales, 299–300
   credits sales, 288
   notes receivable, 289, 296–299
   receivables policy, 304
   receivables turnover, 300
   receivables turnover ratio, 300
   write-offs, 292
Spears & Cantrell, 372
SpongeBobSquarePants, 392
SportChek, 73, 301
Sport Mart, 73, 301
Sports Canada Corp., 317
Standard & Poor's, 428
Starbucks Corporation, 45, 80–81, 178
Statistics Canada, 190, 206
Sun-Rype Products Ltd, 27, 37, 81, 126, 184 226, 282, 324, 373, 422, 476, 519–520, 572–573, 579, 580, 583, 587, 588
Supercuts, 653
Swish Watch Corporation, 80

T

Target, 323
Telus, 447
The Bay. *See* Hudson's Bay Company
The Hockey Company (THC), 257, 281
The Learning Company (TLC), 20, 62, 85
The Source By Circuit City, 218, 270, 364
Thyme Maternity, 181, 189
Tim Hortons, 21, 378, 392
   balance sheet, 22
   income statement, 22
TiVo, 361
Toronto Maple Leafs, 126
Tyco International, 296

V

Verizon, 85. *See also* WorldCom

W

Wal-Mart Stores, 251, 253, 323
   income statement, 220
   inventory system, 242
Weiss Ratings, Inc., 605
Wendy's International, 21
West49, 320
WestJet Airlines Ltd., 34, 378, 420
Wolverine World Wide Inc., 269
Wonderful Merchandise & Things, (WMT) Inc
   bank reconciliation, 237–240
   bank statement., 237
   impact of bank errors, 237–240
WorldCom, 85, 105, 194, 400, 605

X

Xerox Corporation, 321

Y

Yahoo!Finance, 205–206, 493
Yahoo! Inc., 219, 396, 659

Z

Zellers, 219, 362

Topical Index

2/10, 245–246

A

Ability to pay, 446–449
Accelerated amortization method,
    386. *See also* Declining-balance
    method
Account balances
    credit balance, 100–101
    debit/credit framework, 52–55
    journal entries, 54
    T-accounts, 53–54, 101
    transaction analysis, 48–51
Accounting. *See also* Accrual basis
    accounting; Cash basis accounting
    and business activities, 3
    careers, 23–24
    defined, 3
    rules, 16–17
Accounting communication. *See*
    Financial statement users
Accounting information. *See also*
    Financial information
    comparability, 192, 591
    consistency, 191
    contracting role of, 191
    governance role of, 190
    relevance, 191, 591
    reliability, 191, 591
    role of auditors and analysts,
        194–195
    users of, 190–191, 194–195
    valuation role of, 191
Accounting methods/policies
    changes in, 597
    comparative, 589–590
    cost principle, 62–63
    income smoothing, 303
    revenue recognition, 104
    segregation of duties, 233
Accounting period
    inventory updates, 242, 257
    sales revenue for, 333
Accounting policies note, 14
Accounting principles
    conservatism principle, 62–63, 93,
        289, 296
    full disclosure principle, 194
    matching principle, 104, 296
    revenue principle, 104
Accounting process
    adjusted trial balance, 145–146,
        156–157

balance sheet, 147, 148
closing journal entries, 149, 150
depicted, 143
dividend accounts, 148–149
income statement, 146–147
notes to financial statements,
    147–148
post-closing trial balance, 149, 151
statement of cash flows, 147–148
statement of retained earnings,
    146–147
Accounting rules
    cost-benefit constraint, 593
    earnings per share, 496
    Financial Accounting Standards
        Board and, 17
    long-lived assets, 393, 394
    unrecorded liabilities, 450–451
Accounting scandals, 296
    cases, 20, 104–105
    fraudulent reporting, 227, 400, 425,
        449–450, 545
Accounting systems
    information systems, 2, 4
    internal controls, 193, 231–232
    for inventory tracking, 231–232
Accounting transaction, 45. *See also*
    Transaction analysis
Accounting year. *See* Fiscal year
Account names, 44, 45
Accounts, 7, 52
    permanent, 149
    reconciliation of, 235–240
    temporary, 148–149
Accounts payable, 7, 43
    changes in, 532
    as current liability, 430–431
    in inventory control, 244
    recording, 99, 103
Accounts receivable, 289–299
    in accrual-based accounting, 91
    aging of, 294–295
    allowance method, 289–295
    assets, 6
    bad debt estimation, 293–295
    and cash flow, 535, 545
    changes in, 531–532
    days to collect, 301
    defined, 288
    demonstration case, 304–306
    direct write-off method, 296, 308
    factoring arrangement, 299
    gross *vs.* net, 292
    management practices, 299–302

recording, 97, 102
reporting, 295–296
for sales, 247
for sales discounts, 249
uncollectible account recovery,
    292–293
write-offs, 290, 292, 304–305, 308
Accrual adjustments
    dividends payable, 141–142
    income tax expense, 141, 155
    interest payable, 139
    interest receivable, 139, 154
    purpose, 132–133
    wages expense, 140, 155
Accrual basis accounting
    adjustments in, 131
    for expenses, 102–103
    interest received, 297
    matching principle, 104
    revenue principle, 104
    for revenues, 101–102
Accrued interest, demonstration case,
    452–453
Accrued liabilities
    defined, 431
    interest payable, 433
    payroll, 431
    payroll deductions, 432
    PST and GST payable, 433
    taxes, 432
Accrued payroll, 431
Accumulated amortization, 136–138,
    154, 381, 386, 390, 528
Accumulated deficit, 491
Acquisition costs
    and book value, 383
    intangible assets, 392
    tangible assets, 379–381
Additional information note, 14
Additions, 382–383
Adjunct-liability account, 444
Adjusted financial statements, 130–132
Adjusted trial balance, 145–146,
    156–157
Adjusting entries, 133
    bad debt, 295
    for depreciation, 383
    interest received, 297
    unearned revenue, 434
    vs. cash accounts, 142
Adjusting journal entries, 133, 142
Adjustments
    accrual, 132–133, 139–142
    "aggressive" companies, 143

in credit balance, 101
deferral, 132, 133–142
defined, 131
demonstration case, 152–158
ethics of, 142–143
need for, 131–132
purpose, 130
steps, 133–134
Adverse audit report, 194
Advertising and promotion expenses, 8
Aging of accounts receivable, 294–295
Allowance for doubtful accounts,
    291–295, 302–303
Allowance method, 290–292
Allowance method for accounts
    receivable, 289–295
Allowances
    purchase returns and, 244
    sales returns and, 247–248, 249
Amortizable cost, 384
Amortization, 136–138
    accumulated, 528
    basic idea of, 383
    bond discount, 443
    bonds issued at discount, 443
    book value, 383
    cash flow, 397
    changes in estimates, 405
    defined, 136, 383
    demonstration case, 400–403
    effective-interest method, 443,
        455–459
    and income tax, 388–389
    of intangible assets, 393–394
    and matching principle, 383
    not applied to land, 384
    reporting, 377
    taxes, 388–389
Amortization expense
    calculating, 383–388
    and cash flows, 530, 535
    deferral adjustment, 136–138
    double-declining-balance formula,
        385
    impact of differences in amortization
        methods, 397–399
    for intangible assets, 530n
    for partial year, 387
    reporting, 383–384
    revised, 405
    straight-line formula, 385
    units-of-production amortization
        formula, 386
    updating, 390
Amortization methods
    declining-balance method, 386–387,
        387–388
    kinds of, 384–388
    straight-line method, 385–386,
        387–388, 389, 401, 443, 590
    summary of, 387–388

units-of-production depreciation, 386,
    388
Amortization schedules, 385, 386, 387,
    398
Analysts, 194–195
Annual earnings releases, 203
Annual report, 4, 13–14, 204–205
Annuity
    future value of, 637–638
    present value of, 638–639
Annuity due, 637
Articles of incorporation, 482
Asset accounts, 53
Asset cost, 380–381, 384
Asset impairment losses, 389, 402
Assets
    accounts receivable, 6
    on balance sheet, 6
    capitalized costs, 92
    carrying value, 136
    cash, 6
    conservatism in reporting, 62–63, 93
    debt-to-asset ratio, 200, 201, 209
    defined, 5
    inventories, 6
    other, 6
Asset-turnover ratio, 200, 201, 209,
    396–397, 583–584, 594
Assurance statements, 13–14
Auditors, 14, 16, 194, 605
    internal, 234
Auditors' report. See Independent
    auditors' report
Authorized number of shares, 482–483

B

Bad debt
    allowance method, 289–295
    cost, 288
    direct write-off method, 296, 308
    effects of misestimating, 302–303
    reporting, 295
    write-off, 290, 292
Bad debt costs, 288–289
Bad debt estimation
    aging of accounts receivable method,
        294–295
    compared to write-off, 295
    impact of, 302–304
    percentage of credit sales method,
        293–294
Bad debt expense, 293
    and income smoothing, 303
    recording, 291–292
Balance sheet, 5–7, 42–44
    account names, 44, 45
    account (side-by-side) format, 60, 61
    accounts payable, 43
    adjusted, 132
    amortization expense, 383
    asset accounts, 6

basic accounting equation, 5, 46–48,
    527
cash, 43
and cash flows from financing
    activities, 538–539
and cash flows from investing
    activities, 537–538
cash flows from operating activities,
    529
chart of accounts, 44, 45
classified, 42–44
comparative format, 13, 14, 195,
    196, 526
consolidated, 654
content, 5–7
contributed capital, 43
current assets, 43
current liabilities, 43
demonstration cases, 21–22, 63–65
effects of transaction focus, 61–63
expenses on, 94
and financial performance, 578–579
furnishings and equipment, 43
information for users, 42–44
intangible assets, 393
inventory on, 330–331
liabilities, 7
long-term assets, 43
long-term liabilities, 43
notes payable, 43
preparation of, 61, 147, 148, 157
purpose, 5
ratio analysis, 200–201
relation to other statements, 12–13
retained earnings, 43
separate entity assumption, 5
set-up, 5
shareholders' equity, 7
start-up transactions, 42–44
and statement of cash flows,
    526–527
unit of measure assumption, 42
users of, 17
Bank errors, 235, 239–240
Bank loans, 430
Bank reconciliation
    and bank errors, 235
    in bank statements, 234–240
    bounced cheques, 236
    defined, 235
    demonstration case, 254
    depositors' errors, 236
    electronic funds transfers (ETFs), 236
    illustrated, 238
    interest deposited, 236
    need for, 235–236
    service charges, 236
    and time lags, 235
Bankruptcy, 85, 605
Bank service charges, 236, 239
Bank statements

deposits in transit, 235, 237–238
electronic funds transfers (ETF), 236
impact of errors, 239–240
outstanding cheques, 235, 238
reconciling account records, 236–240
recording transactions, 238–239
Bar-code readers, 242
Basic accounting equation, 5, 46–48, 527
Basic earnings per share, 491–492, 496, 585
Beginning inventory, 257, 333
Beginning-of-year cash balance, 11
Black, Conrad, 38, 105
Board of directors, 190, 194–195
Bond amortization schedule, 458, 459
Bond certificate, 438, 440
Bond market, 438
Bonds payable, 438–445
    amortization, 443
    carrying value, 442, 444
    demonstration case, 452–454
    early debt retirement, 444–445, 476–477
    issued above or below face value, 439–441
    issued at discount, 441–443
    issued at face value, 438–439
    issued at premium, 441, 443–444
    issue price, 441
    market interest rate, 441
    present value, 441
    stated interest rate, 439
    usage of term, 438
Book value, 136, 441, 444
    bonds payable, net of discount, 442
    and depreciation, 399
    of long-lived asset, 383
    premium bonds, 444
    vs. market value, 61–62
Borrowing. See Line of credit
"Bottom line," 10, 87, 104
bounced cheques, 236
Braxton, Toni, 85
"Break even," 8
Buffet, Warren, 489
Business activities, 2–3. See also Transaction analysis
    balance sheet accounts, 42–44
    costs, 92
    effect on income statement, 94–103
    operating activities, 240–241
    operating results across industries, 252–253
    reporting financial results of, 4–5
    rule of accrual, 89
    tracking information, 41
    unethical, 104–105
Business Corporations Act (Ontario), 482
Business model, 195–197

Business opportunities, fraud and, 192
Business organization
    corporation, 2
    forms of, 2
    partnership, 2, 480, 500, 502–503
    sole proprietorships, 2, 500, 501
Business valuation, 62–63

C

Callability, 450
Canada Pension Plan (CPP), 432
Canada Revenue Agency
    amortization, 388–389
    direct write-off method, 296
Canadian Business Corporations Act (CBCA), 482, 484, 485
Canadian Institute of Chartered Accountants (CICA), 17, 335, 591
    on reporting cash flows, 17, 525
Canadian Intellectual Property Office (CIPO), 392
Canadian Securities Administrators (CSA), 194, 205, 207
Capital-acquisitions ratio, 542, 583, 589
Capital Cost Allowance (CCA), 388
Capital intensive business, 378
Capitalized costs, 92, 98–99, 379–380, 381, 399–400
Capitalized expenses, 127
Capitalized interest, 381
Capital lease, 396, 450
Carrying value, 136. See also Book value
Cash
    additional, 541
    assets, 6
    on balance sheet, 6, 11
    defined, 234
    delayed receipt of, 288
    net income vs., 103
    reconciliation of accounts, 235–240
    and sales revenue, 531
    for suppliers, 532, 533, 535
Cash basis accounting, 88–89
Cash collection, as condition of revenue principle, 104
Cash control reporting
    bank reconciliation, 235–236
    bank statements, 236–240
    demonstration case, 254–256
    reconciling documents, 240
Cash coverage ratio, 543–544, 583, 589
Cash-coverage ratio, 543–544, 583, 589
Cash dividends, 486
    demonstration case, 497–498
Cash equivalents, 524
Cash flows. See also Statement of cash flows
    amortization and, 397
    capital-acquisitions ratio, 542
    cash coverage ratio, 543–544, 583, 589

converting sales revenues to, 532, 535
    direct reporting, 525, 534–536, 547
    from financing activities, 12, 524–525, 538–539, 543–544
    indirect reporting, 11, 525, 534, 546
    from investing activities, 12, 18–19, 524, 542
    from operating activities, 12, 18, 88–93, 524, 525, 541–542
    quality-of-income ratio, 544–545
    reporting, 524, 525, 528–537
    seasonal changes, 541–542
Cash purchases, 381
Cash receipts, reconciled with bank deposit slips, 240
Changes in estimates, 405
Chart of accounts, 44, 45, 88
Classified balance sheet, 42–44
Closing journal entries, 149, 150
Common shares
    authorized shares, 482–483
    Canadian ownership, 481
    cash dividends, 485–487
    defined, 484
    demonstration case, 496–497
    earnings per share, 492
    issuance of, 484, 496–497
    issued shares, 482
    outstanding shares, 483
    par value, 484
    preferred shares vs., 489–490
    reissuance of stock, 484
    return on equity, 493–494
    stock dividends, 485
    stock splits, 488–489
    transactions, 484–485
    treasury shares, 483
    voting shares, 482–483
Common-size analysis. See Vertical analysis
Comparability, 192, 591
Comparative balance sheet, 13, 14, 196, 526
Compensation expense, 432
Competitors, as benchmark, 197
Compound interest, 638
Comprehensive income, 596
Conservatism, 62–63, 93, 289, 296
Consignment inventory, 332
Consistency, 191, 591
Consolidated financial statements, 653–654
Construction in progress, 376
Contents included note, 14
Contingent liability, 450–451
Contra-account, 137–138
Contra-asset account, 291–293
Contracting role, of accounting information, 191

Contra-liability account, 442
Contributed capital, 7, 43, 94, 481, 538
Convertibility, 450
Copyrights, 392
Corporate life cycles, and financial
    performance, 544
Corporations
    advantages, 481
    authorized shares, 482–483
    common stock transaction, 484–485
    defined, 2
    diluted earnings per share, 495–496
    dividend decision, 485
    dividend *vs.* reinvestment, 485
    early debt retirement, 444–445
    ease of ownership participation, 481
    equity financing, 481–484
    equity *vs.* debt, 494–495
    financing strategies, 543
    issued shares, 482
    legal entity, 481–482
    means of financing, 481
    outstanding shares, 483
    ownership of, 481–483
    parent corporation, 53
    preferred shares, 489–491
    private companies, 480
    public companies, 3, 481
    reasons for stock dividends, 489
    retained earnings restrictions, 495
    stock options, 495–496
    stock repurchase, 482, 485–486
    stock splits, 488–489
    sufficient returned earnings, 487
    treasury shares, 483
Cost-benefit constraint, 593
Cost flow assumption
    and generally accepted accountings,
        344
    inventory costing, 335–340
Cost of goods sold. *See also under*
    Inventory entries
    changes in inventory and, 532
    converted to cash for suppliers, 532,
        533, 535
    defined, 333
    determination, 257
    impact of inventory errors, 347–348
    on income statement, 333
    and last-in, first-out method, 337–338
    lower of cost or market (LCM),
        343–344
    in periodic inventory systems,
        257–258
    in perpetual inventory system, 340,
        352–353
    and specific identification method,
        336
    in weighted average cost method,
        338–339 340–341, 349–350,
        352–353

Cost of goods sold account, 242
Cost of goods sold equation, 257–258,
    333–334
Cost of goods sold expense, 8
Cost principle, 62–63, 379, 391
Costs. *See also* Acquisition costs
    amortizable, 384
    of bad debt, 288
    capitalized, 92, 379–389
    on income statement, 98
    incurred, 86
    of maintenance, 382
Credit, 53–55, 94
    trade-offs, 288–289
Credit analysts, 194–195
Credit balance, 100–101
Credit card discount, 299
Creditors. *See also* Financial statement
        users
    avoiding fraudulent reporting, 207
    financial information for, 130
    financing, 7
    use of auditors' report, 19
    use of financial statements, 17–19,
        191
Credit purchase, 381
Credit rating agencies, 428
Credit transactions, 94
Crosby, Sidney, 46
Cross-sectional analysis, 197–198
Cumulative dividend preference,
    490–491
Current assets, 43, 528
Current dividend preference, 490
Current liabilities, 43, 528
    accounts payable, 430–431
    bank loans, 430
    corporate income taxes, 432
    and current ratio, 446–447
    defined, 430
    line of credit, 430
    long-term debt, 433–434
    notes payable, 435–437
    operating leases, 450
    overdraft, 425
    sales taxes payable, 433
    unearned revenue, 434
Current ratio, 446–447, 583, 587, 594

D

Days to collect, 301
Days to sell, 345–346
Debit, 53–55, 94
Debit/credit framework, 52–55
Debt financing
    equity financing *vs.*, 494–495
    methods of, 437
Debt-to-asset ratio, 200, 201, 209, 583,
    588, 594
DECIDE approach to transaction
    analysis, 48–51

revenues and expenses, 94– 99
Declaration date, 486
Declared dividends, 10
Declining-balance method, 386–387,
    387–388, 398
Deferral adjustments
    depreciation expense, 136–138
    effects, 136
    prepaid insurance, 134–136, 154
    prepaid rent, 134–136
    purpose, 132
    supplies expense, 133–134
    unearned revenue, 138–139, 153
Deferred charges, 393
Depletion, 395
Deposits in transit, 235, 237–238
Depreciation. *See* Amortization
Diluted earnings per share, 495–496
Direct method for reporting cash flows,
    11, 525, 534–536, 547
Directors, 190, 194–195, 205
Direct write-off method, 296, 308
Discontinued operations, 596
Discount bonds, 439, 441–443
Discount rate, 441
Dividend accounts, 148–149
Dividends
    declared, 10
    defined, 7
    expenses *vs.*, 142
    financial statement information and,
        17–19
    share ownership, 482
Dividends in arrears, 490
Dividends payable, 142
Dividends received, 656
Documentation, of activities, 234
Dot.com companies, 541
Double-declining-balance amortization,
    386, 401–402
Drabinsky, Garth, 425
Duality of effects, 46–48

E

Earned revenues, 89
Earnings forecasts, 195
Earnings per share (EPS), 491–492, 582,
    585
    calculation of, 491–492
    diluted, 495–496
    evaluation of, 492
    and price/earnings ratio, 590–591
    and stock repurchase, 496
Ebbers, Bernie, 105
EBITA (earnings before interest, taxes,
    and amortization), 399
EDGAR, 38
Effective-interest method, 443
    bond discount, 456–458
    bond premium, 458–459
    characteristics, 455–456

Effective-interest rate, 441
Efficiency ratios, 581
Electronic funds transfers (ETFs), 236
Employment Insurance (EI), 432
Ending inventory, 257, 333
    impact of errors in, 347–348
End-of-year cash balance, 11
Equity. *See also* Common shares;
        Shares
    authorized number of shares, 482
    characteristics, 480–483
    classes of shares, 482
    earnings per share, 492
    issued shares, 482
    outstanding shares, 483
    preferred shares, 489–491
    return on, 493–494, 496, 582, 585
    treasury stock, 483
    voting shares, 482
    vs. debt, 494–495
Equity financing, 192
Equity method of investment, 652,
        654–656
Estimates, changes in amortization,
        405
Ethics
    of adjustments, 142–143
    capitalized costs, 127, 399–400
    cases, 38–39, 82–83, 127–128,
        185–186, 226–228, 325–327,
        374–375, 424–425, 476–477,
        520–521, 573–574, 605
    chief financial officer, 424–425
    early bond retirement, 476
    fraudulent transactions, 573
    and income smoothing, 302–303
    inventory costing methods, 341
    inventory theft, 282–283
    stock repurchase, 520
    violation of matching principle,
        104–105
    violation of revenue principle,
        104–105
Expenditures. *See also* Costs
    costs of long-lived assets, 381
    expenses *vs.*, 87
    maintenance, 382
Expense account, 94
Expense recognition, changes in, 545
Expenses, 101–103
    accounting summary, 102–103
    accrual-based measurement, 92–93
    adjusting, 132–133
    capitalized costs, 98–99
    compared to expenditures, 87
    in DECIDE approach, 97–99
    dividends *vs.*, 142
    expenditure *vs.*, 87
    on income statement, 8–9, 86–87
    prepaid, 92
    recording, 94, 103

research and development, 392, 393
    in transaction analysis model,
        94–99
Extraordinary items, 596
Extraordinary repairs, 382–383

F
Face value, 444
    bonds issued above, 439–441
    bonds issued at, 438–439
    defined, 439
Factoring receivables, 299
Federal surplus, 142
Financial Accounting Standards Board
        (FASB), 17
Financial information. *See also*
        Accounting information annual
        reports, 204–205
    conveying, 20
    electronic filing of, 205
    for investors and creditors, 130
    investor Websites, 205–206
    press releases, 203–204
    quality of, 591–592
    quarterly reports, 204–205
    sources of, 203–206
    Web sites, 205–206
Financial instruments, 445
Financial leverage, 494–495
Financial misrepresentation
    and full disclosure principle, 194
    incentives for, 192–193
Financial reporting
    accounts receivable, 295
    accrual basis accounting, 90–93
    amortization, 377
    bad debt, 295
    capital cost allowance, 388–389
    cash control, 234–240
    conservatism in, 62–63
    controls, 232
    cost-benefit constraint, 593
    of costs, 92–93
    demonstration case, 105–108,
        546–548
    at Enron, 449–450
    environment, 190–195, 206–207
    financing activities, cash flows from,
        524, 538–539
    fraudulent, 104–105, 545
    full disclosure principle, 194
    investing activities, cash flows from,
        524, 537–538
    matching principle, 103, 104
    non-cash activities, 541
    objectives, 591–593
    operating activities, cash flows from,
        524–525, 528–537
    results from financial statements,
        4–17
    revenue principle, 104

revenues, 90–91
    role of auditors and analysts,
        194–195
    for users of information, 190–191
Financial statement analysis
    and business model, 195–197
    cross-sectional analysis, 197–198
    earnings per share, 499
    impact of inventory costing methods,
        347
    liquidity tests, 582–583, 586–588
    and long-lived assets, 397–399
    misrepresentation by management,
        192–194
    net income, 544–545
    profitability tests, 582, 583–586
    quality of user information, 591–592
    ratio analysis for, 198–202
    return on equity, 499
    role of auditors and analysts,
        194–195
    solvency tests, 583, 588–589
    time-series analysis, 197
    user needs, 190–191
Financial statements
    adjustments to, 133–142
    assurance statements, 13
    consolidated, 653–654
    defined, 2
    and Financial Accounting Standards
        Board, 17
    impact of inventory errors, 347–348
    kinds of, 4–5
    negative amounts expressed in, 11
    notes to, 14, 205
    preparation, 146–148
    public disclosure, 205
    relationships among, 12–13
    reporting results from, 4–17
Financial statement users
    balance sheet, 17
    defined, 2
    ethical reporting, 20
    income statement, 17
    notes and other reports, 19
    statement of cash flows, 18–19
    statement of retained earnings,
        17–18
Financing activities
    cash flows from, 12, 524–525
    defined, 2
    reporting cash flows, 538–539
Finished goods inventory, 331
First-in, first-out (FIFO) method
    cost of goods sold, 342–343
    defined, 336
    demonstration case, 349–350
    financial statement effects, 340–342
    impact on financial statement
        analysis, 347
    inventory costing, 336–337

last-in, first-out method *vs.*, 337–338
in perpetual inventory system, 352–353
Fiscal year, 4
Fixed assets. *See* Long-lived assets; Tangible assets
Fixed-asset-turnover ratio, 396, 403, 404, 584, 594
Fixed dividend rate, 489
FOB (free on board) destination, 246n, 332
FOB (free on board) shipping point, 246n, 332
Footnotes. *See* Notes to financial statements
Franchises, 392
Fraud, 82, 104, 203. *See also* Ethics
avoiding, 206–207
business opportunities and, 192
opportunity to commit, 193
personal greed and, 192–193
rationalization of, 193–194
Fraudulent reporting. *See* Accounting scandals
Free cash flow, 541
Full disclosure principle, 194
Future value
of an annuity, 637–638
annuity table for $1, 646
defined, 634
of a single amount, 635
table for $1, 644

G
Gains, 94
excluded from net income, 596
on income statement, 86
Generally accepted accounting principles (GAAP), 16–17, 61, 191, 192
accrual basis accounting, 89
amortization expense, 382
and auditors, 194
changes in accounting estimates, 405
changes in accounting methods, 597
cost flow assumptions, 344
and direct write-off method, 308
and goodwill, 392
long-lived assets, 382
lower of cost or market valuation, 344
Generally accepted auditing standards (GAAS), 16
Going concern assumption, 593
"Going public," 484
Goods available for sale, 333
Goods in transit, 332
Goodwill, 333, 392
Gottlieb, Myron, 425

Governance role, of accounting information, 190
Grass, Martin, 105
Greed, and fraud, 192–193
Gross accounts receivable, 292
Gross profit, 250, 333
Gross profit percentage, 251, 252–253, 582, 585
Growth investment, 485
GST payable, 433

H
Handler, Elliot, 2
Handler, Ruth, 2
Horton, Tim, 21
HST (harmonized sales tax), 433

I
Impairment losses, 389
Income before income tax expense, 87
Income investment, 485
Income statement, 8–10, 17
accrual basis accounting, 90–93
additional items, 596–597
adjusted, 132
amortization expense, 384, 393
and bankruptcy, 85
bond retirement, 445
business purpose, 86
cash basis accounting, 88–89
cash flows from operating activities, 530, 534–536
chart of accounts, 88
concepts, 103–104
cost of goods sold, 333, 535
demonstration case, 105–108
effect of business activities, 94–103
expenses, 10–11, 86–87
extraordinary items, 596
and financial performance, 578–579
gains or losses, 86
impairment losses, 389
income tax expense, 87
information for users, 86–87
modified, 197
multi-step, 250–252
net income, 10, 103
non-operating transactions, 86
non-recurring items, 596
operating activities, 8, 9
operating income, 86–87
preparation, 146–147, 148–149, 157
purpose, 8
ratio analysis, 198–200
revenues, 8, 86–87
set-up, 8
special items, 596
statement of cash flows, 526–527, 534–535
users of, 17, 103–104

Income taxes payable, 141, 155
Income tax expense, 87, 141, 155, 533
Income trusts, 480n
Incurred costs, 86
Incurred expense, 89, 139
Independent auditors' report, 14, 16–17, 19, 205
Independent verification, 234
Indirect method for reporting cash flow, 11, 525, 534, 546
Initial public offering (IPO), 484
Insurance expense, 134–136
Intangible assets
accounting rules, 393–394
acquisition of, 392
amortization, 393–394, 530n
cash flows from investing activities, 538
defined, 378
disposal of, 394
kinds of, 391–392
of knowledge-based companies, 394
limited life, 393
maintenance costs, 394
optimal level of investment, 395
self-constructed, 392
unlimited life, 394
Interest
capitalized, 381
compound, 638
on notes payable, 435–436
periods, 639
rate, 639
recording, 297–298
Interest deposited, 236
Interest earned, 297–298
Interest payable, 139
Interest receivable, 139, 154
Internal control, 193
cash control reporting, 234–240
computer systems and, 232
concept of, 232
credit card discounts, 299
defined, 232
demonstration case, 254–256
documentation of activities, 234
and employee responsibility, 233
gross profit percentage, 251–252
impact of operating cycles, 252–253
independent verification, 234
inventory control, 242–243
limitations of, 234
multi-step income statement, 250–252
need for, 231–232
and operating activities, 240–241
operating results of merchandisers, 253
principles of, 232–234
for protection, 232

purchase discounts, 245–246
purchases, 244
restricted access, 234
sales, 247
sales discounts, 248–249
sales-related transactions, 249
sales returns and allowances,
     247–248, 249
segregation of duties, 233
transportation costs, 244
International Accounting Standards
     Board (IASB), 17, 395
Inventory, 330
     on balance sheet, 6
     beginning, 333
     below recorded cost, 343
     changes in, 532
     consignment, 332
     days to sell, 345–346
     defined, 330
     ending, 333
     errors in ending inventory, 347–348
     goods in transit, 332
     of manufacturers, 331
     of merchandisers, 330
     monitoring, 243
     purchase discounts, 245–246
     purchase returns and allowances,
          244
     purchases, 244
     reporting, 243, 330–332
     sale of, 246–247
     shrinkage of, 242–243
     theft of, 282–283
     transportation costs, 244
Inventory account, 242, 244
Inventory control/management
     bar-code readers, 242
     demonstration case, 254–256
     goals, 330
     interpreting changes, 344–346
     periodic system, 242
     perpetual system, 242
     product innovation in, 330
     roles of, 241
     systems compared, 242–243
Inventory costing methods
     cost flow assumptions, 335–339
     demonstration case, 349–350
     financial statement effects, 340–342
     first-in, first-out method, 336–337,
          590
     impact on financial statement
          analysis, 347–348
     last-in, first-out method, 337–338
     lower of cost or market valuation,
          343–344
     specific identification method, 336
     weighted average cost method,
          338–339, 349–350

Inventory costs, 332
     cost flow assumptions, 335
     factors affecting, 330
Inventory tracking, 231–232
Inventory-turnover analysis, 344–346
Inventory-turnover ratio, 344–346, 583,
     586–587
Investing activities
     asset accounts, 6
     cash flows from, 12, 18–19,
          537–538, 542
Investments
     for corporate control, 652, 653–654
     for corporate influence, 652,
          654–656
     growth, 485
     income, 485
     passive investment methods, 652,
          657–661
     trading securities, 653, 660–661
Investor information Web sites,
     204–206
Investors
     avoiding fraud, 206–207
     cash flows from operating activities
          and, 541
     financial information for, 130
     and price/earnings ratio, 590–591
     use of auditor's report, 19
     use of financial statements, 17–19,
          191
Involuntary disposal, 390
Issued shares, 482
Issue price, 441

J

Journal entries, 54–55
     adjustments to, 133, 142
     closing, 149, 150
     for expenses, 103
     for revenues, 101–102
     stock dividends, 489
Joyce, Ron, 21

K

Knowledge-based companies, intangible
     assets of, 394
Kozlowski, Dennis, 296
Kumar, Sanjay, 105

L

Land, indefinite useful life of, 384
Land improvements, 378
Last-in, first-out (LIFO) method, 335
     demonstration case, 349–350
     financial statement effects, 340–342
     first-in, first-out method vs., 337–338
     impact on financial statement
          analysis, 347
     inventory costing, 337–338

not allowed for calculating income
     tax, 341
in perpetual inventory system, 340,
     352–353
Leases, 395–396, 450
Ledger, 52–54
Levin, Carl, 573
Liabilities
     ability to pay current amount,
          446–447
     ability to pay future amounts,
          447–449
     on balance sheet, 5, 7
     classification of, 430
     common features of debt, 449
     contingent, 450–451
     and credit ratings, 428–429
     decisions involving, 429–430
     defined, 5
     employee-related, 432
     long-term, 437–445
     measurement of, 430
     repayment, 445–449
     unrecorded, 450–451
Liability account, 54
Licensing rights, 392
Limited liability partnerships (LLPs),
     480n
Limited-life assets, 393
Line of credit, 430, 446
Liquidity, 583
     quick ratio, 583, 587–588
Liquidity, defined, 446, 583
Liquidity ratios, 583–584
     current ratio, 583, 587, 594
     inventory turnover, 583, 586–587
     receivables turnover, 582, 586
Loan covenants, 190, 192, 450, 495
Loan terms, 450
Long-lived assets
     accounting rules, 393, 394
     acquisition of, 379–381, 392–394
     alternative depreciation methods,
          384–388
     amortization, 393–394
     amortization/expense, 383–384
     book value, 383
     capitalized costs, 381
     capitalized interest, 381
     capital leases, 396
     defined, 378
     demonstration case, 400–403
     disposal of, 390–392, 394
     effectiveness of management
          discussion, 395–397
     impact of amortization differences,
          397–399
     impairment losses, 389
     kinds of, 378
     maintenance costs, 382

operating lease, 395
optimal level of investment, 395
tax depreciation, 388–389
Long-term assets, 43
Long-term debt, 430
and cash flow, 539
current portion, 433–434
Long-term liabilities, 43, 437–445
bonds payable, 432–445
debt financing, 437–438
early retirement of, 444–445
Losses, 94
asset impairment, 389, 402
excluded from net income, 596
on income statement, 86
Lower of cost or market (LCM), 343–344

M

Maintenance costs, 382, 394
Management
decisions on long-lived assets, 395–396
decisions on receivables, 288–289
factoring receivables, 299
income smoothing by, 303
inventory costing options, 341
inventory decisions, 330
misrepresenting results, 192–194
receivables turnover analysis, 300–301
segregation of duties, 233
use of financial statements, 190
Management accounting, 190
Management discussion and analysis (MD&A), 205, 541
Management information systems. *See* Accounting systems
Management's statement of responsibility, 13–14
Manufacturing companies, 240, 288, 289. *See also* Inventory
Market interest rate, 441
Market value, 61
Market value methods for passive investments, 652, 657–661
Matching principle, 104, 296
and acquisition costs, 383
and bad debt, 295
bond liability, 443
and depreciation, 136–137
Materiality, 331
Matson, Harold "Matt," 2
Maturity, debt retirement before, 444–445
Maturity date, 296
Merchandise inventory, 330
Merchandisers
credit card discounts, 299
demonstration case, 254–256

gross profit margin, 251–252, 253
impact of operating cycles, 252–253
inventories, 330
inventory tracking and control, 241–243
multi-step income statement, 250–252
operating activities, 240–243
purchase discounts, 245–246
purchase returns and allowances, 244
purchases, 244
retail, 240
sales discounts, 248–249
sales-related transaction account, 249
sales reporting, 247
sales returns and allowances, 247–248, 249
transportation costs, 244
wholesale, 240, 246
Minkow, Barry, 104
Misrepresentation. *See* Financial misrepresentation
Modified income statement, 197
Multi-step income statement, 250–252

N

n/30, 245–246
Natural resources, 395
Net accounts receivable, 292
Net assets, 393
Net cash flow, 11
Net change in cash, 11
Net income
adjustment, 530
cash *vs.*, 103
defined, 8
evaluated, 544–545
excluding gains and losses, 596
on income statement, 10, 87
and retained earnings, 10
Net loss, 8
Net method, for purchase discounts, 246n
Net profit margin, 582, 584–585
Net-profit-margin ratio, 200, 202, 209
New York Stock Exchange, 197
"Nigerian barge" transaction, 573
Non-cash activities, 541
Non-operating transactions, 86–87
Non-recurring items, 596
Notes payable, 7, 43
as current liability, 435–437
Notes receivable, 289
accounting for, 296–299
establishing, 297
interest formula, 297
origin of, 296
recording interest earned, 297–298

recording interest received, 298
recording receipt of interest and principal, 298
uncollectible, 298–299
Notes to financial statements, 205, 347
preparation, 147–148
types of, 14
users of, 19
NSF (not sufficient funds) cheques, 236

O

Operating activities, 86, 524
accrural-based measurement, 90–93
assets, 6
cash-based measurement, 88–89
cash flows from, 12, 18, 88–93, 524, 525, 528–537, 541
changes in management of, 545
on income statement, 8, 86–89
kinds of businesses, 240–243
reporting cash flows, 528–537
schedule, 530, 531
Operating cycle, 288
current liabilities, 430
impact of financial results, 252–253
and internal control, 240–241
for manufacturing company, 240, 288, 289
for merchandising company, 240
for service company, 240
Operating income, 86–87
Operating lease, 395, 450
Ordinary annuity, 637
Ordinary repairs, 382
Other assets, 6
Other current liabilities, 434
Outstanding cheques, 235, 238
Outstanding shares, 483
Overdraft, 430
Owners' equity
benefits, 482
common stock dividends, 485–486
common stock transactions, 484–485
in corporations, 480–481
partnership, 500, 502–503
preferred stock dividends, 490–491
retained earnings restrictions, 495
return on equity, 493–494
sole proprietorship, 480, 500, 501
and stock repurchase, 496
Ownership, transfer of, 246

P

Pacioli, Luca, 16
Parent company, 653–654
Partnership, 2, 480, 500, 502–503
Par value, common share, 484
Payment date, 486
Payroll deductions, 432

Percentage of credit sales method, 293–294
Periodic inventory system, 242, 257–259
Permanent accounts, 149
Perpetual inventory system
 defined, 242
 first-in, first-out method, 340, 352–353
 last-in, first-out method, 340, 352–353
 merits of, 243–244
 periodic system *vs.*, 242–243, 258–259
 recording purchases, 244
 sales journal entries, 247
Ponzi, Charles, 82
Ponzi scheme, 82
Post-closing trial balance, 149, 151
Predictive value, 592
Preferred shares
 cumulative dividend preference, 490–491
 current dividend preference, 490
 defined, 489
 dividends, 490–491
 vs. common shares, 489–490
Premium bonds, 440, 441, 443–444
Prepaid expenses, changes in, 533, 535
Prepaid insurance, 134–136, 154
Prepaid rent, 92, 134–136
Present value
 of an annuity, 638–639, 641–642
 annuity table for $1, 647
 applications of, 639–643
 of bonds, 441
 bonds payable, 455–456
 defined, 634
 of a single amount, 635–637, 640–641
 of a single amount and an annuity, 632–643
 table for $1, 645
Press releases, 203–204
Price, as condition of revenue principle, 104
Price/earnings ratio, 590–591
Principal, 296
Principal at maturity, 298
Prior periods, 197
Private companies, 480
Private placement, 437, 438
Profitability ratios, 581 583–586
 asset-turnover ratio, 582, 583–584, 594
 earnings per share, 582, 585
 fixed-asset-turnover ratio, 582, 584, 594
 gross percentage profit, 582, 585
 net profit margin, 582, 584–585

quality of income, 582, 586
 return on equity, 582, 585
Pro forma numbers, 204
Property, plant, and equipment, 6, 538
Property and equipment account, 136–138
"Pro rata basis," 487
PST (provincial sales tax), 433
Public company, 3, 481
Publicly issued debt certificates, 437, 438
Purchase discounts, 245–246
Purchase orders, matching of supplier invoices with, 240
Purchase returns and allowances, 244
Purchases, 244

Q
Quality-of-income ratio, 544–545, 582, 586
Quarterly reports, 204–205
Quick ratio, 583, 587–588

R
Ratio analysis. *See also* Liquidity ratios; Profitability ratios; Solvency ratios
 asset-turnover ratio, 200, 201, 209, 396–397, 583–584, 594
 averages in, 200
 capital-acquisitions ratio, 542
 cash coverage ratio, 543–544, 583, 589
 debt-to-asset ratio, 200, 201, 209, 583, 588, 594
 demonstration cases, 207–209, 594
 earnings per share, 491–492
 framework for, 582
 goal of, 198
 inventory-turnover ratio, 345
 net-profit-margin ratio, 200, 202, 209
 price/earnings ratio, 590–591
 purpose, 578
 quality-of-income ratio, 544–545, 582, 586
 quick ratio, 583, 587–588
 receivables-turnover ratio, 300–301
 return on equity, 493–494, 496, 582, 585
 summary of, 200, 203
 times-interest-earned ratio, 448–449, 543
 vertical analysis, 200–201
Raw materials inventory, 331
Receivables. *See also* Accounts receivable
 accounting for, 289–299
 factoring, 299
 impact of estimation, 302–303
 management decisions, 288–289

management practices, 299–302
 uncertainty about, 287
Receivables policy, 304
Receivables-turnover ratio, 300–301, 582, 586
Record date, 486
Recording
 amortization, 136–138
 bad debt expense, 291–292
 bonds payable, 438
 cost principle, 62
 disposal of assets, 390
 for expenses, 94, 103
 intangible assets, 392
 interest earned, 297–298
 interest received, 298
 items recorded, 62–63
 liabilities, 430
 matching principle, 104
 noted payable, 435–437
 of purchases, 244
 receipt of interest and principal, 298
 revenue principle, 104
 revenues, 101–102
 revenues and expenses, 101
 unearned revenue, 434
 write-downs, 389–390
Relevance, 191, 591
Reliability, 191, 591
Rent expense, 134–136
Research and development expenses, 392, 393
Residual claim, 482
Residual value, 384
Restricted access, 234
Retail industry, 190
Retail merchandisers, 240. *See also* Merchandisers
Retained earnings, 10, 43–44, 528. *See also* Statement of retained earnings
 on balance sheet, 7
 and cash dividends, 487
 and cash flow, 538
 dividends declared and, 10
 reduced on stock dividend, 487
 reporting negative earnings, 491
 restrictions on, 495
Retroactive treatment, 597
Return-on-assets (ROA) ratio, 495
Return on equity (ROE), 493–494, 496, 582, 585
Revenue account, 94
Revenue principle, 104
 violation of, 104–105
Revenue recognition
 accrual basis accounting, 90–91
 changes in, 545
 conditions for, 91
 principles, 104

Revenue recognition policy, 104
Revenues
   accounting summary, 101–102
   accrual-based measurement, 90–91
   adjusting, 131–142
   DECIDE approach, 95–97
   earned, 89
   on income statement, 8–9, 86–87
   recording, 94, 101–102
   reporting, 90–91
   timing of, 91
   in transaction analysis model, 94–99
   unearned, 90–91, 138–139, 434
Rigas, John, 104
Rule of accrual, 89

S

Sales, 246–247
Sales agreement, 246
Sales growth, 544
Sales returns and allowances, 247–248,
   249
Sales revenue, 8–9, 531
   for accounting period, 333
   contra-revenue account, 247, 249
   converted to cash flow, 532, 535
   credit card discounts, 299
   journal entries, 247
   returns and allowances, 247–248
   sales discounts, 248–249
Sales taxes payable, 433
Sarbanes-Oxley Act (SOX), 194, 232
Seasonality, 541–542, 544
Seasoned new issues, 484
Securities Acts, 194
Securities and Exchange Commission
   (SEC), 226, 227, 573
   and fraudulent reporting, 207
   reporting bad debt, 295
   stock repurchase, 485–486
Security, 450
SEDAR (System for Electronic
   Document Analysis and Retrieval),
   37–38, 205
Segregation of duties, 233
Self-constructed intangible assets, 392
Self-constructed tangible assets, 381
Seniority, 450
Separate entity assumption, 5
Service charges, 236
Service companies, 240–241, 252
Shareholders' equity
   on balance sheet, 5, 7
   decisions affecting returns, 496
   retained earnings restrictions and,
     495
   stock options and diluted earnings
     per share and, 495–496
   stock repurchase and, 496
   and stock splits, 488

Shareholders' equity account, 53
Shareholders' rights, 482
Shares. *See also* Equity
   benefits of ownership, 482
   sale of, 660
   trading securities, 653, 660–661
   transfer of ownership, 481
Shrinkage of inventory, 242–243
Sleeman, John H., 482
Sole proprietorships, 2
   corporations *vs.,* 480–481
   owners' equity, 480, 500
Solvency, 583
Solvency ratios, 583, 588–589
   capital-acquisitions ratio, 583, 589
   cash-coverage ratio, 583, 589
   debt-to-assets ratio, 583, 588, 594
   times-interest-earned ratio, 583,
     588–589
Specific identification method, 335, 336
Stakeholders, 190
Statement of cash flows, 11–12,
   18–19
   balance sheet, relationship to,
     526–527
   classifications in, 523–525
   condensed, 524
   content, 12
   financial results reported, 541–544
   focus of, 523
   format for, 540
   income statement, relationship to,
     526–527
   income taxes paid, 540
   interest, 540
   interpreting, 541–544
   need for, 523
   non-cash activities, 541
   preparation, 147–148, 526–527
   purpose, 11
   set-up, 11
   users of, 18–19
Statement of retained earnings, 10–11,
   17–18
   content, 10
   preparation, 146–147, 157
   purpose, 10
   set-up, 10
   users of, 17–18
Stock analysts, 194–195
Stock dividends, 489
   compared to stock splits, 489
   demonstration case, 497–498
   reasons for offering, 489
   value of, 489
Stock options, 495–496
Stock ownership
   transfer, 481
Stock price, 191
   and earnings per share, 492

   relation to earnings, 590–591
Stock purchases, 481
Stock repurchase, 496–497, 520
   demonstration case, 496–497
   and earnings per share, 496
   reasons for, 485–486
   and return on equity, 496
Stock splits, 488–489
Straight-line amortization method,
   385–386, 387–388, 398, 401, 405,
   443, 590
   bonds at discount, 443
Straight-line rate, 385
"Stuffing the channel," 300
Subsidiary company, 653–654
"Substance over form," 441
Suppliers, 532, 533, 535
Supplies, 92, 133–134
Supplies expense, 93, 133–134

T

T-accounts, 53, 56–57
   in account balances, 100
   in adjustments, 134–135, 138–139,
     144, 145, 156
   cost of goods sold, 334
   summarizing transactions, 59
   in transaction analysis, 53–54
Tangible assets
   accounting rules, 393, 394
   acquisition of, 379–381
   amortization expense, 383–384
   amortization methods, 383–388
   capitalized costs, 380
   capital leases, 396, 445
   cash purchase, 381
   costs incurred, 380–381
   credit purchase, 381
   defined, 378
   disposal of, 391
   evaluating use of, 396–397
   impairment losses, 389
   maintenance costs, 382
   operating lease, 395
   optimal level of investment, 395
   self-constructed, 381
   tax depreciation, 388–389
Tax depreciation, 388–389
Taxes
   accrued, 432
   amortization, 388–389
   sales tax, 433
   on sole proprietorship, 480, 500
Technology companies, intangible
   assets of, 394
Temporary accounts, 148–149
Time lags, 235
Time-period assumption, 592
Time period reporting, 4, 8
Time-series analysis, 197

Times-interest-earned ratio, 448–449, 543, 583, 588–589
Time value of money, 634
Trade accounts and notes receivable, 289
Trademarks, 392
Trade names, 392
Trading securities, 653, 660–661
Transaction analysis, 44–60
    accounting transaction, 45
    basic accounting equation, 46–48
    business activities, 44
    debit/credit framework, 52–55, 94–102
    defined, 44
    duality of effects, 46–48
    effects on balance sheet, 61–63
    identifying transactions, 44–46
    journal entries method, 54–55
    kinds of events, 45–46
    systematic approach, 48–51, 55–59
    T-accounts, 53–54
Transaction analysis model, 54
Transportation costs, 244
Treasury shares, 480
Trend analysis, 481, 578

Trial balance
    defined, 59
    unadjusted, 59–60

U

Unadjusted trial balance, 59–60, 100–101
Uncollectible account recovery, 292–293
Understandability, 591
Unearned revenues, 90–91, 138–139, 153, 434
Unit of measure assumption, 42
Units-of-production amortization method, 386, 388
Unqualified audit report, 194
Unrealized holding gains or losses, 657
Useful life, 384, 399, 405
Utilities expense, 92

V

Valuation role, of accounting information, 191
Vertical analysis, 200–201, 219, 578n
Voting rights, 482, 489

W

Wages expense, 140, 155
Wall Street, 197
Web sites, investor information, 205–206
Weighted average cost method, 338–339, 340–341, 349–350, 352–353
Wholesale merchandisers, 240, 246
Workers' Compensation, 432
Work in process inventory, 331
Write-downs, 389–390
Write-offs, 290, 292, 304–305, 308
    compared to estimates, 295
    reporting, 295

Y

Year-end (fiscal year), 4
Year-over-year change, 578
Yield, 441

Ratios Used for Financial Analyses

Ratio	Basic Computation	Chapter
Tests of Profitability		
a. Asset turnover	$\dfrac{\text{Net sales revenue}}{\text{Average total assets}}$	5
b. Fixed asset turnover	$\dfrac{\text{Net sales revenue}}{\text{Average net fixed assets}}$	9
c. Net-profit-margin	$\dfrac{\text{Net income}}{\text{Net sales revenue}}$	5
d. Gross profit percentage	$\dfrac{\text{Net sales revenue} - \text{Cost of good sold}}{\text{Net sales revenue}}$	6
e. Return on equity	$\dfrac{\text{Net income}}{\text{Average stockholders' equity}}$	11
f. Earnings per share	$\dfrac{\text{Net income}}{\text{Average number of shares of common stock outstanding}}$	11
g. Quality of income	$\dfrac{\text{Net cash flows from operating activities}}{\text{Net income}}$	12
Tests of Liquidity		
h. Receivables turnover (and days to collect)	$\dfrac{\text{Net credit sales revenue}}{\text{Average net receivables}}$	7
i. Inventory turnover (and days to sell)	$\dfrac{\text{Cost of good sold}}{\text{Average inventory}}$	8
j. Current ratio	$\dfrac{\text{Current assets}}{\text{Current liabilities}}$	10
k. Quick ratio	$\dfrac{\text{Cash} + \text{short-term investments} + \text{accounts receivable}}{\text{Current liabilities}}$	13
Tests of Solvency		
l. Debt-to-assets	$\dfrac{\text{Total liabilities}}{\text{Total assets}}$	5
m. Times-interest-earned	$\dfrac{\text{Net income} + \text{Interest expense} + \text{Income tax expense}}{\text{Interest expense}}$	10
n. Cash coverage	$\dfrac{\text{Net cash flows from operating activities} + \text{Interest paid} + \text{Income taxes paid}}{\text{Interest paid}}$	12
o. Capital acquisitions	$\dfrac{\text{Net cash flows from operating activities}}{\text{Cash paid for property, plant, and equipment}}$	12

Conceptual Framework for Financial Accounting and Reporting

PRIMARY OBJECTIVE OF EXTERNAL FINANCIAL REPORTING
To provide useful economic information to external users (particularly investors and creditors) for decision making (assessing future cash flows) [Ch. 5]

ELEMENTS OF FINANCIAL STATEMENTS
Asset—economic resource with probable future benefits [Ch. 2]
Liability—probable future sacrifices of economic resources [Ch. 2]
Shareholders' Equity—financing provided by owners and operations (residual interest to owners) [Ch. 2]
Revenue—increase in assets or settlement of liabilities from ongoing operations [Ch. 3]
Expense—decrease in assets or increase in liabilities from ongoing operations [Ch. 3]
Gain—increase in assets or settlement of liabilities from peripheral activities [Ch. 3]
Loss—decrease in assets or increase in liabilities from peripheral activities [Ch. 3]

QUALITATIVE CHARACTERISTICS OF FINANCIAL INFORMATION
To be useful, information should possess:
Relevance—be capable of making a difference in decisions [Ch. 5]
 - feedback value (assess prior expectations)
 - predictive value (extrapolate into the future)
 - timeliness (available to help with decisions)
Reliability—can be relied upon [Ch. 5]
 - representational faithfulness (represents reality)
 - verifiability (can be verified independently)
 - neutrality (unbiased)
Comparability and consistency—information should be comparable across companies and consistent over time [Ch. 5]
Understandability—information should be understandable by readers if they have a reasonable grasp of business, economics, and accounting and they study the information with diligence [Ch. 13]

ASSUMPTIONS
Separate entity—activities of the business are separate from activities of the owners [Ch. 1]
Unit of measure—accounting measurements are in the national monetary unit [Ch. 2]
Time period—the long life of a company can be reported over a series of shorter time periods [Ch. 13]
Going concern (continuity)—entity will not go out of business in the near future [Ch. 13]

PRINCIPLES
Historical cost—cash equivalent price on the transaction date is used initially to measure elements [Ch. 2]
Revenue recognition—record revenue when earned, measurable, and realizable [Ch. 3]
Matching—record expenses in the same period as the revenues they help to generate [Ch. 3]
Full disclosure—provide all information sufficiently important to influence a decision [Ch. 5]

CONSTRAINTS
Conservatism—exercise care not to overstate assets and revenues or understate liabilities and expenses [Ch. 2]
Materiality—relatively small amounts not likely to influence decisions are to be recorded in the most cost-beneficial way [Ch. 8]
Cost-benefit—benefits to users should outweigh costs of providing information [Ch. 13]